Decisions of the Comptroller General of the United States
by United States. General Accounting Office

Decisions of
The Comptroller General
of the United States

VOLUME 58

OCTOBER 1, 1978, TO SEPTEMBER 30, 1979

UNITED STATES
GENERAL ACCOUNTING OFFICE

U.S. GOVERNMENT PRINTING OFFICE
WASHINGTON : 1980

For sale by the Superintendent of Documents, U.S. Government Printing Office
Washington, D.C. 20402

COMPTROLLER GENERAL OF THE UNITED STATES
Elmer B. Staats

DEPUTY COMPTROLLER GENERAL OF THE UNITED STATES
Robert F. Keller

GENERAL COUNSEL
Paul G. Dembling *

DEPUTY GENERAL COUNSEL
Milton J. Socolar

ASSOCIATE GENERAL COUNSELS
F. Henry Barclay, Jr.
John J. Higgins
Richard R. Pierson

---

*Retired November 3, 1978.

Contents

Compiled in the
OFFICE OF THE GENERAL COUNSEL
Index-Digest Section
Stasia V. Hayman
Supervising Attorney-Advisor

v

Preface

This volume is the fifty-eighth in a series of annual volumes entitled "Decisions of the Comptroller General of the United States," which has been published since the establishment of the General Accounting Office by the Budget and Accounting Act, 1921. Decisions are rendered to heads of departments and establishments and to disbursing officers pursuant to 31 U.S. Code 74, and to certifying officers pursuant to 31 U.S.C. 82d. Decisions in connection with claims are issued in accordance with 31 U.S.C. 71. In addition, decisions on the validity of contract awards are rendered to interested parties.

The decisions included in these volumes are presented in full text and represent about ten percent of the total number rendered annually. Generally, decisions are selected for publication on the basis of their future value as precedent and on the widespread applicability of the issues involved.

All decisions contained in the annual volumes are available in advance of their consolidation into the annual volume through the circulation of individual decision copies and through the issuance of monthly pamphlets. The last pamphlet for each quarterly period includes quarterly index digests and citation tables. In addition, the last pamphlet for the annual period includes a complete cumulative index digest with citation tables for all of the decisions to appear in the annual volume.

To further assist in the research of matters coming within the jurisdiction of the General Accounting Office, ten consolidated indexes to the published volumes have been compiled to date, the first being entitled "Index to the Published Decisions of the Accounting Officers of the United States, 1894–1929," the second and subsequent indexes being entitled "Index Digest of the Published Decisions of the Comptroller" and "Index Digest—Published Decisions of the Comptroller General of the United States," respectively. The second volume covered the period from July 1, 1929, through June 30, 1940. Subsequent volumes have been published at five-year intervals. The period in the last volume was extended to September 30, 1976, to comport with new fiscal-year statutory requirements so that the new commencing date for future volumes will be October 1.

Decisions appearing in the published annual volumes should be cited by volume, page number and year issued, *e.g.*, 58 Comp. Gen. 810

(1979). Decisions of the Comptroller General which do not appear in the printed volumes should be cited by the appropriate file number and date, *e.g.*, B–194701, September 28, 1979.

Procurement law decisions issued since January 1, 1974, whether or not included in these volumes, are also available in published form from commercial sources.

COMPTROLLERS GENERAL OF THE UNITED STATES

1921 To Date

Name	State ·	Date of commission	Expiration of service
Elmer B. Staats	Kansas	Mar. 4, 1966	
Joseph Campbell	New York	Mar. 18, 1955	[1] July 31, 1965
Lindsay C. Warren	North Carolina	Aug. 1, 1940	[1] Apr. 30, 1954
Fred H. Brown	New Hampshire	Apr. 7, 1939	[2] June 19, 1940
J. Raymond McCarl	Nebraska	June 29, 1921	June 30, 1936

COMPTROLLERS OF THE TREASURY

1894–1921

Walter W. Warwick	Ohio	Sept. 1, 1915	June 30, 1921
George E. Downey	Indiana	May 16, 1913	Aug. 31, 1915
Robert J. Tracewell	Indiana	July 26, 1897	May 15, 1913
Robert B. Bowler	Ohio	Oct. 1, 1894	Aug. 4, 1897

1817–1894

First Comptrollers

Robert B. Bowler	Ohio	May 6, 1893	Sept. 30, 1894
Asa C. Matthews	Illinois	May 10, 1889	May 14, 1893
Milton J. Durham	Kentucky	Mar. 20, 1885	Apr. 22, 1889
William Lawrence	Ohio	July 15, 1880	Mar. 24, 1885
Albert G. Porter	Indiana	Mar. 5, 1878	June 10, 1880
Robert W. Taylor	Ohio	Jan. 14, 1863	[3] Feb. 25, 1878
Elisha Whittlesey	Ohio	Apr. 10, 1861	[3] Jan. 7, 1863
William Medill	Ohio	Mar. 26, 1857	Apr. 30, 1861
Elisha Whittlesey	Ohio	May 31, 1849	Apr. 30, 1857
James W. McCulloh	Maryland	Apr. 1, 1842	May 31, 1849
Walter Forward	Pennsylvania	Apr. 6, 1841	Sept. 13, 1841
James N. Barker	Pennsylvania	Feb. 23, 1838	Apr. 19, 1841
George Wolf	Pennsylvania	June 18, 1836	Feb. 28, 1838
Joseph Anderson	Tennessee	Mar. 3, 1817	June 30, 1836

[1] Retired.
[2] Resigned.
[3] Died in office.

Second Comptrollers

Name	State	Date of commission	Expiration of service
Charles H. Mansur	Missouri	May 27, 1893	Sept. 30, 1894
Benj. F. Gilkeson	Pennsylvania	May 23, 1889	June 5, 1893
Sigourney Butler	Massachusetts	Apr. 22, 1887	May 26, 1889
Isaac H. Maynard	New York	June 2, 1885	Apr. 1, 1887
William W. Upton	Oregon	Oct. 1, 1877	June 1, 1885
Cyrus C. Carpenter	Iowa	Jan. 7, 1876	Sept. 30, 1877
John M. Brodhead	New Hampshire	May 29, 1863	Jan. 23, 1876
James M. Cutts	District of Columbia	Oct. 1, 1857	May 11, 1863
John M. Brodhead	New Hampshire	Feb. 11, 1853	Oct. 8, 1857
Edward J. Phelps	Vermont	Oct. 1, 1851	Feb. 13, 1853
Hiland Hall	Vermont	Nov. 27, 1850	Sept. 10, 1851
Albion K. Parris	Maine	June 18, 1836	Nov. 28, 1850
James B. Thornton	New Hampshire	May 27, 1830	June 30, 1836
Isaac Hill	New Hampshire	Mar. 21, 1829	May 24, 1830
Richard Cutts	Massachusetts	Mar. 6, 1817	Mar. 21, 1829

Comptrollers of the Treasury

Name	State	Date of commission	Expiration of service
Joseph Anderson	Tennessee	Feb. 28, 1815	Mar. 3, 1817
Ezekiel Bacon	Massachusetts	Feb. 11, 1814	Feb. 28, 1815
Richard Rush	Pennsylvania	Nov. 22, 1811	Feb. 10, 1814
Gabriel Duvall	Maryland	Dec. 15, 1802	Nov. 21, 1811
John Steele	North Carolina	July 1, 1796	Dec. 14, 1802
John Davis	Massachusetts	June 26, 1795	June 30, 1796
Jonathan Jackson	Massachusetts	Feb. 25, 1795	Sept. 1, 1795
Oliver Wolcott, Jr.	Connecticut	June 17, 1791	Feb. 2, 1795
Nicholas Eveleigh	South Carolina	Sept. 11, 1789	Apr. 16, 1791

x

DEPUTY COMPTROLLER GENERAL OF THE UNITED STATES

1971 To Date

Name	State	Date of commission	Expiration of service
Robert F. Keller	Maryland	[1] July 13, 1971	

ASSISTANT COMPTROLLERS GENERAL OF THE UNITED STATES

1921-1971

Robert F. Keller	Maryland	Sept. 29, 1969	July 12, 1971
Frank H. Weitzel	District of Columbia	Jan. 18, 1954	[3] Jan. 17, 1969
Frank L. Yates	West Virginia	May 1, 1943	[3] June 29, 1953
Richard N. Elliott	Indiana	Mar. 6, 1931	[3] Apr. 30, 1943
Lurtin R. Ginn	....do	June 30, 1921	[3] Nov. 11, 1930

ASSISTANT COMPTROLLERS OF THE TREASURY

1894-1921

Charles Marshall Foree	Kentucky	Sept. 1, 1915	June 30, 1921
Walter W. Warwick	Ohio	May 24, 1913	Aug. 31, 1915
Leander P. Mitchell	Indiana	Jan. 18, 1808	[3] Dec. 6, 1912
Edward A. Bowers	Connecticut	June 6, 1895	Dec. 24, 1897
Charles H. Mansur	Missouri	Oct. 1, 1894	Apr. 16, 1895

. [1] Title changed to Deputy Comptroller General of the United States.
[3] Died in office.
[3] Retired.

October 1, 1978–September 30, 1979

TABLE OF DECISION NUMBERS

LIST OF CLAIMANTS ETC.

TABLES OF STATUTES, ETC., CITED IN DECISIONS OF THE COMPTROLLER GENERAL OF THE UNITED STATES

UNITED STATES STATUTES AT LARGE

For use only as supplement to U.S. Code citations

UNITED STATES CODE

See also, U.S. Statutes at Large

CONSTITUTION OF THE UNITED STATES

PUBLISHED DECISIONS OF THE COMPTROLLERS GENERAL

DECISIONS OF THE COMPTROLLERS OF THE TREASURY

DECISIONS OVERRULED OR MODIFIED

OPINIONS OF THE ATTORNEYS GENERAL

DECISIONS OF THE COURTS

Compensation—Overtime—Fair Labor Standards Act—Compensatory Time

Employee of the National Security Agency covered by Fair Labor Standards Act (FLSA) overtime pay requirements pursuant to solicitation by agency volunteered to work overtime. He knew that in lieu of overtime compensation he would receive compensatory time off under 5 U.S.C. 5543. He is not entitled to additional pay under FLSA, since he is also entitled to overtime pay under title 5, U.S. Code, equal to or greater than his FLSA entitlement. In such cases regulations provide that employee may voluntarily accept compensatory time as full remuneration for overtime performed.

Compensation—Overtime—Compensatory Time—Overtime   v.   Compensatory Time

National Security Agency solicited nonexempt employee under FLSA to volunteer to work overtime supervising cleaning crews in restricted area with understanding he would receive compensatory time off in lieu of overtime. No funds were available to pay overtime, and overtime would not have been performed without a volunteer willing to accept compensatory time off. There is no violation of the Fair Labor Standards Act, 29 U.S.C. 201 *et seq.* (Supp. IV, 1974), in giving compensatory time off under such circumstances.

In the matter of Richard P. Barnitt—Overtime Compensation, October 2, 1978:

By letter of November 15, 1977, Serial N41/0664, with enclosures, Mr. W. Smallets, Chief, Finance and Accounting, National Security Agency, requested an advance decision regarding the entitlement of Mr. Richard P. Barnitt to overtime compensation under the provisions of the Fair Labor Standards Act (FLSA), 29 U.S.C. §§ 201 *et seq.* (Supp. IV, 1974). Mr. Barnitt is a nonexempt employee under FLSA. His entitlement to overtime under title 5, United States Code, is equal to or greater than his entitlement under FLSA.

The record shows that between May 5, 1974, and August 9, 1975, and between September 21, 1975, and March 20, 1976, the claimant worked overtime supervising cleaning crews in a restricted area. The overtime was solicited by the agency and worked with the understanding that the claimant would receive compensatory time off in lieu of overtime. There were no funds available to pay overtime for this work and in the absence of a volunteer supervisor willing to receive compensatory time off in lieu of overtime, the area was not cleaned.

Mr. Barnitt now claims overtime compensation for the overtime which he worked. He contends that under FLSA he cannot be required to take compensatory time off. Thus, he urges that since he was

1

never given an opportunity to choose between overtime and compensatory time off, he is entitled to overtime.

Under the provisions of 29 U.S.C. § 204(f) the Civil Service Commission is authorized to administer the provisions of the Fair Labor Standards Act. Accordingly, by letter of February 27, 1978, we requested a determination from the Commission's Pay Policy Division with regard to Mr. Barnitt's entitlement to overtime compensation. In its reply, dated April 12, 1978, the Commission stated that it has held that there is no violation of FLSA in similar situations, where employees worked overtime with the understanding that they would receive compensatory time off as no funds to pay overtime were available. Thus, it found Mr. Barnitt was not entitled to overtime.

Overtime for Federal employees is authorized by title 5, United States Code, and by the Fair Labor Standards Act for nonexempt employees. An employee's entitlement to overtime may be based on title 5, FLSA, or both.

Section 5542 of title 5, U.S.C., provides in pertinent part as follows:

(a) For full-time, part-time and intermittent tours of duty, hours of work officially ordered or approved in excess of 40 hours in an administrative workweek, or (with the exception of an employee engaged in professional or technical engineering or scentific activities for whom the first 40 hours of duty in an administrative workweek is the basic workweek and an employee whose basic pay exceeds the minimum rate for GS–10 for whom the first 40 hours of duty in an administrative workweek is the basic workweek) in excess of 8 hours in a day, performed by an employee are overtime work and shall be paid for, except as otherwise provided by this subchapter, at the following rates:
(1) For an employee whose basic pay is at a rate which does not exceed the minimum rate of basic pay for GS–10, the overtime hourly rate of pay is an amount equal to one and one-half times the hourly rate of basic pay of the employee, and all that amount is premium pay.

*   *   *   *   *   *   *

The Fair Labor Standards Act at section 207 of title 29 U.S.C. contains the following pertinent provision:

(a)(1) Except as otherwise provided in this section, no employer shall employ any of his employees who in any workweek is engaged in commerce or in the production of goods for commerce, or is employed in an enterprise engaged in commerce or in the production of goods for commerce, for a workweek longer than forty hours unless such employee receives compensation for his employment in excess of the hours above specified at a rate not less than one and one-half times the regular rate at which he is employed.

There are no provisions for compensatory time off under FLSA. However, title 5 permits compensatory time off in lieu of overtime at section 5543(a) which states:

(a) The head of an agency may—
(1) on request of an employee, grant the employee compensatory time off from his scheduled tour of duty instead of payment for an equal amount of time spent in irregular or occasional overtime work; and
(2) provide that an employee whose rate of basic pay is in excess of the maximum rate of basic pay for GS–10 shall be granted compensatory time off from his scheduled tour of duty equal to the amount of time spent in irregular or occasional overtime work instead of being paid for that work under section 5542 of this title.

The Civil Service Commission has issued instructions in Attachment 1 to FPM Letter 551–6, dated June 12, 1975, covering the use of compensatory time off where Title 5 and FLSA overlap. Paragraph A1d(2) of Attachment 1 states that compensatory time off may be substituted for overtime pay if an employee's entitlement to overtime under title 5 is equal to or greater than his entitlement to overtime under FLSA. As stated earlier, the record in the present case shows that Mr. Barnitt's entitlement to overtime under title 5 is equal to his entitlement under FLSA. Therefore, there was no requirement under FLSA that he must receive overtime pay. And, there was no prohibition against giving Mr. Barnitt compensatory time off at his request in lieu of overtime pay.

Mr. Barnitt's contention that he is entitled to overtime pay is apparently based on the fact that he was not given a choice between receiving overtime pay or taking compensatory time off as is provided in applicable NSA regulations and para. A3b(2) of Attachment 1 to FPM Letter 551–6. However, FPM Letter 551–6 does not address situations where no funds are available for payment of overtime and employees are invited to work overtime for time off only. As stated earlier, the Civil Service Commission has determined that under such circumstances there is no violation of FLSA if an employee is not given a choice between overtime pay and compensatory time off.

Consistent with the Civil Service Commission report of April 12, 1978, we find that the claim of Mr. Barnitt is not compensable under the Fair Labor Standards Act, 29 U.S.C. §§ 201 *et seq.*

〔 B–191388 〕

Statutes of Limitation—Claims—Date of Accrual—Compensation Payments—Back Pay

Employee of Federal Aviation Administration alleges he was detailed to a higher grade position from July 1968 to July 1969. Employee's claim is barred by the statute of limitation which precludes consideration of a claim not received in our Office within 6 years after the date first accrued. Claim accrues on the date services in question were performed, not on the date that *Turner-Caldwell* was decided. 50 Comp. Gen. 607 and 34 Comp. Gen. 605, distinguished.

In the matter of Richard C. Clough—Claim of Backpay for Detail and Wrongful Classification, October 3, 1978:

This action concerns an appeal by Richard C. Clough from the denial by our Claims Division of his claim for a retroactive promotion and backpay between grades GS–14 and GS–15, from July 26, 1968, to July 7, 1969.

The record shows that Mr. Clough first filed claim for backpay with General Accounting Office (GAO) by letter dated May 28, 1976, received June 2, 1976. Our Claims Division denied this claim on the grounds that since it was not received in GAO within 6 years after the date it first accrued, the claim was barred by the statute of limitations of 31 U.S.C. 71a (Supp. V, 1975).

Mr. Clough requested reconsideration on the ground that his claim was timely filed because it first accrued on December 5, 1975, as the result of our decision in the *Matter of Turner-Caldwell*, 55 Comp. Gen. 539 (1975), and 34 Comp. Gen. 605 (1955). The Claims Division advised Mr. Clough that on reconsideration his claim was again denied as not timely filed.

Mr. Clough has appealed the settlement of the Claims Division, specifically requesting a decision as to the meaning of the phrase the "date the claim first accrued" with respect to a claim for backpay under 5 U.S.C. 5596 (1976). For the following reasons, we find that in this context, the "date the claim first accrued" refers to the date on which the work in question was performed.

In our decision, *Matter of Marie Grant*, 55 Comp. Gen. 785 (1976), we ruled that the *Turner-Caldwell* criteria for promotion and backpay applied retroactively to extended details to higher-grade positions, but only to claims filed within the 6-year period applicable to claims cognizable by our Office, as specified in 31 U.S.C. 71a. In subsequent cases involving claims for retroactive promotion and backpay for details which took place prior to the date of the *Turner-Caldwell* case we have uniformly calculated the 6-year period, for the purposes of the running of the above-cited statute of limitation, from the date of the actual performance of the work. Moreover, in cases in which we have granted backpay pursuant to *Turner-Caldwell*, we excluded from computation that period of the detail which occurred more than 6 years prior to the date on which the claim was received in our Office. See *Matter of Sam Friedman et al.*, B–189690, February 16, 1978; *Matter of Freddie L. Baker*, B–190841, February 15, 1978; and *Matter of Donald B. Sylvain*, B–190851, February 15, 1978.

It is apparent that in cases similar to that of Mr. Clough we consider the date of performance of the work to be the date of accrual of the claim. This interpretation is suggested by our decision in *Marie Grant*. If Mr. Clough's reasoning were correct, then all similar claims based on retroactive application received in our Office after *Turner-Caldwell* would accrue on December 5, 1975, and all would become barred on the same date, 6 years later. We did not so hold in the *Marie Grant* case, rather we stated simply that such claims would be subject to the usual 6-year statute of limitation.

Mr. Clough asserts that our decisions 50 Comp. Gen. 607 (1971) and 34 *id*. 605 support his reasoning. In 50 Comp. Gen. 607, and 34 *id*. 605, we considered situations in which an agency determination of the validity of the claim was statutorily required in order for the claim to be payable. Under those circumstances, we held that the claim does not accrue, for purposes of the running of the statute of limitations, until a determination of the validity of the claim by a designated agency. Our decision in *Turner-Caldwell* constitutes no such administrative determination of the validity of Mr. Clough's claim. Accordingly the holdings in 50 Comp. Gen. 607, and 34 *id.* 605, are not applicable to the circumstances in Mr. Clough's case.

In 29 Comp. Gen. 517 (1950) we held that for the purpose of computing the statute of limitations for claims filed in our Office: "the date of accrual of the right which now is asserted * * * was the particular [day] on which the services for which extra compensation * * * is claimed were rendered." This interpretation refutes the claimant's contention that the date of accrual did not occur until a later time, i.e., the day on which the Government refused to pay for the services rendered. This reasoning obviously supports the position of the Claims Division in the instant case, and Mr. Clough's reliance on this case for support is misplaced.

Accordingly, the Claims Division properly determined that Mr. Clough's claim accrued on the dates of his detail. Since it was filed more than 6 years later, the claim is barred, and the action of the Claims Division is sustained.

[B–191921]

Interest—Back Pay—Statutory Authority Required

Pursuant to 5 C.F.R. 713.217, Securities and Exchange Commission (SEC) adjusted employee's complaint of discrimination by agreement to authorize retroactive promotion and accompanying backpay plus interest. The SEC has no authority to allow payment of interest. It is well-settled rule of law that interest may be assessed against Government only under an express statutory authority and neither Equal Employment Opportunity Act of 1972 nor the incorporated provisions of title VII provide express authorization of interest against Government.

In the matter of Gene A. Albarado—Interest on Backpay Arising Out of Discrimination Complaint, October 4, 1978:

This action is in response to a request dated May 5, 1978, from Mr. Lawrence H. Haynes, Comptroller of the Securities and Exchange Commission (Commission), for a decision as to whether the Commission may authorize the payment of interest to Mr. Gene A. Albarado, an employee of the Commission, in connection with an award of backpay.

The record shows that on April 6, 1977, Mr. Albarado filed an Equal Employment Opportunity complaint alleging that the Commission had engaged in discrimination against him.

On April 8, 1978, Mr. Albarado and the Commission agreed upon an adjustment of Mr. Albarado's discrimination complaint pursuant to 5 C.F.R. 713.217 and a memorandum was signed setting forth the terms of the informal settlement of the complaint. The terms of the adjustment provided that Mr. Albarado would be granted a retroactive promotion and accompanying backpay for the period September 26, 1976, to April 10, 1977. In a memorandum dated April 18, 1978, the terms of informal adjustment of Mr. Albarado's complaint were amended to include the payment of interest on the backpay award, provided that the General Accounting Office determines that the payment of such interest is proper.

The Equal Employment Opportunity Act of 1972, Public Law 92–261, 86 Stat. 111, amended title VII of the Civil Rights Act of 1964, 42 U.S.C. 2000e *et seq.*, to prohibit discrimination in Federal employment on the basis of race, color, religion, sex, or national origin. Subsection 2000e–16(b) of title 42 provides in pertinent part that the Civil Service Commission shall have the authority to enforce the provisions of title VII with regard to Federal employees through appropriate remedies including reinstatement or hiring of employees with or without backpay, as will effectuate the policies of title VII and shall issue such rules, regulations, orders, and instructions as it deems necessary and appropriate to carry out its responsibilities.

The Commission's regulations implementing title VII provisions pertaining to complaints of discrimination are found in Part 713 of title 5, C.F.R. Those regulations give each Federal agency broad authority to take remedial action in discrimination cases. Section 713.221 of title 5, C.F.R.. provides in pertinent part as follows:

(c) The decision of the agency shall require any remedial action authorized by law determined to be necessary or desirable to resolve the issues of discrimination and to promote the policy of equal opportunity, whether or not there is a finding of discrimination. * * *

See also 5 C.F.R. 713.271(b).

Concerning the payment of interest in connection with a backpay award, it is a well-settled rule of law that interest may be assessed against the Government only under an express statutory or contractual authorization. *Fitzgerald* v. *Staats*, 578 F.2d 435 (D.C. Cir. 1978); 45 Comp. Gen. 169 (1965); and 54 *id.* 760 (1975). Neither the Equal Employment Opportunity Act of 1972 nor the incorporated provisions of title VII provide an express authorization of interest against the Government. In the absence of an express provision in title VII allowing interest in claims against the Government, there is no basis to allow the payment of interest under title VII. *Fischer* v. *Adams*, 572 F.2d 406 (1st Cir. 1978); *Richerson* v. *Jones*, 551 F.2d 918, 925 (3d Cir. 1977). Thus, there is no authority for the Commission to authorize the payment of interest in connection with the adjustment of Mr. Albarado's discrimination complaint.

In accordance with the above, the Commission may not pay Mr. Albarado interest in his award of backpay.

【 B–143189 】

Concessions—Contracts—Modification—Consideration

Secretary of Interior has determined, and General Accounting Office (GAO) concurs, that provision in standard National Park Service concession contract requiring concessioner to furnish accommodations at reduced rates to Federal employees in parks on official business is not in best interest of Government, despite reduced cost, because of risk and appearance of improper conflict of interest. Although generally vested contract rights may not be waived without consideration, GAO will not object to elimination of clause in question where cost saving is determined to be outweighed by adverse effect on Government of clause. 40 Comp. Gen. 234, distinguished.

In the matter of Elimination from Standard National Park Service Concession Contract of Federal Employee's Discount Provision, October 11, 1978:

The Secretary of the Interior requested our opinion on the legality of the unilateral elimination, by the Department of the Interior, of the Federal and State employees' discount provision from National Park Service (NPS) concession contracts now in force. That provision in the standard contract reads as follows:

SEC. *15. Accommodations for Government Employees.* The Concessioner shall furnish (available transportation within the (area)(park) free of charge, and other) accommodations at reduced rates, to Federal and State employees visiting the (area)(park) on official business and to the employees of the (area)(park) away from their regularly assigned stations, upon the presentation of proper credentials. Payments made by such employees in the absence of such credentials shall be without prejudice to a refund upon later submission thereof.

The question arises because this Office has held that the same discount provision is a requirement in the interest of the Government and that the Secretary of the Interior has no authority "to unilaterally relieve the concessioner of the contract obligation, in the absence of adequate consideration therefor moving to the Government." 40 Comp. Gen. 234, 239 (1960). This opinion was premised upon the well established rule that, without a compensating benefit to the United States, Government agents and officers have no authority to dispose of the money or property of the United States, to modify existing contracts, or to surrender or waive vested contract rights. 35 Comp. Gen. 56, 59 (1955); 40 *id.* 234, 239 (1960); *Christine* v. *United States*, 237 U.S. 234 (1915); *Pacific Hardware* v. *United States*, 49 Ct. Cl. 327, 335, 337 (1914).

Under present practice, the discount provision here in issue may represent a monetary benefit to the United States. *See* 40 Comp. Gen. 234, *supra.* Federal employees receiving a subsistence allowance while on official business in national parks will, where the discount provision is in force, incur lower daily expenses. *See* 5 U.S.C. § 5702 (1976). This benefits the Government since its reimbursement to employees on official business will be lower.

The Secretary now urges that the discount provision is detrimental to proper administration of NPS concessions, as it presents both the risk and appearance of an improper conflict of interest. Our Office for a number of years, as a matter of policy, has forbidden its officials from taking advantage of the discount. In a letter dated June 7, 1963 (B–151705), this Office, in commenting on the discount clause of the standard concession contract, noted that while there were no legal grounds for disallowing its inclusion in the contract,

> * * * it is questionable in any event whether it is desirable or appropriate to authorize or require a park concessioner to provide a service free of charge or at a reduced rate to either a Federal or State employee * * *.

Implicit reference is made to the potential for improper influence of Government officials that inheres in a situation where a regulated entity confers monetary benefits upon the officials charged with the duty to regulate it.

The Secretary cites the concern expressed in a Joint Report by the Committee on Government Operations and the Committee on Small Business (H.R. Rep. No. 869, 94th Cong., 2d Sess. 46 (1976)) which his Department shares. The Joint Report cites with approval the following portion of an earlier House Government Operations Committee report:

> * * * Government employees who, on behalf of the Government, exercise supervisory responsibilities over private interests should avoid both any actual conflict of interest, and also the appearance of any conflict of interest which might arise by receiving from such private interests any personal favors, gifts, or perquisites in connection with the performance of their official duties. Such favors tend to create in the employee a sense of personal obligation to the company or person providing it which may be inconsistent with his primary responsibility to the public interest.
>
> Moreover, the furnishing of such accommodations and the acceptance thereof by Government officials in the performance of their official duties could violate the conflict-of-interest laws. H.R. Rep. No. 88–306, 8 (1963).

The Committees ultimately recommended that

> [t]he Secretary of the Interior * * * promptly publish regulations prohibiting National Park Service concessioners from providing discounts for food and lodging to Federal employees or their families, notwithstanding any provision in existing concession contracts or permits.

Clearly, then, there are competing considerations involved in this decision:

(a) the monetary benefits which will accrue to the Government from operation of the discount provision, and

(b) the interest of the Government in avoiding the appearance of conflicts of interests and in maintaining public confidence in the Government.

Vested contract rights would be of little value to the United States if they could be arbitrarily waived by Government agencies. This was the guiding principle in the formulation of our 1960 opinion and is no less valid today. However, a studied administrative determination that the elimination from a contract of a vested right of the United States would, on balance, be "in the best interest" of the United States, would not be inconsistent with that principle.

Our opinion of 1960 dealt exclusively with the question of unilateral waiver where the Interior Department perceived that "there is no indication that the practice [embodied in the discount clause] is not fully consistent with the best interest of the United States * * *." 40 Comp. Gen. 234, 235. That opinion was not dispositive of the issue now before us, since the Interior Department has now taken the position that the retention of the discount provision would not be "in the best interest" of the United States.

An arbitrary determination that a contract right was not in the best interest of the United States would, of course, be entitled to no weight, nor would it be permissible to relinquish a vested contract right of the United States merely because it was of relatively little value. However, agencies may give recognition to other than purely financial interests of the United States in deciding whether there is a benefit to the United States in relinquishing a contract right. In this case, there is ample basis for a finding by the Department that, as the Secretary says: "[t]he few dollars saved by the Government are far outweighed by the inimical nature of a contractual provision which permits Government employees who have responsibility for regulating the operations of private enterprises to receive financial benefits from the regulated industry." It might be said that the discount provision is, in effect, against public policy.

In accordance with the foregoing, we would not be required to object to the elimination by the Interior Department of the discount provision from concession contracts now in force. We assume that there will be no objection from the contractor.

[B–149858]

Commerce Department—National Bureau of Standards—Working Capital Fund—Impairment—Definition

National Bureau of Standards finances operations in part by charges to users of its services, paid into Working Capital Fund. Earned net income of the Fund must be paid into Treasury annually. except that it "may be applied first to restore any prior impairment" of the Fund. 15 U.S.C. 278b (1976). Impairments contemplated by this provision are operating losses. Bureau may not retain profits to offset increased costs—caused by inflation—of replacing equipment or facilities, nor can Bureau calculate depreciation of equipment and facilities based on replacement cost.

In the matter of Definition of "Impairment" in 15 U.S.C. 278b(f), October 12, 1978:

This decision is in response to a memorandum from David S. Nathan, Controller of the Department of Commerce, asking whether the term "prior impairment" as used in 15 U.S.C. § 278b(f) could include impairment caused by inflation.

The National Bureau of Standards, Department of Commerce (NBS), performs services for the United States Government, State or municipal governments, and others. It is authorized to charge for these services based on fixed prices or costs. 15 U.S.C. §§ 273, 275 (1976). NBS finances its activities with a working capital fund established by statute. The statute requires that the amount of any earned net income resulting from the operation of the working capital fund (NBSWCF) at the close of each fiscal year be paid into the general fund of the Treasury. However, prior to such deposit, the net income may be applied first to "restore any prior impairment of the fund." 15 U.S.C. § 278b(f) (1976).

Equipment or facilities acquired for carrying out functions of NBSWCF are capitalized to the fund and their cost allocated by including an amount for depreciation, in fees charged users. However, due to inflation, the amounts recovered are insufficient to permit replacement of the equipment or facilities at the end of their useful lives. Therefore, the Controller asks whether the phrase "to restore any prior impairment" can be interpreted to mean impairment caused by inflation, and whether the NBSWCF may retain profits to offset increased costs in replacing equipment or facilities. For the following reasons, our answer is no to both the questions asked.

The inquiry assumes that the increased cost of equipment is the result of inflation and not attributable to other factors (*e.g.*, product improvement) and also that NBS will still have a need for the equipment or facility at the end of its useful life (*i.e.*, that it will in fact be replaced). Such assumptions might not be warranted in every case. However, we direct the following discussion to those cases where such assumptions are correct.

"Impairment" is not a word of art with a well-defined meaning in the practice of accounting. The dictionary definition of "impair" is to "make worse; to diminish in quantity, value, excellence or strength; to do harm to." *Webster's Third New International Dictionary of the English Language, Unabridged* (Springfield, Mass.. G&C. Merriam Co., 1966), p. 1031. While it could be argued that the Congress, by appropriating a specific amount of money to establish a working capital fund, intended that the amount in the fund be periodically redetermined to reflect changes in the value of the dollar (up or down) so that the buying power of the fund could remain constant *vis-a-vis* price levels on the date of its establishment, we doubt that the Congress would impose such a complex accounting requirement on agencies without expressly stating such an intention. Thus we doubt that the impairment contemplated was the lessening of the value of the fund by means of a lessening in the value of the dollar. However, this is in effect what NBS is suggesting in its proposal.

The NBSWCF was initially established by the Deficiency Appropriation Act of 1950, approved June 29, 1950, 64 Stat. 279, and funded in the amount of $3 million. (As a result of subsequent appropriations by the Congress, the NBSWCF is now capitalized in the amount of $24.3 million.) Subsequently, this provision was amended and added to the Organic Act of the NBS (Act of March 3, 1901, ch. 872, 31 Stat. 1449), by section 2 of the Act of August 3, 1956, ch. 906, 70 Stat. 959 (1956 Act), 15 U.S.C. § 278b (1976).

Section 3 of the NBS Organic Act, as amended by the 1956 Act, provides in pertinent part as follows:

> The bureau shall exercise its functions for the Government of the United States and for international organizations of which the United States is a member; for governments of friendly countries; for any State or municipal government within the United States; or for any scientific society, educational institution, firm, corporation, or individual within the United States or friendly countries engaged in manufacturing or other pursuits requiring the use of standards or standard measuring instruments * * *. 15 U.S.C. § 273 (1976).

Section 7 of the Organic Act, as amended by the 1956 Act, requires the Secretary of Commerce to:

> * * * charge for services performed under the authority of section 273 of this title, except in cases where he determines that the interest of the Government would be best served by waiving the charge. Such charges may be based upon fixed prices or costs. The appropriation or fund bearing the cost of the services may be reimbursed, or the Secretary may require advance payment subject to such adjustment on completion of the work as may be agreed upon. 15 U.S.C. § 275a (1976).

Section 12 of the Organic Act, as amended by the 1956 Act, provides in pertinent part that:

> (d) Credits.
> The fund may be credited with advances and reimbursements, including receipts from non-Federal sources, for services performed under the authority of section 273 of this title.
> (e) Cost defined.
> As used in this chapter, the term "cost" shall be construed to include directly related expenses and appropriate charges for indirect and administrative expenses.
> (f) Distribution of earnings; restoration of prior impairment.
> The amount of any earned net income resulting from the operation of the fund at the close of each fiscal year shall be paid into the general fund of the Treasury: *Provided*, That such earned net income may be applied first to restore any prior impairment of the fund. 15 U.S.C. § 278b (1976).

In explaining the addition of subsections 12(d), (e) and (f) to the NBS Organic Act, the report of the Senate Interstate and Foreign Commerce Committee, states in pertinent part that:

> Subsection (d) will also provide authority, not now provided, to make payments to the fund in advance of performance of services. This authority will

enable the Bureau to avoid shortages in operating cash without receiving additional appropriations to increase the working capital. During periods of emergency increases in program activity, the Bureau has been faced with a serious shortage of operating cash which occasionally has necessitated delays in payment of vouchers for services received.

Subsection (e) presents a more general definition of the term "cost" than is presently incorporated in the authority for the use of the fund. The act which originally established the working capital fund provided that reimbursements shall include handling and related charges, reserves for depreciation of equipment and accrued leave, and building construction and alterations directly related to the work for which reimbursement is made. Subsection (e) will permit the inclusion of any or all of these elements in the determination of costs of services performed but would not preclude the charging of other items. Accordingly, the accounting system to be followed in connection with the use of the working capital fund would be left to the administrative discretion of the Department of Commerce, subject, of course, to the requirements of the Bureau of the Budget, the Treasury Department, and the Comptroller General.

Since a significant part of the work performed by the Bureau would be paid for on the basis of fixed prices or fees, the procedure for handling surpluses or deficits in the capital of the fund is needed. Subsection (f) provides for the depositing of any earned net income in the general fund of the Treasury after first restoring any deficit in working capital due to prior operating losses. S. Rep. No. 1171, 84th Cong., 1st Sess., p. 4 (1955).

Thus the "impairment of the fund" contemplated appears to be the operating losses sustained by providing services to other agencies at a fixed price which might not recover the total cost of performing the service. See also *Hearings before a Subcommittee of the Senate Committee on Interstate and Foreign Commerce on S. 2060*, 84th Cong., 1st Sess. 8 (1955). Furthermore, this interpretation is consistent with the earlier law and legislative history dealing with the operation of working funds. For example, Congress imposed on the Bureau of Engraving and Printing Fund, established under section 2 of the Act of August 4, 1950, ch. 558, 64 Stat. 409, the following requirement:

(e) Any surplus accruing to the fund in any fiscal year shall be paid into the general fund of the Treasury as miscellaneous receipts during the ensuing fiscal year: *Provided, That any such surplus may be applied first to restore any impairment of the capital of the fund by reason of variations between the prices charged for work or services and the amount determined to be the actual cost of performing such work or services.* [Italic supplied.] 31 U.S.C. § 181a (1970).

Also, when the Treasury General Supply Fund was reconstituted into the General Services Administration General Supply Fund by section 109 of the Federal Property and Administrative Services Act of 1949, approved June 30, 1949, ch. 288, 63 Stat. 382, the Congress provided in pertinent part that:

(e) Annual audit; surplus; report to Congress.

The Comptroller General of the United States shall make an annual audit of the General Supply Fund as of June 30, and there shall be covered into the United States Treasury as miscellaneous receipts any surplus found therein, all assets, liabilities, and prior losses considered, above the amounts transferred or appropriated to establish and maintain said fund, and the Comptroller General shall report to the Congress annually the results of the audit, together with such recommendations as he may have regarding the status and operations of the fund. 40 U.S.C. § 756 (1970).

Section 109 of the 1949 Act originated in S. 2020 as reported by the Senate Committee on Expenditures in the Executive Departments. See

H.R. Rep. No. 935, 81st Cong., 1st Sess. 33 (1949). In commenting on section 109, the report of the Senate Committee on Expenditures in the Executive Departments states, in pertinent part as follows:

(e) This subsection alters the previous requirement that all surplus in the fund, as determined in the annual audit by the Comptroller General, must be covered into the Treasury as miscellaneous receipts, by permitting losses incurred by the fund in prior years, as well as all assets and liabilities, to be considered in ascertaining the amount of such surplus. *This change takes cognizance of the fact that such prior losses represent impairments of the fund capital, unless made good from earnings, and also will counteract any tendency to establish prices at too high a level.* Also, there is added the requirement that the Comptroller General report to the Congress annually the results of the audit. Such reports, and his recommendations as to the status and operations of the fund, should be helpful to the Congress in its consideration of supply activities. [Italic supplied.] S. Rep. No. 475, 81st Cong., 1st Sess. 11 (1949).

See also the Civil Service Commission revolving fund established by the Third Supplemental Appropriation Act of 1952, Act of June 5, ch. 369, 66 Stat. 107. Thus it is clear that the Congress, prior to adoption of the 1956 Act, used "impairment" to indicate the detriment to the working capital fund if reimbursements based on fixed fees failed to recover the full cost of providing the service. We therefore find no basis for NBS to retain profits in order to offset increased replacement costs.

The Deficiency Appropriation Act of 1950, *supra*, establishing the NBSWCF, required that "reimbursements" recovered for the services provided include "reserves for depreciation." See 64 Stat. 279. When the NBSWCF was incorporated into the NBS Organic Act in 1956, the definition of "cost" provided in 15 U.S.C. § 278b(e) (1976) was clearly intended to permit the inclusion of "reserves for depreciation" as required by the 1950 Act. See S. Rep. No. 1171, *supra*, p. 4, and H.R. Rep. No. 2809, 84th Cong., 1st Sess.. p. 4 (1955). The question now is, what method of depreciation accounting is required for depreciating equipment and facilities capitalized into the NBSWCF. In turn, if the value ascribed to the item depreciated can be stated in terms of replacement cost, then amounts could be retained in the NBSWCF equal to the replacement value. The NBSWCF could then, by including in its charges to users an element based on replacement cost, achieve the same objective sought to be achieved by the proposal to retain profits—*ie.*, the accumulation of amounts sufficient to replace equipment or facilities at current, inflated, values. However, such a procedure is not authorized.

Generally, depreciation is a means by which a cost *incurred* is allocated over the useful life of the asset. In Paton and Paton, *Asset Accounting* (New York; MacMillan Co., 1952) pp. 236–237 it is stated that:

* * * the primary purpose of depreciation accounting is the orderly charging of plant costs to operation; that recognizing depreciation, like the acknowledgment of other costs, has as its principal objective reasonable income accounting *rather than the accumulation of funds for replacement.* [Italic supplied.]

See also Eldon S. Hendriksen, *Accounting Theory*, rev. ed. (Homewood, Ill.; Richard D. Irwin, Inc., 1970), in which the author states "historical acquisition cost" is the most common method for valuing plant and equipment. Hendriksen, *id.*, p. 363. Furthermore, see 2 GAO Policy And Procedures Manual for Guidance of Federal Agencies § 12.5(d), concerning acquisition cost.

We believe that the term "cost," absent something in the law or its legislative history indicating otherwise, means historical cost, and not replacement cost. Thus, when capitalizing fixed assets in the fund, the value of the asset is determined by historical cost (*e.g.*, acquisition cost) and it is this value that depreciation allocates over the useful life of the asset.

In a similar circumstance, we indicated in our Report to the Congress, entitled "Examination of Financial Statements—Bureau of Engraving and Printing Fund For Fiscal Years 1974 and 1975—Shows Need for Statutory Authority To Increase Capitalization," FOD 76–22, March 7, 1977, that the Secretary of the Treasury lacked authority to charge fees for services of the Bureau which included a surcharge based on replacement costs of equipment (even though he possessed express authority to establish reserves for depreciation based on original cost or appraised value). Further, he could not retain in the fund such surcharges as collected. The Congress subsequently in effect authorized such a surcharge and its retention. Treasury, Postal Service, and General Government Appropriation Act. 1978, Pub. L. No. 95–81, July 31, 1977, 91 Stat. 342.

Consequently, should it be deemed necessary for NBS to include in its fees cost items which include a factor for increased replacement costs of equipment due to inflation, specific statutory authority should be obtained. Without such authority, additional appropriations for the NBSWCF, as authorized by 15 U.S.C. § 278b(a) (1976), must be requested.

〔 B–114874 〕

Postal Service, United States—Mails—Government—Registered Mail

Neither the Government Losses in Shipment Act, 40 U.S.C. 726 (1970), nor the Government's general self-insurance policy prohibits Federal agencies from using registered mail where administratively determined necessary in order to obtain the "special" service of greater protection in the handling and delivery of mail rather than to obtain the insurance coverage also offered.

Postal Service, United States—Mails—Government—Insured Mail

Federal agencies are prohibited from using insured mail under both 40 U.S.C. 726 and the Government's self-insurance policy since insured mail provides no "special" or "additional" service in addition to the indemnity offered. 3 Comp. Gen. 391 and 22 Comp. Gen. 832, modified.

In the matter of Government Losses in Shipment Act—Purchase of Postal Insurance, October 13, 1978:

The Administrator, General Services Administration (GSA), requests our decision as to whether the Government Losses in Shipment Act, 40 U.S.C. §§ 721 *et seq.* (1970), prohibits Federal agencies from purchasing postal insurance to obtain indemnity, unless specifically required by law.

Under the Federal Records Management Amendments of 1976, Pub. L. No. 94–575, October 21, 1976, § 2(a)(2), 90 Stat. 2725, 44 U.S. Code 2904, the Administrator of GSA is responsible for providing Federal agencies with guidance and assistance in the creation, maintenance, use and disposition of records. Pursuant to this authority, GSA recently examined the use of insured and registered mail by Federal agencies and concluded that, unless specifically required by law, agencies should not obtain indemnity by purchasing postal insurance. This conclusion was based both on the well-established policy that the Government is its own insurer and on the requirements of the Government Losses in Shipment Act (40 U.S.C. § 726).

GSA has proposed to the United States Postal Service (USPS) certain changes in USPS fees and procedures which would discourage Federal agencies from obtaining postal insurance, including the suggestion that USPS establish a separate fee schedule that would eliminate any charge for indemnity insurance from the registered mail services provided Federal agencies. If implemented, GSA projects that these changes could save the Government up to $1.9 million annually.

USPS, however, does not entirely agree with either GSA's basic position or its proposals. Even though it recognizes that it is the policy of the Federal Government to self-insure against the risk of loss, and concedes that the extra cost for insured mail provides a low limit of liability and only a minimal degree of protection above that given ordinary mail, USPS maintains nevertheless that registered mail continues to provide a valuable and necessary service to many agencies. This service is the feature of "secure" mail service which provides not only added protection in handling but evidence of mailing and delivery as well. According to USPS, this is the primary purpose of registered mail, with the indemnity feature being of secondary importance. Thus while USPS agrees that Federal agencies should not use insured mail, it does not agree that these agencies should also cease using registered mail. USPS apparently believes that the "security" offered by registered mail is the overriding factor in favor of its continued use by Federal agencies.

With respect to the Government Losses in Shipment Act, USPS cites our decisions at 3 Comp. Gen. 391 (1923) and 22 Comp. Gen. 832 (1943) to support the argument that the Act does not apply to the purchase of postal insurance. USPS also points out that, even though it has been considering the feasibility of selling indemnity as a separate feature of registered mail, it does not believe that it can legally offer such service to only Federal mailers, as GSA proposes, but must make any new fee structure that it develops applicable to all registered mail users.

Against this background, the question presented is whether the Federal Government's self-insurance policy, in conjunction with the specific restraints imposed by the Government Losses in Shipment Act, prohibits Federal agencies from using either insured or registered mail, unless otherwise authorized by law.

It is a well-settled policy that the Government will not insure its property, but will assume its own risks of loss. 13 Comp. Dec. 779 (1907) ; 19 Comp. Gen. 211 (1939) ; 55 *id.* 1321 (1976). This policy arose because it was felt that the magnitude of the Government's resources makes it more advantageous for the Government to carry its risks than to have them assumed by private insurers at rates sufficient to cover all losses, to pay the insurer's operating expenses (including agency or broker's commissions) and to leave such insurers a profit. See, *e.g.*, 55 Comp. Gen. 1343, 1345 (1976). Thus, it has been held consistently that appropriated moneys are not available for the payment of insurance premiums on Government-owned property in the absence of specific statutory authority for the payment of such premiums. 17 Comp. Gen. 419, 421 (1937) ; 21 *id.* 928, 929 (1942) ; 34 *id.* 175, 177 (1954).

Exceptions to the rule have been recognized in situations where the reasons for the rule were not applicable. Thus, exceptions have been allowed where the economy sought under the rule would be defeated ; sound business practice indicates that a saving can be effected ; or services or benefits not otherwise available can be obtained by purchasing insurance. 55 Comp. Gen. 1321, 1323 ; B–151876, April 24, 1964.

In addition, section 4 of the Government Losses in Shipment Act, 40 U.S.C. § 726, provides in pertinent part :

[N]o executive department, independent establishment, agency, wholly owned corporation, officer, or employee shall expend any money, or incur any obligation, for insurance, or for the payment of premiums on insurance, against loss, destruction, or damage in the *shipment of valuables* except as specifically authorized by the Secretary of the Treasury. * * * [Italic supplied.]

This prohibition, like the general policy, is based on the theory that the Government's vast resources make it far more economical for it to assume its own risks of loss than to pay for insurance coverage from private sources. See S. Rep. No. 738, 75th Cong., 1st Sess. 6 (1937). With respect to this prohibition, we have indicated that services which incidentally include in their costs a charge for insurance, but whose principal goal is to minimize the risks of loss, damage or destruction to the valuables being shipped, may be obtained since such services are compatible with the objectives of the Act. See 34 Comp. Gen. 175.

In response to GSA's proposed changes in the Government's use of insured and registered mail, USPS believes that neither the general policy against the Government's purchase of insurance nor the Government Losses in Shipment Act clearly prohibits the use of either of these services. To support this position, as noted above, USPS relies on our decisions at 3 Comp. Gen. 391 and 22 Comp. Gen. 832.

In our 1923 decision (3 Comp. Gen. 391), we held that despite the Federal policy against the Government's purchase of insurance, parcel-post insurance was not of the general class at which this policy was directed, since parcel-post insurance could be considered "more as an additional service performed by one branch of the Government, the Post Office Department, for the other branches of the Government." Moreover, we also noted that the purchase of this insurance was justified by the increased security the mail received during handling and delivery.

The Government Losses in Shipment Act became law on July 8, 1937. In our 1943 decision (22 Comp. Gen. 832), we considered whether the purchase of postal insurance contravened the Act's prohibition against the procurement of insurance in the shipment of "valuables" (as defined by the Act). We concluded that since "postal insurance involves not only indemnity against loss or damage but a special service which minimizes the risk of loss," the procurement of such insurance did not contravene the provisions of the Act. Thus, as indicated in these decisions, the principal justification for the exception to the Government's practice of self-insurance was the "additional" or "special" service offered in conjunction with the insurance and which presumably provided greater care in the handling and delivery of the mail as a means of minimizing the risk of loss.

GSA points out, however, that the Postal Reorganization Act, 39 U.S.C. § 101 *et seq.* (1970), abolished the Post Office Department, formerly an Executive department, and replaced it with the United States Postal Service, an independent establishment within the Executive branch. As a consequence, Federal agencies are now treated as USPS customers. This development, in GSA's opinion, has materially altered that special relationship between the "branches" of Government which our earlier decisions—now relied on by USPS—found significant. GSA argues that it is no longer accurate to characterize the relationship as "one branch" of the Government performing a service for "the other branches," and therefore implies that reconsideration of our earlier decisions is warranted.

Regardless of the status of USPS with regard to other Government agencies, it nevertheless appears that insured mail provides a service only slightly beyond that offered for ordinary mail. This is borne out, as GSA observes, by the instruction in USPS Postal Service Manual § 162.74 that all insured mail is to be dispatched as ordinary mail and handled as such while in transit. Thus, only the indemnity feature of this service distinguishes it from ordinary mail. USPS does not appear to dispute this.

We conclude, therefore, that since insured mail offers no "special" or "additional" service apart from the indemnity feature, the general rule requiring the Government to self-insure prohibits its use unless a particular situation falls within one the exceptions noted in 55 Comp. Gen. 1321, *supra*, or unless otherwise specified by law. See in this connection our report entitled "Federal Agencies Could Do More to Economize on Mailing Costs," GGD–75–99, August 25, 1975, page 6. We further conclude that due to this absence of any "special" or "additional" service, the Government Losses in Shipment Act (40 U.S.C. § 726) also prohibits the use of insured mail in the shipment of "valuables"—definited in 40 U.S.C. § 729(a) and 31 C.F.R. § 262.1. To the extent they are inconsistent with this decision, 3 Comp. Gen. 391 and 22 Comp. Gen. 832 are hereby modified.

On the other hand, insurance is not the only feature offered by registered mail since it also provides "added protection for valuable and important mail plus evidence of mailing and delivery." Postal Service Manual § 161.11. Thus registered mail provides "special" or "additional" service, in addition to indemnity in case of loss. In appropriate cases, the use of registered mail may enable the Government to obtain protective features not otherwise available.

Finally, the Government Losses in Shipment Act does not bar the use of registered mail since the insurance obtained through this service is only incidental to the safeguards it provides to minimize the risks of loss, damage or destruction in the shipment of valuables. See, *e.g.*, 34 Comp. Gen. 175.

Accordingly, while registered mail should not be used for the sole or primary purpose of obtaining indemnity, we conclude that neither the self-insurance rule nor the Government Losses in Shipment Act prohibits Government agencies from using registered mail as a means of safeguarding important or valuable mail, if the use of registered mail for such purpose is administratively determined to be necessary.

【 B-167553 】

Taxes—Federal Payments in Lieu of Taxes—To Units of Local Government—Deduction Propriety

Payments to units of local government under section 2(a)(1) of the Payments in Lieu of Taxes Act of 1976, 31 U.S.C. 1601–1607, are to be reduced only by the amounts of payments actually received by the units of local government under the statutes specified in section 4 of the Act, 31 U.S.C. 1604. Thus, Federal revenues paid to a State under the statutes in section 4 and distributed by the State directly to a school district without being received or acted upon by a unit of local government should not be deducted from payments to that unit of local government under section 2(a)(1) of the Act, 31 U.S.C. 1602(a)(1). Payments to other single or special purpose districts should be treated in a similar manner.

States—Federal Payments in Lieu of Taxes—Distribution to Units of Local Government

Federal revenues paid to a State under the statutes in section 4 of the Payments in Lieu of Taxes Act of 1976, 31 U.S.C. 1604, and distributed by the State to a unit of local government, which unit is required by State law to pass these revenues directly to a financially independent school district, should not be considered "received" by the unit of local government, and should not be deducted from payments to that unit of local government under section 2 of the Act, unless that unit is legally responsible for provision of school services and has collected other tax revenues for that purpose. Payments passed through to other special or single purpose districts should be treated in a similar manner.

In the matter of Computation of statutorily mandated reductions in payments in lieu of taxes, October 16, 1978:

This is in response to a request dated August 3, 1978, from the Deputy Solicitor, Department of the Interior, for a decision concerning whether payments to units of local government under the Payments in Lieu of Taxes Act of 1976, Pub. L. No. 94–565, 31 U.S.C. §§ 1601–1607 (1976), October 20, 1976, 90 Stat. 2662 (the Act) must be reduced pursuant to section 2(a)(1) of the Act, 31 U.S.C. § 1602 (a)(1), with respect to two specific kinds of payments to States.

The questions which we have been asked to decide are:

1. If Federal revenues paid to a State under one of the statutes in section 4 of the Act are distributed by the State government directly to a school district, should the Secretary deduct the amount of the revenues distributed to the school district in computing in-lieu payments to the county within which it is located?
2. If Federal revenues paid to a State under one of the statutes in section 4 of the Act are distributed by the State government to counties, but the counties are obligated under State law to pass on the revenues to school districts, should the Secretary consider the revenues to have been "received by" the counties within the meaning of section 2(a)(1) of the Act and therefore deduct that amount in computing in-lieu payments to the counties?

In fiscal year 1977 the Bureau of Land Management (BLM) answered "yes" to both questions quoted above, and certified payments under the Act, but this position has since been challenged by officials of several States. Prior to certifying payments for fiscal year 1978, the instant request was submitted by the Deputy Solicitor.

The relevant provisions of the Act state in pertinent part:

Section 1, 31 U.S.C. § 1601, provides:

Effective for fiscal years beginning on and after October 1, 1976, the Secretary is authorized and directed to make payments on a fiscal year basis to each unit of local government in which entitlement lands (as defined in section 6 [section 1606 of this title]) are located. Such payments may be used by such unit for any governmental purpose. The amount of such payments shall be computed as provided in section 2 [section 1602 of this title].

Section 2, 31 U.S.C. § 1602, states:

(a) The amount of any payment made for any fiscal year to a unit of local government under section 1 [section 1601 of this title] shall be equal to the greater of the following amounts——

(1) 75 cents for each acre of entitlement land located within the boundaries of such unit of local government (but not in excess of the population limitation determined under subsection (b)), *reduced (but not below 0) by the aggregate amount of payments, if any, received by such unit of local government during the preceding fiscal year under all of the provisions specified in section 4 [section 1604]*, or

(2) 10 cents for each acre of entitlement land located within the boundaries of such unit of local government (but not in excess of the population limitation determined under subsection (b)).

In the case of any payment under a provision specified in section 4 which is received by a State, the Governor (or his delegate) shall submit to the Secretary a statement respecting the amount of such payment which is transferred to each unit of local government within the State. [Italic supplied.]

The underscored portion of section 2 is the subject of the instant inquiry.

Section 6(c) of the Act, 31 U.S.C. § 1606(c), defines "unit of local government" as follows:

(c) "unit of local government" means a county, parish, township, municipality, borough existing in the State of Alaska on [October 20, 1976], or other unit of government below the State which is a unit of general government as determined by the Secretary (on the basis of the same principles as are used by the Bureau of the Census for general statistical purposes). Such term also includes the Commonwealth of Puerto Rico, Guam, and the Virgin Islands.

According to Department of the Interior regulations published at 42 F.R. 51580, September 29, 1977 (to be codified as 43 C.F.R. Part 1881), "unit of general government" has been defined as follows:

(b) (1) "Unit of general government" means a unit of that type of government which, within its state, is the principal provider of governmental services affecting the use of entitlement lands. Those services of government include (but are not limited to) maintenance of land records. police protection, fire protection, taxation, land use planning, search and rescue and road construction. Ordinarily, a unit of general government will be a county. However, where a smaller unit of government is the principal provider of governmental services affecting the use of public lands within a state, the smaller unit, even though within a larger unit of government, will be considered a general unit of government and will receive payments under the Act. These units of general government will ordinarily be "towns" or townships within states where county governments are nonexistent or nearly nonexistent. The term "unit of general government" also includes:

(i) Governments with the functions of a unit of general government in that state combined with another type of government such as city, township, parish, borough or county. e.g., a city and county as in the City and County of Denver.

(ii) Cities located outside of any of the units of general government for that state and administering functions commonly performed by those units of general government.

(iii) Alaskan boroughs in existence on October 20, 1976.

(iv) The Governments of the District of Columbia, Puerto Rico, Guam and the Virgin Islands.

(2) *The term "unit of general government" excludes single purpose or special purpose units of local government such as school districts or water districts.* 43 C.F.R. § 1881. 0–5 [Italic supplied.]

Question One

As stated previously, the first question asked by the Deputy Solicitor was whether payments to States under section 4 of the Act, which the State passed directly to a school district, should be deducted from section 2(a)(1) payments to a unit of local government.

BLM's decision to deduct payments made by States directly to school districts depends upon its interpretation of the intent of Congress, and on certain policy considerations. Thus, in his letter of August 3, the Deputy Solicitor stated:

The Bureau's action was based upon the following arguments:

1. The position is consistent with the intent of Congress. Departmental replies to the concerned State officials pointed out that the House report on the bill which was enacted stated that revenues from several of the statutes in section 4 must be used for schools and roads within counties, but it did not state that such payments would not be deducted simply because they were transferred directly to school districts rather than through a county to a school district. H.R. Rep. No. 94–1106, 94th Cong., 2d Sess. 14–16 (1976).

2. Not to deduct such payments would be inequitable towards States that distribute the section 4 revenues which must be used for schools by providing for their transfer to school districts through the counties in which the districts are located.

3. The purpose of the section 4 deductions would be negated if States were able to change their systems for distributing section 4 revenues so that all such revenues would be distributed to single–purpose entities such as school districts and highway commissions without any distribution to counties. The ten statutes cited in section 4 concern revenue sharing which represents a form of compensation to local governments in view of the tax-free status of federal lands. It appears that Congress, in requiring the deduction in section 2(a)(1), intended to avoid a duplicate payment to units of local government for the tax-free status of federal lands located within their boundaries. It appears, therefore, that a revenue sharing payment to a school district located within a county is tantamount to a payment to the county itself—the county receives the benefits of the payment in the same fashion as if it had received the payment itself and been required to pass it on to the school district.

He continues that:

Arguments which can be made against the Department's position are as follows:

1. School districts may be independent political entities and therefore revenue sharing payments received by them without passing through the county government are not "received by such unit of local government" (i.e., the county) as is required by section 2(a)(1). In connection with this, it should be noted that the Act requires a unit of local government to be a "unit of general government" (43 U.S.C. § 1606(c)) [sic] and the regulations implementing the Act expressly exclude school districts from the definition of "unit of general government" (43 CFR § 1881.0–5(b)(2). 42 Fed. Reg. 51581 (1977)). The words of the Act seem clear: Payments to counties are to be reduced by the amount of payments under section 4 received by *that* unit of local government.

2. The legislative history shows that Congress recognized that payments received under the statutes in section 4 would not be transferred by the State to counties in many cases, but that counties would nevertheless receive the benefits. * * *

We have analyzed the provisions of the Act and have reviewed its legislative history, and we believe that the Federal revenues paid to a State under the statutes listed in section 4 of the Act, and distributed by the State directly to a school district without being received or acted upon by a local government unit, should not be deducted from payments to that unit under section 2(a)(1) of the Act.

It is clear from the history of the Act, that the statute's primary purpose was to reimburse local governments for the direct and indirect burdens placed upon them by the presence of large amounts of Federal lands that are not subject to State or local taxation. Although Federal payments were being made to States or local governments under existing legislation out of receipts from timber, grazing, or mineral leases, Congress believed that these payments were distributed so as to provide an inequitable and inadequate share to local governments. H.R. Rep. No. 94-1106, 94th Cong., 2d Sess., 4-6.

In order to remedy the perceived inadequacies of existing statutes (which are included in the list in section 4 of the Act), the formula of section 2(a)(1) was provided for calculating payments based on the amount of entitlement lands in each unit of local government, subject to a ceiling based on population. Recognizing the potential for the duplication of payments received under the statutes listed in section 4 of the Act, the formula provides for the deduction of the "aggregate amount of payments, if any," received by the local government under these statutes, and requires the Governor of each State to submit to the Secretary of the Interior a statement respecting the amount of payment to his State under a section 4 statute "which is *transferred* to each unit of local government within the State." [Italic supplied.]

We believe that this language evidences a clear intent by the Congress to reduce section 2(a)(1) payments to local governments only by the amount of section 4 funds actually and directly received by them, as was in fact stated by both the House and the Senate Committees on Interior and Insular Affairs:

To whom should the payments be made?
Under existing programs for sharing public land revenues, the Federal government returns a percentage of revenues to the States, which are then distributed to state and local governments according to State law and the requirements of the Federal statutes. For example, while receipts from timber production and grazing on national forest lands are passed on to the counties, mineral leasing receipts are paid to the States for use for schools and roads. Some States pass on a percentage of mineral leasing receipts to counties and others do not, although there are indirect benefits to local governments from most of these funds.

H.R. 9719 requires that *any payments* under the ten statutes set forth in section 4 that *are actually received by a unit of local government arc to be deducted from payments under this Act*. The Committee realized that in most cases only a small percentage of mineral leasing revenues produced within a county are returned to that county by the State, and to preclude penalizing these counties the Committee determined that *only those monies actually received by the local government should be deducted*.

Moreover, the Committee believes that payments under H.R. 9719 should go directly to units of local government since it is the local governments that assume the burden for the tax immunity of these lands. The Committee does not believe

these new payments should be restricted or earmarked for use for specific purposes and the bill allows these payments to be used for any governmental purpose.
   It is the general purpose local governments which are the taxing authorities
and the units responsible for providing services and which should be the recipients
of these payments * * * [Italic supplied.] *Id.*, at 11–12. See also, S. Rep. No. 94–
1262, 94th Cong., 2d Sess., 15.

   Further support for this conclusion is seen in the following explanation of section 4, which is contained in the Section-by-Section
Analysis in H.R. Rep. No. 94–1106:

   Section 4 sets forth certain public laws under which units of local government
now receive a percentage of revenues from natural resource lands. These payments would not be affected by this Act. However, payments made under section
2 of this Act would be reduced by the amount of payments *actually received* by
units of local government from these programs. * * * [Italic supplied.] H.R. Rep.
No. 94–1106, at 14.

   The Deputy Solicitor has expressed concern that it might be inequitable to treat States with independent school districts differently
than States which provide such services through units of local government. He also fears that States might change their systems for
distributing section 4 revenues so that all such revenues would be distributed directly to single-purpose local governments, thereby negating the purpose of section 4. On the first point, we note that both House
and Senate Reports recognize that there are variations in the way
different States designate responsibility for various services but nevertheless chose to rely on the Secretary's discretion in defining "units of
local Government" which would be subject to the deduction provisions.
As to the second concern, if its fears materialize, the Department may
wish to bring them to the attention of the Congress for remedial action.

Question Two

   With respect to whether section 4 payments distributed by States
to units of local government to be passed by them to school districts
should be deducted from section 2(a)(1) payments, the basis stated
for BLM's deduction of these funds from local government payments
is as follows:

   The Bureau of Land Management deducted such payments in computing in-lieu
payments to counties for fiscal year 1977. The basis for this position is the express language of section 2(a)(1), requiring a reduction for section 4 federal
revenue payments "received by such unit of local government." The position has
been expressed also in paragraph 4 of the "Supplementary Information" portion
of the notice of final rulemaking for the Act. 42 Fed. Reg. 51581 (1977). The only
argument in opposition to this position appears to be that money is not actually
"received by" a county in cases where the county is legally obligated to act as a
mere conduit in passing on the funds to a school district.

   Unlike the situation described in our answer to your first question,
here section 4 payments are in fact "received by" the local governments
prior to being passed on to the school districts, and a literal reading
of the Act would require that all such sums be deleted from payments
to units of local government. We do not believe, however, that this

literal approach would carry out the intent of Congress that only those funds actually received by and available to local governments to carry out their own responsibilities be deducted from section 2 payments to these general government entities.

The concern that local governments were not receiving sufficient funds under existing legislation to meet their legitimate, varied needs was included in the list of shortcomings of section 4 funding contained in the Senate report on H.R. 9719, the bill that was enacted as the Payments in Lieu of Taxes Act:

(4) The percentages of revenues and fees shared under the various provisions of law are not based on any rational criteria. As a result they vary from 5 to 90 percent, depending on the program and agency involved.

(5) Even in the few instances when a local government's share of the various revenues and fees is sufficient to meet service demands arising from the Federal lands and to approximate the loss of ad valorem tax revenues which would otherwise be generated by those lands, too many of the revenue sharing provisions restrict the use of funds to only a few governmental services—most often the construction and maintenance of roads and schools. Yet, local governments are called upon to provide many other services to the Federal lands or as a direct or indirect result of activities on the Federal lands. These services include law enforcement; search, rescue and emergency; public health; sewage disposal; library; hospital; recreation; and other general local government services. It is only the most fortunate of local governments which is able to juggle its budget to make use of those earmarked funds in a manner which will accurately correspond to its community's service and facility needs.

(6) Many of the revenue sharing provisions permit the States to make the decisions on how the funds will be distributed. In far too many States, the result has been that the funds are either kept at the State level and not distributed to local governments at all or are parcelled out in a manner which provides shares to local governments other than those in which the Federal lands are situated and where the impacts of the revenue and fee generating activities are felt. S. Rep. No. 94–1262, at 9.

From this language it is obvious that the Congress was concerned that section 2(a)(1) funds should be distributed to the local governments, who then were to make the necessary decisions on how to distribute them to meet their internal needs. We can find no support in the Act, the Committee reports, or the floor debates to lend credence to BLM's view that payments "received by such units of local goverment" means something less than "actually received by" such units and available to them for obligation and expenditure to carry out their own responsibilities, thereby reducing the financial burdens caused by inadequate tax revenues due to the tax-exempt status of Federal lands in their geographical area. For this reason, we do not believe that Congress intended payments to local governments under the Act to be reduced by amounts that, by virtue of State law, merely pass through these governments on their way to politically and financially independent school districts which alone are responsible for providing the services in question.

On the other hand, where a local government serving as a "conduit" for section 4 revenues is, by State law, responsible for providing school services and collects taxes from local residents for that purpose, we believe Congress intended that the local government's section 2 payments should be reduced by the amount of section 4 revenues passed through to the schools, since in the absence of the in-lieu payments, the total costs of providing these services would be borne by the local unit's tax revenues. Other single purpose districts would normally be treated in the same manner.

The questions submitted are answered accordingly.

〔 B–191861 〕

Compensation—Periodic Step–Increases—Eligibility

Pursuant to Public Law 94–484, health professionals are appointed in the National Health Service Corps for short-term employment in designated health manpower shortage areas. Such employees are given excepted appointments of not more than 4 years under civil service regulations. They are eligible for within-grade salary increases under 5 U.S.C. 5335 on same basis as term employees. See B–164031(4).50, October 26, 1972.

In the matter of National Health Service Corps Civilian Employees—Within-Grade Salary Increases, October 20, 1978:

The Department of Health, Education and Welfare (HEW) through its Acting Assistant Secretary for Personnel Administration, has requested our opinion as to whether certain employees appointed to the National Health Service Corps are eligible for within-grade salary increases under 5 U.S.C. 5335 (1976).

The Health Professions Educational Assistance Act of 1976, Public Law 94–484, 90 Stat. 2243, 42 U.S. Code 201 note, established, within the Public Health Service, the National Health Service Corps consisting of certain regular and reserve officers of the Public Health Service, and other civilian personnel appointed by the Secretary of HEW. These civilian employees, which include nurses, medical social workers, speech and hearing specialists, and physicians, are given Schedule A excepted service appointments for periods not to exceed 4 years pursuant to 5 C.F.R. 213.3116(b)(10) (1978). The length of their appointment is based on the needs of the Public Health Service, the length of Government-supported training, and the matched interest of the individual and the host community.

Under 5 U.S.C. 5335 (1976) an employee paid on an annual basis and occupying a permanent position within the General Schedule is entitled to within-grade salary increases in pay. A "permanent position" is defined by 5 C.F.R. 531.402(d) (1978) as "one filled on a permanent basis, that is an appointment not designated as temporary by law and not having a definite time limitation." Since positions in the National Health Service Corps are limited to no more than 4 years such positions are not considered "permanent" as defined in 5 C.F.R.

531.402(d). However, 5 C.F.R. 316.305 provides that term employees (those appointed under certain circumstances for a period of more than 1 year but not more than 4 years) are eligible for within-grade salary increases.

In our decision B-164031, October 26, 1972, we held that hearing examiners appointed pursuant to the authority contained in the Supplemental Appropriation Act, 1972, Public Law 92-184, 85 Stat. 627, were eligible for within-grade salary increases. We based our holding on the fact that 5 C.F.R. 316.305 (1972) authorized within-grade salary increases for term employees appointed pursuant to 5 C.F.R. 316.301 (1972). Although the hearing examiners in question were appointed pursuant to Public Law 92-184 and not 5 C.F.R. 316.301, we held there was no reason to deny them within-grade increases since the type of appointment given and the basis for the time limitations applied were similar under both authorities. In both instances appointments were for not more than 4 years and the need for such employees was for a limited period. For similar reasons we believe that civilian employees of the National Health Service Corps appointed for not more than 4 years are eligible for within-grade salary increases during their period of appointment.

[B-192061]

Contracts—Protests—Procedures—Bid Protest Procedures—Time for Filing—"Adverse Agency Action" Effect

Protest filed with General Accounting Office (GAO) more than 10 working days after receipt by protester of notice that another firm has been selected for award, despite pending protest filed with agency, is untimely since selection constituted adverse agency action as defined in GAO Bid Protest Procedures.

Contracts—Protests—Withdrawal—Oral—Protests Filed With Agency—Written Confirmation/Acknowledgment Recommended

Where written protest filed with agency is orally withdrawn, agency should seek written confirmation from protester or should, in writing, acknowledge withdrawal. In absence of such a writing in the record, GAO cannot resolve dispute concerning alleged oral withdrawal of protest.

In the matter of Sono-Tek Corporation, October 20, 1978:

Sono-Tek Corporation (Sono-Tek) protests the award of a contract by Brookhaven National Laboratory (Brookhaven) to Foster-Miller Associates, Inc. (Foster) under request for proposals (RFP) No. CPT 78-1 for the development of heating equipment.

Brookhaven is a Federally owned facility operated by Associated Universities, Inc. under prime management contract No. EY-76-C-02-0016 with the U.S. Department of Energy (DOE). This Office does not ordinarily review the award of subcontracts by Government prime contractors, except in limited circumstances. *See Optimum Systems,*

Inc., 54 Comp. Gen. 767 (1975), 75–1 CPD 166. One of the exceptions to our general policy is those awards made "for" DOE by prime management contractors who operate and manage DOE facilities. *See Cohu, Inc.*, B–191264, September 6, 1978, 57 Comp. Gen. 759, 78–2 CPD 175; *Fiber Materials, Inc.*, 57 Comp. Gen. 527 (1978), 78–1 CPD 422. Since Brookhaven is operated "for" DOE, the protest falls within our subcontract award review policy. It is, however, untimely.

The RFP was issued on November 15, 1977, with February 6, 1978, as the closing date for receipt of proposals. Proposal evaluation results showed that out of seven offerors, Foster scored highest with 815 points out of a possible 1,000 points and Sono-Tek scored fourth with 589 points. Brookhaven's evaluation panel recommended Foster for award in a report dated March 3, 1978. By letter of April 3, Sono-Tek filed a protest with DOE, objecting to the proposed award and alleging that a "covert relationship" existed between Foster and "certain key" employees of Brookhaven and that Brookhaven's evaluation panel lacked the technical competency essential for proper evaluation of the proposals. DOE forwarded the protest to Brookhaven.

The DOE Brookhaven Area Office contends that on April 14, 1978, one day after it received Sono-Tek's protest, it was telephonically advised by Sono-Tek that the letter was not to be considered a protest. Brookhaven further contends that it therefore advised Sono-Tek that it would proceed with the award in light of the withdrawal. Sono-Tek, however, contends that it did not rescind its written protest and believed that the protest was being considered.

By letter of April 28, 1978, Brookhaven advised Sono-Tek of the proposed award to Foster. On May 24, Sono-Tek received a copy of a May 19 letter from DOE to a Congressman which indicated that the Sono-Tek protest was not being considered in light of the alleged telephonic withdrawal. Sono-Tek contends that this was its first notice of Brookhaven's action on its protest. Sono-Tek filed its protest with this Office on June 2, 1978.

Section 20.2(a) of our Bid Protest Procedures, 4 C.F.R. 20.2(a) (1978), states:

> If a protest has been filed initially with the contracting agency, any subsequent protest to the General Accounting Office filed within 10 days of * * * initial adverse agency action will be considered * * *.

Adverse agency action is defined as any action or inaction which is prejudicial to the position taken in a protest filed with an agency. 4 C.F.R. 20.0(b). The Procedures further provide that in cases where a protest has not been filed with the contracting agency, a protest must be filed with this Office within 10 days of the protester's learning of the grounds for protest. *See* 4 C.F.R. 20.2(b)(2).

Under DOE's version of the facts, there was in effect no protest filed with it, so that in accordance with 4 C.F.R. 20.2(b)(2), Sono-Tek's protest here would be untimely because Sono-Tek clearly knew of its grounds for protest not later than April 3, some 2 months prior to the filing of its protest with this Office.

The protest is also untimely under Sono-Tek's version of the facts, since we believe it received notice of "initial adverse agency action" on its protest when it received Brookhaven's April 28 letter advising of the selection of a firm to provide the required services and requesting disposition instructions for Sono-Tek's proposal. Sono-Tek asserts that the letter should not be regarded as notice of adverse agency action because 1) the notice of contractor selection does not imply "that an award had been made or was in the process of being made"; 2) Sono-Tek believed its protest was still pending; and 3) it regarded the agency making award as DOE and not Brookhaven. We find these reasons to be without merit.

Adverse agency action need not be an actual award. As indicated above, adverse agency action is any action which is prejudicial to the protester's position, such as the opening of bids, 52 Comp. Gen. 821 (1973), or "the rejection of a bid despite the pendency of a protest * * *." 4 C.F.R. 20.0(b). Here, of course, Sono-Tek was clearly placed on notice that its proposal had been rejected despite what it claims to have viewed as its still pending protest. Moreover, Sono-Tek knew both from the solicitation itself and from Brookhaven's April 28 letter that it was Brookhaven as prime contractor and not DOE that was conducting the procurement and awarding the contract.

Sono-Tek also submits that if its protest is regarded as untimely, it should be considered "for good cause shown" as provided in 4 C.F.R. 20.2(c). The "good cause" exception to our timeliness rules is limited to circumstances where some compelling reason beyond the protester's control prevents the filing of timely protest. 52 Comp. Gen. 20 (1972). We find nothing in the record to warrant invoking this exception. *Hammer Security Service of California, Inc.—Reconsideration*, B–190056, April 4, 1978, 78–1 CPD 265.

Although it does not affect the outcome here, we are concerned over DOE's willingness to act on the basis of an oral withdrawal of a written protest. Oral communications often give rise to differing understandings as to exactly what was said or intended, and as a result we believe all matters of significance should be reduced to writing. When they are not, generally we are unable to resolve disputes concerning alleged oral statements. For example, when a protestor asserts that it filed an oral protest with an agency but the agency denies it, we have been unable to conclude that in fact the oral protest had been made. *See, e.g., Marion Health and Safety, Inc.*, B–186451, August 3, 1976,

76–2 CPD 121; *Continental Electronics Corp.*, B–183891, June 23, 1976, 76–1 CPD 399. Similarly, in the situation presented in this case, we would be unable to conclude that there was an oral withdrawal of the written protest without some written confirmation in the record. This confirmation could take the form of a letter from the agency to the protester acknowledging the oral withdrawal. The latter, of course, would serve to place the protester on notice of the agency's interpretation of the oral conversation.

The protest is dismissed.

〔B–193052〕

Contracts—Payments—Advance—Prohibition—Applicability

Payments to State under Federal contract for telephone services, executed by contracting officer of the United States and obligating annual appropriations of National Guard, are subject to statutory prohibition against advance payments contained in 31 U.S.C. 529.

Telephones—Contract for Services—Federal-State Agreements—Advance Payments—Legality

Advance payment of capital cost of telephone equipment under contract for telephone services with State would be in violation of 31 U.S.C. 529, even though a State is the recipient, since services to be provided by State are commercial in nature.

In the matter of National Guard Bureau—Request for Advance Decision, October 20, 1978:

By letter dated September 25, 1978, the Chief, National Guard Bureau (NGB), of the Departments of the Army and the Air Force, has requested our decision as to the legality of making certain advance payments for telephone communication services under proposed contracts ("Federal-State Agreements") with various State governments.

NGB has provided the following background information to our Office:

Typically, the USPFO [United States Property and Fiscal Officer] and the State Adjutant General enter into a Federal-State Agreement for telephone services to be funded by Federal annual Operations and Maintenance funds. * * * Then, pursuant to the Federal-State Agreement, the State enters into a second contract with a telephone company for the phone services. Until recently, the payments to the telephone companies have been on a monthly basis after the services have been received. However, the telephone companies have developed a new leasing scheme whereby monthly charges may be greatly reduced (typically by 12 per cent) if the State pays the telephone company's (lessor's) entire capital costs for equipment at *commencement of the lease.* * * *

This leasing arrangement of the telephone equipment is called "tier-pricing," and, as explained in our decision in *General Telephone Company of California,* 57 Comp. Gen. 89 (1977), 77–2 CPD 376, consists of the following:

The Tier Pricing concept of rate making essentially divides the total cost of providing service into the categories of capital recovery [basic charge or] Tier A, generally considered fixed costs, and on going operating costs Tier B, such as maintenance and administration which are considered variable.

This leasing method requires the lessee to pay, upon completion of installation of the telephone equipment, a basic charge which represents the entire capital recovery costs for the equipment installed under the lease. The lessee acquires no legal or equitable interest in the title to the equipment, having at most the limited right to physical possession for a period of years. The lessee also has no interest in the residual value of the equipment whether or not services are maintained for the full term of the lease or upon its conclusion.

Relevant provisions of the proposed "Federal-State Agreements" are as follows:

This Agreement by and between the United States of America hereinafter called the GOVERNMENT, represented by the Contracting Officer executing this Agreement, and the State of _____, hereinafter called the STATE, covering the telephone communications service at _____ Military Department Complex in said State with the assistance of funds appropriated by the Congress of the United States for the GOVERNMENT contribution to the cost of said service.

Whereas, it has been determined that it would be in the best interest of the GOVERNMENT and the STATE to upgrade and improve the telephone communications system at _____ Military Department Complex to provide a level of service which meets current and foreseeable future requirements;

Whereas, the GOVERNMENT has indicated its intent to pay the cost of the required commercial telephone equipment and facilities; and

Whereas, pursuant to existing GOVERNMENT directives, it is necessary that an Agreement governing joint utilization of the telephone system be entered into before funding assistance may be provided.

NOW, THEREFORE, in consideration of the mutual promises and undertakings of the parties, hereinafter set forth, it is hereby agreed as follows:

ARTICLE 1. The STATE Agrees:

1. To submit to the GOVERNMENT, for review and approval, plans and cost estimates for the installation of a Dimension 400 PBX system complete with all allied equipment and options to meet GOVERNMENT requirements.

2. To contract all work, material, and services required to carry out this Agreement.

3. To contract in accordance with the laws of such STATE, and under those regulations within the Armed Services Procurement Regulation which are applicable to Federally-assisted programs. All such contracts and change orders and contract modifications shall be subject to prior approval by the GOVERNMENT.

4. To permit inspection of the system by representatives of the GOVERNMENT.

5. To supervise and be responsible for the continued provision of service authorized under this Agreement.

6. To furnish certificates and invoices, satisfactory to the GOVERNMENT, for the GOVERNMENT's cost of service as set forth in Appendix "A" of this Agreement.

7. To maintain an accounting system for the total cost of the system acceptable to the GOVERNMENT.

8. The STATE agrees that in return for funds paid to it by the GOVERNMENT, it shall be monetarily accountable and shall reimburse the GOVERNMENT a proportionate share of the funds expended for capital equipment in the event the telephone company fails or refuses to provide the subject services. That is to say, the term of the Agreement years shall be divided into the capital investment and this amount shall be multiplied times the remaining years of the contract term at that time when the telephone company fails or refuses to provide communication services and this amount shall be reimbursed to the FEDERAL GOVERNMENT.

ARTICLE II.   The GOVERNMENT Agrees:

  1. To contribute Federal funds, subject to the availability of such funds, to support the initial installation of the system, all AUTOVON charges, all recurring and toll charges except those recurring and toll charges incident to Training Site and Service Contract administration and charges of any nature that are funded through Inter Service Support Agreements or funded from other than Federally appropriated funds.

  2. To make payment direct to the commercial communications carrier all costs incurred by the State in furnishing such services, supplies and equipment under this agreement. Further, it is the mutual intent of the parties that at that time when the STATE has incurred these costs the Federal grants funds shall be deemed STATE funds subject to STATE laws and regulations pertinent thereto.

Appendix A of the contract contains the "Tier A" capital recovery expenses for the equipment allocable to and payable by the Government.

Advance payments generally are prohibited by the provisions of 31 U.S.C. § 529 (1970), which provides as follows:

  No advance of public money shall be made in any case unless authorized by the appropriation concerned or other law. And in all cases of contracts for the performance of any service, or the delivery of articles of any description, for the use of the United States, payment shall not exceed the value of the service rendered, or of the articles delivered previously to such payment. * * *

As NGB acknowledges, we held in *General Telephone Company*, *supra*, specifically with regard to telephone communication service "tier-pricing," that "any leasing scheme which obligates the Government to pay the contractor's entire capital cost at the outset of the lease is contrary to the statutory limitations of 31 U.S.C. § 529."

NGB, however, advances two lines of reasoning to support the conclusion that the "Federal-State Agreements" do not violate the prohibition against advance payments. First, it is argued that the "Federal funds pass to the State and become State funds prior to, or concurrent with, the payments to the telephone company [and thus] State, not Federal law, governs these expenditures." Second, the fact that a State, and not a private contractor, is the recipient of these advance payments in this case is urged as a distinguishing feature.

With regard to NGB's first argument, we stated in 42 Comp. Gen. 631 (1963):

  Article I, section 8, of the United States Constitution confers on the Congress the power to provide for the organizing, arming, and disciplining the militia, and for governing such part of them as may be employed in the service of the United States, reserving to the States, respectively, the appointment of the officers and the authority of training the militia according to the discipline prescribed by Congress. In conformity with that authority Congress has enacted laws providing for the supplies necessary to uniform, arm, and equip the National Guard, and has provided funds for that purpose by annual appropriations.

In this case, as there, the moneys so appropriated by Congress are being disbursed by a finance officer of the United States pursuant to Federal statutes and regulations. The purchase by the United States of the telephone communication services from the State, acting through its subcontractors, is to be consummated under a Federal contract executed by a contracting officer of the United States, and payment is to be effected by a check drawn on and paid by the Treasurer of the United States from funds on deposit in the United States Treasury. Such contractual payments by the United States from Federal annual appropriations for National Guard operations and activities are not grants to the State. See 42 Comp. Gen., *supra.* Rather, as the contract is for the use of the United States, obligating appropriated funds of the United States, 31 U.S.C. § 529, by its very terms, is controlling since the "Federal-State Agreements" would bind the United States to an advance of Federal public moneys to a contractor, a State government, for the performance of a service. In view thereof, it cannot be said that the appropriated funds allocated for the operation of the National Guard are not subject to the statutory prohibition against advance of public moneys contained in 31 U.S.C. § 529.

Secondly, NGB questions whether, in view of the fact that a State is the proposed recipient of the advance payments, "is this not an authorized exception to 31 U.S.C. § 529, based on the rationale of the decision in 57 Comp. Gen. 399 (1978) and the prior decisions cited therein?" In that case, we held that advance payments to a State for rental of State-owned land was not in contravention of the prohibition against advance payments in 31 U.S.C. § 529 since a State was the recipient. An examination of that decision, however, along with the others cited therein, reveals that this exception to the prohibition against advance payments has only been invoked where the State was furnishing noncommercial services reasonably available only from the State. 39 Comp. Gen. 285 (1959) (sewer service charge) ; B–118846, March 29, 1954 (expenses of State Water Commissioner administering Indian irrigation project pursuant to court order) ; B–109485, July 22, 1952 (repair, operation, and maintenance of roads in conjunction with permanent transfer of Federal roads to County) ; B–65821, May 29, 1947 (State court fees and other items of expenses required to litigate in State courts in compliance with the requirements of State law) ; B–36099, August 14, 1943 (lease of State lands) ; and B–35670, July 19, 1943 (State forest fire prevention and suppression services). We have never applied this exception to situations where the proposed services to be contracted for and provided by a State are generally and commercially available in the marketplace. We do not believe that such an extension of this exception is warranted or justified. If a State, as a contractor, enters the domain of commerce, by proposing to provide services that are freely and readily available in the commercial marketplace, it must also be subject to the same laws governing private providers of such services.

Accordingly, the advance payments may not be made for the leasing of the telephone services in question.

[B–191806]

Contracts—Protests—Timeliness—Filing in Other Than General Accounting Office—Agency Consideration of Untimely Protest—Dismissal by GAO

Procuring agency's consideration on the merits of protest not filed within the time limits established by General Accounting Office's (GAO) Bid Protest Procedures does not preclude GAO from dismissing protest when subsequently filed with it. Protest of cancellation of IFB initially filed with procuring agency more than 10 working days after protester knew the basis therefor, but filed with GAO 4 days after agency's denial of protest, is dismissed.

In the matter of Virginia Abrasives Corporation, October 23, 1978:

On January 19, 1978, the General Services Administration (GSA) issued invitation for bids (IFB) No. CHN–FT–78–028 for 54 items of coated abrasives. The procurement was totally set aside for those firms which qualified as labor surplus area (LSA) concerns "at the time of bid opening and time of award" either by submitting with their bids evidence that they were "certified eligibile" by the Department of Labor (DOL) or by agreeing to substantially perform the contract in areas designated as "labor surplus" by the DOL as of the proposed date of award. In the latter instance, the bidder was required to identify in its bid the geographical areas in which it proposed to perform the contract.

At the time of issuance of the IFB, DOL had identified 1,171 geographical areas as eligible for LSA set-aside consideration. Virginia Abrasives Corporation (VAC), along with four other bidders, bid upon 17 items (1–5, 9–12, 13–15, 17–18 and 22–24). VAC's bid did not contain evidence of certification and the designated production area, Petersburg, Virginia, had not been classified as a labor surplus area by DOL. Thus VAC was determined to be ineligible for award. One other bidder was also ineligible for award as it provided neither a certification nor did it designate where the work would be done. Of the three remaining bidders one, Industrial Abrasives Co. (IAC), was initially eligible since it submitted evidence that it had been "certified eligible" by DOL. However as a result of the change in regulations described below it too became ineligible.

On the same day that bids were opened in the instant case, DOL published new regulations governing eligibility for LSA set-asides superseding the previous regulations contained in 29 Code of Federal Regulations (CFR) Part 8. The new regulation reduced the number of eligible LSA's from 1,171 to 453. The new regulations also removed the certification program upon which IAC had solely relied to qualify pursuant to the terms of the IFB. Thus, although IAC would have been an eligible bidder at the time of bid opening it could not have been an eligible bidder at the time of award, i.e., on or after March 3, 1978, since in accordance with the IFB provisions, it had to qualify as a labor surplus area concern at time of award.

The remaining two bidders were eligible for award since both had designated areas which were on the old and new lists of labor surplus areas. However, neither of these bidders bid on one item and only one of them bid on four other items at prices averaging 36 percent higher than the previous year's contract. On the remaining 12 items, the low eligible bid ranged from three to 35 percent higher than the previous year's contract.

In view of the effect which the new DOL regulations had upon competition, the contracting officer cancelled the set-aside IFB and resolicited on an unrestricted basis. VAC, the low bidder for these 17 items, protested the cancellation to GSA.

VAC has not disputed the contracting officer's assertions that three of the five bidders (including VAC) were not eligible for award under the original solicitation and that the prices offered by the two remaining eligible bidders averaged 20 percent higher than the previous year's contract. VAC's primary desire appears to be to protect its low bid from competition upon resolicitation: it suggested to GSA that "the award be based on the prices as originally submitted by all companies." (In fact, upon resolicitation, VAC was underbid by IAC, whose prices were on the average 2 percent lower than the previous year's contract.)

GSA has argued that not only was the cancellation of the IFB and resolicitation a proper exercise of discretion, but that VAC's protest of the cancellation of the original solicitation was untimely. We agree.

VAC received notice of the cancellation of the solicitation on March 27, 1978, and protested to the agency by letter dated April 11, 1978. The agency denied VAC's protest by letter dated April 19, 1978. Within 4 days of its receipt of this letter, VAC filed a protest with our Office.

Section 20.2(a) of our Bid Protest Procedures, 4 C.F.R. part 20 (1977), provides that when a protester initially files its protest with the contracting agency, that protest must be timely filed. In this case, the applicable period for timely filing, as noted in section 20.2(b)(2), is within 10 working days after the basis for protest is known. VAC knew of the basis for its protest on March 27, 1978, but did not send its letter of protest to the agency until April 11, 1978, or more than 10 working days after the basis of the protest was known. Consequently, VAC's protest to our Office is untimely.

VAC argues that since GSA responded to its protest on the merits, despite its untimeliness, our timeliness rules have in effect been waived. However, a procuring agency cannot waive the procedures established by our Office which govern our consideration of bid protests. Therefore, an agency's consideration on the merits of a protest not filed within the time limits established by our procedures does not preclude our later dismissal of a protest filed with us. We also note that the circumstances of this case are similar to those in *Western Filament Inc.*, B–192148, September 25, 1978, 78–2 CPD 226, in which we upheld an agency's cancellation of an IFB and resolicitation following the March 3, 1978 change in labor surplus policy.

[B–191130]

Contracts—Data, Rights, etc.—Status of Information Furnished-— Unsolicited Proposals—Value Engineering Proposals

Claimant's unsolicited value engineering proposal recommending that Defense Logistics Agency require the faucets it procures be constructed of zinc-based material constitutes mere suggestion and is not within the exclusive list of intellectual property which can be purchased by the Department of Defense under 10 U.S.C. 2386 (1976).

Estoppel—Against Government—Not Established

Since agency officials had no authority to contract for purchase of suggestion, doctrine of estoppel is not for application.

In the matter of Claim of A Better Way, Inc., October 24, 1978:

A Better Way, Inc. (ABW) has submitted claims for $25,896.90 and $3,500 for several unsolicited Value Engineering (VE) proposals which were submitted by ABW under the provisions of Armed Services Procurement Regulation (ASPR) (now Defense Acquisition Regulation (DAR)) § 1–1708 (1976 ed.). The case turns on whether the Court of Claims' decision in *Grismac Corporation* v. *United States*, 556 F.2d 494 (Ct. Cl. 1977) is controlling.

On May 20, 1976 ABW began submitting to the Defense Logistics Agency (DLA) the first of several unsolicited VE proposals. All except one of them deal with the material used in fabricating faucet handles used on lavatories and sinks purchased by DLA.

At that time, DAR/ASPR 1–1708 (1976 ed.) provided for consideration of an unsolicited VE proposal with regard to a supply or service for which the proposer company did not have a current contract. Such proposals under the regulation must have provided for reduction of costs without impairing essential functions or characteristics of the supply or service. The Government could purchase an unsolicited VE proposal; however, the contract price could not exceed 20 percent of the savings.

To date, DLA has accepted and contracted for three of ABW's unsolicited VE proposals covering sinks or faucets under four National Stock Numbers (NSN). The instant claims arise out of three VE proposals dated March 18, 1977, and one dated July 8, 1976, concerning sinks or faucets under four other NSN's.

ABW's VE proposals concerned the fact that DLA's purchase descriptions required that faucet handles be made of chrome-plated brass. ABW proposed that chrome-plated zinc alloy faucet handles would meet the Government's minimum needs; foster more competition due to the nonavailability of brass to some lavatory suppliers; and reduce the costs of the faucets significantly. ABW's proposals are grounded on the fact that the plumbing industry has long recognized the interchangeability of brass and zinc alloy in faucet handles. The Federal Specifications, under which purchase descriptions were issued, merely allowed, but did not require, zinc alloy to be substituted for brass on a procurement by procurement basis. Consequently, the effect of ABW's proposals was to have the Government make mandatory what had been a permissive use of zinc alloy for faucet handles.

DLA initially rejected ABW's three VE proposals of March 18 because the agency determined that its earlier acceptance and purchase of similar VE proposals from ABW regarding the material to be used in faucet handles entitled it to use the idea for other faucets in the supply system. The agency changed that determination when it was informed by ABW that it had been advised by a DLA VE official to submit separate VE proposals for each NSN item affected. DLA then proceeded to evaluate the proposals. DLA finally rejected the VE proposals by letter dated November 29, 1977, which indicated that in view of the *Grismac* decision handed down on May 18, 1977, DLA had no legal authority for compensating persons for suggestions made.

ABW's July 8, 1976 VE proposal was ultimately rejected for the same reason. However, prior to DLA's January 24, 1978 rejection of the VE proposal, DLA discovered that management authority for the item affected had been transferred to the General Services Administration (GSA). It is reported that GSA takes the position that it has no authority to compensate anyone for an unsolicited VE proposal and suggests that DLA pay ABW.

In reports submitted to this Office in connection with the March 18 and July 8 VE proposals the contracting officer takes the position that ABW's claims not be paid in both instances because DLA lacks the authority to pay for unsolicited ideas. In the case of the July 8 proposal, rejection of the claim is also urged because the actual benefit, if any, was bestowed upon GSA rather than DLA. In connection with the March 18 proposals the contracting officer maintains that DLA had a right to use this idea because it had been purchased under earlier VE proposals from ABW. DLA Headquarters takes the position that the claims must be decided without the benefit of *Grismac* v. *United States, supra,* because that case was decided under an earlier version of DAR/ASPR 1–1708 (1976).

The first issue to be decided is whether *Grismac* is applicable here, because, as DLA points out, the DAR/ASPR provision which was interpreted and applied in *Grismac* was an earlier version and not the same as DAR/ASPR 1–1708 (1976 ed.). It is our view, as discussed below, that *Grismac* was decided on a ground which makes the DAR/ASPR provision immaterial.

In *GKS, Inc.*, B–187593, June 26, 1978, 78–1 CPD 461, we considered the rationale on which *Grismac* was decided. We held that the court relied on the prohibition implicit in 10 U.S.C. § 2386 (1976) that only intellectual property specified in that section could be purchased with appropriated funds. 10 U.S.C. § 2386 (1976) allows Department of Defense officials to purchase the following types of intellectual property:

*   *   *   *   *   *   *

"(1) Copyrights. patents, and applications for patents.
"(2) Licenses under copyrights, patents, and applications for patents.
"(3) Designs, processes, and manufacturing data.
"(4) Releases before suit is brought, for past infringement of patents or copyrights."

Both Grismac's and GKS' proposals were held to be outside the scope of 10 U.S.C. § 2386 (1976), because they were actually suggestions and not classifiable as copyrights, patents, designs, processes, or manufacturing data. Grismac, for example, had recommended various changes in the size and grade of plywood used in wooden pallets serving as bases for storing and handling boxed ammunition. We find that the proposals made by ABW in this case to be mere suggestions and also not within the rubric of 10 U.S.C. § 2386 (1976).

However, DLA maintains that the provisions of DAR/ASPR 1–1708 (1976 ed.) (this section has been deleted by Defense Procurement Circular 76–9, August 30, 1977) which specifically provided for the submission of unsolicited VE proposals supplies the regulatory authority for payment which was lacking when the *Grismac* case was decided. The regulation in effect during *Grismac* merely provided that unsolicited proposals could be purchased on a case by case basis in accordance with 10 U.S.C. § 2386 or Part 9 of ASPR, (a section which concerned rights in technical data).

We do not believe that the existence of DAR/ASPR 1–1708 (1976 ed.) has any effect on the *Grismac* holding. Although the court searched the regulations for provisions which could be interpreted as permitting the purchase of unsolicited ideas, the decision was firmly based on 10 U.S.C. § 2386 (1976) which, of course, supersedes any inconsistent regulation purporting to govern this subject. In this regard the court states in pertinent part:

The trial judge does not advert in his opinion to § 2386 (though it is mentioned in the findings). He deduces authority to contract, which implicitly he agrees is necessary if plaintiff is to recover, from a melange of ASPR provisions. Should statutory authority be lacking, ASPR could hardly supply it, but no doubt a long established ASPR provision interpreting a statute would aid us in construing that statute should we find an ambiguity. * * * *Id.* at 498

Although DAR/ASPR 1–1708 (1976 ed.) did provide a more elaborate scheme for the submission and approval of unsolicited VE proposals, it does not specifically provide that mere suggestions which do not meet the criteria set forth in 10 U.S.C. § 2386 (1976) could be purchased by the agency. It is clear, therefore, that the *Grismac* case, which holds that 10 U.S.C. § 2386 (1976) prohibits Defense Agencies from expending appropriated funds for the purchase of suggestions, governs this matter despite the existence of DAR/ASPR 1–1708 (1976 ed.). See *Grismac, supra.*

As in this case, the protester in *GKS, supra,* argued that the Government was estopped to deny the existence of an agreement to pay the company for its VE proposal. In that case, we stated that the protester, in order to establish an estoppel, had to meet the threshold requirement that the agreement to be established must be within the scope of the authority of the responsible Government officials. *Emeco Industries, Inc.* v. *United States,* 485 F. 2d 652 (Ct. Cl. 1963). As the court stated in *Grismac, supra,* at page 499 :

* * * Defendant's officials, high or low in the Department of Defense, did not have authority to make express contracts obligating appropriated funds for the purchase of suggestions * * *.

Accordingly, a case for estoppel cannot be made in this instance. The claims are therefore denied.

〔 B–191949 〕

General Accounting Office—Jurisdiction—Contracts—Options

Rule that General Accounting Office (GAO) will not question under Bid Protest Procedures manner of exercise of option applies only to protest filed by incumbent contractor complaining that option in its contract should have been exercised. Protest by firm interested in competing for requirement covered by contract option will be considered.

Contracts—Options—Not to be Exercised—Requirements to be Resolicited

Where purchase option price was not evaluated in awarding initial contract but added by subsequent contract modification, procedures followed in exercising purchase option should comport as much as possible with competitive procurement norm. Interested suppliers should be afforded adequate notice and fair opportunity to have products and prices evaluated and normally this should be accomplished through competitive procurement.

Procurement—Solicitation for Informational Purposes—Demonstration Tests—Unduly Restrictive of Competition—Computers, etc. Acquisition

Procedures established for potential suppliers to demonstrate equipment were unduly restrictive because agency made no apparent effort either to examine whether acceptability of equipment could be established through simulation testing techniques as requested by protester or to attempt to provide access to Government equipment to facilitate testing. GAO recommends that protester be permitted to show acceptability of equipment, particularly in view of alleged successful performance of recent similar contract with other agency.

In the matter of KET, Incorporated, October 27, 1978:

KET, Incorporated protests the issuance and terms of a notice issued by the Internal Revenue Service (IRS) and published in the Commerce Business Daily (CBD) seeking firms willing to perform a demonstration test of plug-to-plug memory equipment compatible with central processing units (CPU) in operation at the IRS.

The May 3, 1978, CBD notice read as follows:

70—MEMORY, compatible with Control Data Corporation (CDC) 3500 CPU, [in accordance with] the following requirements:
1. Proposed memory must be plug-to-plug compatible with existing CDC 3500 CPU's. No software or hardware changes, however minor, will be allowed.
2. Proposed memory must be demonstrated at a site other than the IRS by 1 Jul 78, and the demonstration test must be conducted on a CDC Model 3514–4 CPU. The Government shall be provided sufficient documentation on the program(s) (*e.g.*, source listings) to determine the validity of the demonstration test. Further, offerors shall provide copies of the program(s) to the Government for the purpose of conducting a "head-to-head" test between the respondent's memory and the existing CDC memory.
3. Respondents * * * will be required to develop test program(s) which * * * produce hardcopy output which will enable the Government to determine memory timing/throughput rates.

    *   *   *   *   *   *   *

The request is for information and planning purposes only. The Government does not intend to award a contract on the basis of this request, nor will the Government pay for information provided in response to this request.

This matter is the subject of a suit filed by KET in the Federal District Court for the District of Columbia, in which KET seeks to enjoin the IRS from awarding any contract for or exercising existing options to purchase CDC 3500 memory except upon the basis of a fully competitive solicitation for such memory. A temporary restraining order, preventing the Government from proceeding in this matter before October 30, 1978, or until the matter could be earlier considered, was issued by the United States Court of Appeals for the District of Columbia. The case is for consideration under § 20.10 of our Bid Protest Procedures, upon requests for our opinion by both the District Court and Court of Appeals. *See, e.g., Dominion Engineering Works, Ltd., et al.*, B–186543, October 8, 1976, 76–2 CPD 324.

By way of background we note that KET previously protested sole source procurement from CDC for various equipments but has been frustrated in its attempts to compete for IRS's requirements. In denying a prior protest by KET we took special note of IRS's advice "that it is making every reasonable effort to minimize the competitive advantage which CDC may enjoy on the follow-on solicitation." We have assumed that the above CBD notice is in furtherance of that advice even though the request was for information and planning purposes.

As we view the CBD Notice, the IRS required only a general demonstration of capability. It did not delineate specific tests to be performed. Moreover, the test programs were to be written by the manufacturer. Any test would have sufficed, provided it was reasonably adequate to validate the various functions performed by the proposed replacement memory and provided it permitted the IRS to determine timing and throughput rates from the resulting hardcopy data. Copies of the programs and related documentation were to be provided to permit the IRS to generate comparable data using its existing Control Data memory, for purposes of comparison.

Until this case came on for hearing in the District Court on KET's motion for a temporary restraining order, KET believed, and maintained before our Office, that the IRS's purpose in conducting the demonstration for information and planning was misleading and that, in fact, the Notice of Demonstration was contrived as a means of assuring that a new contract be awarded to Control Data on a sole-source basis. In addition to challenging the demonstration procedure adopted by the IRS as amounting to improper prequalification, KET argued that in the unusual circumstances presented here the IRS should have facilitated the demonstration by allowing it to demonstrate the acceptability of its product through simulation, or by making available one of the CDC 3500s in use at the IRS.

KET states that it is the leading third-party vendor specializing in Control Data compatible equipment. It is the offspring of International Time Sharing Services (ITSS), formed to provide engineering support of ITSS Control Data 3000 series equipment. KET states that its 5350 memory was designed to support the CDC 3500 and has been proven in applications supporting CDC 3300 equipment through minor changes to interface logic required to slow down the memory to meet the lower speed of the CDC 3300. Except for speed, KET explains, there is little difference between the CDC 3500 and 3300 equipment.

KET has at no point questioned the IRS's right to require that it be satisfied that proposed equipment will meet its needs, including benchmarking of equipment. However, the protester argues that its product has been fully proven through use of memory testing equipment which it has developed. This includes, we understand, substantial operating time supporting an in-house but smaller CPU configured to emulate performance characteristics of the CDC 3500. Central processing units are expensive. Simulation, KET argues, is an entirely appropriate and proper means of demonstrating equipment compatibility, at least in regard to normal applications.

Not only does KET contend that simulation should have been permitted, but it argues that the IRS could have taken advantage of the facilities and services provided by the Federal Computer Performance Evaluation and Simulation Center (FCPESC). At the very least, KET believes, the IRS could have attempted to obtain the use of these facilities or it could have recognized, as the Air Force has done, that circumstances may preclude economical duplication of testing facilities by other Governmental and private organizations. In this regard, the Department of the Air Force has stated that it will permit nongovernmental users to test equipment at Air Force facilities on a workload permitting basis, when: (1) required services are not reasonably available through private industry sources, (2) testing can be performed without additional manpower, (3) the Government is reimbursed for all direct and indirect costs, and (4) the business requesting the test indemnify the Government against certain types of losses. *See* Notice, 43 Federal Register 22030, adding part 835 to 32 CFR. ch. 7C.

Prior to KET's filing of its complaint in the District Court, the contracting officer sought to argue that the Notice of Demonstration was "not a solicitation for goods or services [but] was only a request for demonstrations of memory units compatible with the CDC 3500 CPU's currently installed" at IRS. IRS's stated purpose in requiring the demonstration involved nothing more than a desire to simply test the market, *i.e.*, "to [try] to discover if there is other compatible memory." In this connection IRS counsel acknowledged that:

* * * Should the results of this demonstration indicate that compatible memory is available, and should the [IRS] develop a requirement for such momory, present plans call for the [IRS] to conduct a competitive procurement * * *. "Supplemental Legal Memorandum" dated and submitted to GAO on August 11, 1978.

Throughout, KET has contended that the IRS was being less than candid because the current contract with CDC would expire on October 31, 1978, unless some action were taken. As documents received in our Office since the case was filed in the District Court indicate, IRS counsel knew or should have known that in fact no responses were received to the Notice of Demonstration from any potential offeror. Moreover, on August 15, 1978, the Contracting Officer executed Determination and Findings (D & F) to justify the exercise of options to purchase the existing CDC equipment in connection with a request for a Delegation of Procurement Authority from the General Services Administration (GSA).

As indicated, KET takes exception to the exercise of the options, asserting that it could compete were it only given a fair opportunity.

While we do not review contract administration matters pursuant to our bid protest procedures, we pointed out in *H.G. Peters & Company*,

B–183115, September 27, 1976, 76–2 CPD 284, that we will consider protests against the exercise of contract options when it is alleged that such action is or would be contrary to applicable regulatory provisions governing the exercise of options. Moreover, this Office considers protests which assert that a procuring activity's actions in modifying or extending a contract violate the statutory requirement for competitive procurements and deprive the protester of its right to compete for the Government's business. *American Air Filter Co.—DLA request for reconsideration*, 57 Comp. Gen. 567 (1978), 78–1 CPD 443; *Intermem Corporation*, B–187607, April 15, 1977, 77–1 CPD 263.

As first revealed in Court, IRS intends to purchase the existing Control Data equipment by exercising purchase options under the existing contract, in *lieu* of competing its requirement. The reasonableness of option prices should be determined at the time the option is to be exercised, as a matter of sound procurement practice, just as any bid must be evaluated for price reasonableness before award. Admittedly, the Federal Procurement Regulations (FPR) contain no provision comparable to Defense Acquisition Regulation (DAR) § 1–1505, which directs steps to be taken by a contracting officer before an option is exercised. Specifically, DAR §§ 1–1505(d), (e) *require* that exercise of the option be justified on the basis of the results of a new solicitation, *unless*: (1) an informal market survey or examination or readily ascertainable established prices *clearly* indicate that better terms cannot be obtained, or (2) the time available is so short that option terms can be shown to be the best available, considering factors such as market stability and available time, and the usual duration of such contracts. In the absence of specific regulations relating to the exercise of options, the statutory and regulatory mandate that awards be made competitively imposes, we believe, several fundamental requirements which should have been applied in this instance.

In analogous circumstances we have recently stated, concerning the application of the competition statute to contract modifications, that:

> The impact of any modification is in our view to be determined by examining whether the alteration is within the scope of the competition which was initially conducted. Ordinarily, a modification falls within the scope of the procurement provided that it is of a nature which potential offerors would have reasonably anticipated under the changes clause. *American Air Filter Co.—DLA Request for Reconsideration, supra.*

Whether sufficient concern for competition is shown in exercising an option depends in our view on the circumstances from which the option arose as well as upon the actions taken by the Government in determining that it should be exercised. In those instances where the option price was not evaluated in making the initial award but was only added by a subsequent modification to the contract, the procedures followed in exercising the option should comport, as much as possible, with the competitive norm of Federal procurement. This requires that potentially interested suppliers be afforded adequate notice of and a fair opportunity to participate in the evaluation of their products and prices. See, *e.g.*, *General Electrodynamics Corporation—Reconsideration*, B–190020, August 16, 1978, 78–2 CPD 121.

Moreover, pricing normally can be adequately assessed only through competition. *Olivetti Corporation*, B–187369, February 28, 1977, 77–1 CPD 146. Regarding the use of prequalification techniques in connection with the exercise of an option, we have held that an agency is not required necessarily to solicit prices to ascertain whether to exercise an option provided it can fairly determine without doing so that no other firm could meet one or more of its essential requirements. *Consolidated Airborne Systems, Incorporated*, B–177758, July 10, 1974, 74–2 CPD 15.

We recognize that we have expressed doubt about, or have discouraged, the use of option testing procedures. See, for example, the concern we expressed as to whether it would be "sound procurement policy for the Government to put itself in a position where bids are requested solely for the purpose of determining whether an available option price can be bettered." 41 Comp. Gen. 682, 687 (1962). However, we believe that the better and sometimes only effective method of determining whether the exercise of an option is appropriate is to submit the requirement to the test of competitive bidding. *See*, *e.g.*, B–173141, October 14, 1971. Where competition is solicited for such purposes, of course, offerors should be advised of the purpose for which pricing is sought. B–173141, *supra;* B–173376, August 16, 1971.

Although, as the IRS states, the CDC contract was initially awarded in 1970, the purchase option credits—and indeed, the installation of CDC 3500 equipment—resulted from Modification 42 issued in 1974. KET suggests that the modification was itself improper, citing our decisions in *American Air Filter, supra*. Regardless of the propriety of the action taken in 1974, it is clear that the purchase option pricing is not the result of or tested by a competitive procurement.

Even though in this case the D & F never quite says so, it is clear that IRS seeks to justify the exercise of the CDC option on the basis of the absence of competition because of KET's (or anyone else's) failure to respond to its request for a demonstration. If this is not what was meant, the D & F is deficient because no relative cost justification was included—only a finding by the contracting officer that to exercise the purchase option this year would save the Government

$530,000 over what it would pay CDC if such action were taken next year. KET states that IRS would save substantially more than that by leasing KET equipment and that it would be less expensive for the Government to lease or buy KET equipment now than it would be to exercise the CDC options. The IRS evidently has not done a market (*i.e.*, price) analysis, and in any event, does not contend otherwise.

Concerning the reasonableness of the demonstration requirement, the IRS denies any intent to unduly restrict competition. It asserts that because of prior unfortunate experiences with unproven peripheral equipment it believes it can consider only equipment which is in its opinion fully proven.

In KET's view, the IRS' actions are little more than a disguised attempt to eliminate it from consideration. On August 31, 1978, KET was awarded a contract by the Walter Reed Army Institute of Research (Walter Reed) to install KET 5350 memory to support a CDC 3500 located at the Walter Reed Army Medical Center in Washington, D.C. The KET equipment has been installed. KET's counsel stated in the District Court that this equipment is now operating as intended. Had the IRS been interested only in surveying the market without immediate procurement ramifications, it could have agreed (as it has not) to extend the testing period so that KET could make use of the CDC 3500 located at Walter Reed. Moreover, KET complains, it made every reasonable effort to locate a CDC 3500 which it could use to perform the demonstration test. As stated before our Office, KET has always been willing to purchase CDC 3500 operating time as required to satisfy any doubt the IRS may have regarding its equipment.

We do not find it surprising that KET has not previously demonstrated or tested the KET 5350 on a CDC 3500, notwithstanding that the 5350 memory was designed for CDC 3500 applications. We hardly would expect manufacturers to purchase a mainframe to test every memory application they seek to develop. Not only are mainframes expensive, but the CDC 3500 apparently is not in current production. As KET states, approximately 50 units were manufactured by Control Data. Of the 40 units KET has been able to locate, 19 are controlled by the United States, *eleven of which are operated by the IRS*. Thirteen units not operated by the United States are located outside the United States. The remaining 8 are used by state governments, or by commercial and nonprofit organizations. By the extended IRS deadline of July 31, 1978, KET was unable to come to an agreement with any known CDC 3500 operator as to terms under which KET could have installed and demonstrated its 5350 memory.

The IRS dismisses KET's contentions that KET 5350 memory is compatible with CDC 3300 series equipment, and in any event believes that there is significant difference between CDC 3300 and CDC 3500 compatible memory. As far as the IRS is concerned, only actual operating experience on a CDC 3500 exactly like those used by the IRS will suffice and compatibility with the CDC 3500 cannot be established by simulation. In its opinion, demonstration of the memory on any other equipment or in any other testing environment could demonstrate at most that the equipment works only with that equipment or in that environment.

The IRS seems to believe that it is sufficient that it simply *claim* that it possesses a reasonable basis for requiring the demonstration test or in insisting that simulation not be permitted. In our view the IRS has not carried its evidentiary burden once KET established— as we believe it has—*prima facie* support for its contention, in effect, that the demonstration procedures followed were unduly restrictive of competition. As we noted in *American Air Filter Co.—DLA Request for Reconsideration, supra:*

> While we believe that an agency's opinion regarding technical facts is entitled to consideration, a conclusion by technical personnel regarding the legal implications of their findings carries no more weight than any other conclusion of law.

Although we do not suggest that it is improper for the IRS to insist that KET, or others, demonstrate by benchmark testing during the course of procurement that products perform as claimed, it normally may be acceptable for a manufacturer in KET's position to "prove" its equipment through simulation testing techniques. Simulation and related disciplines, including scaling and modeling, are a part of the engineer's stock-in-trade. *Cf., e.g., Applied Science & Technology Index*, v. 66, No. 8, 79–80 (September 1976); *id.*, 1331–1332 (1977); *Bibliography of Selected Rand Publications*, "Computer Simulation" (Rand, 1972). We cannot accept uncritically the IRS's contention that in no case is simulation acceptable *regardless of how good it may have been*, particularly where the actual equipment for determining the acceptability of competing products was either unavailable or the agency was unwilling to make it available.

In our opinion, an agency seeking in good faith to foster maximum competition at least would have: (1) explored the possibility of permitting simulation data in *lieu* of actual CDC 3500 experience or insist that firms demonstrate satisfactorily that simulation data could provide assurance of equipment acceptability; (2) supported its refusal to consider CDC 3300 operating data by identifying the specific differences in capability which would have to be shown to be met, and how those differences could be shown to have been overcome satisfactorily; (3) provided a fuller explanation of its reasons for refusing to permit its own equipment to be used in conducting such a test, including scheduling information showing that possible use of the equipment was fairly considered but in fact was not possible. In the circumstances, IRS has given the appearance of creating unduly restrictive testing requirements designed to frustrate the statutory requirement that maximum competition be obtained in awarding Government contracts. In any event, we understand that at this time KET is able to demonstrate its equipment in operation at Walter Reed and we think it should be permitted to do so before IRS purchases the equipment from CDC.

Although the IRS must be held accountable for its failure to diligently pursue a competitive follow-on contract, or to properly evaluate the purchase options, IRS's actions have left it without a contract for necessary services and equipment. In our opinion, the IRS should negotiate with Control Data to extend the term of the existing contract, for such time as is reasonably required to permit a competitive procurement action to be conducted. In this connection, we note that by letter of October 20, 1978, GSA has granted a delegation of procurement authority to IRS to extend the existing lease on a month-to-month basis, but not for more than 6 months, in order to accomplish the competitive acquisition of the memory and disk subsystems. The authority granted by GSA requires, as a minimum, that KET plug compatible products be adequately considered. Moreover, inasmuch as GSA has refused to accede to IRS's request for authority to exercise the subject purchase option, IRS cannot properly do so. We believe our decision of today is consistent with this GSA action.

The protest is sustained.

[B-133316]

Appropriations—Deficiencies—Anti-Deficiency Act—Expenditures Beyond Administrative Control

Agency is prohibited by Anti-Deficiency Act from making payments in excess of funding limitations. Fact that limitations must be exceeded to make contract payments because of fluctuation in currency exchange rates, and not through fault of agency, does not justify exceptions to Act. In such situation, agency must ask Congress for deficiency appropriation.

In the matter of Currency Exchange Rate Fluctuations, October 31, 1978:

The Department of the Army has requested our opinion as to whether a violation of 31 U.S.C. 665 (1970), the so-called Anti-Deficiency Act, occurs when, in connection with contract payments to be made in foreign currency, a statutory or regulatory funding limitation is exceeded due to fluctuations in the exchange rates for the foreign currency.

The statute provides that :

(a) No officer or employee of the United States shall make or authorize any expenditure from or create or authorize an obligation under any appropriation or fund in excess of the amount available therein ; nor shall any such officer or employee involve the Government in any contract or other obligation, for the payment of money for any purpose, in advance of appropriations made for such purpose, unless such contract or obligation is authorized by law.

* * * * * * *

(h) No officer or employee of the United States shall authorize or create any obligation or make any expenditure (A) in excess of an apportionment or re-apportionment, or (B) in excess of the amount permitted by regulations pre-scribed pursuant to subsection (g) of this section.

The Army reports that :

The problem arises from the minor construction, repair and maintenance of real property facilities where there are statutory or regulatory limitations or both on the obligation and expenditure of funds for such purposes * * * [A]t the time of entering into the contract, the amount of the contract is within both the statutory and any applicable limitations associated with the work in ques-tion. The contract requires payment in local [foreign] currency. Local currency is purchased at the time such currency is required to make payment to the con-tractor. At some point either during performance of the contract or before final payment to the contractor, due solely to a change in the exchange rate for local currency, payment of the full contract price to the contractor will result in exceeding either the regulatory or the statutory limitation or both.

The Army believes that the statute is not violated in the above situa-tion as it "speaks in terms of an officer or employee of the United States making or authorizing an obligation under an appropriation or fund in excess of the amount available therein" and "certainly no one in the Army could be charged with having authorized or created an obligation or made payment of any sum in excess of the limitation or limitations" as the situation is the result of the workings of the international currency market which the contracting officer could not influence. The Army concludes that :

[I]t is our position that even though ceilings subject to [31 U.S.C. 665] may be exceeded, as long as the fund limitation at the appropriation level is observed and the increase in price is caused solely by devaluation of the dollar, payments may be made under the contract and no reports of violation of [31 U.S.C. 665] need be processed. In such situations, it is difficult to believe the Congress in-tended to have individuals assume responsibility for exceeding limitations where those individuals are not in a position to influence the real cause of the limita-tions being exceeded.

We cannot agree with the Army's position. The statute prohibits an officer or employee of the United States from making "an expenditure * * * in excess of the amount available" under an appropriation. The Army now proposes to make payments in excess of the appropriation available because ceilings imposed by statute or regulation issued pur-suant to 31 U.S.C. 665(g) have been exceeded through no fault of its contracting officers. However, 31 U.S.C. 665 says nothing about why sufficient funds are no longer available; nor is it significant that the contracting officers are not at fault. The statute flatly prohibits such payments from being made.

As the Army suggests, when a contracting officer finds that the dollars required to continue or make final payment on a contract will exceed a statutory limitation he may terminate the contract, provided the termination costs will not exceed the statutory limitations. Alternatively, the contracting officer may issue a stop work order and the agency may ask Congress for a deficiency appropriation citing the currency fluctuation as the reason for its request. In this regard, we note that the general problem of exchange rate fluctuation was the subject of a recent report by this Office entitled "Better Program Management Through Eliminating Exchange Rate Gains and Losses from DOD Budget Process," ID–78–33, April 7, 1978. In the report, we recognized that contracts written in foreign currency had a significant effect on the budget process and stated "that the present method of seeking supplemental appropriations and reprogramming authority is not timely in dealing with the problems caused by fluctuations in the currency rates and it affects the orderly implementation of approved programs." We concluded that "[i]t would be desirable to provide for an alternative funding method to eliminate from the budgetary process exchange rate losses that are not predictable and have adversely affected Defense programs. This would also insure that the Department of Defense does not supplement its appropriations through gains derived from floating currency exchange rates." We recommended that:

* * * the Secretary of Defense seek legislative authority to initiate an alternative funding method to eliminate exchange rate gains and losses from the Department of Defense's budgetary process. Such legislation should require that the Secretary of Defense provide the Congress with an annual accounting of exchange rate transactions by country. The Department of Defense would continue to be responsible to its oversight committees for justifying program expenditures covered by the foreign currency transactions.

We note that Title III of the Department of Defense Appropriation Act, 1979. Public Law 95–457, approved October 13, 1978 (92 Stat. 1233), provides $500,000,000 for transfer by the Secretary of Defense to or from certain appropriations available to the Department of Defense for fiscal year 1979 and thereafter "in order to maintain the budgeted level of operations * * * and thereby eliminate substantial gains and losses to such appropriations caused by fluctuations in foreign currency exchange rates * * *." Thus, it appears that the problems referred to in our report and which have been of concern to the Army should not arise in the future.

[B–191838]

Bids—Buy American Act—Buy American Certificate—Acceptance—Not Reviewable by GAO—Exceptions

General Accounting Office (GAO) will review protest challenging successful bidder's intended compliance with representation in its Buy American Certificate that domestic end products will be supplied where basis of protest is that successful bidder's bid samples indicated that it is offering other than domestic end products.

Bids—Buy American Act—Foreign Product Determination—Sample Submitted—Review by GAO

GAO review of information considered proprietary, including detailed cost breakdown, submitted by successful bidder in response to protest, indicates that cost of domestic components contained in and product offered by successful bidder exceeds 50 percent of total cost of components. Successful bidder was therefore properly evaluated by agency as offering domestic end product under Buy American Act.

In the matter of New Britain Hand Tools Division, Litton Industrial Products, Inc., November 1, 1978:

New Britain Hand Tools Division, Litton Industrial Products, Inc. (Litton), protests the award to American Kal Enterprises, Inc. (American Kal) of Items 5 and 7 under invitation for bids (IFB) No. FTAN–E5–10016–A–3–7–78, issued by the General Services Administration, Federal Supply Service. The IFB solicited bids for requirements contracts to supply various socket wrench sets.

Item 5 is a ⅜ inch square drive socket wrench set consisting of 23 chrome plated components to be furnished in a box. Item 7 is a ½ inch square drive socket wrench set consisting of 20 chrome plated components also to be furnished in a box. For each of these items, the bidders were required by the solicitation to submit two bid samples from the production of the manufacturer whose product is to be supplied.

Litton requests that we find the award to American Kal to be in violation of the Buy American Act, 41 U.S.C. § 10a-d (1976), and that we set aside the award. Specifically, as to Item 5, Litton alleges that components 16 and 17 (½ inch and %₁₆ inch U-joint sockets respectively) of American Kal's bid samples were marked "Kal-Japan" which, along with the other components so marked (at least 15 of the 23 components) indicate that the cost of the foreign components offered in American Kal's bid samples exceeded 50 percent of the cost of all of the components. American Kal and the agency maintain that components 16 and 17 of the sample were marked "Kal" rather than "Kal-Japan" and are of domestic origin. As to Item 7, Litton points to the fact that 17 of the 20 components of that set were also marked "Kal-Japan" (the remaining 3 components, a 9 inch and a 14½ inch hinged handle, and a ratchet, were simply marked "Kal") and questions whether American Kal will comply with its Buy American Certificate (SF 33, para. 7) by supplying domestic end items.

Under Executive Order 10582, December 17, 1954, articles, materials and supplies shall be considered to be of foreign origin if the cost of foreign products used in them constitutes 50 percent or more of the cost of all component products used in them. Under this order, a Buy American Act differential must be applied if the end product to be furnished (1) is not manufactured in the United States or (2) is manufactured in the United States but consists of foreign components which make up 50 percent or more of the total component cost. *Blodgett Keypunching Company*, 56 Comp. Gen. 18 (1976), 76–2 CPD 331. We have recognized tool kits as end products for Buy American Act purposes. *Imperial Eastman Corporation—Thorsen Tool Company*, 53 Comp. Gen. 726 (1974), 74–1 CPD 153.

We have held that where a bidder excludes no end products from its Buy American Certificate and does not otherwise indicate it is offering anything other than domestic end products, acceptance of its bid, if otherwise responsive, results in an obligation on its part to furnish domestic end products, and compliance with that obligation is a matter of contract administration which has no effect on the validity of the contract award. 50 Comp. Gen. 697 (1971); *Becker Instruments & Photographic Optics*, B–185411, July 14, 1976, 76–2 CPD 43.

However, Litton, in effect, alleges that in the bid samples, furnished as part of its bid, American Kal indicated that it was offering other than a domestic end product. Accordingly, we have considered the matter.

We have examined one of the two bid samples for each item at a conference held in connection with this case, and we have been furnished a detailed breakdown of the component costs of the two socket wrench sets. Further, American Kal has submitted details which it considers proprietary concerning the bid samples, its subcontractor relationships and sources of supply, including specific purchase orders and bank commitments. Also included were the sources of supply of one of American Kal's subcontractors, Dellacor Co., Inc., alleged by Litton to be an affiliated firm merely assembling imported Japanese components supplied to it by American Kal.

We find, as to Item 5, that components 16 and 17 were simply marked "Kal" in the bid samples without country of origin indicated as alleged by Litton. We further find, based on our inspection of the information considered by American Kal to be proprietary, including a detailed cost breakdown, that these components, as well as component 21, a U-joint, are of American origin, and that their cost along with 3 of the other admittedly American made components (½ inch, $\frac{9}{16}$ inch and $\frac{5}{8}$ inch Thorsen deep sockets) and the American metal box, exceed 50 percent of the cost of all of the components of the Item 5 socket wrench set. As to Item 7, we find, also based on our inspection of the proprietary information furnished by American Kal, that the 9 inch and 14½ inch hinged handles and the ratchet questioned by Litton are of American origin and that the forged ratchet handle subcomponents are produced by American firms. The cost of these components to American Kal, as represented to us, along with the metal box, exceeds 50 percent of the cost of all of the components of the Item 7 socket wrench set. We find no basis for Litton's allegation that Dellacor Co., Inc. merely assembles imported Japanese components supplied to it by American Kal.

Based on the record before us, we conclude that the two items offered by American Kal were properly determined to be domestic end products.

Accordingly, the protest is denied.

[B–192295]

Officers and Employees—Promotions—Retroactive—Administrative Delay

Employee grieved due to delay in processing promotion papers. Grievance Examiner found that although promotion papers reached personnel office and were acted upon by classification officers prior to beginning of new pay period, grievant's papers were not approved by Personnel Officer until after beginning of new pay period. Grievance Examiner concluded that classification officer acted for Personnel Officer and ordered retroactive promotion. Award may not be implemented since agency regulations delegate authority to approve promotions to Personnel Officer and he has not further delegated that authority in writing.

In the matter of Douglas C. Butler—Retroactive Promotion, November 1, 1978:

This action is at the request of Leonard L. Nahme, Director, Office of Finance, U.S. Patent and Trademark Office, Department of Commerce, for an advance decision concerning their authority to implement a grievance decision awarding a retroactive promotion to an employee of that office, Douglas C. Butler.

Mr. Butler was one of three employees who were recommended for promotion to grade GS–13 Patent Examiner. While their promotion papers were logged in the Personnel Office on the same day, the effective dates of the promotions varied in that one was effective on January 16, 1977, and the other two were effective on January 30, 1977. The two employees whose promotions were made effective on January

30, 1977, filed grievances to have the effective dates made retroactive to January 16, 1977.

In a "Decision on Formal Grievance" dated March 29, 1978, the Deciding Official, the Deputy Assistant Commissioner for Patents, decided in favor of Mr. Butler. The essential portion of his decision is set forth below:

Under the circumstances of this case, I agree with the Grievance Examiner that the approval of the promotion by the classification officer must be deemed to be the act of the Personnel Officer and hence of the authorizing official. The record in this grievance file shows that the promotion of Charles E. Frankfort was approved by Classification Officer Smith on January 18, 1977, whereas the promotion of Douglas C. Butler was approved by Classification Officer Jeter on January 12, 1977. Since January 16, 1977 is the proposed effective promotion date, it is apparent that the Patent and Trademark Office does not have authority to authorize a retroactive promotion to Charles E. Frankfort because his promotion was not approved by the authorized official prior to the proposed effective promotion date. Moreover, I am not aware of any nondiscretionary agency regulation, policy or collective bargaining agreement provision or right granted by statute which mandates that promotion take place by a specific date which would also authorize retroactive promotion.

Since a retroactive promotion was not recommended for Mr. Charles E. Frankfort, no further consideration will be given here to his attempt to obtain a retroactive promotion.

Mr. Nahme questions whether it is proper to grant backpay to Mr. Butler for the period January 16–30, 1977, as required by the grievance award. He states that while the Grievance Examiner found that the Classification Officer had approved Mr. Butler's promotion on January 12, 1977, the record shows that the *Personnel Officer* did not approve the promotion until January 30, 1977. Mr. Nahme argues that the authority for final approval of promotions had not been delegated to the Classification Officer. He states that:

Department of Commerce Administrative Order (DOC AO) 202–250, entitled "Delegation of Authority for Personnel Management" sets forth those DOC officials to whom authority for personnel management is delegated. Appendix A to this agency regulation notes that this authority has been delegated to the following:

"Commissioner
Deputy Commissioner
Assistant Commissioners (statutory)
Assistant Commissioner for Administration
Personnel Officer"

The approval authority for personnel actions including promotions is also set forth in DOC AO 202–250 and in pertinent part states:

SECTION 4. FINAL APPROVAL OF PERSONNEL ACTIONS.

.01   Personnel actions involving accessions, changes in employment status, and separations of employees will become legally valid on the effective date specified on CD–251, "Notification of Personnel Action," or other document specified by the Civil Service Commission or General Accounting Office for a similar purpose, upon approval (individually or on "cover sheets") of the CD–251 or equivalent documents, or other document approved by the Director of Personnel, by *one of the appointing officers* listed in Appendix A of this order, or by some other person to whom authority has been delegated under paragraph 3.01 of this order * * *. [Italic supplied.]

As indicated above, some other person in addition to those noted in Appendix A may have delegated authority to approve personnel actions. This authority has not been so delegated to other persons.

As a general rule a personnel action may not be made retroactive so as to increase the rights of an employee to compensation. We have made exceptions to this rule where administrative or clerical error (1) prevented a personnel action from being effected as originally intended, (2) resulted in nondiscretionary administrative regulations or policies not being carried out, or (3) has deprived the employee of a right granted by statute or regulation. See 55 Comp. Gen. 42 (1975); 54 id. 888 (1975), and decisions cited therein. The parties agree that the second and third exceptions are not applicable to this case.

With respect to delays or omissions in processing of promotion requests that will be regarded as administrative or clerical errors that will support retroactive promotion, applicable decisions have drawn a distinction between those errors that occur prior to approval of the promotion by the properly authorized official and those that occur after such approval but before the acts necessary to effective promotions have been fully carried out. See 54 Comp. Gen. 538 (1974); B–183969, July 2, 1975; and B–184817, November 28, 1975. The rationale for drawing this distinction is that the individual with authority to approve promotion requests also has the authority not to approve any such request unless his exercise of disapproval authority is otherwise constrained by statute, administrative policy, or regulation. Thus, where the delay or omission occurs before that official has had the opportunity to exercise his discretion with respect to approval or disapproval, administrative intent to promote at any particular time cannot be established other than by after-the-fact statements as to what that official states would have been his determination. After the authorized official has exercised his authority by approving the promotion request, all that remains to effectuate that promotion is a series of ministerial acts which could be compelled by *writ of mandamus*.

In the instant case the Grievance Examiner found that the act of the Classification Officer must be deemed to be the act of the Personnel Officer, and that finding was approved by the deciding official. Such a finding is tantamount to finding that the Classification Officer was an official having been delegated the authority to approve promotions. The Department of Commerce Administrative Order DOC AO 202–250, section 4 provides that approval of personnel actions may be exercised by one of the officials listed in Appendix A of that order or "* * * by some other person to whom authority has been delegated under paragraph 3.01 * * *." Paragraph 3.01 is set forth below:

Authority is hereby further delegated to officers and employees who are listed in Appendix A of this order, *and to such other employees of the Government as may be specified in this order or designated or approved by the Director of Personnel in writing*, to administer and conduct personnel management activities and process personnel actions in both the Department and Field Service, subject to the limitations and authorizations outlined in this order. [Italic supplied.]

The other provisions of the order are not capable of being interpreted as delegating to the Classification Officer the authority to approve promotions. Thus, unless the Director of Personnel has made the delegation in writing as required by DOC AO 202–250, section 3.01, the grievance award would be in violation of valid agency regulations and, as such, unenforceable. B–180010.11, March 9, 1977. Mr. Nahme on behalf of the agency states that no further delegations were made.

Accordingly, since there exists no administrative error which would form the basis for a retroactive promotion, we hold that the grievance award may not be implemented.

[B–192316]

Contractors—Defaulted—Reprocurement—Standing

Prior General Accounting Office (GAO) decision held that once contracting officer decides to conduct new competition for reprocurement he may not automatically exclude defaulted contractor from that competition. Prior GAO decision did not hold that defaulted contractor has automatic right to resolicitation. 56 Comp. Gen. 976 clarified.

Contracts—Default—Reprocurement—Defaulted Contractor—Not Solicited—Repurchase v. New Competition

Army's contention, that every defaulted contractor has clearly demonstrated his nonresponsibility as matter of fact and law, is without merit. Because it is necessary to view factual context within which default occurs, it would be improper to lay down rule that defaulted contractor need not ever be considered in reprocurement.

Contracts—Default—Reprocurement—Restrictive Specifications—Justification

Because of relatively short period of time in which reprocurement contract for critically needed item had to be consummated and because offerors solicited were familiar with contractual requirements, GAO finds no abuse of discretion by contracting officer in limiting reprocurement competition to prior producers.

Contracts—Protests—Conflict in Statements of Contractor and Contracting Agency

Protester failed to meet its burden of proof on its allegations about its ability to supply urgently needed items in less time than offerors Army had solicited since only evidence on matter consisted of conflicting statements between Army and protester.

In the matter of Ikard Manufacturing Company, November 1, 1978:

Ikard Manufacturing Company (Ikard) protests the United States Army Missile Materiel Command's limiting of the reprocurement action for a part used in the Nike Missile System after its contract to produce this part had been terminated for default. The Army restricted the reprocurement to offerors who had previously produced the part. Because Ikard had failed to deliver any quantities of the part, it was deemed not to qualify as a prior producer.

On March 22, 1977, the Army awarded to Ikard contract DAAHO1–77–C–0335 which called for 1,050 each Fastener, Flap at a total contract price of $14,595. Delivery was required on August 19, 1977, 130 days after award. Ikard, however, did not deliver on this date and the Army modified the contract, extending the delivery date to November 30, 1977. When Ikard again did not deliver, the Army issued a "show cause" letter on December 5, 1977. Ikard responded to the Army's letter on December 14, 1977. After reviewing the reasons given by Ikard for failing to deliver on time, the Army decided to forbear from terminating for default and further extended the delivery date to April 30, 1978. When Ikard still did not deliver, the Army issued a termination for default letter on May 25, 1978.

The Army states that because of Ikard's failure to deliver after 425 days from the award of the contract to it, there was at the time of termination a critical need for the part because of a zero balance in the Army's inventory and unfilled back orders with past due delivery dates from various missile installations. Consequently, the Army's requirement for the part was upgraded from a low priority to a high priority.

On June 13, 1978, the Army issued request for proposals (RFP) No. DAAHO1–78–R–0888 for the 1,050 Fasteners called for under the terminated contract. The closing date for receipt of proposals was June 26, 1978. Because the closing date was less than 15 days from the date of issuance, the solicitation was not synopsized in the Commerce Business Daily. See Armed Services Procurement Regulation (ASPR) § 1–1003.1(c)(iv) (1976 ed.). The following price proposals were received by the Army on June 26, 1978:

Precision Specialty Corporation	$18,375.00
Special Projects Machine and Tool	12,600.00
Die and Tool Products, Inc	12,253.50

In a letter dated June 30, 1978, and received by us on July 5, 1978, Ikard protested any award under the RFP on the basis that the Army by restricting the RFP to only three firms prevented free and open competition. Further, Ikard stated that as a result of the restriction, it was prevented from submitting a quote or offer even though in its opinion it could have been the most responsive offeror to the RFP.

The Army on August 25, 1978, awarded contract No. DAAHO1–78–C–1155 to Die and Tool Products, Inc., for the production of the needed part. The award was made pursuant to ASPR § 2–407.8 (b) (3) (i) (1976 ed.) which permits award during the pendency of a bid protest when it is properly determined that the items being procured are urgently required. By a letter dated the same date, the Army notified Ikard of the award.

Ikard alleges that the cause of its failure to deliver was difficulties with a particular subcontractor and that at the time the Army terminated its contract it had just received the last subcontractor item. Therefore, according to Ikard, at the time of termination all materials required for the manufacture of the contract part were "in-house." Ikard contends that the Army was aware of this situation. Ikard, then, questions the necessity of the reprocurement solicitation to prior producers because it could make delivery of the required part earlier than any other manufacturer and at a more reasonable price.

The Army acknowledges that a limited procurement is not a preferred procurement method. Nevertheless, the Army states that a limited procurement was justified here because of the zero balance of the contract part and because of the time involved in ordering the documentation needed to solicit by formal advertising. The Army also states that it has no intention of making the item sole source or noncompetitive for future requirements. With regard to Ikard's contention that it had all the materials needed for manufacture in-house at the time of termination, the Army states that Ikard did not provide sufficient evidence that it could be responsive to the requirements in the reprocurement solicitation.

In response to the Army, Ikard argues that it is good common judgment that if a manufacturer has all the materials for the part on hand and if some of these materials require a long leadtime for delivery from subcontractors, the manufacturer having the materials on hand can deliver the required quantity of parts earlier than someone having to start from "scratch." Ikard disputes the Army's contention that it lacked sufficient evidence that Ikard could be responsive to the requirements of the reprocurement solicitation. Ikard contends that the Army had complete knowledge of the fact that it had in-house all the parts and materials required for manufacture. Ikard alleges that it informed the Army of this situation during an April 13, 1978, meeting and by a letter dated April 21, 1978.

The Army contends that our decision in *PRB Uniforms, Inc.*, 56 Comp. Gen. 976 (1977), 77–2 CPD 213, to the extent that it appears to hold that a defaulted Government contractor has an "automatic right" to be resolicited, is inconsistent with relevant ASPR provisions and with the intent of Congress as expressed in 10 U.S.C. § 2202 under which ASPR was promulgated. The Army refers to subparagraphs (a) and (b) of ASPR § 8–602.6 which is entitled "Repurchase Against

Contractor's Account." These subparagraphs provide in pertinent part as follows:

(a) *Where the supplies or services are still required after termination, repurchase* of supplies or services which are the same as or similar to those called for in the contract *shall be made against the contractor's account* as soon as practicable after termination. Such repurchase shall be at as reasonable a price as practicable considering the quality required by the Government and the time within which the supplies or services are required. * * * [Italic supplied.]

(b) If the repurchase is for a quantity not in excess of the undelivered quantity terminated for default, the requirements of 10 U.S.C. 2304(a), with respect to formal advertising, are inapplicable. However, the PCO may use formal advertising procedures. If the PCO decides to negotiate the repurchase contract, he may either (1) use any authority listed in 3-201 through 3-217 (10 U.S.C. 2304(a)(1)-(17)), as appropriate, or (2) if none of those authorities to negotiate is used, the contract shall identify the procurement as a repurchase in accordance with the provisions of the default clause in the defaulted contract. * * *

The Army argues that in electing not to resolicit Ikard it acted strictly in accordance with the broad discretion lawfully conferred under ASPR § 8-602.6 and in strict furtherance of the stated congressional purpose for which the regulation was promulgated. The Army points out that nowhere does ASPR § 8-602.6 require resolicitation of a defaulted contractor. The Army further states that no court or administrative board has ever held that resolicitation of a defaulted contractor is a prerequisite in reprocurement action. Therefore, it is the Army's position that a defaulted contractor's automatic "right" to resolicitation is clearly nonexistent under the established law of Government contracting.

In *PRB Uniforms, Inc., supra,* we held that while the statutory requirement that contracts be let after competitive bidding is not applicable to reprocurements, once the contracting officer decides that it is appropriate to conduct a new competition for the reprocurement, *he may not automatically exclude the defaulted contractor from that competition.* Otherwise, such exclusion would constitute an improper premature determination of nonresponsibility. We also pointed out that our prior cases stating that the defaulted contractor could be disregarded as a source of supply either arose out of a proper sole-source reprocurement or were essentially predicated on the nonresponsibility of the defaulted contractor for the repurchase contract. Our decision, then, dealt essentially with whether a defaulted contractor could be regarded as *per se* nonresponsible for the reprocurement contract.

The Army states that its contracting officers usually do not terminate defaulting contractors even when they have a clear right to do so, unless they conclude that they have no reasonable expectation of obtaining the needed supplies from the defaulting contractor. In this regard, the Army argues that as a general rule a defaulted contractor has clearly demonstrated his nonresponsibility as a matter of fact and law. A requirement that contracting officers resolicit a defaulted contractor is in the Army's opinion an unwarranted invasion of their broad discretion to reprocure upon such terms and conditions as are appropriate.

We note, however, that the boards of contract appeals do not exclude a defaulted contractor from participation in the reprocurement process regardless of the circumstances. See *World-Wide Development Co., Inc.,* ASBCA Nos. 16608, 16717, 73-2 BCA 10, 249, affirmed on reconsideration 74-1 BCA 10, 474; *Tom W. Kaufman Co.,* GSBCA 4623. It is true that these decisions concern the Government's requirement to mitigate its damages before assessing the defaulted contractor with any excess costs for reprocurement. Nevertheless, we believe they do stand for the proposition that because it is necessary to view the factual context within which a default occurs, it is improper to lay down any hard-and-fast rule that a defaulted contractor need not ever be considered in a reprocurement.

With regard to the contracting officer's right to reprocure upon such terms and in such a manner as he deems appropriate, we have recently held that the contracting officer does indeed have considerable latitude in determining the appropriate method of reprocurement, provided his actions are reasonable and consistent with the duty to mitigate damages. See *Hemet Valley Flying Service, Inc.,* 57 Comp. Gen. 703 (1978), 78-2 CPD 117. It is only when the contracting officer decides to conduct a *new competition* for the reprocurement that he cannot choose to ignore the regulatory provisions applicable to competitive procurements. *Hemet Valley Flying Service, Inc., supra.* Consequently, we see no basis for the Army's contention that our decisions in this area are inconsistent with the relevant ASPR regulations concerning reprocurement following default.

We do not, however, believe that the protested procurement is objectionable. Because of the relatively short period of time in which a contract for the critically needed quantity of parts had to be consummated and because the offerors that were solicited were familiar with the contractual requirements, we find no abuse of discretion by the contracting officer in limiting the reprocurement competition to prior producers. See *Nationwide Building Maintenance, Inc.,* B-186602, December 9, 1976, 76-2 CPD 474. This Office will take no exception to the actions of the contracting officer in the absence of any indication that he abused his discretion by limiting competition. See *Non-Linear Systems, Inc.; Data Precision Corporation,* 55 Comp. Gen. 358 (1975), 75-2 CPD 219. We have in the past also indicated that the Government's interest in obtaining maximum competition is to be weighed against a bona fide administrative determination that the exigencies of a particular procurement are such that the delay involved in obtaining maximum competition would adversely affect the Government's interest. 36 Comp. Gen. 809 (1957).

As to Ikard's allegations that it could have supplied the urgently needed parts in much less time than the offerors whom the Army solicited, the record shows only conflicting statements of fact between the Army and Ikard. The protester has the burden of affirmatively proving its case. This burden has not been met where the conflicting statements of the parties constitute the only evidence. *A. J. Fowler*, B-191636, October 3, 1978.

Accordingly, Ikard's protest is denied.

[B-192455]

Officers and Employees—Promotions—Career-Ladder—Retroactive Promotions—Backpay

Promotion of employee in career-ladder position was delayed because the promotion request was clerically misplaced before it reached the authorized official. Arbitrator's finding of administrative mistake does not itself provide a basis for award of backpay to grievant. In the absence of a nondiscretionary requirement mandating promotion within a particular time frame or in accordance with specified criteria, loss of promotion request prior to approval by authorized official does not constitute such administrative error as will support award of retroactive promotion and backpay.

Officers and Employees—Promotions—Career-Ladder—Promotions Not Mandatory

Provision of negotiated agreement calling for consistent and equitable application of merit promotion principles does not constitute a nondiscretionary agency policy requiring agency to make promotions at any specified time or under specified criteria. The inclusion of a provision in a negotiated agreement does not automatically make it nondiscretionary for purposes of the Back Pay Act. A nondiscretionary provision for such purposes is defined at 5 C.F.R. 550.802(d) to mean one requiring an agency to take prescribed action under stated conditions or criteria. 55 Comp. Gen. 42 is distinguished.

In the matter of John Cahill—Arbitration Award of Retroactive Promotion and Backpay, November 1, 1978:

By letter dated July 18, 1978, the Federal Labor Relations Council (FLRC) requested a decision as to the legality of the arbitration award rendered September 16, 1976, in *American Federation of Government Employees, Local 2327 and Social Security Administration, Philadelphia District* (Quinn, Arbitrator), FLRC No. 76A–144. The award of retroactive promotion and backpay was granted by the arbitrator as a remedy for the failure of the Social Security Administration (SSA) to timely process Mr. John Cahill's promotion request.

The FLRC had initially, on June 7, 1977, denied the agency's petition for review of the award because it failed to meet the Council's requirements for review set forth in 5 C.F.R. § 2411.32. Subsequent to the Council's denial of review, we issued a decision in *Matter of*

Janice Levy, B–190408, December 21, 1977, which invalidated an arbitrator's award issued under similar circumstances. Based on that decision, the SSA asked the FLRC to reconsider its denial of review in the present case.

The Council granted the agency's request for reconsideration and accepted its petition for review of the arbitrator's award. In its letter of July 18, 1978, the Council stated:

> * * * The Council determined that the agency's request for reconsideration should be granted and its petition for review of the arbitrator's award accepted because of the apparent precedential significance of your decision in *Janice Levy* to the facts of this case and because of the apparent departure in *Janice Levy* from the general principle established in previous decisions of your Office that a provision in a negotiated agreement, if otherwise proper, becomes a nondiscretionary agency policy for purposes of applying the provisions of the Back Pay Act of 1966.
>
> Because, as indicated, this case involves an issue within the jurisdiction of your Office and since the Council is uncertain, in light of the decision in *Janice Levy*, as to the applicability of prior Comptroller General decisions to the facts of this case, we request your decision as to whether the arbitrator's award in this case violates applicable law or appropriate regulation. * * *

The facts in Mr. Cahill's case are not in dispute. The arbitrator found that the grievant met the requirements for a career-ladder promotion from GS–7 to GS–9 as of November 23, 1975. He was recommended for promotion by his Branch Manager and the required request for promotion action was prepared in September 1975 in the SSA District Office in Philadelphia. The request was forwarded to the SSA Regional Staff for processing and forwarding to the Regional Personnel Office of the Department of Health, Education, and Welfare (HEW) where final authority to approve promotion requests rests. However, neither the SSA Regional Staff nor the HEW Regional Personnel Office has any record of receiving Mr. Cahill's promotion request. After an investigation into the processing delay and an administrative determination that there was no authority to effect Mr. Cahill's promotion on a retroactive basis, he was prospectively promoted to GS–9 effective February 1, 1976.

Mr. Cahill grieved his failure to be timely promoted and the matter was submitted to arbitration. By award dated September 16, 1976, the arbitrator awarded Mr. Cahill a retroactive promotion to GS–9 with backpay, effective November 23, 1975, having specifically found:

> * * * All the facts in this case lead to an administrative mistake at the Receiving Department of the Regional Personnel Office (RPO). The Grievant met the contractural and regulatory requirements for a merit promotion. The properly completed and timely-filed request for personnel action "fell through a bureaucratic crack" that is, was probably clerically misplaced. When the mistake was noted the Grievant was promoted—but no one was able to pinpoint the administrative cause(s) ("bureaucratic crack") and no retroactivity was awarded.
>
> The facts before us, the testimony and exhibits introduced indicate a violation of Article 6 (Merit Promotion), Section 1. The merit promotion principles were not applied in a consistent manner and the Grievant was not treated with equity because someone misplaced the proper and timely request for personnel action. * * *

Section 1 of article 6 of the labor-management agreement found to be violated by the arbitrator is as follows:

> *Section 1.* The Employer and the Union mutually agree that the purpose and intent of the provisions contained herein is to implement the Region's Merit Promotion Plan, which will help insure that merit promotion principles are applied in a consistent manner, with equity to all employees.

As noted above, the arbitrator in the instant case found that an administrative error had resulted in the grievant's not being promoted effective November 23, 1975; that the merit promotion principles were not applied in a consistent manner and the grievant was not treated with equity; and, therefore, that article 6, section 1 of the collective-bargaining agreement had been violated. In Mr. Cahill's case, as in the *Janice Levy* case, the misplacing of the grievant's promotion request occurred before the authorized official had exercised his authority to approve or disapprove the promotion. With respect to delays or omissions in processing a promotion request that will support a retroactive promotion and an award of backpay under 5 U.S.C. § 5596, we explained in *Janice Levy, supra,* page 8:

> With respect to delays or omissions in processing of promotion requests that will be regarded as administrative or clerical errors that will support retroactive promotion, applicable decisions have drawn a distinction between those errors that occur prior to approval of the promotion by the properly authorized official and those that occur after such approval but before the acts necessary to effective promotion have been fully carried out. The rule is as stated in B–180046, quoted above. See also 54 Comp. Gen. 538 (1974); B–183969, July 2, 1975; and B–184817, November 28, 1975. The rationale for drawing this distinction is that the individual with authority to approve promotion requests also has the authority not to approve any such request unless his exercise of disapproval authority is otherwise constrained by statute, administrative policy or regulation. Thus, where the delay or omission occurs before that official has had the opportunity to exercise his discretion with respect to approval or disapproval, administrative intent to promote at any particular time cannot be established other than by after-the-fact statements as to what that official states would have been his determination. After the authorized official has exercised his authority by approving the promotion request, all that remains to effectuate that promotion is a series of ministerial acts which could be compelled by *writ of mandamus.* In that category of case, administrative intent can be ascertained with certainty and retroactive promotion as a remedy for failure to accomplish those ministerial acts is appropriate.

We believe that the reasoning of the *Levy* decision is equally applicable to the case now before us. Since the arbitrator's award here is predicated upon clerical or administrative error prior to action by the authorized official, it is contrary to applicable authorities, except to the extent that the authorized official's exercise of discretion to approve or disapprove the grievant's promotion request is limited by statute, regulation, or collective-bargaining agreement. As we recognized in *Janice Levy*, while employees have no vested right to promotion at any specific time, an agency, by negotiation of a collective-bargaining agreement or by promulgation of a regulation, may limit its discretion so that under specified conditions it becomes mandatory to make a promotion on an ascertainable date. See, for example, 54 Comp. Gen. 403 (1974); 54 *id.* 538 (1974); 54 *id.* 888 (1975); 55 *id.* 42 (1975); and B–180010, August 30, 1976. In those cases, however, in contrast to the present case, the negotiated agreements contained specific provisions requiring promotions to be made under specified conditions.

Since the arbitrator found that the misplacing of Mr. Cahill's promotion request resulted in a violation of article 6, section 1 of the negotiated agreement, the question remaining for decision is whether that provision constituted a nondiscretionary provision so as to support an award of a retroactive promotion with backpay based on the violation. The FLRC originally refused to review the Cahill award based on its understanding that, under 54 Comp. Gen. 312 (1974) and later decisions of the Comptroller General, a violation of a collective-bargaining agreement coupled with a determination that but for that violation the grievant would have been promoted at an earlier date provides a proper basis for retroactive promotion and award of backpay. We note that this was essentially the basis for the Council's refusal to review the award in the *Janice Levy* case. Notwithstanding our decision in the *Levy* case, it appears from the above-quoted language of the Council's July 18, 1978, letter to this Office that there is still some question as to the effect under the Back Pay Act, 5 U.S.C. § 5596, of an arbitrator's determination that an agency has violated a provision of a negotiated agreement. Specifically, we refer to the Council's statement that the *Levy* decision is an "apparent departure * * * from the general principle established in previous decisions of your Office that a provision in a negotiated agreement, if otherwise proper, becomes a nondiscretionary agency policy for purposes of applying the provisions of the Back Pay Act of 1966."

We have held that an agency may bargain away its discretion and thereby make a provision of a collective-bargaining agreement a nondiscretionary agency policy, if the provision is consistent with applicable laws and regulations. The violation of such a mandatory provision in a negotiated agreement which causes an employee to lose pay, allowances or differentials may be found to be an unjustified or unwarranted personnel action under the Back Pay Act, 5 U.S.C. § 5596, thus entitling the aggrieved employees to retroactive compensation for such violation of a negotiated agreement. 54 Comp. Gen. 1071, 1073 (1975); 55 *id.* 171, 173 (1975); 55 *id.* 405, 407 (1975); 55 *id.* 427, 429 (1975).

Thus, we are fully committed to upholding awards of backpay for violations of mandatory provisions in negotiated agreements. However, as we stressed in the *Levy* case, not every violation of a collective-bargaining agreement will support a retroactive promotion and award of backpay. The violation must be of a provision in a collective-bargaining agreement amounting to a nondiscretionary agency policy. Our prior decisions in this area have not held that any provision, by the mere fact of its inclusion in a collective-bargaining agreement, becomes a nondiscretionary policy for purposes of awarding backpay.

In *John H. Brown*, 56 Comp. Gen. 57 (1976), we specifically addressed the suggestion that any provision in a collective-bargaining agreement becomes a nondiscretionary agency policy. The arbitrator in that case had directed that a special achievement award be given the grievant as a remedy for the agency's violation of a clause in the agreement providing the awards shall be used exclusively for rewarding employees for the performance of assigned duties and that the awards program shall not be used to discriminate or effect favoritism. In holding that the agreement did not change the granting of awards into a mandatory agency policy, we stated at 56 *id.* 59:

> In recent decisions this Office has attempted to give meaningful effect to the labor-management program established under Executive Order 11491 and to arbitration awards rendered thereunder if such awards are consistent with laws, regulations and our decisions. 54 Comp. Gen. 312, 320 (1974). We have held that provisions in collective bargaining agreements under the Executive Order may become nondiscretionary agency policies and, if the agency has agreed to binding arbitration, that the arbitrator's decision is entitled to the same weight as the agency head's decision would be given. *Id.* at 316. But we further stated therein that our decision "should not be construed to mean that any provision in a collective bargaining agreement automatically becomes a nondiscretionary agency policy," and we added that "[w]hen there is doubt as to whether an award may be properly implemented, a decision from the Council or from this Office should be sought." *Id.* at 319, 320.

Any doubt as to the nature of contractual violations that will support awards of backpay is resolved by the Civil Service Commission's amended backpay regulations found in title 5, Code of Federal Regulations, Part 550, Subpart H (1978). At 5 C.F.R. § 550.802(d), the term "nondiscretionary provision" is defined to mean:

> * * * any provision of law, Executive order, regulation, personnel policy issued by an agency, or collective bargaining agreement that requires an agency to take a prescribed action under stated conditions or criteria.

Although that regulation was not adopted by the Commission until March 25, 1977, well after the Cahill award was rendered, it primarily restates the standards of specificity applied in our decisions rendered under the Back Pay Act. Under that definition, action which should or should not be taken, as well as the conditions and criteria under which that action should or should not be taken, must be prescribed in the collective-bargaining agreement or in agency regulations or policies. Thus, while an arbitrator may appropriately find that an agency's actions were "inequitable" and hence contravened general language of a negotiated agreement calling for equitable treatment of all employees, that violation does not itself provide a basis for award of backpay, even when the arbitrator finds that the inequitable actions resulted in a loss of pay.

In the instant case, although the arbitrator found that clerical error in failing to process the grievant's promotion request in timely fashion resulted in a violation of article 6, section 1 of the negotiated agreement, he did not find, nor do we believe he properly could find, that article 6, section 1, specifically required promotions to be made within any prescribed time frame or in accordance with any stated conditions or criteria. Nothing in that provision limits or qualifies the discretion of the HEW Regional Personnel Office to approve or disapprove promotions or requires the agency to make promotions within any specified time period. Hence, this case is clearly distinguishable from those cases, such as 55 Comp. Gen. 42, *supra*, where the agency and the union had agreed upon a specified time frame for promotions under stated conditions.

Accordingly, since article 6, section 1, does not constitute a nondiscretionary agency policy, the award of a retroactive promotion and backpay to Mr. Cahill was improper.

Under the circumstances of this case, we believe that collection of overpayments of backpay made to Mr. Cahill in satisfaction of the arbitration award would be against equity and good conscience and not in the best interests of the United States. In particular, we refer to the facts that the issue of Mr. Cahill's entitlement was appealed through proper administrative channels and was deemed finally settled as of July 7, 1977, that payment was made to Mr. Cahill and received by him in good faith satisfaction of the award, and that the Council's determination denying the SSA's petition for review of the award apparently was based in part on its uncertainty as to the import of our prior decisions under the Back Pay Act. Accordingly, Mr. Cahill's indebtedness to the United States as a result of overpayments received pursuant to the arbitration award is waived pursuant to the provisions of 5 U.S.C. § 5584 and 4 C.F.R. Part 91.

[B-192516]

Contracts—Payments—Contractor v. Surety—Payment to Contractor

Army, although a mere stakeholder, became liable to Miller Act surety where surety notified Army of unpaid claims against contractor and asserted its prior rights to contract retainages, but where through clerical error, Army mailed final payments to contractor rather than to surety as agreed by all parties. Surety may be paid upon submission of evidence that all outstanding claims have been paid and surety assigns to Government any right it may have to recoup erroneous payments made to contractor.

In the matter of American Fidelity Fire Insurance Co., November 8, 1978:

The Department of the Army, Finance and Accounting Center, Indianapolis, Indiana, has requested a decision as to whether the claim of a bonding company should be paid. The American Fidelity Fire Insurance Company (American Fidelity) has filed claims for $5,413.15 and $1,303.96 under Army contracts DAKF48–76–C–A011 and DAKF48–77–C–0013 for modifications to buildings at Fort Hood, Texas. American Fidelity was surety under Miller Act (40 U.S.C. § 270) performance and payment bonds furnished by the prime contractor, H. C. Hodge General Contractors (Hodge). The record indicates the following sequence of events.

On May 10, 1977, counsel for American Fidelity advised the contracting officer that certain claims from subcontractors under DAKF 48–76–C–A011 had been received. Because Hodge had not paid these suppliers, the surety requested that all further payments to the contractor be withheld pending further instructions. On June 6, 1977, the surety advised the contracting officer of the contractor's failure to make payments under DAKF48–77–C–0013 and made the same request concerning further payments by the Army under the second contract.

On June 16, 1977, the contracting officer received a letter from Hodge stating that "all monies due or to become due under [contract –0013] have been assigned to American Fidelity." On June 17, 1977, an identical letter was received from Hodge concerning contract –A011.

In letters dated July 13, 1977, the contracting officer advised both the contractor and the surety that the Government considered itself a mere stakeholder in this instance. The contracting officer commented that the assignments did not qualify under the Assignment of Claims Act, 31 U.S.C. § 203, 41 U.S.C. § 15 (1970). It was suggested to both parties that the Army make checks for final payment payable to Hodge and send them to the surety in care of its counsel. The contracting officer requested the contractor and the surety to consent in writing to the proposed procedure. The contractor consented to this payment method.

According to the record, the contracts were completely performed by Hodge. Final payment request and contractor release forms were completed by the contractor, through the surety's attorneys. (The release forms executed by the contractor on September 18, 1977, provided that payment was to be to Hodge and American Fidelity.)

In a letter dated September 26, 1977, surety's counsel returned all necessary forms to the contracting officer with the request that final payment be made jointly to Hodge and American Fidelity and mailed to surety's attorney. Ultimately the surety authorized the final payment checks to be made payable to Hodge and mailed to American Fidelity.

On November 14, 1977, the contracting officer requested that the Army finance office send final payment under both contracts to the contractor and listed the mailing address as that of the surety's attorney. Final payment vouchers dated November 21, 1977, specify payment to H. C. Hodge, but the contractor's mailing address is indicated.

From December 19, 1977, until mid-January of 1978, the record indicates that the procurement agent made numerous phone calls in a futile attempt to locate Hodge. American Fidelity was also unsuccessful in its attempts to contact the contractor following his receipt of the checks. The record indicates, however, that at some point the checks were indorsed and cashed by H. C. Hodge.

By letter of January 19, 1978, American Fidelity made demand for immediate payment in the amount of the final payments under both contracts.

While the surety is no longer claiming the rights of an assignee, we note our agreement with the Army's determination that the attempted assignments were improper, since American Fidelity does not qualify as a "financing institution" under the Assignment of Claims Act. Regardless, the central issues here involve the rights of a surety and the obligations of the Government as a stakeholder. As stated in *Home Indemnity Co.* v. *United States*, "[t]he rights of the surety in the final contract payment have long been recognized." 376 F.2d 890, 892 (1967). In accordance with the decision of the Court of Claims in that case, immediately upon notification by American Fidelity that Hodge was in default on payments due to various subcontractors, the Army owed a higher duty of care to the surety in regard to the contract retainages.

The facts of *Home Indemnity* are substantially similar to those presented here. The surety in that case notified the contracting officer of the unpaid claims of subcontractors and requested that no further contract payments be made to the contractor. The contract was fully performed and final payment was claimed by both the contractor and the surety. In pertinent part, the court in *Home Indemnity* stated:

> When the contract involved here was completed, the Government was the stakeholder of the final payment or security for which there were two contending claimants, the surety and the contractor. In view of [the surety's] equitable rights in the fund, which were superior to those of the contractor, the Government had no right as a stakeholder to settle the question unilaterally by paying the fund to the contractor.

In the instant case, the Army contends that, in mailing the final payment checks to Hodge, it did not attempt to "settle the question unilaterally." Rather, it is the Army's position that the checks were improperly mailed due to a "clerical inadvertence" for which it should not be held liable. While we agree that the Army's purpose was not to settle the question unilaterally, we must conclude that under the circumstances the Army's intention is irrelevant. Our decision here must turn on the effect of the Army's action in mailing the checks to the contractor's address.

In looking to the result of the Army's clerical error, it would appear that the facts of the instant case almost parallel those of *Newark Ins. Co.* v. *United States*, 169 F. Supp. 955, 144 Ct. Cl. 655 (1955). In that case the court stated:

> If it is made to appear that the Government's officials, after due notice of the facts giving rise to an equitable right in the [surety], and of the [surety's] assertion of such a right, paid out *without a valid reason* for so doing, the money in question to someone other than the [surety], the surety will be entitled to a judgment. 169 F. Supp. 955, 957. [Italic supplied.]

Based upon the cases discussed, it is our conclusion that the Army paid funds to Hodge in which American Fidelity had a prior right and, therefore, that the Government is liable to the surety in the amount of the final payments made under both contracts, provided of course, that the surety has not been able to retrieve such payments from the contractor.

As a general rule, for a payment bond surety to share in contract retainages, it must first pay all legitimate claims of the laborers and materialmen irrespective of the limits of its bond. *American Fidelity Fire Insurance Co.* v. *United States*, 206 Ct. Cl. 570, 575, 513 F.2d 1375, 1378 (1975); B-163427, March 1, 1968; B-161093, April 6, 1967; B-155504, November 16, 1965. Moreover, *Home Indemnity, supra*, is consistent with this rule. American Fidelity may be paid the contract retainages as a payment bond surety when it submits reasonable evidence to the Army that it has paid all the outstanding claims under the contracts and assigns to the Government any right it may have to recoup the final contract payments which erroneously were sent to the contractor.

[B-190429]

Courts—Judgments, Decrees, etc.—Interest—Authority

Wrongful death judgment against United States for $373,431, apportioned equally by court among four heirs, is subject to interest limitations in 31 U.S.C. 724a (applied as it existed at time of judgment, prior to 1977 amendment), since each judgment beneficiary received severable and distinct amount less than $100,000. This decision is modified (extended) by 59 Comp. Gen. ———— (B-193927, Feb. 13, 1980).

Courts—Judgments, Decrees, etc.—Appeals—Dismissal

Since a purpose of first proviso of 31 U.S.C. 724a was to provide compensation to a successful plaintiff whose judgment payment was delayed solely because the United States appealed and lost, interest may be allowed on a wrongful death judgment against the United States where the Government filed notice of appeal and appeal was subsequently dismissed by stipulation of the parties because the Government did not pursue its appeal. B–145389, April 18, 1961, is overruled.

In the matter of *Vaillancourt* v. *United States*—Payment of Interest on Judgment, November 14, 1978:

The plaintiff in *Vaillancourt* v. *United States*, United States District Court, Northern District of California, has requested reconsideration of the settlement action of our Claims Division, dated July 19, 1977, which disallowed interest on the judgment awarded to her.

The original suit was a wrongful death action brought pursuant to the Federal Tort Claims Act, 28 U.S.C. §§ 1346(b), 2671–2680. The Plaintiff, Mary T. Vaillancourt, suing individually and as guardian ad litem for her three children, alleged negligence on the part of the Palo Alto Veterans Administration Hospital resulting in the death of her husband, Roger F. Vaillancourt, a patient at the hospital. On September 30, 1976, the Court entered judgment for the plaintiffs in the amount of $373,431. The California wrongful death law requires a lump-sum judgment. California Code of Civil Procedure § 377; *Cross* v. *Pacific Gas and Electric Co.*, 60 Cal. 2d 690, 388 P. 2d 353 (1964). California law also requires that the award be apportioned among the various heirs in accordance with their separate interests. The Court's Memorandum and Order accompanying the judgment apportioned the award as follows: "Mary T., wife, 25%; Gail A., daughter, 25%; Joan Marie, daughter, 25%; and Marie Cecile, daughter, 25%." Thus, the amount payment to each was $93,357.75.

On October 13, 1976, the plaintiffs forwarded a certified copy of the judgment to our Claims Division along with a demand that interest be applied in favor of the plaintiffs from the date of the judgment. On December 3, 1976, the United States filed a Notice of Appeal in the Ninth Circuit Court of Appeals. We understand that the Government prepared an appellate record but did not further prosecute the appeal. The appeal nevertheless remained pending in the Court of Appeals until the parties filed a stipulation to dismiss the appeal on October 21, 1977. On June 29, 1977, the Department of Justice submitted the judgment to us for payment, certifying that no proceedings for review of the judgment would be taken. At that time, we were not aware that the appeal had been filed and was still pending. On July 19, 1977, we issued settlement for the principal amount of the judgment, without interest.

The Attorney for the plaintiffs has requested that we reconsider our position that no interest is payable on the judgment in this case.

Interest on judgments under the Federal Tort Claims Act is generally authorized by 28 U.S.C. § 2411(b) as follows:

Except as otherwise provided in subsection (a) of this section, on all final judgments rendered against the United States in actions instituted under section 1346 of this title, interest shall be computed at the rate of 4 per centum per annum from the date of the judgment up to, but not exceeding, thirty days after the date of approval of any appropriation Act providing for payment of the judgment.

Our authority to pay interest is limited, however, by the permanent indefinite appropriation established by 31 U.S.C. § 724a, which at the time of the judgment provided in pertinent part as follows *:

There are appropriated, out of any money in the Treasury not otherwise appropriated, and out of the postal revenues, respectively, such sums as may on and after July 27, 1956 be necessary for the payment, not otherwise provided for, as certified by the Comptroller General, of final judgments, awards, and compromise settlements (not in excess of $100,000, or its equivalent in foreign currencies at the time of payment, in any one case) which are payable in accordance with the terms of sections 2414, 2517, 2672, or 2677 of Title 28, together with such interest and costs as may be specified in such judgments or otherwise authorized by law: *Provided*, That, whenever a judgment of a district court to which the provisions of section 2411(b) of Title 28 apply, is payable from this appropriation, interest shall be paid thereon only when such judgment becomes final after review on appeal or petition by the United States, and then only from the date of the filing of the transcript thereof in the General Accounting Office to the date of the mandate of affirmance (except that in cases reviewed by the Supreme Court interest shall not be allowed beyond the term of the Court at which the judgment was affirmed): *Provided further*, That whenever a judgment rendered by the Court of Claims is payable from this appropriation, interest payable thereon in accordance with section 2516(b) of Title 28 shall be computed from the date of the filing of the transcript thereof in the General Accounting Office * * *.

Thus, with respect to district court judgments, at the time of the entry of the judgment in this case, the law governing interest on judgments greater than $100,000 differed from that governing judgments of less than $100,000. On judgments exceeding $100,000, interest was not contingent on any appeal and was payable from the date of the judgment pursuant to 28 U.S.C. § 2411(b). Under 31 U.S.C. § 724a, interest on judgments not in excess of $100,000 was payable only when such judgments became final after review on appeal or petition by the United States.

It has been our position that, in suits involving more than one plaintiff, the $100,000 limitation is to be applied not to the aggregate amount of the judgment but to the amounts due each individual judgment creditor. This view is consistent with Congress' purposes in establishing the permanent indefinite appropriation, which were to provide for

*The $100,000 limitation was removed by Pub. L. No. 95-26 (May 4, 1977), 91 Stat. 61. Although we believe the plaintiff's entitlement to interest should be governed by the law as it existed at the time of the judgment, the result here, as discussed *infra*, would be the same in either case.

the prompt payment of judgments without awaiting a special appropriation, and to reduce interest costs to the Government. H.R. Rep. No. 2638, 84th Cong., 2d Sess. 72 (1956). Also, this position has been supported by the courts. Thus, in *United States* v. *Maryland ex. rel. Meyer*, 349 F.2d 693 (D.C. Cir. 1965), the court held that the limitation applied with respect to "each individual who recovered a severable and distinct amount not in excess of $100,000." 349 F. 2d at 695. See also, *United States* v. *Varner*, 400 F.2d 369 (5th Cir. 1968) ; 40 Comp. Gen. 307 (1960).

California law allows for only one judgment in a wrongful death action. Its purpose, to expedite litigation, bears no relationship to the purposes of 31 U.S.C. § 724a. Thus, where under California law, a severable and specific award in a final judgment, payable only to a particular claimant, is less than $100,000, it constitutes a judgment "in any one case" as that expression is used in 31 U.S.C. § 724a. Here, since the awards apportioned by the court were each for $93,357.75, an amount less than $100,000, they must be treated as four "judgments not exceeding $100,000." Therefore, entitlement to interest is governed by the first proviso of 31 U.S.C. § 724a. *United States* v. Maryland *ex. rel. Meyer, supra.*

Under the first proviso of 31 U.S.C. § 724a, interest is payable only when the judgment has "become final after review on appeal or petition by the United States, and then only from the date of the filing of the transcript thereof in the General Accounting Office to the date of the mandate of affirmance." The question thus becomes whether the filing of a notice of appeal by the Government, and the subsequent dismissal of that appeal, can be deemed to satisfy the statutory condition. We considered essentially the same question in B–145389, April 18, 1961, and concluded that interest was not payable since the statute contemplated an actual review on the merits. Our conclusion was stated as follows:

> Under the statute your claim for interest would be allowable only on the basis that the Government's action in filing a notice of appeal on November 28, 1960, which was dismissed on January 19, 1961, constituted a "review" and an "affirmance" by the Court of Appeals. The issuance of a mandate of affirmance presupposes a review of the merits and the mere dismissal of the notice of appeal in no sense indicates such action has taken place. In your case, there having been no "review" of the merits and no mandate of affirmance having been issued, interest is not payable under [31 U.S.C. § 724a]. * * *

Upon careful reconsideration, we now believe our 1961 decision was incorrect.

Prior to the enactment of 31 U.S.C. § 724a in 1956, interest on district court judgments was governed by 28 U.S.C. § 2411(b), *supra*, and was not contingent upon an appeal by the Government. The purpose of the first proviso of § 724a was to make interest provisions for district court judgments consistent with those for the Court of Claims. The proviso was explained in detail in a statement prepared by the Bureau of the Budget (now Office of Management and Budget), as follows:

> The present situation with respect to the payment of interest is undesirable in two respects—first, the Government, because of the delay in making appropriations, bears the expense of interest which could be saved if appropriations were available for payment of the judgments when rendered; and second, there is a wide variance between the provisions of law respecting the payment of interest on judgments rendered by the district courts as compared with those rendered by the Court of Claims. Interest is paid on Court of Claims judgments only when the United States appeals and then only from the date when the transcript of the judgment is filed with the Treasury Department to the date of the mandate of affirmance. Interest is paid on judgments of the district courts, regardless of whether the Government appeals, from the date of the judgment to a date not later than 30 days after the making of an appropriation for payment of the judgment.
>
> It is believed that the provision for the payment of interest in cases where the Government appeals, as now prescribed by law with respect to judgments in the Court of Claims, is fair and equitable and need not be disturbed. If this belief is correct, it would follow that interest should be paid on judgments of the district courts on the same basis. If interest on judgments of the district courts were placed on the same basis as the Court of Claims, interest on district court judgments not appealed by the United States would be eliminated entirely. In district court cases which are appealed by the Government, interest would be eliminated from the date the judgment was rendered to the date the plaintiff filed a transcript thereof with the proper Government agency, and from the date of the mandate of affirmance to the time when a specific appropriation could be secured for the payment of the judgment. Hearings on Supplemental Appropriation Bill, 1957. Before Subcommittees of the House Committee on Appropriations, 84th Cong., 2d Sess., pt. 2, at 888 (1956).

The interest provision for judgments of the Court of Claims, upon which the first proviso of 31 U.S.C. § 724a was patterned, is found at 28 U.S.C. § 2516(b) and also contains the "mandate of affirmance" language.

Thus both statutes use the term "mandate of affirmance," a term which normally presupposes a review on the merits. *See, e.g.*, Fed. R. App. Proc. Rule 41. A literal reading of the statutory language would therefore seem to support our 1961 decision. However, in adopting this literal construction, we now believe the 1961 decision overlooked the purpose of the interest provisions.

We have researched the legislative histories of both statutes—31 U.S.C. § 724a and 28 U.S.C. § 2516(b)—and have found no indication that Congress considered the application of those provisions to a situation where the Government appealed from an adverse judgment and, after considerable delay, later consented to withdraw the appeal. To be sure, one of the purposes of the first proviso of section 724a was to reduce interest costs to the Government. This was accomplished by virtue of the fact that the first proviso is considerably more restrictive than 28 U.S.C. § 2411(b) which would have governed had the proviso not been enacted. It is clear that Congress, had it so desired, could have eliminated post-judgment interest entirely. Since it chose not to do so, it is significant and proper to examine the reasons why Congress authorized interest in cases where the Government appealed and lost.

Section 724a was originally enacted on July 27, 1956, as section 1302 of the Supplemental Appropriation Act of 1957, 70 Stat. 678, 694. Prior to that time, with few exceptions, payment of a judgment against the United States required a specific congressional appropriation, a process which involved considerable delay since it could not be initiated until the judgment had become final. The rationale of 28 U.S.C. § 2411(b) was to compensate the plaintiff for the delay in receiving payment occasioned by the Government, *i.e.*, the need to request and receive a specific appropriation. The enactment of section 724a made funds immediately available for the payment of judgments not in excess of $100,000 in most cases. The first proviso recognized the one situation—an appeal by the Government—in which actions of the Government could still produce a significant delay in payment. It seems clear that the purpose of this proviso, as stated by the Comptroller of the Treasury in an 1899 decision concerning the corresponding Court of Claims provision, was "no doubt to compensate claimants for the loss suffered by delay in receiving payment, when the delay is not justified by the result of the appeal." 5 Comp. Dec. 893, 897 (1889). (*)

In this context, it seems clear that the essential purpose of the first proviso is equally served by the allowance of interest in a case where the Government appeals and simply does not prosecute the appeal. "The want of justification in an appeal is as clearly shown by a dismissal of the appeal as it would be by an affirmance of the judgment." 5 Comp. Dec. at 898. Since the essence of the first proviso is the delay occasioned by the action of the Government, and since the filing of a notice of appeal effectively prevents prompt payment, it would in our opinion be highly anomalous to allow interest where the Government vigorously but unsuccessfully prosecutes the appeal but to deny it where the Government for whatever reason decides not to prosecute the appeal and withdraws it. The effect is the same—the original judgment in favor of the plaintiff stands. Accordingly, B–145389, April 18, 1961, is hereby overruled.

The final question is the determination of the proper beginning and ending dates for interest computation. A certified copy of the orig-

___

(*)When the Court of Claims interest provision was originally enacted in 1863 (12 Stat. 766, the predecessor of 28 U.S.C. § 2516(b)), it was contemplated that indefinite appropriations would be made for the payment of final Court of Claims judgments. In fact this was not done until the enactment of section 724a in 1956 (and, for judgments greater than $100,000, the 1977 amendment made by Pub. L. No. 95–26), hence the historic "inconsistency" in the entitlement to post-judgment interest between 28 U.S.C. §§ 2411(b) and 2516(b).

inal judgment was filed with GAO by plaintiff's counsel by letter dated October 13, 1976, received by GAO October 18, 1976. Although the appeal was not formally dismissed until October 21, 1977, the Justice Department submitted the judgment for payment on June 29, 1977, certifying in its transmittal letter that no proceedings for review of the judgment would be taken. Pursuant to 28 U.S.C. § 2414, whenever the Attorney General determines that no further review will be sought, "he shall so certify and the judgment shall be deemed final." It was this determination which effectively rendered the judgment final for payment purposes and which permitted GAO to certify it to the Treasury Department for payment.

In accordance with the foregoing, an additional settlement will be issued for interest at the rate of 4 percent from October 18, 1976, through June 29, 1977.

[B–191489]

Equipment—Automatic Data Processing Systems—Selection and Purchase—Third Party Market—Master Terms and Conditions Program

Protest that certain provisions of Master Terms and Conditions (MTC) program, for procuring brand name automated data processing equipment (ADPE) from vendors in addition to the original equipment manufacturers, are restrictive of competition is denied, since provisions were determined to be minimum needs of Government and protester has not shown that determination was unreasonable, or that provisions unduly restrict competition.

Equipment—Automatic Data Processing Systems—General Services Administration—Responsibilities Under Brooks Act

Protest that MTC violates Brooks Act mandate that Administrator of General Services Administration procure ADPE in economic and efficient manner is denied, since Administrator is given discretion to develop and implement ADPE procurement policies so long as policies are not contrary to law or otherwise detrimental to Government's interest, and protester has not shown either condition.

In the matter of Federal Leasing, Inc., November 14, 1978:

Federal Leasing, Inc. (FLI) has protested the General Services Administration's (GSA) use of the Master Terms and Conditions (MTC) in two procurements for automated data processing equipment (ADPE), request for proposals (RFP) No. CDPR–DOOOO5N and RFP No. CDPR–DOOOO7N. FLI contends that certain MTC provisions restrict competition.

The MTC program was initiated in 1972 to encourage competition in the procurement of brand name ADPE where the equipment is available from sources in addition to the original equipment manufacturer (OEM). The MTC sets forth requirements such as bid bonds, performance bonds, acceptance testing, established maintenance requirements, evaluation criteria, and acceptable price plans that the Government has determined are necessary when procuring from non-OEM sources (also known as the third-party market). Participants in the MTC program are required to agree to the terms and conditions each fiscal year, after which they are eligible for award on any MTC procurement for which they submit a proposal during the fiscal year. According to GSA, 95 vendors, including FLI, have signed the MTC in this fiscal year, without taking exception to any terms or conditions. Sixteen contracts have been awarded during that time, with an average of 10 vendors submitting proposals on each RFP.

FLI has not argued that anything peculiar to the two protested procurements is restrictive of competition, but rather that certain MTC provisions which are present in all MTC procurements are restrictive. According to FLI, its experience regarding the use of the MTC in a previous GSA ADPE procurement led it to believe that the MTC is restrictive of competition. We note that FLI is not protesting the use of the MTC as a procurement vehicle, but only the use of certain provisions of the MTC, and their nonnegotiability.

FLI contends that the following MTC provisions restrict competition:

1. The requirement that maintenance and hardware rental be offered as a package.

2. The required inclusion of maintenance credit provisions for malfunction of rental equipment.

3. The requirement that defective installed equipment be replaced by the contractor at no additional cost.

FLI also argues generally that GSA will not negotiate on any MTC provisions and that this forces vendors to accept terms and conditions without meaningful review of the requirements. According to FLI, such an approach violates the Brooks Act (40 U.S.C. § 759 (1976)) mandate that GSA "* * * coordinate and provide for the *economic and efficient* purchase, lease and maintenance of automated data processing equipment by Federal Agencies." [Italic provided by protester.]

The MTC provisions that FLI objects to reflect GSA's determination of its needs in procuring ADPE from the non-OEM market. Government procurement officials who are familiar with the conditions under which supplies, equipment or services have been used, and are to be used, are generally in the best position to know the Government's actual needs. Consequently, we will not question an agency's determination of what its minimum needs are, or what will satisfy those needs, unless there is a clear showing that the determination has no reasonable basis. *Herley Industries, Inc.*, B–186947, September 30, 1977, 77–2 CPD 247; *Jarrell-Ash Division of the Fisher Scientific Company*, B–185582, January 12, 1977, 77–1 CPD 19; *Johnson Controls, Inc.*, B–184416, January 2, 1976, 76–1 CPD 4. Also, though needs should be determined so as to maximize competition, we will not interpose our judgment for that of the agency unless the protester shows by clear and convincing evidence that the agency's judgment is in error and that a contract awarded on the basis of those needs would be by unduly restricting competition, a violation of law. See, e.g., *Joe R. Stafford*, B–184822, November 19, 1975, 75–2 CPD 324.

FLI has objected to the MTC requirement that non-OEM offerors offer maintenance or certify its availability from the OEM for the system's life. FLI contends that competition would be enhanced if non-OEM vendors could compete for equipment contracts, without offering maintenance. FLI argues that for almost all of the equipment acquired through the MTC, there are OEM ADP schedules that provide for maintenance of Government equipment. FLI states that while these schedules are for maintenance of Government equipment, it has "never heard of a manufacturer refusing maintenance under the Schedule so long as the third party has authorized repair and maintenance." Consequently, the Government can procure its maintenance requirements separately.

In addition to our general legal standards regarding minimum needs, we have held that a determination to procure possibly divisible portions of a total requirement by means of a "package" approach, rather than by separate procurements, is within the discretion of the contracting agency and will not be disturbed by our Office in the absence of a clear showing that it lacked a reasonable basis. See, e.g., *Allen and Vickers, Inc.; American Laundry Machinery*, 54 Comp. Gen. 445 (1974), 74–2 CPD 303.

According to GSA, separate equipment and maintenance solicitations are undesirable for the following reasons. A separate maintenance solicitation could not be issued until the least cost ADPE proposal had been selected, since the Government would not know its exact maintenance needs until then. Then there might be no acceptable maintenance offers, and the Government would have selected ADPE, but would have no maintenance source.

While FLI might be correct in its argument that the Government usually would have no trouble procuring maintenance separately, it has not shown that the determination to procure maintenance and equipment together to ensure adequate maintenance is unreasonable or unduly restrictive of competition. In fact, if, as FLI asserts, OEMs rarely refuse maintenance under their schedules, we do not understand how the requirement that the third party obtain a certificate to that effect restricts competition.

FLI has objected to the MTC requirement of maintenance credit for equipment malfunction. If the equipment is inoperative, through no fault of the Government, for a continuous period of 8 hours in a 24-hour period, then a credit is applied to the monthly rental payments. According to FLI, this escalates the interest rate that can be obtained from financing institutions when assigning contract rights, and thus escalates the price that must be charged to the Government. It is FLI's contention that often the Government's risk is not great enough to justify the price increase and that the Government should assess the alternatives. GSA feels that the provision is necessary to protect the Government from having to pay for services which it has not received.

Again, FLI has not shown that this provision is unreasonable or restrictive of competition. FLI's objections appear to be on the order of a disagreement over the business judgment of GSA.

FLI's final specific objection to the MTC is that the provision requiring the replacement of defective equipment at the contractor's cost may be inappropriate because the Government can bear the risk, and the equipment has a history of reliability. GSA's response is that the provision provides the Government needed protection over the life of the system, and that the vendor is protected from default based on equipment failure and the potential of an assessment of excess reprocurement costs.

It is our opinion that this objection also amounts to a disagreement over a question of business judgment. FLI certainly has not shown that GSA's determination is unreasonable.

Concerning FLI's general argument that the MTC is nonnegotiable, inhibits vendor/user communication, and thus violates the Brooks Act mandate quoted above, GSA maintains that the MTC was established for, and has generally achieved its goal of, fostering competition by permitting the third-party market to compete on the brand name procurements. GSA argues that the provisions of the MTC are necessary to provide the Government with adequate protection in ADPE procurements with non-OEM vendors. GSA contends that user/vendor communication is not inhibited, since vendors are generally permitted to meet with the user agency for site inspection and other technical purposes. GSA has stated that ample opportunities have existed for FLI and other vendors to present objections and alternatives to the MTC. GSA's position is that the development and use of the MTC fall within the range of discretion granted to the Administrator of GSA by the Brooks Act.

In *Comdisco, Inc.*, B–181956, February 13, 1975, 75–1 CPD 96, we stated that:

The Federal Property and Administrative Services Act, as amended, 68 Stat. 377, authorizes the Administrator of General Services "to the extent that he determines that so doing is advantageous to the Government in terms of economy, efficiency, or service," to "prescribe policies and methods of procurement" and to "procure and supply personal property and nonpersonal services for the use of executive agencies * * *." 40 U.S.C. 481. The Administrator's specific authority to coordinate and provide for the economic and efficient purchase, lease and maintenance of ADP equipment was added by the Brooks Act, *supra*, 40 U.S.C. 759. We have held that these provisions vest in GSA broad authority over Government procurement of ADP equipment, 47 Comp. Gen. 275 (1967); 48 *id.* 462 (1969); 51 *id.* 457 (1972), and that in light of this authority, GSA could develop and implement policies regarding the award of Schedule contracts so long as the policies are not contrary to law or otherwise detrimental to the Government's interest. See B–168971, May 21, 1969.

We then went on to hold that GSA's refusal to negotiate a Schedule contract with a third-party vendor was a proper exercise of this authority because the third-party market did not usually provide the full range of maintenance and repair services required by GSA. In the present case, GSA has insisted on the use of the MTC program in non-OEM procurements for the protection of legitimate Government interests similar to those we found acceptable in *Comdisco*. FLI has not shown how this is contrary to law or detrimental to the Government's interests.

Accordingly, the protest is denied.

[B–192858]

Pay—Medical and Dental Officers—"Variable Incentive Pay"—Agreement—Renegotiation

An existing Variable Incentive Pay (VIP) agreement under 37 U.S.C. 313 may not be renegotiated to a lesser commitment by executing a second VIP contract, even if it had been received by the proper officials. Terms of the first VIP contract are binding on the parties and where officer does not complete active service agreed to, he is subject to the refund provisions of the contract, 37 U.S.C. 313, and the regulations requiring repayment of amounts received for which service was not performed.

Public Health Service—Commissioned Personnel—Active Service Obligation—Failure to Complete—Entitlements

A commissioned officer of the Public Health Service who does not complete a term of active service to which he agreed in writing may be divested of entitlement to lump-sum annual leave and travel and transportation entitlements in accordance with regulations promulgated by the Public Health Service under 37 U.S.C. 501(g) and paragraph M6457 of 1 Joint Travel Regulations, promulgated under 37 U.S.C. 404(b) and 406(c).

In the matter of John P. Manges, MD, November 14, 1978:

This action is the result of an appeal by Dr. John P. Manges, Jr., of a settlement of our Claims Division dated September 1, 1977. In the settlement, Dr. Manges' claim for the payment of transportation expenses, the shipment of household goods, and the lump-sum payment for unused leave incident to his separation from active duty with the Commissioned Corps of the Public Health Service in June 1977, was denied.

On July 23, 1973, Dr. Manges was recalled to active duty as a medical officer with the Public Health Service and assigned as a resident in internal medicine at the University of Vermont. On July 1, 1975, he was transferred to the Public Health Service Indian Hospital in Santa Fe, New Mexico. As a result of his assignment to the University of Vermont he incurred an active duty obligation of 2 years for training received outside the Public Health Service.

On August 7, 1975, he executed a Variable Incentive Pay (VIP) contract for 4 years and was authorized a VIP payment of $9,000 effective July 1, 1975, to coincide with the completion of his initial residency. He was also paid $9,000 for the second year of this contract.

Dr. Manges requested release from active duty with a termination date effective on the completion of his obligated term of active duty resulting from his training at the University of Vermont. Since Dr. Manges did not fulfill the 4-year VIP contract which he had executed on August 7, 1975, he was divested of entitlement to transportation for himself and his dependents, shipment of household goods, and lump-sum payment for unused annual leave in accordance with Public Health Service regulation, Commissioned Corps Personnel Manual (CCPM) CC 22.2, Instruction 3, Section H.5.

Dr. Manges in requesting payment of these allowances indicates that on signing the VIP contract for 4 years he realized that he would receive the lower rate of $9,000 per year until he satisfied his obligation resulting from his residency at the University of Vermont. He states that although he realized this, he was not aware that the contract once executed was not renegotiable to a lesser commitment.

Dr. Manges states that in June of 1976 his career plans had altered and that he planned to leave the Public Health Service on completing his 2-year obligation resulting from his residency. Thus, on June 17, 1976, he executed the annual recertification indicating that he intended to serve only 1 additional year rather than 3 years required under his original VIP contract. The VIP for this year would be $9,000 under either the first or second contract for the year commencing July 1, 1976. Dr. Manges says that he assumed that this action cancelled the remaining portion of the first VIP agreement and that he had entered into a new contract with only a 1-year obligation.

The Public Health Service report on this matter states that the second VIP contract executed by Dr. Manges on June 17, 1976, was never received in their headquarters. Dr. Manges has submitted a copy of the contract and statements from witnesses in support of his statement that he did execute the agreement in June 1976. Dr. Manges also contends that since the original contract he signed made no provision to the effect that the contract was not renegotiable, he was justified in assuming that it could be renegotiated. He also refers to other situations existing during his tenure with the Public Health Service which he believes contributed to the decision to deny him the benefits claimed. However, we do not feel that a listing of these factors has any bearing on his entitlement to the claimed benefits.

Under 37 U.S.C. 313 (1976) and regulations promulgated pursuant thereto by the Secretary of Health, Education, and Welfare, a medical officer of the Public Health Service who is otherwise eligible and executes a written active duty agreement will receive incentive pay for completing a specified number of years of continuous active duty. Upon acceptance of the written agreement by the Secretary or his designee, he may be paid an amount not to exceed $13,500 for each year of the agreement, in addition to any other pay and allowances to which he is entitled.

This statute also provides that an officer who does not complete the service for which he received the VIP payment, will be required to refund any amounts received in accordance with regulations promulgated by the Secretary. There is no provision authorizing the renegotiation of a VIP agreement that has been executed and approved.

Apparently no authority exists whereby the Public Health Service can require a commissioned officer to remain on active duty. Consequently, 37 U.S.C. 501(g) (1976) and paragraph M6457 of 1 Joint Travel Regulations (JTR) which authorize a lump-sum payment for unused annual leave on separation and travel and transportation allowances, respectively, are used to provide additional incentives for an officer to serve the complete period of active duty to which he had agreed.

Under 37 U.S.C. 501(g) a commissioned officer of the Public Health Service may be paid a lump-sum payment for unused annual leave under certain circumstances, with the approval of the Surgeon General. It has been the practice of the Surgeon General to disapprove applications for the lump-sum payment made by officers who do not serve the entire period of duty to which they agreed. See PHS Personnel Instruction 3, dated July 13, 1976, CC22.2, Section H, paragraph 5. Since the Congress specifically provided approval authority to the Surgeon General in connection with the payment for unused annual leave, it is our conclusion that regulations providing for a divestiture of this entitlement are within the scope of the statute.

Likewise, 1 JTR, M6457, provides similar authority in connection with entitlement to travel and transportation allowances for himself and his dependents and household goods when a member voluntarily leaves the service prior to the expiration of a period that he agreed in writing to serve. This restriction is apparently issued under the authority of the Secretary concerned to prescribe conditions and limitations under which such travel and transportation allowances accrue. 37 U.S.C. 404(b) and 406(c) (1976). See 41 Comp. Gen. 767 (1962).

In Dr. Manges' case he executed a contract by which he agreed to serve 4 years from the date of that contract. It is true that for the first 2 years of that contract he could only receive $9,000 per year because of the obligated service. However, the fact that he executed a 4-year contract would have entitled him to substantially higher payments during his third and fourth year under the contract.

Furthermore, a VIP contract is not renegotiable and clearly states on its face that penalties will be imposed in accordance with service policies. See also PHS Personnel Instruction 3, July 13, 1976, CC22.2, Section F, paragraph 5. The subsequent contract executed by Dr. Manges in June 1976, even if received at Commissioned Corps headquarters would not have served to renegotiate his initial agreement. It also appears that he should have been aware that the second contract had not been received or was invalid, when he received the orders authorizing the second year's installment of VIP. The orders clearly stated that the payment would be for 1 year of a 4-year agreement.

Moreover, a memorandum dated May 10, 1976, to all medical and dental officers clearly stated that officers who voluntarily terminate their agreements prior to the date their current agreement expires will be divested of entitlement to transportation for themselves and dependents, shipment of household goods, and lump-sum payment for unused annual leave. This statement was issued as a clarification of the policy, and was not a new policy.

The indications in the record that the Indian Health Service was aware at a relatively early date that Dr. Manges intended to terminate his active service in June 1977, in our view, have no bearing on his entitlement to the lump-sum payment and the travel and transportation allowances.

While it is unfortunate that Dr. Manges was not aware that he would be divested of the claimed entitlements until just prior to his separation, the contract and the pertinent regulations should have put him on notice that he would be divested of these entitlements.

Accordingly, it is our view the actions of the Public Health Service were proper in the circumstances and the denial of Dr. Manges' claim by our Claims Division must be sustained.

[B-165731]

General Accounting Office—Jurisdiction—Contracts—Nonappropriated Fund Activities—Foreign Military Sales

General Accounting Office (GAO), despite prior decisions holding otherwise, will undertake bid protest type reviews concerning propriety of contract awards under Department of Defense (DOD) foreign military sales (FMS) program. Change in position is based on recognition that appropriated funds are utilized in FMS procurements and that, in view of significant dollar amounts involved, area is appropriate for review. 55 Comp. Gen. 674 is modified. Other decisions, to the contrary, are overruled or modified, as appropriate.

In the matter of Procurements Involving Foreign Military Sales, November 16, 1978:

The General Accounting Office during the past 2 years has declined to consider private party complaints concerning procurements made by Department of Defense (DOD) components pursuant to the Arms Export Control Act, formerly known as the Foreign Military Sales Act, 22 U.S.C. §§ 2751 *et seq.* (1976). This declination has been grounded in the perception that foreign military sales (FMS) procurements do not involve the use of appropriated funds, and thus are not subject to review under our Bid Protest Procedures, 4 C.F.R. Part 20 (1978).

For some time, however, we have been aware that at least some aspects of FMS procurements have been viewed as involving the use of appropriated funds. *See*, e.g., *Hughes Aircraft Co.* v. *United States*, 534 F. 2d 889 (Ct. Cl. 1976) ; Graham, "The General Accounting Office and Foreign Military Sales," 19 A.F.L. Rev. 76, 84–7 (1977) ; 43 Fed. Reg. 4010 (1978). Moreover, the significant growth of FMS (from fiscal year (FY) 1970 sales of $953 million to FY 1977 sales of $11.2 billion and an estimated $13.2 billion for FY 1978), coupled with continuing requests, despite our declining to consider bid protests in the FMS area, that we review FMS procurements, suggest that such procurements are appropriate for review under our general audit authority, *cf.* 40 Fed. Reg. 42406–07 (1975), as a concomitant to our ongoing audit reviews in the FMS area. *See*, e.g., our report entitled *The Department of Defense Continues to Improperly Subsidize Foreign Military Sales*, FGMSD–78–51, August 25, 1978. Accordingly, we have thoroughly reconsidered our position and, after taking into account the views of DOD, have concluded for the reasons which follow that in the future this Office will consider private party complaints in connection with FMS procurements.

Under the FMS program, the President and DOD enter into agreements with eligible foreign governments and international organizations to sell them defense articles and defense services. Sales can be either from DOD stocks or on a cash sale basis whereby the United States Government, in effect, acts as the agent of the buying customer in dealing with the United States selling company. The United States is also authorized under certain circumstances to finance the sales.

Foreign military sales are transacted under authority of Pub. L. No. 90–629, 82 Stat. 1320, October 22, 1968, as amended by the Foreign Military Sales and Assistance Act, Pub. L. No. 93–189, 87 Stat. 730, December 17, 1973, and the International Security Assistance and Arms Export Control Act of 1976, Pub. L. No. 94–329, 90 Stat. 738, June 30, 1976, *codified at* 22 U.S.C. §§ 2751 *et seq.* (1976) (the Act). The pertinent provisions of the Act that bear upon the jurisdictional question concerned are sections 22(a), 22(b), and 23 of the Act which respectively provide:

§ 2762. [§ 22(a)]. Procurement for cash sales; * * *

(a) Except as otherwise provided in this section, the President may, without requirement for charge to any appropriation or contract authorization otherwise provided, enter into contracts for the procurement of defense articles or defense services for sale for United States dollars to any foreign country or international organization if such country or international organization provides the United States Government with a dependable undertaking (1) to pay the full amount of such contract which will assure the United States Government against any loss on the contract, and (2) to make funds available in such amounts and at such times as may be required to meet the payments required by the contract, and any damages and costs that may accrue from the cancellation of such contract, in advance of the time such payments, damages, or costs are due. Interest shall be charged on any net amount by which any such country or international organization is in arrears under all of its outstanding unliquidated dependable undertakings, considered collectively. The rate of interest charged shall be a rate not less than a rate determined by the Secretary of the Treasury taking into consideration the current average market yield on outstanding short-term obligations of the United States as of the last day of the month preceding the net arrearage and shall be computed from the date of net arrearage.

(b). [§ 22(b)]. The President may, if he determines it to be in the national interest, issue letters of offer under this section which provide for billing upon delivery of the defense article or rendering of the defense service and for payment within one hunded and twenty days after the date of billing. This authority may be exercised, however, only if the President also determines that the emergency requirements of the purchaser for acquisition of such defense articles and services exceed the ready availability to the purchaser of funds sufficient to make payments on a dependable undertaking basis and submits both determinations to the Congress together with a special emergency request for authorization and appropriation of addiitonal funds to finance such purchases under this Act. Appropriations available to the Department of Defense may be used to meet the payments required by the contracts for the procurement of defense articles and defense services and shall be reimbursed by the amounts subsequently received from the country or international organization to whom articles or services are sold.

§ 2763. [§ 23]. Credit Sales

The President is authorized to finance procurements of defense articles and defense services by friendly foreign countries and international organizations on terms requiring the payment to the United States Government in United States dollars of—

   (1) the value of such articles or services within a period not to exceed twelve years after the delivery of such articles or the rendering of such services; and

(2) interest on the unpaid balance of that obligation for payment of the value of such articles or services, at a rate equivalent to the current average interest rate, as of the last day of the month preceding the financing of such procurement, that the United States Government pays on outstanding marketable obligations of comparable maturity, unless the President certifies to Congress that the national interest requires a lesser rate of interest and states in the certification the lesser rate so required and the justification therefor.

In order to carry out these provisions, the President, by Executive Order No. 11958, January 18, 1977, 42 Fed. Reg. 4311, delegated the responsibility of administering all of section 22(a) and all the functions of section 23, except the certifying of a rate of interest to the Congress as provided for by paragraph (2) of that section, to the Secretary of Defense. Under this grant of authority, the Secretary has established the Foreign Military Sales Trust Fund to manage funds received from foreign customers. *See* U.S. Department of Defense, Military Assistance and Sales Manual, Pt. III, para. 2b and 3, Change 17, February 1, 1978, and DOD Instructions 2140.1, 2140.3 and 2110.29. Funds deposited into the FMS Trust Fund are required by the terms of 31 U.S.C. § 725s (1970) to " * * * be deposited into the Treasury as trust funds with appropriate title * * *." Section 725s further provides that " * * * all amounts credited to such trust fund accounts are appropriated and shall be disbursed in compliance with the terms of the trust * * *." Pursuant to this section, funds received from foreign customers are deposited in Treasury account 97–11X8242, "Advances, Foreign Military Sales." Funds are then either disbursed directly from the Fund, for contracts that directly cite the Fund as a source of funding, or are transferred from the Trust Fund to a DOD appropriation account and then disbursed.

We first considered the question of our bid protest jurisdiction over FMS procurements under section 22(a), 22 U.S.C. § 2762(a), in *Teledynamics Division of AMBAC Industries* (Teledynamics), 55 Comp. Gen. 674 (1976), 76–1 CPD 60. The protest concerned the award of a non-competitive contract by the Department of the Navy. The Navy challenged our jurisdiction to render an authoritative decision on the merits of the protest because the contract costs were charged against the Navy's FMS Trust Fund that consisted of payments made by foreign governments. We agreed that we had no jurisdiction in the matter because the contract did not involve payments from appropriated funds:

From the foregoing record it is sufficiently clear that this contract will not involve payments from appropriated funds. It is well established that this Office is without authority to render authoritative decisions with respect to procurements which do not involve expenditure of appropriated funds. B–171067, March 18, 1971. Our bid protest jurisdiction is based upon our authority to adjust and settle accounts and to certify balances in the accounts of accountable officers under 31 U.S.C. 71, 74 (1970). Where we do not have such settlement authority over the account concerned, we have declined to consider protests on the grounds that we could not render an authoritative decision on the matter. *See Equitable Trust Bank*. B–181469, July 9, 1974, 74–2 CPD 14 and *Reloo, Inc.*, B–183686, May 5, 1975, 75–1 CPD 276. 55 Comp. Gen. at 675.

In *Keco Industries, Inc.*, B–184911, B–185174, June 1, 1976, 76–1 CPD 352, we extended this rationale by refusing to take exception to the award of a contract involving payments from nonappropriated funds merely because appropriated funds may be used by the procuring agency for processing and administering the contract.

In *Consolidated Diesel Electric Company*, B–177450, January 6, 1977, 77–1 CPD 7, we further extended our holding in *Teledynamics* by expressing the view that, even though payments to a contractor under a section 22(a) sales contract were initially made from a United States Army appropriation that later was reimbursed by funds furnished by the foreign customer, this was an insufficient use of appropriated funds to provide us with jurisdiction given the mere incidental and temporary charging of the Army appropriation pending reimbursement.

We reached a similar result in *Aerosonic Corporation*, B–187765, June 13, 1977, 77–1 CPD 424, where we declined jurisdiction over a protest involving a transaction under section 22(b) of the Act on the ground that "* * * the use of appropriated funds serves merely as a temporary convenience for what is essentially a purchase ultimately paid for from nonappropriated funds * * *."

In *Verne Corporation*, B–188332, June 2, 1977, 77–1 CPD 386, we declined jurisdiction over a protest involving a sale of defense articles financed pursuant to section 23 of the Act. We stated:

While in the instant case the United States Government is the nominal contractor, * * * the funds for this procurement are borrowed by the Government of Gabon and will be repaid to the United States Government.

Section 22(b) of the Act authorizes the President (and, by his delegation to the Secretary of Defense, DOD) to use "appropriations available" to DOD to meet payments required by the contracts for the procurement of certain qualifying defense articles and services. The foreign customer is given up to 120 days after the date of billing upon delivery of the defense article or rendering of the defense service to reimburse the DOD appropriation account fully. The Act's language clearly makes DOD appropriations available for meeting contract payments; those appropriations represent accounts which are subject to our settlement authority under 31 U.S.C. § 71 (1970) and our authority to certify balances in the accounts under 31 U.S.C. § 74. Even though there is an eventual reimbursement of those funds by the foreign government, "there can be no question that * * * regular DOD/

* * * appropriated funds were intended to be used, and were so used, in the first instance." *Hughes Aircraft Co.* v. *United States, supra* at 909. In *Hughes*, the Court of Claims expressly held a section 22(b) transaction as one financed with appropriated funds and assumed jurisdiction on that basis. We now believe that the court's position is the better one, and that the temporary use of the appropriated funds should not defeat our jurisdiction.

Accordingly, *Aerosonics Corporation, supra*, and other decisions relying on the rationale of that case are overruled.

It is less clear that Congress envisioned that United States appropriations would be expended in connection with section 22(a) cash sales. While the section 22(b) delayed payment method authorizes initial outlays from DOD appropriations, section 22(a) requires the foreign customer to provide initial and advance funding. The intent of Congress is that all expenses related to section 22(a) procurements be charged to the foreign customer, H.R. Rep. No. 93–664, 93d Cong., 1st Sess. 46 (1973). Section 22(a), on its face, authorizes the President (and, by his delegation to the Secretary of Defense, DOD) "without requirement for charge to any appropriation or contract authorization otherwise provided" in effect to act as a procurement agent for eligible foreign customers, once the foreign customer promises, by means of providing the United States Government with a "dependable undertaking" (1) to pay the full amount of FMS contracts thereby assuring the United States Government against any loss on the contract and (2) to make sufficient funds available in advance to meet payments required by the contract and damages and costs that may accrue from the cancellation of the contract.

The first sentence of the present version of Section 22(a) was originally enacted under the Foreign Military Sales and Assistance Act, Pub. L. No. 93–189, § 25(3), 87 Stat. 730, December 17, 1973. The Senate report accompanying the measure explained how the section is to operate:

> Under this authority the U.S. Government, in effect, acts as the agent of the buying country in dealing with the U.S. selling company.
>
> *   *   *   *   *   *   *
>
> The principal changes from existing law [section 22 of the Foreign Military Sales Act] are a specific requirement that the arrangements provide for payment by the foreign country of a pro rata base of the administrative expense for the sales program * * *. S. Rep. No. 93–189, 93d Cong., 1st Sess. 15 (1973).

Pub. L. No. 94–329, *supra*, added the second sentence to section 22(a) providing for charging interest "on any net amount by which any purchasing country or international organization is in arrears under all of its outstanding unliquidated dependable undertakings to finance its procurement, considered collectively." H.R. Rept. No. 94–

1144, 94th Cong., 2d Sess. 26 (1976) *reprinted in* [1976] U.S. Code Cong. & Ad. News 1402.

From the foregoing, it is clear Congress envisioned the section 22(a) program to be self-sufficient and to exist without benefit of United States fiscal participation. To assure the fiscal integrity of the section 22(a) program, moreover, Congress provided in 22 U.S.C. § 2777(a) that cash payments received from foreign customers be available solely for payments to suppliers and refunds to purchases and not for financing credits and guarantees. *See* S. Rep. No. 90–1632, 90th Cong., 2d Sess. (1968) *reprinted in* [1968] U.S. Code Cong. & Ad. News 4478.

DOD maintains that we should not exercise bid protest jurisdiction over procurements involving section 22(a) accounts because there is no requirement that DOD use its appropriation accounts as bookkeeping vehicles for collecting funds and making disbursements. DOD states:

Hence, payments under contracts entered into under authority of section 22(a) legally could be accomplished without the use of either United States appropriation accounts or a United States disbursing officer, i.e., payments could be made directly from a foreign country to a contractor or by use of an intermediary financial institution, by way of letters of credit or otherwise.

However, as indicated above, under DOD procedures funds received from foreign customers under section 22(a) are normally deposited into the FMS Trust Fund, a fund initially established pursuant to 31 U.S.C. § 725s (1970) as amended by Pub. L. No. 94–273 and Pub. L. No. 94–502, 31 U.S.C.A. 725s (1978 Supp.). That section provides, in pertinent part:

The funds appearing on the books of the Government and listed in subsections (b) [sic] and (c) of this section shall be classified on the books of the Treasury as trust funds. All moneys accruing to these funds are hereby appropriated, and shall be disbursed in compliance with the terms of the trust. Hereafter moneys received by the Government as trustee analogous to the funds named in * * * this section, not otherwise herein provided for, * * * shall likewise be deposited into the Treasury as trust funds with appropriate title, and all amounts credited to such trust-fund accounts are hereby appropriated and shall be disbursed in compliance with the terms of the trust * * *.

The House Report on the measure that became 31 U.S.C. § 725s explained that even though "the moneys are not Government moneys, and in no way enter into the fiscal program of the Government, * * *" the provision was constitutionally necessary because "[o]nce moneys are covered into the Treasury, regardless of the nomenclature that may be applied to the account in which they are deposited, they are bound by the constitutional inhibition that 'no money shall be drawn from the Treasury but in consequence of appropriations made by law.'" H.R. Rep. No. 1414, 73d Cong., 2d Sess. 11 (1934).

Thus, in a technical sense, amounts in the FMS Trust Fund are appropriated funds, even though they are not annually appropriated by

Congress and not subject to direct Congressional control. *Cf. Fortec Constructors*, 57 Comp. Gen. 311 (1978), 78–1 CPD 153.[1]

Moreover, given the current high dollar level of annual FMS procurements, we believe this is an area which should be reviewed under the authority of 31 U.S.C. §§ 53(a), 53(c), 54 and 60 (1970). The importance of review in this area is pointed up by our recent efforts which have resulted in significant findings. *See*, for example, our reports *Loss of Accounting Integrity in Air Force Procurement Appropriations*, FGMSD–77–81, November 1, 1977, and *The Department of Defense Continues to Improperly Subsidize Foreign Military Sales*, *supra*.

Therefore, our Office in the future will review, upon request of prospective contractors and other interested parties, the propriety of awards and proposed awards made by DOD personnel acting under authority of section 22(a) of the Act. *Teledynamics* and the line of cases resulting from it are modified accordingly.

We find little impediment to reviewing section 23 transactions. Section 23 of the Act is used to provide credit financing of the procurement of military items by foreign countries on credit terms of up to 12 years. According to DOD, there is no such thing as a section 23 "sale":

> Contrary to popular misconception, we do not make credit sales under section 23. A credit "transaction" under section 23 is in fact a separate agreement involving a credit or loan agreement substantially identical in form to those used by commercial banks. This agreement is separate and apart from the purchase arrangement which may be an FMS sale under section 21 [purchase from DOD stock] or section 22 or a direct sales contract between the borrowing country and the United States supplier. When the borrowing country is billed for payments due as a result of such sales, it is that country's option either to request a disbursement from the section 23 credit agreement or to provide its own funds or a mix of both.

It is clear that a section 23 credit agreement involves use of funds, specifically appropriated by Congress to finance credit sales. *See* Foreign Assistance and Related Programs Appropriations Act, 1978, Pub. L. No. 95–148, Title II, 91 Stat. 1235. Thus, just as section 22(b) transactions are subject to review because appropriated funds are involved in short-term financing, sales financed under section 23 also are subject

---

[1] It should be noted that we do not consider the FMS Trust Fund analagous to the Commissary surcharge funds discussed in *Fortec*. In *Fortec*, we considered the surcharge to be a continuing appropriation established for the purpose of generating funds for commissary construction. The funds involved in *Fortec* are properly characterized as a kind of Federal Fund Account in which the Government credits receipts which it collects, owns, and uses solely for its purposes. Comptroller General, *Terms Used in the Budgetary Process*, 15 (PAD–77–9 July 1977). In contrast, amounts deposited in trust funds are collected and used by the Federal Government for carrying out specific purposes and programs according to the terms of a trust agreement or statute. *Id.*, at 15. Amounts deposited into the FMS Trust Fund are, in reality, foreign customers' funds that are administered by the United States Government only in a fiduciary capacity.

to review. Moreover, given our decision to review both 22(a) and 22(b) procurements, it is of no relevance, insofar as our review authority is concerned, that it may not be known during the contract formation stage if the contract is to be funded by moneys made available pursuant to the section 23 credit arrangement. *Verne Corporation, supra,* is overruled.

Finally, we point out that one question concerning our reviews of FMS procurements has been the applicability of the Armed Services Procurement Act of 1947, 10 U.S.C. 2301 *et seq.* (1976) and the Armed Services Procurement Regulation/Defense Acquisition Regulation (ASPR/DAR) to those procurements. The ASPR/DAR, however, now explicitly provides that it is applicable to FMS procurements. *See* ASPR/DAR 1–102, 6–1300 *et seq.*, particularly 6–1302. Although the regulation provides a specific exception for FMS procurements from the general requirement for competition, see ASPR/DAR 3–210.2(xviii) and 6–1307, allowing sole source contracting at the request of the foreign government, the overall applicability of the regulatory provisions governing DOD's appropriated fund procurements provides uniform standards for our reviews.

[B–192759]

Officers and Employees — Promotions — Temporary — Detailed Employees

Employee was detailed from her excepted service position to higher grade competitive service position for 2 years without prior approval from Civil Service Commission. Commission Rule VI requires that employee serving under excepted appointment shall be assigned to competitive service position only with prior approval of Commission. Therefore, although employee was improperly placed in overlong detail she may not receive retroactive temporary promotion. Our *Turner-Caldwell* and *Rankin* decisions make it clear that if certain regulatory requirements concerning an employee's entitlement to retroactive temporary promotion are not met there is no entitlement to retroactive temporary promotion.

In the matter of Merle H. Morrow—Retroactive Temporary Promotion, November 17, 1978:

The Honorable Eleanor Holmes Norton, Chair, Equal Employment Opportunity Commission (EEOC), has requested a decision as to whether Ms. Merle H. Morrow, who is employed by EEOC in an excepted service position as an attorney-adviser, GS–905–13, is entitled to a retroactive temporary promotion for having been detailed to perform the duties of an equal opportunity specialist, GS–160–14, a position in the competitive service.

Chair Norton states that on June 24, 1974, Ms. Morrow was detailed on a temporary part-time basis (20 hours per week) to perform the duties of an equal opportunity specialist. After 1 year Ms. Morrow served in the equal opportunity specialist position full-time rather than part-time. Ms. Morrow's detail was effected without the knowledge or approval of EEOC's Personnel Office and upon learning of Ms. Morrow's detail the Director of Personnel ordered its termination.

Ms. Morrow filed a grievance requesting backpay as provided for in Federal Personnel Manual (FPM) Supplement 990–2, Book 550, Subchapter S8–6c(6)(e), June 16, 1977, which states in part:

An employee who is detailed beyond 120 days to a higher grade position without Civil Service Commission approval, is entitled to retroactive temporary promotion with backpay for the period beginning with the 121st day of the detail until the detail is terminated. Entitlement is conditional upon the employee meeting the usual placement requirements * * * (Comptroller General decisions: 55 Com. Gen. 539 (1975) and B–183086, March 23, 1977).

The Director of Personnel, EEOC, denied Ms. Morrow's grievance because EEOC had never requested nor received Civil Service Commission approval for appointing Ms. Morrow to a competitive service position as required by Rule VI, Section 6.5, of the Commission's regulations. That rule states:

Assignment of excepted employees

No person who is serving under an excepted appointment shall be assigned to the work of a position in the competitive service without prior approval of the Commission.

Chair Norton concludes that:

Ms. Morrow appears to be locked into a "Catch-22" situation. She is entitled to backpay under Chapter 550 because prior approval for the detail was not received. However, we have denied these benefits because prior approval for the detail from the excepted to the competitive service was not secured and the detail was, thereby, deemed "illegal." From my reading of Chapter 550 it appears that Ms. Morrow is entitled to backpay because she was detailed to a higher grade position, for a period longer than 120 days, without prior approval of CSC. Your decision, B–183086, *In Re Reconsideration of Turner-Caldwell* (March 23, 1977) is instructive, but does not address the excepted-competitive service complication. * * *

In 56 Comp. Gen. 427, our *Turner-Caldwell* decision referred to above by Chair Norton, we stated the rule concerning whether an employee was entitled to a retroactive temporary promotion for being placed on an overlong detail as follows:

* * * we adhere to the view that under the detail provisions of the FPM, an agency head's discretion to make a detail to a higher grade position lasts no longer than 120 days, unless proper administrative procedures for extending the detail are followed. We further affirm that a violation of these provisions is an unjustified or unwarranted personnel action under the Back Pay Act, 5 U.S.C. § 5596 (1970), for which the corrective action is a retroactive temporary promotion and backpay, as set forth in our decision 55 Comp. Gen. 539, *supra*. It is necessary, however, that the employee satisfy the requirements for a retroactive

temporary promotion. In this connection, certain statutory and regulatory requirements could affect the entitlements of an employee otherwise qualified for corrective action as a result of an improper extended detail. * * *

It may be true, as Chair Norton points out, that Ms. Morrow finds herself in a "Catch-22" situation, but our *Turner-Caldwell* decision, cited above, makes clear that not every improperly extended detail automatically requires that an award of a retroactive temporary promotion be made to the employee so detailed. In our decision *Matter of William Rankin, Jr.*, 56 Comp. Gen. 432 (1977), we held that an employee who was detailed to a GS-17 position from a lower grade position for approximately 11 months without prior Civil Service Commission approval was not entitled to a retroactive temporary promotion because Commission regulations require that the Commission give its prior approval before a promotion to the supergrade position may be effected. The situation here is similar to that in *Rankin* in that the Commission never gave its prior approval to Ms. Morrow's assignment to the competitive service position as was required by Rule VI.

Since the Commission's prior approval of such an assignment was required by the regulations, Ms. Morrow may not be granted a retroactive temporary promotion.

[B-90867]

Experts and Consultants—Compensation—Overtime

Although an expert or consultant is not entitled to overtime compensation, if he is employed on a per diem basis he may be paid his rate of basic compensation for work on days outside his prescribed tour of duty, provided his compensation within any biweekly pay period does not exceed the rate of basic pay for level V of the Executive Schedule. Since the compensation of experts and consultants under 5 U.S.C. 3109 is set by administrative action under 5 U.S.C. 5307, it is subject to the limitation on compensation imposed by 5 U.S.C. 5308 which, by virtue of 5 U.S.C. 5504, is applicable on a pay-period basis.

In the matter of Jerome E. Hass—Compensation of Consultants, November 21, 1978:

By letter dated November 7, 1977, an authorized certifying officer for the Department of Energy has raised a question concerning the pay entitlement of Mr. Jerome E. Hass.

On July 2, 1977, Mr. Hass was appointed as a consultant to the Federal Energy Administration (FEA). He was given a temporary appointment with a regular tour of duty at a rate of pay of $161 per day. During the period of his appointment, Mr. Hass worked in excess of 10 days per pay period and claims compensation for each day worked at the rate of $161 per day. We are asked whether Mr. Hass is entitled to compensation for work in excess of 10 days per pay period.

The authority of the FEA to secure the services of experts and consultants is contained at section 7(b) of Pub. L. No. 93-275:

(b) The Administrator may employ experts, expert witnesses, and consultants in accordance with section 3109 of title 5 of the United States Code, and compensate such persons at rates not in excess of the maximum daily rate prescribed for GS-18 under section 5332 of title 5 of the United States Code for persons in Government service employed intermittently.

The basic authority of 5 U.S.C. § 3109 which that provision implements is as follows:

(b) When authorized by an appropriation or other statute, the head of an agency may procure by contract the temporary (not in excess of 1 year) or intermittent services of experts or consultants or an organization thereof, including stenographic reporting services. Services procured under this section are without regard to—

    (1) the provisions of this title governing appointment in the competitive service;
    (2) chapter 51 and subchapter III of chapter 53 of this title; and
    (3) section 5 of title 41, except in the case of stenographic reporting services by an organization.

However, an agency subject to chapter 51 and subchapter III of chapter 53 of this title may pay a rate for services under this section in excess of the daily equivalent of the highest rate payable under section 5332 of this title only when specifically authorized by the appropriation or other statute authorizing the procurement of the services.

While subsection 7(b) of Pub. L. No. 93-275 gives the FEA authority to compensate experts and consultants at the maximum rate of pay for grade GS-18, the FEA set Mr. Hass' pay at a rate $21.72 per day below the maximum daily rate of pay for GS-18.

An expert or consultant is not entitled to overtime compensation but, when employed on a per diem basis, is entitled to the daily rate prescribed in his appointment documents for each day of service regardless of the number of hours worked. 46 Comp. Gen. 667 (1967), 28 *id.* 328 (1948), and 27 *id.* 776 (1948). The designation of a regular tour of duty in his appointment documents does not necessarily preclude an expert's or consultant's receipt of compensation at the agreed daily rate for work performed outside of that tour of duty. However, there are aggregate compensation considerations that may limit the flexibility to use expert and consultant services for more than 10 days in any pay period.

Pay rates for the statutory pay systems, including the General Schedule, are fixed and adjusted under the pay comparability provisions contained at chapter 53, subchapter I, of title 5 of the United States Code. Section 5308 limits the amount of compensation that employees may receive as follows:

Pay may not be paid, by reason of any provision of this subchapter, at a rate in excess of the rate of basic pay for level V of the Executive Schedule.

That language was adopted in conference with the broad purpose noted in the conference report, No. 91–1685, December 9, 1970, as follows:

Section 5308 of the conference substitute provides that an employee whose rate of pay is adjusted under the provisions of sections 5301–5307 may not be paid at a rate in excess of the rate of pay for level V of the Executive Schedule (now $36,000).

Among others, the limitation of section 5308 applies to individuals paid under the major statutory pay systems, including those in the uniformed services and the Foreign Service. See Executive Order No. 12087, October 7, 1978.

Section 5307 referred to in the conference report and contained in chapter 53, subchapter I, provides for the pay of employees whose rates of pay are fixed by administrative action to be adjusted based on increases in the General Schedule rates of pay. The following language from the conference report, cited above, makes it clear that, with the very precise exceptions of certain congressional employees and wage board employees, 5 U.S.C. § 5307 applies to all pay set by administrative action:

The first feature of section 5307(a) is that it authorizes adjustments to be made in the rates of pay of employees of the legislative, judicial, and executive branches of the Government of the United States and of the government of the District of Columbia (except employees whose pay is disbursed by the Secretary of the Senate or the Clerk of the House) whose rates of pay are fixed by administrative action pursuant to law, and are not otherwise adjusted by the President under section 5305 of title 5, United States Code, as enacted by the conference substitute.

*	*	*	*	*	*	*

The provisions of section 5307(a) are general in nature and all inclusive insofar as applicable administrative pay-fixing authorities are concerned, except as to certain employees of the Senate and the House of Representatives and wage board employees. Similar provisions in prior pay legislation were general in nature and, in addition, contained authorizations relating to specific administrative pay-fixing authorities.

To illustrate, section 211 of the Federal Salary Act of 1967, Public Law 90–206, included a specific authorization under subsection (a) to adjust the rates of pay of U.S. Attorneys and Assistant U.S. Attorneys whose salaries are fixed by administrative action of the Attorney General under 28 U.S.C. 548.

Thus, the limitation of section 5308 is imposed not only upon individuals paid under the statutory pay systems, but upon individuals whose pay is set by administrative action and subject to adjustment under 5 U.S.C. § 5307. We note that the pay of those congressional employees excepted from section 5307 is otherwise limited by a separate statute. See 2 U.S.C. §§ 60a–1 and 60a–2. In 56 Comp. Gen. 375 (1977) we recognized that the limitation of section 5308 extends to employees whose rates of pay are derived from the General Schedule. In that case the pertinent section of the Farm Credit Act provided that the compensation of Deputy Governors "shall not exceed the maximum scheduled rate of the General Schedule." Since, under that section, the pay of Deputy Governors is set by administrative action and subject to adjustment under the provisions of 5 U.S.C. § 5307, it is paid by reason of a provision within subchapter I of chapter 53 and is within the purview of 5 U.S.C. §5308. Similarly, we have recognized that the pay of an expert or consultant hired pursuant to 5 U.S.C. §3109 is fixed by administrative action and subject to adjustment under 5 U.S.C. § 5307. *Matter of Carlyle P. Stallings*, B–131259, July 6, 1976. For this reason it, too, is within the scope of the limitation upon pay imposed by 5 U.S.C. § 5308.

In the case of experts and consultants, we find that the limitation on pay imposed by 5 U.S.C. § 5308 is to be applied on a pay-period basis just as it is applied to the broad spectrum of employees whose pay is adjusted by reason of the pay comparability provisions of title 5 of the United States Code. Subsection 5504(b) of title 5 sets forth the computational rules to be used when it is necessary to convert an annual rate of basic pay to a basic hourly, daily, weekly, or biweekly rate. Because 5 U.S.C. § 5504(a) provides that the pay period for an employee subject to that subsection covers two administrative workweeks, payroll units throughout the Government were advised by the Comptroller General's memorandum B–50870, November 17, 1958, as follows:

> Section 15 of the Federal Employees Salary Increase Act of 1958, 72 Stat. 214, amended section 604(d) of the Federal Employees Pay Act of 1945, as amended, 5 U.S.C. 944 [now 5 U.S.C. § 5504] by providing a new method of computation of pay. For all pay computation purposes affecting officers and employees, subject to section 604(d) * * * the annual basic rate of pay is divided by 2080 * * * to derive an hourly rate. The hourly rate is multiplied by 80 to derive a biweekly rate.

Experts and consultants are not within the category of individuals excluded from the definition of "employee" in 5 U.S.C. § 5541(2) so as to be exempt from either the pay period requirements or the computational rules of 5 U.S.C. § 5504. Since they are required to be paid on a biweekly basis, the limitation imposed upon their pay by 5 U.S.C. § 5308 is applicable to them on a pay-period basis. While it could be argued that the language of 5 U.S.C. § 3109 authorizing experts and consultants to be paid at a "rate not in excess of the daily equivalent of the highest rate payable under 5 U.S.C. 5332," requires application of the limitation only on a daily basis, the effect of that language is merely to permit experts and consultants to be paid at a daily rate regardless of the number of hours worked within any one day. It does not exempt experts and consultants from the biweekly limitation upon pay imposed by 5 U.S.C. § 5308. To hold otherwise would single out experts and consultants as the only category of employees within the purview of 5 U.S.C. § 5308 not limited on a biweekly or monthly basis to the pay for level V of the ExecutiveSchedule and would permit them to be compensated considerably more per year than other employees whose pay is adjusted on the basis of the pay comparability provisions of title 5. Such a result would be clearly at odds with the broad congressional intent to limit the pay of the vast majority of Federal employees to the rate of basic pay for level V. We note that the result of this decision is to treat experts and consultants in much the same manner as regular employees whose receipts of compensation for work in excess of 10 days per pay period are limited by virtue of the biweekly limitation imposed upon their pay by 5 U.S.C. § 5547.

For the reasons stated above, an expert or consultant may only be compensated an amount which does not cause his total compensation for any biweekly pay period to exceed the biweekly rate of pay for level V of the Executive Schedule. In Mr. Hass' case, he may be paid his full salary of $161 for the 11th day of work performed within any pay period. If he should work a 12th day within any pay period he may be paid only such amount as does not cause his biweekly pay to exceed the biweekly pay for level V, and he may not be paid any amount should he work on the 13th or 14th day within any pay period. For the same reason, an expert or consultant compensated at the maximum daily rate for GS–18 would not be entitled to any compensation for work in excess of 10 days within any pay period.

Because the question of application of 5 U.S.C. § 5308 to experts and consultants has not been previously addressed by decisions of this Office, payments made to an expert or consultant prior to the date of this decision in excess of the biweekly amount payable for level V of the Executive Schedule need not be collected. Such overpayments are waived under the authority of 5 U.S.C. § 5584.

[B–148581, B–189651, B–190650]

Purchases—Purchase Orders—Purchase Order v. Intra-Army Order—Department of Defense Procurement From Post Exchanges, etc.

Department of Defense nonappropriated fund instrumentalities, although instrumentalities of the United States, differ from regular Governmental activities in that they are self-supporting, do not receive moneys appropriated by Congress and thus are not subject to requirements of the Armed Services Procurement Act. In light of differences, from appropriation and procurement standpoint, between regular Governmental activities and nonappropriated fund instrumentalities (NAFIs), Army's procurement of goods and services from NAFIs is tantamount to procurement from non-Governmental, commercial sources, so that regular purchase/delivery order, and not Intra-Army order, should be used.

Post Exchanges, Ship Stores, etc.—Sales to Department of Defense—Propriety

Since basic mission of Department of Defense (DOD) nonappropriated fund instrumentalities (NAFIs) is to promote moral and welfare of military personnel and dependents, as a general proposition sale by NAFIs to regular DOD operating activities would be regarded as outside scope of NAFIs' proper functions except where circumstances require that agency obtain goods or services from NAFI and such requirement is properly documented and justified as sole-source procurement.

Purchases—Improper, etc.—Disregard of ASPR/DAR

Army's purchase of $40,000 worth of mattresses from Army and Air Force Exchange System, in lieu of following normal procurement procedures, is contrary to applicable law and regulations. Since record indicates Army has obtained and received benefit of mattresses, payment may be made on *quantum valebant* basis upon ratification of purchase by appropriate contracting official. Similarly, where record is not sufficient to indicate propriety of Army's obtaining services from NAFIs, payment for services may be made on *quantum meruit* basis pending resolution of the matter.

In the matter of Obtaining Goods and Services from Nonappropriated Fund Activities Through Intra-Departmental Procedures, November 21, 1978:

This decision is in response to requests from a United States Army Finance and Accounting Officer, for advance decisions in three related cases. All three cases involve the propriety of certifying for payment vouchers in favor of nonappropriated fund instrumentalities, specifically the Ansbach (Germany) Military Community's BOQ/VOQ/BEQ Fund (B–148581), the Heilbronn Area Club System (B–189651), and the Army and Air Force Exchange Service (AAFES) (B–190650), and the use of intra-Army orders for obtaining goods and services from those nonappropriated fund instrumentalities.

The goods and services were provided to different Department of the Army operating activities, with the nonappropriated fund initially financing the cost of providing the goods or services. In two cases (B–148581 and B–189651), the goods and services were provided pursuant to an Intra-Army Order for Reimbursable Services (Department of the Army Form 2544). In the third case (B–190650), only a Purchase Request and Commitment was utilized.

B–148581 involves the providing of custodial services to common use areas of BOQ (Bachelor Officers Quarters), VOQ (Visiting Officers Quarters) and BEQ (Bachelor Enlisted Quarters) buildings by employees of the nonappropriated fund. Under Army regulations, the cleaning of such areas is the responsibility of the operating activity and is to be paid for out of appropriated funds. The BOQ/VOQ/BEQ Fund used its own employees to clean the common use areas pursuant to the Intra-Army Order and billed the Army operating activity for that work.

B–189651 involves the cost of laundry and dry cleaning incurred by an officers club, a non-appropriated fund activity. The club in question is designated an officers essential mess. Army regulations provide that appropriated funds will be used to defray certain costs of essential messes. Pursuant to the Intra-Army Order, the club arranged and paid for the laundry and dry cleaning services and now seeks reimbursement from appropriated funds.

In B–190650, a Purchase Request and Commitment for 700 mattresses was submitted directly to the Army and Air Force Exchange Service-Europe (AAFES) instead of to the servicing procurement office as required. AAFES accepted the purchase request, delivered the mattresses, and billed the Army.

In each case, the Finance and Accounting Officer (FAO) questioned the propriety of an appropriated fund activity obtaining goods or services from a nonappropriated fund instrumentality (NAFI) by means of an Intra-Army order. The FAO believes that when appropriated funds are utilized to procure goods or services from a NAFI, a contract or purchase order, "processed through a Purchasing and Contracting Officer," should be used so that there will be "sufficient safeguards * * * to preclude the misappropriation of appropriated funds." According to the FAO, a "reimbursable order is not reviewed by a Purchasing and Contracting Officer and does not contain appropriate safeguards to preclude possible misappropriation of appropriated funds." He also questions whether a NAFI can "be considered an installation or activity of the Army and therefore be a party to an Intra-Army Order" or is actually "a party outside the Government."

The Department of the Army takes the position that NAFIs are Department of Defense (DOD) activities, that they have been judicially recognized as being instrumentalities of the Government, and that there is:

* * * no reason why the NAFIs should be considered for this limited purpose [using intra-Army orders for reimbursable services] to be other than the governmental instrumentalities they are classified as for all other purposes.

The Army further states that if NAFIs are not regarded as Government entities, the following "undesirable results" may arise:

(1) NAFIs "would be placed in direct competition with commercial sources, contrary to Department of Defense policy." Moreover, because NAFIs "Have certain benefits flowing from their categorization as Government agencies, that direct competition might unduly favor the NAFI."

(2) A contract would be required for an appropriated fund activity to order goods or services from a NAFI. "Resolution of disputes under that contract would be awkward at best, and at the worst could result in the Government suing an entity generally considered to be part of the Government."

It is clear that DOD and the Army consider NAFIs to be Government entities. For example, Army Regulation 230–1, para. 1–4(a) states:

NAFIs authorized by this regulation are instrumentalities of the U.S. Government * * *.

It is also clear that NAFIs have been considered to be Government instrumentalities in a variety of situations. *See*, e.g., *Standard Oil Company of California* v. *Johnson*, 316 U.S. 481 (1942); *United States* v. *State Tax Commission of Mississippi*, 412 U.S. 363 (1973) and 421 U.S. 597 (1975); *United States* v. *Howell and Cochran*, 318 F. 2d 162 (9th Cir. 1963); *Harlow* v. *United States*, 301 F. 2d 361 (5th Cir. 1962), *cert. denied*, 371 U.S. 814 (1962), *rehearing denied* 371 U.S. 906 (1962); *Rizzoto* v. *U.S.*, 298 F. 2d 748 (10th Cir. 1961). This Office has also observed that "the Army and Air Force Exchange Service is a Government instrumentality which functions as an agency of the Army and Air Force * * *," 49 Comp. Gen. 578, 580 (1970), and the Congress, although not explicitly authorizing the establishment of NAFIs, has recognized their existence and provided certain specific provisions regarding them. *See*, for example, the Nonappropriated Fund Instrumentalities Act, approved June 19, 1952, ch. 444, 66 Stat. 138, as amended, codified in part at 5 U.S.C. 2105(c) (1976), which specifies that employees of such Department of Defense NAFIs are not to be regarded as employees of the United States for purposes of the civil service laws, but that "the status of these nonappropriated fund activities as Federal instrumentalities" is not affected.

Although the NAFIs are recognized as being Government activities, they differ significantly from other Governmental activities, particularly with respect to budgetary and appropriation requirements. The NAFIs are generally self-supporting; they do not receive moneys appropriated by the Congress, *Aetna Insurance Company* v. *O'Keefe*, 356 F. 2d 660, 662 (5th Cir. 1966), and have not been depositing their receipts into the Treasury. *Swift-Train Company* v. *United States*, 443 F. 2d 1140, 1141 (5th Cir. 1971). Generally, the contractual obligations of the NAFIs are not regarded as obligations of the United States, *Standard Oil Company of California* v. *Johnson*, *supra; Jaeger* v. *United States*, 394 F. 2d 994 (D.C. Cir. 1968); *G. L. Christian and Associates* v. *United States*, 312 F. 2d 418 (Ct. Cl. 1963), *rehearing* 320 F. 2d 345, *cert. denied*, 375 U.S. 954 (1963), although in 1970 the Tucker Act was amended by Public Law 91–350 to permit suits directly against the United States in connection with contracts of post exchanges (but not other NAFIs). *See* 28 U.S.C. 1346, 1491 (1976); *Hopkins* v. *United States*, 513 F. 2d 1360 (Ct. Cl. 1975).

Moreover, since the NAFIs do not directly receive appropriated funds for their purchasing operations, but instead are self-supporting, the requirements of the Armed Services Procurement Act, 10 U.S.C. 2301 *et seq.* (1976) and the implementing provisions of the Armed Services Procurement Regulation/Defense Acquisition Regulation (ASPR/DAR) are not applicable to NAFI procurements. *See* B-178786, July 16, 1973. Consequently, procurements conducted by or on behalf of NAFIs are not subject to most of the requirements governing the procurements of the Defense Department; neither have they been subject to review by this Office under our Bid Protest Procedures, 4 C.F.R. Part 20 (1978).

We believe that it is these differences, rather than the status of NAFIs as Government instrumentalities, which must be controlling here. In all three cases, what is involved is the transfer of moneys from the Army's appropriation accounts to the accounts of the NAFIs over which there is no direct control either by the Congress (through the appropriation process) or this Office (through the account settlement authority of 31 U.S.C. 71, 74 (1970)). Thus, for all practical purposes from an appropriation and procurement standpoint, the obtaining of goods and services from a NAFI is tantamount to obtaining them from non-Governmental, commercial sources.

This does not mean that Defense Department NAFIs must now compete with regular commercial contracting services. NAFIs exist to help foster the morale and welfare of military personnel and their dependents. DOD Directive 1330.2; Army Regulation 230-1. Providing regular Defense Department operating activities with goods or services is not directly related to that purpose. This is particularly so with respect to the resale NAFIs such as the exchanges, which operate for the purpose of selling goods and services primarily to military personnel and dependents; they are not expected to sell to the "Government" itself. Thus, as a general proposition, we would view the sale of goods and services by NAFIs to regular Governmental operating activities to be outside the scope of the NAFIs' proper functions. Accordingly, as a general rule there should be no competition between NAFIs and commercial sources simply because NAFIs are not in the business of supplying the Government with its procurement needs.

We recognize, however, that there may be circumstances where, as a practical matter, procurement through a NAFI may be necessary. For example, there may be organizational or functional reasons which dictate the impracticability of having services furnished by other than a NAFI. There may also be extreme exigency situations where only a NAFI can provide urgently required goods or services. In such cases, appropriate sole-source justifications should be prepared, and, in light of the discussion above, regular purchase orders, i.e., DD Form 1155, should be utilized rather than intra-agency orders.

With the above in mind, we turn to the three specific situations presented for decision. In B-190650, the submission of the mattress requirement to the Exchange Service, and the Exchange's acceptance of the purchase request, was clearly improper. As indicated, the Exchange Service is not authorized to engage in selling merchandise to regular Army activities. Moreover, the submission of the purchase request to the Exchange Service instead of to the procurement office resulted in a clear circumvention of the Armed Services Procurement Act and the ASPR/DAR since more than $40,000 worth of mattresses was obtained by the Army, with payment to be made from appropriated funds, without regard to the dictates of those statutory and regulatory requirements.

The record does not provide a sufficient basis for us to reach any conclusion regarding the propriety of the Army's obtaining services from the NAFIs in the other two cases. In B-148581, it is reported that under Army Regulation 420-81 custodial services of BOQ/BEQ common use areas are to be performed by Army civilian employees or by contract, that a U.S. Army Europe supplement to the regulation provides that the custodial services "may be accomplished by other than [Army] personnel using appropriated funds," and that the supplement is interpreted to mean the NAFI can perform the services with its own employees and then be reimbursed with regular Army funds. The record is silent, however, as to why U.S. Army Europe finds it necessary to allow such a procedure or why that procedure was followed in this case. If indeed it is impracticable for the Army to make separate cleaning arrangements for common use areas of the billeting facilities, the use of BOQ/VOQ/BEQ Fund employees on a reimbursable basis would not be objectionable, provided the need to obtain those services from the Fund was properly documented and was ordered (via DD Form 1155) in accordance with the discussion above.

Similarly, in B-189651, it is reported that various Army regulations permit appropriated fund support for officers and enlisted clubs under certain circumstances, including when officers clubs are designated as essential messes. However, it is not reported why these regulations, dealing with custodial and janitorial services (which, as defined in Army Regulation 420-81, do not appear to encompass laundry/dry cleaning), permit the Army to reimburse an officers club for laundry and dry cleaning expenses, or why, if charge to the Army appropriation account is appropriate, the Army cannot procure directly the laundry and dry cleaning services for which it may be responsible.

Accordingly, since we view the purchase of the mattresses through the Exchange Service to be improper, the need to procure the cleaning and laundry services through NAFIs to be unjustified on the present record, and in any event the use of Intra-Army orders in lieu of regular purchase orders to be inappropriate, the vouchers based on those transactions may not be paid and will be retained in this Office. By separate letter, we are requesting the Secretary of the Army to advise us regarding the basis for having the NAFIs provide those cleaning and laundry services to regular Army activities. We are further informing the Secretary that in the interim, in light of the lengthy period of time that has elapsed since the goods and services were provided to the Army and since the Army has apparently had the use and benefit of these goods and services, NAFI providers may be paid on a *quantum meruit/quantum valebant* basis provided the purchases are ratified by an appropriate contracting official of the Army. *Monitor Products Company, Inc.*, B–182437, July 27, 1976, 76–2 CPD 85.

Finally, the FAO questions whether SF 1034, Public Voucher For Purchases And Services Other Than Personal, is the appropriate vehicle for effecting payment in light of Army Regulation 37–103, which indicates that SF 1080, Voucher For Transfers Between Appropriations and/or Funds, should be used for transactions involving NAFIs. In view of our holding above that purchases from NAFIs are tantamount to purchases from commercial entities, we believe the appropriate voucher form is the SF 1034.

[B–191671]

Quarters Allowance—Occupancy of Quarters—Child Support Payments by Separated or Divorced Member—Basic Allowance for Quarters

The basic allowance for quarters at the with dependent rate is not payable to a member living in adequate single-type Government quarters and paying child support to an estranged or divorced spouse when that spouse is also a service member and assigned to adequate family-type Government quarters. 45 Comp. Gen. 146, overruled in part.

Quarters Allowance—Basic Allowance for Quarters (BAQ)—Rate Payable—Child Support Payments by Separated or Divorced Member

A member paying child support to divorced or estranged spouse who is also a member of the uniformed services is not entitled to an increase in basic allowance for quarters based upon the child support if the former or estranged spouse and child are provided adequate family-type quarters by the Government. 45 Comp. Gen. 146, overruled in part.

In the matter of Basic allowance for quarters for separated or divorced members, November 27, 1978:

We have for consideration the letter of April 4, 1978, from the Acting Assistant Secretary of Defense (Comptroller), requesting a determination of Basic Allowance for Quarters (BAQ) entitlements when spouses, who are both members of the uniformed services and have a child, are divorced or separated.

Under the pay and allowance system applicable to members of the uniformed services either housing in kind is provided or an allowance for housing is paid. Housing provided must be adequate for the member and dependents, and if such housing is not provided to a member who has dependents, BAQ is paid at the with dependent rate—a larger allowance than BAQ at the without dependent rate.

When a member is divorced and does not have custody of the children of the marriage, a BAQ at the with dependent rate may be paid if the member provides support for his dependents in the form of alimony and child support. Similar payments may be allowed prior to divorce on the basis of agreements under which the member pays for the support of his dependents.

Several cases have arisen in the past in which the dependents of a divorced or separated member are provided housing by the Government not as a result of the status of the member claiming BAQ, but as a result of the status of the other spouse. Under applicable law and regulations, it has generally been held that a member may not be paid BAQ at the with dependent rate when the dependents who would justify such payment are quartered in Government housing at no expense. This rule has been applied even when the alimony or support payments made by the claiming member are not diminished.

In this context question 1 as presented by the Department is as follows:

1. May basic allowance for quarters (BAQ) at the with dependents rate be paid to a member who is paying court–ordered child support to a former spouse who is a service member and has custody of their child under the following circumstances:
a. When the members are divorced and the former spouse and dependent child are assigned adequate family-type Government quarters and the member *is* assigned to adequate single-type Government quarters?
b. When the members are divorced and the former spouse and dependent child are assigned adequate family-type Government quarters and the member *is not* assigned to adequate single-type Government quarters?

The statute which grants service members entitlement to BAQ expressly states that:

* * * a member * * * who is assigned to quarters of the United States * * * appropriate to his grade, rank, or rating and adequate for himself, and his dependents, if with dependents, is not entitled to a basic allowance for quarters. * * * 37 U.S.C. § 403(b) (1976).

Under 37 U.S.C. 403(j) the President has issued regulations which establish the basic rules for paying BAQ. Those regulations, as contained in Executive Order No. 11157, June 22, 1964, as amended, are set out in a note under 37 U.S.C. 301. Section 403 of the Executive order provides in pertinent part:

SEC. 403. (a) Any quarters of housing facilities under the jurisdiction of any of the uniformed services in fact occupied without payment of rental charges (1) by a member and his dependents, or (2) by a member without dependents, or (3) by the dependents of a member on field duty or on sea duty or on duty at a station where adequate quarters are not available for his dependents, shall be deemed to have been assigned to such member as appropriate and adequate quarters, and no basic allowance for quarters shall accrue to such member under such circumstances * * *.

Regulations providing more specific rules are contained in Chapter 2, Part 3, of the Department of Defense Military Pay and Allowances Entitlements Manual.

Neither Executive Order No. 11157, as amended, nor our decisions have interpreted 37 U.S.C. 403(b) as entitling a member to payment of BAQ at the with dependent rate when Government quarters occupied by the dependents at no expense are furnished incident to an entitlement other than the member's entitlement. Thus, in 45 Comp. Gen. 146 (1965), which is cited in the submission, Government quarters occupied by the member's dependents as a result of the wife's remarriage to another member were considered to have been furnished by the Government within the terms of 37 U.S.C. 403(b) at least during the period when the member claiming BAQ was furnished Government quarters. However, 45 Comp. Gen. 146 allowed the BAQ at the with dependent rate during a short period when he was not furnished single Government quarters. It appears that this rule was predicated upon the wording of section 403(a) of Executive Order No. 11157, as amended. That section does not specifically deny BAQ to a member during a period when Government quarters are not furnished. However, those provisions apply to all members with dependents and assume that the member and dependents would reside together if possible. We do not believe that it must be applied to cases in which there is a marital separation, since such application would result in rules which may not be justified by the facts involved.

Therefore, when both spouses or former spouses are on active duty in the uniformed services and the spouse who has custody of the child (or children) is furnished Government family quarters, the other spouse is entitled to either Government single quarters or a BAQ at the without dependent rate. To the extent 45 Comp. Gen. 146 states a different rule it will no longer be followed. The first question is answered accordingly.

We are aware that alimony and support payments required of the spouse who does not have custody of the child or children may not be decreased by virtue of the fact that the other spouse or former spouse is furnished Government family quarters. However, alimony and support payments are predicated at least to some extent on the needs of the wife and children and are subject to change based upon changing circumstances. We believe it is incumbent upon the member who is liable for such payments to have support agreements or orders written in a manner which will provide appropriate adjustments when the spouse and children are furnished Government quarters at no cost to either spouse.

Questions 2 and 3 are as follows and will be answered jointly.

2. Would the answers to 1.a. and 1.b. be the same for the period of court-ordered separation prior to a final divorce decree?
3. Would the answers to 1.a. and 1.b. be the same for the period of voluntary separation prior to a final divorce decree?

The extent of the couple's estrangement does not change the result of the decision. Both members retain their statutory right either to adequate quarters or to an allowance. When separate quarters can adequately fulfill the members' needs the BAQ cannot be paid. Nor does separation affect the entitlement to BAQ when the member with custody is assigned to quarters and the member paying support is not. On that basis questions 2 and 3 are answered in the affirmative.

[B–191936]

Armed Services Procurement Regulation—Advertised Procurements—Small Business Set-Asides—Unreasonable Prices—Reduction by Negotiation Propriety

Negotiation with sole bidder for reasonable prices after small business restricted advertisement resulted in unreasonable bid is not authorized by law.

In the matter of Crown Laundry and Cleaners, November 28, 1978:

On February 23, 1978, Moody Air Force Base (Moody), Georgia, issued Invitation for Bids (IFB) F09607–B0005 as a small business restricted advertised procurement for laundry service for the base linen exchange and hospital for the period of May 1, 1978, to April 30, 1979. The 4th amendment to the IFB changed the delivery time from 3 days per week to 2 days per week. This amendment was acknowledged by George A. Belleau, President of Crown Laundry and Cleaners (Crown), on April 14, 1978. At bid opening on April 14, 1978, the only bid received was from Crown for $70,485.67. By letter of April 20,

1978, Crown alleged a mistake, stating that amendment 4 was overlooked and that the bid was predicated on 3-day pickup and delivery services. Crown revised its bid to $63,412.80 on the basis of the 2-day pickup and delivery service.

The contracting officer states that Crown was contractor for the services for the period from May 1, 1977, through April 30, 1978, at an estimated total cost of $49,868.10, which was competitive with the only other bid of $49,972.10. IFB F09607-78-B0005 reportedly had no appreciable change in quantities, but deletes the requirement for tablecloths estimated at $3,600. Current quantities of the new requirement were used with the prior contract unit prices less the tablecloth requirement to arrive at the Government estimated cost of $46,170.20. Compared with Crown's revised bid of $63,412.80, an increase of $17,242.60, nearly 35 percent, is indicated.

On April 21, 1978, the contracting officer determined in accordance with Armed Services Procurement Regulation (ASPR) section 2-404.2(e) (now the Defense Acquisition Regulation) to reject the one bid received as unreasonable. And pursuant to ASPR section 2-404.1 (b) (vi) it was further determined to cancel the IFB after bid opening for the reason that the small business restricted advertised procurement did not provide competition which was adequate to insure reasonable prices.

The laundry service was readvertised under IFB F09607-78-B0009, without the small business restriction. Bids were received from Crown and National Linen Service (National), in the respective amounts of $45,913.01 and $42,305.08. Therefore, on resolicitation, Crown was not the low bidder.

Crown contends that the contracting officer, having established a precedent to restrict laundry service to small business, erred in not recommending "that he be permitted to enter into negotiations with Crown Laundry, (ASPR) 3-215, which would have been in the best interest of the Government."

ASPR section 3-215 provides for negotiation after advertising and ASPR section 3-215.1 permits negotiation if the bid prices received after *formal advertising* are determined to be unreasonable. ASPR section 3-215.2 provides that negotiation authority under ASPR section 3-215 *shall not* be used unless the bid prices received after *formal advertising* are determined to be unreasonable.

Formal advertising is defined in section 2-101 of ASPR and means procurement by competitive bids and awards as prescribed in Section II of ASPR. However, small business procurement is prescribed in Section I of ASPR. Section 1-706.2 provides that contracts for total or partial set-asides whether entered into by conventional negotiation or by "Small Business Restricted Advertising" are negotiated procurements, "* * * and shall cite as authority 10 U.S.C. 2304(a)(1) in the case of a unilateral determination * * *." The implementing regulation is published in section 3–201 of ASPR.

Section 3–201.3 of ASPR provides that in the event of a small business set-aside, Section 3–201 authority shall be used in preference to any other authority in Section III, Part 2. Section 3–201.3 further provides that:

> The authority of this paragraph shall not be to negotiate a reasonable price with a low responsible small business bidder whose bid has been determined by the contracting officer to be an unreasonable bid under Small Business Restricted Advertising procedures.

Consequently, negotiation with Crown as proposed by Crown for a reasonable bid price would be contrary to law.

The protest is denied.

[B–192670]

General Accounting Office—Jurisdiction—Contracts—Contracting Officer's Affirmative Responsibility Determination—General Accounting Office Review Discontinued—Exceptions

It is General Accounting Office's (GAO) policy not to review protests against affirmative determinations of responsibility unless fraud is alleged or solicitation contains definitive responsibility criteria which allegedly have not been applied.

Contracts—Protests—Contracting Officer's Affirmative Responsibility Determination—General Accounting Office Review Discontinued—Exceptions—Definitive Responsibility Criteria

Whether bidder satisfies agency intent to subcontract to minority business enterprise 20 percent of total value of subcontracts under procurement or complies with what agency views as best effort to obtain such percentage is definitive responsibility criterion reviewable by GAO.

Bidders — Qualifications — Definitive Responsibility Criteria — Minority Subcontracting Requirement

Contracting officer's determination was supported by objective evidence received from Minority Business Enterprise Subcontracting Evaluation Committee which recommended that potential awardee be found responsible in area of Minority Business Enterprise Subcontracting Program. GAO has no objection to determination in view of facts of record and absence of evidence from protester demonstrating that determination lacked reasonable basis.

In the matter of Mayfair Construction Company, November 28, 1978:

Mayfair Construction Company (Mayfair) protests the award of a contract pursuant to invitation for bids (IFB) No. 10–0054–8 issued by the National Aeronautics and Space Administration (NASA). The IFB called for mechanical and electrical installation on Mobile Launcher Platform No. 2 at the John F. Kennedy Space Center.

Mayfair alleges that Algernon-Blair Industrial Contractors, Inc. (Algernon), the low bidder and awardee, received the award under the instant procurement because NASA waived, subsequent to bid opening, the "minority contractor subcontracting requirements" ("requirements"). Mayfair believes that such waiver gave Algernon an unfair advantage. In addition, Mayfair suggests that Algernon's efforts to satisfy these "requirements" were insufficient. Also, Mayfair contends that had it not followed these "requirements," Mayfair would have been able to submit a lower bid than that which was submitted by Algernon. Further, it is Mayfair's apparent position that these "requirements" are mandatory, nonwaivable, and call for at least 20 percent of the total value of all subcontracts resulting from the instant procurement to be performed by minority business enterprises.

The IFB contains two clauses which concern what Mayfair refers to as "minority contractor subcontracting requirements." The first is Article 8—*MINORITY BUSINESS ENTERPRISE CONSTRUCTION SUBCONTRACTING* (May 1976)—which provides, in pertinent part:

(a) It is the policy of the Government that minority business enterprises shall have the maximum practicable opportunity to participate in the performance of Government contracts.
(b) The Contractor agrees to use his best efforts to carry out this policy in the award of his subcontracts to the fullest extent consistent with the efficient performance of this contract. * * *
(c) In keeping with national policy, it is NASA's objective that a vigorous procurement program of actively seeking out and soliciting minority firms be accomplished at the prime Contractor and subcontractor levels to ensure their equitable participation in this construction effort. It is NASA's intent that at least twenty percent (20%) of the total value of all subcontracts resulting from this prime contract shall be awarded to minority business enterprises as defined above. * * *

The second is found in the Additional Instructions and Conditions Section, paragraph 30, entitled *PRE-AWARD SURVEY*. This paragraph, besides setting forth what is expected of the apparent low bidder during the preaward survey, provides, with respect to minority subcontracting, the following:

A separate Minority Business Enterprise Subcontracting Program Plan shall [, at the time of the preaward survey,] be submitted in writing consisting of but not limited to:
(a) A summary of the corporate program for the employment of minority business enterprises. This summary shall include how this program will be carried out on this contract if award is made.
(b) A report and verification of the company's efforts to achieve the 20 percent minority subcontracting goal. This shall include but not be limited to solicitation procedures, the number of minority firms solicited and their response.

(c) The total work to be subcontracted, including a list of all proposed sub-contractors both minority and non-minority subcontractors, and their plant addresses. This list shall include:

    (i) The value of each subcontract.
    (ii) A summary description of work to be performed.
    (iii) A written certification of the bona fide status of each proposed minority subcontractor.
    (iv) Schedule of awards.

Essentially, Mayfair's protest is directed at NASA's affirmative determination of Algernon's responsibility. It is our Office's policy not to review protests against affirmative determinations of responsibility unless either fraud is alleged on the part of procuring officials or the solicitation contains definitive responsibility criteria which allegedly have not been applied. See *Central Metal Products, Incorporated*, 54 Comp. Gen. 66 (1974), 74–2 CPD 64; *Yardney Electric Corporation*, 54 Comp. Gen. 509 (1974), 74–2 CPD 376. This policy was adopted by our Office because, normally, responsibility determinations are based in large measure on the general business judgment of the procuring officials and, being subjective, are not readily susceptible to reasoned review. *Central Metal Products, Incorporated, supra;* and *Keco Industries* v. *United States*, 492 F. 2d 1200, 1205 (1974). However, in situations where the question of responsibility revolves around a bidder's meeting or failing to meet certain specific and objective responsibility criteria expressed in the solicitation, we will review, to the extent possible, the determinations of the procuring officials to see if the specified responsibility criteria have been met. See *Yardney Electric Corporation, supra.*

In the present case, it is our view that the 20-percent minority subcontracting requirement in the first quoted provision specified a goal and not a quota and that the subcontracting program plan, report and verification requirement and other requirements of the second quoted provision set down preconditions of performance and, thus, definitive responsibility criterion. *Cf. Contra Costa Electric, Inc.*, B–190916, April 5, 1978, 78–1 CPD 268. Therefore, since Mayfair's allegations call into question whether NASA adequately considered Algernon's ability to perform in accordance with this requirement, the question of Algernon's responsibility is properly for review by our Office.

The record discloses that the Minority Business Enterprise Subcontracting Evaluation Committee (Committee) conducted a preaward survey of Algernon which, among other things, concerned the 20-percent minority subcontracting goal and the amount of effort expended by Algernon to achieve such goal. The Committee advised that Algernon's Minority Plan (Plan) indicated that it had solicited 37 minority firms and that seven of those submitted a bid. Also, the Plan indicated that all but one of the responding minority firms were not competitive. Consequently, the Committee requested Algernon to re-contact minority firms whose type of work was in either the steel, steel erection or electrical area. Algernon acceded to this request and advised NASA in a letter dated July 27, 1978, of the following:

> We have talked to Keystone, Fandion & Sons and New World Construction concerning the fabrication and/or erection on this project. Keystone has advised us that due to the nature of the job they did not prepare a subcontract proposal for erection services * * *. We have attempted to work with Fandion & Sons to see if they could find their error in their previous estimate to us. This has been to no avail * * *. We have also attempted to work with New World Construction and have been somewhat successful in working the contract out with him due to the price variation * * *.
>
> We have also attempted to work out the electrical with Fischbach & Moore and their minority contract. The price differential at the present time is somewhat in excess of $80,000, so we have not been successful in this attempt.

Based on the foregoing, the Committee recommended to the contracting officer that Algernon be found responsible in the area of the Minority Business Enterprise Subcontracting Program. It is apparent from the record that the contracting officer concurred with the Committee and considered this information, together with that obtained during the remainder of the preaward survey, adequate to support an affirmative determination of responsibility.

Our Office will not object to a contracting officer's determination unless it is shown to be without a reasonable basis. See *Leasco Information Products, Inc., et. al.*, 53 Comp. Gen. 932 (1974), 74–1 CPD 314. In this instance, there was objective evidence before the contracting officer relevant to the definitive responsibility criterion. This in itself is sufficient to satisfy our Office's review standard. The relative quality of the evidence is a matter for judgment by the contracting officer, not our Office. See *Yardney Electric Corporation, supra.*

Accordingly, Mayfair's protest is denied.

[B-192354]

General Accounting Office—Jurisdiction—Contracts—Disputes—On Questions of Law—Facts Undisputed

Protest against termination of contract is appropriate for review by General Accounting Office (GAO) where there are no material facts in dispute and only question concerning propriety of termination is one of law.

Claims — Assignments — Contracts — Bar Against Assignment — Waiver When in Interest of Government

Although assignment of Government contract may violate Anti-Assignment Act, Government can recognize assignee as successor in interest if in best interests of United States.

Contracts—Novation Agreements—Rule

Contract "A" with Federal Aviation Administration (FAA) provided that it would run concurrently with contract "B" (also with FAA), and would expire upon expiration or termination of a contract "B." Contract "B" was subsequently novated with FAA's approval. Since general legal effect of contract novation is extinguishment of contract and substitution of new one, resulting in discharge of transferor, FAA view that novation of contract "B" operated to cause expiration of contract "A" under cited provision was not improper.

Small Business Administration—Authority—Small Business Concerns—Allocation of 8(a) subcontracts

Determination to set aside procurement under section 8(a) of Small Business Act is matter for contracting agency and Small Business Administration, not GAO.

In the matter of Vialease Corporation, November 29, 1978:

On July 2, 1976, the Federal Aviation Administration (FAA) awarded contract No. DOT–FA–NA–5218 to Vialease Corporation (Vialease) for the lease of a parcel of land adjacent to the viaduct at Washington National Airport until October 31, 1980. The land was to be used to conduct a rental car operation and provide a public parking facility. The rental car operation was the subject of contract No. DOT–FA–NA–5145, between Vialease and the FAA, which was also to expire on October 31, 1980.

Contract No. –5218 provided in article II.B:

The period of this Contract DOT–FA–NA–5218 has been established to coincide with the expiration date of Contractor's contract DOT–FA–NA–5145 with the Government for operation of a car rental concession at the Airport; and further, the Parties understand and agree that this Contract DOT–FA–NA–5218 shall expire immediately upon expiration or termination of Contractor's aforementioned concession Contract DOT–FA–NA–5145.

Contract No. –5145 was novated by Vialease to Dollar Rent-A-Car Systems, Inc. (Dollar), on December 16, 1977, with the FAA's approval. On March 22, 1978, Vialease requested the FAA's approval to assign contract No. –5218 to Corporate Fleet Management, Inc. (CFM). The FAA denied the request by letter of April 25 in which the FAA also directed Vialease to vacate the property leased under contract No. –5218 by June 30. The basis for that advice was that since contract No. –5145 was novated to Dollar, Vialease was no longer considered to be operating a rental car concession under that contract, and contract No. –5218 accordingly expired by operation of article II.B thereof, set out above. Vialease was subsequently advised that the FAA proposed to lease the property that had been involved in contract No. –5218 to Parkington, Inc., for the period beginning July 1, 1978.

Vialease has filed a protest in our Office against the FAA's actions. Vialease contends that the termination of contract No. –5218 was improper, and the contract should therefore be reinstated, with compensation to Vialease for alleged loss of revenue since July 1. In addition, Vialease argues that the FAA should then approve the assignment of the contract by Vialease to CFM. Vialease further contends that, in any case, the FAA cannot properly award a lease contract to Parkington on a sole-source basis without affording Vialease the opportunity to compete.

In a report on the protest, the FAA contends that the termination of contract No. –5218 is not appropriate for our review because it involves a matter of contract administration. See in this connection *Kaufman DeDell Printing Inc., Reconsideration*, B–188054, October 25, 1977, 77–2 CPD 321. The FAA suggests that the dispute over the propriety of the contract termination is, therefore, a matter for review under the procedures set forth in the contract's "Disputes" clause.

Our Office does not generally rule upon matters cognizable under a "Disputes" clause. *Precision Service & Sales Co.*, B–186139, April 16, 1976, 76–1 CPD 263. However, there are no material facts in dispute here for resolution under such clause. There exists only a question of law to be resolved on the basis of the facts of record, i.e., whether the novation of contract No. –5145 operated to terminate contract No. –5218 pursuant to article II.B thereof. Therefore, we will consider the issue presented. 53 Comp. Gen. 167 (1973).

We note here that the FAA's report also suggests that Vialease's performance under contract No. –5218 was not satisfactory, and the contract could have been terminated for default. However, it is clear from the record that the contract was terminated under article II.B, and not for default.

The transfer of a Government contract is prohibited by the Anti-Assignment Act, as amended, 41 U.S.C. § 15 (1976). However, the prohibition is intended for the Government's protection; therefore, the Government may treat a contract as annulled by an assignment or recognize the assignment as the circumstances in a particular case may warrant. See B–173331, August 19, 1971; 32 Comp. Gen. 227 (1952). Thus, the FAA could properly recognize Dollar as the new contractor, as it did here by approving the novation agreement, since such recognition obviously was determined to be in the best interests of the United States. See B–173331, *supra;* compare *Vertical Aviation Transport Systems, Inc.*, ASBCA No. 18266, 74–1 BCA § 10,617.

In its report, the FAA justifies the termination of contract No. -5218 under article II.B, as follows:

> The novation of Contract DOT-FA-NA-5145 to Dollar resulted in a substitution of parties and the termination of all interest of Vialease in and under that contract. As a result, Vialease's right to continue performance under the contract was effectively terminated by the approved novation agreement.

The legal effect of a novation as the term is generally used is the substitution of a new agreement or obligation for the old one, which is thereby extinguished or discharged. Simpson on Contracts § 206 (2d ed., 1965); Corbin on Contracts §§ 1293, 1297 (1952).

Thus, and notwithstanding that the Government may have properly exercised its discretion to recognize Dollar as Vialease's successor in interest under contract No. -5145, the novation operated to extinguish that contract and to substitute a new contract between the FAA and Dollar, albeit with the same contractual provisions as in the discharged contract. On that basis, we cannot disagree with the FAA view that the novation was tantamount to an "expiration or termination" of contract No. -5145 to cause the expiration of contract No. -5218 under article II.B thereof.

In view of the above, the matter of whether the FAA should have approved the assignment of contract No. -5218 to CFM is academic.

In regard to the proposed award of a contract to Parkington, Inc., on a sole-source basis to lease the same land involved in contract No. -5218, the FAA advises in its report that the contract will be awarded pursuant to section 8(a) of the Small Business Act, 15 U.S.C. § 637(a) (1976). That section authorizes the Small Business Administration (SBA) to enter into a contract with any Government procuring agency, and the contracting officer of such agency is authorized "in his discretion" to let the contract to the SBA under such terms and conditions as may be agreed upon by the SBA and the procuring activity. It is clear, therefore, that the determination to set aside a procurement and to award a contract under section 8(a) is a matter within the sound discretion of the contracting agency and the SBA. *Communicology, Inc.; Ocean Technology, Inc.*, B-191486, B-191581, April 18, 1978, 78-1 CPD 302.

The protest is denied.

[B-192668]

Contracts—Protests—Timeliness—Negotiated Contracts—Solicitation Improprieties

Protest after award that terms of request for proposals (RFP) did not permit open competition is untimely. Under General Accounting Office (GAO) Bid Protest Procedures, protests based on apparent improprieties in RFP must be filed before closing date for receipt of proposals.

Contracts—Protests—Procedures—Bid Protest Procedures—Time for Filing—Date Basis of Protest Made Known to Protester

Protest that, regardless of terms of RFP, preferential treatment previously given other firms precluded fair consideration of any proposal protester might submit is untimely. Protester knew basis for protest when it received RFP, and did not file protest within 10 working days thereafter as required by GAO Bid Protest Procedures.

Contracts—Protests—Persons, etc. Qualified to Protest—Interested Parties—Potential Subcontractors

Prospective offeror which did not timely protest terms of RFP and chose not to submit proposal is not "interested party" to protest later that awardees received preferential treatment from Government. Class of parties eligible to protest alleged preferential treatment consists essentially of disappointed offerors. No such parties have protested or indicated that protester is authorized to protest on their behalf.

Contracts—Protests—Conferences—Request Denied—Protest Not for Consideration on the Merits

Where merits of protest are not for consideration because some issues are untimely and protester is not interested party to raise others, no useful purpose would be served by holding bid protest conference.

In the matter of Die Mesh Corporation, November 29, 1978:

Die Mesh Corporation has protested the awards of contracts for the design of electric and hybrid passenger vehicles to four companies. The protester alleges essentially that (1) the procurement was not open because all interested parties were not given an opportunity to submit proposals, and (2) there was preferential treatment by the Government in that several of the contractors have previously received electric vehicle contracts; one of the contractors lacks adequate facilities and some of its principals were previously associated with another company which received an electric vehicle design study contract; and another of the contractors is a foreign company, and should not be receiving U.S. taxpayers' dollars.

While Die Mesh repeatedly complains of various actions by the Department of Energy, the procurement was actually conducted by the California Institute of Technology's Jet Propulsion Laboratory under a prime contract (No. NASA 7–100) with the National Aeronautics and Space Administration (NASA). The relief requested is that the project be stopped and a thorough investigation conducted.

In its September 18, 1978, report to our Office, NASA asserts that Die Mesh is not an interested party to protest, and that this subcontract protest is not for consideration in any event under the standards enunciated in *Optimum Systems, Inc.*, 54 Comp. Gen. 767 (1975), 75–1 CPD 166, where our Office stated that we would review subcontract protests only in certain limited circumstances. Also, NASA questions the timeliness of the protest.

As for the protester's first argument, NASA points out that the procurement was synopsized in the Commerce Business Daily on October 25, 1977, that by letters of October 28, 1977, 342 organizations and individuals were invited to a presolicitation conference, and that 177 copies of the request for proposals (RFP) were issued on January 31, 1978. In this regard, Die Mesh has stated that it was perfectly capable of submitting a proposal under the RFP, but believed that it would have been futile to do so in light of the preferential treatment given to certain companies in previous procurements.

If the protester's argument is that the terms of the RFP did not permit full and free competition, or precluded Die Mesh from competing, it is untimely, because under section 20.2(b)(1) of our Bid Protest Procedures, 4 C.F.R. Part 20 (1977), protests based upon apparent improprieties in an RFP must be filed prior to the closing date for receipt of proposals. If the protester's argument is that regardless of the terms of the RFP, any proposal it submitted would not receive fair consideration in light of the preferential treatment previously given other firms, it is again untimely, because Die Mesh knew this basis for protest when it received the RFP, and protests other than those based upon solicitation improprieties must be filed within 10 working days after the basis for protest is known or should have been known, whichever is earlier. Section 20.2(b)(2), Bid Protest Procedures.

As for the allegation that the successful offerors received preferential treatment, NASA points out that by choosing not to submit a proposal, Die Mesh effectively removed itself as an interested party to protest these issues, because even assuming that preferential treatment occurred, the protester could not have been hurt by it. Die Mesh responds that it has an interest in the procurement because it has been "intricately involved" in electric vehicle development for a number of years and was a vocal proponent of the Electric and Hybrid Vehicle Research, Development and Demonstration Act.

We have stated that to protest the award of a Government contract is "a serious matter." *Cessna Aircraft Company et al.*, 54 Comp. Gen. 97, 111 (1974), 74-2 CPD 91. Protests often delay the Government's procurement of necessary goods and services, and sometimes have a very substantial economic impact not only on the protester but also on other involved parties. We therefore believe, as indicated in section 20.1(a) of our Bid Protest Procedures, that a party must be "interested" in order to have its protest considered by our Office. Determining whether a particular party is sufficiently interested involves consideration of the party's status in relation to the procurement (e.g., prospective bidder or offeror; bidder or offeror eligible for award; bidder or offeror not eligible for award; nonbidder or nonofferor) and the nature of the issues raised. See, generally, *American Satellite Corporation*, B–189551, April 17, 1978, 78–1 CPD 289.

Where the issues raised in a protest involve which of several competing bidders or offerors should properly have received the award, we believe that, in general, a party which would not be eligible for award in any event is not sufficiently interested to protest. See, for example, *Kleen-Rite Janitorial Service, Inc.*, B–178752, March 21, 1974, 74–1 CPD 139 (company which is not eligible 8(a) firm is not interested party to protest amount of contracts let to specific 8(a) firm); *DoAll Iowa Company*, B–187200, September 23, 1976, 76–2 CPD 276 (large business protesting agency's determination that awardee under total small business set-aside has capacity to perform contract); *Elec-Trol, Inc.*, 56 Comp. Gen. 730 (1977), 77–1 CPD 441 (nonbidding party, with mere expectation of receiving subcontract award, protesting evaluation of bids on prime contract); *Comspace Corporation*, B–189516, October 17, 1977, 77–2 CPD 296 (suspended firm alleging Government negotiated with it in bad faith and protesting awards to another offeror); and *American Satellite Corporation, supra* (prospective subcontractor protesting that there was insufficient competition for prime contract award).

In some instances, a nonbidding entity has been considered sufficiently interested to protest concerning which bidder or offeror should properly have received the award. Many of these cases involve some type of organization which, although not a competitor for the contract, arguably has a substantial economic interest in the outcome of the procurement. For example, a parents' association was held to be an interested party to protest the award of a contract for operation of a day care center where its members' fees accounted for approximately 15 percent of the total operation cost of the center, and nearly one-third of the contract price. *Department of Labor Day Care Parents Association*, 54 Comp. Gen. 1035 (1975), 75–1 CPD 353. As pointed out in that decision, other such cases have involved labor unions and civic and trade associations. Also, as noted in *Elec-Trol, supra*, in some instances a subcontractor may be sufficiently interested to protest a prime contract award.

However, it is not enough merely to be an individual employee of a disappointed bidder or offeror (*Dale Chlouber*, B–190638, December 20, 1977, 77–2 CPD 484), two concerned taxpayers (*A. Kenneth Bernier and C. J. Willis*, B–186502, July 19, 1976, 76–2 CPD 56), a concerned citizen (*Patti R. Whiting*, B–187286, September 29, 1976,

76–2 CPD 298), a consultant who is concerned about Government procurement matters but does not represent any participant in the protested procurement (*Kenneth R. Bland, Consultant*, B–184852, October 17, 1975, 75–2 CPD 242), or a former Government purchasing agent concerned about whether adequate supplies will be furnished to the Government under the protested contract (*Barbara L. Bayliss*, B–188751, July 6, 1977, 77–2 CPD 8).

In the present case, the protester states it is concerned about electric vehicle development but chose not to submit a proposal in this procurement. It is evident that the direct and substantial economic interests at stake are not those of Die Mesh, but rather those of offerors which participated in the procurement and did not receive awards. As indicated in *American Satellite Corporation, supra*, Die Mesh's interests are too remote for it to be considered an interested party because there are other intervening parties with more direct and substantial interests. Stated another way, we believe the interests involved in the procurement are adequately protected by limiting the class of parties eligible to protest to disappointed offerors (and, possibly, specially interested organizations or subcontractors). No such parties have protested, nor is there any indication that they have authorized Die Mesh to protest on their behalf.

In its August 16, 1978, letter of protest, Die Mesh requested a "full and open hearing." In this regard, the conferences held pursuant to section 20.7 of our Bid Protest Procedures are informal meetings; our Office does not conduct formal hearings in bid protest cases. See *Julie Research Laboratories, Inc.*, 55 Comp. Gen. 374, 387–388 (1975), 75–2 CPD 232. The merits of the present protest are not for consideration, and we believe no useful purpose would be served by holding a conference in this case. See *Rushton Industrial Construction*, B–191825, June 12, 1978, 78–1 CPD 427.

In view of the foregoing, it is unnecessary to decide whether this subcontract protest is properly for consideration under the criteria of *Optimum Systems, supra*.

The protest is dismissed.

[B–191321]

Appropriations—Permanent Indefinite—Judgments—Availability for Retirement and Insurance Deductions

Employee recovered judgment in U.S. District Court providing for backpay and specifically calling for payment of Government's contribution to Civil Service Retirement Fund. Where judgment specifically provides for payment of Government's contribution to Civil Service Retirement Fund or similar funds, that contribution may be paid from Judgment Fund created by 31 U.S.C. 724a.

Appropriations—Judgments—Agency Appropriations—Availability for·Retirement and Insurance ·Deductions

Where judgment entered in favor ·of employee calls for payment of backpay, but does not specifically mention or provide for ·payment of Government's contribution to Civil Service Retirement Fund, that contribution may be paid from agency appropriations. B–124720, May 15, 1961, overruled.

In the matter of Dr. Katsura Fukui—Payment of Judgment, November 30, 1978:

This matter. arises from a request for the certification of a judgment for· payment from the Judgment Fund created by 31 U.S.C. § 724a.

By letter of December 13, 1977, from Ms. Barbara Allen Babcock, Assistant Attorney General, Civil Division, Department of Justice, the "Stipulation of Compromise and Dismissal," in *Katsura Fukui* v. *Secretary of the Air Force, et al.*, Civil Action No. 75–5208–G, United States District Court for the District of Massachusetts, was submitted to this Office for certification and payment. Under the terms of the Stipulation, plaintiff Fukui was to be paid the net amount of $26,691, and $2,009 was to be deposited on plaintiff's behalf as his contribution to the Civil Service Retirement Fund. Additionally, $2,009 was to be deposited in the Civil Service .Retirement Fund as the Government's or employer's contribution.

During the review of the stipulation prior to certification, our decision B–127420, May 15, 1961, was considered. In that decision we held that no appropriation was available to pay the Government's contribution to the Civil Service Retirement Fund where such contribution became due incident to backpay awarded in a Court of Claims Judgment. Because we believed that it was desirable to reexamine that decision, we certified that part of the Stipulation calling for the payment to plaintiff Fukui and for the payment of his contribution to the Civil Service Retirement Fund. This decision considers whether or not the remainder of the Stipulation may be certified for payment.

The act of July 27, 1956, as amended by chapter XIV of Public Law 95–26, May 4, 1977, 91 Stat. 61, 96, 31 U.S.C. § 724a, provides, in pertinent part that:

There are appropriated, out of any money in the Treasury not otherwise appropriated, such sums as may be necessary for the payment, not otherwise provided for, as certified by the Comptroller General, of final judgments, awards, and compromise settlements, which are payable in accordance with the terms of sections 2414, 2517, 2672, 2677 of Title 28, together with such interest and costs as may be specified in such judgments or otherwise authorized by law * * *.

There is no question that the amounts owed to plaintiff Fukui under the terms of the Stipulation were payable from the above appropriation. These were in fact paid from it, including Mr. Fukui's contribution to the Civil Service Retirement Fund.

A review of B–124720, May 15, 1961, shows that the judgment involved there was silent regarding payment of the Government's contribution. That is not the case here, because the Stipulation specifically calls for the payment of the Government's contribution. We believe that that specific provision distinguishes the instant case from our prior holding. Since there is no specific restriction in 31 U.S.C. § 724a barring the payment, when a judgment or compromise generally qualifies for payment under 31 U.S.C. § 724a, if it provides for payment of the Government's contribution to the Civil Service Retirement Fund, or any similar fund, that payment may be made from the Judgment Fund created by that section. This holding also satisfies the literal requirements of 5 U.S.C. § 8384(a)(1) (1976) that the Government's contribution be paid "from the appropriation or fund used to pay the employee" and it is not in conflict with the theory that the Judgment Fund may be used only for payments to or on behalf of a judgment creditor.

Although the specific issue raised in the instant case is thus settled, we believe that the basic holding of B–124720, May 15, 1961, must be reexamined. The specific provision calling for payments into the Civil Service Retirement Fund, 5 U.S.C. § 8334 (1976), provides, in pertinent part, that:

(a)(1) The employing agency shall deduct and withhold 7 percent of the basic pay of an employee, 7½ percent of the basic pay of a Congressional employee, a law enforcement officer, and a firefighter, and 8 percent of the basic pay of a Member. An equal amount shall be contributed from the appropriation or fund used to pay the employee or, in the case of an elected official, from an appropriation or fund available for payment of other salaries of the same office or establishment. * * *

Under normal circumstances, an employee's salary and the Government's contribution to the Civil Service Retirement Fund are paid at the same time, and there are no obstacles to making both payments from the same "appropriation or fund." The problem arises when an employee receives backpay either because he is reinstated following a termination or his salary is retroactively adjusted.

Most retroactive payments are made under one of the following statutes, the Back Pay Act of 1966, 5 U.S.C. § 5596 (1976); the Veterans Preference Act, 5 U.S.C. § 7701 (1976); or Title VII of the Civil Rights Act of 1964 as amended, 42 U.S.C. § 2000e–16 (Supp. II, 1972). Under all three of these Acts, when an employee is restored or his salary is adjusted, the service of the employee is valid service, at the adjusted pay rate, for all purposes. Once the employee's contribution to the Civil Service Retirement Fund is made, the Government's obligation to pay an annuity, if the employee eventually otherwise qualifies, arises. That obligation is not impaired or diminished because the Government fails to make its equal contribution to the Retirement Fund. The only consequence of the failure of the Government to contribute is that unfunded liability of the Civil Service Retirement Fund is increased.

In B–124720, May 15, 1961, with the judgment silent as to payment of the Government's contribution, we held that it could not be paid from the agency's regular appropriations because appropriations are not available for the payment of judgments unless specifically authorized, and because that appropriation was not the same one that was used to pay the employee's salary. We no longer believe that either reason is valid.

Since the judgment did not provide for the payment of the Government's contribution, it is not truly part of the judgment. The Government's obligation to pay its contribution to the Civil Service Retirement Fund does not arise from the judgment, but from the fact that the employee receives full retirement credit for the service effected by the judgment. Therefore, since the payment is not part of the judgment, the rationale that regular appropriations are not available for the payment of judgments does not apply.

Additionally, we no longer believe that the language of 5 U.S.C. § 8334 requiring that the Government's contribution come from the appropriation or fund used to pay the employee's salary must be read that restrictively. If a payment of backpay is made following an administrative finding or settlement under any of the remedial provisions cited above, then the employee's salary and the Government's contribution will actually be paid from the same appropriation. Although that would not be literally true if the retroactive salary payment was paid from the Judgment Fund appropriation created by 31 U.S.C. § 724a, and the Government's contribution was paid from the agency's appropriation, we believe that it would comport with the expressed intent of the Congress. In Public Law 91–93, October 20, 1969, 83 Stat. 136, the Congress made it clear that increases in the unfunded liability of the Civil Service Retirement Fund were not to be permitted. That Act added subsections (f) and (g) to 5 U.S.C. § 8348. Subsection (f) provides that any statute authorizing new or more liberal annuity payments, extension of retirement coverage to new groups, or increases in the pay used to compute retirement benefits would be deemed to authorize appropriations to the Civil Service Retirement Fund to fund the new liability thereby created. Subsection (g) authorizes the Secretary of the Treasury to transfer money from the Treasury to the Retirement Fund at the end of each fiscal year to pay the interest on the unfunded liability as well as the cost of military service credit. Taken together, these provisions express a congressional mandate limiting further increases in the unfunded liability of the Retirement Fund. See Senate Report 91–339, 91st Cong., 1st Sess., August 1, 1969. We believe that the above materials provide a more than sufficient basis for revising our interpretation of 5 U.S.C. § 8334(a)(1). In arriving at the above conclusion, we did not overlook the fact that Public Law 91–93 did not require a change from a static normal cost to a dynamic cost projection.

We also note that when B–124720, May 15, 1961, was decided, neither the Court of Claims nor the United States district courts could render complete relief to a separated employee. Under 28 U.S.C. § 1491 as it was then written, the Court of Claims could only award money judgments; it could not order that an employee be restored. The opposite was true for the district courts; they could order employees restored but could not award money judgments for backpay. The Court of Claims which entered the judgment involved in B–124720, May 15, 1961, could do nothing but enter a money judgment in favor of the separated employee; they could not order that he be restored to duty. This is no longer the case. Now the Court of Claims may order that an employee be reinstated, and the district courts may award backpay, up to its jurisdictional limit. See section 1 of Public Law 92–415, August 29, 1972, 86 Stat. 652, and Public Law 88–519, August 30, 1964, 78 Stat. 699, 28 U.S.C. § 1346.

In the circumstances we now believe that under the above rule, an agency appropriation generally available for salaries and expenses may be used to pay the Government's contribution to the Civil Service Retirement Fund as part of retroactive relief given to an employee by the courts. The appropriation to which the payment should be charged should be the appropriation that would have been charged had the agency made the payment when it was originally due. If, because of the amount of time involved in the retroactive relief, more than one appropriation is involved, the charge should be apportioned among all of the appropriations covered.

In summary, B–124720, May 15, 1961, is overruled and will no longer be followed. If an otherwise qualifying judgment awards an employee backpay and specifically provides for the payment of the Government's contribution to the Civil Service Retirement Fund or similar funds, then that contribution must be paid from the Judgment Fund created by 31 U.S.C. § 724a. If the judgment is silent as to payment of the Government's contribution, then that contribution shall be paid from the agency's appropriations.

〔B–191871〕

Contracts—Negotiation—Two-Step Procurement—Technical Proposal Acceptability—Acceptance Propriety—Protest Timeliness

While protester might have known prior to opening of step-two bids that competitor's technical proposal was determined acceptable under step one of two-step procurement, protest alleging unacceptability of competitor's technical proposal filed after bid opening is timely since protester did not know specific grounds of protest until after bid opening. Protester is not required to file Freedom of Information Act request to discover grounds for protest before step-two bid opening.

Bids—Two-Step Procurement—Technical Proposals—Acceptability

Agency is not obligated to reject step-one technical proposal which does not include material required by solicitation, since applicable regulations permit agency to request omitted information and to determine acceptability of proposal after submission of that information.

Bids—Two-Step Procurement—Technical Proposals—Deviations— Susceptible of Correction

Contracting officer's acceptance of technical proposal submitted under first step of two-step procurement was proper exercise of discretion since proposal was determined susceptible of being made acceptable and there is no evidence that determination was unreasonable or made in bad faith. In determining acceptability of proposal, contracting officer may consider all circumstances, including magnitude of changes needed as well as whether Government time and effort and accompanying technical risk can be justified by resulting increase in price competition.

Contracts—Negotiation—Two-Step Procurement—First Step— Purpose

Step one of two-step procurement is qualifying rather than competitive phase which contemplates qualification of as many sources as possible.

Contracts—Negotiation—Competition—Discussion With All Offerors Requirement—Technical Transfusion or Leveling

Allegation that agency tranfused to other offeror protester's solutions to problems relating to accessibility and material is without merit as agency has denied telling competitor of protester's solutions and record shows that protester's accessibility solution was not unique and material it intended to use was known to agency and to industry prior to issuance of RFTP.

Bids—Two-Step Procurement—Specifications—Revision—Propriety

Specification changes made to enhance competition and which reflect agency's actual minimum needs are not improper merely because they were advantageous to one offeror.

Contracts—Awards—Small Business Concerns—Set-Asides— Administrative Determination

Decision as to whether particular procurement should be set aside for small business is within discretion of contracting agency.

Contracts—Protests—Timeliness—Issues Not Related to Protest Basis—First Raised at Conference on Protest

Protest allegation first raised at bid protest conference is untimely since it was neither made within 10 working days after basis of protest was known nor related to issues timely filed.

In the matter of Guardian Electric Manufacturing Company, November 30, 1978:

This protest primarily involves the validity of the Army's determination that Bendix Corporation's (Bendix) technical proposal was susceptible of being made acceptable, and therefore qualified for discussions under step one of a two-step formally advertised procurement.

Background

On February 1, 1978, the United States Army Aviation Research and Development Command (Army) issued a Request for Technical Proposals (RFTP) as the first step of a two-step formally advertised procurement. The RFTP requested technical proposals for two configurations of a grip assembly for use in Black Hawk and Cobra Army helicopters. The pilot controls the aircraft through these grip handle assemblies which are located at the end of the helicopter's control "stick." In addition to providing a grasping surface, the grip contains several switch assemblies which control important functions like communications and gun firing.

By the amended closing date of March 6, technical proposals were received from Bendix and Guardian Electric Manufacturing Company (Guardian), the protester. The technical proposals were evaluated and discussions held with both firms. Also during the evaluation period, four amendments were issued to the RFTP which, among other things, changed some of the switch assembly requirements, relaxed some tolerances and clarified the specifications.

On April 14, 1978, after the Army determined that both proposals were technically acceptable, a step-two invitation for bids (IFB) was issued to each firm with bid opening scheduled for May 1. Bendix submitted the low bid at $459,746.29, while Guardian bid $467,588.00. Guardian then filed a request to the Army under the Freedom of Information Act, 5 U.S.C. 552 (1976), for access to the Bendix proposal. Upon receiving the information, Guardian filed the instant protest. We have received and considered submissions from Guardian, the Army and Bendix in connection with this matter.

Basically, it is Guardian's position that Bendix's proposal, as initially submitted, was nonresponsive as it was not in the required format and technically unacceptable since Bendix proposed a grip to be manufactured out of a butyrate material, and the proposed design did not provide for access to the switch assemblies. Instead of rejecting Bendix's proposal, the protester complains, the Army held discussions with Bendix and transfused Guardian's solutions to the access and material problems to Bendix, thereby enabling that firm to prepare a second proposal which could meet the Army's requirements. In addition, Guardian contends that the procurement should have been set aside for small business and alleges that even with the Army's "help" the final Bendix proposal is unacceptable because it contains an ambiguity regarding the material to be used in manufacturing the grip. All this leads Guardian to the conclusion that it has submitted the only technically acceptable proposal and that the Bendix proposal should have been rejected and sole-source negotiations conducted with it.

Timeliness of the Protest

The Army argues that Guardian's protest, which was not filed until after bids were opened on May 1, is untimely under our Bid Protest Procedures. It is the agency's view that when the step-two IFB was issued on April 14 Guardian should have known that the Bendix technical proposal, which constituted Guardian's only competition, was determined to be acceptable and should have taken steps to obtain the information needed to protest the agency's action. It appears that the Army favors a rule in two-step procurements that would require a protester to request access to a competitor's proposal or other information within 10 days from the date it knew that the proposal was determined to be acceptable under step one.

Although Guardian may have been aware that Bendix's technical proposal had been accepted when it was not approached for negotiations pursuant to Defense Acquisition Regulation (DAR) § 2-503.1 (h) (1976 ed.) and the IFB was issued, it is significant that the agency did not issue any public notice that indicated Bendix could participate in step two and that the Bendix proposal was not available for public inspection. Thus, at that time Guardian could not have been aware of the specific grounds of protest without filing some type of request for information with the agency.

Our Bid Protest Procedures do not provide any specific time limit for filing such requests and we do not believe that the agency's proposed rule is appropriate for use in two-step procurements. We held in *Hyster Company*, 55 Comp. Gen. 267 (1975), 75-2 CPD 176, that our Office will consider protests against agency action under step one of a two-step procurement even if filed after bid opening under step two as long as the protester does not have a prior opportunity to know the specific basis of protest. In *Hyster Company, supra*, as in this case, the protester did not request information concerning a competitor's technical proposal until after bid opening under the second step. We believe that it would be disruptive of the two-step procurement process, which does not provide for public availability of technical proposals (*see* DAR § 2-503.1(c)(i)), to require protesters to attempt to obtain information regarding competing technical proposals during the procurement process prior to the opening of step-two bids. This is not inconsistent with our holdings in *Access Corporation*, B-189661, February 3, 1978, 78-1 CPD 100, and *Ingersoll-Rand Company*, B-189071, October 3, 1977, 77-2 CPD 254, where arguments raised after bid opening under step two were determined untimely because in both *Access* and *Ingersoll-Rand* the protesters were or should have been aware of the specific bases of protest at the close of step one.

Responsiveness and Acceptability of Bendix Proposal

Guardian contends that Bendix's technical proposal, as initially submitted, was "materially nonresponsive" to the specific requirements of the RFTP as well as technically unacceptable and should have been rejected pursuant to DAR § 2–503.1(e) which states that any proposal which modifies or fails to conform to the essential requirements or specifications of the RFTP shall be considered nonresponsive and categorized as unacceptable. More specifically, Guardian argues that the Bendix proposal was nonresponsive because it was not accompanied by a separate, bound, detailed and contractually binding specification as required by paragraph 6b(1) of the RFTP and did not include detailed engineering drawings and narrative descriptions of the design approach and of its proficiency in grip design and manufacture as required by RFTP paragraphs 6b (2), (3) and (4).

The Army acknowledges that the Bendix proposal, as originally submitted, lacked the items listed by the protester. However, it takes the view that these items were in the nature of administrative details and did not prevent the Bendix proposal from being classified under DAR § 2–503.1(e)(ii) as reasonably susceptible of being made acceptable with additional information which would not change the basic proposal.

It is clear that these deficiencies could be cured by the submission of additional information. Thus, under DAR § 2–503.1(e), the agency was not obligated to reject the Bendix proposal and properly could request that Bendix submit the missing material for subsequent evaluation. *See*, e.g., 51 Comp. Gen. 85 (1971).

Similarly, we do not believe that the technical deficiencies in Bendix's initial proposal required rejection of that proposal. The purchase description contained in the RFTP provides:

3.3.1 *Design and Construction.* * * * The head modules shall be removable for access to the switches and wiring connections contained therein. A means shall also be provided for removing -and replacing switches in the main body section. * * *

3.5 *Maintainability.* The grip assembly is designed to permit ease of maintenance at field level, including replacement of switches, wiring and associated parts without damage, and without the use of special tools and techniques.

In response to this requirement Bendix proposed to mold the grip body without a removable section for access to three of the switch assemblies. Instead Bendix indicated that switches could be removed by heating the grip and pulling them out with a suitable tool.

The Army was not satisfied with this approach and informed Bendix of its views during discussions held with Bendix in mid-March. Bendix then revised its design to include an access panel in front of the grip body below the switches.

The purchase description in the RFTP did not require that the grips be molded of a particular material, but specified that the grips must meet certain criteria regarding weight, strength, resistance to moisture, etc. Bendix, in its initial proposal, indicated that it intended to mold its grip from a butyrate material. It was the Army's view that this material would not meet the specified performance criteria and Bendix was so informed. Bendix then altered its design to provide for the use of glass filled polypropylene.

Guardian asserts that Bendix's initial proposal was technically unacceptable because, as indicated above, it did not provide for access to the switch assemblies as required by the RFTP and proposed to mold the grip from butyrate which is an unacceptable material. Since these deficiencies go to the very heart of Bendix's proposed grip design and could not be cured without a major proposal rewrite and redesign, Guardian urges that the proposal could not be classified as reasonably susceptible of being made acceptable pursuant to DAR § 2–503.1(e)(ii) but should have been rejected as unacceptable pursuant to DAR § 2–503.1(e)(iii).

In support of its position Guardian points to the evaluation record where it is indicated that the initial Bendix proposal was found to be "unacceptable" because of the proposed use of butyrate and the lack of accessibility. Further, in this connection Guardian notes that evaluation memoranda which concern the classification of Bendix's proposal "as susceptible of being made acceptable" appear to deal only with "administrative deficiencies" which pertain to the form of the proposal rather than the technical deficiencies relating to the use of butyrate and lack of accessibility.

Here Guardian notes that there are only three categories under DAR § 2–503.1(e); namely, (i) acceptable, (ii) susceptible of being made acceptable, and (iii) unacceptable. Thus, Guardian concludes that since the record shows that the Army actually determined that the Bendix proposal was "unacceptable," DAR § 2–503.1(e)(iii) mandated its rejection.

Although Guardian is correct in its observations regarding the use of the term "unacceptable" in the evaluation memoranda we do not believe agency technical personnel used the term to indicate that the total proposal was unacceptable. The record shows that they merely considered Bendix's approach to the material to be used and to accessibility to be unacceptable. Even though the contracting officer's memorandum for record does not specifically list the technical deficiencies in the Bendix proposal, we cannot conclude that he was unaware of the technical problems when the determination to hold discussion with Bendix was made. It is clear from the record and the actions of the agency that although the Bendix proposal was unacceptable in certain respects, the initial proposal, as an entity, was considered susceptible of being made acceptable under DAR § 2–503.1(e)(ii) and qualified for discussions.

The two-step formal advertising procedure ·described in DAR § 2–501, *et seq.* combines the benefits of competitive advertising with the flexibility of negotiation. *Page Airways*, B–185166, July 29, 1976, 76–2 CPD 95, and cases cited therein. The first step of the procedure contemplates the qualification of as many technical proposals as possible under negotiation. 50 Comp. Gen. 346 (1970). This procedure requires that first step technical proposals comply with the basic requirements of the specification, but does not require compliance with all specification details. 51 Comp. Gen. 85, *supra.* Our Office has held that questions as to whether technical proposals submitted under two-step procedures are deficient and whether they are reasonably susceptible of being made acceptable without major revision are basically matters requiring the judgment and expertise of technically qualified personnel. *METIS Corporation*, 54 Comp. Gen. 612 (1975), 75–1 CPD 44. We will ordinarily accept the considered judgment of the procuring agency's specialists and technicians as to the adequacy of a technical proposal, unless it is clearly shown that the agency action was erroneous, arbitrary, or not made in good faith. *Coastal Mobile and Modular Corporation*, B–183664, July 15, 1975, 75–2 CPD 39.

In this instance Guardian argues that the Army's action in not rejecting the initial Bendix proposal was arbitrary and unreasonable. It is Guardian's view that the defects regarding material and accessibility could not be rectified by the submission of additional data or clarifying language. Rather, Guardian insists that these defects concerned essential performance characteristics and that their correction required a major redesign.

There is no question that the changes required to make the Bendix proposal acceptable in the areas of material and accessibility were of a substantial nature and did relate to the basic design offered by Bendix. However, we do not believe the agency is in every instance prevented from conducting discussions with an offeror whose proposed design is deficient in these respects. Here, although some changes in the grip design were needed to qualify Bendix for the step-two competition the agency reports that these changes did not represent a significant amount of effort or technical risk for the Government. It is our view that the determination of whether changes needed to qualify a proposal under step one of a two-step procurement are so basic as to require it to be rejected is one which must be made in light of all the facts and circumstances. The matters to be considered are not just related to the magnitude of the changes versus the basic design of the proposal but whether those changes and the time and effort needed to effectuate them as well as the accompanying technical risk can be justified by the resulting increase in competition under step two.

In view of the fact that price competition would have been eliminated (DAR § 2–503.1(e) repeatedly expresses concern over the preservation of price competition) if the Bendix proposal were rejected and since the agency viewed technical risk as slight, we do not believe that the Army abused its discretion in judging Bendix's proposal as susceptible of being made acceptable despite its technical shortcomings. *See generally* 51 Comp. Gen. 372 (1971). Nor do we share Guardian's concern over the fairness of permitting Bendix to improve its weaker proposal. Step one of a two-step procurement is a qualifying rather than competitive phase which contemplates the qualification of as many sources as possible. 50 Comp. Gen. 346 *supra*; 51 Comp. Gen. 372, *supra*. Proposals are classified as either acceptable or unacceptable on their own merits and are not in competition with other proposals submitted. *Struthers Electronics Corporation*, B-186002, September 10, 1976, 76-2 CPD 281.

Technical Transfusion

Guardian maintains that its solutions to the problems of accessibility and material were improperly transfused to Bendix by the Army during discussions. In support of its position Guardian directs our attention to *Procurement Consultants, Incorporated*, B-181779, December 10, 1974, 74-2 CPD 321, where we defined technical transfusion as the conveying, either directly or indirectly, during negotiations of a better approach or solution to a problem by the Government negotiators.

In regard to the accessibility problem, Guardian alleges that the Army directed Bendix to provide an access cover which was functionally similar to that proposed by the protestor. Although Guardian does not contend that the use of an access cover for switch removal is unique, it expresses "suspicion" that, given the number of options available to solve this problem, Guardian would "choose" this option after discussion with Army personnel. Further, Guardian notes that Bendix in its initial proposal suggested that if its design, which required the use of heat guns and clamps for switch removal was unacceptable, it would add a removable section to the body. Thus, Guardian concludes Bendix had no intention of using an access cover and only decided to do so at the behest of the Army.

There is no evidence in the record to indicate that Bendix was ever told by the Army to use an access cover. Bendix specifically denies it was so advised and the Army technical evaluator specifically denies mentioning anything to Bendix regarding an access cover. In addition, the Army has produced affidavits from its entire evaluation team which deny that any information from Guardian's proposal was given to Bendix.

Further, Guardian admits that there is nothing unique or special about the use of an access door and Guardian even concedes that Bendix's proposed use of the access cover is not the same as Guardian's design. Thus there does not appear to have been any transfusion in regard to the use of an access cover.

In connection with the choice of material from which the grip is to be molded, Guardian claims that its proposed use of glass filled polypropylene was improperly transfused to Bendix. In this instance Guardian points to a March 16, 1978, letter to Bendix where the Army informs that firm that its proposed use of butyrate is not acceptable and states "* * * possibilities inherently narrow down to a few engineering quality glass filled thermoplastics." It is further noted that Bendix subsequently altered its proposal to provide for the use of glass filled polypropylene. The Army replies that the use of glass filled thermoplastics was well known in the industry prior to the issuance of the RFTP. In fact, the Army has submitted a transcript of a talk given in 1976 by an official of Guardian concerning the use of such material in grip manufacture. The agency also directs our attention to the fact that it only suggested the use of glass filled thermoplastics, rather than polypropylene, the specific type of glass filled thermoplastic used by Guardian.

The protester counters that there is no requirement that transfused information be of a proprietary nature and argues that information disclosed to the public prior to the negotiation still may not be transfused from one offeror to another during negotiation.

We do not believe the statements made by agency personnel regarding the use of "glass filled thermoplastics" constitute technical transfusion. This information given to Bendix was, by the admission of all parties, publicly available. Further, the statements by agency evaluators were general in nature in that they pertained to a class of materials, "glass filled thermoplastics," which could be used. They did not convey Guardian's particular solution, the use of glass filled polypropylene, to Bendix. Technical transfusion implies that an approach or solution is taken from one offeror's proposal and given to another offeror. 51 Comp. Gen. 621 (1972); *Applied Management Sciences, Inc.*, B–184654, February 18, 1976, 76–1 CPD 111. In this instance, where the record indicates that the Army evaluators were aware of the use of thermoplastics in grip manufacture independently of and prior to the submission of Guardian's proposal and contains affidavits from the involved Army employees which state that no information from the Guardian proposal was given to Bendix, we are unable to conclude that the agency's suggestion that Bendix could use glass filled thermoplastics constitutes transfusion of Guardian's proposed approach.

Specification Changes

Guardian complains that the Army revised its specifications and relaxed its requirements as an improper inducement for Bendix to remain in the competition. In this regard the protester notes that despite the Army's initial misgivings, Bendix was able to convince the Army to issue amendments to the RFTP altering the requirements for some of the switch assemblies. It is Guardian's view that these changes were not necessary nor in the Government's best interest, but were solely an accommodation to Bendix. It is the agency's position, however, and the record indicates that these amendments were issued to add new supply sources for the switches and thus to enhance competition. Accordingly, since the revised specifications appear to reflect actual agency needs and provide for a broader competitive base, we do not find their use to be improper merely because the result was advantageous to Bendix. Consequently, we have no basis to object to the agency's amending the specifications.

Small Business Set-Aside

Guardian contends that it has discovered an irregularity in the agency's determination that this procurement should not be a small business set-aside. The protester states that in reviewing the documents included in the agency's report submitted in connection with the protest it noted that although the contracting officer concluded that adequate small business sources were not known, the file reveals that of 15 firms on the proposed bidders list, 12 were small businesses. The agency responds that its determination was made according to the applicable regulations and was concurred in by the Small Business Administration representative.

We think it is important to note that the presence of a number of small business firms on a proposed bidders list, alone, is not an assurance of reasonable competition. For example, of the 23 firms solicited for this procurement, two responded and only one, Guardian, was a small business. In any event, we have long held that while it is the policy of the Government to award a fair proportion of its total purchases to small business, there is nothing in the Small Business Act or the implementing regulations which mandates that any particular procurement be set aside for small business. The decision whether a procurement should be set aside is within the authority and discretion of the contracting agency. *General Electrodynamics Corporation*, B–190020, January 31, 1978, 78–1 CPD 78; *See Kinnet Dairies, Inc.* v. *Farrow*, 580 F. 2d 1260 (5th Cir. 1978).

Alleged Ambiguity of Bendix Proposal

During the conference held in this Office in connection with the protest on August 22, 1978, Guardian first raised a question regarding a possible ambiguity in Bendix's final proposal. Guardian directed our attention to the drawings submitted with the Bendix proposal which specify that the grip will be molded of "PPO Glass Filled Polypropylene." Guardian states that there is no such substance as "PPO Glass Filled Polypropylene." Rather there is a material known as polyphenylene oxide (PPO) and a material known as polypropylene (PP). These materials have different characteristics, according to the protester. One may be acceptable while the other may not. Thus, Guardian concludes the Army is confused as to what is being offered and has arbitrarily accepted a proposal which contains a patent ambiguity in a critical design characteristic.

The Army denies that the ambiguity is of any significance and replies that this allegation is untimely raised. It is the agency's view that Guardian should have been aware of the alleged ambiguity in the Bendix drawings sometime soon after May 5, 1978, when the protester was permitted to inspect the Bendix proposal. Guardian maintains that this allegation is merely additional evidence to support its earlier timely raised contentions as to the unacceptability of the Bendix proposal.

Guardian attempts to relate the "PP vs. PPO" issue to its earlier contention regarding the proportion of glass to plastic to be used by Bendix. This issue was spawned by an Army memorandum included in the agency's protest report which incorrectly stated that Bendix intended to use a polypropylene material containing 55 percent glass. The Army has subsequently admitted that the statement in the memorandum was erroneous and no evidence exists in the Bendix proposal or the evaluation record to substantiate the statement. Bendix maintains that it never intended to offer material with such a glass to plastic ratio. Consequently, Guardian's argument that such a proportion of glass to plastic would not meet the Army's needs was rendered moot.

Further, the protester explains that it set forth its suspicion about the vague material specification in its May 26 protest submission but could not explore the issue until the Army filed its protest report. Apparently, Guardian refers to the following statement on page 8 of its May 26 submission:

In its second proposal, Bendix retreated from its intended use of butyrate and instead proposed to mold the grips out of either PPO (polyphenylene oxide) or glass-filled polypropylene.

This statement appears to be a mere statement of fact. Nowhere in the submission is there an indication that Guardian viewed this use of material as improper or that such use was to be a ground of protest. Since Guardian had been provided the Bendix proposal, which included the drawings with the disputed notation, prior to filing its protest we fail to understand why Guardian would need the protest report to "explore this issue." As far as we can tell the report makes no mention (other than that included in the Bendix drawing) of the use of "PP vs. PPO" as the material from which the grips would be molded.

As a general rule, we have viewed the timeliness of specific grounds of protest raised after the filing of a timely initial general protest as dependent upon the relationship the later-raised bases bear to the initial protest. *See Kappa Systems, Inc.*, 56 Comp. Gen. 675 (1977), 77–1 CPD 412; *Annapolis Tennis Limited Partnership*, B–189571, June 5, 1978, 78–1 CPD 412. Where the later bases have presented new and independent grounds for protest, we have considered that they must independently satisfy the timeliness criteria of our Bid Protest Procedures, 4 C.F.R. Part 20 (1978). *See State Equipment Division of Secorp National, Inc.*, 55 Comp. Gen. 1467 (1976), 76–2 CPD 270; *Consolidated Airborne Systems, Inc.*, B–184369, October 21, 1975, 75–2 CPD 247. Conversely, where the later bases have merely provided additional support for earlier timely raised objections, we have considered these additional arguments in our evaluation of the protest. *Kappa Systems, Inc., supra*. In this connection, our Bid Protest Procedures provide:

[b] (2) * * * bid protests shall be filed not later than 10 [working] days after the basis for protest is known or should have been known, whichever is earlier. 4 C.F.R. § 20.2(b) (2) (1978).

We do not believe it is reasonable to conclude that the protester's "PP vs. PPO" argument provided support for its position regarding the glass to plastic ratio of Bendix's material. The fact that Bendix could supply either PP or PPO as a material has nothing whatever to do with the ratio of glass to plastic in a particular material. In fact, Guardian's glass to plastic ratio argument, which has been rendered moot, was based on the premise that PP would be used. Also the basis for Guardian's "PP vs. PPO" contention was available to it long before the basis for its glass-to-plastic argument became available in the protest report.

Similarly, we see no relation to Guardian's complaint that the agency is accepting an ambiguous proposal and an earlier reference in the protester's May 26 submission that Bendix proposed to use "PPO (polyphenylene oxide) or glass-filled polypropylene" in a factual statement which did not indicate in any manner that it constituted a basis for protest.

The information needed for Guardian to set forth its position relating to the alleged ambiguity was available to it in early May, more than 10 days prior to the date the issue was raised on August 22. Consequently, we must conclude that this basis of protest is untimely and need not be considered.

The protest is denied.

[B-192669]

Pay—Retired—Death of Member—Court Determination

A claim by a retired Navy member's wife for the member's retired pay accruing during the 7-year period from the date of his disappearance to the date he was declared dead by a State court may not be allowed since retired pay is payable only during the member's life and there is no showing whether he was alive after his disappearance or evidence of when he actually died, and the State court determination appears to be presumptive only and does not establish that the member lived for 7 years.

In the matter of Retired pay—presumption of death, December 1, 1978:

This decision is the result of an appeal of a settlement by our Claims Division dated July 31, 1978, denying a wife's claim for her husband's retired pay for the period January 1, 1970, through November 26, 1976.

A retired member of the Navy disappeared from the Veterans' Administration Hospital, Seattle, Washington, on November 26, 1969, after having been diagnosed as suffering from a fatal disease. Apparently the disease was in its advanced stage at the time the member disappeared. His retired pay was suspended effective January 1, 1970. No information concerning his whereabouts or existence has been received since his disappearance. On March 25, 1977, the Superior Court of the State of Washington for Kitsap County held a hearing for the purpose of adjudicating intestacy and heirship and in the matter of his estate. The Court in connection with that hearing issued an order stating that the member had died intestate on November 26, 1976, leaving property in the State of Washington subject to probate. There is no indication that the United States was represented at that hearing.

The retired pay of a retired member of the armed services accrues only during the life of the member. 48 Comp. Gen. 706 (1969). Payment of such pay is generally authorized to be made only to the retired member, except that upon his death the amount accrued but unpaid may be paid to his beneficiary as provided by 10 U.S.C. 2771. Therefore, the fact of the member's death and the date of death must be established before payment may be made on such claim. We have also held that retired pay may not be paid for any period subsequent to the last day on which the member is known to have been alive, when the actual date of death is not established by competent evidence. 14 Comp. Gen. 411 (1934).

In cases where a judicial decree declares that a person is presumed to be dead on a designated date, such a decree does not establish that the person concerned lived for any fixed period or that his life did not end immediately after his unexplained absence. See *David* v.

Briggs, 97 U.S. 628 (1878). Further, even a statutory presumption of death does not purport to create a conclusive presumption that the individual died at the end of the 7-year period, nor does it preclude the introduction of evidence to show that death occurred earlier. *Peak* v. *United States,* 353 U.S. 43, 45–46 (1957).

In settling similar missing persons' cases we have said that in the absence of an applicable Federal statute, we will give great weight to the determinations of the State courts under State statutes, particularly where the United States has been represented in the State court and the pertinent issues are presented to the court. See B–187165, September 16, 1976. However, where the only basis presented to us for payment of a claim for retired pay of a missing member is a State court decree entered on the basis of presumptive evidence in a proceeding to which the United States is not a party, we have followed the rule that the United States is not necessarily bound by such a decree. See *Privett* v. *United States,* 256 U.S. 201 (1921); *United States* v. *Candelaria,* 271 U.S. 432 (1926). In the absence of further proof in such cases that the member was alive after the date of disappearance, we have found such claims too doubtful for us, the accounting officers of the Government, to allow. In such cases the claimants are left to pursue their claims in the Federal courts. See for example B–176008, September 18, 1972, and B–173649, August 31, 1971.

Accordingly, in view of the lack of specific information relating to the continued life of the decedent and in view of his condition at the time he disappeared, subject claim is too doubtful for us to allow. Therefore, the Claims Division's action disallowing the claim is sustained.

〔 B–189778 〕

Officers and Employees—Transfers—Relocation Expenses— Eligibility

Employees of Postal Service contract compliance unit were transferred to General Services Administration (GSA) incident to a transfer of function. They are not eligible for relocation expenses under 5 U.S.C. 5724 and 5724a since those sections restrict reimbursement to employees of an agency. The term "agency," as defined in 5721(1) and 5 U.S.C. 105, excludes the United States Postal Service. Therefore, individuals who transfer to or from the Postal Service are not eligible for relocation expenses under 5 U.S.C. 5724 and 5724a.

In the matter of Postal Service Employees—Relocation incident to transfer of function to GSA, December 4, 1978:

The Administrator, General Services Administration, asks whether an agency may refuse to reimburse an employee for relocation expenses because of budget considerations and, if an agency cannot, whether an employee may effectively waive reimbursement of those expenses.

The Administrator states that the questions arise due to the transfer of a Postal Service contract compliance function to the General Services Administration (GSA) effective April 1, 1976. The transfer was accomplished by Order No. 1 (Revised) dated January 20, 1976, of the Acting Director, Office of Federal Contract Compliance Functions, United States Department of Labor. As a result of the transfer of function, GSA was required to offer employment to 67 Postal Service employees. To help accommodate the transfer of function, GSA's personnel ceiling was increased by the Office of Management and Budget by a total of 25 positions. The Administrator states that because of personnel ceiling limitations and budget constraints, each of the transferees was advised that "if more than twenty-five employees accept the GSA offer, a reduction-in-force will be highly probable." However, all of the 67 employees were offered positions with GSA at their existing salary. Also, the Postal Service provided each employee with an offer of a Postal Service position, which usually was at a lower salary rate. Apparently, 27 employees accepted the GSA offer of employment and all were able to be accommodated because of GSA employee turnover and retirements.

The Administrator states that since this action had not been planned for, there was no money in the budget to pay for other benefits for the 27 employees. Although the Postal Service transferred some funds for salaries and retirement contributions and the Office of Management and Budget allowed GSA to request additional funds, insufficient funds were available to enable GSA to pay all the necessary expenses. Accordingly, GSA advised each employee that it would not be able to pay appropriate relocation expenses because of its budget situation.

The Administrator presents two questions for our resolution. The first question is whether the authorization and approval of expenses incurred incident to an employee's transfer is within an agency's discretion in order that such expenses may be withheld due to budget considerations. The second question presented is whether an employee may effectively waive appropriate reimbursement for transfer related expenses.

Although not raised by GSA, we believe that a threshold question is whether an employee who transfers or is transferred to or from the Postal Service is eligible for reimbursement of relocation expenses. Sections 5724 and 5724a (1976) of title 5, United States Code, which authorized payment of relocation expenses, are limited by section 5721(2) to apply only to "an individual employed in or under an agency." The term "agency" is defined in section 5721(1) as including an "Executive agency," which under 5 U.S.C. § 105 includes an "independent establishment." However, the latter is defined at 5 U.S.C. § 104 as follows:

> For the purpose of this title, "independent establishment" means—
> (1) an establishment in the executive branch (*other than the United States Postal Service* or the Postal Rate Commission) which is not an Executive department, military department, Government corporation, or part thereof, or part of an independent establishment * * *. [Italic supplied.]

Since the Postal Service is not an "agency" within the meaning of 5 U.S.C. § 5721(1), it follows that an employee of the Postal Service is not covered by the provisions of 5 U.S.C. §§ 5724 and 5724a, and is not entitled to relocation expenses thereunder upon transfer to an agency covered under those sections. Rather, the situation here is analogous to that of a new employee who, unless he qualifies as a man-power shortage category employee, must bear the expenses of report-ing to his first duty station. Thus, the subject employees are not eligible for reimbursement of relocation expenses under 5 U.S.C. §§ 5724 and 5724a.

In view of the above we find it unnecessary to answer the questions presented by the GSA Administrator. However, we note that the question pertaining to "budget constraints" was addressed in a deci-sion of this Office, *David C. Goodyear*, 56 Comp. Gen. 709 (1977). In *Goodyear* we held that budget constraints cannot form the basis for denying an employee relocation expenses once his transfer has been found to be in the Government's interest.

[B–191293]

Mileage—Travel by Privately Owned Automobile—Dependents— Evacuation

Employees of Padre Island National Seashore and their families were ordered to leave the island and travel to a place of safety due to the threat of a hurri-cane. If the agency determines that an evacuation in fact occurred under its regulations, employees would be entitled to mileage for dependent transportation by private automobiles incident to the evacuation.

In the matter of Veldon A. Chapman and others—Travel Expenses— Hurricane Evacuation, December 4, 1978:

This decision responds to the request of Levi E. Lopez, an authorized certifying officer of the Department of the Interior, National Park Service, Southwest Region, concerning the claims of three employees, Rudy G. Fichtner, Veldon A. Chapman, and H. Wayne Norton, for the reimbursement of expenses related to the evacuation of their dependents from Padre Island. Mr. Lopez disallowed the claims on the basis that an evacuation did not take place since no household goods or personal effects were removed from the island.

The employees work at the Padre Island National Seashore where they are required to live in Government furnished quarters as a condition of employment. The record shows that the three employees and their families were directed to leave Padre Island and take up temporary residence at the Hilton Inn, located approximately 40 miles from the island headquarters, when hurricane Anita threatened to strike the island on August 31, 1977. The employees were given radios and Government automobiles and were instructed to remain in duty status and maintain continuous radio communications with headquarters which is located some 16 miles from the employees' residences and out of the park boundary. The wives of the employees drove privately owned vehicles to and from the Hilton Inn.

As a result of this temporary evacuation, claims for the expenses of the employees' families were submitted and denied for the reason set forth above. Mr. Lopez has treated the incident as an official order to the employees to leave the island and travel to the Hilton Inn on temporary duty rather than an authorized evacuation. He concludes that only the employees are entitled to mileage and per diem allowances for the temporary duty.

The Padre Island National Seashore operates under a Hurricane Preparedness Plan, approved by the Southwest Regional Office on September 30, 1976. This Plan prescribes procedures to be followed by the National Seashore employees and their families in situations when a hurricane strike is imminent. Pertinent provisions of the Plan provide for the evacuation of families to the mainland well in advance of a storm to insure their safety.

Section V of the Preparedness Plan, Relocation of Families Living in Government Quarters, stipulates that park employees and dependents living in Government housing on Padre Island will be evacuated and provided with temporary quarters within a 50 mile radius of park headquarters. The section further provides that park employees living in private housing on the mainland may evacuate at their own discretion, but will not be placed on per diem. Rates of per diem allowed are designated as the same rates applicable to a change of duty station. The Plan also recognizes the possibility that some employees will be assigned duties at a duty station other than the place of evacuation and therefore will be separated from their families.

Title 5, United States Code, section 5725, provides the authority for transportation at Government expense of the immediate family of a Government employee when an official determination by proper authority is made that emergency evacuation of families is required. No provision is made in section 5725 for subsistence and we are unaware of any other authority that would authorize such payments including the per diem set forth in the evacuation plan. Staff personnel at agency headquarters in Washington, D.C., advise that they know of no such authority. In accordance with Part 347, Chapter 16, Paragraph 4 of the Departmental Manual criteria for evacuation is as follows:

> The immediate family of an employee may be evacuated because of military or other reasons which create imminent danger to life or property, or adverse living conditions which seriously affect health, safety, or accommodations of the family. They may also be evacuated when an employee is transferred or assigned to duty at places where his immediate family is not permitted to accompany him for above reasons.

It is indicated that the three employees and their families were officially ordered to leave the island and travel to the Hilton Inn because of the threat of a hurricane. Whether an evacuation in fact occurred would primarily be a matter for determination within the agency under the authority of 5 U.S.C. 5725, *supra*. If the agency determines that the employees were evacuated in accordance with the applicable agency regulations then the employees would be entitled to reimbursement for mileage for transportation of their families by private automobiles for the round-trip distance between their residences on Padre Island and the evacuation point. As stated above, no travel per diem or other form of subsistence expense reimbursement is authorized under 5 U.S.C. 5725. However, in addition to mileage for family transportation under 5 U.S.C. 5725 the employees are entitled transportation and per diem for themselves under the Federal Travel Regulations if they were required to perform duty away from their duty station on Padre Island.

The evacuation plan should be reviewed and modified to conform with this decision.

[B–192238]

Quarters Allowance—Basic Allowance for Quarters (BAQ)—Assigned to Government Quarters—Partial Allowance Entitlement

A Navy member assigned Government single-type quarters (barracks), and who is ineligible for regular basic allowance for quarters (BAQ) under 37 U.S.C. 403(b), is entitled to "partial" BAQ under 37 U.S.C. 1009(d). Neither the member's temporary duty status, between permanent duty stations, nor his pay grade (E–4, less than 4 years' service, or below) precludes him from receiving partial BAQ.

In the matter of Seaman Recruit Steve R. Knerr, USN, December 4, 1978:

This action is in response to a letter dated January 31, 1978, from the Officer in Charge, Navy Finance Office, Orlando, Florida, requesting our decision as to the propriety of paying partial basic allowance for quarters (BAQ) to Seaman Recruit Steve R. Knerr, USN, 211–

52–4357, while on temporary duty under instruction. This request was approved by the Department of Defense Military Pay and Allowance Committee and forwarded to us as submission No. DO–N–1294.

Apparently doubt has arisen as to Mr. Knerr's entitlement to partial BAQ because he is in pay grade E–4 (less than 2 years' service) or lower and he was performing the temporary duty between permanent duty stations. Rule 16, Table 3–2–3, Department of Defense Military Pay and Allowances Entitlements Manual (DODPM), precludes payment of BAQ in such circumstances.

Section 403(a), title 37, United States Code (1976), authorizes BAQ at rates prescribed under 37 U.S.C. 1009 (1976) to a member of a uniformed service who is entitled to basic pay. However, sections 403 (b) and (c) basically disallow BAQ to a member who is assigned adequate Government furnished quarters, or is on field or sea duty.

Sections 1009 (a) and (b), title 37, United States Code, permit the President to make upward adjustments in monthly basic pay and basic allowances for subsistence and quarters "Whenever the General Schedule of compensation for Federal classified employees * * * is adjusted upwards," at the same percentage increase as in the General Schedule. Section 1009(c) permits the President, whenever he determines it to be in the best interest of the Government, to allocate the increase among the elements of compensation on other than an equal percentage basis. When such a method of allocation is chosen, section 1009(d) authorizes payment of amounts termed by the services as "partial BAQ" to certain members without dependents.

Section 1009(d) states:

Under regulations prescribed by the President, whenever the President exercises his authority under subsection (c) to allocate the elements of compensation specified in subsection (a) on a percentage basis other than an equal percentage basis, he may pay to each member without dependents who, under section 403 (b) or (c), is not entitled to receive a basic allowance for quarters, an amount equal to the difference between (1) the amount of such increase under subsection (c) in the amount of the basic allowance for quarters which, but for section 403 (b) or (c), such member would be entitled to receive, and (2) the amount by which such basic allowance for quarters would have been increased under section (b)(3) if the President had not exercised such authority.

The legislative purpose behind this section was to pay partial BAQ to members without dependents who are ineligible for full BAQ under 37 U.S.C. 403(a), due to their assignment to Government quarters (barracks and bachelor quarters), or because they are on field or sea duty, since it is recognized that the value of the quarters furnished them in such cases is less than the regular BAQ forfeited. 56 Comp. Gen. 894, 897 (1977).

No distinction between assignment to temporary or permanent duty station for the purpose of determining eligibility for partial BAQ was made in the law nor appears in the legislative history, nor is the member's pay grade a factor in this case. In this regard the restrictions in Rule 16, Table 3–2–3, DODPM, apply only to regular BAQ, not partial BAQ.

Accordingly, since Mr. Knerr was apparently assigned to Government quarters during his temporary duty and was not receiving regular BAQ, he is entitled to partial BAQ.

【 B–149685 】

Small Business Administration—Loans—Sale—Federal Financing Bank

Small Business Administration (SBA) does have authority to issue certificates to Federal Financing Bank (FFB) evidencing ownership of group of SBA loans. Proposed financing arrangements, as well as SBA's current procedure of selling individual loans to FFB with recourse, is sufficiently similar from legal standpoint to financing arrangements our Office has approved in past. Also, SBA has same authority to sell loans to FFB with recourse as it has to sell to other purchasers.

Small Business Administration—Loans—Disaster—Direct Sale

SBA is not authorized under existing legislation to sell direct disaster loans to Federal Financing Bank on guaranteed basis either individually or collectively. In absence of specific statutory authority or clear expression of congressional intent that SBA does have such authority to sell direct disaster loans in this manner, which, if allowed, could result in establishment of unlimited contingent liability against SBA without any congressional restraints, our Office cannot approve proposed procedure. Moreover, SBA's proposal to sell these loans with 100 percent guarantees is not consistent with its statutory authority to guarantee maximum of 90 percent of loans made in first instance by participating lending institutions.

In the matter of Authority of SBA to sell disaster and nondisaster loans to Federal Financing Bank, December 5, 1978:

This decision to the Administrator of the Small Business Administration (SBA) is in response to his request for our concurrence in SBA's position concerning two separate, but related, questions. The first question involves SBA's authority to issue certificates to the Federal Financing Bank (FFB) evidencing ownership of a group of SBA loans. The second question concerns SBA's authority to sell direct disaster loans to FFB and to guarantee payment of principal and interest at a rate which may be in excess of the rate paid to SBA by the borrower.

With respect to the first question, SBA maintains that issuance of these certificates evidencing ownership of a group of direct SBA loans merely represents a change of procedure to accommodate FFB's accounting. In past sales to FFB, SBA has transferred title to individual loans and debentures, although the actual loan documents have been held by SBA "acting as bailee for the purchaser." If the proposed change of procedure is made, SBA would continue to hold and service the loans as is now being done.

The Federal Financing Bank was established pursuant to the Federal Financing Bank Act of 1973, approved December 29, 1973, Pub. L. No. 93–224, 87 Stat. 937, 12 U.S.C. §§ 2281 *et seq.* (1976). As stated in section 2 of the Act, 12 U.S.C. § 2281, the purpose of the legislation was to assure coordination of Federal and federally assisted borrowing programs

with the overall economic and fiscal policies of the Government, to reduce the cost of Federal and federally assisted borrowings from the public, and to assure that such borrowings are financed in a manner least disruptive of private financial markets and institutions.

The authority of Federal agencies to finance their operations through FFB is set forth in section 6(a) of the Act, 12 U.S.C. § 2285 (a) as follows:

Any Federal agency which is authorized to issue, sell, or guarantee any obligation is authorized to issue or sell such obligations directly to the Bank.

Also, section 18 of the Act, 12 U.S.C. § 2296, specifically provides that:

Nothing in this chapter shall be construed as authorizing an increase in the amounts of obligations issued, sold, or guaranteed by any Federal agency which issues, sells, or guarantees obligations purchased by the Bank.

In accordance with these provisions, the authority of SBA, as well as other Federal agencies, to issue, sell, or guarantee obligations purchased by FFB is neither greater nor less than its authority to issue, sell, or guarantee obligations to other purchasers.

As stated in SBA's submission, our Office has on several occasions upheld the authority of SBA to sell to private investors, with recourse, debt instruments representing loans SBA had made to small business investment companies (SBICs) pursuant to the Small Business Investment Act of 1958, 15 U.S.C. §§ 661 *et seq.* (1976). Thus, in 44 Comp. Gen. 549 (1965) we upheld SBA's authority to sell loans originally made directly by SBA to SBICs, with recourse, to private financial institutions, pursuant to what was then section 303(b) of the Small Business Investment Act of 1958, 15 U.S.C. § 683(b). Also see 45 Comp. Gen. 253 (1965), and 45 *id.* 370 (1965), in which we again upheld and, to some extent, enlarged SBA's authority to sell SBIC debt instruments to private investors, with SBA's guarantee.

Our position in these decisions was based on the broad authority granted to the Administrator in sections 5(b)(2) and 5(b)(7) of the Small Business Act, 15 U.S.C. §§ 634(b)(2) and (b)(7) (1976), and made applicable to functions under the Small Business Investment Act of 1958 by section 201 thereof, 15 U.S.C. § 693 (1976), to sell debt instruments on such terms and conditions as he determines to be reasonable. Pursuant to section 5(b)(2), the Administrator may:

under regulations prescribed by him, assign or sell at public or private sale, or otherwise dispose of for cash or credit, in his discretion and upon such terms and conditions and for such consideration as the Administrator shall determine to be reasonable, any evidence of debt, contract, claim, personal property, or security assigned to or held by him in connection with the payment of loans granted under this chapter, and to collect or compromise all obligations assigned to or held by him and all legal or equitable rights accruing to him in connection with the payment of such loans until such time as such obligations may be referred to the Attorney General for suit or collection.

Section 5(b)(7) further provides that the Administrator may:

in addition to any powers, functions, privileges, and immunities otherwise vested in him, take any and all actions * * * determined by him to be necessary or desirable in making, servicing, compromising, modifying, liquidating, or otherwise dealing with or realizing on loans made under the provisions of this chapter * * *

Again, on March 15, 1971, SBA requested our approval of its proposed sale of guaranteed SBIC debentures to a group of underwriters for resale to private investors. The proposed plan involved SBA's purchase of $30 million of newly issued debentures from SBICs pursuant to section 303(b) of the Small Business Investment Act, 15 U.S.C. § 683(b). These debentures would be immediately sold, with SBA's guarantee of payment of principal and interest according to the terms of the instrument, to private investors by means of an underwritten public offering. If any of these debentures either went into default or if SBA experienced other difficulties in regulating the SBICs that had issued the debentures, SBA was authorized to substitute another debenture out of a pool of identical debentures, worth approximately $25 million, created by SBA specifically for this purpose. It was contemplated that debentures would be sold initially at face value to investors by a group of underwriters in denominations of $10,000 or multiples thereof. SBA's submission further explained the proposed arrangement as follows:

While an actual sale of the guaranteed debentures will occur and ownership of the debentures will vest in the purchasers. physical possession of the debentures will be given to a custodian bank, acting on the holders' behalf under a bailment agreement pursuant to which holders will have the right to withdraw debentures from bailment by demanding delivery thereof. The purchaser will receive a certificate stating the SBA guaranty. * * * SBA will act as servicing agent for the holders and receive payment from the SBIC's. SBA will remit to the holders the periodic interest payments (and the final repayment of principal) in the amounts and on the dates specified on the debentures (which will be the same for all debentures, whether originally sold or thereafter substituted.)
In summary, the proposed sale is a sale with recourse against SBA of SBIC debentures, which is essentially the same as previously approved guaranteed sales programs.

In our decision B-149685, March 25, 1971, we concluded that:

* * * the proposed sale and guarantee of debentures comes within the scope of 45 Comp. Gen. 370 and our earlier decisions and is within the statutory authority of the Small Business Administration, provided that it does not exceed any pertinent statutory limitations and the budgeted program levels.

Our decisions in the cases cited above only involved SBA loans made to SBICs under the Small Business Investment Act, whereas the present question presumably applies to loans made under the Small Business Act as well. However, the precedent established in those decisions is obviously applicable to the instant situation since our decisions in those cases were based on the broad language in sections 5(b)(2) and 5(b)(7) of the Small Business Act, authorizing the Administrator to sell and otherwise deal with loans made under the Act in such a manner and on such terms and conditions as he determines to be reasonable.

Based on the information available to us concerning this question, including SBA's submission as well as additional information informally provided to us by SBA's Office of General Counsel, it appears that the proposed sale of these certificates to FFB is in many, if not all, respects analogous to the procedure we approved in our decision B–149685, March 25, 1971.

First, in both the procedure approved in our decision of March 25, 1971, as well as that involved here, title to the individual loans would be transferred to the purchaser, although in both instances physical possession of the debt instruments would remain with a bailee holding the instruments on behalf of the purchaser. In the prior case, a designated bank was to be the bailee, while in the instant proposal the SBA would be the bailee. In both cases certificates would be issued to the purchaser indicating the transfer of title to the individual loans and setting forth SBA's guarantee assuring payment thereof, which guarantee could be satisfied by cash payment or loan substitution. Finally, in both situations, SBA would act as the loan servicing agent for the purchaser and would receive payments from the borrower and remit the appropriate amounts of principal and interest to the purchaser.

The prior decision involved SBA's authority to sell specific individual loans, whereas here SBA is proposing to sell certificates "evidencing ownership of a group of Small Business Administration loans." However, it does not appear that this difference alone dictates a different result, provided that the certificates refer to specific designated loans and actually represent a passing of title thereto. Although SBA was unable to furnish us with a sample certificate since, pending our decision, they have not yet been prepared, we were informally advised that these certificates will in fact refer to specific loans and, when transferred to FFB, will represent a transfer of ownership of the loans to FFB.

These certificates would thus be distinguishable from participation certificates issued pursuant to the Participation Sales Act, 12 U.S.C. § 1717(c) (1976), which represent a beneficial interest in an underlying pool of loans. In no real sense can it be said that a purchaser of a participation certificate issued under 12 U.S.C. § 1717(c) has gained title to any of the underlying loans. This distinction has legal significance since, pursuant to the Participation Sales Act, SBA (as well as other named agencies) can only issue participation certificates to the extent authorized in its annual appropriation act. 12 U.S.C. § 1717 (c)(4). (If the transfer of certificates herein proposed to be issued and sold by SBA could be construed to constitute borrowing rather than a sale of assets, which, based on the record before us, does not appear to be the case, SBA would require specific statutory budget authority in order to engage in such transactions, regardless of whether these certificates are considered to be participation certificates.)

Essentially, we agree with the position set forth in SBA's submission that the proposed procedure is basically the same from a legal standpoint as the arrangement that SBA is currently using to sell loans to FFB on an individual basis. In accordance with the foregoing, and since SBA has the same authority to sell debt instruments to FFB as it does to other purchasers, it is our view that, while the practice SBA is proposing here as well as its present method may vary somewhat from the types of financing arrangements we have upheld in the past, we do not believe that any such differences that may exist are so substantial from a legal standpoint as to prohibit implementation of the proposed financing arrangement. Naturally, the same limitation expressed in our decision B–149685, March 25, 1971, that the sale not exceed pertinent statutory limitations and budgeted program levels, is applicable to the instant procedure.

Although we concur in SBA's position that it does have authority under its existing legislation to implement the proposed procedure, this is not to say that we in any way concur in or approve of the desirability from a policy standpoint, of engaging in this type of financing arrangement. To the contrary, we believe that it would be preferable not to extend this arrangement that was originally established, by statute, for the Farmers Home Administration (Pub. L. No. 93–135), to SBA. In our view, the primary, if not only, reason, behind SBA's proposal is the reduction of the apparent size of the SBA budget. We believe that this action could hamper congressional budgetary control over the program. In two of our recent reports, we have addressed these proposed practices and set forth the policy of the General Accounting Office on this matter.

In our report entitled "Revolving Funds: Full Disclosure Needed for Better Congressional Control" (PAD–77–25 dated August 30, 1977), we noted on p. 59:

The effect of congressional control on financing programs * * * depends on what is meant by congressional control. A broad interpretation of the term includes the Congress' *ability to effectively determine* both on an aggregate basis and on an individual program basis, what *budget levels will be for a given fiscal year*. Congressional control also involves the Congress' ability to effectively monitor how far its dictates (as expressed in authorizing legislation, appropriations acts, and associated hearings or other oversight activities) are being carried out. Thus the term congressional control encompasses the *closely related budget control and oversight control*. [Italic supplied.]

Congressional control is not an absolute. For instance, a high degree of it can be very useful or may be unnecessary. It may be exercised over the amount of budget authority a program is to receive, the amount of outlays it may have during a fiscal year, program parameters, etc. The Congress may or may not choose to exercise control over specific programs for a number of reasons. Likewise, the Congress may choose a form of financing for a program with the possible result of obscuring the program's financial impact on the budget totals. Finally, the Congress may enact legislation, aimed at exerting strong control, only to have its intent distorted by administrative regulations.

On page 60 we stated :

Programs over which the Congress has little budgetary control also tend to be programs over which the Congress has diminished oversight control. They do not need to justify past performance to continue receiving funds for operations. Due to the nature of congressional operations, it is likely that a program * * * whose *total level of activity is largely hidden* (by the netting process) *would tend to avoid close annual committee oversight*. This would not be if the program totally depended on the Congress for annual financing and if the program's full financial impact were reflected in the budget totals. [Italic supplied.]

We concluded on page 88 :

The fundamental objective of the Congressional Budget Act of 1974 was to establish a process through which the Congress could systematically consider the total Federal budget and determine priorities for allocating budget resources. We believe this process achieves its maximum effectiveness when the budget represents as complete as possible a picture of the financial activities of Federal agencies.

More specifically, in our report entitled "Government Agency Transactions with the Federal Financing Bank Should be Included on the Budget" (PAD–77–70, August 3, 1977), we addressed the sale of certificates of beneficial ownership to FFB. Certificates of beneficial ownership (CBOs) are very similar, if not identical, to the certificates referred to in SBA's submission.

On page 11 of the report, we stated that CBOs should be considered agency borrowing :

2. FFB purchase of Certificates of Beneficial Ownership. Because CBOs are not presently considered agency debt, FFB's purchase of this paper raises the level of Federal indebtedness. We believe that CBOs should be considered agency borrowing since the original loan remains in the hands of the agency. If one adopts this view, the level of Federal indebtedness is unchanged, but its composition is changed. Agency debt is swapped for Treasury debt.

On page 19 we summarized the CBO effect on outlay totals :

4. *FFB purchase of CBOs*. If current treatment of these transactions continues, FFB purchase of this paper would be reflected on the budget as FFB loan outlay. If these securities were treated as agency obligations (as we believe they should be), they would be included in the outlays of the agency selling the paper when the proceeds were loaned out. Either way, outlays would be increased by the amount of agency lending.

On page 22 we addressed the need for full disclosure including CBOs.

If the activities of lending agencies are not properly reflected in individual program or functional accounts, it is difficult to see how the budget process can properly allocate Federal resources among Federal credit programs, between credit programs and direct expenditure programs, and, ultimately between the public and private sectors of the economy.

The way FFB affects the meaning of Federal outlays and deficits is not solely a function of its off-budget status. The problem with the way Federal credit assistance going through FFB is reflected in the budget results from the combined effects of FFB's off-budget status and other deviations of actual from recommended budget treatment of these activities.

For example, FFB purchases of on-budget agency obligations are properly reflected in the budget now because of the way that borrowing is reflected in the budget and because these agencies are on the budget. If off-budget agencies which currently engage in debt transactions (borrow) with FFB were placed on the budget, their lending and direct expenditure activity would be reflected on the budget in their respective accounts, regardless of the budget status of FFB.

If CBOs were given the recommended budget treatment—namely, if sales of these securities were treated as borrowing rather than asset sales which reduce loan outlays—then FFB purchase of these issues would be reflected in the accounts of the borrowing agencies, regardless of the budget status of FFB.

The combined effects of eliminating the off-budget status of agencies that borrow from FFB to finance lending and of proper budget treatment of CBOs would bring a considerable amount of lending and direct expenditures, currently occurring outside of the budget, onto the budget.

Asset sales to FFB are currently properly treated in the selling agency's account. When these securities are sold to FFB, a problem arises because the Federal Government retains possession of the loans and overall outlays are understated by the amount of FFB purchases. If FFB remains off the budget, this problem will continue to exist unless the Federal Government's continued ownership of the paper is reflected as an outlay in the account of the agency selling the paper. It might be argued that since the Federal Government still retains possession of the asset, the best place to reflect this is in the agency account. This treatment would increase the agency's outlays and would technically be at variance with recommended budget practices.

And on page 25, we recommended that the Congress require that "CBOs be treated as agency obligations and, therefore, be treated in the Federal budget as borrowing."

In summary it is our view that the SBA proposed practices would be contrary to the need for full disclosure and inclusion in the budget totals.

Moreover, although our prior decisions concerning proposed financing arrangements by SBA, particularly B–149685, March 25, 1975, did not discuss this type of policy consideration, it appears that when individual loans are "sold" to FFB under the current procedure, which was based on our decision of March 25, 1975, SBA retains at all times actual possession of the loan and all related documents, services the loan and merely forwards to FFB the payments it receives from the borrower. Accordingly, since SBA's current procedure for selling individual loans to FFB contains some of the same flaws that were the concern of the criticism set forth in the above-quoted audit reports, we believe that, to some extent, the current manner in which SBA is conducting its "refinancing" activities could be the subject of similar criticism from a policy standpoint.

SBA's second question involves the agency's authority to sell to FFB direct disaster loans made by SBA pursuant to the provisions of section 7(b) of the Small Business Act, 15 U.S.C. § 636(b) (1976), subject to a full SBA guarantee. In its submission, SBA says, in support of its position:

> Although there is no ceiling on these loans, the direct loans made under this section are, in fact, limited by the Agency's appropriation. The guaranty authority is not limited but, as a practical matter, very few lenders are willing to participate with the Agency in such loans.
> The proposed sale to FFB would be made subject to the Agency's guaranty. In prior discussions with SBA personnel, members of your staff expressed concern with the fact that, in theory, such sales of disaster loans could result in subjecting the Agency to unlimited liability, without Congressional restraints. In any sales of disaster loans, we will state in our Budget Request the dollar amount of disaster loans to be sold and note that we have reduced our appropriation request accordingly. Thus, unlimited liability could not be created by such sales. We are of the opinion that both §§ 5(b)(2) and 5(b)(7) are applicable to these disaster loans, since these sections refer to loans made "under this Act," and "under the provisions of this Act."

Under subsections 7(b)(1)–(8) of the Small Business Act, SBA makes various types of disaster loans. We have been advised informally that SBA is here primarily concerned with its authority to sell physical and economic injury loans made pursuant to subsections 7(b) (1) and (2). Pursuant to these subsections, SBA is authorized

> to make such loans (either directly or in cooperation with banks or other lending institutions through agreements to participate on an immediate or deferred basis) as the Administration may determine to be necessary or appropriate * * *.

On the basis of language in section 7(a) of the Small Business Act, 15 U.S.C. § 636(a) (1976), identical to that quoted above from section 7(b), our Office has upheld SBA's authority to carry out a loan guarantee program. 51 Comp. Gen. 474 (1972); B–140673, October 12, 1959. Accordingly, we are not questioning SBA's authority to guarantee disaster loans made to eligible borrowers by participating lending institutions.

The issue is whether this authority to guarantee disaster loans made by lending institutions necessarily includes authority to guarantee direct loans made by SBA in the first instance and then sold to FFB, with recourse against SBA. There are several considerations.

First, under section 7(b) of the Small Business Act, SBA's authority to make disaster loans on a deferred basis, which is the basis for its authority to make guaranteed loans, is limited by statute to a maximum of 90 percent of the balance of the loan outstanding at the time of disbursement. Therefore, assuming that SBA is authorized to sell these direct disaster loans with its guarantee, it follows that its guarantee authority in connection with such a sale is also limited to the

90 percent statutory maximum. This would be true whether SBA were selling a direct disaster loan to FFB or to some other purchaser, since the statute makes no distinction between purchasers. It is our understanding that SBA's proposal would involve a 100 percent guarantee of the full face amount of the obligations sold to FFB, whether the loans are sold individually or collectively by mean of certificates of ownership. This financing arrangement would violate the 90 percent limitation, discussed above. (SBA is legally authorized to sell its SBIC debentures, with a 100 percent guarantee, since there is no similar statutory limitation in the Small Business Investment Act of 1958 on the percentage SBA can guarantee.)

In addition to the foregoing, there is another consideration which leads us to disapprove the proposed procedure. SBA states in its submission that its guarantee authority under section 7(b) is unlimited although, as a practical matter, very few lenders have been willing to participate with SBA in making such loans. Moreover, SBA states that while there is no ceiling on its disaster loan authority, direct loans are in fact limited by the agency's appropriation.

If SBA's position is upheld by our Office, the consequences could be very significant. SBA would be able to sell direct disaster loans to FFB with its guarantee and thereby to replenish its disaster loan revolving fund so as to enable it to make new disaster loans and repeat the process indefinitely. Notwithstanding SBA's argument that in its Budget Request it would state the dollar amount of disaster loans to be sold and would note that it had reduced its appropriation request accordingly, this procedure, if allowed, could theoretically build up an unlimited contingent liability against the United States, without any effective congressional restraints. We do not believe for the reasons set out below, that in authorizing SBA to establish a disaster loan program, Congress was aware of or intended such a result.

We agree with SBA that its authority to make physical and economic injury disaster loans under sections 7(b)(1) and (2) is not subject to any statutory ceiling. This is not to say, however, that there are no limitations on its authority to sell direct disaster loans that would be fully guaranteed by SBA.

Ceilings were established in Pub. L. No. 89–409, 80 Stat. 132, approved May 2, 1966 (15 U.S.C. 633), on the "total amount of loans, guarantees, and other obligations or commitments," which could be outstanding at any one time for the different programs funded out of the business loan and investment revolving fund. However, no ceiling was established on the funding of the disaster loan programs funded out of a separate disaster loan revolving fund. The House and Senate Reports on the legislation that was ultimately enacted as Pub. L. No.

89–409 explained the basis for establishing the disaster loan fund to operate in this manner as follows:

In order to prevent the breakdown of SBA's regular business loan program by the overriding needs of the disaster loan program, a separate revolving fund for the physical disaster loan programs has been provided in this bill.

Since it is impossible to predict the extent of the need for funds to meet physical disaster requirements no authorization ceiling has been placed on the disaster loan fund. For humanitarian reasons the Congress has always been ready to provide the necessary funds to meet disaster loan needs.

If a ceiling were placed on disaster loans, it is possible that the ceiling might be reached at a time when Congress was not in session. *Therefore, even with funds available, loans could not be made until Congress returned to raise the ceiling.*

Funds for the use by SBA in its disaster loan program would still be subject to the restrictions placed on the program by the Bureau of the Budget and by the Appropriations Committees of the Congress. [Footnote omitted, Italic supplied.] H.R. Rep. No. 1348 and S. Rep. No. 1057, 89th Cong., 2d Sess. 4, 5 (1966).

The foregoing explanation reflects the legislative view that disaster loans would primarily, if not exclusively, be made, on a direct rather than guaranteed basis. Otherwise the statement that "even with funds available, loans could not be made until Congress returned to raise the ceiling" would have no meaning since it is not legally necessary that funds be available in order to guarantee a loan made by a participating lending institution. (We have informally been advised by SBA that 10 percent of the total amount of a guarantee is charged against the monies in its revolving funds.) Likewise, the reference in the explanation to restrictions placed on the program by the appropriations committees presumably means the amount of money appropriated to the disaster loan revolving fund which, with respect to loan guarantee authority, is of course no restriction at all.

It is not surprising that Congress held this view, since the primary purpose of Pub. L. No. 89–409 was to provide for a separate fund for disaster loan needs in order to avoid the total disruption that had previously occurred in SBA's business loan program because of the vast amount of money SBA had diverted out of its revolving fund to make direct disaster loans. See H.R. Rep. No. 1348 and S. Rep. No. 1057, *supra*, 2, 3. A review of the debate on the legislation in the House of Representatives further supports the view that Congress did not expect or intend that, with the passage of Pub L. No. 89–409, SBA would be involved to any significant extent in guaranteeing disaster loans, whether made in the first instance by a participating lending institution or directly by SBA, to be subsequently sold with SBA's full guarantee. See 112 Cong. Rec. 7311–7329 (1966).

The Small Business Act was recently amended, with the enactment of Pub. L. No. 95–89, 91 Stat. 553, approved August 4, 1977, to modify the approach previously used by Congress in budgeting for SBA. That legislation authorized funding for SBA by establishing specific line item authorizations for individual loan and guarantee programs for fiscal years 1978 and 1979. These line item authorizations established maximum amounts of direct loans, immediate participation loans, and guaranteed (or deferred participation) loans that SBA was authorized to make in fiscal years 1978 and 1979. Although an overall ceiling was established for disaster loans made pursuant to subsections 7(b) (3)–(8) no similar ceiling was placed on SBA's authority to make fiscal and economic injury disaster loans under sections 7(b)(1) and (2). This was explained in S. Rep. No. 95–184, 4, 19 (1977) as follows:

> Ceilings were not placed on physical and economic injury disaster loans since there is no method possible to anticipate the level of demand for these programs. By leaving the authorizations open ended for these two programs, there will not be a need to legislate a supplementary authorization each time a disaster occurs.
>
> *   *   *   *   *   *   *
>
> The Committee bill does not provide for a specific dollar authorization for the 7(b)(1) and 7(b)(2) disaster programs in that the loan demand for these programs cannot be accurately estimated. Instead such funds are authorized to be appropriated as may be necessary to operate the 7(b)(1) and 7(b)(2) disaster programs.

Certainly, as stated in SBA's submission, "as a practical matter very few lenders are willing to participate with the agency in such loans." In fact, based on information contained in recent hearings before the House Committee on Small Business, it appears that as of June 30, 1975, in excess of 99 percent of the total amount of all disaster loan funds disbursed and outstanding had been made on a direct rather than guaranteed basis. See "Federal Natural Disaster Assistance Programs;" Hearings before the Subcommittee on SBA and SBIC Authority and General Small Business Problems of the House Committee on Small Business, 95th Cong., 1st Sess. 503 (1977). Moreover, our review of the legislative history of Pub. L. No. 95–89 which, in essence, adopted the same approach to the physical and economic injury disaster loan program as was established in Pub. L. No. 89–409, did not reveal anything to indicate that Congress intended that SBA be authorized to guarantee disaster loans without limitation.

In light of the very real possibility that SBA could, if its authority is upheld in this matter, establish an unlimited contingent liability against the United States, without any congressional restraints whatsoever, our Office cannot approve the proposed procedure in the absence of a specific statutory authorization or, at the very least, a clear indication that Congress intended that SBA have such authority. Neither is present here.

Moreover we do not believe that the situation would be different in any significant respect whether SBA sells its direct disaster loans individually or collectively by means of certificates representing ownership of a group of SBA loans.

For these reasons, we cannot concur in SBA's opinion that it is authorized to implement this proposal as now constituted to sell direct disaster loans to FFB with SBA's full guarantee.

〔 B-190392, et al. 〕

Contracts — Specifications — Military—Restrictive—Procurement Method Coding of Spare Parts—Sole-Source Suppliers

Coding of spare parts to require sole-source procurement under "approved source" system within contemplation of Armed Services Procurement Regulation (ASPR) 1-313(1976 ed.) cannot be used to preclude consideration of offers from previously unapproved sources which could otherwise qualify.

Contractors — Responsibility—Determination—Relative v. Adequate Basis of Qualification—Validity of Relative Basis

Disqualification of firm from competition on basis that another may furnish superior quality is invalid prequalification procedure.

Armed Services Procurement Regulation—Basic Ordering Agreements—Limitations on Use

Procuring activity's use of basic ordering agreement (BOA) to exclude previously unapproved suppliers that may be capable of furnishing acceptable products and to effect sole-source procurements with BOA contractor contravenes ASPR 3-410.2(c)(1) (1976 ed.) prohibition against using BOA in any manner to restrict competition.

Advertising—Commerce Business Daily—Publication Requirement—Prior to Ordering Under Basic Ordering Agreement—Spare Parts Procurement

Procuring activity is required, absent circumstances not applicable here, to publish spare parts procurement synopses in Commerce Business Daily (CBD) in timeframe prescribed by ASPR 1-1003.2 (1976 ed.) ; neither fact that items are deemed critical aircraft parts nor that agency now posts CBD synopses letters in bid room relieves agency of obligation to promptly synopsize proposed procurements.

In the matter of Rotair Industries; D. Moody & Co., Inc., December 13, 1978:

Rotair Industries (Rotair) and D. Moody & Co., Inc. (Moody) have protested the procurement procedures used by the Department of the Navy (Navy), Navy Aviation Supply Office, Philadelphia, Pennsylvania, in awarding a series of orders (set forth below) to Sikorsky Aircraft, Division of United Technologies Corporation (Sikorsky), under Basic Ordering Agreement (BOA) No. N00383-77-A-7503.

The orders for procurement of H-3 and H-53 helicopter parts were issued pursuant to the Department of Defense (DOD) Joint Regulation on the High Dollar Spare Parts Breakout Program identified within the Navy as Navy Materiel Instruction (NAVMATINST) 4200.33A, March 1969.

The protesters cite as evidence of a continuing course of conduct by the Navy the following orders awarded to Sikorsky under the aforementioned BOA during the period of September 1977 through July 1978:

GAO REFERENCE	ORDER NO.	COMMERCE BUSINESS DAILY PUBLICATION	PROPOSED AWARD DATE	AWARD DATE
B-190392_____	0438	8-24-77	-------	9-12-77
B-191211_____	0784	1-13-78	1-19-78	1-27-78
B-191299_____	0872	2-10-78	2-17-78	5-3-78
B-191309_____	0516	11-2-77	11-7-77	11-7-77
	0537	11-3-77	11-11-77	11-11-77
		12-5-77	-------	-------
B-191400_____	0901	2-28-78	3-1-78	3-1-78
B-191454_____	0904	3-8-78	3-13-78	5-3-78
B-191509_____	0930	3-20-78	3-22-78	5-3-78
	0932	3-20-78	3-22-78	5-3-78
	0938	3-20-78	3-22-78	5-3-78
	0941	3-20-78	3-20-78	3-20-78
	0943	3-20-78	3-20-78	3-20-78
	0947	3-20-78	3-20-78	3-20-78
	0951	3-20-78	3-20-78	3-20-78
B-191510_____	0934	3-20-78	3-20-78	5-3-78
B-191585_____	0952	3-24-78	3-30-78	5-3-78
	0989	3-24-78	3-30-78	5-3-78
B-191605_____	0978	3-29-78	4-4-78	5-3-78
B-191641_____	0960	4-5-78	4-3-78	4-3-78
	0962	4-5-78	4-3-78	5-3-78
	1000	4-4-78	4-13-78	5-3-78
B-191666_____	1008	4-7-78	4-13-78	Canceled
	1010	4-7-78	4-13-78	5-3-78
	1029	4-6-78	4-14-78	5-3-78
B-191733_____	1059	------	4-20-78	5-3-78
B-191845_____	1085	5-1-78	5-4-78	7-7-78
	1087	5-1-78	5-4-78	7-7-78
	1101	5-1-78	5-4-78	7-7-78

Rotair Protest

Rotair essentially contends that the procedures used by the Navy in procuring helicopter parts are unduly restrictive of competition. More specifically, counsel for Rotair states that despite the firm's experience in supplying parts for other Government agencies and private industry and repeated requests to the Navy, the firm has been denied an opportunity to qualify as an approved parts supplier. Counsel for the protester asserts that the Navy's lack of procedure for qualifying additional suppliers, continued use of restrictive procurement method coding on orders, and failure to promptly publicize orders in the Commerce Business Daily (CBD) prior to award as required by Armed Services Procurement Regulation (ASPR) (now Defense Acquisition Regulation) § 1–1003.2 (1976 ed.) result in virtually automatic procurement of orders under Sikorsky's BOA on a noncompetitive basis.

The Navy, however, contends that pursuant to ASPR § 1–313 (1976 ed.) a part for military equipment is to be bought from the original manufacturer of the equipment (i.e., Sikorsky) or its supplier unless or until a determination has been made that the part can be bought competitively. Section 1–313 provides for the procurement of parts as follows:

(a) Any part, subassembly or component (hereinafter called "part") for military equipment, to be used for replenishment of stock, repair, or replacement, most be procured so as to assure the requisite safe, dependable, and effective operation of the equipment. (Items procured as spare parts are governed by the "DoD High Dollar Spare Parts Breakout Program" described in the DoD Joint Regulation AR 715–22, NAVMATINST P4200.33, AFR 57–6, MCO P4200.13, DSAM 4105.2.) *Where it is feasible to do so without impairing this assurance, parts should be procured on a competitive basis*, as in the kind of cases described in (b) below. However, where this assurance can be had only if the parts are procured from the original manufacturer of the equipment or his supplier, the procurement should be restricted accordingly, as in the kind of cases described in (c) below.

(b) *Parts that are fully identified and can be obtained from a number of known sources, and parts for which fully adequate manufacturing drawings and any other needed data are available with the right to use for procurement purposes* (or can be made so available in keeping with the policies in Section IX, Part 2) *are to be procured on a competitive basis.* In general, such parts are of a standard design configuration. They include individual items that are susceptible of separate procurement, such as resistors, transformers, generators, spark plugs, electron tubes, or other parts having commercial equivalents.

(c) Parts not within the scope of (b) above generally should be procured (either directly or indirectly) only from sources that have satisfactorily manufactured or furnished such parts in the past, unless fully adequate data (including any necessary data developed at private expense), test results, and quality assurance procedures, are available with the right to use for procurement purposes (or can reasonably be made so available in keeping with the policies in in Section IX, Part 2) to assure the requisite reliability and interchangeability of the parts, and procurement on a competitive basis would be consistent with the assurance described in (a) above. In assessing this assurance, the nature and function of the equipment for which the part is needed should be considered. Parts qualifying under this criteria are normally sole source or source controlled parts (see MILSTD 100) which exclusively provide the performance, installation and interchangeability characteristics required for specific critical applications. To illustrate, acceptable tolerances for a commercial television part may be far less stringent than those for a comparable military radar part, permitting competitive procurement of the former but not of the latter. The exacting performance requirements of specially designed military equipment may demand that parts be closely controlled and have proven capabilities of precise integration with the system in which they operate, to a degree that precludes the use of even apparently identical parts from new sources, since the functioning of the whole may depend on latent characteristics of each part which are not definitely known.

(d) When an award is made to a source that has not previously produced the item, the cognizant Government inspection activity and the appropriate contract administration office should be notified by the procurement contracting office that the contractor will be producing the item for the first time. [Italic supplied.]

NAVMATINST 4200.33A establishes uniform procedures relating to procurement of spares and repair parts, requires screening of spare parts which account for a preponderance of procurement dollars in order to determine the optimum method for their procurement, and provides that parts be assigned a procurement method code (PMC) which indicates their procurement status. PMC1 denotes that the items are already competitive. PMC3 denotes that items are procured directly from the actual manufacturer or vendor, including a prime contractor which is the actual manufacturer. PMC5 indicates that parts continue to be purchased from a prime contractor which is not the actual manufacturer. PMC2 and 4 indicate that parts have been determined for the first time to be suitable for competitive procurement and direct purchase, respectively. NAVMATINST 4200.33A, paragraph 1–201.12.

The Navy's regulation is implemented by Military Standard (Mil-Std)–789B, Procurement Method Coding of Replenishment Spare Parts, May 15, 1970, designed for incorporation in prime contracts for equipment, which provides a procedure for obtaining contractors' recommendations concerning methods of procuring selected spare parts. NAVMATINST 4200.33A, paragraph 5–203.1. In developing these codes, first preference is for open competitive procurement, then purchase from designated approved sources, and finally, noncompetitive procurement from a source other than the actual manufacturer. Mil-Std–789B, paragraph 4.1.1.

Rotair does not take exception to the DOD Breakout Program, but asserts that the Navy uses procurement method coding, CBD publication, and the Sikorsky BOA in such a manner as to discourage and restrict competition and to avoid its obligation to obtain maximum competition on parts procurements in violation of ASPR §§ 1–313, 1–1003, and 3–410.2(c) (1976 ed.).

Both procurement method coding and placing orders under a BOA are procedures which prequalify products and competitors and restrict competition for the Navy's parts procurements. The question, however, is whether the procedures or the manner in which they are applied are unduly restrictive of competition.

The general rule is that prequalification of offerors is an undue restriction on competition. *D. Moody & Company, Inc., et al.*, 55 Comp. Gen. 1, 11 (1975), 75–2 CPD 1. We have, however, tentatively approved special agency procedures which limit competition to offerors which have previously entered into certain types of agreements with the procuring activity. See *Department of Health, Education, and Welfare's use of basic ordering type agreement procedure*, 54 Comp. Gen.

1096 (1975), 75–1 CPD 392; *Department of Agriculture's use of master agreements*, 56 Comp. Gen. 78 (1976), 76–2 CPD 390 (hereinafter cited as *Agriculture II*).

The validity of any procedure which limits the extent of competition depends upon whether the restriction serves a bona fide need of the Government. Such restrictions include those essential to assure procurement of a satisfactory end product, *Department of Agriculture's use of Master Agreement*, 54 Comp. Gen. 606, 609 (1975), 75–1 CPD 40 (hereinafter cited as *Agriculture I*), or to determine the high level of quality and reliability assurance necessitated by the criticality of the product, 50 Comp. Gen. 542, 545 (1971); 36 *id.* 809, 818 (1957). Use of restrictive procedures will not be sanctioned merely because obtaining maximum competition is administratively burdensome; rather, a showing that the exigencies of the procurement in question are such that the Government's interests would be adversely affected by the delay necessary to obtain maximum competition is required. *Agriculture I, supra*, at 610. Basic characteristics of approved, albeit restrictive, procedures are that they function so that 1) no firm which is able to provide a satisfactory product is necessarily precluded from competing on procurements of that item, and 2) a firm may become eligible to compete at any time it demonstrates under applicable procedures that it is able to furnish an acceptable item which meets the Government's needs. *Id.* at 609. We have, therefore, found improper the use of restrictive procedures under which an offeror's disqualification would not be based on a finding that it could not provide a satisfactory product. *Ibid.* Moreover, even a prequalification system for which there may be valid reasons would be rendered invalid by a lack of regulation and procedures for its use. 53 Comp. Gen. 209, 212 (1973).

The Navy takes the position that procurement method coding is a reasonable exercise of procurement authority and a system of approved sources within the contemplation of ASPR § 1–313(c), citing our decisions in *Mercer Products & Manufacturing Co.*, B–188541, July 25, 1977, 77–2 CPD 45, and 52 Comp. Gen. 546 (1973). The Navy's contracting officer further states that the time required to review and change a PMC makes such action impracticable for in-progress, replenishment-purchase transactions; that, until a PMC is changed, procurement in accordance with the assigned PMC is mandatory; and that, because the parts in question were so coded as to require procurement from Sikorsky, there was no need to issue solicitations and no improper prequalification of Sikorsky.

We believe that the Navy's reliance on the above-cited decisions is misplaced. In both decisions, we expressly stated that ASPR § 1–313 (c) does not prohibit the submission and consideration of proposals from previously unapproved sources which could otherwise qualify under procedures established by the Joint DOD Regulation on the Spare Parts Breakout Program (here, NAVMATINST 4200.33A). See also *Mercer Products & Manufacturing Co.—Reconsideration*, B–188541, October 4, 1977, 77–2 CPD 260. Contrary to the Navy's interpretation, we held that the *type of qualification procedure* used by the procuring activity was consistent with the regulatory provision and that an offeror could properly be required to furnish data and samples for examination and testing as a prerequisite for award because award could be limited to approved sources. 52 Comp. Gen. 546, 548–49 (1973). In so doing, we noted that the use of a qualification procedure for determining approved sources was recognized as an appropriate way to qualify new sources. *Ibid;* B–176256, November 30, 1972.

We are unable to concur with the Navy's characterization of the nature of PMC's and their effect on procurement of parts so coded. We believe that ASPR § 1–313 does not constitute a mandate to effect sole-source awards regardless of the capability of producers which have not previously supplied the parts in question. Reliability assurance and interchangeability of parts may also be obtained through competitive negotiation procedures. B–166435, July 1, 1969. In our decision in 50 Comp. Gen. 184, 189 (1970), we indicated that to preclude competitive procurement of parts on the basis of the assignment of a certain PMC without regard to the willingness or ability of other sources to produce the parts would contravene the concept of "maximum practical competition." We concluded in that case that designating parts "engineering critical," a standard similar to that used in procurement method coding, had perpetuated an unjustified sole-source position, and recommended that the procuring activity institute a qualification test program to determine the acceptability of parts offered by alternate sources. *Id.* at 191.

The Navy is required by ASPR § 1–313(a) to procure parts so as to assure the requisite safe, dependable, and effective operation of equipment, and contends that the relevant issue is whether the protester can furnish parts, including necessary quality assurance services, required by the procuring activity. Lack of adverse reports about items furnished to others by Rotair, the Navy believes, does not provide adequate assurance that parts procured from Rotair will be satisfactory. The Navy says that, even though Rotair can furnish the data and quality assurance procedures used by Sikorsky in approving the parts, it must have Sikorsky assurance and inspection because Sikorsky may have information and may be doing something unknown to the Navy that contributes to the reliability of the parts.

However, the Navy does not know that Sikorsky is doing any more than Rotair is prepared to do. Even if Sikorsky, by virtue of its position, possesses knowledge superior to Rotair, the standard is not whether Rotair has the same qualifications as Sikorsky, but whether it is capable of furnishing parts that will provide for the safe, dependable and effective operation of the helicopters. The Navy has adduced no evidence to show that Rotair is incapable of providing the requisite assurances, has concluded only that Rotair may provide services somehow different from those furnished by Sikorsky, and has excluded Rotair from competition on a general finding of the protester's relative qualification. Rotair's disqualification as a potential supplier is not predicated on a finding that the firm could not provide satisfactory inspection and quality assurance services, but that Sikorsky may furnish services of a superior quality. Exclusion of prospective competitors on these bases constitutes an invalid prequalification procedure which is unduly restrictive of competition. *Agriculture I, supra*, at 609; *Agriculture II, supra*, at 80.

Evaluation of inspection and quality assurance procedures pertains to contractor responsibility, i.e., Rotair's ability to perform the work. Resolution of a contractor's responsibility by an unauthorized preselection method is contrary to full and free competition contemplated by applicable procurement law and regulations. Such a prequalification procedure, coupled with inadequate CBD synopsizing in furtherance of prequalification, results in an unwarranted restriction on competition in both formally advertised and negotiated procurements. 52 Comp. Gen. 569, 572 (1973).

Prequalification based on matters of responsibility is particularly objectionable as applied to small business concerns, including the protesters here, because a procuring activity is otherwise required, upon finding a small business concern nonresponsible as to capacity, to so notify the Small Business Administration (SBA) in order to afford SBA an opportunity to issue a certificate of competency. ASPR § 1–705.4(c) (1976 ed.); ASPR § 1–705.4(c), Defense Acquisition Circular (DAC) No. 76–15, June 1, 1978.

Therefore, we conclude on the basis of the present record that the continued exclusion of Rotair from competition on the basis that Sikorsky may have information and may be doing something unknown to the Navy which contributes to the reliability of the parts is not justified.

Nature and Use of Basic Ordering Agreements

A BOA is a written instrument of understanding between a procuring activity and a contractor which shall apply to future procurements between the parties during the term of the BOA. It includes descriptions of the supplies to be furnished when ordered and the method for determining the prices the contractor will be paid. It states the terms and conditions of delivery or the method for their determination, lists the activities which are authorized to issue orders under the BOA, and specifies the circumstances under which an order becomes a binding contract. ASPR §§ 3–410.2(a)(1) and (2) (1976 ed.).

A BOA may be used to expedite procurement where specific items, quantities, and prices are not known when the BOA is executed and where procurement of parts under a BOA can be administratively and financially advantageous because the procedure reduces both the amount of inventory kept on hand and the administrative time required to place items in a production status. ASPR § 3–410.2(b). The content and use of such agreements are subject to a number of limitations. A BOA is not a contract; it cannot provide or imply that the Government agrees to place future orders or contracts with the BOA contractor. Most important, it cannot be used in any manner to restrict competition. ASPR §§ 3–410.2 (a)(1) and (c)(1). The issuance of orders under a BOA is restricted as follows:

> (2) Supplies or services may be ordered under a basic ordering agreement *only* under the following circumstances:
>
> (i) If it is determined *at the time the order is placed* that it is impracticable to obtain competition by either formal advertising or negotiation for such supplies or services; or
>
> (ii) *If after a competitive solicitation of quotations or proposals from the maximum number of qualified sources* (see 3–101), other than a solicitation accomplished by use of Standard Form 33, it is determined that the successful responsive offeror holds a basic ordering agreement, the terms of which are either identical to those of the solicitation or different in a way that could have no impact on price, quality or delivery, and if it is determined further that issuance of an order against the basic ordering agreement rather than preparation of a separate contract would not be prejudicial to the other offerors.
>
> In situations covered by (ii), the choice of firms to be solicited shall be made in accordance with normal procedures, without regard to which firms hold basic ordering agreements; firms not holding a basic ordering agreement shall not be precluded by the solicitation from proposing or quoting; and the existence of a basic ordering agreement shall not be a consideration in source selection. ASPR § 3–410.2(c). [Italic supplied.]

As mentioned above, the Navy contracting officer states that, because the parts were assigned a restrictive PMC which required procurement from Sikorsky, no solicitations were issued and the orders were subject to a BOA provision allowing negotiation of prices within a monetary limitation after the orders were issued. Because no solicitations were issued, ASPR § 3–410.2(c)(2)(ii), *supra*, is not applicable here. Consequently, placement of orders under the Sikorsky BOA was proper only if the determination required by ASPR § 3–410.2(c) (2)(i) was validly made at the time the orders were placed. The validity of that determination is, however, subject to the proscription that a BOA "shall [not] be used in any manner to restrict competition." ASPR § 3.410.2(c)(1).

We have recently held that conducting informal competition for an order to be issued under one of several BOA's without issuing an adequate written solicitation was a procedure at variance with fundamental principles of Federal negotiated procurement. *Tymshare, Inc.*, 57 Comp. Gen. 434, 437 (1978), 78–1 CPD 322. The Navy contends that the *Tymshare* decision should be distinguished from the instant procurements because (1) the services being purchased were fully competitive and not required to be procured from a single source, (2) no formal solicitation was issued, and (3) informal negotiations were only conducted with two BOA contractors. We find the Navy's distinctions to be without substantial differences from the facts obtaining in the Tymshare procurement. The Navy has conceded that no solicitation was issued or deemed necessary for the instant parts procurements. The orders were issued exclusively to Sikorsky under the firm's BOA, subject to price negotiation after their issuance. For these reasons, we believe that the BOA was used in a manner to restrict competition. Furthermore, in light of the Navy's disqualification of Rotair on a relative qualification basis, we are unable to conclude that a determination requisite to issuance of orders under the BOA was validly made at the time the orders in question were placed.

Finally, Rotair contends that the Navy's failure to timely synopsize its orders in the CBD precludes the protester from submitting offers for the Navy's consideration, unduly restricts competition for these requirements, and further demonstrates the Navy's preference for sole-source procurement from Sikorsky. Timely synopsis is required by ASPR § 1–1003.2 in order to allow potential bidders or offerors an opportunity to compete. Of the orders listed above, six were synopsized in the CBD on or after the proposed date of award, 20 were published from 1 to 9 days prior to the proposed award date, and 42.8 percent of the latter group were published less than 4 days before the proposed date of award.

The Navy defers issuance of BOA orders for which it mails synopses to the CBD until 15 days after the date the synopses are mailed. The Navy states that its synopsis procedure was developed in recognition of the exception provided in ASPR § 1–1003.1(c)(iv) (Defense Procurement Circular (DPC) No. 76–9, August 30, 1977), that ASPR § 1–1003.2 is not mandatory and that the procedure consumes the maximum time compatible with its procurement needs and applicable procurement law and regulations.

We do not agree with the Navy's interpretation of the regulatory provisions upon which the agency's synopsizing procedure was developed. ASPR § 1–1003.1(a) requires, absent expressly enumerated circumstances not applicable here, that every proposed procurement which may result in an award exceeding $10,000 be timely synopsized. When feasible, synopses should be published no later than 10 days prior to placement of BOA orders. ASPR § 1–1003.2 (DPC No. 76–9,

August 30, 1977). The Navy's synopsizing procedure ostensibly assumes that synopsis of replacement parts orders is never feasible within the 10-day timeframe. However, even the fact that replacement aircraft parts are deemed critical safety items does not relieve the procuring activity of its obligation to timely synopsize such procurements in accordance with the pertinent procurement regulations. *Rotair Industries*, B–189021, December 21, 1977, 77–2 CPD 487.

ASPR § 1–1003.1 states:

(c) The following need not be publicized in the Synopsis * * *

*   *   *   *   *   *   *

(iv) procurement (whether advertised or negotiated) which is of such urgency that the Government would be seriously injured by the delay involved in permitting the date set for receipt of bids, proposals, or quotations to be more than 15 calendar days from the date of transmittal of the synopsis or the date of issuance of the solicitation, whichever is earlier.

That exception contemplates those occasions when the Government's requirements are so urgent as to necessitate unusually rapid receipt of pricing and technical submissions for expedited evaluation and award. Under the circumstances, the procuring activity is not required to synopsize the procurement. In other words, ASPR § 1–1003.1(c) (iv) is an exception from the synopsis requirement, not from the requirement concerning the time of publicizing synopses. Both the feasibility language and the exception cited are intended to establish exceptions to an otherwise required course of conduct, not to become a regular course of conduct or procurement system.

The Navy has advised our Office that "although not required by the Armed Services Procurement Regulation [the procuring activity] has begun posting copies of its letters to the Commerce Business Daily in the * * * Bid Room," and asserts that interested firms will thereby be able to review CBD synopses 15 days prior to the issuance of BOA orders. ASPR § 1–1002.4 provides for public display of solicitations as follows:

A copy of each solicitation for an unclassified procurement in excess of $2,500 which provides at least ten calendar days for submission of offers *shall* be displayed at the contracting office, and, if appropriate, at some additional public place from the date issued until seven days after bids or proposals have been opened. [Italic supplied.]

Notwithstanding the fact that posting notices is consistent with DOD's policy to increase competition by publicizing procurements, ASPR § 1–1001, and may result in competition for the Navy's parts procurements, it does not relieve the Navy of its obligation to promptly synopsize proposed parts procurements in the CBD as well.

Rotair also takes exception to the Navy's use of "Number note" 46, rather than Note 33, in synopses of the BOA orders in question. See ASPR § 1–1003.9(b)(5) and (d). We agree with the protester that reference to a note which advises potential contractors that the synopsis is published solely for informational purposes and that solicitation documents are not available is inappropriate. ASPR § 1–1003.2 expressly provides that orders against BOA's are to be timely synopized to afford concerns an opportunity to prepare bids or offers. We believe that the Navy's reference to Note 46 merely evidences further use of the BOA in a manner to restrict competition in violation of ASPR § 3–410.2(c)(1). We cannot, however, agree that Note 33 is applicable to these synopses because it pertains to procurements for which solicitations have been issued. Consequently, we believe that neither note is applicable to these synopses.

Moody Protest

Moody, a small business concern, also protests the Navy's CBD synopsizing procedure, contending that failure to allow 10 days' advance notice from the publication of synopses before orders are issued violates the Small Business Act, 15 U.S.C. § 637(e) (1976), and ASPR § 1–1003.2. Counsel for Moody asserts, and the Navy concedes, that Moody's position is different from Rotair's because Moody would be offering parts which were former Government surplus articles, i.e., parts previously furnished by an approved contractor. Nevertheless, the Navy states that surplus offers require time-consuming review which makes delay of the entire procurement process unrealistic for the few surplus material offers that might be received and suggests that by reviewing CBD notices posted in the procuring activity's bid room or employing a bid service to do so, Moody and other surplus dealers would have ample time to submit offers or give notice of their intention to do so within a reasonable time. The Navy contracting officer states that if Moody indicates that it has a supply of the parts being procured and wants to submit an offer, order issuance will be further deferred, within reason.

While the Navy may legitimately be concerned about the circumstances in which a part became surplus, that concern alone is insufficient to preclude procurement of surplus parts from surplus dealers. *D. Moody & Co., Inc.*, 56 Comp. Gen. 1005, 1007 (1977), 77–2 CPD 233. Procuring activities are not required in every instance to ascertain the existence of surplus dealers, assuming surplus parts are acceptable, before using a BOA. Timely publication of CBD synopses in accordance with ASPR § 1–1003.2 is, however, required and if an alternate source offers the same item being procured under the BOA, the Government is required to include the source if surplus parts are determined to be acceptable. *Id.* at 1008.

Attempts to substitute posting notices in the bid room for prompt CBD synopses are, for the reasons stated above, equally inappropriate and ineffective with regard to prospective surplus–dealer competitors. Similarly, the Navy's synopsizing procedure in conjunction with the agency's use of the Sikorsky BOA constitutes, under the circumstances of the procurements in question, an undue restriction on surplus parts competition for the Navy's parts procurements.

For the reasons stated above, we find that the Navy's disqualification of Rotair, CBD synopsis procedure, application of procurement method coding, and use of the Sikorsky BOA with regard to the instant aircraft parts procurements unduly restrictive of competition. Accordingly, the protests are sustained. Because the orders under the BOA have been substantially completed, no remedial action is appropriate. We recommend, however, that procedures for effectively qualifying alternate suppliers, including surplus dealers, be established and implemented, that synopsizing procedure be amended to provide notice requisite to allow and encourage competition for future parts procurements, and that basic ordering agreements be used in a manner consistent with the regulatory requirements.

[B–193109]

Contracts—Labor Stipulations—Nondiscrimination—"Affirmative Action Programs"—Commitment Requirement

No award may properly be made under solicitation that does not contain current affirmative action provisions required in federally financed contracts or subcontracts since such omission is material, and readvertisement is required.

Indian Affairs—Contracting With Government—Preference to Indian Concerns

Indian Self-Determination and Education Assistance Act does not require award to Indian-owned economic enterprises because statute and regulations call for preference "to the greatest extent feasible," thus conferring broad, discretionary authority. Approval or disapproval by Department of Interior of proposed subcontract awards will not be disturbed by General Accounting Office unless arbitrary, capricious, or in violation of law or regulation.

In the matter of Department of the Interior—request for advance decision, December 22, 1978:

The Department of the Interior, Bureau of Indian Affairs, requests an advance decision on whether it would be proper to approve a subcontract award to either of two competing firms where the low bidder, a non-Indian-owned firm, did not certify compliance with the Arizona Plan—an affirmative action program—and where the next low bidder, an Indian-owned firm, bid in excess of the amount of money available for the project.

Pursuant to a contract awarded to Alchesay High School District No. 20 (Alchesay), Whiteriver, Arizona, Alchesay is responsible for the design, construction, and equipment of a complete school facility. Under a subcontract with an architect, the new Alchesay High School was designed and the architect administered the bidding process and conducted the bid opening. Alchesay selected option "B" as the best combination for consideration. Okland Construction Company, Inc. (Okland) was the low bidder at $6,900,000 and Chuska Development Co.'s (Chuska) bid was $7,539,371.

Interior reports that after bid opening it was discovered that Okland did not certify the Arizona Plan but Chuska's bid did contain that certification. However, Interior also reports that it was advised that the Arizona Plan may no longer be required; therefore, certification of the Arizona Plan may be inconsequential.

Finally, Interior notes that Public Law No. 93–638, the Indian Self-Determination and Education Assistance Act, 25 U.S.C. § 450e(b)(2) (1976), requires award of subcontracts to Indian preference eligible firms such as Chuska. Interior also notes that Chuska is ready to negotiate if the award is made to it—presumably Chuska would alter its price which is now about $300,000 over budget of $7,221,553. Alchesay, however, recommends award be made to Okland.

In this factual context, Interior raises these questions:

1. If award is made to the low bidder, may the Arizona Plan requirement be waived?

2. Does Public Law 93–638 require that award be made to Chuska, even though its bid was very high?

3. Should Alchesay be advised that the project must be readvertised?

We requested the views of Okland, Chuska, Alchesay and its architect, and the Arizona Department of Education. Responses from that request and the record provided by Interior form the factual basis for our decision.

The solicitation contained form CS–132 (SF 2/72), which provides, in pertinent part, as follows:

BID CONDITIONS—ARIZONA PLAN

All Bidders must comply with the provisions of the Arizona Plan incorporated in Part I of these bid conditions or the affirmative action program set forth in Part II of these bid conditions to be considered responsible bidders, and hence eligible for award of a contract for this project.

*   *   *   *   *   *

Part I: To be eligible for award of a prime contract on this project, a bidder who will himself perform work on the project in one or more trades with respect to which he is a participant in the Arizona Plan * * * must execute and submit as part of his bid the following certification, which, as executed and submitted, shall be deemed a part of the contract specifications for the project * * *.

(A two-page certification followed this paragraph and at the end the bidder's authorized representative was required to sign.)

> Part II: A. Coverage. The provisions of this Part II requiring the submission of an affirmative-action plan shall be applicable to any prime contractor bidder with respect to whose prime contract any work will be performed thereunder in any trade by a contractor or subcontractor who is not (at the time of bid opening for the prime contract) a participant, with a labor organization for which there are [Office of Federal Contract Compliance (OFCC)]—approved minority utilization goals, in the [Arizona] Plan as to the trade or trades.

(At the end of Part II, the bidder's authorized representative was' required to sign a commitment to an affirmative action plan meeting the criteria of Part II.)

> Part IV: Responsiveness and Responsibility. Any EEO submission required to be made by the prospective prime contractor pursuant either to Part I or Part II of these "Bid Conditions" which is material and which will govern the EEO performance of contractors and/or subcontractors during the term of performance of this project must be made as a part of the bid to the Owner. Failure to submit a Part I certification and/or a Part II affirmative action plan (or certification) as applicable will render the bid *nonresponsive.* * * *
> Part V: Compliance and Enforcement. Following is a list of trades for which there are OFCC-approved goals of minority manpower utilization for the geographic area:
> No trade commitments of goals and timetables. [Footnotes omitted and italic supplied.]

Okland did not execute and submit part I or part II with its bid. Nevertheless, Okland asserts that since it is compliant with the Arizona Bid Conditions, there is no necessity for waiver of these conditions and its bid is thus responsive to the contract requirement. Okland states that our Office has found that the fact that a solicitation expressly directs a bidder to sign a certificate agreeing to comply with an affirmative action plan (AAP) is not decisive of the issue of whether a bid is responsive if the bidder fails to execute the directed certification. Citing *Astro Pak Corporation/Diversified Chemical Corp.*, B–183536, August 8, 1975, 75–2 CPD 97, and *Armor Elevator Company, Inc.*, B–190572, March 30, 1978, 78–1 CPD 250, Okland contends that our Office has recognized that a bidder may make the requisite commitment to AAP requirements in ways other than that specified in the solicitation, and that execution of the certification as required by the contract specification was not essential. This is so "[b]ecause Astro Pak [was] not a signatory to the Greater Las Vegas Plan"; however, the test for responsiveness of a bid with regard to AAP compliance must be measured not by the presence of a certificate, but "by its commitment to the solicitation's affirmative action requirements." Therefore, in Okland's view, the issue is whether Okland has demonstrated its commitment to the solicitation's AAP requirements.

Okland submitted the affidavit of its president as evidence of the company's commitment to the Arizona Plan and all Federal and State

AAP requirements. As stated therein, Okland is currently completing a project in Whiteriver, Arizona, as a subcontractor for construction of the Whiteriver Indian Health Facility. In that project Okland is contractually committed to the Arizona Plan and all Federal AAP requirements. Okland has also committed itself to AAP's in the State of Arizona by filing with the city of Phoenix, Arizona, its AAP on October 1, 1978. In addition, Okland is now and has been a member of the Associated General Contractors of America (AGC), affiliated with the Utah Chapter. As stated in the affidavit, Okland is currently a signatory with several other State chapters of the AGC, all of which are bound to Federal and State AAP requirements, and Okland is signatory to AGC agreements with affiliated trade unions, which union agreements provide for compliance with State and Federal AAP.

In summary, Okland contends that it has a deep commitment to the Arizona Plan as well as all Federal and State AAP requirements. In Okland's view, therefore, Okland has demonstrated "its commitment to the solicitation's affirmative action requirements," its bid is responsive to the solicitation's AAP requirements and Okland is entitled to award of the contract.

Chuska contends that Okland's bid must be rejected as nonresponsive for failure to execute and certify part I and/or part II of the Bid Conditions—Arizona Plan.

I. Current Affirmative Action Specification

We note that the Department of Labor, Office of Federal Contract Compliance Programs, on April 7, 1978, published in 43 *Federal Register* 14899, "Goals and Timetables for Female and Minority Participation in the Construction Industry," which were to be included in all federally assisted construction contracts and subcontracts for which invitations for bids or other solicitations or amendments were issued on or after May 8, 1978. Since the Alchesay solicitation was issued on June 30, 1978, the following goals and timetables were applicable to the instant procurement:

Women—Nationwide Timetable	Goal (percent)
From April 1, 1978 until March 31, 1979	3.1
From April 1, 1979 until March 31, 1980	5.1
From April 1, 1980 until March 31, 1981	6.9

Minority Utilization—State of Arizona		
Timetable	Trade	Goal (percent)
Until further notice	All	25.0–30.0

Also published on April 7, 1978, at 43 *Federal Register* 14894, was the new standard notice provision to be included in federally assisted construction contracts and subcontracts in excess of $10,000. Unlike the outdated form used in the Alchesay solicitation, the new notice provision does not require separate execution and certification and potential contractors commit themselves to the requirements of affirmative action simply by submitting a properly executed bid or proposal. Moreover, the outdated form did not contain the current required goals and timetables applicable to women. Furthermore, the outdated form appears to permit potential contractors, which would be subject to part II, to escape any trade commitments of goals and timetables. Thus, the outdated form would not be an acceptable substitute for current requirements.

II. *Okland's Commitment to Affirmative Action*

Okland's contention—that its past conduct is evidence of its commitment to the Alchesay solicitation's affirmative action goals contained in the outdated form—is academic since that solicitation's goals are ambiguous and incomplete. And Okland's contention—that its contractual commitment to the Arizona Plan on another project is evidence of its contractual commitment to the Arizona Plan on the instant solicitation—is without merit because (1) the projects are independent, and (2) Okland's failure to execute and submit the required form would not result in a legal commitment to the required, specific goals and timetables (50 Comp. Gen. 844 (1971); *Northeast Construction Company* v. *Romney*, 485 F. 2d 752 (D.C. Cir. 1973)).

We considered a substantially similar situation in *McKenzie Road Service, Inc.*, B–192327, October 31, 1978, 78–2 CPD 310. There, McKenzie's low bid was rejected for failure to acknowledge an amendment which incorporated the current minority manpower utilization goals and timetables. McKenzie argued that the amendment would not have affected its price and the failure to acknowledge the amendment should be waived as a minor informality. We concluded that (1) the amendment was material because it added new provisions for female and minority participation—notwithstanding McKenzie's contention that it always has followed equal employment opportunity guidelines, and (2) McKenzie's failure to acknowledge the amendment or otherwise indicate a commitment in its bid to be bound by the specific goals and timetables rendered McKenzie's bid nonresponsive since a bidder's commitment must be determined from the bid as submitted. Compare *Mayfair Construction Company*, B–186278, August 10, 1976, 76–2 CPD 148, where, unlike here, use of affirmative action clause different from that prescribed by the Department of Labor was upheld because the clause used was substantially similar to that prescribed by Labor.

Okland contends that the omitted new minority utilization goals and timetables are not material because they would have no effect on the price Okland bid. By letter dated November 29, 1978, Okland agreed to meet all the appropriate requirements at no additional cost.

Since it has been held that minority manpower utilization goals and timetables are material elements of a solicitation, a bidder, such as Okland, may not be permitted, after the time for bid opening, to agree to accept a material alteration in its bid. The integrity of the competitive bidding system would be destroyed if the apparent low bidder could in effect withdraw its bid—by not agreeing to the material addition—after prices are revealed contrary to the terms of the solicitation.

III. Constitutionality of Specific Goals

Okland argues that the constitutionality and enforceability of the Arizona Plan are seriously in question. Okland states that in the very recent case of *Associated General Contractors of California, et al.* v. *Secretary of Commerce, et al.*, Civil No. 77–3738–AAH (C.D. Cal. filed October 20, 1978), the court addressed the question of the permissibility of "racial quotas" to promote employment of minority group contractors in light of the Supreme Court's decision in *Regents of the University of California* v. *Bakke*, 46 U.S.L.W. 4896 (1978); the court concluded that while affirmative action is permissible, "racial quotas are impermissible and unconstitutional" and, therefore, "the 10% race quota [1] [is] not a constitutionally acceptable means of promoting the Congress' legitimate interest in promoting employment in the construction industry among minority group members." Okland also cites *Montana Contractors' Association, et al.* v. *Secretary of Commerce* (D. Mont., filed November 24, 1978) as evidence that racial quotas are unconstitutional. Okland concludes that its lack of compliance with an unconstitutional requirement could not be a basis for refusing award of the contract to Okland.

We note that the minority business enterprises provision has been the subject of conflicting United States District Court decisions. See *Constructors Association of Western Pennsylvania* v. *Kreps*, 441 F. Supp. 936 (W.D. Pa., 1977). Accordingly, our Office has taken the position that we will not review protests concerning compliance with that provision until the litigation is finally resolved. *Solar Electrical Construction Corporation*, B–191531, April 25, 1978, 78–1 CPD 319. Similarly, we do not believe it appropriate for our Office to consider the constitutionality of specific minimum goals in affirmative action programs prior to that issue's final resolution by the courts. See *Inter-Con Security System, Inc.*, B–186347, B–185495, March 7, 1977, 77–1 CPD 165. Accordingly, we will not consider this aspect of the matter.

---

[1] 42 U.S.C. § 6705(f)(2) (1976) (the minority business enterprises provision).

IV. Conclusion

In summary, regarding Interior's first and third questions, we must conclude that (1) the solicitation as issued did not contain all the current AAP requirements, (2) the omission was material and prejudiced the interest of the Government (see 50 Comp. Gen. 844, *supra*), and (3) award may not properly be made under the defective solicitation; thus, readvertisement is required.

V. Indian Preference Requirement of Public Law 93–638

Interior's second question essentially requests our views on whether contract awards under Public Law 93–638 grant programs must be made to Indian-owned firms even when the price would be substantially higher than award to a non-Indian-owned firm. While our conclusion above makes this issue academic here, we comment on this question since it is likely to arise on resolicitation of the instant procurement or in the future.

The Indian Self-Determination and Education Assistance Act provides in pertinent part that,

Any contract [or] subcontract * * * pursuant to this Act * * * shall require that to the greatest extent feasible * * * preference in the award of subcontracts * * * shall be given to Indian organizations and to Indian-owned [51 percent] economic enterprises * * *. 25 U.S.C. § 450e(b)(2) (1976)

Interior's implementing regulation at 25 C.F.R. § 277.28 (1977), entitled "Indian Preference," provides that:

(b) Any contract made by the Bureau with a State or school district shall provide that the contractor shall, to the greatest extent feasible, give preference in the award of subcontracts to Indian organizations and Indian-owned economic enterprises.

To the same effect, the solicitation provided as follows:

In accordance with the provisions of Public Law 93–638, preference will be given to 51 percent Indian Owned Economic Enterprises to the maximum extent feasible in the awarding of any contract or subcontracts pursuant to this advertisement.

Okland has advised that its research has not surfaced any legal precedents or case law which explains or amplifies the meaning of the statutory and regulatory language "to the greatest extent feasible." Okland contends that while there is a delineated preference for Indian subcontractors in 25 U.S.C. § 450e(b)(2), just as there is a preference for small business set-asides under 15 U.S.C. § 644 (1976), the elements of fair competition and reasonable price must play a part in the contracting officer's decision to award.

Okland does not contend that a nonpreferred bidder whose price is a few dollars lower than a preferred bidder should receive award of the contract because such an interpretation would clearly thwart the legislative intent of the statute and effectively remove the Indian preference; however, if there is a significant price differential between a preferred and a nonpreferred bid, the weight in favor of the preferred bidder may be overcome.

In our view, the language "to the greatest extent feasible" confers broad discretionary authority, and, therefore, Public Law 93-638 does not require award to Indian-owned firms. When our Office reviews agency determinations made pursuant to such authority, we will not disturb them unless they are arbitrary, unreasonable, or violative of law or regulation. See *Department of the Interior—request for advance decision*, B-188888, December 12, 1977, 77-2 CPD 454 (the quantum of evidence required for an offeror to establish Indian descent and tribal enrollment). Accordingly, we would review Interior's approval or disapproval of proposed subcontract awards to non-Indian economic enterprises under that standard, which must also be applied by the contractors in the first instance.

By regulation published prior to any resolicitation or by solicitation provision, Interior should definitize the preference that Indian enterprises will receive in this and future procurements because bidders cannot compete on an equal basis as required by law unless they know in advance the basis on which their bids will be evaluated. 36 Comp. Gen. 380, 385 (1956).

[B-192502]

Experts and Consultants—Leaves of Absence—Accrual

Expert appointed on an intermittent basis is not entitled to leave even though he was compensated for 80 hours per pay period for substantially the full term of his employment. His work was assigned on a project basis and the hours at which he worked were largely within his discretion. Since he was not required in advance to report at a definite and certain time within each workweek, he is not entitled to leave as a part-time employee with an established regular tour of duty. He is not entitled to leave as a de facto full-time employee since he was not required to work a standard workweek.

In the matter of Copp Collins—Annual and Sick Leave, December 26, 1978:

This matter involves Mr. Copp Collins' claim for crediting of annual and sick leave for the period from June 30, 1977, to May 26, 1978, during which he served under an excepted appointment as an expert with the Energy and Minerals Division of the General Accounting Office.

Mr. Collins was appointed as an expert under the authority of 5 U.S.C. § 3109 (1976), as implemented by 31 U.S.C. § 52c (1976), and Pub L. No. 94-440, 90 Stat. 1439. His appointment, effective June 30, 1977, was designated as "Excepted Appointment—Intermittent," and was limited to a period not to exceed 130 working days in a service year. The following notation was included on the Standard Form 50 effecting his appointment:

Ineligible for Health Benefits, Annual or Sick Leave or any other Benefits provided by law for Government employees except as specifically provided.

Effective January 9, 1978, his appointment as an expert was converted to an excepted appointment not to exceed June 29, 1978.

Notwithstanding the above notation, Mr. Collins claims entitlement to both annual and sick leave on the basis that he:

* * * was a de facto fulltime employee during the entire period from June 30, 1977 to April 22, 1978, and a part-time, temporary Expert employee from April 23, 1978 to May 26, 1978, but with ample extra time built up that [he] could receive administrative or "comp" time to make that latter period fulltime * * *.

In support of the contention that he is entitled to leave credits, Mr. Collins has prepared and submitted time sheets showing that, with the exception of the last three pay periods, he worked 80 hours per pay period throughout the term of his employment. In addition to the 80 hours per pay period for which he was compensated, Mr. Collins' time sheets show that he worked an additional 235.5 hours in the evenings, overnight, and on weekends and holidays.

An expert or consultant whose services are secured on an employment rather than an independent contract basis under the authority of 5 U.S.C. § 3109 is entitled to annual and sick leave insofar as he is eligible under the applicable provisions of chapter 63, subchapter I, title 5, of the United States Code (1976). The mere fact that an expert may have been compensated for an aggregate of 80 hours per pay period does not itself establish his entitlement to leave benefits. Under 5 U.S.C. § 6301 (1976) the annual and sick leave provisions apply generally to employees as defined in 5 U.S.C. § 2105 (1976) and to individuals employed by the government of the District of Columbia, except those categories of employees specifically excluded from coverage by subsections 6301(2)(B)(i)–(xii). Subsection 6301(2)(B) (ii) specifically excludes from entitlement to annual and sick leave.

(ii) a part-time employee who does not have an established regular tour of duty during the administrative workweek * * *.

As used in this context the term "part-time employee" includes employees hired on an intermittent or when-actually-employed basis. *Matter of John W. Matrau, et al.*, B–191915, September 29, 1978; 32 Comp. Gen. 206 (1952). It extends to experts and consultants serving on an intermittent basis. 35 Comp. Gen. 638 (1956).

With regard to Mr. Collins' assertion that he is entitled to leave benefits by virtue of having worked 80 hours per pay period, we have specifically held that part-time employees, including those appointed on an intermittent or when-actually-employed basis, are not entitled to leave benefits even though they might actually work full-time, unless their work is pursuant to a regular tour of duty prescribed in advance. 31 Comp. Gen. 215 (1951). In fact, the contention that a person who works the annual equivalent of a 40-hour workweek is not a part-time employee but is entitled to leave benefits regardless of whether he has a regular tour of duty was specifically found to be without merit by the Court of Claims in *Lemily, et al.* v. *United States*, 190 Ct. Cl. 57 (1969). There the court stated:

> Plaintiffs' contention that a person who works the annual equivalent of a 40-hour week is, by definition, not a part-time employee under the Act, is without merit.
>
> The standard personnel forms (S.F. 50) by which plaintiffs were employed neither guaranteed nor required any particular amount of work. Finding 23, *infra*. Suffice to say, the forms expressly noted that plaintiffs were only to be paid "when-actually-employed."
>
> The legislative history of the 1951 Act, previously discussed, makes it abundantly clear that the government employee for whom Congress fashioned the generally applicable leave benefits was one who was *required* to regularly put in the standard 40-hour workweek. A "basic workweek" is so defined in the Civil Service Regulations. 5 C.F.R. § 25.211 (Rev. as of Jan. 1961). Thus, the annual and sick leave allowances provided in the 1951 Act are stated in terms of days, or fractions thereof, "for each full bi-weekly pay period." The regular 40-hour workweek is implicit in that arrangement.
>
> In general, the full-time employee to whom the provisions of the 1951 Act are applicable is one regularly required to put in the standard workweek, not a when-actually-employed employee who happens to work the annual equivalent of a 40-hour week.

Under the above decisions, notwithstanding that Mr. Collins was compensated for 80 hours per pay period, he is entitled to crediting of annual and sick leave only insofar as he had an established regular tour of duty during the administrative workweek. In this connection we have specifically recognized that the mere designation of an employee's appointment as "intermittent" is not conclusive of the question of his entitlement to annual and sick leave if his actual service differs and is not in fact intermittent but is performed pursuant to a regularly scheduled tour of duty. *Matter of Julia McCarthy and others*, B–183813, June 20, 1975, and *Matter of Kenneth L. Nash*, 57 Comp. Gen. 82 (1977).

In 31 Comp. Gen. 581 (1952) we construed the requirement that the employee have an established tour of duty as contemplating a "definite and certain time, day and/or hour of any day, during the workweek when the employee regularly will be required to perform duty." In 32 Comp. Gen. 490 (1953) we amplified that definition, holding that a part-time employee is entitled to benefits under the leave act only if he serves under an established tour of duty for each of the two administrative workweeks in each biweekly pay period. The holdings in these two decisions are reflected in the Civil Service Commission's instructions at Book 630, subchapter S2–3a(4) of Federal Personnel

Manual Supplement 990–2. Consistent with those decisions we held in *Kenneth L. Nash, supra*, that an Immigration and Naturalization Service inspector whose position was designated "intermittent" was nonetheless entitled to annual leave benefits as a part-time employee having an established regular tour of duty where he was routinely issued a form scheduling his work at specific times and dates for each of the two workweeks of the next pay period. Compare *John W. Matrau, et al., supra*, denying leave benefits to intermittent employees who were given tentative schedules on a weekly basis as a matter of personal convenience.

Mr. Collins does not specifically claim that he had an established regular tour of duty while serving as an expert with the Energy and Minerals Division. Rather, the time sheets that he prepared suggest that his working hours in large part were determined by the demands of the particular tasks on which he was working and were within his discretion. The time sheets show that Mr. Collins worked 8 hours a day during regular duty hours from Monday through Friday of both administrative workweeks of the pay period for only 7 of the 24 pay periods of his appointment. During all 24 pay periods he worked various hours outside regular duty hours.

Mr. Collins worked on two separate projects while employed with the Energy and Minerals Division. One dealt with coal and the other with biomass and solid waste. In connection with his work on the coal research project, Mr. Collins was given his assignment on a job basis. The schedule by which he performed that assignment was a matter within his own judgment and, except for occasional instances in which he was specifically asked to be present at the office, he was not required by his supervisors to report for work at any particular time. While Mr. Collins was assigned to work in the area of biomass and solid waste during the latter part of his appointment, he was not required to work in accordance with any particular schedule. Essentially, it was Mr. Collins, not the Energy and Minerals Division, who determined when and how long he would work. Officials of the Energy and Minerals Division were aware that Mr. Collins was reporting to work on substantially a full-time basis for an extended period. However, while that awareness may raise some question as to the propriety of designating his initial appointment as "intermittent," mere awareness of even strictly routine work performance does not establish that an employee had a prescribed regular tour of duty where, in fact, he was not required by his agency to perform duty at any particular times.

Since Mr. Collins was not scheduled by the Energy and Minerals Division to work at a definite and certain time, day and/or hour of any day, during each of the two administrative workweeks in each biweekly pay period, he is not entitled to leave benefits as a part-time employee having an established regular tour of duty. And, consistent with the above-quoted language from *Lemily, supra*, since Mr. Collins was not regularly required to put in a standard workweek, we find no merit to Mr. Collins' contention that he is entitled to leave benefits as a "de facto fulltime employee."

Accordingly, Mr. Collins' claim for accrued leave is disallowed.

[B–193099]

Social Security—Medicare, Medicaid, etc.—Reduction in Federal Share—Waiver

Under section 1903(g) of the Social Security Act, 42 U.S.C. 1396b(g), as amended, the Secretary may waive otherwise required reductions in Medicaid payments to a State if he finds that the State's showing for the last quarter of calendar year 1977 was (1) on its face, satisfactorily in compliance with specified statutory requirements and (2) valid (*i.e.*, actually in compliance with those requirements). In order to have a satisfactory showing, subsection 1903(g)(1)(D) requires an annual on-site evaluation by the State. Even though the State of Colorado may have complied with the other requirements, the Secretary has no authority to grant it a waiver of reductions since he has been unable to validate the State's compliance with that subsection.

In the matter of Medicaid—Utilization Control—State of Colorado, December 26, 1978:

This decision responds to a request by the Secretary of Health, Education, and Welfare (HEW) for an opinion as to whether, under the circumstances he presents, he must reduce the payment made to the State of Colorado as a result of its failure to satisfy the utilization control provisions of the Medicaid program set forth in section 1903 (g) of the Social Security Act (42 U.S.C. § 1396b(g) (1976)), as most recently amended by section 20(a) of the Medicare–Medicaid Anti-Fraud and Abuse Amendments, Pub. L. No. 95–142, 91 Stat 1205, October 25, 1977.

Section 1903(g) of the Social Security Act, as amended, provides in pertinent part as follows:

(g) Decrease in Federal medical assistance percentage. (1) Subject to paragraph (3), with respect to amounts paid for the following services furnished under the State plan after June 30, 1973 (other than services furnished pursuant to a contract with a health maintenance organization as defined in section 1876), the Federal medical assistance percentage shall be increased as follows: After an individual has received care as an inpatient in a hospital (including an institution for tuberculosis), skilled nursing facility or intermediate care facility on 60 days, or in a hospital for mental diseases on 90 days (whether or not such days are consecutive), during any fiscal year, which for purposes of this section means the four calendar quarters ending with June 30, the Federal medical assistance percentage with respect to amounts paid for any such care furnished thereafter to such individual in the same fiscal year shall be decreased by a per centum thereof (determined under paragraph 5)) unless the State agency responsible for the administration of the plan makes a showing satisfactory to the Secretary that, with respect to each calendar quarter for which the State submits a request for payment at the full Federal medical assistance percentage for amounts paid for inpatient hospital services (including tuberculosis hospitals), skilled nursing facility services, or intermediate care facility services furnished beyond 60 days (or inpatient mental hospital services furnished beyond 90 days), there is in operation in the State an effective program of control over utilization of such services; such a showing must include evidence that—

* * * * * * * *

(D) Such State has an effective program of medical review of the care of patients in mental hospitals, skilled nursing facilities, and intermediate care facilities pursuant to 1902(a) (26) and (31) whereby *the professional management of each case is reviewed and evaluated at least annually by independent professional review teams.* [Italic supplied.]

* * * * * * * *

It is the requirement for an annual review and evaluation which gives rise to the instant problem. While Colorado's showing under the above-quoted provision was "facially satisfactory," the Secretary, under subsection 1903(g)(2), 42 U.S.C. § 1396b(g)(2), is required to validate, in a timely manner, the State's showing. Colorado was the only State which the Secretary found lacking. In essence, he found that Colorado was probably in compliance with most requirements within the last calendar quarter of 1977 but that he could not validate the State's compliance with the annual review requirement of subparagraph (D), quoted above except for reviews completed in the last calendar quarter. (We note that the new subparagraph (4)(B) of subsection 1903(g), added by section 20(a) of the Medicare–Medicaid Anti-Fraud and Abuse Amendments, *supra*, in effect defines the annual review requirements, but the refinements of this new subparagraph are not an issue in this case.)

The Secretary asks specifically:

May I find Colorado's showing for the quarter ending December 31, 1977, valid and thus waive reductions for prior 1977 quarters even though I have been unable to validate Colorado's pre-October 1 review dates?

This question grows out of section 20(a) of the Medicare–Medicaid Anti-Fraud and Abuse Amendments, *supra*, to section 1903(g) of the Social Security Act, as amended, which added the following provision to subsection 1903(g):

(3)(A) No reduction in the Federal medical assistance percentage of a State otherwise required to be imposed under this subsection shall take effect—
(i) if such reduction is due to the State's unsatisfactory or invalid showing made with respect to a calendar quarter beginning before January 1, 1977;
(ii) before January 1, 1978;
(iii) unless a notice of such reduction has been provided to the State at least 30 days before the date such reduction takes effect; or
(iv) due to the State's unsatisfactory or invalid showing made with respect to a calendar quarter beginning after September 30, 1977, unless notice

of such reduction has been provided to the State no later than the first day of the fourth calendar quarter following the calendar quarter with respect to which such showing was made.

(B) The Secretary shall waive application of any reduction in the Federal medical assistance percentage of a State otherwise required to be imposed under paragraph (1) because a showing by the State, made under such paragraph with respect to a calendar quarter ending after January 1, 1977, and before October 1, 1977, is determined to be either unsatisfactory under such paragraph or invalid under paragraph (2), if the Secretary determines that the State's showing made under paragraph (1) with respect to the calendar quarter ending on December 31, 1977, is satisfactory under such paragraph and is valid under paragraph (2).

The Secretary describes the problem with the Colorado utilization control program as follows:

> All States made a facially satisfactory showing with respect to the December quarter, including all twenty-two penalty-liable States. However, when we attempted to validate those showings by examining review reports on file at the State agencies for all reported calendar 1977 reviews, we were unable to validate the pre-October 1, 1977, review dates reported by Colorado on its December showing. Due to the methodology used by Colorado in its pre-October reviews, we were able to validate only review dates during the December quarter (October 1, 1977, through December 31, 1977). We were able to validate *all* 1977 review dates reported by all other States on their December 31, 1977, showings, and have accordingly waived the 1977 reductions of the other twenty-one penalty-liable States.

> I am deeply distressed by these findings concerning Colorado. Section 1903(g) (3)(B) appears to authorize a waiver of 1977 reductions *only if* I determine that a State's showing with respect to the quarter ending December 31, 1977, is satisfactory *and valid*. Because I have been unable to validate the pre-October 1 review dates reported by Colorado, I have been unable to validate its December showing with respect to the annual onsite review requirement.

> However, it is also apparent that, beginning in the December, 1977 quarter, Colorado has made great efforts to implement a review process that meets Federal requirements, and I have been able, based on evidence presented by the State during the validation survey, to validate all but two of the review dates reported by Colorado for reviews completed during the December quarter. It seems to me that any reasonable postulation of the intent of the conditional waiver provision has therefore been served, and I have no desire to penalize Colorado if I am not required by statute to take these reductions. (Footnote omitted.)

The Secretary apparently has concluded that he is required by section 1903(g) to reduce Colorado's Medicaid payment. His argument against doing so appears to rest upon a theory that Colorado, although not in strict compliance with the requirements of subsection 1903(g), as amended, has made satisfactory progress and should not be penalized. He provides the following summary of his reading of subsection 1903(g), as amended:

> Thus, to be satisfactory under the statute, a State's showing for the quarter ending December 31, 1977, would apparently need to demonstrate that the State conducted the required inspection sometime during calendar 1977 in every facility requiring inspection by December 31, 1977, (or alternatively, that the State met the conditions specified in 1903(g)(4)(B) for excusing failures to perform 100 percent of required inspections).

We agree with the Secretary's reading of section 1903(g), as amended by section 20(a) of the Medicare–Medicaid Anti-Fraud and

Abuse Amendments. Further, we are unable to find any support in the legislative history of this amendment for the conclusion that Colorado's utilization control compliance posture at the end of 1977 as described by the Secretary met the conditions set by the Congress in passing the Medicare–Medicaid Anti-Fraud and Abuse Amendments for waivers of Medicaid payment reductions otherwise necessary.

The annual inspection requirement for all cases to which such subsection 1903(g) applies requires that compliance be determined for each quarter. Inspections may be conducted in a single quarter or spread out over a year. From the Secretary's letter, it appears that none of Colorado's reported inspections conducted in the first three quarters of 1977 could be validated due to the methodology used. Accordingly, Colorado would have had to redo all inspections in the last quarter to be in compliance at the end of 1977. This it did not do. The statutory system established by Congress in section 1903(g) does not authorize the Secretary to waive the reductions unless the State's showing is both satisfactory and valid. If, as in this case, the Secretary cannot validate the showing by the end of the final quarter, he must impose the reductions.

The legislative history of the amendments to section 1903(g) provides no support for a contrary reading. The reasons for adding the paragraph providing a waiver of the reduction of State payments are described in H.R. Rep. No. 95–393 (II), July 12, 1977, at pp. 84–85:

The "Social Security Amendments of 1972" (Public Law 92–603) added section 1903(g) to the Social Security Act. This section requires a one-third reduction in Federal matching payments under medicaid for long-term stays in institutional settings, unless a State demonstrates that it has an adequate program of control over the utilization of institutional services. The program must include a showing that:
(1) The physician certifies at the time of admission and recertifies every 60 days that the patient requires inpatient institutional services.
(2) The services are furnished under a plan established and periodically reviewed by a physician.
(3) The State has a continuous program of utilization review whereby the necessity for admission and continued stay of patients is reviewed by personnel not directly responsible for care of the patient, not financially interested in a similar institution, or, except in the case of a hospital, employed in the institution.
(4) The State has a program of independent medical review for SNF's, ICF's, and mental hospitals whereby the professional management of each case is subject to independent annual review. The section further requires the Secretary to conduct sample onsite surveys of institutions as part of his validation procedures.
The committee notes that this section was to go into effect on July 1, 1973, as an incentive payment for States showing a satisfactory program of utilization control. States which did not make the requisite showings were automatically to be subject to the reduced Federal matching rate. Despite the clear intent of the law and extensive evidence developed by the Subcommittee on Oversight and Investigations as well as the Comptroller General of the United States, that a large number of States failed to meet the requirements, HEW indicated that it was reluctant to impose the reductions. The first reduction actually to be imposed under this authority was announced to take effect July 1977. During the

intervening 4-year period the committee has on a number of occasions, both during hearings and in a report prepared by the committee, indicated its concern that HEW had failed to fulfill its responsibilities.

On June 8, 1977, HEW announced that it would reduce July 1977 Medicaid payments to 20 States by a total of $142 million (Actual application of these announced reductions was delayed by Public Law 95–59 until October 1977). *These reductions were to take effect, because the States failed, during the first quarter of 1977, to conduct annual medical reviews of patients in long-term care facilities.* The Department further announced that it had under review the potential disallowance of $378 million of fiscal year 1975 funds for failure to have adequate utilization controls in place, based upon validation requirements. The committee is encouraged that the Department has begun to aggressively implement the congressional mandate. However, in view of past inaction on the part of HEW, it feels that the sudden reduction in Federal funds for past years activities could have a severe and unanticipated impact on affected State Medicaid programs. [Italic supplied.]

The House and Senate versions of the bill that went to conference on the Medicare–Medicaid Anti-Fraud and Abuse Amendments had two different approaches to lessen the "severe and unanticipated impact" of the then pending reductions in State Medicaid payments. The conference committee report (H.R. Rept. 95–673 at 47) describes the Senate version as an "unconditional waiver" of reductions through 1977; the House version is described as providing additional time for States to achieve compliance by the end of 1977:

29 CONDITIONS FOR WAIVER OF PAST PENALTIES FOR FAILURE TO PERFORM REQUIRED REVIEW OF INSTITUTIONAL CARE (SECTION 20)

House bill.—The House bill allows States additional time to meet the requirements of the current law concerning review of care delivered in long-term care institutions, by providing that if a State is in compliance for the calendar quarter ending December 31, 1977, the Secretary shall waive all previously assessed reductions which would otherwise be imposed on those States that failed to fulfill the requirements of the law during previous periods.

Senate amendment.—The Senate amendment provides for unconditional waiver of all reductions in medicaid payments due to an unsatisfactory or invalid showing made with respect to a calendar quarter beginning prior to January 1, 1978.

The conference committee went on to explain its reconciliation of these two provisions (see subsection 1903(g)(3)(A) as quoted *supra*) as follows [*id.* at 47]:

Conference Agreement.—The conference agreement provides that all penalties assessed against States for unsatisfactory or invalid showings made with respect to calendar quarters beginning prior to January 1, shall be waived unconditionally. It further provides that if a State is in compliance with the requirements of the law for the calendar quarter ending December 31, 1977, the Secretary shall waive all penalties for unsatisfactory or invalid showings for quarters occurring in 1977; if the State is not in compliance on December 31 and past penalties are imposed, the penalty will be determined by taking into account the proportion of medicaid patients in homes that were not reviewed to all medical patients in homes to be reviewed.

Congress incorporated the absolute waiver objective of the Senate-passed bill for all quarters prior to 1977, while the House approach was used to reward compliance by the end of 1977. The Secretary's question concerns his inability to validate the State's showing in 1977, the period to which the House approach applies. The House Committee report [*id.* at 85] describes this approach as requiring "full compliance."

> The committee has approved an amendment which would give States an additional 6 months to demonstrate full compliance with the law. The committee emphasizes that this is in no way to be viewed as a retrenchment or a lack of resolve on its commitment to effective utilization control and medical audit programs. It fully expects and intends that during this extension period all States will take the necessary actions to bring them into full compliance.

> *   *   *   *   *   *   *   *

> The Secretary is required to waive application of all or part (as is appropriate) of any decrease otherwise required to be imposed with respect to cases of noncompliance occurring prior to October 1, 1977, if he determines that the State makes a satisfactory showing, and the showing is valid, that it is in full compliance with the law for the last quarter of calendar year 1977. The committee has left to the Secretary's discretion the amount of the decrease which may be waived. It fully expects that where previous violations of the law have been of sufficient magnitude, the Secretary may impose a portion of the penalty. *In cases where the State is not able to show a satisfactory program that is validated by the Secretary, the committee expects that all previous reductions will be taken.* [Italic supplied.]

We read carefully the correspondence, dated August 16, 1978, enclosed with the Secretary's letter, from Senators Herman E. Talmadge, Chairman of the Senate Subcommittee on Health, and Floyd K. Haskell and Representative Paul G. Rogers, Chairman of the House Subcommittee on Health and the Environment, to Representative Timothy E. Wirth about the congressional intent behind the penalty waiver provision of Pub. L. No. 95–142, *supra.* They all indicate that the Congress intended "to wipe the slate clean" of deficiencies in the first three quarters of 1977 as long as the State conducted "*regularly scheduled*" inspections during the last quarter of 1977. All agree that no State was expected to review all the facilities in the State in only one quarter. It therefore appears that the writers feel that the Secretary need not require reviews for any facility for which an inspection could not be performed during the last quarter of 1977.

All these Congressmen participated in writing the waiver amendment in question and of course their views are entitled to great respect. However, the official legislative history, quoted previously, which was written contemporaneously with congressional consideration of the waiver amendment, gives a very different picture of congressional intent. The concept of an unconditional waiver, originally proposed by the Senate, was rejected, except for quarters ending prior to calendar 1977. As the House committee report explains, and the Conference report reiterates (both quoted *supra*), "The Committee has approved an amendment which would give States an additional 6 months to demonstrate full compliance with the law." It appears that the only way for Colorado to "wipe the slate clean" of previously assessed reductions was to demonstrate conclusively by the end of 1977 that it had completed reviews of all of its facilities to which the review requirement applies.

We therefore conclude, on the basis of the statute and the legislative history, that the Secretary must make all the statutory reductions if he finds that Colorado did not complete all required reviews during 1977. Colorado does not qualify for the waiver of previously assessed reductions if it was not in compliance by the end of calendar 1977.

Accordingly, the Secretary's specific question is answered in the negative.

[B-191401]

Officers and Employees — Transfers — Relocation Expenses— Temporary Quarters—Subsistence Expenses—Reasonableness of Meal Costs

Transferred employee, who was authorized temporary quarters subsistence expenses allowance, agreed to pay mother-in-law $22.50 for room and board of three children. Agency determined that expenditure of $12 per day for food was unreasonable since statistical data showed that reasonable expenditure would be $7.74 per day. Agency determination is reversed since agency failed to consider fact that $12 amount was reached by preparing a sample week's shopping list using actual market prices, that his mother-in-law prepared the three meals, and that employee negotiated rate with his mother-in-law in good faith.

Officers and Employees — Transfers — Relocation Expenses— Temporary Quarters—Reasonableness of Amount Claimed

Transferred employee who was authorized temporary quarters subsistence expenses allowance agreed to pay mother-in-law for room and board of his three daughters. Agency determination that $10.50 per day for rooms was unreasonable is reversed as arbitrary. We find rate was reasonable since $10.50 was considerably less than commercial rate, mother-in-law experienced inconvenience by staying with neighbor, except when she prepared meals, cleaned house and chaperoned children, children expended large amount of utilities, and employee negotiated rate in good faith.

In the matter of Richard E. Nunn—Temporary Quarters Subsistence Expenses, December 27, 1978:

This action is in response to a letter from Mr. W. Smallets, Chief, Finance and Accounting, Central Security Service, National Security Agency (NSA), requesting a decision as to whether the NSA properly denied a portion of the claim of Mr. Richard E. Nunn for temporary quarters subsistence expenses (TQSE) allowance attributable to room and board expenses paid to his mother-in-law for his three daughters, and whether NSA is using proper methods in the settlement of similar claims. The request was forwarded to us by the Per

Diem, Travel and Transportation Allowance Committee and has been assigned PDTATAC Control No. 78–9.

The record indicates that Mr. Nunn was transferred to Fort George G. Meade, Maryland, from Harrogate, England, effective August 3, 1977. Incident to this transfer TQSE was authorized by Travel Order No. MP 7 MH 124–77. The record further indicates that Mr. Nunn and his wife stayed at a Howard Johnson's Motor Lodge in Wheaton, Maryland, from August 2, 1977, to August 24, 1977, and that his three daughters stayed at their grandmother's house for the period August 2, 1977, through August 24, 1977. In consideration of his three daughters staying at his mother-in-law's house and receiving their meals there, Mr. Nunn agreed to pay his mother-in-law $7.50 per day per child with $4 attributable to food and $3.50 attributable to lodging.

Mr. Nunn filed a claim with NSA for $474, the amount that he paid his mother-in-law for room and board for his three daughters. The payment was based on the $7.50 daily rate less certain meals that the children had with their parents. Thereafter NSA requested Mr. Nunn to provide documentation in support of the $7.50 per day per child amount and, after receiving his response, allowed Mr. Nunn's claim to the extent of $283.96 and denied the rest as in excess of that which was reasonable.

Mr. Nunn also filed a claim of $1,237.19 for the expenses incurred by him and his wife which was allowed to the extent of $1,192.72. That portion of Mr. Nunn's claim which was denied and which was attributable to expenses incurred by him and his wife does not appear to be in dispute and is therefore not addressed in this decision.

Mr. Nunn in a letter to NSA stated that the food amount of $4 per day per child figure was subdivided into charges of $1 for breakfast, $1 for lunch, and $2 for dinner, and was arrived at by preparing a typical week's shopping list using local market prices and an amount for the energy and labor costs associated with food preparation. He further stated:

Generally speaking, the food and cost of its preparation averaged $10.00 a day and $2.00 was included for ancillary incidentals for the whole job. This divided by three people was arbitrarily factored into a 1+1+2 figure based on a reasonable estimate that the dinner value was quite a bit higher than breakfast or lunch. It may be that it should have been estimated at $1.25, $1.25 and $1.50 respectively, but since it was a late exception when the children ate out with us * * * and she agreed to a $2 dinner decrement, I knew the cost advantage was in my (and the government's) favor.

In defense of the lodging cost of $3.50 per day per child Mr. Nunn stated:

Determining the factors used for room costs were a lot easier. My mother-in-law actually moved out of the house to reside with an elderly friend down the street, and only came home to cook the meals, clean, and chaperone if necessary.

In actual fact the children took over her two-bedroom home for over ¾ month. I agreed to pay for a prorated (¾) share of a month's house payment, ½₂ taxes, and ¾ of a month's worth of the gas, sewer, electricity, water and trash disposal services at amounts commonly averaged to the house for that time of the year * * *.

The three-week board estimate included cleaning labor, approximated $253. This was rounded off to $231, which amounts to $10.50 per day, and allotted in even ⅓ increments to each child at a cost of $3.50 each.

Mr. Nunn in his letter to NSA additionally stated that the $4 per day per child amount for food and the $3.50 per day amount per child for lodging was the lowest his mother-in-law would agree to and that he negotiated the lowest price possible since it was apparent that they would be exceeding their daily maximum and that the excess would be at his own expense.

Paragraph C13000 of Volume 2, Joint Travel Regulations (2 JTR) (Change 133, November 1, 1976), authorizes, under proper circumstances, the payment of subsistence expenses of an employee and his dependents while occupying temporary quarters when the employee is transferred to a new permanent duty station. Also, reimbursement may be made only for actual subsistence expenses incurred not to exceed the maximum amount allowable, provided these are incident to occupancy of temporary quarters and are reasonable. 2 JTR para. C13005 (Change 138, April 1, 1977).

It is the responsibility of the employing agency, in the first instance, to insure that such expenses are reasonable. Since this is primarily a question of fact, depending upon the particular circumstances of the case, this Office gives great weight to the agency's determination of what is reasonable, inasmuch as it is more familiar with the particular situation. While we have the right to review the circumstances of each case and make an independent determination as to the reasonableness of the subsistence expenses claimed, we will not substitute our judgment for that of the agency, in the absence of evidence indicating the agency's determination as to the reasonableness was clearly erronous, arbitrary or capricious. *Matter of Gordon S. Lind*, B–182135, November 7, 1974.

In 52 Comp. Gen. 78, 82 (1972) we considered the reimbursement of amounts paid to relatives for food and lodging and stated in part:

* * * we have allowed reimbursement for charges for temporary quarters and subsistence supplied by relatives where the charges have appeared reasonable: that is, where they have been considerably less than motel or restaurant charges. It does not seem reasonable or necessary to us for employees to agree to pay for lodging in motels or meals in restaurants or to base such payments to relatives upon maximum amounts which are reimbursable under the regulations. Of course, what is reasonable depends on the circumstances of each case. The number of individuals involved, whether the relative had to hire extra help to provide lodging and meals, the extra work performed by the relative and possibly other factors would be for consideration. * * *

The NSA in denying Mr. Nunn's claim determined that a food expenditure of $12 per day for his three daughters was unreasonable and determined that a total cost of $178 for 23 days or $7.74 per day was reasonable. The NSA based this figure on Bureau of Labor statistics data which showed a typical family of three on a high-cost budget would spend $8.10 per day. Also, NSA states that since settlement of Mr. Nunn's claim it obtained a Department of Agriculture booklet entitled "Your Money's Worth In Food" and the November 1977 statistical data sheet, "Cost of Food at Home Estimated for Food Plans at Four Cost Levels." The latter publication using a moderate cost plan reflects a food cost of $7.35 per day for a family of three.

Although NSA based its determination that $12 per day on food was unreasonable on statistical data showing that a reasonable expenditure would be much less, we believe that NSA erroneously failed to consider that Mr. Nunn arrived at the $12 figure by preparing a sample shopping list using actual market prices, that his mother-in-law prepared the meals for his three daughters, and that Mr. Nunn negotiated this rate in good faith with his mother-in-law. Based on these facts, we believe that $12 per day for food was a reasonable expenditure. Therefore, the agency determination on this item is reversed.

After considering Mr. Nunn's claim of $10.50 per day for the lodging expenses of his three daughters NSA allowed Mr. Nunn's claim to the extent of $73.26 for lodging and $32.50 for utilities. Although Mr. Nunn's claim was based on a flat rate, NSA settled the claim on a separate room and utilities charge basis apparently due to Mr. Nunn's explanation of how the charge was arrived at. Without sufficient explanation NSA determined that a $100 per month rate for the rooms or $73.26 was reasonable and that a rate of $32.50 for utilities was reasonable. The amount of $32.50 for utilities was one-half of the amount that Mr. Nunn had used in arriving at a lodging rate of $10.50 per day. The NSA apparently based its decision on the belief that the utility amount was an estimate because Mr. Nunn did not supply the actual receipts for the utilities used during the period in question.

The record in the instant case lacks a proper basis to support NSA's determination that the amount claimed for lodging was unreasonable under the circumstances. The NSA has given insufficient reasons why it considers $10.50 per day unreasonable and why it considers $3.33 per day for lodging ($100.00 monthly rate) plus $1.48 per day for utilities to be reasonable. Therefore, we have considered the various factors upon which the lodging cost was based. We agree that mortgage costs are fixed and do not change with the number of residents and, therefore, are usually not an accurate measure of the value of lodging. However, in this case we note that had Mr. Nunn's three daughters stayed in motel rooms, it would have probably cost an amount in excess of $33 per day. Thus, the $10.50 per day is a rate which is one-third of that which would have been expended had Mr. Nunn's three daughters stayed at the motel. In addition we believe that Mr. Nunn negotiated in good faith with his mother-in-law for a rate of $10.50 per day since that rate was the lowest she would accept. Moreover, the fact that the three girls were staying at their grandmother's is just one factor to be considered. *Lind, supra.* Another factor to be considered is that Mr. Nunn's mother-in-law stayed with a neighbor during her granddaughters' occupancy of her house. Additionally it is apparent that any utility charges during the period in question are attributable to Mr. Nunn's daughters and not to his mother-in-law. We believe that the inconvenience experienced by Mr. Nunn's mother-in-law, the cost of utilities, the apparent good faith negotiation on Mr. Nunn's part, and the comparative low cost of the lodging justify a conclusion that the $10.50 per day rate was reasonable in the absence of evidence to the contrary.

Accordingly, Mr. Nunn's reclaim voucher should be paid if otherwise correct.

[B–192253]

Compensation—Reassignments—Two-Step Increases—Entitlement

Three employees were reassigned under competitive procedures to a position at the same GS grade having greater promotion potential. Reassignment to a position at the same GS grade where a promotion is only potential or expected some time after reassignment falls short of an actual promotion or transfer to a "higher General Schedule position" under 5 C.F.R. 531.204(a). Consequently, the reassignment did not entitle the three employees to a two-step increase under 5 U.S.C. 5334(b).

In the matter of John E. Hansen, et al.—Claim for backpay, December 27, 1978:

This decision is on claims filed by the National Treasury Employees Union, Atlanta, Georgia, on behalf of John E. Hansen, George F. Dickinson, Jr., and Michael McGee, for backpay as employees of the United States Customs Service, Miami, Florida.

The employees are of the opinion that upon the reassignment they were entitled to an increase in basic pay of not less than two step increases. They rely on 5 C.F.R. § 531.204(a) as the authority for their opinion.

The principal issue is whether the claimants' reassignment was a "transfer from one General Schedule position to a higher General Schedule position" within the meaning of Civil Service Commission regulation 5 C.F.R. § 531.204(a). If it was, the claimants were entitled to the minimum two-step increase in pay provided by 5 U.S.C. § 5334 (b), the legislative provision implemented by this regulation.

The notification of personnel actions, issued in October 1977, show that the employees were reassigned under the Customs Service Merit Promotion Plan from their positions as Dog Handler, GS–301, grade GS–7, to Customs Inspector, GS–1890, grade GS–7. The pay rate (step) within grade GS–7 was the same before and after reassignment. The personnel actions changing the claimants' positions specifically state the nature of the action is a "Reassignment," which means a change of an employee, while serving continuously in the same agency, from one position to another without promotion or demotion. Federal Personnel Manual (FPM) Supplement 990–2, Book 531, subchapter S2–2(j). The positions were "filled below full performance level," and if certain conditions were subsequently met, the claimants would be entitled to promotion through GS–9 without further competition.

Although the reassignment did not result in an immediate rise in General Schedule grade or salary, the Union argues that the claimants were transferred to a "higher General Schedule position" within the meaning of 5 C.F.R. § 531.204. The main reason for this view is that subsequent to their reassignment the claimants could anticipate promotion from Customs Inspector, GS–7, as trainees to GS–9, after they reached full performance capability and without competing for the promotion. This promotion potential or "journeyman" grade of GS–9 for Customs Inspector is more favorable than the GS–7 "journeyman" level for Dog Handler. As a further indication that the claimants' reassignment was to a higher level position, the Union observes that the claimants competed for their reassignment under the Customs Service Merit Promotion Plan.

In the ordinary sense of the term, the reassignment might be regarded as a transfer to a "higher General Schedule position," under the language used in 5 C.F.R. § 531.204(a). However, this regulation was issued to implement the statutory language in 5 U.S.C. § 5334(b), which provides for a minimum two-step pay increase only when a General Schedule employee is "promoted or transferred to a position in a higher *grade*." [Italic supplied.] The term "grade" in that section is defined by 5 U.S.C. §§ 5331(a) and 5102(a)(5) to mean a class of sufficiently equivalent positions in terms of difficulty, responsibility, and qualification requirements to be placed "within one range of rates of basic pay in the General Schedule." As shown in the General Schedule chart at 5 U.S.C. § 5332, each grade in the ascending order GS–1 to GS–18 is "one range" of "rates" or steps. A "grade," in other words, is one of the General Schedule levels ("one range of rates") between "GS–1" and "GS–18."

The fact that claimants competed for their reassignment under the Merit Promotion Plan does not change the result. Chapter 335, Subchapter 2, Requirement 1(a)(1), of the FPM provides that plans under a merit promotion program must apply to a reassignment to "a position with known promotion potential." This requirement covered the claimants' reassignment. However, reassignment to a position where a promotion is only potential or expected some time after reassignment, such as in the claimants' case, falls short of an actual promotion or transfer to a higher General Schedule grade at the time of the reassignment.

The employees did not receive a "higher grade" within the meaning of 5 U.S.C. § 5334(b), since they remained within the same General Schedule range of rates, that is the GS–7 grade level, after their reassignment. Consequently, we are unaware of any basis for a two-step increase. The claims are disallowed.

[B–157586]

Family Allowances—Separation—Eligibility Basis—Base Closure— "Enforced" Separation

Where a base closure plan requires the transfer, using Government-furnished transportation, of dependents to the sponsor's next permanent duty station, while the sponsor remains behind to implement base closure, "enforced" separation exists within the contemplation of 37 U.S.C. 427(b)(1), and the granting of Family Separation Allowance, Type II, is authorized.

In the matter of Family Separation Allowance, Type II, December 28, 1978:

This action is in response to a letter dated January 19, 1978, from H. M. Trost, Disbursing Officer, Morocco—U.S. Naval Training Command, FPO New York 09544, requesting our decision as to the propriety of granting Family Separation Allowance Type II (FSA–II) incident to a base closing. The request was approved by the Department of Defense Military Pay and Allowance Committee, and forwarded to us on July 28, 1978, as submission No. DO–N–1299.

The request arose from the planned phaseout of the United States Naval Training Command, Kenitra, Morocco, in September 1978. The base closure plan, promulgated pursuant to Office of the Chief of Naval Operations notice number 5450, dated May 2, 1977, required that dependents vacate Government quarters, at the convenience of the Government, but not later than June 30, 1978. It was stated that members' dependents would be furnished Government transportation to the next permanent duty station, and that there would be an enforced separation, as military members would be required to remain in Morocco to implement the base closure.

Section 427(b), title 37, United States Code, which authorizes FSA–II, provides in pertinent part:

> Except in time of war or national emergency hereafter declared by Congress, and in addition to any allowance or per diem to which he otherwise may be entitled under this title, including subsection (a) of this section, a member of a uniformed service with dependents (other than a member in pay grade E–1, E–2, E–3, or E–4 (4 years' or less service)) is entitled to a monthly allowance equal to $30 if—
>
> (1) the movement of his dependents *to his permanent station or a place near that station* is not authorized at the expense of the United States under section 406 of this title and his dependents do not reside at or near that station; [Italic supplied.]

Given a strictly literal reading, section 427(b)(1) would seem to permit FSA–II payments only when movement *to* the member's present permanent station, or a place nearby, is not authorized at Government expense under 37 U.S.C. § 406. However, when the purpose of FSA–II is considered, a different conclusion is required.

The legislative history of the section shows that it originated in a Department of Defense proposal, and was enacted by section 11(1) of the Uniformed Services Pay Act of 1963, Public Law 88–132 (October 2, 1963), 77 Stat. 210, 217. Congress' rationale for enacting the section was that:

> * * * enforced separations of servicemen from their families cause added household expenses where the member is absent for any extended period of time. This condition results in an inequity as compared with those members whose dependents are authorized to accompany them. The extra expenses include such matters as home and automobile maintenance, increased child care costs, etc. S. Rep. No. 387 (Aug. 5, 1963) at p. 25; [1963] U.S Code, Cong. & Aid. News p. 925.

The inequity results from the necessity of the service members maintaining two "households," one for themselves, and one for their dependents who are prevented from traveling with the members, concurrently, and residing at or near their permanent stations. The situation where the enforced separation is due to military orders (volition of the Government) must be distinguished from the one where the separation is of the member's own choice; FSA–II, may be granted only for the former. 43 Comp. Gen. 332, 347 (Question 18) (1963).

There is nothing in the legislative history of the section to indicate that Congress intended to distinguish between barred transit *to* the permanent duty station of the member, and departure *from* the permanent duty station, on Government orders, as affecting eligibility for FSA–II.

In an analogous situation, a question was raised as to eligibility for FSA–II, beginning on the date of dependent's departure, where the member's dependents had been furnished transportation from that station pursuant to paragraph M7105 of the Joint Travel Regulations. Paragraph M7105 authorized transportation of dependents from an overseas area prior to the termination of the sponsor's overseas tour of duty when the Secretary of the service concerned, or a higher authority, determined their return to be in the national interest. We held, in effect, that a determination pursuant to this section has the effect of converting the station for affected members into a restricted duty station, necessitating the maintenance of two "households." Hence, if otherwise proper, the granting of FSA–II in those circumstances was determined to be appropriate. 43 Comp. Gen. 332, 348, *supra.*

Due to lack of necessary services, residence by dependents at the present duty station in Morocco is barred by the base closing plan, and an enforced separation is the result. Government-furnished transportation is apparently authorized only to the next duty station or the United States. In such circumstances, the enforced separation is at the behest of the Government only. The result is inequitable treatment as contemplated by the Congress in enacting section 427(b). Thus, based on the facts presented, FSA–II is payable to otherwise eligible members with dependents in these circumstances.

[B–189756]

Bids—Mistakes—Withdrawal—Evidence of Error—Degree of Proof Less Than for Correction

Where agency had knowledge of alleged mistake in bid after bid opening but before award, and bidder submitted evidence, which could reasonably support its claim of mistake, but agency denied bidder's request for withdrawal because under applicable regulation it found that evidence was not "c'ear and convincing." agency should not have awarded contract at bid price, but should have referred doubtful matter to General Accounting Office (GAO) for determination as to whether withdrawal could be allowed under less stringent criteria applied by GAO.

General Accounting Office—Jurisdiction—Contracts—Mistakes—Withdrawal v. Correction of Bid

Authority under Federal Procurement Regulations 1–2.406–3 in Executive agencies to determine mistake in bid cases in certain well-defined situations does not divest GAO of authority to review administrative determinations and to decide doubtful cases.

In the matter of Murphy Brothers, Inc.—Reconsideration, December 28, 1978:

The Federal Highway Administration (FHWA) requests that we reconsider our decision B–189756, March 8, 1978, in which we held that Murphy Brothers, Inc. (Murphy) was entitled to relief for a mistake in its bid on contract DOT–FH–10–3148.

In our prior decision, we held that no contract was consummated at the award price because an error in Murphy's bid had been brought to FHWA's attention after bid opening but before award. FHWA refused to permit withdrawal of the bid. Under the circumstances, and because the contract work had been substantially completed so that rescission was not feasible, we held that Murphy was entitled to relief on a *quantum valebant* or *quantum meruit* basis.

FHWA contends that our decision was erroneous. The agency argues that its refusal to provide relief was reasonable because Murphy had not presented clear and convincing evidence that an error had been made. FHWA believes its decision should have been upheld by our Office unless we could find that it was unreasonable. As explained below, we believe FHWA has misconstrued this Office's role and standards of review in cases of mistake in bid alleged prior to award.

In our earlier decision we held that Murphy should have been allowed to withdraw its bid because of a mistake in the bid. We did not find that Murphy's bid should have been corrected prior to award, as Murphy had requested. In this respect, FHWA's reliance on our decisions holding that an agency determination concerning correction of a mistake in bid will be questioned only if there is no reasonable basis for the determination, such as 51 Comp. Gen. 1 (1971), is misplaced. Our review is circumscribed by the reasonableness of the agency determination only in cases involving corrections of bids and not where the question, as here, is whether bid withdrawal should have been allowed.

Because procedures among Federal agencies for resolving mistake in bid claims were inconsistent, this Office agreed that the General Services Administration (GSA) should promulgate regulations allowing administrative resolution in certain well-defined cases. 38 Comp. Gen. 177 (1958). We believed this would minimize delays in contract awards by allowing agencies to determine clear-cut cases. Consistency in administrative determinations was to be attained by requiring agencies to find "clear and convincing evidence" of a mistake in bid before allowing a bidder to withdraw its bid, and clear and convincing evidence of a mistake as well as of the bid intended before allowing correction.

Consequently, the Federal Procurement Regulations § 1–2.406–3 (1964 ed.) now provide, in pertinent part:

(a) Heads of executive agencies are authorized, in order to minimize delay in contract awards, to make the administrative determinations described below, in connection with mistakes in bids alleged after opening of bids and before award * * *

＊   ＊   ＊   ＊   ＊   ＊   ＊

(1) A determination may be made permitting the bidder to withdraw his bid where the bidder requests permission to do so and clear and convincing evidence establishes the existence of a mistake * * *.

*   *   *   *   *   *

(3) A determination may be made permitting the bidder to correct his bid where the bidder requests permission to do so and clear and convincing evidence establishes both the existence of a mistake and the bid actually intended * * *. If the evidence is clear and convincing only as to the mistake, but not as to the intended bid, a determination permitting the bidder to withdraw his bid may be made.

(4) If the evidence does not warrant a determination under paragraphs (a), (1), (2), or (3) of this section, a determination may be made that a bidder may neither withdraw nor correct his bid. * * *

*   *   *   *   *   *

(e) Nothing contained in this § 1–2–406–3 shall deprive the Comptroller General of his statutory right to question the correctness of any administrative determination made hereunder nor deprive any bidder of his right to have the matter determined by the Comptroller General should he so request. All doubtful cases shall be submitted to the Comptroller General for advance decision in accordance with agency procedures * * *.

Implicit in the delegation and in the regulatory provisions is the recognition that agencies have been delegated authority to make determinations in clear-cut cases, subject to our authority to review the administrative determinations. In other words, where there is clear and convincing evidence of a mistake, for example, the agency may act accordingly and permit relief. Similarly, where there is clearly no evidence at all to support an allegation that a mistake has been made, the agency may not permit relief. In other cases, however, where the bidder submits some evidence to the agency which reasonably supports the allegation of error but the evidence is not "clear and convincing," the matter is to be submitted to this Office for determination. *See* e.g., B–153639, September 4, 1964.

Moreover, it is also clear that the FPR standard of "clear and convincing evidence" applies only to administrative determinations by Executive agencies, such as FHWA—in approving the procedure for Executive agencies to determine certain mistake in bid claims in accordance with that standard, we did not adopt that particular standard for our reviews. Rather, in reviewing mistake in bid claims, we have long recognized that the degree of proof required to justify withdrawal of a bid before award is in no way comparable to that necessary to allow correction of an erroneous bid. 36 Comp. Gen. 441, 444 (1956) ; 52 *id.* 258, 261 (1972).

Thus, when a bidder requests that it be allowed to correct its bid because of mistake, this Office does require the bidder to show, by "clear and convincing evidence," the intended bid, and when we review an agency determination in this particular area, we sustain the administrative decision unless we find that decision unreasonable. 41 Comp. Gen. 160, 163 (1961) ; 53 *id.* 232, 235 (1973).

In contrast, when we consider cases concerning withdrawal of a bid, we apply a different standard, allowing withdrawal whenever it reasonably appears that an error was made. 36 Comp. Gen. 441, 444, *supra;* 51 *id.* 1, 3, *supra.* In this regard, in view of the longstanding general rule that acceptance of a bid with knowledge of an error therein does not consummate a valid and binding contract, 36 Comp. Gen. 441, 444, *supra; Ruggiero* v. *United States*, 420 F. 2d 709, 713 (Ct. Cl. 1970), we have held that where the Government undertakes to bind a bidder to its bid, after notice of a claim of error by the bidder, the Government "virtually undertakes the burden of proving that there was no error or that the bidder's claim was not made in good faith." 36 Comp. Gen. 441, 444, *supra.* If that burden is not satisfied, we will find that the bidder cannot be held to the contract purportedly awarded.

In the instant case, Murphy submitted worksheets to FHWA in support of its claim that it had committed an error in its bid. While we agree with FHWA that Murphy's intended bid was not discernible from the face of its worksheets, Murphy would have been allowed by this Office to withdraw its bid since the worksheets provided evidence which could reasonably support Murphy's claim that a mistake was made. *Cf. Ruggiero* v. *United States, supra.* While FHWA had authority to determine that the worksheets were not "clear and convincing evidence" of a mistake in bid so as to permit that agency to allow Murphy to withdraw its bid, FHWA should have first referred to this Office for resolution the doubtful question of whether a mistake was made. B–153639, *supra.* Once the matter was brought here, however, FHWA's determination that Murphy's evidence was insufficient for that agency to allow Murphy to withdraw its bid in no way foreclosed this Office from making an independent determination under the less stringent criteria applied in accordance with the legal precedent referred to above.

Thus, while FHWA is correct in stating that it could not permit withdrawal, we find our previous action in this matter to be appropriate under the circumstances. Accordingly, our previous decision is sustained.

〖 B–191989 〗

Travel Expenses—Fares—Taxicabs—Between Residence and Headquarters—Outside Regular Working Hours

Paragraph 1–2.3e of the Federal Travel Regulations (FTR) was not intended to authorize payment of taxicab fares where the use of public transportation is merely inconvenient. Commuting on other than the employee's regular schedule involves a degree of additional inconvenience and for an employee who regularly uses public transportation, the most common form of inconvenience is variation in bus or train schedules. The requirement of FTR para. 1–2.3e of infrequency of scheduled public transportation is not satisfied by a mere showing that public transportation is not as readily available as at the height of rush hour.

Travel Expenses—Fares—Taxicabs—Between Residence and Headquarters—Outside Regular Working Hours

The authority of FTR para. 1–2.3e to reimburse taxicab fares when an employee who is dependent on public transportation is required to work overtime is intended to be exercised only in limited situations under stringent agency controls. An employee with a Monday-through-Friday workweek required to work overtime on weekends until 5:30 p.m., and to commute from work in the early evening hours corresponding to the time he normally commutes from work to home, may not be authorized taxicab fare on the sole basis that in the winter his travel occurs after sunset. Such factors as added risk and curtailment of public transportation would be for consideration.

In the matter of Virginia Goodman—Taxicab fares between office and residence in case of necessity, December 29, 1978:

By letter dated May 8, 1978, Ms. Vera Herzog, Authorized Certifying Officer, ACTION, has requested a decision concerning application of the Federal Travel Regulations (FPMR 101–7) para. 1–2.3e (May 1973) to the taxicab fare claims of three ACTION employees. The three employees, Virginia Goodman, Arnita Gaskins, and Lucretia LaRoche, worked overtime on weekends in January of 1978. Ms. LaRoche also worked overtime on Saturday and Sunday, August 21 and 22, 1976, and on the prior Thursday and Friday. On the weekends for which claims are submitted, the employees worked overtime at their regular places of business between 8 a.m. and 5:30 p.m. On Thursday and Friday, August 19 and 20, 1976, Ms. LaRoche remained at ACTION headquarters until 7:15 p.m., 2 hours beyond the end of her regular workday. Each claims taxicab fare for all or a part of the distance between the office and her residence upon completion of overtime work.

In claiming reimbursement for taxicab fares totaling $8.60 incurred on Saturday, January 14, and Sunday, January 15, 1978, Ms. Goodman states that the express bus by which she normally commutes from work on weekdays, and which delivers her to a stop one block from her residence, does not run on weekends. She explains that she took a taxicab from work rather than traveling by two non-express buses to avoid the five-block walk from the bus stop to her home. Ms. Gaskins claims reimbursement for taxicab fare of $9 plus a tip of $1 for Saturday, January 7, 1978, and for fares of $7 plus tips of $1 each for January 14 and 15, 1978, for transportation between her office and residence. Although she offers no explanation for the $2 difference between the fares claimed, Ms. Gaskins explains that on weekdays she takes a train to a bus stop and waits 40 minutes to catch a bus that lets her off four blocks from her residence. On weekends the connecting bus comes every hour and 15 minutes. On weekdays, Ms. LaRoche takes a bus to the end of the bus line and travels by carpool from there to her residence. Ms. LaRoche claims taxicab fares of $2.70 for each of seven trips from the end of the bus line to her residence on August 19, 20, 21, and 22, 1976, and on January 7, 14, and 15, 1978. Each of the three claimants states that the area in which she lives is unsafe and each claims to have taken a taxicab for reasons of personal safety.

The certifying officer disallowed the claims, having determined that the circumstances of transportation did not meet the conditions of entitlement as set forth at FTR para. 1–2.3e, which provides as follows:

> e. *Between residence and office in cases of necessity.* Reimbursement for the usual taxicab fares paid by an employee for travel between office and home may be authorized or approved incident to the conduct of official business at an employee's designated post of duty when the employee is dependent on public transportation for such travel incident to officially ordered work outside of regular working hours and when the travel is during hours of infrequently scheduled public transportation or darkness. Agencies are expected to establish stringent administrative controls at sufficiently high levels which ensure that reimbursements are authorized only when justifiable and when all circumstances set forth herein are met.

With respect to Ms. Goodman's and Ms. Gaskins' claims, the certifying officer states that she is unconvinced that the justifications offered demonstrate that public transportation was other than inconvenient. Ms. LaRoche's claim was disallowed since her transportation by taxicab was over a segment of the journey for which public transportation would not have been available in the course of her normal weekday commuting.

The record indicates a difference of opinion within ACTION regarding the proper interpretation of FTR para. 1–2.3e. The submission is accompanied by a letter dated May 11, 1978, from the Deputy Director, Office of Administration and Finance, characterizing the certifying officer's disallowance of the claims as evidencing an overly literal construction of the regulation to preclude payment of taxicab fares.

The authority of FTR para. 1–2.3e to pay taxicab fares is a limited exception to the well-established rule that an employee must bear the cost of commuting between his residence and official duty station. His personal responsibility extends to all commuting between home and office even though the total cost of such transportation may be increased by the requirement to perform additional work outside regular duty hours. Thus, in *Matter of Richard E. Bollinger and Adam E. Muckenfuss*, B–189061, March 15, 1978, and *Matter of George F. Clark*, B–190071, May 1, 1978, we held that the claimants could not be reimbursed mileage for commuting between their homes and their regular places of duty to perform additional work on nonworkdays or after regular working hours.

Paragraph 1–2.3e was not intended to authorize payment of taxicab fares where use of public transportation is merely inconvenient. Most any employee who finds it necessary to commute to or from work on other than his regular schedule is subjected to a degree of inconvenience that he does not normally encounter. For an employee who regularly uses public transportation, the most common form of inconvenience is a variation in bus or train schedules. The fluctuation in frequency of public transportation service that occurs in response to rush-hour commuting demands is in itself no more than inconvenience and, in the context of the phrase, "infrequently scheduled public transportation," the requirement of infrequency is not satisfied by a mere showing that public transportation is not as readily available as at the height of rush hour. The use of taxicabs based on infrequency of scheduled public transportation could be based on factors such as an unusual risk of harm to the employee, and unreasonable and lengthy delays because of curtailment of service.

As drafted, the regulation is directed specifically at the transportation situation of an employee who is required to stay late to perform overtime work after his regular duty hours. The term "hours of darkness" contemplates the situation in which an employee is faced with the necessity to use public transportation during late evening hours when few people are using public transportation. If literally construed, the regulation would permit payment of the taxicab fare of an employee whose regular workday ends at 4:30 p.m. and who, in the winter months of early sunset, works overtime until 5:30 p.m. Reimbursement of taxicab fares clearly was not contemplated under such circumstances. Absent unusual circumstances, we consider it beyond the authority of agencies under FTR para. 1–2.3e to reimburse an employee's taxicab fare for transportation on weekdays during those early evening hours when much of the employed population is commuting from work.

We do not intend to suggest that taxicab fares may not be paid for commuting in the early evening hours of weekend days in connection with overtime work. We stress merely that the fact that such commuting may occur on weekends after sunset in the winter months normally is not itself a sufficient basis to authorize reimbursement under para. 1–2.3e. The fact that, in some areas, transportation is curtailed on Saturdays or Sundays is certainly a factor for consideration in determining whether to authorize taxicab fares.

Because of the variation of local conditions it is not possible for our Office, by decision, to state other than general concepts, such as set forth above, for the operation of the regulation. The regulation by its terms cautions agencies to establish stringent administrative controls in exercising their responsibilities thereunder. Determinations by agencies under it will not be questioned by this Office unless clearly outside the scope of the regulations as interpreted in this decision.

The submitted cases present situations on which reasonable persons could disagree as to the application of the regulation. With the exception of Ms. LaRoche's claim for taxicab fares for 2 days in August of 1976 the three claimants' use of taxicabs occurred after hours of darkness on weekend days, but during early evening hours, corresponding to the times they commute home from work on weekdays; i.e., 5 :30 p.m. The claimants state that they live in unsafe areas and took the taxicabs for personal safety. Further, there was a curtailment of transportation on the days in question.

Ms. LaRoche's claim is for taxicab fares only from the end of the bus line to her residence. From Monday through Friday she normally commutes this distance by carpool which, understandably, does not operate other than on the carpool members' usual commuting schedule. Apparently there is no public transportation available for this segment of the trip and it is for this reason that the certifying officer concluded that Ms. LaRoche was not dependent on public transportation for the travel for which she claims reimbursement. The certifying officer's determination comports with the specific language of FTR para. 1–2.3e. However, the purpose of the regulations was to provide for the transportation at Government expense of employees who, by reason of overtime work requirements, cannot as a practical matter commute to and from work other than by taxicab. An employee who does not own a car, who has no public transportation available to her and who commutes on her regular workdays as a carpool rider is in as untenable a transportation posture with respect to overtime work requirements as any employee who normally rides a bus not scheduled to run at the time he finishes work. We believe that the taxicab fares of such individuals may be paid under FTR para. 1–2.3e where clearly warranted.

In the circumstances, if after administrative review it is concluded that approval of the claims is proper under the regulation as interpreted in this decision, they may be certified for payment.

[B-192805]

Fees—License, Permit, etc. Fees—State—Federal Agency Liability

Section 404(t), Federal Water Pollution Control Act, as amended, requires Federal agencies to comply with State substantive or procedural requirements governing discharge in navigable waters of dredged material to same extent as "any person." Section 67, Pub. L. No. 95–217. Federal agencies must get permits if required by State for activity in question, whether or not State has taken over from United States administration of program for issuance of dredging permits. In present case, however, Wisconsin permit requirement does not pertain to dredging activities. Therefore, section 404(t) does not apply and permit fee may not be paid.

In the matter of Payment of State permit fee by Federal agency under section 404(t), Federal Water Pollution Control Act, January 4, 1979:

This is in response to a request for an advance decision from an authorized certifying officer of the Forest Service, United States Department of Agriculture (Forest Service), regarding payment of a $75 fee to the Wisconsin Department of Natural Resources (DNR) for the processing of a permit under Wis. Stat. Ann. §§ 30.28, 31.29 (*Supp* 1978, West). DNR contends that it is empowered to collect a permit fee from the Forest Service under the authority of § 404(t) of the Federal Water Pollution Control Act (WPCA), 33 U.S.C.A. § 1344(t), as added by § 67(b) of the Clean Water Act of 1977, Pub. L. No. 95–217, 91 Stat. 1566, 1606. For the reasons set forth below, we find that, without a clearer basis to conclude that a private person engaging in the same activity planned by the Forest Service would be subject to a State requirement governing the discharge of dredged or fill material, the permit fee may not be paid.

The Forest Service plans to construct an impoundment to create a wildlife flowage in the Chequamegon National Forest (Chequamegon) on the East Fork feeder to Lynch Creek in Sawyer County, Wisconsin. This construction will create a wetland where none previously existed. As a result of this construction, incidental discharges of dredged and fill material may flow into Lynch Creek.

Section 404(t), added by the 1977 Amendments, is the final portion of the section of the WPCA dealing with the discharges of dredged and fill material into navigable waters. It provides:

Nothing in this section shall preclude or deny the right of any State or interstate agency to control the discharge of dredged or fill material in any portion of the navigable waters within the jurisdiction of such State, including any activity of any Federal agency, and each such agency shall comply with such State or interstate requirements both substantive and procedural to control the discharge of dredged or fill material to the same extent that any person is subject to such requirements. This section shall not be construed as affecting or impairing the authority of the Secretary [of the Army] to maintain navigation.

Section 404(t) was enacted in response to the decisions in *Environmental Protection Agency* v. *California,* 426 U.S. 200 (1976) and *Minnesota* v. *Hoffman,* 543 F. 2d 1198 (8th Cir. 1976); *cert. denied* 430 U.S. 977 (1977). S. Rep. No. 95–370, 67–68 (1978). In *Environmental Protection Agency* v. *California, supra,* the issue arose under the 1972 Amendments to the WPCA. Under the law, a State which qualified could assume from the Federal Government the role of regulating the discharge of pollutants (other than dredged or fill material) into navigable waters. Pub. L. No. 92–500, 86 Stat. 880. The question in *EPA* was whether Federal installations discharging water pollutants into navigable waters in a State with a federally approved program were required to secure permits from the State.

Section 313 of the WPCA (33 U.S.C. 1323) then provided that Federal installations "shall comply with Federal, State, interstate, and local requirements respecting control and abatement of pollution to the same extent that any person is subject to such requirements * * *." Pub. L. No. 92–500, 86 Stat. 875. The Court, finding no clear congressional mandate, concluded that the quoted language, while it required Federal installations to comply with State substantive requirements, did not require them to obtain State permits.

Minnesota v. *Hoffman, supra,* involved the discharge into navigable waters by the Corps of Engineers of dredged material. Discharge of dredge spoil was specifically excepted from the system of pollution discharge regulation discussed in *Environmental Protection Agency, supra,* under which a State could assume the Federal regulatory role. The 1972 version of section 404 required that a permit be secured from the Corps of Engineers by anyone seeking to discharge dredged spoil into navigable waters. The state of Minnesota argued that the Corps was required by section 313 of the 1972 version of the act, quoted in part above, to comply with State water quality control standards with respect to the Corps' own dredging operations in State navigable waters.

Rejecting this contention, and relying in part on *Environmental Protection Agency, supra,* the Court of Appeals stated that it found no "clear Congressional mandate" in the 1972 version of section 404 that the dredging operations of the Corps be subject to State control. Rather, the Court found the overriding congressional intent in the 1972 Amendments to be that these dredging activities necessary for the maintenance of commerce not be "unreasonably impeded." 543 F. 2d at 1206. The Court therefore held that Minnesota's substantive water pollution standards were not aplicable to the Corps' dredging activities.

The 1977 Amendments to the WPCA, which, as discussed above, were intended to overcome the effect of these two decisions, changed the quoted language of the 1972 version of section 313 to require that Federal officers, agents, and employees—

shall be subject to, and comply with, all Federal, State, interstate, and local requirements, administrative authority, and process and sanctions respecting the control and abatement of water pollution in the same manner, and to the same extent as any nongovernmental entity * * *. Section 61(a). Pub. L. No. 95–217, 33 U.S.C. 1344(a).

As amended by the 1977 Amendments, section 313 goes on to say, more specifically, that—

The preceding sentence shall apply (A) to any requirement whether substantive or procedural (including any recordkeeping or reporting requirement, any requirement respecting permits and any other requirement, whatsoever) * * *.

In addition, the 1977 Amendments added section 404(t). Since the *Minnesota* decision held that section 313 did not apply to the Corps' own dredging activities, the Congress added subsection (t) to section 404, the section of the act dealing specifically with dredging activities and permits. While section 404(t) does not (as does section 313, as amended) specifically mention permit requirements as among the requirements with which Federal facilities must comply, it qualifies the word "requirements" with the same phrase, "substantive and procedural," which is said in section 313 to include "requirements respecting permits."

The purpose of the 1977 Amendment to section 404 was—

to insure that the dredge and fill activities of the U.S. Army Corps of Engineers are carried out in compliance with State, local, or interstate substantive or procedural requirements. S. Rep. No. 95–370, *supra*, 67.

Although the legislative history speaks in terms of activities of the Corps (presumably because it was the Corps' activities which were at issue in *Minnesota* and also because most of the Federal dredge and fill operations in navigable waters are conducted by the Corps), section 404(t) says that activities of all Federal agencies are covered.

A separate amendment to section 404 by the 1977 Amendments establishes a program, analogous to that in section 402 for other forms of pollutants, whereby the States can, upon qualifying, assume responsibility from the Corps for issuance of dredge and fill permits in their own navigable waters. Wisconsin has not done so. 33 U.S.C. 1342.

In an opinion recommending that this matter be submitted to our Office, counsel for the Department of Agriculture concedes that, if the State of Wisconsin had a federally approved program whereby it had assumed responsibility for issuance of permits for dredging activities in navigable waters, the Forest Service would have had to secure such a permit. (This is not because the Forest Service is discharging dredged spoil—it is, rather, building an impoundment—but by virtue of section 404(f)(2), 33 U.S.C. 1344(f)(2), which says that a federally approved State program must cover discharges of dredged or fill material which are incidental to an activity either introducing a new use of navigable waters, or impairing the reach, circulation, or flow of such waters.)

The mandate of section 404(t) that Federal agencies comply with State requirements does not depend on whether the State has assumed the Corps' regulatory responsibility. Federal facilities are unconditionally required by section 404(t) to obtain State permits, if the State has a requirement to control discharge of dredged or filled material. (See in this connection section 510 of the Act, 33 U.S.C. § 1370, which says that except as expressly provided, the FWPCA does not prevent the States from adopting or enforcing pollution control standards more stringent than the Federal standards under the Act and does not impair or affect any right or jurisdiction of the States with respect to their waters.)

Accordingly, if the State of Wisconsin had a law governing dredging and filling which would require anyone doing what the Forest Service proposes to get a permit, the Forest Service would also be required to get a permit. In this case, however, counsel for the Forest Service apparently denies that such a State requirement exists:

> The present wording of the Wisconsin statutes is aimed at the effect of the impoundment, and not at the "discharge" effect. The fee is for the statutory purpose of reviewing and processing the transformation of the stream from basically public recreational use (boating) to a wildlife purpose (wetland creation). The Wisconsin statute creating the fee requirement is not essentially relevant to the congressional direction in section 404(t), and the demand [for a permit] is not supported by it.

We understand the position of the Forest Service to be that if the State had a program regulating dredging and filling activities, and requiring a permit for those engaging in such activities, the Forest Service would be required to obtain such a permit, whether the State program was federally approved or based solely on State law. However, the Forest Service asserts that Wisconsin has neither a federally approved program nor a State program which covers the kind of incidental discharge of dredge or filled material taking place here.

The State assessment of the fee in question is based on sections 30.28 and 31.39, Wisconsin Statutes. Section 31.39 gives the State authority to charge a fee for carrying out its duties under sections 31.02 to 31.38. Those sections deal generally with State regulation of dams and bridges affecting navigable waters. Those seeking to construct or operate dams on navigable waters must get State permits. Sections 31.04, .05, .07. But, among the permit requirements in chapter 31, we find no explicit reference to control of the discharge of dredged or fill material.

Similarly, section 30.28 of the Wisconsin Statutes gives the State authority to charge a fee for carrying out its duties under sections

30.10 to 30.37. None of those sections clearly requires a State permit for the discharge of dredged spoil. Section 30.12 requires a permit for the deposit of material upon the bed of any navigable water "where no bulkhead [*i.e.*, shore] line has been established" or beyond a bulkhead line. But it seems reasonably clear that section 30.12 is not a water pollution control requirement, which is what section 404(t) of the WPCA contemplates, but a requirement intended to preserve navigability.

While ordinarily we do not question the interpretation by a State of its own laws, in this case the Forest Service has raised what appears, on the present record, to be a valid objection to the State's claim that its law is, by virtue of section 404(t), applicable to the Forest Service's planned construction. Accordingly, the fee may not be paid.

[B-188693]

Appointments—Informal, Irregular, etc.—Voidable *v.* Void

Civil Service Commission (CSC) directed cancellation of employee's temporary appointment at GS-6 level because of violation of CSC requirements. Since employee had basic qualification for appointment and appointment was not contrary to law it was voidable only and corrective action as ordered by CSC is prospective only. Employee is entitled to all benefits of position to which appointed until separated or transferred. Modified in part by 58 Comp. Gen. 734.

In the matter of Cherrold W. Seabrook—Compensation for period of improper appointment, January 5, 1979:

This action involves a request for a decision by Mr. Preston David, Executive Director, Equal Employment Opportunity Commission (EEOC), regarding the entitlement to compensation of an employee, Ms. Cherrold Williams Seabrook, during a period of employment under an improper appointment.

As a result of a personnel management evaluation conducted in March 1976, the Civil Service Commission (CSC) found that violations of Civil Service restrictions had occurred in the temporary appointment of Ms. Seabrook to the position of Secretary (Typing), GS-318-6, and the CSC ordered the appointment terminated. The period of the improper appointment was August 4, 1974, to May 8, 1976. Ms. Seabrook was converted to reinstatement under merit staffing to the position of Equal Employment Technician, GS-301-5, on May 9, 1976. Additionally, it is noted that Ms. Seabrook was initially appointed in EEOC without a break in service from the Office of Minority Business Enterprise (OMBE), where she was serving under a career appointment as a Clerk-Stenographer, GS-312-5.

By virtue of the temporary status of the employee with EEOC during the period involved, decision is requested as to whether the employee is entitled to pay at the GS–6/2 level for the time worked under the improper appointment. EEOC advises that Ms. Seabrook performed the duties of the GS–6 position during the period involved in a highly satisfactory manner and had no knowledge of any improprieties in her appointment.

In the alternative, EEOC suggests that, if we determine that any erroneous payments of pay were made then a waiver of the erroneous payment of compensation under 5 U.S.C. 5584 would be for application. The agency states that there is no evidence of fraud, misrepresentation, fault or lack of good faith on the part of the employee in the improper appointment.

Ms. Seabrook qualified for appointment to a secretarial position, but upon examination of the appointment the Civil Service Commission determined that she was not qualified for appointment at the GS–6 level and ordered her appointment terminated. Failure to conform to the Civil Service Commission regulation did not make the appointment void *ab initio* but merely voidable. 37 Comp. Gen. 483 (1958). Until action is taken to correct a voidable appointment, the employee holds the position and is entitled to all the benefits thereof. Action taken to correct the appointment or place the employee in a position which complies with the applicable regulations is prospective only.

For the reasons stated, no overpayment is involved in this case and the employee is entitled to service credit for the time spent in the grade GS–6 position.

[B–189782]

Compensation—Wage Board Employees—Prevailing Rate Employees—Entitlement to Negotiate Wages

Section 704(b)(B) of Pub. L. No. 95–454, Civil Service Reform Act of 1978, allows prevailing rate employees whose labor-management contract provisions are covered by section 9(b) of Pub. L. No. 92–392 to negotiate these contract provisions without regard to the restrictions in 5 U.S.C. 5544. Accordingly, decisions 57 Comp. Gen. 259 (1978) and 57 *id.* 575 are overruled insofar as they invalidated certain contract provisions concerning overtime for section 9(b) employees. Likewise, B–191520, June 6, 1978, and 56 Comp. Gen. 360 (1977) are overruled to the same extent.

In the matter of Department of the Interior—Labor-Management Wage Agreements Negotiated under Section 9(b) of Pub. L. No. 92–392—Effect of Civil Service Reform Act of 1978, January 5, 1979:

Section 704 of the Civil Service Reform Act of 1978, Pub. L. No. 95–454, October 13, 1978, 92 Stat. 1218, 5 U.S. Code 5343 note, provides special authority for the continued negotiation of wages and related matters by those employees, principally in the Department of Interior and the Department of Energy, who have traditionally negotiated such matters and who are covered by the savings clauses of section 9(b) of Pub. L. No. 92–392, August 19, 1972. The purpose of this decision is to determine the effect of Section 704 on our decisions B–189782, February 3, 1978, 57 Comp. Gen. 259, and B–191520, June 6, 1978.

Prior to the enactment of Section 704, the Honorable Richard R. Hite, Deputy Assistant Secretary of the Department of the Interior, by letter of August 28, 1978, requested a clarification of decision B–189782, June 23, 1978 (57 Comp. Gen. 575), which modified the implementation of our February 3 decision (57 Comp. Gen. 259). Since the Deputy Assistant Secretary's request involves a labor-management relations matter, interested parties were informed of his submission and comments were received from James M. Peirce, President, National Federation of Federal Employees, and from Charles H. Pillard, President, International Brotherhood of Electrical Workers, who had also requested a decision on the matter.

BACKGROUND

In our February 3 decision we stated that, although section 9(b) of Pub. L. No. 92–392, August 19, 1972, 5 U.S.C. § 5343 note, governing prevailing rate employees, exempts the wage-setting provisions of certain bargaining agreements from the operation of that law, section 9(b) does not exempt agreement provisions from the operation of other laws or provide independent authorization for agreement provisions requiring expenditure of appropriated funds not authorized by any other law. Accordingly, certain negotiated labor-management provisions relating to overtime pay which had been in effect for many years were held to be invalid.

We noted in that decision that the contract provisions in question had been negotiated over a long period and that our decision was the first one stating they were illegal. Therefore, to cushion the impact of our decision, we authorized the Department of the Interior to delay its implementation of the decision and we suggested that the Bureau of Reclamation might wish to request legislation permitting the continued negotiation of the contract provisions in question.

On June 23, 1978, in B–189782 (57 Comp. Gen. 575), we modified our February 3 decision, postponing the date of its implementation by authorizing the Department of the Interior to continue to negotiate or to renegotiate the contract provisions in question until the end of the Second Session of the 96th Congress. If Congress had taken no action by that time, the February 3 decision was to become fully effective as to all agreements on that date.

The Comptroller General's authority to render advance decisions to heads of agencies and to certifying and disbursing officers on matters involving appropriated funds is found in 31 U.S.C. §§ 74 and 82d. It is clear that under Title VII of the Civil Service Reform Act, 92 Stat. 1191, the Comptroller General may not overrule a specific arbitration award or a decision of the Federal Labor Relations Authority made thereon. However, with those exceptions, the Comptroller General retains the authority to render decisions on the legality of expenditures of appropriated funds. Accordingly, this Office has the jurisdiction to issue a decision to the Deputy Assistant Secretary.

OPINION

The Civil Service Reform Act of 1978 (5 U.S.C. 1101 note) specifically addresses the legality of negotiated contract provisions arrived at under section 9(b) of Pub. L. No. 92–392. Section 704 of the Civil Service Reform Act of 1978 states:

Sec. 704. (a) Those terms and conditions of employment and other employment benefits with respect to Government prevailing rate employees to whom section 9(b) of Public Law 92–392 applies which were the subject of negotiation in accordance with prevailing rates and practices prior to August 19, 1972, shall be negotiated on and after the date of the enactment of this Act in accordance with the provisions of section 9(b) of Public Law 92–392 without regard to any provision of chapter 71 of title 5, United States Code (as amended by this title), to the extent that any such provision is inconsistent with this paragraph.

(b) The pay and pay practices relating to employees referred to in paragraph (1) of this subsection shall be negotiated in accordance with prevailing rates and pay practices without regard to any provision of—

(A) chapter 71 of title 5 United States Code (as amended by this title), to the extent that any such provision is inconsistent with this paragraph;

(B) subchapter IV of chapter 53 and subchapter V of chapter 55 of title 5, United States Code; or

(C) any rule, regulation, decision or order relating to rates of pay or pay practices under subchapter IV of chapter 53 or subchapter V of chapter 55 of title 5, United States Code.

The following statement in the Conference Report on the Civil Service Reform Act of 1978 describes the purpose of Section 704:

CERTAIN COLLECTIVE BARGAINING AGREEMENTS

Section 704(d) of the House bill provides certain savings clauses for employees principally in agencies under the Department of the Interior and the Department of Energy who have traditionally negotiated contracts in accordance with prevailing rates in the private sector of the economy and who were subject to the savings clauses prescribed in section 9(b) of Public Law 92–392, enacted August 19, 1972.

The Senate contains no comparable provision.

The conference report adopts the House provision with an amendment.

As revised, section 704(d) overrules the decision of the Comptroller General in cases number B–L89782 (sic) (Feb. 3, 1978) and B–L9L520 (sic) (June 6, 1978), relating to certain negotiated contracts applicable to employees under the Department of the Interior and the Department of Energy. This section also provides specific statutory authorization for the negotiation of wages, terms and conditions of employment and other employment benefits traditionally negotiated by these employees in accordance with prevailing practices in the private sector of the economy.

Section 704(d)(1) authorizes and requires the agencies to negotiate on any terms and conditions of employment which were the subject of negotiations prior to August 19, 1972, the date of enactment of Public Law 92-392. Section 704(d)(1) may not be construed to nullify, curtail, or otherwise impair the right or duty of any party to negotiate for the renewal, extension, modification, or improvements of benefits negotiated.

Section 704(d)(2) requires the negotiation of pay and pay practices in accordance with prevailing pay and pay practices without regard to chapter 71 (as amended by this conference report), subchapter IV of chapter 53, or subchapter V of chapter 55, of title 5, United States Code, in accordance with prevailing practices in the industry. Conference Report No. 95-1272, 95th Cong., 2d Sess. 159 (1978).

By virtue of section 704(b)(B), prevailing rate employees whose labor-management contract provisions are covered by section 9(b) of Pub. L. No. 92-392, may negotiate the contract provisions without regard to subchapter V of chapter 55, title 5, United States Code. Subchapter V contains 5 U.S.C. § 5544, pertaining to overtime pay for prevailing rate employees, which provision was the subject of our February 3 decision. Accordingly, our decision of February 3, 1978, is overruled insofar as it invalidated certain overtime contract provisions of employees who negotiate their wages pursuant to section 9(b) of Pub. L. No. 92-392.

Our decision B-191520, June 6, 1978, relied in part on the rationale in the February 3 decision and held invalid certain other contract provisions concerning overtime pay for prevailing rate employees. The June 6 decision likewise is overruled insofar as it invalidated the contract provisions of employees who negotiate their wages pursuant to section 9(b) of Pub. L. No. 92-392. The arbitration award overruled and the contract provisions held invalid in our June 6 decision may be reinstated insofar as the applicable contract provisions were covered by section 9(b) of Pub. L. No. 92-392. Our prior decision in 56 Comp. Gen. 360 (1977) is also overruled insofar as it pertains to overtime provisions negotiated under section 9(b).

The Deputy Assistant Secretary has also asked many other questions as to what contract provisions may or may not be negotiated under the stay order contained in our earlier decision of June 23, 1978. Our stay order was intended to preserve the status quo for employees covered by section 9(b) until the Congress had had a chance to consider this matter. Since the Congress, by passing Section 704, has acted on the matter, our stay order will no longer be necessary. Accordingly, the Deputy Assistant Secretary's questions must now be viewed in light of the recently passed Civil Service Reform Act of 1978. In view of the date the submission, the many difficult issues raised by the Act have not been addressed by the interested parties. Moreover, the questions asked are very broad and we are not acquainted with the factual background essential for a thoroughly considered decision. Therefore, we shall not render a decision on these issues until a request has been made by an appropriate party concerning the specific facts involved and the matter has been fully briefed by all those interested.

[B-191737]

Equal Employment Opportunity—Spanish-Speaking Program—Establishment

The Spanish-Speaking Program was establshed as a component of the Federal Equal Employment Opportunity Program by presidential proclamation on November 5, 1970. Under 42 U.S.C. 2000e–16(b), the Civil Service Commission promulgated Federal Personnel Manual letter 713–18, January 23, 1973, making the Spanish-Speaking Program a special emphasis area within the Federal EEO program. Accordingly, the Bureau of Mines, within the Department of Interior, is authorized to institute a Spanish-Speaking EEO program.

Appropriations—Availability—Training—Equal Employment Opportunity Programs

In the absence of specific authority in statute or regulations, appropriated funds may not be expended to procure entertainment for Federal employees. Hence agencies without specific authority may not procure entertainment such as live ethnic music and artistic presentations, characterize it as training and present it in connection with EEO programs. We will not question past agency characterizations of EEO program entertainment as training; however, all future entertainment expenses whether or not in connection with EEO programs will not be allowed.

Agents—Government—Government Liability for Acts Beyond Authority—Contract Execution

Department of Interior questions the legality of appropriated fund expenditure by Bureau of Mines, a subordinate agency, where EEO officer, who lacked delegated procurement authority, procured services of contractors and payment was eventually made for services rendered. Agreements violated the prohibition against the provision of entertainment from appropriated funds and included payments for premiums on insurance coverage of art objects exhibited incident to National Hispanic Heritage Week, contrary to the longstanding policy of Government to assume its own risks of loss and not to purchase commercial insurance. The employee has been advised of the limits of his authority. In view of the special facts and circumstances involved, we believe no useful purpose will be served by taking exceptions to these payments.

In the matter of Bureau of Mines—Live Entertainment for National Hispanic Heritage Week, January 5, 1979:

This action involves a request from Mr. Larry E. Meierotto, Deputy Assistant Secretary, United States Department of Interior, for a ruling on the legality of two vouchers paid by the Bureau of Mines, a subordinate agency of the Department. The vouchers are BV # 8681 for insurance premiums in the amount of $109.50 in favor of L. E. Harris Agency, Inc., and BV # 8687 for theatrical performance fees in the amount of $275 in favor of Sonia Castel.

The facts and circumstances surrounding these payments are as follows. Pursuant to a Joint Resolution approved by Congress on September 17, 1968, 36 U.S.C. § 169f (1976), the President of the United States issued Proclamation 4516, on August 31, 1977, 3 CFR 41 (1978), proclaiming the week beginning September 11, 1977, as National Hispanic Heritage Week. The Secretary of the Interior promulgated a memorandum dated August 31 1977, subject: "Hispanic Heritage Week," implementing the Presidential Proclamation by announcing a Department Program in honor of Hispanic Week.

In previous years the Bureau of Mines co-sponsored activities for this week with the Department and its other sub-agencies. In 1977, however, responding to criticism that the Bureau's Spanish Speaking Program was not sufficiently visible, Mr. Ronald Shelton, Equal Employment Opportunity Officer for the Bureau, arranged with the Equal Employment Opportunity Commission (EEOC) to co-sponsor a joint program on a cost sharing basis at Columbia Plaza, Washington, D.C., where major elements of both agencies are located. Mr. Shelton explained his actions as follows:

> The Bureau's cultural performances for observance of National Hispanic Heritage Week were arranged through the District of Columbia Department of Recreation. Ms. Sonia Castel, Department of Recreation, arranges such cultural events for the entire D.C. area. However, because she acts as a cultural clearinghouse that is a public service, the billing cannot be handled through the DC Dept. of Recreation. Therefore, she uses Stage Directions to handle the business end of all her arrangements. Stage Directions or Ms. Castel make no profits from their activities.

Ms. Castel referred them to, and worked with, a non-profit organization called "Stage Directions" which develops such programs on a fee basis. Negotiations followed which led to Mr. Shelton's requisition through Stage Directions for performers to present traditional music while showing the relevance of the music to the Hispanic culture and to coordinate an exhibition of art objects created by Hispanic artists. Through Ms. Castel, Mr. Shelton requisitioned insurance coverage from the L. E. Harris Agency, Inc., on the art objects included in the exhibition.

Pursuant to Part 205 of the Bureau of Mines Manual, Mr. Shelton is delegated requisitioning authority; however, he does not have procurement authority. Moreover, he entered into the agreements described above without the concurrence of the Bureau of Mines Contracting Officer.

We are advised that the agreements were duly performed in accordance with their terms and conditions. Ms. Castel, who continued to assist Mr. Shelton in arranging the program, paid Stage Directions $275 on October 3, 1977, the share of the contract price attributable to the Bureau of Mines. She explained her action to the Bureau of Mines as follows:

> I was professionally embarrassed by your agency's delay in payment; I personally paid the amount of two-hundred-seventy-five dollars ($275) to Stage

Directions for your share of your joint program with EEOC. I made this payment because it was due and owing for services rendered and needed to be paid.

Ms. Castel had also personally deposited $100 with the L. E. Harris Agency, Inc., for insurance premiums to provide coverage for the art objects. She subsequently billed the Bureau of Mines for the Stage Directions payment and also advised that her deposit would not be returned until the insurance agency received payment.

The Bureau of Mines finally paid the two vouchers on December 21, 1977. However, the Department of Interior has questioned the legality of the payments. The specific issues raised by the Department of Interior are as follows:

1. Since the various laws, acts, publications, etc., concerning the Bureau of Mines Equal Employment Opportunity funding are so general, particularly concerning the Spanish-Speaking Program, is the Spanish-Speaking Program to be considered as an integral part of the Bureau's Equal Employment Opportunity Program?

2. If your answer to question 1 above is affirmative, are the types of entertainment and exhibit expenses we paid in the enclosed vouchers proper for the Spanish-Speaking Program?

3. Since Mr. Shelton did not have procurement authority, is the legality of these contracts and subsequent payments in question?

AUTHORITY FOR THE SPANISH SPEAKING PROGRAM

The first question concerns whether the Bureau of Mines may legally fund the Spanish Speaking Program under its Equal Employment Opportunity Program. By virtue of the authority contained in 5 U.S.C. § 1301 *et. seq.*, 3301, 3302 and 7301, governing the appointment, examination, selection and regulation of conduct of Federal employees, the President announced on November 5, 1970, the initiation of a 16 point program to assist Spanish-Speaking American citizens to obtain employment in the Federal Service and thereby assure full application of the Federal Service EEOC program to this group.

Pursuant to the authority contained in 42 U.S.C. § 2000e–16(b), to promulgate regulations covering the Federal Service Equal Employment Opportunity Program, the Civil Service Commission implemented the President's 16 point program through the issuance of Federal Personnel Manual Letter No. 713–18, dated January 23, 1973, Subject: "Equal Employment Opportunity—Implementing the Spanish-Speaking Program." The purpose of this letter was to specifically advise Federal officials that the Spanish-Speaking minority is included in the disadvantaged minority group that the EEO program is designed to assist. In addition, the FPM letter provides guidance for use by agency officials in developing agency EEO affirmative action measures to accommodate the special needs of the Spanish-Speaking employees and prospective employees. Finally the letter cautions that the Sixteen Point Program is not to be viewed as a separate equal employment opportunity program, but as a special emphasis effort within the context of a total EEO program.

In accordance with our general practices we solicited the views of the Civil Service Commission on this issue. The Commission's General Counsel has formally advised us that the Spanish-Speaking Program has been incorporated into the Federal Service Equal Employment Opportunity Program since 1970. In view of the above and our own analysis of the law, we are of the opinion that the Bureau of Mines Spanish-Speaking Program is a legitimate component of that agency's EEO Program.

LEGALITY OF ETHNIC MUSIC AND EXHIBIT PROGRAM

Next, Interior questions whether the Bureau of Mines may have exceeded its legal authority by the expenditure of appropriated funds for the "entertainment and exhibit" programs. At the outset, we note that it is a general principle of law that funds appropriated for Government departments and agencies may not be used for entertaining individuals except as specifically authorized by law. 47 Comp. Gen. 657 (1968) ; 43 *id.* 305 (1963). Entertainment has been defined as a source or means of amusement, a diverting performance, especially a public performance, as a concert, drama or the like. *People* v. *Klaw*, 106 N.Y.S. 341, 351 (1907). Also, entertainment denotes that which serves for amusement and amusement is defined as a pleasurable occupation of the senses, or that which furnishes it, as dancing, sports, or music. *Young* v. *Board of Trustees of Broadwater County High School*, 4 P. 2d 725, 726 (1931). Thus, if Interior has properly characterized these expenditures as entertainment, there would be no authority to expend appropriated funds.

The Bureau of Mines Program for Hispanic Week consisted, according to the record before us, of several different elements. At 2:30 p.m. on Wednesday, September 14, 1977, there was a presentation made in the Columbia Plaza cafeteria which was available to all employees. Following introductions by the Directors of the Equal Employment Opportunity offices of EEOC and the Bureau of Mines, and opening remarks by the chairperson of the EEOC, Mr. Patrick Apodaca, Associate Counsel to the President, addressed the gathering. Thereafter there was a 1 hour lecture-demonstration of South American folk music by two musicians from Argentina. According to the materials presented us,

their program has two aims; first, to make American audiences of all ethnic backgrounds aware of the richness and variety of Argentina's musical contribution to the world; and second, to explain and to enlighten their audience on the study of folk music. Their explanations of the geographic and demographic factors which contribute to each folk form is both educational and famous. * * *

At the end of these proceedings, there was a reception honoring Mr. Apodaca. We assume that any refreshments served were paid from private funds or from appropriations specifically available for entertainment purposes. The use of Federal funds not specifically available for this purpose would, of course, be unauthorized.

On Friday, September 16, there were two separate programs offered. At noon, in the Plaza area, 12 musicians and a guest singer from Puerto Rico provided a 2-hour concert of traditional and popular music typical to various Caribbean and Latin American countries. We are advised that the different ethnic contributions (Spanish, European, African and Native American) to the music of Latin America were emphasized. In addition, the group performed some of their own original music. This group performed outdoors so that the employees were able to participate in this program during their lunch hour. We are advised that "the purpose of this program was to expose the agency employees to the richness of the musical traditions of the majority of Spanish-Americans. For most participants, this was a unique opportunity to expand their awareness of Latin American popular musical tradition."

Later in the afternoon, in one of the rooms in Columbia Plaza, after remarks by Mr. Shelton and the Director of the Bureau of Mines, a slide presentation on Hispanic Americans was given. This activity was not part of Interior's inquiry.

In addition, there was a slide presentation developed by the audio-visual department of EEOC shown continuously in the main lobby. Also there was an Hispanic art and ceramics exhibit by five artists. The exhibit was open for 2 hours a day during Hispanic Week with one artist available each day to discuss his or her work with visitors. The information we were provided stated:

> We hope that this program served to expose many people to the fine arts and in particular to the contributions made to the fine and plastic arts by Spanish-Americans.

As noted above, under our decisions, appropriated funds may not be expended to provide entertainment for employees except when specifically authorized by statute or implementing regulations. See, for example, 43 Comp. Gen. 305, *supra.* When we analyze within the context of our decisions the artistic presentations which were components of the Bureau of Mines Hispanic Week, they seem very similar to the kinds of activities which we have consistently characterized in the past as "entertainment." We recognize that there may be some confusion regarding the kinds of activities which are authorized to commemorate Hispanic Week and similar occasions, or which could be carried out under any agency's EEO program, and that some agencies in the past have expended appropriated funds to provide entertainment characterized as training in connection with EEO programs. While we accept without question past agency characterizations that this entertainment-type activity was EEO training or, at least, an authorized part of its EEO program and we will not take exception to any such past expenditures by the Bureau of Mines or other agencies, we feel that no similar expenditures in the future should be incurred unless made in strict conformance with statute or applicable Civil Service Commission regulations.

UNAUTHORIZED PROCUREMENT ACTION

We note that as part of the overall EEO package procured by Mr. Shelton, there was insurance coverage, in the amount of $300 each for thirteen paintings and three sculptures, for a total of $4,800. It is a longstanding policy of the United States to assume its own risks of loss and not to purchase commercial insurance coverage. 55 Comp. Gen. 1196 (1976); 39 *id.* 145 (1959); and 21 *id.* 928 (1942). Thus we must hold that this insurance coverage should not have been obtained.

While Mr. Shelton as the Bureau of Mines' Equal Employment Opportunity Officer had authority to approve requisitions, he had not been delegated authority to enter into procurement action on behalf of the Government. Notwithstanding this lack of authority, Mr. Shelton entered into a procurement agreement purportedly on behalf of the Bureau of Mines for the ethnic music presentations and for insurance coverage of the art objects.

It is a general principle of law that an agent of the Government must have actual authority in order to bind the United States, and individuals entering into contractual arrangements with the United States are charged with the responsibility of ascertaining the authority of the agent to act for the Government. The contractor must assume the risk if the employee does not have the authority to enter into the contract on behalf of the Government. The contractor's remedy where the employee lacks authority will be against the unauthorized agent, in this case, Mr. Shelton. It is our understanding that Mr. Shelton has been made aware of the extent of his authority.

Thus, not only did Mr. Shelton enter into agreements which involved improper use of appropriated funds, but he had no authority to enter into any kind of agreements on behalf of the United States. Nonetheless, the contracts have been performed and payment made. We have determined not to take exception to payments made in the past by other agencies, and we see no useful purpose in doing so in his case.

[B-191445]

Officers and Employees—Transfers—Relocation Expenses—House Sale—Prior to Official Notice of Transfer

Residence selling expenses in anticipation of transfer from Hawaii may be reimbursed where illness of employee's wife did not permit her to continue to live in Hawaii. There was a compelling reason for the transfer in the Government's interest at the time the expenses were incurred, and travel orders based on this compelling reason were subsequently issued authorizing expenses. Accordingly, there was substantial compliance with requirement that there be an administrative intention to transfer the employee when the real estate expenses are incurred. *James A. Colyer*, B-182840, February 18, 1975, modified.

Officers and Employees—Transfers—Relocation Expenses—House Sale—Actual Residence at Time of Official Transfer Requirement

Entitlement to reimbursement for sale of residence incident to a transfer requires (under para. C14000.1-1 of 2 Joint Travel Regulations and para. 2-6.1 of Federal Travel Regulations) that it be the employee's actual residence when he is first definitely notified of the transfer. There was substantial compliance where illness of the employee's wife required living in an apartment pending notice of a transfer and where the employee had not entirely vacated the house before the transfer notice. Reimbursement for sales expense is allowable but subject to deduction of any previous reimbursement for lease termination expenses.

In the matter of Joseph L. White—Expenses of Sale of Residence in Anticipation of Transfer, January 8, 1979:

This decision responds to a request submitted by John D. Graham, Chief, Accounting and Finance Division, Defense Property Disposal Service, Defense Logistics Agency, Department of Defense, concerning the claim of Mr. Joseph L. White for reimbursement of real estate expenses in the amount of $1,632.95. The matter was forwarded to our Office by the Per Diem, Travel and Transportation Allowance Committee, PDTATAC Control No. 78-11.

The issue is whether Mr. White may be reimbursed for the expenses of selling his house when prior to actual notice of the transfer Mr. White had entered into the contract of sale, had incurred selling expenses, and had moved with his wife into an apartment.

Mr. White, a civilian employee of the Defense Logistics Agency, was transferred to Honolulu, Hawaii, in November 1975. He purchased a house in Honolulu in February 1976. His wife became seriously ill, and Army medical officers at Hickam Air Force Base determined, during March 1976 or shortly thereafter, that the environment in Hawaii was destructive to her health. Mr. White made plans to return to the mainland and entered into a contract for the sale of his residence on May 24, 1976. He received oral notice on July 6, 1976, that he would be transferred to the mainland. He received formal written travel orders changing his permanent duty station to Battle

Creek, Michigan, on July 20, 1976, and, because of his wife's illness, he was released on that date from his commitment to serve 3 years in Hawaii.

Settlement day for closing the sale and transferring ownership of his Honolulu residence was July 23, 1976. However, Mr. White had moved from his house to an apartment in Honolulu on about June 21, 1976. The move was required because of his wife's illness. Living in the apartment was temporary until he could close the sale of his residence in Honolulu and return to the mainland. Although he and his wife lived in the apartment, he did not fully vacate his residence until July 15, 1976. They evidently remained in the apartment until August 12, 1976, when they departed from Hawaii.

The file contains a receipt dated May 7, 1976, showing Mr. White's payment of $550 to a realtor as a portion of his broker's fee or commission evidently for services performed by May 24, 1976, when the buyer signed a sales contract to purchase the residence. The file also includes the sales contract which provided for an additional $700 brokerage fee for services rendered, evidently before May 24, 1976.

The Defense Property Disposal Service disallowed the sales expenses because the contract of sale was signed before the employee was notified of the transfer. An additional reason for the disallowance was that Mr. White had moved into an apartment prior to being notified of his transfer.

By memorandum of February 24, 1978, Headquarters, Defense Logistics Agency, recommended reimbursement to Mr. White for expenses incurred for the sale of his residence in Honolulu. Two reasons are given in support of the recommendation. First, although Mr. White had contracted for the sale of his residence before he received formal notice of his transfer, we held in *James A. Colyer*, B–182840, February 18, 1975, that this circumstance does not disqualify a civilian employee from entitlement to reimbursement. Second, Mr. White apparently satisfied the condition for entitlement in paragraph C14000.1–1, Volume 2 of the Joint Travel Regulations (JTR), that the dwelling must be the actual residence of the employee when he is first definitely informed of the transfer.

We agree that a contract to sell a residence before definite notice of a transfer does not in itself disqualify an employee from reimbursement for relocation expenses incurred in the sale of purchase of a residence. See 48 Comp. Gen. 395 (1968).

However, this decision announced a limitation concerning the time the employee incurs real estate expenses in anticipation of his transfer. It held that reimbursement is authorized only if there in an administrative intention to transfer the employee clearly evident at the time the real estate expenses were incurred. See also 52 Comp. Gen. 8

(1972); 53 *id.* 836 (1974); 54 *id.* 993 (1975); and 57 *id.* 447 (1978). In recent cases, reimbursement has been denied when there was no clear evidence of an administrative intention to transfer the employee at the time the real estate expenses were incurred and the employing agency does not find that the sale or purchase of the residence was incident to the transfer. Further, agencies have broad discretion in deciding whether the sale or purchase was incident to the transfer. *Samuel V. Britt*, B–186763, October 6, 1976; *G. F. McBride*, B–187088, February 3, 1977; *Joan E. Marci*, B–188301, August 16, 1977.

James A. Colyer, supra, conflicts with the decisions discussed above. In *Colyer* it was stated that for long-distance transfers there was no need for a finding that the sale is incident to the transfer and that the only requirement was the employee's occupancy of the residence when there is notice of the transfer, even though the selling expenses were incurred before the employee anticipated a transfer. *Colyer* is, therefore, modified to the extent it is inconsistent with the above cases.

When Mr. White incurred the real estate expenses, there were compelling reasons in the Government's interest for a transfer and these reasons were the basis for subsequently issuing travel orders approving the real estate expenses. Where such a compelling reason leads the employee to believe he will be transferred and he actually is transferred, we have held that there is substantial compliance with the requirement for a clearly evident intention to transfer him. See B–170800, December 22, 1970.

We find that the reasons for the transfer in this case were compelling when military doctors determined that Mrs. White could not continue to live in Hawaii. The alternative to a transfer was Mr. White's separation from the service and return to his former residence in the continental United States at Government expense. Serious illness in the employee's immediate family, when found to exist by a responsible command official and verified by a physician, is an adequate reason for release from the employee's 3-year commitment to serve overseas. Paragraph C4009–2b of 2 JTR.

We conclude that the military doctors' finding that Mrs. White could not live in Hawaii constituted substantial compliance with the requirement that there be a clearly evident intention to transfer at the time real estate expenses are incurred.

The final question in this case is whether the residence sold in Hawaii was Mr. White's actual residence when he was first definitely informed of the transfer as required by paragraph C14000.1–1 of 2 JTR and paragraph 2–6.1 of FTR. It is to be noted that because of Mrs. White's illness Mr. and Mrs. White had lived in an apartment since approximately June 21, 1976, when Mr. White was orally informed on July 6, 1976, that he would be transferred. Since living in the apartment was required because of Mrs. White's illness and was only temporary pending reassignment, there was substantial compliance with the residence requirement. *Jesse A. Greer*, B–189122, November 7, 1977. Also, the administrative report indicates that the residence to be sold was not entirely vacated until after definite notice of the transfer. Consequently, reimbursement is not prohibited because of temporarily living in the apartment.

Reimbursement of the selling expenses may be paid, subject to deduction for any amount already reimbursed for expenses incurred to terminate the apartment lease. Reimbursement of expenses for only one residence transaction at the old official station is permitted. B–177343, March 7, 1973.

[B–188552]

Officers and Employees—Transfers—Relocation Expenses—Taxes

The real estate listing agreement signed by a transferred employee incident to sale of his residence at his old duty station required payment of 6 percent commission on selling price, plus the applicable gross receipts tax on the commission. Employee may be reimbursed for the tax paid to the broker under para. 2–6.2a, Federal Travel Regulations, if it is customary in area for tax to be passed through to seller. Tax should be viewed as part of cost of services rendered by real estate broker, since it is neither levied on property nor included in purchase price. 54 Comp. Gen. 93 (1974) distinguished.

In the matter of David R. Wiser—Real Estate Commission—Taxes, January 10, 1979:

By letter dated March 7, 1977, Edwin J. Fost of the Drug Enforcement Administration (DEA), Department of Justice, requested an advance decision as to whether Mr. David R. Wiser, an employee of DEA, is entitled to be reimbursed for the tax he paid on the broker's commission when he sold his home in Albuquerque, New Mexico, incident to his transfer to Miami, Florida.

By Travel Order B–0271, April 29, 1976, Mr. Wiser was transferred from Albuquerque to Miami. His broker's commission and other expenses associated with the sale of his residence in Albuquerque have been reimbursed. However, DEA disallowed the amount of $118.58 of the broker's fee, representing a 4¼ percent tax on the commission. This was done on the basis of our decision B–171878, August 4, 1974, published at 54 Comp. Gen. 93. Mr. Wiser has reclaimed the $118.58 on the ground that the cited decision is not applicable to the sale of a residence and that the fee (tax) is charged by all real estate firms. The Federal Travel Regulations (FTR), FPMR 101–7 (May 1973), in paragraph 2–6.2a allows reimbursement of a broker's fee or real estate commission paid by the employee for services in selling his residence, but not in excess of the rates generally charged for such services in the locality of the old official station.

The claimant's contract or listing agreement with his real estate broker states in pertinent part:

I agree to pay Broker a commission of 6 per cent of the selling price plus applicable New Mexico Gross receipts tax on said commission * * *.

We note that this listing agreement appears to be a standard agreement that was prepared by the Albuquerque Board of Realtors. The gross receipts tax referred to is imposed by the State of New Mexico and the city of Albuquerque upon the real estate broker and is measured by the amount of the commission earned from a sale. According to a letter dated July 21, 1976, from Pioneer National Title Insurance, the $4\frac{1}{4}$ percent tax on the realtor's commission is charged by all real estate firms in Aubuquerque.

In our decisions concerning reimbursement of taxes paid in connection with the relocation of an employee, we have attempted to determine whether or not the tax is a transfer tax and hence reimbursable under FTR para. 2–6.2d. Cf. B–178943, September 17, 1974, and 54 Comp. Gen. 93 (1974). In doing so we look to the local interpretation of the tax in question, rather than viewing the tax from the perspective of its impact on the employee and then applying a national standard. 54 Comp. Gen. 93 (1974).

We do not believe that the above cases are applicable here. In those cases, the tax was included in the purchase price of a residence and was measured by the value of the property. Since the tax was, in effect, levied on the property we had to determine whether or not it was a transfer tax within the meaning of the FTR. In the instant case, however, the tax is levied neither on the property nor on either party to the sale, but on the value of services performed by a third party, the real estate broker. As such, we believe it is more appropriate to treat the tax imposed here as part of the cost of the services rendered by the broker incident to the sale of the house rather than as a tax on the property.

As stated above, under FTR para. 2–6.2a, a transferred employee may be reimbursed for the amount of real estate broker's commission paid on the sale of his home, but not more than the amount generally charged in the locality. According to the letter from Pioneer Title Insurance, all the real estate brokers in Albuquerque pass on the gross receipts tax as part of the commission charged. Also, as we noted above, the listing agreement is a standard form agreement, and provides for the pass-through of the tax.

Accordingly, unless it is determined by the appropriate office of the Department of Housing and Urban Development that it is not customary in Albuquerque for the real estate broker to charge the seller the gross receipts tax in addition to the broker's commission, Mr. Wiser may be reimbursed for the amount claimed.

[B-191201]

Transportation—Freight—Charges—More Than One Rate Applicable

Where either of two rates may be applied the shipper is entitled to the rate which produces the lowest charges on the shipment.

In the matter of Yellow Freight System, Inc., January 15, 1979:

Yellow Freight System, Inc., requests review by the Comptroller General of the final action taken by the General Services Administration (GSA) pursuant to Section 201(3) of the General Accounting Office Act of 1975, 49 U.S.C. 66(b) (Supp. V, 1975). GSA withheld $1,840.26 from other moneys due the carrier to collect an overcharge discovered in the freight charges billed and paid on a less-than-truckload mixed shipment weighing a total of 8,309 pounds moving from West Yermo, California, to Camp Lejeune, North Carolina, under Government bill of lading No. K–0730126, issued on March 19, 1975.

Yellow Freight contends that GSA used an improper basis in computing the overcharge and requests repayment of $763.46. Yellow Freight contends that the radio repair outfits contained in the shipment should be rated as a truckload of 12,000 pounds under item 147850 of National Motor Freight Classification 100–A, and that the charges on them should be computed at the truckload rate of $13.46 per hundred pounds published in Rocky Mountain Motor Tariffs ICC RMB 120–A and 521. (In its initial billing the carrier used a minimum weight of 20,000 pounds in computing those charges.) On all the other articles contained in the shipment, Yellow Freight contends that the charges should be computed at the same less-than-truckload rates as used in the initial billing.

GSA contends that a less-than-truckload rate of $14.07 per hundred pounds provided in item 2000 of Rocky Mountain Motor Tariff Bureau U.S. Government Quotation ICC RMB 33 (RMB 33) which applies on shipments weighing between 5,000 and 9,999 pounds should be used on all of the articles in the 8,309-pound shipment.

The $14.07 rate applies on freight all kinds except those articles named in item 1225. Radio repair outfits are not named in item 1225.

Among other things, item 100 of Quotation RMB 33 provides as follows:

NOTE 1—THE CLASSES RULES AND REGULATIONS, ESTIMATED AND MINIMUM TRUCKLOAD OR VOLUME WEIGHTS, SHIPPING AND PACKING REQUIREMENTS, ALLOWANCES AND PRIVILEGES, OR OTHER PROVISIONS OR CONDITIONS PUBLISHED IN THIS QUOTATION, ABBROGATE AND SUPERSEDE THOSE IN THE GOVERNING PUBLICATIONS IN CONFLICT.

Note 1 of item 100, by its terms, provides for the replacement of the ratings published in the National Motor Freight Classification 100–A on shipments ratable under Quotation RMB 33. The quotation, which contains the less-than-truckload rates, is a self-contained rate authority which produces lower charges than those available under the motor freight classification and the carrier's published tariffs.

When either of two rate authorities may be applied to compute the charges on a given shipment, the shipper is entitled to application of the rate which produces the lower charges. *Emery Air Freight Corp.* v. *United States*, 499 F. 2d 1255 (Ct. Cl. 1974) ; *Union Pacific R.R.* v. *United States*, 163 Ct. Cl. 473 (1963) ; *Union Pacific R.R.* v. *Ore-Ida Potato Products, Inc.*, 252 F. 2d 505 (9th Cir. 1958).

Since Quotation RMB 33 is not dependent upon the ratings in the National Motor Freight Classification, and since the charges computed under Quotation RMB 33 are lower than the charges computed under tariffs ICC RMB 120–A and 521, the charges computed under Quotation RMB 33 are for application.

The charges computed by the GSA thus appear proper and the settlement action is sustained.

[B–193045]

Contracts—Protests—Procedures—Bid Protest Procedures—Time for Filing—Significant Procurement Issue Exception

Protester argues that bid rejection as nonresponsive for failure to comply with mandatory prebid site inspection requirement was improper, on basis that prebid site inspection is not appropriate responsiveness criterion. Agency contends that protest is untimely, since it was not filed prior to bid opening. However, since agency states that requirement is now standard in all of its IFB's, protest presents principle of widespread interest for consideration under "significant issue" exception to General Accounting Office's timeliness rules.

Contracts—Specifications—Site Visits

Where bid does not take exception to Government's requirements, bidder's failure to make mandatory prebid site inspection does not justify bid rejection as "nonresponsive," since acceptance of bid would effectively bind bidder to perform at bid price in accordance with advertised terms and specifications. Purpose of site inspection provision must be viewed as warning bidders that site conditions could affect performance cost and bidders therefore assume risks of increased performance cost caused by observable site conditions, and to protect Government from necessity of permitting bid withdrawal or claims after contract award.

In the matter of Edw. Kocharian & Company, Inc., January 15, 1979:

Invitation for bids (IFB) No. DMA 800–78–B–0052 was issued on September 7, 1978, by the Defense Mapping Agency (DMA) to replace four air-handling units at the DMA Topographic Center. Paragraph 11 of an addendum to Standard Form 22, "Instructions to Bidders," was entitled "SITE INSPECTION" and provided:

A site inspection in connection with work covered under this solicitation is *MANDATORY*. Prospective bidders shall inspect the site of the proposed work to inform themselves of all general and local conditions that may affect the work or cost thereof, to the extent such information is reasonably obtainable. The site will be available for inspection, by appointment, Mondays thru Fridays, between the hours of 7:00 a.m. and 2:00 p.m. Bidders shall contact Mr. William E. Shimmel * * * to make the necessary appointment. * * *

CAUTION: *FAILURE ON THE PART OF THE BIDDER TO MAKE THE MANDATORY SITE INSPECTION WILL RESULT IN REJECTION OF HIS BID AS NONRESPONSIVE.*

Bids were opened on September 27, and Edw. Kocharian & Company, Inc. (Kocharian), was the apparent low bidder. However, it was determined that Kocharian did not comply with the site inspection requirement, and the contracting officer proposes to reject the bid as nonresponsive. Kocharian has filed a protest in our Office against such proposed action.

Kocharian contends that it in fact fulfilled the solicitation's site inspection requirement. Kocharian states that it did not receive a complete IFB until Friday, September 22. In view of the short time left to inspect the site and prepare a bid, a Kocharian representative visited the site on Saturday, September 23, at which time, Kocharian states, "he was able to make an inspection sufficient to assure himself of the type of construction of the interior." That inspection consisted of a view of the building from the door, accompanied by the security officer on duty.

Kocharian further argues that even absent a site inspection the rejection of its bid as nonresponsive would be improper, notwithstanding the warning in the IFB quoted above. Kocharian contends that its bid represents an objective, unequivocal offer to perform the required work at the bid price. Kocharian states:

* * * unless a bidder takes exception to, or otherwise manifests an intention not to be bound to perform the contract in strict accordance with the requirements of the contract then the bid is not non-responsive. * * * if a bid constitutes a definite and unqualified offer to meet the substantive terms of the solicitation, i.e., those that could affect price, quality, quantity or delivery, then the bid is responsive. * * *

Kocharian further states:

* * * The sole effect of a bidder's failure to conduct a pre-bid site inspection in the face of this mandatory language would be to provide the government with a defense, should, during the course of performance, claims be presented for equitable adjustments under the Changes or the Differing Site conditions clause where the matter in issue could have readily been ascertained through a pre-bid site inspection. * * *

Thus, it is Kocharian's position that a failure to perform a prebid site inspection is not relevant to the responsiveness of a bid, i.e., that it would in no way diminish the responsibility of a firm offering to perform the contract in strict accordance with the invitation's specification to in fact do so.

In a report on the protest, DMA first argues that the protest, which DMA characterizes as being against the inclusion in the IFB of a mandatory site inspection provision, is untimely under section 20.2(b)(1) of our Bid Protest Procedures, 4 C.F.R. part 20 (1978), since it was filed after bid opening and, therefore, should not be considered on the merits. That provision in our Procedures requires that protests based on alleged improprieties in an IFB which are apparent prior to bid opening be filed by that date. DMA argues that by having failed to protest the requirement Kocharian accepted it as a valid responsiveness matter and, therefore, should be estopped from protesting its application.

However, the report indicates that mandatory prebid site inspection is now a standard requirement in all IFB's issued from DMA's Engineering Division, Facilities Engineering Office. Therefore, we consider the issue as characterized by DMA to present a principle of widespread interest. On that basis, even if untimely filed, we will consider the merits under section 20.2(c) of our Procedures as involving an issue "significant to procurement practices or procedures." See 52 Comp. Gen. 20 (1973).

We note here that it is the contracting officer's opinion that the September 23 site visit by Kocharian does not constitute a valid site inspection under the IFB requirement, although the reason therefor is not provided. Although we recognize that the visit took place on other than a day specified in the IFB and did not involve the named DMA representative, we are not convinced that Kocharian did not comply with at least the intent of the requirement. However, this issue is academic since, for the reasons discussed below, we must agree with the protester that even if it had not inspected the site at all it would be improper for DMA to reject its bid as nonresponsive.

In regard to the propriety of the subject provision, DMA contends that a site inspection could affect price, quantity, quality or delivery and as such is a material requirement and, therefore, a legitimate responsiveness criterion. DMA concedes that, as Kocharian contends, the standard site inspection clause essentially operates as a defense to subsequent contractor claims, but argues:

* * * the intention of the Agency in requiring a mandatory site inspection was addressed to affirmative contract formation principles rather than preserving a possible defense.

It was our intention that the contract be interpreted based on *informed* mutuality of assent, devoid of waivers which could possibly involve us in avoidable claims. * * *

* * * we sought a contract based on fully informed, intelligent mutuality of assent, rather than mutuality based on a promise instinct with a waiver.

In this regard, the report also states the following reasons for making mandatory prebid site inspection a standard IFB requirement.

[1] Experience has proven that only if the prospective contractor visits the site can he become familiar with all aspects of the job which may influence his bidding.

[2] It is literally impossible to depict in drawings all of the details of existing conditions that the contractor has to work around during various phases of construction. Only site inspection will confirm and identify these conditions.

[3] The site inspection will identify, first-hand, the working conditions, enable the contractor to make a realistic bid package, and minimize misunderstandings and change orders during the period of the contract.

[4] Site inspections will also give the contractors a feel for the lost time, which may be experienced by his mechanics in getting to the job site due to security procedures. This lost time would also be reflected in his bid package.

Finally, DMA cites as support for its view a number of our decisions in which we indicated that failure to perform a *non*mandatory site inspection would not affect a bidder's eligibility for award; DMA suggests that the "implicit corollary" of those decisions is that failure to perform a *mandatory* site inspection is a proper ground for bid rejection.

Defense Acquisition Regulation (DAR) § 18–204 (1976 ed.) advises procuring agencies that appropriate provisions should be made for bidders to inspect construction sites. Paragraph 2 of Standard Form 22, "Instructions to Bidders," included in the DMA solicitation, urges bidders to visit the construction site to ascertain the nature and location of any factors which could affect the work or the cost thereof, and warns that failure to do so will not relieve bidders of the responsibility to properly estimate the difficulty or cost of successfully performing the work. (Note that the *mandatory* site inspection provision was contained in an addendum to this paragraph.)

As DMA points out, we have considered protests involving solicitations that reflect such advice by containing provisions that strongly suggest that bidders inspect the worksite before submitting bids. See, for example, *Southern Industrial Laundry d/b/a Alabama Laundries and Linen Supply*, B–191095, April 21, 1978, 78–1 CPD 310, and B–170294, October 5, 1970. In resolving those protests, we indicated that the failure to attend a site inspection was not sufficient reason to reject a bid. We have also considered a protest where a prebid site inspection was mandatory, although we there found that the Government nevertheless intended to consider a bid for award even though the bidder may have failed to inspect the site. See 52 Comp. Gen. 955 (1973).

In both situations, we stated that provisions giving bidders the opportunity to visit a worksite and urging them do do so are designed to warn bidders that site conditions could affect the cost of contract performance and to protect the Government from the necessity of permitting the withdrawal of a bid submitted by a firm that failed to inspect, or a claim by such firm after award of the contract.

The test to be applied in determining the "responsiveness" of a bid, however, is whether the bid as submitted is an offer to perform, without exception, the exact thing called for in the invitation. 49 Comp.

Gen. 553, 556 (1970). If the test is met, the bidder is effectively bound to perform in accordance with the invitation's requirements, see 42 Comp. Gen. 464 (1963), and we do not see how a failure to make a prebid site inspection would define or limit that obligation. To the extent that a site inspection affects the bidder's price, as DMA argues, it does so only in the context of that price's reflection of the bidder's business judgment as to his performance cost; it does not affect the obligation to perform at the price bid.

In fact, we see no difference between the above-stated purposes for recommending prebid site inspections and those proferred by DMA for making the inspection mandatory, notwithstanding that DMA distinguishes its rationale in the present case as being based on a desire for "informed, intelligent mutuality of assent" as opposed to "mutuality based on a promise instinct with a waiver." Whether expressed in mandatory terms or not, the provision is viewed as advising bidders that they bear the risk of problems that could have been resolved by a reasonable prebid site inspection. See 52 Comp. Gen. 389, 391 (1972).

We understand how DMA could draw the "implicit corollary" it suggests from our decisions in this area. However, since the issue was never directly decided in the cited cases, we reject the view that they support DMA's position in the present protest. In fact, we have in dictum cited our decision in 52 Comp. Gen. 955 (1973) for the proposition that the Government cannot make attendance at a prebid site inspection a mandatory condition of submitting a bid. See *Southeastern Services, Inc., and MC&E Service and Support Co., Inc.*, B-183108, June 16, 1975, 75-1 CPD 366.

In view of the above, the prebid site inspection requirement provides no basis for disqualifying Kocharian from the competition. Compare our similar view regarding attendance at scheduled preproposal conferences. See 50 Comp. Gen. 355 (1970).

The protest is sustained, and award should be made to Kocharian under the IFB, if otherwise appropriate. In addition, we are advising DMA by separate letter of our view concerning mandatory prebid site inspections in relation to "responsiveness."

[B-193270]

General Accounting Office—Jurisdiction—Subcontracts

Where prime contractor is conducting competitive procurement designed to develop second source for subsystem and after proposals are received Government encourages prime to consider alternate proposal from licensee of subsystem contractor, participation by Government is sufficient under *Optimum Systems* standard for General Accounting Office (GAO) to hear protest by potential second source against cancellation of solicitation and proposed award of subcontract to licensee.

Contracts—Negotiation—Source Selection—Preprocurement v. Procurement Actions—Review by GAO—Prime Contractor Procurement

Argument that choice of licensing proposal as opposed to proposals for development of second source was preprocurement action under *Maremont Corporation,* 55 Comp. Gen. 1362, to preclude GAO review is found to be without merit since Government and prime contractor were not determining minimum needs so much as they were comparing alternative proposals for meeting those needs.

Contracts—Protests—Subcontractor Protests—Timeliness

While protester knew alternative method was being considered at least 2 months prior to final decision being made, protest is timely where filed within 10 working days of final decision because to have protested earlier would have been premature.

In the matter of Singer Company, Inc., Kearfott Division, January 17, 1979:

Singer Company, Inc., Kearfott Division (Singer), protests actions taken by McDonnell Douglas Corporation, McDonnell Douglas Astronautics Company (MDAC), in connection with MDAC's performance of its prime contract with the Department of Defense (DOD). This prime contract is for the design, development and furnishing of AN/DSW–15 Cruise Missile Land Attack Guidance Sets and Navigation/Guidance Equipment for the AGM–86–B Air Launched Cruise Missile.

Singer's protest challenges the cancellation of three requests for proposals (RFP's) issued by MDAC to develop a second source for the Cruise Missile inertial guidance subsystem and the choice of a licensing approach instead to fulfill the requirement.

Because of various issues raised, this decision is limited solely to the jurisdiction of our Office to hear the protest and the timeliness of Singer's protest under our Bid Protest Procedures (4 C.F.R. part 20 (1978)).

The first issue for resolution is whether our Office should exercise jurisdiction, so as to rule on the merits of the protest, since the protest is against the award of a subcontract by a Government prime contractor.

Generally, the contracting practices and procedures employed by prime contractors—who are normally acting as independent contractors—in the award of subcontracts are not subject to the statutory and regulatory requirements governing direct procurements of the Federal Government. 49 Comp. Gen. 668 (1970). However, we will consider protests by subcontractors under certain limited circumstances, including where the active or direct participation of the Government in the selection of a subcontractor has the net effect of causing or controlling the rejection or selection of potential subcontractors, or of significantly limiting subcontractor sources. *Optimum Systems, Incorporated*, 54 Comp. Gen. 767 (1975), 75–1 CPD 166. Both Singer and the Government procuring activity, the Joint Cruise Missile Project Office (JCMPO), agree that, if our Office is to entertain the protest, our jurisdiction would be founded under that criterion.

The following history is relevant. MDAC was awarded the above-noted prime contract in 1975 by DOD with Litton Industries, Inc., Guidance and Control Systems Division (Litton), Woodland, California, as the subcontractor for design and production of the inertial guidance subsystem.

On January 14, 1977, DOD established the JCMPO to manage the Cruise Missile Program and to direct the development of both the Navy and Air Force versions of the missile. One of the policies to be followed by JCMPO was to encourage subsystem/second-source competitive procurement by which major Cruise Missile subsystems would be procured from two contractors who would be competing with each other for a portion of the total production order.

In late 1977, MDAC sent requests to industry for planning information concerning the cost to the Government of developing and qualifying an alternate production source or a "second source." Following evaluation of the information submitted by industry, MDAC briefed JCMPO regarding its proposed second-source competition which envisioned competition through either a form, fit and function approach of redevelopment of the system utilizing new technologies. The second-source development, through the demonstration phase, would be funded by the subcontractors themselves. MDAC requested JCMPO approval of this approach, but JCMPO advised that, since it had no control over how MDAC or its potential subcontractors expended their funds, such approval or disapproval would be presumptuous.

On March 17, 1978, MDAC issued three RFP's to a number of prospective offerors. Each RFP was for a portion of the inertial guidance subsystem, i.e., computer subsystem, power subsystem and reference measuring unit.

At a briefing with offerors held on March 24, 1978, MDAC advised that it would obtain commitments from JCMPO, prior to authorizing a supplier to proceed, that:

1. establish JCMPO intent to fund and support FSD (Full Scale Development) if the Competitive Evaluation Phase System development is successful;

2. confirm JCMPO policy that development of a second-source system is required and will be actively supported through FSD and full production; and

3. confirm that JCMPO plans do not include procurement of Cruise Missile Guidance Systems from any source other than MDAC and that the Guidance System developed during this program will be the only second-source system considered for Cruise Missile application.

Because of numerous complaints received from offerors, JCMPO advised MDAC, on April 6, 1978, that it would fund the second-source competition and, therefore, it wished to review the source selection criteria and written procurement plan for the second-source solicitations and also to review and approve the proposed source selection.

During May 1978, several discussions were held between JCMPO and MDAC regarding the status of the second-source competition, the alternate vendor technical approaches and how MDAC would evaluate the responses to the RFP's.

In this same time period, May 1978, following preliminary contacts by Litton during March and April regarding the possibility of licensing production of Litton's equipment to another manufacturer, JCMPO met with Litton on several occasions to explore acquisition alternatives to MDAC's second-source competition.

During these discussions, it became evident that, while Litton was willing to license another contractor to produce most of the components of the guidance system, it was unwilling to license production of the gyroscopes and accelerometers, two essential components of the subsystem. Litton suggested that Litton Systems, Canada, Limited (Litton-Canada), Litton's Canadian division, could supply these components to the second-source contractor. It was determined that the licensing of another contractor would require too long a leadtime at an unreasonable cost for such a contractor to reach production capability.

The discussions then turned to the possibility of licensing Litton-Canada as the second source for the entire inertial guidance subsystem as a less expensive, lower risk alternative to the MDAC second-source competition. On June 27, 1978, JCMPO visited Litton-Canada to review its capabilities and facilities. Subsequently, a Memorandum of Agreement (MOA) was drafted between JCMPO and Litton to establish Litton-Canada as the second source for the guidance subsystem. The purpose of the MOA was to:

a. agree on steps to establish a dual-source capability for cruise missile guidance and control components in Litton-Canada including the necessary transfer of technology from Litton Guidance and Control Division;

b. assure independent competition in pricing between Litton-Canada and Litton Guidance and Control Division;

c. preclude royalty charges or license fees to the Government;

d. limit profits charged to the Government; and

e. provide for Litton capitalizing equipment needed to achieve production capability with an appropriate capital investment incentive for inclusion in applicable procurements.

Returning now to the MDAC second-sources competitions, on August 4, 1978, MDAC presented JCMPO with its methodology, requirements and approach being utilized in the second-source RFP's.

On August 11, 1978, JCMPO requested that MDAC include the licensing approach in its evaluations and on August 31, 1978, MDAC advised JCMPO of its conclusions regarding the second-source RFP responses and its preliminary evaluation of the licensing approach. Also, in the early part of September, Litton-Canada submitted an unsolicited proposal to MDAC to produce the inertial guidance subsystem under license from Litton. Between September 7–14, 1978, JCMPO reviewed MDAC's evaluation of the technical proposals under the RFP's. On September 15, 1978, in a presentation to JCMPO, MDAC advised that none of the second-source offerors offered as low a risk at minimal cost as the licensing approach and on October 13, 1978, MDAC, with the concurrence of JCMPO, decided no awards would be made under the RFP. By letter of October 16, 1978, MDAC advised the offerors of the above decision and on October 20, 1978, Singer protested the cancellation of the RFP to our Office.

JCMPO, MDAC and Litton all have taken the position that the involvement of JCMPO in these proceedings was not sufficient to invoke the jurisdiction of our Office under the standards enunciated in *Optimum Systems, supra*, and its progeny.

JCMPO contends that its actions in the instant matter are comparable to the actions of the National Aeronautics and Space Administration (NASA) in *Structural Composites Industries, Inc.* (SCI), B–184938, October 28, 1975, 75–2 CPD 260, affirmed, 55 Comp. Gen. 1220 (1976), 76–1 CPD 417, wherein we declined to take jurisdiction of the subcontractor protest. In that decision, NASA's prime contractor, Rockwell International, was attempting to procure gas storage pressure tanks for the space shuttle. Rockwell and NASA developed a specification which SCI maintained mandated the selection of another firm as the subcontractor.

Our holding in the decision, based on the above facts, stated as follows:

* * * NASA denies that it either suggested, approved or directed a sole-source award to Brunswick or directed that the award not be split. While we recognize that SCI strongly disputes NASA's position with respect to the foregoing matters, we do not believe on the basis of the record that SCI has carried the burden of proof to establish that NASA's involvement or alleged bias justifies our consideration of the protest under the first *Optimum Systems* standard.

We do not find *Structural Composites Industries, Inc.* controlling in this case. Moreover, while numerous other cases are cited by

JCMPO, Litton and Singer, we do not find any controlling in the present factual situation. We believe JCMPO's involvement was more substantial than merely approving the prime's selection of a subcontractor, the offered equipment or the subcontractor's experience. *Flair Manufacturing Corp.*, B–187870, December 14, 1976, 76–2 CPD 486; *Lyco–ZF*, B–188037, January 17, 1977, 77–1 CPD 36; *Industrial Boiler Co.*, B–187750, February 25, 1977, 77–1 CPD 142; *William M. Bailey Company, Industrial Products Division*, B–190682, December 8, 1977, 77–2 CPD 447; and *Teledyne Brown Engineering*, B–186221, May 21, 1976, 76–1 CPD 336, affirmed, December 15, 1976, 76–2 CPD 489.

Here, MDAC had surveyed the industry concerning possible costs involved, in a second-source competition and then had issued RFPs to numerous prospective contractors and received proposals. While MDAC was in the process of evaluating these responses, JCMPO asked MDAC to evaluate the licensing approach, following discussions between JCMPO, Litton and Litton–Canada which lasted from March 1978 to August 1978. MDAC had not been involved in these meetings.

Therefore, it appears that without encouragement from JCMPO, MDAC would not have considered Litton–Canada to be an acceptable source under a licensing arrangement in view of its relationship to Litton, the second primary source. In fact, Litton must have recognized that MDAC would not have considered a proposal from Litton–Canada without JCMPO's prior approval, since Litton initially approached JCMPO rather than MDAC with the idea of using Litton–Canada under a licensing arrangement. Also, because of JCMPO's discussions with Litton, JCMPO knew that the use of the licensing approach would necessarily limit the number of firms to which Litton would license to only Litton–Canada.

The basis of the protest is that it was unfair to compare Litton–Canada's proposal to the RFP proposals. While the parties and our Office have not found any past decisions directly on point with the instant factual situation, we believe the actions of JCMPO were sufficient to meet the test of *Optimum Systems, supra.*

However, JCMPO also argues that our Office should not review the merits of the protest because the actions of both MDAC and JCMPO were merely "preprocurement" actions under our decision in *Maremont Corporation*, 55 Comp. Gen. 1362 (1976), 76–2 CPD 181. In *Maremont*, our Office held that the conduct of "side by side" tests of American and Belgian machine guns by the U.S. Army was not a procurement such as to require compliance with applicable procurement rules and regulations but was a preprocurement action to determine the Army's minimum needs. JCMPO contends that the MOA is not a Government contract because it did not procure anything and was not entered into by a designated contracting officer, but was merely a "preprocurement" document which establishes the basis for future competitions between Litton and Litton–Canada.

There has been much discussion in the briefs submitted to our Office as to whether this factual situation was comprised of two separate and distinct acquisition approaches, licensing and second-source competition, or was a single procurement action to determine an alternate contractor for the inertial guidance subsystem. We believe the facts before our Office, when viewed from the standpoint of MDAC, show that MDAC was attempting to fulfill the mandate of JCMPO for a second source, when interrupted by the introduction of the possibility of a licensing arrangement by JCMPO.

While JCMPO takes the position that the RFP's and the MOA were merely attempts to define the minimum needs of the program (i.e., the technical approach to be utilized, either a form, fit and function approach or licensing), it appears the JCMPO and MDAC were not determining minimum needs so much as they were comparing alternative proposed methods of meeting those needs. We believe it is appropriate for our Office to review the merits of such a protest.

Finally, JCMPO has challenged the timeliness of Singer's protest under our Bid Protest Procedures by arguing that Singer knew or should have known that licensing was being considered as an alternative to the second-source competition more than 10 working days prior to the filing of its protest with our Office on October 20, 1978. JCMPO cites *Brandon Applied Systems, Inc.*, 57 Comp. Gen. 140 (1977), 77–2 CPD 486, as authority for the proposition that a protest should be filed if the protester's interests are being directly threatened under a then-relevant factual scheme. JCMPO states that Singer had knowledge that the licensing approach was being explored by JCMPO as early as June 2, 1978, when an interview with the head of JCMPO was published in an industry publication and certainly no later than July 28 or July 29, 1978. On July 28, 1978, a congressional source from Singer's State wrote to JCMPO inquiring as to consideration being given to licensing. On July 29, 1978, the head of JCMPO visited Singer's facilities and was shown charts by Singer comparing licensing with Litton–Canada and other acquisition approaches. Therefore, JCMPO concludes that Singer knew of the possibility of the utilization of the licensing approach to Singer's detriment by July 29, 1978, and should have protested within 10 working days thereafter.

However, JCMPO admits, and the record reflects, that a decision to cancel the RFP's and choose the licensing approach was not made until October 13, 1978, with the offerors being notified of the decision by letter of October 16, 1978. In a letter of September 18, 1978, JCMPO advised a congressional source that JCMPO was considering both alternatives but that "no decision will be made until full consideration is given to all possibilities."

Since no decision had been made prior to October 13, 1978, we believe a protest filed by Singer prior to that time would have been premature under our Procedures, since no action had been taken adverse to Singer. *Accountor Systems USA, Ltd.*, B–192337, August 18, 1978, 78–2 CPD 131; *Clifford Industries, Inc.*, B–191075, February 8, 1978, 78–1 CPD 107; and *Imperial Products Company, Incorporated*, B–188297, May 12, 1977, 77–1 CPD 340. Accordingly, we find the protest of Singer to be timely. *Tosco Corporation*, B–187776, May 10, 1977, 77–1 CPD 329.

For the foregoing reasons, we will proceed to consider the protest on the merits, in accordance with our Bid Protest Procedures, upon receipt of a report responsive to the protest from JCMPO.

[B–192941]

General Accounting Office—Jurisdiction—Contracts—Defaults and Terminations—Review of Procedures Leading to Award

Although General Accounting Office (GAO) normally will not consider protests of decisions to terminate contracts for convenience of the Government, GAO will consider protest against termination of contract based on an alleged impropriety in the award process.

Contracts—Awards—Propriety—Premature Bid Opening

Termination of contract is not justified where purchasing agent prematurely opened all bids in private to ascertain if bids contained necessary papers, low bid was first received and opened, and all bids were kept in purchasing agent's exclusive possession until formal bid "opening," since evidence clearly indicates that no bidder was prejudiced by premature opening.

Contracts—Termination—Convenience of Government—Propriety of Termination—Reinstatement of Contract Recommended

Termination of contract is not justified by improper evaluation of options under invitation for bids in violation of Defense Acquisition Regulation 1–1504(c)(ii) where there is no evidence that bidders submitted unbalanced bids or that bidders would have submitted lower base bids had options not been evaluated, where no bidder was prejudiced by evaluation, and where awarded contract would result in lowest cost to Government. However, since it appears option provisions should not have been included in solicitation, it is recommended that agency not exercise options in reinstated contract.

In the matter of Safemasters Company, Inc., January 22, 1979:

Safemasters Company, Inc. (Safemasters) has protested the decision of Defense Supply Service–Washington (DSS–W) to terminate its contract awarded under invitation for bids (IFB) No. MDA 903–79–B–0020 due to the premature opening of all bids and the evaluation of options in violation of Defense Acquisition Regulation (DAR) § 1–1504(c)(ii) (1976 ed.).

The IFB was issued by DSS–W on August 21, 1978, for the repair and maintenance of safes and related security services on a yearly basis. The IFB required bidders to submit prices for an initial 1-year period and for two 1-year options. The IFB provided that options would be evaluated in determining the low bid. Bids were to be opened at 10 a.m. on September 20, 1978.

Three bids were submitted in response to the IFB. The first bid received was Safemasters' at 8:48 a.m. Safemasters' bid was then taken by the DSS–W purchasing agent to the DSS–W mailroom where it was opened to ascertain whether the bid contained all necessary papers. Safemasters' bid was placed back into its envelope and clocked in at 8:54 a.m. The bid was then placed into the DSS–W purchasing agent's envelope, carried back to the purchasing agent's desk and placed in the DSS–W contract folder where it remained until bid opening.

The second bid to be received was submitted by Mosler Safe Co. (Mosler). Mosler's bid was delivered to the head of the purchasing branch at DSS–W who in turn delivered the bid to the purchasing agent. Mosler's bid was clocked in at 9:02 a.m. by Mosler's representative and was delivered to the purchasing agent sometime between 9:02 a.m. and 9:49 a.m. At 9:50 a.m. the purchasing agent opened Mosler's bid to ascertain whether it contained all necessary papers, after which it was placed back into its envelope and placed into the DSS–W contract folder. Mosler's bid remained in the possession of the purchasing agent until formal bid opening at 10:00 a.m.

The last bid to be received was from A–1 Lock & Safe Service, Inc. (A–1). The bid was clocked in by A–1's representative at 9:18 a.m. and delivered to the purchasing agent at 9:44 a.m. At 9:45 the purchasing agent opened the A–1 bid to ascertain whether it contained all necessary papers after which it was placed back into its envelope and then into the DSS–W contract folder where it remained until bid opening.

Formal bid opening took place as scheduled at 10:00 a.m. on September 20, 1978, in the DSS–W conference room. The three bids were as follows:

Bidder	For basic year	First option year	Second option year	Total price as computed by DSS–W
Safemaster	$93,343.44	$97,615.47	$102,012.33	$292,971.24
A–1	121,677.75	(¹)	(²)	436,712.59
Mosler	127,630.30	133,688.17	140,624.37	401,942.14

¹ 15 percent increase.
² 25 percent increase.

Bid opening was attended by three representatives from each bidder, the purchasing agent, the purchasing agent's team leader, the contracting officer and the chief of the purchasing office. After all bids were disclosed one of the representatives from Mosler asked whether the procedures for bid opening had changed, since it was apparent that the bids had been opened prior to the scheduled time. The purchasing agent told the Mosler representative that the procedures had not changed but that bids were opened solely to assure that all necessary papers had been included. No other questions or statements were made regarding the premature opening of the bids.

The contract was awarded to Safemasters on September 20, 1978, and shortly thereafter A–1 filed a protest with our Office. On September 21, 1978, the Deputy Director for Acquisition directed the chief of the purchasing office to terminate Safemasters' contract due to the premature bid opening and the improper evaluation of options under the solicitation. On September 22, 1978, the contracting officer notified Safemasters by telephone that DSS–W intended to terminate Safemasters' contract for the convenience of the Government.

On September 25, 1978, Safemasters protested to our Office the proposed termination of its contract and at the same time filed a motion for a temporary restraining order and a preliminary injunction in the United States District Court for the District of Columbia. On September 26, 1978, Safemasters' motion for a temporary restraining order was denied but a hearing was not held on the preliminary injunction. Thereafter DSS–W terminated Safemasters' contract and A–1 withdrew its protest with our Office. On October 24, 1978, Safemasters and DSS–W filed a stipulation of dismissal dismissing Safemasters' complaint without prejudice, which was approved by the court on October 25, 1978.

Safemasters alleges that DSS–W's decision to terminate Safemasters' contract due to the premature bid opening was unjustified in light of our decisions which hold that cancellation of a solicitation is not proper where bids have been prematurely opened but no bidder has been prejudiced. *See, e.g., Boyd Lumber Corporation*, B–189641, October 21, 1977, 77–2 CPD 315 and cases cited therein; 34 Comp. Gen. 395 (1955). Safemasters asserts that DSS–W's decision to terminate rather than suspend performance, as provided by DAR § 2.407.8(c), in order to allow Safemasters to pursue its protest against the proposed termination with our Office, constitutes an abuse of discretion. Safemasters further asserts that it is a well established rule of administrative law that an administrative decision based on an erroneous interpretation of law cannot stand. Accordingly, Safemasters requests that we rule that DSS–W acted improperly in terminating its contract and that DSS–W should reinstate the terminated contract rather than resolicit its needs.

DSS–W, on the other hand, argues that while no bidder was actually prejudiced by the premature opening, preservation of the integrity of the competitive bidding system required that Safemasters' contract be terminated and DSS–W's needs resolicited. DSS–W characterizes the premature opening circumstances here as more "suspicious" than those in *Boyd Lumber Corporation, supra*, where the bidders, after the premature opening, were given an opportunity to confirm or revise their bids prior to bid opening; here no such opportunity was given to the bidders and DSS–W personnel did nothing after becoming aware of the premature opening. DSS–W states that it believes termination of Safemasters' contract was the only course of action which would erase any suspicion of irregularity undoubtedly raised in the minds of the bidders.

DSS–W also asserts that termination was proper since the solicitation provided that option year prices would be evaluated in making award in violation of DAR § 1–1504(c), which provides:

The option quantity may be considered in the evaluation for award of a firm fixed-price contract, a fixed-price contract with economic price adjustment provisions, or such other types of contracts as may be approved by Departmental procedures, if, before issuance of the solicitation, it has been determined by the Chief of the Purchasing Office that:

(i) there is a known requirement which exceeds the basic quantity to be awarded, but either (A) the basic quantity is a learning or testing quantity and there is some uncertainty as to contractor or equipment performance. or (B) due to the unavailability of funds, the option cannot be exercised at the time of award of the basic quantity; *provided* that in this latter case there is reasonable certainty that funds will be available thereafter to permit exercise of the option; and

(ii) realistic competition for the option quantity is impracticable once the initial contract is awarded and hence it is in the best interests of the Government to evaluate options in order to eliminate the possibility of a "buy-in" (1–811). This determination shall be based on factors such as, but not limited to, substantial startup or phase-in costs, superior technical ability resulting from performance of the initial contract, and long pre-production lead time for a new producer.

In such cases, the solicitation shall contain an Evaluation of Options provision substantially as set forth in 7–2003.11(b).

In addition, DAR § 1–1502(b) provides that:

Option clauses shall not be included in contracts, and option provisions shall not be included in solicitations, if:

(i) the supplies or services being purchased are readily available on the open market;

(ii) the contractor would be required to incur undue risks (*e.g.*, the price or availability of necessary materials or labor is not reasonably foreseeable);

(iii) an indefinite quantity contract or requirements contract is appropriate except that options for continuing performance may be used in such contracts;

(iv) market prices for the supplies or services involved are likely to change substantially; or

(v) the option quantities represent known firm requirements for which funds are available unless (A) the basic quantity is a learning or testing quantity and there is some uncertainty as to contractor or equipment performance, and (B) realistic competition for the option quantity is impracticable once the initial contract is awarded.

DSS–W states that a determination under DAR § 1–1504(c) allowing the evaluation of options cannot be made because realistic competition for the option quantities would be practical. DSS–W notes that the very nature of the safe maintenance business is such that it would not require substantial startup or phase-in cost, or superior technical ability resulting from performance of the initial contract.

Finally, DSS–W asserts that a contracting officer may terminate a contract whenever he determines that termination is in the best interest of the Government and that the termination is valid absent a showing of bad faith.

Generally, we do not consider protest against determinations to terminate contracts for the convenience of the Government. However, where an alleged impropriety in the award process is the basis of the Government's decision to terminate, our Office will review whether the contract award was valid and proper. *Electronic Associates, Inc.*, B–184412, February 10, 1976, 76–1 CPD 83. In so doing, we are not limited to a consideration of whether the termination was the result of bad faith. (In this regard, we point out that bad faith is not the only basis upon which a termination for convenience may be challenged. For example, a termination may be regarded as an abuse of discretion. *See National Factors, Inc.* v. *United States*, 492 F. 2d 1383, 1385 (Ct. Cl. 1974); *see also Art Metal—U.S.A., Inc.* v. *Solomon, et al.*, Civil Action No. 78–1660 (D.D.C., October 6, 1978).) Rather, our review under these limited circumstances is for the purpose of determining whether the termination was justified given the facts of the original contract award.

We do not believe that DSS–W's termination of Safemasters' contract was justified. As Safemasters argues, our decisions clearly indicate that resolicitation of the Government's needs is not required nor justified when bids have been prematurely opened but no bidder has been prejudiced. *See Boyd Lumber Corporation, supra*, and 34 Comp. Gen. 395, *supra*. In the instant case, it is clear that no bidder was prejudiced. Safemasters' bid was the first submitted and did not leave the possession of the DSS–W purchasing agent. It was therefore impossible for Safemasters, the low bidder, to have obtained any advantage by the premature opening of the other bids. DSS–W's argument that termination was necessary to protect the integrity of the competitive bidding system since the bidders were not given the opportunity to revise or confirm their bids is misdirected. Whether a bidder was given an opportunity to confirm or revise its bid prior to bid opening is merely a factor in determining whether a bidder has been prejudiced. Where the facts clearly indicate that no bidder has been prejudiced we do not believe that a failure to ask bidders to confirm or revise their bids justifies resolicitation. Furthermore, we think that the competitive system is normally better protected by making an award once bids have been opened, rather than resoliciting, where there has been an irregularity which did not result in prejudice to any bidder. *See Spickard Enterprises, Inc. et al.*, 54 Comp. Gen. 145, 147 (1974), 74–2 CPD 121; *GAF Corporation et al.*, 53 Comp. Gen. 586, 592 (1974), 74–1 CPD 68.

With regard to DSS–W's assertion that the improper evaluation of options justified termination of Safemaster's contract, we note the following. When a solicitation requires the submission of option prices which are not to be evaluated in determining the low bidder, a bidder might attempt to "buy in" to the total procurement by submitting a low basic quantity price in hope of recovering its costs upon the Government's exercise of significantly higher priced options. *See, e.g., R&R Inventory Service, Inc.*, 54 Comp. Gen. 206, 209 (1974), 74–2 CPD 163. Additionally, since a bidder must guarantee an option price without assurance that the option will be exercised, a bidder might submit a higher item price for an option than it would if bidding on a firm basic quantity instead. *See, e.g.,* 1 R. Nash & J. Cibinic, Federal Procurement Law 743 (3rd ed. 1977). On the other hand, if the solicitation provides that options will be evaluated, a bidder might submit an unbalanced bid in order to obtain a disproportionately high price for the basic contract period, thereby obtaining, in effect, use of Government funds more properly allocated to the option periods, or in order to benefit from a high basic price in the event the Government fails to exercise the options. *See Mobilease Corporation*, 54 Comp. Gen. 242 (1974), 74–2 CPD 185.

These potential problems are dealt with to some extent by DAR Part 15, which places limitations on the use and evaluation of options. For example, DAR § 1–1505 provides that options should not be exercised unless "exercise of the option is the most advantageous method of fulfilling the Government's needs, price and [other] factors considered." Additionally, DAR § 1–1504(c)(ii) provides that options may be evaluated in making award only if (1) there is a "known requirement" which exceeds the basic quantity but either the basic quantity is a learning or testing requirement or due to the unavailability of funds the option cannot be exercised at the time of award and (2) realistic competition for the option quantity is impracticable once the initial contract is awarded.

In light of DSS–W's statement that it can obtain realistic competition for its subsequent needs, we agree that the solicitation should not have provided that options would be evaluated in making an award. Furthermore, in view of DSS–W's statement, it does not appear that the solicitation should have contained option provisions at all. *See* DAR § 1–1502(b). However, we do not believe that the improper evaluation of options in this instance justifies termination of Safemasters' contract. It does not appear that the evaluation or use of option periods had any effect on the award. Examination of the three bids submitted does not indicate that any of the bidders submitted unbalanced bids, or otherwise attempted to benefit in the event the Government failed to exercise the options. As noted above, the three bids were evaluated by DSS–W as follows:

Bidder	For basic year	First option year	Second option year	Total price as computed by DSS–W
Safemasters	$93, 343. 44	$97, 615. 47	$102, 012. 33	$292, 971. 24
A–1	121, 677. 75	(¹)	(²)	436, 712. 59
Mosler	127, 630. 30	133, 688. 17	140, 624. 37	401, 942. 14

¹ 15 percent increase.
² 25 percent increase.

As can be seen, each bidder submitted a bid which provided for a basic year price and higher prices for the option years. Although each bidder increased the option year prices by different percentages, each bidder increased the second option year price by approximately the same percentage that it increased the first option year price. There is no indication that any bidder attempted to "front load" its bid in order to benefit in the event the Government failed to exercise the options. Additionally, Safemasters' bid is low whether evaluated on the basic year, the basic year plus the first option year, or the basic year plus both option years.

Although in *Mobilease Corporation, supra,* we held that an award under a solicitation which did not comply with DAR § 1–1504(c)(ii) was improper we do not believe our holding is directly applicable to this situation. In *Mobilease,* the Government issued an IFB for the rental of relocatable office buildings for a 2-year period with three 1-year options while a permanent facility was being constructed. Under the IFB, which required evaluation to be on the total 5-year period, Mobilease was not the low bidder. However, Mobilease was the low bidder on the initial 2-year period and remained low when evaluated on the first two 1-year options (3 and 4 year periods). It was only after the evaluation of the third 1-year option (5 year period) that Mobilease was no longer the low bidder. Mobilease protested the award alleging that the awardee's bid was unbalanced.

In considering Mobilease's protest, we determined that the question implicitly raised was whether options could be properly evaluated under the then-applicable Armed Services Procurement Regulation (ASPR) § 1–1504(d)(ii). We held that the evaluation of options and subsequent award were improper since the Government had failed to make the requisite findings under ASPR § 1–1504(d)(ii). Specifically, the Government had failed to determine that there was a "known requirement" for the full 5-year period and failed to determine with a reasonable certainty that funds would be available to permit the exercise of the options. Since there was no "known requirement" for the full 5-year period, it was not clear that award to someone other than Mobilease would result in the lowest cost to the Government.

In this case, Safemasters is the low bidder under all possible situations, award to Safemasters will result in the lowest cost to the Government, and no bidder was prejudiced by the option evaluation.

Based on the foregoing, we do not believe that termination of Safemasters' contract was justified. Accordingly, we believe that DSS–W should reinstate Safemasters' terminated contract. However, since it appears that the option provisions should not have been included in the solicitation, we believe that the options in the reinstated contract should not be exercised.

[B–192114]

National Guard—Death or Injury—While on Training Duty—Injury Within Scope of Duties

A National Guard member is in a travel status for medical and disability entitlements for injury incurred while traveling to and from active duty training when he leaves his living quarters with the intention of going directly to the place where ordered to perform such duty and such travel status continues upon completion of his tour when he returns directly from his place of duty to his home until he has entered his living quarters.

In the matter of Medical and disability entitlements—National Guard personnel, January 25, 1979:

This action is in response to a letter dated June 5, 1978, from the National Guard Bureau, Departments of the Army and the Air Force, requesting a decision regarding medical and disability entitlements for National Guard personnel injured while traveling to or from duty under sections 503, 504, and 505 of title 32, United States Code.

The question presented in the submission involves when and where travel status begins and ends in certain situations where the members were either proceeding to or from their duty station without deviation or delay. The cases in question include:

(a) A member of the Ohio Air National Guard (ANG) was ordered under section 503, *supra*, to report at 5:30 a.m., for annual training (AT) during the period February 10 through February 24, 1978. At 5 a.m., on February 10, 1978, the member proceeded from his house, walked down the exterior steps, slipped and fell on ice causing injury to his hand.

(b) A member of the New York ANG was ordered under section 503, *supra*, to full-time training duty (FTTD) from 12:01 a.m., August 15 through 12 p.m., August 19, 1977. On returning home at 8:30 p.m., on August 19, the member slipped and fell on his driveway area resulting in a fractured hand.

(c) A member of the Washington ANG ordered under section 503, *supra*, to FTTD for one (1) day, October 18, 1977, returned from duty on this day at 8:30 p.m. When the member attempted to open his electric garage door, he found it inoperative. He attempted to lift the door manually and while doing so he suffered severe back injury requiring orthopedic surgery.

Section 204, title 37, United States Code, provides in pertinent part as follows:

> (h) A member of the National Guard is entitled to the pay and allowances provided by law and regulation for a member of the Regular Army or the Regular Air Force, as the case may be, of corresponding grade and length of service, whenever he is called or ordered to perform training under section 502, 503, 504, or 505 of title 32—
>
> *　　　*　　　*　　　*　　　*　　　*　　　*
>
> (2) for any period of time, and is disabled in line of duty from injury *while so employed.* [Italic supplied.]

Subsection 318(2) of title 32, United States Code, also provides benefits to members of the National Guard who are disabled in line of duty from injury while so employed.

Paragraph 4b, Section B, Air Force Regulation (AFR) 168–6, September 3, 1974, provides that Reserve and National Guard personnel who incur an injury in line of duty while on active duty (including active duty for training) or while traveling to and from such duty may be provided medical care including rehospitalization for the injury until the disability cannot be materially improved.

Line of duty determinations and investigations of members of the ANG incurring an injury while on tours of active duty training are made in accordance with AFR 35–67, August 14, 1964, as changed by Change A, of April 20, 1965, and Change B of December 2, 1968. Paragraph 2a, Section A, of this regulation provides that all determinations are "in line of duty" unless the injury resulted from the person's own misconduct, occurred while in desertion status, occurred while absent without authority, or existed prior to service.

We are not aware of any specific rulings by either this Office or the courts with regard to when travel commences and terminates for members of the Reserve components or the National Guard when they are ordered to active duty or active duty for training or the equivalent. However, we have found analogous situations in cases involving the award of workmen's compensation for injuries.

As a general rule, injuries sustained by workmen while going to and from work are not compensable. See 99 CJS 232. However, where an employment contract covers a period of going to and from work, injury incurred during such travel may be compensable. 99 CJS 233.

Since a member of a Reserve component or the National Guard who is disabled while traveling to active duty or its equivalent is considered to have incurred the injury in line of duty while so employed (see *Adams* v. *United States*, 127 Ct. Cl. 470 (1954) and 33 Comp. Gen. 599 (1954)), such situations must be considered analogous to an employee who is compensated for traveling to and from his employment.

In this regard ample authority exists concluding that such an employee on departing his residence is considered to be "in the course of his employment" even if he sustains injury while walking down his own outside stairs or slips in his driveway. See *Cohen v. Central Home Furniture Co. et al.*, 23 A 2d 70 (1941) ; *Bitker Cloak & Suit Co., et al. v. Miller, et al.*, 6 NW 2d 664, 665, (1942) ; *Eaton v. Webster Motors of Glen Falls, Inc., et al.*, 39 NYS 2d 32 (1943) ; *In the Matter of Fred T. Craik and Dept. of Agriculture*, 12 ECAB 28 (1960) ; and *Black River Dairy Products, Inc., et al. v. Dept. of Industry, Labor & Human Relations, et al.*, 207 NW 2d 65 (1973).

Based upon the foregoing, we have concluded that a member entering on active duty begins a travel status when he leaves his living quarters with the intention of going directly to the place where ordered to perform such duty and such travel status continues upon completion of his tour when he returns directly from his place of duty to his home until he has entered his living quarters.

Accordingly, if the facts in the cases presented show that the member had left his residence with the intention of traveling directly to his place of duty, in contrast to merely preparing to depart or, on return, that he had proceeded directly to his residence without deviation, a finding of disabled in the line of duty by injury while so employed would be appropriate.

Doubtful cases may be submitted to this Office for decision.

〔 B–192318 〕

Contracts—Federal Supply Schedule—Awards—Propriety

Where vendor under Federal Supply Schedule (FSS) contract apprises procuring activity shortly before award that it offers "middle of the line" equipment and procuring activity only has specifications for vendor's "top of the line" equipment, procuring activity, in attempt to reduce procurement costs, should have attempted to obtain specifications from vendor or General Services Administration and determine if "middle of the line" equipment would satisfy Government's legitimate needs. However, since vendor should have advised agency of middle of line equipment earlier in the procurement process and offered equipment met agency's minimum needs and has been delivered and installed, award will not be disturbed.

Contracts—Federal Supply Schedule—Bid Evaluation Factors—Price Differentials—Labor Surplus Areas—Addition of 6% or 12%

Federal Procurement Regulations provide that Buy American Act differential of 12 percent be applied to price of foreign-origin products where concern submitting low domestic bid or offer will substantially perform contract in labor surplus area. A 12-percent Buy American Act differential should not be applied where vendor under FSS contract produced equipment in labor surplus area facility but facility was closed before purchase order was issued for equipment because regulations contemplate contract performance in labor surplus area after issuance of purchase orders so as to help achieve regulatory objective of fostering employment in such area.

Purchases—Purchase Orders—Federal Supply Schedule—Prices—Procurement at Lowest Price Requirement

Purchase of least costly dictating and transcribing systems which satisfied legitimate need of various field offices, as determined by agency, was proper procurement practice.

In the matter of Dictaphone Corporation, January 25, 1979:

This protest by Dictaphone Corporation (Dictaphone) involves the procurement of dictating and transcribing equipment (D/T equipment) by the Federal Bureau of Investigation (FBI) for five FBI field offices, namely, Baltimore, Milwaukee, Newark, San Diego, and Washington, D.C.

The FBI made a detailed evaluation of the D/T equipment offered by each vendor under General Services Administration's (GSA) Federal Supply Schedule (FSS) contracts to determine which vendor offered D/T equipment which would satisfy the FBI's legitimate needs. As a result of this analysis, the FBI determined that only Dictaphone and Lanier Business Products and Oxford Industry (Lanier) offered acceptable products. In evaluating the cost of the D/T equipment, the FBI added a 6-percent Buy American Act differential to the prices offered by Lanier.

A schedule of the offered prices, less discount and trade-in, follows:

Field Offices	Dictaphone	Lanier
Baltimore	$24, 476. 34	$23, 248. 12
Milwaukee	14, 864. 82	13, 406. 05
Newark	36, 101. 50	41, 874. 90
San Diego	12, 742. 34	10, 591. 20
Washington	[1] 31, 407. 51	30, 735. 97

[1] Does not include price of three Dictaphone central recorders.

The FBI purchased D/T equipment for the Baltimore, Milwaukee, San Diego, and Washington field offices from Lanier. The D/T equipment for the Newark field office was purchased from Dictaphone. We have been advised that the vendors have delivered and installed the equipment.

Dictaphone protests in substance as follows:

1. Dictaphone's "top of the line" model 260 equipment was compared to Lanier's "middle of the line" Regent model equipment. The FBI failed to evaluate Dictaphone's model 255 equipment, which is less costly than model 260 equipment and is comparable to the Lanier Regent equipment, even though the FBI had information concerning model 255 equipment before award.

2. Lanier offered equipment which lacked certain essential features such as voice-operated relays (VOR), buffered storage VOR, or audio time delays.

3. Dictaphone made an offer and in July 1977 was awarded an FSS contract. Dictaphone proceeded to manufacture the D/T equipment here involved at a facility located in a labor surplus area until the facility was closed in November 1977. Therefore, a 12-percent instead of a 6-percent Buy American Act differential should have been applied to the prices of Lanier's equipment since Dictaphone's equipment was manufactured under Government contract in a labor surplus area. Entitlement to Buy American Act preferences is determined at the time a vendor submits an offer for an FSS contract and not at the time purchase orders are issued under such contract. See section 1–6.104.4 (1964 ed. circ. 1) of the Federal Procurement Regulations (FPR). If vendors were required to produce products in a labor surplus area after the issuance of a purchase order under an FSS contract, virtually every vendor in a labor surplus area would not be entitled to a Buy American Act preference because the products could not be manufactured in time to meet the short delivery schedule of FSS contracts. Besides, purchase orders are not contracts which must be performed in a labor surplus area in order to qualify for a 12-percent Buy American Act differential.

4. Dictaphone was asked to offer prices for three central recorders for the Washington Field Office (WFO), which Lanier did not have to offer since three Lanier central recorders were already installed at WFO. This placed Dictaphone at a competitive disadvantage; moreover, Dictaphone should not have been asked to quote these prices and the prices should not have been included in the cost comparison since Dictaphone equipment is compatible with Lanier recorders already installed at WFO.

5. If a 12-percent Buy American Act differential had been properly applied to Lanier's offered prices and the three Dictaphone central recorders were excluded from the calculations, Dictaphone's total offer for the five FBI field offices would be low.

In response to Dictaphone's protest, the FBI states that Dictaphone and Lanier were contacted on June 22, 1978. Both vendors were apprised of FBI equipment needs and existing FBI equipment available for trade-in. Dictaphone and Lanier were requested to submit only trade-in allowances by June 28, 1978. They were further advised that award would be made prior to June 30, 1978.

The FBI states further that the FSS contracts involved were due to expire on June 30, 1978. A sharp price increase was anticipated, and the FBI field offices were urgently in need of the D/T equipment.

The FBI goes on to assert that Dictaphone made a timely submittal setting forth trade-in allowances; however, it made no mention of its model 255 equipment. On June 28, 1978, Dictaphone orally provided information concerning such equipment but the information was incomplete. Although Dictaphone's GSA contract was amended on May 13, 1978, to include model 255, the FBI had no record of ever having received the amendment concerning model 255 equipment. Approximately 3 weeks before award, Dictaphone demonstrated its equipment and provided clarifying information to FBI representatives, but it made no mention of its model 255 equipment.

According to the FBI, Lanier and other vendors were not expected to offer equipment with certain features. Vendors were advised that the equipment which satisfied the FBI's legitimate needs would be procured under FSS contracts.

With regard to the Buy American Act differential, the FBI states that applicable regulations provide that the 12-percent differential requested by Dictophone is applied only where the low domestic offeror will substantially perform the contract in a labor surplus area. A 6-percent Buy American Act differential was applied to Lanier's offered prices because Dictaphone was not manufacturing model 260 D/T equipment in a labor surplus area at the time the purchase orders were issued. Consequently, Dictaphone would not substantially perform the contract in a labor surplus area. See FPR §§ 1–1.801(c) (1964 ed. amend. 192), 1–1.802–1 (1964 ed. amend. 192), 1–6.104.4 (1964 ed. circ. 1). In this regard, the FBI states that purchase orders issued under an FSS contract are contracts which must be substantially performed in a labor surplus area if a 12-percent Buy American Act differential is to be applied to the prices of foreign origin products. See FPR § 1–1.208 (1964 ed. amend. 9).

The FBI also contends that the WFO utilizes three Lanier central recorders. The Lanier recorders are not compatible with Dictaphone equipment. Therefore, three Dictaphone central recorders were considered in the evaluation of equipment for WFO. If Dictaphone had offered the low cost system for WFO, WFO's central recorders would have been transferred to an office utilizing compatible Lanier equipment.

The FBI contends that it did not receive complete data concerning Dictaphone's model 255 equipment in time for it to be evaluated. The record shows that shortly before award the FBI was aware that Dictaphone offered model 255 equipment. Under the circumstances, we think that the FBI should have attempted to obtain information from Dictaphone or GSA concerning the features and capabilities of the model 255 equipment so that a determination could be made as to whether the equipment would satisfy the FBI's legitimate needs at any of the five field offices. However, since the vendor should have advised the agency of its middle of the line equipment earlier in the procurement process and the offered equipment met the agency's minimum needs and has been delivered and installed, the award will not be disturbed.

There is no merit to Dictaphone's assertion that the Lanier D/T equipment lacked certain essential features or components, such as VOR, buffered storage VOR, or audio time delays, as the FBI determined from Lanier's descriptive literature that its equipment met its needs.

We agree with the FBI concerning the application of a 6-percent Buy American Act differential to the prices offered by Lanier. To be more specific, the applicable provisions of the FPR provide as follows:

1–6.104–4   Evaluation of bids and proposals.

* * * * * * *

(b) * * * Each foreign bid shall be adjusted for purposes of evaluation by adding to the foreign bid (inclusive of duty) a factor of 6 percent of that bid, except that a 12 percent factor shall be used instead of a 6 percent factor if the firm submitting the low acceptable domestic bid is a * * * labor surplus area concern (as defined in * * * 1–.801 * * *

§ 1–1.801 Definitions.

* * * * * * *

(c) The term "labor surplus area concern" means a concern that together with its first-tier subcontractors *will perform substantially in a labor surplus area.*

(d) The term "perform substantially in labor surplus areas" means that the costs incurred on account of manufacturing, production, or appropriate services in labor surplus areas exceeded 50 percent of the contract price.

§ 1–1.802 Labor surplus area policies.

§ 1–1.802–1 General policy.

It is the policy of the Government to award appropriate contracts and grants to, and to execute agreements with, eligible labor surplus area concerns and to encourage prime contractors to place subcontracts with concerns which *will perform substantially in labor surplus areas.* [Italic supplied.]

In our opinion, the applicable regulations make it clear that in order for a 12-percent Buy American Act differential to be applied to a foreign offer or bid, the low domestic offeror or bidder must be willing and able to perform the contract substantially in a labor surplus area. The obvious objective of these regulatory provisions is to foster employment in such areas.

As indicated above, Dictaphone was awarded a GSA FSS contract in July 1977. After award, Dictaphone proceeded to manufacture the D/T equipment here involved at a facility located in a labor surplus area until that facility was closed in November 1977, or before the FBI issued purchase orders for D/T equipment. We view each FBI purchase order as a contract because it is by issuance of purchase orders that an FSS contract becomes effective. FPR § 1–1.208 (1964 ed. amend. 9). It follows then that the FBI procurement of Dictaphone D/T equipment would not help relieve unemployment in a labor surplus area, because Dictaphone's facility in a labor surplus area has been closed. Therefore, we do not agree with Dictaphone that the critical date for determining applicability of the Buy American differential is the date of award of the FSS contract. Consequently, Dictaphone is not entitled to have a 12-percent Buy American Act differential applied to the price of Lanier's foreign-origin D/T equipment since the application of the differential would not have its required impact on unemployment in a labor surplus area.

The requirement that each purchase order will be substantially performed in a labor surplus area before a 12-percent Buy American Act differential will be applied to the price of foreign-origin end products does not bar a vendor in a labor surplus area from providing products from inventory, since there is a reasonable presumption that the stock drawn from inventory will be replenished. The replenishment of inventory stock will create a demand for services and material and, thereby, accomplish the regulatory objective of helping to relieve unemployment in a labor surplus area. Therefore, we do not agree with Dictaphone's argument that the Buy American preference cannot relate to the date of the purchase order because the products could not be manufactured in time to meet the short delivery schedule of FSS contracts.

Finally, it was proper for the FBI to purchase the lowest-priced D/T system for each of its field offices which satisfied its legitimate needs. *Cf. Lanier Business Products, Inc.; Mid-Atlantic Industries, Inc.*, B–187819, August 24, 1977, 77–2 CPD 143. Moreover, even if the price of three Dictaphone central recorders were deducted from Dictaphone's offered price for the WFO, Lanier's offered price for the WFO would still be low. See schedule of offered prices, *supra.*

Based on the foregoing, the protest is denied.

[B-192462]

Contracts—Awards—Legality—Award Not Plainly or Palpably Illegal—Procurement v. Sales Contracts

Where Government administrative error in sale of surplus property results in notice of award to second highest bidder, award is unauthorized.

Sales—Legality—Surplus Sales—Statutory Presumption of Validity—Applicability—Contract v. Property Interest

Under solicitation which provides that title will not pass until removal of property from Government control, 40 U.S.C. 484(d) does not raise conclusive presumption of compliance with surplus sale procedures required by law, since property was not removed.

Estoppel—Against   Government—Not   Established—Surplus Sales—Cancellation of Erroneous Award

Government is not bound by its agents acting beyond their authority and contrary to law, and the United States is not estopped to deny the authority of its agents.

In the matter of Charlie Driesbock Machine Tools, January 26, 1979:

Charlie Driesbock Machine Tools (Driesbock) protests the cancellation of surplus sale contract No. 60–8050–032 for item 165 awarded to Driesbock under sale invitation No. 60–8050 issued by the Defense Property Disposal Region (DPDR) Pacific Sales Office in Hawaii.

On June 20, 1978, bids were opened. Ten bids were received for item 165, a horizontal boring machine located on the island of Guam. On the abstract of bids, the bid of Driesbock in the amount of $3,333.33 was circled to denote it as the high bid. The bid of Greer Machinery Company, Inc. (Greer), in the amount of $6,756 on the abstract was misread as $675.60. As a result of that misreading, item 165 was awarded to Driesbock, the second high bidder, on June 23, 1978. DPDR states that the erroneous award was discovered on July 3, 1978, and by letter of July 6, 1978, Driesbock was advised that the contract was being canceled and that payment for the item would be returned. The item has not been removed from Government control.

Driesbock protests cancellation of the contract stating that it sold item 165 for $27,500 on the basis of the award and that it has committed air fare to Guam to conclude the sale which represents an additional expense of over $1,300. Driesbock states that it will be sued for breach of contract if it fails to deliver the item to its customer.

The Defense Logistics Agency (DLA) has indicated that over the years it has followed 36 Comp. Gen. 94 (1956) which held that where the highest bid for the purchase of Government surplus sold under competitive bidding procedures is solicited, but through an administrative error award has been made to the second highest bidder, the interest of the United States, as well as the duty of the contracting officer to award such contracts to the highest bidder, requires that such unauthorized award be set aside and award made to the highest bidder. (Our Office recently has sustained that holding in *William D. Garrett*, B–192592, November 16, 1978, 78–2 CPD 350.) Now, in light of *Fink Sanitary Service, Inc.*, 53 Comp. Gen. 502 (1974), 74–1 CPD 36, applying estoppel against the Government in an erroneously awarded procurement contract, DLA proposes that the estoppel principle be applied in a situation where a sale contract is awarded to the second high bidder by mistake. In that connection, DLA notes that estoppel was considered in a sale situation in *Leonard Joseph Company*, B–182303, April 18, 1975, 75–1 CPD 235, and was denied there because one of the essential elements for estoppel was missing. See also, *Metalsco, Incorporated*, B–187882, March 9, 1977, 77–1 CPD 175, another sale situation where estoppel was considered and denied. Thus, our Office has considered estoppel against the Government in sales as well as procurement situations. DLA also focuses attention on 40 U.S.C. § 484(d) (1976) which states:

Validity of deed, bill of sale, lease, etc.

A deed, bill of sale, lease or other instrument executed by or on behalf of any executive agency purporting to transfer title or any other interest in surplus property under this subchapter shall be conclusive evidence of compliance with the provisions of this subchapter insofar as concerns title or other interest of any bona fide grantee or transferee for value and without notice of lack of such compliance.

We do not believe that 40 U.S.C. § 484(d) is applicable. That subsection raises a conclusive presumption of the validity of the sale "insofar as concerns title or other interest of any bona fide grantee or transferee for value and without notice of lack of such compliance." The terms "grantee" and "transferee" refer to holders of a property interest as opposed to a contractual interest. See *Black's Law Dictionary* (4th ed. 1968). In *Turney v. United States*, the Court of Claims ruled that section 25 of the War Surplus Act of 1944, 58 Stat. 780, 50 U.S.C. App. § 1634 (1946), a precursor to 40 U.S.C. § 484(d), operated to give valid title to the purchasers of certain radar equipment despite the fact that Government agents had exceeded their authority in selling the radar as disposable surplus. 126 Ct. Cl. 202, 115 F. Supp. 457 (1953). The court specifically stated that if the surplus property sale did not pass ownership to the property, the purchaser never acquired title and could not recover. 126 Ct. Cl at 213, 214; 115 F. Supp. at 463. It is evident from *Turney* that the event which gives a purchaser the rights of a grantee or transferee and triggers application of 40 U.S.C. § 484(d) is the passage to the purchaser of reputed title to the surplus property. See also *United States* v. *Jones*, 176 F. 2d 278 (9th Cir. 1949); *East Tennessee Iron & Metal Co.* v. *United States*, 218 F. Supp. 377 (E.D. Tenn. 1963).

The notice of award in this case specifically conditions the passage of title upon payment by the buyer of the balance due ($422.23) and removal of the surplus property. Sale by reference pamphlet, Part 2, paragraph 7 (January 1978), incorporated into the IFB, provides in pertinent part:

Unless otherwise provided in the Invitation, title to the property sold hereunder shall vest in the purchase as and when removal is effected * * *.

The boring machine in this case was never removed from Government possession by Driesbock. Therefore, title did not pass, and 40 U.S.C. § 484(d) is not applicable to raise a conclusive presumption of compliance with the requirements stated elsewhere in 40 U.S.C. § 484.

We also believe that estoppel is inappropriate. In the present case we are concerned with a sales contract. Our Office has frequently held that where the highest bid for the purchase of Government surplus sold under competitive bidding procedures has been solicited, but through administrative error award was made to the second highest bidder, the interests of the United States, as well as the duty of the contracting officer to award such contracts to the highest bidder, require that such unauthorized award be set aside and award made to the highest bidder. *E.g.*, 36 Comp. Gen. 94, *supra; William D. Garrett, supra; Metalsco, Inc., supra; Leonard Joseph Co., supra.* The rationale of these decisions is that a contracting officer has no authority to award a surplus sale contract to other than the highest responsive, responsible bidder and that an award to another party is illegal and a nullity, conferring no rights on the contractor against the Government. *Cf.* 53 Comp. Gen., *supra*, at 507.

We recognized the contract in *Fink, supra*, as creating rights in the contractor, because that case involved a procurement contract award which was improper as opposed to "plainly or palpably illegal" under the standards prescribed in 52 Comp. Gen. 215 (1972). This Office has not applied the standard of plain or palpable illegality for procurement contracts to the area of sale contracts, and we are unaware of any court having done so. The standards for procurement contracts were reached to remove the contractor from what the Court of Claims termed "an unfortunate dilemma :"

> If he questions the award and refuses to accept it because of his own doubts as to possible illegality, the contracting officer could forfeit his bid bond for refusing to enter into the contract. The full risk of an adverse decision on validity would then rest on the bidder. If he accedes to the contracting officer and commences performance of the contract, a subsequent holding of non-enforceability would lead to denial of all recovery under the agreement even though the issue of legality is very close ; and under the doctrine of quantum meruit there would be no reimbursement for expenses incurred in good faith but only for any tangible benefits actually received by the defendant. *United States* v. *Mississippi Valley Generating Co.*, 364 U.S. 520, 566 n. 22 (1961) ; *Clark* v. *United States*, 95 U.S. 539, 542 (1877). It is therefore just to the contractor, as well as to the Government to give him the benefit of reasonable doubts and to uphold the award unless its invalidity is clear. *John Reiner & Co.* v. *United States*, 163 Ct. Cl. 381, 386, 325 F. 2d 438, 440 (1963).

The party to a sale contract does not suffer such a dilemma. The purchaser does not have to incur expenses to begin performance, with the possible exception of arranging removal. In this regard we note that Driesbock alleges to have committed $1,300 air fare to Guam to conclude the sale. It is not clear from the record, however, whether the $1,300 was incurred by Driesbock in reliance upon the notice of award or was incurred in the course of Driesbock's participation as a bidder. In any event, we are not persuaded that the "plain and palpable illegal" test should be applied to the sales contracts so as to protect purchasers such as Driesbock from incurring removal cost. Of course, once the property is removed, 40 U.S.C. § 484(d) operates to pass valid title.

Based on the above, the contract in this case is unauthorized and illegal. It is well settled that one who purports to contract with the United States assumes the risk that the official with whom he deals is clothed with actual authority to enter the alleged contract, and that the United States is not bound by its agents acting beyond their authority and contrary to law. *Federal Crop Insurance Corp.* v. *Merrill*, 332 U.S. 380, 384 (1947) ; *Jackson* v. *United States*, 213 Ct. Cl. 354, 359, 551 F. 2d 282, 285 (1977). Moreover, the United States is not estopped to deny the authority of its agents. 213 Ct. Cl. at 359, 551 F. 2d at 285. We believe that until title vests in the purchaser pursuant to 40 U.S.C. § 484(d), the purchaser must bear the risk that the official has actual authority to enter the sale contract, and that the United States is not estopped to deny an unauthorized award by its agent. Although we did discuss estoppel in conjunction with sales contracts awarded to other than the high bidder, we have never held the Government estopped to deny the illegality of such contracts. We simply stated that the requirements for estoppel are not present, never reaching the issue whether the Government can be estopped to deny the illegality of the contract.

In light of our decision that the contract is illegal and the Government cannot be estopped to deny its illegality, we do not find it necessary to discuss potential Government liability for damages to Driesbock under the contract. See *Peck Iron & Metal Co.* v. *United States*, 204 Ct. Cl. 381, 496 F. 2d 543 (1974); *Freedman* v. *United States*, 162 Ct. Cl. 390, 320 F. 2d 359 (1963). The unauthorized contract creates no rights in Driesbock against the Government.

Accordingly, the interests of the United States as well as the duty of the contracting officer to award contracts for which bids were solicited to the highest bidder require that the unauthorized award to Driesbock be set aside and award made to the highest bidder, Greer.

[B-193379]

Environmental Protection and Improvement—Clean Air Act—State and Local Air Quality Regulations—Federal Compliance

In the absence of express Presidential exemption, the 1977 Amendment to section 118 of the Clean Air Act requires Federal facilities to abide by State and local laws regarding abatement and control of pollution, to same extent an nongovernmental entity, including obtaining permits and paying associated fees. Therefore Air Force must pay permit fee to municipal air pollution control authority for operation of equipment which would be subject to municipality's air pollution control regulations if operated by nongovernmental entity.

In the matter of Obligation of Federal Facility under Clean Air Act to Pay Fees for Sacramento County Environmental Protection Permits, January 26, 1979:

The Deputy Director, Plans & Systems, United States Air Force, has forwarded a request by the Accounting and Finance Office of the 323d Flying Training Wing, Mather Air Force Base, California (Mather AFB), for an advance decision on whether Mather AFB must pay filing and operating permit fees for certain equipment (*e.g.*, gasoline storage tanks, boilers, and paint spray booths) to the Air Pollution Control District, Sacramento County, California (APCD). The Accounting and Finance Officer is an authorized certifying officer and has a voucher before him for payment in the amount of $2,082.50.

The Accounting and Finance Officer has been informed by the APCD that it interprets the 1977 Amendment to section 118 of the Clean Air Act (Act), Pub. L. No. 95–95, section 116, 91 Stat. 711 (1977), classified to 42 U.S.C. § 7418, as making Mather AFB subject to all local requirements for the control and abatement of air pollution, including the obtaining of permits. Under Rule 70 of the APCD Rules and Regulations, a fee schedule is established for required permits. The Accounting and Finance Officer asks whether the APCD interpretation of this amendment is correct.

Additionally, he asks that we examine certain bases of exemption from the local regulations requiring permits or fees, if we decide that Federal agencies and departments, such as Mather AFB, are subject to local regulation. The specific bases of these exemptions advanced by the Accounting and Finance Officer are:

(a) A statement in Air Force regulations (AFR 19-1, Attachment 2, paragraph (i)) that the Air Force "presently has no obligation" to obtain operating permits from State or local Governments although it must comply with emission limitations, which the Accounting and Finance Officer reads as an exercise of the President's authority under section 118(b) of the Act allowing him to exempt military equipment from compliance with section 118; and

(b) APCD's past practice of including Federal agencies within an exemption from paying permit fees given to State and local agencies.

In interpreting statutes, the first step is to look at the words by which the legislature undertook to give expression to its intent. Section 118, as amended, reads in pertinent part:

> Each department, agency and instrumentality of the executive, legislative, and judicial branches of the Federal Government (1) having jurisdiction over any property or facility, or (2) engaged in any activity resulting, or which may result, in the discharge of air pollutants, and each officer, agent, or employee thereof, shall be subject to, and comply with, all Federal, State, interstate, and local requirements, administrative authority, and process and sanctions respecting the control and abatement of air pollution in the same manner, and to the same extent as any, nongovernmental entity. The preceding sentence shall apply (A) to any requirement whether substantive or procedural (including * * * any requirement respecting permits and any other requirement whatsoever) * * *.

We believe that the plain meaning of this statute is consistent with the APCD interpretation. The legislative history supports this conclusion.

The 1977 Amendment to section 118 of the Clean Air Act was enacted primarily to subject Federal agencies and departments to all procedural and substantive requirements regarding air pollution control and abatement promulgated by State and local governmental units. The Clean Air Act Amendments originated in the House of Representatives as H.R. 6161. H.R. Rep. No. 95-294, 12-13 (1977), which accompanied H.R. 6161, says that section 118 of the existing Clean Air Act constituted a waiver of sovereign immunity and that Federal facilities were required to comply with all State and local air pollution requirements, both substantive and procedural. Even more revealing is the additional statement that "This provision is intended fundamentally to overrule the Supreme Court's ruling in *Hancock* v. *Train* * * *."

In *Hancock* v. *Train*, 426 U.S. 167 (1976), the Supreme Court ruled that section 118 of the Clean Air Act did not subject Federal installations to State and local permit requirements. The Court said that "the Clean Air Act does not satisfy the traditional requirement that such intention [to bind the United States] be evinced with satisfactory clarity." The Court then specifically advised that, if the Congress intended that the United States be bound, "it need only amend the Act to make its intention manifest." *Id.* at 198. Clearly, the Committee heeded this advice.

The Senate Report on a similar amendment to section 118 was in accord with the House Report. S. Rep. No. 95–127, 57–58. Additionally, the Senate Report explicitly stated that the intent of the language in the amendment requiring Federal compliance with both substantive and procedural requirements was to include requirements to obtain operating and construction permits and to pay reasonable service charges. *Id.* at 58.

Since Federal facilities are required to obtain State and local permits, Mather AFB must do so, unless there be some special basis for exemption. Section 118(b) of the Clean Air Act, as amended, 91 Stat. 711 (1977), authorizes the President to exempt any emission source of any Executive department from State and local regulations for a period of 1 year. Additionally, the President may issue regulations exempting classes of Armed Forces equipment uniquely military in nature. In either case the sole criterion in the law is that "he determines it [the exemption] to be in the paramount interest of the United States."

The former exemption authority—for any particular emission source in the Executive branch—existed prior to the 1977 Amendment. The latter exemption, for uniquely military equipment of the Armed Forces, did not. Compare section 5, Pub. L. No. 91–604, 84 Stat. 1689 with section 116(a), Pub. L. No. 95–95, 91 Stat. 711.

President Carter has issued Executive Order 12088, 43 Fed. Reg. 47707 (October 13, 1978), which sets forth the guidelines for agencies seeking exemptions pursuant to section 118(b) of the Act. As opposed to the previous practice of delegating the authority to grant exemptions to department heads (see section 5, Executive Order 11752, 3A C.F.R. 240, 244 (1973)), the President has retained this authority. The

President has stated that he will personally review each request for exemption. Statement on signing Executive Order 12088, 14 Weekly Comp. of Pres. Doc. 1769 (October 16, 1978).

We find no indication that the President has acted personally to exempt the emission sources at Mather AFB or the classes of equipment,* nor does the the Accounting and Finance Officer cite any specific exemption action. He suggests only that paragraph (i), Attachment 2, AFR 19–1, may constitute an exemption, under the President's authority to issue regulations exempting uniquely military property from compliance with section 118.

Air Force Regulation 19–1 properly directs Air Force bases to comply with all local procedural and substantive requirements regarding air pollution. (Section A.2.a (14).) This directive appears to be contradicted by Attachment 2, paragraph (i), which states that the Air Force need not obtain permits from State or local Governments for facilities which emit pollutants but comply with emission limitations. Paragraph (i) of Attachment 2 in effect restates the holding in *Hancock* v. *Train, supra*, which, as discussed above, is no longer the law by virtue of the amendment to section 118 of the Act. We note that in the first paragraph of Attachment 2, certain provisions of the Clean Air Act are referred to by outdated United States Code references. These Code references are to the classification used prior to the August 7, 1977, effective date of the Amendments to the Act, which resulted in a reclassification of the Act from 42 U.S.C. § 1857 *et seq.* to 42 U.S.C. § 7401 *et seq.* See note at Pub. L. No. 95–95, section 1, 91 Stat. 685 (1977). It thus appears that Attachment 2 did not take into account the changes brought about by the 1977 amendment to section 118.

Moreover, paragraph (i) of Attachment 2 does not purport to be a Presidential exemption; it does not cite a Presidential determination that an exemption is in the paramount national interest and is not limited either to a specific emission source or to uniquely military property. We therefore find no basis to conclude that paragraph (i) exempts Mather AFB from payment of the fees.

Finally, the fact that the APCD may in the past have considered that Federal facilities were exempt from paying permit fees is not significant. As Federal facilities were previously exempt from the requirement of obtaining permits (*Hancock* v. *Train, supra*), the APCD lacked legal authority to impose fees. Alternatively, even assuming that the APCD, after enactment of the 1977 amendments, had authority to charge Federal facilities a permit fee, but decided as a

---

*From the description provided, it does not appear that the equipment is "uniquely military," as it must be to qualify for the exemption.

matter of policy to include Federal facilities in its stated exemption for State and local governmental agencies, there is no legal principle precluding the APCD from changing this policy.

Accordingly, the voucher may be certified for payment.

[B–193087]

Contracts—Protests—Procedures—Bid Protest Procedures—Time for Filing—Sole-Source Procurement

Protest concerning sole source nature of a procurement filed more than 2 months after notice of intent to make contract award was published in the Commerce Business Daily is untimely under GAO Bid Protest Procedures, 4 C.F.R. 20.2 (b)(2) (1978). Even if initial protest had been filed with procuring agency, protester delayed too long in pursuing matter with General Accounting Office—more than 2 months after publication.

Advertising—Commerce Business Daily—Information—Constructive Notice—Date Determination—Publication v. Mail Receipt Date

Where protester has actual notice of award of contract after timely receipt of Commerce Business Daily in ordinary course of business within a reasonable time after publication and mailing, timeliness of protest may be measured from date publication is received, allowing a few days for mailing and receipt of the CBD. Prior decisions are clarified to allow for reasonable time for protester to receive publication in ordinary course of business. B–182318, Jan. 27, 1975, and other cases following rule established therein, modified.

In the matter of Delphi Industries, Inc., January 30, 1979:

Delphi Industries, Inc., (Delphi) protests the award of a letter contract F08635–78–C–0027 for missile containers on a sole-source basis to Metric Systems Corporation (Metric). Delphi contends that the Air Force should have solicited competition for this procurement because Delphi is a current manufacturer of missile containers.

The Air Force's intent to make a sole source award to Metric was publicized in the July 24, 1978, issue of the Commerce Business Daily (CBD). Specifically this notice identified the containers and quantity involved and provided that "letter contract is being issued sole source to Metric Systems Corp. * * *." In our opinion, this publication constituted notice to Delphi of the basis for protest. *Delta Scientific Corporation*, B–184401, August 3, 1976, 76–2 CPD 113. Subsequently, the September 18 issue of the CBD announced that the contract had been awarded to Metric on August 11.

The Air Force argues in its report that the protest to this Office is untimely under our bid protest procedures because on the basis of either synopsis date Delphi exceeded the 10 days in which to file the protest. 4 C.F.R. § 20.2(b)(2) (1978). Delphi's only response to the Air Force's position concerns the second synopsis. The protester argues that it received the September 18 issue of the CBD on September 21 and its protest was filed within 10 days after receipt of the publication. However, as indicated above we think the basis for protest should have been apparent to Delphi from the first synopsis in July.

Delphi has stated in a letter to its Senator, which was forwarded to this Office by the Senator, that after the July synopsis it called the procuring activity and "inquired what was going on" and "protested that we wanted some of this action * * *." However, Delphi has not argued here that a timely protest was filed with the Air Force on the basis of the July synopsis. We therefore must conclude from the record before us that Delphi's protest to this Office in October, more than 2 months after the July synopsis, is untimely. Even if Delphi were to argue that a timely initial protest was lodged with the Air Force on the basis of the July synopsis, we think Delphi delayed too long in pursuing the matter with this Office more than 2 months after it "protested" to the Air Force, since that agency's inaction itself would have constituted adverse agency action on the protest. 4 C.F.R. 20.0(b) ; 52 Comp. Gen. 792 (1973) ; *Illitron*, B–192309, August 7, 1978, 78–2 CPD 100.

The protest, therefore, is dismissed as untimely filed.

This protest suggests the need for clarification of our prior decisions following the rule established in *Del Norte Technology, Inc.*, B–182318, January 27, 1975, 75–1 CPD 53. We held in that decision that publication of award information of a sole source procurement in the CBD is constructive notice thereof to all concerned. That case involved a situation where the protester waited more than 30 days after publication to protest. However, we did not intend to deny potential protesters a reasonable period necessary to receive the publication, since the CBD generally is sent by mail. Where, as here, the protester receives the publication in the ordinary course of business a few days after the date of publication, the timeliness of any protest will be measured from the date the publication is received.

[B–192499]

Transportation—Automobiles—Authority

Employee transferred in August 1977 from San Diego, California, to Denver, Colorado, drove to new station. Although authorized the use of a second automobile, his wife and children traveled by air and shipped the second car by commercial carrier. The transportation costs of the dependents and automobile plus per diem are less than the constructive entitlement of the dependents' travel by automobile. In the absence of specific statutory authorization required by 5

U.S.C. 5727(a), employee's claim for the cost of shipping his privately owned vehicle from San Diego to Denver may not be paid.

In the matter of Timothy A. Towns—Reimbursement of Cost of Shipping Privately Owned Vehicle, January 31, 1979:

This is in response to a request for a decision regarding the claim of Timothy A. Towns, an employee of the Internal Revenue Service, for reimbursement of the cost of shipping his privately owned vehicle incident to his transfer from San Diego, California, to Denver, Colorado.

The record shows that Mr. Towns was transferred from San Diego to Denver effective August 15, 1977, and was authorized the use of two privately owned vehicles because his reporting date was earlier than his family's relocation date. Mr. Towns completed his travel from San Diego to Denver by automobile and was reimbursed for mileage and per diem. However, although authorized the use of a second automobile, his wife and three children completed their travel by air, and shipped the second car by commercial carrier.

Mr. Towns has been reimbursed for air fare and per diem for the travel of his family, but his claim of $150 for the cost of shipping the second automobile was denied by the agency. In seeking reimbursement, Mr. Towns points out that the cost of transporting his family by air plus the cost of shipping the second car are less than the constructive cost of travel by automobile for his wife and three children. Since the Government would realize an overall savings, he believes he is entitled to his actual expenses not to exceed the constructive cost of travel by the second automobile. He also notes that the method of transportation used was more beneficial to his family since, at the time of the move, the ages of his children were 4 years, 2 years, and 10 months.

The transportation of privately owned vehicles at Government expense in connection with a transfer between duty stations is prohibited by 5 U.S.C. 5727(a) (1976) in the absence of specific authorization by statute. While 5 U.S.C. 5727(b) does permit transportation of privately owned vehicles at Government expense in connection with assignments to duty, or return from duty, at posts outside the continental United States, there is no authority which permits reimbursement for the cost of shipment of an automobile within the continental United States. B-186115, February 4, 1977.

Accordingly, the prohibition in 5 U.S.C. 5727(a) applies, and Mr. Towns' claim for the cost of shipping his car within the continental United States may not be paid.

[B–193326]

Compensation—Negotiation—Prevailing Rate Employees—Pay Increase Ceiling—Applicability

Pay adjustment limitation of section 614(a) of Public Law 95–429 applies only to those employees whose pay is adjusted by one of methods listed in that section. Since the pay of employees who negotiated their wages under section 9(b) of Public Law 92–392 is not adjusted pursuant to any of the methods listed, the section 614(a) limitation does not apply to them.

In the matter of Department of the Interior—Pay adjustment limitation, February 1, 1979:

This action is in response to a request for an advance decision submitted by Mr. John F. McKune, Director of Personnel of the Department of the Interior, concerning the 5.5 percent pay adjustment limitation or "pay cap" enacted by section 614(a) of the Treasury, Postal Service, and General Government Appropriation Act, 1979, Public Law 95–429, October 10, 1978, 92 Stat. 1001, 1018. The question presented is whether the pay cap applies to those prevailing rate employees who, through collective bargaining, negotiate their wages with the Department of the Interior. In accordance with our "Procedures for Decisions on Appropriated Fund Expenditures in Federal Labor-Management Relations Program," 4 C.F.R. Part 21, 43 F.R. 32395–96, July 27, 1978, interested parties were served, and we have considered the comments and views of those parties that were provided to us.

Section 614(a) of Public Law 95–429, provides that:

No part of any of the funds appropriated for the fiscal year ending September 30, 1979, by this Act or any other Act, may be used to pay the salary or pay of any individual in any office or position in an amount which exceeds the rate of salary or basic pay payable for such office or position on September 30, 1978, by more than 5.5 percent, as a result of any adjustments which take effect during such fiscal year under—

   (1) section 5305 of title 5, United States Code;
   (2) any other provision of law if such adjustment is determined by reference to such section 5305; or
   (3) section 5343 of title 5, United States Code, if such adjustment is granted pursuant to a wage survey (but only with respect to prevailing rate employees described in section 5342(a)(2)(A) of that title).

It is important to note that although the first part of this provision refers to the part of "any individual in any office or position," the remainder of the section limits the restriction only to salary adjustments made under specific statutory provisions.

The employees involved here are those covered by section 9(b) of Public Law 92–392, August 19, 1972, 86 Stat. 564, 574, 5 U.S.C. § 5343 note, which provides that:

The amendments made by this Act shall not be construed to—

   (1) abrogate, modify, or otherwise affect in any way the provisions of any contract in effect on the date of enactment of this Act pertaining to the wages, the terms and conditions of employment, and other employment benefits, or any of the foregoing matters, for Government prevailing rate employ-

ees and resulting from negotiations between Government agencies and organizations of Government employees;

(2) nullify, curtail, or otherwise impair in any way the right of any party to such contract to enter into negotiations after the date of enactment of this Act for the renewal, extension, modification, or improvement of the provisions of such contract or for the replacement of such contract with a new contract; or

(3) nullify, change, or otherwise affect in any way after such date of enactment any agreement, arrangement, or understanding in effect on such date with respect to the various items of subject matter of the negotiations on which any such contract in effect on such date is based or prevent the inclusion of such items of subject matter in connection with the renegotiation of any such contract, or the replacement of such contract with a new contract, after such date.

As generally construed, this section has been held to mean that the employees covered by it negotiate their wages through the collective-bargaining process, rather than having them set through prevailing rate surveys. *Matter of Department of the Interior*, 57 Comp. Gen. 259 (1978).

The importance and intent of section 9(b) was recently affirmed by section 704 of Public Law 95–454, October 13, 1978, 92 Stat. 1111, 1218, which provides that:

(a) Those terms and conditions of employment and other employment benefits with respect to Government prevailing rate employees to whom section 9(b) of Public Law 92–392 applies which were the subject of negotiation in accordance with prevailing rates and practices prior to August 19, 1972, shall be negotiated on and after the date of the enactment of this Act in accordance with the provisions of section 9(b) of Public Law 92–392 without regard to any provision of chapter 71 of title 5, United States Code (as amended by this title), to the extent that any such provision is inconsistent with this paragraph.

(b) The pay and pay practices relating to employees referred to in paragraph (1) of this subsection [read as subsection (a) of this section] shall be negotiated in accordance with prevailing rates and pay practices without regard to any provisions of—

(A) chapter 71 of title 5, United States Code (as amended by this title), to the extent that any such provision is inconsistent with this paragraph;

(B) subchapter IV of chapter 53 and subchapter V of chapter 55 of title 5, United States Code; or

(C) any rule, regulation, decision, or order relating to rates of pay or pay practices under subchapter IV of chapter 53 or subchapter V of chapter 55 of title 5, United States Code.

In order to determine whether the pay limitation found in section 614(a) of Public Law 95–429, applies to the employees covered by section 9(b) of Public Law 92–392, it must be determined whether the manner in which their wages are adjusted is included in those specified in section 614(a). Section 614(a)(1) refers to pay adjustments made under 5 U.S.C. § 5305, which establishes the system of yearly comparability adjustments for the General Schedule pay system. Section 614(a)(2) includes pay adjustments made with reference to 5 U.S.C. § 5305. The wages of section 9(b) employees are in no way tied to 5 U.S.C. § 5305; therefore, neither 614(a)(1) nor (2) applies.

Section 614(a)(3) refers to wage adjustments of prevailing rate employees that are made pursuant to wage surveys conducted under

5 U.S.C. § 5343. As stated above, the wages of employees covered by section 9(b) are set or adjusted through the collective-bargaining process, not pursuant to wage surveys. Therefore, the method used to adjust the wages of section 9(b) employees is not included within those listed in section 614(a). See also B–193573, January 8, 1979.

Accordingly, the 5.5 percent pay adjustment limitation or "pay cap" imposed by section 614(a) of Public Law 95–429 does not apply to employees whose wages are negotiated under section 9(b) of Public Law 92–392.

With respect to the jurisdictional aspects of this case, we have held herein that the pay increases in question are not made under the authority of 5 U.S.C. § 5343—a part of subchapter IV of chapter 53 of title 5 as it relates to the language of section 704 of the Civil Service Reform Act of 1978. Also, this case does not involve premium pay as authorized in subchapter V of chapter 55 of that title, but involves a generally applicable appropriation limitation which, within its terms, is applicable to all funds appropriated for fiscal year 1979. Since we have general authority to consider expenditures of appropriated funds except where that authority is specifically denied or limited, we have authority to issue a decision in this matter. It is noted, however, that with respect to pay rates and practices negotiated under labor agreements by the employees and agencies concerned, we have, in 58 Comp. Gen. 198 (B–189782, January 5, 1979), held inapplicable any limitations in the provisions of title 5, United States Code, mentioned in section 704 of the Civil Service Reform Act of 1978 or our decisions issued under those provisions.

[B–193197]

Officers and Employees—Training—Expenses—Reimbursement

Where an employee is sent on a 2-year training assignment overseas under 5 U.S.C. 4109 and is authorized to have his immediate family accompany him, his entitlements to travel and transportation allowances at Government expense on their behalf are limited to those allowances specifically prescribed in that section not to exceed employee's estimated aggregate per diem payable, rather than those prescribed for permanent change-of-station assignments, since assignments for training purposes only are not permanent duty assignments. Since the terms "nontemporary storage of household goods" and "shipment of privately owned vehicles" are not allowances prescribed in that section, neither they, nor related costs, i.e., round-trip travel to pick up a shipped vehicle at port of debarkation, may be reimbursed under that section.

In the matter of Mr. Michael G. Pond, February 5, 1979:

This action is in response to correspondence dated September 11, 1978, with enclosures (reference Serial: N41/400), from the Chief, Finance and Accounting, Central Security Service, National Security

Agency (NSA), requesting an advance decision as to the propriety of making payment on a voucher in favor of Mr. Michael G. Pond, an employee of that agency, representing reimbursement for round-trip transportation costs incurred in traveling to and from his residence to a port terminal to pick up his privately owned vehicle (POV) in conjunction with return travel from an overseas station to the United States in 1978. This correspondence was forwarded to this Office by second endorsement of the Per Diem, Travel and Transportation Allowance Committee dated October 12, 1978, and has been assigned PDTATAC Control No. 78–41.

The submission states that the employee was sent by NSA on a 2-year training assignment overseas at the United States Army Institute for Advanced Russian and European Studies in Garmisch, Germany. Following completion of that training the employee performed return permanent change of station (PCS) travel from there to Fort George G. Meade, Maryland, under authority of Travel Orders TP8G0015, issued April 11, 1978. Subsequent to completion of the travel, but incident thereto, he performed travel from his residence in Millersville, Maryland, to Bayonne, New Jersey, and return, to pick up his POV which had been shipped from Germany.

The submission points out that over the past few years there has been a great deal of correspondence and numerous discussions both in-house and with other Government agencies relative to the scope of benefits to which employees on training assignments are entitled. The question has been whether the movement of employees to and from the United States Army Institute at Garmisch, Germany, for training is or is not a PCS move so as to entitle such employees to all PCS benefits, including nontemporary storage of household goods and shipment of a POV.

As background, enclosed with the submission were copies of miscellaneous correspondence relating to the matter of these entitlements. It seems that in 1974 NSA was authorized by the Civil Service Commission to send a limited number of employees overseas for training on a PCS with limited benefits. This authority apparently was continued on an annual basis through fiscal year 1977. In 1978, NSA sought an extension of that authority. In so doing, the specific point was raised concerning the range of PCS benefits which are payable, referring to the changes made to Volume 2 of the Joint Travel Regulations (JTR) by change 138, April 1, 1977.

According to the submission, NSA, prior to that change, had been authorizing payment of nontemporary storage of household goods and shipment of POV's for students on in-country training assignments because the Table of Eligibility in Appendix F of 2 JTR did not specifically prohibit these entitlements. Change 138, however, changed the language used to describe these training assignments and specifically stated that they were not to be considered a PCS.

A response memorandum dated April 12, 1978, from the Office of the Assistant Secretary of Defense to NSA, advised that movement of dependents and household goods on an employee training assignment was not to be considered a PCS move and the employee was not entitled to PCS allowances. A further response memorandum dated May 25, 1978, also from the Office of the Assistant Secretary of Defense, and enclosing a letter dated May 4, 1978, from the United States Civil Service Commission, granted a further extension of authority to send immediate families, household goods and personal effects of NSA employees undergoing language training in foreign countries.

Apparently, certain NSA officials considered the response of May 25, 1978, to be noncommittal on the question of entitlement to nontemporary storage and POV shipments in connection with training. By memorandum dated June 5, 1978, addressed to the Per Diem, Travel and Transportation Allowance Committee, NSA requested that they be permitted to waive the limitations of 2 JTR relating to travel and transportation entitlements while an employee is attending training courses. By response memorandum dated June 15, 1978, the Committee denied the request for waiver.

In spite of that denial, there is still disagreement as to whether there exists a basic entitlement to nontemporary storage of household goods and shipment of a POV in these cases. Therefore, the following questions are presented for resolution:

a. As presently written, does the exception granted by the U.S. Civil Service Commission, to 5 U.S.C. 4109, include authority for nontemporary storage and shipment of POV's to and from the training site mentioned herein?

b. May the language in Enclosure 5 [the letter from Director, Bureau of Training, United States Civil Service Commission to the Deputy Assistant Secretary of Defense, dated May 4, 1978] be interpreted as authorizing nontemporary storage and shipment of POV's?

c. If the answers to the preceding questions are in the negative, is this Office correct in denying claims for travel to and from ports to deliver and pick up vehicles in connection with movement to and from the overseas training site?

In addition to those specific questions the submission goes on to state that they have other problem cases which are the reverse of Mr. Pond's situation. Apparently, they have employees who are being transferred from one overseas area to another (an Inter Theatre Transfer (ITT)), with a CONUS stopover when such transfer requires attendance at a course of language training at the Defense Language School, Monterey, California. It is stated that the basic orders are issued reflecting an ITT with training and PCS orders are issued authorizing travel to the language school. Upon completion of the training, new PCS orders are issued for travel from the school to the new overseas location. The submission states that on PCS's as ordered, employees are being authorized the full range of PCS allowances, including per diem for dependents, miscellaneous expense allowances, and temporary quarters subsistence expenses. It is the view of the finance and accounting officer that those enumerated expense items are not payable; however, in light of the before-mentioned controversy the matter is considered unclear. As a result, a decision is also requested on this point.

Payment of travel and transportation expenses relating to periods of training is governed by the provisions of 5 U.S.C. 4109 (1976), which provide in pertinent part:

(a) The head of an agency, under regulations prescribed * * * may—

*　　*　　*　　*　　*　　*　　*

(2) pay, or reimburse the employee for, all or part of the necessary expenses of the training * * * including among the expenses the necessary costs of—
(A) travel and per diem instead of subsistence * * *;
(B) transportation of immediate family, household goods and personal effects, packing, crating, temporarily storing, draying, and unpacking * * * when the estimated costs of transportation and related services are less than the estimated aggregate per diem payments for the period of training * * *;

Regulations implementing the above provisions for civilian employees of the Department of Defense are contained in Volume 2 of the Joint Travel Regulations (JTR). Paragraph C3052 of the regulations (change 78, April 1, 1972), which were in effect at the time Mr. Pond commenced his training assignment, provided in part:

2. OTHER THAN TEMPORARY DUTY ASSIGNMENT
a. *General.* To the extent of the authority provided in 5 U.S. Code 4109, which allows transportation of an employee's family and household goods in lieu of per diem payments, the conditions in subpars. b and c will apply. * * *
b. *Transportation of an Employee's Family and Household Goods.* If the estimated cost of round-trip transportation of an employee's immediate family and household goods between the employee's official duty station and the training location is less than the aggregate per diem payments that the employee would receive while at the training location, such round-trip transportation at Government expense may be authorized in lieu of per diem payments. Such transportation will be in accordance with the provisions of this volume relating to permanent change-of-station movement (see par. C4102).
c. *Employee's Election to Type of Movement.* Consideration may be given an election of the employee concerned to be authorized a temporary duty assignment or a permanent change-of-station movement if allowable upon comparison of costs indicated in subpar. a. An initial determination to authorize a permanent change-of-station movement may be changed to a temporary duty assignment any time prior to the beginning of transportation. After transportation begins, the entitlement of the employee and obligations of the Government become fixed and cannot be changed thereafter (89 Comp. Gen. 140).

Notwithstanding the language contained in the before-quoted JTR provisions, especially the reference in subparagraph c to a permanent change of station movement as the alternative to a temporary duty assignment, it is clearly evident from the law that all assignments for training purposes are in fact similar in many aspects to temporary duty assignments, i.e., assignments which contemplate travel either to another PCS location following training, or return to the same PCS location, at the time the orders are issued. However, because of the length of the training assignments, it was determined and congressionally approved that it would be in the Government's interest as well as that of the individuals concerned to permit the employee's family to accompany him at Government expense under certain circumstances, a benefit not authorized for TDY travel. It must be recognized that travel for training is not ordinary TDY or PCS travel but is in a class by itself. The authority for payment of the costs of such travel is derived from 5 U.S.C. 4109 by reference to the provisions of chapter 57 of that title. That section provides travel benefits similar to those authorized for temporary duty, but provides limited benefits for long term training assignments.

The authorized parameters of dependents travel for this type of assignment contained in subsection 4109(a)(2)(B) are "transportation of immediate family, household goods and personal effects, packing, crating, temporarily storing, draying, and unpacking," but only "when the estimated costs of transportation and related services are less than the estimated aggregate per diem payments for the period of training."

Because of the use of the term "permanent change-of-station movement" in subparagraph C3052–2c, difficulties in establishing employee entitlements arose and became the subject of decisions by our Office. While none of those decisions involved the question of entitlement to nontemporary storage of household goods, or shipment of POV's, our decisions are universal in disallowing claims for PCS type of expenses incurred by employees while on training assignments which were other than "transportation of immediate family, household goods and personal effects, packing, crating, temporarily storing, draying, unpacking," when the employee elected to have his family accompany him and such move was administratively approved.

In 1976, in conjunction with decision B–185281, May 24, 1976, involving a claim for temporary quarters subsistence expense by a Government employee as an incidence of a training assignment, a letter of the same date was addressed to the Executive of the Per Diem, Travel and Transportation Allowance Committee, directing their attention to the fact that a number of employees were being authorized benefits incident to training assignments which were erroneous. Further, that the erroneous authorization seemed to emanate from the use of the term "permanent change-of-station" in paragraphs C4102(1) and C3052 of Volume 2 of the JTR's. We requested that since training assignments under 5 U.S.C. 4109 were not in fact PCS's, the term "permanent change-of-station" used therein be deleted to avoid any misunderstanding as to an employee's entitlements while on such an assignment. The removal of that phrase was accomplished in change 138, April 1, 1977.

We have reviewed these amended JTR provisions, and find them to be in accord with the law and our decisions limiting the entitlements of employees on training assignments to those enumerated in 5 U.S.C. 4109. This, of course, would not include nontemporary storage of household goods or shipment of POV's since those terms are not used in that section. The exception issued by CSC for training of a limited number of employees at overseas sites is to permit payment of travel and transportation costs authorized in 5 U.S.C. 4109 without regard to the limitation imposed by clause (a)(2)(B) of that section under which travel and transportation costs may not exceed the travel and per diem in lieu of subsistence costs authorized to be paid by clause (a)(2)(A). Authority for making such exception is contained in 5 U.S.C. 4102 as delegated to the CSC by section 401(a) of Executive Order No. 11348, April 20, 1967.

Therefore, questions a. and b. are answered in the negative and question c. is answered in the affirmative. As the foregoing relates to Mr. Pond's claim, not only may he not be reimbursed for his round-trip travel to pick up his POV, but since he was not entitled to ship it at Government expense, the costs which may have been incurred by the Government for such shipment are to be recovered from him. See 56 Comp. Gen. 85 (1976).

With regard to the additional question asked concerning an employee's entitlement to the full range of PCS allowances where his permanent duty station is overseas and where he receives PCS orders to CONUS for training and upon completion of that training receives PCS orders to a new overseas permanent duty station, the fact that it is the reverse of Mr. Pond's situation, in our view, is a distinction without a difference and that dependent's travel and transportation to the training location are limited by the provisions of 5 U.S.C. 4109. However, see in this connection, paragraph C4502–3 of Volume 2 of the JTR's (change 138, April 1, 1977). In this regard, it is to be noted that the entitlements of employees affected by such transfers are quite complex. In such circumstances, we do not believe that a question in this area can properly be answered in the absence of presentation of a factual situation to this Office. Since the submission indicates the existence of such a case, it is suggested that it be submitted here for resolution.

[B-139703]

Tennessee Valley Authority—Condemnation Proceedings—Fees— Expert Witnesses

Generally, fees and expenses of expert witnesses appointed by the court in land condemnation proceedings, whether on motion of the court or at request of a party, are considered to be expenses of litigation and are therefore pursuant to Rule 706, Federal Rules of Evidence, payable by the litigating agency. However, where Tennessee Valley Authority (TVA) is the litigating agency, courts have held that costs in condemnation case cannot be assessed against TVA. Courts have also held that costs may not be assessed against the condemnee. Since neither party may pay such costs, if court so orders, the Administrative Office of the United States Courts may pay litigation expenses from Judiciary appropriations. 52 Comp. Gen. 621 (1973) will no longer be followed.

In the matter of Payment of court-appointed expert witness— land condemnation proceedings, February 6, 1979:

The Deputy Director, Administrative Office of the United States Courts, has requested our decision as to the availability of Judicial Branch appropriations for the payment of compensation and expenses to Mr. Tom Seagroves, a court-appointed expert witness. Mr. Seagroves testified on the valuation of land to be taken by the Federal Government in a condemnation action initiated by the Tennessee Valley Authority (TVA), *United States ex rel. TVA v. 190 Acres of Land*, 404 F. Supp. 1392 (E.D. Tenn. 1975). The expenses involved, which were allowed by the Court, total $531.10 and cover the appraisal fee, per diem for one day in court, and transportation costs. For reasons set forth below, we conclude that Judicial Branch appropriations are available for such payment.

BACKGROUND

Mr. Seagroves was appointed by the Court in order to provide the jury with an impartial witness because the court felt that it was not in the best interest of justice to expect lay persons, as jurors, to undertake to reconcile the widely divergent opinions of expert witnesses offered by the respective counsel. (E.D. Tenn., No. CIV-4-74-40, Order of March 13, 1975.) The appointment was made by the Court under its inherent power to do so, and prior to the effective date of the Federal Rules of Evidence (enacted on January 2, 1975, effective 180 days later on July 2, 1975). 404 F. Supp. 1392.

The Federal Rules of Evidence became effective before the case went to trial (on July 28, 1975) and applied to proceedings then pending. Pub. L. No. 93-595 (January 2, 1975), 88 Stat. 1926. Rule 706(b) specifically provides that compensation for the services of independent expert witnesses appointed by the court "is payable from funds *which may be provided by law* in * * * proceedings involving just compensation under the fifth amendment." [Italic supplied.]

In a Memorandum and Order dated July 31, 1975, the court, noting that Rule 706(b) was now effective, directed TVA to pay the compensation and expenses of the expert witness. TVA filed a motion urging the Court to reconsider and set aside the Memorandum and Order, arguing that Rule 706(b) does not authorize the taxation of court-appointed experts' fees against either TVA or the United States in "just compensation" cases, but, as in criminal cases, merely authorizes payments of such amounts out of the Judiciary's appropriations. Plaintiff's Brief in Support of Motion to Reconsider and Set Aside Memorandum and Order on Taxation of Costs, at 2.

In October, 1975, the Court vacated and set aside the July 31 Order and directed the Administrative Office of the United States Courts to pay the expert witness compensation and expenses from the Judiciary's current (fiscal year 1976) appropriation "for necessary travel and miscellaneous expenses." The Administrative Office advised the court that it had no funds available from which to pay the fee and expenses of the expert witness. Subsequently, after a reconsideration of the October Order, the Court entered an Order on August 2, 1976, requiring the Director of the Administrative Office to show cause why he should not be held in contempt of Court for failing to comply with the October Order. Thereafter, the Administrative Office requested this decision.

SUMMARY OF POSITIONS

In its submission, the Administrative Office maintains that the compensation of the expert witness is an expense of litigation governed by Federal Rule of Evidence 706(b) and as such, is payable by the litigating agency rather than from funds appropriated to the Judicial Branch. The Administrative Office believes TVA should pay the fees of the court-appointed witness in this case because the litigation was initiated and prosecuted by TVA attorneys.

The Department of Justice, whose opinion was solicited in this matter, agrees with the Administrative Office that fees of expert witnesses appointed under Rule 706(b) are expenses of litigation payable by the litigating agency (normally, but not always, the Justice Department). However, in this particular case, since the expert witness was appointed before the Federal Rules of Evidence were enacted into law and "[u]nder [the court's] inherent power so to do * * * as an aid to the Court in discharging its official duty," the Department believes that the Administrative Office should pay the compensation of the witness as an expense of maintenance of the courts.

TVA aso submitted extensive comments. TVA agrees with the Department of Justice that the Administrative Office should pay the fees in this case. However, TVA disagrees with the Department's more generalized conclusion that the costs of experts appointed by the court under Rule 706 in condemnation cases should be paid by the agency initiating and litigating the action. Citing prior decisions of this Office, TVA argues that such expenses are in all cases expenses of maintenance of the courts and as such should be paid by the Administrative Office from funds appropriated to the Judiciary.

QUESTIONS PRESENTED

The questions presented in this case are as follows:

1. The effect of Rule 706(b), Federal Rules of Evidence, with respect to the source of funds for the payment of fees in condemnation cases;

2. Whether the compensation of a court-appointed expert witness in a land condemnation case is a litigation expense chargeable to the parties, or an expense chargeable to Administrative Office (Judiciary) appropriations.

DISCUSSION

Prior to the enactment of Rule 706 of the Federal Rules of Evidence, Pub. L. No. 93–595, Jan. 2, 1975, 88 Stat. 1938, it was our view that expenses incurred by a court on its own motion to provide services deemed necessary to determine a matter before it were properly chargeable to funds appropriated to the Judiciary. 52 Comp. Gen. 621 (1973).

The enactment of the revised Rules of Evidence has provided us with guidance from Congress on the compensation of court appointed expert witnesses in Rule 706. That rule provides, in pertinent part, as follows:

Rule 706. Court Appointed Experts

(a) Appointment. The court may on its own motion or on the motion of any party enter an order to show cause why expert witnesses should not be appointed, and may request the parties to submit nominations. The court may appoint any expert witnesses agreed upon by the parties, and may appoint expert witnesses of its own selection. An expert witness shall not be appointed by the court unless he consents to act. A witness so appointed shall be informed of his duties by the court in writing, a copy of which shall be filed with the clerk, or at a conference in which the parties shall have opportunity to participate. A witness so appointed shall advise the parties of his findings, if any; his deposition may be taken by any party; and he may be called to testify by the court or any party. He shall be subject to cross-examination by each party, including a party calling him as a witness.

(b) Compensation. Expert witnesses so appointed are entitled to reasonable compensation in whatever sum the court may allow. *The compensation thus fixed is payable from funds which may be provided by law in criminal cases and civil actions and proceedings involving just compensation under the fifth amendment.* In other civil actions and proceedings the compensation shall be paid by the parties in such proportion and at such time as the court directs, and thereafter charged in like manner as other costs. [Italic supplied.]

In civil actions generally, the costs of expert witnesses are to be charged "in like manner as other costs"—i.e., treated as litigation expenses and divided among the litigants in whatever way the court directs. The Rule recognizes, however, that this cannot be done in two situations—criminal and condemnation cases.

Condemnation actions differ from other civil actions in that costs cannot be assessed against the condemnee. The reason for this is as follows:

> The general principle with regard to costs in land condemnation cases is based on Rule 71A(1), Fed. R. Civ. P. which provides that "costs [in such cases] are not subject to Rule 54(d)." (Rule 54(d) provides generally that all costs shall be allowed to the prevailing party.) In clarifying the intent of Rule 71A(1), the Advisory Committee on Rules in its Notes states that "Costs shall be awarded in accordance with the law that has developed in condemnation cases." This implements the established rule that the condemnor (i.e. the United States) may not recover its costs against the condemnee, since to charge the latter with the cost of taking would violate the constitutional prohibition against the taking of private property without just compensation. *Grand River Dam Authority* v. *Jarvis*, 124 F. 2d 914 (10th Cir., 1942). 55 Comp. Gen. 1172, 1173 (1976).

Therefore, where the Federal Government is the condemnor, costs of a court-appointed witness must be borne in some manner by the Government.

While this necessarily affects the available sources of funds for payment (by eliminating one of the parties), it does not change the nature of the expense. Further, the Rule makes no distinction between expert witnesses appointed by the court on its own motion or upon request by one of the parties. We therefore agree with the Justice Department and the Administrative Office of the Courts that the Rule was intended to treat expert witness costs as litigation expenses rather than court expenses. Our prior decision in 52 Comp. Gen. 621 (1973), rendered before clarification on this point by the Rule, will no longer be followed.

Generally, litigation in land condemnation cases is conducted by the Department of Justice. Where the Department of Justice has control over the institution of proceedings, all expenses necessarily incurred by the Government in preparing and prosecuting its case are properly chargeable to appropriations made available to the Justice Department for this purpose. However, where another Government agency or entity has specific authority to resort to litigation in the performance of its duties, the expenses of such proceedings, including special fees, when ordered by the court to be paid, are payable from the appropriations of that agency. 15 Comp. Gen. 81 (1935); 46 *id.* 98 (1966). Even where the Justice Department prosecutes the case on behalf of an agency that has such specific authority, we have held that that agency rather than the Department of Justice should bear the expenses of the litigation. 38 Comp. Gen. 343, 344 (1958).

Thus, as a general proposition, we concur with the Department of Justice and the Administrative Office of the Courts that fees of expert witnesses appointed by the Court under Rule 706 in condemnation cases are properly payable by the Department of Justice as expenses of litigation where Justice is the litigating agency. It follows that, where Justice is not the litigating agency, the agency that actually prosecutes the case should bear the expenses.

In *United States ex rel. TVA* v. *Pressnell*, 328 F. 2d 580 (6th Cir. 1964), the Court held that although TVA "may cause" condemnation proceedings to be instituted, the proceedings are actually instituted by the United States which is the real party in interest and the actual condemnor of the property. The Court stated that it could find "no authority for assessing costs against one who is not the condemnor in the proceeding" and therefore concluded that the cost of such proceedings could not be assessed against TVA. *Id.* at 582.

The basic authority for the taxation of costs in the Federal courts is 28 U.S.C. § 1920 (1976). Pursuant to 28 U.S.C. § 2412, a judgment for costs as enumerated in § 1920 may be taxed against the United States when it is a party in any civil action. Costs so assessed are payable from the permanent indefinite appropriation established by 31 U.S.C. § 724a. However, the judgment must—

* * * be limited to reimbursing in whole or in part the prevailing party for the costs incurred by him in the litigation. 28 U.S.C. § 2412 (1976).

The District Court here noted (404 F. Supp. at 1393) that 28 U.S.C. § 2412 does not authorize such payment in an eminent domain proceeding. *United States ex rel. TVA* v. *Easement and Right-of-Way*, 452 F. 2d 729 (6th Cir. 1971).

There is also no basis for charging the fees in the present case to the Justice Department since the Justice Department had no role in the litigation.

In these unusual circumstances, i.e., where neither party to the proceeding can properly be charged with the litigation expense, if the Court orders the Administrative Office of the United States Courts to bear the expense, the Administrative Office would be authorized to make payment out of its appropriation for "Travel and Miscellaneous Expenses."

[B-190401]

Advertising—Advertising v. Negotiation—Negotiation Propriety—Protest Timeliness

Protest allegation that negotiated procurement should have been formally advertised which is raised after closing date for receipt of proposals is untimely under General Accounting Office Bid Protest Procedures and therefore not for consideration.

Contracts—Negotiation—Evaluation Factors—Point Rating—Differences Significance

Where solicitation does not require award to be made in accordance with results of numerical point scoring of proposals, agency is not required to award contract to offeror whose overall proposal is rated two points higher than competing proposal.

Contracts—Negotiation—Evaluation   Factors—Additional   Factors—Not in Request for Proposals

Where source selection official, after taking into account all evaluation criteria, i.e., both price and technical factors, finds proposals to be "tied" and is unable to make a selection, he properly may consider other factors which are rationally related to specific procurement involved, and such consideration does not violate general rule that awards are to be based on established evaluation criteria.

Contracts—Awards—Equal or Tie Bids/Offers—Evaluation— Additional Criteria for Consideration—Change of Contractor Impact

Source selection official's consideration of incumbency status of one offeror and of disruptive effect of changing contractors is reasonable under circumstances where proposals are viewed as "tied" and official seeks appropriate discriminators on which to base award selection.

Contracts — Awards — Equal or Tie Bids/Offers — Evaluation — Additional Criteria for Consideration—Labor Surplus Area Concern Status

Solicitation provision permitting firm's status as labor surplus area concern to be considered in case of tie bids is intended for use primarily in formal advertising and in negotiated procurements where award is to be made on basis of price. Where, however, proposals are "tied" based on evaluation of both technical and price factors, consideration of labor surplus area concern status would not be improper and would not involve violation of Maybank Amendment.

Contracts — Awards — Labor Surplus Areas — Qualification of Bidder/Offeror—Administrative Determination—Improper

Agency's reliance on offeror's claim to be labor surplus area concern by virtue of performing contract to be awarded in area of substantial unemployment was improper where Department of Labor (DOL) had removed designated area from list of such areas several months prior to evaluation and award and so informed Federal agencies. Fact that agencies were notified through monthly notices instead of revision to DOL's formal publication referenced by applicable agency regulation does not change fact that agency had duty to verify offeror's claim and in so doing to seek out latest available information. 45 Comp. Gen. 471, distinguished.

Contracts — Negotiation — Changes, etc. — Reopening Negotiations — Failure to Reopen — Not Materially Prejudicial

Agency's actions allowing one offeror, during so-called "pre-award survey," to make its proposal more favorable by offering earlier starting date constituted discussions and should have resulted in new request for best and final offers from other offeror in competitive range. However, agency's actions, while procedurally deficient, appear not to have been materially prejudicial since record suggests that earlier starting date was not significant factor in selection decision.

Contracts — Negotiation — Awards — Propriety — Evaluation of Proposals

Since selection decision may have been influenced by erroneous view that awardee was labor surplus area concern, recommendation is made that source selection official reconsider his decision. If it is determined that award should have been made to protester, it is further recommended that contract be terminated and award made to protester.

In the matter of Group Hospital Service, Inc. (Blue Cross of Texas), February 6, 1979:

Group Hospital Service, Inc. (Blue Cross of Texas) of Dallas, Texas (GHS) with its proposed subcontractor, Management Data Communications Corporation of Rosemont, Illinois, protests the award of a contract to Mutual of Omaha Insurance Company of Omaha, Nebraska (Mutual) by the Office of Civilian Health and Medical Program of the Uniformed Services, Department of Defense, Denver, Colorado (OCHAMPUS) for the implementation and operation in the State of Texas of a CHAMPUS fiscal intermediary system as the result of request for proposals (RFP) No. MDA–906–77–R–0031. GHS contends that award of the contract was not made in accordance with the criteria set forth in the RFP and that the contract services should have been procured by means of formal advertising, rather than negotiation. GHS requests this Office "to cancel" the award to Mutual and have the contract awarded to GHS.

CHAMPUS is a health benefits program administered by the Secretary of Defense. The fiscal intermediary contractor provides services necessary to receive, adjudicate and pay health benefit claims from eligible beneficiaries and providers to beneficiaries of the program on an area basis, usually a single state or group of states. The contractor is required to perform substantial administrative and automated data processing (ADP) tasks.

The RFP, as originally issued, required proposals to be received by October 12, 1977, and provided for a one year period of contract performance from February 1, 1978, through January 31, 1979, with an option for an additional year. After receipt of initial proposals, no written or oral discussions were held with any offeror. Amendment No. 1, dated November 3, 1977, was issued which changed the contract period to March 1, 1978, through February 28, 1979, and added a second option year. Best and final offers were required by November 16, 1977. Four proposals were received as a result of the solicitation, and all were found to be technically acceptable.

The offers were reviewed by a Source Selection Evaluation Board (SSEB) and a Source Selection Advisory Council (SSAC). On December 14, 1977, the Council recommended to the Source Selection Authority (SSA), Director, OCHAMPUS, that Mutual be awarded the contract. However, further evaluation of the Mutual and GHS proposals was directed due to their competitive closeness. (The highest ranked proposal was eliminated from the competition for other reasons.) During the evaluation and negotiation period, Mutual offered to accept a no-cost termination of its then current cost contract with OCHAMPUS for fiscal intermediary services in Texas and to start performance under the new contract on January 1, 1978. The Council, on December 28, 1977, again recommended award to Mutual; the SSA approved the recommendation on that date. The contract, effective January 1, 1978, was executed by the contracting officer on January 9, 1978, and by Mutual on January 13, 1978. The option for the first follow-on year has been exercised.

Section D of the RFP set forth the following four major technical evaluation criteria in descending order of importance: administration, utilization/peer review, claims processing and payment, and management capability. Price was considered less important than the technical evaluation. Paragraph D-1 provided that:

> These proposals shall be evaluated on the basis of the offeror's demonstrated performance or its plan for accomplishment of each function, with greater weight being accorded actual performance criteria.

Numerical scoring of proposals resulted in a 4-point advantage for Mutual in the technical area (with a 3-point advantage to Mutual in the most important category of administration) and, in recognition of GHS's lower prices, a 6-point advantage for GHS in the price area, with a resulting combined score of 768 to 766 in favor of GHS. The proposal of another offeror, Blue Cross of California, was assigned a somewhat higher score, but the SSAC recommended against acceptance of that proposal. The SSAC also viewed GHS and Mutual as virtually tied, but recommended that award be made to Mutual. The SSAC's rationale is explained in its December 14, 1977 memorandum to the SSA as follows:

> The Source Selection Advisory Council has completed its evaluation * * * and has determined that all proposals are technically acceptable. * * *
> * * * Mutual of Omaha and Blue Shield of California tied for the top ranking in the category of Administration; however, [the GHS] score was only three (3) points less than that of the top offerors. The category of Claims Processing and Payment was also demonstrative of the keen competition that prevailed between the top three offerors. Although that applicable portion of the proposal submitted by Blue Cross Blue Shield of Texas was excellent, Mutual of Omaha and Blue Shield of California are currently OCHAMPUS' two largest contractors with excellent systems in actual operation which accounts for the slight difference in scores. * * *
> In summation, the SSAC is of the opinion that the scoring process has resulted in a rank-order for the top three offerors that is too close to depend completely on for the final decision. * * *
> Therefore, the SSAC has considered several additional factors in arriving at its final recommendation. First, Blue Shield of California's production capacity must be reviewed since they have just recently been awarded the high-volume Florida/Puerto Rico contract. Award of this contract to their existing business could seriously impair their ability to effectively perform, thereby jeopardizing not one, but four, contracts. Furthermore, award to Blue Shield of California would give them 50% of the existing OCHAMPUS business which could be a serious disadvantage in assuring effective control of the OCHAMPUS program. Therefore, it is recommended that award should not be made to Blue Shield of California.

Only two points marked the difference between the 2nd and 3rd offerors. BC/BS of Texas submitted an excellent proposal including a price that would result in a first-year price reduction of $207,030 when compared with Mutual of Omaha. The latter is, of course, the incumbent contractor for the State of Texas and is an effective performer. Although the SSAC feels that BC/BS of Texas could also do an effective job the disruptive aspects necessitated by the change-over of contractors could be detrimental to both provider and beneficiary relations which have just recently been redressed. In addition, it is estimated that a considerable portion of the $207,030 savings could be lost in transition costs charged by the losing contractor. Therefore, it is in the best interest of the Government to accept the most responsive offer price and other factors considered, and the SSAC recommends that award be made to Mutual of Omaha.

As previously indicated, the SSA did not accept this recommendation, but directed further evaluation, after which the SSAC again recommended that Mutual be awarded the contract. The SSAC's later memorandum stated, *inter alia*:

2. After considerable discussion it was mutually agreed that this competitiveness dictated additional discussion with these two offerors to assure full understanding of the proposals. A list of twelve questions were prepared for a formal interview. These questions were designed to (1) cover the major factors that affect the fiscal intermediary process; and (2) uncover any weaknesses which could not be ascertained by reading the proposals.

3. Attached as exhibits I and II are the pre-award survey reports on Mutual of Omaha and Blue Cross/Blue Shield of Texas. Although no significant weaknesses were noted as a result of these surveys, the following positive factors are noted:

A. Mutual of Omaha has an experience base which ably reflects their long-term tenure as an OCHAMPUS contractor. This base is further substantiated by excellent training programs which are structured to maintain high quality assurance standards.

B. Blue Cross/Blue Shield of Texas has availability to a much broader statistical base relative to reasonable charges, physicians profiles, hospital reimbursement, and UR [Utilization Review] and PR, [Peer Review], as a result of their operation in Texas.

C. Blue Cross/Blue Shield of Texas has clearly demonstrated that the 23 sub-offices will have trained personnel to handle beneficiary relations. This also is a positive factor for provider relations except that the current physician participation rate experienced by the Medicare program is 65% to 70% which is comparable to the low rate currently experienced by OCHAMPUS.

D. Although Blue Cross/Blue Shield of Texas misinterpreted the question on control of the ADP system, their technical proposal discusses tighter controls than other offerors employing the same ADP system.

E. The incumbent made a firm statement that they would accept a firm fixed-price contract immediately vice 1 March 1978. Assuming a start-work date of 1 January 1978, OCHAMPUS could save approximately $34,000 over the next two months (75,000 claims x ($5.70–$5.25)).

$5.70=Cost reimbursement negotiated claim rate
$5.25=Range 1 firm fixed price.

4. In summation the SSAC is of the opinion that, although the formal interviews clarified certain facts, no substantial weaknesses were found to exist. Therefore the award recommendation to Mutual of Omaha Insurance Company is reaffirmed based on the following factors:

A. The factors determined to fall outside the normal evaluation process which were discussed in the 14 December 1977 memorandum; or

B. A determination that the evaluation process (inclusive of the pre-award surveys) has resulted in tie bids. This would necessitate award to Mutual of Omaha Insurance Company since they are located in a labor surplus area and have claimed preference as a labor surplus area concern. Exhibit III is an excerpt from their business proposal which clearly substantiates their claim.

The evaluation process justifies the latter determination and it is the recommendation of the SSAC that award be made to Mutual of Omaha Insurance Company based on the proposal received, price and other factors considered inclusive of the labor surplus preference.

The SSA, in accepting the recommendation of the SSAC, did not specify any particular reason for his action. His memorandum merely references the SSAC's December 14 and 28 memoranda and states that Mutual "is hereby selected for award."

GHS enumerates several reasons why it believes the award to Mutual was improper:

1. GHS received a higher combined technical and price proposals score but award was still made to Mutual because of the "incumbency" of Mutual and the associated convenience to the Government in not having to change contractors, which was not in accordance with the award evaluation criteria set forth in the RFP.

2. Award was also made to Mutual because Mutual was believed to be a labor surplus area concern which was not, in fact, so.

3. Award to Mutual did not result in the lowest ultimate cost to the Government as GHS's proposal price was $201,810 less than Mutual's for the contract year with additional savings for the option years.

4. The contract services should have been procured by means of formal advertising rather than negotiation.

5. GHS was not afforded the opportunity to discuss a change in the contract start date to January 1, 1978, or revise its proposal in that regard after Mutual offered the earlier start date.

Thus, GHS essentially protests 1) OCHAMPUS' failure to make award on the basis of the numerical scoring results and the lower costs associated with the GHS proposal and 2) its decision to rely instead on Mutual's incumbency and labor surplus area concern status. (The assertion that the procurement should have been formally advertised is untimely and will not be considered since it relates to an alleged solicitation deficiency and therefore should have been made prior to the initial closing date for receipt of proposals. *See* 4 C.F.R. 20.2(b)(1).)

Point scores are often used by agencies in the evaluation of proposals. When a solicitation sets forth a precise numerical evaluation formula and provides that award will be made on the basis of the high score, the highest scored acceptable proposal should be selected for award. *Telecommunicaitons Management Corporation*, 57 Comp. Gen. 251 (1978), 78–1 CPD 80. In most cases, however, a solicitation will indicate the relative weights of the evaluation criteria, but will not explicitly provide for award on the basis of a numerical score.

In such cases, award need not be made to the offeror whose proposal receives the highest number of evaluation points, since point scores need not determine the outcome of a competitive source selection, but are merely guides for decisionmaking by source selection officials whose job it is to determine whether technical point advantages are worth the cost that might be associated with that higher-scored proposal. *See Grey Advertising, Inc.*, 55 Comp. Gen. 1111 (1976), 76–1 CPD 325 and cases cited therein. *Telecommunications Management Corp.*, supra, 57 Comp. Gen. at 254.

In this case, despite the 4-point scoring advantage Mutual had in the technical area and the overall 2–point scoring advantage in favor of GHS, and despite the OCHAMPUS assertions, in response to the protest, that Mutual was selected for award on the basis of its technical superiority, the record clearly reflects that both the SSAC and the SSA viewed the two competitors as essentially equal overall. Under such circumstances, and since the RFP did not mandate award in accordance with the results of point scoring, there was no requirement that award be made to GHS merely because of the higher total point score assigned its proposal *vis-a-vis* the Mutual proposal.

Where competing proposals are regarded as essentially equal technically, cost or price, even when designated as a relatively unimportant evaluation factor, usually becomes the award determinant. *See,* e.g., *Computer Data Systems, Inc.*, B–187892, June 2, 1977, 77–1 CPD 384, *aff'd on reconsideration* August 2, 1977, 77–2 CPD 67; *Bunker Ramo Corporation*, 56 Comp. Gen. 712 (1977), 77–1 CPD 427, *aff'd on reconsideration* B–187645, August 17, 1977, 77–2 CPD 124. Here, however, the situation is somewhat different. The Mutual and GHS proposals were not viewed as equal technically; rather, they were viewed as "a tie" on the basis of the overall scoring, that is, on the basis of both technical *and* price considerations. In other words, although there was a lower cost associated with the GHS proposal, there was more technical value associated with the Mutual proposal. It was only when the more technically advantageous but more costly Mutual proposal was compared with the less costly but less technically advantageous GHS proposal on an overall basis that OCHAMPUS determined that the competing proposals were virtually equal. This evaluation approach is similar to others where there is a numerical cost/ technical trade-off. *See Corbetta Construction Co.*, 55 Comp. Gen. 201 (1975), 75–2 CPD 144 and *TGI Construction Corporation, et al.*, 54 Comp. Gen. 775 (1975), 75–1 CPD 167, where cost/quality ratios were computed, and *Bell Aerospace Company*, 55 Comp. Gen. 244 (1975), 75–2 CPD 168, where the technical point scores were "normalized" to reflect the dollar value of technical point spreads between competing proposals. The situation is unusual, however, because the SSA found himself unable to make a reasoned judgment that the cost premium involved in making award to Mutual would or would not be justified in light of the technical superiority of Mutual's proposal. *See Grey Advertising, Inc.*, 55 Comp. Gen. 1111, 1118–20 (1976), 76–1 CPD

325. Under these circumstances, and given the low relative weight assigned to price as an evaluation factor, we do not believe the SSA was required to select GHS on the basis of that offeror's lower price.

Since application of the RFP evaluation criteria produced a "tie" in the sense that the SSA found himself without a clear choice on the basis of the technical cost considerations reflected in the point scoring, the SSA logically had to find an appropriate discriminator on which to make a rational selection. Consequently, he was presented with and took into account two factors—the disruptive effects and cost consequences of not awarding to the incumbent contractor, and the status of one offeror as a labor surplus area concern—which were not explicitly encompassed by the evaluation criteria delineated in the RFP.

We often have expressed the view that solicitations should contain a listing of all significant evaluation factors along with an indication of their relative importance, and that an award based on an agency's failure to adhere to those factors is improper. *See Francis & Jackson, Associates,* 57 Comp. Gen. 244 (1978), 78–1 CPD 79, and cases cited therein; 50 Comp. Gen. 59 (1970); *BDM Services Co.,* B–180245, May 9, 1974, 74–1 CPD 237. When, however, competing proposals are measured against the evaluation factors established for the procurement and the selection official, in the good faith exercise of the discretion vested in him, is unable to discern an appropriate choice on the basis of that evaluation, we think that official properly may take into account other factors which are rationally related to a selection decision for the particular procurement involved. Thus, what must be determined here is whether the award to Mutual is rationally supportable on the basis of the two additional factors considered by OCHAMPUS.

Incumbency frequently, but not always, confers certain competitive advantages upon an incumbent contractor. Obviously, if those advantages routinely are taken into account in proposal evaluation and source selection, incumbent contractors usually will have an edge over their competitors, with the consequence that the fresh approaches and new ideas proposed by non-incumbents may be lost to the Government and something less than maximum competition will be realized. *See,* for example, *Burns and Roe Tennessee, Inc.,* B–189462, July 21, 1978, 78–2 CPD 57, where the source selection official chose to stay with the long-term incumbent contractor rather than take a chance on the unsupported promises for a more efficient and less costly operation offered by a non-incumbent. Because of the possible detrimental effect on competition an undue concern with incumbency can have, contracting agencies do, at times, attempt to avoid evaluation results which reflect such concern. *See, e.g., Rockwell International Corporation,* 56 Comp.

Gen. 905 (1977), 77-2 CPD 119, and *Consultants and Designers, Incorporated*, B-186391, April 29, 1977, 77-1 CPD 294, where the cost of phasing in a new contractor was either not considered or considered apart from the basic cost evaluation, and *Grey Advertising, Inc., supra*, where the selection official determined that an offeror's higher point score reflected the "natural advantage" of incumbency rather than any meaningful technical superiority and that a lower scored proposal should be selected for award.

However, because incumbents often can offer real advantages to the Government, those advantages are often taken into account in proposal evaluation, and we have uniformly held that such action is proper since the Government is not required to equalize the "natural" advantages arising out of incumbency. *Burroughs Corporation*, 57 Comp. Gen. 109 (1977), 77-2 CPD 421; *Houston Films, Inc.*, B-184402, December 22, 1975, 75-2 CPD 404; *H. J. Hansen Co.*, B-181543, March 28, 1975, 75-1 CPD 187.

Under the circumstances here, we find nothing improper with OCHAMPUS considering both the "disruptive" effects of changing contractors on provider and beneficiary relations, a matter of some concern to OCHAMPUS in view of an earlier problem in that area, and the cost involved in transferring the claims processing function from one contractor to another. These seem to be reasonable matters for a selection official to consider, particularly when application of the designated evaluation factors does not enable that official to make a selection.

With respect to the consideration of labor surplus area concern status, we note that the RFP clause relied on by OCHAMPUS, which is set forth at Defense Acquisition Regulation (DAR) 7-2003.13, refers to bids, bidders, and tie bids and thus appears to have been written for use in formally advertised procurements, where the term "tie bids" would refer to a precise dollar and cents tie in bids either as submitted or as evaluated. Although DAR 3-501(b) Section B (ix) provides for use of the clause in negotiated procurements, we believe that use is limited primarily to situations where award is to be made on the basis of price. Other use of the clause, such as to break technical evaluation "ties," could result in a violation of the Maybank Amendment, which precludes the use of appropriated funds by the Department of Defense for the payment of a price differential to alleviate labor surplus situations. *See Maybank Amendment*, 57 Comp. Gen. 34 (1977), 77-2 CPD 333.

Here, of course, award was not to be made on the basis of price, but neither was there a finding of technical equality. Rather, the "tie" proposals reflected cost as well as technical factors, so that it is clear that the higher cost of the Mutual proposal is associated with the higher technical quality of the proposal. Thus, it cannot reasonably be said that an award to Mutual based on labor surplus considerations would involve payment of a price differential in violation of the Maybank Amendment.

The problem here is not that labor surplus status was taken into account, but that, as alleged by the protester, Mutual was regarded as a labor surplus area concern when in fact it was not.

The record shows that Mutual in its proposal claimed to be a labor surplus area concern on the basis of its incurring costs of more than 50% of the contract price in an area of substantial unemployment, which it identified as the Omaha Labor Area. The record does not indicate that OCHAMPUS sougth to verify Mutual's claim.

At the time of this procurement, "labor surplus areas" were listed in a Department of Labor (DOL) publication entitled "Area Trends in Employment and Unemployment." The January, February 1977 issue of this publication listed the Omaha Labor Area as an area of substantial unemployment. During 1977, the publication was updated periodically by a DOL press release and notices to State employment security offices and Federal agencies. A notice dated March 1977 advised that the Omaha Labor Area was no longer designated as an area of substantial unemployment. However, the March, April 1977 edition of "Area Trends in Employment and Unemployment" which did not include the Omaha Labor Area as an area of substantial unemployment, was not published and distributed by DOL until late January 1978, after award to Mutual had been made.

The provisions of DAR 1–801.2 in effect during the procurement defined a "labor surplus area" as a geographic area which at time of award is classified by DOL as an area of persistent or substantial unemployment and listed as such by DOL in its publication "Area Trends in Employment and Unemployment." OCHAMPUS takes the position that inasmuch as that publication did not actually change the classification of the Omaha Labor Area from one of substantial unemployment until the publication and distribution of the March, April 1977 issue in late January 1978, Mutual was, in fact, a labor surplus area concern when award was made to it. In support of its position, OCHAMPUS relies on our decision 45 Comp. Gen. 471 (1966), where the contracting officer received the latest issue of "Area Trends," which changed an offeror's eligibility for labor surplus area concern status, one day after award. We found that although the awardee was not a labor surplus area concern at the time of award as a consequence of the new "Area Trends" listing, the award itself was proper because it was made in accordance with the information contained in the latest issue of the applicable DOL publication which had been or should have been received by the procuring activity prior to the time the relevant determination had to be made.

We do not agree with OCHAMPUS. Although the DAR provision referred to the "Area Trends" publication, DOL's own regulations provided only that "the Secretary of Labor will publish at regular intervals a list of * * * areas of persistent or substantial unemployment." 29 C.F.R. 8.6 (1977). Further, we are advised by DOL that changes to the "Area Trends" listings were made through monthly notices, including the March 1977 notice entitled "CLASSIFICATION CHANGES AFFECTING * * * AREAS OF SUBSTANTIAL OR PERSISTENT UNEMPLOYMENT * * *" which DOL informally advises was sent to all Federal agencies. Thus, this case differs substantially from 45 Comp. Gen., *supra*, where there had been no updates to "Area Trends" and where the contracting officer reasonably relied on the most recent issue of that publication that he had any reason to know about. Here, we believe the "Area Trends" publication must be viewed as having been periodically updated by the March 1977 and succeeding notices issued by DOL, that OCHAMPUS should have known of this updated information or should have sought it out to verify Mutual's claim instead of automatically relying on it, and that the Omaha area was not, at the time of award to Mutual, an area of substantial unemployment. Consequently, we find that Mutual properly could not be viewed as a labor surplus area concern on the award date.

With respect to the final issue, the record shows that during the subsequent evaluation directed by the SSA, Mutual verbally offered to accept a no-cost termination of its existing contract and to begin immediate performance under the new contract to be awarded. This was followed by a confirming telephone conversation and telegram, in which Mutual stated it "is in a position to implement immediately under the [new] contract." The second SSAC memorandum to the SSA referred to Mutual's offer and pointed out that an award to Mutual by January 1, 1978, instead of March 1, 1978, would result in approximate savings of $34,000, the difference between what Mutual would be paid under its existing contract and under the new contract. Award was made effective January 1. GHS objects that it was not given the opportunity to offer an earlier start date.

It is not clear from the record before us just what GHS was given the opportunity to offer. The second SSAC memorandum, quoted above in pertinent part, states that a list of 12 questions was prepared for further discussions with GHS and Mutual. We have not been furnished a copy of that list; however, the confirming telegram from Mutual referred to "the OCHAMPUS verbal questionnaire" and the OCHAMPUS request for "anything we wished to add favoring our receiving this award." If GHS were also given the same response opportunity, it would have been given the same opportunity as was given Mutual to make its offer more attractive. We do not understand, however, how GHS could have made its offer appear more favorable by offering an earlier starting date, since it appears that the earlier date was beneficial to OCHAMPUS only in light of a no-cost termination of the existing Mutual contract and since it further appears that Mutual offered to accept a no-cost termination only in connection with award of the new contract to it and not to a competitor.

Nonetheless, we find OCHAMPUS' actions in this regard to be procedurally deficient. First of all, although OCHAMPUS characterizes its additional discussions with GHS and Mutual as preaward surveys, it is clear that the discussions were for the purpose of further exploring offeror understanding of requirements and ferreting out possible weaknesses, all with a view toward providing a meaningful discriminator for selection of a contractor. As such, the discussions should have been treated as a new round of competitive negotiations, as envisioned by DAR 3–805, and should have been concluded by a request for new best and final offers. *See*, e.g., *The Human Resources Company*, B–187153, November 30, 1976, 76–2 CPD 459.

Second, even if the discussions initially properly could have been viewed as merely preaward survey contacts, Mutual's offer to make its proposal more desirable by beginning contract performance 2 months earlier than the start date indicated in the RFP, and OCHAMPUS' willingness to consider that offer, constituted additional competitive range discussions, thereby requiring additional discussions with GHS. *New Hampshire-Vermont Health Service*, 57 Comp. Gen. 347 (1978), 78–1 CPD 202; *University of New Orleans*, 56 Comp. Gen. 958 (1977), 77–2 CPD 201; *Bristol Electronics, Inc., et al.*, 54 Comp. Gen. 16 (1974), 74–2 CPD 23. Consequently, OCHAMPUS should have reopened negotiations, issued an RFP amendment indicating its willingness to accept the earlier start date, and requested new best and final offers. *Union Carbide Corporation*, 55 Comp. Gen. 802, 807 (1976), 76–1 CPD 134. While GHS may not have been able to offer an earlier starting date, since Mutual had been given an opportunity to make its offer more attractive, GHS was also entitled to an opportunity to improve its proposal in any way it deemed appropriate. *PRC Information Sciences Company*, 56 Comp. Gen. 768 (1977), 77–2 CPD 11.

The question remains as to what, if any, remedial action is appropriate in light of the deficiencies noted in this case. When an offeror is improperly denied the opportunity to submit a revised proposal, we often recommend that negotiations be reopened so that the impropriety can be corrected. *See*, e.g., *Bristol Electronics, Inc., et al., supra; Union Carbide Corporation, supra.* Similarly, when a source selection decision, or evaluation upon which the decision is based, is subject to question, we will recommend that the selection official reconsider his decision. *See New Hampshire-Vermont Health Service, supra; Bell Aerospace Company*, 55 Comp. Gen. 244 (1975), 75–2 CPD 168; *see also Lockheed Propulsion Company, et al.*, 53 Comp. Gen. 977 (1974), 74–1 CPD 339. However, when it appears likely that little or no prejudice resulted from such deficiencies in the procurement process, we see no reason to disturb an award or recommend other corrective action with respect to the procurement under review. *See Fiber Materials, Inc.*, 57 Comp. Gen. 527 (1978), 78–1 CPD 422; 52 Comp. Gen. 161 (1972); *Data 100 Corporation—Reconsideration*, B–185884, October 21, 1976, 76–2 CPD 354.

Here, we doubt that GHS was materially prejudiced by the agency's consideration and acceptance of Mutual's offer to advance the contract start date. Although the Mutual offer and its benefits were discussed in the SSAC's second memorandum, the SSAC's final recommendation referenced only two factors: Mutual's incumbency and Mutual's status as a labor surplus area concern. Thus, we find it unlikely that the advantage to OCHAMPUS of the earlier starting date played a significant role in the SSA's decision. Consequently, we do not believe we would be warranted in recommending the reopening of negotiations on the basis of this particular deficiency.

The situation is less clear, however, with respect to the effect of Mutual's perceived labor surplus area concern status on the selection decision. On the one hand, OCHAMPUS' erroneous view of Mutual as a labor surplus area concern could be regarded as immaterial since under the circumstances we believe the selection decision properly could have been based on the incumbency considerations alone. On the other hand, the SSAC's first memorandum recited the advantages of retaining the incumbent contractor, but the SSA declined to make a decision on the basis of that memorandum and instead ordering further evaluation. It was on the basis of the second memorandum, which recommended award to Mutual in part on the basis of labor surplus considerations, that resulted in the selection decision.

It is possible, of course, that if labor surplus status had not been mentioned and the SSA merely had been informed that the subsequent evaluation produced no additional meaningful award discriminators, he at that time might have accepted the SSAC recommendation to award to Mutual solely on the basis of the firm's incumbency. Such a conclusion on our part, however, would only be conjectural; on the basis of the record, we can only conclude that the selection decision may have been influenced by the SSAC's belief that Mutual was a labor surplus area concern. Accordingly, we are recommending that the SSA reconsider his selection decision without regard to any labor surplus considerations. We are further recommending that, should the SSA conclude GHS should have been selected for award, the Mutual contract be terminated for the convenience of the Government as soon as it is feasible to do so and that award be made to GHS for the remainder of the first year option period. In either case, in light of the deficiencies in the procurement, we are also recommending that the second-year option not be exercised.

This decision contains a recommendation for corrective action to be taken. Therefore, we are furnishing copies to the Senate Committees on Governmental Affairs and Appropriations and the House Committees on Government Operations and Appropriations in accordance with section 236 of the Legislative Reorganization Act of 1970, 31 U.S.C. 1176 (1976), which requires the submission of written statements by the agency to the Committees concerning the action taken with respect to our recommendations.

The protest is sustained.

[B–192796, B–192827, B–193062]

Agents—Of Private Parties—Authority—Contracts—Signatures—Time for Submitting Evidence

Where authority of signer of bid is questioned by contracting agency, burden rests on bidder to submit necessary documentation to demonstrate such authority. Preferably, such evidence would be included on Standard Form 129 which would be on file prior to bid opening. However, furnishing evidence after bid opening is not legally prohibited. In absence of timely submission of probative evidence, protester has failed to satisfy its burden to substantiate authority of signer of bid.

Agents—Of Private Parties—Authority—Contracts—Evidence to Establish—Administrative Determination

Question of signer's authority is essentially factual determination to be made upon consideration of all relevant evidence.

Contracting Officers—Determinations—Erroneous—Estoppel

Prior actions of contracting officials cannot estop Government's rejection of nonresponsive bid.

Contracts—Protests—Timeliness—Basis of Protest—Date Made Known to Protester—Doubtful

Where record does not contain probative evidence concerning awareness of protest basis, any doubt as to date on which knowledge was or should have been obtained should be resolved in favor of protester. Therefore, matter of award is considered on merits.

Contracts—Protests—Moot, Academic, etc. Questions

Protest against Army making award when aware of protest, which Army denies, is rendered moot since record indicates protest was filed with General Accounting Office after award.

Bids—Responsiveness—Test to Determine—Unqualified Offer to Meet All Solicitation Terms

Bid accompanied by letter which sets forth unqualified bid price and alternate approach bid price is responsive since Army's acceptance of bid as submitted would have effectively bound bidder to perform in accordance with terms and conditions of the invitation for bids. Alternate approach is merely an offer to be accepted or rejected by Army.

Bids—Prices—Reasonableness—Administrative Determination

Contracting officer's determination that successful offeror's price was reasonable will not be disturbed unless it is unreasonable or there is showing of bad faith or fraud.

In the matter of Forest Scientific, Inc., February 9, 1979:

Forest Scientific, Inc. (Forest) has protested the rejection of its bid pursuant to invitation for bids (IFB) No. DAAA22–78–B–0519, issued by the Department of the Army, Watervliet Arsenal (Army), on April 25, 1978, for housing, elevating mechanisms. The Army, citing the Armed Services Procurement Regulation (ASPR) (now the Defense Acquisition Regulation) § 2–404.2(2) (1976 ed.), rejected Forest's bid for lack of a valid signature by an authorized official of the firm.

In addition to IFB–0519, Forest has filed two other protests with our Office which question the rejection of Forest's bid by the Army for lack of a valid signature. The first, B–192796, concerns IFB No. DAAA22–78–B–0540 and the second, B–193062, concerns IFB No. DAAA22–78–B–0521. In the former, we note that there are initials beneath the "signature—Anthony Saginario" on Forest's bid while, in the latter, there are no initials. It is our view that the facts in all three instances are sufficiently analogous and that the issues raised with respect to the rejection of Forest's bids are the same. Accordingly, we will specifically consider B–192827 (IFB–0519) which will also be dispositive of the remaining protests.

ASPR § 2–404.2(a) provides:

Any bid which fails to conform to the essential requirements of the invitation for bids shall be rejected.

The IFB incorporated by reference standard form 33A, March 1969, which provides, in paragraph 2(b), that:

Each offeror shall furnish the information required by the solicitation. The offeror shall sign the solicitation and print or type his name on the Schedule and each Continuation Sheet thereof on which he makes an entry. Erasures or other changes must be initialed by the person signing the offer. Offers signed by an agent are to be accompanied by evidence of his authority unless such evidence has been previously furnished to the issuing office.

Forest's major contention is that a company can delegate to its employees the authority to act on its behalf and that such action would be binding on the company. Moreover, Forest believes that the personal signature of an owner or executive who is specifically authorized to bind his company is not necessary as long as the employee designated to act on behalf of the company is delegated the authority to sign the owner's or executive's name. Further, it appears that Forest is taking the position that such employee does not have to be listed on Standard Form 129, "Bidder's Mailing List Application." Notwithstanding, Forest argues that Anthony Saginario's name was signed by an authorized employee, Francine Garofalo, who is listed on form 129. We note that this argument was first made approximately 2 months after Forest's protest was filed with our Office and after award had been made. In addition, Forest is of the opinion that form 129, executed on September 23, 1976, is now obsolete since, if it was in force at this time, it would include the names of two additional authorized employees. Also, Forest, in its comments to the Army's report, questions for the first time the award of a contract, notwithstanding Forest's protest concerning rejection of its bid, to Ruoff and Sons, Inc. (Ruoff) whose bid was allegedly nonresponsive to the IFB and was 40 percent higher than the price quoted by Forest.

Form 129, dated September 23, 1976, provides that two persons, Anthony Saginario (President) and Francine Garofalo (Secretary), are authorized to sign bids in the name of Forest. The Army advises that initially Forest's bid "appeared proper which resulted in normal processing of the bid (i.e., a check on a possible mistake in bid and preaward survey)." A review of the bids received resulted in a letter dated May 31, 1978, which listed the amount of each bid and requested that Forest examine its bid since it appeared that the bid may be in error. In a June 16, 1978 letter, Forest confirmed its initial bid and this letter was personally signed by Anthony Saginario. Subsequently, the Army became cognizant of another procurement where initials were placed next to the signature of Anthony Saginario indicating that such signature was in effect a proxy signature. [See *Forest Scientific, Inc.*, B-192742, September 13, 1978, 78-2 CPD 201, involving Forest's protest essentially questioning the Army's rejection of its bid as nonresponsive on the basis of Forest's utilization of a proxy signature. Forest's position was that "it may authorize whomever the firm wishes to represent the Company." Our Office found that Forest's protest was untimely filed.] Then, the Army examined Forest's instant bid to determine whether or not a proxy signature was utilized by Forest. The Army concluded that such was the case and rejected Forest's bid.

The record indicates that in a July 25, 1978, letter Anthony Saginario stated: "* * * I have not signed an IFB or RFP in at least eight years * * *." In addition, the Army advises that it suggested, even prior to the instant cases, that Forest execute a new form 129 giving the names of all persons presently authorized to sign bids for Forest. To date, the Army advises that Forest has not filed an updated form 129.

We agree with Forest that a company can delegate to its employees the authority to act on its behalf and thus bind the company. However, we believe that the contracting activity must be made aware of the signer's authority either by form 129 filed prior to bid opening or sufficient evidence submitted when the signer's authority is questioned. To do otherwise would unnecessarily hinder the procurement process and potentially damage the integrity of the bidding system, since this would keep open the question of the bid's validity.

The burden rests on each bidder to submit the necessary documentation to demonstrate the authority of the signer. In this instance, Forest alleged, approximately 2 months after its initial protest and after award, that the signer was authorized since she was listed on form 129. However, this is merely an allegation, with no documentation to support it. Thus, Forest has failed to satisfy its burden to substantiate the authority of the signer. See *New Jersey Manufacturing Company, Incorporated*, B–179589, January 23, 1974, 74–1 CPD 25. Had the necessary information been submitted at the time when the signer's authority was first questioned, and deemed sufficient, Forest's bid would have been valid. See B–146348, December 8, 1961.

With respect to Forest's contention that form 129 is obsolete, we disagree. Until the time that form 129 is amended or revoked by the potential bidder it is valid. Consequently, it is up to the potential bidders to keep form 129 current and advise the procuring agency of any changes.

We have indicated that the absence of evidence existing before bid opening may make it difficult for the bidder to establish to the contracting officer's satisfaction that the individual signer of the bid was authorized to do so at the time of bid opening. *Square Deal Trucking Company, Incorporated*, 49 Comp. Gen. 527 (1970). Therefore, we encourage the submission of such evidence prior to or at bid opening to avoid potential challenges and problems of substantiating the authority of the signer. See *New Jersey Manufacturing Company, Incorporated, supra*. However, the evidence required to establish the authority of the signer of a bid to bind a corporation may be presented after bid opening. *Corbin Sales Corporation*, B–182978, June 9, 1975, 75–1 CPD 347. In this regard, it is our view that a bid signed by an agent should be rejected, as here, where proof of agency is not timely submitted. See *New Jersey Manufacturing Company, Incorporated, supra*. The evidence required to establish the authority of a signer of a bid to bind a corporation is for the determination of the contracting officer. See *General Ship and Engines Works, Inc.*, 55 Comp. Gen. 422, 426 (1975), 75-2 CPD 269; *Atlantic Maintenance Company*, 54 Comp. Gen. 686, 692 (1975), 75-1 CPD 108.

The record before our Office reflects that the contracting agency acted reasonably in concluding that Forest's bid was nonresponsive since Forest did not prove the signer's authority and, therefore, the signature did not bind Forest to the terms and conditions of the bid.

The fact that for the past 8 years a proxy signature was used by Forest does not change our opinion. The record indicates that the Army first became aware of Forest's utilization of proxy signatures in May 1978. Therefore, the past acceptance by the Army of Forest's bids was without knowledge of such practice. In any event, prior erroneous actions by contracting officials cannot estop the Army from rejecting Forest's instant bid as nonresponsive since it was required to do so by law. See *A. D. Roe Company, Inc.*, 54 Comp. Gen. 271 (1974), 74-2 CPD 194; *Prestex Inc.* v. *United States*, 320 F. 2d 367 (1963). Accordingly, Forest's protest regarding the rejection of its bid is denied.

Concerning Forest's last contention, the questioning of the award of a contract, our Bid Protest Procedures (Procedures) require that protests "be filed not later than 10 [working] days after the basis for protest is known or should have been known, whichever is earlier." 4 C.F.R. § 20.2(b)(2) (1978). The matter of the August 17, 1978, award of contract should have been known by Forest prior to the October 20, 1978, date it first raised this issue with our Office. However, we note that the record does not contain any probative evidence to indicate such awareness. In addition, we have been informally advised that the Army did not publish notice of the award in the Commerce Business Daily and the protester believes that its first awareness of award occurred when it received the Army's report. In cases as this, we have held that any doubt as to the date on which knowledge was or should have been obtained as to a protest basis should be resolved in favor of the protester. See *Ampex Corporation*, B-190529, March 16, 1978, 78-1 CPD 212. Therefore, we will consider the matter on the merits.

Forest initially questions the ethics of the Army in making an award when it was aware that Forest was protesting the rejection of its bid. In response, the Army submitted a supplemental statement of the contracting officer which provided, in pertinent part:

> This Contracting Officer did not make an award to Ruoff and Sons at a time when he was aware that Forest Scientific was protesting rejection of its bid. Award was made on 17 August 1978 and Forest Scientific protested to GAO by a letter dated 25 August 1978. This Arsenal was initially advised of their protest orally by our higher headquarters on or about 30 August 1978.

Our Bid Protest Procedures, 4 C.F.R. § 20.4 (1978), provide:

When a protest has been filed before award the agency will not make an award prior to resolution of the protest except as provided in the applicable procurement regulations. In the event the agency determines that award is to be made during the pendency of a protest, the agency will notify the Comptroller General.

The record indicates that award was made on August 17, 1978, and Forest's protest letter, dated August 25, 1978, was received by our Office on August 30, 1978, *after* award. Accordingly, Forest's protest is not a before-award protest as specified in 4 C.F.R. § 20.4, *supra*, but an after-award protest, rendering this issue moot.

Forest makes the allegation that Ruoff submitted a bid that was nonresponsive to the IFB since the "bid was modified to the extent that the price offered was contingent upon the Government supplying inspection equipment which was clearly defined in the IFB as the contractor's responsibility." The Army disagrees with Forest and states:

Ruoff and Sons, Inc. was awarded this contract on the basis of a responsive bid wherein all provisions of the IFB were met. In addition to its responsive bid, Ruoff and Sons sent a letter which submitted for our consideration a price reduction of $1.00 per item if it were allowed to use Government gauges listed on page 27 of the solicitation which were presently in their possession for use on another Government contract. A modification dated 25 October 1978 has been entered into by mutual agreement of both parties to allow this $1.00 reduction per item for use of the gauges; however, the bid accepted was responsive to the basic solicitation.

Ruoff's bid was accompanied by a letter, both dated May 16, 1978, which provided, in pertinent part:

We submit for your consideration a price of $147.00 EA for item 0001AB and $145.00 EA for item 0001AC based on using Government gauges listed on page 27 which are presently in our possession for use on Contract DAAA22–77–C–0253. All other conditions remain the same.

It is clear that Ruoff's letter did not qualify Ruoff's bid. Therefore, the Army's acceptance of Ruoff's bid as submitted effectively bound Ruoff to perform in accordance with the advertised terms of the solicitation, which provide that it is the contractor's responsibility to provide inspection equipment. In addition, it is our view that Ruoff's letter makes it clear that Ruoff's offer to reduce its price if it was permitted to use Government gauges, already in its possession, was merely an offer of an alternative approach that the Army could accept or reject. See *Nordam Division of R. H. Siegfried, Inc.*, B–187031, January 4, 1977, 77–1 CPD 3. As stated above, the initial contract, awarded August 17, 1978, was modified on October 25, 1978, to incorporate this alternate approach. Accordingly, this aspect of Forest's protest is denied.

Finally, Forest questions the reasonableness of the award price ($147 per item), which is 40 percent higher than that quoted by Forest

($87.50 per item). In support of its position, that Ruoff's price was reasonable, the contracting officer states:

The Government estimate for this procurement was $76,145.00 for all 485 items or $157.00 each.
This estimate was based on the following procurement history of this item:

QUANTITY	AWARDEE	COST/UNIT	DATE
266	Ruoff & Sons_____	$165	February 1978
144	Ruoff & Sons_____	$128	June 1977
192	Ruoff & Sons_____	$139	December 1976
343	MKB._____	$187	August 1975

Based on the Government estimate and the history involved, it was deemed the price was fair and reasonable.

Whether or not a bid price is reasonable is a matter of administrative discretion which our Office will not question unless it is unreasonable or there is a showing of bad faith or fraud. See *Reza Seyyedin Art and Film Production*, B–191470, August 21, 1978, 78–2 CPD 138; and *Support Contractors, Inc.*, B–181607, March 18, 1975, 75–1 CPD 160. We have recognized that the agency may base its determination of price reasonableness on a Government estimate, past procurement history, current market conditions, or other relevant factors, including any which may have been disclosed by the bidding. See *Westinghouse Electric Corporation*, 54 Comp. Gen. 699 (1975), 75–1 CPD 112.

In this circumstance, there has been neither a showing of bad faith or fraud, nor, in view of the prior procurement history and Government estimate, can we say that such determination was unreasonable. Accordingly, our Office will not object to the contracting officer's finding that Ruoff's price was reasonable.

For the foregoing reasons, Forest's protest is denied.

[B–183576]

General Accounting Office—Procedure—Litigation

It is the policy of the General Accounting Office to decline ruling on matters in litigation. Hence, no action will be taken on questions of whether Variable Reenlistment Bonus payments may be made to members of the Armed Forces who (1) cancelled enlistment extension agreements on the basis of erroneous advice that they were not eligible for the previously authorized Variable Reenlistment Bonus, 37 U.S.C. 308 (1970), and (2) executed new enlistment extension agreements in order to become eligible for the new Selective Reenlistment Bonus, 37 U.S.C. 308 (1976), since those questions are the subject of pending litigation in the Federal courts.

Gratuities—Selective Reenlistment Bonus—Computation—Multiplier—Effective Date

Selective Reenlistment Bonus payments for extensions of enlistments, authorized by 37 U.S.C. 308 (1976), must be based on the award level multiplier in effect on the date the extension agreement is executed rather than on the date the extension agreement becomes operative, in accordance with the Supreme Court's decision in *United States* v. *Larionoff*, 431 U.S. 864 (1977), concerning the similar Variable Reenlistment Bonus. 50 Comp. Gen. 515, B–175846, Oct. 4, 1972, and similar cases are overruled.

Gratuities—Enlistment Bonus—Basis for Payment

If an individual enlists in a Reserve component under the Delayed Entry Program with a concurrent commitment to serve in a Regular component for a period of at least 4 years in a skill designated as critical, the award level of the enlistment bonus authorized by 37 U.S.C. 308a (1976) must be fixed on the date of enlistment in the Delayed Entry Program, rather than on the date of entry on active duty. Payment of the bonus must, however, be contingent on the member's qualifying and serving in his designated military specialty. *United States* v. *Larionoff*, 431 U.S. 864 (1977) ; 52 Comp. Gen. 105 (1972).

In the matter of Department of Defense Military Pay and Allowance Committee Action No. 542, February 14, 1979:

This action is in response to a letter dated May 11, 1978, from the Assistant Secretary of Defense (Comptroller) requesting an advance decision concerning the payment of enlistment and reenlistment bonuses to members of the Armed Forces in the circumstances described in Department of Defense Military Pay and Allowance Committee Action No. 542, enclosed with the submission.

Background

In the Committee Action it is noted that former 37 U.S.C. 308(a) and (b) provided for a Regular Reenlistment Bonus (RRB) for a first reenlistment or extension of enlistment, determined by multiplying an enlistee's monthly pay at the time of the expiration of this initial enlistment by the number of years agreed to in the reenlistment or extension agreement. That bonus program was augmented in 1965 through the enactment of section 3 of Public Law 89–132, 79 Stat. 545, 547, by the Variable Reenlistment Bonus (VRB) program (37 U.S.C. 308(g), now repealed). The purpose of the VRB program was to encourage members with skills that were in short supply ("critical skills") to reenlist or extend. The VRB was to be a multiple of the RRB. The multiple was to be determined under prescribed regulations by the critical need for the skill and was to be revised from time to time. The statutory authority for the VRB program was repealed effective June 1, 1974, by the Armed Forces Enlisted Personnel Bonus Revision Act of 1974, Public Law 93–277, 88 Stat. 119. The VRB and RRB were thereby replaced with the current Selective Reenlistment Bonus (SRB) program, now codified in 37 U.S.C. 308 (1976).

It is further noted in the Committee Action that regulations governing individual eligibility for the VRB were set forth in Department of Defense Instruction 1304.15, dated September 3, 1970. Those regulations, as applied, required calculation of the VRB using the multiple in effect when the reenlistment or extension became operative. Thus, it is said, an enlistee who signed a 2-year extension for advanced training in a critical skill some time prior to the expiration of his current enlistment would sometimes find that when his extension became operative, his skill was no longer critical and his multiple was zero, or the multiple in effect when he executed his extension agreement, *e.g.*, four, was reduced when his extension became operative, e.g., two. Also, an enlistee who began to serve a 2-year extension in a critical skill after June 1, 1974, which extension was agreed to prior to that date, found himself disentitled by the repeal of the VRB program when his extension became operative.

It is further noted that this situation gave rise to the case of *United States* v. *Larionoff*, 431 U.S. 864 (1977), wherein the United States Supreme Court concluded that the regulations were contrary to the manifest purposes of Congress in enacting the VRB program, and hence invalid, insofar as they required the amount of a VRB to be determined by reference to the award level in effect at the time the member began to serve the extension, rather than at the time he agreed to it. The Supreme Court ruled that because Congress intended to provide at the reenlistment decision point a promise of a reasonably certain and specific bonus for extending service in the Armed Forces, the members in the affected class were entitled to VRB's determined according to the multiples in effect at the time they agreed to extend their enlistments, not the award levels in effect when the extension agreements became operative.

It is indicated that the Supreme Court's ruling required a recomputation of many thousands of VRB entitlements. That ruling has also given rise to a number of questions concerning bonus payments.

First of all, it is said that after June 1, 1974, the date the VRB program was replaced by the SRB program, a significant number of enlisted personnel opted for an SRB by terminating their original extension agreements and executing reenlistment contracts for 3 or more years, or executing a second extension agreement. Some portion of this group received an SRB less than the VRB and RRB they would have received but for the fact that their original extension agreements were cancelled. A question thus arises as to whether authority exists to pay such members VRB and RRB, and if so, by what computation formula.

Secondly, it is said that the objective of the SRB is essentially the same as the VRB, that is, to increase the number of reenlistments in critical military specialties and attain adequate career manning in those designated specialties. In light of the Supreme Court's ruling in *United States* v. *Larionoff*, *supra*, a question has arisen as to whether SRB payments for extensions of enlistments should also be based on the date the extension agreement is executed.

Third, it is noted that under 37 U.S.C. 308a (1976) a person who initially enlists in an Armed Force for a period of at least 4 years, in a skill designated as critical, may be paid an enlistment bonus in an amount prescribed by the Secretary of Defense, but not more than $3,000. It is said that this enlistment bonus is a recruiting incentive offered to influence individuals to enter the service concerned either by immediate entry on active duty or through the Delayed Entry Program (DEP). Under the DEP, an individual may delay entry into the Regular component for a specific period of time by enlisting in a Reserve component. Questions have arisen as to the proper treatment to be accorded an individual entering the DEP for ultimate service in a designated critical skill, since the bonus amount may change or the skill may even be removed from the critical skill list between the time the individual enters the DEP and the time he actually enlists in the Regular component of the service concerned. Except for the Army, the services have taken the position that entitlement to the bonus may vest as of the date the individual enters the DEP because, at that time, he has committed himself to serve and been promised a bonus after meeting all other prerequisites. The Army position, however, is that entitlement to the bonus should be fixed on the date the individual enlists in the Regular component of the service concerned, contingent upon the successful completion of advanced training.

In view of the foregoing, five specific questions relating to the VRB, the SRB, and the enlistment bonus have been submitted for resolution.

I. Variable Reenlistment Bonus

The first question presented in the submission is:

1. Is a member in the following circumstances now entitled to a Variable Reenlistment Bonus (VRB) to the extent that it exceeds the Selective Reenlistment Bonus (SRB), 37 U.S.C. 308, paid to him?

a. On 30 April 1974 he executed an extension of enlistment for two years to become operative on 1 October 1974 and his rating or Navy Enlisted Classification (NEC) was VRB eligible at the time he executed the extension.

b. On 1 October 1974 he cancelled his extension to either execute a new agreement to extend his enlistment or to reenlist, in either case, to become SRB eligible.

c. If the answer to the aforesaid question is affirmative, would the VRB entitlement be based on the original two year extension (30 April 1974), or the number of years agreed to in order to become SRB eligible?

Subsequent to our receipt of the request for an advance decision, we were informed by the Department of Justice that the legal issues presented in the first question are a subject matter of litigation in the case of *James Thomas Edmonds, Jr., et al.* v. *United States*, a class action filed in the United States District Court, District of South Carolina, Civil Action No. 75–1624, and several related cases. In particular, we have been advised that there has been no ruling on the issue of whether RRB and VRB payments may be made on the basis of an extension of enlistment that was cancelled in the manner described, or the issue of whether members who opted for an SRB in these circumstances may all properly be regarded as belonging to one class or subclass. We have been further advised that the litigation may be protracted.

We have also received and considered a brief primarily concerning question "1," submitted by attorneys representing plaintiffs in this litigation.

It is a longstanding rule that this Office will not act on matters which are in the courts during pendency of litigation. Since the eventual outcome of the litigation may fully resolve the first question submitted, we decline to answer that question at this time. If, at such time as these court cases have been finally decided, it is the view of the Department of Defense that the issues presented by the first question have not been fully resolved, the question may be resubmitted to this Office for further consideration.

II. Selective Reenlistment Bonus

The second and third questions presented in the submission are:

2. Under *Larionoff*, should SRB payments for extensions of enlistments be based on the multiple in effect on the date the extension agreement is executed, or on the date the extension agreement becomes operative?
3. If it is determined that SRB payments should be based on the date the extension agreement is executed, would such a determination have a retroactive effect to the inception of the SRB program (i.e., 1 June 1974)?

Subsection 308(a) of title 37, United States Code (1976), provides as follows with respect to the payment of the SRB:

(a) A member of a uniformed service who—
(1) has completed at least twenty-one months of continuous active duty (other than for training) but not more than ten years of active duty;
(2) is designated as having a critical military skill by the Secretary of Defense, or by the Secretary of Transportation with respect to the Coast Guard when it is not operating as a service in the Navy;
(3) is not receiving special pay under section 312a of this title; and
(4) reenlists or voluntarily extends his enlistment in a regular component of the service concerned for a period of at least three years;
may be paid a bonus, not to exceed six months of the basic pay to which he was entitled at the time of his discharge or release, multiplied by the number of years, or the monthly fractions thereof, of additional obligated service, not to exceed six years, or $15,000, whichever is the lesser amount. Obligated service in excess of twelve years will not be used for bonus computation.

Subsection 308(e) further provides that the SRB program shall be administered under regulations prescribed by the Secretary of Defense for the Armed Forces under his jurisdiction, and by the Secretary of Transportation with respect to the Coast Guard when it is not operating as a service in the Navy.

Implementing regulations issued by the Secretary of Defense are contained in Department of Defense (DOD) Instruction 1304.22, June 3, 1975, as amended. Section III of Enclosure 2 to DOD Instruction

1304.22 (change 1, December 1, 1976) provides in pertinent part as follows with respect to SRB eligibility:

III. *Criteria for Individual Member Eligibility*

A. *General Eligibility.* An enlisted member is eligible to receive a Selective Reenlistment Bonus if he meets all of the following conditions:

* * * * * * *

> 4. Attains eligibility prior to the effective date of termination of awards in any military specialty designated for termination of award. (Member must attain eligibility prior to the effective date of a reduction of award level to be eligible for the higher award level.* * *)

And further with respect to the reduction or termination of SRB:

E. *Maintenance, Reduction, and Termination of Awards*

* * * * * * *

When a military specialty is designated for reduction or termination of award, an effective date for reduction or termination of awards shall be established and announced to the field at least 30 days in advance. All awards on or after that effective date in a military specialty designated for reduction of award will be at the level effective that date. No new awards will be made on or after the effective date in a military specialty designated for termination of award.

Those provisions are nearly identical to the language of the VRB regulations scrutinized in *United States* v. *Larionoff*, *supra*, in which the Supreme Court concluded (at page 877, 431 U.S.):

* * * We therefore hold that insofar as the Defense Department regulations required that the amount of the VRB to be paid to a service member who was otherwise eligible to receive one be determined by the award level as of the time he began to serve his extended enlistment, they are in clear conflict with the congressional intention in enacting the VRB program, and hence invalid. Because Congress intended to provide at the re-enlistment decision point a promise of a reasonably certain and specific bonus for extending service in the Armed Forces, Larionoff and the members of his class are entitled, as the Court of Appeals held, to payment of VRB's determined according to the award levels in effect at the time they agreed to extend their enlistments.

As is noted in the Committee Action, the SRB was established to accomplish the same purpose as the VRB, that is, to induce members with critical skills to extend their service in the Armed Forces. It is therefore our view that the Supreme Court's reasoning in the *Larionoff* case is applicable to the SRB program. While we have previously held differently concerning the VRB, to the extent our decisions conflict with the Supreme Court's decision in *Larionoff*, our decisions should no longer be followed. See for example, 50 Comp. Gen. 515, 518 (1971), and B–175846, October 4, 1972. Accordingly, in answer to question "2," SRB payments for extensions of enlistments must be based on the multiple in effect on the date the extension agreement is executed rather than on the date the extension agreement becomes operative.

Concerning question "3," the construction of the SRB statute provided in answer to question "2" is an original construction applicable from the effective date of the statute. Accordingly, question "3" is answered in the affirmative.

III. Enlistment Bonus Under the Delayed Entry Program

The fourth and fifth questions presented in the submission are:

4. Does a member's entitlement to an enlistment bonus under 37 U.S.C. 308a become fixed on (a) the date the member enlists in a reserve component under the Delayed Enlistment Program (DEP), or (b) the date the member enlists in the regular component of the service concerned, or (c) whichever of those two dates is more advantageous to the member?

5. Would the answer to Question 4 be the same if the individual entered the DEP prior to the inception of the bonus program and enlisted in the regular component of the service concerned after the bonus program had been implemented?

Under delayed enlistment or entry programs, a qualified individual is generally authorized to enlist in a Reserve component of one of the Armed Forces with a concurrent commitment to enter on active duty in a Regular component at a future date, at which time he will receive specialized training in the career field of his choice and serve in that career field upon the successful completion of training. In general, service regulations provide that in the event the enlistment option, school course, or training for which an applicant enlists is cancelled or for some other reason becomes unavailable, the applicant may secure a discharge from the DEP. Otherwise, however, the applicant is generally obligated to enter on active duty, and he may be subject to disciplinary action under the Uniform Code of Military Justice if he fails to honor his obligation in this respect.

· Subsection 308a(a) of title 37, United States Code (1976), provides as follows with respect to the payment of an initial enlistment bonus:

(a) Notwithstanding section 514(a) of title 10 or any other law, under regulations prescribed by the Secretary of Defense, or by the Secretary of Transportation with respect to the Coast Guard when it is not operating as a service in the Navy, a person who enlists in an armed force for a period of at least four years in a skill designated as critical or who extends his initial period of active duty in that armed force to a total of at least four years in a skill designated as critical, may be paid a bonus in an amount prescribed by the appropriate Secretary, but not more than $3,000. The bonus may be paid in a lump sum or in equal periodic installments, as determined by the appropriate Secretary.

Neither DOD Instruction 1304.22 nor the other Defense Department directives governing payment of the enlistment bonus prescribe a method for computing the award level for individuals who enlist through the DEP. However, section XII of Army Regulation 601–210 (change 6, July 28, 1976) directs that the following provision be included in the Statements of Enlistment of an individual who becomes a member of the Army Reserve through the DEP:

If I subsequently enlist in the Regular Army for an option for which an enlistment bonus is authorized, has been authorized in the past, or may be authorized in the future, I will be entitled to the bonus only if it is authorized at the time of my enlistment in the Regular Army.

Thus, as is noted in the Committee Action, under this procedure an individual who enters the Army Reserve through the DEP, chooses an option for which an enlistment bonus is then authorized, and incurs an active duty obligation of at least 4 years, may subsequently receive a bonus in a reduced amount or no bonus at all. On the other hand, it is also possible under these procedures that an individual who enlists in the Army through the DEP may later receive a totally gratuitous bonus award which was not authorized at the time he made his service commitment.

In our view, the rationale of the *Larionoff* case is for application in this situation, i.e., the award level of the enlistment bonus must be fixed on the date the member enlists in a Reserve component under the DEP with a concurrent commitment to serve for a period of at least 4 years in a skill designated as critical. Hence, a subsequent increase or decrease in the award level for the critical skill may not operate to increase or decrease the amount of the bonus payable to the member after he has obligated himself to serve the required 4 years of active duty. Any regulatory provision to the contrary is therefore ineffective and invalid. Of course, payment of the enlistment bonus thus fixed in amount must also be contingent on the member qualifying and serving in his designated military specialty. See 52 Comp. Gen. 105 (1972). Question "4" is answered accordingly.

It is recognized that the enlistment bonus procedure which is determined to be invalid has been included in the Statement of Enlistment which individuals entering the Army's DEP are required to sign. However, as stated in *United States* v. *Larionoff, supra*, at page 869, 431 U.S., the entitlement of service members to pay and allowances depends upon law and regulation and not on ordinary contract principles. Thus, inclusion of the wording in question in an enlistment document signed by the member provides no basis for computing payments in a manner not permissible under the controlling statute.

Consistent with our answer to question "4," question "5" is answered in the affirmative. If a member entered the DEP prior to the inception of the bonus program, he could gain no entitlement to an enlistment bonus simply by later entering on active duty as he was already obligated to do anyway under the terms of the DEP enlistment. In that situation, the bonus could not have been an inducement to enlist; hence, payment of the bonus would constitute a totally gratuitous and improper award. Compare *United States* v. *Larionoff, supra*, at page 876, 431 U.S.

Conclusion

It is our view that the Supreme Court's reasoning with respect to the VRB in the *Larionoff* case is for application to the SRB and enlistment bonus programs authorized by 37 U.S.C. 308 and 308a, and we therefore hold that SRB and enlistment bonus payments must be based on the award levels in effect on the date a member executes the appropriate enlistment, reenlistment, or extension documents in order to qualify for that particular bonus. We recognize that this ruling may require a recomputation of some SRB and enlistment bonus payments that have been made in the past, and that it may be determined that some members are in debt on account of erroneous overpayments of bonus monies received. Such members may receive consideration for waiver of the claims against them, pursuant to 10 U.S.C. 2774 (1976).

[B-192365]

Compensation—Increases—Quality Increases—Retroactive

Action erroneously filed a supervisor's insufficiently documented recommendation of a Quality Step Increase (QSI) for an employee, thus causing a delay in the granting of the QSI. Retroactive granting of the QSI may not be made since Action had discretion to grant it and employee had no vested right to it at a particular time under statute or agency regulation.

In the matter of Carolyn Whitlock—Retroactive Quality Step Increase, February 14, 1979:

This action concerns a request from the Director of Personnel, Action, for an official ruling as to whether Action may retroactively grant a Quality Step Increase (QSI) to Carolyn Whitlock, the State Program Director in Action's New York Regional Office.

Ms. Whitlock was recommended for a QSI on her performance evaluation which was submitted in December 1976. Her supervisor used an obsolete rating form. Action personnel accepted and filed the form in her official personnel folder insufficiently documented. No follow-up was done to obtain the appropriate documentation for the QSI which would have required the Office Head and the Director of Personnel's signatures. Later her supervisor prepared the correct documentation and necessary approvals were obtained. Action does not wish to penalize Ms. Whitlock for the failure of its personnel to correctly complete her promotion package. However, while Action believes its delay in processing the QSI was an unjustified or unwarranted personnel action under the Back Pay Act of 1966, 5 U.S.C. 5596 (1976), it is uncertain as to whether it may grant Ms. Whitlock a QSI with backpay for the retroactive period.

The awards statute and implementing regulations vest discretion in agencies to make awards and their determinations will not be upset except for a clear showing of abuse of discretion. *Shaller* v. *U.S.*, 202 Ct. Cl. 571 (1973), cert. denied 414 U.S. 1092. We believe the same principle applies to the awarding of QSI under 5 U.S.C. 5336. Thus, an agency has discretion to approve or disapprove a QSI. See *John H. Brown*, 56 Comp. Gen. 57 (1976).

We have long held that the granting of promotions is a discretionary matter within the province of the administration of the agency involved, 54 Comp. Gen. 263 (1974). Also, the effective date of a change in salary resulting from administrative action is the date action is taken by the administrative officer vested with necessary authority or a subsequent date specifically fixed by him. 21 Comp. Gen. 95 (1941); B-186649, January 3, 1977. As a general rule, retroactive promotions are not sanctioned by our Office. 33 Comp. Gen. 140 (1953). In addition an administrative change in salary may not be made retroactively effective in the absence of specific statutory authority to do so. B-186649, *supra*. However, where an administrative or clerical error prevented a personnel action from taking effect as originally intended, deprived an employee of a right granted by statute or regulation, or resulted in the failure to grant a nondiscretionary administrative regulation or policy, we have held that the promotion or corrective action with back pay can be granted retroactively since the agency error constituted an unjustified or unwarranted personnel action and was compensable under the Back Pay Act, 5 U.S.C. 5596. 54 Comp. Gen. 69 (1974); 55 *id.* 42 (1975); B-186916, April 25, 1977.

In this case Ms. Whitlock did not have a vested right pursuant to statute or agency regulation to a QSI until the appropriate Action officials approved the recommendation and, therefore, it cannot be said that she underwent an unjustified or unwarranted personnel action because her promotion was delayed beyond the date when she first became eligible for the QSI. B-186649, *supra.* Accordingly, the QSI may not be granted retroactively.

[B-193533]

Property—Private—Damage, Loss, etc.—Military Personnel and Civilian Employees' Claims Act of 1964

Military Personnel and Civilian Employees' Claims Act of 1964 provides that claim may be allowed only if use of employee's property under the particular circumstances was reasonable, useful, or proper, and if damage to employee's property was not caused wholly or partly by employee's negligence. Settlement is final and conclusive if statutory conditions are met. Claim of National Labor Relations Board employee, for damage to motor vehicle resulting from accident where other participant in accident is compensated under Federal Tort Claims Act, is not cognizable under Military Personnel and Civilian Employees' Claims Act since settlement under Federal Tort Claims Act amounts to determination of employee's negligence.

In the matter of Erma Dees—Claim under Military Personnel and Civilian Employees' Claims Act of 1964, February 15, 1979:

Ms. Mary Ann Hawkins, an authorized certifying officer of the National Labor Relations Board (NLRB), has asked whether an employee's claim under the provisions of the Military Personnel and Civilian Employees' Claims Act of 1964, as amended (the Act), 31 U.S.C. §§ 240–243 (1976), can be paid "when negligence is a factor and the employee carries no insurance." We were informally advised by the certifying officer that the claim was submitted to her by the Tort Claims Officer, the NLRB designee for settling claims of this type, who approved payment pending a determination by our Office of the stated issue.

According to the information submitted, on April 25, 1978, the date of the accident, Ms. Erma Dees, a cooperative student employee, was engaged in conducting a representative case election for the NLRB in Xenia, Ohio. While on her way to lunch, the employee entered an intersection controlled by what she "presumed" to be a yellow caution light, and struck the left side of a vehicle entering the intersection from the right. As a result of the accident, the local police charged the employee with "Disobeying Traffic Light."

The other participant in the accident is being compensated for the damage to his vehicle of $326.06 under the provisions of the Federal Tort Claims Act. The employee has no insurance to cover the damage to her vehicle and has filed a claim with the NLRB in the amount of $980.46.

Section 3(b)(1) of the Act, 31 U.S.C. § 241(b)(1), authorizes the head of a Federal agency or his designee to settle and pay claims of up to $15,000 for loss of or damage to an employee's personal property incident to the employee's service. Additionally, this section provides that the decision should be made "subject to any policies the President may prescribe * * * and under such regulations as the head of an agency * * * may prescribe."

31 U.S.C. § 242 provides:

> Notwithstanding any other provision of law, the settlement of a claim under sections 240 to 243 of this title is final and conclusive.

Accordingly, our Office has no jurisdiction to render decisions relative to the *merits* of a claim under the Act. B–187913, February 9, 1977; B–180994, June 12, 1974. However, it is proper for our Office to consider the threshold question of whether a claim is properly cognizable under the Act. B–190106, March 6, 1978. As stated in 47 Comp. Gen. 316, 318 (1967), settlement is final and conclusive "if made in accordance with the provisions of the . . . act and applicable regulations." See also B–187913, *supra*.

The last sentence of 31 U.S.C. § 241(b)(1), *supra*, provides as follows:

> * * * If the claim is substantiated *and the possession of that property is determined to be reasonable, useful, or proper under the circumstances*, the claim may be paid * * *. [Italic supplied.]

The certifying officer states that at the time Ms. Dees was using her private car "GSA vehicles were available." This suggests that maybe her use of her own property under those circumstances was not "reasonable, useful, or proper." Whether this statutory test was met is, of course, a matter for determination by the claimant's employing agency, and such a determination would not be subject to review by this Office.

The Act further provides that a claim may be allowed only if the loss or damage "was not caused wholly or partly by the negligent or wrongful act of the claimant, his agent, or his employee." 31 U.S.C. § 241(c)(3). A claim which does not meet this test is not properly "cognizable" under the Act. As indicated above, the other participant in the accident filed a claim with the NLRB under the Federal Tort Claims Act and is being compensated under that claim for the damage to his vehicle. Allowance of a claim under the Federal Tort Claims Act must be based on the "negligent or wrongful act or omission" of the employee. 28 U.S.C. § 2672 (1976). It is impossible for the employee to be negligent for purposes of the Federal Tort Claims Act and not negligent for purposes of the Military Personnel and Civilian Employees' Claims Act. Accordingly, the agency's determination that the claimant was negligent—evidenced by the Federal Tort Claims Act settlement—precludes allowance of the claim by virtue of 31 U.S.C. § 241(c)(3), and payment in these circumstances would not be proper.

[B–193741]

Contracts—Mistakes—Purchase Orders—Erroneous Quotation

Contracting officer's error detection and verification obligation with regard to mistake in quotation alleged after performance is measured by standards applicable to mistake in oral bid alleged after award. Advice by contracting officer that supplier's oral quotation appeared low in conjunction with request for verification was sufficient to communicate both existence and nature, to extent known, of suspected mistake. Post-verification performance in accordance with purchase order creates binding contract and no price adjustment may be authorized on basis of error. Price disparity of about 35 percent does not reflect unconscionable bargain.

In the matter of Los Angeles Chemical Co., February 15, 1979:

The United States Forest Service (USFS) has forwarded for our consideration an appeal from its denial of a claim by the Los Angeles Chemical Company (LACC) based on a mistake in bid alleged after award.

The facts are not in dispute. On March 15, 1978, a USFS contracting officer solicited oral quotations from three potential suppliers for 175 gallons of weed killer for delivery to the USFS in Jackson, Wyoming. The following oral quotations were received:

	Per gallon
Supplier A	$63.00
Supplier B	65.30
LACC	41.40

In view of the price disparity, the contracting officer contacted LACC by telephone and requested verification of its quotation. LACC was advised that the reason for the request was that its price "appeared low." LACC confirmed its quotation. A purchase order was issued to LACC at the quoted price on March 17 and the weed killer was delivered on May 16. LACC subsequently advised the contracting officer by letter received on or about May 19 that its quotation had been in error due to the use by LACC of an outdated manufacturer's price list. LACC stated that the error was not discovered until May 15 when it received an invoice from the manufacturer charging LACC $57.86 per gallon for the weed killer. LACC requests an adjustment in its contract price to $59.86 per gallon, i.e., its cost plus approximately $2 per gallon transportation. The USFS denied LACC's request.

The general rule applicable to mistakes in bid alleged after award is that the sole responsibility for the preparation of a bid rests with the bidder and that unless the mistake is mutual or the contracting officer is on actual or constructive notice of the mistake, the bidder must bear the consequences of its mistake. *Security Systems, Inc.—Reconsideration,* B–190865, July 19, 1978, 78–2 CPD 48; *Porta-Kamp Manufacturing Company,* 54 Comp. Gen. 545 (1974), 74–2 CPD 393. Where an error is apparent or where there is reason to believe that an error has been made, a contracting officer is required to request verification of the bid. See *A. L. M. Construction Company,* B–191630, June 8, 1978, 78–1 CPD 424. Proper verification requires that in addition to requesting confirmation of a bid price, the contracting officer must appraise the bidder of the mistake which is suspected and the basis for such suspicion. *C. F. Tyler & Sons, Inc.,* B–186433, July 7, 1976, 76–2 CPD 16; *General Time Corporation,* B–180613, July 5, 1974, 74–2 CPD 9. The contracting officer's duty to seek verification is discharged if the bidder knows the basis for the request for verification. *Atlas Builders, Inc.,* B–186959, August 30, 1976, 76–2 CPD 204. Verification following such notice will result in an enforceable contract. *Frank Black, Jr., Incorporated,* B–191647, June 26, 1978, 78–1 CPD 463. Where, as here, an error in a quotation is alleged after the formation of the contract, we think the extent of the contracting officer's obligation of error detection and verification may be measured by these same standards.

We think that the contracting officer's advice to LACC that its price for weed killer appeared low in conjunction with the request for verification was sufficient both to convey to LACC that an error was suspected and, to the extent known, the nature of the error. Furthermore, we do not think that the price disparity was so great that the contracting officer should have been on notice that LACC's verification of its price was also in error or would result in an unconscionable bargain. See *Frank Black, Jr., Incorporated, supra; J. D. Shake Construction Co., Inc.*, B–190623, April 25, 1978, 78–1 CPD 318.

Therefore, LACC's acceptance through performance of the purchase order resulted in a contract binding as to price and no adjustment may be authorized.

[B–189901]

Contracts—Payments—Surety of Defaulted Contractor—"Unexpended Contract Balance"—Entitlement of Surety

Surety which completes defaulted contract pursuant to takeover agreement with Government is entitled to priority to contract retainages under performance bond over trustee in bankruptcy, assignee bank and Internal Revenue Service.

In the matter of C. G. Grant Construction Corp., February 21, 1979:

This case concerns the sum of $80,923.12 which constitutes the final payment under Bureau of Mines (BOM) contract No. K0144080 and which is being withheld by BOM pending resolution of the conflicting demands for payment.

On March 21, 1974, the Bureau of Mines, Department of the Interior (BOM), entered into a contract with the C.G. Grant Construction Corp. (Grant) for construction of the Keyser Valley Strip Mine Area reclamation project in Lackawanna County, Pennsylvania. In accordance with the terms of the contract, Grant and the American Empire Insurance Company (Surety) executed performance and payment bonds.

On August 28, 1974, Grant filed a voluntary petition in bankruptcy and on September 8, 1974, Grant formally defaulted on the contract by notifying BOM that it was unable to fulfill contract obligations.

On July 25, 1974, Grant had assigned its rights under the contract to Hanover National Bank (Hanover) and on August 27, 1974, BOM reviewed the assignment and found it to be "proper and in order."

On August 21, 1974, the Surety sent a telegram to BOM stating that there were unpaid creditors and requesting that BOM make no further payments to Grant without the Surety's consent.

Shortly after Grant defaulted the Surety undertook completion of the remaining work under the contract. Although a formal takeover agreement between the Surety and the Government was not entered into until February 27, 1975, the Surety received regular progress payments beginning on September 15, 1974 (progress payment No. 9).

Work on the project was satisfactorily completed and on July 31, 1975, the Surety received the final progress payment (No. 23).

The unexpended funds, which are retained by BOM, are comprised of the following amounts:

1. Retainage (10 percent) of progress payments 1 through 6 amounting to $10,665.77.
2. Withheld progress payments 7 and 8 in the full amounts totaling $63,541.16.
3. Uncommitted contract balance of $6,716.19.

Under the terms of the takeover agreement the unexpended funds are labeled the "contract fund" and are defined as "funds payable under the contract including all retained percentages and earned but unpaid progress estimates which are presently owing, but have not been paid to the defaulted contractor."

Claims to the contract fund have been filed by the Trustee in Bankruptcy, the assignee bank (Hanover), the Surety, and the Internal Revenue Service (IRS) for unpaid taxes.

The claim of the assignee is clearly inferior to the claim of the completing surety. *National City Bank of Evansville* v. *United States*, 143 Ct. Cl. 154 (1958). Likewise, a completing surety has priority over a trustee in bankruptcy. 8 Comp. Gen. 58 (1928) ; *United States* v. *National Surety Co.*, 254 U.S. 73 (1920).

Regarding the priority as between the Surety and IRS, the Surety takes the position that since it spent more to complete the contract than is available from the contract balance, it is entitled to the remainder of the contract fund. According to figures submitted by the Surety, it expended $489,626.03 to complete the contract. That figure is composed of $92,247.12 under the payment bond and $397,378.91 under the performance bond. Since the Surety has received only $224,266.33, payment of the entire amount remaining in the contract fund ($80,923.12) would not fully reimburse the Surety for the cost of completing the contract.

IRS argues that because of the nature of the contract funds remaining, namely funds retained by BOM to assure that laborers and materialmen are paid and progress payments retained while the contractor was still performing, the Surety's claim is under the payment bond and not the performance bond. Therefore, since the Government may set off debts due it by a contractor from funds retained and due a Surety pursuant to payments under a payment bond, IRS is entitled to the contract fund. *United States* v. *Munsey Trust Company*, 332 U.S. 234 (1947). As of June 1, 1978, the outstanding tax liability of Grant, including interest, was $92,388.38.

A performance bond surety which undertakes to complete the remaining work left by a defaulted contractor is entitled to the funds in the hands of the Government without any setoff. *Trinity Universal Insurance Co.* v. *United States*, 382 F. 2d 317 (5th Cir. 1967) ; *United States Forest Service-Request for Advance Decision*, B–192237, January 15, 1979. IRS's contention that the claim is actually under the payment bond rather than the performance bond has been found to be without merit by the courts. In *Aetna Casualty and Surety Company* v. *United States*, 435 F. 2d 1082 (5th Cir. 1970), the Court of Appeals noted that to follow the above reasoning would make ineffective the rule enunciated in *Trinity, supra.*

The court made no distinction regarding the makeup of the contract retainage and stated:

> * * * Here, however, the stipulation shows that Aetna expended in performance sums "in excess of receipts and in excess of the contract price." What defendant really wishes us to think is that a Surety who has issued both performance and payment bonds, and who completes a contract to avert a default, incurs expense under its payment bond, not under its performance bond, to the extent the costs are attributable to payments to labor and materialmen. The stipulation here fails to state that the costs of performance were for labor and material, but defendant wishes us to assume they were. Suppose they were, and in such cases no doubt usually they are, defendant's gloss would suck all the meaning out of the Trinity rule, and leave it an empty shell. * * *

Accordingly, we find that the Surety is entitled to the entire contract fund free from setoff.

[B–192696, B–194037, B–194103]

Contracts — Protests — Subcontractor Protests — Interested Party Requirement

General Accounting Office will consider protest by subcontractor that requirement in prime contract solicitation directly affects subcontractor and is unduly restrictive of competition.

Contracts — Protests — Subcontractor Protests — Timeliness — Prime Contract Specifications — Allegedly Restrictive

Protest of Navy's allegedly restrictive approach to subcontracting is timely where protester learned of approach after bid opening and filed protest within 10 working days thereafter.

Contracts—Subcontracts—Minority Subcontracting

Navy did not act illegally or improperly in considering the use of only first tier minority subcontractors in measuring contractor's compliance with minority subcontracting goal in prime contract, since administration of subcontracting programs essentially is matter within discretion of Navy.

Contracts — Specifications — Restrictive — Subcontractor Selection—Second-Tier Subcontractor Status—Minority Subcontracting

Policy of requiring compliance with minority subcontracting clause at first tier subcontractor level is not unduly restrictive and does not foreclose lower tier minority subcontracting.

Contracts—Subcontractors—Listing—Bidder Responsibility v. Bid Responsiveness

Solicitation requirement for identifying minority subcontractors after bid opening was for purpose of determining bidder responsibility, not to prevent bid shopping. Consequently, rejection of bid which did not contain commitment to particular subcontractors would be improper.

Contracts—Subcontracts—Minority Subcontracting—Prime Contract Requirements—Minority Status—Establishment Methods

Where solicitation allows contractors to rely on written representations of subcontractors to determine their minority status, reliance on a letter from subcontractor to Navy is proper.

Bidders—Qualifications—Failure to Submit Information Before Bid Opening—Bidder Responsibility Information—Minority Status of Identified Subcontractor

Since minority status of proposed subcontractors is matter of bidder responsibility, Navy properly refused protesters' request to determine, prior to bid opening, minority status of particular potential subcontractor.

In the matter of Donald W. Close Co. and others, February 27, 1979:

These cases concern the Navy's policy of considering only first tier subcontractors in determining the prime contractor's compliance with a specified percentage goal (11 percent) for minority subcontracting. We conclude that the Navy has a reasonable basis for its policy.

The first protest, B–192696, concerns Invitation for Bids (IFB) No. 68248–76–B–6035 issued by the Navy for equipment-installation and building construction at the Naval Submarine Base Bangor in Bremerton, Washington. Donald W. Close Co. and Wright, Inc. protested as potential subcontractors for this project, and were joined in the protest by Hoffman Construction Company, the second low bidder on the prime contract. Close later protested IFB Nos. N68248–76–B–6046 and N68248–77–B–7099, issued for other work at the same facility. The work under these IFBs is related to the Trident submarine program.

The IFBs required the apparent low bidder, prior to award, to submit its plan for complying with a minority subcontracting program and to identify in the plan the minority subcontractors with which firm commitments had been made.

The protesters believe that Pacific Ventures, Inc., the low bidder under IFB 68248–76–B–6035, originally planned to use Close as a first tier electrical subcontractor with Wright, a minority-owned firm, as a second tier subcontractor, but arranged to subcontract with Rosenden Electric, Inc., a minority-owned electrical subcontractor, and so indicated in its plan, when it learned that the Navy would consider only first tier subcontracts in measuring compliance with the minority utilization goal. The protesters thus object to the Navy's willingness to consider only first tier subcontractors in connection with that goal.

In addition, Close, Wright, and Hoffman protest the award to Pacific because Pacific allegedly changed its intended subcontractors after bid opening. The protesters assert this is tantamount to "bid shopping" which rendered Pacific's bid nonresponsive.

The Navy suggests that Close and Wright should not be regarded as "interested parties" within the meaning of 4 C.F.R. § 20.2(a) (1978), our Bid Protest Procedures, because they only "had a mere expectance of receiving a subcontract." However, where a firm is precluded from receiving a subcontract because of allegedly unduly restrictive provisions in a prime contract solicitation, we regard the firm as an interested party to protest those provisions. *See Abbott Power Corporation*, B–186568, December 21, 1976, 76–2 CPD 509. Here, Close and Wright claim to have lost subcontracting opportunities as a result of the Navy's approach to its minority subcontracting program; we believe they are interested parties under 4 C.F.R. § 20.2(a).

The Navy believes the protests are untimely because they were not filed within 10 days after the basis for protest was known or should have been known, as required by our Bid Protest Procedures, 4 C.F.R. § 20.2(b)(2). The prime contractor, Pacific, after discussions with the Navy, submitted its minority subcontracting plan by letter dated July 28, 1978. Its plan named Rosenden as the minority electrical subcontractor. The Navy argues that Close and Wright knew or should have known at that point that they were no longer being considered for the electrical subcontracting work, thereby rendering untimely this protest filed more than 10 working days thereafter.

However, there is no evidence in the record that either Close or Wright received a copy of this letter from Pacific to the Navy, and the affidavit of Close states that its first knowledge of the Navy's approach was from telephone conversations on August 14 with Pacific and the Navy. Since the protests were received within 10 days of these telephone conversations, they were timely filed. The Navy suggests additional reasons for regarding the protests of Wright and Hoffman as untimely. However, since those protests raise no issues other than those raised by Close, the Navy's reasons are academic.

The solicitation contained a bidding information document, which gave notice of the minority subcontracting program and stated:

For the purpose of this program, the term "subcontract" includes all construction, alterations, repairs, materials, supplies, and service work contracted for *by* the prime contractor in the prosecution of the work. [Italic supplied.]

However, in yet another portion of the solicitation, the general provisions, this notice was repeated but the underlined word, by, was omitted. The protesters argue that the notice in the general provisions does not make any distinction between different tiers of subcontractors.

Although it may not have been clear to the protesters from the general provisions that the Navy would insist that the minority subcontracting goal was to be satisfied at the first tier level, there can be little doubt from the bidding information document which specifically defines the term subcontract as a contract awarded *by* the prime contractor. A second tier subcontract, by definition, is not awarded by the prime contractor. The requirement in the bidding information document that the goal be met by the prime contractor's subcontract awards is more specific than the general provisions and it is a well established principle of contract interpretation that a specific provision will prevail when there is a conflict between that provision and a more general one. *Total Leonard, Inc.*, 56 Comp. Gen. 307 (1977), 77–1 CPD 62.

Moreover, we point out that even if the protesters were misled by the solicitation, there is no indication that the prime contract bidders, to the extent any of them might have been misled, suffered any prejudice as a result of the alleged solicitation defect such as would warrant cancellation and readvertising. *See Union Carbide Corporation*, 56 Comp. Gen. 487 (1977), 77–1 CPD 243.

The protesters also object that measuring compliance with the minority subcontracting goal through first tier subcontracts only would result in discrimination in favor of the largest, best-financed minority enterprises with the least need of the program. The protesters assert that the Navy's approach encourages the general contractor not to incur the added expenses and risks of contracting directly with a greater number of minority firms for smaller portions of the work.

The Navy states that its insistence on satisfying the minority subcontracting goals at the first tier level is the only practical way to administer the program. We understand that shortly after contract award, the Navy requests the prime contractor to provide a copy of each minority subcontract so that the Navy can verify compliance with the minority subcontracting plan submitted previously. We further understand that if there is an unjustified deviation from that plan, a termination for default could result. The Navy suggests that since lower level subcontractors are not in privity with the Government, and are not subject to the Government's enforcement sanctions, there could be difficulty in its obtaining those lower level subcontracts to verify compliance with the minority subcontracting plan.

We do not completely understand the Navy's rationale, since it is not clear to us why the taking into account of minority subcontractors below the first tier level would bring about the problems mentioned. It would seem that it should be the prime contractor's responsibility to provide the Navy with whatever the Navy reasonably needs to measure the prime's compliance with its own minority subcontracting program, so that the Navy would not have to concern itself with the problems associated with a lack of privity.

Nonetheless, we cannot say that the Navy's approach is illegal or improper. How the Navy chooses to administer its minority subcontracting program is a matter within the discretion of the Navy, subject only to basic Federal procurement principles requiring contracting officials to act in good faith, maintain the integrity of the competitive system, and not unduly restrict competition. While the protests, in effect, allege such an undue restriction on competition because certain subcontractors are excluded as a result of the Navy's approach, we note that no firm is, in fact, precluded from possible participation as a subcontractor in these procurements because of the Navy's approach. Rather, it is the prime contractor, in determining how it will comply with the minority subcontracting program requirements, that decides whether to subcontract with a minority firm for work in one category (such as electrical) or another. One prime contractor may choose to achieve the program goal by engaging minority subcontractors in two particular categories; another prime may select minority firms for work in two other categories; still another prime may subcontract directly with minority firms in three or four work categories. In short, it is solely as a result of the prime contractor's approach to meeting the minority subcontracting goal that determines which firms will have opportunities to participate in the procurement. While in some geographical areas at any given time a prime contractor may not have a significant choice because of the limited availability of qualified minority firms, that by itself does not, in our view, render the Navy's approach overall to be unduly restrictive.

Moreover, we also point out that lower tier minority subcontracting is not foreclosed by the Navy's policy, since nothing precludes awards of lower tier subcontracts to minority firms. In fact, clause 108(d)(6) of the contract requires the prime contractor to include the provision at Defense Acquisition Regulation 7–104.36(a) in its subcontracts; that provision requires the first tier subcontractor to use "best efforts" to insure minority participation in lower tier subcontracts.

With regard to the allegation of bid shopping, we point out that the General Services Administration imposes a subcontractor listing requirement to prevent bid shopping (selecting subcontractors after bid opening), but there is no general policy against bid shopping, and other agencies generally do not prohibit the practice. Here, the minority subcontractor listing requirement is not related to preventing bid shopping, but is part of the requirement for the apparent low bidder to show after bid opening how it intends to insure that a certain percentage of subcontracted work will be performed by minority-owned firms. As such, and since bidders were not required to identify or to commit themselves to particular subcontractors in their bids, the subcontractor information was required for use by the Navy in determining bidder responsibility, and was not related to bid responsiveness. Thus, the Pacific bid could not properly be rejected because it did not include a commitment to particular subcontractors. *Dubicki & Clarke, Inc.*, B–190540, February 15, 1978, 78–1 CPD 132.

Protesters also question the basis for regarding Rosenden Electric as a minority subcontractor. They claim the only basis given was a letter to the Navy from Rosenden dated March 31, 1976, in which Rosenden claimed that it was a minority firm. However, the solicitation provides that "* * * [C]ontractors may rely on written representations by subcontractors regarding their status as minority business enterprises in lieu of an independent investigation." In relying on the March 31 letter from Rosenden, the Navy and Pacific complied with the terms of the solicitation regarding the status of minority subcontractors.

Close also objects to the Navy's refusal, prior to bid opening, under IFB N68248–76–B–6046 and IFB N68248–77–B–7099, to determine whether Rosenden is a qualified minority firm. As indicated above, compliance with the minority subcontracting requirements of the solicitation is a matter of bidder responsibility, which is to be determined after bid opening and prior to award. There is no assurance, of course, that Rosenden's status before bid opening would be the same after bid opening. *See Harper Enterprises*, 53 Comp. Gen. 496 (1974), 74–1 CPD 318. Thus, Rosenden's minority status prior to bid opening would not necessarily be relevant to the post bid opening determination of responsibility, which would have to be based on the information current at that time. Therefore, the Navy did not act improperly in refusing to determine prior to bid opening whether Rosenden is a qualified firm.

The protests are denied.

[B–193899]

Bidders—Debarment—*De Facto*—Nonresponsibility Determination *v. De Facto* Debarment

Grantee's refusal to permit award of subcontract to particular firm is tantamount to negative determination of responsibility with respect to that firm, which under circumstances is not *de facto* debarment without due process of law or improper prequalification or other undue restriction on competition.

Bidders—Qualifications—Prior Unsatisfactory Service—Dispute Pending

Under Federal law, firm may be found nonresponsible even though dispute concerning allegedly improper performance of prior contract for similar work has not been resolved.

Bidders—Qualifications—Prior Unsatisfactory Service—Affiliated Concerns

Firms acting as joint venturers are answerable for acts done by their co-venturers, or other agents, and may be found nonresponsible because of deficient performance by joint venture in prior procurement.

In the matter of Howard Electric Company, February 27, 1979:

Howard Electric Company (Howard) complains that it was improperly disqualified from participating as a subcontractor to the Weaver Construction Company (Weaver). Weaver is prime contractor to the Colorado State Department of Highways (Colorado), a grantee under Federal Highway Administration (Development of Competitor) grant 1 70–3 (83). The grant supports work on the Eisenhower Memorial Tunnel.

According to Howard, 1) the prime contract requires Colorado's approval of all subcontracts; 2) Weaver intended to subcontract with Howard; 3) Colorado refused to approve award of a subcontract to Howard; and 4) the basis for Colorado's action is an unresolved dispute relating to delay on another contract on which the prime contractor, a joint venture consisting of Howard and another firm, was assessed liquidated damages.

Howard urges that Colorado acted arbitrarily and capriciously in advising Weaver that no subcontract could be awarded to Howard because of its performance on that prior contract. The complainant views Colorado's act as contrary to "the Federal norm of competitive bidding" and as a *de facto* debarment without due process of law. Moreover, Howard complains, Colorado violated 23 C.F.R. § 635.108 (1978) by improperly imposing prequalification procedures and Office of Management and Budget (OMB) Circular A–102 (Attachment O) by unduly restricting competition at the subcontract level.

We find no merit to the complaint. Neither the "Federal norm," the regulations cited by Howard, nor anything else of which we are aware was violated by the grantee's actions in this case. As stated by Howard, the grantee had a contractual right to concur or not concur with any decision to subcontract, and the negative decision was based on the performance problems encountered under a prior contract. In effect, it would appear that the grantee's decision was tantamount to a negative determination of responsibility with respect to Howard. Under Federal law, such a determination may be made on the basis of what the Government sees as the contractor's prior inadequate performance even if the contractor disputes the Government's position and the dispute is unresolved. *See*, e.g., *United Office Machines*, 56 Comp. Gen. 411 (1977), 77–1 CPD 195; *Halo Optical Products, Inc.*, B–178573, B–179099, May 17, 1974, 74–1 CPD 263. Moreover, while *de facto* debarment could result from repeated negative responsibility determinations, *see* 43 Comp. Gen. 140 (1963), or even from a single negative determination if it is part of a long-term disqualification attempt, *see Myers & Myers, Inc.* v. *United States Postal Service*, 527 F. 2d 1252 (2nd Cir. 1975), all that is alleged here is a one-time disqualification, which under the circumstances appears to have a reasonable basis and does not constitute a denial of due process. *See* 51 Comp. Gen. 551 (1972).

23 C.F.R. 635.108 prohibits the approval of a requirement or procedure for the "prequalification, qualification or licensing of contractors * * * which, in the judgment of the [Federal Highway] administrator, may operate to restrict competition" or prohibit the submission by or consideration of a bid from "any responsible contractor." OMB Circular A–102 imposes a general requirement for competition. We fail to see how the grantee's actions in this case contravene either requirement. A good faith nonresponsibility determination does not, in and of itself, unduly restrict competition and does not involve the approval of a prequalification procedure.

Finally, Howard believes it should not be prevented from contracting on the basis of what the joint venture may have done. However, the common law rule is well settled that persons acting as a joint venture are answerable for acts done by their co-venturers or other agents. 68 C.J.S. *Partnership* § 183 (1950); Restatement of Agency (2d) § 20

(1957). In this regard, we point out that Federal law permits debarment of all known affiliates of a debarred concern or individual where circumstances warrant. 51 Comp. Gen. 65 (1971).

The complaint is summarily denied.

[B-192344]

Mileage—Travel by Privately Owned Automobile—More Than One Employee Traveling—Reimbursement Basis

Where an employee utilizes a privately owned vehicle as a matter of personal preference when such use is not determined to be advantageous to the Government, the employee's total reimbursement for the travel is limited to the total constructive cost of appropriate common carrier transportation. In the computation of the constructive costs, the employee is not entitled to include the cost by common carrier of transporting other Government employees who accompany the employee on the trip to determine maximum reimbursement when there is no order or administrative approval of additional payment.

In the matter of James W. Shores—Two Government Employees Traveling in Privately Owned Vehicle, February 28, 1979:

Mr. James W. Shores, by letter dated May 31, 1978, requests reconsideration of a settlement by the Claims Division of this Office, Z-2707005, May 23, 1978, which disallowed the employee's claim for additional reimbursement in the amount of $38.87 for expenses incurred as a result of travel performed between Washington, D.C. and Cleveland, Ohio, as an employee of the Patent and Trademark Office.

The record reveals that Mr. Shores was authorized to travel by privately owned vehicle (POV) from Washington, D.C. to Cleveland, Ohio to attend a meeting by Travel Authorization 76–68, September 18, 1975. The travel authorization provided that the reimbursement of mileage could not exceed the round trip air fare to Cleveland ($80.73) plus taxis and/or limousines. On the trip to Cleveland, another Government employee, Mr. John MacIvor, travelled as a passenger in Mr. Shores' POV.

In the travel voucher submitted for his trip to Cleveland, Mr. Shores included in the constructive cost statement the taxis and common carrier air fare costs that Mr. MacIvor would have incurred had he flown commercially to Cleveland. The Office of Finance in the Patent and Trademark Office suspended $38.87 from Mr. Shores' reimbursement with the explanation that costs for common carrier transportation saved by the use of a POV when more than one employee travels in the same vehicle cannot be included in a comparative cost statement. On review, our Claims Division agreed with the agency's determination and rejected the employee's contention that since his transportation of Mr. MacIvor resulted in savings to the Government, the passenger's constructive costs should be included in his comparative cost statement.

In Mr. Shores' request for reconsideration, the claimant took specific objection to the characterization of his requested additional reimbursement as "hypothetical expenditures." Although we recognize that all expenses claimed by Mr. Shores were actually incurred during his trip to Cleveland, we note that the Federal Travel Regulations (FTR), (FPMR 101-7) provide a limitation to the maximum amount of actual expenses which may be reimbursed when an employee utilizes his POV in lieu of a common carrier for his personal preference. Pursuant to paragraph 1-4.3 of the FTR, where an employee uses a POV as a matter of personal preference when such use is not determined to be advantageous to the Government, the employee's total reimbursement for the travel is limited to the total constructive cost of appropriate common carrier transportation including constructive per diem by that method of transportation.

With regard to the computation of the constructive costs, we have consistently held that an employee who is authorized to travel by POV on a mileage basis, cost limited to that by common carrier, is not entitled to include the cost by common carrier of transporting other employees who accompany the employee on the trip to determine maximum reimbursement when there is no order or administrative approval of additional payment. B-134115, November 6, 1957. See also B-143098, June 27, 1960, and 22 Comp. Gen. 572 (1942). In that connection it has been held that an order limiting the mileage to the cost of travel by common carrier, in the absence of qualifying language, can be construed to mean only the cost of common carrier for one person, even though accompanied by several other official travelers. 22 Comp. Gen. 572 (1942). Therefore, since there is no qualifying language in the travel order of Mr. Shores, the comparison between the cost of mileage and common carrier travel must be made on the basis of only one person traveling by common carrier.

Generally, however, our Office has no objection to a travel order authorizing the use of constructive common carrier costs of all travelers to arrive at the maximum reimbursement when such action is specifically administratively directed and approved. B-158046, January 11 and April 5, 1966. In the instant case, there was no administrative approval of a more beneficial basis for reimbursement.

Accordingly, since Mr. Shores' travel order authorized reimbursement not to exceed the cost of transportation by common carrier for one person and approval for reimbursement on any other basis was administratively denied upon reclaim, our Office is without legal authority to direct payment of the sum reclaimed. Therefore, the action of our Claims Division in disallowing Mr. Shores' claim is sustained.

[B-192581]

Contracts — Protests — Timeliness — Small Business Set-Aside — Withdrawal—By Amendment

Where protester received amendment to invitation for bids (IFB) less than 3 hours before bid opening and filed protest within 10 working days of receipt, protest is timely under 4 C.F.R. 20.2(b)(2) (1978) as protester did not have reasonable opportunity to file protest before bid opening.

Contracts — Awards — Small Business Concerns — Set-Asides — Eligibility—Unacceptable

Bidder on total small business set-aside which certifies it is small and that large business concern will manufacture, inspect, package, and ship supplies indicates that it intends to furnish supplies manufactured or produced by large business without small business making significant contribution to manufacture or production of contract end item. Therefore, bid would be nonresponsive under small business set-aside and bidder is not prejudiced by withdrawal of set-aside by amendment allegedly issued too close to time set for bid opening.

Bids — Invitation for Bids — Cancellation — Not Required — Set-Aside Erroneous — Withdrawal by Amendment

While bidders, actual or potential, may have been misled as to competition contemplated by inadvertent set-aside provision in IFB, any possible adverse impact on competition does not require corrective action in view of exposure of prices and inadvertent nature of deficiency.

Contracts — Awards — Small Business Concerns — Set-Asides — Withdrawal — Procedural Compliance

Where contracting officer erroneously and inadvertently fills out small business set-aside determination, small business set-aside withdrawal procedures are not for application. In any event, pre-bid-opening withdrawal of small business set-aside by contracting officer was subsequently approved by small business specialist.

In the matter of Culligan, Inc., March 6, 1979:

Culligan, Inc. (Culligan), protests award of a contract under invitation for bids (IFB) No. N00104–78–B–0888, issued on July 3, 1978, as a total small business set-aside by the Navy Ships Parts Control Center, Mechanicsburg, Pennsylvania. The IFB solicited bids for two items of ion exchange resins used to purify water in nuclear reactors. Bid opening was scheduled for 11:15 a.m. on July 31, 1978. At 8:33 a.m. on that date and after Culligan had already submitted its bid, Culligan received amendment A0002 withdrawing the small business set-aside.

When bids were opened as scheduled, Culligan was second low bidder. The bids were as follows:

	Item 1	Item 2	Business size
Diamond Shamrock Corp	$67.22	$79.00	Large.
Culligan	69.20	80.30	Small.
Rohm & Haas Co	69.48	79.85	Large.
Illinois Water Treatment Co	74.00	83.50	Small.
Ionics, Inc	81.10	91.40	Large.
Bio-Rad Laboratories	99.54	111.22	Small.

If the small business set-aside had not been withdrawn, Culligan would have been in line for award, assuming its bid was responsive. As will be discussed, Culligan's bid was nonresponsive.

On August 9, 1978, the procuring activity and this Office received a mailgram from Culligan protesting award to any other company but Culligan, alleging that the "last minute" amendment to the IFB materially altered the pricing consideration as a result of the inclusion of large business in the competitive environment. Further, Culligan contends that amendment AOOO2 should be null and void since it was issued so late as to deprive Culligan of an opportunitty to reassess its bid.

In accordance with Defense Acquisition Regulation (DAR) § 2–407.8(b)(3)(1) (1976 ed.), partial award has already been made to Diamond Shamrock Corp. for the procurement of item 1 because that item is urgently required by the procuring activity.

Amendment AOOO2 was issued July 24, 1978, and mailed July 27, 1978, after the contracting officer discovered that he had erroneously set aside the procurement for small business. At the time the contracting officer was preparing the solicitation, he was also preparing solicitations for the procurement of 45 other nuclear-type chemicals, all of which are procured under small business set-asides. The contracting officer inadvertently made a unilateral determination to set aside the subject procurement. Nevertheless, having intended that the procurement be unrestricted, the Navy also solicited bids from large businesses. In fact, in past procurements the Navy had never set aside these resins, because the procuring activity believed that only large business concerns manufactured them. Culligan has submitted bids for the resins under prior unrestricted procurements. With the exception of Bio–Rad Laboratories, all of the bidders, including Culligan, proposed in the subject procurement to supply resins produced by a large business concern. We note that Bio–Rad Laboratories, a small business concern, also certified that it is a manufacturer of the resins.

Initially, there is a question as to the timeliness of Culligan's protest. Generally, to be timely, a protest must be filed before bid opening if it is based on alleged improprieties in the solicitation which are apparent prior to bid opening. GAO Bid Protest Procedures, 4 C.F.R. § 20.2(b)(1) (1978). Culligan received amendment AOOO2 on July 31, 1978, before bid opening, but did not file its protest until 7 working days later. Under the circumstances of this case, where Culligan knew its basis for protest less than 3 hours before bid opening, we believe that § 20.2(b)(1) is inapplicable because Culligan did not have a reasonable opportunity to file its protest before bid opening.

In cases other than those covered by § 20.2(b)(1), bid protests must be filed not later than 10 working days after the basis for the protest is known or should have been known. 4 C.F.R. § 20.2(b)(2) (1978). Since Culligan's protest was filed within 10 working days after receipt of amendment A0002, it is timely under § 20.2(b)(1).

With regard to the effect of the "last minute" issuance of amendment A0002 to the IFB, DAR § 2–208(c) (1976 ed.) requires that if information contained in an amendment is necessary for bidders in submitting bids on the invitation or where the lack of such information would be prejudicial to uninformed bidders, no award shall be made unless the amendment is issued in sufficient time to permit all prospective bidders to consider the information in submitting or modifying their bids. However, no corrective action is required where, as discussed below, a bidder is ineligible for award and, therefore, suffers no prejudice by its failure to receive the information. See B–159454, August 17, 1966.

This Office has consistently held that where a bid on a total small business set-aside fails to establish the intention of the bidder to furnish products manufactured or produced by small business concerns, the bid is nonresponsive and the bidder is ineligible for award. *Aluminum Alloys Corporation*, B–189550, October 20, 1977, 77–2 CPD 310; *American Amplifier and Television Corporation*, 53 Comp. Gen. 463, 465 (1974), 74–1 CPD 10. A small business may subcontract work to a large business concern as long as the small business makes a significant contribution to the manufacture or production of the contract end item. *Fire & Technical Equipment Corp.*, B–191766, June 6, 1978, 78–1 CPD 415. However, if an examination of the bid by a contracting officer indicates that the bidder intends to furnish contract end items manufactured by a large business concern, the bid is properly rejected as nonresponsive. B–175337, January 3, 1973; B–170114, February 24, 1971.

Culligan certified that it was a small business concern and that the resins would be manufactured by a small business concern, but also stated that the resins would be manufactured, inspected, packaged and shipped by Ionac Chemical Company, Division of Sybron Corporation, which, according to the contracting officer, is a large business concern. Culligan has not contested this fact. It is apparent from the bid that Culligan did not intend to make a significant contribution to the manufacture of the contract end item, and rejection of Culligan's bid under the unamended IFB as nonresponsive would have been required. See B–175337, *supra;* B–170114, *supra.* Therefore, since Culligan was not prejudiced by the "last minute" issuance of amendment A0002 withdrawing the set-aside, no corrective action is warranted.

While we are not unmindful that bidders, actual or potential, may have been misled as to the competition anticipated, any possible adverse impact on competition must be weighed against the fact that prices have been exposed and the deficiency here resulted from inadvertency. Therefore, we do not believe corrective action would be appropriate.

This Office has frequently held that after a small business set-aside has been withdrawn, the proper procedure is to resolicit so that all eligible bidders may have an opportunity to compete. *Lawrence W. Rosine Company*, 55 Comp. Gen. 1351 (1976), 76–2 CPD 159. However, in this case, bids have been exposed, there has been adequate competition and the bids are considered reasonable. *See Culligan, Incorporated, Cincinnati, Ohio*, 56 Comp. Gen. 1011, 1013 (1977), 77–2 CPD 242. Therefore, we do not recommend resolicitation of the procurement.

However, in the future, the procuring activity should adhere to DAR § 2–208(b) (1976 ed.), relating to amendments of invitations for bids, which provides that before an amendment is issued, the period of time remaining until bid opening and the need for extending such period by postponing the time set for bid opening must be considered; also, where only a short time remains before the time set for bid opening, consideration should be given to notifying bidders of an extension of time by telegram or telephone and such notification should be confirmed in an amendment.

With regard to the contention that the amendment should be considered null and void, presumably because withdrawal was not properly effected, the DAR prescribes procedures for the making and withdrawal of small business set-asides. DAR § 1–706.1(b) (1976 ed.) provides in part that a procurement shall be set aside when such action is determined to be in the interest of assuring that a fair proportion of Government procurement is placed with small business concerns. The contracting officer intended no such determination in this case since he believed that only large business concerns manufactured the resins. The fact that large concerns also were solicited further evidences that the contracting officer inadvertently made the procurement a set-aside. Since the set-aside was made through inadvertence and the contracting officer intended the procurement to be unrestricted, the procedures pertaining to the withdrawal of set-asides are not for application. See *Groton Piping Corporation and Thames Electric Company*, B–185755, April 12, 1976, 76–1 CPD 247. At any rate, we note that after amendment A0002 was issued the contracting officer informally sought and received approval of the withdrawal from the small business specialist. Further, if the amendment was considered null and void, as urged by Culligan, as noted previously, Culligan would not have been eligible for award as a small business.

Accordingly, Culligan's protest is denied.

[B-178551]

Courts—Judgments, Decrees, etc.—Payment—"Final Judgment" Requirement

Judgments against the United States awarding back pay under the Back Pay Act but not indicating the dollar amount to be paid are nevertheless money judgments against the United States and therefore payable from the permanent appropriation established by 31 U.S.C. 724a. However, since an agency's computation of back pay is subject to judicial review, a judgment without a dollar amount cannot be considered "final" for purposes of certification for payment until General Accounting Office has been furnished the agency's computation together with written indication, administrative or judicial, that the plaintiff will accept the amount in satisfaction of the judgment.

Appropriations — Permanent Indefinite — Judgments — Against Government

Even though the agency or unit head is the nominal defendant in an employment discrimination suit under Title VII of the Civil Rights Act of 1964, as amended, a suit under 42 U.S.C. 2000e–16 is nevertheless a suit against the United States. Judgments against the Federal Government in Title VII actions are therefore payable from the permanent appropriation established by 31 U.S.C. 724a.

In the matter of Payment of judgments under Back Pay Act and Title VII of Civil Rights Act, March 7, 1979:

This decision is the result of two questions which have arisen in recent months. The questions involve the source of funds for the payment of judgments and awards against the United States in various contexts, and hence are treated together.

For the most part, judgments against the United States are paid from the permanent indefinite appropriation contained in 31 U.S.C. § 724a (1976), as amended by Pub. L. No. 95–26 (May 4, 1977), 91 Stat. 61, 96, set forth in pertinent part below:

There are appropriated, out of any money in the Treasury not otherwise appropriated, such sums as may be necessary for the payment, not otherwise provided for, as certified by the Comptroller General, of final judgments, awards, and compromise settlements, which are payable in accordance with the terms of section 2414, 2517, 2672, or 2677 of Title 28 * * *.

The questions to be considered are whether judgments and awards in the following situations are payable from the indefinite appropriation or from agency appropriations ("otherwise provided for").

(1) Judgments under the Back Pay Act which direct the payment of back pay but which do not specify the dollar amount to be paid.

(2) Judgments under Title VII of the Civil Rights Act of 1964, 42 U.S.C. 2000e, as amended.

1. Judgments involving the Back Pay Act.

The Back Pay Act entitles employees of agencies specified in the Act to back pay where the employee "is found by appropriate authority under applicable law, rule, regulation, or collective bargaining agreement, to have been affected by an unjustified or unwarranted personnel action." 5 U.S.C. § 5596 (1976), as amended by section 702 of the Civil Service Reform Act of 1978, Pub. L. No. 95–454 (October 13, 1978), 92 Stat. 1111, 1216 (5 U.S.C. 5596(b)). Implementing regulations are found at 5 C.F.R. §§ 550.801 *et seq.* The regulations recognize a court of competent jurisdiction as an "appropriate authority" under the Act. 5 C.F.R. § 550.803(c). Actions are brought in the Court of Claims or in the district courts. One of the more common situations is a claim of wrongful termination or dismissal and the remedy sought is reinstatement plus back pay.

It is clear that a covered judgment which awards back pay and specifies the amount to be paid is payable, upon becoming final, from the permanent judgment appropriation. See 31 U.S.C. § 724a, *supra;* 28 U.S.C. §2414; 28 U.S.C. § 2517. It is equally clear, where a judgment orders reinstatement or other corrective action but does not mention back pay, that entitlement to back pay arises from the Back Pay Act rather than from the judgment itself, and in such a case the back pay is payable by the employing agency from its own appropriations.

The more difficult situation is a judgment which directs the payment of "back pay in accordance with the Back Pay Act," or similar language, but does not contain a specific amount. The situation does not arise in a Court of Claims judgment since, under current Court of Claims procedures, the amount is obtained from the employing agency, through the General Accounting Office, prior to issuing the judgment, and then included in the judgment. It does occur occasionally, however, in district court judgments. Examples are *Marr* v. *Lyons*, W.D. Okla., Civil No. 72–286, judgment entered January 18, 1974 (order on related motion reported at 377 F. Supp. 1146); *Van Winkle* v. *McLucas*, S.D. Ohio, Civil No. 4537, judgment entered June 16, 1975 (separate issue reported at 537 F. 2d 246 (6th Cir. 1976), *cert. denied*, 429 U.S. 1093).

It may be argued that a judgment which orders the payment of back pay without including a dollar amount is not a money judgment within the scope of 28 U.S.C. § 2414 and 31 U.S.C. § 724a, but that the payment of back pay in such a case is a part of the administrative action to be taken by the employing agency. Our research has disclosed relatively little judicial guidance. *White* v. *Bloomberg*, 360 F. Supp. 58 (D.Md. 1973), *aff'd.*, 501 F. 2d 1379 (4th Cir. 1974), was a suit for reinstatement and back pay by a discharged Postal Service employee. After determining that the plaintiff was entitled to back pay, without specifying the amount, the District Court found that a judgment against the Postal Service is not "one against the sovereign," and awarded post-judgment interest under 28 U.S.C. § 1961 which mandates interest "on any money judgment in a civil case." The Court concluded:

> Herein, on June 23, 1972, this Court specifically directed payment of back wages from the date of White's discharge to the date of White's reinstatement. The former date was October 30, 1970; the latter, June 29, 1972. The amount of back wages for each and every part of that period up to and including June 23, 1972, and White's rate of pay from and after June 23, 1972, were known on June 23, 1972 and at all times thereafter. So were the facts in connection with the amount earned and received by White from any employment he engaged in between October 30, 1970 and June 23, 1972. Thus, only simple mathematical calculations were required on and after June 23, 1972 to determine the dollar amount of back wages payable by the Postal Service to White. Accordingly, this Court's June 23, 1972 Order constituted a money judgment. 360 F. Supp. at 63.

The Fourth Circuit affirmed on the rationale that post-judgment interest was a normal incident of the Postal Service's power to "sue and be sued in its official name." 501 F. 2d at 1385–86.

Fitzgerald v. *Staats*, 578 F. 2d 435 (D.C. Cir. 1978), *cert. denied*, December 4, 1978, involved an Air Force employee ordered to be reinstated by the Civil Service Commission upon a finding of improper termination. The litigation involved several issues relating to the amount of back pay to be paid. Part of the Court's holding was that 31 U.S.C. § 227, which directs the withholding of debts owed to the United States from final judgments, was not applicable because Fitzgerald was not a judgment creditor. The Court noted:

> The decision of the Commission was not, as Fitzgerald contends, an award of a sum certain in the form of a judgment. It was a ruling that Fitzgerald was entitled to the remedy provided by the Back Pay Act, which, by its terms, requires some non-mechanical calculations. The three opinions of the Comptroller General cited above reveal the extent to which the calculations in the instant case were not self-evident, and thus the extent to which the Civil Service Commission's ruling was not a judgment for a sum certain. 578 F. 2d at 439.

While it seems clear that an award of back pay which does not include a dollar amount is not a "sum certain," we are of the opinion that a judgment ordering the payment of back pay is nevertheless a money judgment. 55 Comp. Gen. 1447 (1976). (*Fitzgerald* did not involve a judgment and thus the source of payment was not an issue.) Where a judgment orders the payment of back pay, that directive is part of the judgment and the judgment is therefore payable from the permanent appropriation.

Further, in our opinion, the language of the Back Pay Act is not sufficient to invoke the "otherwise provided for" exception in 31 U.S.C. § 724a. The Back Pay Act, quoted *supra*, establishes an entitlement to a monetary remedy under specified circumstances, but there is no provision made to authorize payment from agency funds when the entitlement arises as a result of a court's determination rather than administrative action.

It is also our opinion, however, that a judgment for back pay without a dollar amount is not, in and of itself, "final" for purposes of our certification for payment, even though it may be final with respect to plaintiff's right to recover. In order for a judgment to be paid from the permanent appropriation, it must be certified by the Comptroller General to the Treasury Department for payment. 31 U.S.C. § 724a, *supra*. This cannot be done until we have been furnished the amount to be certified for payment, with the assurance that it is not subject to further litigation. Under the back pay regulations, the employing agency must perform the computations. 5 C.F.R. § 550.804(a). It is clear that the agency's calculation is not binding on the plaintiff and is subject to judicial review. *E.g., Burke* v. *Green*, 422 F. Supp. 350, 358 (E.D. Penn. 1976). The Fourth Circuit in *White* v. *Bloomberg*, *supra*, discussed the problem as follows:

> In many cases the court may be able to compute back pay at the time it orders reinstatement. If a particular case presents a complex dispute over computation, the district court has discretionary power to bifurcate the proceedings under Rule 42(b) or Rule 56(c). Indeed, the district court might have done so here had it been asked. Or the district judge may prefer to have the employee and the agency seek agreement on the computation of back pay. If so, he may follow a procedure that has been employed in other Back Pay Act cases, ordering reinstatement and retaining jurisdiction over the back pay issue in case the parties cannot reach an administrative settlement. * * * 501 F. 2d at 1385.

Accordingly, judgments awarding back pay will be certified for payment from the permanent appropriation, but where the judgment does not specify the amount to be paid, we must be furnished the employing agency's computation, together with written indication that the plaintiff will accept the amount in satisfaction of the judgment. If the parties agree on the amount, the written indication may be a separate letter from the plaintiff or the plaintiff's counsel, or may be incorporated into the Justice Department's transmittal letter. If the latter approach is used, the transmittal must plainly state that the plaintiff has agreed to accept the amount computed by the employing agency (or some compromise figure, if that is the case) in satisfaction of the judgment. If the parties are unable to agree, further resort to the court may be necessary. In that event, the amount finally determined to be payable should be specified in an amended judgment or supplemental order.

The point is that the judgment is not final for payment purposes until there is an agreed-upon amount. Disputes over the amount to be paid must be resolved—administratively or judicially—prior to the submission for payment.

2. Judgments under Title VII of the Civil Rights Act.

Title VII of the Civil Rights Act of 1964, 42 U.S.C. §§ 2000e *et seq.*, prohibits employment discrimination. When originally enacted, it did not apply to the Federal Government. It was made applicable to the Federal Government by section 11 of the Equal Employment Opportunity Act of 1972, 42 U.S.C. § 2000e–16.

Title VII actions are brought in the United States district courts, which have broad discretion in fashioning remedies. Monetary awards in Title VII cases, although they may conceivably take the form of damages (*Hodge* v. *Commissioner*, 64 T.C. 616 (1975)), generally represent back pay. The authority of a court to award back pay in a Title VII action is found in section 706 of the Civil Rights Act, 42 U.S.C. § 2000e–5(g), set forth in pertinent part below:

> If the court finds that the respondent has intentionally engaged in or is intentionally engaging in an unlawful employment practice charged in the complaint, the court may enjoin the respondent from engaging in such unlawful employment practice, and order such affirmative action as may be appropriate, which may include, but is not limited to, reinstatement or hiring of employees, with or without back pay (*payable by the employer, employment agency, or labor organization, as the case may be, responsible for the unlawful employment practice*), or any other equitable relief as the court deems appropriate. * * * [Italic supplied.]

In addition, 42 U.S.C. § 2000e–16(c) provides that "the head of the department, agency, or unit, as appropriate, shall be the defendant" in a Title VII suit brought by a Federal employee. The question is thus whether, by virtue of the italic language in 42 U.S.C. § 2000e–5(g), *supra*, in conjunction with the quoted portion of section 2000e–16(c), payment of a judgment for back pay under Title VII is "otherwise provided for" and therefore payable from agency appropriations.

The italic language in 42 U.S.C. § 2000e–5(g), quoted above, was a part of the original 1964 Act; that is, it was enacted at a time when Title VII was not applicable to the Federal Government. Thus it could not have been originally intended to affect the source of funds for the payment of judgments involving the Federal Government. Its intent appears to have been merely to establish that back pay would not necessarily be payable by the employer, but could be payable by an employment agency or labor organization if the court found that the employment agency or labor organization was responsible for the unlawful practice. Thus, it is possible under section 2000e–5(g) for a court to order an employee reinstated with back pay, to be paid by someone other than the employer. But for the italic language, section 2000e–5(g) would have seemed to indicate that back pay would be payable in all instances by the employer.

When Title VII was extended to the Federal Government in 1972, Congress saw no need to repeat entire sections of the existing law. Instead, Congress merely incorporated the applicable portions of the existing procedure by including 42 U.S.C. § 2000e–16(d), as follows:

> The provisions of section 2000e–5(f) through (k) of this title, as applicable, shall govern civil actions brought hereunder.

We find nothing in the legislative history of the Equal Employment Opportunity Act of 1972 to indicate that Congress intended to address the question of whether the judgment would be payable from the indefinite appropriation or by the defendant agency from its own funds. While it is certainly possible to view the defendant agency as the "employer," it is equally possible to read "employer" as the United States. We have also found no explanation in the legislative history of the requirement to designate the agency head as defendant. However, as one court has noted:

Although the commanding officer of the Shipyard was the nominal defendant against whom Richerson's action had to be brought under 42 U.S.C. § 2000e–16(c), in reality Richerson's claim was against the United States. *Richerson* v. *Jones*, 551 F. 2d 918, 925 (3d Cir. 1977).

Accordingly, in the absence of more specific indication that Congress intended Title VII judgments to be treated differently from other money judgments against the United States, it is our view that Title VII judgments fall within the scope of 28 U.S.C. § 2414 and 31 U.S.C. § 724a and are payable from the permanent appropriation.

The portion of the discussion of Back Pay Act judgments, *supra*, dealing with the "finality" for payment purposes of judgments which award back pay but do not contain dollar amounts is equally applicable to Title VII judgments.

It should be noted that a Title VII violation does not necessarily entitle the employee to back pay. Therefore, a Title VII judgment which orders reinstatement without reference to back pay does not automatically result in a charge to agency appropriations.

[B–193065]

Contracts—Awards—Small Business Concerns—Certifications—Competency—Urgency Exception Eliminated

Veterans Administration contracting officer's determination of nonresponsibility, based on preaward survey which concluded that small business concern, otherwise in line for award, does not have capacity to perform required work, must be referred to Small Business Administration for consideration under certificate of competency program since applicable law and regulations no longer allow exception to this requirement based on urgency.

In the matter of Hatcher Waste Disposal, March 7, 1979:

Hatcher Waste Disposal (Hatcher) protests the award of a contract to Mobile Waste Controls (Mobile), doing business as Arkansas Waste Disposal, under invitation for bids (IFB) 598–17–79, issued by the Veterans Administration Medical Center (VA), Little Rock, Arkansas.

The IFB solicited bids for trash removal services to be performed at two VA hospitals in the Little Rock area and at the Little Rock National Cemetery. Bidders could offer to perform these services for a 1-year or 3-year period beginning on October 1, 1978. The IFB was mailed to four prospective bidders with bid opening scheduled for September 21, 1978. However, due to the issuance of amendment No. 1, the date for bid opening was changed to September 26, 1978. Three bids were received, and Hatcher, a small business, offered the low bid to provide the required services for the two VA hospitals for a period of 3 years. Mobile was second low bidder on this item and low bidder for the services to be provided the Little Rock National Cemetery.

On September 28, 1978, the VA conducted a preaward survey of both Hatcher and Mobile. While the survey team found Mobile to be an efficient and well-run company, it questioned whether Hatcher could be ready to perform if awarded the contract. Specifically, the survey team did not believe that Hatcher either owned or had readily available sufficient equipment and facilities to permit it to begin performance on October 1, 1978. Based upon these findings, the contracting officer telephoned Hatcher on September 29, 1978, to indicate that a letter was being sent to it rejecting its bid on the grounds that the lack of equipment on hand was a major deficiency. In other words, Hatcher was determined to be nonresponsible. On that same day, Hatcher filed a protest with our Office.

Hatcher argues that the brief period of time allowed between bid opening and the date for performance is prejudicial to a small business, such as itself, which has to make arrangements to obtain additional equipment. Moreover, Hatcher contends that the preaward survey team chose to disregard all the information it was given explaining the steps Hatcher was taking to get itself ready to begin performance on October 1, 1978, and that this is reflected in its report which is inaccurate and incomplete. Finally, Hatcher maintains that as a small business it had the right to apply for a certificate of competency (COC) from the Small Business Administration (SBA), but was never given the opportunity. This, Hatcher argues, is in violation of the Small Business Act (15 U.S.C. 631 note), as amended by Pub. L. No. 95–89.

The VA candidly admits that there were too few days between bid opening and the time performance was to begin and has stated that steps have been taken to avoid this problem in the future. The VA also admits that the contracting officer failed to request a COC from SBA, but excuses this failure on the grounds that if a referral to SBA had been made the two hospitals would have suffered a disruption in their trash removal services while waiting for SBA to make its determination. The VA points out that attempts were made to negotiate a short term contract for 30 days in order to allow more time for such things as SBA determinations, but that these proved fruitless. Thus, due to the potential health hazard which would result from a disruption of trash services, the VA believes that an emergency existed and that the contracting officer was justified in bypassing SBA and awarding the contract to the second low bidder, Mobile. While conceding, therefore, that there has been a violation of the SBA Act, the VA again states that steps have been taken to avoid this in the future. Finally, in regard to the accuracy of its preaward survey, the VA believes that Hatcher's allegations of incomplete and incorrect findings are not supported by the facts.

The controlling factor in this protest is the contracting officer's failure to refer the question of Hatcher's responsibility to the SBA as required by the Small Business Act, 15 U.S.C. § 637(b)(7) (1976), as amended by Pub. L. No. 95–89, 91 Stat. 557, effective August 4, 1977. Under this act, the SBA is empowered to certify conclusively to Government procurement officials with respect to all elements of responsibility. See *Com-Data, Inc.*, B–191289, June 23, 1978, 78–1 CPD 459.

From the record presented, the VA appears to be arguing that the urgency of maintaining continuous trash removal services for its two hospitals permits an exception to this statutory requirement so long as a level above that of the contracting officer concurs in the decision to make the award to other than the low bidder. Until recently, the Federal Procurement Regulations (FPR) permitted just such an exception. See FPR § 1–1.708–2(a)(1) (1964 ed. amend. 174). However, the Small Business Act, as amended by Pub. L. No. 95–89, makes no exception for urgency as a ground for not referring the question of a small business' responsibility to SBA. Therefore, effective June 14, 1978, FPR was amended to eliminate the urgency exception it had previously allowed. See FPR § 1–1.708–2(a)(1) (1964 ed. amend. 192).

Clearly, then, VA had no basis for not referring the question of Hatcher's responsibility to SBA and has violated the Small Business Act in failing to do so. We have been notified that the VA has recently referred this matter to SBA for possible issuance of a COC, but that SBA has deferred consideration pending our decision. We request, therefore, that SBA proceed in its consideration of whether issuance of a COC is appropriate in this case. If a COC is issued, and Hatcher accepts award for the balance of the contract term, the current contract with Mobile should be terminated for the convenience of the Government. If a COC is not issued or Hatcher refuses such an award, no further action is required.

By letters of today, we are informing the Administrators of Veteran Affairs and SBA of our recommendation.

Accordingly, the protest is sustained.

[B–193316]

Officers and Employees — Transfers — Relocation Expenses — Incident to Change of Official Duty Station

The words "general local or metropolitan area" as used in paragraph 2–1.5b(1) of the Federal Travel Regulations (FTR) are descriptive rather than restrictive. These are general criteria rather than fixed rules to be narrowly applied in all cases involving transfer between official stations which are relatively close to each other. Therefore, it does not follow that for relocation to be incident to transfer of duty station it must invariably result in less commuting time and distance.

Officers and Employees — Transfers — Relocation Expenses — Mileage—Effect on Relocation Determination

Where the old duty station and the new duty station are located 77 miles apart and the employee's residence from which he commuted daily 43 miles to the old station is located midway between the two stations, fact that employee chose to relocate to the new station, rather than continue to commute 45 miles daily, does not preclude a determination that the relocation was incident to the transfer.

In the matter of Harvey Knowles—Relocation Expenses, March 12, 1979:

This action is in response to a letter from H. Larry Jordan, Authorized Certifying Officer, Department of Agriculture. Under 31 U.S.C. 82d (1976), he requests our decision as to whether a claim by Mr. Harvey Knowles for expenses incurred in connection with his transfer of station may be paid.

Mr. Knowles, an employee of the Food and Nutrition Service of the Department of Agriculture, was authorized to change his official duty station from Greensboro, North Carolina, to Raleigh, North Carolina. Travel Authorization No. 17–612–40, dated June 23, 1976, was issued for that purpose. At the time Mr. Knowles' official duty station was changed and apparently during the time his duty station was at Greensboro, he resided in Hillsborough, North Carolina. Hillsborough is located almost equal distance between Greensboro and Raleigh. Greensboro is approximately 43 miles west of Hillsborough and Raleigh is approximately 45 miles southeast of Hillsborough. The official distance between Greensboro and Raleigh by the most direct route is 77 miles. Mr. Knowles sold his residence in Hillsborough and purchased a new residence in Raleigh, about a year after the transfer. The sale and purchase settlement dates were June 15, 1977, and June 16, 1977, respectively. He submitted a travel voucher claiming reimbursement for transportation of household goods, miscellaneous expenses, and expenses for the sale of residence at Hillsborough and purchase of residence in Raleigh. Since paragraph 2–1.5b(1) of the Federal Travel Regulations (FTR) (FPMR 101–7, May 1973) provides that

* * * Ordinarily, a relocation of residence shall not be considered as incident to a change of official station unless the one-way commuting distance from the

old residence to the new official station is at least 10 miles greater than from the old residence to the old official station. * * *

the Food and Nutrition Service believes that the relocation of residence was not incident to his transfer.

Under 5 U.S.C. 5724 and 5724a (1976) travel and transportation and other relocation expenses of transferred employees may be authorized or approved by the head of an agency pursuant to such regulations as the President may prescribe. Implementing regulations are found in chapter 2 of the FTR. Paragraph 2–1.3 of those regulations provides that travel and transportation expenses and applicable allowances are payable in the case of the transfer of an employee from one official station to another for permanent duty provided, among other things, that the new official station is at least 10 miles distant from the old official station and, in case of a relatively short distance relocation, a determination of eligibility is made under the provisions of paragraph 2–1.5b(1) of the FTR.

The regulations do not define "short distance" except that the term is used in paragraph 2–1.5b(1) as follows:

> When the change of official station involves a short distance within the *same general local or metropolitan area*, the travel and transportation expenses and applicable allowances in connection with the employee's relocation of his residence shall be authorized only when the agency determines that the relocation was incident to the change of official station. * * * [Italic supplied.]

In B–175822, June 14, 1972, we held that if the employee in fact commutes daily to his new official station from the newly purchased residence, the fact that the residence is located in the same city as his former residence would not in itself preclude reimbursement of expenses incurred in connection with either real estate transaction. In that decision we stated that the words "general local or metropolitan area" are descriptive rather than restrictive. See also 54 Comp. Gen. 751 (1975) and B–167171, August 8, 1969. We have also held that whether a change of official station involves a "short distance" within the purview of the regulations does not change the standard applicable to all cases that an employee's relocation of residence be "incident to the change of official station." See B–172705, May 21, 1971; B–167171, *supra*. Those decisions also characterize the determinative factors as general criteria rather than fixed rules to be narrowly applied in all cases involving transfer between official stations which are relatively close to each other. Therefore, it does not follow that for relocation to be incident to a transfer of duty station it must invariably result in less commuting time and distance.

Section 2–1.5b is for application where the change of official station is within the same general local or metropolitan area but a hard and fast rule should not be applied. In the present case the distance between the old and the new station was 77 miles. To hold that these communities are in the same general locale or that Greensboro and Raleigh are within the same metropolitan area would appear unreasonable. Further, the fact that the employee chose to commute daily a distance of 43 miles to Greensboro should not preclude him from moving to a residence only 8 miles from the new duty station in Raleigh when the distance between the old and new stations is 77 miles. To require the employee to continue to commute 45 miles or to move his residence at his own expense would be unreasonable.

Since no final determination appears to have been made by the Department of Agriculture as to whether Mr. Knowles' move was incident to his transfer, and since the question has been presented for our determination, we hold that the relocation of residence from Hillsborough to Raleigh was incident to his transfer from Greensboro to Raleigh. Accordingly, Mr. Knowles should be reimbursed allowable relocation expenses in connection with his move. The voucher submitted may be paid if otherwise proper.

[B-164031(5).22]

Appropriations—Fiscal Year—Availability Beyond—Contracts— Two Fiscal Years

Norton Sound Health Corporation annually has entered into contracts with Indian Health Service (IHS), Health, Education, and Welfare, to provide health care services during that fiscal year and desires to carry over into the succeeding fiscal year any unexpended funds to provide for medical services it will render in that year. Although provisions of 25 U.S.C. 13a (1976) make the funds available for 2 years, this authority has been overridden annually by provision in appropriation acts restricting use of funds to current fiscal year unless specifically provided for otherwise in the appropriation act involved. Appropriations made to IHS for fiscal year 1978 contain no such specific provision and funds lapse at end of that year. Appropriation act for fiscal year 1979 makes IHS funds appropriated therein available until the end of fiscal year 1980.

In the matter of Norton Sound Health Corporation, March 14, 1979:

The Norton Sound Health Corporation (NSHC) requests our views on three questions concerning the carryover of funds not obligated under an Indian Health Service (IHS) contract.

The Corporation's Executive Director states that, "Most recently there has been some confusion" within DHEW [the Department of Health, Education, and Welfare] and IHS as to whether such carryover is possible within existing law and regulations." We are asked to resolve the "confusion." As explained in more detail below, only when the applicable appropriations act permits funds to remain available for an additional fiscal year is the carryover of contract funds for health services authorized.

Utilizing funds from the Office of Economic Opportunity, the NSHC was established in 1970 as a private corporation under the laws of the State of Alaska. Starting in 1974, the Alaska Area Native Health Service, a component of the Indian Health Service, Department of Health, Education, and Welfare, began contracting with NSHC, initially for the provision of physician's services. According to NSHC's Executive Director,

That contract has now been expanded to 2 contracts which together encompass responsibility for an entire comprehensive regional health delivery system. The contract vehicle was and is cost-reimbursement type for health service programs.

The Executive Director notes that both the authorizing legislation and the applicable regulations appear to provide some authority for carrying over unexpended fiscal year funds. He notes that there is a continuous growth in complexity in providing health services and that while the program needs of NSHC are never ending, the contracts with HEW are funded on a fiscal year basis. He states that the inability to carry funds over lessens the flexibility of response to normal peaks and valleys in demand for services and otherwise hampers the corporation.

His first question is: "With the above cited Public Health Service Regulations [42 CFR 36.236(e)] being based on Public Law 93–638, can the Indian Health Service Contracting Officer allow carryover of the appropriations for ongoing health services?"

Since the Indian Health Service is administered by HEW, we requested the reviews of the Secretary on this matter. Those views were provided to us in a letter from an Assistant General Counsel. He suggests in his letter that funds under these contracts may be carried over from one year to the next in the event of a cost underrun in a contract which is expected to be renewed from year to year and calls for the performance of services of a continuous nature. He states that it is a practice, not only by the Indian Health Service but of other HEW units, to permit funds obligated by "continuing-type" contracts which were made in one fiscal year but which remain unexpended at the expiration of the contract to be used in performing services in the succeeding fiscal year under the follow-on or renewal contract. HEW's rationale, as stated in the letter, is as follows:

The Comptroller General has long held that a contract obligates the appropriations of the fiscal year in which it is executed provided that it meets a *bona fide* need of that fiscal year. 33 Comp. Gen. 57, 61 (1953), and the decisions cited therein. Where the work under a contract is of a continuing nature, the expiration of the term of the contract does not necessarily mean that any further work to be performed may not be regarded as meeting the needs which prompted the initial contract. If there is a cost contract underrun at the expiration of the initial contract, the period of the contract can be extended to permit the contractor to expend the balance of the estimated cost of the contract. At the conclusion of this period of extension, the Government can enter into a follow-on contract, obligating funds of the then current fiscal year. However by executing a follow-on contract immediately upon the expiration of the initial contract and by authorizing the contractor to continue to use the prior fiscal year's appropriations which had not been completely expended, we would obviate the need for executing two separate contracts, *viz.*, a short-term extension contract and a new follow-on contract. Since there would be no legal objection to executing a short-term extension contract to permit the utilization of the unexpended balance of the initial contract and then executing a follow-on contract which would obligate the funds of the then current fiscal year, there would also be no legal objection to telescoping the process by executing a single follow-on contract under which the contractor would be authorized to utilize both the unexpended balance of the original contract as well as the additional funds obligated by the follow-on contract.

The subject contracts involve, as we understand it, the provisions of the services of physicians and other medical services, during a fiscal year, to a discrete group of eligible individuals. With respect to the particular questions raised by NSHC, for the reasons discussed below, we disagree with HEW's position. It is our view that whether these funds remain available for the provision of health services in a succeeding fiscal year depends entirely upon the language used in the appropriations act.

The basic rule on availability of appropriations is that unless otherwise provided by law, appropriations made for a specific fiscal year lapse at the end of that year and may not be obligated for expenditure in the succeeding fiscal year. See 31 U.S.C. § 712a (1976).

If section 8 of the Indian Self-Determination and Education Assistance Act, Public Law 93–638, January 4, 1975, 88 Stat. 2206, 25 U.S.C. § 13a (1976) stood alone, it would overcome this general statutory restriction on the availability of appropriations. 25 U.S.C. § 13a provides:

The provisions of any other laws to the contrary notwithstanding, any funds appropriated pursuant to sections 13 and 52a of this title, for any fiscal year which are not obligated and expended prior to the beginning of the fiscal year succeeding the fiscal year for which such funds were appropriated shall remain available for obligation and expenditure during such succeeding fiscal year.

However, the provisions of 25 U.S.C. § 13a authorizing the carryover of unobligated and unexpended appropriation have been regularly overridden by a provision which has appeared for many years in annual appropriation acts. That provision states: "No part of any appropriation contained in this Act shall remain available for obligation beyond the current fiscal year *unless expressly so provided herein.*" [Italic supplied.] See, for example, section 305 of Public Law 95–74, July 26, 1977, 91 Stat. 285, 307, known as the Department of the Interior and Related Agencies Appropriation Act, 1978. This provision controls as it is the latest expression of congressional intent on the availability of the appropriation. Where the Congress wanted to overcome this provision, it specifically did so.

With respect to fiscal year 1978, we note that many of the funds appropriated (by Public Law 95–74, *supra*), to the Department of the Interior under the heading of "Indian Affairs, Bureau of Indian Affairs, Operation of Indian Programs," 91 Stat. 292–293, are specifically made available in the Appropriation Act beyond the end of fiscal year 1978. However, in the same act, at 91 Stat. 300–301, appropriations to the Indian Health Service, HEW, do not provide for such a carryover, Accordingly, under the 1978 appropriation act, funds which were not used to provide medical services during fiscal year 1978 may not be used to pay for health care services provided in fiscal year 1979.

The appropriation of the Indian Health Service for fiscal year 1979, contained in the Department of the Interior and Related Agencies Appropriation Act, 1979, Pub. L. No. 95–465, October 17, 1978, 92 Stat. 1296, includes a proviso that funds made available to tribes and tribal organizations through contracts authorized by the Indian Self-Determination and Education Assistance Act of 1975 shall remain available until September 30, 1980. This specific provision satisfies the requirement of the appropriations limitation mentioned above and allows the funds appropriated for fiscal year 1979 to be used thoughout the end of fiscal year 1980. As with the 1978 act, this specific provision would be unnecessary if the Congress did not believe that the appropriation act provision would be controlling.

The Executive Director's second question is: "Would the appropriations act require changes in wording to allow carryover of funds to subsequent years' programs?"

As just noted, if the Congress enacts language such as that contained in the 1979 appropriation act, no change will be necessary.

The Executive Director's final question is: "Would a change in the term period of performance under a cost-reimbursement contract, i.e., performance start up from March 1 to contract completion February 28 allow carryover? Or would this require six (6) months of funding from each of the fiscal year funds involved?"

Obviously, when there is a provision such as that in the fiscal year 1979 appropriation act, a contract from March 1 to February 28 would be authorized. Should the appropriation act, such as the 1978 fiscal year appropriation act, fail to allow for a carryover from one fiscal year to another, a contract for health services entered into on March 1 would have to terminate by September 30, the end of the fiscal year, and a new contract, funded from the next fiscal year's funds, would have to be entered into for the succeeding 6 month period.

[B–192171]

Contracts — Protests — Persons, etc. Qualified to Protest — Interested Parties—Potential Contractors, etc. Not Submitting Bids, etc.—Restrictive Specifications

Submission of proposal is not prerequisite to consideration of protest of restrictive solicitation filed prior to closing date for receipt of proposals.

General Accounting Office—Jurisdiction—Policy Determinations

Bid protest is not appropriate vehicle to question determinations made under OMB Circular A-76 or similar documents since such determinations relate to Executive Branch policy matters.

Contracts—Competitive System—Price Competitiveness—Lease v. Purchase

Solicitation which does not permit consideration of offers to lease to Government equipment needed for entirely new system is unduly restrictive where based solely on earlier analysis of comparative cost to upgrade existing system, because determination that alternative approach is not competitive as to price can only be made by competitive procurement.

In the matter of Peninsula Telephone and Telegraph Co., March 14, 1979:

Peninsula Telephone and Telegraph Co. (Peninsula) protests Navy's RFP N00228-78-R-2127, because it solicits only offers to sell, as opposed to offers to lease, a VHF/UHF communications system to service Trident communications requirements in the Puget Sound area. We find the protest has merit.

The Navy objects to the protest because Peninsula did not submit a proposal. The protester, however, filed its objection before the closing date for receipt of initial proposals, as required by our procedures, 4 C.F.R. § 20.2(a) (1978), and is not required to submit a proposal to retain its "interested party" status under those procedures. We note that, while the protester received oral assurance from the Navy that it would consider lease proposals, the solicitation included the usual warning that the Government would not be bound by oral explanations or instructions given before award. Moreover, offerors were advised that the Government reserved the right to make award without holding discussions (*see* Standard Form 33A, paragraphs 3 and 10g), and the solicitation contained no provision for evaluating lease proposals. To the contrary, offerors were required to agree to certain maintenance and purchase-related terms, indicating that only a purchase was contemplated. Thus, had Peninsula submitted a lease proposal, its offer could have been rejected by the Navy, and it is questionable whether a protest at that point would have been a viable vehicle for the relief Peninsula seeks. Accordingly, we believe Peninsula was free to protest and obtain a formal resolution of its questions without also submitting a proposal.

The Navy concedes that for operational purposes the equipment could be leased, but asserts that the cost of leasing would not have been competitive.

Peninsula contends that Navy ownership of this system would be inconsistent with the requirements set out in Office of Management and

Budget (OMB) Circular A–76, Department of Defense Directive 4100.15, and Office of Telecommunications Policy (OTP) Circular No. 13. These documents establish Government policy outlining when the Government should rely on the private sector to provide supplies and services which the Government might otherwise provide itself. In any case, the determination under these documents whether to provide services in–house is a matter of Executive policy and is outside the scope of the bid protest decisionmaking process. *Rand Information Systems*, B–192608, September 11, 1978, 78–2 CPD 189.

We will consider, however, whether the RFP limiting the procurement to purchase of equipment was unduly restrictive. See *General Telephone Company of California*, B–189430, July 6, 1978, 78–2 CPD 9. In this connection, Peninsula questions the Navy's reliance upon an earlier A–76 analysis to dismiss as too expensive anticipated lease proposals to furnish a new and different system. The earlier analysis, performed in 1976, involved a plan to augment existing facilities by adding new leased supporting systems. The Navy concluded that its needs would be best served were it to upgrade the existing system by purchasing the additional equipment needed. The Navy thinks that this analysis provided an appropriate basis for not soliciting to lease the equipment required by this procurement. Moreover, it believes it has complied with the criteria for determining whether the Government should rent or purchase equipment contained in Defense Acquisition Regulation (DAR) § 1–317. Peninsula disagrees, urging that the question should be determined through price competition. *Cf. Olivetti Corporation*, B–187369. February 28, 1977, 77–1 CPD 146.

We agree with Peninsula. The system now proposed appears to differ from the earlier network in several significant respects. The number of sites served has been reduced, while the locations of others have been changed. Peninsula also says the system as now configured duplicates a significant portion of the telephone network serving the same area. Even, however, if it did not, the Navy does not advance an adequate reason for precluding Peninsula from offering to lease the needed equipment. Regardless of whether the Navy under different circumstances could decide that it required a Government-owned system, or could rely on cost estimates to support planning decisions, it here indicates that *either* approach, lease or purchase, is acceptable. DAR § 1–317 cautions that the Government's requirements may be met best by lease—it does not authorize procurement personnel to disregard competitive procurement techniques where appropriate in determining whether needed equipment should be leased or purchased. Without more, as we noted in *Olivetti*, the contracting officer may not speculate as to whether potential offerors can or would be willing to offer competitive pricing, in the face of another firm's apparent competitive advantage. Well founded as the Government may believe its market survey to be, anticipated pricing may not be asserted as a defense to a restrictive specification where at least one offeror asserts that he can and will offer a lower price if permitted to do so.

The protest is sustained. By separate letter we are today bringing this matter to the attention of the Secretary of the Navy, along with our recommendation that the Navy cancel its solicitation and resolicit its requirement under a solicitation permitting acquisition by either purchase or lease.

[B-193603]

Buy American Act—Applicability—Use Outside United States—Coins Manufactured for Foreign Governments—Metal Purchases

Buy American Act does not apply to Bureau of Mint purchases of metal for use in manufacturing coins for foreign government because such acquisitions are not for public use under terms of Buy American Act.

In the matter of Department of the Treasury—Request for Advance Decision, March 14, 1979:

By letter dated November 29, 1978, the Director of the Mint, Department of the Treasury, has asked for our opinion on the applicability of the Buy American Act, 41 U.S.C. 10a–d (1976), to purchases of metals by the Bureau of the Mint (Mint) for use in manufacturing coins for foreign governments.

In 1874, the Mint was authorized to manufacture coins for foreign governments. Foreign Coinage Act, 31 U.S.C. 367 (1976). The Act provides the Mint may manufacture the coins on a cost reimbursable basis, charging the foreign government an amount equal to the expenses for executing the coins including labor, materials, and use of machinery. The charges are set by the Director of the Mint, with the approval of the Secretary of the Treasury. Manufacturing foreign coins is not to interfere with manufacturing domestic coins.

Usually, orders for foreign coinage are awarded to the Mint following competitive bidding conducted by a foreign central bank or other monetary authority. Thus, the Mint competes for foreign coinage awards with the mints of other countries and private mints.

The Mint Director states that these contracts are generally considered desirable, as foreign coin orders allow the Mint to use effectively excess equipment capacity during slack periods in domestic coin demand. The Director also notes these contracts are beneficial for their effect on United States balance of payments.

In June 1978, after a competitive bidding procedure, the Mint was awarded a contract by the Central Bank of the Dominican Republic for its circulating and numismatic coin requirements for 1978 and

1979. The contract, like the Mint's other contracts of this type, provides that the Mint will act as agent for the Central Bank of the Dominican Republic in buying the necessary metal at the best market price and bill the Central Bank at actual cost.

To acquire the metal needed to fabricate the Dominican Republic's coins, approximately 38,000 pounds of nickel, the Mint issued an invitation for bids. During the course of the procurement, AMAX Nickel, Inc. (AMAX) questioned the Mint regarding the application of the Buy American Act preference in the evaluation of bids offered by foreign suppliers. AMAX indicates that it is the only domestic refiner of pure nickel suitable for coinage. As a result of the questions raised, the Mint canceled the invitation, with resolicitation being withheld pending our resolution of the question.

The Buy American Act provides that:

> Notwithstanding any other provision of law and unless the head of the department or independent establishment concerned shall determine it to be inconsistent with the public interest, or the cost to be unreasonable, only such unmanufactured articles, materials, and supplies as have been mined or produced in the United States, and only such manufactured articles, materials, and supplies as have been manufactured in the United States substantially all from articles, materials, or supplies mined, produced, or manufactured as the case may be, in the United States, shall be acquired for public use. This section shall not apply with respect to articles, materials or supplies for use outside the United States * * *. 41 U.S.C. 10a.

In the Director's view, it is doubtful that the provisions of the Buy American Act would apply to the procurement of coinage material where the material is to be used for foreign coins. The Director suggests that the purchase in question is an implementation of its "business transaction" with a foreign government to provide coinage, rather than an acquisition for "public use" within the terms of the Act.

Moreover, the Director also suggests that even if the metal to be purchased is for public use, the Act is inapplicable because it exempts articles which will be used outside the United States. The Director points out that coinage ordered by a foreign government for its own circulating and numismatic purposes is destined essentially for use in the foreign country.

In addition, the Director notes the Act does not apply where the domestic preference is inconsistent with the public interest. *See* 41 U.S.C. § 10d. As contracts for foreign coinage are awarded after competitive bidding, the Mint Director is concerned that application of a price differential would adversely affect its competitive position with foreign and private mints. In that case, the Director states, not only would the mint lose the benefits to be gained from the order, but also "the very same balance of payments advantage the Buy American Act was designed to achieve would be negated."

On the other hand, AMAX states that the domestic nickel industry is at the low point because of a severe, persistent recession in the industry worldwide, and that nickel is being sold at low prices. It states its refinery is operating below capacity and that the rationale for buy national practices applies in this situation. It alleges that most governmentally owned mints prefer domestic refined metal when it is available and largely exclude foreign-source refined metal. Thus, AMAX states that on the whole it has been foreclosed from foreign procurement for coinage.

Also, AMAX points out that the legislative history of the Foreign Coinage Act, which as noted above first authorized the Mint in 1874 to manufacture foreign coinage, indicates the object of the legislation was to benefit domestic silver mining production and interests (2 Cong. Rec. 768 (1874); *see also*, 14 Op. Atty. Gen. 219 (1873)), rather than to benefit the Mint itself or affect United States balance of payments. AMAX's position is that the Mint was authorized to strike foreign coins as an aid to American suppliers of raw material and that the authority was not granted in order to sustain the Mint. In addition, AMAX argues that to the extent the Mint uses foreign source material, the export benefit to the United States is offset.

The Mint Director indicates that in recent congressional hearings, Congress has been advised of the Mint's view that its foreign coinage program is advantageous, since it provides a means for reimbursement of fixed cost elements which would otherwise have to be borne by the domestic coinage program, and also that it contributes to the favorable side of balance of payments. See *Treasury, Postal Service and General Government Appropriations for Fiscal Year 1979, Hearings Before a Subcomm. of the Comm. on Appropriations House of Representatives*, 95th Cong., 2d Sess. 364 (1978) (statement of Stella B. Hackel).

The Buy American Act provides a competitive preference favoring domestic materials. However, the language of the Act establishes that the preference is not intended to apply across the board to any purchase made by the United States. As the statute indicates, a number of contracts remain unaffected, as the Act applies only to "articles, materials, or supplies acquired for public use" within the United States, unless the head of the agency concerned determines application of the Act to be inconsistent with the public interest, or the cost unreasonable. *See* 41 U.S.C. § 10 and B-168434, April 1, 1970.

The public use requirement is mandatory. Public use is defined by the Act as "use by * * * the United States." 41 U.S.C. § 10c; see *General Electric Company*, 54 Comp. Gen. 791 (1975), 75-1 CPD 176. Thus, if the acquisition of nickel by the Mint does not involve a public use, the Act would not apply to the procurement.

As stated above, the Mint Director suggests that a public use is not involved in the nickel procurement. The Director states the solicitation is an implementation of a "business transaction," drawing a distinction between public and non-public type operations of the Government. In addition, the Director points out that under the Mint's contract with the Central Bank the Mint is acting merely as the purchasing agent for the foreign government in acquiring nickel at the best market price, instead of procuring for public use.

Normally, it can be assumed that most materials which the Government procures for its own use within the United States are subject to the Act. *See* Watkins, L., *Effects of the Buy American Act on Federal Procurement*, 31 Fed. Bar J. 191 (1972). On the other hand, we have recognized that purchases of office trailers and relocatable steel buildings made by a prime contractor for its own use while performing a Government construction contract are not subject to the Act because such trailers and temporary buildings were not items to be delivered to the Government for public use. While we noted that the importation into the United States of the non-domestic trailers and buildings undoubtedly has an adverse impact on the domestic industry, we also found that the purchases were for contractor rather than for Government use, and thereby were not acquired for public use as contemplated by the Act. 51 Comp. Gen. 538 (1972).

In addition, because procurements conducted by state and local authorities under Federal grants do not involve acquisitions either by the United States or for its use, such procurements are not subject to the Act. Thus, in a case concerning a State of California procurement partially funded by a Federal grant, we stated that since the items being procured were for an agency of the state, the Buy American Act does not apply. B–163399, July 9, 1968; *see also* B–168434, *supra*.

In this case, the Mint is buying nickel in the performance of its contract with the Central Bank of the Dominican Republic, although the metal will be used by the United States to fabricate the coins. We do not think the use of the nickel by the Mint under these circumstances is a public use within the provisions of the Act. As the Director points out, in competing for award of a contract and in contracting with a foreign government, the Mint is essentially entering into a competitive business-type transaction, similar in some respects to the arrangement a commercial mint has with its customers. The nickel is to be used to enable the Mint to meet its contractual commitment as agent for the Central Bank. While the Mint Director believes foreign coinage contracts are beneficial to the public, we find this benefit to be incidental to the overall business-type agency arrangements rather than as giving rise to a "public use" within the meaning of the Act. We see nothing in the Act's legislative history which would lead to any other conclusion.

We cannot agree with AMAX that the Mint's procurement of nickel pursuant to arrangements with the Dominican Republic might violate the philosophy of *Ashwander* v. *Tennessee Valley Authority*, 297 U.S. 288 (1936), as an improper "private" operation of the Government. In *Ashwander*, the Supreme Court held that the Tennessee Valley Authority (TVA) has the right to dispose of surplus electric energy, but that the method of disposal must be in the public interest "as distinguished from private or personal ends," (*Id.* at 338) and noted that TVA was not seeking to establish a business having no relationship to the governmental purpose for which it was established (*Id.* at 339–340).

Similarly, the Mint here is not engaged in a function unrelated to its governmental purposes simply because its acquisition of nickel is not for "public use" as defined by the Buy American Act. Rather, the Mint is acting pursuant to law by buying the metal, and it is clear that the purchase does further Government objectives.

While the *Treasury, Postal Service and General Government Appropriation Act of 1977*, Pub L. No. 94–363, July 14, 1976, as AMAX points out, would generally prohibit the expenditure of public funds for the procurement of foreign stainless steel flatware, since the Mint seeks to buy nickel (not flatware) the Act does not apply to the proposed acquisition.

Lastly, we do not believe, as AMAX has alleged, that our decision bears upon the military export program. While the Department of Defense as a matter of policy applies the Buy American Act to purchases in support of Foreign Military Sales (Defense Acquisition Regulation § 6–1302 (1976 ed.)), the Mint chooses not to apply the Act to its foreign coinage program.

In conclusion, we find that the Buy American Act does not apply to purchases of metals by the Mint for use in manufacturing coins for foreign governments for the reasons stated above, and we need not consider whether the purchases are also exempt for the other reasons suggested by the Director.

[B-193824]

Compensation — Additional — Environmental Pay Differential — Basis for Payment

General Services Administration (GSA) questions legality of Federal Labor Relations Council decision requiring payment of environmental differential for "high work." GSA believes payment is unauthorized because of mistakes of fact concerning height of structure and existence of protective wall. Grievance agreement upheld by Council may be implemented since under Federal Personnel Manual the parties may determine entitlement through collective bargaining process. Furthermore, authorization of environmental differential in the present case does not appear to be contrary to law or regulation or to be arbitrary or capricious.

In the matter of General Services Administration, Region 3, and American Federation of Government Employees, Local 2151 — Environmental Differential, March 22, 1979:

This decision is in response to a request dated December 18, 1978, from the Acting Administrator, General Services Administration (GSA), for an advance decision regarding the entitlement of certain employees of GSA, Region 3, to environmental differential. This matter has already been the subject of decisions by the Assistant Secretary for Labor-Management Relations, A/SLMR No. 996, dated March 2, 1978, and the Federal Labor Relations Council, FLRC No. 78A–39, dated November 6, 1978, which directed GSA to pay environmental differential for "high work" pursuant to a grievance settlement agreement. In requesting our decision, GSA states that there have been mistakes of fact and that it has been ordered by the Federal Labor Relations Council to make payments which are without legal or regulatory basis.

BACKGROUND

The facts in this case, as summarized from the prior decisions, are as follows. The union, American Federation of Government Employees, AFL–CIO, Local 2151, filed a grievance in 1974 under the negotiated collective bargaining agreement alleging that there were "hazardous working conditions" which existed at the Central Heating Plant of GSA, Region 3, and which entitled certain employees to environmental differential. To resolve the grievance, GSA conducted a study of conditions at the Central Heating Plant, and the agency reported on February 26, 1976, that an environmental differential in the amount of 25 percent was warranted for work on the roof of the Central Heating Plant under the criteria for "high work." Payment was authorized by GSA on March 8, 1976, for the workers who were exposed to these working conditions. The grievances concerning environmental differential for "dirty work," "hot work," and "toxic chemicals" were submitted to arbitration and were subsequently denied.

Shortly thereafter, GSA reconsidered its decision authorizing environmental differential for "high work" when it was determined that there was a protective wall around most of the heating plant roof and after GSA received an informal advisory opinion from the Civil Service Commission (CSC) (now Office of Personnel Management). As a result, GSA decided that the conditions did not meet the "high work" criteria set forth in Federal Personnel Manual (FPM) Supplement 532–1, Appendix J, and GSA rescinded the pay authorization on June 28, 1976.

The union filed an unfair labor practice complaint alleging that the agency had violated section 19(a) (1) and (6) of Executive Order 11491, as amended. The complaint alleged that when GSA rescinded the grievance settlement agreement authorizing environmental differential pay, the agency interfered with, restrained, or coerced employees in the exercise of their rights and refused to consult, confer, or negotiate with the union as required by the Order. The unfair labor practice charge was heard by an Administrative Law Judge of the Department of Labor who concluded that the agency had properly rescinded the settlement agreement on the basis of the mistake of fact regarding the existence of a protective wall. He recommended that the complaint be dismissed.

However, on review, the decision of the Assistant Secretary of Labor was that the agency had violated section 19(a) (1) and (6) of the Order by unilaterally terminating the authorization of environmental differential. The decision held that the grievance settlement agreement had the same standing as an award by an arbitrator and constituted an extensioin of the negotiated agreement and an established term and condition of employment. Further, his decision held that the payment of environmental differential was not contrary to law and that the informal verbal opinion provided by the CSC did not constitute a policy interpretation which rendered the settlement invalid.

The agency appealed the Assistant Secretary's decision to the Federal Labor Relations Council which rendered its decision, No. 78A–39, on November 6, 1978. The Council held that the decision of the Assistant Secretary was not arbitrary and capricious since (1) the relevant provisions of the FPM were incorporated by reference in the negotiated agreement, (2) the agency had agreed to authorize environmental differential under the grievance settlement, and (3) there was no showing that the CSC had declared the settlement invalid. The decision of the Council sustained the Assistant Secretary's order directing the agency to reinstate the grievance settlement and, "to the extent consonant with law, regulations, and decisions of the Comptroller General," reimburse each affected employee the environmental differential authorized pursuant to the grievance settlement for "high work."

ARGUMENT

The General Services Administration argues that there are two mistakes of fact which preclude the payment of environmental differential under the FPM. As noted above, GSA argues that the existence of a protective wall surrounding the inner roof level where all of the work in question is performed greatly reduces the hazard of working on a high structure. In addition, GSA points out that when the Central Heating Plant was measured in 1978 the area outside the protective wall was found to be 89 feet above ground level and the area inside the protective wall was found to be 95 feet above ground level. Thus, GSA concludes that since the roof is less than 100 feet above ground and since there is a protective wall surrounding the inner roof where all work is performed, the hazard does not exist and payment of environmental differential is not warranted under the regulations.

The union argues that the environmental differential payments are legal since a mistake of fact is not grounds for contract avoidance under the circumstances and that the agency should be estopped from claiming that the agreement was based upon a mistake. In addition, the union contends that the agreement reached in this case was based upon the FPM provisions which allow environmental differential payments to be authorized through labor-management negotiation. Finally, the union argues that the advisory opinion by the CSC in this case was not, and could not, be binding on the agency, citing *Naval Air Rework Facility*, 56 Comp. Gen. 8 (1976).

DISCUSSION AND CONCLUSION

The statutory authority for environmental differential pay for wage schedule employees is contained in 5 U.S.C. § 5343(c)(4) which provides that the CSC shall prescribe regulations for the administration of the prevailing rate system, including regulations which provide "for proper differentials, as determined by the Commission, for duty involving unusually severe working conditions or unusually severe hazards." The regulations promulgated by the CSC are contained in FPM Supplement 532-1, subchapter S8-7 and Appendix J, and they provide guidance to the agencies for the payment of an environmental differential for exposure to various degrees of hazards, physical hardships and severe working conditions. With regard to the local determination of conditions under which a differential could be paid, subchapter S8-7 provided at the time of the grievance herein, as follows:

g. Determining local situations when environmental differentials are payable. (1) *Appendix J* defines the categories of exposure for which the hazard, physical hardships, or working conditions are of such an unusual nature as to warrant environmental differentials, *and gives examples of situations which are illustrative of the nature and degree of the particular hazard, physical hardship, or working condition involved in performing the category. The examples of the situations are not all inclusive but are intended to be illustrative only.*

(2) Each installation or activity must evaluate its situations against the guidelines in appendix J to determine whether the local situation is covered by one or more of the defined categories.

(a) When the local situation is determined to be covered by one or more of the defined categories (even though not covered by a specific illustrative example), the authorized environmental differential is paid for the appropriate category.

(b) When the local situation is not covered by one of the defined categories but is considered to be unusual in nature so as to warrant payment of an environmental differential, a differential may not be paid (except as provided by i below), but action is to be initiated to request the Commission to consider authorizing the payment of an environmental differential.

(3) *Nothing in this section shall preclude negotiations through the collective bargaining process for determining the coverage of additional local situations under appropriate categories in appendix J or for determining additional categories not included in appendix J for which environmental differential is considered to warrant referral to the Commission for prior approval as in (2) above.* [Italic supplied.]

Appendix J to FPM Supp. 532–1 provides, in pertinent part, as follows:

2. High work.
a. Working on any structure at least 100 feet above the ground, deck, floor or roof, or from the bottom of a tank or pit:
b. Working at a lesser height:
(1) If the footing is unsure or the structure is unstable; or
(2) If safe scaffolding, enclosed ladders or other similar protective facilities are not adequate (for example, working from a swinging stage, boatswain chair, a similar support); or
(3) If adverse conditions such as darkness, steady rain, high wind, icing, lightning or similar environmental factors render working at such height(s) hazardous.

In the present case, it is the contention of the agency that the existence of the protective wall and the fact that the roofs are less than 100 feet above ground level preclude payment of environmental differential under the above-cited regulations.

We believe that the present case is controlled by *Naval Air Rework Facility*, 56 Comp. Gen. 8, *supra*. In that decision, the Navy requested our opinion as to the legality of implementing two arbitration awards of environmental differential pay which the Navy had concluded were inconsistent with the applicable regulations. We pointed out that the Civil Service Commission has declined to make determinations regarding specific cases involving the payment of environmental differential and that the CSC has refrained from acting as an appellate source in disputes between agencies and their employees in specific cases. 56 *id.* 8, at 13. In addition, we noted that the regulations authorize the agencies to evaluate local working conditions to determine whether such conditions are covered by the standards (subchapter S8–7g(2)) and permit negotiations through the collective bargaining process for determining the coverage of additional local situations (subchapter S8–7g(3)). Thus, we concluded that the arbitrator could properly determine coverage under the appropriate regulations and that the arbitrator's award would be considered binding absent a finding that it was contrary to applicable law, regulations, or decisions of our Office.

In the present case, we are considering a grievance settlement agreement instead of an arbitrator's award. We note that the Federal Labor Relations Council declined to pass upon or adopt the statement of the Assistant Secretary that a grievance settlement agreement has the same standing as an arbitration award. See FLRC No. 78A–39, footnote 6. Nevertheless, in view of the FPM provisions permitting the parties to determine coverage through the collective bargaining process, we shall consider the settlement agreement under the standards set forth in our decision in B–181498, January 30, 1975. In that decision, we held that where the agency had declined to authorize environmental differential for certain employees, our Office would not substitute its judgment for that of the agency absent clear and convincing evidence negating the information in the agency report or indicating that the agency determination was arbitrary or capricious.

In the present case, the agency's action of unilaterally terminating the authorization of environmental differential has been reviewed by the Assistant Secretary of Labor and the Federal Labor Relations Council. We will not substitute our judgment for that of the Assistant Secretary or the Council where we are unable to conclude that implementation of the grievance settlement agreement is contrary to law or regulation or that the agreement itself is arbitrary or capricious. Assuming all the facts presented by the agency concerning the height of the structure, the degree of the hazard, and the existence of protective devices, we are not convinced that environmental differential cannot be authorized for work under the circumstances in the present case. We note that the applicable regulations clearly state that the examples listed in the categories in Appendix J are illustrative only and are not intended to be exclusive of other exposures under other circumstances. See FPM Supp. 532–1, subchapter S8–7e(1). Furthermore, as provided in subchapter S8–7(g)(3), the regulations allow for negotiations through the collective bargaining process for determining coverage of additional local situations under the categories listed in Appendix J.

To further emphasize the fact that the authorization of environmental differential is left to local determination and is subject to the collective bargaining process, we point out that, subsequent to GSA's action in this case, the CSC revised its regulations concerning local determinations through the collective bargaining process. See **FPM Letter No. 532–89, January 12, 1977.** Those revised regulations have been incorporated into the FPM Supp. 532–1, Inst. 14, May 31, 1978, and they appear in subchapter S8–7(g)(3) as follows with the new material in italic:

(3) Nothing in this section shall preclude negotiations through the collective bargaining process for:

(a) determining the coverage of additional local situations under appropriate categories in Appendix J *and application of Appendix J categories to local work situations. For example, local negotiations may be used to determine whether a local work situation is covered under an approved category, even though the work situation may not be described under a specific illustrative example.*

(b) determining additional categories not included in Appendix J for which environmental differential is considered to warrant referral to the Commission for prior approval as in (2), above. *For example, labor and management may negotiate locally whether to submit a joint request for a new environmental differential category or a different percentage differential for an existing category to the Commission through either of their respective headquarters.* [Italic supplied.]

Accordingly, we affirm the decisions of the Assistant Secretary of Labor and the Federal Labor Relations Council and conclude that the order to reinstate the grievance settlement agreement authorizing payment of an environmental differential for "high work" may be legally implemented.

〔B-194141〕

Bids——Mistakes——Price——Modification Error

Bidder alleging after bid opening, but before award, that late telegraphic bid modification that further lowered its already low bid was sent to procuring activity by mistake, is entitled to submit evidence of alleged mistake for consideration under applicable regulations to determine if bid can be corrected or withdrawn.

In the matter of Jaybil Industries, Inc., March 22, 1979:

Jaybil Industries, Inc. (Jaybil), low bidder on invitation for bids (IFB) N62477–77–B–0269 issued by the Chesapeake Division, Naval Facilities Engineering Command (Navy), protests the Navy's acceptance of its late telegraphic bid modification on the basis that the telegram was sent by mistake.

The IFB solicited bids for storm windows to be installed at the United States Naval Academy and Naval Station, Annapolis, Maryland. Bid opening was scheduled for 3 p.m., January 18, 1979. Seven bids were received, and when opened, Jaybil's bid of $509,572.40 was low.

At 8 p.m. that evening, the procuring agency received over its telex machine a message from Jaybil which reduced that company's bid by $20,000. Although this modification was received some 5 hours after the time scheduled for bid opening, the Navy determined that under the provisions of paragraph 7(d) of the IFB's "Instructions to Bidders" and Armed Services Procurement Regulation/Defense Acquisition Regulation (ASPR/DAR) § 7–2002.2 (1976 ed.) it was authorized to accept a late modification of an otherwise successful bid which makes the terms of that bid more favorable to the Government.

Yet, when informed that its bid was low at the reduced price of $489,572.40, Jaybil notified the Navy that the bid modification had been a mistake and that the original price of $509,572.40 was the one actually being offered.

According to Jaybil, on the afternoon of January 18, 1979, it had intended to reduce by $20,000 a bid being submitted on a project at Fort Bragg, North Carolina, under which bid opening was scheduled for January 19, 1979. However, a secretary inadvertently picked up the file for the Annapolis project and as a result sent the telegram to the wrong base. The telegram was filed with Western Union at 2:06 p.m., less than an hour before bid opening. Jaybil claims that at approximately 4 p.m. the error was discovered and Western Union was immediately telephoned in order to cancel the telegram. The Western Union office in Washington, D.C., the destination point, assured Jaybil that it had not yet received the telegram and when it did that it would take steps to stop delivery. Yet, as noted above, the Navy received Jaybil's message directly over its telex line at 8 p.m. and later accepted the late bid modification under paragraph 7(d) of the IFB's "Instructions to Bidders" and ASPR/DAR § 7–2002.2.

Jaybil argues that this bid modification was a mistake due entirely to human error and as a result that it should not be bound by such an erroneous modification but awarded the contract at the price originally bid. The Navy, on the other hand, maintains that not only is it authorized under the IFB and the applicable regulation to accept Jaybil's late bid modification, but that it would also be detrimental to the integrity of the competitive bidding system to allow a low bidder to decide after bid opening whether its bid reduction should be applied or not. However, Jaybil has indicated that it will not accept the contract award unless it is made at the original bid price.

It is well established that the Government may consider and accept a late telegraphic bid modification from an otherwise successful bidder if the modification is favorable to the Government and will not prejudice the other bidders. See 38 Comp. Gen. 674 (1959); 40 *id.* 466 (1961); ASPR/DAR §§ 2–303.1, 7–2002.2; Federal Procurement Regulations § 1–2.305 (1964 ed. amend. 118). However, the regulations also contemplate the possible correction or withdrawal of a bid where a mistake in bid is alleged after opening but prior to award. See ASPR/DAR § 2–406.3.

In this regard, ASPR/DAR § 2–406.3(a) provides in pertinent part:

(a) The Departments are authorized to make the following administrative determinations in connection with mistakes in bids, other than apparent clerical mistakes, alleged after opening of bids and prior to award.

*   *   *   *   *   *   *

(3) When the bidder requests permission to correct a mistake in his bid and clear and convincing evidence establishes both the existence of a mistake and the bid actually intended, a determination permitting the bidder to correct the

mistake may be made; provided that, in the event such correction would result in displacing one or more lower bids, the determination shall not be made unless the existance of the mistake and the bid actually intended are ascertainable substantially from the invitation and the bid itself. If the evidence is clear and convincing only as to the mistake, but not as to the intended bid, a determination permitting the bidder to withdraw his bid may be made.

(4) When the evidence is not clear and convincing that the bid as submitted was not the bid intended, a determination may be made requiring that the bid be considered for award in the form submitted.

Likewise, our Office has also permitted the correction of an error in bid prior to award if the bidder submits "clear and convincing evidence" (1) that a mistake was made, (2) the nature of the mistake, and (3) the bid price actually intended. 53 Comp. Gen. 232 (1973); *Michigan Electric*, B–190446, March 23, 1978, 78–1 CPD 229.

In addition, our Office has held that where the Government undertakes to bind a bidder to its bid, after notice of a claim of error by the bidder, the Government virtually undertakes the burden of proving that there was no error or that the bidder's claim was not made in good faith. 36 Comp. Gen. 441 (1956); *Murphy Brothers, Inc.—Reconsideration*, 58 Comp. Gen. 185 (1978), 78–2 CPD 440. If, therefore, the Government fails to meet this burden, we will find that acceptance of the bid does not consummate a valid and binding contract.

The authority to correct mistakes alleged after bid opening but prior to award has been delegated to the procuring agency and the weight to be given to the evidence in support of an alleged mistake is a question of fact to be considered by the administratively designated evaluator of evidence, whose decision will not be disturbed by this Office unless there is no reasonable basis for the decision. *John Amentas Decorators, Inc.*, B–190691, April 17, 1978, 78–1 CPD 294.

In the present case, the Navy has not processed the alleged mistake in accordance with the applicable regulations. We note that ASPR/DAR § 2–406.3(e)(1) provides that where a mistake in bid is alleged prior to award, the contracting officer is to advise the bidder to make a written request, supported by pertinent documents, indicating its desire to either modify or withdraw the bid. In this connection, the above regulation provides:

* * * The request must be supported by statements (sworn statements if possible) concerning the alleged mistake and shall include all pertinent evidence such as bidder's file copy of the bid, the original worksheets and other data used in preparing the bid, subcontractor's quotations, if any, published price lists, and any other evidence which conclusively establishes the existence of the error, the manner in which it occurred, and the bid actually intended. ASPR/DAR § 2–406.3(e)(1).

The Navy, therefore, should first notify Jaybil that it must not only submit a written request indicating whether it wants to correct or withdraw its bid, but that it must also support such request with documents that show that the telegraphic modification was in fact sent by mistake. Upon receipt of Jaybil's documented request, the Navy should then process it in accordance with the appropriate regulations to determine whether the evidence supports correction or withdrawal.

By letter of today, we are informing the Secretary of the Navy of our recommendation.

Accordingly, the protest is sustained.

[B–193180]

Contracts — Specifications — Tests — First Article — Waiver Denied — Incumbent Contractor

Waiver of first article approval testing requirement is matter within the discretion of procuring agency and will not be questioned by General Accounting Office without showing that decision was arbitrary or capricious. Agency's decision not to waive first article approval testing for incumbent contactor is not arbitrary or capricious where solicitation contains a more stringent testing specification than previous year's contract and only vendor of essential ingredient in required item has had break in production that can reasonably be considered to have effect on manufacturing processes.

Contracts—Specifications—Tests—Waiver—Invitation Provision

Bidder's potential eligibility for waiver of first article testing does not preclude addition of evaluation factor for such testing, absent determination that waiver will be granted.

In the matter of BEI Electronics, Inc., March 23, 1979:

BEI Electronics, Inc., Defense Products Division (BEI), protests the proposed contract award to MB Associates (MBA) under invitation for bids (IFB) N00019–78–B–0006 for 50,000 MJU–8/B decoy flares issued by the Department of the Navy, Naval Air Systems Command (NAVAIR). BEI, the incumbent contractor, maintains that NAVAIR has improperly refused to waive first article preproduction testing for it. BEI argues that NAVAIR's actions are unreasonable and contrary to the solicitation. The solicitation provided that in the event NAVAIR elected to conduct first article approval testing, the bid would be evaluated by adding $12,485 to the bid price whereas no adjustment would be made to each bid qualifying for waiver. BEI would be the low evaluated bidder if first article testing were waived for it.

The solicitation was issued on June 21, 1978, and bid opening occurred on August 15, 1978. By letters dated October 11, 1978, the Navy requested that the bidders extend their bids because the Navy was still conducting an evaluation of the need for first article testing. BEI protested on October 12, 1978, objecting to NAVAIR's delay in awarding it the contract and requesting us to direct NAVAIR either to award it the contract or to cancel the solicitation and resolicit bids. Subsequently, NAVAIR determined that it would require first article testing for both BEI and MBA.

The material facts are not in dispute. BEI was the contractor under the prior year's contract for production of 4,000 MJU–8/B decoy flares. That contract required flares to be subjected to first article approval testing in accordance with Purchase Description AS–2627, Revision A, that examined, among other things, the flares' infrared static and air stream output. NAVAIR then twice revised the testing specification. Revision B increased the static and airstream output requirements. Revision C incorporated a longer wavelength spectra band in addition to the spectra band required in Revision B and increased the infrared output test grain sample size for first article approvals from twenty to fifty units.

According to NAVAIR, the changes to the testing specification were made after NAVAIR received complaints from the fleet that all decoy flares were not performing satisfactorily in actual use. NAVAIR also reports that it made an additional change to the Purchase Description, which is not apparent on the record because the change constituted classified information.

BEI's flares under the prior contract initially failed first article approval testing in May 1978 but passed the testing in August 1978 after BEI made certain adjustments in burning rate. BEI claims that as a result of these changes, the flares satisfy the requirements of both Revision A and the static and airstream requirements of Revision C. BEI delivered the 4,000 flares to NAVAIR on September 19, 1978; to date, NAVAIR reports, only 336 flares have been used.

On August 18, 1978, a fire and explosion occurred in the screening room of Hart Metals, one of BEI's suppliers and the only known producer of atomized magnesium, an important ingredient of decoy flares.

In October 1978, BEI received a purchase order for the manufacture of 200 MJU–8/B decoy flares. We have been advised that BEI delivered these items to the Navy testing facility at China Lake, California, on October 31, 1978, where they are being used for various missile testing.

On these facts, BEI alleges that the contracting officer's refusal to waive first article approval testing with respect to it in accordance with Section D–3 of the solicitation, "Waiver of First Article Approval," is improper because BEI was in production on the MJU–8/B decoy flare under the prior year's contract. BEI claims that NAVAIR's refusal to exercise waiver of first article approval testing for it constitutes an improper change in the IFB's evaluation scheme. BEI's argument is that as the only incumbent contractor providing the identical product to the Government, it was the only prospective contractor who could benefit from the waiver provision and thus reasonably anticipated NAVAIR would waive first article approval testing for it and priced its bid accordingly. BEI also claims NAVAIR improperly evaluated its bid because the language of Section D–3(c) of the solicitation gives it an absolute entitlement to have its bid evaluated without the addition of first article testing costs regardless of whether NAVAIR actually conducts the testing. Lastly, BEI claims that there is no reasonable basis for NAVAIR's refusing to waive first article approval testing for it because its flares made to the same manufacturing specification as would be required under this contract passed first article testing under the prior year's contract; that under that contract its flares passed production lot testing, and the 200 flares delivered to the China Lake facility have performed satisfactorily.

Section D–3 of the solicitation provides:

    *   *   *   *   *   *   *

(b) **Where supplies identical or similar to those called for in the Schedule have been previously furnished by offeror or quoter and have been accepted by the Government, the requirement for first article approval may be waived by the Government. * * ***

(c) If the Government determines that offeror or quoter is eligible to have the first article approval tests waived, the offer or quotation will be evaluated excluding first article approval. The Government reserves the right to make an award excluding first article approval. * * *

Defense Acquisition Regulation (DAR) Part 19 (1976 ed.) explains the purpose of first article testing and presents the factors to be considered by the procuring agency in determining whether first article testing is required. In particular, DAR 1–1902 provides:

(a) A requirement for first article approval is designed to assure that the contractor can furnish a product that is satisfactory for its intended use and, therefore, minimizes risks for both the contractor and the Government. In determining whether first article approval is to be required, consideration shall be given to increased cost and time of delivery by reason of the test, the risk to the Government of foregoing such tests, and the availability to the Government of other less costly methods of achieving the desired quality. First article approval tests are particularly appropriate when:

(1) the interest of the Government requires assurance that a product is satisfactory for its intended use when the product—

(A) has not been previously furnished by the contractor to the Government; or

(B) has been previoulsy furnished by the contractor to the Government but there have been subsequent changes in processes or specifications, or production has been discontinued for an extended period of time; or

(C) is described by a performance specification; * * *.

(b) Except in unusual procurements, first article approval tests shall not be required in contracts:

    *   *   *   *   *   *   *

(iv) For suplies covered by complete and detailed technical specifications, unless the technical or performance requirements are so novel or exacting that it cannot reasonably be anticipated that such supplies will meet the technical or performance requirements without first article approval. * * *

At the outset, we disagree that NAVAIR's refusal to waive first article approval testing constituted an improper change in the IFB evaluation scheme. While BEI implies that it relied on the presence of the waiver clause in the IFB to submit a higher bid than it would have had the IFB not contained the clause, in *Libby Welding Company, Inc.*, B–186395, February 25, 1977, 77–1 CPD 139, we explained this type of clause:

does no more than reserve to the Government the right to waive first article testing for any bidder found to be qualified for such a waiver. While prior acceptance by the Government of identical or similar supplies is a requirement for first article waiver, we do not believe that acceptance automatically requires the Government to waive first article testing * * *.

Our determination in *Libby Welding Company, supra,* was upheld in *Libby Welding Cb. v. United States,* 444 F. Supp. 987 (D.D.C. 1977). Thus, the mere presence of the clause, which clearly states that the requirement for first article approval *may* (but not will) be waived, conferred no special rights on BEI nor did it provide BEI with a reasonable basis to maximize its bid price in certain expectation that NAVAIR would exercise waiver. See *Met-Pro Water Treatment Corporation,* 54 Comp. Gen. 39, 43 (1974), 74–2 CPD 29. It follows that a bidder's *potential* eligibility for waiver does not preclude the addition of the state evaluation factor for first article testing absent a determination that the waiver in fact will be granted. Moreover, we do not believe NAVAIR departed from the stated evaluation scheme in the IFB. While it is true that DAR 1–1903(b) (1976 ed.) prohibits use of a waiver of first article approval testing clause when it is known that first article approval would be required of all bidders, the record clearly reveals NAVAIR did not decide against exercising waiver until October 17, 1978, over 2 months after bid opening. The record further shows that the contracting officer included the clause in the solicitation in June based on the possibility that BEI might qualify for waiver but that changes in the specification and disruption of a subcontractor's production led NAVAIR's technical personnel to recommend first article testing be conducted. Accordingly, the inclusion of the clause in the IFB for the purposes of bid evaluation was not improper.

With respect to BEI's contention that NAVAIR has no reasonable basis to refuse waiver of first article approval testing, we consider an agency's determination not to waive first article approval testing to be a matter of administrative discretion which will not be questioned by this Office unless there is a clear showing that the decision was arbitrary or capricious. See *Homexx International Corporation,* B–192034, September 22, 1978, 78–2 CPD 219. Here, while BEI has presented considerable evidence to demonstrate its eligibility for waiver of first article testing, we believe that NAVAIR's refusal to waive first article approval testing was a reasonable and proper exercise of administrative discretion.

The record indicates that BEI initially failed first article approval testing on the MJU–8/B decoy flare under the prior contract and, further, that decoy flare manufacturers consistently fail initial first article testing. NAVAIR explains that the failures are to be expected in light of the MJU–8/B flare manufacturing process which involves the mixing of atomized magnesium and other highly volatile pyrotechnic ingredients. In this regard, NAVAIR states that the IFB contains a functional specification and that it cannot reasonably be anticipated that the flares will meet the specification's requirements without first article approval:

> * * * the history of decoy flares has clearly shown that the difficulties which surface concerning decoy flares are not minor but would involve the "guts" of the flares, the IR output which relates to the burning of the flare. In fact, the mixing of the ingredients is an art and not a science. * * * It is impossible to describe in precise detail the exact percentage of each ingredient to be mixed. This is where the art of mixing becomes so important and makes the procurement of decoy flares unusual under ASPR 1–1903(b) because the "performance requirements are so novel or exacting * * *" (ASPR 1–1902(b)(iv).

Further, it is undisputed that NAVAIR changed the testing specification after the award of the prior contract to BEI. The increase in test samples from twenty to fifty grains without a corresponding change in the rejection criteria increased the possibility of rejection. However, even assuming that the twenty first article samples that were submitted by BEI for first article approval testing in the prior contract met Revision C's infrared and static output requirements, the critical point is that BEI's flares were never tested to the new and more stringent fifty sample test.

In this respect, BEI contends that the increase of thirty test samples is not significant because its flares have been accepted by NAVAIR after passing production lot testing and are, along with the 200 flares delivered to the Navy's China Lake facility, being used by NAVAIR. We are not convinced that these events alone require NAVAIR to waive first article approval testing. NAVAIR asserts that the fact that an item satisfies production lot testing does not necessarily mean it would pass first article approval testing, because first article testing in this instance is more extensive and stringent than production lot testing, and is done on a smaller quantity than production lot testing to let the Government know at the earliest time whether a contractor can furnish a product satisfactory for its intended use. In this situation the Government cannot wait until the first production lot has been completed and thus accept the risk of production lot testing failure.

Finally, NAVAIR reports that Hart Metals has not returned to regular production since it suffered the fire and explosion. NAVAIR states that it cannot be certain that Hart's atomized magnesium produced following this break in production will be of the same composition or quality as before. While it is true that DAR Part 19 does not directly address whether a supplier must be requalified in the event of a break in its production, it is not written so narrowly as to preclude NAVAIR from examining Hart's break in production in determining whether to waive first article approval. The purpose of this testing is to show at the earliest possible time that the contractor can produce a satisfactory product. Should a change or disruption occur that can reasonably be considered to have an effect on the manufacturing processes, the regulation states that first article approval tests are particularly appropriate. Since atomized magnesium produced by Hart following the disruption in its production will be used in decoy flares produced under the proposed contract, it is not inappropriate for NAVAIR to want to conduct tests as early as possible to determine if there is a problem with the flare's atomized magnesium or the mixing of their ingredients.

In summary, despite the fact that BEI had recently produced decoy flares that have passed production lot testing and some had actually been successfully used, we believe that NAVAIR did not act unreasonably in requiring first article approval testing. The regulation governing waiver of first article testing allows the procuring agency discretion in determining whether to exercise waiver but does suggest circumstances when first article approval tests are particularly appropriate. Three such circumstances are present here. The IFB contains a changed testing specification, making it more difficult for contractors to pass first article testing, the IFB uses a functional specification to describe the flare, and there has been a break in production of the only vendor of an essential ingredient which can reasonably be considered to have an adverse effect on the manufacturing process.

On the basis of the above, the protest is denied.

[B-127474]

Leaves of Absence — Holidays — Employees Receiving Premium Compensation

Department of the Navy asks if the intent of 56 Comp. Gen. 551 (1977) requires deduction of leave credited under 54 Comp. Gen. 662 (1975) but unused as of April 19, 1977, and whether related claims unresolved between the dates of the two decisions are valid. Such leave recredited prior to April 19, 1977, remains available for use. The determination in 56 Comp. Gen. 551 to forego collection action for lump-sum payments made for leave recredited, and not to require correction of leave records for recredited leave taken pursuant to 54 Comp. Gen. 662, did not validate all claims that arose or were presented for payment between the dates of the two decisions. Rather, it was to inform agencies that corrective action would not be required for actions allowing claims taken prior to April 19, 1977, pursuant to 54 Comp. Gen. 662.

In the matter of Holiday premium pay—Leaves of absence—Excused absence, March 27, 1979:

The Office of Civilian Personnel, Department of the Navy, seeks clarification regarding the application of 56 Comp. Gen. 551 (1977) which overruled the ruling in 54 Comp. Gen. 662 (1975). The 1975 decision held that certain employees receiving premium pay under 5 U.S.C. 5545(c)(1) should have leave restored to them which was charged to them for absences on holidays. In the 1977 decision we held that an employee in receipt of annual premium pay under 5 U.S.C. 5545(c)(1) (1970) at a rate determined in accordance with 5 C.F.R. 550.144(a) who performed work on holidays or was charged annual leave for holidays falling within his regularly scheduled tour of duty is not entitled to holiday premium pay or restoration of annual leave charged. Such employee may be excused without charge to leave if his agency determines his services are not required on a particular holiday.

Specifically, we have been asked the following questions:

(1) Is any leave recredited under 54 Comp. Gen. 662 which remained to an employee's account on 19 April 1977 to be deducted as of that date?

(2) If the answer to question (1) above is in the negative, is all leave recredited based on 54 Comp. Gen. 662 to remain for credit and use, irrespective of 56 Comp. Gen. 551?

(3) For those employees whose leave accounts were not adjusted in accordance with 54 Comp. Gen. 662 prior to 19 April 1977, does there exist any legal basis to now credit their leave accounts?

Although the situation in question (1) was not addressed in 56 Comp. Gen. 551, there was no intent that such leave be deducted effective April 19, 1977. On the contrary such leave remains for credit and use. Questions (1) and (2) are answered accordingly.

With regard to claims paid pursuant to the decision in 54 Comp. Gen. 662 (1975), we stated in 56 Comp. Gen. 551 (1977):

* * * Since such payments or use of leave were made pursuant to 54 Comp. Gen. 662, no action is necessary and the employees may be considered properly to have been paid or to have taken leave. Also, inasmuch as there has been considerable confusion in this area, those employees who were not charged leave for absences on holidays *prior to the date* of this decision may be regarded as having properly been excused from duty on such days. [Italic supplied.]

The above determination did not validate all claims that arose or were presented for payment between the dates of the two decisions, February 5, 1975, and April 19, 1977. Rather, it was meant to inform agencies which had relied upon the 1975 decision and had recredited leave and made lump-sum payment on claims or authorized leave to be taken, that recovery of money paid or correction of leave records would not be required. See B-192815, February 26, 1979. The decision of February 26, 1979, suggests that leave restored under 54 Comp. Gen. 662 would remain available for use after April 19, 1977, the effective date of 56 Comp. Gen. 551.

Thus, if an employee's claim was allowed and leave restored prior to April 19, 1977, no action is to be taken by the agency to correct leave records. However, if the leave was not recredited prior to April 19, 1977, neither the decision in 54 Comp. Gen. 662, nor the decision in 56 Comp. Gen. 551, provides authority for recredit of leave thereafter.

Accordingly, question three is answered in the negative.

[B-193352]

Compensation — Overtime — Work in Excess of Daily and/or Weekly Limitations

Army hospital has two work shifts: 0500–1330 and 1100–1930. Employees on 1100–1930 shift, who periodically work regular shift 1 day and 0500–1330 shift next day, claim overtime compensation for work in excess of 8 hours. Definition of "day" for purposes of overtime compensation is not limited to calendar day but may be any 24-hour period. See 42 Comp. Gen. 195 (1962). Thus, since Army agreed through negotiated agreement to treat workday as 24-hour period from start of shift, employees who work more than 8 hours during 24-hour period but not on same calendar day are entitled to overtime compensation.

In the matter of Council and Washburn — Entitlement to Overtime Pay, March 27, 1979:

This action is in response to a request for an advance decision from Lieutenant Colonel D. I. Walter, Finance and Accounting Officer, Headquarters XVIII Airborne Corps and Fort Bragg, Department of the Army, Fort Bragg, North Carolina, concerning a number of backpay claims for overtime submitted by both Wage Board and General Schedule employees (and former employees) of the Food Service Division, Womack Army Hospital, MEDDAC, Fort Bragg, North Carolina. The issue presented for decision is the entitlement to overtime pay of these employees who frequently worked two 8-hour shifts within a 24-hour period but not within the same calendar day.

The report from the Army states that over a period of several years the Food Service Division scheduled its employees to an "early/late" tour of duty involving two overlapping shifts, 0500 to 1330 and 1100 to 1930 daily. The report states further that approximately four times per pay period, employees who worked the 1100 to 1930 shift one day would work the 0500 to 1330 shift the following day. The Army forwarded to our Office two claims which are apparently representative of other claims it has received. The claim of Richard Council has been computed by the Army for the period from 1971 to 1976 at an average of 25 hours of overtime per pay period, while the claim of Betty L. Washburn has been computed for the period from 1971 to 1976 at generally between 20 and 25 hours of overtime per pay period.

The overtime claims of the employees are based upon a provision in the contract agreements between Headquarters XVIII Airborne Corps and Fort Bragg and AFGE Local 1770 which have been in effect without material change since 1971 and which provide, in pertinent part, as follows:

> No employee in the unit shall be required to work more than eight (8) hours in his basic workday without compensating such at the existing compensatory time off rate or overtime rate of pay for all hours worked in excess of eight (8) hours. *For purposes of this section, the basic work day is considered to be elapsed 24 hours from the starting time of his shift;* however, this does not apply to 24-hour shift employees who voluntarily and mutually exchange or split shifts with approval of their supervisor. [Italic supplied.]

The report from the Army states that applying the above-quoted language literally would result in 6 hours overtime entitlement for a Food Service Division employee on the second day, but the Army questions the validity of these back pay claims in view of regulations contained in the Federal Personnel Manual and our decision in 42 Comp. Gen. 195 (1962). The report concludes by posing two questions: (1) is there any overtime entitlement when an agency follows a 5 workday, Sunday to Saturday, midnight to midnight scheduling and an employee does not work more than 8 hours in a day or 40 hours in a week; and (2) does our decision in 42 *id.* 195, *supra*, or any law or regulation concerning the use of a calendar day or a Sunday through Saturday workweek override a locally negotiated contract provision which appears to the contrary.

With regard to overtime entitlement, 5 U.S.C. § 5542(a) (1976) provides, in pertinent part, as follows:

> For full-time, part-time and intermittent tours of duty, hours of work officially ordered or approved in excess of 40 hours in an administrative workweek, or * * * in excess of 8 hours in a day, performed by an employee are overtime work * * *.

The above-quoted section is applicable to General Schedule employees, and Wage Board employees are covered under a substantially similar provision contained in 5 U.S.C. § 5544 (1976). The law concerning the scheduling of hours of work and basic workweeks is contained in 5 U.S.C. § 6101 (1976), which provides, in pertinent part, as follows:

> (a)(2) The head of each Executive agency, military department, and of the government of the District of Columbia shall—
> (A) establish a basic administrative workweek of 40 hours for each full-time employee in his organization; and
> (B) require that the hours of work within that workweek be performed within a period of not more than 6 of any 7 consecutive days.
> (a)(3) Except when the head of an Executive agency, a military department, or of the government of the District of Columbia determines that his organization would be seriously handicapped in carrying out its functions or that costs would be substantially increased, he shall provide, with respect to each employee in his organization, that—
> (A) assignments to tours of duty are scheduled in advance over periods of not less than 1 week;

(B) the basic 40-hour workweek is scheduled on 5 days, Monday through Friday when possible, and the 2 days outside the basic workweek are consecutive;
(C) the working hours in each day in the basic workweek are the same;
(D) the basic nonovertime workday may not exceed 8 hours;
(E) the occurrence of holidays may not affect the designation of the basic workweek; and
(F) breaks in working hours of more than 1 hour may not be scheduled in a basic workday.

In our decision in 42 Comp. Gen. 195, *supra*, we considered the question of whether the 8-hour day and the 40-hour week are defined as a calendar day (midnight to midnight) and a calendar week (Sunday through Saturday). We held that, since there may be problems involving employees with uncommon tours of duty which create the need for flexibility, any 24-hour period may be treated as a "day" and any consecutive 7 day period may be treated as a "week" although *when administratively feasible* the Sunday through Saturday week and the midnight to midnight day should be used. 42 *id.* 195, at 200. Subsequently, we held in 57 Comp. Gen. 101 (1977) that our Office would have no objection to the Department of Agriculture adopting a 24-hour period other than midnight to midnight as a "day" where the administrative workweek involved two shifts within the same calendar day.

In the present case we believe that where the agency has adopted the definition of a "day" as set forth in the negotiated agreement cited above, employees who work more than 8 hours in a "day" are entitled to overtime compensation even though not more than 8 hours of work are performed in any 1 calendar day. See 57 Comp. Gen. 101, *supra;* and 42 *id.* 195, *supra.*

The Army has also asked whether there is any law or regulation concerning the definition of a "day" or "workweek" which would override the negotiated agreement provision cited above. We have reviewed the applicable laws and regulations and we find nothing which would preclude the Army from adopting the definition of a "day" as set forth above. Furthermore, under the provisions of sections 6101 and 5542(a) of title 5, United States Code, the agency has the authority to establish work schedules and order and approve overtime. Through the negotiated agreement, it appears that the agency exercised its statutory authority by defining a workday as the 24-hour period beginning with the employee's shift and, in effect, authorizing overtime work where the employee worked more than 8 hours during a 24-hour period. See, for example, 55 Comp. Gen. 405 (1975).

Accordingly, we conclude that the Food Service Division employees are entitled to overtime compensation for work in excess of 8 hours during a "day" as defined in the negotiated agreement.

[B-193861]

Federal Judicial Center — Contracts — Competitive Negotiation Where Practicable Requirement

Although Federal Judicial Center (FJC) is exempt from 41 U.S.C. 5 (1976) and civilian agency procurement statutes do not apply to FJC, examination of FJC's enabling legislation shows Congress' intent that FJC enter into contracts by "negotiation." Further, maximum practicable competition should be obtained as matter of sound Federal procurement whenever contracts utilizing appropriated funds are to be awarded. Therefore, FJC should award contracts by using competitive negotiation where practicable.

Equipment — Automatic Data Processing Systems — Acquisition, etc. — Brooks Act Applicability — Federal Judicial Center Procurements

Federal Judicial Center (FJC), as establishment in judicial branch, is "Federal agency" as term is used in Brooks Act, 40 U.S.C. 759 (1976). Since no law expressly exempts FJC from Brooks Act, FJC must comply with Brooks Act and General Services Administration's implementing regulations in all automatic data processing equipment procurements.

In the matter of Federal Judicial Center, March 27, 1979:

This decision results from our current survey of the Federal Judicial Center's (FJC) activities. Incident to the survey, a question arose on (1) whether the FJC is exempt from Public Law No. 89–306, the Brooks Act, and (2) whether the FJC must procure ADP equipment and services in compliance with the Federal Procurement Regulations and competitive procurement statutes.

In sum, the FJC maintains that it is exempt from the requirements of the Brooks Act because (1) the legislative history of 28 U.S.C. § 620(a) (1976)—establishing the FJC—shows Congress' intent that the FJC be exempt from the Brooks Act, (2) the goal of the Speedy Trial Act of 1974, 18 U.S.C. § 3161–74 (1976), can only be realized if the FJC is free from the time delays of the General Services Administration (GSA) regulations concerning ADP equipment procurement, and (3) when the FJC's claim of exemption was placed before the GAO in a bid protest, the GAO did not express disagreement with that claim. The FJC's detailed rationale, our legal analysis, and our conclusion are presented below.

I. BACKGROUND

The FJC's purpose is "to further the development and adoption of improved judicial administration in the courts of the United States." 28 U.S.C. § 620(a) (1976). The FJC was established as a research and development organization with the general functions of supporting the Federal judiciary through independent research, education and training of judicial and parajudicial personnel, and the application of innovative technology to court management. 28 U.S.C. §§ 620 (b)(1)–(4), 623(a)(5) (1976).

In addition, Congress established a seven-man board of directors, permanently chaired by the Chief Justice of the Supreme Court, and Congress directed that proposals be evaluated for possible application of data processing and system techniques to the administration of the Federal courts. 28 U.S.C. § 623(a)(5). The reason for the mandate appears in the legislative history:

> The computer revolution, sweeping the financial and industrial enterprises of our Nation, has thus far made little headway in the courts. Claims of unprecedented efficiency for the courts in the age of the computer, on the one hand, and fears of "mechanized justice" and "trial by computer," on the other, have been voiced in various circles, but it is apparent to your committee that an objective evaluation of the potential of data processing systems in the work of the courts is a necessity. By its very nature as a center for the study of court administration, the Federal Judicial Center is an appropriate medium for such an evaluation. S. Rep. No. 781, 90th Cong., 1st Sess. at 2416.

In light of this mandate, the FJC developed a comprehensive local court management information and research system and purchased two minicomputers to conduct pilot projects in two district courts. In fiscal year 1974, the minicomputer specifications were approved by GSA and the FJC was advised to proceed with solicitation of bids based on these specifications. Once the responses were received and a vendor selected, award was made independent of GSA but with GSA's full approval. Since then, the FJC has made sole-source ADP awards without GSA involvement.

II. THE FJC'S POSITION ON EXEMPTION FROM THE BROOKS ACT AND COMPETITIVE PROCUREMENT REQUIREMENTS

A. The FJC was given specific statutory exemption from 41 U.S.C. § 5 (1976), which requires that a Government agency, including one in the judicial branch, must obtain needed supplies and services by means of formal advertising:

> The Board is authorized—
> (3) to contract with and compensate government and private agencies for research projects and other services, without regard to section 3709 of the Revised Statutes, as amended (41 U.S.C. § 5), and to delegate such contract authority to the Director of the Federal Judicial Center, who is hereby empowered to exercise such delegated authority.

The Senate report on this section states:

> It is contemplated that much of the research and analysis stimulated by the Center will be conducted by independent contractors, providing services on either a voluntary or a for-profit basis. The nature of these services will be varied and often custom tailored to the needs of the Center. *To require that the Center employ the methods of advertising, bidding, and acceptance promulgated for Government contracts generally might mean impairment of the Cen-*

ter's ability to negotiate effectively for the services it needs. In many instances, is may be that few or no enterprises exist that are capable of meeting the Center's requirements without detailed negotiation and special improvisation. S. Rep. No. 781, 90th Cong., 1st Sess. 2411. [Italic supplied.]

Although the FJC's enabling legislation does not specifically exempt it from GSA control over ADPE procurement, the FJC contends that such legislation should be read *in pari materia* with duties of FJC's Board and the Brooks Act.

Under traditional principles of statutory construction, in the FJC's view, the three statutory provisions should be read together and each provision should be construed in connection with every other provision so as to produce a harmonious whole. Since, in the FJC's view, both the Center's enabling legislation and the Brooks Act contain provisions that deal with the same subject matter (ADPE) and since the two provisions are in apparent conflict, the FJC argues that the ambiguity must be resolved in a manner which gives effect to the latest legislative expression and still leaves an area of effective operation for the earlier expression. *International Union of Elec. Radio and Mach. Workers, AFL–CIO* v. *NLRB*, 280 F. 2d 757 (D.C. Cir. 1960). The FJC states that although it very well may have been Congress' original intent to include every Federal agency within the scope of the Brooks Act, it must be remembered that the legislation creating the FJC was not passed until 1967, 2 years later. Given the legislative history of the FJC's statutory functions, the duties of its Board, and the grant of a statutory exemption from other procurement regulations, it is evident to the FJC that Congress has changed its position and exempted the FJC from the Brooks Act.

Moreover, in the FJC's view, its exemption from the Brooks Act would not frustrate the purpose of that act because once ADP is adapted for use in the Federal courts, the Administrative Office will assume general management and budgetary responsibilities for it. Then the Brooks Act would properly require GSA involvement in further computer procurement and maintenance. By this construction neither is emasculated.

The FJC also contends that there is ample legislative history showing Congress' strong desire that the FJC remain an independent organization in order to carry out its statutory responsibilities. By statute, the FJC is responsible only to Congress, the Judicial Conference of the United States and its Board of Directors. In the FJC's view, to require that another administrative agency control all ADPE, in effect and in practice, destroys the very independence that Congress so zealously provided.

B. The FJC further argues that the Speedy Trial Act of 1974, 18 U.S.C. § 3161–74 (1976), clearly recognizes the need for broad-based planning by each Federal district court to meet a 3-month criminal case processing goal and the FJC is required to play a substantial role in this planning process.

The FJC states that its computer-based local court information system (Courtran II) is the only system that has the capacity and potential to significantly assist the Federal judiciary in meeting the information-gathering, monitoring and research demands of the Speedy Trial Act, and thus is the only method by which the FJC can meet its statutory responsibilities under that act. Under the demands of the Speedy Trial Act, the FJC believed that some procurement of ADPE had to be completed immediately. Obviously, this could not have been completed if the FJC were bound to the time delays of GSA regulations concerning ADPE procurement.

Further, in 1975, the FJC advised the House Appropriations Committee of its view that it was exempt from the Brooks Act and that it would proceed with Courtran II without regard to the Brooks Act. At the same time, the FJC proposed that its appropriation bill be amended to specifically provide that the FJC was exempt from the Brooks Act. The FJC's proposal, however, was never introduced because, the FJC reports, the appropriate subcommittee chairman thought it unnecessary.

C. On July 30, 1975, a formal protest was filed with our Office. The FJC's award of a contract to the Digital Equipment Corporation for the majority of the computer equipment needed to support Courtran II development and subsequent pilot implementation. In responding to the protest, the FJC specifically raised the issue of exemption from the Brooks Act. The protestor withdrew the protest after receiving the FJC's response and our Office subsequently closed our file on the entire matter. The FJC states that although our Office did not expressly support the claim of exemption from the Brooks Act, this claim was squarely placed before GAO in our response to the protest and GAO did not in any way express disagreement with that claim.

D. In October 1976 the Administrative Office wrote to the GSA questioning an FJC contract with Bird Engineering Research Associates for software development and analysis relating to juror selection by the Federal courts. GSA responded stating, among other things, that the Brooks Act gave GSA exclusive authority to provide automated data processing equipment, including software, to Federal agencies, and expressed the opinion that the FJC contract was in violation of the GSA regulations and was not authorized.

In a very strongly worded reply to GSA, Judge Hoffman completely disagreed with GSA's conclusion and presented the FJC's claim of exemption.

Judge Hoffman requested that GSA contact him if, after reviewing his letter and attachments, any question remained concerning the exemption. GSA did not respond to Judge Hoffman's letter and the FJC proceeded with the Bird contract.

From this event, the FJC concludes that GSA concurs in its exemption claim.

III. ANALYSIS

A. *The FJC's Requirement to Procure Competitively.*

First, we note that the Administrative Office has the primary authority and duty to purchase equipment and supplies for the FJC. 28 U.S.C. § 604(a)(9) (1976). Second, we note that the Administrative Office would be required to comply with the requirements of competitive procurement in general since the Administrative Office is not exempt from the provisions of 41 U.S.C. § 5 (1976), the statute requiring competition in Government procurements. 5 Comp. Gen. 717 (1926). Third, we note that (1) the FJC has limited procurement authority for "research projects and other services," and (2) Congress expressly exempted the FJC from the provisions of 41 U.S.C. § 5. 28 U.S.C. § 624 (1976). Some research projects could necessitate utilizing ADP equipment or services which would be considered a part of the research project. To the extent that the ADP equipment is part of the research project, FJC should procure subject to the Brooks Act and implementing regulations. See "The Applicability of the Brooks Act, etc.," *infra.*

Regarding "research projects," the question arises as to whether the FJC's practice of purchasing and installing equipment in the Federal district courts would be considered a research project. Unquestionably, the FJC's first attempt to solve a problem at the Federal district court level could be considered a research project. It seems obvious that the application of the pilot solution to the same problem at other Federal district courts would not be considered a research project. Of course, the facts will determine whether a problem in one court is so substantially similar to a problem in another court that it is the same problem. Since the FJC's independent procurement authority is limited to research projects and other services, it would appear that the Administrative Office would be the procurement agency for equipment to be installed in nonpilot-project courts.

From the language of the referenced statutes, it could be concluded that in the FJC's direct procurements, the FJC could award contracts without competition. Note that the general statutes applicable to civilian agency procurements refer only to GSA and other executive agencies and, thus, would not be applicable to a judicial agency. 41 U.S.C.

§ 251–260 (1976); *CSA Reporting Corporation*, 54 Comp. Gen. 645 (1975), 75–1 CPD 70. The legislative history of the FJC's exemption from 41 U.S.C. § 5 clearly shows Congress' intent that the FJC be exempt from the requirements of formal advertising so that the FJC could enter into contracts by "negotiation." S. Rep. No. 781, *supra*, at 2411. However, in our judgment, the maximum practicable competition should, as a matter of policy, be obtained whenever contracts utilizing appropriated funds are to be awarded. See 51 Comp. Gen. 57, 61 (1971), involving the Atomic Energy Commission, which was similarly exempt from the requirements of 41 U.S.C. § 5. We recognize that in many instances the practicalities of the situation may impose severe limits on the amount of competition obtainable. *Id.* Consequently, it is our view that the FJC's award of a contract without competitive negotiation, where practicable, would be violative of sound Federal procurement policy.

B. *The Applicability of the Brooks Act to ADP Procurements by or for the FJC.*

Our decision at 55 Comp. Gen. 1497 (1976) held that the Brooks Act authorized GSA to procure ADP equipment for the Administrative Office or to delegate its ADP procurement authority to that Office. The rationale for our conclusion in 55 Comp. Gen. 1497 was simply this: (1) 40 U.S.C. § 759(a) authorizes and directs GSA to coordinate and provide for the purchase, lease and maintenance of ADP equipment by "Federal agencies"; and (2) the term "Federal agency" is defined in 40 U.S.C. § 472(b) to include any establishment in the judicial branch of the Government.

Since the Administrative Office and the FJC are establishments in the judicial branch, both would fall within the literal coverage of the Brooks Act, GSA's implementing regulations (41 C.F.R. part 101–36), and the scope of our decision at 55 Comp. Gen. 1497, *supra.*

Accordingly, ADP procurements by or for the FJC must be in accord with the Brooks Act and GSA's implementing regulations. We note that it is not uncommon for GSA to issue a delegation of procurement authority conditioned in part on the requirement that the procuring agency conduct a competitive procurement. We would suggest that in the future GSA so condition any delegation of procurement authority to FJC. Moreover, such a conditional delegation would be consistent with the Brooks Act because Congress contemplated that GSA would actually make the necessary ADP purchases for Federal agencies and GSA is governed by the competitive procurement regulations.

We reach the above conclusion after thorough analysis and consideration of the FJC's position. With regard to the FJC's first basis for the exemption claim—the statutory construction of the Brooks Act and its enabling legislation—we note that the basis for the FJC's position is that the two laws conflict. We find no conflict in the laws since the Brooks Act unquestionably covers all judicial branch agencies and no law specifically or expressly exempts the FJC from that coverage. Further, no passage of the FJC enabling act's legislative history shows congressional intent to exempt the FJC from the Brooks Act. Accordingly, the principles of statutory construction relied on by the FJC are not applicable.

On the other hand, we refer to another well-recognized principle of statutory construction overlooked by the FJC: the legislative history of a statute may be considered in determining the intention of Congress only (1) when the language of the statute is not clear, or (2) when its literal application would produce an absurd result. See *LTV Aerospace Corporation*, 55 Comp. Gen. 307, 317 (1975), 75–2 CPD 203, and the cases and decisions cited therein. Here, the language of the Brooks Act is literally broad enough to encompass the FJC and the FJC admits that its enabling legislation does not expressly exempt it from the Brooks Act. Moreover, we have reviewed the legislative history involved and we can find no support for the FJC's view. Further, a construction of the statutes including the FJC within Brooks Act coverage would be in accord with Congress' intent and would not produce an unreasonable burden on the FJC. We arrive at the latter conclusion after due consideration of the important and pressing work of the FJC relative to other Federal agencies and their programmatic ADP needs which must be satisfied in compliance with the Brooks Act. We also note that the congressional list of agencies exempt from requirements applicable to "Federal agencies" has been amended twice since the passage of the FJC's enabling legislation and Congress did not exempt the FJC. 40 U.S.C. § 474 (1976).

With regard to the FJC's second basis for exemption—Speedy Trial Act "demands"—the FJC cannot point to a single passage in that act or its legislative history exempting it from the Brooks Act. We note that the requirements of the Speedy Trial Act were to be met on a phase-in schedule over more than 4 years. In other urgent programs of national importance, agencies have complied with the Brooks Act and implementing regulations. See, e.g., *PRC Computer Center, Inc., et al.*, 55 Comp. Gen. 62 (1975), 75–2 CPD 35 (the Federal Energy Administration (FEA) procurement of ADP services for use in combating the "energy crisis" was subject to the Brooks Act). Therefore, in our view, Speedy Trial Act demands do not provide any support for the FJC's exemption claim. Further, the fact that a House Appropriations Subcommittee took no action on the FJC's proposal—

to amend its 1975 supplemental appropriations bill to specifically exempt the FJC from the Brooks Act—does not support the FJC's position. First, that fact does not overcome the Brooks Act's clear and unambiguous language encompassing the FJC. Second, where Congress is requested to revise existing law and no action is taken, a valid inference could be drawn that Congress did not intend to exempt the FJC from the Brooks Act. See *Wage rate coverage of offsite work under Federal-Aid Highway Act of 1956, as amended*, B–185020, December 28, 1978, 78–2 CPD 439.

Regarding the FJC's third basis for exemption—our handling of an FJC bid protest—when a protester withdraws its protest and requests that we close our file (B–194650) on the matter, that is precisely what we do. Our action is not a decision on the merits of the protest and usually the agency is so advised. Here, we closed the file at the protester's request without any consideration of the protest's merits. Similarly, we do not regard the FJC's fourth basis for exemption—GSA's failure to rebut the FJC's claim—as supportive of the exemption claim. GSA's views of record contain its conclusion that the FJC is covered by the Brooks Act.

C. *The Effect of the FJC's Past Noncompliance.*

In view of the circumstances of the FJC's past ADP procurements and its firm belief that it was exempt from the Brooks Act, we do not question the validity of such contracts. See *PRC Computer Center, Inc., supra* (FEA relied on GSA's authorization to proceed with an ADP procurement); B–115369, May 31, 1978 (the Department of Transportation relied on the Office of Management and Budget's authorization to proceed with an ADP procurement).

IV. CONCLUSION

Future FJC ADP procurements must be in compliance with the Brooks Act and GSA regulations and all future FJC procurements should be competitively negotiated, where practicable.

By letter of today, we are advising the Director of the FJC and the Administrator of GSA of our recommendation.

This decision contains a recommendation for corrective action to be taken. Therefore, we are furnishing copies to the Senate Committees on Governmental Affairs and Appropriations and the House Committees on Government Operations and Appropriations in accordance with section 236 of the Legislative Reorganization Act of 1970, 31 U.S.C. § 1176 (1976), which requires the submission of written statements by the agency to the committees concerning the action taken with respect to our recommendation.

[B-193710]

Appropriations—Typographical Errors—Enrolled Act Controlling

Public Law 95–480 appropriates $36,606,000 for the Office of Inspector General, Department of Health, Education, and Welfare, despite convincing evidence in legislative history showing that each House of Congress passed bill appropriating $1,000,000 less and that figure in enrolled bill was the result of typographical error. Enrolled act, signed by the Speaker of the House of Representatives and the President of the Senate, and approved by the President of the United States, is conclusive evidence of the contents of a law passed by Congress.

In the matter of HEW Office of Inspector General — Amount of Appropriation, March 28, 1979:

This decision is in reply to an inquiry from the Assistant Director, Accounting Operations, Bureau of Government Financial Operations, Department of the Treasury, concerning the actual amount appropriated to the Office of the Inspector General (Inspector General), Department of Health, Education, and Welfare (HEW), by the Departments of Labor and Health, Education, and Welfare Appropriations Act, 1979. The act, as passed by the House of Representatives and the Senate (H.R. 12929, 95th Cong.), contained an appropriation of $35,606,000 for the HEW Inspector General. However, the enrolled act (Public Law 95–480), signed by the Speaker of the House of Representatives and the President of the Senate, and approved by the President of the United States, appropriated $36,606,000 for the same office. The question is whether the Department of the Treasury has the legal authority to transfer to the account of the Inspector General $36,606,000, as contained in the enrolled act instead of $35,606,000, contained in the act as it passed the two Houses of Congress. For the reasons given in this decision, we hold that the higher amount is the actual sum appropriated.

In response to our request for the views of the Secretary of Health, Education, and Welfare, we received a reply from the HEW Acting Assistant Secretary for Management and Budget, which stated, in part:

In answer to your letter of December 29, 1978, the $36,606,000 included for the Inspector General in the enrolled bill is in error. A typographical error was made in preparing the enrolled bill. The correct number is $35,606,000 which was both our FY 1979 request and the amount allowed by the House and Senate Labor-Health, Education, and Welfare Subcommittees. This amount is clear from the legislative history including the reports of the House and Senate Appropriations Committees, the Conference Report, and the printed copies of the bill as it moved through both Houses. The only place where the higher number appears is the enrolled bill.

The Labor-HEW appropriations bill for fiscal year 1979, H.R. 12929, was reported from the House Committee on Appropriations on June 1, 1978. The bill contained an appropriation of $35,606,000 for the HEW Inspector General. In the accompanying report the committee stated:

The bill includes $35,606,000, the amount requested and an increase of $8,876,000 over the amount available for 1978. * * * (H.R. Rept. No. 95–1248, 95th Cong., 2nd Sess. 98 (1978).)

H.R. 12929 was passed by the House of Representatives on June 13, 1978, still containing an appropriation of $35,606,000, for the HEW Inspector General.

The bill was reported from the Senate Committee on Appropriations on August 16, 1978. It too contained an appropriation of $35,606,-000 for the Inspector General. In reporting the bill, the committee stated:

The Committee recommends an appropriation of $35,606,000, an increase of $8,876,000 over the comparable fiscal year 1978 level. This is the same as the President's budget and the House allowance. (S. Rept. No. 95–1119, 95th Cong., 2nd Sess. 132 (1978).)

On September 27, 1978, the Senate passed H.R. 12929 containing an appropriation of $35,606,000 for the HEW Inspector General.

The House and Senate versions of H.R. 12929 were not in agreement on matters other than the amount of the appropriation and the bill was referred to a conference committee. The conference committee report of October 6, 1978, was agreed to by each House on October 12, leaving disagreement on only one Senate amendment, not here pertinent. In the Congressional Record of October 12. 1978, two tables were printed, showing the appropriations contained in H.R. 12929 as agreed to by the conferees. Each table indicated an appropriation of $35,606,-000 for the HEW Inspector General. *See* 124 Cong. Rec. S18433, H.12483 (Daily ed. October 12, 1978). On October 14, 1978, the House agreed to a reworded Senate amendment resulting in final passage of the bill.

Although it is not entirely clear from the record, it appears that in enrolling H.R. 12929, a typographical error was made and the appropriation for the HEW Inspector General was increased to $36,606,000. The Speaker of the House and the President of the Senate did not notice the error and signed the enrolled bill. The enrolled bill was approved by the President of the United States on October 18, 1978, who apparently also did not notice the error, and the enrolled bill became Public Law 95–480.

This situation does not arise frequently but there are some decisions of the Attorney General, the Comptroller General, and the Supreme Court of the United States which are pertinent. The Attorney General decision involved an appropriation act which directed the Secretary of the Treasury to pay funds to one R. W. Thompson as provided for in an agreement with the Menominee Indians. The Indians objected to the payment, claiming that the act as it passed Congress contained a proviso, not contained in the enrolled act, which would have allowed them to veto the payment. The Attorney General decided against the Indian claim and instructed the Secretary of the Treasury to pay Thompson. In his decision, the Attorney General stated:

We cannot go behind the written law itself for the purpose of ascertaining what the law is. An act of Congress examined and compared by the proper officers, approved by the President, and enrolled in the Department of State, cannot afterwards be impugned by evidence to alter and contradict it. It imports the absolute verity of a record, at least in so far that no extrinsic proof can be received to erase one thing from it or to interpolate another into it. If there be an apparent conflict between the journals and the law as finally approved and enrolled, the journals have no claim to superior authenticity. (9 Op. Att. Gen. 1, 3 (1857).)

The Supreme Court decision involved the application of a tariff act. Several importers claimed that the act could not be enforced against them because the enrolled act did not contain an entire section contained in the act as passed by the Congress and was thus not a law of the United States. The Supreme Court rejected this contention. In the Court's words:

The signing by the Speaker of the House of Representatives, and by the President of the Senate, in open session, of an enrolled bill, is an official attestation by the two houses of such bill as one that has passed Congress. It is a declaration by the two houses, through their presiding officers, to the President, that a bill, thus attested, has received, in due form, the sanction of the legislative branch of the government, and that it is delivered to him in obedience to the constitutional requirement that all bills which pass Congress shall be presented to him. And when the bill, thus attested, receives his approval, and is deposited in the public archives, its authentication as a bill that has passed Congress should be deemed complete and unimpeachable. As the President has no authority to approve a bill not passed by Congress, an enrolled act in the custody of the Secretary of State, and having the official attestations of the Speaker of the House of Representatives, of the President of the Senate, and of the President of the United States, carries, on its face a solemn assurance by the legislative and executive departments of the government, charged, respectively, with the duty of enacting and executing the laws, that it was passed by Congress. * * * (*Field* v. *Clark*, 143 U.S. 649, 672 (1892).)

The Court went on to conclude:

We are of opinion for the reasons stated, that it is not competent for the appellants to show, from the journals of either house, from the reports of committees or from other documents printed by authority of Congress, that the enrolled bill designated H.R. 9416, as finally passed, contained a section that does not appear in the enrolled act in the custody of the State Department. (*Id.* at 680.)

Public Law 95–480, Signed by the Speaker of the House of Representatives and the President of the Senate, and approved by the President of the United States, appropriates:

For expenses necessary for the Office of the Inspector General, $36,606,000 * * *.

Under *Field* v. *Clark*, and the 1857 Opinion of the Attorney General, the enrolled act, so signed and approved, is conclusive evidence of the law passed by Congress. Committee reports, the Congressional Record, or any other congressional printed material should not be used to show that the enrolled act differs from the act as passed by the Congress. Thus, we conclude that the Departments of Labor and Health, Education, and Welfare Appropriations Act, 1979, appropriated $36,606,000 to the HEW Inspector General.

This case differs significantly from previous decisions in which courts and this Office have looked to the whole statute or to the legislative history and have corrected obvious printing errors in acts of Congress. In *Fleming* v. *Salem Box Co.*, 38 F. Supp. 997 (D. Ore. 1940), and *Ronson Patents Corp.* v. *Sparklets Devices, Inc.*, 102 F. Supp. 123 (E.D. Mo. 1951), typographical errors in acts of Congress were apparent on the face of the statute. In each instance the court corrected the error in order to effectuate the true congressional intent.

In B–127507, December 10, 1962, we were faced with a statute authorizing the Department of Agriculture to purchase certain land for the Superior National Forest. One of the tracts to be purchased was described by the statute as section 12, Township 63 North, Range 14 West. The statute could not be executed as printed, however, because the designated section was already included within the national forest. Faced with this ambiguity, we examined the legislative history and discovered that Congress intended to authorize purchase of section "13" but this was erroneously printed as "12." We therefore interpreted the statute as authorizing purchase of section 13.

In another instance, referred to in an attachment to the Department of the Treasury inquiry, our General Counsel was faced with an Appropriation Act which appropriated money for the payment of claims and judgments as set forth in Senate Document 94–163, 94th Congress. An examination of that document revealed that it did not deal with claims and judgments. The statute as printed, therefore, could not be fulfilled. The legislative history indicated that Congress intended to refer to Senate Document 94–164, and that the reference to 94–163 resulted from a typographical error. Our General Counsel decided that the claims and judgments could be paid as if there was no error in the act.

In the present instance, the typographical error is not apparent on the face of the statute, nor is this an instance where compliance with the statute as printed is impossible. The appropriation of $36,606,000 for the HEW Inspector General is clear and unambiguous.

Although we decide that Public Law 95–480 appropriated the full $36,606,000 stated in the enrolled act, we believe that this appropriation resulted from a typographical error and was not intended by Congress. Accordingly, we are sending a copy of this decision to the House and Senate Appropriations Committees for whatever corrective legislation they may deem appropriate.

[B–189884]

Contracts — Negotiation — Cost, etc. Data — "Truth-In-Negotiation" — Exceptions to Cost or Pricing Data Requirement — Applicability to Fixed-Price Incentive Contracts

Plain language of Truth in Negotiations Act, legislative history of Act, regulatory implementation, and history of implementation all support application of adequate price competition exemption to requirement for submission of certified cost or pricing data to fixed-price incentive contracts. 46 Comp. Gen. 631 and 53 Comp. Gen. 5, overruled in part.

Contracts—Cost, etc. Data—Requirement to Furnish

Agency properly did not require proposed awardee to submit certified cost or pricing data since such data need not be submitted where price is based on adequate price competition. Adequate price competition was achieved where request for proposals permitted award to other than low-priced offeror, price was substantial evaluation factor (30 percent), price evaluation did not have effect of eliminating price as evaluation factor, two proposals were in competitive range, and Government made award to best technical proposal for the dollar.

Contracts—Protests—Conferences—Request Denied

Request for conference is denied, since Bid Protest Procedures do not explicitly provide for conference on reconsiderations of decisions, and matter can be resolved without conference.

In the matter of Serv-Air, Inc.—Reconsideration, March 29, 1979:

Serv-Air, Inc. (Serv-Air), has requested reconsideration of our decision in *Serv-Air, Inc.*, 57 Comp. Gen. 827 (1978), 78–2 CPD 223, which denied its protest of the award of a contract for the operation and maintenance of Vance Air Force Base, Oklahoma (Vance), to Northrop Worldwide Aircraft Services, Inc. (Northrop).

Original Decision and Grounds for Reconsideration

Serv-Air's grounds for protest were as follows:

1. The technical evaluation criteria were designed to give special weight to recent experience rather than the quality of services offered.

2. The system of price evaluation is inherently defective because it penalizes offerors for cost-saving techniques, regardless of the soundness of the techniques, by subtracting points from proposals whose target cost falls outside a predetermined range from the Government estimate.

3. The application of the price evaluation formula "leveled widely divergent" price proposals, thus eliminating price as an evaluation factor, and rendering the solicitation noncompetitive as to price.

4. In the absence of adequate price competition, the Department of the Air Force (Air Force) was required to obtain certified cost or pricing data, which it did not do.

5. The Air Force failed to disclose in the RFP or during negotiations preferences for specific methods employed by the incumbent to accomplish certain tasks, thus making equal technical competition impossible.

6. Oral discussions concerning both technical and price proposals should have been held, and, even if oral negotiations were not required, the written negotiations were so inadequate as to not constitute "meaningful discussions."

Serv-Air states that its request for reconsideration "is limited solely to the legal issue of whether the fixed price incentive contract awarded by the Air Force to * * * Northrop * * * was invalid because the Air Force did not obtain certified cost or pricing data in accordance with the Truth in Negotiations Act (10 U.S.C. § 2306(f) [1976])."

In our original decision, we held that the Air Force was not required to obtain certified cost or pricing data because adequate price competition was achieved in the procurement, and the Truth in Negotiations Act, 10 U.S.C. 2304(a), and Defense Acquisition Regulation (DAR) then Armed Services Procurement Regulation (ASPR) § 3–807.3(b) (1976 ed.) do not require the data where adequate price competition is achieved.

Serv-Air had made two basic arguments concerning the lack of adequate price competition. First, Serv-Air argued that because the request for proposals (RFP) stated that "lowest price will not necessarily receive the award," the requirement of DAR § 3–807.1(b)(1)(a)(iii) (1976 ed.), that adequate price competition exists only if award is to be made to the offeror submitting the "lowest evaluated price," could not be satisfied. Serv-Air also argued that price was totally eliminated as an evaluation factor, even though it was to be weighted 30 percent, because "widely divergent" price proposals were leveled and scored so near the maximum that "differences between them were lost."

We stated, quoting *Shapell Government Housing, Inc. and Goldrich and Kest, Inc.,* 55 Comp. Gen. 839, 848 (1976), 76–1 CPD 161, that "we believe the language 'lowest *evaluated* price' [italic supplied] should be defined to include all of the factors in the award evaluation." Therefore, adequate price competition can still exist where award will not be made to the offeror with the lowest price, so long as price is a substantial factor in the prescribed evaluation criteria and more than one offeror was in the competitive range.

Regarding Serv-Air's argument that price was eliminated as an evaluation factor because widely divergent proposals were leveled, we found that the greatest variation in any of the components of the two price proposals was approximately 5 percent, and that the proposals were therefore not widely divergent. We noted that the two price proposals were scored very closely, with Serv-Air receiving 270 points and Northrop receiving 276.6 points, out of a possible total of 300 points. While Serv-Air's proposal was slightly lower in price, Northrop received a higher rating for "cost realism" and was, therefore, rated slightly higher. We then stated that "[w]e see nothing improper in two closely priced proposals being scored closely in a price evaluation."

In conclusion, we found that the factors specified in DAR § 3–807.1(b)(1) were present here, that there was adequate price competition, and that the Air Force properly did not obtain certified cost or pricing data from Northrop.

Price Evaluation Formula

While Serv-Air has limited the request for reconsideration to one issue, it has made numerous specific arguments. As in the original decision, Serv-Air again attacks the reasonableness and validity of the stated evaluation criteria and their application. Serv-Air contends that the only incentive in the price evaluation was to estimate the Air Force's predetermined estimate and come as close to that estimate as possible, and that estimate was based on prior cost experience with Northrop. Serv-Air also argues that the determination that Northrops' price was more favorable to the Government, even though it was higher than Serv-Air's, is "incomprehensible."

Serv-Air further contends that the procurement penalized cost-saving proposals, and that low offered price was an irrelevant factor in the price evaluation method. According to Serv-Air, the Air Force had no basis for assuring that the Northrop price was fair and reasonable. Serv-Air concludes that "[t]he price evaluation procedure used by the Air Force is so inimical to competitive procurement that it should not be allowed to stand."

As we stated in our original decision, all arguments and allegations concerning the propriety of the evaluation criteria and their application were untimely. We looked only at the narrow question of whether price was eliminated as an evaluation factor in this procurement to resolve the adequate price competition issue. Serv-Air has not specified any errors of law or fact or presented any new facts or arguments concerning the timeliness of these matters. Therefore, we affirm our original determination that we would not consider the propriety and application of the evaluation scheme.

Application of the Adequate Price Competition Exemption to Fixed-Price-Incentive Contracts

In the original protest, concerning the absence of adequate price competition, Serv-Air mentioned in a footnote that " '[a]dequate price competition' does not normally exist where an incentive contract is involved. *Televiso Electronics, Inc.*, B–159922, 46 Comp. Gen. 631, 645 (1967)." Serv-Air did not, however, argue or develop the point, but rather went on to argue that the factors comprising adequate price competition were not present for the reasons discussed in the first section of this decision. Consequently, we did not specifically address this argument.

In the request for reconsideration, Serv-Air has now fully developed the argument. Serv-Air contends that the provisions of the Truth in Negotiations Act and DAR § 3–807.3(b), which permit exemptions from the general requirement for certified cost or pricing data, cannot be applied where an incentive contract is used. Serv-Air relies primarily on 46 Comp. Gen., *supra*, and 53 *id*. 5 (1973). Serv-Air has quoted the following from 46 Comp. Gen., *supra*, at 644–5:

> The legislative history of the statutory provision discloses that one of its primary purposes was to require full, complete, and accurate data and disclosure by both parties in pricing discussions of incentive contracts in particular, including fixed-price incentive contracts, and to require the contractor to certify to the cost figures in hand at the time of negotiation for target price. As stated in H. Rept. No. 1638, 87th Cong., 2d Sess., the provision does two things: "It requires by law a full disclosure in negotiations and its requires a readjustment of target prices, before final settlement and cost sharing, so that the incentive profit over the normal profit will be the product of the contractor's action in performance rather than artificial pricing in negotiations for target price."
>
> * * * * * * *
>
> While the first sentence of FPR 1–3.807.3(f) provides that cost or pricing data should not be requested when there is adequate price competition (see also ASPR 3–807.3(c) [now DAR § 3–807.3(a)], in *the light of the legislative history of the statute, which serves as the basis for the data requirements set forth in both ASPR 3–807.3 and FPR 1–3.807–3*, it is our opinion that FPR 1–3.807–3(f) *could not have been invoked to dispense with the requirement for cost or pricing data once it was decided that an incentive-type contract was to be awarded.* To apply such provision to justify failure to obtain such data in the case of an incentive contract such as involved here would be contrary to the intent of the statute * * *. [Italic supplied.]

The following is quoted by Serv-Air from 53 Comp. Gen., *supra*, at 8:

> "* * * award could not have been made prior to the submission of cost or pricing data * * * See 46 Comp. Gen. 631 (1967), wherein we held that a *finding of adequate price competition could not serve as a basis to dispense with the requirement for cost or pricing data where award of a fixed-price-incentive contract was contemplated.*" B–177847, 53 Comp. Gen. 5, 8 (1973). [Italic supplied.].

Our holding in 53 Comp. Gen., *supra*, appears to have been based solely on 46 Comp. Gen., *supra*, which, in turn, was based, in part, on an interpretation of the legislative history of the Truth in Negotiations Act. Despite the interpretation in the earlier decision, we feel it is unnecessary to resort to the legislative history of the act to resolve the question of whether the adequate price competition exemption applies to fixed-price-incentive (FPI) contracts. The clear language of the statute does not exclude FPI contracts from the adequate price competition exemption and provides, in pertinent part, that:

> (f) A prime contractor, or any subcontractor, shall be required to submit cost or pricing data under the circumstances listed below, and shall be required to certify that, to the best of his knowledge and belief, the cost or pricing data he submitted was accurate, complete and current—
> (1) Prior to the award of *any negotiated prime contract* under this title where the price is expected to exceed $100,000 * * * [Italic supplied.]
> *Provided*, That the requirements of this subsection need not be applied to contracts where the price negotiated is based on adequate price competition. * * *

Since 46 Comp. Gen., *supra*, did rely on legislative history, however, we have reexamined the legislative history of the act. We are unable to find support for the proposition that application of the adequate price competition exemption to FPI contracts is contrary to the intent of the act.

While abuses in incentive contracting did provide the original impetus behind the act, as asserted by Serv-Air, these abuses were primarily in the area of *noncompetitive* procurements. See, generally, Senate Report No. 1884, 87th Cong., 2d Sess., p. 3. The classic situation concerning the advocates of the act was where the Government and a large firm negotiated target costs on a one-to-one basis, with the firm knowing its true costs and the Government having no such knowledge. See, e.g., Roback, *Truth in Negotiating: The Legislative Background of P.L. 87-653*, 1 Pub. Cont. L. J. 3, 7–8 (1968). In such cases, where the pressures of competition were not present to ensure fair and reasonable prices, the Government needed protection.

The only portion of legislative history specifically cited in 46 Comp. Gen., *supra*, is H. Rept. No. 1628, 87th Cong., 2d Sess. The "provision" it refers to is H.R. 5532 § (g), the first version of the bill, which applied only to incentive contracts, and contained no exemptions from the requirement for certified data. It is our opinion that such legislative history does not support the view that the exemptions of the act do not apply to all contracts, including incentive contracts.

The Senate version of the bill, which was enacted, extended the certified cost of pricing requirements equally to all forms of negotiated contracts. The exemption for adequate price competition was also added, and there is no indication that it was not to apply to all forms of contracts. Clearly, if Congress had intended to single out incentive contracts for special treatment, it could have done so, particularly considering the House version which did so single out incentive contracts with no exemptions. We can only conclude that it was the intent of Congress to treat all types of contracts equally, both for the requirement for submission of certified cost or pricing data and for the exemptions to that requirement.

The requirements discussed above have been implemented by DAR § 3–807.3. Even though the act applies only to the Department of Defense, the National Aeronautics and Space Administration, and the Coast Guard, the Federal Procurement Regulations (FPR) have incorporated the requirements at FPR § 1–3.807–3. The present version of both DAR and FPR follows the statute in applying the requirement and exemptions equally to all types of negotiated contracts over $100,000. The histories of change in both ASPR and FPR indicate that a conscious decision was made to apply the requirements and exemptions equally to all forms of contracts.

The first version of ASPR § 3–807.3 implementing the act, issued in Defense Procurement Circular (DPC) No. 12, October 16, 1964, essentially required certified cost or pricing data without exemptions, when incentive contracts or anything other than a firm-fixed-price (FFP) contract was used, subject to waiver only in exceptional cases where the Secretary (or, in the case of a contract with a foreign government or agency thereof, the head of a procuring activity) authorizes such waiver and states in writing his reason for such determination. The version of FPR § 1–3.807–3 in existence at that time was similar in substance.

On November 30, 1967 (DPC #57), the ASPR provision was revised to substantially its present form, treating all types of contracts equally and applying exemption to all. The provision provided that:

3–807.3 *Cost or Pricing Data.*

(a) The contracting officer shall require the contractor to submit, either actually or by specific identification in writing, cost or pricing data in accordance with 16–206 and to certify, by use of the certificate set forth in 3–807.4, that, to the best of his knowledge and belief, the cost or pricing data he submitted was accurate, complete, and current prior to:

(i) the award of any negotiated contract expected to exceed $100,000 in amount;

(ii) the pricing of any contract modification expected to exceed $100,000 in amount to any formally advertised or negotiated contract whether or not cost or pricing data was required in connection with the initial pricing of the contract;

(iii) the award of any negotiated contract not expected to exceed $100,000 in amount or any contract modification not expected to exceed $100,000 in amount to any formally advertised or negotiated contract whether or not cost or pricing of the contract, provided the contracting officer considers that the circumstances warrant such action in accordance with (d) below;

unless the price negotiated is based on adequate price competition, established catalog or market prices of commercial items sold in substantial quantities to the general public, or prices set by law or regulation. The requirement under (i) and (ii) above may be waived in exceptional cases where the Secretary (or, in the case of a contract with a foreign government or agency thereof, the Head of a Procuring Activity) authorizes such waiver and states in writing his reasons for such determination.

The plain language of the provision, then, changed from treating all non-FFP contracts separately and not applying the exemptions to them to treating all types of contracts in the same manner. While the change in language alone is sufficient to support application of the exemptions to incentive contracts, the "history" of the change also adds support.

In referring to the proposed changes, a memorandum from the Office of the Assistant Secretary of Defense for Installations and Logistics, dated September 27, 1965, to the Chairman of the ASPR Committee states that:

The above changes would be consistent with the requirements of the statute and I recommend that they be adopted.

A January 20, 1966, memorandum from the ASPR staff to the Chairman of the ASPR Committee stated:

In addition to revised 3–807.3(a)(i) and (ii) being more consistent with the requirements of the statute, the changes permit more flexible application of the requirements on cost reimbursement type contracts.

A memorandum of August 25, 1966, from the United States Air Force ASPR Committee member to the Chairman of the ASPR Committee stated that:

We concur with the elimination of the mandatory requirement for cost or pricing data and a certificate on contracts under $100,000. Because this is one area where *ASPR went beyond the law*, it has been a constant source of friction with industry. [Italic supplied.]

By letter of September 15, 1966, to the Chairman of the ASPR Committee, our Office approved of these proposed changes in ASPR § 3–807.3(a).

It is clear that the ASPR Committee felt that § 3–807.3, as originally promulgated, had gone beyond the statute by requiring certified cost or pricing data for all non-FFP contracts, regardless of dollar amount, and by not permitting application of the statutory exemptions. The FPR was revised in 1969, and followed the ASPR revision, treating all types of contracts equally. 34 F.R. 2660, February 27, 1969. It seems clear that both ASPR and FPR were deliberately changed to permit application of exemptions, including adequate price competition, to all types of contracts, including incentive contracts.

Thus, both the clear language of the present regulations and the history of changes in them demonstrate that the adequate price competition exemption is applicable to all types of contracts, including incentive contracts.

Recently, we found that certified cost or pricing data was not required because adequate price competition was present where a cost-plus-fixed-fee contract was awarded. *U.S. Nuclear, Inc.*, 57 Comp. Gen. 185 (1977), 77–2 CPD 511. Also, we found that adequate price competition existed and, therefore, certified cost or pricing data was not required and award could properly be made on the basis of initial proposals, where a cost-plus-award-fee contract was awarded. 52 Comp. Gen. 346 (1972). The earlier version of ASPR and FPR grouped these contract types with incentive contracts and did not permit application of exemptions to them. With the changes in the regulations, we have already recognized that the exemptions apply to cost–type contracts, and we see no reason that they should not apply equally to incentive contracts. In concluding on this point, we observe distinguishing aspects to the cases relied on by Serv-Air. In 46 Comp. Gen., *supra*, unlike here, a prior version on FPR specifically excepting incentive contracts from exemption was applicable. In 53 Comp. Gen., *supra*, the request for cost or pricing data was made in the conducting of negotiations to enhance competition rather than award to the protesting offeror on an initial proposal basis by invoking the adequate price competition exemption. In any event, to the extent that the above cases are in conflict with this decision, they are overruled.

Adequate Price Competition

Serv-Air objects to our interpretation of the requirements for adequate price competition, as specified in DAR § 3–807.1(b)(1), and our application of them in this case.

"Adequate price competition" is defined in DAR § 3–807.1(b)(1) in the following manner:

(1) **Adequate Price Competition.** a. Price competition exists if offers are solicited and (i) at least two responsible offerors (ii) who can satisfy the purchaser's (e.g., the Government's) requirements (iii) independently contend for a contract to be awarded to the responsive and responsible offeror submitting the lowest evaluated price (iv) by submitting price offers responsive to the expressed requirements of the solicitation. Whether there is price competition for a given procurement is a matter of judgment to be based on evaluation of whether each of the foregoing conditions (i) through (iv) is satisfied. Generally, in making this judgment, the smaller the number of offerors, the greater the need for close evaluation.

Serv-Air disagrees with our interpretation of "lowest evaluated price" as including all of the factors in the award evaluation as long as price is a substantial evaluation factor. Serv-Air reiterates its position in the original protest, that "lowest evaluated price" means that award must be made to the low-priced offeror. According to Serv-Air, *Shapell Government Housing, Inc. and Goldrich and Kest, Inc.*, *supra*, does not support our interpretation, because the decision is distinguishable.

Serv-Air argues that in *Shapell*, while award was made to a higher-*priced* offeror, its offer was evaluated as the *low cost offer* based on evaluated considerations of quality, durability, maintainability and life cycle cost. Serv-Air contends that here the Air Force made no attempt to evaluate probable cost to the Government or to determine whether the Air Force was getting the best deal for the dollar.

Serv-Air argues that in applying the criteria to this procurement our decision (1) ignores how price was evaluated; (2) ignores the fact that offering the lowest price was not a factor in the price evaluation; and (3) makes the adequate price competition exemption depend solely on the formality of whether price is a stated "substantial" evaluation criterion. Serv-Air states that it clearly offered the lowest price to the Government.

According to Serv-Air, our decision makes the basis for exemption from the Truth in Negotiations Act the same as the basis for award of most negotiated contracts and thereby makes the act inapplicable to most negotiated procurements. Since DAR § 3–807.3(f) states that where adequate price competition exists "cost or pricing data shall not be requested," Serv-Air contends that our decision makes the act mandatorily inapplicable except in two extreme circumstances: (1) only one proposal within a competitive range is received, or (2) the stated evaluation criteria make price an insubstantial evaluation factor.

Regarding Serv-Air's disagreement with our interpretation of lowest evaluated price and our reliance on *Shapell*, we feel that the distinctions pointed out by Serv-Air are only partially accurate and, in any event, do not preclude our interpretation in this case or in other circumstances. Serv-Air's assertion that the award in *Shapell* was made to the low cost offeror is in error. Award was made to a higher-priced, higher technically rated offeror. Award was made on the basis of lowest dollar per technical quality point ($/q.p.) ratio. The ratio was obtained by dividing an offeror's total technical score into its price. It is this concept of selecting the offeror proposing the best technical deal for the dollar that is embodied in the definition of lowest evaluated price as including all factors in the award evaluation. The competitive pressures of one or more additional offerors in the competitive range force offerors to "trade off" between cost and technical factors in order to offer the best possible proposal at a "fair and reasonable price."

Here, offerors knew that technical factors were going to be more important than price, but that price would be important. They also knew that a low price would receive more points, as long as it was reasonable. Therefore, they had the incentive to offer the best technical proposal at a fair and reasonable price. The result was that award was made to a substantially higher-rated technical proposal that cost only 5.5 percent more at most. If the price evaluation formula that Serv-Air claims is inimical to competition is discarded and a comparison is made between the proposals on a pure best technical proposal for the dollar basis, as in *Shapell*, the effectiveness of the competition here becomes even more clear. Assuming the worst circumstances for Northrop's proposal by using its ceiling price, and the best circumstances for Serv-Air's by using its target price, Northrop's $/q.p. ratio is $27,381 and Serv-Air's is $30,201. Of course, the spread is likely to be even greater, since both circumstances are not likely to occur. It is our opinion that award was made on the basis of lowest evaluated price, as that term is defined in *Shapell*.

Regarding Serv-Air's assertion that our decision ignored how price was evaluated, we agree that it did not address the propriety of the evaluation scheme, since that issue was clearly untimely. We did, however, examine the price evaluation to a limited extent to determine if adequate price competition was achieved. Serv-Air's contention that the decision ignored the fact that lowest price was not an evaluation factor is incorrect. Low price was evaluated positively by the "assumption of risk" criteria. Additionally, low *evaluated* price, as defined above, was the basis for award.

While Serv-Air states that our decision makes the adequate price competition exemption depend solely on the formality of whether price is a stated "substantial" evaluation criterion, in fact the decision dealt in some detail with the issue of whether price had been eliminated as an evaluation factor even though it was a stated criterion. The determination of whether there is price competition for a procurement is a matter of judgment to be based on the evaluation of whether the conditions set forth in DAR are present. The determination is made after proposals are received but prior to award, so that the factual circumstances may be examined. 52 Comp. Gen. 346, *supra*. DAR § 3–807.1(b)(1).

Price must be a *stated* substantial evaluation factor and must also *actually* be a substantial factor in the evaluation. Serv-Air seems to be implying that 30 percent weighting is not a substantial evaluation factor. We feel that it is substantial, since we found that adequate price competition existed in 52 Comp. Gen. 346, *supra*, and cost was weighted only 20 percent in that case.

Regarding Serv-Air's contention that our decision makes the basis for the exemption the same as the basis for award of most negotiated contracts and thus mandatorily inapplicable to most negotiated contracts, we feel that our decision merely recognizes that adequate price competition often exists in a negotiated environment, even though award is made to a higher-priced, higher technically rated proposal. Since Government procurement laws and regulations require maximum feasible competition, many procurements are competitive, and certified cost or pricing data would not be necessary in appropriate cases. Of course, as we stated above, that determination is a matter of judgment to be based on the application of the criteria stated in DAR § 3–807. 1(b)(1) to the facts of each procurement and the competitive environment. See 53 Comp. Gen., *supra.*

We note that, while DAR § 3–807.3(e) makes application of the exemption mandatory where adequate price competition has been determined to exist as Serv-Air contends, the judgmental nature of that determination introduces a considerable range of discretion into the application of the exemption.

Request for a Conference

Serv-Air requested a conference on this reconsideration because of the importance of the case. Our Bid Protest Procedures do not explicitly provide for conferences in these circumstances, 4 C.F.R. § 20.9 (1978). We believe a request for a conference should be granted only where the matter cannot be resolved without a conference. In our judgment, this is not such a case. See *International Business Machines—Reconsideration,* 56 Comp. Gen. 875 (1977), 77–2 CPD 97; *Dubie-Clark Company, Patterson Pump Division—Request for Reconsideration,* B–189642, April 6, 1978, 78–1 CPD 274.

Conclusion

In view of the foregoing, our decision in *Serv-Air, Inc., supra,* is affirmed.

〔B–190462〕

Federal Claims Collection Act of 1966 — Compromise, Waiver, etc. of Claims—Collection Expense Excessive

Under Federal Claims Collection Act of 1966, 31 U.S.C. 951–953, Department of the Interior need not pursue collection action in cases of underpayments of $1 or less of reclamation fees paid by coal mine operators pursuant to Surface Mining Control and Reclamation Act of 1977. Further, it is General Accounting Office policy that refunds of overpayments of $1 or less should not be made unless specifically claimed.

In the matter of Department of the Interior—Disposition of Reclamation Fee Under- and Overpayments of $1 or less, March 29, 1979:

The Department of the Interior (Department) has requested our decision concerning the treatment of under- and overpayments of $1 or less of reclamation fees which coal mine operators are required to pay quarterly to the Secretary of the Interior (Secretary) under section 402 of the Surface Mining Control and Reclamation Act of 1977 (Act), Pub. L. No. 95–87 (August 3, 1977), 91 Stat. 445, 30 U.S.C.

1232. The Department asks whether it may forego both the collecting of underpayments and the refunding of overpayments on these small amounts. The Department seeks to establish these minimum amounts because the costs of collection activity or refund processing significantly exceed the sums to be collected or refunded in cases of $1 or less. For the reasons that follow, we conclude that the Department (1) need not initiate collection activity for underpayments of $1 or less, and (2) need not refund overpayments of $1 or less unless a specific claim is made therefor.

The fees collected under section 402 of the Act are for deposit into the Abandoned Mine Reclamation Fund (Fund), a trust fund established on the books of the Treasury by section 401, 30 U.S.C. 1231. The Fund is available, upon appropriation, for a number of purposes as specified in section 401. The amount of a reclamation fee is determined by multiplying the tonnage of coal produced by a coal mine operator times the applicable fee per ton of the type of coal produced. Section 402(a). Coal mine operators must complete a Coal Production Reclamation Fee Report (Form OSM 837–1) on which the operator must list the number of tons of each type of coal produced and calculate the applicable fee. The operators then return the form along with their remittance to the Department, which deposits the remittance directly into the Fund. Among other checks, the fee collection system provides for automated verification of these calculations which has disclosed a large number of under- and overpayments of $1 or less as summarized 'below:

Underpayments of $1.00 or less by Mine Operators:

	Number
4th Qtr CY* 1977	243
1st Qtr CY 1978	142
2nd Qtr CY 1978	280
Total, (3 quarters)	665

Overpayments of $1.00 or less by Mine Operators:

4th Qtr CY 1977	119
1st Qtr CY 1978	66
2nd Qtr CY 1978	95
Total	280

* Qtr CY—Calendar Year Quarter.

Pending our decision, the Department has withheld action on underpayments and refunds of overpayments of $1 or less.

The under- and overpayments of $1 or less have virtually no effect on the reclamation program which has collected $105 million for the three quarters listed above and may also be presumed insignificant to the operators. As stated previously, the cost of collecting underpayments or refunding overpayments of $1 or less significantly exceeds the sums involved.

The Federal Claims Collection Act of 1966, 31 U.S.C. §§ 951–953 (1976), places the responsibility in the administrative agencies for collecting debts determined to be due the United States which arise as a result of their activities. This includes the authority to compromise, terminate or suspend collection action in specified circumstances. Regulations implementing the Federal Claims Collection Act, in particular 4 C.F.R. § 104.3(c) (1976), provide that the head of an agency or his designee may terminate collection activity and consider the agency's file closed when it is likely that the cost of further collection action will exceed the amount recoverable.

As the Department notes, the question at hand involves the determination not to initiate collection action at all, whereas the termination and suspension provisions of the Federal Claims Collection Act and regulations, strictly speaking, would seem to imply situations where collection action has already begun. Nevertheless, we believe the Department's proposal is within the scope of the authority conferred by that Act. Under the Federal Claims Collection Act and regulations, it is clear that the Secretary could terminate collection action on underpayments of $1 or less on a case-by-case basis on the grounds of diminishing returns. The purpose of the termination provision was to permit an agency to avoid spending more money to collect a debt than the debt itself is worth. In our opinion, a reasonable application of the statute should further permit a categorical determination that collection costs will always exceed the amount recoverable in cases of $1 or less. Certainly construing the statute in light of its purpose supports this result.

In B–188000, October 12, 1977, we concluded that, by virtue of the termination authority in the Federal Claims Collection Act, collection action "need not be pursued" on overpayments of tropical differentials to "unknown individuals" employed by the Justice Department where that department had determined that the costs of identifying and locating the employees and determining the amounts of overpayments might well exceed the ultimate recovery. See also B–184947, March 21, 1978. Thus, the actual commencement of collection action has not always been considered a prerequisite to the exercise of termination authority.

We have stated in the past that we would not object to the establishment by an agency of any reasonable minimum amount for the pursuit of debt claims of a given type "where cost studies indicate that such action is warranted." The minimum amount so established would be subject to review by this Office under our regular audit authority, e.g., 31 U.S.C. § 67. 55 Comp. Gen. 1438 (1976) ; B–115800/ B–117604, August 17, 1976. We think it may safely be presumed, without cost studies, that in cases of $1 or less collection costs will always exceed the amount recoverable. Accordingly, we concur with the Department that there is no need to pursue collection action with respect to underpayments of reclamation fees in amounts of $1 or less.

In the case of reclamation fee overpayments, the Federal Claims Collection Act, of course, has no application. However, we are not aware of any law which requires the Department, on its own initiative, to refund such overpayments. Rather, the practice of making refunds in the absence of a specific claim is based on public policy. As a general proposition, we believe that the concept of diminishing returns is relevant in the case of refunds also. In A–12900, February 11, 1942, we said :

> The General Accounting Office has long advocated that credit balances less than $1 should not be refunded unless claim is made by the remitters, for the reason that the cost of issuing the checks drawn in payment and the handling * * * [is] not commensurate with the amounts involved.

Accordingly, it is our view that refunds in amounts of $1 or less should not be made, unless a specific claim is made by the operator. It may be desirable to include a statement to this effect in the Form OSM 837–1 instructions or in appropriate regulations.

[B–192411]

Transportation—Rates—Special Agreements—Special v. Tariff Rates

United States and carrier may contract independently of tariff filed with State regulatory commission although, in absence of contract, tariff applies. Government officers have no authority to contract for interstate or intrastate transportation at rates higher than those available to the general public for the same or similar services.

Transportation—Rates—Intrastate—Applicability

Rates and charges in intrastate tariff are "otherwise applicable" within meaning of alternation provision in tender.

In the matter of Hilldrup Transfer & Storage Co., March 29, 1979:

Hilldrup Transfer & Storage Company (Hilldrup) requests review of deduction action taken in November 1978, by the General Services Administration (GSA) to recover an overcharge collected by Hilldrup on a shipment of household goods owned by Captain Joseph G. Raker, USAF. See 49 U.S.C. 66(b) (Supp. V, 1975). The shipment was picked up by Hilldrup's agent at Key West, Florida, on Government bill of lading No. K–1025376 (GBL) on July 6, 1976, and delivered to Callaway, Florida, on July 12, 1976.

Freight charges of $2,465.90 were collected by the carrier. They are derived from Government and Military Rate Tender No. 1–H, I.C.C. No. 35 (Tender 1–H). The overcharge of $494.02 is the difference between the $2,465.90 collected and freight charges of $1,971.88 derived from Florida Household Goods Carriers' Bureau Tariff 13, HG–FPSC 13 (Tariff 13), GSA's audit basis. Most of the overcharge represents a bridge charge of $4 per 100 pounds, found in item 150 of Tender 1–H and applicable to transportation performed through Islamorada, Florida, and points south and west in the Florida Keys.

Hilldrup and GSA state that the issue involving GBL K–1025376 is present in similar intrastate Florida shipments transported by Hilldrup and other carriers.

Hilldrup contends that the audit action is unfair in the context of the circumstances surrounding the assessment of the bridge charge on intrastate traffic traversing the Florida Keys. Hilldrup explains that without the bridge charge the carrier would have had to transport the household goods shipment at a loss because the imposition of weight restrictions by the Florida Department of Transportation on bridges in the Florida Keys reduced payloads, requiring a drastic change in the carrier's method of operation. A provision similar to the bridge charge in Tender 1–H was added to the interstate commercial tariffs, but, according to Hilldrup, none was added to the intrastate commercial tariff because the "vast majority of the shipments moving to and from the Key West area are for the account of the Department of Defense."

Hilldrup also contends that the rates and charges in Tender 1–H are applicable despite the fact that they are higher than those derived from the intrastate tariff. It argues that military traffic is covered by a detailed set of rules found in a Tender of Service that requires a performance different from that required by the intrastate tariff. It also states that the GBL requirement for extended storage-in-transit (SIT) constitutes a different service than that contemplated by the intrastate tariff. Hilldrup explains that the intrastate tariff limits SIT to 60 days whereas the Government requires 90 days SIT and can extend it up to 180 days, thereby substantially increasing the potential tenure of common carrier liability.

GSA contends that Tariff 13, the intrastate tariff, is applicable to this shipment for three reasons. First, GSA relies on item 23 of Tender 1–H which provides that the tender will not apply for a carrier where the total charges accruing under the tender exceed the total charges otherwise applicable for that carrier for the same services. Second, GSA refers to its regulations naming the terms and conditions governing the use of GBLs. One of those terms provides that a shipment made on a GBL "shall take a rate no higher than that chargeable had the shipment been made on the uniform straight bill of lading * * * provided for commercial shipments." 41 C.F.R. 101–41.302–3(c)(1978). Third, GSA argues that Section 22 of the Interstate Commerce Act, as amended, 49 U.S.C. 22 (Supp. V, 1975), which permits carriers to transport property for the United States free or at reduced rates, does not authorize officers of the Government to contract for transportation at rates higher than those available to the general public for the same services.

We note first that under paragraph 6001 of Department of Defense Regulation 4500.34–R, a carrier who wants to participate in the through GBL method of transporting household goods must:

> (1) Submit a Tender of Service to HQ MTMC. [Headquarters, Military Traffic Management Command]
> (2) Receive approval of its Tender of Service by the Commander, MTMC.
> (3) Submit a Letter of Intent to each shipping office it wishes to serve.
> (4) Be qualified by the ITO. [Installation Transportation Officer]
> (5) Be listed in the Personal Property Carrier Approvals Printout(s) and supplements thereto published and disseminated by HQ MTMC.
> (6) Have a published tariff on file with the Interstate Commerce Commission, State regulatory body for intrastate service, or an accepted Uniform Tender of Rates and/or Charges for Transportation Services on file at HQ MTMC.

The Tender of Service names the qualifications required of the carrier, contains carrier service and performance requirements and sets forth the mutual understandings between the carrier and DOD.

Tender 1–H is the accepted Uniform Tender of Rates referred to in paragraph 6001(6) of the DOD regulation. It sets forth in detail the rules, regulations, rates and charges governing shipments of military household goods between points in the United States. Although the tender states on its cover sheet that for the carriers named in the tender, it "* * * names reduced rates under authority of Section 22 of the Interstate Commerce Act * * *," it is not restricted to interstate traffic but applies to the intrastate traffic of many carriers including Hilldrup.

Tariff 13 is the intrastate tariff referred to in paragraph 6001(6) of the DOD regulation. It is published under Florida law which requires intrastate carriers to publish and file rates and prohibits carriers from deviating from them.

Tender 1–H applies to Hilldrup's intrastate Florida shipments. In its absence, intrastate tariff rates ordinarily would apply by operation of law. *Alabama Highway Express, Inc.* v. *United States*, 146 Ct. Cl. 594 (1959). The court there cited *Pub. Utilities Comm'n of California* v. *United States*, 355 U.S. 534 (1958), for the holding that state laws could not prohibit carriers from transporting Government property at lower rates agreed to by the parties. See also *United States* v.

Georgia Public Service Comm'n, 371 U.S. 285 (1963). It is also clear that the United States can contract to pay higher rates than the regularly filed tariff rates where the Government obtains services and privileges not extended to commercial shippers. *Alabama Highway Express, Inc.* v *United States*, 146 Ct. Cl. at 600; and *Greyhound Corporation* v. *United States*, 124 Ct. Cl. 758 (1953). Both cases involved intrastate shipments. In the former case, the carrier refused to agree to an alteration provision similar to item 23 of Tender 1–H; in the latter case, the carrier agreed to furnish buses that it had no duty at law to provide to the public generally. See also *United States* v. *Louisville & Nashville R.R. Co.*, 221 F. 2d 698 (6th Cir. 1955); *United States* v. *Missouri Pac. R.R.*, 56 Ct. Cl. 341 (1921); *Southern Pacific Co.* v. *United States*, 62 Ct. Cl. 649 (1926). In B–177939, November 6, 1973, we recognized the existence of a special benefit where the carrier furnished specialized equipment to meet the peculiar needs of the Government.

The existence of Tender 1–H, however, cannot preclude the applicability of intrastate rates for similar services. It long has been the rule that officers of the Government have no authority to contract for interstate or intrastate transportation at rates higher than those available to the general public for the same or similar service. See 57 Comp. Gen. 584 (1978). Indeed, item 23 of Tender 1–H is a recognition of that fact.

The Letter of Intent, referred to in paragraph 6001(3) of the DOD regulation, was filed with the ITO U.S. Naval Air Station, Key West, Florida, and shows that Hilldrup agreed to participate in the traffic at rates and charges shown in Tender 1–H and this was acknowledged and accepted by the ITO. In the "Tariff or Special Rate Authorities" block of the GBL is the notation "MGRT 1H" [Tender 1–H]. Although the parties intended that Tender 1–H apply, under item 23 of the tender Hilldrup agreed that the rates and charges therein would not apply if the total charges thereunder exceeded the total charges otherwise applicable for the same service. Compare B–190757, July 28, 1978.

While the primary question is whether the services and privileges offered to the United States under Tender 1–H are substantially similar to those available to the general public under the intrastate tariff, we first must consider whether Hilldrup would have been required by Florida law to transport the shipments for the Government at the rates and charges published in Tariff 13.

In *United States* v. *Carter*, 121 So. 2d 433 (Fla. 1960) the Supreme Court of Florida, citing, among other cases, *Pub. Utilities Comm'n of California*, supra., could be construed to have held that the pertinent sections of Florida Statutes, F.S.A. 323.08, 323.09, 323.19, among others, requiring intrastate carriers to publish and file rates, and prohibiting any deviation from those rates, do not apply to transportation of Government property or household goods of servicemen. But the precise issue considered by the court was whether the state regulatory commission could prohibit common carriers from entering into any agreement (like the one in Tender 1–H) with the United States for the transportation of Government property and servicemen's household goods at any rate except as approved by the commission. The issue of whether carriers could be required to transport this traffic at rates and charges applicable to the public generally was not raised or considered.

The court adopted the rationale of *Public Utilities Comm'n of California*, recognizing the Government's policy of negotiating rates to to effect savings in transportation costs, and further noting that the economies were for the benefit of all of the people. 121 So. 2d at 436. In view of this rationale, we cannot attribute to the court an intention to deprive the United States of the operation and protection of Florida's laws where to do so would discriminate against the United States with reference to commercial shippers. Furthermore, no opinion is an authority beyond the point actually decided, and the court did not consider the question whether the United States, as any commercial shipper, is entitled to the published intrastate tariff rates where its officers decided that they were most advantageous to the Government. See *United States* v. *Rias*, 524 F. 2d 118 (5th Cir. 1975), and *United States* v. *Cocke*, 399 F. 2d 433, 452 (5th Cir. 1968), cert. denied 394 U.S. 922. We conclude that the rates and charges published in Tariff 13 were "otherwise applicable" within the meaning of item 23 of Tender 1–H, provided the services offered by the tender and tariff were similar. That question depends on whether the Government received in Tender 1–H any additional benefits or privileges not available to the public in Tariff 13.

This is a breakdown of the freight charges derived from Tariff 13 and Tender 1–H which shows the components of the overcharge:

	Tariff 13	Tender 1–H	Difference
Linehaul charges	$1,345.58	$1,272.00	($73.58)
Shipment charge		39.00	39.00
Bridge charge		480.00	480.00
Packing charges	593.80	644.90	51.10
Extra Pickup	20.00	20.00	----------
Appliance Service	12.50	10.00	(2.50)
Total	$1,971.88	$2,465.90	$494.02

Except for the bridge charge and the shipment charge, the tender and tariff cover the same services.

Hilldrup states that the addition of the bridge charge of $4 per 100 pounds to the tender was a necessary measure to compensate the carrier for the additional costs of operation resulting from the bridge weight restrictions. By admission of the carrier the additional charge of $480 on this shipment, due to assessment of the bridge charge, is a consequence of action apparently taken by the Florida Department of Transportation. No benefit or privilege was granted to the Government by the change in Hilldrup's method of operations. Hilldrup was saddled with the same from and to Key West, Florida, whether the shipment was tendered under Tariff 13 by a member of the general public or by the Government.

The shipment charge is contained in item 12 of Tender 1–H; Tariff 13 does not contain a similar charge. However, note 2 in item 12 provides: "This additional assessment charge is not related to physical services performed by or for the carrier * * *." Since the shipment charge is not related to the carrier's performance of a physical service we question whether it is a transportation charge. See 52 Comp. Gen. 612, 613 (1973).

Hilldrup argues that the Tender of Service requires a performance different from that required by the intrastate tariff. But the Tender of Service is not a tariff and Section 1A.2a of the Tender of Service reads: "I understand that this is a Tender of Service and not a Rate Tender." See also, *Trans Ocean Van Service* v. *United States*, 426 F. 2d 329, 335 (Ct. Cl. 1970), in which the Court stated that the Tender of Service does not purport to quote rates or to provide rates or formulae for the computation of freight charges. Thus, performance required by the Tender of Service is immaterial to the question whether the two rate authorities, Tender 1–H and Tariff 13, cover the same services.

Hilldrup's argument that the GBL requirement for extended SIT constitutes a different service from that contemplated by the intrastate tariff is untenable. Aside from the fact that Captain Raker's household goods were not stored in transit, both tariff and tender provide charges for SIT services. The fact that Hilldrup's potential liability for loss and damage may be made more extensive under the tender than under the tariff is irrelevant because a common carrier's liability for loss and damage is distinct from the shipper's liability for freight charges [*Alcoa S.S. Co.* v. *United States*, 338 U.S. 421 (1949); *National Trailer Convoy, Inc.* v. *United States*, 345 F. 2d 573 (Ct. Cl. 1965)] and is not an additional benefit or privilege relating to freight charges.

We agree with GSA that under item 23 of Tender 1–H and under the terms of the GBL, Tariff 13 provides the lowest applicable charges on the shipment transported by Hilldrup under GBL No. K–1025376.

In these circumstances and since Hilldrup has the burden of affirmatively proving its case, 57 Comp. Gen. 155 (1977), GSA's deduction action was correct and is sustained.

[B-193283]

Contracts — Specifications — Qualified Products — Listing — Capability to Deliver Listed Product—Contractor Responsibility and/or Contract Administration Matter

Whether contractor will deliver qualified end product listed on Qualified Products List (QPL) is matter relating to affirmative determination of offeror's responsibility and to contract administration. General Accounting Office does not review affirmative determination of responsibility in absence of showing of fraud or allegations that definitive responsibility criteria in solicitation were misapplied, and does not review matters of contract administration.

Bidders — Qualifications — Qualified Products Procurement— Bidder v. Product Qualification

Qualified Products List (QPL) requirement in solicitation relates to qualification of specific products and does not concern qualification of individual offerors. Therefore, QPL requirement does not constitute definitive responsibility criterion.

In the matter of American Athletic Equipment Division, AMF Incorporated, March 29, 1979:

Invitation for bids (IFB) No. DLA400–78–B–2074–0001 and request for proposals (RFP) No. DLA400–78–R–2883 were issued by the Defense General Supply Center, Defense Logistics Agency (DLA), Richmond, Virginia, for the procurement of military stopwatches, National Stock Number (NSN) 6645–00–126–0286, in accordance with Military Specification MIL–S–14823. The soliciations required that the stopwatches be qualified end products under the applicable Qualified Products List (QPL). While Z.A.N. Co. (ZAN) was not listed as a qualified manufacturer of these items, it proposed to furnish qualified products of another manufacturer. Awards were made under both solicitations to ZAN as the low, responsible offeror.

American Athletic Equipment Division, AMF Incorporated (AMF), has filed a protest against the awards, contending than ZAN is not an authorized distributor under the QPL, has no intention of furnishing a qualified end product, and is otherwise nonresponsible. In this regard, AMF has submitted an affidavit to the effect that ZAN's subcontractor quotation from its proposed supplier, submitted to DLA during the preaward surveys conducted, specifies delivery of a non-QPL product. AMF further states that the contracting officer, prior to award, should have determined that ZAN had the authority and capability to provide the qualified stopwatches offered in its bid.

In *D. Moody & Co., Inc.; Astronautics Corporation of America*, 55 Comp. Gen. 1 (1975), 75-2 CPD 1, we noted that:

The QPL procurement process is a two step process: the first step is the process of qualifying the product and the second step is the agency's procurement of the qualified product. These steps are mutually exclusive, and a firm which passes the tests qualifying the product need not be the same firm that bids the qualified product. In this connection, we have consistently held that the mere listing of a product on a QPL does not relieve a contractor from its obligaton of delivering an item which meets the specifications.

We therefore concluded that valid bids may be submitted in QPL procurements by bidders other than manufacturers or distributors.

Here, an examination of ZAN's bid and proposal indicates that ZAN offered without exception to furnish the QPL product in compliance with the specifications. The question whether ZAN will in fact furnish a QPL product in conformity with the specifications in the course of its performance of the contracts relates to the contractor's responsibility and to matters of contract administration. The contracting officer made affirmative determinations of responsibility before awarding the contracts and is also taking steps to assure monitoring of the performance of the contracts to insure delivery of conforming products. Our Office does not review affirmative determinations of responsibility in the absence of a showing of fraud on the part of procuring officials or allegations that definitive responsibility criteria were misapplied.

In this connection, AMF argues that the QPL requirement in the solicitations constituted a definitive responsibility criterion. We disagree. The purpose of the QPL system is to allow the Government to efficiently procure items on which substantial testing would be required by permitting extensive tests needed to show that the particular product will meet the Government's requirements to be conducted prior to the actual procurement action. The QPL, therefore, concerns the qualification of a *product*. Definitive responsibility criteria, however, are solely concerned with the qualifications of an *offeror*. Such special standards of responsibility limit the class of offerors to those meeting specified qualitative and quantitative qualifications necessary for adequate contract performance, e.g., minimum experience requirements. *Haughton Elevator Division, Reliance Electric Company*, 55 Comp. Gen. 1051 (1976), 76-1 CPD 294. There are no such questions presented here.

Moreover, whether ZAN in fact performs in accordance with the requirements of the contract is a matter of contract administration and is not for our consideration. *Virginia-Maryland Associates*, B-191252, March 28, 1978, 78-1 CPD 238.

In view of the foregoing, the protest is dismissed.

[B-193587]

Voluntary Services—Officers and Employees—Waiver of Portion or All of Statutory Salary

Some members of the United States Metric Board desire to waive their compensation while other members desire to accept it but return it as a gift to the Board. Here the statute authorizes payment of Board members at a rate not to exceed the daily rate currently being paid grade 18 of the General Schedule. Such pay is not considered salary fixed by or pursuant to statute which would preclude waiver. Also, since statute authorizes acceptance of gifts and donations, members may make gifts of their salary to the agency. However, the members would be liable for the income tax on such salary and would be entitled only to the limited deduction for charitable contributions prescribed by the Internal Revenue Service. 57 Comp. Gen. 423 and 54 *id.* 393, distinguished.

In the matter of United States Metric Board—Waiver of Compensation, April 2, 1979:

By letter of November 17, 1978, Mr. Malcolm E. O'Hagan, Executive Director, United States Metric Board (Board), requested our opinion concerning the legality of members of the Board waiving their compensation or in some cases accepting their compensation and then returning it as a gift to the Board.

Our Office has consistently held on the basis of court decision that it is contrary to public policy for an appointee to a position in the Federal Government to waive his ordinary right to compensation or to accept something less when the salary for his position is fixed by or pursuant to legislative authority. 54 Comp. Gen. 393 (1974); 27 *id.* 194 (1947); 26 *id.* 956 (1947); *Glavey* v. *United States*, 182 U.S. 595 (1900); *Miller* v. *United States*, 103 F. 413 (S.D. N.Y. 1900). In *Miller*, the court held such waiver to be against public policy since the willingness of one person to waive his compensation would exclude from competition all other candidates who were not willing or unable to take the position for less than the salary fixed by Congress. In addition, the United States Supreme Court, in *Glavey*, stated the opinion that if waiver of compensation fixed by Congress were permitted, "salaries for public officers would be under the control of the Executive Department of the Government."

Waiver of compensation, however, has been permitted in certain circumstances. In 27 Comp. Gen. 194 (1947) we held that the person occupying a position could waive his right to all or part of the compensation if there was some applicable provision of law authorizing the acceptance of services without compensation. In that case the law permitting the employment of experts and consultants on a temporary or intermittent basis provided that such employment should be without regard to civil service and classification laws and fixed only the maximum rate of compensation that could be paid.

The issue, therefore, is whether the Metric Conversion Act of 1975 (15 U.S.C. 205a–k (1976)) provides authority to permit waiver of compensation by members appointed to the Board. Section 205g of title 15, United States Code, authorizes the Board to accept gifts and personal services. Section 205g reads as follows:

The Board may accept, hold, administer and utilize gifts, donations and bequests of property, both real and personal, and personal services, for the purpose of aiding or facilitating the work of the Board.

Compensation for members of the Board is authorized by 15 U.S.C. 205h. That section is in pertinent part as follows:

Members of the Board who are not in the regular full-time employ of the United States shall, while attending meetings or conferences of the Board or while otherwise engaged in the business of the Board, *be entitled to receive compensation at a rate not to exceed the daily rate currently being paid grade 18 of the General Schedule* (under section 5332 of Title 5), including traveltime. [Italic supplied.]

In addition, members of the Board are allowed travel expenses including per diem in lieu of subsistence under 5 U.S.C. 5703. Section 205h is specific in stating that payments are not to render members of the Board employees or officials of the United States for any purpose.

In the above waiver situations the controlling factor is whether the salary to be waived is set by or pursuant to statute, i.e., set by Congress. Every salary of anyone who is paid by the Government in a sense is set pursuant to statute. This is so since the Government may not make any payment without statutory authorization. As indicated above, our cases do not preclude waiver in all cases. In the present situation, the language of 15 U.S.C. 205h sets a maximum rate of compensation entitlement for Board members. Where the statutory authorization of the salary of an individual who is to render services to the United States merely sets a maximum limit for that salary, then the salary of that individual is not considered to be fixed pursuant to statute within the meaning of our cases. Therefore, assuming other conditions are satisfied, such individuals may waive their salaries. Also, we do not read section 205h as fixing the compensation which each Board member must be paid. Accordingly, Board members may agree to serve without compensation and thereafter they would be estopped from asserting any valid claim for compensation on account of the service performed. Compare 57 Comp. Gen. 423 (1977); 54 *id.* 393 (1974).

The Executive Director's letter also inquires whether members of the Board may accept compensation and then return it as a gift to the Board. Since 15 U.S.C. 205g authorizes the Board to accept gifts and donations there is nothing to prevent members of the Board from making gifts of some or all of the salary to the Board. These gifts are allowable as long as they are made for the purpose of aiding or facilitating the work of the Board. 15 U.S.C. 205g. Of course, the members will be liable for the income tax on their salary and will be entitled only to the limited deduction for charitable contributions prescribed by the Internal Revenue Service.

[B-190672]

Travel Expenses — Temporary Duty — Family Accompanying Employee

Employee of the Drug Enforcement Agency, who was married while at a temporary duty (TDY) station overseas, claims reimbursement for wife's travel between TDY stations and her per diem at TDY stations. Employee is not entitled to reimbursement as there is no authority to pay travel expenses of dependent of an employee to or from a TDY station or to pay per diem to the dependent at a TDY station.

Travel Expenses — Overseas Employees — Transfers — Failure to Report at New Duty Station

Employee, who was transferred from Ankara, Turkey, to Detroit, Michigan, resigned in Washington, D.C. during a debriefing and did not report at Detroit, is not entitled to reimbursement of traveling expenses of himself and wife under relocation travel order since such obligation does not arise until the transfer is consummated by the employee's entrance on duty at his new official station. The employee's travel expenses to Washington do not have to be collected since his travel may be considered temporary duty travel incident to his debriefing.

Travel Expenses—Overseas Employees—Separation—Failure to Negotiate Transportation Agreement—Reimbursement Entitlement

Local hire overseas who did not sign a transportation agreement at the time of hire is not entitled to reimbursement of transportation expenses to his home of record in the United States at the time of his separation.

In the matter of Joseph Salm—Travel Expenses, April 4, 1979:

The Chief of the Accounting Section, Office of Controller, Drug Enforcement Administration (DEA), U.S. Department of Justice, has requested a decision concerning reimbursement of certain travel expenses incurred by Mr. Joseph G. Salm, a Special Agent of the DEA, and his wife.

The record shows that on May 20, 1974, Mr. Salm was appointed to the position of Special Agent for the DEA and assigned to the Beirut district office. At the time of Mr. Salm's appointment he was residing in Beirut, Lebanon. In November 1975, all nonessential Government personnel were removed from the Beirut station. Mr. Salm was then sent to the DEA regional office in Ankara, Turkey, on a temporary basis. On April 3, 1976, while on temporary duty assignment in Egypt, Mr. Salm married Helena Baraibar Camunas in Alexandria. A DEA cable dated May 28, 1976, authorized Mrs. Salm to accompany her husband from Cairo to Ankara with her belongings. This travel was accomplished on June 2, 1976.

On June 19, 1976, Mr. and Mrs. Salm traveled from Ankara incident to a change of duty station to Detroit, Michigan. En route to Detroit Mr. Salm stopped off in Washington, D.C., for a debriefing period. On July 12, 1976, after the debriefing period, Mr. Salm resigned his position effective July 31, 1976, and never did report to

Detroit. The travel authorization was amended to provide for the trip from Ankara to Mr. Salm's home of record, Eugene, Oregon. After the debriefing period in Washington, D.C., the claimant and his wife departed on July 12, 1976, for Boston, Massachusetts, in lieu of his home of record.

Mr. Salm submitted three vouchers. The initial voucher, dated June 4, 1976, indicates use of a Government Travel Request for transportation of Mr. and Mrs. Salm and her personal effects from Cairo, Egypt, to Ankara. The second voucher, dated June 29, 1976, is a claim for reimbursement of expenses incident to documentation of the marriage and per diem for Mrs. Salm to and while at Ankara. The third voucher, dated November 5, 1976, claims travel expenses relating to the permanent change of station.

Mr. Salm objected to the disallowance of travel expenses and per diem for his spouse and the DEA's refusal to pay the final voucher regarding permanent change-of-station travel. Based on these objections, the Accounting Section of the DEA reviewed all three vouchers to ensure compliance with the travel regulations governing travel expenses for a spouse acquired after assignment abroad. The Accounting Section concluded that Mrs. Salm did not meet applicable travel regulations concerning a dependent spouse and that agency officials had been in error in authorizing any payments for her travel while accompanying her husband. In accordance with this determination, the voucher of November 5, 1976, was reevaluated and travel and subsistence expenses for Mrs. Salm disallowed. Reimbursement for Mrs. Salm's travel had been previously made including cost of marriage documents, and Mrs. Salm's travel from Cairo to Ankara with baggage costs. After adjustment these travel costs totaled $602.24. The DEA requested remission of the amount. The other voucher request for reimbursement of expenses regarding Mrs. Salm was not paid.

Mr. Salm asked the DEA to obtain an opinion as to the legal validity of their action since all travel had been authorized by the DEA Personnel Director through specific travel orders. Unfortunately, these orders were based on the mistaken belief that certain provisions of the Foreign Affairs Manual (FAM) applied to DEA.

Initially, there appears to have been some confusion regarding the travel regulations governing DEA employees and dependents overseas. The FAM, Volume 6, Uniform State/AID/USIA Foreign Service Travel Regulations were promulgated pursuant to 22 U.S.C. § 1136. The FAM covers travel and related expenses for all Foreign Service officers and Foreign Service Reserve officers of the Department of State, the Agency for International Development, and the U.S. Information Agency. The FAM has statutorily been extended to cover certain employees of other agencies where the agency head has authority to pay allowances and benefits similar to those authorized under the Foreign Service Act of 1946. In such cases, the Federal Travel Regulations (FTR) do not apply to these personnel.

The DEA received authorization in their appropriation act in 1976 to apply certain provisions of the Foreign Service Act, 22 U.S.C. § 1136(9), (10), and (11) to DEA employees overseas. The intent of this request for authorization was to provide DEA employees certain benefits not available to employees who travel under the provisions of 5 U.S.C. §§ 5721 *et seq.*, the statutory basis for the FTR. The authorization was limited to three concerns: employee and dependent travel expenses for rest and recuperation; temporary duty assignment; and family visitation in certain specified instances. See Appropriations Act of 1975 for Justice Department, 88 Stat. 1195. However, the FAM provision (6 FAM 126.8) authorizing transportation of a newly acquired spouse (overseas) which was originally thought to be determinative, has not been made applicable to the DEA in any subsequent appropriations legislation.

The FTR do not include a provision similar to that in the FAM travel regulations. Mr. Salm's permanent duty station was Beirut. Subsequently, he was placed on temporary duty status in Ankara and other stations in the region. In fact Mr. Salm married while on temporary duty in Egypt. There is no authority in the FTR to pay the traveling expenses of Mrs. Salm from Egypt to Ankara. Furthermore, there is no authority to authorize per diem to the spouse at the temporary duty station of an employee.

Therefore, the claim for Mrs. Salm's travel and incidental expenses relating to her establishment at the temporary duty station is disallowed.

The remaining claim for reimbursement of expenses incurred upon transfer of official headquarters is governed by 5 U.S.C. § 5724 and the FTR, which provide for the transfer of an employee at Government expense when in the interest of the Government. However, the obligation does not arise until the transfer actually is consummated by the employee's entrance on duty at his new official station.

While Mr. Salm traveled from his old duty station at Ankara he did not report for duty at his new duty station in Detroit, resigning while at Washington, D.C., during a debriefing. The subsequent change of duty station to Eugene, Oregon, the home of record of Mr. Salm at his request may not be considered as altering the purpose for which the original transfer order was issued. See B–160397, December 2, 1966. This is so because Mr. Salm was a local hire with whom no agreement for transportation entitlement had been negotiated. We assume that

Mr. Salm did not meet the eligibility criteria prescribed by para. 2–1.5h
(3)(b) of the FTR for a transportation agreement. Since Mr. Salm
had not signed a transportation agreement he was not entitled to transportation at Government expense to his home of record at the time of
his separation from his overseas duty station.

Therefore, since Mr. Salm did not report for duty at Detroit he
is not entitled to travel and transportation expenses under travel authorization B–0350 as amended for his travel beyond Washington or
for any travel for his wife. The expenses paid for his travel to Washington do not have to be collected since it may be considered temporary
duty travel incident to his debriefing.

Action on the claim should be taken in accordance with the foregoing.

[B–193399]

Timber Sales — Contracts — Modification — Mutual Mistake—Reformation of Contract

Bidder is justified in placing reasonable reliance on estimates stated in purchaser
road credit portion of timber sale contract; if, as here, agency negligently states
unreasonable estimate for road clearing, mutual mistake as to accuracy of estimate exists and reformation of contract to allow additional compensation for
doing required clearing work is proper. Prior denial of claim is reversed; decision in B–193399, Dec. 5, 1978, overruled.

In the matter of Sierra Pacific Industries — Reconsideration, April 5, 1979:

Sierra Pacific Industries (Sierra) requests reconsideration of our
decision in *Sierra Pacific Industries*, B–193399, December 5, 1978,
78–2 CPD 390, in which we denied the firm's claim of $13,804 for
road-clearing work done in connection with Cook Timber Sale under
Department of Agriculture contract No. 017753. The basis of Sierra's
request for reconsideration is that the legal principle of mutual mistake allows reformation of the contract and payment of the claim.

As indicated in the previous decision, Sierra was required to construct certain roads for hauling logs as part of the timber sale. The
purchaser road credit limit for road No. 28N02 was $127,902, of which
$6,960 was allotted for clearing land which the contract specified as
being an estimated six acres. When Sierra constructed road No. 28N02,
it alleged that it cleared 17.9 acres, resulting in costs exceeding the
allotted amount for clearing by $13,804. The agency does not dispute
that the contract specified an estimated six acres for clearing, nor does
it dispute that this amount was an error—apparently typographical.

In initially denying Sierra's claim, we pointed out that the prospectus for the timber sale under item 7 put bidders on notice that

estimates were not guaranteed and that the contract contained detailed specifications for road No. 28N02. Based on this admonition and "since this figure [approximate acreage for clearing] could easily be determined from these specifications" we held that reformation was not proper.

The decision was in accordance with our decision in B–176649, January 24, 1973. In that case we were asked to grant reformation of a timber sale contract because a clerical error by the agency resulted in the road construction credit being reduced from $50,560 to $36,230. We declined to find reformation an appropriate remedy by pointing out that common industry practice was for bidders to examine all contract forms and appraisal forms as well as to physically inspect the timber sale site before submitting bids. Thus, we concluded that the amounts for road credits were treated simply as estimates and not solely relied on by bidders.

However, a recent decision of the Court of Claims indicates that reformation would be appropriate under the circumstances of this case.

In *Timber Investors, Inc. v. United States*, No. 61–75 (Ct. Cl. November 15, 1978), the court had occasion to consider the legal principle of mutual mistake in regard to the road construction aspect of a timber sale contract. The court noted that a mutual mistake justifying reformation would exist where the purchaser and the Forest Service believed that the estimates were reasonably accurate and where, in fact, performance showed unreasonably inaccurate estimates due to a mistake on the Forest Service's part. There is a mutual mistake because both parties are mutually mistaken as to the accuracy of the estimates. This is so, noted the court, even though the prospectus warned potential bidders that estimates were not guaranteed because the Government is not insulated from liability where contract estimates are grossly erroneous due to negligence on the Forest Service's part. See *Timber Investors, Inc.* v. *United States, supra,* note 4 at page 5, and citations therein.

In concluding its discussion of the legal principle of mutual mistake as it relates to road construction estimates, the court stated:

* * * under the purchaser road credit provision the Forest Service estimates the cost of the road construction work to be performed. Contractors have no say in the matter. Successful purchasers of Forest Service timber must perform the road construction work called for by the timber sale contract at the estimated cost price set forth by the Forest Service. Under these circumstances, the contract representation * * * would lead reasonable and prudent bidders to view the * * * contract work and cost estimates, as reliable and reasonably accurate. It would also serve to justify reliance by a timber purchaser and/or road contractor on such estimates as being reasonably accurate. *Id.* at page 10.

Thus, the court stated that reliance by the bidder on the Forest Service's estimates is justified and that an egregious error, as here, in the estimates will support reformation. See also *Morgan Roofing Company*, 54 Comp. Gen. 497 (1974), 74–2 CPD 358, in which reformation was allowed where prior to award a Government representative indicated to a roofing contractor that a certain roof was not included in the work to be performed even though the specifications in the solicitation, which was in the contractor's possession, clearly showed that work on this roof was to be part of the contract.

Accordingly, the prior decision is reversed and the claim may be paid upon verification by the agency of the costs incurred by reason of the excess acreage which was cleared. However, payment should be limited to an amount which would not result in displacement of the second high bidder.

[B–193561]

Pay—Retired—Reservists—Erroneous Notification of Eligibility—What Constitutes

The written communication required by 10 U.S.C. 1331(d) as notice to a member of a Reserve component of an armed force advising that he has completed the years of service requirement for retired pay at age 60 need not be in any specific format. So long as the notice is from an authorized activity of his military service and uses appropriate words advising him that he has completed the service requirements for such retired pay at age 60, such notice satisfies the requirements of 10 U.S.C. 1331(d) so as to invoke 10 U.S.C. 1406, thereby preventing denial of retired pay due to administrative error.

Pay—Retired—Reservists—Eligibility

The exceptions to the invocation of 10 U.S.C. 1406, preventing denial of retired pay entitlement due to erroneous written notice of entitlement, are limited to cases of direct fraud or misrepresentation on the part of the person to whom the notice is sent. Where the evidence fails to show that the member caused his service record to be altered or induced the erroneous notice to be sent, the statutory exceptions have not been met. A showing that the member possibly should have had reasonable doubt as to the propriety of the notice is insufficient to serve as a basis to deny entitlement to retired pay at age 60, if he is otherwise qualified.

In the matter of Lieutenant Colonel William P. Cassedy, USAFR, April 9, 1979:

This action is in response to a letter dated November 17, 1978, with enclosures, from the Principal Deputy Assistant Secretary of the Air Force (Financial Management), requesting an advance decision concerning the entitlement of Lieutenant Colonel William P. Cassedy, USAFR, FV793065/578–50–6260, to receive non-Regular retired pay under the provisions of chapter 67 of title 10, United States Code. The request has been assigned Air Force submission No. SS–AF–1308 by the Department of Defense Military Pay and Allowance Committee.

The submission indicates that, under the provisions of 10 U.S.C. 1406 (1976), a person who receives notification as provided for in 10 U.S.C. 1331(d) (1976) of entitlement to non-Regular retired pay from the service concerned is entitled to that pay even though he does not in fact have sufficient service (20 years) for such retirement. Apparently Colonel Cassedy received correspondence from the Air Force which purportedly advised him that he had fulfilled the service requirement for eligibility to receive retired pay at age 60. As a result, he is asserting his right to retired pay.

The submission expresses doubt as to whether the correspondence in question constituted official notification since it was not in the form provided in Department of Defense Directive 1340.7, and the record indicated that Colonel Cassedy had reason to believe that such correspondence was in error. Therefore, we are asked to resolve the following questions:

a. Where the Secretary of Defense has provided for format and procedure for notifications under 10 U.S.C. 1331(d) in DOD Directive 1340.7, may a notification which does not meet the requirements of * * * [that directive] be considered official under 1331(d) so as to invoke the provisions of 10 U.S.C. 1406?

b. If the answer to a, above, is affirmative, in the instant case, is the letter dated August 11, 1969 from Headquarters, Air Reserve Personnel Center, to Lieutenant Colonel William P. Cassedy, USAFR Retired, an official notification under 10 U.S.C. 1331(d) which invokes the provisions of 10 U.S.C. 1406?

c. If the answer to b, above, is affirmative, is Lieutenant Colonel William P. Cassedy entitled to retired pay under Sections 1331 and 1401 of Title 10, as a result of the invocation of the provisions of Section 1406, notwithstanding the fact that he has only 14 years, 2 months and 3 days of satisfactory service under Section 1331. * * *

Section 1331(a) of title 10—which was derived from Title III of the act of June 29, 1948, ch. 708, 62 Stat. 1087–1091—provides in pertinent part:

(a) * * * a person is entitled, upon application, to retired pay computed under section 1401 of this title, if—
(1) he is at least 60 years of age;
(2) he has performed at least 20 years of service computed under section 1332 of this title;
(3) he performed the last eight years of qualifying service while a member of any category named in section 1332(a)(1) of this title, but not while a member of a regular component, the Fleet Reserve, or the Fleet Marine Corps Reserve; and
(4) he is not entitled, under any other provision of law, to retired pay from an armed force or retainer pay as a member of the Fleet Reserve or the Fleet Marine Corps Reserve.

In 1966, subsection (d) was added to section 1331 of title 10, by section 1 of the act of October 14, 1966, Public Law 89–652, 80 Stat. 902, which reads as follows:

(d) The Secretary concerned shall provide for notifying each person who has completed the years of service required for eligibility for retired pay under this chapter. The notice must be sent, in writing, to the person concerned within one year after he has completed that service.

The same law also added a new section 1406 to chapter 71 of title 10, which provides in pertinent part:

§ 1406. *Limitations on revocation of retired pay*

After a person * * * has been notified in accordance with section 1331(d) of this title that he has completed the years of service required for eligibility for retired pay under chapter 67 of this title, the person's eligibility for retired pay may not be denied or revoked on the basis of any error, miscalculation, misinformation, or administrative determination of years of service performed as required by section 1331(a)(2) of this title, unless it resulted directly from the fraud or misrepresentation of the person. The number of years of creditable service upon which retired pay is computed may be adjusted to correct any error, miscalculation, misinformation, or administrative determination and when such a correction is made the person is entitled to retired pay in accordance with the number of years of creditable service, as corrected, from the date he is granted retired pay.

The Navy Department in its report of June 6, 1966, on the need for H.R. 5297 which became Public Law 89-652, stated that the complicated method of computation of service creditable for retirement under chapter 67:

* * * usually leaves the reservist in serious doubt as to whether he has in fact passed the 20-year milestone. The services, by a variety of administrative procedures, have attempted to keep the reservist informed of his progress and his completion of the years of service required. In some cases, however, reservists have received erroneous information or have miscomputed their years of service and in reliance thereon have reduced their Reserve participation only to find upon reaching retirement age that they have not in fact met the 20 years of service requirement. When the errors are not discovered until at or near retirement age the reservists no longer have time to renew their participation and acquire the necessary additional service. Page 3 of H. Rept. No. 1689, and page 2 of S. Rept. No. 1693, 89th Cong., 2nd. Sess.

The primary purpose of Public Law 89-652, *supra*, as shown by its legislative history, was to mandate that every person who has completed 20 years of creditable service be notified in writing of that fact as provided for by the Secretary concerned, within 1 year following completion of such service. And, if administrative error is made, in the absence of fraud or misrepresentation on his part, he may not be denied chapter 67 retirement benefits at age 60, if all other conditions for qualification have been met.

Based on the Secretarial notice requirement in 10 U.S.C. 1331(d), Department of Defense Directive 1340.7 (March 29, 1967) was issued setting forth the notification policy to be followed by the services. Basically, that directive reiterated the provisions of 10 U.S.C. 1331, as amended, and the newly enacted 10 U.S.C. 1406. Additionally, it makes provision for the format of the notification, and makes the following statements regarding the purpose for its use:

F. In view of the restrictions on denial or revocation of eligibility for retired pay * * * suitable controls and procedures shall be established to avoid errors, miscalculations, misinformation, and erroneous administrative determinations.
G. The notification shall be issued in the name of an official having general responsibility for administering the controls and procedures referred to in F., above, and shall be authenticated by the handwritten signature of the officer or employee immediately responsible for the determination of the eligibility of the member being notified.

The reported facts show that Colonel Cassedy, by orders dated August 1, 1969, was transferred from the Ready Reserve to the Retired Reserve in the grade of lieutenant colonel, effective that date. He did not receive a letter in the format prescribed in Directive 1340.7, but by letter dated August 11, 1969, from Headquarters Air Reserve Personnel Center, signed by the Director, Personnel Actions, enclosing those orders, he was advised in part as follows:

> You have fulfilled the service requirements for eligibility to receive retirement pay when you reach 60 years of age. Approximately six months before your 60th birthday we will furnish you further information and forms in order that you may apply for this pay benefit.

The pertinent language of 10 U.S.C. 1331(d) is that the Secretary "shall provide for notifying each person" and the "notice must be sent, in writing * * * within one year." Section 1406 provides that after a person "has been notified in accordance with section 1331(d) * * * the person's eligibility for retired pay may not be denied or revoked on the basis of any error."

It is evident that the law requires that the member be notified. However, it contains nothing which requires the notice to be in any specific form, only that the notice inform the member of the fact of completion of years of service for chapter 67 retirement purposes. Implicit in that requirement is that the words used in the notice are such that a reasonable person would understand their import. Considering the purpose for the law, it is our view that if an individual receives a written communication from one who has apparent responsibility for the issuance of such notice and the notice uses words advising the recipient that he has completed the service requirements for eligibility for retired pay at age 60, such written notice satisfies the requirements of 10 U.S.C. 1331(d), so as to invoke the provisions of 10 U.S.C. 1406. The August 11, 1969 letter to Colonel Cassedy meets these criteria. Accordingly, questions a. and b. are answered in the affirmative.

Air Force correspondence with Colonel Cassedy, before the erroneous letter of August 11, 1969, apparently advised him that he would not be able to qualify for retirement under chapter 67 of title 10. In effect, question c. asks whether such prior knowledge on his part would negate the August 11, 1969 letter and preclude him from receiving benefits at age 60.

The file shows generally that Colonel Cassedy performed creditable service as an enlisted member with the Mississippi National Guard in 1934. In 1942 he enlisted in the United States Army and served on active duty in that capacity and as a Reserve officer until 1945, when he was released. He remained assigned to the Officer Reserve Corps until 1949 when he was transferred to the Inactive Air Reserve and was ineligible to earn service retirement points. In 1953, he was returned to an active status, and while he did participate between then and 1956, he apparently did not earn enough points on an annual basis to be credited with any years of satisfactory service. It further appears that between 1956 and 1962 he did not participate in the Reserve program even though he was in an active status. On April 20, 1962, he was again assigned to an inactive status.

During the period from 1962 to 1968, Colonel Cassedy and the Air Reserve Personnel Center corresponded regarding his Reserve status and qualification for retirement pay. By letter dated July 25, 1962, he was apparently notified that he had a mandatory separation date of November 7, 1970, and even if he succeeded in qualifying for satisfactory years of service from April 20, 1962, to November 7, 1970, the maximum number of creditable years of service he could achieve would be 16 years, 8 months and 2 days.

In April 1962, the member, having previously received notification of assignment to the inactive Reserve, was granted a waiver for the purpose of assignment to the Judge Advocate General's Department of the Army and served in that organization from April 20, 1962, until April 19, 1965. It is reported that at the completion of that service he had to his credit, 11 years, 2 months and 3 days of satisfactory service for retirement qualification purposes.

By letter dated May 9, 1966, the member was again notified of his inability to complete the service requirements prior to his mandatory separation date in 1970 to make him eligible for retired pay at age 60. In letters to him dated September 17 and October 7, 1968, which apparently were in response to an earlier inquiry by him concerning the possibility of his promotion to the grade of colonel, he was advised that he would be ineligible for such a promotion when the colonel selection board next convened in 1970, because that board would only consider those with a promotion service date prior to June 30, 1966, and his service date was July 30, 1966. He was also advised that the unit vacancy board would be convened in November 1970, but not until after he was mandatorily separated on November 6, 1970. He was also apparently told in the same correspondence that on that date he would have a choice of either assignment to the Retired Reserve or complete separation from his Reserve status. On July 17, 1969, the Air Reserve Personnel Center received an application from him for transfer to the Retired Reserve "without pay" to be effective August 1, 1969. It is indicated that Colonel Cassedy's annotations on that application show that he was fully aware of the fact that the assignment to the Retired Reserve was without eligibility for retired pay at age 60. At that point, he had only completed 14 years, 2 months and 3 days of satisfactory service.

Based on the foregoing, it is contended that in spite of the fact that the member received the letter of August 1, 1969, containing erroneous retirement information, he was well aware that he was not eligible for retired pay at age 60.

In rejoinder, the member made two principle assertions. First, when he received the August 11, 1969 letter, he thought that there had been a correction of an earlier mistake regarding the creditableness of certain of the years of service already performed. Second, under the law and regulations in effect in 1969 he could have secured additional years of service in grade with the Selective Service after transfer to the Retired Reserve until his 60th birthday; that there was sufficient time between August 1969 and December 20, 1975 (his 60th birthday) to acquire all of the additional years of creditable service needed for retirement eligibility even though it would have inconvenienced him, but he refrained from doing so because of the August 11, 1969 letter.

The pertinent language in 10 U.S.C. 1406 permitting denial or revocation of an erroneous notification of eligibility, is when "it resulted directly from the fraud or misrepresentation of the person." The term "fraud" is defined as the "intentional perversion of truth in order to induce another to part with something of value or to surrender a legal right" and "misrepresentation" is defined as giving "a false or misleading representation of." Webster's Seventh New Collegiate Dictionary (1963).

The clear connotation of those terms is that they require a positive act on the part of an individual with intent to achieve an improper end or gain unjust enrichment. The points raised concerning the information provided Colonel Cassedy over several years' time suggest that he may have had reasonable grounds to believe that he did not have sufficient time to qualify for retirement pay as of the date he was placed in the Retired Reserve and possibly should have had doubts as to the propriety of the August 11, 1969 notice. However, such arguments fall far short of the criteria stated in the law. There is no evidence of record to show that the member in any way induced or caused his record of creditable service, which record was maintained by the Air Force, to be altered or confused or the erroneous statement concerning retirement eligibility to be introduced into the letter sent to him. That is, there is no showing of "fraud or misrepresentation" on his part. Therefore, it is our view that the error made was purely administrative and the resulting situation in this case was of the type which the Congress sought to prevent by enactment of 10 U.S.C. 1406. Accordingly, question c. is answered in the affirmative, subject, of course, to the adjustment limitation authorized in the last sentence of 10 U.S.C. 1406.

[B-193241]

Contracts—Negotiation—Specifications Unavailable — Basis for Exception to Formal Advertising—Offeror Assistance in Defining Needs

"Exception 10" negotiating authority for National Aeronautics and Space Administration (NASA) computerized information processing system has been justified because: (1) NASA needed offerors' approaches to work requirements to evaluate proposed acceptability and to assist in defining reasonable needs for service unlike negotiated procurement in *Informatics, Inc.*, B–190203, March 20, 1978, 78–1 CPD 215, where procuring agency intended to evaluate offerors' approaches only as part of responsibility evaluation and not as part of proposal evaluation; and (2) there is no indication NASA ever formally advertised prior procurements for similar system unlike prior advertised procurement history in *Informatics* decision. B–190203, Mar. 20, 1978, modified in part.

Contracts—Specifications—Restrictive—Minimum Needs Requirement—Administrative Determination—Reasonableness

Two-month phase-in period is appropriate limitation where it appears that phase-in period will cost less than longer phase-in and it is speculative that higher performance cost will necessarily follow 2-month phase-in when nothing in record of experience supports that view.

In the matter of International Computaprint Corporation, April 10, 1979:

International Computaprint Corporation (ICC) has protested the issuance of request for proposals (RFP) W10–20668/HWE–2 by the National Aeronautics and Space Administration (NASA). NASA issued the RFP on July 18, 1978, for the "personnel, services and supplies necessary to support the operation of the NASA Scientific and Technical Information Facility" on a cost-plus–award-fee basis. ICC contends that the procurement should have been issued under formal advertising procedures. Further, ICC insists that the RFP's stated "phase-in period" unnecessarily restricts competition because the period is too short. For the reasons set forth at length below, we reject ICC's grounds of protest.

Background

By Determination and Findings (D&F) dated December 16, 1977, NASA's contracting officer for the procurement found that:

The proposed contract will require the contractor selected to continue with the performance of the above facility and associated services and be responsible for a wide-ranging complex of highly specialized documentation and information functions; and the production of scientific and technical information and NASA technology utilization products which must be coordinated and integrated at multiple points and levels to insure control and continuance of activities without disruption to the program. This will involve a comprehensive direct access computerized information system necessitating high-speed input processing, publication preparation, search and retrieval, and dissemination of information from world-wide aerospace and aeronautics subject matter to the world-wide aerospace and aeronautics scientific community on demand and at scheduled intervals. These activities are dependent upon keeping abreast of scientific information and technology, as well as, possessing a high degree of competence in documentation techniques, information services, microfiche production, computer operations, management information systems, system design and programming, process and method improvement, and quality assurance.

Formal advertising is neither feasible nor practicable for this procurement because it is impossible to describe in precise detail or by definite drawings and specifications the exact nature of the work to be performed. Information that will be obtained during some phases of this effort will be used to determine the depth of consideration to be given to other phases. Through negotiations the Government is afforded an opportunity to evaluate in detail the contractor's technical capability, his understanding of the work to be performed, and other associated factors that are essential to the proposed procurement.

Based on these findings the contracting officer determined that the procurement was properly for the negotiated procurement method, as follows:

On the basis of the above findings, I hereby determine that this proposed procurement is for services for which it is impracticable to secure competition by formal advertising. Specifically, it is impossible to draft adequate specifications or any other detailed description for the required services.

Upon the basis of the Determination and Findings above, I hereby decide that this contract will be negotiated pursuant to 10 U.S.C. 2304(a)(10) ["exception 10" negotiating authority] and paragraph 3.210-2(xiii) of the NASA Procurement Regulations.

RFP

The tasks outlined in the above D&F were described in the "Statement of Work and Work Breakdown Structure" section of the RFP (pages 4–119 through 4–163). For example, at page 4–161 the RFP described requirements for the contractor to furnish "ADP support with Government-furnished equipment," as follows:

The Contractor shall provide the tasks described below:

Computer Operations

The Contractor shall operate installed ADP equipment and associated hardware listed in the "Facility Contract" on a 24-hour basis and, where necessary, shall provide installation and start-up and/or changeover support for such ADP equipment and for other equipment provided by NASA. The Contractor shall provide equipment maintenance for those items listed in Attachment Number 4, hereto. He shall provide all end products and services specified by the Scientific and Technical Information Branch and the Technology Utilization Branch under this contract. * * *

This task shall include * * * (1) input processing control; (2) computer scheduling; (3) magnetic tape/disk library; and, (4) output processing control.

Data Entry * * *

Operating System Programming * * *

Discontinued and Off-Line Files * * *

The RFP also contained evaluation criteria under which proposals were to be "numerically weighted and scored." For example, with respect to the "ADP support" requirements described above, the evaluation criteria provided that proposals would be evaluated for:

Demonstrated understanding and competence in the approach for (1) ADP support; (2) systems study; (3) systems support; and, (4) systems development. The approach must show a high degree of familiarity with advanced computer applications, on-line systems, communications networks, remote data entry, computerized photocomposition, and hardware/software interfaces. The plan should also demonstrate an understanding of the special ADP problems associated with (1) maintaining high system reliability associated with extremely large files with interrelated indexes and hierarchial file structure * * * ("Mission Suitability Factors," Technical Operations Plan, page 3–10).

Propriety of Negotiation

ICC insists that the "product is clearly defined in the existing specifications submitted to each prospective bidder [and that] the approach actually consists of an offeror's ability to adequately staff and maintain existing NASA facilities and to provide technical manpower to carry forward the development of new programs." ICC further argues:

Since the procurement document and accompanying specifications clearly define the products desired, and since the MISSION SUITABILITY FACTORS constitute an adequate means of determining an offeror's understanding of the work, the method of approach cannot be a valid basis for a negotiated procurement.

By contrast, NASA continues to insist its description of work tasks does not describe its needs with sufficient specificity to permit formal advertising. As stated by NASA:

* * * the RFP does not give detailed step-by-step instructions for every task but rather requires offerors to present their own approach for accomplishing many of the tasks. Since no two offerors will be alike in their approach to performance of these tasks, there is no common basis sufficient to permit formal advertising. Moreover, in order for the SEB to discover and evaluate how each offeror proposes to accomplish the tasks, written proposals and discussions with offerors in the competitive range are necessary.

* * * The statement of Work is not a "how to perform" instruction. The RFP here goes beyond the agency's use of negotiated procurement merely to determine an offeror's "understanding" of the requirements. Rather, many parts of the Statement of Work require the offeror to present a *plan as to what he will do* in order to accomplish the tasks. The manning level and skill mix for most WBS areas will vary from offeror to offeror. * * *

Throughout the RFP, in those sections devoted to proposal preparation and evaluation (pages 3–4 to 3–19), there are many areas, too numerous to reiterate here, where offerors are requested to provide a plan or approach as to how a certain portion of the work will be accomplished. We maintain that a reading of these sections clearly demonstrates the need for the SEB to evaluate the variety of different approaches submitted by the competitors. Moreover, we believe you will find reasonable our judgment that we could not describe our needs with sufficient specificity to permit formal advertising.

Analysis

Both ICC and NASA agree that the precedent established by *Informatics, Inc.*, B–190203, March 20, 1978, 78–1 CPD 215, offers guidance in resolving this issue.

In that case—which also involved a protest against the use of the negotiated procurement method—we made certain observations about when "exception ten" negotiating authority may be properly employed. As we said in that case: "In general, the fact that a procurement is for 'complex' supplies or services does not *per se* preclude the use of formal advertising. * * * the hope of minimizing * * * difficulties through negotiations does not authorize procurement by negotiation unless it is impossible to draft a specification adequate for advertising."

The questioned negotiated procurement in *Informatics* was for the preparation and extraction of patent data via a computerized information system. The procuring agency (the Department of Commerce) admitted: (1) complete specifications for the work products ("input" and "output") were set forth in the RFP; (2) no technical evaluation factors, or any other evaluation factors other than the total evaluated price, were identified in the solicitation; (3) prior solicitations for similar services had been formally advertised; and (4) the agency wanted to evaluate the offeror's "in-between proposed actions" (that is, the actual approach for ADP support) *only* as part of a responsibility evaluation and not as a part of a proposal evaluation leading to a judgment as to the comparative merits of the approach.

In rejecting Commerce's claim that it could properly invoke "exception ten" negotiating authority given the above admissions, we concluded:

> Where there are specifications adequate enough to permit competition, the desire to conduct discussions with offerors to assure their understanding of the specifications or to cover matters traditionally related to responsibility (such as the "in-between" technical approach here) cannot, in our opinion, authorize a negotiated procurement. See *Cincinnati Electronics Corporation*, 55 Comp. Gen. 1479 (1976), 76-2 CPD 286.

ICC views the quoted statement as applying to NASA's procurement here. Specifically, ICC apparently believes that NASA should not be able to justify "exception ten" negotiating authority by pointing to— among other things—its proposed proposal evaluation of offerors' approaches for ADP support.

It must be remembered that our quoted remarks regarding the evaluation of "in-between technical approaches" for furnishing ADP support were said in a context where the procuring agency had determined that these approaches were not needed to determine the technical acceptability of a proposal or to assist the agency in defining its reasonable needs for the service. Moreover, they were said in a procurement (as was the case in *Cincinnati Electronics Corporation, supra*), where there was a history of formal advertising under prior solicitations for similar products and services. To the extent, however, that the quoted remarks may give the impression that the evaluation of proposed approaches for ADP support may never be used in proposal evaluation or in assisting an agency to define its reasonable needs for a product or service such that the proposed evaluation supports "exception 10" negotiating authority, the remarks are expressly modified.

Based on our analysis, it may well be that NASA and Commerce may have reached diametrically opposed technical judgments about the need for offerors to assist in the definition of reasonable needs for ADP support. Nevertheless, we will not substitute our opinion for that of a procuring agency in matters involving technical complexity and judgment even where other governmental units may advance differing technical judgments on similar matters so long as the particular agency judgment in question is reasonably founded. See *E. I. du Pont de Nemours & Company*, et al., B-190611, September 22, 1978, 78-2 CPD 218. Based on our review of the record, we cannot question NASA's stated rationale for reviewing—as a matter of proposal evaluation—the offerors' proposed approaches for—among other things—ADP support in an attempt to obtain offerors' assistance in defining its reasonable needs for the service. Specifically, we cannot question NASA's technical judgment that the varying possible approaches for ADP support are so divergent that it is impossible to draft adequate specifications suitable for insuring fair and equal competition on a common basis under the advertised procedure.

"Phase-In Period"

ICC contends that the "two month phase-in period" for the contract is too short a period given the "contemplated" 62-month contract period* and that this short period necessarily gives the incumbent contractor for the services an unfair advantage—therey resulting in increased costs to NASA and arbitrary restriction of competition.

NASA insists that a 60-day phase-in period provides sufficient time around which offerors can propose effective phase-in plans. NASA further argues:

   (1) Prior solicitations for similar services have included 60 days for phase-in and no prior complaint from industry has been received;
   (2) Six offerors in addition to the incumbent offeror have submitted proposals—therefore indicating that the stated phase-in period is not restricting competition;
   (3) No point scoring advantage accrues to the incumbent because the phase-in factor is only rated for acceptability, not points;
   (4) Increasing the phase-in period should tend to increase costs rather than decrease costs as ICC suggests.

In reply to NASA's arguments, ICC still insists that it would be "far more costly to 'slap together' an organization to meet the 60 day start-up requirement [which] will lead to poor quality work, which then forces overstaffing to meet the requirements."

We have recognized that firms may enjoy a competitive advantage by virtue of their incumbency but that the advantage may be questioned only if the competitive advantage enjoyed results from unfair action by the Government. *Amdahl Corporation*, B–192588, December 15, 1978, 78–2 CPD 417, and cases cited in text. The competitive advantage accruing to an incumbent in this procurement is not the result of "unfair action" but simply results from the reasonable need of NASA to evaluate nonincumbent offerors' approaches to, and costs of, taking over an ongoing operation.

---

*Actually, NASA only firmly committed itself in the RFP to a 12-month contract ending on July 31, 1980; performance past that date depended on NASA's exercise of option rights.

As to the length of the phase-in period, ICC has not questioned NASA's observations that a 2-month phase-in period has not been the subject of complaint under earlier similar contracts—thus indicating that historical experience supports the reasonableness of NASA's phase-in period. Although ICC does not dispute that a 60-day phase-in period is less costly than a longer period, it contends that it will result in increased costs during the performance of the contract as a consequence of a hastily arranged work organization. We will not question an agency's determination of what its actual minimum needs are unless there is a clear showing that the determination has no reasonable basis. *Informatics, Inc., supra.* Here the agency has determined its minimum needs in terms of reduced costs. ICC disagrees only as to the ultimate cost. However, it is speculative in this case that higher performance cost will necessarily follow from a short phase-in period. Nothing in the record of experience has been cited to support that view. Accordingly, we do not find the 60-day phase-in requirement in this case exceeds the Government's needs.

Protest denied.

[B-193427]

Details—Compensation—Higher Grade Duties Assignment—Excessive Period

Employee, who was temporarily promoted to higher grade position for 120 days, was returned to former grade but was then immediately detailed to same higher level position for additional 132 days. Under *Turner-Caldwell* decisions employee must be detailed to higher level position without compensation of higher level position for 120 days before entitlement to temporary promotion begins on 121st day. Therefore, the period the employee served on temporary promotion may not be included in computation of detail.

In the matter of Donald L. Bressler—Detail to Higher Graded Position, April 10, 1979:

This action is in response to the request for an advance decision from Fred L. Hayes, a certifying officer of the National Park Service, Rocky Mountain Regional Office, U.S. Department of the Interior, reference W1819 (RMR)AF, concerning the claim of Mr. Donald L. Bressler, an employee of the Denver Service Center, National Park Service, to a retroactive temporary promotion with backpay for the period of time he served as Acting Associate Manager of the Denver Service Center. The question presented for decision is whether the period of a temporary promotion which immediately precedes a detail may be included in computing the length of the detail.

The agency report states that effective March 28, 1976, Mr. Bressler was given a temporary promotion from Deputy Associate Manager, grade GS–14, to the position of Acting Associate Manager, grade

GS–15, for a period not to exceed 120 days. On July 25, 1976, Mr. Bressler's temporary promotion was terminated by a "Change to Lower Grade" personnel action. However, it appears that on that same day Mr. Bressler was informally detailed back to the grade GS–15 position and that he performed the duties of that position through December 3, 1976, when he was selected for the position of Associate Manager. The agency questions whether Mr. Bressler may be retroactively promoted for the entire period of the informal detail from July 25 through December 3, 1976, a period of 132 days.

Our Office has held that where an employee is detailed to a higher graded position and the agency fails to seek Civil Service Commission approval to extend the detail for a period beyond 120 days, the agency must award the employee a retroactive temporary promotion and backpay if he continues to perform those higher grade duties. *Turner-Caldwell*, 55 Comp. Gen. 539 (1975), affirmed at 56 *id.* 427 (1977). In the present case, the agency has not questioned whether Mr. Bressler was actually detailed to a higher graded position, and, in response to our request, the agency has submitted additional evidence which tends to establish that Mr. Bressler was detailed to the position of Associate Manager during the period from July 25 through December 3, 1976.

The question presented by the agency is whether Mr. Bressler is entitled to a retroactive temporary promotion with backpay for the entire period of the detail; that is, whether Mr. Bressler's temporary promotion for 120 days serves the same purpose as a 120-day detail. As noted above, our *Turner-Caldwell* decisions hold that an employee must be temporarily promoted retroactive to the 121st day of an extended detail which has not been approved by the Civil Service Commission. However, we believe that there must first be a period of 120 days where the employee has been detailed and has not been compensated at the higher level. See *Marvin R. Dunn*, B–192437, September 20, 1978. Since a detail and a temporary promotion are separate and distinct personnel actions, we do not believe the period of the temporary promotion to a position in which the employee is later detailed is includable in computing the length of the detail for the purposes of our *Turner-Caldwell* decisions. Therefore, we conclude that Mr. Bressler's entitlement to a retroactive temporary promotion would begin on the 121st day following the commencement of the detail on July 25, 1976.

Accordingly, Mr. Bressler's claim may be allowed only to the extent consistent with the above discussion if otherwise proper.

〔B–193853〕

Contracts — Protests — Procedures — Bid Protest Procedures— Time for Filing—Mailgram Transmission of Protest

Mailgram protesting alleged improprieties in request for proposals, whose receipt was recorded by General Accounting Office (GAO) after closing date for receipt of proposals, is untimely and ineligible for consideration where mailgram did not evidence a date of transmission at least 3 days prior to final date for filing a protest. 4 C.F.R. 20.2(b)(3).

Contracts — Protests — Procedures — Bid Protest Procedures— Time for Filing—Time of Receipt Establishment

GAO Bid Protest Control Unit time/date stamp is *prima facie* evidence of time of receipt of bid protest at GAO, and absent affirmative evidence to the contrary to show actual timely receipt, time/date stamp controls.

In the matter of Linguistic Systems, Incorporated, April 10, 1979:

Linguistic Systems, Incorporated (Linguistic) protests various alleged improprieties in request for proposals No. F 33657–79–R–0078, issued by the Wright–Patterson Air Force Base, Ohio. The date set for receipt of proposals was December 29, 1978.

The protest was sent to the General Accounting Office (GAO) by mailgram addressed to the Bid Protest Control Unit and was transmitted by the Postal Service to Washington, D.C. on December 29, 1978, at 1:06 a.m. The protest was recorded as received by the GAO Bid Protest Control Unit at 9:35 a.m. on January 4, 1979.

Our Bid Protest Procedures require that a protest based upon alleged improprieties in a request for proposals be "filed" prior to the closing date for receipt of proposals. 4 C.F.R. 20.2(b)(1) (1978). The term "filed" means receipt in GAO. 4 C.F.R. 20.2(b)(3). Thus the protest on its face was not timely.

However, protester has furnished a statement from the Postmaster in Washington, D.C. advising that in the normal course of business, the mailgram should have been received at the Postal Service's Washington, D.C. mailgram terminal at 1:22 a.m. December 29, 1978; that it should have been forwarded to the Government Mails Section shortly after 4 a.m. the same date; and would have been dispatched to GAO no later than 9 a.m. that day. The Postmaster further advises that a search of his records indicated neither a record of delayed mail nor a record of returned mail.

By way of background, ordinary mail, including mailgrams, is not time and date stamped as received by the GAO central mailroom. Consequently, the first documentation of the receipt of a protest by GAO is the Bid Protest Control Unit's time/date stamp. Thus, it is impossible to determine whether or not this protest was physically present in GAO prior to the December 29 closing date, and the absence of a Postal Service record to indicate delayed mail is not persuasive of its actual receipt by GAO. For example, although the mailgram *should* have been received in Washington at 1:22 a.m., there is no record to show that it actually was dispatched to GAO at 9 a.m. Moreover, the Postal Service advises that once a mailgram is delivered to its Government Mails Section, it enters the ordinary uncontrolled mailstream for first class mail, so that it cannot be determined whether an individual item of mail actually arrived at its intended destination on a particular date. The time/date stamp must therefore be considered *prima facie* evidence of the time of receipt at this Office.

For that reason, our Bid Protest Procedures have anticipated that in the normal course of business an indeterminate amount of time will necessarily transpire between dispatch of a mailgram and receipt by our Bid Protest Control Unit, the address specified in our Bid Protest Procedures, *supra.* Accordingly, those procedures specify that any protest received by this Office after the prescribed time limits [December 29, 1978, in this instance] shall not be considered unless it was sent by mailgram not later than the third day prior to the final date for filing a protest, with the only acceptable evidence to establish the date of transmission by mailgram being the automatic date indication appearing on the mailgram. 4 C.F.R. 20.2(b)(3).

Thus, offerors electing to submit a protest by mailgram are clearly placed on notice that if a mailgram is dispatched 3 days or more prior to the date for filing a protest, consideration of the protest is assured, whereas dispatching of a mailgram less than 3 days prior to the filing date places the risk of late receipt upon the protester. Our Bid Protest Procedures therefore caution protesters to submit their protests in the manner which will assure earliest receipt, 4 C.F.R. 20.2(b)(3), and we have charged protesters with the responsibility for making sure a protest is filed in a timely manner. *Somervell & Associates, Ltd.*, B–192426, September 18, 1978, 78–2 CPD 208.

In a similar vein, where a bidder or offeror is required to submit a bid or proposal to an office designated by the solicitation within a contracting agency by a specified time, he is responsible for allowing sufficient time to permit a mailed bid or proposal to pass through a contracting agency's central mailroom and reach the specified office by the indicated time. See *Lectro–Magnetics, Inc.*, 56 Comp. Gen. 50 (1976), 76–2 CPD 371. We believe this principle is no less applicable to protests submitted through the mails to this Office.

The time limitations prescribed in GAO Bid Protest Procedures are not regarded as waivable technicalities, as their purpose is to provide expeditious consideration of bid protests without unduly burdening Government procurements. See *California Computer Products*,

Inc.—Reconsideration, B–193437, February 22, 1979, 79–1 CPD 391. As a consequence, we have strictly enforced the time limitations set forth in our procedures and have dismissed protests as untimely without any consideration of their merits when the filing deadlines have not been met. Thus we have dismissed protests that were only 1 day late, *Lemont Shipbuilding and Repair Company*, B–180104, January 21, 1974, 74–1 CPD 20; that were late due to the mailing time required from Saigon, South Vietnam, *Johnson Associates, Inc.*, 53 Comp. Gen. 518 (1974), 74–1 CPD 43; when the protester was unaware of the time limitations, *DeWitt Transfer and Storage Company*, 53 Comp. Gen. 533 (1974), 74–1 CPD 47; when a protester sought additional clarification from the contracting agency after the agency's initial denial of the protest, *A. C. Manufacturing Company*, B–186298, August 9, 1976, 76–2 CPD 137; and even where the protester was inadvertently misled by the contracting agency, *Mr. Scrub Car Wash Systems, Inc.*, B–186586, July 9, 1976, 76–2 CPD 29. Recently we even declined to consider a protest that was filed one minute late. *Somervell & Associates, Ltd., supra.* Moreover, we have infrequently invoked the "significant issue" exception to these time limitations (4 C.F.R. 20.2 (c)), since that exception relates only to the presence of a "principle of widespread interest," 52 Comp. Gen. 20 (1972), which is not found in most cases, *see, e.g.*, 53 Comp. Gen. 412 (1973), and have yet to invoke the "good cause shown" exception also provided in 4 C.F.R. 20.2(c). *See, e.g., Somervell & Associates, Ltd., supra;* 52 Comp. Gen. 20 *supra.*

Since this late mailgram protest was not transmitted 3 days prior to the date for filing and absent any affirmative evidence to show actual timely receipt of the protest, we consider the protest to be untimely filed and not for consideration on the merits.

[B–192908]

Contractors — Responsibility — Contracting Officer's Affirmative Determination Accepted—Exceptions—Not Supported by Record

Allegation that low bidder is nonresponsible is not considered since General Accounting Office does not review affirmative determinations of responsibility except where fraud is shown or failure to meet definitive responsibility criteria is alleged, neither of which is present here.

Bids—Responsiveness—Unqualified Offer to Meet All Solicitation Terms

Contention that low bid is nonresponsive since work called for by solicitation cannot be performed at level of effort reflected by bid price is meritless since test of whether bid is responsive is whether bid constitutes an offer to perform, without exception, the exact thing called for in solicitation and low bid does not take exception to solicitation.

Contracts—Awards—Small Business Concerns—Acceptability of Large Business on Basis of Lower Price—Partial Set-Aside Dissolved

Small business concern's unwillingness to accept set-aside quantity at substantially lower, allegedly below cost, bid of large business upon which non-set-aside quantity was awarded properly resulted in dissolution of set-aside. Even if it were proven that large business bid below cost, that in itself would not bar award to that firm, and under partial set-aside procedure Government's obligation is simply to reserve a portion of its needs for award to small business firms at the same price obtained for the unrestricted portion.

In the matter of Fiber Materials, Inc., April 12, 1979:

This protest concerns an Air Force two-step procurement of missile nosetips, half of which were set aside for small business concerns. Two firms competed for this award: Fiber Materials, Inc. (FMI), a small business, and AVCO Corporation, Systems Division (AVCO), a large business. AVCO's step-two bid was less than half of FMI's. FMI has protested the award of the non-set-aside portion to AVCO, as well as the dissolution of the partial set-aside and award of that quantity to AVCO, after FMI refused to take the set-aside quantity at AVCO's bid price. FMI contends that AVCO's bid was below cost, and that the firm was therefore not responsible, its bid was nonresponsive, and that the set-aside program was circumvented. Other issues raised by FMI but abandoned after a bid protest conference at our Office will not be considered.

The first-step request for technical proposals (RFTP) was for the purchase of an initial quantity of 60 nosetips and option year quantities totaling 476 nosetips over fiscal years 1979, 1980, and 1981. AVCO and FMI were the only firms who responded to the RFTP and both were found by the Air Force to have submitted acceptable technical proposals. The Air Force then issued an invitation for bids to AVCO and FMI for the nosetips as the second step of the procurement. The bids were as follows:

AVCO

ITEM NO.	ITEM	UNIT PRICE	ITEM PRICE
0001	60 EA CCNTs*	$15,000	$900,000
0002	1 LOT DATA	N/A	20,000
0003	105 EA CCNTs (FY '79)	11,142.90	1,170,000
0004	1 LOT DATA (FY '79)	N/A	10,000
0005	180 EA CCNTs (FY '80)	9,900	1,782,000
0006	1 LOT DATA (FY '80)	N/A	17,000
0007	191 EA CCNTs (FY '81)	10,890	2,080,000
0008	1 LOT DATA (FY '81)	N/A	20,000
Total price			$5,998,995

FMI

ITEM NO.	ITEM	UNIT PRICE	ITEM PRICE
0001_____	60 EA CCNTs*_____	$36, 256	$2, 175, 360
0002_____	1 LOT DATA_____	N/A	280, 560
0003_____	105 EA CCNTs (FY'79)___	22, 898	2, 404, 290
0004_____	1 LOT DATA (FY'79)_____	N/A	224, 070
0005_____	180 EA CCNTs (FY'80)___	23, 121	4, 161, 780
0006_____	1 LOT DATA (FY'80)_____	N/A	325, 440
0007_____	191 EA CCNTs (FY'81)___	26, 664	4, 710, 824
0008_____	1 LOT DATA (FY'81)_____	N/A	391, 743
Total price_____			$14, 674, 067

*Carbon-carbon nosetips

The Air Force compared AVCO's bid to the Government's estimate and found that while AVCO's bid was lower than the Government estimate, it was reasonable. The Air Force then awarded the non-set-aside portion to AVCO. In accordance with the solicitation provisions prescribed by Defense Acquisition Regulation (DAR) § 1–706.6(d) (1976 ed.), FMI was offered the remaining set-aside portion at the prices bid by AVCO, which as we have noted were less than half of FMI's.

FMI protested, contending that AVCO's bid on the non-set-aside portion was substantially below cost and that a small business such as FMI could not afford to produce the nosetips at AVCO's bid price. Therefore, FMI argued, acceptance of AVCO's bid would circumvent the Air Force's decision to set-aside half of the procurement for small businesses. FMI further alleged that the contracting officer was required to reject AVCO's bid as a "buy-in"; that AVCO's bid was nonresponsive since AVCO could not comply with the specifications at the level of effort reflected by AVCO's bid; and that AVCO was nonresponsible since the work could not be performed at AVCO's bid price. FMI refused to accept the set-aside quantity at the prices bid by AVCO. Since no firms, other than AVCO, then responded to a request for technical proposals for the remaining quantity, the Air Force awarded the remaining quantity to AVCO.

The three issues before us—that the small business set-aside procedure has been circumvented, AVCO is not responsible and its bid is nonresponsive—flow from the premise that AVCO submitted a below cost bid. In support of its position that AVCO's bid was below cost, FMI has submitted evidence of how FMI arrived at its bid price. FMI has also submitted evidence of the preproduction costs of AVCO and FMI under an experimental program. FMI maintains that most of the material costs are fixed because of the small number of suppliers capable of supplying the qualified material specified by the solicitation: therefore, FMI's material costs should approximate AVCO's. FMI also maintains that the nosetip specifications are such that they inhibit, if not preclude, the introduction of newer cost savings techniques.

In its initial report to our Office, the Air Force stated:

* * * Under competitive bid conditions the Government is not privy to the bidder's cost data; accordingly, the relationship of AVCO's price to its expected cost cannot be determined. However, AVCO's bid price is in line with the Government estimate and there is no evidence that the Government estimate is inaccurate. * * *

The Air Force submitted a second report after the conference was held in this protest, in which it advises:

* * * we have again reviewed the procedures employed to develop the [Air Force] estimate and the resultant estimate itself, and we can find no fault with either. As noted in the contracting officer's statement, the Government estimate was based on actual experience on the pilot production program and an industry survey by the AFML [Air Force Materials Laboratory] to access efficiencies and savings which could be anticipated in a large scale production program. We believe this approach to be valid and the estimate as derived provides a reasonable basis for assessment of the bids submitted in response to the invitation. Further, our review showed that the estimate considered the total nosetip and its fabrication and was based on the best available information. FMI has submitted no evidence to support its conclusion that the Government's estimate is unreasonable. Instead, its contention is based solely on the fact that the estimate is below the amount FMI considers to be realistic and which it bid in response to the solicitation. * * *

AVCO, which participated in the protest as an interested party, asserts that it bid "according to its continuing bidding policies, that is, a reasonable expectation to accomplish the effort with a resulting reasonable profit."

We have reviewed FMI's presentation together with the Government estimate and are unable to conclude with certainty that the Government estimate is incorrect or that AVCO's bid was below cost. However, for the reasons given below we do not believe that the Air Force's acceptance of AVCO's bid, even if it was below cost, violated applicable procurement law or regulations.

Our Office has often stated that acceptance of a below cost bid is not legally objectionable. *Homexx International Corporation*, B-192034, September 22, 1978, 78-2 CPD 219; *Allied Technology, Inc.*, B-185868, July 12, 1976, 76-2 CPD 34. In fact, rejection of a below cost bid requires finding that the bidder is nonresponsible. *Consolidated Elevator Company*, B-190929, March 3, 1978, 78-1 CPD 166. The Air Force determined that AVCO was responsible, and this Office does not review affirmative determinations of responsibility unless fraud on the part of procuring officials is shown or it is alleged that definitive responsibility criteria have not been met, neither of which is present in this case.

With regard to FMI's contention that the Air Force was required to reject AVCO's bid as nonresponsive since AVCO allegedly could not comply with the specifications at the level of effort reflected by AVCO's bid, we note that a bid is responsive if it constitutes an offer to perform, without exception, the exact thing called for in the solicitation. *Vintage Services, Inc.*, B–190445, January 11, 1978, 78–1 CPD 25. Since AVCO has not taken exception to the terms of the solicitation its bid is clearly responsive.

Finally, FMI argues that acceptance of AVCO's bid effectively circumvented a partial small business set-aside, because FMI cannot afford to produce these items at AVCO's price and therefore FMI was compelled to refuse the set-aside.

Nothing in the Small Business Act, 15 U.S.C. § 631 *et seq.* (1976), requires that a particular procurement be set aside for small business and such a decision rests with the procuring agency. *Tidewater Protective Services, Inc., and Others*, 56 Comp. Gen. 115, 123 (1976), 76–2 CPD 462. The partial small business set-aside provisions which are part of this IFB simply contemplate that a portion of the procurement will be reserved for small business firms who will be given the opportunity of contracting with the Government "at the highest unit price for each item awarded on the non-set-aside." If acceptance of AVCO's bid on the non-set-aside portion is not legally objectionable, then all the Air Force is obligated to do is offer FMI the set-aside quantity at AVCO's bid price.

The protest is denied.

[B–192996]

Contracts — Specifications — Failure to Furnish Something Required—Information—Delivery—Transportation Mode

Under an invitation for bids which requires a bidder to supply information relating to point of origin and mode(s) of transportation for delivery of contract items F.O.B. origin, and to load items on carrier's vehicle, failure of bidder to furnish all or some of transportation data did not render bid nonresponsive. Where solicitation requires delivery F.O.B. origin, information concerning mode of transportation can be acquired by the Government after bid opening because bidder signed Standard Form 88 committing itself to deliver to designated points at Government's option, and information is extrinsically verifiable and is not under bidder's control.

Bids — Two-Step Procurement — Second Step—Deviating From First Step

Information furnished by bidder under second step solicitation requiring transportation data for F.O.B. origin bids, which indicated that contract item's shipping weight exceeded the specification's maximum weight for highway transport, does not render bid nonresponsive. Bidder's proposal under step one, which was incorporated in its step-two bid, proposed to furnish item capable of disassembly to meet requirement, which was permitted by the Government's specification.

Bids—Evaluation—Incorporation of Terms by Reference

Bidder's failure to submit entire soliciation package does not render bid non-responsive where portions of package submitted unambiguously incorporate by reference material terms and conditions of solicitation.

Contracts—Specifications—Failure to Furnish Something Required—Invitation to Bid Attachments

Bidder's insertion of N/C (no charge) or a price next to each line item representing data items described on forms not returned with bid package obligates bidder to supply data items in accordance with specifications.

Contracts—Protests—Procedures—Bid Protest Procedures—Time for Filing—Contract Award Notice Effect

Protest concerning award to alleged nonresponsive bidder filed within 10 days of receipt of notice of award is timely filed even though protester had prior knowledge of alleged nonresponsiveness of competitor's bid, since grounds for protest arose only upon receipt of notice of award.

Bids—Acceptance Time Limitation—Omitted from Invitation

Statement in solicitation that bids would be rejected if they allowed less than number of days specified in "Offer" portion of Standard Form 33 (SF 33) does not establish a minimum bid acceptance period where SF 33 is not altered to establish a minimum period which would eliminate the option provided bidders to offer less than a 60-day acceptance period.

In the matter of International Harvester Company, April 12, 1979:

International Harvester Company (International) protests the award of a contract to Caterpillar Tractor Co. (CAT) under invitation for bids (IFB) No. DAAK70–78–B–0411 issued by the Army. The IFB, the second step in a two-step procurement, requested offers for the manufacture and delivery of 177 Rough Terrain Container Handlers with top-handlers.

International maintains that CAT's bid is nonresponsive for five reasons: (1) CAT's bid contemplates shipment by only *one mode* of transportation even though the solicitation provides for delivery of contract items on an F.O.B. origin basis and provides the Government with the option of deciding the most economical mode of transportation for delivery; (2) the item described in CAT's bid does not comply with the payload weight limitation for highway transport; (3) the firm's bid does not offer to supply the required data items; (4) CAT altered the bid acceptance period in its bid after bid opening; (5) the bid acceptance period in CAT's bid is ambiguous.

For the following reasons, we deny the protest.

Bids were solicited on an F.O.B. origin basis. Because delivery points were unknown, the costs of transporting supplies to destination would not be evaluated for award. The F.O.B. point for delivery on F.O.B. origin bids was specified as F.O.B. carrier's equipment, wharf or freight station at the Government's option.

The solicitation stated in clause B.16, entitled "Transportation Data for F.O.B. Origin Offers," that "the Government will ship the contract items using that mode of common carrier and the type and size of equipment which will result in the lowest overall transportation cost." Because shipment might be made utilizing a variety of modes and sizes of common carrier's equipment, the Government required submission of transportation characteristics, including the type and size of carrier's equipment. The protester maintains that by providing the information sought from bidders under this clause, bidders were *offering* a choice of transportation modes to the Government. Unlike International and one other bidder which listed rail *and* truck transport for their F.O.B. origin point(s), CAT listed only one mode of transportation (motor) from its plant and one mode of transportation (rail) from its subcontractor's plant. International argues that a bidder's failure to provide information regarding *more than one mode* of transportation nullifies the Government's right of choice because of the absence of alternative data. The protester also refers to other clauses in the solicitation which reaffirm the requirement that the Government have complete freedom of choice between multiple modes of shipment.

We basically disagree with the purpose and effect attributed by the protester to clause B.16. In our opinion, the bidder's *offer* to deliver at the points designated by the Government arises from the express statement to that effect in its signed offer on Standard Form 33 (SF 33) and is not perfected by providing information under clause B.16. The protester attributes too much significance to the act of providing information required by this clause. B.16 expressly states that the information would be used by the Government at the time of shipment in selecting the mode, type and size of common carrier equipment. We think it is clear that the Government did not intend to require a further affirmative offer to deliver as designated.

Although CAT may not have provided complete information concerning transportation modes, we do not construe this deficiency as limiting its offer in SF 33 to furnish the items at the designated points, that is "F.O.B. carrier's equipment, wharf or freight station at the Government's option." This information may be acquired by the Government after bid opening because the availability of a particular mode of transportation is extrinsically verifiable and is not under the bidder's control. 42 Comp. Gen. 434 (1963); *Beta Systems, Inc., et al.*, B–184413, February 18, 1976, 76–1 CPD 109.

The protester argues that the solicitation establishes a maximum weight limitation of 72,000 pounds for highway transport of the trucks deliverable under the contract but that CAT bid a nonresponsive shipping weight of 78,100 pounds. To support its allegation of a maximum shipping weight limitation, the protester refers to clause 3.1.2.1 of the applicable military specification for the item. This provides:

3.1.2.1 *Highway transport*. The truck shall be transportable on semitrailer(s) * * *. Limited disassembly of the truck * * * is acceptable to meet height, width, length and weight requirements.

*   *   *   *   *   *   *

Weight—the maximum payload weight for highway transport shall not exceed 72,000.

CAT's technical proposal, submitted under step one, responded directly to this specification and was incorporated in its step two bid. CAT designed its trucks with the capability for disassembly to meet this weight limitation for highway transport. CAT's step-one proposal stated, "The 5,700 lb. slab counterweight, and two of the 1,800 lb. corner counterweights that fit into pockets within the rear bumper may be left on the truck and still have a weight less than the 72,000 lb. payload * * *." However, CAT's response to the invitation's requirement in the second step for shipping data (clause B.16) described the truck as weighing 78,100 pounds. The protester believes that CAT therefore does not contemplate disassembly of its trucks for shipment purposes. It argues that the Government would have to bear the expense of disassembly if it chooses delivery by motor carrier.

In our opinion, CAT did not qualify its bid regarding the cost of preparing the trucks for delivery. We take this position because the solicitation required the contractor to provide, at its bid price, delivery F.O.B. origin, carrier's equipment, wharf or freight station and to be responsible for loading the trucks on the carrier's vehicle. Moreover, the bidder executed SF 33, expressly offering delivery at the designated points. We believe CAT thus committed itself to meet any weight limitation incident to the mode of transportation selected by the Government, as long as the truck's design permits compliance with the weight limitation, as it does in this case. Moreover, the 78,100 pounds stated in CAT's bid was furnished in the context of rail shipment. Apparently, rail transportation can accommodate a truck weighing 78,100 pounds and we therefore find no inconsistency in CAT's bid.

The protester cites prior decisions of this Office in which the shipping data furnished with the bid indicated that the bidder would not comply with other specifications. For example, see B–163181, February 7, 1968 and B–161984, January 29, 1968. The present case, however, is distinguishable because we have concluded that the shipping information does not necessarily conflict with the design requirement to which the bidder has committed itself.

The protester argues that by CAT's failure to submit DD Form 1423, "Contract Data Requirements List," and DD Form 1664, "Data Item Description" with its bid, CAT avoided any obligation to supply data in accordance with the detailed requirements contained in those forms. Although the protester concedes the fact that CAT inserted a bid price or N/C (no charge) for each data item listed in the bid schedule, it argues that, nevertheless, CAT's offer does not indicate that these data items would comply with the forms' data item description. International states that CAT's contract contemplates something less than the data described in the solicitation.

The protester argues that bidders were required to return these forms with their bids because item 4 of the bid schedule states, "Data in accordance with Contract Data Requirements List, DD Form 1423, * * * Marked Exhibit 'A' hereto and made a part hereof, individually priced per following data items." Contrary to the protester's assertion, this language does not expressly require a bidder to attach the DD Forms to its bid. Rather, the forms were attached to the IFB by the Government and marked Exhibit A for identification purposes. Moreover, paragraph 2 of the General Provisions merely requires a bidder to sign the solicitation and print or type its name on the bid schedule and continuation sheets.

Generally, where the bidder fails to return the entire solicitation package, the bid must be submitted in a form so that the Government's acceptance creates a valid and binding contract requiring the bidder to perform in accordance with all the material terms and conditions of the invitation. *International Signal and Control Corp., et al.*, 55 Comp. Gen. 894 (1976), 76-1 CPD 180. A responsive bid must not deviate from the material terms and conditions of the invitation. *See* 49 Comp. Gen. 538 (1970); 49 *id.* 289 (1969).

In this case, CAT signed and returned SF 33. This form listed all of the documents comprising the IFB, including "Sec. M List of Documents and Attachments." Section M specifically listed the "Data Requirements List, DD 1423," as part of the IFB. DD Forms 1664 describe in more detail each data item listed on the DD 1423's. The use of the words "In compliance with the above" on Standard Form 33, in conjunction with the documents' listing which comprises the invitation package, incorporates the entire package by reference, making a signed bid responsive even though portions of the solicitation are not physically returned. 49 Comp. Gen. 538, *supra.* This is so even though the references to the material provisions are general and can be identified only through an examination of the complete IFB. *Armada, Inc.—Reconsideration*, B-189409, April 17, 1978, 78-1 CPD 288.

In this connection the protester urges that CAT's bid did not unambiguously incorporate the amended DD Forms 1423, because both the amended as well as the original DD 1423's, as issued by the Government, were dated July 31, 1978. Consequently, the protester argues that unless a bidder submitted the amended DD Forms 1423 with its bid, the Government could not be certain which forms were offered by the bidder. The record, however, shows that the original DD Forms 1423 were dated May 1, 1978; the amended forms are dated July 31, 1978. In any event, we think the Government would be in a position to prove which forms were sent with the amendment to the solicitation.

Furthermore, even though the data item descriptions in the schedule are generally worded, CAT's insertion of N/C or a price next to each line item is evidence of its intent to be bound by the solicitation's requirements, and absent a material requirement to do more, obligates CAT to furnish the data items. 45 Comp. Gen. 221 (1965); *Storage Technology Corporation—Reconsideration*, 57 Comp. Gen. 395 (1978), 78–1 CPD 257.

International also contends that CAT took exception in its step-one proposal to two of the data requirements. However, these items were deleted by an amendment.

The protester also alleges that CAT's bid was nonresponsive because it indicated a bid acceptance period of less than 60 days. International contends that CAT's bid was altered after bid opening in an attempt to make the bid responsive but that the alteration succeeded only in making the bid ambiguous. The agency, however, argues that this basis for protest is untimely raised because the protester was aware of the alleged nonresponsiveness more than 10 working days before filing its protest. Timeliness, however, is measured from the time the protester learns that the agency has accepted or intends to accept an allegedly nonresponsive bid, since it is at that time, rather than when the alleged nonresponsiveness is discovered, that grounds for protest arise. *See Carco Electronics*, B–186747, March 9, 1977, 77–1 CPD 172. Thus, the protest filed here within 10 days after the protester received notice of the award to CAT is timely. 4 C.F.R. § 20.2 (b)(2)(1978).

The threshold issue is whether the solicitation contained a minimum bid acceptance period. The agency claims it did not because of inadvertent error. The protester states that an *informational* copy of the IFB for step two contained a clause entitled "Minimum Acceptance Period" which expressly stated that bids offering less than 60 days for acceptance would be considered nonresponsive. The IFB, as finally issued, contained the statement that bids would be rejected if they allowed less than the number of days specified in the "Offer" portion of SF 33. Nevertheless, a minimum acceptance period was not included in this IFB because the "Offer" portion of SF 33 was not revised in accordance with Defense Acquisition Regulation (DAR) 2–201(a)(C)(xviii). That regulation provides that a minimum bid acceptance period must be inserted in the "Offer" portion of SF 33 and that the form must be altered to eliminate the option provided bidders to offer less than 60 days.

In our opinion, it would be incongruous to construe the IFB as requiring a minimum bid acceptance period merely because one section of the IFB refers to a nonexistent minimum period in another section. The language in SF 33 that a bid will remain open for "60 calendar days" if no other time is specified by the bidder merely presents an option to the bidder to offer less than a 60-day acceptance period. 47 Comp. Gen. 769, 771 (1968). Ordinarily, nothing in the

"Offer" portion of SF 33 prevents a bidder from providing an acceptance period greater or less than 60 days. 47 Comp. Gen., *supra*. Moreover, we think the preliminary informational copy of the IFB cannot be given effect where the official solicitation as finally issued otherwise provides. Although the protester cites several prior decisions in which we found a minimum acceptance period to exist, the decisions are distinguishable because there was other language in the solicitations which justified imposing a specific minimum period for bid acceptance; such language is not present in this case.

Thus, we conclude that the period for bid acceptance was not made a material requirement in this procurement. The other issues raised in this regard assume the materiality of the bid acceptance period and, therefore, are academic.

For the reasons stated, the protest is denied.

[B–192574]

Contracts—Protests—Procedures—Bid Protest Procedures—Time for Filing—Significant Procurement Issue Exception

First ground of protest is held to be timely, notwithstanding agency objections, since initial protest letter—timely received—questioned exclusion from competitive range as well as making other assertions. Other grounds of protest relating to effect of Public Law 95–89 on rights of small business and to indirect allegation of pattern of abuse of public exigency negotiating authority are considered "significant" under General Accounting Office's (GAO) Bid Protest Procedures and for review even if untimely filed.

Contracts—Negotiation—Evaluation Factors—Factors Other Than Price—Experience

Based on review of record, GAO cannot take exception to Army's technical evaluation of protester's proposal—especially given complexity of procurement—or specific judgment that protester's proposal did not demonstrate understanding of requirements. Consequently, exclusion of protester's higher priced proposal (compared to initial and final prices proposed by awardee) from competitive range is not questioned. Furthermore, GAO finds that request for proposals did call for experience information found lacking in protester's proposal.

Contracts—Negotiation—Competition—Competitive Range Formula—Small Business Proposals—Nonapplicability of COC Procedure

Agencies are not prohibited from making relative assessments of responsibility-related factors in determining competitive range without regard to certificate of competency procedure. Rejection of protester's proposal from competitive range cannot be regarded as tantamount to nonresponsibility finding as found by GAO in 52 Comp. Gen. 47 (1972).

Contracts—Negotiation—Competition—Competitive Range Formula—Award Entitlement

Mere fact that offeror is in competitive range does not necessarily ensure award to offeror given negotiating opportunities afforded all competitive offerors and flexibility inherent in negotiated method.

Contracts—Negotiation—Public Exigency—Priority Designation Purchases

Determination and findings (D&F), although relying on expired QRC designator for negotiation authority, also recites additional 02 priority designator. 02 priority designator is fact of record lending support for negotiation under Defense Acquisition Regulation 3–202.2(vi). Moreover, GAO cannot question continued validity of 02 designator.

Contracts—Negotiation—Public Exigency—Justifiction for Negotiation—Sufficiency—Priority Designation

Consistent GAO position that mere citation of certain "priority designators" authorized negotiation under "public exigency" statutory exception was founded on two suppositions. First, that designators were symbols for facts which would demonstrate exigency and—in terms of 10 U.S.C. 2310(b)—"clearly and convincingly" establish that formal advertising would not have been feasible; second, that designators would be cited in good faith. Recent observations of House Committee on Government Operations have severely undermined assumptions.

Contracts — Negotiation — Determination and Findings — Public Exigency—Priority Designation—Acceptance by GAO

Because of observations that raise serious questions about propriety of use of priority designator as substitute for facts justifying use of "public exigency" negotiating authority, GAO recommends regulatory change. If change is not made by start of 1980 fiscal year, GAO informs Secretary of Defense that, in event future year D&F's are subject of protests, D&F's reciting only priority designators for competitively negotiated procurements involving formal proposals, contemplated discussions, and evaluations will be held invalid.

Contracts — Negotiation — Awards — Procedural Requirements—Noncompliance

Army's failure to give GAO required preaward notice is procedural defect not affecting validity of award. Nonetheless, Secretary of Army is informed of failure.

In the matter of Electrospace Systems, Inc., April 13, 1979:

Table of Contents

This protest questions the award of an Army contract for the "Quick Look II" system. For the reasons set forth at length below, we cannot question the award.

Background

On November 18, 1977, the contracting officer, United States Army Electronics Command, Fort Monmouth, New Jersey, executed a Determination and Findings (D&F) supporting the negotiation of a contract for the "Quick Look II" system. The D&F reads:

Upon the basis of the following findings and determination, the proposed contract described below may be negotiated without formal advertising pursuant to the authority of 10 U.S.C. § 2304(a)(2), as implemented by paragraph 3–202.2 (vii) of the Armed Services Procurement Regulation.

Findings

1. The U.S. Army Electronics Command proposes to procure by negotiation Quick Look II Systems as follows: ten each Airborne Systems and one each Ground Support System. Pertinent ancillary items will also be procured. The proposed procurement will also provide for an up to 100% option provision for the hardware items. The estimated cost of the proposed procurement is $15,000,000.

2. Procurement by negotiation of the above described property and services is necessary because the Quick Look II program is assigned an 02 priority and is part of Electronic Warfare QRC No. 41.

3. Use of formal advertising for the procurement described above is impracticable because Electronic Warfare QRC 41 has been assigned this procurement.

Determination

The proposed procurement is for services and property for which the public exigency will not permit the delay incident to formal advertising.

RFP

Under this D&F the Army issued request for proposals (RFP) DAAB07–78–R–2703 on February 24, 1978, for a "fully militarized airborne emitter location–identification system * * * which will detect, parametically identify and locate emitters," known as Quick Look II. Specifically, the RFP called for—in the Army's words—ten "highly specialized items." The RFP further informed prospective offerors that award would be made to that responsible offeror who submitted the lowest fixed-price proposal provided the proposal was technically acceptable as evaluated under the "Technical Factors and Sub-Factors" part of the RFP.

Those technical factors and subfactors were set forth at length in the RFP as follows:

D. 3 Technical Factors and Sub-factors to be Evaluated.

FACTOR A—PRODUCTION ENGINEERING

a. *Production Evaluation.*—The offeror shall describe the nature and extent of effort and contractual obligations required by the Production Evaluation Provision. He will enumerate the extent and amount of engineering and related efforts allocated in the proposal to accomplish the required initial and continuing technical data reviews and to implement any changes or corrections to the hardware and/or technical data found essential during the reviews.

The offeror shall describe detailed procedures to be employed or actions taken to resolve or correct conflicts, errors or deficiencies of the nature shown by the following examples of some of the conditions that could be uncovered or encountered:

(1) The omission of a dimension or the inclusion of an incorrect tolerance on a component part drawing, precluding practical assembly of the part into the next assembly.

* * * * * * *

b. *Experience.*—Very strong emphasis will be placed on offeror experience in the evaluation for contract award. Failure to meet experience requirements will cause rejection of the offer.

The offeror shall furnish evidence including complete details of recent (within the past two years) experience in the integration of large multiple minicomputer-based systems. A key task in the contractual effort is the integration of mini-computers, some contractor-built minicomputer equipment, and other hardware with Government furnished software. Since any such integration involves hardware and software, requirement for experience in system integration as stated above shall include experience in the design and development of such systems with data link operation, both hardware and software.

The offeror shall completely detail his experience and expertise in the fabrication and test of airborne Electronic Intelligence (ELINT) equipments utilizing phase interferometer direction finding techniques as well as spiral antennas.

The offeror shall also provide complete details of his experience with systems requiring pre and postflight test procedures, flight testing, antenna and tempest test facilities and measurement experience and automatic test equipment.

In evaluating the proposals, strong emphasis also will be placed on the offeror's record of past performance for jobs of comparable complexity. Consideration will be given to the degree to which offeror has met requirements including technical, and delivery requirements.

Seven amendments were issued to the RFP, the last of which extended the date for receipt of proposals to May 15, 1978. On May 15, 1978, a total of five proposals—including proposals from Electrospace Systems, Inc. (ESI), and UTL Corporation—were received. Technical evaluation of the proposals then began. The initial evaluation of technical proposals was completed on July 14, 1978, with the result that two proposals—including the proposal of ESI—were judged unacceptable and excluded from the competitive range for the procurement. On July 26, 1978, the contracting officer sent a letter to ESI informing the company of his determination. Thereafter, the Army completed negotiations with competitive range offerors and awarded a contract to UTL on December 21, 1978.

Timeliness Issue

The Army has argued that ESI's grounds of protest—discussed below—are untimely filed.

As to the first ground of protest, GAO received ESI's August 7 letter of protest within 10 working days from the company's receipt of the Army's letter rejecting its proposal. Since the letter specifically protested the rejection of its proposal as well as asserted that ESI had the capability to do the required work and that the Army rejection reasons were "irrelevant," we consider the company's protest against the rejection of its proposal to be timely filed, even though the specific complaints about the Army's evaluation were later received.

Assuming, without deciding, that the other grounds of protest are untimely filed, we nonetheless find the issues raised to be "significant" under 4 C.F.R. § 20.2(c) (1978) and otherwise for consideration since the bases of protest affect a class of procurements (those negotiated under 10 U.S.C. § 2304(a)(2)) as well as the purported rights of small business offerors generally in negotiated procurements under the 1977 Public Law.

Propriety of Exclusion From Competitive Range

ESI initially protested its exclusion from the competitive range to our Office. Throughout its protest ESI has insisted that several details included in the Army's description of the reasons for excluding ESI from the competitive range are considered confidential and should not be publicly disclosed. Neither the Army nor any interested party has contested this restriction. Consequently, we are necessarily constrained in our discussion of the facts relating to the exclusion.

The Army's reasons for rejecting ESI's proposal were originally set forth as a list of eight "proposal deficiencies" in the July 26, 1978, letter to ESI. Of these eight deficiencies, ESI considers the vast majority as relating to the "RFP's requirement to describe the offerors' experience in this field of technology." Further, ESI contends that the evaluation criteria relating to experience were construed "so narrowly as to virtually preclude offerors who had not previously participated in the developmental or initial production contracts for the Quick Look II system."

As explained by ESI:

> The agency's basic description of ESI's deficiencies is set forth in Item 1 [of the July 26 letter]: The proposal failed to demonstrate the ELINT experience necessary to deliver a QUICK LOOK II system which will fulfill the Government's requirements. Literally, only a prior producer could satisfy this test. This view is confirmed by the detailed descriptions listed under Item 1.
>
> For example, Item 1(b) required ESI to have experience in interfacing *several* minicomputers and a *sophisticated microprogrammed* computer, *like the C–9537 monitor-controller*. The italicized portion of this language represents requirements not contained in the solicitation criteria. Schedule D.3, A(b) contains no requirement for experience with the C–9537 monitor-controller, or even like devices. It merely requires experience in minicomputer equipment and systems. There is similarly no requirement for experience in "sophisticated microprogrammed computers." These represent additional evaluation criteria "interpreted into" the solicitation after the proposals were submitted.
>
> * * * * * * *
>
> Similar examples of imposing experience requirements more restrictive than the solicitation can be found in Items 1(a), 1(c), 1(d), and 1(h). The solicitation required experience with "spiral antennas" and with "phase interferometer direction finding techniques." *See* Schedule D.3, A(b). Yet Item 1(d) required

ESI "to demonstrate experience and expertise needed to integrate the spiral antennas *into the QUICK LOOK II phase interferometer DF system.*" [Italic supplied.]

*   *   *   *   *   *   *

Moreover, the antenna experience was required to be with "the Quick Look II spiral antennas" (*see* Item 1(c)) instead of merely spiral antennas as required by the solicitation.

The manner in which the agency interpreted the solicitation's requirement for experience with "jobs of comparable complexity" also is overly restrictive (*see* Schedule D.3, A(b)). Item 1(h) engrafted the additional requirement that there be experience with "*ELINT* systems of comparable complexity."

Item 7 of the deficiencies required demonstration of production capability for all major components.

*   *   *   *   *   *   *

Similarly, Item 6 required experience in producing microwave phase interferometer DF systems while the solicitation requirements (Schedule D.3A(b)) required only experience in equipment utilizing these systems.

*   *   *   *   *   *   *

Two of the criteria on which ESI's proposal was rejected do not have any foundation in the solicitation. There are no requirements for experience in the areas covered by Item 1(e) or requirements to list personnel with expertise listed in Item 8. These were apparently added to the criteria by the agency after the proposals were submitted.

*   *   *   *   *   *   *

It is apparent from the foregoing that the criteria by which ESI's proposal was evaluated were different, and more restrictive, than the criteria expressed in the solicitation. Perhaps it is permissible to engraft normative interpretations on an offeror's technical approach to the problem (*e.g.,* where one technical approach is superior or more feasible than another's). But to engraft normative requirements on *experience listing* requirements is totally without justification. In the case of a technical approach, a completely new design concept may be required to achieve feasibility. But in the case of experience listing, all that may be required is a more detailed description of jobs already listed in the solicitation.

*   *   *   *   *   *   *

If the offeror had known in advance the agency's restrictive interpretation of the criteria, it would have been a simple matter of adding details and highlights to jobs already described in order to satisfy the agency's desires. *In this particular case, however, we believe only the prior producers of Quick Look II could have satisfied the after-the-fact restrictions the agency placed on proposals.* [Italic supplied.]

The narrow construction of the evaluation criteria complained of related, in ESI's view, to the Army's insistence that ESI's proposal simply did not contain the information which demonstrated "that ESI was * * * responsive to the RFP."

As explained by the contracting officer:

The protestor, in attempting to justify his position, states that ESI was not rejected due to inferior technical approaches, using as a basis for this the fact that the agency's rejection letter does not specify evaluation factor D.3.A.a * * * Production Evaluation. A look at the Technical Factor Matrix shows that, in fact, ESI received an "acceptable" rating for this factor; however, this is only one of six Production Engineering factors. Of these six, ESI received twice as many "unacceptable" and "unacceptable but susceptible to being made acceptable" as it did "acceptable" ratings. Furthermore, this factor, D.3.A.a., does not, despite the protestor's claim, "involve all the engineering and technical skills represented by the contract work." A reading of the solicitation requirements bears this out. ESI is again missing the point that viewing the solicitation as a whole, the proposal submitted contained a number of material deficiencies, the cumulative effect of which was to render the proposal unacceptable. The rejection letter lists these major deficiencies. It does not contain, nor was it intended to contain, an exhaustive list of every deficiency uncovered, but simply those which, taken together, are sufficiently substantial to render the proposal unacceptable absent a major revision or complete rewrite. The rejection letter was not the evaluation, but was intended to be indicative of the basis for finding the proposal unacceptable.

To this argument, ESI has replied that the alleged informational deficiencies in its proposal could not have properly been cited for reasons to exclude its proposal under applicable GAO precedent. As stated by ESI:

> The Army argues that proposals may be excluded for informational deficiencies, cited *Servrite International, Ltd.*, 76–2 CPD 325 (1976). This is only true, however, when the deficiencies "are so material as to preclude any possibility of upgrading the proposal to an acceptable level." *Servrite*, 76–2 CPD at 5. Therefore, the question is not whether there were informational deficiencies, but whether they could be corrected.
>
> Your office has elaborated on this test by providing the following guidelines: "* * * In determining whether allegedly 'informational' deficiencies in a submitted proposal are of such nature that an agency, within the reasonable exercise of its discretion, may exclude that proposal from the competitive range, our Office has, at times, looked at the following factors: (1) how definitely the RFP has called for the detailed information, the omission of which was relied on by the agency for excluding a proposal from the competitive range, * * *; (2) the nature of the 'informational' deficiencies, e.g., whether they tended to show that the offeror did not understand what it was required to do under the contract or merely made the proposal inferior but not unacceptable, * * *; (3) the scope and range of the proposal 'informational' deficiencies, e.g., whether the offeror had to essentially rewrite its proposal to correct the deficiencies, * * *; (4) whether only one offeror was found to be in the competitive range * * *; and (5) whether a deficient but reasonably correctable proposal represented a significant cost savings, * * *."

In reply, the Army maintains that the above criteria for excluding an informationally deficient proposal were, in fact, satisfied in the circumstances of this case. As stated by the contracting officer:

> The protestor has listed five factors which your Office has at times considered in determining whether exclusion of a proposal from the competitive range involved an unreasonable exercise of agency discretion * * *. These factors are: (1) how definitely the RFP has called for the detailed information, the omission of which was relied upon by the agency for excluding a proposal from the competitive range; (2) the nature of the "informational" deficiencies; (3) the scope and range of the proposal's "informational" deficiencies; (4) whether there was only one offeror in the competitive range; and (5) whether a deficient but reasonably correctable proposal represented a significant cost savings. With regard to (1), (2), and (3), both the Administrative Report and this Supplemental Report have clearly demonstrated that the RFP did definitely call for the information here involved (1), that ESI did not *in its proposal* demonstrate an understanding of what it would be required to do under the contract (2), and that ESI would have had essentially to rewrite its proposal to correct the deficiencies (3). As protestor notes, the fourth criterion is not applicable here. With regard to the fifth, ESI's proposal did not represent a significant cost savings (as has been noted, only one offeror submitted a higher-priced proposal than did ESI); furthermore, ESI did not submit a "deficient but reasonably correctable proposal" so that cost savings could not have been considered in any case. There is no basis for determining what ESI's costs would have been, had its proposal been acceptable from a technical standpoint.

Analysis

Competitive range determinations necessarily involve the exercise of a considerable range of administrative discretion. See *Magnetic Corp.*

of America, B–187887, June 10, 1977, 77–1 CPD 419. Moreover, it is not our function to evaluate proposals, and we will not substitute our judgment for that of the procuring agency as to the adjectival ratings or numerical scores to be assigned proposals. *PRC Computer Center, Inc., et al.*, 55 Comp. Gen. 60 (1975), 75–2 CPD 35. We will not question competitive range determinations—particularly where, as here, the procurement involves complex technical matters unless they are clearly lacking in rational support. See, for example, *Plessey Environmental Systems*, B–186787, December 27, 1976, 76–2 CPD 533.

In analyzing the propriety of ESI's exclusion, we will follow the guidelines of the *PRC Computer Center* decision, *supra*, which are described under the headings listed below.

Did the RFP Specifically Call for the Information Which the Army Found Lacking in ESI's Proposal?

We have held that a "specific" call for information may consist of no more than a general request which obviously was intended to elicit specific responses. See *PRC Computer Center, Inc., supra*, at page 73.

Based on this general principle, we conclude that the RFP did specifically call for the information which the Army found lacking in ESI's proposal. We offer the following specific comments regarding the deficiencies listed in the Army's July 26 letter (as later supplemented) to ESI.

Computer Experience

We view these experience requirements—including experience with the C–9537 device (descriptively referred to by the Army as a sophisticated microprogrammer)—as a general call for specific experience in the described areas. Moreover, we cannot contest the Army's stated position that the technical description of the system and the general description of the required experience should have placed a reasonably prudent offeror on notice that the necessary experience required here also involved an offeror's experience with interactive computers.

Spiral Antennas

Here again we view the RFP's generally described spiral antenna experience requirements as specifically calling for the kind of experience information which was found wanting in the ESI proposal. Specifically, we cannot question the Army's position that the RFP's antenna experience requirements described a specialized experience closely related to the described technical requirements of the system and that the phrase "Quick Look II"—as used in the evaluation of ESI's proposal—was nothing more than a descriptive reference to the system as such without in any way implying that only prior specific experience with Quick Look II was necessary.

Jobs of Comparable Complexity

We must agree with the Army's position that there was a general call for specific information under this title. We further find no basis to question the Army position that the requirement for description of "ELINT systems of comparable" complexity is reasonably and specifically found in the RFP—even though the finding is dependent on a reading of cumulative requirements.

Microwave Phase Interferometer DF Systems

We cannot disagree with the Army's position that cumulative RFP requirements, reasonably read, specifically called for the information found lacking in ESI's proposal.

Personnel Experience Requirements

Again we find a specific call for the kind of information the Army found lacking in ESI's proposal; in so finding, moreover, we disagree with ESI's interpretation of the Army's evaluation.

How Important Were the Informational Deficiencies?

Based on a complete review of the record, we cannot take exception to the Army's technical evaluation of ESI's proposal, especially given the complexity of the information being evaluated. Further, we cannot disagree with the Army's specific technical decision that the cumulative deficiencies showed that ESI "did not demonstrate an understanding of what it would be required to do under the contract." Nor can we disagree with the Army's related technical judgment that these informational deficiencies— together with other deficiencies— meant that a major revision of ESI's proposal would be required to correct the deficiencies; hence, even if cost savings * were present in ESI's proposal, the savings were not for consideration. See 52 Comp. Gen. 382 (1972).

Was There Only One Other Offeror in the Competitive Range?

ESI acknowledges this was not the case here.

Based on the above reasoning, we cannot question the Army's decision to exclude ESI's proposal from the competitive range.

---

*The award price of UTL's contract was considerably below the price ESI proposed for the work; further, UTL's initial price was also below ESI's price.

ESI has raised two additional grounds of protest, namely: (1) whether the certificate of competency (COC) procedure of the Small Business Administration (SBA) applies to the rejection of its proposal; and (2) whether the procurement was properly negotiated.

COC Procedure

Arguing in the alternative that the standards regarding informational deficiencies should not be considered the appropriate legal measure of the correctness of the Army's actions here, ESI argues that the RFP criteria involved here are all responsibility-related and, thus, under section 501 of Public Law No. 95–89, 91 Stat. 561, August 4, 1977 (15 U.S.C. 637), which specifically gave the SBA authority to certify, with respect to "all elements of responsibility," any small business concern to receive and perform a specific Government contract, SBA should review ESI's "exclusion from award."

Both the Army and ESI agree that *SBD Computer Services Corporation*, B–186950, December 21, 1976, 76–2 CPD 511 (which also involved the question of the propriety of excluding a small business' proposal from a competitive range), provides insights into this issue. In that decision we held:

SBD's contention that its proposal was rejected for reasons related to its responsibility, i.e., its capacity to perform the contract, is based on various decisions of this Office, cited by SBD, in which matters bearing on capacity to perform, including offeror experience, are treated as matters of responsibility. The decisions cited, however, involved either formal advertising, *see* 52 Comp. Gen. 647 (1972) ; 52 *id.* 87 (1972) ; 38 *id.* 864 (1959), or a situation in which it appeared that while technical evaluation criteria dealing with capacity were set forth in an RFP, the agency did not expect to receive different technical approaches but only offers indicating that the work to be performed would "conform to the best practices of the industry, and be of a quality acceptable to the Government * * *." 52 Comp. Gen. 47, 53 (1972).

In many other cases, we have recognized that contracting agencies may properly utilize evaluation factors which include experience and other areas that would otherwise be encompassed by offeror responsibility determinations when the needs of those agencies warrant a comparative evaluation of those areas. See 53 Comp. Gen. 388 (1973) ; 52 *id.* 854 (1973) ; *Design Concepts, Inc.*, B–184754, December 24, 1975, 75–2 CPD 410; *Home and Family Services, Inc.*, B–182290, December 20, 1974, 74–2 CPD 366.

ESI argues:

This case is squarely within the *SBD Computer* example given. The experience-listing factors were not used in weighing ESI's technical approach *vis-a-vis* others' since ESI's technical approach was acceptable, the only rating given. Instead, the factors were used to reject ESI's offer as not meeting the solicitation requirements (virtually identical to rejecting a bid for non-responsiveness). If this result was a violation of the Small Business Act prior to the 1977 amendments [see 40 Comp. Gen. 106 (1960) involving as advertised procurement in which GAO held that a small business' compliance with experience requirements was to be decided under COC procedures and could not be made a matter of bid responsiveness] *a fortiori* it is a violation of the amended act. We would further point out that the Small Business Act relates equally to negotiated as well as advertised procurements. Since no exception is provided in the act for negotiated procurements, the agency's distinction would violate the act.

Responsibility involves, among other things, a prospective contractor's organization, technical experience, knowledge, skills, "know-how," technical equipment, and facilities. 45 Comp. Gen. 4, 7 (1965). Assuming, without deciding, that all the evaluation factors here (or at least the ones under which ESI was ranked as unacceptable) are responsibility-related, that fact does not necessarily mean that the Army was precluded, *per se*, from using these considerations as proposal evaluation factors even considering the 1977 legislative changes.

ESI, like other small businesses (see, for example, the arguments raised in *Design Concepts, Inc.*, *supra*), apparently believes that a negotiated contract must be awarded to any small business offeror which submits the lowest priced proposal under a solicitation so long as the offeror is responsible—has the minimum competency to do the work.

ESI's position fails to recognize the flexibility inherent in the negotiated procurement method. As we stated in 50 Comp. Gen. 110, 113 (1970), quoting from B–152306, September 15, 1967:

"The 'competitive negotiation' contemplated by Public Law 87–653 [10 U.S.C. 2304(g)] is clearly distinguishable from 'competitive bidding' or price competition under the formal advertising for bids statutes. While the rigid rules applicable to formally advertised procurements generally require award to the lowest (price) responsive, responsible bidder, the flexibility inherent in the concept of negotiation permits an award to be made to the best advantage of the Government, 'price and other factors considered.' Negotiation permits, and indeed requires, the contracting officials of the Government to consider these 'other factors' of the procurement, which, in a proper case, may result in an award to one offeror as opposed to another less qualified offeror submitting a lower price. * * *"

Since neither 10 U.S.C. § 2304(g) nor applicable regulations in any way restrict the "other factors" that may be used by agencies in selecting the proposal having the greatest value to the Government, we have not prohibited procuring agencies from using responsibility–related factors in making *relative* assessments of the merits of competing proposals. There is no indication on the face of Public Law 95–89 or in the legislative history of the law that Congress intended to eliminate this long-standing practice as far as the evaluation of small business proposals are concerned. Thus, neither the cited precedent (40 Comp. Gen., *supra*) of advertised procurements nor the 1977 Public Law prevents the relative–assessment evaluation of responsibility-related information contained in small business proposals.

Of course, where an agency—in the guise of a relative–assessment of responsibility-related factors—seeks to reject a small business proposal as unacceptable even though there was no indication that the small business (which had previously secured a COC from SBA on a nearly identical procurement) had not met the needs of the procuring agency under a "best practice of the industry" RFP evaluation standard, the rejection will be held to be tantamount to a nonresponsibility finding if the *final* prices for selection purposes show that the small business is lowest in price. See 52 Comp. Gen. 47 (1972). Here, however, there is no indication in the record that ESI had ever obtained a COC for work of identical complexity or that ESI met the expressed needs of the Air Force for the work in question. Moreover, the Air Force's needs were not listed under a "best practice of the industry" standard. (Indeed, at several points in its protest, ESI has insisted that only a "prior producer" of the items being sought—which ESI is not—could meet the needs of the RFP as interpreted by the Army.) Finally, and of significant importance, ESI's price was higher than the initial (and final) prices of the small business concern ultimately awarded the contract.

Although there is no way to have known whether the initial and final price advantage of the selected small business offeror would have been overcome had ESI been permitted to submit a final price, ESI would have been permitted to submit a final price only on the assumption that the COC procedure is applicable for the purpose of placing a small business offeror in the competitive range. In short, the COC procedure is not for application in determining whether a small business shall be placed in the competitive range for a given procurement.

Propriety of Negotiation

Finally, ESI contends that the procurement was improperly negotiated for several reasons mainly having to do with the "Electronic Warfare QRC" number listed in the D&F. ESI contends that this "QRC" number had expired and that it could not, therefore, justify negotiation under the cited "exigency" exception.

In reply, the Army argues that the "02 priority [designator]" assigned the procurement independently justified negotiation of the requirement under DAR § 3–202 (1976 ed.) which provides:

3–202   Public Exigency
3–202.1 *Authority.* Pursuant to the authority of 10 U.S.C. 2304(g)(2) purchases and contracts may be negotiated if—[in terms of the cited statute] "the public exigency will not permit the delay incident to advertising."
3–202.2 *Application.* In order for the authority of this paragraph 3–202 to be used, the need must be compelling and of unusual urgency, as when the Government would be seriously injured, financially or otherwise, if the supplies or services were not furnished by a certain date, and when they could not be procured by that date by means of formal advertising. When negotiating under this authority, competition to the maximum extent practicable, within the time allowed, shall be obtained. The following are illustrative of circumstances with respect to which this authority may be used:
    (1) supplies, services, or construction needed at once because of fire, flood, explosion, or other disaster;

    *   *   *   *   *   *

    (vi) purchase request citing an issue priority designator 1 through 6, inclusive, under the Uniform Material Movement and Issue Priority System (UMMIPS):

(vii) purchase requests citing "Electronic Warfare QRC Priority" as the priority designator.

3–202.3 *Limitation.* Every contract negotiated under the authority of this paragraph 3–202 shall be accompanied with a determination and findings justifying its use, signed by the contracting officer and prepared in accordance with the requirements of Part 3 of this Section III, except that in the case of a contract resulting from a purchase request citing an issue priority designator 1 through 6 or the priority designator "Electronic Warfare QRC Priority," the determination and findings need only cite the designator or "Electronic Warfare QRC Priority" as justification. * * *

In reply to the Army's position, ESI argues:

(1) The D&F does not rely on the priority designator;

(2) The cited priority designator had in fact expired or had never been properly established in the first place;

(3) The priority designator does not, in itself, justify negotiation under the statutory authority (10 U.S.C. § 2303(a)(2) (1976)) which authorizes negotiation when the "public exigency" will not permit the delay incident to advertising since the statute requires that both exigency and impracticality of advertising be found prior to negotiation.

Analysis

Although finding 3 in the above D&F recites that it is impracticable to negotiate because "QRC 41 has been assigned this procurement" and the implementing DAR paragraph (3–202.2(vii)) cited is concerned with "QRC" authority, we cannot overlook the "02 priority" designator cited in finding 2. Finding 2, in our view, is a fact of record in the D&F lending support for negotiation under DAR § 3–202.2(vi) even though not specifically cited.

As to the actual validity of the priority designator for this procurement, the Army has furnished us classified documentation which reasonably supports the continued validity of the designator for this procurement. In any event, we cannot disagree with the view of the contracting officer that the procurement regulations do not require that he investigate the authority of a priority designator before relying on it to commence a negotiated procurement.

Finally, we have repeatedly observed that negotiating under "priority designators 01 through 06" is consistent with the statutory authority involved. As we said in B–167389(1), February 12, 1970:

You have additionally alleged that there was no justification for the Air Force's use of the "public exigency" exception (10 U.S.C. 2302(a)(2)) as the basis for negotiating this contract. However, the contracting officer executed the required "Determination and Findings" (D&F) on February 25, 1969, reciting the fact that the purchase request cited a priority designator of 01 under the Uniform Materiel Movement and Issue Priority System (UMMIPS). ASPR 3–202.2(vi) provides that one of the circumstances authorizing negotiation under the public exigency exception is a procurement in which the purchase request cites a UMMIPS priority designator 01 through 06. Furthermore, ASPR 3–202.3 specifically provides that the D&F need only cite the issue priority designator as justification for undertaking procurement by negotiation. See our decisions 45 Comp. Gen. 374 (1966) and B–166886, August 7, 1969, indicating our approbation of this procedure. [See also, for example, *Bristol Electronics, Inc.*, B–190341, August 16, 1978, 78–2 CPD 122; *Ampex Corporation*, B–190529, March 16, 1978, 78–1 CPD 212.]

Implicit in our approving negotiation when only priority designators "01 through 06" are cited were two suppositions. First, that the priority designators were symbols for a series of facts which, if taken together and elaborated in detail, would not only demonstrate exigency but also satisfy the requirement of 10 U.S.C. § 2310(b) for a "written finding * * * [setting forth] facts and the circumstances that * * * clearly and convincingly establish * * * that formal advertising would not have been feasible and practicable." * Second, we presumed that the designators would only be cited in good faith.

Both these suppositions have recently been questioned in House Report No. 95–1677, October 2, 1978, entitled "Procurement Practices at the U.S. Army Communications and Electronics Materiel Readiness Command." In this report—issued by the Committee on Government Operations—the committee observed:

C. Loopholes in the defense acquisition regulations (formerly ASPR) [page 15 of the Report]

During our review of Army procurement practices, the subcommittee observed significant loopholes in the defense acquisition regulations (DAR's). These loopholes need to be closed in order to limit the opportunity for game-playing in the award and administration of Government contracts. Specific areas of abuse concerned the: (i) frequent use of urgent priority codes to go competitive negotiated when formal advertisement is as quick or quicker, * * *.

1. Urgent Priority Codes.—Procurement regulations need tightening to avoid the indiscriminate use of urgent priority designator codes as the justification for not using advertised solicitations.

For example, CERCOM has avoided using formal advertising by citing an "02" priority as justification. This is permitted by the procurement regulations. However, as shown in the Army report on the award of the Modem 522 Radio Tele-typewriter [the subject of GAO's decision in *Bristol Electronics, Inc.*, *supra*] the formal advertised method would have been quicker than the competitive negotiations method utilized. Loopholes such as this should be closed. Encouraging formal advertising in the award of contracts is a good method for ensuring that minority and small business are treated fairly and that the Government gets the best price. At our review date, the Office of Assistant Secretary of the Army (ASA) (RDA) had not made any proposals for changes to the procurement regulations designed to stop the indiscriminate use of priority designator codes.

It is the subcommittee's opinion that when formal advertising is as quick or quicker, (DAR's) exception 3–202.2 "Public Exigency" cannot be used.

Also in appendix 9 of the Report (page 58) the following observation (contained in a letter from the Chairman of the Committee to the Secretary of the Army) was made concerning the negotiation of this procurement:

The command is about to award a contract for what is termed the "Quick Look II"—a surveillance device—by competitive negotiation. The rationale initially given for utilizing competitive negotiation is that the procurement is

---

*Such a finding, of course, is made final by 10 U.S.C. § 2310(b).

of such urgency that it must be made by a method quicker than formal advertising. However, no determination was made that formal advertising would cause an unacceptable delay.

    ＊   ＊   ＊   ＊   ＊   ＊   ＊

In many of the instances examined by the subcommittee in which the command utilized the urgency rationale to avoid formal advertising, it turned out that the formal advertising method would have been quicker than the method the command actually utilized. And, in this instance, it seems clear that the competitive negotiation method being used will actually take longer than if the award was formally advertised. It is obvious that delays will occur if the Government has to review the capability of numerous offerors to perform as in the case of negotiated competitive procurements whereas only the lowest bidder need be reviewed in the case of formal advertising.

It makes little sense to permit contracting officers to cite urgency as the reason for deviating from normal procedures and then allow them to use an exception which actually takes longer.

It is clear that these observations raise serious questions about the propriety of the use of a priority designator as a substitute for the facts justifying the use of the "public exigency" authority. Specifically, the competitive negotiation method selected here and in other procurements—requiring formal proposals, competitive range determinations, competitive discussions, final offers and a series of time-consuming evaluations—would take at least as long—or longer—than if the procurements had been formally advertised. Moreover, in *Bristol Electronics, Inc., supra*, another competitively negotiated Army procurement made under an "urgency" rationale, we also noted:

＊＊＊ the procurement was officially negotiated and awarded under the urgency exception [; however,] a subsequent Army investigative report [suggested] that the procurement was negotiated to keep incompetent companies from competing— a reason which does not justify negotiation—＊ ＊ ＊.

For this reason, we are recommending that DAR § 3–202.3 be amended to eliminate—insofar as competitively negotiated procurements involving formal proposals, contemplated discussions and evaluations are intended—the provision which recites that where a purchase request carries a "priority designator 1 through 6" or a "QRC" priority designator the D&F need only cite the designator as authority for negotiation. We are further informing the Secretary of Defense that if the recommended amendment is not enacted prior to the end of the current fiscal year, we will not give future force and effect to the provision; therefore, in the event future fiscal year D&F's are the subject of protests, we will find invalid any D&F's which, as here, merely cite a priority designator as authority for "public exigency" competitive procurements involving formal proposals, contemplated discussions, and formal evaluations without further detailed findings as to why the urgently required goods or services could not be obtained as quickly under formal advertising. Nevertheless, since the current D&F citing an "02" priority designator validly authorized negotiation under existing regulation and GAO precedent, we cannot question the award made.

Award Notice To GAO

Although the Army failed to give GAO preaward notice of the award to UTL as required by DAR § 2-407.8(b)(2), this procedural defect did not affect the validity of the award. Nonetheless, we are bringing this failure to the attention of the Secretary of the Army.

Protest denied.

[B-192528]

Officers and Employees—Back Pay Act—Applicability—Federal Dependents' Schools Employees

Persons employed to work at Federal dependents' schools are subject to all laws pertaining to Government employment except those for which an exemption is expressly authorized under 20 U.S.C. 241(a) (1976); therefore, school employees are covered by the Back Pay Act of 1966, 5 U.S.C. 5596.

Officers and Employees—Federal Dependents' Schools Employees—Civil Service Laws—Applicability

Under 20 U.S.C. 241(a), persons "may" be employed to work at Federal dependents' schools without regard to certain civil service laws, including those pertaining to the General Schedule pay rates, but the provisions of such laws may nevertheless be extended to school employees by operation of administrative directives and contract clauses.

Personal Services—Contracts—Federal Dependents' Schools Employees—Compensation—Rate Establishment

Section IV, Army Procurement Procedure, directed that a clause be included in dependents' school personal service employment contracts reserving to school officials the right to amend the rate of pay in conformity with the pay schedules of Department of the Army civilian employees performing similar duties; hence, the Fort Rucker Elementary School Board had the right to adopt a policy of having all clerical, janitorial, and other non-teaching positions at the school classified and equated to comparable civil service positions for pay purposes.

Compensation—Increases—Retroactive—Increases Withheld During Wage Freeze

The Fort Rucker Elementary School Board adopted a policy in 1969 of paying school support personnel on an equivalent basis with Federal General Schedule (GS) and wage board (WG) employees, but support personnel pay was "frozen" between April 1974 and March 1977 as the result of an erroneous opinion by Army procurement officials that there could be "no such thing as a GS/WG equated contract employee." The support personnel therefore suffered an unjustified or unwarranted personnel action within the terms of the Back Pay Act, 5 U.S.C. 5596, and are entitled to backpay for cost-of-living and step increases withheld from them.

In the matter of Fort Rucker Elementary School Employees, April 20, 1979:

This action is in response to a letter dated July 14, 1978 (file reference ATZQ–RM–FA), with enclosures, from Major B. G. Poole, FC, Finance and Accounting Officer, Fort Rucker, Alabama, requesting an advance decision as to the propriety of making payments on vouchers totalling $21,562.00, representing retroactive pay increases covering the period from April 1974 to March 1977 for civilian employees holding non-teaching positions with the Fort Rucker Elementary School. The request was forwarded here by the Office of the Comptroller of the Army by letter dated July 31, 1978 (DACA–FAF–C).

The request for an advance decision concerns the eligibility of employees holding administrative, clerical and custodial positions with the Fort Rucker Elementary School to receive retroactive salary and wage adjustments for the years 1974–1977, so as to make their pay rates conform to directives which were applicable to most other Federal employees during that period.

It is indicated that all of the individuals concerned were employed at the school on the basis of annual personal service contracts. Each contract contained the following clause relating to pay rates:

> The rate of pay as shown herein has been certified by the Fort Rucker Elementary School Board as fair and equitable and in general accord with the pay schedules for similar positions in selected comparable public school systems in surrounding localities. *However, the right is reserved by the Elementary School Board, Fort Rucker to amend the rate of pay,* either by increases or decreases, to include retroactive adjustments if pay schedules in selected comparable public school systems are changed, or if verification of certification requirements cause rate of pay changes, or *if existing pay schedules for Department of the Army civilian employees performing similar duties on the same installation are changed.* [Italic supplied.]

This clause was included in each school employment contract as directed by section IV, Army Procurement Procedure (1969 ed., Rev. 6, superseded), issued by the Secretary of the Army.

It is further indicated that effective July 1, 1969, the Fort Rucker Elementary School Board adopted a policy of having all clerical, janitorial, and other non-teaching positions classified and equated to comparable civil service positions. Under this policy and the above–quoted provision concerning pay rates, school support personnel were paid on an equivalent basis with Federal General Schedule (GS) and wage board (WG) employees, and they were given equivalent cost–of–living increases and step increases authorized for civil service employees. The policy was followed continuously from July 1969 until April 1974.

However, on April 12, 1974, the President signed Executive Order No. 11777 to provide pay raises for Federal employees, and the support personnel of the Fort Rucker Elementary School were denied the benefits of that order. It does not appear that this was the result of a policy revision or any other action taken by the school board. Rather, it appears that certain Army procurement officials reviewed the matter and concluded that the employees were not then, and never had been, entitled to be paid on the same basis as Federal GS and WG civil employees. Essentially, those procurement officials were of the opinion that there could be "no such thing as a GS/WG equated contract employee," and that the contract employees' pay rates should instead be set in accordance with Army Procurement Procedure § 4–5603(c) (1969 ed., Rev. 6, superseded), which provided:

> (c) Contracts shall be negotiated on the basis of and shall provide for a rate of pay which is in general accord with pay schedules for similar positions in selected comparable school systems in the state in which the dependents school is located.

On the basis of local wage surveys, it was estimated that Fort Rucker Elementary School support personnel were being paid at rates which exceeded the pay schedules for persons holding similar positions in comparable school systems in the State of Alabama. Army procurement authorities concluded that the employees were not eligible for a pay increase under Executive Order No. 11777, April 12, 1974, and thereafter the pay rates of administrative, clerical, and custodial positions at the school remained "frozen" until March 1977.

It appears that this action caused some controversy, and eventually led to the issuance of the following directive on March 3, 1977, by the Secretary of the Army concerning the Fort Rucker Elementary School:

> Non-certified support personnel in the case of "blue collar" employees are to be paid salaries comparable to Wage Board personnel, to include pay-adjustments when applicable. In the case of clerical employees, non-certified support personnel are to be paid salaries comparable to the Civil Service General Schedule, to include pay-adjustments when applicable.

It appears that the clerical, janitorial, and other non-teaching positions at the school were then, again, classified and equated to comparable civil service positions. It also appears that on April 26, 1978, the school board passed a resolution that the affected employees be granted the pay raises that were withheld from them in the interim period from April 1974 to March 1977.

The submission presents a number of questions concerning the propriety of granting those retroactive pay increases. In effect, it is questioned whether the Army Secretary's March 3, 1977 directive or the school board's April 26, 1978 resolution may properly be given retroactive application. In that connection, it is also questioned whether this would require a modification of the personal service contracts covering the years 1974–1977, and if so, whether modifications may lawfully be made to completed contracts in succeeding fiscal years. However, for the following reasons we find it unnecessary to address those questions or concerns.

Section 6 of Public Law 874, 81st Congress, ch. 1124, 64 Stat. 1100, 1107, approved September 30, 1950, as amended, and codified as 20 U.S.C. § 241 (1976), directs that schools be provided for children living on Federal property when no local educational agency is able to provide suitable comparable free public education for such children.

Section 6 as originally enacted contained no provision relating to the employment of personnel required to operate those schools. However, amending legislation subsequently authorized such personnel to be employed under conditions exempting them from certain of the civil service laws and regulations applicable to most other Federal employees. With respect to such exemptions, 20 U.S.C. § 241(a) (1976) provides in pertinent part as follows:

> * * * For the purpose of providing such comparable education, personnel may be employed and the compensation, tenure, leave, hours of work, and other incidents of the employment relationship *may* be fixed without regard to the Civil Service Act and rules and the following: (1) chapter 51 and subchapter III of chapter 53 of title 5; (2) subchapter I of chapter 63 of title 5; (3) sections 5504, 5541 to 5549, and 6101 of title 5; (4) sections 3305(b), 3306(a)(2), 3308 to 3318, 3319(b), 3320, 3351, 3363, 3364, 3501 to 3504, 7511, 7512 and 7701 of title 5; and (5) Chapter 43 of title 5. * * * [Italic supplied.]

This provision, as codified, is derived from section 2 of Public Law 89–77, 79 Stat. 243, July 21, 1965. The legislative history of Public Law 89–77 indicates that the provision was enacted as the result of draft legislation submitted to Congress by the Secretary of the Army, who at the time stated, "Based upon the Department's experience in operating section 6 schools, it is highly desirable that the personnel practices for instructional personnel be patterned after those usually encountered in the teaching profession rather than those which have been developed for the Federal service as a whole." See Senate Report No. 311, June 9, 1965.

It is therefore to be noted that this provision was intended to apply primarily to members of the teaching profession, in recognition of the fact that instruction schedules do not coincide with civil service work-hour and leave policies. Thus, even though under 20 U.S.C. § 241 (a) persons employed in clerical, custodial, and other non–teaching positions "may" also be exempted from certain civil service laws, a review of the contracts of the support personnel in question discloses that most were required to work under a civil service type of schedule and were made subject by provisions of contract to the Annual and Sick Leave Act of 1951, as amended, chapter 63 (subch. I) of title 5, United States Code, from which they could have been exempted.

Furthermore, it is also to be noted that the above-quoted provision of 20 U.S.C. .§ 241(a) does not authorize the exemption of persons employed in connection with "section 6" schools from every provision of title 5 of the United States Code. In particular, while such employees "may" be exempted from the General Schedule pay rates contained in subchapter III of chapter 53, title 5, no similar exemption is expressly authorized with respect to the Back Pay Act of 1966, codified as 5 U.S.C. § 5596.

This Office has consistently held that "section 6" school employees are subject to all statutes pertaining to Government employment except those for which an exemption is expressly authorized. 52 Comp. Gen. 291 (1972). See also decisions B–138773, May 15, 1959; B–183804, November 14, 1975; B–187881, October 3, 1977. Thus, "section 6" school employees are covered by the Back Pay Act, 5 U.S.C. § 5596. See decision B–192568, December 8, 1978. Moreover, we recognize that the exempted provisions of title 5 may be extended to "section 6" school employees by operation of administrative directives and contract clauses.

Insofar as here pertinent, the Back Pay Act, 5 U.S.C. § 5596, authorizes payment of compensation to employees who, on the basis of an administrative determination or a timely appeal are found by appropriate authority to have been affected by an unjustified or unwarranted personnel action that has resulted in the withdrawal or reduction of all or a part of the pay, allowances, or differentials. The Comptroller General is an "appropriate authority" to determine whether an employee has suffered a withdrawal or reduction of pay as the result of an unjustified or unwarranted personnel action under applicable law or regulation, and to grant appropriate relief. 5 C.F.R. § 550.803(d) (1978).

In the present case, it appears that the entire controversy was the result of disagreements among various Army authorities with respect to the proper interpretation of somewhat inconsistent provisions of the Army Procurement Procedure. It is our view that under the Army Procurement Procedure the right was reserved to the Fort Rucker Elementary School Board to amend the rate of pay of school employees, and that the school board had the right to adopt a policy of having all clerical, janitorial, and other non-teaching positions classified and equated to comparable civil service positions. Moreover, it appears that such policy was adopted by the school board in 1969. Our view is that the policy was mandatory and remained in effect during the period here in question, notwithstanding the action of the procurement officials. We therefore find that under the applicable provisions of law and regulation, and the mandatory policy, all of the employees in question were entitled to be paid on the basis of Federal civil service pay rates after July 1, 1969, and that they were affected by unjustified and unwarranted personnel actions from April 1974 to March 1977 through the withdrawal of cost-of-living increases and step increases authorized for civil service employees.

Accordingly, we hold that the employees in question are entitled to backpay under 5 U.S.C. § 5596, to be computed in accordance with 5 C.F.R., part 550, subpart H. The submitted vouchers are returned for further processing consistent with the holding in this decision.

[B-182608]

Leaves of Absence—Forfeiture—Retirement—Disability

Employee scheduled use of annual leave which was subject to forfeiture prior to his retirement. However, he did not use scheduled annual leave as he was on extended sick leave pending disability retirement. Forfeited leave may be restored under 5 U.S.C. 6304(d)(1)(C), since neither statutory language nor legislative history indicates that annual leave which is not used as result of extended sick leave pending disability retirement may not be restored under 5 U.S.C. 6304(d)(1)(C).

In the matter of Forfeiture of Annual Leave, April 23, 1979:

By letter dated September 13, 1978, Mr. Thomas S. McFee, Assistant Secretary for Personnel Administration, Department of Health, Education, and Welfare (HEW) has requested an advance decision as to whether an employee of the Social Security Administration (SSA) may be restored forfeited annual leave under 5 U.S.C. § 6304 (d)(1)(C) where such leave was scheduled pending the effective date of the employee's approved disability retirement.

In the case presented, the Civil Service Commission (Commission) approved the disability retirement application of the employee on October 27, 1976. Subsequently, on November 15, 1976, the employee began a period of approved sick leave prior to his disability retirement which was not to be effective until more than a year later, i.e. January 17, 1978. The agency counseled the employee to schedule in advance the annual leave he would earn during the 1977 leave year in order to avoid forfeiture of accrued annual leave in excess of the maximum permissible carryover under 5 U.S.C. § 6304(a). This was accomplished on November 17, 1976. After the employee retired he filed a claim for the restoration of the scheduled 208 hours of annual leave which he had forfeited.

Forfeited annual leave can be restored under the circumstances set forth in 5 U.S.C. § 6304(d)(1) as added by section 3 of Public Law 93–181, December 14, 1973, 87 Stat. 705 which provides:

> (d)(1) Annual leave which is lost by operation of this section because of—
> (A) administrative error when the error causes a loss of annual leave otherwise accruable after June 30, 1960;
> (B) exigencies of the public business when the annual leave was scheduled in advance; or
> (C) sickness of the employee when the annual leave was scheduled in advance;
>
> shall be restored to the employee.

The Commission has issued implementing regulations and guidelines pursuant to 5 U.S.C. § 6304(d)(2) and 6311, which appear in Federal Personnel Manual Letter 630–22, January 11, 1974. The regulations, but not the guidelines, have been codified in Subpart C, Part 630, Title 5, Code of Federal Regulations. Concerning the scheduling in advance requirement the Commission's regulation at 5 C.F.R. 630.308 provides as follows:

> Beginning with the 1974 leave year, before annual leave forfeited under section 6304 of title 5, United States Code, may be considered for restoration under that section, use of the annual leave must have been scheduled in writing before the start of the third biweekly pay period prior to the end of the leave year.

Agency officials authorized to restore annual leave under subsection 6304(d)(1)(C) questioned the propriety of restoring the leave since it was known in advance that the employee would not be able to use it. Accordingly, the agency requested an opinion from the Commission as to the appropriateness of restoring forfeited leave under subsection 6304(d)(1)(C) where the employee knew prior to his scheduling the leave in advance that his disability retirement had been approved.

On May 16, 1978, the Chief of the Commission's Pay and Policy Division, Bureau of Policy and Standards, advised the HEW that in his opinion it was not appropriate to restore to the employee the forfeited annual leave under subsection 6304(d)(1)(C). The opinion is in part as follows:

> * * * The guidance issued for the implementation of P.L. 93–181 contained in FPM Letter 630–22 states on page 7:
> "Sickness, i.e., a medical or physical condition for which a grant of sick leave would be approved, is not in itself a basis for permitting annual leave to be forfeited and subsequently restored for later use. Management still has the responsibility to schedule or reschedule the use of annual leave to avoid forfeiture even though an absence period because of sick leave occurs during the year. This is especially true where it is known in advance that a medical or physical condition will require an absence prior to the end of the leave year."
> Inasmuch as the Social Security Administration had foreknowledge of the employee's pending disability retirement at the time the annual leave was scheduled, it is apparent that the annual leave was not scheduled *to avoid forfeiture*, as required under FPM Letter 630–22. Use of the annual leave in 1977 was not precluded as a result of illness, as the employee had the option of substituting annual leave for sick leave at any time. Absent any other relevant circumstances, restoration of the forfeited annual leave is not warranted.

However, the Commission advised the HEW that the forfeiture of annual leave in this situation may have been the result of administrative error if written agency regulations required counseling the employee with regard to the forfeiture of annual leave and the employee was erroneously advised to forfeit the annual leave and apply for restoration. In view of its administrative regulation requiring the counseling of employees with regard to the restoration of leave the agency held that the annual leave was forfeited due to administrative error and restored the leave to the employee under subsection 6304(d)(1)(A). The HEW now asks us to determine the proper basis on which the employee's forfeited leave may be restored.

We believe that the Commission has adopted a restrictive view of the scheduling requirement of subsection 6304(d)(1)(C) which is not required by either the statutory language or legislative history.

The legislative history shows that Congress intended that section 6304(d)(1) would authorize the restoration of leave lost through no fault of the employee. There was concern that an employee should not be able to carry over additional leave on his own volition. H.R. Rep. No. 93–456, 93rd Cong. 1st Sess. 4 (1973). Accordingly, the Congress provided that annual leave should be scheduled in advance if it was to be restored under that provision. Page 6 of H.R. Rep. No. 93–456, *supra*.

With regard to the Commission's view that the employee involved here had the option of substituting annual leave for sick leave, the legislative history shows that Congress specifically rejected the view that an employee should be required to use annual leave while he is sick in order to avoid loss of annual leave. On page 5 of H.R. Rep. No. 93–456, it is stated that such view ignored the basic purpose of annual leave, which is to give an employee time for vacation or other *purposes not related to illness*.

We note further, that by section 1 of Public Law 93–181, *supra*, Congress amended 5 U.S.C. § 5551 to authorize a lump-sum payment for all of the annual leave standing to the credit of an employee at the time of his separation from the service. Previously, such lump-sum payment was limited to 30 days of annual leave or the number of days of annual leave carried over to the employee's credit at the beginning of the leave year in which the entitlement to payment occurred, whichever was the greater. The Congress intended that this removal of the prior restrictions on lump-sum compensation for annual leave would eliminate situations where an employee would take an extended period of annual leave just prior to the date of separation from Government service. Congress perceived that such use of annual leave just prior to an employee's separation had resulted in administrative difficulties as a position vacancy is not created until an employee is actually off the agency's rolls. See page 6 of H.R. Rep. 93–456, *supra*.

It would appear incongruous with that intent of Congress to construe the leave restoration provisions of section 3 of Pub. L. 93–181, section 6304(d)(1)(C) so narrowly as to preclude the restoration of annual leave scheduled by an employee who is on extended sick leave pending disability retirement. To require such an employee to interrupt his use of sick leave in order to use annual leave to avoid forfeiture thereof under 6304(a) would extend the length of time such an employee would remain on the agency's rolls prior to his retirement, a situation which the Congress has considered to be undesirable.

In view of the above, it is our belief that forfeited annual leave may be restored under 5 U.S.C. § 6304(d)(1)(C) where such leave has been scheduled in advance in accordance with 5 C.F.R. 630.308, notwithstanding such leave may have been scheduled subsequent to the approval of the employee's disability retirement. Regarding the scheduling requirement as it applies to cases in which the employee is on extended sick leave at the end of a leave year, compare *Matter of Robert T. Good*, B–182608, February 19, 1976.

In accordance with the above, as the record indicates that the employee in question properly scheduled his annual leave which was subject to forfeiture, the agency may properly restore such leave pursuant to 5 U.S.C. § 6304(d)(1)(C).

[B–194251]

Details—Compensation—Higher Grade Duties Assignment—Military Position Duties

A retired civilian employee of the Air Force claims retroactive temporary promotion and accompanying backpay under *Turner-Caldwell*, 56 Comp. Gen. 427 (1977), incident to details to higher grade military positions. There is no entitlement to backpay as the employee could not have been temporarily promoted into the military position. The *Turner-Caldwell* remedy is only available where the employee was able to satisfy requirements for a retroactive temporary promotion.

In the matter of Mrs. M. Virginia Conklin, April 23, 1979:

This action concerns an appeal by Mrs. M. Virginia Conklin, a retired civilian employee of the Department of the Air Force, of the action of our Claims Division on September 13, 1978, which disallowed her claim for retroactive promotion and backpay incident to details to higher grade positions.

During the period in question Mrs. Conklin was employed in the Housing Referral Office at George Air Force Base, California, as a clerk stenographer GS–4. Mrs. Conklin states that during the period from September 2, 1971, to February 2, 1972, she was detailed to the position of NCOIC (Non Commissioned Officer in Charge) in the Housing Referral Office and that for the periods February 2 to March 3, 1972, and July 1 to July 23, 1972, she was detailed to the position of Housing Referral Officer.

The record supports her contention that, at least for most of the period she claims backpay, she was either detailed to or performing the functions of the NCOIC or Housing Referral Officer while in grade GS–4. However, during those periods both the NCOIC and Housing Referral Officer positions were allocated, graded and assigned as military positions only. While Mrs. Conklin recognizes that fact, she has claimed a retroactive promotion and accompanying backpay on the basis of an evaluation of the equivalent civilian grade of the positions, GS–8 and GS–9, for the military positions NCOIC (senior master sergeant) and Housing Referral Officer (captain) respectively. Her claim is based on decisions of our Office and implementing Civil

Service Commission guidance, that employees who are detailed to higher grade positions for more than 120 days without Civil Service Commission approval are entitled to a retroactive temporary promotion with backpay for the period beginning with the 121st day of the detail until the detail is terminated. *Matter of Marie Grant*, 55 Comp. Gen. 785 (1976); *Matter of Reconsideration of Turner-Caldwell*, 56 Comp. Gen. 427 (1977); and CSC Bulletin No. 300–40, May 25, 1977.

On March 20, 1978, the Air Force denied Mrs. Conklin's claim on the basis that the position involved had not been classified to a grade or pay level. On September 13, 1978, our Claims Division also disallowed Mrs. Conklin's claim on the basis that the positions for which she claims a retroactive temporary promotion and backpay were military positions and were not established or classified to a civilian grade or pay level.

Mrs. Conklin has appealed this denial of her claim on the basis that both the NCOIC and Housing Referral Officer positions were officially established and classified military positions and that there is no requirement for entitlement under *Turner-Caldwell* or CSC Bulletin No. 300–40 that the detailed position be a civilian position.

Our decision in *Turner-Caldwell* was construing 5 U.S.C. § 5596 (1976) which provides backpay for an unjustified or unwarranted personnel action that resulted in the withdrawal or reduction of all or a part of an employee's pay. That decision is applicable only in those extended detail situations where there exists a properly classified and established position to which the detailed employee may be promoted. It is a well established rule that an employee may not be promoted to a position which has not been classified. *Matter of Walter F. Ray and Joseph D. Elam*, B–187847, January 25, 1977; and *United States* v. *Testan*, 424 U.S. 392 (1976). Furthermore, the employee must have been able to satisfy other applicable requirements for a retroactive temporary promotion. *Reconsideration of Turner-Caldwell*.

In this regard CSC Bulletin No. 300–40, May 25, 1977, which was issued by the Civil Service Commission to provide assistance to agencies in the proper application of our *Turner-Caldwell* decisions, provides in paragraph 4 in part as follows:

* * * For purposes of this decision, *the position must be an established one, classified under an occupational standard to a grade or pay level.* As the decision notes, the Supreme Court recently ruled in *United States* v. *Testan* that classification actions upgrading a position may *not* be made retroactive so as to entitle an incumbent to backpay. Care must be taken to distinguish between employee claims based on details to higher graded positions, and to claims based on a classification action; only the former may be considered for retroactive correction under the decision. [Italic in the original.]

We are aware of no statutory authority which would allow an employee in the civil service who is temporarily assigned to perform the duties of a military position to be promoted into that military position. Thus, we have held that since civilian employees who are temporarily assigned to a military position could not have been temporarily promoted to those positions, corrective action under our *Turner-Caldwell* line of decisions would not be applicable. B–183086, July 12, 1977. Thus, employees temporarily assigned to higher grade military positions may not be given retroactive temporary promotions to the equivalent civilian grade. *Id.* and *Matter of Donald R. Konrady*, B–193555, January 26, 1979.

The remedy which was available to Mrs. Conklin while she was performing the duties of the military positions was to file a position classification appeal to have her position classification reviewed and possibly upgraded. See 5 Code of Federal Regulations, Part 511, Subpart F. However, that remedy is available only while the employee is performing the higher level duties and may not be applied retroactively.

In view of the above, there is no authority to grant Mrs. Conklin a retroactive temporary promotion and backpay. Accordingly, Mrs. Conklin's claim is denied and the action taken by our Claims Division is sustained.

[B–192454]

Contracts—Negotiation—Changes, etc.—Written Amendment Requirement—Noncompliance

Request for proposals (RFP) required Tempest certified equipment. After receipt of best and final offers, agency determined that no offeror proposed technically acceptable system that could meet Tempest certification requirement. Agency then deleted requirement but did not notify competitors and other qualified offerors. General Accounting Office (GAO) views relaxation of requirement as substantial change in agency's needs and agency's failure to amend RFP violated applicable procurement regulations and sound procurement policy.

Contracts—Negotiation—Requests for Proposals—Specification Requirements

Contention that RFP specified only off-the-shelf equipment is without merit where RFP states that if any item in the performance specification precludes off-the-shelf equipment, offeror is requested to proposed solution for evaluation.

Contracts—Negotiation—Evaluation Factors—Criteria — Acceptability of Proposal

Protester argues that awardee's proposal did not describe how proposed equipment will satisfy each specification as required by RFP. While agency report does not respond to this protest basis, GAO reviewed awardee's proposal and observes that explanation was provided for each specification. In view of award, agency obviously viewed awardee's description as complaint. After reviewing both protester's and awardee's explanations, GAO has no basis to disturb agency's determination.

Contractors—Responsibility—Contracting Officer's Affirmative Determination Accepted—Exceptions—Not Supported by Record

Protest that awardee is not capable of meeting search time of 4 seconds as stated in its proposal is matter related to awardee's responsibility. GAO will not consider merits of protest against agency's affirmative responsibility determination, absent circumstances not preesnt here.

Contracts—Negotiation—Evaluation Factors—Evaluators—Technical Competence—Standard of GAO Review

Protester, after reviewing qualifications of agency's sole technical evaluator, challenges his technical competency. Where protester essentially contends that an evaluator is appointed in bad faith, prior decisions indicated that GAO will make subjective judgment on evaluator's qualifications. Absent such allegation, GAO's standard of review is whether technical evaluation is rationally based. Here, after considering merits of protester's contentions, GAO has no basis to conclude that technical evaluation was not reasonably based.

Contracts—Negotiation—Evaluation Factors—Delivery Provisions, Freight Rates, etc.

Protester contends that awardee cannot meet delivery schedule and should not have received favorable evaluation for proposed timely delivery. Proposals must be evaluated as submitted; therefore, GAO has no basis to question awardee's point score for proposed timely delivery. Further, awardee's capability to deliver timely is matter relating to agency's affirmative determination of responsibility and, in circumstances, will not be questioned by GAO.

Contracts—Negotiation—Offers or Proposals—Best and Final—Technically Unacceptable

Contention that protester proposed timely delivery in initial proposal but was not afforded proper point score is without merit where offeror's best and final offer stated that required paper tape punch could not be timely delivered.

In the matter of CompuScan, Inc., April 26, 1979:

CompuScan, Inc. protests the Defense Communication Agency's (DCA) award of contract No. DCA200–78–C–0023 to Sperry Univac, a division of the Sperry Rand Corporation (Univac), for the lease of up to 50 Optical Character Recognition (OCR) Terminals and maintenance support for use at multiple locations worldwide. The initial award was for 20 terminals with maintenance in the amount of $4,212,640. CompuScan essentially contends that (1) Univac's technical proposal was improperly evaluated and did not offer to meet mandatory solicitation requirements, (2) Univac's proposed delivery schedule was unrealistic and, thus, improperly evaluated, and (3) CompuScan's proposed delivery schedule should have received more points in the evaluation scheme. CompuScan requests that DCA terminate Univac's contract, reject Univac's unacceptable proposal, reevaluate the remaining proposals, and make a new award.

I. EVALUATION OF UNIVAC'S TECHNICAL PROPOSAL

The request for proposals (RFP), as amended, revealed that proposals would be evaluated by considering technical sufficiency (including engineering design, software, maintenance, and human engineering), delivery schedule, and price. The amended RFP disclosed that technical sufficiency was the most important factor and it was more than twice as important as either delivery or price, and delivery was more important than price.

CompuScan contends that Univac's proposal was not technically acceptable because the equipment offered did not satisfy these mandatory RFP requirements: (a) Tempest certification prior to award; (b) off-the-shelf equipment; (c) complete description of how the system would work, and (d) capability of searching 8,000 plain language addresses (PLA) on line.

A. Tempest Certification Prior to Award

The amended RFP expressly provided that the OCR device or system must receive Tempest certification prior to contract award. CompuScan believes that Tempest tests are vital to the security of any sensitive information contained in messages processed through the system and to prevent or suppress any compromising emanations from leaking to potential enemies. CompuScan states that systems can only be said to meet Tempest requirements when they have been tested to the appropriate Government specification in a certified laboratory, and the tests show that all required results have been met. In this regard, the RFP stated that the OCR device or system shall meet Tempest requirements of the National COMSEC/EMSEC Information Memoranda (NACSEM) 5100 series.

CompuScan notes that Univac's proposal states that its equipment is Tempest certified, but elsewhere requests $50,000 for software development; from this, CompuScan concludes that Univac did not have the required software at the time of award and obviously Univac could not have passed the Tempest requirements as a complete system, since such tests must be made on an actual operating, total-tested system with integrated hardware and software in place.

CompuScan learned, pursuant to the Freedom of Information Act (5 U.S.C. 552) that the person who performed the technical evaluation stated:

My basic evaluation criteria were for a complete system meeting all technical specifications with Tempest certification to follow at a later date if necessary.

CompuScan concludes that the "basic evaluation criteria" used by the evaluator failed to meet the ground rules and requirements laid down by the solicitation and that his error resulted in a grossly unfair award to Univac.

In response, DCA reports that none of the offerors could meet the specification calling for Tempest certification; accordingly, the Government had to delete this requirement and provide for alternate testing and certification procedures.

In reply, CompuScan first notes that at no time prior to contract award was CompuScan ever notified of any change in the ground rules which called for Tempest-certified systems. CompuScan disagrees with DCA's decision to delete that requirement as a peril to the security of the communications of our Armed Forces. CompuScan also contends that if there was no requirement for Tempest, the RFP should have been amended to permit CompuScan to have proposed an alternate system at a fraction of the cost. In addition, CompuScan notes that many other OCR manufacturers could have submitted offers and the Government would have saved millions of dollars.

Secondly, CompuScan argues that while the Univac system does not meet the Tempest requirement, the CompuScan system does. Compu-Scan states that its equipment has been Tempest-certified and has passed all tests on an individual basis and on a system based with hardware and software in place and that the test results are available at SCOCE, a subsection of the National Security Agency. CompuScan further states that its systems have been shipped to Government agencies, such as the Defense Intelligence Agency (DIA).

CompuScan states that the Tempest certification for its system was approved by DIA in April 1978 and filed with SCOCE by the testing laboratory, National Scientific Laboratories, on April 25, 1978.

In rebuttal, DCA reports that the contracting officer informally deleted the Tempest requirement prior to award when evaluation of proposals demonstrated that no offeror had a Tempest-certified system which met all other requirements. DCA reports that UNIVAC must meet Tempest levels of NACSEM 5100 but Univac's minicomputer had not passed Tempest testing.

DCA further reports that CompuScan has no Tempest certification for a system configured to meet the RFP's performance requirements and that the user military department has not certified even the unacceptable CompuScan system. In that regard, DCA states that Com-puScan was "nonresponsive" to the RFP because its offered system (which could meet the delivery date) could not meet the requirements for expandability from 500 to 8,000 PLA, and for a paper punch speed of 110 characters per second (CPS); CompuScan could only ofer a system meeting the specifications approximately a month after the required initial delivery date. DCA contends that Univac agreed to meet the required delivery date with a responsive system; thus, rather than being unfairly treated, CompuScan was given every conceivable advantage and kept in the competition and was not being rejected initially as being "nonresponsive."

Finally, DCA argues that "prerequisite software" does not require the software's existence prior to award; in fact, CompuScan also would have had to modify software to expand 500–PLA to 8,000–PLA capability.

Defense Acquisition Regulation (DAR) § 3–805.4 (1976 ed.) governs the manner in which changes in Government requirements are to be communicated to offerors and potential offerors. It provides that when, either before or after receipt of proposals, changes occur in the Government's requirements or a decision is made to relax a requirement, such change shall be made in writing as an amendment to the RFP. It also provides that no matter what stage the procurement is in, if substantial changes are made, a new solicitation should be issued and any other qualified firms should be added to the mailing list. Here, because of the RFP's manatory Tempest–certification–prior–to–award requirement, competition was narrowly restricted and excluded all OCR manufacturers who could not meet that requirement. In these circumstances, the decision to relax that requirement was a substantial change and should have been communicated to all offerors and all other qualified potential offerors in a new solicitation. By not doing so, DCA violated the DAR.

We note that DCA's informal decision to relax that requirement was based on its conclusion that CompuScan's proposed equipment was not acceptable. DCA's conclusion is based on CompuScan's revised technical proposal dated June 28, 1978, which stated as follows:

> CompuScan can ship Systems containing 500 PLAs by July 1978. We can ship Systems containing 8000 PLAs within four (4) months after Award of Contract. Similarly, we can ship Paper Tape Punches with a speed of 75 CPS by July 1978. We can ship Paper Tape Punches with a speed of 110 CPS within four (4) months after Award of Contract.

Since the RFP required (1) "the capability to expand to at least 8000 PLA's" (amendment dated April 17, 1978); (2) a "high speed (110–300 CPS paper tape punch" (paragraph 4.1, section "F," part II, RFP); and (3) delivery at the rate of four systems in the month of September 1978, CompuScan's delivery compliant proposal was clearly technically unacceptable. Nevertheless, while that establishes that CompuScan would not be entitled to award under the RFP, that did not provide a basis for DCA to ignore the applicable DAR requirements to amend the solicitation and provide all qualified offerors an opportunity to compete because CompuScan and others may have been able to meet the RFP's technical requirements with non-Tempest-certified equipment at lower cost. Accordingly, this aspect of the protest is sustained.

B. "Off-the-shelf" equipment

CompuScan contends that the RFP specified only off-the-shelf equipment. The relevant portion of the RFP states:

> Development: This specification is to be met with off-the-shelf equipment. If any item in this performance specification precludes off-the-shelf equipment, the vendor is requested to propose a solution for evaluation.

CompuScan argues that since Univac's proposal requested $50,000 for software development, Univac could not have had the required off-the-shelf equipment. CompuScan also states that until a few days before the deadline for submission of offers, Univac was negotiating with CompuScan to buy software for this system and Univac informed CompuScan that it did not have any software package of its own that would meet the RFP requirements.

CompuScan's argument is without merit because the RFP, as quoted above, expressly permitted offerors "to propose a solution for evaluation" when off-the-shelf-equipment would not satisfy the requirement.

C. Functional Description of System

The RFP's Instructions for Preparation stated that the vendor must describe how the proposed equipment will satisfy each paragraph or subparagraph of the specifications and statements that the vendor is fully compliant with the requirements of paragraph or word-for-word parroting of paragraphs would not be acceptable. CompuScan contends that Univac's proposal fails to comply with this instruction since Univac supplies general puffery about its hardware with no description at all about how the software works. Univac also states that it will meet the RFP's requirements, but does not describe how it would do it.

As an example, CompuScan points to one part of the RFP which describes the message formatting, editing, and file updating requirements of the system. CompuScan contends that Univac's proposal addresses none of these specific technical points but simply states that Univac is competent and describes in general terms the proposed hardware, by saying, "Univac offers you speed, power, reliability, availability and opportunity for future growth at a sensible price," and "Univac's proposed system is fully competitive, both in costs and in high standards of the components proposed." CompuScan argues that Univac's failure to describe the software makes its proposal unacceptable.

Although the DCA report does not address this basis of protest, DCA provided a copy of Univac's proposal which we reviewed. We note that in response to paragraph 7 of the specifications entitled "Specific Requirements—Software," Univac devotes five full pages of its proposal describing how its software would meet the RFP's requirements. Whether Univac's description complied with the RFP's description requirement is primarily a matter of proposal evaluation. Here, DCA, in view of the award to Univac, obviously concluded that Univac's software description and other specification descriptions were compliant. In our review of DCA's determination, our Office will not substitute our judgment and will not disturb DCA's determination unless it is shown to be arbitrary or in violation of procurement statutes or regulations. See *Ads Audio Visual Productions, Inc.*, B–190760, March 15, 1978, 78–1 CPD 206. After considering Univac's and CompuScan's explanations in their proposals, we have no basis to disturb DCA's determination.

D. Capability to Expand to at Least 8,000 PLA's Efficiently

The amended RFP stated that the file shall contain as a minimum 500 PLA's and associated RI's "with the capability to expand to at least 8,000 PLA's and associated RI's." In this regard, CompuScan states that the system must be capable of searching 8,000 PLA's on line; since 8,000 PLA's have an average of 40 characters each, the total size of the PLA table will exceed 300,000 characters. CompuScan contends that Univac proposed to meet this requirement by means of a cassette unit which can read and write at a rate of 600 characters per second and can search at 120 inches per second; therefore, a complete search of 300,000 characters will require 500 seconds, not 4 seconds, as stated by Univac. CompuScan concludes that it would take about 30 hours using the Univac proposed equipment to look up all the PLA's on a given 200-address message, worst case, which is far slower than the manual system.

In response, DCA reports that in its estimate, at the maximum utilization rate, the Univac system could perform the required tasks in only a very few minutes. Univac contends that the CompuScan estimates are wrong, in part, because CompuScan erroneously assumed a serial search and a single tape read.

CompuScan is not contending that Univac failed to propose a system capable of satisfying the RFP's expansion requirement. CompuScan is contending that Univac's system cannot and will not be able to perform in the time stated in Univac's proposal. Because Univac stated that its proposed system could perform certain tasks within certain time constraints, its proposal was evaluated on that basis and award was made on that basis. The awardee is contractually bound to provide a system that will perform as offered under penalty of breach of contract. Under our Bid Protest Procedures, we do not consider matters of contract administration relating to whether the awardee will deliver the proposed system. Neither do we consider matters related to affirmative determinations of responsibility, that is, whether the awardee can deliver the proposed system, with the exception of alleged fraud or bad faith, which is not the case here. *Virginia-Maryland Associates*, B–191252, March 28, 1978, 78–1 CPD 238. Accordingly, this basis of protest is dismissed without consideration on the merits.

E. Alleged Improper Technical Evaluation of CompuScan's Proposal Relative to Univac's

Consistent with the RFP's disclosed evaluation factors, DCA used a weighted evaluation scheme and the two offerors' proposals received the following scores:

Factors	RFP's Weight	Univac	CompuScan
[60] Technical			
Sufficiency_____		[58]	[57]
Engineering Design__	21	20	(*)
Software_____	17	16	16
Maintenance_____	13	13	(*)
Human Engineering_____	9	9	(*)
[25] Delivery_____	25	25	10
[Timely delivery gets maximum ½ point penalty per day of delay]			
[15] Price_____	15	15	13. 2
[100] Total_____	100	98	80. 2

*Not disclosed in record.

CompuScan argues that Univac's proposal:
- (a) did not have a Tempest-certified system;
- (b) did not have the prerequisite software;
- (c) presented parroting of phrases and puffery, rather than the required technical discussion and description; and
- (d) required up to 30 hours to process a single message.

From this, CompuScan concluded that it is beyond comprehension how Univac was awarded a score of 58 points out of 60 for technical sufficiency, as compared with CompuScan's 57 points. CompuScan believed, therefore, that the technical evaluation was improper and must not have been performed by anyone with technical competence. After some effort, CompuScan learned that the technical evalution was performed by one Navy ensign, whose "most significant civilian and military education included High School, Radioman School, Teletype Maintenance School, Speedkey Operator School and Cryptographic School;" he also was an experienced teletype repairman and radioman.

CompuScan essentially contends that the evaluation of a highly technical and complex computer terminal system:

(1) that employs advanced state-of-the-art techniques in the field of optical character recognition and telecommunications microprocessor message processing;

(2) that is to be used by the Navy (and later by the Air Force) in bases all over the world to transmit a large part of their communications traffic;

(3) that requires the most advanced techniques to suppress any compromising emanations and radiation in order to protect the security of the messages from the enemy; and

(4) that is supposed to process and to protect communications affecting the national security of the United States,

requires the technical evaluation of a skilled electrical engineer with a deep expertise in computers and not someone whose technical training does not go beyond the repair of a radio or a teletype machine.

DCA reports that its technical evaluator had over 15 years' experience in Navy Communications, was a Senior Chief Radioman, was Chief-in-Charge at the Naval Telecommunication Center at Agnano, Italy (18 months) (and while there used an operational CDC MENS II, a stand-alone OCR), had a tour at Communications Area Master Station (Norfolk) as Analysis Officer dealing with hardware and software aspects of the major automated message processing system intalled there, and his hobbies include minicomputer-software programming.

In response, CompuScan contends that a CDC MENS II OCR is extremely simple and elementary and belongs to an earlier technological generation; it not only lacks a computer, but it has almost nothing to do with the new intelligent terminal containing a built-in computer with sophisticated storage devices. CompuScan also contends that a hobby of computer software programming does not adequately replace engineering schooling, training, and experience in Stand-Alone Intelligent Terminals and computer technology required to evaluate a multimillion dollar procurement that affects the security and the vital interests of the United States and its Armed Forces.

In reply, DCA reports that the CDC MENS II is functionally the same as the OCR required by the specification and it employs a CDC 1700 (32K byte) computer and two 1.5 byte disk drives plus a paper tape punch and printer. DCA also points out that the specification was directed toward off-the-shelf equipment. DCA states that the offeror's systems must meet essential operational requirements including man-machine interface and the evaluator's background lent itself explicitly to the evaluation of those aspects.

With regard to the qualifications of the technical advisers and evaluators, as a general rule, we will not become involved in appraising the qualifications of contracting agency personnel. See *Ads Audio Visual*

Productions, Inc., supra; Joseph Legat Architects, B–187160, December 13, 1977, 77–2 CPD 458. Further, we have held that the important and responsible positions held by agency evaluators constitute a *prima facie* showing that they are qualified and with nothing more than a protester's unsubstantiated allegations regarding an evaluator's qualifications, we would have no basis to examine or question the evaluator's qualifications. *Ads Audio Visual Productions, Inc., supra.*

In the matter of *Dikewood Service Company*, 56 Comp. Gen. 188 (1976), 76–2 CPD 520, the protester challenged, as unusual, the number of changes made to the composition of the technical evaluation board personnel and alleged that well–qualified individuals were removed in favor of less qualified individuals. GAO investigators reviewed the personnel files of the individuals concerned and interviewed all but one of the evaluators. We concluded that all persons concerned were well qualified and we found no substantial difference between the qualifications of the evaluators removed from the board and those who remained. We are unaware of any decision concluding that an evaluator was not qualified.

The *Dikewood Service Company* decision and other decisions represent this Office's implicit recognition that (1) agencies have a statutory– and regulatory–based duty to fairly evaluate proposals, and (2) technically qualified agency personnel are required to perform the evaluation.

The *Dikewood Service Company* decision and other decisions of this Office may have led protesters to believe that we would generally conduct an audit of an evaluator's qualifications to determine his or her competency to evaluate particular proposals; however, we believe that the audit approach should be reserved to situations where a protester has made some showing of bad faith in the appointment of an evaluator. Here, there has been no such showing. In this case, we will not audit to subjectively judge the evaluator's qualifications. Instead, we will employ a more objective standard, i.e., we will review the technical evaluation to determine whether it is rationally based. Here, the objective standard is the better approach because it matters not whether the evaluator is qualified "on paper"; what matters is the reasonableness of the evaluation. Furthermore, we note that, as in agency affirmative determinations of responsibility, performance and costly contractual changes may be required to compensate for such improper technical evaluations; therefore, it is in an agency's own interest to select qualified evaluators and perform proper evaluations.

To apply the objective test here, we must look to the protester's specific contentions of improper technical evaluation. Each was discussed at length above and none was found to be improper. Accordingly, we have no basis to question the technical evaluation.

II. UNIVAC'S DELIVERY SCHEDULE

CompuScan notes that only one contractor, Univac, stated that it could deliver as scheduled, and thus obtained the maximum points (25) for delivery. CompuScan argues that, in light of all of the above facts, there was no way in the world for Univac to make any of the deliveries required and it should have been penalized 25 points for this factor.

When an offeror proposes to meet the Government's required delivery schedule, its proposal is acceptable and deserving of an appropriate score. When award is made based on that offeror's proposed delivery schedule, the Government has the right to demand delivery as scheduled in the contract. The awardee must deliver as required by the contract or be in breach. Accordingly, to the extent that CompuScan's contention relates to Univac's capability to deliver as proposed, the matter relates to responsibility. Where, as here, the contracting agency has affirmatively determined that an offeror is responsible, our Office will not object, absent limited circumstances not present here. *Unitron Incorporated*, B–191273, July 5, 1978, 78–2 CPD 7 (successful bidder's capability to meet delivery requirement was not to be questioned in similar circumstances). Therefore, this aspect of CompuScan's protest is dismissed.

III. COMPUSCAN'S DELIVERY SCHEDULE

CompuScan argues that it did not state that delivery would be 30 days late but its initial proposal stated that it was capable of performing all the requirements of the solicitation including all delivery schedules. Again, in its cover letter of its best and final offer, it stated, "CompuScan can deliver one system in July 1978, one system in August 1978, four systems in September 1978, and two or more systems per month thereafter."

We note that although CompuScan stated in one section of its best and final offer that it could meet the delivery requirement in another section, it stated that it could not deliver paper tape punches with the required speed until after the RFP required delivery. DCA interpreted CompuScan's specific exception to the delivery requirement as overriding its prior general offer to timely deliver. We cannot disagree with the reasonableness of DCA's interpretation.

IV. CONCLUSION AND RECOMMENDATION

Protest sustained in part. We conclude that DCA's relaxation of mandatory RFP requirements without notifying all potential offerors violated the provisions of DAR § 3–805.4. By letter of today, we are bringing this matter to the attention of the Director, DCA, so that corrective action can be taken to avoid this impropriety in future procurements. Further, we are recommending that the contract with Univac be limited to the 20 basic systems in the award and that the optional 30 systems, if required, be the subject of a fully competitive procurement.

We may not recommend any additional corrective action because at the time the matter was ready for our Office to consider the merits, under the contract's terms, the contract was to be 40 percent complete (DCA advised that Univac was on schedule) and, because of the contractor's need to incur costs for the balance of the items required under the contract in order to meet delivery requirements, the cost of termination for convenience relative to the total price of the contract was too high. Accordingly, a termination for convenience recommendation would not be in the best interests of the Government.

[B–194088]

Contracts—Protests—Court Solicited Aid—No Protest Pending

In response to request by U.S. District Court concerning litigation whose subject matter is not involved in any pending General Accounting Office (GAO) case, GAO furnishes opinion to court as to whether Commerce Department violated applicable law and regulations in canceling request for proposals.

General Accounting Office — Jurisdiction — Contracts — Court-Solicited Assistance—Scope of Review—No Protest Pending

In regard to court's request for GAO opinion on issues in lawsuit, GAO sees no obligation to keep plaintiff informed of staff resources used by GAO in arriving at opinion. Whether audit resources should be used is matter for internal GAO determination.

Contracts—Protests—Court Action—Preliminary Injunction—Granted—Court Request for GAO Opinion

GAO agrees with plaintiff that in furnishing opinion to court on matter which is not subject of any GAO case, court's findings and conclusions in issuing preliminary injunction should be carefully considered.

Contracts—Negotiation—Requests for Proposals—Cancellation—Guidelines—Availability

Examining propriety of RFP cancellations is essentially accomplished on case-by-case basis, as Federal Property and Administrative Services Act of 1949 and Federal Procurement Regulations provide virtually no specific guidance as to when RFP can or should be canceled.

Contracts—Negotiation—Requests for Proposals—Cancellation—In-House Government Performance

Section 601 of Economy Act does not appear to be applicable to Commerce Department's cancellation of RFP and determination to proceed with work in-house, as record does not indicate any inter- or intra-departmental orders for work and services involved.

Departments and Establishments—Commercial Activities—Private v. Government Procurement—Cost Comparison

Section 601 of Economy Act does not require Commerce Department to perform comparative cost analysis of plaintiff's proposal versus cost of doing work via Commerce—U.S. Postal Service agreement, because Economy Act does not apply to agreement for furnishing property or services between Postal Service and executive agencies.

Office of Management and Budget—Circulars—No. A–76—Statute v. Circular—Judicial Enforcement

GAO view is that OMB Circular A–76, March 3, 1966, as revised—statement of Executive branch policy which does not have force and effect of law—does not create right of action in disappointed bidder to sue in Federal Courts to enforce its provisions.

Contracts—Negotiation—Requests for Proposals—Cancellation—Reasonable Basis—Changed Conditions, Needs, etc.

GAO does not agree with belief agency acted wholly without reasonable basis in cancelling RFP where cost data underlying sole offeror's proposal had never been fully audited, requirements were reduced, agency made some attempt to ascertain if reduced work could be performed at less cost in-house, agency believed in-house costs would be lower than costs of informal "offers" it was receiving for reduced work submitted by sole offeror, and agency was concerned over amount of time being consumed in resolving how work would be performed.

Contracts—Negotiation—Changes, etc.—Written Amendment Requirement—Noncompliance—Not Prejudicial

Substantial changes in scope of work prior to termination of negotiations should have been issued as written amendment to RFP. However, it is difficult to see prejudice to sole offeror where it was on actual notice of changes in requirements. FPR 1–3.805–1(d) did not require agency to amend RFP and seek revised proposal based on further changes in requirements after negotiations with sole offeror had been terminated and Government had decided to perform work in-house.

Federal Procurement Regulations—Applicability—Services "Procured" from Postal Service

GAO does not agree with Plaintiff's contentions in U.S. District Court litigation that Commerce Department, in canceling RFP, violated numerous provisions of Federal Procurement Regulations (41 C.F.R. 1–1.000 *et seq.* (1978)) including sections 1–1.009–1(e), 1–1.1001, 1–2.404–1, 1–3.210, 1–3.302(c), 1–3.804, 1–3.805–1(b), and 1–3.802(c)(2).

In the matter of United States District Court for the District of Columbia, April 26, 1979:

Table of Contents

I. Introduction

In an order dated March 20, 1979, in the case of *ADVO-System, Inc.* v. *Juanita M. Kreps, et al.*, Civil Action No. 79–0257, which preliminarily enjoined the Department of Commerce (DOC) from proceeding with certain work pertaining to the 1980 census, the United States District Court for the District of Columbia (Gesell, J.) requested our Office—

* * * to inquire into and determine whether or not the Department of Commerce, through the Bureau of the Census, has complied with all applicable statutes and regulations in its rejection of plaintiff's proposal governing an APOC (Advanced Post Office Check) for the 1980 Census and in its subsequent decision to perform all or part of the APOC itself or in combination with the United States Postal Service.

The plaintiff's January 25, 1979, complaint had essentially sought declaratory and injunctive relief in 2 areas—the first, relating to DOC's allegedly unlawful cancellation of a request for proposals (RFP) for APOC and determination to proceed with the work within the Government, and the second relating to DOC's alleged misappropriation of proprietary information which ADVO had revealed in its proposal or during discussions. It appears that the ultimate relief sought as to the first of these areas is a permanent injunction compelling DOC to retract its cancellation of the RFP and resume negotiations in good faith with the plaintiff.

The preliminary injunction was granted only as to the first area, and, as we understand the court's order and accompanying memorandum opinion, it is only as to this area that our views are requested. This matter is not the subject of any protest or other case before our Office. This opinion has been prepared solely in response to the court's request.

Our opinion is based upon the pleadings and supporting papers filed with the court as well as the following submissions: (1) a letter from DOC dated March 30, 1979, accompanied by a legal memorandum and copies of some 31 supporting documents, and a letter dated April 13, 1979, from DOC including an additional legal memorandum, and (2) letters from ADVO's counsel dated March 28, 1979, with enclosures, April 4, 1979, with enclosures including a partial transcript of the hearing before the court on March 16, 1979, and April 23, 1979, with enclosures.

Finally, the court's opinion states that the issues must be resolved with the utmost dispatch and DOC has urged our Office to expedite our opinion.

II. Scope of Review

ADVO has presented several arguments relating to how our Office should go about furnishing a response to the court. A summary of these points and our comments on each follow.

ADVO: The court's memorandum opinion clearly states that the court's knowledge of ongoing GAO audit work in this area was one of the reasons this matter was referred to GAO. The court clearly contemplated that GAO's report would consist in part of an audit finding. Yet, at an informal conference called by GAO on March 27, 1979, the GAO attorney handling the case indicated that the court's request is being handled in a manner similar to a bid protest and as an entirely separate matter from ongoing GAO audit work. To follow this approach would represent a failure by GAO to discharge its full responsibilities under the doctrine of primary jurisdiction.

Comment: At the March 27, 1979, meeting, which incidentally was attended by a GAO auditor familiar with the APOC procurement, ADVO was never advised that input from GAO auditors would be excluded from our response to the court. Rather, ADVO was told that the court, in our view, was requesting a legal opinion and that whatever assistance our auditors could provide to our legal staff in this connection was purely an internal GAO matter. We see nothing in the court's order and opinion suggesting that we should keep ADVO informed of how we go about arriving at our response to the court. Neither do we find any specific indication that the court is requesting a GAO audit "report" or "finding."

ADVO: As a matter of judicial-administrative comity under the doctrine of primary jurisdiction, GAO should carefully consider the preliminary findings and conclusions which the court reached in issuing the preliminary injunction.

Comment: In 52 Comp. Gen. 198 (1972) we advised the Court of Appeals for the District of Columbia Circuit of our independent views and conclusions on a protest notwithstanding certain pre-existing findings and conclusions of the U.S. District Court in the same case. However, there the Court of Appeals order made it plain that the District Court's opinion on the merits should not be considered by our Office. In the present case, we agree with ADVO that the court's findings and conclusions should be carefully considered and we have so considered them.

ADVO: The court is not asking GAO to determine whether DOC's violation of OMB Circular A-76 would give a disappointed bidder or offeror a legal cause of action. Rather, it is asking whether DOC complied with the circular. It is ultimately up to the court to decide the legal issues.

Comment: The court's order asks our Office to inquire into and determine whether DOC has complied with all applicable statutes and regulations. In addition, ADVO bases its case in large measure on DOC's alleged violation of the circular. We see no specific indication in the court's order and memorandum opinion that our inquiry is to exclude legal questions related to this point.

III. Background

One of the major difficulties in this case is that the various negotiation sessions between DOC and ADVO apparently were not transcribed and there is not much in the way of detailed contemporaneous memoranda or notes memorializing what transpired in these meetings. The controversy thus has been reduced to a disagreement between the parties with each side relying to a large extent on after-the-fact recollection of what was said or done months earlier. While it could be said that many of the facts are controverted, it might be as accurate to say that the facts are simply unclear or confused. In this regard, ADVO charges DOC with taking inconsistent positions in its various submissions and sees DOC's failure to adequately substantiate certain facts—particularly its cost estimates—as critical to the outcome of the case. To some degree, at least, the court agreed with ADVO's view in issuing the preliminary injunction.

In contrast, after reviewing the record we believe the legal issues are of overriding importance. Accordingly, we think that for the purposes of this opinion, a very general description of the factual situation and the parties' factual allegations is sufficient.

RFP No. 7-35030, issued August 1, 1977, sought proposals for residential mailing lists (about 52 million addresses) and for other work, described as "(Optional) Updating activities, including verification of lists with U.S. Postal Service." The latter was, or evolved into, the APOC work in controversy here. The overall effort procured under the RFP is in support of DOC's plans to conduct part of the 1980 census by mailing questionnaires to respondents.

Several proposals were received in September 1977. Exactly what transpired over the next year is not entirely clear. ADVO alleges a substantial, unwarranted delay by DOC in evaluating the proposals. In any event, contracts for the first part of the work were awarded in October 1978 to ADVO and two other companies. In the meantime, DOC had provided ADVO in August 1978 with what it describes as a "briefing package"—a description of the APOC work. This apparently was not issued in the form of an amendment to the RFP. Also, by letter dated September 12, 1978, DOC told ADVO that it was the only offeror interested in and qualified to perform the APOC work. In this regard, the court's memorandum opinion describes ADVO as the country's largest bulk mailer which through its long experience has developed a method to maintain and update its national address list through the use of postal carrier routes.

DOC states that its representatives conferred frequently with ADVO over the next several months ADVO submitted a proposal dated December 1, 1978, to perform the APOC work.

On December 12, 1978, there was a meeting between the parties. The full scope of what was discussed is not clear. DOC indicates that, as a result of the meeting, it had increased concern about ADVO's cost and schedule for performing APOC. DOC also indicates that at this time it was reconsidering its APOC plans and was reducing the APOC workload by about 40 percent. The agency states that ADVO was provided with a 4-page "preliminary outline" of the reduced requirements on December 19, 1978. ADVO admits this. There is no indication that this document was issued as an amendment to the RFP.

Also, at about this time, DOC undertook to visit ADVO's plant to audit cost data. However, a dispute developed. ADVO maintained in a letter from its counsel dated December 22, 1978, that DOC was demanding access to unrelated cost information rather than auditing the cost data contained in the December 1, 1978, proposal. There was a delay of several weeks before the audit was resumed on or about January 8, 1979.

On January 11, 1979, the parties met again. DOC asserts that at this time it presented a complete outline of the reduced APOC requirements to ADVO. It does not appear from the record that this was issued in the form of an amendment to the RFP. ADVO contends it was told, for the first time, that it was in competition with the Census Bureau to perform the APOC work. ADVO evidently made an oral offer to perform the reduced APOC work at a figure variously described as an estimated $6.3 to $6.7 million (DOC) or a cost slightly in excess of $6 million (ADVO). DOC states that ADVO was told its cost was considered by DOC to be high or too high.

There is a dispute as to who terminated the meeting and how. In general, ADVO maintains that DOC refused to negotiate in good faith. DOC contends ADVO terminated the meeting. Also, DOC states that on January 11, 1979, it terminated its audit at ADVO's plant prior to its completion.

On January 12, 1979, DOC apparently advised ADVO in a telephone call that DOC estimated it could do the APOC work in-house for about $5 million. ADVO asserts it was told that, unless it agreed to perform the work for $5 million, DOC would terminate negotiations. ADVO states it tried to ascertain what the $5 million estimate was composed of and to arrange another meeting, but that DOC was not responsive to these requests.

DOC further states that on January 12, 1979, ADVO was telephonically requested by the contracting officer to submit its "best price" by 3 p.m. on that date and that ADVO did not respond by 3 p.m. There are also statements in the record by DOC that ADVO failed to furnish a revised offer within 2 days or within 1 week after the January 11, 1979, meeting. There is no indication in the record that DOC at any time sent ADVO a written request for its "best and final" offer by a specific cutoff time. ADVO states that it made an oral, revised offer ᴄf $5.9 million in a telephone conversation with a Census Bureau official on January 14, 1979.

By message dated January 18, 1979, the contracting officer advised ADVO that negotiations with it for the APOC work were being terminated in order that preparations for Government performance of the effort could proceed.

Yet another meeting between the parties was held on January 22, 1979. ADVO states that DOC again refused to explain how its $5 million estimate was calculated.

By letter dated January 24, 1979, ADVO's counsel submitted what he described as a "new and final offer" of $5,792,315. This 3-page letter does not make any reference to the RFP or state that it is being furnished in response to any DOC document. Rather, it makes reference to prior ADVO offers and conversations with DOC officials. It contains a very brief description of some APOC work and a dollar figure broken down into several price and cost elements and profit. This offer was rejected by a DOC letter dated February 1, 1979.

Also, in January 1979, two basic documents were generated by DOC concerning its estimate of the cost of performing the APOC work within the Government—a 1-page memorandum dated January 10, 1979, and a 2-page memorandum dated January 30, 1979. Each contains an estimate broken down into certain elements of work.

ADVO's position is essentially that these estimates are nothing more than numbers on a piece of paper derived from oral statements of various individuals and unsupported by any documentary evidence. A deposition of the individual who compiled the January 10 estimate does indicate that there was very little in the way of documentary back-up at that time. DOC for its part maintains that the January 10 estimate was the product of a systematic, coordinated effort in that various operating areas within the Census Bureau which would be responsible for performing the APOC work were required to submit cost figures to a central point, i.e., the individual who assembled them into the estimate. DOC also points out that the January 10 estimate was based on the same reduced requirements which were discussed with ADVO at the January 11, 1979, meeting.

In addition to challenging specific cost elements, ADVO attacks the January 10 and January 30 estimates as being inconsistent in that both arrive at totals of about $5 million whereas (ADVO contends) the latter was based on a further reduction in the requirements reflected in a January 29, 1979, scenario which lengthened the work schedule. ADVO states it can perform the work per this scenario for less than $5 million. DOC does not dispute the basis of the January 30 estimate but does dispute ADVO's contention that it can perform the work for less than $5 million.

Also, ADVO has called attention to an audit report by our Office (B–78395, November 9, 1978, GGD–79–7) which was critical of the Census Bureau's planning for the 1980 Census in certain respects, such as budgeting for certain work based upon inaccurate or inadequate data.

Finally, there is also a dispute over the urgency of the procurement. DOC maintains, essentially, that it is operating under a tight schedule in trying to conduct the 1980 census and that the APOC work is interrelated with the schedule of other necessary operations and procedures. In an April 11, 1979, affidavit, the Acting Director of the Census Bureau states that there is a grave risk inherent in any further delay in implementing the APOC. ADVO questions DOC's assertion of urgency contending that the agency has made no showing why the scheduling of various operations cannot be relaxed. In addition, the plaintiff maintains that as of January 1979 urgency could not have been a valid basis for canceling the RFP since the agency was at that time relaxing the APOC schedule by several months. ADVO also claims that, while the agency now asserts urgency, it has not previously made this argument before the court.

IV. Cancellation of an RFP—General Principles

The general statutory requirements for procurements conducted by executive agencies are set forth in Title III of the Federal Property and Administrative Services Act of 1949, as amended, 41 U.S.C. § 251 et seq. (1976). 41 U.S.C. § 252(c) describes the circumstances in which contracts may be negotiated and 41 U.S.C. § 254 describes certain other requirements pertaining to negotiated contracts. However, the statute does not address the circumstances in which a solicitation in a negotiated procurement can or should be canceled. Similarly, the Federal Procurement Regulations (FPR), which implement the procurement provisions of the 1949 Act, provide virtually no specific guidance on the subject of canceling an RFP. (All references to the FPR in this opinion are to the provisions contained in 41 C.F.R. § 1–1.000 et seq. (1978) except as otherwise noted.)

The law concerning canceling RFP's thus consists of caselaw. In general, our Office has said that we will not object to an agency's decision to cancel an RFP unless the protester shows that the decision, in light of the facts and circumstances of the particular procurement, clearly lacked a reasonable basis. See *Federal Leasing, Inc., et al.*, 54 Comp. Gen. 872 (1975), 75–1 CPD 236; *Semiconductor Equipment Corporation*, B–187159, February 18, 1977, 77–1 CPD 120, affirmed May 4, 1977, 77–1 CPD 301. The United States Court of Appeals for the District of Columbia Circuit has held that the cancellation of an RFP is objectionable if it is found to be "irrational." *Air Terminal Services, Inc.* v. *Department of Transportation*, 515 F. 2d 1014 (1975).

V. Plaintiff's Contentions and GAO Comments

The plaintiff has presented numerous contentions of errors on the part of DOC buttressed by scores of citations to what it sees as the applicable law and precedent. While we have considered the entire record, we believe the following discussion—consisting of summaries of the plaintiff's key contentions and our comments on each—is sufficient.

ADVO: The Economy Act of 1932, June 30, 1932, 47 Stat. 382, implicitly required DOC to perform a comparative analysis of the costs of the ADVO proposal versus the costs of performing the work within the Government.

Comment: Section 601 of the Economy Act of 1932, 31 U.S.C. § 686(a) (1976), states essentially that an executive department or independent establishment within the Government, or any bureau or office thereof, may place orders for certain supplies or services with any other such entity if various conditions are satisfied and provided, "That if such work or services can be as conveniently or more cheaply performed by private agencies such work shall be let by competitive bids to such private agencies." Section 601 covers both the inter- and intra-departmental furnishing of work or services on a reimbursable basis when not otherwise specifically authorized by statute. See generally *Washington National Airport, et al.*, 57 Comp. Gen. 674 (1978).

In our opinion, section 601 of the Economy Act has no applicability to the present case. As far as performance of work within DOC is concerned, there is no indication in the record that this is being accomplished by intra-departmental order on a cost-reimbursable basis. (In other words, the Census Bureau has not issued a purchase order to some other bureau or office within DOC for the performance of the APOC work in lieu of procuring the same work from the private sector.) Even if section 601 were applicable to the present case, it must be noted that it refers to procuring work from the private sector by competitive bidding. DOC's attempt to conduct a competitive procurement under RFP 7–35030 has shown that there is only one interested prospective contractor for the APOC work—ADVO. Sustaining ADVO's position based upon the section 601 proviso would not result in the competition envisioned by the statute, but in a *de facto* sole-source award.

Further, insofar as any agreement between DOC and the Postal Service is concerned, it must be noted that section 601 does not apply to the Postal Service. See 39 U.S.C. § 410 (1976), which provides in part that "* * * no Federal law dealing with public or Federal contracts, property, works, officers, employees, budgets, or funds * * * shall apply to the exercise of the powers of the Postal Service." 39 U.S.C. § 410 includes certain exceptions to this broad exemption but section 601 of the Economy Act is not among them.

Further, 39 U.S.C. § 411 (1976) provides:

Executive agencies * * * are authorized to furnish property, both real and personal, and personal and nonpersonal services to the Postal Service, and the Postal Service is authorized to furnish property and services to them. The furnishing of property and services under this section shall be under such terms and conditions, including reimbursability, as the Postal Service and the head of the agency concerned shall deem appropriate.

The statutory language makes no reference to a requirement for comparison of the costs of an executive agency—Postal Service agreement for the furnishing of property or services and the costs of procuring such property or services from the private sector. It appears to confer broad discretion on executive agencies insofar as determining the appropriateness of entering into such arrangements with the Postal Service is concerned.

For the foregoing reasons, we see no merit in the plaintiff's argument that DOC is violating 31 U.S.C. § 686(a).

ADVO: FPR § 1–2.404–1 governs the cancellation of Government contract solicitations. Although FPR § 1–2.404–1 by its terms addresses cancellations of invitations for bids, GAO decisions recognize that it also governs cancellations of negotiated procurement solicitations.

Comment: As ADVO recognizes, the language of FPR § 1–2.404–1 is directed only at cancellations of solicitations in formally advertised procurements. Our Office has noted in various cases that the principles reflected in FPR § 1–2.404–1 (and the corresponding provision in the Armed Services Procurement Regulation (ASPR)) may be equally applicable to cancellations of RFP's. See, for example, *California Stevedore and Ballast Company*, B–186873, January 24, 1977, 77–1 CPD 47 (RFP cancellation considered in light of ASPR § 2–404.1 (1975) principle that IFB can be cancelled where all bids are at unreasonable prices) and *Microfilm Communication Systems, Incorporated*, B–180465, September 4, 1974, 74–2 CPD 140 (FPR § 1–2.404–1(b)(2) principle that IFB can be canceled where supplies or services are no longer required applied to RFP cancellation).

ADVO's assertion, however, that FPR § 1–2.404–1 "governs" the cancellation of RFP's is an overstatement. As already noted, the FPR's are silent on the specific subject of canceling RFP's. The propriety of such cancellations is reviewed on a case-by-case basis. We have indicated that the possible justifications for canceling an RFP are not necessarily limited to the grounds stated in FPR § 1–2.404–1 or ASPR § 2–404.1. See *Federal Leasing, Inc.*, 54 Comp. Gen., *supra*, at 877.

ADVO: FPR § 1–2.404–1 and numerous GAO decisions make clear that the Government must establish a "compelling reason" in order to justify canceling a solicitation.

Comment: The Government is required to have a compelling reason to reject all bids in a formally advertised procurement basically because of the evils inherent in the public exposure of bidders' prices and the resultant creation of an auction atmosphere in a resolicitation for the same or similar requirements. See generally 52 Comp. Gen. 285 (1972).

In a negotiated procurement there is normally no public disclosure of the proposals which are received. In addition, in the present case the Government plans to perform the work in-house and there is no resolicitation in which ADVO might be disadvantaged vis-a-vis other competitors. ADVO's repeated citation, therefore, of cases applying the "compelling reason" standard to cancellations of IFB's is not germane to the inquiry whether DOC acted unreasonably or irrationally in canceling the present RFP.

ADVO: FPR §§ 1–2.404–1(b), 1–3.302(c) and 1–3.305 required DOC, prior to canceling the RFP, to make a written determination setting out the facts and circumstances justifying the decision to cancel. No such written determination was made.

Comment: As already discussed, FPR § 1–2.404–1 applies by its terms only to cancellations of IFB's. FPR § 1–3.302 states in pertinent part:

* * * [T]he following determinations in connection with the negotiation of contracts are required to be made in writing supported by written findings as specified in § 1–3.305:

* * * * * * *

(c) The determination required by section 303(b) of the Act (41 U.S.C. 253(b)) that it is in the public interest to reject all bids; * * *

We believe FPR § 1–3.302(c) is referring to the situation where a negotiated procurement is initiated after all bids have been rejected in an advertised procurement. See FPR § 1–3.214. This has nothing to do with the situation in the present case where a negotiated procurement was initiated and the agency ultimately decided to terminate negotiations with the sole remaining offeror and cancel the RFP. We see no violation by DOC of the aforementioned sections of the FPR's in the present case.

ADVO: An agency's failure to comply with OMB Circular A–76 is an independent basis for judicial review when raised by a disappointed bidder.

Comment: OMB Circular No. A–76, issued March 3, 1966, revised August 30, 1967, October 18, 1976, and June 13, 1977, describes itself as containing:

* * * basic policies to be applied by executive agencies in determining whether commercial and industrial products and services used by the Government are to be provided by private suppliers or by the Government itself * * *.

By way of background, our Office's position on protests alleging violations of the circular was stated as follows in B–161862, September 14, 1967:

The question whether a department or establishment of the Executive branch of the Government may properly perform "in house" the type of operations here concerned, or should contract with commercial companies for such services, is not covered by any specific statute of which we are aware, or regulation or instruction issued pursuant thereto, which would place the resolution of such questions within the decision functions of the General Accounting Office. The directives incorporated in Bureau of the Budget Circular No. A–76, are matters of Executive policy, prescribed by the Bureau of the Budget as the agent of the President designated by Executive Order No. 8248 of September 8, 1939, to assist the President in the formulation and administration of the fiscal program of the Government and to advise the executive departments and agencies in the areas of administrative organization and practice. See 43 Comp. Gen. 217; also 42 Comp. Gen. 640, wherein we concluded, in reference to the predecessor Bureau of the Budget Bulletin No. CO–2, as follows:

"Thus, the propriety of a determination by an executive agency as to whether services or products should be obtained under contract with private enterprise or through the use of Government-owned facilities is not a matter permitting of a ruling in terms of legal rights and responsibilities. We therefore find no legal basis for objection to the proposed administrative action, and we must decline to rule upon the policy question involved, which we deem to be a matter for resolution within the executive branch."

To our knowledge, the Federal courts have not explicitly held that OMB Circular A–76 is enforceable in a private civil action filed by a disappointed bidder or offeror. None of the authorities cited by ADVO directly so hold. *American Federation of Government Employees* v. *Dunn,* 561 F. 2d 1310 (9th. Cir., 1977) and *American Federation of Government Employees* v. *Hoffmann,* 427 F. Supp. 1048 (N.D. Ala., 1976) were unsuccessful suits by labor organizations attempting to prevent contracting-out of services. In *Dunn,* the court pointed out that, unlike a disappointed bidder, the appellants were not within the zone of interest protected by the Service Contract Act and therefore lacked standing. In *Hoffmann,* the court pointed out that cases involving complaints by disappointed bidders concerning the bidding and award process prescribed by ASPR were an exception to the normal proscription against judicial interference in the procurement process, but that the facts of the plaintiff's case did not involve disappointed bidders or any fairly comparable situation. In addition, ADVO cites the apparently unreported opinion in *J.E.T.S. Waescherie-Gmbh* v. *Stetson,* Civil Action No. 77–1901 (D.D.C., November 11, 1977), as stating merely that, in the event of a failure to follow "OMB and DOD regulations" by the Air Force in the future, the court would have jurisdiction to enjoin the providing of mess attendant services in-house. It appears to us that these precedents offer only very limited support—either by implication or possibly in *dicta*— for the proposition that a disappointed bidder or offeror has a cause of action for violation of the circular.

ADVO has argued that the circular must be read in conjunction with the Economy Act, *supra,* and the Office of Federal Procurement Policy (OFPP) Act, 41 U.S.C. § 401 (1976). As discussed *supra,* the Economy Act is not applicable to the present matter. As far as the OFPP Act is concerned, the 1966 circular and the first revision in 1967 were issued prior to the existence of OFPP. The OFPP Act was enacted in 1974 and authorizes the OFPP Administrator to prescribe policies, regulations, procedures, and forms in accordance with applicable law which shall be followed by executive agencies in their procurement of certain goods and services. See 41 U.S.C. § 405. The 1976 and 1977 revisions to the circular followed, which essentially dealt with retirement costs of Federal employees as a factor in comparative cost analyses. To our knowledge, the Administrator has never issued the 1966 circular, as revised, as a binding policy or regulation under the authortiy of 41 U.S.C. § 405.

We note that on March 29, 1979, a complete revision of the circular, replacing the 1966 circular and all subsequent amendments, was announced by OFPP and OMB and will presumably become effective in the near future. It is unnecessary to consider the legal status of the new circular as the events at issue here preceded it. However, as a matter of information section 11 of the new circular provides a procedure for appealing determinations made by agencies under it, and states in part: "This procedure does not authorize an appeal outside the agency or a judicial review."

In our opinion, the edition of the circular in question here does not create a private right of action in a disappointed bidder or offeror. Initially, our Office's view, as indicated *supra*, has consistently been that Executive orders or directives which are not specifically authorized by statute and which are essentially directed at insuring the efficient operation of the Executive branch are matters of executive policy and do not have the force and effect of law. In accord with this view is *Independent Meat Packers Ass'n.* v. *Butz*, 526 F. 2d 228 (8th Cir., 1975), *cert. denied*, 424 U.S. 966 (1976), where it was held that a district court erred in holding that the Secretary of Agriculture had failed to comply with OMB Circular A-107. The circular implemented an executive order which the court found was not authorized by statute but rather was intended primarily as a managerial tool to implement the President's personal economic policies.

A somewhat similar result occurred in *Manhattan-Bronx Postal Union* v. *Gronouski*, 350 F. 2d 451 (D.C. Cir., 1965), *cert. denied*, 382 U.S. 978 (1966), where postal employees tried unsuccessfully to enforce an executive order not issued pursuant to statute which directed agencies to recognize employee organizations selected by a majority of employees. The court held that the Executive order represented a formulation of broad policy which imposed no hard and fast directives on the many different kinds of Federal employees, found no violation of the order in the way the Postmaster General applied it in the particular circumstances involved, and said that, even if the Postmaster General's action was not in compliance with the order, it did not follow that the appellants could obtain judicial intervention.

Moreover, in the present case, even if OMB Circular A–76 had the force and effect of law, it does not expressly grant a private right of action and the inference of such a right is not undertaken lightly. *Acevedo* v. *Nassau County, New York*, 500 F. 2d 1078 (2d. Cir., 1974). The circular contains seemingly mandatory provisions as to what executive agencies "must" or "shall" do in deciding whether to perform work in-house or contract out and goes into some detail as to how cost comparisons are to be conducted. Notwithstanding this ostensibly precise and binding quality, the circular, like the executive order considered in *Manhattan-Bronx Postal Union*, is obviously a broad policy formulation, containing considerable precatory language and leaving a range of discretion to individual agencies as to how its provisions should be applied in any particular situation. For example, in the circular's various directions to executive agencies, the word "should" appears in excess of 40 times and the word "may" in excess of 10 times.

It is our view that to hold the circular gives a disappointed offeror an implied right of action would be a highly significant development, the consequences of which cannot be accurately predicted. Since the circular's preference is for contracting out as opposed to in-house performance, numerous suits by private parties asserting that various in-house Government activities should be contracted out are certainly conceivable.

Considering all the foregoing circumstances, it is our opinion that ADVO does not have a right of action under OMB Circular A–76.

ADVO: DOC's violation of OMB Circular A–76 is the best evidence of the unlawful cancellation of the RFP in violation of FPR § 1–2.404–1, because, in the absence of a proper cost analysis, there is simply no basis for concluding that ADVO's proposed price was unreasonable. The factual issue of whether a valid cost analysis preceded the cancellation has already been decided, because the court has stated it certainly appears that an adequate determination was not made that the work could be performed at less expense within the Government.

Comment: FPR § 1–2.404–1, as already indicated, is not directly applicable. Moreover, whether a "violation" of the circular occurred is not the issue. The issue is whether, in light of pertinent precedent, DOC's action in terminating negotiations with ADVO and canceling the RFP is shown to be totally unreasonable or irrational. This is a heavy burden for a plaintiff or protester to bear, because the agency reserved the right in the RFP to reject any and all offers and it is well established that the contracting agency enjoys a broad range of discretion in deciding whether to cancel an RFP.

ADVO's case is based, in large measure. on the theory that, since DOC has failed to substantiate its $5 million estimate for doing the work within the Government, it necessarily follows that DOC has no reasonable basis for determining that ADVO's offer of about $5.8

million was unreasonably high and therefore that the agency erred in terminating negotiations. This theory is based upon several faulty premises.

The first premise is that ADVO and DOC are in competition to perform the APOC work and that, while ADVO has substantiated the merits of its proposal, DOC has not substantiated the merits of its. DOC, however, is the contracting agency, not an offeror. It is fundamental in negotiated procurement that the burden is, initially, on each offeror to affirmatively demonstrate the merits of its proposal. The merits of a proposal are not automatically assumed and it is not up to the contracting agency to prove that the proposal is unsatisfactory or that some other alternative is better than the proposal. See *Julie Research Laboratories, Inc.*, 55 Comp. Gen. 374, 383–384 (1975), 75–2 CPD 232. What ADVO has done in the present case is to reverse this burden and to assert that it is up to DOC to prove by a preponderance of the evidence that its "proposal" is better than ADVO's.

Related to this is the erroneous premise that the only possible justification for terminating negotiations with ADVO in the present case would be a fully supported determination by DOC which demonstrates convincingly that ADVO's proposal is unreasonably high in price. In this connection, we believe it is extremely important to bear in mind ADVO's posture in this procurement—that of the sole offeror to perform the APOC work. ADVO is a party seeking a *de facto* sole-source award.

In this regard, our decision in *Telectro-Mek, Inc.*, B–185892, July 26, 1976, 76–2 CPD 81, is pertinent. There, the Navy experienced difficulty in obtaining "cost or pricing data" (a breakdown of an offeror's price into separate cost elements checked by the agency to verify price reasonableness) from a sole-source supplier. Ultimately, the Navy investigated and found another supplier offering a lower price and awarded it a sole-source contract. We denied the protest and Telectro-Mek was unsuccessful in subsequent litigation (*Telectro-Mek, Inc. v. Middendorf*, D.D.C., Civil Action No. 76–736, unreported opinion, December 9, 1976).

ADVO points out that its September 1977 proposal was prepared in a competitive environment and that it furnished cost or pricing data in its December 1, 1978, proposal. In addition, DOC in the present case does not have a lower-priced offer from another supplier. Balanced against these considerations, however, is the fact that ADVO has never, as far as we can determine, presented anything which could be described as a genuine proposal for the reduced APOC requirements. The December 1, 1978, proposal, which is in excess of $12 million, was submitted before the scope of the work was reduced. The purported "offers" for the reduced work of about $6 million on January 11, 1979, and $5.9 million on January 14, 1979, were mere oral statements. As for the written offer of about $5.8 million dated January 24, 1979, in our opinion it is impossible to tell what DOC would have been contracting for and on what terms and conditions had it accepted this "proposal." The letter does not state it is being furnished in response to the RFP or any identifiable statement of DOC requirements.

The issue, then, as we see it, is whether DOC was acting in a totally unreasonable or irrational fashion in breaking off negotiations with ADVO in a situation where

—it had received a formal proposal (December 1, 1978) from a sole offeror but had never completed its audit of the cost data associated with that proposal

—it had reduced the work requirements

—it had made at least some attempt to estimate what it would cost to perform the reduced requirements within the Government (January 10, 1979)

—it had never received any formal offer for the reduced requirements from the sole offeror

—it believed its in-house costs would be lower than the cost of the informal "offers" it was receiving from the sole offeror, and

—it was becoming increasingly concerned about the amount of time being consumed in definitizing which party would perform the work.

We believe it is difficult to say that the agency was being totally unreasonable in deciding to cancel the RFP in these circumstances. As for the court's statement that an adequate determination of in-house costs was not made by DOC, we believe this statement was made in the context of ADVO's legal arguments that OMB Circular A–76, the Economy Act, and various provisions of the FPR's required certain cost analyses by DOC. The court noted that ADVO's legal arguments were highly technical and did not conclusively rule on them.

ADVO has also argued that after-the-fact rationalizations about possible additional grounds for canceling the RFP should not be given any weight. Our approach is to look to whether, in light of the record, the agency's action has any basis supporting it, not simply to examine the basis which the agency advanced at the time it took the action. See, for example, *Torco Corporation*, B–187776, May 10, 1977, 77–1 CPD 329.

The foregoing is not to say that DOC's conduct of the procurement should be regarded as a model of effective negotiated procurement procedure. The reduction of the scope of the work appears to have been substantial and should have been issued in the form of a written amendment to the RFP. The lack of a written request for a "best and final" offer from ADVO was another deficiency in this procurement. Oral requests of this nature generate misunderstandings which produce litigation. *Cf. Kappa Systems, Inc.*, 56 Comp. Gen. 675, 684–686

(1977), 77–1 CPD 412, and decisions discussed therein. In addition, a conclusion that DOC's cancellation of the RFP is not legally objectionable or that it meets a minimum standard of legal sufficiency should not be confused with a conclusion that the decision to perform APOC within the Government represents a wise management decision as a matter of policy.

ADVO: By not following OMB Circular A–76, DOC has deviated from established procurement policy within the meaning of FPR § 1–1.009–1(e) and there is no evidence that DOC has complied with FPR § 1–1.009–2 which sets forth specific procedures for authorizing deviations.

Comment: FPR § 1–1.009 deals with "deviations," which FPR § 1–1.009–1(e) describes as including a situation "When a policy or procedure is prescribed, use of any inconsistent policy or procedure."

We believe this provision is referring to policies or procedures contained in the various sections of the FPR's, not to all other procurement policies or procedures in existence. This is clear from a reading of FPR § 1–1.009 as a whole and also from the specific reference in FPR § 1–1.009–2 to "* * * deviations from the Federal Procurement Regulations * * *." OMB Circular A–76 is not part of the FPR's.

ADVO: DOC cannot rely on a claim that "urgency" precludes reopening negotiations with ADVO when the existence of any urgency was created by DOC's own extensive delay in evaluating the APOC proposals.

Comment: In *Datapoint Corporation*, B–186979, May 18, 1977, 77–1 CPD 348, cited by ADVO in this connection, the question was whether reopening negotiations was a practicable remedy where the Government had made an improper award by accepting a nonconforming proposal. In *Minjares Building Maintenance Company*, 55 Comp. Gen. 864 (1976), 76–1 CPD 168, the question was whether negotiations should have been reopened to incorporate a new Service Contract Act wage determination in order to assure that all offerors were competing on an equal basis. Neither case is particularly apposite here as the present case does not involve an improper award to another offeror or the question whether ADVO was accorded an equal opportunity to compete vis-a-vis other offerors. DOC and the Postal Service are not "offerors."

ADVO: It is clear that the contracting officer never made any independent determination of the propriety of canceling the RFP, but merely complied with the Census Bureau's desires.

Comment: The record shows that a Census Bureau official, by memorandum dated January 18, 1979, "requested" the contracting officer to advise ADVO that the RFP was canceled. The fact that this may have initiated the action which led to the cancellation does not establish that the contracting officer did not make his own independent determination before carrying out the cancellation itself. The contracting officer's January 18, 1979, notice of cancellation to ADVO does not state that he was taking the action based on instructions from someone else.

ADVO: DOC failed to conduct meaningful discussions with ADVO in violation of FPR §§ 1–3.804 and 1–3.805–1(a). DOC's ultimatum that ADVO perform the APOC contract at the same price as DOC's estimate was not negotiations but "procurement blackmail."

Comment: The Government may disclose its estimate to an offeror during negotiations and use it as a negotiating tool. *Airflote, Inc.*, B–181701, November 6, 1974, 74–2 CPD 242. Moreover, the FPR's do not prohibit the Government from telling an offeror its price is considered to be too high nor do they proscribe hard bargaining by the Government. None of the decisions cited by ADVO in this connection support its contention that DOC violated the FPR's.

ADVO: DOC acted unreasonably in giving ADVO less than one working day within which to submit its offer on substantially revised requirements.

Comment: The plaintiff's argument on this point is undercut by several factors. First, ADVO admits that it knew as early as December 19, 1978, that the scope of the work might be reduced. Second, ADVO states that in the January 11, 1979, meeting it made an offer to perform the reduced work. Third, ADVO on at least one occasion has questioned whether DOC in fact ever established a best and final offer deadline of 3 p.m. on January 12, 1979. Fourth, ADVO made what it describes as revised offers several times after January 12 and these were apparently given some consideration by the contracting agency. Fifth, ADVO continually stresses its unique knowledge and expertise and alleges it knows more about performing the APOC work than DOC does.

Considering all these circumstances, we have difficulty seeing any prejudice to ADVO. It should be noted that in a number of cases best and final offers have been requested within extremely tight time limits. See 50 Comp. Gen. 202, 205 (1970); *Martin Widerker, Eng.*, 55 Comp. Gen. 1295 (1976), 76–2 CPD 61. Finally, the cases cited by ADVO are not in point. 45 Comp. Gen. 651 (1966) involved an advertised procurement. In *ABC Food Service, Inc.*, B–181978, December 17, 1974, 74–2 CPD 359, the issue involved one offeror's failure to receive the request for best and final offers due to the Government's error. Here, though the agency did not follow proper procedures in closing out negotiations, ADVO knew enough to know they were being closed out.

ADVO: FPR § 1–3.802(c)(2) (FPR amend. 194, September 1978) requires that RFP's state the relative importance of cost, technical and other factors and GAO decisions have held that, when such factors are changed, offerors must be given an opportunity to submit revised proposals. The present RFP weighted cost at only 20 percent in relation to the other factors. In canceling the RFP, DOC made cost the sole evaluation criterion without giving ADVO the opportunity to submit a revised proposal.

Comment: The authorities relied on by ADVO in this connection, like others it cites, deal essentially with ensuring an equal opportunity to compete for all offerors participating in an ongoing negotiated procurement. The cancellation of the RFP did not result in the evaluation factors being changed to the advantage of some offerors without ADVO having the opportunity to compete based upon the revised factors. With the termination of negotiations with ADVO, there was no longer any ongoing procurement and, as discussed elsewhere, DOC and the Postal Service are not "offerors" in competition with ADVO.

ADVO: The Postal Service stands on the same footing vis-a-vis both DOC and ADVO as any private competitor. 41 U.S.C. § 23 (1976). The Postal Reorganization Act of 1970, 39 U.S.C. § 101 *et seq.* (1976), makes clear that Congress intended the Postal Service to be an independent establishment with powers equivalent to a private business enterprise.

Comment: 41 U.S.C. § 23 states in pertinent part:

All orders or contracts * * * placed with Government-owned establishments shall be considered as obligations in the same manner as provided for similar orders or contracts placed with commercial manufacturers or private contractors * * *.

The statute deals with the subject of whether an order or contract of the type described constitutes as obligation of appropriated funds. The issue, however, is not whether a DOC order to the Postal Service would be an obligation but the Postal Service's status as a recipient of such an order. Aside from 41 U.S.C. § 23, ADVO cites decisions from the 2nd., 3rd., 7th., and 8th. Circuits holding that the Postal Service is not immune from state garnishment proceedings. In this regard, the fact that the Postal Service might be treated as a private business enterprise for some purposes does not establish that it is like a private business enterprise for all purposes. If Congress in enacting the Postal Reorganization Act of 1970 had intended that the Postal Service be like any private bidder or offeror when offering to perform work for an executive agency, the provision in the Act codified at 39 U.S.C. § 411, *supra*, would be meaningless surplusage. In addition, FPR § 1-1.209 defines "procurement" as the acquisition of property or services from "non-Federal sources" and 39 U.S.C. § 201 states that the Postal Service is "an independent establishment of the executive branch of the Government of the United States."

ADVO: DOC violated FPR § 1-3.805-1(d) by failing to give ADVO the opportunity to submit a revised proposal after reducing the scope of the APOC work in January 1979. This action is particularly egregious because the Postal Service is being given the opportunity to submit a proposal on the revised requirements.

The regulation states in pertinent part:

When, during negotiations, a substantial change occurs in the Government's requirements or a decision is reached to relax, increase, or otherwise modify the scope of the work or statement of requirements, such change or modification shall be made in writing as an amendment to the request for proposals, and a copy shall be furnished to each prospective contractor.

As far as changes in the Government's requirements prior to the termination of negotiations with ADVO are concerned, ADVO does not deny that it received what DOC calls a "preliminary outline" of the revised requirements on or about December 19, 1978, nor that it received what DOC calls a "complete outline" during the January 11, 1979, meeting. As discussed *supra*, we believe the reduction in the scope of the work should have been issued as a written amendment to the RFP. However, as also previously discussed, it is difficult to see prejudice to ADVO where it was aware of the revision in the Government's requirements and submitted what it describes as revised offers in response to the revised requirements. In any event, FPR § 1–3.805–1(d) is primarily directed at insuring an equal opportunity to compete among offerors in an ongoing negotiated procurement. See, in this regard, *International Finance and Economics*, B–186939, January 27, 1977, 77–1 CPD 66 (level of effort in RFP substantially reduced without any amendment to RFP or notice to offerors); *Computek, Inc., et al.*, 54 Comp. Gen. 1080 (1975), 75–1 CPD 384 (significant changes in quantity and other terms and conditions made during negotiations with one offeror were not communicated to other offerors).

As far as any other changes in the Government's requirements after negotiations with ADVO were terminated, the Postal Service, as already indicated, is not a prospective contractor or offeror within the meaning of the regulations. Thus, the numerous cases cited by ADVO in support of the proposition that all offerors in a negotiated procurement should have an equal opportunity to compete and to submit revised proposals in response to changes in the Government's requirements (e.g. *Computek, supra*) are inapposite. FPR § 1–3.805–1(d) does not require that changes in requirements made after negotiations with a sole offeror have been terminated and the Government has decided to proceed with the work in-house be issued as a written amendment to the RFP and that the sole offeror be provided with an opportunity to submit another revised proposal.

ADVO: DOC is seeking the furnishing of certain services by the Postal Service, but did not publicize this procurement as required by FPR § 1–1.1001.

Comment: For reasons already indicated, the "procurement" in question is not a procurement within the meaning of the FPR's.

ADVO: DOC's sole-source procurement from the Postal Service violates FPR § 1–3.210(a)(1) because more than one source is available to furnish the services. DOC failed to prepare a determination and findings as required by FPR § 1–3.210(b).

Comment: For reasons already discussed, these regulations and the numerous decisions cited by ADVO dealing with sole-source procurements are inapplicable to DOC's "procurement" of services from the Postal Service.

VI. Conclusion

Based on the record before us, we find no substantive violations of applicable law and regulations by DOC in terminating negotiations with ADVO, canceling the RFP and proceeding to perform the work within the Government.

[B–194400]

Appropriations—Obligation—Interagency Agreement

Fiscal year 1978 funds obligated by Bureau of Alcohol, Tobacco and Firearms under Economy Act agreement with Air Force must be deobligated at the end of of fiscal year 1978 to extent that Air Force has not incurred valid obligations under agreement during fiscal year. Air Force has validly obligated funds only to extent that performance by contractor satisfies *bona fide* need of fiscal year 1978.

Departments and Establishments—Services Between—Reimbursement—Research and Development Costs

Under Economy Act agreement providing that contractor of Air Force is to provide research and development work and technical support to Bureau of Alcohol, Tobacco and Firearms, with Air Force paying for work and then being reimbursed by Bureau, only work actually performed by contractor during fiscal year 1978 satisfies *bona fide* need of that year. Work done by contractor during fiscal year 1979 may not be paid for from fiscal year 1978 funds.

In the matter of Bureau of Alcohol, Tobacco and Firearm—Payments Under Interagency Agreement, April 27, 1979:

This decision is in response to an inquiry from an authorized certifying officer of the Bureau of Alcohol, Tobacco and Firearms (Bureau), Department of the Treasury, seeking our opinion on whether a voucher may be legally certified for payment. The voucher, submitted by the Space and Missile Systems Organization, United States Air Force (Air Force), seeks reimbursement, to be charged against fiscal year 1978 funds, for expenditures incurred through January 31, 1979, under an interagency agreement between the Bureau and the Air Force. For the reasons indicated below, it is our opinion that the voucher may not be certified for payment from fiscal year 1978 funds.

The interagency agreement (designated Tatf–78–B–117 and accepted by the Air Force on September 23, 1977) states that it was entered into under the authority of the Economy Act of 1932, as amended, 31 U.S.C. § 686 (1976). Under the agreement, Aerospace Corporation, pursuant to a cost-plus-a-fixed fee contract with the Air Force, was to perform research and development work and provide technical support to the Bureau in connection with the National Explosives Tagging Program. The Air Force was to pay Aerospace for this work, and was to be reimbursed by the Bureau.

The agreement indicated that the estimated cost of the work to be done by Aerospace during fiscal year 1978 was $2,025,000, and that the Bureau was obligating $225,000 of fiscal year 1977 funds and $1,800,000 of fiscal year 1978 funds to cover this estimated cost. The agreement specified that the period of performance by Aerospace was to be October 1, 1977, through September 30, 1978.

Another interagency agreement between the Bureau and the Air Force, designated Tatf–79–3, was accepted on October 2, 1978. Under this agreement Aerospace Corporation was to continue its work for the Bureau for the period October 1, 1978, through September 30, 1979. The Air Force was to pay Aerospace for this work and was to be reimbursed from the Bureau's fiscal year 1979 funds. The estimated cost of the work to be performed by Aerospace during fiscal year 1979 was stated to be $1,500,000.

The voucher seeks reimbursement under the fiscal year 1978 interagency agreement for work done by Aerospace Corporation during fiscal year 1979. The certifying officer asks the following specific question:

> Since the performance period is fixed as 10/1/77 through 9/30/78 by the agreement is it permissible to use a one year appropriation obligated on 9/30/78 and prior to pay for research and development services received during January 1979 * * * or should the obligation balance on September 30, 1978 covering research and development work not yet performed as of that date be deobligated?

Section 601 of the Economy Act of 1932, as amended, 31 U.S.C. § 686 (1976), provides that one Federal agency may place orders with another Federal agency for materials, supplies, equipment, work, or services, and may pay for such orders either in advance or by reimbursement upon performance. The statute permits the Department of the Treasury, and four other named agencies, to place such orders even though the requisitioned Federal agency can only fulfill the order by contracting with a nongovernmental source.

All orders placed under the authority of the Economy Act are subject to the limitation contained in section 1210 of the General Appropriations Act, 1951, 31 U.S.C. § 686–1 (1976), which provides:

> No funds withdrawn and credited pursuant to section 686 of this title, shall be available for any period beyond that provided by the Act appropriating such funds.

Under this provision, fiscal year appropriations obligated by Economy Act agreements must be deobligated at the end of the fiscal year, to the extent that the performing agency has not completed performance or incurred valid obligations under the agreement during the fiscal year. See *HUD–Corps of Engineers Flood Insurance Studies*, B–167790, September 22, 1977; *Interagency Agreement—Administrative Office of the U.S. Courts*, 55 Comp. Gen. 1497, 1499 (1976); 39 *id.* 317, 318–19

(1959); 34 *id*. 418, 421–22 (1955). *See generally*, 31 Comp. Gen. 83 (1951). In the present case, the fiscal year 1978 funds, obligated by the Bureau in fulfillment of the 1978 interagency agreement, should have been deobligated at the end of fiscal year 1978 to the extent that the Air Force had not incurred valid obligations under the agreement.

The work done by Aerospace for the Bureau was performed as part of a contract between Aerospace and the Air Force. It is therefore necessary to determine whether, under this contract, the Air Force validly obligated fiscal year 1978 funds for work performed and to be paid for during fiscal year 1979.

Section 1 of the Surplus Fund-Certified Claims Act of 1949, 31 U.S.C. § 712a (1976), provides that one-year funds may be used only to pay for expenses incurred during the fiscal year or to fulfill contracts properly made within the fiscal year. In interpreting this statute, we have long held that in order to obligate a fiscal year appropriation for payments to be made in a succeeding year, the contract imposing the obligation must not only have been made within the fiscal year to be charged, but the contract must also have been made to meet a *bona fide* need of that fiscal year. *E.g.*, 33 Comp. Gen. 57, 61 (1953). It follows that the Air Force has validly obligated funds under the 1978 interagency agreement only to the extent that performance by Aerospace Corporation meets a *bona fide* need of fiscal year 1978.

As we stated above, the fiscal year 1978 interagency agreement specifies that Aerospace Corporation is to perform over the period October 1, 1977, through September 30, 1978. Attached to the agreement is a Statement of Work, which, we assume, became part of the Aerospace contract with the Air Force. The Statement of Work sets forth the general objectives of the work Aerospace was to perform and also the specific tasks for fiscal year 1978 "to be completed prior to September 30, 1978." These tasks are for the most part continuations of the work Aerospace had performed for the Bureau under a fiscal year 1977 agreement. As part of the work, Aerospace was to submit to the Bureau monthly progress reports and statements of costs incurred. In addition, it was to submit, by September 1, 1978, a draft final report which was to document and summarize the results of the work accomplished during the year.

The fiscal year 1979 interagency agreement stated that the period of performance was to be October 1, 1978, through September 30, 1979. It contained a Statement of Work which was nearly identical to that in the fiscal year 1978 agreement, except that it set forth specific tasks "to be completed prior to September 30, 1979." Under the 1979 agreement, Aerospace was to submit its draft final report to the Bureau by September 1, 1979.

As we view the interagency agreements, and the resulting contractual provisions between Aerospace and the Air Force, the 1978 agreement covered whatever work was actually performed by Aerospace during fiscal year 1978, and the 1979 agreement covers whatever work is actually performed during fiscal year 1979. Under the 1978 agreement, the Bureau obligated funds to pay the estimated cost of work to be performed by Aerospace during fiscal year 1978 only. Funds to pay for work to be performed during fiscal year 1979 were obligated by the 1979 agreement. Therefore, only the work performed by Aerospace during fiscal year 1978 was done under the 1978 agreement and satisfied a *bona fide* need of fiscal year 1978. Work performed during fiscal year 1979 was done under the 1979 agreement, and does not meet a *bona fide* need of fiscal year 1978.

The interagency agreements are akin to "level of effort" contracts, in which the contractor is paid for the work it is able to perform, or the work actually ordered by the Government, during the contract period. Under such a contract, the Government may obligate the full estimated cost when the contract is entered into. However, as we stated in *Recording obligations under EPA cost-plus contract*, B-183184, May 30, 1975:

> * * * The actual level of effort furnished apparently represents full performance during a fiscal year and delimits the Government's liability therein. Consequently, any amount initially recorded as obligated in excess of the actual level of effort called for by work orders could not remain as an obligation for that year. Since the contract and its funding operate on a single fiscal year basis, the carryover (upon exercising the option to renew) into a succeeding fiscal year of any "surplus" level of effort as described would be precluded under the *bona fide* needs principle and related statutory restrictions. * * *

We conclude that only the work performed by Aerospace during fiscal year 1978 satisfies a *bona fide* need of that year. Under the interagency agreement, the Air Force has only validly obligated whatever funds are necessary to pay for the work performed by Aerospace during fiscal year 1978. Any fiscal year 1978 funds, obligated by the Bureau under the interagency agreement and by the Air Force under its contract with Aerospace, which were not needed to pay for work performed during fiscal year 1978 should have been deobligated as of October 1, 1979. The Air Force voucher, therefore, may not be certified for payment from fiscal year 1978 funds.

Although the question was not raised by the certifying officer, we note that fiscal year 1977 funds were obligated by the Bureau to reimburse the Air Force under the fiscal year 1978 interagency agreement. Under the *bona fide* need principles discussed above, fiscal year 1977 funds were not available to pay for work performed by Aerospace in fiscal year 1978. To the extent that these funds were not otherwise validly obligated during fiscal year 1977 they lapsed at the end of the year. The Bureau must adjust its accounts so that only fiscal year 1978 funds are used to pay for work performed during fiscal year 1978, and only fiscal year 1979 funds are used to pay for work performed during fiscal year 1979.

[B-193487]

Contracts — Protests — Procedures — Bid Protest Procedures — Time for Filing — Contract Award Notice Effect

Protest filed less than 10 days after protester learned that agency accepted proposal which showed incomplete development of equipment offered is timely even if protester previously suspected nonconforming nature of equipment.

Contracts—Negotiation—Requests for Proposals—Specification Requirements—Waiver

Requirement for operational prototype restricted offerors to propose existing equipment components capable of demonstrating essential solicitation requirements. Offeror's prior model did not meet requirement for operational prototype where solicitation expressly sought equipment capable of computational capabilities beyond prior model's capacity.

Contracts — Competitive System — Price Competitiveness — Determination Basis

Assertion that protester was not prejudiced because it would have been unable to be price competitive had it known that procuring activity would relax requirements is rejected. Pricing may only be determined through competition.

Contracts — Negotiation — Awards — Erroneous — Remedial Action Recommended

Air Force should review whether requirement should be resolicited. At minimum, it should reopen competition to accord protester a reasonable opportunity to meet its relaxed, actual requirements, assuring that all parties are permitted to compete on equal basis. Erroneously awarded contract should be terminated if protester is selected for award.

In the matter of System Development Corporation, May 1, 1979:

The System Development Corporation (SDC) protests award to Control Data Corporation (Control Data) under RFP No. F19628-79-R-0084 issued by the Air Force Computer Acquisition Center, Hanscom Air Force Base. The solicitation was issued to support an Air Force Weapons Laboratory (Kirtland Air Force Base) requirement for a Fourth Generation Advanced Computer System which could significantly enhance data processing capabilities at the Weapons Laboratory. (The Air Force facilities involved will be referred to collectively as the "Air Force.")

Essentially, SDC complains that the award was improper, and indeed, that the contract was void *ab initio*, because Control Data offered equipment for which an "operational prototype" did not exist at the time the proposal was submitted. The protester states that it did not offer the system proposed by Control Data (the Star 100A), or other equipment in a similar state of development because SDC understood that an operational prototype was required at the time proposals were to be submitted and that the Star 100A was not available for benchmarking. SDC also asserts that Control Data was not required to perform a preproposal Live Test Demonstration (LTD or preproposal benchmark) as anticipated by the RFP. SDC further argues that it was required to agree that the equipment it proposed would achieve a 95 percent minimum effectiveness level, while Control Data was permitted to propose equipment having an effectiveness level of only 93 percent.

We have concluded that the Air Force awarded the contract to Control Data without regard to the mandatory requirement that the offeror have an operational prototype of the equipment by the due date for proposals and that the protester was denied equal treatment in this regard and was prejudiced thereby.

SDC's protest is for consideration on a request for our opinion by Judge Gerhard A. Gesell, stemming from a suit for injunctive and declaratory relief filed by SDC in the United States District Court for the District of Columbia (*System Development Corporation* v. *John C. Stetson, et al.*, Civil Action No. 79–0829). See, *e.g.*, *KET, Incorporated*, 58 Comp. Gen. 38 (1978), 78–2 CPD 305. Contract performance was initially stayed by the court, under a temporary restraining order and the Air Force has since agreed not to proceed pending receipt of our decision.

I

As background, this procurement of a fourth generation advanced computer system began several years ago. In August of 1975 the Air Force requested industry comments on a draft RFP. A second draft was released for comment in March 1977. The solicitation was formally announced on July 12, 1977, with a closing date for receipt of initial proposals set for September 29, 1977. Several amendments followed, including an amendment No. 3, dated September 23, 1977, which extended the date for initial proposals to January 30, 1978.

Because SDC is not a hardware manufacturer, it surveyed a number of potential vendors, in anticipation of the RFP, to identify potential subcontractors on whom it might rely to meet the hardware portion of the Air Force requirement. Several vendors responded, including Control Data. After reviewing Control Data's response, SDC requested clarification, inquiring as to:

How soon can a STAR 100A be available for a Live Test Demonstration with and without the full CDC 6600 front-end interface?

By letter dated August 17, 1977, Control Data advised SDC that:

A STAR 100A will be available for benchmarks in May, 1978. The front end interface is demonstrable now.

As SDC points out, paragraph 56 of the RFP dealt with the format of proposals. Paragraph 56:4–2 stated that offerors, as a part of their proposals, were required to:

Provide the necessary LTD documentation and information required in accordance with the following items * * *.

a. Source program compilation listings and assembly listings of all the Benchmark Programs to be used during the conduct of the LTD. * * *.

*   *   *   *   *   *   *

c. The output products from the execution of the Benchmark Programs.

*   *   *   *   *   *   *

This requirement for data, particularly subparagraph (c), cannot be literally met unless a benchmark is performed prior to submission of proposals with the equipment being offered. This was in addition to a formal LTD required after submission of proposals. Recognizing this, SDC wrote the Air Force for clarification. The Air Force responded on September 14, 1977, stating:

The Contractor must execute the Live Test Demonstration prior to submission of his proposal in order to produce information needed for inclusion in his proposal. The [offeror] must also execute the Live Test Demonstration subsequent to proposal submission and in the presence of designated Government representatives. This second execution is part of the technical evaluation of the submitted proposals.

The Air Force further stated:

During the execution of the LTD prior to proposal submission, the contractor may use whatever technique he chooses. During the execution of the LTD *subsequent* to proposal submission, the designated Government representatives present * * * will utilize stopwatches and their recordings will constitute the official timings.

Based on Control Data's statement that the STAR 100A system would not be available for benchmarking until May of 1978, long after the original or extended closing date for receipt of initial proposals, SDC concluded that it could not frame its proposal around the STAR 100A. SDC turned to Cray Research, Inc. (Cray) and submitted an offer based on use of the Cray Model 1 system (Cray 1). The Cray 1 has a well-established performance history.

SDC and Control Data submitted proposals. Control Data based its proposal on the STAR 100A system. Although Control Data apparently ran portions of the benchmark sometime before it performed the post-proposal LTD, it did not furnish benchmark data with its proposal. Instead it stated that simulation tests showed that an existing system, the CDC STAR 100, would meet the Air Force's requirements when upgraded to the STAR 100A through the addition of a new scalar processor. Control Data stated in its initial proposal that:

Control Data *estimates* that the CDC STAR 100A computer system will exceed six times the multiprogramming capability [of existing equipment]. *Because the * * * STAR 100A system is being constructed at the time of this proposal* submission, the reported multiprogramming values are *estimated* on the basis of the computer's design specifications. Verification of these *estimates* will take place on an actual * * * STAR 100A computer system when the LTD is conducted. [Italic supplied.]

Control Data concedes that the essential difference between the STAR 100 and STAR 100A is the substitution of the new scalar processor accompanied by certain timing changes required to enhance memory performance. Indeed, Control Data stated in its proposal that, "The principal feature of the CDC STAR 100A Central Processor Unit is the integration of an LSI high-speed scalar processor with the vector processor of the CDC Star 100," and that, "The scalar processor is physically contained in a stand–alone cabinet attached to the vector processor cabinet." The scalar processor had been designed. The parts were ordered and construction of the first unit had begun. However, a scalar processor had not been completely assembled by January 30, 1978, the extended date for submission of proposals.

Not only is it admitted that Control Data did not perform a complete preproposal benchmark, but in SDC's view, the STAR 100A was unacceptable under other terms of the solicitation which dovetail with the proposal LTD requirement.

The solicitation contained certain mandatory specifications which were required to be met if proposals were to receive further consideration. Specifically, paragraph 3.2, a mandatory provision, required:

> At the time of the proposal submission, the system(s) proposed must consist of hardware components and software selected from announced, commercially available ADP equipment and software. Equipment must be a production model or at least an operational prototype. * * *.

A similar requirement was included in paragraph 48 of the specifications, requiring that all but software for certain interface and FORTRAN extensions "consist of components, hardware and software selected from announced commercially available ADP systems" and repeating that equipment was to "be a production model or at least an operational prototype." Read in context with the LTD documentation to be furnished at the time proposals were submitted and with the first sentence of paragraph 3.2, it is clear that there was to be at least an operational prototype of the equipment at the time of proposal submission.

II

Before turning to a detailed examination of the merits of SDC's protest, we will deal with the threshold issue raised by the Air Force and Control Data, both of which assert in large measure that SDC's protest is untimely. It is our policy to give our opinion in an untimely protest where a court has asked for it. See, *e.g.*, *Control Data Corporation*, 55 Comp. Gen. 1019 (1976), 76–1 CPD 276; *Dynalectron Corporation, et al.*, 54 Comp. Gen. 1009 (1975), 75–1 CPD 341. However, we believe a discussion of the timeliness of this protest is appropriate because we would not be inclined to recommend remedial relief if the protest were untimely filed.

The respondents maintain SDC knew of Control Data's role in the procurement long before SDC's initial protest was filed with the Air Force on January 18, 1979. In their view, SDC slept on its rights until advised on January 12, 1979, that award had been made to Control Data. The Air Force denied the protester relief in part because SDC unjustifiably delayed filing the protest.

SDC admits that it knew by mid-December 1978 that Control Data was competing for this requirement. By then it had received a copy of our decision in an earlier protest filed by Control Data. See *Control Data Corporation*, B-193487, December 12, 1978, 78-2 CPD 408. In fact, SDC representatives inquired with this Office in early December seeking information regarding the status and basis of Control Data's protest.

The Air Force and Control Data believe that SDC knew of Control Data's interest in the procurement much earlier. Both refer to an internal Air Force memorandum memorializing a May 12, 1978 meeting among representatives of SDC and Cray and Air Force personnel. The respondents also refer to information published in trade journals, which had carried articles indicating that Control Data had offered the STAR 100A system.

SDC concedes that it believed it was competing with Control Data, possibly among others. However, according to SDC:

Whatever SDC may have thought, inferred, suspected, deduced, or read, it did not know prior to the oral notification of award * * * that the Air Force had determined to make an award in derogation * * * of the solicitation.

SDC points out that the Defense Acquisition Regulation (DAR) § 3-507.2(a) prohibits disclosure of the identity of persons participating in a negotiated procurement until award is made. At no time, according to SDC, did the Air Force admit that Control Data was a participant. Thus, in SDC's view, it lacked the kind of specific knowledge which is necessary to start the time running for filing a protest. *VAST, Inc*, B-182844, January 31, 1975, 75-1 CPD 71.

We agree. Prior to receiving the award notification, SDC knew with certainty only that the STAR 100A was being developed and that Control Data had indicated equipment could not be made available to SDC for benchmarking until May 1978. SDC did not know and had no way of knowing that a prototype scalar processor had not been built, or that a preproposal benchmark had not been performed, until it learned for the first time on January 29, 1979, that Control Data had qualified its initial proposal. Only then did SDC know that the Air Force knew from the outset that Control Data sought to meet the initial proposal requirements by offering data derived through simulation and that the Air Force acquiesced in this action.

The memorandum of the May 12, 1978 meeting between the Air Force, SDC and Cray representatives indicates that the protester was aware that the delays in the procurement schedule were permitted to obtain maximum competition and that this action was taken on the basis of knowledge gained by the Air Force from its visits to a competitor's plant. However, the memorandum provides no evidence as to the stage of development of the STAR 100A or of the fact that the Air Force was allowing Control Data the opportunity to develop a key component to the point of an operational prototype. As the protest developed—not before—it was revealed that the first STAR 100A scalar processor consisted on January 30, 1978, of a design and an assorted collection of unassembled parts.

III

The Air Force and Control Data advance a number of reasons to support their position that the Control Data proposal properly was considered for award. According to the Air Force, the solicitation required announced, commercially available equipment that was at least an operational prototype (paragraphs 3.2 and 48) and execution of the LTD prior to proposal submission in order:

* * * to (1) preclude the offering one of a kind systems; (2) to discourage costs of a research and development effort; and (3) to assure the Air Force that the offeror would and could provide standard hardware and software from the start of and throughout the contract term.

The procuring activity believed that Control Data's proposal met the purposes of the solicitation requirements.

The Headquarters Air Force decision in the initial protest concluded that acceptance of Control Data's proposal, in effect, relaxed the literal language of the solicitation. It recommended no corrective action except that the language used be clarified for purposes of future procurements. Control Data, on the other hand, has chosen to defend its acceptability under the terms of the solicitation as written.

In our view, solicitation paragraphs 3.2 and 48 imposed a dual test. On the one hand, hardware components and software offered were required to be "announced, commercially available." Further, the equipment offered was to exist at least in an "operational prototype" form at the time proposals were submitted and it was clear that an LTD was to be performed prior to submission of proposals.

The meaning of the phrase "announced, commercially available" was considered in our decision *Intermem Corporation*, B-188910, December 15, 1977, 77-2 CPD 464, which coincidentally was decided prior to the closing date set in this case for receipt of initial proposals. We held that a solicitation requirement for "announced, commercially available" ADP equipment was met by an offeror whose equipment was commercially available and whose sales force was offering the equipment for sale. A published announcement (*e.g.*, through trade journals) was unnecessary to show that the vendor had offered the equipment for sale to the public.

We were then aware, as the parties here are aware, that ADP equipment usually is manufactured on receipt of an order—it is not the kind of product which can be literally ordered "off-the-shelf." "Commercially available" connotes only that the equipment can be acquired in the commercial marketplace, importing the notion that it is available for delivery within a reasonable time.

We believe the STAR 100A was announced. It was announced in trade publications as early as 1976, and it was offered to SDC in August of 1977.

It is less clear that the STAR 100A was commercially available by January 30, 1978, *i.e.*, that Control Data was by then in a position to accept orders for commercial deliveries in the ordinary course of business. Control Data maintains that it was—that it had completed all design work and had proven its design through simulation on the earlier model STAR 100 equipment. Simulation as we have noted, normally may be acceptable to "prove" ADP equipment. *KET, Incorporated, supra.* As our decision in *KET* illustrates, there are occasions when an ADP equipment manufacturer may offer a product for sale even though the product itself has never been built.

However, the solicitation stated that the Air Force required a production model or at least an "operational prototype." We agree with the respondents that the phrase "operational prototype" must be taken in context with "production model," because both terms are used in paragraph 3.2. As these terms are used, an "operational prototype" refers to something less than a "production model," but something more than a design "proven" through simulation. The Air Force admits that "prototype" is defined by Air Force convention as "A model suitable for evaluation of design, performance and production potential." No evidence has been submitted showing that "operational prototype" has meaning as a term of art in the ADP field. Although we agree with Control Data that simulation may be sufficient to prove an ADP equipment design (after *KET, Incorporated, supra*), we believe the phrase "operational prototype" must be given its plain meaning. The dictionary defines "operational" as ready for or in a condition to undertake an intended function. The term "operational prototype" in our view refers to an original model after which the product is to be patterned, which exhibits the characteristics of the product *essential* to evaluation of its design and performance. The apparent purpose for adding an "operational prototype" requirement is to assure that the suitability of the equipment could be tested.

Control Data maintains, however, that the STAR 100A did exist at least as an operational prototype in the form of the STAR 100. In this connection, the Air Force asserts that:

> * * * in considering the criteria for a production model or operational prototype * * * [consideration was given to] the fact that the hardware for the STAR 100A * * * was being completed. Subsequent [discussions] established * * * that the STAR 100A was not a new generic model computer system, but was actually an enhancement of the STAR 100 system which was marketed commercial equipment being used in an operational environment. The basic architectural design established for the STAR 100 was retained in the STAR 100A. The vector processor, the input/output, maintenance control unit, high capacity disk stations, and the software (operating system, FORTRAN, the I/O system and cyber link software) were substantially unchanged from the 100 to the 100A. The STAR 100 was * * * operated to demonstrate the performance and production potential of the 100A.

We do not agree that an earlier model reasonably can be taken as an "operational prototype" of a new generation machine merely because it was possible to create a simulation model on it, even if it shares many attributes with the proposed new generation of equipment. ADP systems are unique in their ability to be used themselves as a tool to simulate other systems, even other ADP systems, through software redesign, in other than so-called "real" time, or otherwise. In our view, the "operational prototype" requirement was not met unless the STAR 100 was capable of demonstrating the salient qualities sought by the Air Force while operating in the configuration which Control Data proposed in its offer.

In this regard, the Air Force's specifications provided at paragraph 1.1 that:

> These performance specifications define the resources necessary to support the computational requirements of the Air Force Weapons Laboratory * * *. The requirements of the [Air Force] identify the need for computer system capabilities that exceed the computational capability of a single Control Data Corporation * * * 6600 by a factor of eighty.

Ability to process work at high speed was clearly of the essence. The equipment proposed was required to demonstrate an arithmetic computational capability of twenty times that for a single existing Control Data 6600 and a multiprogramming capability exceeding six times that of earlier equipment. Each offeror's final proposal was required to include that number of units (but not more than four) which the LTD showed would be necessary to satisfy these requirements.

Although it was computational time—speed—which the new scalar processor and enhanced memory would provide, it was speed in certain types of operations which Control Data could demonstrate only through simulation. The scalar processor was described in Control Data's proposal as a separate hardware component. It appears, therefore, that the STAR 100 could not be used to evaluate the speed of the STAR 100A in an operational mode, and reasonably cannot be viewed as satisfying the requirement for an operational prototype.

IV

Control Data asserts that its proposal was properly considered, because Control Data should have been treated as being within the competitive range, regardless of whether an operational prototype STAR 100A existed on January 30, 1978. We disagree.

Paragraphs 3.2 and 48 together with the provision for a proposal LTD clearly limited consideration of proposals to offers of equipment for which an operational prototype existed on the closing date for receipt of initial proposals. Had an operational STAR 100A prototype existed on January 30, 1978, Control Data could have been permitted to submit evidence of that fact during discussions, as indeed it evidently attempted to do. It is in our view quite another thing to allow Control Data to turn back the clock—to demonstrate that equipment which had not existed earlier did exist later as an operational prototype. A procuring activity is afforded reasonable latitude in defining the competitive range; it cannot use that authority in effect to waive a significantly restrictive solicitation requirement with regard to one party, without advising others of that fact or resoliciting its requirement to permit competition by others who may have been excluded from the procurement because of the requirement. *See* DAR § 3–805.4; *cf. Computer Network Corporation, et al.*, 56 Comp. Gen. 245 (1977), 77–1 CPD 31.

This point is fundamental. The effect of what was done goes to the scope of the competition obtained. It affects the ground rules by which other participants—here, SDC—thought they were bound, ground rules which may have left others believing that they were precluded from the competition, or had only limited options because the equipment they might have offered did not appear to qualify. *Annandale Service Co.; Austin Carbonic Co., Inc.*, B–181806, December 5, 1974, 74–2 CPD 313; *Corbetta Construction Company of Illinois, Inc.*, 55 Comp. Gen. 201 (1975), 75–2 CPD 144, modified in part, 55 Comp. Gen. 972 (1976), 76–1 CPD 240.

We also have considered whether the Air Force, in effect, announced that offerors could propose equipment which would meet the "operational prototype" requirement after the due date for initial proposals, but we have concluded that this significant deviation from the mandatory requirements was not made clear. In this connection, Amendment 5, transmitted by letter of May 17, 1978, changed the procurement's projected schedule of major events. The amendment permitted offerors to perform the post-proposal LTD beginning on October 2, 1978, an extension from the previous requirement that the LTD be performed within 2 weeks after initial proposals were submitted in January. The letter accompanying this amendment advised offerors that:

2. The amendment now provides that offerors must be prepared to perform the LTD by 2 October 1978. This extension to 2 October 1978 does not preclude an earlier competitive range determination, if appropriate, based on the Government's assessment of offerors' progress toward meeting the LTD requirement and all other factors indicating whether the offeror can successfully compete for award of the contract. The change in dates has been determined to be in the best interest of the Government and is based on an evaluation of the urgency of operational requirements in comparison to the potential benefits to the Government of maintaining competition in this procurement.

Moreover, the amendment provides:

42. PROJECTED SCHEDULE OF MAJOR EVENTS

The following milestone schedule for this project is provided for planning purposes only and the dates reflected are subject to change:

Event	Date
Begin Live Test Demonstration	2 Oct. 1978
Contract Award	15 Dec. 1978
ADPS Installation	16 June 1980

It is clear that the time for performing the post-proposal LTD was substantially extended because the Government sought to obtain the benefit of increased competition. This was announced by amendment to the solicitation "for planning purposes only." Had the Air Force intended to remove the mandatory restriction for an operational prototype existing at the time initial proposals were submitted, we think it was required to say so forthrightly in the interest of obtaining the best deal for the public through competition. This amendment does not make it sufficiently clear to us that the mandatory requirement for an operational prototype by the proposal due date had been relaxed. Any such purpose was concealed.

Moreover, we can see no justification for requiring that the equipment exist as an operational prototype on or before the closing date for receipt of initial proposals. Such a requirement might be reasonable where time is of the essence and it is essential to assure minimum difficulty in running the benchmark—considerations which in our view justify SDC's belief that this "mandatory" requirement was intended to be taken seriously. The Air Force, however, has not sought to support its need for the "operational prototype" requirement on this basis, arguing instead that the requirement was included to assure that the equipment proposed was not a "one of a kind" system, that the Government was not incurring research and development costs, and that the equipment and software was commercially available and would be fully supported as a commercial product. This need was met by requiring that only announced, commercially available hardware and software be offered, and that the system be demonstrated during the benchmark. *Cf. Telefile Computer Products, Inc.*, B-186983, October 28, 1977, 77-2 CPD 328. In our view, the solicitation's insistence on an operational prototype imposed an unnecessary and thus, undue, additional restriction on competition.

V

In SDCs view, award to Control Data should be viewed as void *ab initio*, and that in any event, the Control Data contract should be terminated and award directed to SDC. We disagree, although we believe the Air Force should take necessary action to provide all offerors an equal basis to compete.

As the Air Force points out, the Court of Claims and this Office have taken the view that once a contract comes into existence it should not be canceled, that is, regarded as void *ab initio*, even if it were improperly awarded, unless the illegality of the award is "plain" or "palpable." *John Reiner & Co.* v. *United States*, 325 F. 2d 438 (Ct. Cl. 1963); *Warren Brothers Roads Co.* v. *United States*, 355 F. 2d 612 (Ct. Cl. 1965); 52 Comp. Gen. 215 (1972). We have indicated that the essential test in determining whether these criteria are met is whether the award was made contrary to a statute or regulation due to some improper action or inaction by the contractor, or whether the contractor was on direct notice that the procedures followed were inconsistent with statutory or regulatory requirements. 52 Comp. Gen., *supra; Fink Sanitary Service, Inc.*, 53 Comp. Gen. 502 (1974), 74–1 CPD 36. We have also pointed out that cases in which contractor action resulted in an illegal award involved instances where award would not have been made but for the contractor's improper conduct. *Lanier Business Products*, B–187969, May 11, 1977, 77–1 CPD 336.

Were the protester to prevail with its view that the contract is void, it would be necessary, at a minimum, to conclude that Control Data did not in good faith believe that it had complied with the essential purposes of the mandatory requirements of the solicitation. In our opinion, the record does not provide sufficient proof to support such a conclusion.

We cannot review on our present record the questions which SDC has raised regarding whether the LTD results were fairly and properly evaluated, and whether Control Data's system offered the Government the lowest proposed life-cycle cost. Assuming, however, that the Control Data proposal was the lowest life-cycle cost proposal meeting the Air Force's actual requirements, we cannot recommend that the Air Force substitute an award to SDC, because Control Data was entitled to and could participate in a properly conducted procurement for the Air Force's actual requirements. Award to SDC would be justified only if the Air Force's requirements were as stated in the solicitation and SDC should have received award based on that competition.

The Air Force's decision on the initial protest concluded that other forms of relief would not be justified because the record did not demonstrate that anyone was prejudiced. Responding, SDC suggests that it might have itself offered the STAR 100A, had it known that the Air Force did not require an existing operational prototype. Moreover, SDC observes, it might have been able to offer an enhanced Cray system. Asked at the conference held in this case whether SDC could offer different Cray equipment were the procurement resolicited, SDC personnel responded uncertainly, but stated that as a minimum SDC might offer enhanced software. Presumably SDC would consider the desirability of formulating a proposal which utilizes the STAR 100A equipment.

Nevertheless, the Air Force believes:

It is highly unlikely SDC could have obtained the CDC [Control Data] machine for this procurement in light of CDC's involvement. And if it could have obtained the CDC machine, it is difficult to see how SDC could have been cost competitive with CDC using CDC's own machine. Thus, there is no other equipment which SDC could have realistically obtained, at any time during the acquisition process, other than the Cray I machine upon which it based its proposal.

Control Data has not stated that it would refuse to provide the STAR 100A to SDC. At best it might have proved awkward for Control Data to argue that it would not have while maintaining the STAR 100A was commercially available equipment. Moreover, it is not uncommon for a firm to compete for subcontract work, offering its equipment to multiple vendors or permitting vendors to offer that equipment even though it does so itself.

Regarding the Air Force's second point, that SDC could not have been competitive as to price with Control Data, the Air Force assumes (but has offered no evidence) that SDC could not have furnished software which would have enhanced the life-cycle cost effectiveness of the STAR 100A. Further, whether a proposal would be competitive as to price should be determined through competition. *Olivetti Corporation of America*, B–187369, February 28, 1977, 77–1 CPD 146; *Peninsula Telephone and Telegraph Co.*, 58 Comp. Gen. 324 (1979), 79–1 CPD 176.

We are not in a position on the present record to determine whether other firms may have been excluded from competing due to the operational prototype requirement. (SDC states that a third firm considered competing for this requirement, but did not submit a proposal because it believed it could not satisfy the requirements of paragraphs 3.2 and 48. However, no protest has been lodged by any other firm.) The Air Force, therefore, should determine in the first instance whether there should be a resolicitation. At a minimum, however, we believe the Air Force should revise its requirement to reflect its actual needs and reopen negotiations to permit SDC to revise its proposal to reflect the relaxed requirements. The erroneously awarded contract should be terminated if SDC is selected for award on the basis of revised proposals. This, in our opinion, would serve to protect the integrity of the competitive procurement process. *Southeastern Services, Inc., et al.*, 56 Comp. Gen. 668 (1977), 77-1 CPD 390 and *Dyneteria, Inc.—Reconsideration*, B-187872, August 22, 1977, 77-2 CPD 134. It would assure that potential offerors have an opportunity to respond on the same basis and thereby protect the public interest in obtaining maximum competition.

Although Control Data argues that relief should not be permitted because it would in effect make the procurement an auction, we note that Control Data was not in line for award under the mandatory provisions of the solicitation as written.

Because of our recommendation that the Air Force take appropriate corrective action to assure that SDC has an appropriate opportunity to revise its proposal with the knowledge it now has gained regarding the Air Force's actual requirements, we believe it is unnecessary to reach SDC's contention that the Air Force relaxed the minimum effectiveness level requirement. Whatever course of action the Air Force takes should permit SDC (and Control Data) to submit a new best and final offer, allowing it to respond knowing that a 95 percent effectiveness level is not mandatory.

[B-193562]

Pay—Retired—Foreign Employment—Congressional Consent—Pub. L. 95-105—Prospective Application

Section 509 of the Foreign Relations Authorization Act, Fiscal Year 1978, granting consent of Congress to the acceptance of foreign civil employment by certain officers of the United States, as required by Article I, section 9, clause 8 of the Constitution, cannot be retroactively applied to retirement pay withheld from an officer for a period he was employed by a foreign state without such consent which occurred prior to the effective date of section 509.

Military Personnel—Acceptance of Foreign Presents, Emoluments, etc.—Foreign Government Employment—Retired Pay Adjustment—Pub. L. 95-105 Effect

The consent of Congress to the acceptance of foreign civil employment and compensation by certain retired members of the uniformed services, as required by Article I, section 9, clause 8 of the Constitution, is granted in section 509 of the Foreign Relations Authorization Act, Fiscal Year 1978, which consent is conditioned upon approval of the employment by the Secretary of State and the Secretary of the service concerned. Such approval is only effective prospectively from the date it is granted and may not be made retroactively to authorize foreign employment and compensation received before the approval is granted. However, once approval is granted withholding of retired pay may be terminated and the payment of retired pay resumed on the date of approval.

Military Personnel—Acceptance of Foreign Presents, Emoluments, etc.—Foreign Government Employment—Prohibition

The withholding of retired pay from a member of the uniformed services employed by a foreign government without the consent of Congress is based on the constitutional requirement for congressional consent to the receipt of emoluments from a foreign government, which requirement cannot be ignored. Substantial effect is given the constitutional mandate by withholding retired pay in an amount equal to the foreign emoluments received. The basis for the rule is that the emoluments are deemed accepted on behalf of the United States.

Pay—Retired—Foreign Employment—Congressional Consent— Pub. L. 95–105—Prospectice Application

As with the constitutional provision prohibiting retired military officers from accepting emoluments from foreign governments without congressional consent. section 509 of the Foreign Relations Authorization Act, Fiscal Year 1978, which grants such consent, is silent as to any sanctions to be applied. Thus, the rule that retired pay is to be withheld in the amount of the foreign emoluments received is applicable to the law when approval is not granted. However, when approval is granted the legislative history is clear that Congress intended withholding of retired pay to terminate and payment of retired pay be resumed effective on the approval date.

Pay—Retired—Withholding—Foreign Employment

Amounts of retired pay withheld from members of the uniformed services who accept foreign employment without congressional consent as required by the Constitution should be treated as though the members had no entitlement to them and should not be "held in trust" for them pending possible future congressional consent to their receipt.

Military Personnel—Acceptance of Foreign Presents, Emoluments, etc.—Foreign Government Employment—Prohibition—Military Allowances—Status

The prohibition against receipt of emoluments "of any kind whatever" from a foreign government by retired member of the uniformed services, under Article I, section 9, clause 8 of the Constitution, includes forms of compensation other than salary, such as free transportation, household goods shipments, housing allowances, etc. To determine the amount to be withheld from a member on account of such emoluments, they should be fairly valued considering the actual value of the emolument received.

In the matter of Retired uniformed services members receiving compensation from foreign governments, May 3, 1979:

By letter of November 16, 1978, the Assistant Secretary of the Navy (Financial Management) requested our opinion regarding the proper disbursement of funds withheld by the Department of the Navy from the retired pay of Lieutenant Commander Harry Bigham, USN (Retired), pursuant to our decisions applying the prohibition of Article I, section 9, clause 8 of the Constitution of the United States. The matter has been assigned number SS–N–1309 by the Department of Defense Military Pay and Allowance Committee.

Commander Bigham is a retired Regular officer of the United States Navy. In October 1976, he became an employee of Saudi Arabian Airline (SAUDIA) as a result of the transfer of employees from Trans World Airlines, his prior employer, to SAUDIA. SAUDIA is a corporation owned by the Kingdom of Saudia Arabia.

His tenure with SAUDIA placed him in contravention of the Constitution, Article I, section 9, clause 8, which provides:

No Title of Nobility shall be granted by the United States: And, no Person holding any Office of Profit or Trust under them, shall, without the consent of the Congress, accept of any present, Emolument, Office, or Title, of any kind whatever, from any King, Prince, or foreign state.

Retired Regular officers are members of the military service of the United States. *United States* v. *Tyler*, 105 U.S. 244 (1881), *Hooper* v. *United States*, 164 Ct. Cl. 151 (1964), and *Puglisi* v. *United States*, 564 F. 2d 403, 410 (Ct. Cl. 1977), *cert. denied*, 435 U.S. 968 (1978). Therefore, they are considered to be covered by the provision's prohibition against foreign employment without congressional consent and are subject to withholding of their retired pay in an amount equal to the amounts received from the foreign government. B–178538, October 13, 1977.

In August 1977, Commander Bigham petitioned the Secretary of the Navy and the Secretary of State for approval of his foreign employment pursuant to authority delegated to them by Congress in section 509 of the Foreign Relations Authorization Act, Fiscal Year 1978, Public Law 95–105, August 17, 1977, 91 Stat. 844, 859–860, 37 U.S.C. 801 note. Approval was granted to Commander Bigham by the Secretary of State on September 27, 1977, and by the Secretary of the Navy on March 30, 1978. The letters of approval did not specifically determine an effective date for the consent. In fact, Commander Bigham had been working for SAUDIA over a year prior to the effective date of section 509 of the Authorization Act which granted the approval authority to the Secretaries. The Navy has been withholding Commander Bigham's retired pay in order to equal the salary earned for the period of employment prior to the effective date of the approval.

The Assistant Secretary indicates that several issues have arisen concerning the application of section 509 of the Authorization Act and the amounts to be withheld from the retired pay of Commander Bigham and other members who have not secured approval of their foreign employment.

To resolve the Bigham case and the cases of those similarly situated, the Assistant Secretary of the Navy requests responses to several specific questions. Question (1) is—

(1)(a) As a matter of statutory construction, could the consent granted by a Department Secretary pursuant to the authority delegated by Congress in Section 509 of the Foreign Relations Authorization Act, Fiscal Year 1978 be retroactive or must it operate prospectively only?

(b) If in your opinion consent to foreign employment could apply retroactively, what, if any, limits would pertain to such application, e.g., (i) consent retroactive to the date of submission of the request for approval; (ii) consent retroactive to the effective date of the Foreign Relations Authorization Act, Fiscal Year 1978; or (iii) consent retroactive to the date employment began even if such date predated the effective date of the Foreign Relations Authorization Act?

Sections 509(a) and (b) of the Authorization Act provide in part as follows:

(a) Subject to the condition described in subsection (b) the consent of Congress is granted to—
(1) any retired member of the uniformed services,

*   *   *   *   *   *   *

to accept any civil employment (and compensation therefor) with respect to which the consent of Congress is required by the last paragraph of section 9 of article I of the Constitution of the United States, relating to acceptance of emoluments, offices, or titles from a foreign government.

(b) No individual described in subsection (a) may accept any employment or compensation described in such subsection unless the Secretary concerned and the Secretary of State approve such employment.

In our decision B–175166, April 7, 1978, after considering the language and legislative history of section 509, we held that it is prospective only and could not be construed as granting congressional consent to foreign employment which took place prior to its enactment, August 17, 1977.

As to whether the Secretaries' approval may be made retroactive to some date prior to such approval but on or after the effective date of the law, section 509(b) provides that no individual subject to its terms "may accept any [foreign government] employment or compensation" unless the Secretaries "approve such employment." The report of the Committee on International Relations, House of Representatives, states that section 509(b) specifies that the Secretaries' approval "is necessary prior to acceptance of foreign government employment." H.R. Report No. 95–231, 95th Cong., 1st Sess. 20 (1977). See also the remarks of Senator Thurmond to the same effect concerning S. 1351, a similar bill which he introduced in the Senate. 123 Cong. Rec. S6147 (daily ed., April 21, 1977).

Therefore, in answer to question (1)(a), it is our view that the consent granted under section 509 of the Authorization Act operates prospectively only. However, as with the constitutional provision no specific sanction is applied when an individual accepts compensation in contravention of the law. Thus, it would appear that in instances where an individual accepts employment and compensation therefor and does not obtain secretarial approval, the position this Office has taken that in order to give substantial effect to the Constitutional prohibition retired pay in an amount equal to that received from the foreign government should be withheld, would continue to be applicable.

However, while the law is silent concerning any sanctions to be applied, the legislative history of the law does supply information concerning the intent of Congress when approval is granted, at least in the cases of individuals employed by foreign governments at the time the legislation was considered. In that regard, House Committee on Foreign Relations Report No. 95–231, 95th Cong., 1st Sess., Foreign Relations Authorization Act, FY 1978, pages 20–21, states in part as follows:

> The committee is particularly concerned with problems facing American citizens currently employed by foreign governments, who are subject to the constitutional provision contained in Article I, section 9, clause 8 of the Constitution of the United States. But for the enactment of this section, and under a 1974 ruling of the Comptroller General, the individual's foreign salary would be set off against his retirement pay. It is the intention of the committee, that if such an employee obtains the approval specified in subsection (b) of this section, no reductions will be made from retirement benefits payable after such approval is granted. Given the unique circumstances applying to such individuals, the committee expects that the Secretary of State and the Secretary concerned will give expeditious consideration to the requests for such approval.

In view of this statement in the Committee Report it seems that the Committee and the Congress intended that if approval was granted, deductions from retired pay would cease at the time such approval was granted.

Accordingly, in instances where an individual secures the required approval, withholding of his retired pay may be discontinued effective the date when both Secretarial approvals have been granted.

In addition, it is our information that the Secretarial approval in certain instances has been delayed not because of considerations concerning the propriety of the employment itself, but rather due to questions concerning what effect section 509 of the Authorization Act would have on an individual's retired pay. If the Secretaries concerned determine such was the case and in those cases approve the employment effective no earlier than the date the application was received we would raise no objection.

In view of the answer to question (1)(a), no answer is necessary to question (1)(b).

Questions (2) and (3) are as follows:

> (2) Under your prior decisions, withholding of pay would result where the consent to the acceptance of foreign employment has not been obtained, or if, as in the instant case, consent is later obtained but you determine that such consent cannot be given retroactive application. It is not clear on what theory and authority withholding of a retired member's statutory entitlement to retired pay is based. Therefore, it is requested that the basis and authority for the withholding be specifically addressed.
>
> (3)(a) Based on the response to question (2), please elaborate on the nature of the withholding. Would the funds be treated as earned by the member, such that an obligation is recorded but the disbursing officer would be required to hold the funds in a trust account pending possible approval or consent by Con-

gress, or should the matter be treated as if there were no entitlement and no special treatment given the funds.

(b) If, in response to question (1), it is determined that retroactive approval could be granted, then once approval is obtained, could the disbursing officer release all funds previously withheld from the retired member?

We have held, in considering the language of the constitutional provision, that actions contrary to its mandate may not be ignored even though the Constitution itself does not provide for a specific sanction. Thus, we held that substantial effect can be given the provision by withholding retired pay from a member who accepts foreign employment in violation of its prohibition in an amount equal to the present or emoluments received from the foreign government. See 44 Comp. Gen. 130, 131 (1964). See also B–178538, October 13, 1977, where the basis for and amount of the withholding were carefully reviewed and it was stated in part:

> It is our view that the rule expressed in 44 Comp. Gen. 130, *supra*, is more in line with the intent of the constitutional provision and does in fact give substantial effect to the prohibitions contained therein. That is, the constitutional provision states that without congressional consent a person holding an office of profit or trust under the United States may not accept "any present, Emolument, Office or Title * * *." We have previously stated the applicable rule in terms of withholding retired pay in amounts equal to those received from the foreign government. The basis for such rule is that the emoluments are accepted on behalf of the United States. Our conclusion that a retired member does not lose h's status by the acceptance of emoluments from a foreign state likewise is predicated on the same basis. *Cf.* 5 U.S.C. 7342.

We note also that Congress was aware of our interpretation of the sanction required by the constitutional provision at the time it enacted section 509 of the Authorization Act. Had it been considered that our interpretation was improper, Congress could have taken that opportunity to change or remove the sanction. It did not do so, except of course for those individuals for whom approval of their employment is granted under section 509. As we stated in our response to question (1), when approval is not granted retired pay should be withheld in an amount equal to that which is received from the foreign government. However, when an individual accepts employment with a foreign government and has made timely application for approval, retired pay need not be withheld once approval has been granted and payment of retired pay may be resumed on approval.

Question (2) is answered accordingly.

Regarding question (3)(a), as is stated in answer to question (1), if approval is granted to foreign employment under section 509 of the Authorization Act, it is not retroactively effective. Thus, the funds withheld should be treated as if there were no entitlement to them and they should be given no special treatment.

In view of our other answers, question (3)(b) is answered in the negative.

Question (4) is as follows:

(4) (a) In your prior decisions, withholding in an amount equal to the salary received from the foreign source was authorized to be withheld. However, as discussed in 44 Comp. Gen. 130 (1964), the language in the Constitution covers more than acceptance of salary. Therefore, is it correct to withhold pay in amounts equal to other elements of compensation such as free or reduced transportation, household goods shipments at employer expense, housing allowances, etc.?

(b) If it is determined that additional elements of compensation must be taken into consideration in determining the amount of the withholding, values based on best estimates furnished by the retired members will be placed on these elements. Due to the inflated cost of housing overseas, this item will be valued at either the actual cost in the foreign country or the fair market value of comparable housing prevailing at the retired member's last address for pay purposes, whichever is lower. Would you concur in this method of valuation? If not, what method of calculating the amounts to be withheld would be appropriate?

The constitutional provision prohibits the acceptance by public officers of presents, emoluments, office or title, "of any kind whatever" from a foreign state. We have held that that wording requires the broadest possible scope and application. See 49 Comp. Gen. 819, 821 (1970), and B–178538, October 13, 1977. Thus, forms of compensation other than salary would fall within the prohibition, and question (4) (a) is answered in the affirmative.

Concerning the issues raised in question (4) (b) as to the value to be placed on nonmonetary elements of compensation, we believe such value should be set fairly, considering the actual value of the compensation received. The proposed method of evaluation is acceptable provided that the estimates furnished by the retired members are reviewed for obvious errors. Questionable cases may, of course, be submitted to our Office for decision.

[B–192907]

Bids—Buy American Act—Price Differential—Reasonableness—Domestic Material Costs

Despite fact that agency questions data it obtained to determine unreasonableness of cost of domestic materials, agency states that information provided by first and second low bidders regarding the nondomestic construction material they proposed to use was sufficient for cost comparison to proceed.

Bids—Buy American Act—Foreign Product Determination—Cost Information—Bidder's Failure to Provide—Bid Responsive

If bidder fails to supply data concerning domestic prices, it takes the risk that procuring agency will not be able to verify fact that domestic prices are unreasonable. However, where agency is able to obtain prices on comparable domestic material, as here, bid need not be rejected because of bidder's failure to provide data regarding domestic prices.

Bids—Buy American Act—Construction Contracts—Statement of Foreign Materials

General Accounting Office (GAO) decision in 51 Comp. Gen. 814 (1972) is distinguishable. Unlike bids of first and second low bidders, bid in that case did not include information pertaining to portion of nondomestic material to be used. Sufficient information as to nondomestic material offered was submitted here by low bidders.

Contractors — Responsibility — Contracting Officer's Affirmative Determination Accepted—Exceptions—Not Supported by Record

GAO does not review protests of affirmative determinations of responsibility except in limited circumstances which are not present here. Moreover, once contract is awarded, compliance with solicitation provision cited by protester is matter of contract administration, which is not for resolution by GAO.

In the matter of C. R. Fedrick, Inc., May 4, 1979:

BACKGROUND

C. R. Fedrick, Inc. (Fedrick) protests the bids of Hitachi America Ltd. (Hitachi) and Nissho-Iwai American Corporation (Nissho) on invitation for bids (IFB) No. DC–7339 issued by the Bureau of Reclamation, Department of the Interior (Interior). The IFB is for the furnishing and installation of motor-driven pumping units and discharge valves at pumping plants located at Hacienda and Twin Lakes, Nevada.

The three low bidders are:

Hitachi	$6, 568, 440
Nissho	6, 625, 000
Fedrick	7, 247, 600

The Government estimate is $6,959,900. No award to date has been made by Interior.

The IFB included Bureau of Reclamation form 7–1532 (6–68) entitled "Representations By Bidders Pursuant To 'Buy American Act.'" The top portion on the front of this form stated that, except as noted below, the bidder represented that all construction materials used would be domestic materials conforming to the clause entitled "Buy American" of the IFB's General Provisions (Standard Form 23–A). Immediately following this language, space was provided for noting each item of nondomestic construction material the bidder intended to use, the quantity of such material and the cost of its delivery to the jobsite. The lower portion of the front of the form asked for a listing of the lowest-costing domestic material that was comparable to the items of nondomestic material noted by the bidder.

Hitachi noted a quantity of "21 sets" of "motor driven pumping unit" at $2,677,290 as the nondomestic construction materials that it intended to furnish. An engineering fee of $195,310 was also listed.

Nissho's nondomestic construction materials were noted as eight sets of pumping units (39 units) and eight sets of metal piping supports and valves at $3,080,000 and $695,000, respectively. Neither Hitachi nor Nissho listed any lowest-costing, comparable domestic material. Hitachi put the words "Not Applicable" on this portion of form 7–1532. Nissho stated "No domestic material available to us."

ARGUMENTS

Fedrick alleges that the bids of Hitachi and Nissho are nonresponsive because of their failure to: (1) specifically identify the nondomestic construction materials intended to be supplied and (2) list lowest-costing domestic material comparable to the nondomestic material. Fedrick argues that Hitachi's reference to 21 sets of motor-driven pumping units is ambiguous because there is no way one can determine from this description how many pumping *units* are to be supplied, their precise type, or the cost of each individual pumping unit. With regard to Nissho, Fedrick admits that the description is more specific, but asserts that it is still not enough. Even assuming, *arguendo*, that Nissho's description of its nondomestic material is adequate, Fedrick contends that the phrase "No domestic material available to us" makes it impossible for Interior to make a cost comparison.

Fedrick takes the position that form 7–1532 *requires* the bidder to supply information regarding the cost of comparable domestic material. Furthermore, this information must be identical to the information specified on the form for the nondomestic material that the bidder intends to supply. Fedrick points to paragraph (b)(2) on the back of the form which provides that the bidder shall include data, based on a reasonable canvass of suppliers, demonstrating that the cost of domestic construction material would exceed by more than 6 percent the cost of comparable nondomestic construction material. Fedrick notes, moreover, that the lower portion of the front of the form is set up for the bidder to provide the name of each item of comparable domestic material, the quantity of such material, and its cost if delivered to the jobsite. Thus, Fedrick believes that it is clear from the language of the form that any bidder proposing the use of nondomestic materials must provide reliable evidence supporting such use including the results of the bidder's canvass of domestic suppliers.

Fedrick has furnished our Office with letters that it received from domestic pump manufacturers concerning the contacts that they had with Hitachi and Nissho. Fedrick asserts that these letters demonstrate that while Nissho and Hitachi did request quotes from these manufacturers for some pumps, they did not seek quotes for all the pumps required by the IFB. In support of this assertion, Fedrick suggests that these letters indicate that Hitachi's contacts were for the purpose of obtaining quotes on the smaller, less expensive pumps only. According to Fedrick, Hitachi did not seek price quotes for pumping plants 1B, 2B, and Hacienda which required the largest, most expensive pumps. As to Nissho, Fedrick avers that while the manufacturers which Nissho contacted indicated a willingness to provide price quotes, no further effort was made by it to obtain any quotes.

Interior takes the position that the failure of Hitachi and Nissho to furnish data regarding the cost of comparable domestic construction material is inconsequential and not prejudicial to the other bidders. Interior states that the Buy American Act, 41 U.S.C. § 10a–10d (1976), requires that only domestic construction materials be used in construction contracts unless the head of the department finds that it would unreasonably increase costs to do so. Interior asserts that the Federal Procurement Regulations (FPR) on the Buy American Act speak in terms of "findings" and "determinations" which can only be made by the Government itself. Moreover, paragraph (b)(1) on the back of the form states that bids offering the use of additional non-domestic construction material may be acceptable if the *Government* determines that use of comparable domestic construction material is impracticable or would unreasonably increase cost. Consequently, Interior argues that even if Hitachi and Nissho had filled in the bottom portion of form 7–1532, the Government would still have the obligation to check the data provided against an independent canvass of domestic suppliers.

Interior also states that it determined that both Hitachi and Nissho furnished sufficient information on the top portion of form 7–1532 for it to proceed with a cost comparison. Further, Interior indicates that it believed that this information was sufficient to preclude any change by Hitachi and Nissho after bid opening which would affect their relative standing. Interior then contacted five domestic suppliers of pumps and requested price quotations. For the 21 units that Hitachi listed, Interior received quotes of $3,981,523 and $4,000,000. For the 39 units that Nissho listed, Interior received quotes of $3,800,000 to $4,330,000 from one source (depending on terms of delivery, drawings required and special conditions), $4,301,464 and $4,863,393 from the other source.

Based on its historical records, Interior had estimated the cost of furnishing 21 domestic pumping units to be $2,880,000. As to Nissho's 39 units, Interior's estimated cost for furnishing comparable domestic materials had been $4,000,000. However, Interior states that the pumping units required by the IFB are not stock units and, therefore, are unique. As such, their exact cost cannot be determined. After reviewing all bids submitted and the quoted costs from domestic pump manufacturers, Interior concluded that its estimated costs were somewhat low. Using just the bids submitted and the domestic quotations for comparison, Interior found the cost of Hitachi's and Nissho's nondomestic construction materials to be substantially less than the cost of similar domestic construction material and thus acceptable under the Buy American Act.

In response, Fedrick argues that it would be prejudicial for the Government to supply information to supplement the nonresponsive bids of Hitachi and Nissho by its own survey. In Fedrick's opinion, reliance by the contracting officer on his own survey undermines the integrity of the competitive bidding system and acts to Fedrick's detriment. Fedrick asserts that a meaningful comparison of the cost of domestic material to nondomestic material can only be done within the context of the bidding process itself. When the cost of comparable domestic material is determined after bid opening. Fedrick believes that it is impossible to evaluate whether the domestic material could have been obtained at a lesser cost. Therefore, Fedrick concludes that in order to have cost comparisons of similar items under similar circumstances, a bidder who proposes to use nondomestic construction materials must submit, as required by form 7–1532, the results of his own survey of domestic suppliers of the materials.

In further support of its position, Fedrick calls attention to the fact form 7–1532 is designed in such a manner that the bidder supplies the same information for domestic material as for nondomestic material. When the information regarding the cost of comparable domestic materials is supplied, Fedrick claims that a ready comparison can be made by the contracting officer through *verification* rather than independent price inquiries. In Fedrick's view, this verification could easily be accomplished by the contracting officer calling the listed sources of comparable domestic material. Also, Fedrick contends that the difficulties Interior stated it encountered in determining whether the domestic materials in its survey were similar to the listed nondomestic materials would not have existed had Hitachi and Nissho properly completed the form at the time they submitted their bids.

Fedrick further emphasizes the problems it believes are associated with a post-bid-opening survey of domestic suppliers by pointing out that Interior's survey contradicted the Government's estimates that were based on historical costs. Fedrick argues that any survey made under noncompetitive conditions gives questionable results. If Interior had used its own estimates to make the cost comparison, Fedrick observes that the cost of comparable domestic construction material would have been found to be *lower* than the cost of the nondomestic construction material proposed by Hitachi and Nissho. Fedrick asserts that any subjectiveneses involved in making a cost comparison using information obtained after bid opening is removed when all the required information is provided by the bidder with his bid. Furthermore, Fedrick contends that in view of the requirements of the Buy American Act, it is good policy to require bidders who propose the use of nondomestic construction material to demonstrate clearly, in accordance with the instructions on form 7–1532, that their nondomestic construction materials would cost less than comparable domestic materials.

Finally, Fedrick urges that the use of information obtained after bid opening defeats the purpose of form 7–1532. In Fedrick's opinion, if the failure to furnish information on the lower portion of the front of the form does not render a bid nonresponsive, this portion of the form will become meaningless. Bidders will never supply information on the cost of comparable domestic material. Instead, they will wait for a survey to be made after bid opening by the contracting officer, where there are no pressures of competition and where the effect of inflation is already known. Fedrick concludes that if our Office decides that the bids of Hitachi and Nissho are responsive, form 7–1532 will have to be changed since a significant portion of it will never be filled out.

Hitachi asserts that its bid was responsive, as a matter of law, to the specifications. Hitachi refers to our decisions which hold that unless something on the face of the bid, or specifically made a part thereof, either limits, reduces or modifies the obligation of the prospective contractor to perform in accordance with the terms of the invitation, the bid is responsive. See 49 Comp. Gen. 553 (1970) and 57 id. 361 (1978). Hitachi states that once the bids were opened, it was contractually obligated to perform the work described by the IFB specifications at the price stated in its bid. In this regard, Hitachi believes that in its bid it properly identified the nondomestic material it proposed to use and a price for such items.

GAO ANALYSIS

FPR § 1–18.603–1 provides: (1) that a "determination" be made that the cost of each item of nondomestic construction material offered in the bid plus 6 percent be less than the cost of comparable domestic construction material; and (2) that the bid be the lowest after adding, for evaluation purposes, 6 percent of the cost of the nondomestic construction material. All costs involved in delivery to the construction site are to be used in computing the cost of both domestic and nondomestic construction material. Further, the computations are to be based on costs on the date of bid opening. See FPR § 1–18.603–2.

The language of the Buy American Act provision that must be included in solicitations for construction work is set forth in FPR § 1–18.604. Paragraph (b)(2)(1) of this prescribed provision states that where the bidder alleges that the use of domestic construction material would unreasonably increase cost, data is to be included, based on a reasonable canvass of suppliers, which demonstrates that the cost of each item of comparable domestic construction material would exceed by more than 6 percent the cost of the nondomestic construction material offered by the bidder. Form 7–1532 provides space at the bottom of the front portion for the bidder to list this data.

While the language of the FPR mandated provision indicates that the bidder is to provide data to demonstrate that the use of comparable domestic construction material would unreasonably increase costs, we do not, however, believe that the failure of a bidder to furnish such data is always fatal. Paragraph (b)(1) of this provision also provides that bids offering the use of nondomestic construction material *may* be acceptable for award *if the Government* determines that the use of comparable domestic construction material is impracticable or would unreasonably increase cost or that domestic construction material is commercially unavailable. Consequently, it is our opinion that regardless of whether the bidder furnishes data on the cost of comparable domestic material, the Government is still obligated to perform a cost comparison on the nondomestic construction materials offered by the bidder.

We note that Interior questions the data upon which it determined that the cost of comparable domestic construction material was unreasonable because it was not possible to create the same competitive conditions that existed at the time of bid opening. Interior states that the system established by the regulations for making Buy American Act determinations calls for a considerable amount of subjective judgment by the contracting officer in establishing the cost of the comparable domestic material. Where the prices of the nondomestic versus domestic material are close, as is the case here, Interior expresses the concern that the result of the required cost comparison will depend on the subjectivity of the contracting officer in analyzing the data available.

Despite the foregoing, Interior does indicate that the information given by Hitachi and Nissho regarding the nondomestic construction material they proposed to use was sufficient for the cost comparison to proceed. In this regard, we think that if a bidder fails to supply data concerning domestic prices, it takes the risk that the procuring agency will not be able to verify the fact that domestic prices are unreasonable. However, where the agency is able to obtain prices on comparable domestic material, as Interior was able to do here, we believe that a bid need not be rejected because of bidder's failure to provide data regarding domestic prices.

Fedrick cites 51 Comp. Gen. 814 (1972) in support of its contention that the failure to supply data demonstrating that the cost of comparable domestic materials would exceed by more than 6 percent the cost of nondomestic materials offered is a failure that goes to the responsiveness of a bidder's bid. That decision involved in part a protest against a bid that did not include information pertaining to the portion of nondomestic materials that the bidder proposed to use. In addition, the protested bid failed to provide any data to demonstrate that the cost of domestic material would exceed by 6 percent the cost of the bidder's nondomestic material. Fedrick argues that our decision in that case makes it clear that bidders are required to provide both information concerning the amount of nondomestic material to be used and supporting data to demonstrate the unreasonableness in cost of comparable domestic material.

Hitachi asserts that 51 Comp. Gen. 814 is distinguishable. Unlike Hitachi's bid, the bid in that case did not include information pertaining to the portion of nondomestic material to be used. According to Hitachi, if such failure had been permitted to be waived, the bidder could have identified the quantity of nondomestic construction material to be used subsequent to bid opening in a manner most advantageous to itself and prejudicial to other bidders. In clear contrast to that situation, Hitachi claims that its bid committed it both as to quantity and price of the nondomestic materials it proposed to use.

We agree with Hitachi's position. Because both Hitachi and Nissho filled out the top portion of form 7–1532, we conclude that sufficient information was submitted by both bidders to preclude any change after bid opening which would affect their relative standing among the other bidders. As to any data that a bidder submits based upon its canvass of domestic suppliers, the Government would still have an obligation to check the bidder's data against its own independent canvass of suppliers and its own cost estimates. Furthermore, any data supplied by a bidder would be subject to bias and thus suspect. Therefore, in view of the fact that the Government's obligation remains the same whether or not the data on the bottom of the front of form 7–1532 is provided, the controlling aspect of whether a bid meets the requirements of the Buy American Act pertains to the information required by the top portion of the front of form 7–1532.

THE RESPONSIBILITIES OF HITACHI AND NISSHO

Fedrick also alleges that the bids of Hitachi and Nissho must be rejected on the grounds that neither company is a responsible bidder.

Fedrick refers to Special Provision 1.2.9 of the IFB entitled "Performance and Supervision of Work By Contractor," which requires the contractor to perform on the site and with his own organization and forces on his payroll, work equivalent to at least 20 percent of the total amount of construction work at the site. Fedrick claims that while Hitachi and Nissho are large Japanese-controlled manufacturers or suppliers of a variety of equipment including pumps, they are not construction firms engaged in civil construction in the United States. Fedrick argues that the only logical implication from the background of these two companies is that they will have to rely completely on other firms for the installation of the pumps that they furnish. In addition, Fedrick claims with respect to Hitachi's pumps that the State of Nevada has had significant problems with them on other similar projects.

This Office does not review protests of affirmative determinations of responsibility unless either fraud is alleged on the part of procuring officials or the solicitation contains definitive responsibility criteria which allegedly have not been applied. *Central Metal Products, Inc.*, 54 Comp. Gen. 66 (1974), 74-2 CPD 64. Neither exception is present here. Furthermore, once the contract is awarded, compliance with Special Provision 1.2.9 of the IFB is a matter of contract administration which is for resolution by the contractor and the Government, and not this Office. *Thorsen Tool Company*, B-188271, March 1, 1977, 77-1 CPD 154.

CONCLUSION

The protest is denied.

[B-189154]

Compensation — Withholding — Debt Liquidation — Withholding Prohibited

Government may not withhold current salary to satisfy general debts owed by employee and may not setoff against employee's retirement account until employee withdraws contribution or claims annuity. Government has right to setoff indebtedness administratively against annuity payments or refund of retirement contribution based upon common-law right long recognized by our Office and the courts.

Set-Off — Statutes of Limitation Effect — Employee Retirement Funds

Government's right to setoff indebtedness againt annuity payments or refund of retirement contribution is not subject to statute of limitations on court action by Government contained in 28 U.S.C. 2415. Legislative history shows no intention to limit Government's right to setoff indebtedness administratively without resort to courts.

In the matter of Collection of Debts — Statute of Limitations on Administrative Setoff, May 8, 1979:

The Honorable Alan K. Campbell, Director, Office of Personnel Management (formerly Civil Service Commission), has requested our opinion as to whether the provisions of 28 U.S.C. § 2415 (1976), or any other general statute of limitations, in any way limits an agency's authority to setoff claims by that agency or another agency against money it holds for an individual.

In order to answer this question properly, we shall first discuss the general authority of the Government to collect its debts and then proceed to the issue of the effect of the statute of limitations.

DEBT COLLECTION AND SETOFF

Our Office is vested with broad authority to settle claims by the Government of the United States or against it and to superintend the recovery of debts due the United States. See 31 U.S.C. §§ 71 and 93 (1976). Claims procedures are found in title 4 of the "General Accounting Office Policy and Procedures Manual for Guidance of Federal Agencies." In addition, under the Federal Claims Collection Act of 1966, 31 U.S.C. §§ 951–953 (1976), the Comptroller General and the Attorney General are jointly charged with promulgating standards for collecting and compromising claims of the United States. The Federal Claims Collections Standards are contained in 4 C.F.R. Parts 101–105 (1978). Agencies are required to take aggressive action to collect all claims of the United States (4 C.F.R. § 102.1), including collection by offset as prescribed in 4 C.F.R. § 102.3. In collecting claims by offset agencies are instructed to use the cooperative efforts of other agencies, and all agencies are enjoined to cooperate in this endeavor. See 4 C.F.R. § 102.3.

Under 5 U.S.C. § 5514, a Government agency may use the setoff procedure against an employee's current salary to collect a debt which arises from an erroneous payment made by the agency to or on behalf of the employee. Also, under 5 U.S.C. §§ 5705 and 5724(f), agencies may setoff against current salary to collect unused advances for travel and transportation expenses. However, our Office has long held that the Government cannot withhold current salary of employees to satisfy general debts owed to the Government without the employee's consent. 29 Comp. Gen. 99 (1949); 24 id. 334, 338 (1944). Collection of such debts may be made after the employee's separation by offset against his final salary check or lump-sum payment for leave. See 29 Comp. Gen. 99, *supra*, and decisions cited therein.

We have also held that monies held in an employee's retirement account are not available for setoff until he is separated and withdraws his contribution or until he qualifies for a retirement annuity. 39 Comp. Gen. 203 (1959). However, we have long held that once such funds become payable, the amount may be applied in liquidation of the employee's indebtedness to the United States. 39 Comp. Gen. 203, *supra;* 27 *id.* 703 (1948) ; 21 *id.* 1000 (1942) ; and 16 *id.* 161 (1936). Such action is accomplished by the filing of a request with the Office of Personnel Management under the procedures set forth in Federal Personnel Manual Supplement 831-1, Subchapter S19.

It is also well recognized that the Government has the common–law right which belongs to every creditor to apply the appropriated monies of his debtor, in his hands, to extinguish the debts of that debtor. *United States* v. *Cohen*, 389 F. 2d 689 (5th Cir. 1967). See also *United States* v. *Munsey Trust Co.*, 332 U.S. 234, 239 (1947) ; *Gratiot* v. *United States*, 40 U.S. 336, 370 (1841) ; and *Avant* v. *United States*, 165 F. Supp. 802 (E.D. Va. 1958). This principle has been consistently followed by this Office as well. See 49 Comp. Gen. 44 (1969) ; 46 *id.* 178, 182 (1966) ; and 41 *id.* 85 (1960).

STATUTE OF LIMITATIONS

With the enactment of Pub. L. 89–505, July 18, 1966, 80 Stat. 304, Congress for the first time imposed a general statute of limitations on civil actions brought by the United States. See 28 U.S.C. § 2415. The law provides in section 2415(a) that every action for money damages brought by the United States which is founded upon any contract express or implied in law or fact shall be forever barred unless the complaint is filed within 6 years after the right of action accrues. Similarly, section 2415(d) imposes a 6-year statute of limitations on actions brought by the United States to recover money erroneously paid to a Federal employee or member of the uniformed service.

However, the Congress preserved the right of offset or counterclaim in section 2415(f) of title 28, United States Code, which provides as follows:

(f) The provisions of this section shall not prevent the assertion, in an action against the United States or an officer or agency thereof, of any claim of the United States or an officer or agency thereof against an opposing party, a co-party, or a third party that arises out of the transaction or occurrence that is the subject matter of the opposing party's claim. A claim of the United States or an officer or agency thereof that does not arise out of the transaction or occurrence that is the subject matter of the opposing party's claim may, if time-barred, be asserted only by way of offset and may be allowed in an amount not to exceed the amount of the opposing party's recovery.

DEPARTMENT OF JUSTICE OPINION

With regard to the application of a statute of limitations on setoff actions we have been advised that the Department of Justice, by letter of September 29, 1978, has sent the Office of Personnel Management a memorandum opinion signed by Mr. John M. Harmon, Assistant Attorney General, Office of Legal Counsel. The opinion concludes that where judicial enforcement of a debt is barred by 28 U.S.C. § 2415, the debt may not be collected by administrative offset. The opinion refers to "administrative offset" as merely a "prejudgment attachment device," and the opinion states that if there is no possibility of obtaining a judgment on the debt, administrative offset would be inappropriate and could not be used. The Assistant Attorney General recognizes that, under the provisions of 28 U.S.C. § 2415(f), the Government may assert a time-barred claim by way of offset against the claim of an opposing party which does not arise out of the same transaction or occurrence, but such offset may not exceed the recovery of the opposing party on its claim. Furthermore, if the Government's time-barred claim arises out of the same transaction or occurrence as the opposing party's claim, the Government may assert its claim without any limitation on recovery. However, the opinion states that where a person seeks to dispute an offset, his action does not constitute a claim against the United States.

The Justice memorandum opinion states that the statute of limitations was intended to allow repose to stale debts except where the debtor initiates and prevails in a claim against the United States arising out of the same or a different transaction or occurrence, and that allowing administrative setoff of time-barred debts where the debtor has not filed a claim would render the statute completely ineffective. Finally, the opinion refers to two court decisions where the offset of time-barred debts against civil service retirement benefits was at issue. The Assistant Attorney General agrees with the court's decision in *Tomakin* v. *United States*, No. C 75 1079 (N.D. Cal. 1975) (unpublished order), which holds that administrative setoff is subject to the 6-year statute of limitations contained in 28 U.S.C. § 2415(a). However, he disagrees with the decision in *Atwater* v. *Roudebush*, 452 F. Supp. 622 (N.D. Ill. 1976) which holds that section 2415 has no application to administrative setoff.

Based upon our review of court decisions, prior decisions of our Office, and the legislative history of the statute of limitations, 28 U.S.C. § 2415, we disagree with the memorandum opinion of the Assistant Attorney General and conclude that section 2415 has no application to administrative setoff. Our reasons are as follows.

DISCUSSION

The general rule is that statutes of limitations applicable to suits for debts or money demands bar or run only against the remedy (the right to bring suit) to which they apply and do not discharge the debt or extinguish, or even impair, the right or obligation, either in law or in fact, and the creditor may avail himself of every other lawful means of realizing on the debt or obligation. See *Mascot Oil Co.* v. *United States*, 42 F. 2d 309 (Ct. Cl. 1930), affirmed 282 U.S. 434; and 33 Comp. Gen. 66 (1953). See also *Ready-Mix Concrete Co.* v. *United States*, 130 F. Supp. 390 (Ct. Cl. 1955).

As shown above, the inherent right of administrative setoff by the Government was recognized by the courts and our Office long before the enactment of the statute of limitations contained in 28 U.S.C. § 2415. This statute of limitations applies specifically to civil actions brought by the United States. The statute also contains an exception in section 2415(f) whereby the United States, in an action filed against it, may assert a claim by way of offset or counterclaim. The legislative history of this statute of limitations reveals no clear intention by the Congress to apply this statute to administrative setoff. In fact, it suggests the contrary. In testifying before the House subcommittee which held hearings on the bill, the spokesman for the Department of Justice made the following statement concerning the effect of the bill on offsets and counterclaims:

> The bill will not affect the authority of each agency to offset, on its own books and without resort to the courts, any claim it may have against a person to whom it is about to make a payment based on the same or an unrelated transaction. For example, under 31 U.S.C. 71a, 237, a claimant has ten full years to present to the General Accounting Office a claim against the United States. *We do not intend any diminution of that agency's authority to offset against a claim so presented any debt, however old, such claimant owes to the United States.*
>
> Further, if the Government is sued there is no time bar to the assertion by the Government of claims arising out of the same transaction upon which it is being sued. The only change we are proposing in existing law is with respect to claims which would be time barred under the present proposal in an independent action and which do not arise out of the same transaction upon which the United States is being sued. Under the bill, these latter claims may be asserted only to offset the opposing party's claim in an amount not to exceed such party's recovery. (Hearing on H.R. 13652 before Subcommittee No. 2 of the House Committee on the Judiciary, 89th Cong., 2d Sess., at 8 (1966)). [Italic supplied.]

This statement was adopted in the Committee Reports of both Houses, as evidenced by the following statement from the House Committee Report:

> Subsection (f) of section 2415 contains carefully drafted provisions permitting the Government to assert its claims by way of offset or counterclaim in actions brought against the United States. Where the United States finds itself involved in litigation, it very often is to the interest of the Government to assert claims by way of counterclaim and the provisions of this subsection represent a very practical implementation and classification of the Government's rights in this regard. It is expressly provided that the limitations provided in the section will not prevent the assertion of a claim by the United States against the opposing party in such an action, or a coparty, or a third party when the claim of the United States arises out of the transaction or occurrence that is the subject matter of the opposing party's claim. This merely gives the Government the right to a full hearing of all aspects of the case arising out of the same transaction or

occurrence. When the claim of the United States does not arise out of the transaction or occurrence that is the subject of the opposing party's claim and is time barred, it may only be asserted by the United States to the degree that it offsets the other claim and cannot exceed the amount of the opposing party's recovery.

The testimony at the hearing on the bill noted the fact that this bill does not affect the authority of each agency to offset on its own books and without resort to court any claim it may have against a person to whom it is about to make a payment based on the same or an unrelated transaction. There is a 10-year statute of limitations which applies to claims against the United States filed with the General Accounting Office. This provision is found in title 31 of the United States Code, sections 71a and 237. This bill therefore does not affect that agency's authority to offset a claim presented within that time period any debt which the same claimant owes to the United States.

H.R. Rep. No. 1534, 89th Cong., 2d Sess. 6, 7 (1966). See also S. Rep. No. 1331, 89th Cong., 2d Sess. (1966).

The application of 28 U.S.C. § 2415 to administrative setoff was also raised by the plaintiff in *Atwater* v. *Roudebush, supra,* where the Government was collecting a time-barred Federal Housing Administration debt by setoff against the plaintiff's final salary payment and his retirement annuity. However, the court concluded, based upon the common law doctrine of setoff and the legislative history of the statute of limitations cited above, that, even though the statute barred direct action by the Government to collect the debt, the Government could still recover the debt by administrative setoff against current payments to the debtor. 452 F. Supp. 622, at 632. We agree with the District Court's reasoning and conclusion and must respectfully disagree with the Assistant Attorney General's memorandum opinion.

Finally, we note that the Justice memorandum states that where a person seeks to dispute an offset, his action in so doing does not constitute a claim. We do not agree since we have held that a debtor could, if the debt were collected by means of setoff, assert his right against the United States for the alleged amount, and that such action would constitute a claim which could be submitted to our Office for adjudication on its merits, pursuant to our statutory authority contained in 31 U.S.C. § 71 (1976). See *Matter of Nabisco, Inc.*, B–184506, October 29, 1975. Similarly, we know of no reason why the debtor could not pursue his claim in Federal courts under 28 U.S.C. §§ 1346(a)(2) or 1491 (1976). We note, for example, that the plaintiff in *Tomakin* v. *United States, supra,* asserted jurisdiction for repayment of the money deducted under the authority of 28 U.S.C. § 1346(a)(2). Therefore, we believe that a debtor's action in challenging an offset by asserting his right to the money which has been withheld does constitute a claim against the United States.

Accordingly, we conclude that the statute of limitations contained in 28 U.S.C. § 2415 has no application to the Government's collection of indebtedness through administrative setoff, and we are aware of no other statute which limits administrative setoff. Hence, the Government has the right to collect the indebtedness of its employees by means of setoff against monies owed to the employee even if direct action to collect the debt would be barred by the statute of limitations.

[B-194187]

Leaves of Absence—Annual—Restored—Administrative Error Determination

National Aeronautics and Space Administration (NASA) employee elected to be carried on continuation-of-pay status for 45-day period after job-related injury pursuant to Pub. L. No. 93–416. Contrary to 20 C.F.R. 10.200 *et seq.*, NASA refused to continue his pay but required him to take leave to cover the periods of his absence attributable to the injury. Upon correction of his leave accounts, annual leave subject to forfeiture may be restored under 5 U.S.C. 6304(d)(1)(A) (1976) as leave lost because of administrative error. B–184008, Mar. 7, 1977, and B–182608, Aug. 9, 1977, distinguished.

In the matter of Walter E. Blank—Restoration of Annual Leave, May 9, 1979:

Patrick F. O'Brien, an authorized certifying officer of the National Aeronautics and Space Administration (NASA), Washington, D.C., seeks an advance decision as to whether 34 hours of annual leave may be restored to Walter E. Blank, a NASA Headquarters employee, under Pub. L. No. 93–181, 87 Stat. 705 (1973), 5 U.S.C. § 6304(d) (1)(A) (1976).

The certifying officer asks:

(a) Upon the determination of administrative error by a responsible authority, may forfeited annual leave be restored by operation of 5 U.S.C. 6304(d)(2) if there is also a finding of fault on the part of the employee.

(b) May a finding of fault be made in a case where the employee acknowledged the annual leave taken by initialling his Time and Attendance Record and where he has been regularly advised through the issuance of biweekly Earning and Leave Statements * * * which reflects the amount and type of leave charged to his account during each pay period.

The record shows that Mr. Blank was injured on the job February 2, 1977. He applied for workmen's compensation and his claim, controverted by NASA, was forwarded to the Office of Workmen's Compensation Programs (OWCP), Department of Labor, on April 7, 1977, under the provisions of the Federal Employees' Compensation Act, 5 U.S.C. § 8101 *et seq.* (1976). In April 1978, NASA received a notice from the OWCP that the claim was noncontroverted and that Mr. Blank was entitled to continuation of pay for the period of his disability not to exceed 45 days.

At the time of his injury, Mr. Blank requested that his absence from work attributable to the injury be charged to continuation of pay under 5 U.S.C. § 8118 (1976). Apparently because NASA controverted his claim that the injury was a "job-related, traumatic injury" it denied his request for continuation of pay. His absence from work as a result of the injury was instead charged to 72 hours of sick leave and 34 hours of annual leave. In compliance with the determination by the OWCP that he was entitled to continuation of pay, NASA restored 72 hours of sick leave and 34 hours of annual leave to Mr. Blank's respective leave accounts. However, because of the operation of 5 U.S.C. § 6304(a) (1976), the 34 hours of restored annual leave was forfeited, since Mr. Blank carried forward the maximum allowable 240 hours to the 1978 leave year.

A determination of administrative error has been made by NASA based on its view that the entire period of Mr. Blank's absence attributable to his work-related injury should have been charged to sick leave rather than to annual leave. Because Mr. Blank signed for the annual leave and understood that he had taken the 34 hours of annual leave, the certifying officer questions that determination of administrative error.

What constitutes administrative error under 5 U.S.C. § 6304(d)(1)(A) is a matter within the primary jurisdiction of the agency involved. See *Matter of John J. Lynch*, 55 Comp. Gen. 784 (1976). However, decisions of this Office have construed an administrative error as the failure of an agency to follow written administrative regulations having mandatory effect. In general, an employee entitled to use sick leave who specifically requests to have his absence charged to annual leave may not, in the leave year after the annual leave is granted, have such leave charged instead to his sick leave account. 54 Comp. Gen. 1086 (1976) and 57 Comp. Gen. 535 (1978). However, we do not view Mr. Blank's case as one in which his absence was simply charged to his annual leave rather than his sick leave account, but as a case in which NASA, contrary to a mandatory regulation, refused to carry him in a continued-pay status under 5 U.S.C. § 8118, resulting in improper charges to either leave account.

The Federal Employees' Compensation Act as amended in part by Pub. L. No. 93–416, 88 Stat. 1145 (1974), 5 U.S.C. § 8118 (1976), provides in pertinent part that:

(a) The United States shall authorize the continuation of pay of an employee * * * who has filed a claim for a period of wage loss due to a traumatic injury with his immediate superior on a form approved by the Secretary of Labor within the time specified in section 8122(a)(2) of this title.
(b) Continuation of pay under this subchapter shall be furnished—

   *   *   *   *   *   *   *

(2) for a period not to exceed 45 days; and
(c) An employee may use annual or sick leave to his credit at the time the disability begins * * *.

The Secretary of Labor has promulgated regulations on continuation of pay pursuant to this statute in 20 C.F.R. § 10.200 *et seq.* (1976).

The employing agency can controvert an employee's claim and terminate his pay right under any one of the nine circumstances listed at 20 C.F.R. § 10.202(a) (1976). In all other cases in which the employing agency controverts an employee's right to continuation of pay, 20 C.F.R. § 10.202(b) (1976) specifically provides that the employee's regular pay cannot be interrupted during the 45-day period unless the controversion is sustained by the OWCP and until the employing agency is notified. 20 C.F.R. § 10.202(b) (1976). In this case the OWCP advised NASA that Mr. Blank's claim was noncontroverted and that he should be carried on continuation of pay for a period not to exceed 45 days.

Although 20 C.F.R. § 10.210 (1976) provides that an employee can make an election to have his absence charged to annual or sick leave, the record shows that Mr. Blank did not so elect but, on his original claim form CA–1, chose to have his lost time charged to continuation of pay in accordance with OWCP regulations at 20 C.F.R. § 10.209(a) (1976). In view of his election, and under the regulations discussed above, Mr. Blank was entitled to be carried in a continuation-of-pay status for a 45-day period.

Subsection 6304(d)(1)(A) of title 5 of the United States Code authorizes restoration of lost leave because of an administrative error when the error "causes" the loss. In this case NASA's failure to carry Mr. Blank in a continuation-of-pay status contrary to a mandatory regulation constituted an administrative error that directly caused the loss of his leave. See *Matter of Gerard W. Caprio*, B–190263, July 5, 1978. Since his absence should not have been charged to either leave account, we do not view Mr. Blank's determination to have a portion of his absence charged to annual leave rather than sick leave as precluding restoration of the 34 hours of annual leave under 5 U.S.C. § 6304(d)(1)(A).

Accordingly, pursuant to 5 U.S.C. § 6304(d)(1)(A) (1976), NASA may restore the 34 hours of forfeited annual leave to Mr. Blank's annual leave account. This decision, based on the mandatory effect of the Department of Labor's regulations on continuation of pay, is to be distinguished from cases, including *Matter of Helen Wakus*, B–184008, March 7, 1977, and *Matter of Betty J. Anderson*, B–182608, August 9, 1977, involving annual leave that is properly taken but that is "bought back" under the Federal Employees' Compensation Act.

[B–192221]

Contracts—Protests—Court Solicited Aid

General Accounting Office (GAO) will not consider issues raised in bid protests where same issues are before court of competent jurisdiction except where Court expresses interest in GAO proceedings and defers ruling on merits for purpose of allowing GAO to exercise its expertise as an aid to Court.

Bids—Responsiveness—Responsiveness v. Bidder Responsibility

"Responsibility" is term of art employed in Federal procurement and refers to proposed contractor's ability or "capacity" to perform all contract requirements, while "responsiveness" of a bid concerns whether bidder has unequivocally offered to provide requested items or service in total conformance with terms of invitation for bid. Question of application of regulation requiring bids to materially conform to specifications of invitation for bids is matter of responsiveness.

Contractors—Responsibility—Determination—Review by GAO— Effect of Issuance of Certificate of Competency by SBA—Definitive Responsibility Criteria

Issuance of Certificate of Competency (COC) by Small Business Administration (SBA) will overcome special experience requirements (definitive responsibility criteria) specified in solicitation as COC is conclusive on contracting officers by law, and where record shows SBA fully considered definitive responsibility criteria in determining to issue COC, GAO would not recommend that SBA reconsider decision.

In the matter of J. Baranello and Sons, May 9, 1979:

J. Baranello and Sons (Baranello) protests the award of a contract to PJR Construction Corporation (PJR) under invitation for bids (IFB) No. INY74005 issued by the General Services Administration (GSA) for the repair and improvement of the Federal Building in New York City. Baranello contends that Allied Elevator (Allied), the subcontractor which PJR proposed for the performance of the elevator work, did not meet the experience requirements of the "Competency of Bidder" clause of the IFB.

The gravamen of the protest is the authority of the Small Business Administration (SBA) to issue a Certificate of Competency (COC) to PJR in the face of what Baranello perceives as PJR's failure to comply with definitive responsibility criteria set forth in the solicitation.

As a preliminary matter we point out that the issue in this case is presently before the United States District Court for the Southern District of New York in Civil Action No. 79-595. As a general rule GAO will not consider issues raised in a bid protest where the same issues are before a court of competent jurisdiction. *Alton Iron Works, Inc.*, B-191899, August 30, 1978, 78-2 CPD 156. However, where as here, the Court expresses an interest in the GAO proceedings, particularly where the Court by order defers ruling on the merits for the purpose of allowing GAO to exercise its expertise as an aid to the Court, we will issue a decision on the merits. 53 Comp. Gen. 522 (1974), 74-1 CPD 44; 52 *id.* 706 (1973).

The material facts in this case are not in dispute. Bids were opened on June 8, 1978, with eight bids having been received ranging from

PJR's low bid of $13,447,000 to $15,972,000. Baranello was the second low bidder at $13,449,700.

The solicitation contained the following provision:

13. COMPETENCY OF BIDDER (ELEVATOR)

13.1 The bidder, or the subcontractor whom the bidder will use for performance of the elevator work, shall have had at least three years' successful experience in installing and servicing elevators.

13.2 In addition, the bidder or the subcontractor shall have installed, on at least two prior projects, elevators which are comparable to those required for this project and which have performed satisfactorily under conditions of normal use for a period of not less than one year. To be considered comparable, prior installation shall have not less than the same number of elevators operating together in one group as the largest number in any group specified for this project, except that a group of four may be considered comparable to a larger group specified for this project.

13.3 A list of the prior comparable installations by the bidder or by the subcontractor * * * shall be submitted promptly upon request of the Government.

13.4 The names, addresses, experience, and a statement of the work to be performed by each subcontractor or second-tier subcontractor whom the bidder or the principal subcontractor, as the case may be, will use for performance of minor portions of the installation of elevators, shall also be submitted promptly upon request by the Government.

The IFB also required bidders to submit with their bids the names of the individuals or firms proposed to perform various categories of work by subcontract. Pursuant to that requirement, PJR listed Allied Elevator (Allied) as its proposed subcontractor for 100% of the elevator work required by the specifications while Baranello listed Otis Elevator Company (Otis) as its proposed elevator subcontractor.

By letter of June 9, 1978, Baranello informed GSA of its belief that Allied did not qualify under the "Competency of Bidder" clause, and on June 22, 1978, PJR protested award to any other bidder on the ground that it was the lowest responsive and responsible bidder.

On June 28, 1978, Allied provided the contracting officer with information which it believed indicated that it met the IFB's experience requirements. That letter listed prior elevator installations, the firm's experience and the experience and "know-how" of the firm's principals and employees.

On July 10, 1978, the contracting officer informed PJR that Allied did not meet the requirements of the "Competency of Bidder" clause and instructed PJR to propose a substitute subcontractor. However, the contracting officer's determination in this instance did not consider the experience of Allied's employees, but was based only on the finding that Allied had not previously installed elevator banks of four or more. It was the decision to consider a subcontractor substitution that was the basis for Baranello's initial protest.

Thereafter, the contracting officer conducted an extensive investigation of the competency of Allied's *employees*, and in a letter of October 11, 1978, GSA notified GAO of a second negative determination of Allied's qualifications. That letter also advised that the question of PJR's responsibility was being referred to the Regional Director of the Small Business Administration (SBA) pursuant to the Small Business Act, 15 U.S.C. § 637(b)(7) (1976), *as amended by* Act of August 4, 1977, Pub. L. No. 95–89, § 501 and the Federal Procurement Regulations (FPR) § 1–1.708.2 (1964 ed.). That referral requested SBA to consider whether Allied had the requisite 4-bank installation experience required by subparagraph 13.2 of the "Competency of Bidder" clause.

After thoroughly reviewing Allied's business history and technical competency, SBA found that:

Allied has not installed more than 3 elevators in a single bank in any past job.

SBA thereafter concluded that:

* * * Although Allied's past experience does not qualify the firm in accordance with the Competency of Bidder clause, it must certainly be considered in any evaluation of the firm's technical capability to perform on this procurement. Discussions with several experts in the field of elevator installation revealed that the basic installation of a bank of 4 elevators is extremely similar to the installation of a bank of 2 or three elevators. The difference lies in the complexity of the control system * * *.

In order to gain the additional management level experience in the installation of a bank of 4 elevators and to comply with the requirements of this installation, Allied has retained * * * a consultant * * * [who] is considered thoroughly competent to install elevators in banks of 4 or more * * *.

[Allied's personnel] * * * have had long and diversified experience in the installation and repair of elevators similar to those required by this solicitation. The following summaries are intended to demonstrate that the listed personnel meet the specific requirements of the Competency of Bidder clause and do not represent a complete review of the experience of each man * * *.

Thereafter, SBA recommended issuance of a Certificate of Competency. This recommendation was based on the following premises, among others:

A. Allied and PJR have demonstrated the technical capability to perform on this procurement. The firm has retained a management level consultant with extensive experience in the installation of banks of 4 elevators and over.

B. A review of the past experience of all primary employees that will be used to install the elevators on this job revealed that each individual meets the requirements of the Competency of Bidder clause contained in Section 0100, Special Conditions, paragraph 13.

GSA appealed the recommendation to the Assistant Administrator for Procurement and Management Assistance of SBA pursuant to 13 C.F.R. 124.8–16(c) (1978). In that appeal, GSA submitted extensive comments to SBA in opposition to issuance of a COC. For example, in a letter dated December 15, 1978, the contracting officer contended that SBA unilaterally determined that the installation of a bank of 2 elevators is comparable to installation of a bank of 4, resulting in a modification of specific IFB criteria prejudicial to other bidders and prospective bidders. The letter urged that issuance of a COC to PJR, using Allied as the elevator subcontractor, would exceed SBA's authority to determine responsibility under Section 8(b) of the Small

Business Act, 15 U.S.C. 637(b), and would undermine the workmanship and safety required by the project. Nonetheless on December 28, 1978, the SBA issued a COC certifying PJR to be a responsible contractor as to capacity and credit.

On January 5, 1979, Baranello protested to GAO asserting that the COC was not conclusive on GAO and that award to PJR would be prejudicial to Baranello.

Discussion

"Responsibility" is a term of art employed in Federal procurement and refers to a proposed contractor's apparent "ability" or "capacity" to perform all of the contract's requirements within the limitations prescribed in the solicitation (see *National Technical Services, Inc.*, B–191096, Feb. 16, 1978, 78–1 CPD 138; *Empire Manufacturing Company, Incorporated*, B–180433, February 8, 1974, 74–1 CPD 60), and a contracting officer may not award a Federal contract unless he is able to determine that the prospective contractor is "responsible." FPR § 1–1.1204–1 (1964 ed.). FPR § 1–1.1203 sets forth various standards which a prospective contractor must meet prior to being found responsible and included therein is the following provision:

> When the situation warrants, contracting officers shall develop * * * special standards of responsibility to be applicable to a particular procurement or class of procurements. Such special standards may be particularly desirable where a history of unsatisfactory performance has demonstrated the need for insuring the existence of unusual expertise or specialized facilities necessary for adequate contract performance. The resulting standards shall form a part of the solicitation and shall be applicable to all bidders or offerors. FPR § 1–1.1203–3.

To the extent these "special standards" involve specific and objective responsibility criteria they have been characterized as "definitive responsibility criteria" compliance with which is a necessary prerequisite to award, i.e., they cannot be waived *by the contracting officer*. See *Data Test Corporation*, 54 Comp. Gen. 499 (1974), 74–2 CPD 365; *Oceanside Mortuary*, B–186204, July 23, 1976, 76–2 CPD 74. "Compliance," however, does not necessarily mean literal compliance with the specific letter of such definitive criteria, as a bidder may be able to demonstrate experience equivalent to that specified in the solicitation through the experience of its officers and employees. See *Haughton Elevator Division Reliance Electric Corporation*, 55 Comp. Gen. 1051 (1976), 76–1 CPD 294. In this respect, we believe that the experience requirements set forth in the "Competency of Bidder" clause should be regarded as "definitive responsibility criteria," and we have so regarded them on prior occasions where the same or substantially similar provisions have been included in the solicitation. *E.g., George Hyman Construction Company of Georgia*, B–186279, November 11, 1976, 76–2 CPD 401.

On the other hand, the concept of the *responsiveness* of a bid concerns whether a bidder has unequivocally offered to provide the requested items in total conformance with the terms and specifications of the invitation. This determination must be made from the bid documents as of the time of opening. *Lift Power Inc.*, B–182604, January 10, 1975, 75–1 CPD 13. A bid which takes no exception to the requirements of the invitation is responsive, i.e., it complies with all material requirements of the invitation. FPR § 1–2.301. In other words, where the bidder has promised to deliver exactly what was called for in the invitation, within the time periods specified, and in accordance with the terms and conditions of the invitation, the bid is responsive. Thus the question of the application of regulations requiring that bids *"materially conform* to the specifications" of the IFB is a question of *responsiveness* although whether the bidder is able to perform in accordance with those specifications is a question of responsibility. In this respect the responsiveness of the PJR bid is not in issue, as there is no claim that PJR took exception to any of the terms and conditions of the IFB. The question for consideration is therefore PJR's responsibility.

GAO will not review protests against affirmative determinations of responsibility unless fraud is alleged on the part of procuring officials or the solicitation contains definitive responsibility criteria which allegedly have not been met. *Edmac Associates, Inc.*, B–184469, January 30, 1976, 76–1 CPD 68. Thus, as this protest deals with the precise factors with which this Office is ordinarily concerned in these cases— Allied's alleged inability to met the definitive responsibility criteria— we would normally review Baranello's protest. However, where, as here, a small business has originally been found not responsible because it did not meet the definitive responsibility criteria and the basis for the contracting officer's subsequent affirmative determination of responsibility rests solely on the COC issued by the SBA, there are different considerations involved, since the statutory authority of the SBA to certify the responsibility of a small business bidder is called into question.

Prior to the 1977 amendments, the Small Business Act, 15 U.S.C. § 637(b) (1976), provided that:

(b) It shall * * * be the duty of the [Small Business] Administration and it is hereby empowered, whenever it determines such action is necessary—
(7) to certify to Government procurement officers * * * with respect to the competency, as to capacity and credit, of any small-business concern * * * to perform a specific Government contract. In any case in which a small-business concern * * * has been certified by or under the authority of the Administration to be a competent Government contractor with respect to capacity and credit as to a specific contract, the officers of the Government having procurement * * * powers are directed to accept such certification as conclusive, and are authorized to let such * * * contract to such concern without requiring it to meet any other requirement with respect to capacity and credit.

FPR § 1–1.708–1 defines "capacity" to mean:

the overall ability of a prospective small business contractor to meet quality, quantity and time requirements of a proposed contract and includes the ability to perform, organisation, experience, technical knowledge, skills, "know-how", technical equipment and facilities.

We believe a reasonable reading of the FPR definition of "capacity" cannot be fairly interpreted to exclude "special conditions of responsibility," i.e., the "definitive criteria" in this case. Moreover, the 1977 amendments to the Small Business Act, *supra*, expanded SBA's authority to conclusively determine *all* areas of responsibility, "including, but not limited to capability, competency, capacity, credit, integrity, perseverance, and tenacity * * *."

Under prior versions of the Small Business Act, we have concluded that a COC *will* overcome the special experience requirements specified in a solicitation. *See* 40 Comp. Gen. 106 (1960) ; B–163671, July 18, 1968. Thus we have consistently declined to review SBA determinations of responsibility absent a prima facie showing that such action was taken fraudulently or with such willful disregard of the facts as to imply bad faith. *E.g., Dyneteria, Inc.*, 55 Comp. Gen. 97 (1975), 75–2 CPD 36, because *even if we disagreed* with the SBA's determinations those judgments are *conclusive* on the contracting officers *by law. Electro Systems Corp.*, B–190640, December 14, 1977, 77–2 CPD 462.

Implicit in the foregoing is the conclusive nature of the COC on GAO, because we could *not* recommend the agency find a small business bidder nonresponsible in the face of a COC, notwithstanding any independent conclusions we might reach in a given procurement. Thus, where no question of fraud is involved, our recommendations would be limited to suggesting that the agency request SBA to reconsider its decision if the record indicates that certain vital information bearing on a small business bidder's responsibility had not been considered by SBA. *Kepner Plastic Fabricators, Inc.*, B–184394, June 1, 1976, 76–1 CPD 351. Here there is no suggestion that SBA's determination was taken fraudulently, and the record clearly indicates that SBA considered the definitive responsibility criteria fully in arriving at its determination.

In analoguous situations, i.e, those dealing with the statutory authority of the Secretary of Labor to determine the applicability of the Service Contract Act (SCA), 41 U.S.C. 351 *et seq.* (1976), we have held that:

[T]he Secretary of Labor has been regarded as having primary responsibility for administering and interpreting the SCA, so that to the extent there is a disagreement between DOL [Department of Labor] and the contracting agency over the application of the SCA to a particular contract * * * DOL's views must prevail, "unless they are clearly contrary to law." *B.B. Saxon Company*, 57 Comp. Gen. 501 (1978), 78–1 CPD 410.

Thus, even where we concluded that the Secretary's policy in arriving at his wage rate determinations was questionable in view of the legislative history of the SCA, we nonetheless concluded that the determination *must* prevail because they were not "clearly contrary to law." *The Cage Company of Abilene, Inc.*, 57 Comp. Gen. 549 (1978), 78–1 CPD 430.

We believe the SBA's authority to issue COCs must be similarly viewed. In this respect, we are aware of no limitation on the SBA's authority which would bind that agency to the actual requirements of a Competency of Bidder's clause. Hence, in our opinion, notwithstanding the contracting officer's disagreement over SBA's application of the Competency of Bidders clause to the facts of this case, the issuance of the COC in this case must be viewed as conclusive. Consequently, contracting agencies cannot overcome SBA's statutory authority to make these responsibility determinations as regards to small business concerns by specifying the "special standards" or "definitive criteria" of responsibility in the invitation. *See* 40 Comp. Gen., *supra*.

As a final matter, we note that Baranello refused to extend its bid beyond its December 29, 1978, expiration date. Under these circumstances, this Office would ordinarily consider the challenge to PJR's responsibility as academic and would dismiss the protest. See *Risi Industries, Inc., et al.*, B–191024, April 27, 1978, 78–1 CPD 329. However, rather than seek award of the contract under the IFB, Baranello "amended" its protest to request either that the requirement be readvertised, or that in the alternative, if award were to be made to PJR, "it be a condition of the award that PJR use a qualified subcontractor for elevators other than Allied."

[B–193045]

Bidders—Responsibility *v.* Bid Responsiveness—Site Visits

Where bid does not take exception to Government's requirements, bidder's failure to make mandatory prebid site inspection does not justify bid rejection as "nonresponsive," since acceptance of bid would effectively bind bidder to perform at bid price in accordance with advertised terms and specifications. However, such failure may be considered by contracting officer in determining whether bidder is responsible, i.e., whether bidder is able to so perform. Reconsideration of decision in 58 Comp. Gen. 214.

In the matter of Edw. Kocharian & Company, Inc.—request for modification, May 10, 1979:

The Defense Mapping Agency (DMA) requests that we modify our decision in *Edw. Kocharian & Company, Inc.*, 58 Comp. Gen. 214 (1979), 79–1 CPD 20, in which we sustained a protest by Edw. Kocharian & Company against DMA's rejection of that firm's bid under invitation for bids (IFB) No. DMA 800–78–B–0052.

The IFB, which solicited bids to replace four air-handling units at the DMA Topographic Center, stated that a site inspection was "mandatory," and cautioned that a prospective bidder's failure to make the mandatory site inspection would result in rejection of the bid as nonresponsive. Although Kocharian was the apparent low bidder, the contracting officer determined that the firm did not comply with the site inspection requirement, and proposed to reject the bid as nonresponsive.

We stated in our decision:

* * * provisions giving bidders the opportunity to visit a worksite and urging them to do so [see also Defense Acquisition Regulation (DAR) § 18–204 (1976 ed.)] are designed to warn bidders that site conditions could affect the cost of contract performance and to protect the Government from the necessity of permitting the withdrawal of a bid submitted by a firm that failed to inspect, or a claim by such firm after award of the contract.

The test to be applied in determining the "responsiveness" of a bid, however, is whether the bid as submitted is an offer to perform, without exception, the exact thing called for in the invitation. 49 Comp. Gen. 553, 556 (1970). If the test is met, the bidder is effectively bound to perform in accordance with the invitation's requirements, see 42 Comp. Gen. 464 (1963), and we do not see how a failure to make a prebid site inspection would define or limit that obligation. To the extent that a site inspection affects the bidder's price * * * it does so only in the context of that price's reflection of the bidder's business judgment as to his performance cost; it does not affect the obligation to perform at the price bid.

In fact, we see no difference between the above-stated purposes for recommending prebid site inspections and those proffered by DMA for making the inspection mandatory, notwithstanding that DMA distinguishes its rationale in the present case as being based on a desire for "informed, intelligent mutuality of assent" as opposed to "mutuality based on a promise instinct with a waiver." Whether expressed in mandatory terms or not, the provision is viewed as advising bidders that they bear the risk of problems that could have been resolved by a reasonable prebid site inspection. See 52 Comp. Gen. 389, 391 (1972).

Accordingly, we concluded that the prebid site inspection requirement provided no basis for disqualifying Kocharian from the competition, and recommended that award be made to the firm, if otherwise appropriate. In addition, since we had been advised that mandatory prebid site inspection had become a standard requirement in all IFB's issued from DMA's Engineering Division, Facilities Engineering Office, we advised the Director of DMA of our view by separate letter. The contract subsequently was awarded to Kocharian.

In its request for modification, DMA contends that the test of "responsiveness" as stated in our January 15 decision "is not an absolute test in that many prior decisions rejected protests [against the rejection of bids as 'non-responsive'] concerning other characteristics of an IFB." "Other characteristics" cited by DMA include the failure to provide a bid bond at bid opening; submission of a bid bond improper on its face; and failure to provide descriptive data with a bid even though offering to perform, without exception, the exact thing called for in the IFB. DMA argues that it "cannot discover how * * * the bidders' 'obligations to perform' were diminished or their 'assumptions of risk of performance' were dispelled. Yet they were determined to be non-responsive."

In view thereof, DMA suggests that a prebid site inspection may in fact be an appropriate responsiveness factor notwithstanding the stated test, if determined by the procuring activity to be necessary to the submission of an "informed" bid. DMA concedes that inclusion in an IFB of a mandatory prebid site inspection should not be a standard matter. However, DMA contends that there are circumstances in which such inclusion represents a legitimate exercise of a contracting agency's discretion to determine what is reasonably necessary to meet its needs in the manner most advantageous to the Government. Those circumstances are essentially where DMA can foresee probable delays in performance by contractors who did not visit the construction site before bidding, which are caused by matters that would have been noted in prebid site inspections. Such delays result in otherwise unnecessary cost to the Government due to unavailability of the facility, as well as administrative inconvenience, notwithstanding the contractor's obligation to perform at the contract price. DMA is concerned that, although prebid site inspection does not *necessarily* result in problem-free performance, it reduces the possibility of problems arising by virtue of otherwise unexpected site conditions.

DMA is correct that we have held that certain factors which evidently do not affect a bidder's obligation to perform may have an impact on the bid's responsiveness. However, in each situation cited by DMA there is a consideration not present regarding site inspection.

Waiver of a bid bond requirement or of a failure to submit a proper bid bond would make it possible for a bidder to decide after opening whether or not to have its bid rejected, cause undue delay in effecting procurements, and create, by the necessary subjective determinations by different contracting officers whether waiver is appropriate, inconsistencies in the treatment of bidders. 38 Comp. Gen. 532, 536 (1959). A blanket offer to comply with an IFB's requirements is not sufficient to overcome a failure to supply descriptive literature with the bid, to be used for bid evaluation, because such descriptive literature is necessary for the Government to be able to determine exactly what the bidder is offering, and whether the product offered meets the IFB's specifications. 36 Comp. Gen. 415 (1956). Other factors that similarly may cause the rejection of a bid as nonresponsive involve comparable considerations: failure to submit with a bid a required list of proposed subcontractors (to prevent "bid shopping," 50 Comp. Gen. 839, 842 (1971)): failure to indicate in a bid for construction work that a certain specified minimum percentage of the work will be performed by the bidder's own forces (to prevent "brokering," see 45 Comp. Gen. 177 (1965)); conditioning a bid on payment provisions differing from those contained in the IFB (would modify the legal obligations of the parties concerning payment under the contract, contrary to the express terms of the invitation, 47 Comp. Gen. 496, 499 (1968)).

However, consideration of a bid submitted by a firm that did not inspect the construction site does not pose the same prejudice to the competitive bid system or to the contracting agency's mission as do the above factors. As long as a bidder is given the *opportunity* to visit a worksite and *warned* that site conditions could affect the cost of performance (see DAR § 18–204 (1976 ed.), and paragraph 2 of Standard Form 22, "Instructions to Bidders"), the bid price is in effect presumed by law to include consideration of the effects of observable site conditions. *Blauner Constr. Co. v. U.S.*, 94 Ct. Cl. 503 (1941). Thus, the low bidder who has not inspected the site cannot, without consequences such as forfeiture of a bond or incurring excess reprocurement costs, after bid opening withdraw its bid, or after contract award stop work or claim additional money, by contending that it is encountering or will encounter problems at the site, if such problems would have been mitigated by a prebid site inspection.

We remain of the same view regarding prebid site inspections in relation to "responsiveness" as that expressed in our earlier decision and it is therefore affirmed.

However, in view of DMA's concern as reflected above, and its apparent belief that it is our position that award must be made to the low bidder notwithstanding the bidder's failure to make a prebid site inspection, we offer the following comments.

DAR section 1, part 9 (1976 ed.), entitled "Responsible Prospective Contractors," provides at § 1–902:

General Policy
 * * * The award of a contract to a supplier based on lowest evaluated price alone can be false economy if there is subsequent default, late deliveries, or other unsatisfactory performance resulting in additional procurement or administrative costs. * * *

We believe that such provision reflects the same concern as that expressed by DMA in the instant request. Because of that concern, DAR § 1–902 (1976 ed.) requires that a prospective contractor must demonstrate affirmatively his "responsibility," i.e., the apparent ability to successfully meet the contract requirements, before being awarded the contract. DAR § 1–903 (1976 ed.) prescribes certain minimum standards for responsible prospective contractors. DAR § 1–903.1 (1976 ed.) sets out general responsibility standards, including adequate financial resources; ability to comply with the performance schedule; and satisfactory records of performance and integrity. DAR § 1–903.2 (1976 ed.) provides additional standards for certain contracts, including construction contracts: "the necessary organization, experience, operational controls and technical skills, or ability to obtain them," and "the necessary production, construction, and technical equipment and facilities, or the ability to obtain them."

Thus, the appropriate time to judge whether the firm that did not inspect the construction site before bidding would be able to perform the contract in a timely manner at the contract price is during the responsibility survey. The contracting officer either may decide that failure to inspect is reflected in the bid price to the extent that the firm cannot perform satisfactorily, or he may still find the firm responsible. In fact, the contracting officer may determine a firm that *did* visit the site before submitting its bid to be nonresponsible notwithstanding such visit. To the extent that DMA is concerned that it may determine responsible a firm that did not inspect the site, and the firm may nevertheless encounter problems because of site conditions, we can only point out that the projection of a bidder's ability to perform if awarded a contract is largely within the sound administrative discretion of the contracting officer. The basis therefor is precisely because he is in the best position to assess responsibility, and must bear the consequences of any difficulties experienced by reason of the contractor's inability to perform in the time and manner required. 51 Comp. Gen. 448, 452 (1972). We will not question a contracting officer's determination of nonresponsibility absent a showing of either bad faith or that it lacked a reasonable basis. *Hydromatics International Corporation*, B–181240, September 4, 1974, 74–2 CPD 142.

〔B–193497〕

Contracts—Negotiation—Conflict of Interest Prohibitions—Applicability—Non-Profit Organizations

Where offeror has individual and corporate ties with gas and oil industry, agency rejection of proposal for services to assist agency review of gas curtailment because of organizational conflict of interest is sustained. Offeror's status as not-for-profit, tax exempt organization does not preclude agency determination that conflict of interest does or might exist.

In the matter of Institute of Gas Technology, May 10, 1979:

The Institute of Gas Technology (IGT) protests the refusal by the Department of Energy (DOE) to consider its proposal for award under request for proposals (RFP) No. EB–78–C–01–6363 for technical consulting and management support services to assist the Economic Regulatory Administration review the present natural gas curtailment approach, and, if necessary, the establishment of a modified curtailment priority system for interstate pipelines. DOE disqualified IGT and awarded the contract to another firm because it determined that conflicts of interest existed for IGT and its proposed subcontractor.

The RFP set forth as qualification criteria requirements relating to organizational conflicts of interest. DOE states that it attempted to fully implement the special statutory conflict of interest disclosure requirements applicable to the Department (see 15 U.S.C. § 789 (Supp. 1979) ; 42 U.S.C. § 5918 (Supp. 1979)). To this end, DOE considers that portion of Energy Research and Development Administration (ERDA) (one of DOE's predecessor agencies) Procurement Regulations relating to the avoidance of organizational conflicts of interests to have been applicable to this procurement. Under the above authority, the Department is prohibited from entering into technical and management support service contracts unless it finds, after evaluating all information disclosed by the offeror, that (1) it is unlikely that a conflict of interest would exist, (2) such conflict has been avoided, or (3) it is in the best interest of the United States to do so. See, e.g., 15 U.S.C. § 789(b).

The RFP required the submission of a disclosure statement regarding organizational conflicts of interest, a necessary prerequisite for consideration of the offeror's proposal. According to DOE, due to the sensitivity of the work to be done, the following paragraph was added :

(5) Special Disclosure Regarding Performance of Related Studies For Public or Private Organizations. Offerors are advised that the Department considers the question of natural gas curtailment priorities to be a most sensitive matter requiring the utmost in care to avoid either the possibility of bias or the appearance of bias. It is, therefore, the Government's intent by separate disclosure to ascertain in the fullest extent possible whether offerors have performed any studies for organizations which could be construed in any manner as affecting the offeror's ability to render impartial, technical, sound, and objective assistance or advice. The offer shall, therefore, provide a separate statement which discloses all relevant facts concerning any studies, to include analysis, data collection, and other similar work, dealing either in whole or in part, with natural gas curtailment, energy user priorities, natural gas supplies, natural gas substitution, or related maters, performed during the three years prior to the issuance of this solicitation, presently being performed, or presently being considered for performance in any manner. All such studies are to be disclosed by providing a brief description of the study, whether performed for public or private organizations, together with the identity of the client organization. Offerors are advised to interpret this requirement in the broadest reasonable manner possible should there be any question of applicability of this disclosure requirement to a given situation. In addition, offerors are to briefly describe any corporate financial or other special affiliation of continuous relationship with oil, gas, or energy industry firm or associates thereof.

The Department believes that an actual or potential conflict of interest existed because of IGT's close corporate ties with the natural gas industry. The recommendation to disqualify IGT states that many members of IGT's board of trustees, which governs the organization, and a majority of its executive committee include officials of gas and oil companies. In addition, some gas industry members sponsor research projects through IGT by contributions which totalled $710,-000 in 1977 from 184 corporate members. In this connection, DOE states:

It was and is DOE's belief that IGT's membership of its board of trustees which governs the organization could subtly influence the study on natural gas curtailment priorities. The fact that the board of trustees includes a large number of gas industry officials as well as the gas industry's sponsoring of research through IGT creates the appearance of a conflict of interest and also opens the possibility for gas industry officials to influence the outcome of planned projects in the statement of work in order to gain a more favorable gas allocation. In addition, the relationship of the gas industry and IGT would give rise to the questioning of the validity of the study by those most affected by its outcome. The public perception of this relationship could render the study worthless.

IGT argues that its disqualification is an improper and arbitrary action based upon DOE's faulty interpretation of IGT's purpose and operational constraints. IGT alleges that it is a not-for-profit organization under state law and is required to operate for public rather than private benefit by its charter, state law and the Internal Revenue Service, citing 26 U.S.C. § 501(c)(3). Therefore, it cannot have a conflict of interest in matters pertaining to the public interest. The protester argues further that DOE did not consider fully these constraints or IGT's record of complete freedom of scientific inquiry without improper outside influence on gas matters.

We have recognized that procuring activities have a legitimate interest in protecting the Government from the bias that might result from awarding a contract to a firm having an organizational conflict of interest. See *Planning Research Corporation Public Management Services, Inc.*, 55 Comp. Gen. 911 (1976), 76–1 CPD 202. At the same time, because it is a general policy of the Federal Government to allow all interested qualified parties an opportunity to participate in its procurement in order to maximize competition unless there is a clearly supportable reason for excluding a firm, we recognize that a firm should not be excluded from competition simply on the basis of a theoretical conflict of interest. *PRC Computer Center Inc.; On-Line Systems, Inc.; Remote Computing Corporation; Optimum Systems, Inc.*, 55 Comp. Gen. 60 (1975), 75–2 CPD 35.

Furthermore, the determination as to whether a sufficient possibility exists that an award to a particular firm would result in an organizational conflict of interest must be made by the procuring activity, with which lies the responsibility for balancing the Government's competing interest in (1) preventing bias in the performance of certain contracts which would result from a conflict of interest and (2) awarding a contract that will best serve the Government's needs to the most qualified firm. See *Planning Research Corporation Inc.*, *supra*.

The regulation applied by the agency stated that "The ultimate test should always be: is the contractor placed in a position where its judgment may be biased, or where it has an unfair competitive advantage?" ERDA Procurement Regulations § 9–1.5406(a). We believe the agency's affirmative answer to this question has not been shown to have been an unreasonable abuse of discretion in the circumstances. We do not find unreasonable DOE's determination that the individual and corporate composition of the protester could "subtly influence" the gas curtailment study.

DOE's conclusion does not require, as the protester suggests, that DOE presume that IGT's trustees or executive committee would willfully violate the various fiduciary duties imposed upon them. That the composition of the board of trustees would harm the public perception of the study, rendering it worthless, is viewed as a valid major concern of the agency. In addition, IGT's brochure which IGT offered to us as evidence of the nature of the protester, states that the organization's work is done "in the best interest of the *industry* and the general public." [Italic supplied.] The brochure also states that, for nonsponsored activities, IGT depends on the support of its members, more than half of which are utility companies. We believe that the combination of these factors could call into question IGT's objectivity in performing a contract that could significantly affect the gas industry.

Furthermore, the regulations applied by DOE were designed to avoid placing a contractor in a position where its judgment might be biased, or where there would be an unfair competitive advantage. ERDA PR § 9–1.5402(b) exempts some not-for-profit organizations and educational institutions from those parts of the rules which pertain to unfair competitive advantage except in unusual or specific situations identified by contracting officers. Such organizations are not excepted, however, from the conflict of interest regulations which relate to bias. Thus, the regulations recognize that a not-for-profit organization can have a conflict of interest. In this regard DOE's recent issuance of permanent procedures to avoid organizational conflicts of interest specifically eliminated any further exclusion for firms similar to that in the predecessor ERDA PR. This was explained as follows:

(1) Exclusion of Independent Contract Research Organizations (ICRO) and Universities. It was recommended by some commenters that ICRO's and universities be specifically excluded from OCI coverage. One commenter stated that such organizations should not be excluded from OCI coverage. The Department has adopted the latter position because it believes that ICROs and universities are not immune from being in the position of serving two masters or from gaining an unfair competitive advantage. Neither Pub. L. 95–39 (42 U.S.C. § 5918) nor Pub. L. 95–70 (15 U.S.C. § 789) provides for the exclusion of such organizations and the Department does not believe that such exclusion was the intent of Congress. Additionally, OFPP's (Office of Federal Procurement Policy) revised proposed rule does not exclude such organizations from coverage. 44 Fed. Reg. 2556 (1979).

In addition, we agree with DOE's statement that the fact that IGT is organized under 26 U.S.C. § 501(c)(3) does not prevent application by DOE of its organizational conflict of interest statutes and regulations here.

IGT's allegation that DOE failed to consider fully the statutory and regulatory constraints on IGT to act in the public interest is not supported by the record. The protester submits no evidence for this statement, and we cannot assume that DOE ignored the disclosure statement in IGT's proposal. Moreover, DOE states that the decision to disqualify IGT "was made with a good deal of thought and effort pursuant to the information submitted by IGT."

IGT seeks to avoid future summary rulings by Government procuring agencies that the business affiliations of its trustees or sources of funds are by and of themselves a sufficient basis for its disqualification without complete consideration of all circumstances in specific procurements. We observe that DOE is required to make independent evaluations based on disclosure statements provided for each procurement and to consider the specific circumstances based on all relevant information.

In view of the foregoing, we find it unnecessary to address IGT's protest against disqualification of its subcontractor for failure to comply with the conflict of interest provisions in the RFP.

Protest denied.

[B-193812]

Appropriations—Agriculture Department—Federal Aid, Grants, etc.—State Matching Contributions

Since 1967, Department of Agriculture has interpreted annual appropriation provision requiring "minimum matching by any State of at least 40 per centum" as allowing accumulation of all contributions by a State since 1963 to determine if matching requirement for brucellosis program has been met. For 1979, provision was changed to require matching "by the States" on a 60/40 basis. Agriculture believes this change authorizes aggregation of all State contributions since 1963 rather than on State-by-State basis. Provisions in annual appropriation acts, unless otherwise provided, apply only to that fiscal year and neither language nor legislative history of these provisions support Agriculture's interpretation. However, in view of longstanding practice we will not object to this practice for this year.

In the matter of State Matching Requirement—Brucellosis Eradication Program, May 10, 1979:

The Secretary of Agriculture has requested a decision on whether, to comply with the matching requirement imposed on the States by the act making appropriations for Agriculture, Rural Development and Related Agencies programs for fiscal year 1979, Pub. L. No. 95-

448, October 11, 1978, 92 Stat. 1073, 1076, the contribution of all States from 1963 to date may be aggregated to determine whether, collectively, the States have contributed 40 percent of the total expenditures for the brucellosis eradication program.

Beginning in 1967, identical language contained in annual appropriation acts for fiscal years 1963 through 1978 was interpreted as requiring each individual State to have contributed 40 percent of the cost of the program in that State on a cumulative basis over those years. The 1979 appropriation act made a change in the language of prior appropriation acts with regard to determining the required percentage of the States matching share. For the reasons discussed below, we agree that the effect of the new language is to authorize an aggregation of the contributions of all of the States for the years 1963 to 1979 inclusive in determining whether the requirement for State matching has been met.

Section 11 of the Act of May 29, 1884, as amended, 21 U.S.C. § 114a (1976), authorizes the Secretary of Agriculture, either independently or in cooperation with, among others, the States, to control and eradicate any communicable disease of livestock or poultry, including brucellosis. Pursuant to this authorizing legislation, the Animal and Plant Health Inspection Service of the Department of Agriculture participates with the States in a cooperative program to eradicate brucellosis. For fiscal years 1963 to 1978, Congress appropriated funds for the Department to engage in this program with the following limitation in the appropriation acts:

Provided further, That no funds shall be used to formulate or administer brucellosis eradication programs for the current fiscal year that does not require a minimum matching *by any State* of at least 40 per centum. [Italic supplied.] See, e.g., Pub. L. No. 95-97, August 12, 1977, 91 Stat. 810.

The purpose of the matching funds provision was to accelerate the effort of States that were not contributing enough to the brucellosis eradication program. S. Rept. No. 1407, 86th Cong., 2d Sess., 4 (1960).

In his submission, the Secretary of Agriculture explains that in each State, the cooperative eradication program is a multi-year operation designed to continue until the disease is eradicated. The program's progress in one year directly affects its progress in subsequent years. Further, the disease is highly infectious, and its existence in one State is a threat to other States. Some States, including those with the greatest brucellosis problem, had contributed in early years of the program more than 40 percent of the program cost but were not able to continue 40 percent funding of accelerated programs in later years.

Initially, each State was required to provide its 40 percent matching share on the basis of the cost of the program in that State for each fiscal year. The Secretary states that in 1966 and 1967, several members of Congress initiated an exchange of letters regarding the method the Department should use to compute the matching requirement. In 1967, after a program and legal review, the Department agreed with the Congressmen's recommendations and began to compute the 60/40 cost sharing requirement on a cumulative basis for each State, beginning with fiscal year 1963 (the year the matching provision first became effective). Determining cost on a cumulative basis meant that the Department would consider each State's contributions from 1963 on. If a State had contributed in the aggregate from 1963 to the current fiscal year at least 40 percent of the cost of the brucellosis eradication program in that State, the matching requirement was considered satisfied.

Congress changed the language it had used in the proviso for fiscal years 1963 through 1978 in the appropriation act for 1979, *supra*, 92 Stat. at 1076, to read:

> *Provided further,* That no funds shall be used to formulate or administer a brucellosis eradication program for the current fiscal year that does not require minimum matching *by the States* of at least 40 per centum. [Italic supplied.]

The change in the language of the proviso from "by any State" to "by the States" was explained by the House Committee on Appropriations as follows:

> 8. *Animal and Plant Health Inspection Service.* Language has been carried in the annual appropriation bill for a number of years to require that States provide funds for matching—not otherwise required by law—of at least 40 percent of the cost of the brucellosis eradication program. This provision assures more effective program operations through State cost-sharing, with resulting savings to the Federal budget. The usual language has been slightly modified this year to allow accelerated Federal effort in selected States without being delayed by waiting for State funding to catch up. H.R. Rep. No. 95–1290, 95th Cong., 2d Sess. 108 (1978).

The Secretary of Agriculture contends that the only purpose of the change is to require that the contributions of all States from 1963 to date be aggregated to determine whether collectively they have contributed at least 40 percent of the cost of the total eradication program. This means that as long as the 40 percent matching requirement is met by the States collectively, a State that contributed less than 40 percent, or even nothing at all in any given year, could receive funding from the Department of Agriculture for its brucellosis eradication program.

The matching requirement has been contained in the Department's annual appropriation act which normally applies only to a single year's funds. There is no statutory provision which specifically authorizes cumulation or aggregation of the State's prior years contributions. In addition, the legislative history of the original appropriations act containing the first matching proviso does not indicate an intent to authorize aggregation of a State's contribution nor has the Department made us aware, formally or informally, of any significant legislative history (such as committee reports) in later years in which this practice is discussed and approved.

Nevertheless, the Department of Agriculture has been computing the States' contributions in this manner since 1967. As the Secretary points out, an established rule of statutory construction is that in determining the meaning of statutory language, great deference is to be given to the consistent interpretation thereof by those individuals responsible for the administration of the statute in question. *See, e.g., Udall v. Tallman,* 380 U.S. 1, 16 (1965). Further, according to the Secretary, since 1967, the Department of Agriculture has regularly informed Congress of its policy of cumulating matching funds under the proviso in the appropriation acts, and no objection was made.

The Department of Agriculture now proposes to continue its practice of cumulating matching funds from the inception of the program in 1963 to date except that it feels that it can now aggregate all State contributions as a result of the 1979 language instead of cumulating them on a State by State basis.

We have some difficulty with Agriculture's position. We agree with its view that the change in language in the 1979 appropriation act was intended to permit the Secretary to lump the contributions of all States together (rather than viewing each State's contribution separately) to meet the forty percent matching requirement. This view can be supported by the language and legislative history of that provision. However, nothing in the act or its history specifically indicates that this totaling of all State contributions is to include anything but contributions made in 1979.

There is nothing in the language of the provision which was used for fiscal years 1963 to 1978 inclusive, or in the 1979 provision which authorizes aggregating matching funds over the entire period that the program has been in operation. Further, insofar as we are aware, there is nothing in the committee reports or other cognizable legislative history which indicates an intent that this be done. Although specific committees may have been aware of the practice, there is no evidence in the legislative history that the Congress as a whole was aware that, as a result of the Administration's interpretation, some States were not being required to meet the 40 percent matching requirement for each year that the program was in effect.

Again, we feel that the intent of the modified appropriation language for FY–1979, as expressed in House Report 95–1290, June 13, 1978, "to allow accelerated Federal effort in selected States without waiting for State funding to catch up," is satisfied by aggregating all State contributions for the fiscal year in question instead of requiring each State to supply a full 40 percent of its own program costs in a year when State funds for this purpose may be in short supply.

On the other hand, we recognize that the literal interpretation we are suggesting should be followed, in the absence of evidence of a contrary congressional intent, does not take into account the contributions, over and above the required matching share, which various States may have made in prior years. Under the proposed interpretation and viewing the eradication program as a continuing, multi-year project, it cannot be said that the Federal Government has or will be obliged to assume more than its statutorily limited share of the total costs of the program. For these reasons, and in view of the longstanding administrative practice of aggregating costs and contributions, we will not object to the Secretary's proposed interpretation for fiscal year 1979. However, we urge the Department to seek congressional clarification of the scope of the matching requirement for application in future years.

[B-193608]

Military Personnel — Record Correction — Retirement Status — Disability in Lieu of Years of Service—Income Tax Refund

Where military records are corrected under 10 U.S.C. 1552 to show a portion of taxable retired pay as tax exempt disability retired pay, the claimant may be paid, under 10 U.S.C. 1552(c), the amounts of pay withheld for income taxes by the Air Force in years for which the Internal Revenue Service is barred from making tax refunds by the applicable statute of limitations. However, while 10 U.S.C. 1552(c) provides for certain types of payments pursuant to correction of military records, it does not authorize payment for tax refunds in derogation of the Internal Revenue Code statute of limitations beyond monies withheld for taxes by the military department concerned.

In the matter of Colonel Major T. Martin, USAF, Retired, May 14, 1979:

This action is in response to a letter from Mr. H. Dudley Payne, attorney for Colonel Major T. Martin, USAF, Retired, appealing the April 14, 1978 settlement of our Claims Division which disallowed Colonel Martin's claim for recovery of amounts he paid in State and Federal income taxes as a result of his military retired pay being classified as nondisability during 1960 through 1973. His claim results from correction of his military record under 10 U.S.C. 1552 (1976) to show that he was retired for disability rather than for length of service. On the basis of the following, we sustain the settlement action.

On March 10, 1977, the Secretary of the Air Force, based on the recommendation of the Air Force Board for Correction of Military Records, corrected Colonel Martin's military records to show a disability retirement from the Air Force with a compensable rating of 60 percent retroactive to March 30, 1960. Because of the tax advantage of disability retirement, Colonel Martin received income tax refunds from the Internal Revenue Service for Federal taxes and from the

State of Virginia, his residence for State taxes, retroactive through 1974. However, applicable Federal and State statutes of limitations on refunds barred additional tax refunds for the years 1960 through 1973.

Since he is precluded from receiving further tax refunds, he claims the amounts he indicates he paid in excess taxes during the years 1960–1973 as "pecuniary benefits" payable pursuant to 10 U.S.C. 1552(c). The amounts claimed are $9,022.47 paid in Federal taxes, and $1,523.62 paid in State taxes, plus interest at the rate of 6 percent.

The Air Force has proposed to pay Colonel Martin $571.97, representing the amount the Air Force withheld for Federal income tax from his retired pay during the period 1960–1973. State taxes were not withheld by the Air Force.

The Air Force bases its computation of the amount due Colonel Martin on *Ray* v. *United States*, 197 Ct. Cl. 1, 453 F. 2d 754 (1972), and 52 Comp. Gen. 420 (1973), as the amount actually withheld for taxes. Our Claims Division agreed.

Colonel Martin argues that repayment of the withholding will not adequately compensate him for the excess income taxes he paid as a result of his retired pay being subject to taxation which placed him in a higher tax bracket. He was therefore taxed at a higher rate on his total income (including income other than retired pay) than he would have been had his retired pay been properly sheltered from taxes. His claim for refund of a portion of State and Federal taxes paid is based on the difference between what he paid at the higher tax rate resulting from his retired pay not receiving the disability shelter, and the amount he would have paid if more of his earnings had been tax exempt. He states that the *Ray* case supports his request.

Neither *Ray* nor our decision 52 Comp. Gen. 420 ruled on the issue of whether a tax refund claim barred by the Internal Revenue Code statute of limitations could be granted by applying 10 U.S.C. 1552(c).

The question in this case is, in essence, whether the exposure to increased tax liability when not adequately compensated by refund of the withholding is claimable under 10 U.S.C. 1552.

Under 10 U.S.C. 1552(a) the Secretary of a military department, acting through a civilian board, may correct a military record to correct an error or remove an injustice. Upon such a correction under 10 U.S.C. 1552(c) the department concerned may pay "from applicable current appropriations, a claim for the loss of pay, allowances, compensation, emoluments, or other pecuniary benefits * * *."

In *Ray* the court noted that the withholding refunded to the claimant approximated the money he would have been entitled to had the records been corrected initially. The court stated that the case was "simply a matter of correcting the pay account between the serviceman and the United States. " The claim was not one for a tax refund, but for "pecuniary benefits" wrongfully denied. *Ray* v. *United States*, 197 Ct. Cl. 1, 9.

The "pecuniary benefits" were limited to a refund of the withholding. Overall recalculation of income tax liability, which Colonel Martin requests in his claim, was not an issue before the court. *Ray, supra*, p. 10. The court expressly cautioned against unlimited application of 10 U.S.C. 1552 to provide relief from any perceived wrong flowing from correction of erroneous records. It did not intend to "intimate any roving delegation to us or anyone else, to remedy the indirect consequences of an erroneous record." *Ray, supra*, p. 9. The *Ray* decision focused only on the relationship of the withholding to the retired pay, not to other income sources. *Ray, supra*, p. 8. The court appears to suggest that the overall tax liability problem is an Internal Revenue Service tax matter, not germane to effectuating an administrative remedy under 10 U.S.C. 1552.

In agreeing to follow the holding in *Ray*, we stated in part that we:

* * * have no objection to following the rule in the *Ray* case to the effect that claims for amounts withheld for income tax purposes will be treated as "pecuniary benefits" due the individual within the meaning of 10 U.S.C. 1552(c) rather than a claim for tax refund. However, claims for such amounts should be limited to amounts *withheld* for income taxes in years for which the Internal Revenue Service is barred from making refunds by the applicable statute of limitations. * * * 52 Comp. Gen. 420, 424. [Italic supplied.]

To grant the claimant the tax relief he requests would be to extend the holdings of *Ray* and 52 Comp. Gen. 420 beyond their original intent, and beyond the scope of 10 U.S.C. 1552(c). Therefore, Colonel Martin is entitled only to the money withheld for Federal income taxes by the Air Force for the years 1960–1973. Since no money was withheld for State taxes, he has no valid claim for State tax overpayment from the Air Force.

The 6 percent interest claimed on the money recoverable also may not be allowed. No interest may be allowed in a settlement pursuant to 10 U.S.C. 1552(c) since the statute makes no provision for payment of interest. 52 Comp. Gen. 420, 424.

The settlement by the Claims Division is, therefore, sustained.

[B–194063.2]

Appropriations — Continuing Resolutions — Availability of Funds

Term "current rate for operations" as used in Continuing Resolutions is equivalent to total funds which were available for obligation for program for previous fiscal year. Fiscal year 1979 Continuing Resolution appropriated amount of funds for CETA programs, which, when added to 1978 unobligated balances carried over, equals the total funds that were available for fiscal year 1978, including funds appropriated for fiscal year 1978 by Economic Stimulus Appropriations Act of 1977. B–194063, May 4, 1979, and B–194362, May 1, 1979, distinguished in part.

In the matter of CETA appropriation under 1979 Continuing Resolution, May 14, 1979:

This decision is in response to an inquiry from the Assistant Secretary of Labor for Administration and Management concerning the amount of funds appropriated for Employment and Training Assistance, and Temporary Employment Assistance, by the "Joint Resolution Making continuing appropriations for the fiscal year 1979, and for other purposes," Pub. L. No. 95–482, 92 Stat. 1603, approved October 18, 1978. As expressed by the Assistant Secretary, it is the position of the Department of Labor that the Continuing Resolution appropriated sufficient funds to allow these programs to operate throughout fiscal year 1979 at the "rates of program operations" in effect at the end of fiscal year 1978. For the reasons indicated below, it is our opinion that the fiscal year 1979 Continuing Resolution appropriated only the amount of funds for CETA programs which, when added to unobligated balances carried over from fiscal year 1978, equals the total amount that was available for fiscal year 1978, including funds appropriated for fiscal year 1978 by the Economic Stimulus Appropriations Act of 1977, Pub. L. No. 95–29, 91 Stat. 122, approved May 13, 1977.

The Continuing Resolution, in section 101(a), appropriates:

> Such amounts as may be necessary for continuing the following activities, not otherwise provided for, which were conducted in fiscal year 1978. But at a rate for operations not in excess of the current rate:
>
> *   *   *   *   *   *   *
>
> activities under the Comprehensive Employment and Training Act, *except that such activities shall be continued at a rate for operations not in excess of the lower of the current rate or the rate authorized by S. 2570 as passed the House of Representatives*; * * *. [Italic supplied.]

Upon enactment of the Continuing Resolution, the Department of Labor requested that the Department of the Treasury issue appropriation warrants for fiscal year 1979 in the amounts of $6,769,758,000 for Employment and Training Assistance and $3,474,954,000 for Temporary Employment Assistance. Treasury prepared these warrants and submitted them to this Office for countersignature under the requirement of section 11 of the Act of July 31, 1894, as amended, 31 U.S.C. § 76 (1976), as modified by Department of the Treasury–General Accounting Office Joint Regulation No. 5 (September 16, 1974). Based upon information contained in Treasury workpapers, which accompanied the warrants, we countersigned the warrants.

On March 19, 1979, Labor requested an additional $45,000,000 for the Employment and Training Assistance acccunt. At a meeting held to discuss this request with representatives of Labor, Treasury, and

GAO, it was discovered that the original Labor requests, and the warrants issued, were based on an interpretation of the term "current rate for operations," as used in the Continuing Resolution, which differed from previous GAO interpretations of that term. As a result, it appeared that the warrants already issued for the Employment and Training Assistance and Temporary Employment Assistance accounts might have exceeded the actual amount of funds appropriated by the Continuing Resolution. The Assistant Secretary's request was submitted in response to the concerns expressed by the GAO representatives at this meeting.

In interpreting Continuing Resolutions, we must keep in mind their unique nature. Although they are passed by both Houses of the Congress and approved by the President of the United States and are thus laws of the United States, Continuing Resolutions differ significantly from normal appropriations acts. Continuing Resolutions are intended by Congress to be temporary stop-gap measures enacted to keep existing Federal programs functioning after the expiration of previous budget authority. The Congress resorts to the Continuing Resolution only when there is no regular appropriation for a program, perhaps because the two Houses have not yet agreed on common language, because authorizing legislation has not yet been enacted, or because the President has vetoed an appropriation act passed by the Congress.

In enacting Continuing Resolutions, there is a clear indication that Congress intends and expects that the normal authorization and appropriation process will eventually produce appropriation acts which will replace the budget authority contained in the resolution. Thus, for example, section 102 of the fiscal year 1979 Continuing Resolution provides that funds appropriated for a program by the resolution will no longer be available if the program is later funded by a regular appropriation act, or Congress indicates its intent to terminate the program by enacting an applicable appropriation act without provisions for the program.

Further, Continuing Resolutions are usually enacted in a great hurry toward the end of a session of Congress, and may not be the product of the detailed committee deliberations which produce regular appropriation acts. In sum, Continuing Resolutions are meant to provide only temporary, minimal funding and their language must be interpreted accordingly.

The 1979 Continuing Resolution appropriates sufficient funds to operate activities under the Comprehensive Employment and Training Act (CETA), 29 U.S.C. 801, "at a rate for operations not in excess of the lower of the current rate or the rate authorized by S. 2570 as passed the House of Representatives." In order to determine the amount of funds appropriated by the Continuing Resolution we must ascertain both the "current rate" and the rate authorized by S. 2570.

The S. 2570 rate is more easily determined. The conference committee report on S. 2570 contains a table showing the authorization levels of the bill as it passed the House. The table indicates authorization levels of $4 billion for Title II of CETA, $800 million for Title II, $2.25 billion for Title IV, $500 million for Title VII, and $350 million for Title VIII. The bill further authorized appropriation, under Title VI of CETA, of an amount sufficient to fund jobs for 20 percent of the unemployed in excess of a 4 percent unemployment rate. The Department of Labor has calculated that for fiscal year 1979 this Title VI authorization is equivalent to $3,753,600,000. Therefore, the total rate authorized for fiscal year 1979 by S. 2570 as it passed the House is $11,653,600,000.

Determination of the "current rate" is more difficult. Recently, we have reiterated our position that the term "current-rate," as used in Continuing Resolutions, refers to a sum of money rather than a program level. See *Department of Labor Appropriations under Continuing Resolution*, B–194063 (May 4, 1979); *Elderly Feeding Program under the fiscal year 1979 Continuing Resolution*, B–194362 (May 1, 1979). We stated that it has repeatedly been our position that "current rate" is equivalent to the total appropriation or the total funds which were available for obligation for a program during the previous fiscal year. *Id.*

In those instances in which the program in question has been funded by one-year appropriations in prior years, the current rate is equal to the total funds appropriated for the program for the previous fiscal year. See *Elderly Feeding Program, supra.* In those instances where the program has been funded by multi-year or no-year funds in prior years, the current rate is equal to the total funds appropriated for the previous fiscal year plus the total of unobligated budget authority carried over from prior years. See our letter to Senator William Proxmire, B–152554, October 9, 1970 (116 Cong. Rec. 36298).

According to the "Treasury Combined Statement of Receipts, Expenditures and Balances of the United States" for fiscal year 1978, there was a total of $3,440,930,000 appropriated for Employment and Training Assistance for fiscal year 1978. There were no appropriations for Temporary Employment Assistance. The same statement indicates carryovers into fiscal year 1978 of approximately $1,859,832,000 in unobligated Employment and Training Assistance funds, and about $1,861,241,000 in unobligated Temporary Employment Assistance funds. Using these figures, the total funds available for obligation in fiscal year 1978—the current rate—was about $5,300,762,000 for Employment and Training Assistance and $1,861,241,000 for Temporary Employment Assistance, or a total of about $7,162,000,000.

The Department of Labor argues, however, that part of the funds appropriated by the Economic Stimulus Appropriations Act of 1977, Pub. L. No. 95-29, 91 Stat. 122, approved May 13, 1977, were intended to be advance funding for fiscal year 1978, and that these funds should be included in calculating the current rate. Most of these funds were obligated in fiscal year 1977 for the 1978 program and were thus not carried over into fiscal year 1978 as unobligated budget authority.

The Economic Stimulus Appropriations Act, in Title I, Chapter II, appropriated $2,578,000,000 for Employment and Training Assistance, and $6,847,000,000 for Temporary Employment Assistance, both sums to remain available until September 30, 1978. The legislative history of this act indicates that Congress intended a portion of these funds to be advance funding for fiscal year 1978. Thus, in the report of the House Committee on Appropriations it is stated:

* * * The budget request considered by the Committee includes $1,016,000,000 that was requested by the President in the fiscal year 1978 budget for public service employment under the Comprehensive Employment and Training Act (CETA). Consideration of this 1978 request in fiscal year 1977 is essentially a bookkeeping transaction as far as the budget figures are concerned. The Committee decided to proceed in this fashion in order to provide advance funding for fiscal year 1978 in this bill for public service employment under titles II and VI of CETA. This appropriation account contains the funding for title II of CETA. Funds for title VI are in the Temporary Employment Assistance account. (H.R. Rept. No. 95-66, 95th Cong., 1st Sess. 15-16 (1977).)

Tables included in the reports of the House and Senate Appropriations Committees and in the Congressional Record indicate that $1,016,000,000 of the Employment and Training Assistance appropriation and $4,855,000,000 of the Temporary Employment Assistance appropriation, or $5,871,000,000 of the total CETA appropriation was intended to be advance funding for fiscal year 1978. *See* H.R. Rept. No. 95-66, *supra*, at 20; S. Rept. No. 95-58, 95th Cong., 1st Sess. 19 (1977); 123 Cong. Rec. H2089 (daily ed. March 15, 1977); *id.* S6882 (daily ed. May 2, 1977). Moreover, the legislative history of the Departments of Labor and Health, Education, and Welfare and Related Agencies Appropriations Bill, 1978, H.R. 7555 (95th Cong.), which was incorporated by reference into the fiscal year 1978 Continuing Resolution, indicates that no funds were being appropriated in that bill for public service employment under CETA for fiscal year 1978, because these funds had already been appropriated by the Economic Stimulus Appropriations Act. *See* H.R. Rept. No. 95-381, 95th Cong., 1st Sess. 7 (1977); S. Rept. No. 95-283, 95th Cong., 1st Sess. 8, 10 (1977).

It is clear that substantial portions of the fiscal year 1978 CETA programs were funded by the 1977 Economic Stimulus Appropriations Act. Therefore, in order to ascertain the full amount of funds available for fiscal year 1978 it is necessary to include the advance funding provided in the 1978 Act. Part of these funds, however, are included in the amounts of unobligated budget authority carried over into fiscal year 1978, discussed above. The Department of Labor indicates that of the advance funding, approximately $668,719,000 of Employment and Training Assistance, and $3,010,759,000 of Temporary Employment Assistance funds, were not included in the Treasury Combined Statement as carryovers of unobligated budget authority. Adding these figures to the ones calculated above, the current rate for fiscal year 1978 was about $5,969,481,000 for Employment and Training Assistance and $4,872,000,000 for Temporary Employment Assistance, or a total of $10,841,481,000 for all CETA programs.

The rate authorized by S. 2570 was $11,653,600,000. The current rate was $10,841,481,000. Since the current rate is lower, under section 101(a) of the Continuing Resolution, it represents the maximum rate for operations in fiscal year 1979.

The Treasury Combined Statement, referred to above, indicates that about $238,800,000 in Employment and Training Assistance funds remained unobligated at the end of fiscal year 1978 and were carried over into fiscal year 1979. This carryover must be deducted from the current rate in calculating the amount of funds appropriated by the Continuing Resolution. Otherwise, the 1979 program would be funded at a higher level than the 1978 program, which is prohibited by the language of the 1979 Continuing Resolution, *supra*.

The Continuing Resolution appropriated funds for "activities under the Comprehensive Employment and Training Act." Although in prior years, as indicated above, these activities were funded by two separate appropriations—Employment and Training Assistance, and Temporary Employment Assistance—we interpret the Continuing Resolution as appropriating a single lump-sum amount. The CETA program was restructured by the Comprehensive Employment and Training Act Amendments of 1978, Pub. L. No. 95-524, 92 Stat. 1909 (29 U.S.C. 801 note), approved October 27, 1978. Some CETA programs that were funded under the Temporary Employment Assistance account in fiscal year 1978 apparently are now considered part of the permanent CETA program. Nevertheless, the Continuing Resolution covers both programs under one designation—"activities under the Comprehensive Employment and Training Act." The Department of Labor, in calculating the amounts it requested for appropriation warrants, attempted to adjust the "current rate" to reflect these program changes. Rather than attempting to verify Labor's calculations, and because the language of the Continuing Resolution does not refer to two separate appropriations for CETA, we calculated a single appropriation based on the combined current rate for fiscal year 1978.

This differs from the approach we followed in B-194063 and B-194362, referred to above, in which we calculated separate current rates for two Older Americans Act programs also funded by the 1979 Continuing Resolution. In those decisions, however, the two programs were administered by two different agencies and it would have been impossible to calculate a single lump-sum appropriation for the two programs.

In sum, we conclude that the fiscal year 1979 Continuing Resolution appropriated a total of $10,602,664,000 for activities under CETA—$10,841,481,000 ("current rate") minus $238,800,000 (carry-over funds). To date, appropriation warrants totaling $10,244,712,000 have been issued by Treasury and countersigned by GAO. Should Treasury present an additional warrant for $45,000,000, as requested by Labor, we shall countersign that warrant.

[B-189197]

Compensation—Premium Pay—Sunday Work Regularly Scheduled

Employee's normal 40-hour basic workweek is Monday through Friday, midnight to 8 a.m., in an administrative workweek of Sunday through Saturday. His regularly scheduled administrative workweek includes daily overtime from 11 p.m. to midnight. Working this hour on Sundays does not entitle him to premium pay for the entire shift under 5 U.S.C. 5546(a), since that hour is considered overtime under 5 U.S.C. 5542(a) and 6101 and is thereby excluded. The fact that the employee is entitled to overtime for hours worked over 40 hours under the Fair Labor Standards Act does not operate to change the employee's normal basic workweek as established under 5 U.S.C. 6101 and implementing regulations.

In the matter of James E. Sommerhauser—Sunday premium pay, May 16, 1979:

This action is the result of an appeal of a settlement of our Claims Division dated July 27, 1978, which disallowed the claim of Mr. James E. Sommerhauser for Sunday premium pay incident to his employment at the Puget Sound Naval Shipyard.

Mr. Sommerhauser's contention is that, because he is covered by the Fair Labor Standards Act (FLSA) (29 U.S.C. 207), his overtime hours must be the last hours of his workweek. He believes that the first part of a workday and workweek which falls on Sunday may not be designated as overtime so as to preclude entitlement to Sunday premium pay. For the reasons given below we hold that an agency may designate hours or work other than the last hours of the workweek or workday as overtime hours for a computation of pay entitlement under title 5, United States Code.

The regular third shift at the Shipyard is midnight to 8 a.m. However, when Mr. Sommerhauser and some other employees in his unit are assigned to that shift they are subject to the duty hours prescribed in a memorandum of the Head, Test Engineering Division, Code 2340, dated February 17, 1977. That memorandum designates the "Standard shift hours" for Shift Test Engineers (STE's) as 11 p.m., to 8 a.m., and for Assistant Shift Test Engineers (ASTE's) as 11:24 p.m., to 8 a.m. The records before us do not contain all the details relating to the work schedules of these individuals, but it is stated that STE's and ASTE's assigned to the regular midnight to 8 a.m. shift must report one hour and six-tenths of one hour early, respectively, in order to receive turnover information from the outgoing shift. The Shipyard pays overtime for this hour (and 36-minute) period of work and counts the hours between midnight and 8 a.m. as the employees' non-overtime shift. Overtime which the claimant and other third shift STE's and ASTE's work is either computed under 5 U.S.C. 5542(a) or the FLSA, 29 U.S.C. 207 (1976), whichever provides the more favorable benefit. It is Mr. Sommerhauser's contention that the hour (or 36 minutes) which he works on Sunday night is not overtime but is the first hour of his regularly scheduled tour and that as a result he is entitled to Sunday premium for the whole shift under 5 U.S.C. 5546(a). In support of this view, he notes that overtime payable under the FLSA and implementing regulations is not payable until 40 hours in a week have been worked. As a result he contends that the hour he works on Sunday is paid as regular time. He also urges that overtime under 5 U.S.C. 5542, which is payable for hours worked in excess of 40 hours in a week and 8 hours in a day, must be computed the same way. This would result in the hour worked on Sunday being considered regular time or part of his regular tour of duty thereby entitling him to Sunday premium pay for a shift commencing at 11 p.m. Sunday and ending at 7 a.m. Monday, with overtime payable for 7 a.m. to 8 a.m. on Monday or at the time he completes 40 hours of work.

Sunday premium pay of 25 percent is paid under 5 U.S.C. 5546(a). That provision gives Sunday premium pay to employees who work a regular 8-hour *nonovertime* shift, any part of which falls on Sunday. Overtime compensation is paid under 5 U.S.C. 5542(a) for "hours of work officially ordered or approved in excess of 40 hours in an administrative workweek, or * * * in excess of 8 hours in a day."

Thus the basic question to be resolved is whether the hour worked on Sunday from 11 to 12 may be considered overtime even though it is performed before the 8 hours of the regular tour of duty.

Section 6101 of title 5, United States Code, provides in pertinent part as follows:

(2) The head of each Executive agency, military department, and of the government of the District of Columbia shall—
   (A) establish a basic administrative workweek of 40 hours for each full-time employee is his organization; and
   (B) require that the hours of work within that workweek be performed within a period of not more than 6 of any 7 consecutive days.
(3) Except when the head of an Executive agency * * * he shall provide, with respect to each employee in his organization, that—

   *   *   *   *   *   *   *

   (B) the basic 40-hour workweek is scheduled on 5 days, Monday through Friday when possible, and the 2 days outside the basic workweek are consecutive;

Civil Service regulations issued pursuant to 5 U.S.C. 6101(c) generally reiterate that which is provided in the statute. See 5 C.F.R. 610.111(a). However, 5 C.F.R. 610.111(a)(2) provides as follows:

(2) A regularly scheduled administrative workweek which consists of the 40-hour basic workweek established in accordance with paragraph (a)(1) of this section, plus the period of overtime work, if any, regularly required of each group of employees. * * *

In this regard the pertinent local regulation, NAVSHIPYD PUGETINST 7410.4C, 12 April 1974, provides the administrative workweek of graded and ungraded employees consists of 7 consecutive calendar days, Sunday through Saturday, and that the normal basic workweek (within the administrative workweek) consists of 40 hours on 5 days, Monday through Friday. That regulation also provides that the hours for third shift are midnight to 8 a.m.

Thus it appears that the Shipyard instructions are in accord with the Civil Service Commission regulations. The instruction clearly spells out the administrative workweek and the normal basic workweek. Regularly scheduled overtime for the specific group of employees here in question is not included in that regulation but is established in the memorandum of February 17, 1977, mentioned above.

The law and regulations require that a normal 40-hour basic workweek be established and that hours worked outside of this 40-hour basic workweek are overtime hours. Employees may be assigned to "regularly scheduled administrative workweeks" of more than 40 hours. However, the requirement that the agency designate the 40-hour basic workweek is still applicable in that situation. Hours outside the basic workweek are the designated regular overtime hours. The Court of Claims in *Acuna* v. *United States*, 202 Ct. Cl. 206 (1973), *cert. denied*, 416 U.S. 905, construed these regulations at page 218 as follows:

* * * There is no requirement in the Civil Service Commission's regulation that work regularly scheduled beyond the 40-hour basic workweek be scheduled at

the end of the administrative workweek, after the basic workweek has been completed. The requirement is simply that, once the agency has selected such period, its regulations specify the period by calendar day, etc., regardless of where in the administrative workweek it occurs. * * *

In Mr. Sommerhauser's case it appears that there has been no misunderstanding of what has been designated as the normal 40-hour basic workweek at the Shipyard. Furthermore, the record indicates that both management and the employees have recognized that midnight to 8 a.m. is the regular shift period and that the first hour (or 36 minutes) of work in each workday of third shift STE's and ASTE's is overtime. Thus, the period worked on Sunday is overtime. This is evidenced particularly by leave practices in effect at the Shipyard.

The FLSA, 29 U.S.C. 207, merely provides that overtime will be paid following the completion of 40 hours of work in a week. While it is established that an individual entitled to overtime under both title 5 and the FLSA is to be allowed the computation most favorable to him, we find no merit to the view that the FLSA operates to change the regularly scheduled administrative workweek and the 40-hour basic workweek as determined under the provisions of title 5, United States Code.

Accordingly, the action of our Claims Division in disallowing Mr. Sommerhauser's claim must be sustained.

[B–193602]

Officers and Employees—Transfers—Relocation Expenses—Time Limitation—Mandatory

Transferred employee reported to new duty station on May 4, 1976. He purchased a residence there with settlement on May 5, 1978. He is not entitled to reimbursement of real estate expenses since applicable regulations limit maximum time for settlement to within 2 years. Error of agency in extending initial year to May 5, 1978, provides no authority to modify statutory regulations.

In the matter of William R. Walberg—Relocation—Real Estate Expenses—Time Limitation, May 16, 1979:

ISSUE DECIDED

It is determined here that an error of 1 day made by an agency in granting a 1-year extension of the time limitation for the purchase of a residence incident to a permanent change of duty station provides no authority to reimburse real estate expenses where settlement occurs on such day.

FACTS

Mr. William R. Walberg, an employee of the Department of the Army, was transferred from Fort Lee, Virginia, to Fort Ritchie,

Maryland, under travel authorization approved April 2, 1976. The record shows that he traveled on May 3, 1976, and reported for duty May 4, 1976. The agency granted the employee a 1-year extension of the time limit allowed to complete the purchase of a residence at his new duty station. The agency, in error, stated that all transactions were to be completed by May 5, 1978, whereas they should have made it clear that all transactions were to be completed by May 4 or *before* May 5. The employee signed a real estate contract on April 16, 1978, for the purchase of a residence. Settlement occurred on May 5, 1978.

The employee's claim for real estate expenses has been denied administratively and by our Claims Division on the ground settlement occurred after expiration of the maximum entitlement period. We have been asked to review the disallowance.

OPINION

Chapter 2 of the Federal Travel Regulations (FTR) (FPMR 101–7) (May 1973), which are issued by the General Services Administration, governs the entitlements of civilian employees of the Federal Government to relocation allowances. Para. 2–6.1 provides for reimbursing an employee for the expenses of selling a residence at his old official station and of purchasing a residence at his new station. However, para. 2–6.1(e) of the FTR imposes a time limitation on such sales and purchases, as follows:

e. *Time limitation.* The settlement dates for the sale and purchase or lease termination transactions for which reimbursement is requested are not later than 1 (initial) year after the date on which the employee reported for duty at the new official station. Upon an employee's written request this time limit for completion of the sale and purchase or lease termination transaction may be extended by the head of the agency or his designee for an additional period of time, not to exceed 1 year, regardless of the reasons therefor so long as it is determined that the particular residence transaction is reasonably related to the transfer of official station.

Issued pursuant to 5 U.S.C. § 5724a (1976) which contains the authority for reimbursement of real estate expenses, these regulations have the force and effect of law and may not be waived by any department of the Government in an individual case. See B–189898, November 3, 1977. Similar provisions are contained in paragraph C14000–2 of Volume 2 of the Joint Travel Regulations (JTR) relating to reimbursement of relocation allowances of civilian employees of the Department of Defense.

The FTR and JTR clearly provide that the settlement date on a residence transaction must occur not later than 2 years after the date on which the employee reported for duty at his new station. Agency officials have no authority to grant an exception to that requirement. Thus, since Mr. Walberg reported for duty on May 4, 1976, the maximum period within which his settlement had to occur was May 4, 1978. It is unfortunate that he was misinformed, but it is a well-established rule of law that the Government is neither bound nor estopped by the erroneous or unauthorized acts of its officers, agents, or employees, even though committed in the performance of their official duties. See 56 Comp. Gen. 943, 949 (1977) and cases cited therein.

Accordingly, the disallowance of Mr. Walberg's claim by our Claims Division on September 26, 1978, is sustained.

[B-194634]

Agriculture Department—Farmers Home Administration—Energy Impacted Area Development Assistance Program

Under section 601(a) of the Powerplant and Industrial Fuel Use Act of 1978, a State Governor may designate an impacted area based on his finding that employment in coal or uranium production activities "increased for the most recent calendar year by 8 percent or more from the immediately preceding year." Both the plain meaning of the statute and its legislative history support the view that "the most recent calendar year" is determined with respect to the time of the Governor's finding, and not, with respect to any calendar year since 1975, of 8 percent increased employment. Final regulations of the Farmers Home Administration for the Energy Impacted Area Development Assistance Program should include an amended definition of "base year" consistent with this decision.

In the matter of Federal Assistance for Areas Impacted by Increased Coal or Uranium Production, May 16, 1979:

The Acting General Counsel of the Department of Agriculture had requested our interpretation of a portion of section 601 of the Powerplant and Industrial Fuel Use Act of 1978, Pub. L. No. 95-620, approved Nov. 9, 1978, 92 Stat. 3289, which established Federal assistance for areas impacted by coal or uranium production.

Although there is a second criterion, for purposes of this decision, eligibility for this assistance depends on a determination by the Governor for an area in the State that employment in coal or uranium production activities has increased by 8 percent or more in a base period— defined in the statute as "the most recent calendar year" over the immediately preceding year.

Section 601(a) states in pertinent part:

(a) DESIGNATION OF IMPACTED AREAS.—(1) In accordance with such criteria and guidelines as the Secretary of Agriculture shall, by rule, prescribe, the Governor of any State may designate any area within such State for the purposes of this section, if he finds that—
(A) either (i) employment in coal or uranium production development activities in such areas has increased for the most recent calendar year by 8 percent or more from the immediately preceding year or (ii) employment in such activities will increase 8 percent or more per year during each of the 3 calendar years beginning after the date of such finding;
(B) such employment increase has required or will require substantial increases in housing or public facilities and services or a combination of both in such area; and

(C) the State and the local government or governments serving such area lack the financial and other resources to meet any such increases in public facilities and services within a reasonable time.

The Secretary of Agriculture shall prescribe a rule containing criteria and guidelines for making a designation under this subsection, after consultation with the Secretary of Labor and the Secretary of Energy, not later than 180 days after the effective date of this Act.

*   *   *   *   *   *   *

(3) The Secretary shall, after consultation with the Secretary of Agriculture, approve any designation of an area under paragraph (1) only if—

(A) the Governor of the State making the designation provides the Secretary in writing with the data and information on which such designation was made, together with such additional information as the Secretary may require to carry out the purposes of this section; and

(B) the Secretary determines that the requirements of subparagraphs (A), (B), and (C) of paragraph (1) have been met.

The question presented is whether "the most recent calendar year" as used in section 601(a) means most recent in relation to a governor's designation or the most recent in relation to employment growth in development activities. The Acting General Counsel puts the question as follows:

* * * if the Governor's designation occurred in 1979, could it be based upon an 8 percent employment increase occurring in 1976 over 1975 even though in 1978 (1978 being literally the most recent year to the Governor's designation) there was no 8 percent employment increase over 1977 and in 1977 there was no 8 percent employment increase over 1976?

History of Impact Provision

Senate Bill 977, as introduced in the 95th Congress on March 10, 1977, was a modified version of proposed legislation for expanded use of coal as a substitute for other fossil fuels, which had been considered in the prior Congress. Subsequently, on April 20, 1977, President Carter announced a national energy program which included a proposal to "increase the use of coal by 400 million tons, or 65 percent, in industry and utilities by 1985 * * *." Legislative proposals incorporating the President's National Energy Plan soon followed. As reported by the Senate Committee on Energy and Natural Resources (S. Rep. No. 95–361, 95th Cong., 1st Sess., July 25, 1977) S. 977 was extensively amended. A new section 306(a) was added which provided in pertinent part that—

When the Governor of any State or chairman of any Indian tribe determines that coal production will expand above 1976 production levels in an area which will require the provision of additional public facilities and services or housing, the Governor or chairman may designate such an area within his jurisdiction as an "energy-impacted region." * * *

In discussing the provision, the Senate report stated that—

Section 306 is an attempt to alleviate the significant adverse socio-economic impacts on coalfield communities that are likely to result from the coal conversion program. Eastern Governors, such as John D. Rockefeller IV of West Virginia, and Western Governors, such as Richard Lamm of Colorado, have pointed out in testimony the serious difficulties small communities face in meeting the demand for housing, public facilities and services that will result if the President's goal of 1.2 billion tons of annual coal production is reached. The opening subsection of the new provisions gives Governors and tribal Chairmen the power to designate for special aid energy-impacted regions where coal production is expanding. At 62.

Shortly thereafter, on September 8, 1977, the Senate passed H.R. 5146 which had been amended to incorporate provisions of S. 977, as amended, including a changed section 306, providing for assistance to regions impacted by expanded coal or uranium production. As passed by the Senate, subsection (a) of section 306 of H.R. 5146 read in part as follows:

> When the Governor of any State or chairman of any Indian tribe determines that employment in the coal- or uranium-mining industries and in coal- or uranium-related industries in an area has increased by 8 per centum or more over the 1976 level of employment in coal or uranium mining and coal- or uranium-related industries in the area which will require the provision of additional public facilities and services or housing, the Governor or chairman may designate such an area within his jurisdiction as an "energy-impacted region." * * *

The House had not passed a comparable provision. The conference report on H.R. 5146, October 10, 1978 (H.R. Rep. No. 95–1749, 95th Cong., 2d Sess.), states that the Senate provision on impact assistance, as modified, was adopted as section 601 of the Powerplant and Industrial Fuel Use Act of 1978. It was explained that an energy-impacted region may be designated:

> Whenever a Governor of a State identifies within that State an area or areas to be impacted by energy development such as new or existing coal or uranium producing, processing, and transportation industries and demonstrates to the Secretary that:
> (a) such development has increased employment by at least 8 percent over the prior year directly (i.e., this does not include increases from non-energy activities, such as a shopping center) from coal or uranium production, processing, or transportation, or is projected to increase employment by at least 8 percent annually over the next 3 years from the same activities; * * * At 93.

On October 14, 1978, the Honorable John D. Dingell, Chairman of the Subcommittee on Energy and Power of the House Committee on Interstate and Foreign Commerce, presented to the House of Representatives on behalf of himself and other House conferees an explanatory statement addressed to questions which had arisen about the meaning of certain sections of H.R. 5146 as reported by the Conference Committee. The statement was made prior to acceptance of the conference report. The portion addressed to impact assistance (124 Cong. Rec. H 13121 (daily ed. October 14, 1978)) is as follows:

> The language in section 601(a), titled assistance to areas impacted by increased coal or uranium production, specifies that an area within a State may be eligible for assistance in one of two ways. First, coal or uranium related employment has increased for the most recent calendar year by at least 8 percent from the immediately preceding year.
> The 8-percent criterion was developed in 1977 after examining the employment patterns of 1975 and 1976. The purpose was to provide assistance to communities facing the most severe impacts at that time from expanding coal development. These communities continue to need assistance like that provided in this bill.

Additional communities facing more recent growth impacts may become eligible based on 1976–77 changes in employment levels. The actual employment situation varies greatly not only from State to State, but from county to county. The conferees intend that the Secretary of Agriculture, in prescribing rules on eligibility for assistance, shall permit flexibility, to the greatest degree possible, in qualifying for assistance under this criterion.

* * * * * * *

Once the Governor has designated an area and satisfied the Federal administrative requirements set out in the bill, then the Secretary of Energy, after consultation with the Secretary of Agriculture, must approve the Governor's designation. The conferees also intend that, to the greatest extent possible, these Federal administrative requirements not be unduly complex or burdensome.

The President signed H.R. 5146 on November 9, 1978. The Farmers Home Administration (FmHA) of the Department of Agriculture has responsibility for administration of section 601 activities. Relying on the legislative history of this section, it believes that "most recent calendar year" refers to the time of increase in employment rather than the time of the Governor's designation. We are also told that a contrary interpretation would render ineligible those communities to which Mr. Dingell referred in colloquy prior to House passage of the Act. This includes almost all of West Virginia, where substantial employment increases occurred during 1975, 1976, and 1977 but apparently not in 1978.

The FmHA published proposed regulations for its Energy Impacted Area Development Assistance Program (44 Fed. Reg. 12936, *et seq.*) on March 8, 1979. It provides that an area designated by a Governor must show increased employment of 8 percent or more in the year following a base year or that such employment will increase by 8 percent or more over the base year during each of the next 3 calendar years (section 1948.73(a)). "Base year" is defined in section 1948.53(c) as—

The most recent calendar year determined by the Governor of the appropriate State to be prior to the occurrence of the most significant impact on the designated area. This may be any calendar year selected by the Governor from 1975 to the calendar year preceding the most recent calendar year.

Analysis

The issue before us, in essence, goes to the Governor's discretion to choose which 2-consecutive-year period to look at in determining if an area within the State is eligible for impact aid. FmHA's proposed regulations would authorize the Governor to examine data dating back to 1975 in making a determination. For the reasons discussed below, we do not believe this is permissible.

The original impact provision proposed by the Senate Committee on Energy and Natural Resources based eligibility on increased coal production in an area over 1976 production levels. During floor debate, Senator Randolph offered an amendment to change the criteria from coal production increases to an 8 percent increase in "employment in the coal-mining industry and in coal-related industries." He explained that, among other things, in many communities production might not have increased over 1976 levels due to wil lcat strikes or due to a shift from surface mining to deep mining, but that the need to produce more coal brought more employment to, and had a dramatic impact on those communities. He also explained that, as proposed by the Committee, numerous communities would eventually become eligible for assistance. To target the aid to those most in need, the 8 percent figure was developed from examining coal employment data from the States of West Virginia, Colorado, and New Mexico.

Both as reported by the Committee and as passed by the Senate, the proposed legislation mandated 1976 as the base year. Thus, even had one of these versions been enacted, FmHA's proposed regulations, which authorize a Governor to choose 1975 as the base year, would not have been valid.

Athough the Senate passed H.R. 5146 on September 8, 1977, the Conference Committee did not complete its work until about one year later. Although it does not provide very much comment on the changes it recommended, it seems clear that the Conference Committee intended to restrict even further eligibility for assistance and to decrease the program's size.

In addition to deleting reference to 1976 as the base year in favor of the "most recent calendar year" standard, the Conference Committee suggested, and the Congress and the President accepted, numerous other changes in the program. It changed the Senate-passed language relating to increases in employment in "coal- or uranium-mining industries and in coal- or uranium-related industries" to increases in employment in "coal or uranium production activities."

It also added to the Senate-passed requirement that the increase in employment will "require the provision of additional public facilities and services or housing," the requirement that the State and local governments serving the impacted area lack the financial and other resources to meet these needs. In determining this, increased revenues from severance taxes, royalties, and similar fees which are associated with the increase in development activities are generally required to be taken into account.

The final change recommended by the Conference Committee to which we will refer is its amendment of the appropriation authorization. The Senate-passed measure would have authorized appropriations in the sum of $150,000,000 annually for the 8 years beginning with fiscal year 1978, with unexpended amounts to be available until expended. The final version authorized to be appropriated $60 million for fiscal year 1979 and $120 million for fiscal year 1980. This is a much smaller total authorization of appropriations than in the Senate bill.

While the Conference Committee does not explain its deletion of the reference to 1976 as the base year and substitution of the most recent calendar year and the year preceding it, it does not seem likely in view of the other actions it took that it intended to broaden eligibility over that provided by the Senate-passed bill. We have also reviewed the explanatory statement made by the House conferees quoted above, and do not find it inconsistent with our view of the law and legislative history.

Finally, we do not believe that we can read into the provisions a qualification of the words "the most recent calendar year" to mean the most recent calendar year of increased employment. The words of the statute, when given a normal and unstrained reading, indicate that a Governor may make a finding as to the most recently completed calendar year (since employment information for a year cannot be ascertained with certainty before the end of that particular year), which is then to be compared with the immediately preceding calendar year. To hold, for example, that 1976 could now be compared with 1975 would do violence to the plain meaning of the provision since 1976 is not "the most recent calendar year" prior to 1979—the year in which the finding was made.

FmHA relies in part on the 1978 explanatory statement, quoted above, which was presented to the House by Mr. Dingell on behalf of the conferees, in which it was said that communities could be eligible for impact assistance based on "1976–77" changes in employment levels. The statement, of course, was correct at the time it was made since the legislation was enacted in 1978. A finding in that year relating to the then most recent completed calendar year, 1977, of increased employment over 1976 would have clearly been within the ambit of section 601(a).

Accordingly, we are of the opinion that under section 601(a) a Governor in making an impact designation based on a finding of increased employment may not choose, as FmHA proposes, any year of employment increase starting with any year since 1975 as the base year. The Governor must select the most recent calendar year as compared to the calendar year immediately preceding it. (In the alternative, of course, he may find an adverse impact based on a projected 8 percent employment increase for each of the next 3 calendar years following his finding.) The final regulations promulgated by the FmHA should include a definition of "base year" consistent with this view.

Compensation—Overtime—Training Courses—Outside Regular Tour of Duty—Prohibition—Exceptions

Customs Patrol Officers who attended special training course claim overtime pay under the Fair Labor Standards Act (FLSA) or overtime or night premium pay under title 5, United States Code, for regularly scheduled training sessions conducted after 6 p.m. Where training qualifies under exception to prohibition against payment of premium pay for training in 5 U.S.C. 4109(a), overtime under FLSA or overtime or night premium pay under title 5, United States Code, must be paid. Payment should be made to employees under title 5 or under FLSA, whichever law gives the greater benefit. 38 Comp. Gen. 363 (1958) clarified.

In the matter of Customs Patrol Officers—Entitlement to Overtime and Night Premium Pay During Training, May 18, 1979:

This decision is in response to a request from John A. Hurley, Assistant Commissioner (Administration), U.S. Customs Service, Department of the Treasury, concerning the entitlement of certain Customs Patrol Officers to overtime or night premium pay while they attended the Navy's Sea, Air and Land (SEAL) School.

Our Office has received claims from three Customs Patrol Officers, Donald A. Bambenek II, David A. McDonald, and John H. Spillane, Jr., and the Customs Service is holding similar claims from other patrol officers while it awaits our decision. The question presented for decision is whether these employees are entitled to overtime or night premium pay under title 5, United States Code, or overtime under the Fair Labor Standards Act (FLSA), 29 U.S.C. 201, in light of the general prohibition on the payment of overtime and night premium pay during training contained in 5 U.S.C. § 4109.

The facts presented show that certain Customs Patrol Officers were directed to attend Navy SEAL School or "C-Fist" School so as to receive specialized training to assist them in the performance of their law enforcement duties. The employees contend, and the agency does not dispute, that the training was for more than 40 hours a week and that certain training sessions were conducted after 6 p.m. because the employees were being trained for situations which occur only at night. The employees claim overtime or night premium pay in connection with this training.

Messrs. Bambenek and Spillane have claimed overtime, and Mr. McDonald has claimed night premium pay in connection with this training. With regard to Mr. McDonald's claim, the Customs Service recommends denial of his claim in a report to our Claims Division. The agency points out that 5 U.S.C. § 4109 prohibits the payment of overtime or night premium pay to employees who are selected and assigned for training. The agency recognizes that there are exceptions to this prohibition established under Civil Service Commission regulations, one exception being for training at night for situations which only occur at night. See 5 C.F.R. § 410.602(b)(2). However, the agency argues that the exceptions to the prohibition contained in 5 U.S.C. § 4109 only make the employee eligible for overtime or night premium pay and that it is still within the discretion of the agency to allow or disallow such pay during training. The agency also points out that Mr. McDonald continued to receive premium pay for administratively uncontrollable overtime while in training under the provisions of 5 C.F.R. §§ 410.602(b)(4) and 550.162(c)(2). Therefore, the agency argues that his only entitlement to night premium pay would be for regularly scheduled night duty under 5 U.S.C. § 5545(a) and that this night training was not "regularly scheduled work" within the meaning of the statute. See 5 U.S.C. § 5545(c)(2). The claims of Messrs. Bambenek and Spillane for regularly scheduled overtime under 5 U.S.C. § 5542(a) have been denied by the Customs Service for reasons similar to those cited above.

The agency has also received a claim from the National Treasury Employees Union on behalf of all Customs Patrol Officers who attended SEAL School for overtime compensation under the FLSA. Customs Patrol Officers are covered, i.e.. "nonexempt" employees, under the FLSA. The Customs Service received apparently conflicting reports from the Dallas and Atlanta Regional Offices of the Civil Service Commission concerning overtime entitlement under the FLSA. We requested a report from the Office of Personnel Management (OPM) (formerly Civil Service Commission) concerning the entitlement of Customs Patrol Officers to overtime under the FLSA while attending SEAL School.

The report from the Director of the Compensation Division of OPM, dated February 16, 1979, states that "training" as defined by 5 U.S.C. § 4101(4) is compensable under the FLSA as hours of work but that the prohibition contained in 5 U.S.C. § 4109(a) applies equally to overtime pay under title 5 or under the FLSA. See Federal Personnel Manual Letter 551–3, August 29. 1974. After reviewing the prior determinations of the Dallas and Atlanta Regional Offices of the Civil Service Commission and the report submitted to our Claims Division by the Customs Service (cited above). the Director's report concludes as follows:

After discussions with staff members of the Customs Service, it is our understanding that the Customs Service agrees that the time spent in training at the SEAL and C-Fist Schools meets one or more of the exceptions. In fact. the entire training period may be excepted under 5 CFR 410.602(b)(3) which applies to employees "given training on overtime. on a holiday. or on a Sunday because the cost of the training, premium pay included, are less than the costs of the same training confined to regular work hours . . . ." We believe that once an agency has determined that one of the exceptions applies. the agency does not have discretion to withhold overtime payment under the FLSA. To do so would be to deny payment for time which is hours of work under the FLSA and for which no specific prohibition applies under 5 U.S.C. 4109(a).

The authority for the payment of expenses incident to training is contained in 5 U.S.C. § 4109 which provides, in pertinent part, as follows:

> (a) The head of an agency, under the regulations prescribed under section 4118(a)(8) of this title and from appropriations or other funds available to the agency, may—
> (1) pay all or a part of the pay (except overtime, holiday, or night differential pay) of an employee of the agency selected and assigned for training under this chapter, for the period of training * * *.

Our Office has long held that in view of the above-cited provision overtime or premium pay, holiday pay, or night differential may not be paid to employees for time spent in training unless an exception has been established by the Civil Service Commission (CSC). See 48 Comp. Gen. 620 (1969); 39 *id.* 453 (1959); 38 *id.* 404 (1958); *id.* 363 (1958); and B–168528, January 2, 1970. The exceptions to this prohibition, established by the CSC under the authority of 5 U.S.C. § 4102(b)(1) and Executive Order No. 11348, April 22, 1967, are contained in 5 C.F.R. Part 410, Subpart F, and Federal Personnel Manual, Chapter 410, Subchapter 6.

It appears from the OPM report quoted above that the Customs Service now agrees that this training meets the exception to the prohibition on overtime contained in 5 C.F.R. § 410.602(b)(2) for training at night for situations which occur only at night. The OPM report also raises the question of the applicability of the exception contained in 5 C.F.R. § 410.602(b)(3) for training on overtime, on a holiday, or on a Sunday where the costs of training including premium pay are less than the costs of the same training confined to regular work hours. However, we have no information concerning relative training costs, and we do not believe that it is necessary to consider this question further.

Once it has been determined that the training satisfies one of the stated exceptions to the prohibition on the payment of overtime or premium pay, the question remains whether the Customs Service retained discretion as to whether or not to pay overtime or premium pay for these periods of training. With regard to the entitlement of these Customs Patrol Officers to overtime under the Fair Labor Standards Act, the Office of Personnel Management has advised us that, where the training qualifies under an exception to the prohibition in 5 U.S.C. § 4109(a), the agency may not withhold overtime payment for hours of work under the FLSA. We concur with that determination since, under the FLSA, a nonexempt employee *must* be compensated at overtime rates for work which exceeds 40 hours in a week. See 29 U.S.C. § 207 (1976).

With regard to the entitlement of these Customs Patrol Officers to overtime and night premium pay under title 5, United States Code, we believe that where an agency has selected and assigned an employee to perform training and has determined that the employee shall receive his basic pay for the period of training, the agency has no discretion to deny title 5 overtime or premium pay where the training meets one of the exceptions to the prohibition in section 4109. 38 Comp. Gen. 363, *supra*, clarified.

In the present case, the Customs Patrol Officers were receiving premium pay for administratively uncontrollable overtime and, under the provisions of 5 C.F.R. §§ 410.602(b)(4) and 550.162(c)(2), they continued to receive this premium pay during training. As to their entitlement to any additional overtime or premium pay under title 5, United States Code, we point out that premium pay under 5 U.S.C. § 5545(c)(2) for administratively uncontrollable overtime is in lieu of all other forms of premium compensation, except for regularly scheduled overtime, night, and Sunday duty, and for holiday duty. Although the Customs Service originally denied the claims of the Customs Patrol Officers for overtime and night premium pay on the ground that the work was not "regularly scheduled," it appears that the agency has subsequently determined that the work was scheduled in advance, required to be performed, and assigned and approved by management. Since such work appears to have been scheduled to occur on successive days as evidenced by the training schedules, we agree that the work was "regularly scheduled" for the purposes of entitlement to overtime or night premium pay. See, for example, 48 Comp. Gen. 334 (1968).

Accordingly, payments should be made under title 5, United States Code, or under the FLSA, whichever provides the greater benefit.

[B–192125]

Contracts — Protests — Timeliness — Solicitation Improprieties—Wage Determinations

Oral protest to agency is permissible if stated in fashion that intent to protest is clear. Intent to protest is not evident by statement asserted prior to submission of best and final offer that Service Contract Act wage determination is incompatible with solicitation and will need clarification, and protest, after submission of best and final offer against wage determination *per se*, is untimely.

Contractors — Successors — Wages — Reduction — Job Reclassification—Retained Employees

Successful offeror is not guilty of "wage busting" (practice of lowering employee wages and fringe benefits by successor contractor to become low offeror when incumbent contractor's employees are retained to perform same jobs on successor contracts) if incumbent's retained employees are reclassified to lower paying jobs with different duties and responsibilities. However, where no statute, regulation or statement of policy in existence at time solicitation issued precludes "wage busting," no legal impediment exists to prevent lowering of wages for incumbent employees even if reduction can be categorized as "wage busting."

Contracts—Negotiation—Evaluation Factors—Labor Costs

While offeror is not legally obligated to pay wages paid by incumbent, where such offeror's proposal expressly states labor rates proposed are based on current wage rates for incumbent personnel, contracting officer should take such statement into account in consideration of proposed costs.

Contracts — Cost-Plus — Evaluation Factors — "Realism" of Costs and Technical Approach

Where cost reimbursement contract is awarded on basis of estimated costs, required cost realism determination of proposed costs which is based for most part on Defense Contract Audit Agency's qualified statements and which does not take into account possible disparity between statements in technical proposal and proposal costs is inadequate.

Contracts — Negotiation — Evaluation Factors — Evaluators— Improper Influence, Bias, etc. — Not Established

Suggestion that there may have been impropriety in evaluation of proposals because one member of evaluation team was hired by successful offeror shortly after contract award is not substantiated by record, which indicates only that awardee learned of member's retirement plans and made employment offer only after contract award.

Contracts — Negotiation — Evaluation Factors — Cost Analysis— Inadequate — Corrective Action

Where agency advises option for second year's contract performance will not be exercised but initial contract will be extended only for limited period necessary to solicit and award second year's requirements, General Accounting Office need not recommend other corrective action since agency's intended action is considered reasonable under circumstances.

In the matter of Joule Technical Corporation, May 21, 1979:

Joule Technical Corporation (Joule) protests the award of contract No. N00421–78–C–0051 to Dynalectron, Inc. (Dynalectron) by the Naval Air Station, Patuxent River, Maryland. Joule, the incumbent contractor, contends the award is unlawful because of substantial irregularities in the procurement process including a "nonresponsive" best and final offer by Dynalectron, a defective wage determination incorporated into the request for proposals (RFP), arbitrary evaluations of proposals and a possible conflict of interest by a member of the evaluation team.

The RFP (No. 421–78–R–0003) called for proposals to provide engineering and technical support services on a cost-plus-fixed-fee basis for one year with an option for one additional year. The RFP stated that in the evaluation of proposals, technical capability would be rated at least twice as important as cost, but cautioned offerors that cost (which would be evaluated on basis of cost realism) should not be ignored as the degree of its importance would increase with the degree of equality of the technical proposals. The RFP further provided that award would be made to the offeror whose proposal offered the greatest value in terms of technical approach and price. Final cost evaluation took into account base year estimated costs plus those for both the option year and an alternative option year, and on this basis Dynalectron's offer was found to be $103,178 less than Joule's and was the lowest received. The actual difference between the two offers based on the combination of the base year and the alternative option for the second year was $79,474.

Joule's claim of "nonresponsiveness" in the Dynalectron proposal, as well as its assertion of an arbitrary evaluation by the Navy, are grounded upon what Joule perceives as the personnel supervisory requirements of the RFP, the Dynalectron proposal in this respect, and Dynalectron's asserted misclassification of the employees under a Department of Labor (DOL) wage rate determination. In this regard, Joule claims Dynalectron is guilty of "wage busting" in that it hired Joule's employees at lower wage rates than those paid by Joule.

On January 26, 1978, proposals were received from seven companies, including Joule and Dynalectron, both of which were found to be within the competitive range. Additional information and revised proposals were received on April 24, 1978, and evaluations were completed on May 3, 1978. Because the Navy had been advised by DOL that the Service Contract Act of 1965 (SCA), as amended, 41 U.S.C. 351 *et seq.* (1976), applied, the Navy amended the RFP to include a DOL wage determination and a call for best and final offers by May 25, 1978. After further evaluations, the Navy concluded that the technical proposals of Joule, Dynalectron (scored 92.96 and 92.85 respectively), and five other offerors were essentially equal, and that award should be made on the basis of cost. Award was therefore made to Dynalectron on June 7, 1978, and Joule protested to this Office on June 8, 1978.

The Navy, contending that Joule's objections go to the validity of the wage determination, asserts that the protest is untimely under our Bid Protest Procedures, 4 C.F.R. § 20.2(b) (1978), because it was not filed prior to closing date for receipt of best and final offers. In this respect, Joule states that when it hand delivered its best and final offer on May 25, 1978, it orally informed the Navy that the wage determination was not compatible with the solicitation and would need clarification.

While an oral protest is permissible under Defense Acquisition Regulation (DAR) § 2–407.8 (1976 ed.), it must be stated in such a fashion that the intent to lodge a protest is clear. *Automated Processes Incorporated*, B–181262, September 4, 1974, 74–2 CPD 143. In our opinion, an intent to protest is not evident merely by a statement that a wage determination is incompatible with a solicitation and will need clarification. Thus, questions relating to the DOL wage rate determination *per se* which were apparent from the solicitation are untimely and will not be considered on the merits. However, portions of the protest arise from information available to Joule only after contract award; these portions are timely and will be considered.

The RFP classified various technical personnel required for the contract performance, principally in terms of education and experience. Four technician levels were specified. DOL categories, however, were based on job descriptions and were broken down into three classifications. It was the offeror's responsibility to conform the RFP labor categories to the DOL classifications for the purpose of conforming to the appropriate DOL specified minimum wage rates. A tabulation of the pertinent RFP requirements and the proposal results is as follows:

PROPOSAL SUMMARY

| | | ITEM 0001 | | | ITEM 0004 | |
| | | | Rate | | | Rate |
LABOR CATEGORY	L.O.E.[1]	Joule	Dynalectron	L.O.E.[1]	Joule	Dynalectron
Elect. Tech.						
Level IV [5]	2	$8.00	$7.78 (A)	2	8.40 (5%) [3]	$8.17 (5%)
III	8	7.78 (A)[2]	6.27 (B)	10	8.17 (5%)	6.52 (4%)
II	0	6.27 (B)	5.50 (C)	5	6.58 (5%)	5.50 (0%)
I	0	5.50 (C)	3.75	3	5.78 (5%)	3.75 (0%)
Mech. Tech.[4]						
Level IV	0	8.00	7.30	1	8.40 (5%)	7.30 (0%)
III	2	7.07	6.28	2	7.42 (5%)	6.69 (5%)
II	0	6.00	4.95	3	6.30 (5%)	4.95 (0%)
I	0	5.10	3.75	1	5.36 (5%)	3.75 (0%)

[1] Level of effort as specified in RFP in man-years at 2000 hours per man year. Item 0003 same as Item 0001.
[2] Upper case letters in parentheses are DOL wage classifications for base year.
[3] Percent figures in parentheses are proposed escalation for second year's performance.
[4] No DOL wage rates specified for Mechanical Technicians.
[5] RFP classification.

The basis for the difference between the two cost proposals is clear from the tabulation—Dynalectron and Joule did not conform the RFP labor categories to the DOL wage classifications in the same manner. Obviously Joule conformed the RFP electronic technician labor categories to the DOL classifications one step higher than did Dynalectron, and where no wage rate existed Joule proposed rates that were consistently higher than those proposed by Dynalectron. In addition, other variations are apparent. For example, for the most part, where particular classes of labor were required during the initial contract period. Dynalectron proposed a 5 percent wage increase for each employee after one year's service purportedly based on "current projected living costs," but provided no increase for employees not utilized during the initial contract period. Joule projected 5 percent higher wage rates across the board for the second performance year, without regard to first year utilization. Thus, if we consider only items 0001 and 0004, Dynalectron's projections include no wage increase for 26,000 labor hours used in evalulation and are premised on a significantly lower wage rate for the total 112,000 labor hours specified by the RFP as the level of effort for these items. These differences alone well exceed the $79,474 difference in proposed costs between the two lowest offers for these items.

The difference in job classifications utilized by the two firms is in part explained by the administrative duties assigned by Joule to its lead (Level IV) technicians because the DOL wage determination excluded from its coverage those [among others] technicians with administrative or supervisory responsibility.

The wage rate determination also provided that any class of service employee required in the performance of the contract but not listed in the wage determination was to be classified by the contractor so as to provide a reasonable relationship between such class and those listed in the wage determination with employees to be paid as determined by agreement of the contracting agency, the contractor and the employees. In the absence of such agreement, the question of proper rate was to be submitted to DOL for final determination.

Although the Navy states all offerors but Joule classified the required personnel as did Dynalectron, Joule contends that Dynalectron misclassified the personnel because its two former lead technicians with supervisory duties have been hired at lower wages by Dynalectron for the same duties they performed for Joule. Joule contends that this is a violation of fundamental national labor policy and of the service contract procurement policy as reflected in Policy Letter 78–2, entitled "Preventing 'Wage Busting' for Professionals: Procedures for Evaluating Contractor Proposals for Service Contracts," issued by the Office of Federal Procurement Policy (OFPP), Office of Management and Budget, on March 29, 1978. 43 Fed. Reg. 18805 (May 2, 1978).

"Wage busting" is the practice of lowering employee wages and fringe benefits by a successor contractor as a result of the contractor's effort to be a low bidder or offeror on a Government service contract when the employees continue to perform the same jobs on the successor contract. A successor contractor is not guilty of wage busting when employees are reclassified by the successor contractor to lower paying jobs with different duties and responsibilities. REPORT BY THE COMPTROLLER GENERAL OF THE UNITED STATES, SPECIAL PROCUREMENT PROCEDURES HELPED PREVENT WAGE BUSTING UNDER FEDERAL SERVICE CONTRACTS IN THE CAPE CANAVERAL AREA, HRD–78–49, February 28, 1978.

In this respect, Dynalectron contends its classifications were based on the duties reflected by the solicitation and not upon the practices followed by Joule in its performance of the previous contract. Dynalectron states that while Joule's lead technicians may have been performing supervisory duties, the duties of the Electronic Technician, Level IV specified in the solicitation do not include any supervisory duties, and that it was not its intention that they do so. It further states, and the Navy concurs, that it was the offeror's responsibility to conform the personnel proposed to appropriate wage classes in the wage determination and that Dynalectron reasonably did so.

DOL has excluded from the coverage of the SCA "bona fide executive, administrative or professional personnel," 29 C.F.R. 4.113(a)(2) (1978), although the Act does extend to employees such as a "foreman or supervisor in a position having trade, craft or laboring experience as the paramount requirement." 29 C.F.R. 4.113(b). Complex definitions of "bona fide executive, administrative or professional personnel" promulgated by the Secretary of Labor are contained in 29 C.F.R. 541. As we understand it, it is Joule's position that the Level IV technicians required by the solicitation perform administrative functions which would exclude those persons from the coverage of the Act (apparently this was the basis for Joule's determination that the Level IV technicians did not conform to DOL's Class A classification); that by hiring Joule's employees to perform the same duties as performed for Joule, Dynalectron was bound to conform to the DOL determination in the same manner as Joule, and that by failing to do so, Dynalectron was in violation of the SCA and thus guilty of "wage busting." Joule also asserts that the contracting officer could not have adequately determined the cost realism of Dynalectron's proposal without considering the implications of the SCA violations.

In its original form the SCA permitted DOL to find "prevailing wage rates" which were lower than those being paid by an incumbent contractor under a collective bargaining agreement. As a consequence, competitors were often able to propose lower wages than were being paid by an incumbent so long as they were consistent with the DOL wage rate determinations. *National Labor Relations Board* v. *Burns International Security Services, Inc.*, 406 U.S. 272 (1972). Subsequent amendments to the SCA prohibited successor contractors from paying "less than the wages and fringe benefits * * * provided for in a collective-bargaining agreement as a result of arm's-length negotiations, to which such service employees would have been entitled if they were employed under the predecessor contract * * *." 41 U.S.C. 353(c) (1976). However, no such collective bargaining agreement exists in this case, and hence neither DOL nor Dynalectron was bound by the wages previously paid by Joule to its employees under the predecessor contract.

The Office of Federal Procurement Policy (OFPP) has sought to preclude wage busting for professional employees, a class of people not normally covered by union agreements, by providing for agencies to consider lowered professional employee compensation as indicating a lack of sound management. 43 Fed. Reg. 18805, May 2, 1978. The OFPP procedures are clearly inapplicable to this case, however, because their effective date (April 1, 1978) is subsequent to the December 1977 date the RFP was issued. As a consequence, there is no impediment either in the SCA, in the regulations, or in anything else to prevent a reduction in wages for incumbent employees in this case, even if a reduction can be categorized as "wage busting."

Nonetheless, we do question the efficacy of the contracting officer's cost realism determination. While Dynalectron claimed it had its own employees available for contract performance, it asserted that:

> [I]t is our intention to utilize, to the maximum extent possible, currently assigned [incumbent] employees. This approach recognizes the performance improvement curve of incumbent personnel, a management tool the government has relied upon for many years to forecast cost. The retention of incumbent personnel will result in maximum performance at the lowest cost.
> * * * we have projected the price, wages and pay as realistically as possible. It is Dynalectron's policy to pay * * * wages consistent with the work schedule and the responsibilities assigned to each employee. * * * The labor rates for the contract period are based on the following:
> —"Curent wage rates for incumbent personnel
> —Wage Determination #75–639, Rev. #2
> —Projected Cost Increases * * *."
> We assume that the overall cost evaluation will include accurate, current and realistic estimating practices and that this cost realism will be a part of the government's evaluation.

There is no evidence on the record to suggest that, except for the Level IV technicians, the incumbent's employees were to be reclassified to perform different duties for Dynalectron. Indeed, for Dynalectron to have done so would be inconsistent with the premise in its proposal which recognized "the performance improvement curve of incumbent personnel" and that "retention of incumbent personnel will result in maximum performance at lowest total cost." The familiarity of the incumbent's personnel with the work required as well as the impact on costs resulting from their retention presumably were considered in the proposal evaluation process. Thus, while Dynalectron was not legally obligated to pay the wages paid by its predecessor, we believe that in view of the express language of its proposal the contracting officer's consideration of its proposed costs should have taken into account the wages previously paid to these personnel, not merely the minimum wages specified in the DOL wage rate determination and the offeror claimed conformance thereto.

In this respect, we have reviewed the DCAA audit reports of the cost proposals of both Dynalectron and Joule.

When comparing Joule's proposed labor rates for item 0001 (the base year of the contract) to the most current payroll records at the time of the examination, DCAA found no basis for questioning those costs. DCAA also found that the labor rates proposed for Items 0003 and 0004 (the option period) were based on "current labor rates" plus an escalation. DCAA questioned only the extent of the proposed escalation for the option year, not the base rates themselves. Since the DCAA audit of Joule's proposal was based on actual payroll data, and presumably to some extent the prevailing wage rate for similar personnel in the area, particularly with respect to those jobs not required for the base year (where no actual payroll data existed), we think it was incumbent on the contracting officer to verify through negotiations Dynalectron's proposed labor costs *vis-a-vis* the statements contained in its proposal. *See* 47 Comp. Gen. 336 (1967).

There is no evidence to suggest that the contracting officer questioned the potential disparity between actual payroll data and Dynalectron's proposed labor costs or the significant difference in wage rates it proposed where no payroll data existed. For example, Dynalectron proposed wages at $3.75 per hour for Level I Electronic Technicians, who by the terms of the solicitation were required to have a "minimum of one year's general electronic experience and one year specialized experience on radar and/or test equipment or related systems," with education either in technical school or in the military. These wage rates showed no escalation for the option year ostensibly because no such personnel were required during the initial year's contract performance. Yet DCAA verified that Joule has experienced an average of 7.2 percent annual wage increase for personnel on its payroll at the job site, a rate which appears to be in keeping with general inflationary trends currently experienced in the United States. In addition, the DOL determination listed applicable minimum rates for the base year for other personnel such as typists (Class A) at $4.10 per hour, Class B at $3.87 per hour, file clerks, Class A at $4.31 per hour and Class B at $3.97 per hour, all at higher hourly rates than proposed by Dynalectron for Level I technical personnel.

We believe that where, as here, the award of a contract is ultimately based strictly on costs proposed, a determination of cost realism requires more than the acceptance of proposed costs as submitted. DCAA's audits were admittedly limited in scope and were not considered in conjunction with any technical evaluation. More importantly, however, the DCAA audit report did contain a significant caveat, i.e.,:

Although the cost and pricing data are not adequate in all respects (see paragraph 2, "Special Circumstances Affecting the Examination") the proposal may be considered to be acceptable as a basis for negotiation. [Translation : There were missing items of support for the costs proposed, but based on the data in hand, there was nothing to indicate the proposed costs were not in line with the data examined. Consider this in negotiation].

Paragraph 2 referred to above, includes a statement that:

Although we reviewed the proposal to the extent possible in the circumstances, we were unable to reach a definitive conclusion on the quantitative and qualitative aspects of the proposal * * *.

Also, the DCAA report stated that:

The evaluation disclosed no questioned unsupported or unresolved items which would preclude acceptance of the [Dynalectron] proposal as submitted.

However, in view of the qualifications noted above, we question the extent to which the contracting officer could reasonably rely on the Dynalectron proposal "as submitted," particularly when he was faced with a comparative audit report based on "current labor rates" at substantial variance to those proposed by Dynalectron. Ultimately the contracting officer is responsible for the exercise of the requisite judgments and solely responsible for the pricing decisions. Audit reports are advisory only and at most form the basis for these pricing decisions. DAR 3–801.2(d)(1) (1976 ed.).

The award of cost reimbursement contracts requires the exercise of informed judgments as to whether proposed costs are realistic and it is improper to award such a contract on the basis that such costs are reasonable because they are low *per se* on a comparative basis if the Government fails to adequately measure the realism of such low costs. *See* 50 Comp. Gen. 390 (1970). In this respect, the report submitted by the agency indicates to us that the contracting officer did not perform any cost realism analysis in conjunction with the technical and management proposals, but instead relied solely upon the significantly qualified DCAA audit findings. Also, the record does not show that the contracting officer questioned Dynalectron's application of the DOL wage rate determination in connection with the clearly expressed statements in its proposal that its proposed wage rates were based on current wage rates for incumbent personnel. Neither is there any indication that for those categories of labor where DOL had not issued a wage rate determination, the contracting officer considered the possibility that the wages were unrealistically low (particularly in view of the DCAA finding in its audit of Joule's proposal and the DOL wage rates for clerical type personnel) or that the lack of an inflation escalation factor for those wage rates might reflect on the credibility of the cost proposal. In our view, the contracting officer, when faced with material variances between the competing proposals, should have verified the discrepancies by requesting verification and support for the wage rates proposed by Dynalectron. We do not here suggest that Dynalectron's cost proposal would not ultimately have been found to be realistic, had an analysis been formed. However, in the apparent absence of such an analysis, we must view the contracting officer's cost realism determination as inadequate.

Finally, Joule suggests that there may have been an impropriety in the evaluation of proposals because of its claim that within one week of contract award, one member of the evaluation team was hired by Dynalectron to administer the contract. However, Dynalectron points out it was not until *after* award that it learned of the retirement plans of the party in question and it was at that time that it made its offer of employment. Thus, because of the time sequence involved, Dynalectron in effect claims the employment offer could not have influenced the evaluation process. We have no reason to question the veracity of Dynalectron's statements in this respect, and Joule has offered no evidence to the contrary.

Although we find the cost analysis to have been inadequate, we need not recommend corrective action since we have been advised by the contracting officer that the Navy will not exercise the option for the second year's performance, but will extend the contract for the limited period necessary to resolicit and award on the basis of expanded requirements. We believe such agency action is reasonable under the circumstances. By separate letter of today, we are pointing out to the Secretary of the Navy our concern with regard to the cost analysis.

The protest is sustained in part and denied in part.

[B-192863]

Real Property—Acquisition—Relocation Costs—Uniform Relocation Assistance and Real Property Acquisition Policies Act of 1970

Title II of the Uniform Relocation Assistance and Real Property Acquisition Policies Act of 1970, Pub. L. No. 91–646, 84 Stat. 1894, 42 U.S.C. 4601 *et seq.* (1976), is inapplicable to Federal Government or State agency acquisition of property for a program or project undertaken by a Federal agency or with Federal financial assistance, where property owner is not displaced or relocated as a result of such acquisition.

Real Property—Acquisition—Condemnation Proceedings—Uniform Relocation Assistance and Real Property Acquisition Policies Act of 1970

Title III of the Uniform Relocation Assistance and Real Property Acquisition Policies Act of 1970, Pub. L. 91–646, 84 Stat. 1894, 42 U.S.C. 4601 *et seq.* (1976), sets forth uniform and equitable procedures for the taking of real property by Federal Government or by State agencies receiving Federal financial assistance. Pursuant to section 305, provisions of Title III are mandatory, to the extent practicable, upon States as condition to their receipt of Federal financial assistance. Title III is applicable to acquisition of any interest in real property, including easements, even where acquisition is funded solely by local funds, if underlying program or project is Federally administered or assisted.

Real Property—Acquisition—Reimbursement—Adequacy

Nothing in the Uniform Relocation Assistance and Real Property Acquisition Policies Act of 1970, Pub. L. No. 91–646, 84 Stat. 1894, 42 U.S.C. 4601 *et seq.* (1976) affects long-standing definition of just compensation which requires landowner to be put in as good shape pecuniarily as he or she would have been if property had not been taken. Where taking of easements has, in fact, benefitted remainder of landowner's property which was not taken, accruing benefit is to be set off against value of property interest actually taken. When direct benefits to landowner exceed value of easement taken, no monetary compensation is required. In our view, the Environmental Protection Agency may use any widely accepted appraisal method which takes both direct benefits and damages into account.

Real Property—Acquisition—Reimbursement—Adequacy

Nothing in the Uniform Relocation Assistance and Real Property Acquisition Policies Act of 1970, Pub. L. No. 91–646, 84 Stat. 1894, 42 U.S.C. 4601 et seq. (1976), prevents an owner—who receives Government or State agency offer to purchase real property for no less than appraised fair market value of property— from willingly and knowingly selling property for less than amount offered, and the Government or State agency from purchasing property for lesser amount.

To The Honorable Gillespie V. Montgomery, House of Representatives, and The Honorable John C. Stennis, United States Senate, May 23, 1979:

This is in response to the request submitted jointly by you, Senator John C. Stennis, and former Senator James O. Eastland, that we determine whether the Rankin County (Mississippi) Regional Sewer System is subject to the requirements of section 305 of the Uniform Relocation Assistance and Real Property Acquisition Policies Act of 1970, Pub. L. No. 91–646, 84 Stat. 1894, January 2, 1971, 42 U.S.C. §§ 4601 *et seq.* (1976) (Act), with respect to the acquisition by the System of easements necessary to the construction of sewage and water systems.

In order to assist us in responding to your inquiry, we requested a report from the Administrator of the Environmental Protection Agency (EPA) setting forth the agency's views on this question, and the legal authority for its position. After some initial delay, we received two reports from EPA. This opinion is based on these reports as well as on our interpretation of the Act in light of the facts you outlined in your correspondence with us.

Title II of the Act, which contains the relocation assistance provisions, establishes a uniform policy for the fair and equitable treatment of persons displaced as a result of Federal and federally-assisted programs. See section 201 of the Act, 42 U.S.C. § 4621. Title II of the Act applies only to "displaced persons" as that term is defined in section 101(6) of the Act, 42 U.S.C. § 4601(6).

Your letter states that "the process of securing easements, as well as the actual construction of the sewer system, will not result in any relocation or displacement of persons or businesses or farms." On the basis of this statement, it is obvious that there are no "displaced persons" as a result of the acquisition of the subject easements by the System. For this reason we agree that the provisions of Title II of the Act are inapplicable to the situation you describe. See *Beiard-Poulan Division of Emerson Electric Company* v. *Department of Highways, State of Louisiana*, 441 F. Supp. 866, 872 (W.D. La. 1977). However, this does not make the entire Act inapplicable.

Title III of the Act, which contains the real property acquisition policies provisions, sets forth uniform and equitable nationwide procedures for the taking of real property by the Federal Government or by State agencies receiving Federal financial assistance. Sections 301–304 of the Act, 42 U.S.C. §§ 4651–4654, by their terms apply to Federal agencies acquiring real property for Federal projects. Section 305, 42 U.S.C. § 4655, makes compliance with the provisions of the preceding sections mandatory, to the greatest extent practicable under State law, upon the States and their agencies as a condition to their receipt of Federal financial assistance. Section 101(3) of the Act defines "State agency" to include departments, agencies, or instrumentalities of a State or of a political subdivision of a State. We assume that the Rankin County Regional Sewer System is such a State agency.

Further, the Act is applicable even though only easements are being acquired. Neither section 305 nor any other provision of the Act specifically defines the term "acquisition" or sets forth what types of interests in real property are covered thereby. We believe it clear, however, that the provisions of the Act apply when an easement is being acquired. See, *e.g.*, sections 301(8) and 302(a) of the Act, both of which speak of acquisition of *any* interest in real property. In this regard, at 40 C.F.R. § 4.600, EPA has promulgated a regulation which by its terms makes Title III requirements applicable to the acquisition of easements for EPA administered or EPA assisted projects. See also the unpublished decision in *City of Fayetteville, Arkansas* v. *Harris*, Civil No. F–76–45–C (W.D. Ark., filed August 17, 1977). [Copy eliminated from this publication.]

You point out in your letter that under the applicable law, the subject EPA grant funds cannot be used for land acquisition costs, including the acquisition of easements. You question whether, since only local funds are being used to secure the easements, the provisions of Title III of the Act apply. We believe they do.

The fact that only local funds are being used to acquire the easements is not controlling on the issue of the applicability of section 305, and of the Act as a whole, to such acquisitions. Rather, it is a question of whether the underlying project for which the easements are required is financed in whole or in part by Federal financial assistance. See, *e.g., Lake Park Home Owners Association* v. *H.U.D.,* 443 F. Supp. 6 (S.D. Ohio 1976), where in interpreting the applicability of section 101(6) of the Act the Court stated in pertinent part:

> The pertinent question arising from such language [acquisition of property for a program or project undertaken with Federal financial assistance] is not whether federal monies directly funded the acquisition of the real property involved, but whether the state program or project which resulted in the acquisition was federally assisted. * * * The statute turns on whether there is federal funding of the program or project, not whether the funds can be traced directly to the acquisition of a particular parcel of real estate. *Id.,* at 8–9.

In subsequent letters, we were referred to *Rhodes* v. *City of Chicago, Use of Schools,* 516 F. 2d 1373 (7th Cir. 1975), and *Goolsby* v. *Blumenthal,* 590 F. 2d 1369 (1979), *rehearing en banc, aff'g in part, rev'g in part* 581 F. 2d 455 (5th Cir. 1978), which it was felt might have a bearing on the question presented. The Court in *Rhodes* held that section 305 of the Act "is applicable only when Federal financial assistance is used in or directly supports the property acquisitions," *Rhodes* v. *City of Chicago, supra,* at 1377. In that case, the Federal assistance was merely the broad range of educational assistance which, directly or indirectly, flowed to the city. None of these funds had any particular relationship to the condemnation proceedings involved in that case. In the instant case, even though Federal funds are not "used in" these purchases, the acquisition of easements is, as we understand it, necessary for and directly related to the subject sewer project.

The Court of Appeals in *Goolsby* v. *Blumenthal, supra,* reversed in pertinent part an earlier panel opinion and affirmed the judgment of the district court holding that the Uniform Relocation Act does not apply to projects in which the only Federal involvement is the presence of Federal revenue sharing funds. This decision is based on the terms of the State and Local Fiscal Assistance Act of 1972 (Revenue Sharing Act), 31 U.S.C. § 1221 *et seq.* (1976), which exclude the application of acts not specifically mentioned in the body of the Revenue Sharing Act, 590 F. 2d at 1371. In fact, the Court distinguishes the Revenue Sharing Act from the more customary block grant programs to which the Uniform Relocation Act does apply, 590 F. 2d at 1372. For this reason, we believe this decision is inapplicable to the question presented here.

Thus, *Rhodes* and *Goolsby* are not controlling in this situation, and the System must comply with the provisions of Title III of the Act in acquiring easements for the sewer project. These provisions include, *inter alia*, (1) an agency offer to purchase real property in an amount believed to be just compensation, but in no event less than the agency's appraised fair market value of the property, section 301(3), 42 U.S.C. § 4651(3); (2) reimbursement to the owner of the property of certain expenses incurred incidental to the transfer of title to the agency, section 303, 42 U.S.C. § 4653; and (3) payment of specified litigation expenses resulting from condemnation proceedings where judgment is against the agency, section 304, 42 U.S.C. § 4654.

We recognize that these requirements can result in substantial costs being incurred by the acquiring agency, but are aware of nothing in the legislation or its history that indicates a congressional intent to exempt from the clear requirements of the Act the acquisition of easements for interceptor sewer lines being financed in part by EPA.

In a report to us from the Assistant General Counsel of EPA, the agency has recognized the concerns of State agencies caused by these increased costs, and states that the key to these concerns "is the treatment of betterment in the acquisition of easements." Acquisition of all interests in real property is covered by section 301(3) of the Act, which provides in pertinent part:

> (3) Before the initiation of negotiations for real property, the head of the Federal agency concerned shall establish an amount which he believes to be just compensation therefor and shall make a prompt offer to acquire the property for the full amount so established. In no event shall such amount be less than the agency's approved appraisal of the fair market value of such property. Any decrease or increase in the fair market value of real property prior to the date of valuation caused by the public improvement for which such property is acquired, or by the likelihood that the property would be acquired for such improvement, other than that due to physical deterioration within the reasonable control of the owner, will be disregarded in determining the compensation for the property. * * *

The agency consistently has held that these provisions apply to the acquisition of easements for Federal or federally-assisted projects, see, 40 C.F.R. § 4.600, and in its appraisals has ignored all increases or decreases in the value of the property caused by actual or contemplated acquisition for a public improvement. It now proposes to apply a new policy, and to construe section 301 based on the interpretation set forth in the Uniform Appraisal Standards for Federal Land Acquisitions, which permits the use of a "before and after" method of determining the fair market value of easements.

In its report, EPA provided an illustration of its understanding of the application of the "before and after" method of appraisal where land value increases because of the publicly financed project.

> For example, on January 1, the property value of the land is $100,000. Then, on February 1, a municipality announces a sewer interceptor line construction project to be funded by Federal funds. The land value rises to $120,000 as a result of the announcement. On March 1, the appraisal is made and the fair market value is estimated to be $100,000. The $120,000 figure is not taken into consideration because under 42 U.S.C. § 4651(a) [sic] the $20,000 increase was caused by the announcement of the project. The appraisal also estimates that

after the project is completed, the fair market value of the property will be $135,000. Because there is an increase in property value from $100,000 to $135,000, it is our interpretation that the landowner need not be compensated under Title III of the Act for the acquisition of a sewer easement for the federally funded project. Otherwise, the landowner will receive a windfall. See *Bausman* [sic] v. *Ross*, 167 U.S. 548, 570 (1897). Under this interpretation the vast majority of easement questions under the Act would be eliminated.

This interpretation appears to require EPA to set off against the appraised fair market value of the easement, the amount of increased value it estimates will accrue to the remaining property as a result of the benefit conferred on the property by the program or project, even to the point of eliminating all compensation for the easement.

We would prefer not to comment on the use of any particular appraisal method at this time. It is clear, however, that under this Act landowners are entitled to receive "just compensation." The owner is "entitled to receive the value of what he has been deprived of, and no more. To award him less would be unjust to him; to award him more would be unjust to the public." *Bauman* v. *Ross*, *supra*, at 574–575. This involves consideration of damages on the one hand and benefits on the other. *Aaronson* v. *United States*, 79 F. 2d 139 (D.C. Circuit 1935). As the Supreme Court has stated:

The constitutional prohibition against uncompensated taking of private property for public use is grounded upon a conception of the injustice in favoring the public as against an individual property owner. But if governmental activities inflict slight damage upon land in one respect and actually confer great benefits when measured in the whole, to compensate the landowner further would be to grant him a special bounty. Such activities in substance take nothing from the landowner.

United States v. *Sponenbarger*, 308 U.S. 256, 266–267 (1939). See also *United States* v. *Miller*, 317 U.S. 369, 373–376 (1943) ; *Ark-Mo. Farms, Inc.* v. *United States*, 530 F. 2d 1384, 1386 (Ct. Cl. 1976) ; *Hartwig* v. *United States*, 485 F. 2d 615 (Ct. Cl. 1973) ; *United States* v. *3,317.39 Acres of Land, Jefferson County, Ark.*, 443 F. 2d 104 (8th Cir. 1971) ; *United States* v. *901.89 Acres of Land, Tenn.*, 436 F. 2d 395, 398 (6th Cir. 1970) ; and *6,816.5 Acres of Land, Rio Arriba Co., N.M.* v. *United States*, 411 F. 2d 834 (10th Cir. 1969).

There is nothing in the Uniform Relocation Act which affects this long-standing definition of just compensation which requires that the landowner be put in as good shape pecuniarily as he or she would have been if the property had not been taken. Where the taking of easements has, in fact, benefitted the remainder of the landowner's property which was not taken, the accruing benefit may be set off against the value of the property interest actually taken. When the direct benefits to the landowner exceed the value of the easement taken, no monetary compensation is required. In our view, EPA may use any appraisal method which takes both the direct benefits and the damages into account in determining "just compensation."

Whether or not payment must be made to individual landowners, EPA states that in its construction grant program authorized by Title II of the Clean Water Act, 33 U.S.C. §§ 1281 *et seq.*, as amended, "the process of obtaining easements in compliance with the [Uniform Relocation] Act entails a considerable amount of paperwork and effort for grantees."

For example, the grantee must appraise the value of each individual easement and give the landowner the written results thereof and, where applicable, an offer of money not less than the appraised value. The landowner is statutorily entitled to participate in the appraisal process. These activities entail time, effort, and expense even if no money is paid for the actual acquisition of the easements. EPA suggests that since there are other Federal agencies with similar programs, "a recommendation from your office to the Congress for further study of possible amendment to the legislation would undoubtedly be welcomed by numerous grantees in the EPA program and other similar programs which require the acquisition of easements." We might point out that the only absolutely definitive way of determining whether an individual landowner receives more in benefit than the value of the easement taken is to perform appraisals on each landowner's property. However, if EPA, and any other interested agency, could reliably demonstrate that all landowners under any particular program would be benefitted, an amendment to the Uniform Relocation Act which would relieve grantees of certain responsibilities (such as making individual appraisals) which do not benefit the landowners would appear to be sensible.

A subsequent letter from you raised an additional issue, which in this particular circumstance appears to be in large part moot due to our answers above. Specifically, you ask whether easements (or by extension, any interest in property to be acquired) can be purchased by the State agency for an amount less than the appraised value, where the sellers are willing to accept nominal consideration only. Provided that the acquiring agency meets its obligations under the Act to offer just compensation for the property, we are aware of no statutory prohibition against the consummation of a sale for less than the fair market value if the owner is willing to sell on that basis.

The purpose of the Act's requirements is to protect individual property owners from the superior negotiating position that the Federal Government or State and local Governments (for federally assisted projects) enjoy. Once the property owner receives the Government's offer for the amount which the agency has determined to be just compensation for the property, which amount may be no less than the agency's approved appraisal of the fair market value of the property, the property owner may accept that amount or negotiate for a different amount. In most cases we would assume that a property owner would not be interested in accepting less than the full amount of the Government's offer and any negotiation would be for the purpose of obtaining a higher payment. However, in those situations where the owner knowingly and willingly wants to accept a lesser payment for the property, we see nothing in the Act requiring him to take the full amount proffered by the agency, nor are we aware of anything requiring, in those circumstances, that the agency actually pay the full amount. It would be incumbent, of course, upon the head of the Federal agency involved both as to Federal projects and federally assisted projects over which he has jurisdiction, to assure that pressure is not placed on property owners to accept less than the amounts to which they are entitled. ·

Accordingly, if the Rankin County Sewer System offers to purchase an easement from a real property owner for no less than the approved appraisal of the fair market value of such property, there is nothing in the Act which would prevent that owner, upon receipt of such an offer, from willingly selling the property for less than the amount offered by the System, and the System from buying the easement for the lesser amount.

We trust that this information will be helpful to you.

[B–194278]

Pay—Retired—Foreign Citizenship Effect

A retired Regular Army officer residing in Israel acquired Israeli citizenship by operation of Israeli law, but also remains a United States citizen. While the loss of United States citizenship is inconsistent with status as a retired Regular officer and thus results in loss of status as an officer and loss of entitlement to retired pay, dual Israeli/United States citizenship alone does not require loss of entitlement to retired pay.

Pay—Retired—Foreign Military Service Effect

A retired Regular Army officer residing in Israel who has dual Israeli/United States citizenship is subject to service in the Israel Defense Forces, the Israeli armed force. Such service in a foreign armed force by a retired Regular Officer appears inherently inconsistent with his position as a Regular Army officer, as well as being prohibited (without congressional consent) by Article I, section 9, clause 8 of the Constitution of the United States. Thus, service in the foreign armed force would make his status as a retired Army officer very doubtful. Retired pay may not be paid to him without authorizing legislation.

In the matter of Lieutenant Colonel Thomas E. Snyder, USA Retired, May 25, 1979:

The issue presented by this case is the effect on a retired Regular Army officer's retired pay when he lives in a foreign country, acquires dual citizenship by operation of the foreign country's laws, and serves in the armed forces of the foreign country. We conclude that while dual citizenship would not affect retired pay, service in a military force of the foreign country is incompatible with Regular retired status as well as contrary to a provision of the Constitution. Thus, retired pay must be discontinued when a retired officer becomes a member of the foreign military force.

The matter was presented for decision by the Assistant Secretary of the Army (Installations, Logistics and Financial Matters) and was assigned submission number SS–A–1313 by the Department of Defense Military Pay and Allowance Committee.

Background

The reported facts of the matter are that Lieutenant Colonel Thomas E. Snyder, USA, was retired under 10 U.S.C. 3911 (1976) with over 20 years' service and is residing in Israel. He is a citizen of the United States but automatically acquired Israeli citizenship because of his Jewish heritage and residence in that country. The United States Department of State and Embassy in Israel consider Colonel Snyder to have dual citizenship. Colonel Snyder states that he has not relinquished his United States citizenship but acquired foreign citizenship with no action on his part. He states, however, that as a citizen of Israel he is required to serve in the Israel Defense Forces for a period of 3 or 4 weeks each year. It is not known whether he will receive pay for the time he serves.

Because of our decisions holding in certain cases that loss of United States citizenship is inconsistent with continued military status, which then entails loss of entitlement to retired pay, the Assistant Secretary questions Colonel Snyder's entitlement. He also asks if loss of entitlement to retired pay is not required because of dual citizenship, what is the proper application of Article I, section 9, clause 8 of the Constitution of the United States if he serves in the Israel Defense Forces.

The Assistant Secretary presents the following specific questions:

1. Would Colonel Snyder, an officer of a Regular component, who retired under 10 USC 3911, and who is a citizen of the United States, forfeit his retired pay if he automatically becomes a citizen of Israel by reason of his Jewish heritage and residence in that country?

2. If the answer to question 1 is in the negative, does he forfeit payment of retired pay because of mandatory service in the defense forces of that country for 3 to 4 weeks each year?

3. If the answer to question 2 is in the affirmative, is the forfeiture of pay only during the period of military service or a total forfeiture?

Status of Retired Regular Officers

Retired Regular officers are members of the military service of the United States and are considered as holding an office of profit or trust. See 10 U.S.C. 3075 (1976) and *Puglisi* v. *United States*, 564 F. 2d 403, 410 (Ct. Cl. 1977), *cert. denied*, 435 U.S. 968 (1978); *Hooper* v. *United States*, 164 Ct. Cl. 151 (1964); and *United States* v. *Tyler*, 105 U.S. 244 (1881).

Regular officers retired for years of service, such as those retired under 10 U.S.C. 3911, receive retired pay by virtue of their continuing status as military officers, and loss of that status would entail loss of entitlement to retired pay. 41 Comp. Gen. 715 (1962); 37 *id.* 207, 209 (1957) (question 3); and 23 *id.* 284, 286 (1943).

Loss of United States Citizenship Effect

It has long been our view that retired military officers who receive retired pay by virtue of their continuing military status lose their entitlement to retired pay upon the loss of their United States citizenship. The theory in those cases is that acceptance of foreign citizenship which results in loss of United States citizenship is repugnant to their oath of office and inconsistent with the continuation of their status as officers of the United States. See 37 Comp. Gen. 207, 209 (1957); 41 *id.* 715 (1962), and 10 U.S.C. 3285 (1976). See also 44 Comp. Gen. 51 (1964), and 44 *id.* 227 (1964), to the same effect concerning certain retired enlisted members and members of the Fleet Reserve.

Since apparently Colonel Snyder has not lost his United States citizenship merely by residing in Israel and receiving Israeli citizenship, he would not lose his entitlement to retired pay on that basis. Question 1 is, therefore, answered, no.

We also note, however, that section 349 of the Immigration Nationality Act, June 27, 1952, ch. 477, 66 Stat. 163, 267–268, as amended, 8 U.S.C. 1481 (1976), provides in subsection (a)(3) that a United States national shall lose his nationality by—

entering, or serving in, the armed forces of a foreign state unless, prior to such entry or service, such entry or service is specifically authorized in writing by the Secretary of State and the Secretary of Defense * * *

However, the continued vitality of that provision, at least as it relates to a case such as this, appears questionable in view of the Supreme

Court's decision in *Afroyim* v. *Rusk*, 387 U.S. 253 (1967). In that case the court found unconstitutional another provision of the Immigration and Nationality Act (8 U.S.C. 1481(a)(5)) under which a United States national would lose his citizenship by voting in a political election in a foreign state. In doing so the court held that Congress cannot forcibly take away the citizenship of a United States citizen and that the constitution insures the right of an individual to remain a citizen unless he "voluntarily relinquishes" it.

Apparently Colonel Snyder does not wish to relinquish his United States citizenship and, based on the bare facts presented to us, it appears doubtful that his service in the Israel Defense Forces would be considered tantamount to a voluntary relinquishment of his citizenship. See *Baker* v. *Rusk*, 296 F. Supp. 1244 (C.D. Calif. 1969), and *In re Balsamo*, 306 F. Supp. 1028 (N.D. Ill. 1969). In any event determinations and rulings of law under the Immigration and Nationality Act are matters primarily within the jurisdiction of the Attorney General. 8 U.S.C. 1103(a) (1976). Colonel Snyder would be well advised to seek an authoritative ruling as to the effect on his citizenship of 8 U.S.C. 1481(a)(3) should he serve in the Israel Defense Forces so that he may seek the necessary authorization, if necessary.

Should it be determined that such service would result in loss of his citizenship, our decisions cited previously would apply and he would not be entitled to retired pay on that basis.

Incompatibility of Service in Foreign Armed Force

In addition, whether or not his United States citizenship is affected, there must be considered the obvious inherent incompatibility of a Regular United States military officer serving in a foreign armed force, as well as the explicit prohibition contained in Article I, section 9, clause 8 of the Constitution.

As we understand it the Israel Defense Forces is the integrated land, sea, and air military organization of Israel. Service in the reserve of the Israel Defense Forces appears similar to service in our Army Reserve. That is, members serve regular periods of active duty or active duty for training and are subject to call to active duty at any time during periods of war or national emergency.

By entering into such service Colonel Snyder obviously would become subject to the orders and requirements of the foreign armed force which he would be bound to follow and from which he could not voluntarily withdraw. Thus, he would be placed in a position clearly incompatible with his position as an officer of the United States subject to the laws, regulations and orders of the United States Army, including the Uniform Code of Military Justice (10 U.S.C. 802), recall to active duty (10 U.S.C. 3504), and the requirements of his oath of office (5 U.S.C. 3331).

Also, Article I, section 9, clause 8 of the Constitution of the United States provides that—

* * * no Person holding any Office of Profit or Trust under them [the United States], shall, without the Consent of the Congress, accept of any present, Emolument, Office, or Title, of any kind whatever, from any King, Prince, or foreign State.

The language of that provision is particularly directed against every kind of influence by foreign governments upon officers of the United States. 24 Op. Atty. Gen. 116 (1902).

We have considered cases involving retired members engaging in *civil* employment with foreign government controlled corporations or instrumentalities without congressional consent. In those cases we have not concluded that the retired members lost their military status by the unauthorized acceptance of the emoluments incident to the civil employment. However, we have held that the emoluments received are deemed accepted on behalf of the United States and, therefore, the members' retired pay is to be withheld in an amount equal to such emoluments. 44 Comp. Gen. 130 (1964) and B–178538, October 13, 1977. Unlike this case, however, those cases involved civil employment and the acceptance of a foreign office or title, in addition to emoluments, was not an issue.

Congress has granted conditional consent for retired members of the uniformed services to accept foreign government "civil employment." See Section 509, Foreign Relations Authorization Act, Fiscal Year 1978, Public Law 95–105, August 17, 1977, 91 Stat. 844, 859–860, 37 U.S.C. 801 note. However, that consent does not apply to foreign *military* service and would have no application to this case.

Therefore, since Colonel Snyder does not have congressional consent to the proposed service, in view of the broad language of the constitutional prohibition against accepting a foreign office or title "of any kind whatever" without congressional consent, and the obvious inherent incompatibility involved in a retired Regular officer serving in a foreign armed force, should Colonel Snyder serve in the Israel Defense Forces his continued status as a United States officer would be very doubtful. In those circumstances, without authorizing legislation, we could not approve any further payments of retired pay to Colonel Snyder. Questions 2 and 3 are answered accordingly.

[B–192811]

Leaves of Absence—Annual—Charging—Excess Compensatory Time

Employee, who was erroneously granted compensatory time off in excess of the hours for which he could have received overtime pay under the aggregate salary limitation in 5 U.S.C. 5547, requests recredit of 47 hours of annual leave which agency charged to recover erroneous payments. Payments for the salary paid for excess compensatory time off must be recovered but are subject to waiver under 5 U.S.C. 5584 and 4 C.F.R. Part 91. Employee's annual leave balance may not be charged for compensatory time erroneously granted without employee's consent. Modified (amplified) by 59 Comp. Gen.—(B–196444. Feb. 8, 1980).

In the matter of Edward W. Dorcheus—Overpayment of Compensatory Time, June 5, 1979:

This decision is in response to a request from the Department of Energy (DOE) concerning the claim of Mr. Edward W. Dorcheus, a DOE employee, for restoration of 47 hours of annual leave which was charged by DOE to recoup excess compensatory time off. The issue presented for decision is the method by which an agency may recover hours of compensatory time which have been erroneously granted to and used by the employee.

The report from DOE states that while Mr. Dorcheus was employed at the Federal Energy Administration (an agency which became part of DOE) he was credited with 126 hours of compensatory time between April and June of 1975. The report states further that of these 126 hours of compensatory time, 47 hours were erroneously credited to Mr. Dorcheus since these hours were in excess of the biweekly limitation on premium pay contained in 5 U.S.C. § 5547. Since Mr. Dorcheus had already used all 126 hours of compensatory time, the agency charged the 47 hours to his annual leave account and thereby reduced his personal leave ceiling.

Mr. Dorcheus has requested restoration of the annual leave so as to restore his personal leave ceiling to 350 hours. He states that he was unaware of the limitation on compensatory time, and he argues that he is being further penalized through the reduction in his personal leave ceiling.

Under the provisions of 5 U.S.C. § 5543(a), agencies may grant compensatory time off instead of paying overtime compensation for time spent in irregular or occasional overtime work. However, we have long held that such compensatory time is subject to the aggregate salary limitation contained in 5 U.S.C. § 5547. 37 Comp. Gen. 362 (1957) and 26 *id.* 750 (1947). Under that limitation, employees may be paid premium pay only to the extent that the payment does not cause the employee's aggregate rate of pay for any pay period to exceed the maximum rate for grade GS–15. Also, the hours of compensatory time may not exceed the number of hours for which the employee may receive overtime pay.

In the present case, the agency determined that it had erroneously granted Mr. Dorcheus 47 hours of compensatory time in excess of the aggregate salary limitation, and, citing our decision in 37 Comp. Gen. 362, *supra*, it charged the excess hours which had already been used by Mr. Dorcheus to his annual leave account. In addition, the agency, citing our decision in B–176020, August 4, 1972, denied Mr. Dorcheus' request for waiver of the overpayment of pay since Mr. Dorcheus had sufficient leave to cover the adjustment to his leave account.

In our decision in 37 Comp. Gen. 362, *supra*, the third question presented to our Office was whether excess compensatory time granted and used would be automatically charged to annual leave. In response, we held that the granting of annual leave is a matter of administrative discretion and that the cancellation of excess compensatory time would not automatically convert the time off on excess compensatory leave to annual leave. 37 *id*. 362, at 364, *supra*. See also 45 *id*. 243 (1965). We find no authority, however, for the agency to charge excess compensatory time off to the employee's annual leave balance without his consent. We believe the proper course of action to recover compensatory time erroneously granted is to recoup the amount paid for the compensatory time. Recovery of the salary paid for the compensatory time erroneously taken may be considered for waiver pursuant to the provisions of 5 U.S.C. § 5584 and 4 C.F.R. Part 91. If waiver is not allowed, the employee's annual leave balance could, with his consent, be reduced by the amount of compensatory time erroneously granted and used.

In the present case, the erroneous crediting of compensatory time to Mr. Dorcheus should be considered for waiver. If the overpayment is waived or, alternatively, if Mr. Dorcheus elects to repay to the Government the amount erroneously paid, the charge to annual leave should be recredited to his leave account and his personal leave ceiling should be restored. If Mr. Dorcheus does not agree to repay the amount paid for the compensatory time, such amount may be recovered by means of offset. See 5 U.S.C. § 5514. Our decision in B–176020, *supra*, which was cited by the agency in denying waiver, was concerned with the improper granting of administrative leave and the agency's action to correct the error by charging the absence to annual leave. This decision has no application to compensatory time off which is a form of compensation for services rendered.

Accordingly, action should be taken on the employee's request consistent with the above discussion, if otherwise proper.

[B-194286]

Contracts—Negotiation—Requests for Proposals—Submission Date—Extension—Notice Requirement

Where snowstorm closed agency on original closing date and agency extended closing date for only 24 hours, even though debilitating conditions continued beyond that time, agency should not reject proposal as late because there was no urgency to justify the informal rescheduling of the closing date and interested parties have not alleged or shown premature disclosure of other proposals. In the absence of any urgency, agency abused its discretion in extending closing date without informing prospective offerors of that fact.

In the matter of CompuServe, June 5, 1979:

CompuServe protests the rejection of its proposal under request for proposals (RFP) No. N66032–78–R–0009, issued by the Department of the Navy. CompuServe's hand-delivered proposal has not been evaluated by the Navy because it is considered late. The Navy has retained CompuServe's unopened proposal pending our decision on this protest.

CompuServe maintains that its proposal should be considered because the Navy failed to act reasonably in extending the closing date by only 24 hours without providing prior notice of that fact. In the circumstances, we recommend that the Navy not reject CompuServe's proposal as late.

The material facts are not in dispute. The RFP was issued by the Navy's Automatic Data Processing Selection Office (ADPSO). As amended, the solicitation established Tuesday, February 20, 1979, as the closing date for initial proposals. A heavy snowstorm struck the Washington, D.C. area over the preceding holiday weekend which caused the Government, including ADPSO, to remain closed until Wednesday, February 21, 1979. Communications and transportation were disrupted and were not essentially reinstated until Thursday, February 22, 1979. The Federal Government was open for business on Wednesday, February 21, 1979, although liberal annual leave policy (Condition 2) was in effect for Federal workers and in many instances Federal workers who found roads impassable were granted limited administrative leave. ADPSO reports that less than half its staff attended work that day.

The contracting officer extended the closing date by only 24 hours, until 3:30 p.m., Wednesday, February 21, 1979. Any prospective offeror able to reach ADPSO personnel by telephone at home or the office on the 19th, 20th, and 21st of February was advised of this extension. The Navy, however, made no effort to contact the firms (more than 90) which had been furnished copies of the solicitation. CompuServe states that it made unsuccessful attempts to contact ADPSO but only learned of the extension on Thursday, February 22, 1979, at which time it promptly hand-delivered its proposal.

The Navy's position is that it had authority to reschedule the closing date in the manner that it did. It points to the fact that ten offers were received by the extended February 21, 1979 closing time; and it considers the 24-hour extension as fair because the Government was completely closed for business for only 24 hours. Further, the Navy refers to our decision B–158464, March 28, 1966, as authority for a 24-hour extension. CompuServe, on the other hand, maintains that the Navy acted unreasonably in failing to notify it of the extension and for failing to extend the closing date for a sufficiently long period to permit delivery.

We have held that a procuring agency may extend a closing date for 24 hours without notifying offerors of the extension in the event the Government is closed on the originally scheduled closing date and urgency for the supplies or services does not permit the delay incident to amending the solicitation. *See Falcon Research & Development Co.*, B–188321, May 4, 1977, 77–1 CPD 306 and B–158464, *supra*. However, the facts here are distinguishable. In the former case it was reasonable for the Army to refuse to extend the closing date because of impassable conditions at the offeror's locale where further delays would have created scheduling difficulties for the using activity. In B–158464, *supra*, unlike the present case, all bidders met the extended deadline and we rejected the protester's argument that the low bidder be rejected for not meeting the original opening date. We sanctioned the agency's 24-hour postponement of a bid opening even though bidders were not apprised of the extension, but we expressed our preference for notifying all prospective bidders to whom the original invitation was sent, assuming time would permit.

The Navy explains that it elected to extend the closing date for only 24 hours because it believed the only reasonable course of action available was to grant an automatic extension to compensate for the Government's being closed on February 20, 1979. Yet, the Navy admits that on February 19, 1979, it made the decision to reschedule the closing date for February 22. It only became apparent on February 21, 1979, that so few ADPSO personnel would report to work as to preclude the possibility of informing prospective offerors of the extension. Inasmuch as there was no urgency, the preferable course of action would have been for the Navy to extend the closing date at least until the restoration of normal business conditions and offerors could be notified of the extension.

We believe the Navy abused its discretion by allowing offerors to submit proposals beyond the established closing date of February 20, without making any effort to inform prospective offerors of that fact, in the absence of any urgency. As a result, the protester failed to divine the extended closing date and did not submit its proposal by the next business day. It is essential that the Government conduct its procurements in accordance with clearly defined standards that apply equally to all to ensure fair and impartial treatment. *Phelps-Stokes Fund,* B–194347, May 21, 1979, 79–1 CPD 366. To permit one or more offerors to deliver proposals after the published closing date, without advising prospective offerors of a new cut-off date where time permitted notification thereof, tends to subvert the competitive system.

Ideally, the Navy should now establish a new closing date and allow all offerors an equal opportunity to submit proposals. However, the Navy has evaluated proposals and has notified offerors found to be outside the competitive range. Under these circumstances, we believe that the fairest course of action without doing violence to the competitive procurement system is to consider CompuServe's proposal at this time. The purpose of establishing cutoff dates in negotiated procurements is to eliminate the danger of premature disclosure of information during the course of the competitive process. *Presnell-Kidd Associates,* B–191394, April 26, 1978, 78–1 CPD 324. Here we are satisfied that CompuServe submitted its proposal unaware of information about the other proposals. During the informal conference held to discuss the merits of this case all interested parties in attendance agreed that there was no possibility that CompuServe had been apprised of the contents of the proposals submitted by other offerors. No allegation of disclosure has been raised. Further, those proposals excluded from the competitive range are incapable of being made acceptable and the short additional time allowed CompuServe would not have materially affected their competitive position. Those offerors included in the competitive range will not suffer any significant disadvantage inasmuch as the Navy intends to conduct further negotiations with all such offerors.

The protest, therefore, is sustained.

〔 B–193270 〕

Contracts—Negotiation—Offers or Proposals—Best and Final—Failure to Request—Cancellation of RFP

Contrary to allegations of protester, record reflects that competitive range was established and that negotiations were conducted with offerors. Moreover, in view of establishment of competitive range only 3 days prior to request for cancellation of request for proposals (RFP), receipt of best and final offers at that time would have been useless act.

Contracts—Negotiation—Requests for Proposals—Unsolicited Proposals, etc.—Propriety of Consideration—Assessment, etc. of Procurement Needs

Whether proposal based on licensing arrangement, submitted after date for receipt of initial proposals under ongoing RFP, was solicited or unsolicited is immaterial, because procurement activity is entitled to receive information concerning procurement at any time and utilize that information to assess or reassess its procurement needs.

General Accounting Office—Jurisdiction—Contracts—Negotiation—Sole-Source Basis—Scope of GAO Review

Review of sole-source award by General Accounting Office (GAO) is not confined to specific reasons advanced by contracting activity at time of award, but is to determine if contracting actions comport with statutes and regulations in light of totality of circumstances as they existed at time of award.

Contracts—Negotiation—Sole-Source Basis—Justification—Delay and Technical Risk Factors

While protester argues that it was not permitted to compete on equal basis with sole-source awardee, there was no method whereby any firm could compete because licensing arrangement offered by awardee has been determined to be Government's need and it was only available to awardee. Determination to award sole-source, in view of lower technical risk and schedule requirements, was justified.

Armed Services Procurement Regulation—"Leader Company Procurement"—Compliance—No Other Source of Supply

Where only one firm can supply system deemed necessary, there is no violation of "Leader Company Procurement" regulations (DAR 4–701).

Contracts—Negotiation—Offers or Proposals—Preparation—Costs—Recovery

In view of conclusion that cancellation of RFP and award of sole-source contract was proper, GAO does not find arbitrary or capricious action toward protester-claimant to support claim for proposal preparation costs.

In the matter of Singer Company, Inc., Kearfott Division, June 6, 1979:

Singer Company, Inc., Kearfott Division (Singer), has protested the award of a subcontract by McDonnell Douglas Astronautics Company (MDAC) to Litton Systems Canada Limited (Litton-Canada) as the second source for the Cruise Missile inertial guidance subsystem.

In a previous decision of our Office (*Singer Company, Inc., Kearfott Division*, 58 Comp. Gen. 218 (1979), 79–1 CPD 26), we found the protest to be timely filed and accepted jurisdiction under the standards enunciated in *Optimum Systems, Incorporated*, 54 Comp. Gen. 767 (1975), 75–1 CPD 166. This is a decision on the merits of the protest following development of the matter and a conference with all the parties.

MDAC holds a prime contract with the Department of Defense (DOD) for the design, development and furnishing of AN/DSW-15 Cruise Missile Land Attack Guidance Sets and Navigation/Guidance Equipment for the AGM-86-B Air Launched Cruise Missile. Litton Industries, Inc., Guidance and Control Systems Division, Woodland, California (Litton), is MDAC's subcontractor for design and production of the inertial guidance subsystem.

On January 14, 1977, DOD established the Joint Cruise Missile Project Office (JCMPO) to manage the Cruise Missile Program and to direct the development of both the Navy and Air Force versions of the missile. One of the policies to be followed by JCMPO was to encourage subsystem/second-source competitive procurement by which major Cruise Missile subsystems would be procured from two contractors who would be competing with each other for a portion of the total production order.

In late 1977, MDAC sent requests to industry for planning information concerning the cost to the Government of developing and qualifying an alternate production source or a "second source." Following evaluation of the information submitted by industry, MDAC briefed JCMPO regarding its proposed second-source competition, which envisioned competition through either a form, fit and function approach or redevelopment of the system utilizing new technologies.

On March 17, 1978, MDAC issued three RFP's to a number of prospective offerors. Each RFP was for a portion of the inertial guidance subsystem, i.e., computer subsystem, power subsystem and reference measuring unit.

JCMPO advised MDAC, on April 6, 1978, that it would fund the second-source competition and, therefore, it wished to review the source selection criteria and written procurement plan for the second-source solicitations and also to review and approve the proposed source selection.

During May 1978, several discussions were held between JCMPO and MDAC regarding the status of the second-source competition, the alternate vendor technical approaches and how MDAC would evaluate the responses to the RFP's.

In this same time period, May 1978, following preliminary contacts by Litton during March and April regarding the possibility of licensing production of Litton's equipment to another manufacturer, JCMPO met with Litton on several occasions to explore acquisition alternatives to MDAC's second-source competition.

During these discussions, it became evident that, while Litton was willing to license another contractor to produce most of the components of the guidance system, it was unwilling to license production of the gyroscopes and accelerometers, two essential components of the sub-system. Litton suggested that Litton-Canada, Litton's Canadian division, could supply these components to the second-source contractor. It was determined that the licensing of another contractor would require too long a leadtime at an unreasonable cost for such a contractor to reach production capability.

The discussions then turned to the possibility of licensing Litton-Canada as the second source for the entire inertial guidance subsystem as a less expensive, lower risk alternative to the MDAC second-source competition. A Memorandum of Agreement (MOA) was drafted between JCMPO and Litton to establish Litton-Canada as the second source for the guidance subsystem. The purpose of the MOA was to:

a. agree on steps to establish a dual-source capability for cruise missile guidance and control components in Litton-Canada including the necessary transfer of technology from Litton Guidance and Control Division;

b. assure independent competition in pricing between Litton-Canada and Litton Guidance and Control Division;

c. preclude royalty charges or license fees to the Government;

d. limit profits charged to the Government; and

e. provide for Litton capitalizing equipment needed to achieve production capability with an appropriate capital investment incentive for inclusion in applicable procurements.

On August 4, 1978, MDAC presented JCMPO with its methodology, requirements and approach being utilized in the second-source RFP's.

On August 11, 1978, JCMPO requested that MDAC include the licensing approach in its evaluations and on August 31, 1978, MDAC advised JCMPO of its conclusions regarding the second-source RFP responses and its preliminary evaluation of the licensing approach. Also, in the early part of September, Litton-Canada submitted an unsolicited proposal to MDAC to produce the inertial guidance sub-system under license from Litton. Between September 7–14, 1978, JCMPO reviewed MDAC's evaluation of the technical proposals under the RFP's. On September 15, 1978, in a presentation to JCMPO, MDAC advised that none of the second-source offerors offered as low a risk at minimal cost as the licensing approach and on October 13, 1978, MDAC, with the concurrence of JCMPO, decided no awards would be made under the RFP. By letter of October 16, 1978, MDAC advised the offerors of the above decision and on October 20, 1978, Singer protested the cancellation of the RFP to our Office.

Singer alleges that it was unfair to compare the proposal of Litton to those received under MDAC's RFP and advances numerous arguments to support this contention. Singer contends that there were procedural shortcomings in the MDAC RFP and the reasons given by JCMPO to justify the cancellation of the MDAC RFP and the sole-source award to Litton-Canada are invalid.

Initially, Singer argues that no competitive range was established under the RFP, no negotiations were conducted and there was no common cutoff date for best and final offers.

We believe these three contentions must be viewed in the light of the ultimate outcome of the RFP, namely, the cancellation, which effectively rendered some actions which normally occur in a procurement moot or unnecessary.

However, it does appear that certain firms competing under the MDAC RFP were eliminated from further consideration on October 13, 1978, and were so advised by MDAC, leaving only Singer and two other firms in the competition.

Also, the record reflects that MDAC did discuss Singer's proposal with Singer during May, June and July 1978. Further, since the competitive range was established only 3 days prior to the cancellation of the RFP, it appears that a request for best and final offers under the RFP at that time would have been a useless act.

Singer's major contention in its protest is that it was denied the opportunity to compete on an equal basis with Litton-Canada and that it was improper to compare the two approaches (licensing versus form, fit and function) in making the determination to cancel the RFP and award sole source to Litton-Canada.

Since Litton-Canada's proposal was not submitted until 4 months after the closing date for receipt of proposals under the MDAC RFP, Singer contends the proposal was late and should not have been considered under Defense Acquisition Regulation (DAR) § 3–506 (1976 ed.). JCMPO and Litton argue that as the Litton-Canada proposal was unsolicited, the time constraints of the RFP do not apply to the submission of the proposal. Whether the Litton-Canada proposal was solicited or unsolicited is immaterial. In our view, notwithstanding late proposal provisions, a procurement activity is entitled to receive information concerning a procurement at any time and use that information to assess or reassess its procurement needs.

Therefore, the basic question presented by the protest is whether the ongoing competition based solely on form, fit and function proposals was properly canceled in favor of a sole-source contract based on a licensing arrangement.

At the time the RFP was canceled, MDAC advised the offerors that based on total performance and cost, the proposals submitted were not sufficiently competitive to justify an award. In justifying the sole-source award to Litton-Canada, the Director of the JCMPO stated the Litton-Canada proposal offered the lowest cost and most expeditious scheduling of all the proposals submitted.

Singer argues that these reasons were insufficient to cancel the RFP and make a sole-source award because Singer and the other two offerors in the competitive range had never competed on an equal basis with Litton and, therefore, it was improper to compare the proposals. The major differences in the terms under which the proposals were reviewed were that the Litton-Canada proposal was based on (1) licensing, (2) an accelerated delivery schedule, (3) utilizing Government-owned data not available to Singer, (4) a Capital Investment Incentive Clause, (5) a guaranteed minimum order of 4,000 units, and (6) firm prices, whereas the RFP proposals were on a not-to-exceed price basis.

In addition to the reasons noted above, JCMPO has now advanced other reasons which it contends justify the selection and which our Office should consider under the holding in *Tosco Corporation*, B–187776, May 10, 1977, 77–1 CPD 329. *Tosco* contains the following statement:

> In reviewing a protest against a sole-source award, our Office is concerned with whether the action is supportable and not whether it was properly supported. *The Intermountain Company*, B–182794, July 8, 1975, 75–2 CPD 19. Under this standard, our review is not confined to the specific reasons advanced by the contracting activity at the time. Rather, our inquiry is to determine if the contracting actions taken comport with applicable statutes and regulations, in light of the totality of the circumstances as they existed at the time. Thus, we have held that, even where the reasons advanced by a contracting activity justifying a particular action were erroneous at the time the action was taken, a subsequent statement of different reasons which would have supported the action, if advanced initially, is acceptable. B–172061, August 24, 1971.

While Singer attempts to distinguish *Tosco* on its facts, we hold that the above standard applies to any sole-source award and, therefore, will consider the additional bases now stated by JCMPO. Moreover, in view of the relationship between technical risk and delivery requirements, as discussed below, we are not certain technical risk constitutes an additional basis not previously considered.

JCMPO states that only through the licensing approach can the goal of commonality for the subsystems be obtained. As noted above, dual sources for the major subsystems of the cruise missile is one of the policies to be followed by JCMPO. In the memorandum of January 14, 1977, which established the JCMPO, the Deputy Secretary of Defense noted:

> In conducting the above tasks, the JCMPO is to maximize subsystem/component commonality and quantity buy, to utilize fully joint test and evaluation, to encourage subsystem/second-source competitive procurement, and to otherwise derive maximum benefit from the joint service management of several separable cruise missile programs.

Singer points to a statement by JCMPO, made in October 1978, that "Common should not be read as meaning exactly the same." Therefore, us commonality does not require that the second source produce the identical item the other source is supplying, Singer argues it was improper to award the sole-source contract based on the fact that the design is identical.

While it is true that commonality does not require that an identical item be produced by the second source, it is permissible and within the procuring activity's discretion as to which of two technical approaches it believes will better fulfill the Government's needs.

Here, JCMPO and MDAC found that the lower technical risk presented by the licensing approach would assure meeting the schedule requirements of the program. JCMPO states that it requires the second source to have a capacity of 40 units per month by May 1982. While this constitutes an acceleration over the initial timeframe required in the MDAC RFP of January 1984, the program production schedules furnished our Office show that JCMPO has always had a need for 40 units per month. While Singer argues that it was not permitted to compete on an equal basis, which is true, there was no method whereby any other firm could offer the identical guidance system because of the limited data rights available to the Government. While competition could have been equalized in most of the areas which Singer noted, the licensing arrangement was only available to Litton-Canada and, therefore, it was the only firm which could supply what is now considered necessary to meet the Government's need.

Singer contends that it could meet the 1982 delivery schedule required by JCMPO. JCMPO states that Singer's proposed delivery schedules in response to the MDAC RFP were highly optimistic, especially in view of the fact that the system which MDAC rated the highest of those proposed was the Singer reference measuring unit integrated with the Lear Siegler computer. This combination would require additional time for testing and interfacing of the two units.

MDAC, in its final evaluation of the RFP proposals and Litton-Canada proposal, found that Litton-Canada offered the lowest risk. JCMPO concurred in this finding.

Therefore, while the form, fit and function approach, as embodied in the MDAC RFP, appeared to satisfy the Government's needs at the time the RFP was issued, the complexion of the procurement changed when the possibility of licensing was presented. The lower technical risk, which would better insure delivery within the Government's 1982 schedule and allow competition between Litton and the second source for the production quantities at an earlier date, would justify the sole-source award to Litton-Canada.

We have recognized that noncompetitive awards may be made where the minimum needs of the Government can be satisfied only by one firm which could be reasonably expected to produce the required item without undue technical risk within the required timeframe. *Hughes Aircraft Company*, 53 Comp. Gen. 670 (1974), 74–1 CPD 137.

We believe the above test has been met in the present case. While Singer contends it is improper to compare the delivery schedules of Litton-Canada and Singer since they were not submitted on the same basis, such a comparison is not required. A procuring activity, taking into consideration technical risk, can judge the realism of a proposed delivery schedule and the fact that a prospective contractor claims to be able to comply with the requirement does not relieve the agency of that judgment. See *Hughes, supra.*

Accordingly, since there was nothing improper in the selection of the licensing approach, no purpose would have been served by amending the MDAC RFP and requesting best and final offers. The cancellation of a solicitation is proper where the specifications no longer accurately reflect the needs. See *Praxis Assurance Venture*, B–190200, March 15, 1978, 78–1 CPD 203, and cases cited therein.

Singer also contends that the sole-source award to Litton-Canada violates the provisions of DAR section 4, part 7 (1976 ed.), "Leader Company Procurement," pertinent portions of which read as follows:

4–701 General. Leader company procurement is an extraordinary procurement technique under which the developer or sole producer of an item or system (the leader company) furnishes manufacturing assistance and know-how or otherwise enables a follower company to become a source of supply for the item or system. This technique is used to accomplish one or more of the following objectives:

    (i) shortening the time for delivery;

       *   *   *   *   *   *   *

    (iv) achieving economy in production;
    (v) assuring uniformity and reliability in equipment performance, compatibility or standardization of components, and interchangeability of parts;
    (vi) eliminating problems in use of proprietary data not amenable to other more satisfactory solutions; or
    (vii) effecting transition from development to production and to subsequent competitive procurement of end items or of major components.

4–702 Limitations on Use. Leader company procurement is to be used only when all of the following circumstances are present:

    (i) the leader company possesses the necessary production know-how and is able to furnish the requisite assistance to the follower;
    (ii) no source of supply (other than a leader company) would be able to meet the Government's requirements without the assistance of a leader company;
    (iii) the assistance required of the leader company is limited to that which is essential to enable the follower company to produce the items; and
    (iv) the Government reserves the right to approve contracts between the leader and follower companies.

Singer alleges that the use by JCMPO and MDAC of the leader-follower procurement violates DAR § 4–702(ii) since there are other sources of supply which can furnish a suitable guidance system. In view of the determination to procure the identical system, there is no other source of supply other than Litton or its licensee (because of the limited data rights) that would be able to meet the Government's requirements. Therefore, we find no violation of the regulation.

Singer states that there will be no real price competition between Litton and Litton-Canada since both are part of the same corporate entity and that the Government would assure true competition by having a completely separate firm compete with Litton for the production requirements.

JCMPO advises that it has carefully considered the ramifications from a price standpoint of having the two firms compete against each other and believes that certain provisions in the MOA and the various antitrust statutes afford protection against either firm utilizing anticompetitive practices.

While Singer questions that the antitrust statutes would apply to the present situation, it recognizes that antitrust matters are not for our consideration.

From the record, it appears that JCMPO is satisfied that there will be adequate competition between Litton and Litton-Canada. That such condition will not prevail is purely speculative on Singer's part. In the circumstances, we find no legal basis for an objection to the arrangement set up by JCMPO to provide competition between Litton and Litton-Canada.

Singer also asserts a claim for proposal preparation costs. The standard for determining whether to allow recovery for bid or proposal preparation costs is whether the procurement activity's actions were arbitrary or capricious toward the offeror-claimant. *The George Sollitt Construction Company*, B-190743, September 25, 1978, 78-2 CPD 224. In view of the above, we do not find that JCMPO or MDAC acted arbitrarily or capriciously toward Singer.

The protest and claim are denied.

[B-189756]

Bids—Mistakes—Correction—Delegation of Authority—Finality of Administrative Determinations—Doubtful Cases

Authority under Federal Procurement Regulations 1-2.406-8 in executive agencies to determine whether a mistake in bid case is doubtful and therefore should be referred to General Accounting Office (GAO) does not foreclose GAO from reviewing that determination as well as agency determination regarding sufficiency of bidder's evidence.

Bids—Mistakes—Withdrawal—Availability as Alternative Relief—Correction Request

Where bidder requests permission only to correct bid price, bidder may alternatively be allowed to withdraw its bid if evidence is clear and convincing only as to the mistake, but not as to the intended bid.

In the matter of Murphy Brothers, Inc.—Reconsideration, June 7, 1979:

The Federal Highway Administration (FHWA) requests that we reconsider our decisions, *Murphy Brothers, Inc.*, B–189756, March 8, 1978, 78–1 CPD 182, and 58 Comp. Gen. 185 (1978), 78–2 CPD 440, in which we held that Murphy Brothers, Inc. (Murphy) was entitled to relief for a mistake in its bid on contract DOT–FH–10–3148.

In the original decision, we held that no contract was consummated at the award price because an error in Murphy's bid had been brought to FHWA's attention after bid opening but before award. FHWA refused to permit correction or withdrawal of the bid. Because rescission was not feasible, we granted Murphy relief on a *quantum valebant* or *quantum meruit* basis.

In the first reconsideration, we held that FHWA should have referred the doubtful matter to us for determination as to whether withdrawal could be allowed under less stringent criteria applied by this Office pursuant to decisions of the Court of Claims. We additionally held that FHWA's authority under Federal Procurement Regulations (FPR) § 1–2.406–3 (1964 ed., amend. 165) to determine mistake in bid cases in certain well-defined situations did not divest us of authority to review administrative determinations and decide doubtful cases.

We further stated in that decision that FHWA had authority to determine that the evidence submitted by Murphy was not "clear and convincing evidence" of a mistake in bid so as to permit Murphy to withdraw its bid. The agency now argues that it may also determine whether a case is doubtful and therefore should be referred to this Office. FHWA contends that it made the determination that this was not a doubtful case and implies that because the agency fully complied with the applicable regulations, this Office is precluded from reviewing the agency decision. While admittedly the determination whether a case is doubtful must be made before the agency submits it to this Office, as discussed below, we believe that we are not foreclosed from reviewing that determination as well as the agency determination as to whether a bidder's evidence is clear and convincing.

The authority of various agencies to handle certain mistake in bid questions was agreed to by this Office subject to the express condition that the procedure authorized not operate to deprive a bidder of its right to have the matter determined by this Office. We also reserved the right to question the correctness of agency determinations. 38 Comp. Gen. 177 (1958). Consequently the regulations granting agencies the authority to decide mistake in bid cases acknowledge the authority of this Office "to question the correctness of any administrative determination" under the regulation. (FPR § 1–2.406–3(e)) [Italic supplied.]

The regulation also states that nothing contained therein shall "deprive any bidder of his right to have the matter determined by the Comptroller General should he so request." Although Murphy accepted the award after its allegation of a mistake but prior to the correction thereof, it did not waive any rights to relief since it reserved its right to possible relief from this Office. *See* 49 Comp. Gen. 446 (1970).

Accordingly, we believe we have not exceeded the authority recognized under the regulations to review FHWA's decision not to allow Murphy withdrawal of its bid and not to refer the case to us as doubtful.

The agency has not provided any new information that convinces us that this was not a doubtful case. In our earlier decisions in this case, we observed that the evidence submitted by Murphy made it reasonably clear that a mistake was made. Thus, FHWA's concern that our decisions will encourage bidders to seek bid withdrawals after bid opening "on the slightest pretext of possible mistake" is unfounded.

FHWA also argues that we could not decide that Murphy's bid should have been withdrawn when Murphy sought permission only to correct its bid and never requested to have it withdrawn. We note that FHWA itself decided the issue of withdrawal although Murphy had requested correction, as its response to Murphy's request for correction also denied Murphy permission to withdraw. Murphy reserved "the right to protest the award," which we interpret as objection to FHWA's denial of both correction and withdrawal of its bid. In any event, Murphy did not expressly request withdrawal of its bid in its request for review of the agency decision since the contract award had already been made.

Furthermore, even where a bidder requests permission to correct its bid, an agency may permit the bidder to withdraw its bid if the evidence is clear and convincing only as to the mistake, but not as to the intended bid. FPR § 1–2.406–3(a)(3). Thus, the agency's function is broad enough to grant withdrawal where correction is requested but not allowed. As stated above, we may review the agency's determination. Moreover, we have allowed bid withdrawal where correction was the relief requested. *See* 52 Comp. Gen. 400 (1972).

Our previous decisions are sustained.

[B–193720]

Contracts—Protests—Timeliness—Solicitation Improprieties—Not Apparent Prior to Bid Opening

Bid protest, filed after bid opening, alleging that inclusion of option provision in invitation for bids violated Armed Services Procurement Regulation/Defense Acquisition Regulation (ASPR/DAR) 1–1502(b)(v), is timely since protester was unaware of facts allegedly indicating violation until after bids were opened.

Contracts—Options—Limitations on Use—Military Procurements—Option Quantities Representing Known Firm Requirements—Funding Available

Agency inclusion of solicitation quantity under option provision is unjustified where quantity in provision represents firm requirements for which funds are available. [Reconsideration: B–193720, Aug. 27, 1979.]

Contracts—Termination—Convenience of Government—Recommendation—Resolicitation

Agency's failure to follow ASPR/DAR 1–502(b)(v) raises doubt as to whether Government is receiving items at lowest possible cost and whether integrity of competitive bidding system is being maintained. These considerations form basis for recommendation that contract be terminated for convenience of Government and requirement be resolicited.

In the matter of East Wind Industries, Inc., June 7, 1979:

East Wind Industries, Inc. (East Wind), protests the award of a contract to St. Clair Rubber Company (St. Clair) under invitation for bids (IFB) No. DLA100–78–B–0835, issued by the Defense Personnel Support Center (DPSC), Philadelphia, Pennsylvania.

The IFB solicited bids for 1,268,688 pairs of chemical protective footwear covers. The solicitation was issued on July 24, 1978, as a 50-percent small business set-aside (unrestricted and set-aside portions each consisting of 634,344 pairs) with bid opening scheduled for August 14, 1978. The IFB also requested bidders to submit an offer for an option quantity which would not exceed 100 percent of the unrestricted quantity awarded (634,344 pairs).

By letter dated August 7, 1978, East Wind appealed the small business size standard assigned to the procurement. In order to allow time to resolve this appeal, on August 9, 1978, DPSC issued IFB amendment 0001 which extended the date for bid opening indefinitely. The Small Business Administration Size Appeals Board later denied East Wind's appeal, and on October 2, 1978, DPSC issued IFB amendment 0002 which established October 12, 1978, as the new bid opening date.

When bids were opened on that date, six bids were received for the unrestricted portion as follows:

Bidder	Unit Prices	Option
East Wind	$6.59	$8.21 per pair.
St. Clair Rubber Co	$6.71	$6.71 per pair.
P.F. Inds., Inc	$7.30–$7.92	$7.75 per pair.
Kings Point Mfg. Co., Inc	$8.37/$8.47/$8.77	Price same if option exercised at time of award of basic, otherwise 20 percent higher.
Guida Clothing Co., Inc	$10.00	$11 per pair.
Alamo Mfg. Co., Inc	$15.00	Price 15 percent higher than basic.

Bids were evaluated during November 1978, and a few days before December 13, 1978, East Wind learned that DPSC was planning to make an award to St. Clair for the unrestricted portion (634,344 pairs) plus 399,096 pairs under the IFB's option provision. Thus, on December 14, 1978, East Wind filed a protest with our Office arguing that St. Clair should not be given the award since East Wind was actually the low responsive and responsible bidder on the subject solicitation.

The record indicates that before the IFB in question was issued, the Government's identified requirement for chemical protective footwear covers was for a total quantity of 2,653,488 pairs. Initially, DPSC intended to satisfy this requirement by (1) invoking the 100-percent option on East Wind contract DSA100–77–C–1316 for the total available quantity of 985,704 pairs at a unit price of $6.79; (2) invoking the 100-percent option on East Wind contract DLA100–78–C–0737 for the total available quantity of 399,096 pairs at a unit price of $7.33; and (3) issuing a new solicitation—the instant procurement—for 1,268,688 pairs.

DPSC exercised the option for 985,704 pairs under contract DSA 100–77–C–1316 on July 28, 1978, but did not exercise the option under contract DLA100–78–C–0737 since this option was not scheduled to expire until November 17, 1978. The Government also concedes that it did not exercise this second option because it was concerned with the reasonableness of the price and thus deemed it appropriate to wait until the results of the bid opening for the additional 1,268,688 pairs were known before deciding whether to exercise this option.

After bid opening, DPSC concluded that the most economical way of procuring the remaining quantity needed (1,268,688 pairs plus 399,096 pairs) was to obtain the full amount under the subject solicitation rather than by exercising the option on East Wind's contract DLA100–78–C–0737. In order to accomplish this, the Government decided that it would exercise the IFB's option at the time the unrestricted portion was awarded and by this means obtain the additional 399,096 pairs that it needed.

Under these circumstances, the agency relied on paragraph 6 of IFB clause D52, "Option for Increased Quantity," which provides:

> Offers will be evaluated on the basis of the quantities to be awarded, exclusive of the option quantity, unless the Government elects to exercise the option at the time of award, in which case offers will be evaluated for purposes of award on the basis of the total price for the basic quantity and the option quantity exercised with award.

Thus, even though East Wind offered a lower price than St. Clair on the basic quantity ($6.59 per pair v. $6.71 per pair), when the Government evaluated the bids on the basis of the total price—the price for the basic quantity plus the price for the option quantity—St. Clair was found to be low overall because the price it offered on the option quantity was substantially lower than East Wind's ($6.71 per pair v. $8.21 per pair) and as a result offset East Wind's lower price on the basic quantity.

Based on this determination, DPSC made an award to St. Clair on February 16, 1979, for 1,033,440 pairs of chemical protective footware covers pursuant to Armed Services Procurement Regulation/Defense Acquisition Regulation (ASPR/DAR) § 2–407.8(b) (1976 ed.) which, under certain circumstances, allows an award to be made while a protest is pending.

East Wind argues that the inclusion of the option provision in the IFB was in violation of ASPR/DAR § 1–1502(b)(v) (1976 ed.) which provides:

> (b) Option clauses shall not be included in contracts, and option provisions shall not be included in solicitations, if:
>
> *   *   *   *   *
>
> (v) the option quantities represent known firm requirements for which funds are available unless (A) the basic quantity is a learning or testing quantity and there is some uncertainty as to contractor or equipment performance, and (B) realistic competition for the option quantity is impracticable once the initial contract is awarded.

Under our Bid Protest Procedures, 4 C.F.R. § 20.2(b)(1) (1978), protests based upon alleged improprieties in a solicitation apparent prior to bid opening must be filed in our Office prior to bid opening in order to be considered timely. The agency argues here that if East Wind wished to protest the inclusion of an option provision in the IFB, it should have filed its protest prior to bid opening and its failure to do so makes its protest untimely.

We do not agree. East Wind's concern with the IFB's option provision only arose after bid opening when it learned that the agency planned to exercise the IFB's option clause at the time of award for the exact number of protective covers (399,096 pairs) which it could obtain under the option provision of East Wind's contract DLA100–78–C–0737. This alerted East Wind to the questions of whether DPSC had a known firm requirement for protective covers, had funds available, and finally whether it was proper to include an option provision in the IFB. Under these circumstances, we do not believe that East Wind was required to file its protest with our Office prior to bid opening. Therefore, we will consider the matter.

The issue then is whether there has been a violation of ASPR/DAR § 1–1502(b)(v).

As noted above, ASPR/DAR § 1–1502(b)(v) provides that an option clause will not be used in an IFB if "the option quantities represent known firm requirements for which funds are available." The agency argues that its requirements for protective covers remained uncertain until bids were opened and the prices offered under the IFB could be compared with the price available under the option on East Wind's contract so as to determine which would be the most advantageous to the Government.

From the record presented, however, it appears that DPSC knew the total number of protective covers it wished to procure, but was uncertain over whether part of this quantity should be obtained by invoking the option clause under East Wind's contract DLA100–78–C–0737. Thus, DPSC indicates that it included an option provision in the subject solicitation because it believed that in this way it might be able to obtain a lower unit price for these 399,096 pairs than available under the option on East Wind's contract and as a result achieve a monetary savings for the Government. Clearly, then, the inclusion of an option provision in the IFB was not because DPSC's requirements were uncertain, but because of uncertainty over the best method of fulfilling those requirements. Thus, DPSC did in fact have a firm known requirement at the time the IFB was issued.

DPSC also argues that because of the conflicting directions it received regarding the funds to be used for this procurement, funds were in fact unavailable until after bid opening and that this then was also a basis for including an option provision in the IFB.

DPSC states that at the time the IFB was issued the general practice was to use DPSC's revolving stock funds to procure the items in question. However, at a budget hearing on October 4, 1978, the Office of the Assistant Secretary of Defense (OASD) directed DPSC to obtain funded requisitions from the military services (each of which received separate appropriations for the chemical protective clothing program) prior to taking purchase actions. This, DPSC states, meant that funds from the revolving stock funds were no longer available to purchase the protective covers. However, the services were slow in responding to DPSC's request for funded requisitions. As a result, OSAD decided in December 1978 to allow an award to be made by once again authorizing the use of revolving stock funds.

Thus, in DPSC's opinion, funds were no longer available at the time bids were opened (October 12, 1978) and remained unavailable until the use of revolving stock funds was once again authorized (December 11, 1978).

We have recognized that executive officials have a certain amount of discretion in the reprogramming of funds within an appropriation account and that a decision to shift funds from one program to another may not be questioned unless shown to be wholly arbitrary. *A.R.F. Products, Inc.*, 56 Comp. Gen. 201 (1976), 76–2 CPD 541. However, we do not believe that this is the situation presented here. The record indicates that there was no reprogramming of funds, but rather that the responsible officials had more than one source of funds for this procurement and after encountering some difficulty with getting funded requisitions from the military services decided to use the revolving stock funds which had initially been projected as the source of funds for the procurement and had in fact been used before to make similar purchases. Therefore, not only did DPSC have a known firm requirement, but it also had funds available throughout the entire procurement process. Consequently, the inclusion of an option provision in the IFB was inconsistent with ASPR/DAR § 1–1502(b)(v).

We must determine then whether this improper use of an option provision requires the termination of St. Clair's contract for the convenience of the Government and the resolicitation of the requirement.

A situation analogous to the one presented here is when an agency solicits bids on the basis of estimated quantities. In that situation, the estimated quantities must be compiled from the best information available so that the estimates are a reasonably accurate representation of actual anticipated needs. If the estimates are not reasonably accurate, the evaluation of bids based on those estimates is suspect and may not result in the lowest cost to the Government. Therefore, if during the procurement process it becomes apparent that the estimated quantities do not accurately reflect the agency's actual anticipated needs, the proper procedure is to cancel the solicitation and readvertise. *Union Carbide Corporation*, B–188426, September 20, 1977, 77–2 CPD 204, and decisions cited.

From the facts now known, we are aware that DPSC always intended to purchase 399,096 more pairs of protective covers than the number actually solicited under the IFB. DPSC has admitted that its main reason for including an option provision in the IFB was to determine whether it might get a lower unit price for those 399,096 pairs under the new solicitation than if it invoked the option on East Wind's contract DLA100-78-C-0737. While it is apparent that DPSC was trying to obtain the lowest price possible for the Government, its decision to include an option provision in the IFB resulted in the IFB soliciting bids for a quantity which did not accurately represent DPSC's actual anticipated needs. This raises doubt, therefore, whether the prices received were as competitive as they might have been had the bids received offered prices for 1,033,440 pairs of protective covers rather than for 634,344 pairs plus an unspecified option quantity. In addition, DPSC's improper use of the option provision also brings into question the integrity of the competitive bidding system.

We recommend, therefore, that the contract with St. Clair be terminated for the convenience of the Government and the agency's known firm requirement for protective covers be resolicited. By letter of today, we are informing the Director, Defense Logistics Agency, of our recommendation.

Since this decision contains a recommendation for corrective action, we are furnishing copies of our decision to the Senate Committees on Governmental Affairs and Appropriations and to the House Committees on Government Operations and Appropriations in accordance with section 236 of the Legislative Reorganization Act of 1970, 31 U.S.C. § 1176 (1976), which requires the submission of written statements by the Defense Logistics Agency to those committees concerning the action taken with respect to our recommendation.

Protest sustained.

〔 B-193752 〕

Contracts—Protests—Persons, etc. Qualified to Protest—Interested Parties—Potential Contractors, etc. Not Submitting Bids, etc.—Direct Economic Interest Criterion

Prospective offeror, which chose not to submit proposal, is "interested party" to protest later that request for proposals (RFP) amendment during negotiations has changed work so substantially that agency should cancel RFP and initiate new procurement.

Contracts—Protests—Timeliness—Negotiated Contracts—Changes During Negotiations—Amendment v. Cancellation of RFP

Protest by nonofferor, that RFP amendment has changed work so substantially that new procurement should be initiated, was timely filed within 10 working days after protester received copy of RFP amendment.

Contracts—Protests—Timeliness—Negotiated   Contracts—Unacceptable Proposal

December 1978 protest asserted that changes in RFP are so substantial as to warrant its cancellation. In April 1979, after agency report and conference, protester asserted for first time that sole proposal received was unacceptable. Latter contention—separate basis of protest—is untimely, as protester knew, or should have known, basis for protest in December 1978 or January 1979. Also, protester's initiation of Freedom of Information Act request in April 1979, seeking information regarding evaluation of sole proposal, indicates failure to diligently pursue matter.

Contracts—Negotiation—Requests for Proposals—Cancellation v. Amendment—Substantiality of Changes—Determination to Amend

RFP for design and manufacture of electronic air navigation equipment contemplated that offerors propose individual technical approaches to meeting agency's needs. After negotiations with sole offeror, RFP amendment made changes in equipment configuration, delivery schedule and various technical specifications. Agency position that changes in requirements are not so substantial as to warrant complete revision of RFP (i.e., cancellation and resolicitation) is not clearly shown to have no reasonable basis.

Contracts—Negotiation—Changes, etc.—Scope of Permissible Changes—Solicitation v. Existing Contract

Protester, seeking cancellation of RFP, relies on General Accounting Office decisions which found that modifications to contracts were so substantial that work covered by modifications should have been subject of new procurement. Argument is not persuasive, as scope of changes which may permissibly be made to RFP without requiring cancellation and initiation of new procurement is greater than scope of changes permitted to existing contract.

Contracts—Negotiation—Competition—Adequacy—One Acceptable Proposal

Federal Procurement Regulations sec. 1–3.101 requirement for maximum practical competition in negotiated procurements does not in itself require agency to cancel RFP where only one proposal is received.

In the matter of Cardion Electronics, June 8, 1979:

Table of Contents

Cardion Electronics has protested to our Office concerning request for proposals (RFP) No. LGM–8–7247, issued by the Federal Aviation Administration (FAA).

I. Introduction

The RFP, copies of which were distributed on April 20, 1978, contemplated the award of a fixed-price incentive contract for the design, fabrication, installation and testing of solid state VOR/VORTAC equipment. FAA has described this equipment as a system which combines civilian and military subsystems to provide aeronautical navigation information to aircraft, and which will replace aging vacuum tube-type equipment at hundreds of sites around the country.

The RFP (Enclosure 2, Page 1) stated in part:

> The Technical Proposals shall clearly and fully demonstrate that the prospective offeror has a valid and practical design and engineering solution to the technical problems inherent in the design and engineering of equipment meeting the requirements of the specification. To this end, the technical proposals shall explain why the proposed design, including technical methods and engineering approach, was selected as the solution to such problems. * * * It is essential that the technical proposal shall set forth the offeror's proposed design, including its specific application of "state-of-the-art" scientific theory and engineering techniques, with sufficient particularity * * *.

The RFP evaluation criteria listed "Proposed method of approach" as the most important criterion and stated that it was worth more than one-half the total value of all evaluation criteria.

On May 4, 1978, Cardion and other prospective offerors attended a preproposal conference. On May 17, 1978, Cardion representatives met with FAA officials, and Cardion in its words "* * * proposed that the VORTAC system be separated into its basic components in order to achieve active competition * * *." FAA did not implement this suggestion and there is no indication in the record that Cardion filed a protest with FAA prior to the closing date for receipt of initial proposals (June 1, 1978).

One proposal—submitted by a joint venture consisting of ITT Avionics and Wilcox Electric, Inc. (ITT-Wilcox)—was received. A Cardion message to FAA dated June 1, 1978, stated in part:

> AFTER CAREFUL CONSIDERATION CARDION ELECTRONICS WOULD LIKE TO ADVISE THAT, AT THIS TIME, WE WILL NOT SUBMIT A PROPOSAL FOR THE SUBJECT PROCUREMENT. OUR REASONS ARE AS FOLLOWS:
> 1) CARDION HAS TECHNICAL CAPABILITY, THE PRODUCTION CAPACITY, AND THE FINANCIAL RESOURCES TO RESPOND AS A PRIME CONTRACTOR FOR THE VORTAC PROGRAM. HOWEVER, WE FIND IT PRUDENT NOT TO MAKE A MAJOR PROPOSAL INVESTMENT WITH THE ANTICIPATED LOW PROBABILITY OF BEING CONSIDERED AS THE MOST ACCEPTABLE OFFEROR FOR THE SUBJECT NEGOTIATED PROCUREMENT.
> 2) AS A SUBCONTRACTOR, CARDION HAS NOT BEEN ABLE TO ESTABLISH A SATISFACTORY TEAMING OR SUBCONTRACT ARRANGEMENT WITH ANY OF THE LEADING NAVIGATIONAL AIDS MANUFACTURERS WHICH, IN OUR JUDGEMENT, WOULD BE MUTUALLY BENEFICIAL OR IN THE BEST INTEREST OF THE GOVERNMENT.
> SHOULD THE GOVERNMENT ELECT TO CHANGE THE PROCUREMENT AND SOLICIT SEPARATE TURNKEY SYSTEMS FOR THE VOR AND

THE DME TACAN EQUIPMENTS WE WOULD RECONSIDER OUR DECISION. * * *

In the course of negotiations with ITT-Wilcox, changes in the RFP specifications were made. These were reflected in amendment No. 6 to the RFP, dated September 29, 1978. In December 1978 Cardion requested and received a copy of this amendment from FAA. Cardion protested to our Office on December 19, 1978, asserting that the RFP should be canceled and a new solicitation issued. No award has been made.

II. Procedural Issues

A. Interested Party Requirement

ITT argues that Cardion is not an "interested party" to protest to our Office because (1) Cardion is unable to manufacture a key VORTAC component and thus would not have been eligible for award had it submitted a proposal in June 1978, and (2) Cardion "no-bid" the procurement because of its business judgment of the risks involved, and nothing in the protest relates to or cures the reasons why Cardion elected not to compete.

Under section 20.1(a) of our Bid Protest Procedures, 4 C.F.R. Part 20 (1978), a party must be "interested" in order to have its protest considered by our Office. Whether a party is sufficiently interested depends on its status in relation to the procurement, the nature of the issues raised, and how these circumstances show the existence of a direct and/or substantial economic interest on the part of the protester. See *Die Mesh Corporation*, 58 Comp. Gen. 111 (1978), 78-2 CPD 374.

In *Die Mesh*, we pointed out that a prospective offeror which did not timely protest the terms of the RFP and deliberately chose not to submit a proposal was not an interested party to protest later that the eventual awardees had received preferential treatment from the Government. In that situation, the class of parties eligible to protest as to which of several offerors should properly have received the awards consisted essentially of disappointed offerors (i.e., the parties which had chosen to compete in the procurement and whose direct economic interests would have been affected by the alleged preferential treatment).

In the present case, Cardion is not a nonofferor protesting as to which of several competing offerors should properly receive an award under the RFP. Rather, Cardion is protesting essentially on the basis that the RFP has been so substantially changed that it should be canceled, and that a new procurement reflecting the changed requirements should be initiated. Cardion's protest, or a protest by any other party similarly situated, involves a direct economic interest, i.e., an opportunity for the party to submit a proposal under the new RFP and compete for an award. Unlike *Die Mesh*, there is no other identifiable group of potential protesters whose members arguably have a more direct interest in asserting this basis for protest.

In our view, whether a Cardion proposal under the RFP would have been found unacceptable, or whether Cardion's motivation for not submitting a proposal was its business judgment of the risks involved, are not pertinent to this inquiry. None of the decisions cited by ITT in this connection involved a similar factual situation and we do not regard them as controlling.

We see no reason why Cardion is not sufficiently interested to protest that changes in the RFP are so substantial that the RFP should be canceled and a new procurement initiated.

B. Timeliness

FAA and ITT question the timeliness of the protest in certain respects. Initially, they point out that prior to the closing date for receipt of initial proposals (June 1, 1978), Cardion unsuccessfully requested FAA to break out certain VORTAC components for separate procurement. FAA and ITT view the present protest as an additional and untimely attempt to accomplish the same objective. Also, they note that while Cardion cites a change in the type of contract for VORTAC installation and testing as part of the substantial changes effected by amendment No. 6, the original RFP specifically indicated that the contract type might be changed .

To whatever extent Cardion's protest can be read as objecting to the terms and conditions of the RFP, it is untimely, because protests which are based upon apparent improprieties in an RFP as originally issued must be filed prior to the closing date for receipt of initial proposals. See 4 C.F.R. § 20.2(b)(1). The primary ground of Cardion's protest, however, is that the aggregate of changes in the specifications effected by amendment No. 6 has altered the RFP so substantially that it should be canceled and a new RFP issued. We do not see why this reasonably should have been apparent to Cardion from the contents of the original RFP. The principal ground of protest is not based upon improprieties in the original RFP, but on the way the procurement has been conducted after the closing date for receipt of initial proposals. The applicable timeliness standard in these circumstances is 4 C.F.R. § 20.2(b)(2), i.e., protests other than those based upon apparent solicitation improprieties must be filed within 10 working days after the basis for protest is known or should have been known, whichever is earlier. See, in this regard, *Telos Computing, Inc.,*

57 Comp. Gen. 370 (1978), 78–1 CPD 235; *Computer Sciences Corporation*, 57 Comp. Gen. 627 (1978), 78–2 CPD 85.

ITT maintains, however, that insofar as the protest is based upon amendment No. 6 to the REP, it is untimely because Cardion was aware of the June–September 1978 negotiations between FAA and ITT-Wilcox and the matters covered therein, and did not protest within 10 working days after amendment No. 6 was issued on September 29, 1978. ITT does not explain how Cardion was aware of what was happening in the negotiations.

Cardion does not specifically state to what extent it had knowledge of the negotiations between FAA and ITT-Wilcox. The protester maintains essentially that it was not in a position to protest until it actually received a copy of amendment No. 6. In this regard, FAA states that Cardion requested a copy of the amendment in early December 1978, and in its letter of protest dated December 18, 1978, Cardion states that it received a copy of amendment No. 6 on December 7, 1978.

The identity of offerors in a negotiated procurement and the content of discussions with them normally are not public information prior to award. Thus, where an after-award protest is based on the contents of a competitor's proposal, a protester's reasonable statement as to when it became aware of its basis for protest will be accepted if unrefuted. *Honeywell Information Systems, Inc.*, 56 Comp. Gen. 505 (1977), 77–1 CPD 256; see also *Computer Machinery Corporation*, 55 Comp. Gen. 1151, 1152 (1976), 76–1 CPD 358.

In the present case, the principal basis of protest relates to the extent of changes made in an RFP during an ongoing negotiated procurement. As discussed *infra*, a number of changes were made, involving matters such as equipment configuration, various individual technical specifications, and delivery and test schedules. In these circumstances, for the protester to assert that it was not aware of its basis for protest until it received a copy of RFP amendment No. 6, which formally reflected the scope of the changes, does not seem unreasonable. ITT has not presented any evidence that the protester knew or reasonably should have known about the extent of the changes at an earlier date. Accordingly, we believe the protest on this basis is timely.

Finally, ITT in its April 10, 1979, letter to our Office argues that Cardion's attempt to expand its protest to challenge the sufficiency of the ITT-Wilcox proposal is untimely. ITT refers in this regard to Cardon's April 6, 1979, letter to our Office. There, Cardion noted that FAA representatives at the April 3, 1979 conference in this case stated that the ITT-Wilcox proposal involved a "unique engineering approach." In the protester's view, this raises a substantial question whether ITT-Wilcox's proposal was "responsive." Prior to this time,

Cardion's protest correspondence did not assert that the ITT-Wilcox proposal was deficient or unacceptable. We understand that subsequent to the April 3 conference, Cardion has sought under the Freedom of Information Act information relating to the FAA evaluation of the ITT-Wilcox proposal.

Where a protester files an initial statement of protest in general terms and, within 5 working days after being so requested by our Office, furnishes additional details which appear to assert separate bases of protest not mentioned in the initial filing, we are nonetheless inclined to regard the separate bases as timely filed. See *Kappa Systems, Inc.,* 56 Comp. Gen. 675, 681–684 (1977), 77–1 CPD 412. However, where a protester attempts, after that time, to raise additional and separate bases for protest, such bases must independently satisfy our timeliness requirements. *Annapolis Tennis Limited Partnership,* B–189751, June 5, 1978, 78–1 CPD 412.

In addition, under 4 C.F.R. § 20.2(b)(2), protests must be filed within 10 working days after the basis for protest is known or should have been known, whichever is earlier. Thus, we have held in certain cases that where a protester did not seek within a reasonable period of time information which ultimately revealed a basis for protest, its failure to diligently pursue the matter calls for rejection of its protest as untimely. See, for example, *Loral Electronic Systems Division, Loral Corporation,* B–187779, February 22, 1977, 77–1 CPD 125.

We believe that an allegation that an RFP should be canceled because it has been so substantially changed that it is tantamount to a new procurement is a separate basis of protest from a contention that an RFP should be canceled because the only proposal submitted was unacceptable. It appears to us that the latter basis of protest should have been known to Cardion long before April 1979. In December 1978 Cardion had received from FAA copies of RFP amendment No. 6 and the revised FAA specifications, which indirectly revealed information about the technical approach proposed by ITT-Wilcox. Cardion also knew at that time that the ITT-Wilcox proposal was the only one received. In addition, comments on the protest filed by ITT and Wilcox on January 30, 1979, explicitly asserted that the ITT-Wilcox technical approach was innovative and involved proprietary information, and that participation in the procurement by Cardion would result in prohibited "technical transfusion."

Accordingly, we regard as untimely Cardion's contention that the RFP should be canceled because the only proposal received was unacceptable. In addition, we believe that Cardion had ample opportunity between December 1978 and April 1979 to seek additional information under the Freedom of Information Act, but failed to diligently pursue the matter.

III. Protester's, Agency's, and Interested Parties' Positions

Cardion states that "The gist of our protest is that the FAA should have opened the VORTAC procurement to parties in addition to [ITT-Wilcox] after issuing Amendment 6 to the RFP * * *. The effect of this amendment 6 was to reduce drastically the scope of the VORTAC project and the risk borne by the contractor. The change in the RFP was so substantial that amendment 6 amounted to a new procurement."

The protester has submitted considerable argumentation as to the substantial nature of the technical changes made by amendment No. 6. Cardion repeatedly emphasizes that the cumulative effect of the changes is to greatly reduce the risk involved in contract performance. A summary of these points, along with responses by the FAA and interested parties, follows:

1. Cardion: Single transmitters with dual monitors at all sites have been substituted for the previous combination of single transmitters at some sites and dual transmitters at others. The number of transmitters is reduced by more than 33 percent. Facility Control and Transfer (FCT) equipment is eliminated, at a cost reduction of about $500 per site, and software is simplified. The contractor's design burden is lessened and there is a vast decrease in risk of contract performance.

FAA: Equipment configuration at some sites has been changed, with some cost reduction. However, there is no change in the total number of systems required or in the functional requirements which must be met. The FCT change involves a possible cost reduction of about $200 per site. Even accepting the protester's figure ($500/site, or $450,000), this is hardly a great amount in the context of a possible $100 million procurement. The software change involves no recognizable cost impact.

ITT: Contrary to the protester's view, the requirements are now more complex and riskier. Dual transmitters had been required at some sites for backup capability, i.e., the second transmitter would be needed in case the first failed. The substitution of single transmitters at these sites means that the contractor must supply more sophisticated, higher reliability single transmitter equipment.

Wilcox: The configuration of equipment at one-half of the sites has been changed, but the types of equipment involved at all sites are the same as those required by the original RFP. No new equipment design effort is required by amendment No. 6. The FCT change involves a trifling impact of less than .2 percent of the contract price.

2. Cardion: The Facility Central Processor Unit has been simplified by substituting a commercially available input-output terminal for the previous built-in alphanumeric display or keyboard.

FAA : This is an insignificant change involving perhaps a $200–$300 increase in cost per site.

Wilcox : This change probably involves less than .25 percent of the contract price.

3. Cardion : Amendment No. 6 provides clearer specifications regarding read only memory and support data.

FAA : This is a clarification, not a change in requirements.

Wilcox : A mere clarification with no effect on design or equipment cost.

4. Cardion : The number of monitored signals for environment equipment interface is now defined.

FAA : This is clarification, not a change in requirements.

Wilcox : This probably affects less than .2 percent of the contract price.

5. Cardion : Several changes in Frequency Shift Keying (FSK) transmission have significantly reduced design complexity.

FAA : The basic FSK capability was required by the original specification ; the changes the protester refers to are minor and involve approximately the same degree of design complexity.

Wilcox : These changes have no effect on cost.

6. Cardion : Spectrum requirements for modulation sidebands have been reduced ; the previous requirements are known to be very difficult to meet.

FAA : The relaxation in tolerances is not a major change and is of no consequence in terms of system performance.

Wilcox : Since Cardion has a current FAA contract under which the same relaxation in requirements occurred, it is hard to see how Cardion can claim to be surprised by this change.

7. Cardion : Goniometer sideband spectrum requirements have been reduced, with a tremendous decrease in design risk.

FAA : This is a minor change.

Wilcox : From its previous contract where the same requirements were reduced, Cardion probably had better notice of the FAA's actual needs than any other prospective offeror.

8. Cardion : Frequency deviation ratio tolerance has been reduced, lessening Goniometer design risk.

FAA : See comments on Nos. 6 and 7 ; this is a very insignificant change with negligible effect on design complexity.

Wilcox : This merely corrects a conflict in the specifications.

9. Cardion : The substitution of a programmable keyboard for internal monitor adjustments has clarified ambiguities in the control requirements.

FAA: This is a clarification of the specification, not a change in requirements.

Wilcox: This clarification involves less than .1 percent of the total contract price.

10. **Cardion**: The delivery schedule has been significantly relaxed. For example, the original requirement was 12 units per month during the first 6 months of deliveries; now only 2 or 3 units per month are required. The net effect is an enormous decrease in risk because the contractor is able to gradually deploy its resources and better assess the risks involved in the critical early stage of contract performance.

FAA: Over 1½ years of design and test precede delivery of the first production VORTAC's. The protester's comments concerning the effect on risk of the changes in early deliveries are basically speculative. In the context of a 54-month program, the changes are minor. Overall delivery requirements are probably more stringent, as the initial deliveries of basic and option units are accelerated under amendment No. 6.

ITT: Amendment No. 6 accelerates the schedule for initial deliveries of VORTAC's and VOR's, as well as options.

Wilcox: The protester selectively points out relaxations in the early delivery schedule and ignores the fact that overall delivery requirements have been accelerated.

11. **Cardion**: There have been major changes in installation and test scheduling. Only six units must be installed in the first 5 months, whereas the original RFP called for 48 installations of dual VORTAC's during the same period. In addition, while amendment No. 6 increased the number of monitors, it substantially decreased the number of transmitters and transponders, and production testing for transmitters and transponders is substantially more burdensome than for monitors. The net result is a huge reduction in production testing. Further, reliability demonstration requirements have not been increased.

FAA: The changes in the units comprising the 950 systems are as follows:

	Original Requirement	Amendment No. 6	Difference
VOR transmitters_____	1401	950	—451
VOR monitors_____	1401	1900	+499
TACAN/DME transponders_____	1214	870	—344
TACAN/DME monitors_____	1214	1740	+526
	5230	5460	+230

While the relative difficulty in building these units depends on the individual manufacturer, in our opinion monitors are somewhat more difficult to design and build. In any event, manufacturing and production testing is about the same regardless whether monitors or transmitters/transponders are involved. The protester has made inconsistent statements in its submissions as to whether qualification testing is more demanding under amendment No. 6, at first admitting that it probably is and later claiming it is not. In our opinion, qualification and reliability testing will be somewhat more complex under amendment No. 6.

Wilcox: The protester's assertions are misleading and oversimplified. Amendment No. 6 calls for system testing as opposed to testing of the separate units which make up the systems.

12. Cardion: The contract type for installation and testing work has been changed from firm-fixed-price to cost-plus-fixed-fee, greatly reducing the risk to the contractor.

FAA: This affects only about 10 percent of the estimated contract cost. Under the RFP, cost was not specified as a factor in determining competitive range and was not a primary factor in making a selection.

ITT: This involves only about 3 percent of the total contract price and is *de minimis* in the context of the procurement as a whole.

Wilcox: This affects only about 3.2 percent of the contract price.

13. Cardion: The requirements for spares have been relaxed; spare modules on option items have been reduced from 401 to 156.

FAA: This is not a major change and it does not decrease a contractor's risk.

Cardion advances the following legal theories in support of its position:

(1) *Computek, Inc. et al.*, 54 Comp. Gen. 1080 (1975), 75–1 CPD 384, and other GAO decisions indicate that when significant changes are made in the Government's requirements, the RFP must be amended and the Government must seek "new offerors."

(2) Decisions such as *American Air Filter Company, Inc.*, 57 Comp. Gen. 285 (1978), 78–1 CPD 136, also 57 Comp. Gen. 567 (1978), 78–1 CPD 443, and *Kent Watkins & Associates, Inc.*, B–191078, May 17, 1978, 78–1 CPD 377, establish that where a modification to a contract changes its purpose or nature so substantially that the contract for which the competition was held and the contract to be performed are essentially different, the work covered by the modification should be obtained by a new and separate competitive procurement.

(3) Federal Procurement Regulations (FPR) §§ 1–3.101(c) and 1–3.101(d) (41 C.F.R. § 1–3.101(c), (d) (1978)) require procuring agencies to solicit proposals from the maximum number of qualified sources and to ensure that negotiated procurements are competitive whenever feasible. (Cardion stresses in this regard that the active interest in the protest expressed by three other companies indicates

that a number of concerns might be willing to submit proposals if the RFP is canceled and a new procurement initiated.)

FAA, ITT and Wilcox have responded at length to the protester's legal arguments. ITT and Wilcox also maintain that since the innovative technical approach in their proposal involves proprietary information, participation by Cardion or others in the procurement would involve a prohibited "technical transfusion" of these innovative concepts. They also argue that further delay occasioned by any resolicitation will result in a substantial increase in cost to the Government.

IV. Discussion

FPR § 1–3.805–1(d) states in pertinent part:

When, during negotiations, a substantial change occurs in the Government's requirements or a decision is made to relax, increase, or otherwise modify the scope of the work or statement of requirements, such change or modification shall be made in writing as an amendment to the request for proposals, and a copy shall be furnished to each prospective contractor. * * *

The regulation requires only that notice of changes be given to offerors. In the present case, Cardion is not an offeror. Thus, decisions such as *Computek, supra*— where we found that an agency failed to comply with the regulation and recommended that the competition be reopened and that offerors be notified of changes in the Government's requirements—are easily distinguishable. Contrary to Cardion's view, *Computek* did not recommend that the agency "seek new offerors" but rather that it *seek new offers* from the offerors in the procurement.

The FPR's do not specifically address the subject of whether or when an RFP should be canceled due to changes in the Government's requirements. However, Defense Acquisition Regulation (DAR) § 3–805.4(b) (1976 ed.) does address this point:

(b) The stage in the procurement cycle at which the changes occur and the magnitude of the changes shall govern which firms should be notified of the changes. If proposals are not yet due, the amendment should normally be sent to all firms solicited. If the time for receipt of proposals has passed but proposals have not yet been evaluated, the amendment should normally be sent only to the responding offerors. If the competitive range has been established, only those offerors within the competitive range should be sent the amendment. *However, no matter what stage the procurement is in, if a change or modification is so substantial as to warrant complete revision of a solicitation, the original should be canceled and a new solicitation issued.* In such cases, the new solicitation should be issued to all firms originally solicited, any firms added to the original mailing list and any other qualified firms. [Italic supplied.]

The DAR is not applicable to FAA procurements. However, in the absence of a directly applicable FPR provision, we will use it as a guide. *Iroquois Research Institute*, 55 Comp. Gen. 787, 797 (1976), 76–1 CPD 123.

It is well established that contracting agencies enjoy a broad range of discretion in deciding whether or not to cancel an RFP, and that our Office will not object to an agency's decision in this regard unless it is clearly shown to have no reasonable basis. See *United States District Court for the District of Columbia*, 58 Comp. Gen. 451 (1979), and decisions cited therein. The issue in this case, therefore, can be stated as follows: has Cardion shown that FAA's decision that the changes in requirements are not so substantial as to warrant complete revision of the RFP has no reasonable basis?

Considering the nature of the changes, as characterized by the parties *supra*, we see no basis on the record to answer this question in the affirmative. Insofar as the changes are readily and objectively quantifiable, such as the numbers of transmitters or monitors or the alterations in the delivery schedule, it is by no means obvious or self-evident why they must be regarded as "so substantial as to warrant a complete revision" of the solicitation. If anything, FAA's and ITT-Wilcox's characterizations of the changes as being of the type which might normally occur in negotiations for the acquisition of a major system appears more obvious and reasonable, especially where, as here, the RFP expressly contemplated that each offeror would provide its own design and technical approach to meeting the requirements, and technical approach was the most important evaluation criterion.

The protester's citation of *Frequency Electronics, Inc.*, B–178164, July 5, 1974, 74–2 CPD 8, is not in point. There, the protester objected to the cancellation of an RFP which had called for specific models of electronic equipment. We found no basis to object to the Navy's view that amending the RFP was impracticable, because it was ultimately possible that a considerably different type of equipment might be procured under a new RFP. Whether the FAA in the present case could reach a reasonably based conclusion that the changes in the specification are so substantial as to warrant a complete revision of the RFP is beside the point. The protester, to succeed, must show in effect that FAA would be totally unreasonable if it reached any other conclusion. The protester's presentation falls far short of such a showing.

Insofar as the alleged substantial nature of the changes is premised on the protester's perception of the reduced risk they entail, it must be noted that an individual prospective contractor's perception of the risk is of no especial concern to the Government. The Government's concern is whether its minimum needs will be satisfied at a reasonable price. See *Comten, Inc.*, B–186983, December 8, 1976, 76–2 CPD 468, affirmed March 9, 1977, 77–1 CPD 173. When the Government issues a solicitation, it is required to provide a clear statement of its requirements so that all offerors will be competing on an equal basis (*Fiber*

Materials, Inc., 54 Comp. Gen. 735 (1975), 75–1 CPD 142) but the Government makes no guarantee that each offeror will be facing the same degree of risk; one offeror, due to its superior experience or resources, may well enjoy a competitive advantage over another. *Telos Computing, Inc., supra.* We see little merit, therefore, in the idea that the substantial nature of changes in an RFP should be judged in terms of an individual prospective offeror's perception of their effect on risk.

Cardion has lately introduced an argument akin to detrimental reliance, i.e., that the changes effected by amendment No. 6 relate to the same areas of risk which caused Cardion to forego submitting a proposal in June 1978. However, the contemporaneous documentation (see Cardion's June 1, 1978, "no bid" message to FAA, *supra*) does not substantiate this after-the-fact assertion. If a prospective offeror believes the terms of the RFP involve too much risk, it has a choice of either submitting a proposal in response to the RFP, or protesting prior to the closing date for receipt of initial proposals and specifically challenging those areas of the RFP it believes should be changed. We agree with Wilcox's comments to the effect that the Government cannot conduct its negotiated procurements on a "start and stop" basis, with procurements being halted as various nonofferors change their minds about the degree of risk.

Further, we do not find decisions such as *Kent Watkins* and *American Air Filter, supra,* to be in point. The relevance of these and similar decisions to the present case rests on the theory that in determining whether changes to an RFP are so substantial as to warrant its complete revision, it is pertinent to consider whether such changes—if made to a contract already awarded—would constitute a change so substantial that the work covered by the modification should be the subject of a new procurement. The difficulty with this reasoning is that a change to a contract is not the same thing as a change to an RFP, whether considered from the perspective of the opportunity to compete or from the perspective of the best interests of the Government in satisfying its needs on the most advantageous terms. A contract modification is accomplished in what amounts to a sole-source environment; the Government deals only with the contractor and no other party has an opportunity to compete. A change to an RFP, on the other hand, does not in itself preclude any party which chose to compete in the procurement from competing for the changed requirements, nor is the Government, even if there is only one offeror, locked into a sole-source situation to the same degree in a precontract environment as it is when dealing with a contractor.

Thus, in our view, the scope of changes to an RFP which may be permissible without requiring a new solicitation is greater than the scope of changes permitted to an existing contract. See, in this regard, *Alton Iron Works*, B–183955, August 29, 1975, 75–2 CPD 131, where we stated:

> Alton also questions the propriety of an award for 895 items when the original RFP called for only 418 items. When the contracting officer learned that increased quantities would be needed he negotiated only with Yarway because it was the only offeror submitting an acceptable offer on the lesser quantity. We can find no reason to object to this procedure since ASPR § 3–805.4(b) (1974 ed.) provides, in effect, that changes in the Government's requirements that do not warrant a complete revision of the solicitation and which occur after the competitive range for the procurement has been established need only be conveyed by amendment to those offerers determined to be in the competitive range. * * *

Compare *Kent Watkins, supra,* where we found that a contract modification which doubled contract costs and performance time was in fact an unjustified sole-source award and recommended that the agency conduct a competitive procurement.

Thus, we do not find the "contract modification" line of decisions to be controlling here, and the various court decisions cited by Cardion which deal with cardinal changes are even further afield. The cardinal change cases deal with the rights of the Government and the contractor in a breach of contract situation and are not directly concerned with the subject of when certain work must be the subject of a competitive procurement.

Even if the *Kent Watkins* and *American Air Filter* rationale were to be applied here, it offers no support for the protester's position. In this regard, in our second *American Air Filter* decision, in discussing to what extent a contract can be modified before the statutory requirement for competition comes into play, we stated (57 Comp. Gen., *supra,* at 573):

> The impact of any modification is in our view to be determined by examining whether the alteration is within the scope of the competition which was initially conducted. Ordinarily, a modification falls within the scope of the procurement provided that it is of a nature which potential offerors would have reasonably anticipated under the changes clause.
>
> To determine what potential offerors would have reasonably expected, consideration should be given, in our view, to the procurement format used, the history of the present and related past procurements, and the nature of the supplies or services sought. A variety of factors may be pertinent, including: whether the requirement was appropriate initially for an advertised or negotiated procurement; whether a standard off-the-shelf or similar item is sought; or to whether, e.g., the contract is one for research and development, suggesting that broad changes might be expected because the Government's requirements are at best only indefinite.

By analogy, the scope of changes to an RFP which would be permissible without requiring cancellation and resolicitation would have to be judged in terms of what changes in the RFP prospective offerors might reasonably have anticipated would be made after proposals were received. Cardion and all other prospective offerors were on notice that in this negotiated procurement the RFP explicitly contemplated individual design approaches by offerors. To assert in these circumstances that an RFP amendment incorporating technical changes based on the particular technical approach taken by the sole offeror makes the RFP as amended fundamentally different in purpose or nature from the original RFP is totally unpersuasive.

As for Cardion's argument that the RFP should be canceled because FPR § 1–3.101 requires agencies to seek maximum competition in negotiated procurements, our decision *Environmental Protection Agency—request for modification of GAO recommendation,* 55 Comp. Gen. 1281 (1976), 76–2 CPD 50, is pertinent. There, our Office had sustained a protest and recommended that negotiations be reopened with the six offerors. The agency proposed instead to cancel the RFP, partly on the basis that issuing a new RFP would maximize competition by allowing parties other than the six original offerors an opportunity to submit proposals. Our decision stated (55 Comp. Gen. at 1284–1285) :

[FPR] § 1–3.101(d) (1964 ed. amend. 153) provides that negotiated procurement shall be on a competitive basis to the maximum practical extent. However, we do not believe that this principle, considered in and of itself, necessarily justifies canceling an existing RFP and issuing a new RFP. Unless there is a reasonable basis to believe that continuing the competition under an existing RFP will not lead to the receipt of technically acceptable proposals whose realistic probable costs are considered reasonable, we see no grounds why the RFP should be canceled in the hope of experiencing better results under a new RFP.

A decision to cancel, in other words, should not be undertaken based solely on speculation about possible increased competition under a new RFP and irrespective of the results obtained under the original RFP. In 55 Comp. Gen. 1281, six proposals had been received as opposed to only one in the present case. However, the FAA initiated the current procurement as a competitive one and ITT-Wilcox's proposal was prepared in anticipation of competition. There is no requirement that an agency cancel an RFP solely because only one acceptable proposal is received. See, in this regard, *Cessna Aircraft Company et al.,* 54 Comp. Gen. 97 (1974), 74–2 CPD 91; *cf. Alton Iron Works, supra.*

V. Conclusion

The protest is denied.

❲ B–192795 ❳

Officers and Employees—Transfers—Relocation Expenses—Temporary Quarters—Beginning of Occupancy

If a Federal employee's dependents are returned from overseas to the United States prior to the employee's transfer, subsistence expenses while occupying temporary quarters may not be paid on the basis of the dependents' occupancy of temporary quarters at the time of and in connection with their early return from overseas, since the statutory provision governing the travel of dependents in such circumstances provides only for the reimbursement of the dependents' "transportation expenses" and does not, in addition, authorize payment of subsistence expenses. 5 U.S.C. 5729 (1976).

Officers and Employees—Transfers—Relocation Expenses—Temporary Quarters—Entitlement

If a Federal employee's dependents are returned from overseas to the United States prior to the employee's transfer, temporary quarters subsistence expenses may nevertheless be paid on their behalf when the employee performs his permanent-change-of-station travel, provided that the dependents are required to occupy temporary quarters at the time of and in connection with the employee's transfer. 5 U.S.C. 5724a (1976).

In the matter of Subsistence Expenses While Occupying Temporary Quarters—Early Return of Dependents of Civilian Employees from Overseas Areas, June 14, 1979:

This action concerns subsistence expenses while occupying temporary quarters (TQSE), which are reimbursable relocation expenses payable to a Federal employee when use of temporary lodgings is justified in connection with his transfer to a new permanent duty station. A decision has been requested on the following question:

If dependents are returned from overseas to CONUS prior to the time the PCS transfer is authorized, prior to the time PCS orders are issued, and prior to the time the transportation agreement is signed, may the dependents be included for TQSE purpose when the employee ultimately performs PCS travel?

The request for a decision on this question was submitted by Mr. Joe F. Meis, Principal Deputy, Assistant Secretary of the Air Force (Manpower, Reserve Affairs and Installations), and the request has been assigned Control No. 78–30 by the Per Diem, Travel and Transportation Allowance Committee, Department of Defense.

In the submission it is noted that para. 2–5.2e of the Federal Travel Regulations imposes certain time limitations on the use of temporary quarters for subsistence expense purposes. It is also noted that in decision B–164948, October 18, 1968, involving the early return of an employee's dependents from an overseas duty station, we disallowed payment of per diem in the absence of a related transfer of the employee. It is indicated that because of the above-mentioned regulatory provision and Comptroller General's decision, doubt has arisen as to whether TQSE on behalf of an employee's dependents may be paid in the event of their early return to the continental United States from an overseas duty station, even if the dependents eventually join the employee in temporary quarters upon his subsequent transfer.

I. Temporary Quarters Subsistence Expenses Are Not Payable in Connection With the Early Return of Dependents from Overseas Under 5 U.S.C. § 5729.

With respect to expenses allowable in connection with the early return of a civilian employee's dependents to the continental United

States from a foreign or overseas post of duty, section 5729 of title 5, United States Code (1976), provides as follows:

(a) Under such regulations as the President may prescribe, an agency shall pay from its appropriations, not more than once before the return to the United States or its territories or possessions of an employee whose post of duty is outside the continental United States, *the expenses of transporting his immediate family and of shipping his household goods and personal effects* from his post of duty to his actual place of residence when—

(1) he has acquired eligibility for that transportation; or

(2) the public interest requires the return of the immediate family for compelling personal reasons of a humanitarian or compassionate nature, such as may involve physical or mental health, death of a member of the immediate family, or obligation imposed by authority or circumstances over which the individual has no control.

(b) Under such regulations as the President may prescribe, an agency shall reimburse from its appropriations an employee whose post of duty is outside the continental United States for *the proper transportation expenses of returning his immediate family and his household goods and personal effects* to the United States or its territories or possessions, when—

(1) their return was made at the expense of the employee before his return and for other than reasons of public interest; and

(2) he acquires eligibility for those transportation expenses.

(c) This section does not apply to appropriations for the Foreign Service of the United States. [Italic supplied.]

We have long held that the term "transportation expenses" of an employee's dependents as used in a statute does not include authority for payment of per diem in lieu of subsistence in addition to transportation expenses. See, for example, 25 Comp. Gen. 268 (1945). We have, therefore, expressed the view that the authority for the transportation of an employee's dependents at public expense contained in 5 U.S.C. § 5729 does not, in addition, include authority for the payment of per diem in lieu of subsistence. See decision B–164948, *supra*, and B–172078, March 30, 1971. Moreover, since no statutory authority exists under 5 U.S.C. § 5729 for the payment of any amounts for subsistence, it is also our view that temporary quarters subsistence expenses, TQSE, are not payable in connection with the early return of dependents under that provision of law.

II. Temporary Quarters Subsistence Expenses May Be Paid Under 5 U.S.C. § 5724a if the Dependents Occupy Temporary Quarters When the Employee Is Later Transferred.

Section 5724a of title 5, United States Code (1976), provides that in addition to transportation expenses, an employee may also be authorized reimbursement of all or part of certain relocation expenses incurred in connection with a permanent-change-of-station transfer. Among the relocation expenses authorized to be paid are per diem in lieu of subsistence while en route (subsection (a)(1)), and subsistence expenses of the employee and his immediate family for a period of 30 days while occupying temporary quarters, TQSE, where the new official station is located in the United States, its territories or possessions, the Commonwealth of Puerto Rico, or the Canal Zone (subsection (a)(3)).

Implementing statutory regulations governing the payment of TQSE are contained in chapter 2, part 5, Federal Travel Regulations, FPMR 101-7 (May 1973) (FTR) issued by the General Services Administration. Para. 2-5.2e of those regulations, which is referred to in the submission, provides as follows:

> e. *Time to begin occupancy*. The use of temporary quarters for subsistence expense purposes under these provisions may begin as soon as the employee's transfer has been authorized, and the written agreement required in 2-1.5a(1) has been signed. In order to be eligible for the temporary quarters allowance, the period of use of such quarters for which a claim for reimbursement is made must begin not later than 30 days from the date the employee reported for duty at his new official station, or if not begun during this period, not later than 30 days from the date the family vacates the residence at the old official station, but not beyond the maximum time for beginning allowable travel and transportation.

Thus, under the regulations, the use of temporary quarters for TQSE purposes may not begin until the employee's transfer has been authorized and a required written agreement signed. With respect to the written agreement required of Department of Defense employees, para. C4005-1, Volume 2, Joint Travel Regulations, provides that the minimum service requirement in connection with transfers to and within the United States is a 12-month tour of duty. Other provisions of those regulations prescribe rules for the preparation and disposition of the related written agreement to remain in Government service for the required period.

Once the employee's transfer is authorized and the other conditions of entitlement have been met, his dependents would thereafter be eligible to occupy temporary quarters for TQSE purposes. This is so even if at some earlier date such dependents had received advance transportation under the provisions of 5 U.S.C. § 5729. Their occupancy of temporary quarters at the time of the employee's transfer may properly be viewed as being related to his permanent-change-of-station move. See decision B-170446, January 11, 1971. As previously indicated, however, no additional TQSE payments could be made on the basis of subsistence expenses the dependents might also have incurred while occupying temporary quarters at the time of their early return from overseas, since those expenses could not properly be viewed as having a direct relationship to the employee's transfer under the applicable laws and regulations.

The question presented is answered accordingly.

【 B–177610 】

Federal Credit Unions—Services Furnished By Government

Available space and services may be provided to Federal Credit Union Service Centers if approved by the appropriate officer or agency. 12 U.S.C. 1770 (1976). Also, General Accounting Office will not raise legal objection if credit union is allowed to use desks, chairs, and office machines without charge. However, agency funds are hereafter not available to furnish without charge telephone services for credit union.

In the matter of Federal Services to Employees' Credit Union Service Center, June 15, 1979:

The Director, Fiscal and Accounting Management, United States Forest Service, Department of Agriculture (Forest Service), has requested our decision on whether funds appropriated to the Forest Service are available to finance miscellaneous services provided to a local Forest Service employees' Credit Union Service Center (Credit Union). The Director states that for a number of years, property and services have been provided without charge to its Atlanta Region Credit Union office, including the use of "surplus" Government property (desks, chairs, and office machines) and "telephone installations, FTS lines, and monthly use rates." He questions whether Forest Service appropriations are available for these purposes.

A Federal credit union is a cooperative association organized in accordance with the provisions of the Federal Credit Union Act, as amended, 12 U.S.C. §§ 1751 *et seq.* (1976), for the purpose of promoting thrift among its members and creating a source of credit for provident or productive purposes. 12 U.S.C. § 1752(1). While organized under Federal law and subject to the supervision of the Administrator of the National Credit Union Administration, a Federal credit union is a private organization; its funds are obtained from private sources and are not appropriated by the Federal Government.

However, when organized within the terms of the Federal Credit Union Act, *supra*, Federal employee credit unions may be assigned space in Government-controlled buildings in the community or district in which they do business. 12 U.S.C. § 1770 (1976). Assignment of space, if it is available, is within the discretion of the officer or agency of the United States charged with the allotment of space in the Federal building, and it may be assigned without charge for rent or services. *Id.* The statute reads as follows:

* * * Upon application by any credit union organized under State law or by any Federal credit union organized in accordance with the terms of this Act, at least 95 per centum of the membership of which is composed of persons who either are presently Federal employees or were Federal employees at the time of admission into the credit union, and members of their families, which application shall be addressed to the officer or agency of the United States charged with the allotment of space in the Federal buildings in the community or district in which

such credit union does business, such officer or agency may in his or its discretion allot space to such credit union if space is available without charge for rent or services.

We have held that the kind of services which may be supplied without charge to Federal credit unions under section 1770 includes only those services which are necessary to meet normal space needs. Any special services over and above those normal needs, such as providing security alarm systems, are not authorized to be furnished from Federal appropriated funds. Payment for such services must be provided from funds of the Credit Union, which may contract and pay for the services itself. B-164310, August 28, 1968.

Unlike available space, which must be paid for by the United States whether used by a credit union or not, telephones and telephone service for the credit union would not otherwise be required and would therefore, to some degree, result in additional cost to the United States. We believe that furnishing of telephone service (including installations, FTS lines, and other expenses associated with telephone service) by a Federal agency would fall into the category of special service, the cost of which should be borne by the credit union.

However, under the circumstances, the Department need not bill the credit union for costs of telephone service previously incurred. The credit union should be billed for such costs henceforth.

With regard to the so-called surplus property, the question is more complex. Section 1770 allows agencies controlling allotment of space in Federal buildings to give credit unions "space and services." While the authorization to provide "services" to credit unions may originally have been understood as covering services associated with the space, such as lighting, heat or cooling, and maintenance, in practice certain personal property such as furniture and office machines has also been widely made available. In our report, "Applying a Uniform Policy With Respect to Rental Charges For Credit Unions" (B-164031(4), February 17, 1971), we recognized that Federal agencies commonly provided office furniture and equipment to credit unions without charge. We concluded that the Federal Credit Union Act contained sufficient authority to charge credit unions for space and personal property furnished by Government agencies and we recommended that the Administrator of General Services establish guidelines for use by Federal agencies in determining such charges.

However, on reconsideration, we held that, while we continued to believe that the Act permitted establishment of a policy of "rent" assessments to credit unions, in view of the doubts raised by the legislative history of the 1937 Act "and the resulting need for legislative clarification of the actual wording" of 12 U.S.C. § 1770, we would not pursue the matter without further action by the Congress. B-164031

(4), July 1, 1971. To our knowledge, Congress has taken no further action. Accordingly, we will not raise legal objections to the practice of allowing a Federal employees' credit union to use available Government space or so-called surplus personal property (furniture and office machines) without charge.

〖 B–193805 〗

Travel Expenses—Private Parties—Invitational Travel on Federal Government Business—Foreign Air Carrier Use

Requirement to use U.S. Flag air carriers unless those carriers are "unavailable" applies to Government invitees even though traveler is unaware of statutory provisions and inviting agency fails to make proper travel arrangements. 49 U.S.C. 1517.

In the matter of H. J. Otway—Fly America Act, Application to Government Invitees, June 15, 1979:

This is in response to a request from the Director, Division of Accounting, Office of the Controller, Nuclear Regulatory Commission (NRC), for an advance decision concerning a travel voucher submitted by H. J. Otway, an invitational traveler for the NRC.

The Division Director, who is an authorized certifying officer, forwarded to this Office a copy of the voucher in question. Ordinarily the General Accounting Office will not render an advance decision unless the request is accompanied by an original voucher, properly certified and approved. 22 Comp. Gen. 588 (1943). Where the record shows, however, that the certifying or disbursing officer does have a voucher before him, the question presented may be decided in order to expedite matters. B–193434, November 30, 1978; B–178441, June 18, 1973.

Mr. Otway, an American member of the International Atomic Energy Agency in Austria was invited to confer in Washington by the NRC at the agency's expense for the period March 25–30, 1978. He was not instructed as to how he should arrange air transportation, nor were the administrative facilities of the NRC, which were available, used to arrange travel for Mr. Otway. He made his own travel arrangements and used a foreign air carrier for the segment of his trip from Vienna through Amsterdam to New York. A U.S. air carrier was available for the trip to New York. Upon his arrival in Washington, he was informed of the requirement to use U.S. air carriers, and changed his return trip which included a personal side trip to Albuquerque, New Mexico, so that he returned to Vienna by a route making the greatest practical use of U.S. air carriers.

Mr. Otway was unaware of the requirement to use U.S. air carriers. Because Mr. Otway is not an employee of NRC, the agency feels that he should not be penalized for its failure to give appropriate instructions and to make proper arrangements for the travel.

The requirement for use of certificated U.S. air carriers in international travel is imposed by section 5 of the International Air Transportation Fair Competitive Practices Act of 1974, Public Law 93–623, January 3, 1975, 49 U.S.C. § 1517 (1976), which provides that:

> * * * The Comptroller General of the United States shall disallow any expenditure from appropriated funds for payment of such personnel or cargo transportation on an air carrier not holding a certificate under section 401 of this Act in the absence of satisfactory proof of the necessity therefor. * * *

The law does not differentiate between Government employees and Government invitees. All Government-financed air travel must be on U.S. air carriers unless those carriers are "unavailable." See B–188968, August 8, 1977. There is no provision to relieve a traveler of the penalty for using a foreign flag carrier because of the agency's failure to make appropriate travel plans. The requirement for use of certificated service is mandated by statute and may not be waived. B–186007, November 15, 1976. Therefore, because transportation by certificated U.S. air carriers was available between Vienna and Washington, Mr. Otway may not be allowed the amount of money improperly diverted from U.S. air carriers.

NRC has adopted the mileage proration formula described in 56 Comp. Gen. 209 (1977) for use in determining the amount of the traveler's financial liability. Applying the formula to Mr. Otway's case, his liability for use of a noncertificated air carrier from Vienna to New York is $245.08.

However, Mr. Otway's travel voucher includes an inapplicable round trip air fare of $722; the correct price for the authorized round trip ticket if purchased in Vienna, Austria, is $969.60, or $247.60 more than the amount claimed. Since the penalty is $245.08, Mr. Otway may be allowed $2.52 in addition to the amount claimed on his voucher, if otherwise correct. See 58 Comp. Gen. 298 (1978).

〔 B–193536 〕

Attorneys—Fees—Administrative Investigative Proceedings

As a result of its own investigation of misconduct charges initially made by a private party, Securities and Exchange Commission (SEC) found possible merit to charges against three of eight SEC employees and appointed a hearing examiner who ultimately determined the misconduct allegations to be without merit. SEC may not reimburse attorney's fees incurred by the employee as a cost of providing legal representation, since, upon its determination to further pursue the matter, the case was no longer one in which the Government's interests were aligned with those of the employee in defending charges brought by a third party against the employee for conduct within the scope of his official responsibilities. Compare B–127945, April 5, 1979.

Attorneys—Fees—Agency Authority To Award

Where an SEC investigation of charges of misconduct against three SEC employees was ultimately resolved in favor of the employees, the employees' legal fees may not be reimbursed. Attorney's fees may be awarded to the prevailing party only when there is express authority for the payment of such fees and there is no specific authority for award of attorney's fees in standards of conduct proceedings in the nature of those conducted by the SEC.

In the matter of Securities and Exchange Commission—Reimbursement of Legal Expenses Incident to Internal Investigation, June 18, 1979:

This action is in response to a request for a decision from the Securities and Exchange Commission (SEC) concerning its authority to reimburse reasonable attorney's fees paid by SEC employees incident to an SEC internal inquiry into allegations of misconduct filed against the employees by an outside party.

The request from the SEC states that in the course of administrative proceedings against a securities broker-dealer, a respondent in these proceedings charged that certain SEC employees had violated provisions of title 18 of the United States Code, violated or aided and abetted violations of the SEC Conduct Regulation (17 C.F.R. § 200.-735–1 *et seq.*), and otherwise engaged in improper professional conduct in connection with the administrative proceedings. These allegations were also filed with the Internal Revenue Service, the United States Attorney's Office, and the Ethics Committee of the Bergen County, New Jersey, Bar Association. In addition, the respondent filed four separate lawsuits in United States District Court in which he raised substantially the same charges of misconduct by SEC staff. The SEC and its staff members were represented in these lawsuits by counsel from the SEC's Office of General Counsel, and all of these lawsuits were ultimately dismissed.

Under SEC procedures, the Office of General Counsel conducted an informal inquiry into these allegations of misconduct by three of the SEC employees and, upon the advice of that office, the SEC appointed an impartial hearing officer to conduct a formal inquiry. After a period of about 2 years, these two inquiries were completed, and the SEC accepted the hearing officer's conclusion that the allegations of misconduct were without merit. The SEC closed the matter with no adverse personnel action taken against the employees in question. At least two of the employees involved have requested that the SEC reimburse the legal fees they incurred in retaining private counsel to represent them in connection with the inquiries.

The request from the SEC states further that allegations of misconduct are taken very seriously and that where the allegations are found to have merit, the employee involved may be subject to an adverse personnel action. In addition, violation of the SEC's Conduct Regulation can lead to that person's temporary or permanent disqualification from appearing or practicing before the SEC. See 17 C.F.R. § 200.735–13. Since an employee who is the subject of an inquiry may find his career in jeopardy, the SEC believes it is not unreasonable for the employee to retain private counsel. Where the allegations of misconduct have been found to have been without merit, the SEC believes it is appropriate to reimburse reasonable attorney's fees paid by its employee. The SEC, therefore, asks to be advised whether it has the legal authority to reimburse attorney's fees under the circumstances described above.

The question of whether attorney's fees may be awarded to the successful or prevailing party in a particular proceeding is a matter to be resolved on the basis of whether there is express statutory authority for the payment of such fees. *Alyeska Pipeline Co.* v. *Wilderness Society*, 421 U.S. 240 (1975). There is no specific authority for award of attorney's fees in standards of conduct proceedings in the nature of those conducted by the SEC and we are unable to find that the SEC otherwise has statutory authority to award attorney's fees in administrative proceedings of this type. Compare 15 U.S.C. § 77k(e) and 78i(e). Therefore, we find that the SEC does not have authority to pay the attorney's fees of the employees based upon the fact that the administrative proceedings were resolved in their favor and that the allegations of misconduct were found to have been without merit.

However, we believe there is another aspect of this case that warrants consideration. While the hiring of an outside attorney to represent an employee is generally a private matter between the attorney and the client (55 Comp. Gen. 1418 (1976)), the Government may provide an employee with representation for private litigation when the United States' interest is at stake along with the employee's personal interest. B–130441, April 12, 1978. We have recognized that the Government has an interest in judicial proceedings brought by a private party against a Federal employee in his individual capacity arising out of conduct within the scope of his Federal employment and that the Government may properly provide representation in such proceedings. B–150136, May 19, 1978. Since the United States acts through its employees, advocating the legality of employee actions taken in furtherance of their official duties is in the interest of the Federal Government. Moreover, if agency employees knew that they would have to bear their own representation expenses in actions against them resulting from performance of their jobs, they would discharge their duties and exercise their discretionary functions less vigorously.

Generally, the Department of Justice provides its attorneys to represent employees in litigation under the authority of sections 516, 517, 518, and 547(b) of Title 28, United States Code. These sections charge the Department with the responsibility for representing the United States in all litigation in which it has an interest. The Attorney General interprets these provisions as giving the Department the statutory authority for its policy of representing Federal employees in court actions brought against them in their individual capacity because of acts performed within the scope of their employment. The Department implements this policy in accordance with its statement on representation found at 28 C.F.R. §§ 50.15 and 50.16.

However, the Department will not provide counsel to charged employees in administrative disciplinary proceedings. Subsection 50.15 (a) of its policy statement specifies the kind of proceedings in which the Department *will* provide representation. It states:

> (a) Under the procedures set forth below, a Federal employee (herein defined to include former employees) may be represented by Justice Department attorneys in state criminal proceedings and in civil and Congressional proceedings in which he is sued or subpoenaed in his individual capacities, not covered by § 15.1 of this chapter.

In response to a recent request for the Attorney General's views regarding Department of Justice representation at the agency level in disciplinary and discrimination proceedings, the Assistant Attorney General explained that administrative disciplinary proceedings are not included in subsection 50.15(a) because:

> * * * It is the policy of the Civil Division, in this regard, that none of its attorneys may represent federal agency personnel in disciplinary or Title VII discrimination proceedings for the reason that the Civil Division will be responsible for defending the employing agency in the event the employee brings a civil action challenging the results of the proceeding. Representing the employee at the agency level proceeding would, therefore, create an unacceptable conflict.

In judicial actions in which the Attorney General declines to provide representation, agency appropriations are available to provide representation if otherwise proper. 55 Comp. Gen. 408, 412 (1975). In such cases, the agency must determine that representation is in the Government's interest and that the conduct in question was in furtherance of an agency function. In such cases, where the appropriate determinations have been made, the cost of an attorney may be considered a necessary expense incurred in performing that agency function. 53 Comp. Gen. 301, 306 (1973). Recently, in B–127945, April 5, 1979, we recognized that because of the unavailability of Department of Justice representation an agency may use its appropriations to provide counsel in connection with an administrative hearing of charges of misconduct by an employee in the performance of his official duties where the charges were initiated and pursued by a private party in that administrative forum.

In B–127945 the Nuclear Regulatory Commission (NRC) staff filed a motion for censure for alleged professional misconduct against a private attorney representing certain parties to a licensing-related proceeding. The private attorney filled a motion for disciplinary action against two NRC employees whom he charged with misconduct. In accordance with NRC's Rules of Procedure, the charges were referred to a special board for hearing. The NRC retained private attorneys to defend its employees in the two-party disciplinary proceeding against the charges brought and pursued by the private attorney. In concluding that the NRC could expend its appropriations for the necessary legal services, we stated:

> * * * an agency may properly charge against its appropriation the expenses of defending acts performed within the scope of agency employment. Here, "the NRC Executive Legal Director determined that the employees involved were clearly acting within the scope of their authority." It was therefore in the agency's interest to provide them with legal counsel, and since the Attorney General has declined representation in this type of proceeding, NRC appropriations would be available to supply counsel to the charged staff members.
>
> It was NRC's view that its own attorneys could not defend the charged staff members before the Special Board because their appearances might create conflicts of interest. The NRC's Office of General Counsel could not supply its attorneys because that Office would be responsible for advising the NRC in its review of the Board's decision in the proceeding. Although it is not clear from the Executive Director's letter, we have been advised informally that attorneys from the Office of Executive Legal Director (ELD) could not provide representation because the intervenors who filed misconduct charges contended that ELD attorneys must prosecute all such charges. As a result, when its was necessary for NRC to decide whether to retain outside attorneys, the possibility existed that the Office of ELD would be prosecuting the same case, thus making that Office's representation of the accused attorneys inappropriate.
>
> Accordingly, since providing legal counsel to these NRC employees to defend conduct within the scope of agency employment is in furtherance of the agency's purpose, the NRC could properly expend its appropriations for the necessary legal services. * * *

At the outset of the special proceedings, a determination was made by NRC that the conduct of its staff members was conduct within the scope of their employment and that it was in the interest of the Government to provide them legal representation to defend their actions against the charges brought and pursued by the private attorney. Outside legal counsel was retained by NRC at the outset of the special proceedings. Inasmuch as Department of Justice representation was unavailable and agency staff representation involved an apparent conflict of interest, payment of the legal expenses involved was sustained on the basis consistent with our decisions cited above, holding that the Government may provide legal representation in private litigation against an employee in proceedings arising out of conduct within the scope of his employment. In the prior cases and in the NRC proceeding, the conduct of the Federal employees was brought into issue and pursued by a third party and not by the Government itself.

The SEC case here in issue differs significantly from the NRC case in that the charges of misconduct, while initially raised by an outside party, were pursued not by the outside party but by the SEC on the basis of its independent determination to investigate the conduct of three of its employees. Correspondence received from two of the three SEC attorneys involved indicates that the private respondent in the SEC administrative proceeding against the securities broker-dealer initially made allegations of staff misconduct against at least eight SEC employees. The SEC Office of General Counsel conducted a formal investigation into all of those allegations. With respect to at least one of the employees, the Office of General Counsel initially concluded that there was possible merit to the allegations and recommended that disciplinary action be taken. Because of additional information subsequently obtained, disciplinary proceedings were not in fact instituted but, upon the recommendation of the Office of General Counsel, the SEC appointed an independent hearing examiner to conduct a further inquiry into the matter. It was at this point that the employee retained private counsel. We understand that the other two SEC employees also retained private counsel at this point and that a transcribed hearing was held concerning the conduct of all three. The hearing examiner found the allegations of misconduct to be without merit and recommended that no action be taken with respect to any of the three.

Under these circumstances, the cost of providing counsel may not be considered a proper expenditure of appropriated funds. Upon SEC's determination that the matter should be further investigated with respect to three of the SEC employees, the situation was no longer one in which the Government's interest was aligned with the interests of the three employees against charges pressed by a third party, and thus it was no longer in the Government's interest to provide them with legal counsel. The SEC hearing was a formal agency fact-finding inquiry to determine whether its employees were guilty of misconduct. In fact, at that point, the situation was indistinguishable from that in which an agency itself initiates an investigation into the conduct of its own employees. That the employees were ultimately vindicated does not change the character of the proceeding.

The determination to provide an employee with legal representation is one to be made at the outset of proceedings initiated against him by an outside party based on a determination that the conduct in question was within the scope of his official responsibilities and that it is in the interest of the Government to provide for his representation.

It is not a determination to be predicated on the employee's ultimate success in the particular proceeding.

〔 B–194945 〕

Claims—Assignments—Contracts—Validity of Assignment—Assignee's Right to Payment

Government contractor's secured note, assigning accounts receivable to financial institution, which was executed during the period the instant Government contract was being performed, should be recognized under Assignment of Claims Act. Record includes contractor's schedule of accounts receivable which lists the instant contract account. B–120222, Oct, 27, 1955, modified.

In the matter of General Services Administration—Advance Decision, Assignment of Claims Act, June 19, 1979:

The General Services Administration (GSA) requests an advance decision concerning the proper payee under GSA contract No. GS–02S–29880 with Teltronics Services, Inc. (Teltronics). GSA, having received performance from Teltronics, is now in the position of stakeholder ready to make payment, but is uncertain as to the proper payee. This uncertainty stems from a claim of the Sterling National Bank and Trust Company of New York (Sterling) that it should be the payee by virtue of an agreement in which Teltronics allegedly assigned the proceeds from this Government contract to Sterling. The validity of this assignment under the Assignment of Claims Act of 1940, as amended, 31 U.S.C. § 203 (1976) and 41 U.S.C. § 15 (1976) (hereafter referred to as the Act) is the determinative issue here.

Background

On May 1, 1978, GSA awarded to Teltronics a contract for the installation and maintenance of a communications system at Floyd Bennett Field, Brooklyn, New York. Upon completion of installation, Teltronics submitted to GSA on May 4, 1979, an invoice for payment in the amount of $519,678. Previously, on March 16, 1979, Sterling asserted its claim to any payment under the instant contract by notifying GSA's contracting officer that it was assignee of all Teltronics' accounts receivable. As evidence of this assignment, Sterling submitted a Security and Assignment Agreement, dated July 19, 1976, in which Teltronics agreed to the following terms:

FOR VALUE RECEIVED, and in consideration of loans or extensions of credit made to the Undersigned [Teltronics], as evidenced by any notes, guarantees or other evidence of indebtedness executed by Undersigned, the Undersigned hereby grants a security interest in, sells, assigns, transfers, deposits, pledges and sets over to the Bank [Sterling] all it right, title and interest in and to each and every account of the Undersigned now owned or hereafter arising and all moneys now due or hereafter to become due thereon * * *.

On March 22, 1979, GSA informed Sterling that the assignment was not in compliance with the Assignment of Claims Act and GSA was therefore unable to honor the request for payment. In particular, GSA noted that the 1976 Teltronics/Sterling agreement did not refer to any specific Government contract, was not a certified copy, and was entered into approximately 2 years prior to the date of the contract in question. Sterling resubmitted its notice of assignment on April 3, 1979, and, again, it was rejected by GSA on April 4, 1979, as an assignment not conforming to the requirements of the Act.

Subsequently, Sterling requested a Temporary Restraining Order in the United States District Court for the Southern District of New York. On April 17, 1979, the court entered an order which: (1) restrained GSA from paying Teltronics any funds due under the subject contract; and (2) required any funds which may become payable thereunder to be paid into court. By Order to Show Cause, Sterling commenced a proceeding seeking a preliminary injunction to prevent GSA from paying Teltronics monies due under the contract and to require Teltronics to execute any documents necessary for Sterling to obtain payment directly from the Government. Upon motion of the court and after testimony was heard, the court dismissed the action for lack of subject matter jurisdiction on May 7, 1979.

On May 8, 1979, Sterling renewed its request to GSA that the assignment be recognized. As additional support for its position, Sterling submitted a copy of a corporate resolution of Teltronics, dated July 19, 1976, which authorized the execution of the 1976 assignment. Further, Sterling provided a portion of the transcript of the April 20, 1979 hearing in the previously mentioned court action in which a Teltronics Vice-President testified that the Floyd Bennett Field contract account receivable had been assigned to Sterling.

Upon receipt of this renewed request from Sterling, and having possession of other documents tending to demonstrate the establishment of a line of credit extended to Teltronics during the performance of this contract, GSA sought our advice in this matter. GSA's primary area of concern is that the 1976 security agreement submitted by the bank predated the Government contract by nearly 2 years and is a blanket security agreement which does not necessarily require the Teltronics accounts receivable to be paid to the bank.

Discussion

The Act permits the assignment to a bank, trust company, or other financing institution of monies due under a Government contract.

Assignees, however, must comply with the requirements for written notice of assignments stated in the Act, as follows:

> * * * file written notice of the assignment together with a true copy of the instrument of assignment with (a) the contracting officer or the head of his department or agency; (b) surety or sureties upon the bond or bonds, if any, in connection with such contract; and (c) the disbursing officer, if any, in connection with such contract; and (d) the disbursing officer, if any, designated in such contract to make payment.

The Security and Assignment Agreement of July 19, 1976, between Teltronics and Sterling is best characterized as a blanket security agreement because of its general terms with no reference to any specific contract and because it covers a variety of security interests in the debtor's current and future accounts receivable. Moreover, it predates the instant contract by nearly 2 years and therefore it does not evidence that the bank was providing financing at the time this Government contract was executed or being performed. GSA states that the Act has been interpreted as requiring the assignment to reference a specific Government contract or that there must be a recognition, on an invoice or purchase order, by the contractor that an assignee should be paid monies due under the contract. In this regard, the agency cites *First National City Bank* v. *United States*, 548 F. 2d 928, 212 Ct. Cl. 357 (1977) and prior decisions of this Office. GSA also quotes from the cited court case wherein the court, in effect, stated that under the Act a proper assignee was confined to a lender whose loan was used, or was available for use, in financing the particular Government contract.

However, the question there was whether the set-off protections of the Act were available to the assignee bank. The court noted that Congress did not intend to eat into the Government's normal right of set-off against an assignor more than would be necessary to induce monetary aid in performing a contract. There is no question of set-off in this case, the Government being a mere stakeholder and the contractor demanding direct payment without contesting the authenticity of the assignment of the instant account. We are aware of no requirement for the Government to ascertain the purpose of the loan before recognizing an assignment of contract payments over the contractor's conflicting demands for direct payment. In such circumstances it is enough that the Government assure itself of the assignment's authenticity and its applicability to the contract right involved here. Moreover, the fact that the Government contract may have been only one of many accounts assigned by Teltronics to Sterling would not invalidate an assignment under the Act. In accord with the modern trend away from tying a particular loan to a particular security, the use of a revolving credit financing device has been regarded as acceptable under the Act. *Continental Bank & Trust Co.* v. *United States*, 416 F. 2d 1296, 189 Ct. Cl. 99 (1969).

In this connection, we have held that an assignment of a claim against the Government should specify the particular contract involved, and therefore, that a blanket assignment does not meet the requirements of the Act where the Government seeks to set off a tax indebtedness. *See* B–120222, October 27, 1955. We have noted in one decision that the lack of specificity of a blanket agreement can be cured for purposes of perfecting a valid assignment under the Act when "there are in existence later amendment schedules [specifying the Government contract] signed by the assignor, which purport to be an integral part of the original [blanket] assignment instrument." B–171125, February 4, 1971. GSA has provided us documentation in addition to the 1976 agreement which raises the possibility that there may be sufficient documentation of a valid assignment applicable to the instant contract payment.

It appears from the documents subsequently submitted here by GSA that during the period of performance of the Floyd Bennett Field contract, Sterling loaned Teltronics $1 million. This is evidenced by a secured note dated December 29, 1978, and executed by the Treasurer and Vice-President of Teltronics. By the terms of the note, Teltronics granted a security interest in and assigned all accounts receivable to Sterling. (This note also refers to the 1976 blanket agreement as a matter of collateral security for the loan.) In the documentation we received, a schedule of Teltronics' accounts receivable lists the Floyd Bennett Field contract account. Assuming that GSA concludes that the December 1978 secured note is an authentic document, we believe it should be recognized as an assignment under the Act. Nevertheless, because of the controversy in this matter the bank should be required to indemnify the Government from any claims that might be made by the contractor. The bank may be paid upon satisfaction of these requirements.

〖 B–190420 〗

Pay—Retired—Waiver for Veterans Benefits—Effective Date

A retired Regular Air Force Officer employed in a Federal civilian position whose retired pay was subject to reduction under the Dual Compensation Act, 5 U.S.C. 5532, was advised by the Veterans Administration (VA) on February 23, 1978, that he was entitled to VA disability compensation retroactive to June 26, 1977. The officer filed a waiver of retired pay with the service department, pursuant to 38 U.S.C. 3105, on March 3, 1978. Waiver of retired pay upon notification of entitlement to VA compensation is effective from the earliest date of entitlement to VA compensation; but the additional amount due is payable as VA compensation, and not retired pay. *Matter of Lieutenant Colonel Oliver B. Larson*, 55 Comp. Gen. 1402 (1976), is modified.

In the maitter of Lieutenant Colonel Leo A. Fitzgerald, USAF, Retired, June 26, 1979:

Section 5532 of Title 5, United States Code, requires that the pay of retired military members be reduced upon their acceptance of Federal civilian employment. Section 3104 of Title 38, United States Code, prohibits the concurrent payment of military retired pay and Veterans Administration (VA) pension or compensation benefits. Section 3105 of Title 38, however, authorizes members to receive both retired pay and VA pension or compensation payments so long as they waive entitlement to retired pay in an amount equivalent to the veterans' benefits paid them.

A member gains in two ways by receiving payments characterized as veterans' benefits rather than retired pay: veterans' benefits are not taxable, and should the member become federally employed, veterans' benefits are not subject to reduction by the Dual Compensation Act, 5 U.S.C. 5532 to which retired pay is subject.

The present case involves a retired Regular officer, Lieutenant Colonel Leo A. Fitzgerald, USAF, Retired, whose retired pay was reduced upon his Federal civilian employment. At a later date the VA determined that he was entitled to veterans' compensation payments retroactively as well as prospectively. Upon learning of his new entitlement, he executed a waiver of the appropriate amount of retired pay entitlement. The question we are asked to resolve is whether the proper effective date to be given the waiver is the date it was executed or the date of the earliest entitlement to veterans' benefits.

The request for an advance decision was made by Mr. Ernest E. Heuer, Deputy Chief, Accounting Division, Air Force Accounting and Finance Center. It has been assigned Submission No. DO–AF–1311, by the Department of Defense Military Pay and Allowance Committee and was forwarded to us by letter dated November 20, 1978.

Colonel Fitzgerald retired from the Air Force on October 31, 1966, and has been employed in a civilian position with the Federal Government since July 17, 1967, during which time his retired pay has been reduced under the Dual Compensation Act. On June 26, 1977, he became ill and was hospitalized through August 6, 1977. In September 1977, he returned to his civilian employment and at that time applied to the VA for disability compensation. On February 23, 1978, the VA determined that Colonel Fitzgerald was disabled beginning June 26, 1977, and was entitled to receive VA compensation from that date. However, he was advised that if he elected to receive VA compensation he should return VA Form 21–651, to indicate waiver of that portion of his military retired pay which was equal to his VA disability compensation entitlement since he could not receive both. Colonel Fitzgerald completed and forwarded this form to the VA on March 3, 1978, and his retired pay was reduced in the amount of his VA compensation payment effective May 1, 1978.

The Air Force requests our determination of the effective date of Colonel Fitzgerald's waiver of his retired pay so that it may determine the proper amount of reductions from his retired pay to be made pursuant to the dual compensation provision. The Air Force computes the additional amount Colonel Fitzgerald would be entitled to as $2,535.30 if his waiver of retired pay in favor of VA compensation may be given effect as of June 26, 1977, the earliest date of entitlement to VA compensation, rather than March 3, 1978, the date the waiver was executed.

A valid waiver of retired pay and the payment of VA benefits on the basis of such waiver operates to reduce the legally authorized retired pay by the amount waived and from the effective date of the waiver the retiree ceases to be entitled to retired pay equal in amount to the compensation which he is entitled to receive from the VA. See 36 Comp. Gen. 799 (1951). Disability compensation payable by the VA is not retired pay and accordingly, payments equal in amount to the VA compensation entitlement and received subsequent to the effective date of the waiver are classified as disability compensation and are not subject to reduction under the dual compensation provisions.

Concerning the effective date of a valid waiver of retired pay, we have held that where the VA award of disability compensation, retroactively effective, is delayed administratively, the service department concerned "may not establish an effective date for waiver which would operate to deny the member the full monetary benefit which he would have otherwise received had the award of disability compensation been timely established on or before the date on which he became entitled thereto." See *Matter of Lt. Colonel Oliver B. Larson*, USAF, Retired, 55 Comp. Gen. 1402 (1976).

That case involved a member who had filed a waiver of his retired pay (VA Form 21–651) with the Air Force prior to the beginning date of the retroactive period of a VA award of disability compensation. We believe that this rule should also be applied where the member files his waiver of retired pay upon being advised by the VA of his entitlement to VA compensation. Since the member's right to elect to receive VA compensation does not accrue until the VA makes the determination of compensation entitlement, it is our view that the member need not file the waiver prior to the VA determination of entitlement in order to receive the full benefit of the compensation award with regard to dual compensation reduction.

This view is consistent with the congressional intent to provide retired members the full benefit of a VA award for taxation purposes. In that regard Congress recently amended 38 U.S.C. § 3101 to provide that the filing of a waiver of retired or retirement pay in the amount of VA pension or compensation before the end of the 1-year period from the date of the individual's notification of eligibility for VA compensation shall exempt the retired pay from taxation in the amount of the VA pension or compensation which would have been paid but for the receipt of such pay. See Section 301 of the Veterans' Disability Compensation and Survivors' Benefits Act of 1978, Public Law 95–479, October 18, 1978, 92 Stat. 1560, 1564. The purpose of this legislation was to clarify the intent of the Congress to assure the exemption from taxation of compensation paid in lieu of military retired pay. See H.R. Rep. No. 95–1226, 95th Cong. 2d Sess. pp. 1, 9 (1978).

In view of the above, where a member files a waiver of retired pay in an amount equal to his VA compensation entitlement, such waiver operates to classify as VA compensation the retired pay, equal in amount to the VA compensation, received during the period covered by the award of VA compensation. Thus, retired pay received by Colonel Fitzgerald since June 26, 1977, the beginning date of his VA compensation entitlement, is now to be classified, in an amount equal to the compensation, as VA compensation, so as to be excluded from reduction under the dual compensation provisions.

The Air Force has stated that in accordance with its interpretation of our decision in *Larson* it has adjusted Colonel Fitzgerald's retired pay for the period between the date he had filed the waiver, March 3, 1978, and the date it had adjusted his retired pay, May 1, 1978. In *Larson*, we advised the Air Force to recompute the voucher presented by the member to retroactively adjust under the dual compensation formula of 5 U.S.C. § 5532, the retired pay received by the member from the effective date of the waiver. However, further analysis shows that the additional payment actually due the member would be payable by the VA as compensation and not by the service department.

While the effect of the VA award, retroactive to the earliest date of entitlement, is to decrease the dual compensation reduction from the member's retired pay, this adjustment in the dual compensation reduction is the result of the retired pay, equal in amount to the VA compensation award, being classified as VA compensation. Thus, while the effect of the waiver is to increase that total monetary entitlement of the member, retired pay plus VA compensation, it also operates to reduce the amount payable from the service department as retired pay. Accordingly, the additional amount due the member as the result of retroactively classifying as VA compensation the retired pay received from the earliest date of the VA entitlement would be payable by the VA and not the service department. At this point we must recognize that the VA has full discretion as to whether to make such payment since we have no authority to direct the VA to pay benefits. See 38 U.S.C. § 211(a) (1976). We have no reason to believe, however, that based upon a full analysis of this situation, the VA will come to a contrary conclusion.

To the extent that *Larson* is inconsistent with this decision, it is modified in accordance with the foregoing, and this decision should be followed in the future. While this decision authorizes a retroactive effective date for the waiver of May 1977, the retroactive pay adjustment for a portion (March 3, 1978 to May 1978) of the period made under *Larson* need not be disturbed.

[B–193472]

Pay—Retired—Survivor Benefit Plan—Spouse—Remarriage After Age 60—Loss of DIC Eligibility

A deceased Navy officer's widow was receiving a reduced Survivor Benefit Plan (SBP) annuity because she was also entitled to Veterans Administration Dependency and Indemnity Compensation (DIC). She remarried in 1977 after reaching age 60 and thereby lost entitlement to DIC. Under the new provisions of 10 U.S.C. 1450(k), added by sec. 203 of Public Law 95–397, the full SBP annuity may be restored to her upon repayment of retired pay contributions she received when the SBP annuity was reduced. However, under sec. 210(a) of Public Law 95–397, the full annuity may not be paid for months prior to October 1, 1978.

In the matter of Mrs. Susan E. O'Neill Speed, June 28, 1979:

This case interprets a new statute that would allow certain surviving spouses, whose Survivor Benefit Plan (SBP) annuities have been reduced due to their entitlement to Veterans Administration (VA) Dependency and Indemnity Compensation (DIC), to have their SBP annuities reinstated in full upon loss of entitlement to DIC due to their remarriage. We hold that, while the new provision authorizes the reinstatement of the full annuity upon repayment by the spouse of retired pay refunds received when the annuity was reduced, payment of the full annuity may be made only for months beginning on or after October 1, 1978.

The specific case in question is a request for reconsideration of our Claims Division's settlement and the Navy's action concerning Mrs. Susan E. O'Neill Speed's SBP annuity entitlement as the former spouse of Rear Admiral Edward J. O'Neill, USN (Retired) (Deceased). The request was presented in letters dated March 2 and May 7, 1979, from Mrs. Speed's attorney, John E. O'Neill, Esq.

Admiral O'Neill retired from the Navy in 1957 and participated in the Uniformed Services Contingency Option Act survivor protection program, later renamed the Retired Serviceman's Family Protection Plan (RSFPP). 10 U.S.C. 1431–1446. As required by 10 U.S.C. 1431 and 1436, Admiral O'Neill's retired pay was reduced to cover the cost of his participation in those plans.

In 1973 Admiral O'Neill elected to participate in the new SBP to provide an annuity for his spouse at 55 percent of his retired pay, and he canceled his participation in the RSFPP. This action was authorized by section 3(b), Public Law 92–425, September 21, 1972, 86 Stat. 711 (10 U.S.C. 1448, note). Appropriate deductions were made from his retired pay for the SBP coverage.

In 1975 Admiral O'Neill died, apparently from service-connected causes. His widow, Mrs. Susan E. O'Neill, who was entitled to a full SBP annuity—55 percent of Admiral O'Neill's retired pay—instead was paid a reduced annuity as required by 10 U.S.C. 1450(c) because she was also entitled to DIC from the VA under 38 U.S.C. 411(a). As required by 10 U.S.C. 1450(e) in such a case, the cost of the reduced SBP coverage was calculated and the excess amount which had been deducted from Admiral O'Neill's retired pay for the full SBP coverage was credited to his widow.

On January 29, 1977, Mrs. O'Neill who at that time was over age 60, remarried. As a result, her DIC entitlement was terminated. However, under 10 U.S.C. 1450(b), since Mrs. O'Neill, now Mrs. Speed, remarried after reaching age 60, her eligibility for the SBP annuity was not lost. Since she was no longer receiving DIC, she asked that her SBP annuity be restored to the full amount and offered to repay the refund of retired pay deductions she had received. She also requested payment of all amounts deducted from Admiral O'Neill's retired pay for RSFPP coverage.

Mrs. Speed was found to be entitled to receive the SBP annuity only in the reduced amount. That determination was based on our decision B–181712, April 7, 1975, 54 Comp. Gen. 838, where we noted that unlike the Civil Service survivor annuity plan, under the SBP there was no statutory authority to permit a spouse to repay an amount previously refunded and have the annuity reinstated at the higher level. Therefore, we held that once an SBP annuity was reduced due to DIC entitlement and the deductions refunded to spouse, the reduction was permanent and the full annuity could not be reinstated upon repayment by the spouse of the refunded deductions.

Mrs. Speed's claim for all amounts deducted from Admiral O'Neill's retired pay for RSFPP coverage was denied. That denial was based on section 3(b) of Public Law 92–425 which authorized retired members, such as Admiral O'Neill, to terminate their RSFPP participation and instead participate in the SBP, but specifically provided that, in such cases, the member was not entitled to refund of the deductions in retired pay made for RSFPP coverage.

In his May 7, 1979 letter Mrs. Speed's attorney refers to 10 U.S.C. 1450(k) and asks that it be applied in her case to allow her to repay the refund of retired pay deductions she received and have the full SBP annuity reinstated effective beginning with the date of her loss of DIC entitlement upon her January 29, 1977 remarriage. Section 1450(k) was added by section 203 of the Uniformed Services Survivors' Benefits Amendments of 1978, Public Law 95–397, September 30, 1978, 92 Stat. 843, 846, and provides as follows:

> (k) If a widow or widower whose annuity has been adjusted under subsection (c) subsequently loses entitlement to compensation under section 411(a) of title 38 because of the remarriage of such widow or widower, and if at the time of such remarriage such widow or widower is 60 years of age or more, the amount of the annuity of such widow or widower shall be readjusted, effective on the effective date of such loss of compensation, to the amount of the annuity which would be in effect with respect to such widow or widower if the adjustment under subsection (c) had never been made, but such readjustment may not be made until the widow or widower repays any amount refunded under subsection (e) by reason of the adjustment under subsection (c).

That provision, which was not in effect when our April 7, 1975 decision was rendered, now authorizes widows or widowers in Mrs. Speed's situation to repay the retired pay refund received and have their full SBP annuities reinstated upon loss of DIC entitlement. However, section 210(a) of Public Law 95–397 (10 U.S.C. 1447 note) limits the retroactive effect of various amendments made by that law, including 10 U.S.C. 1450(k), to October 1, 1978, as follows:

> * * * the provisions of this title and the amendments made by this title shall take effect on October 1, 1978, or on the date of the enactment of this Act, whichever is later, and shall apply to annuities payable by virtue of such amendments for months beginning on or after such date.

Therefore, under the newly added 10 U.S.C. 1450(k), Mrs. Speed may now repay the refund she received and have her SBP annuity readjusted to the full annuity. However, under section 210(a) above she is entitled to be paid the full annuity only for months beginning on October 1, 1978, and not for months prior to that date. Upon Mrs. Speed's repayment of the refund she received, the Navy should adjust her annuity payments accordingly.

〔 B–118370 〕

States—Federal Aid, Grants, etc.—Administration—Cost Limitations

The 3 percent administrative overhead and indirect cost limitations of the Pittman-Robertson and Dingell-Johnson Acts, 16 U.S.C. 669e(c) and 777e(c) respectively, apply to costs incurred by an agency or department—a central service activity—of the State whose functions include regularly performing services not for its own constitutent elements but all agencies of the State. Therefore, they do not apply to costs incurred by the Colorado Department of Natural Resources (DNR) in providing services to its Division of Wildlife even though the Division may exercise control over its programs, since for administrative purposes it is a part of DNR and any services provided by DNR to it are of an intra-departmental nature.

In the matter of Administrative Costs Limitation: Pittman-Robertson, Dingell-Johnson Acts, June 29, 1979:

This decision is in response to a request from the Deputy Solicitor, Department of the Interior, for an interpretation of two laws prescribing a limitation on overhead or indirect costs assessed for State central services to grantee agencies. His letter describes the problem as follows:

We would appreciate your advice on the interpretation of a provision of concern to this Department's Fish and Wildlife Service (FWS) Federal Aid program, under the Pittman-Robertson and Dingell-Johnson Acts, 16 U.S.C. § 669 *et seq.* and § 777 *et seq.*, respectively. Section 6(c) of the Pittman-Robertson Act, 16 U.S.C. § 669e(c), provides: [footnote omitted]
"Administrative costs in the form of overhead or indirect costs for services provided by *State central service activities outside of the State agency having primary jurisdiction over the wildlife resources* of the State which may be charged against programs or projects supported by the fund established by Section 669b of this title shall not exceed in any one fiscal year 3 per centum of the annual apportionment to the State." [Italic supplied.]
The problem that has arisen is caused by the recent trend of several states (including Colorado which gives rise to this request) to create a new administrative agency called the Department of Natural Resources (DNR), under which are placed several subordinate agencies, including the Division of Wildlife and the Division of Parks. In the case of Colorado, by statute, 1977 C.R.S. § 24-1-105, and § 24-1-124(3)(h), it would appear that the Division of Wildlife is "the State agency having primary jurisdiction over the wildlife resources of the State" for purposes of 16 U.S.C. § 669e(c).
The State of Colorado's Division of Wildlife is assessed overhead and indirect costs by its parent agency, DNR. In addition, DNR passes on to the Division of Wildlife certain state central service activity costs which are assessed against DNR for costs attributable to DNR and its constituent agencies.
Colorado's Division of Wildlife contends that all indirect and overhead costs assessed against it are per se "outside of the State agency having primary jurisdiction over the wildlife resources of the State" and therefore must be subject to the three percent limitation imposed by section 6(c) of the Pittman-Robertson Act.
On the other hand, this Department's Office of Audit and Investigation believes that while those indirect and overhead costs assessed against the Division of Wildlife are for services provided outside of the agency having primary jurisdiction over wildlife resources, they fail to meet the other statutory criterion, namely that they be provided "by State central service activities."
Prior to the reorganization in Colorado, the agency having primary jurisdiction over wildlife was the Department of Game, Fish, and Parks, directly under the Governor's office. Thus, any indirect and overhead costs billed to that agency were provided by state central service activities and were outside the agency having primary jurisdiction over wildlife. As a result of the reorganization, certain functions of the Department of Game, Fish, and Parks were removed to the DNR. Consequently, if the DNR were not performing those functions, primarily administrative activities, the Division of Wildlife itself would have

to perform them and 16 U.S.C. § 669e(c) would not appear to impose a direct limitation on the extent of these expenditures.

*   *   *   *   *   *   *

We would therefore appreciate your advice as to whether the three percent limitation in section 6(c) of the Pittman-Robertson/Dingell-Johnson Acts. 16 U.S.C. §§ 669e(c) and 777e(c), applies at the Division of Wildlife level, so that all overhead and indirect costs charged to that agency are limited, or at the DNR level, so that only those costs provided by "State central service activities" are subject to the limitation.

Section 6(c) of the Dingell-Johnson Act, 16 U.S.C. § 777e(c), in language essentially identical to that in the Pittman-Robertson Act, except that it applies to the State fish and game department rather than the State agency with jurisdiction over wildlife resources, provides that:

Administrative costs in the form of overhead or indirect costs for services provided *by State central service activities outside of the State fish and game department charged against programs* or projects supported by funds made available under this chapter shall not exceed in any one fiscal year 3 per centum of the annual apportionment to the State. [Italic supplied.]

Sections 6(c) of both the Pittman-Robertson and the Dingell-Johnson Acts were added by the Federal Aid to Fish and Wildlife Restoration Act Amendments of 1970, Pub. L. No. 91–503, §§ 102 and 202, October 23, 1970, 84 Stat. 1099, 1102, 16 U.S.C. 669c, 777e. In explaining the purpose of section 6(c) of the Pittman-Robertson Act, to be added by the 1970 amendments, the House Committee on Merchant Marine and Fisheries said:

Subsequent to the Subcommittee hearings on the legislation, the International Association of Game. Fish, and Conservation Commissioners advised the Subcommittee of its concern over Bureau of the Budget Circular—No. A–87—issued in May of 1968 [now Federal Management Circular 74–4]. The Circular established rules and regulations for determining costs applicable to Federal grants and contracts with State and local government. It applied: to all Federal agencies responsible for administering such programs and was designed to provide the basis for a uniform approach to the problem of determining costs and, at the same time, promote efficiency and better relationships between grantees and their Federal counterparts. The principles to be followed in determining costs were to be applied at the earliest practicable date, but not later than January 1, 1969. with respect to State governments, and January 1. 1970. with respect to local governments.

Upon investigation, your Committee determined that under the new regulations indirect costs could amount to as much as 15 to 20 percent of the total costs of a project. Naturally, this would result in Federal funds being used for administrative costs that ordinarily would have been used for acquisition of lands and field work. Upon further investigation, your Committee discovered that there had been little experience on which to measure the effects of Circular No. A–87. *Several of the States polled indicated indirect costs were running around 1 percent of the total funds apportioned to the State: another State indicated its rate was a flat 2 percent of such funds.*

In view of the foregoing, your Committee determined that a reasonable limitation should be placed on the amount of administrative costs—*in the form of overhead or indirect costs for services provided by State central service activities outside of the State agency having primary jurisdiction over the wildlife resources of the State*—which may be charged against programs or projects supported by the fund established under Section 3 of this Act (Pittman-Robertson fund).

Accordingly, your Committee added a new subsection (c) to Section 6 of the Act to provide that indirect * * * [charges] could not exceed 3 percent of the annual apportionment of such funds to the State in any one fiscal year. (Italic supplied, H.R. Rep. No. 91–1272, pp. 11–12 (1970)).

The Committee explained the purpose of section 6(c) of the Dingell–Johnson Act as follows:

* * * a new subsection (c) would provide that indirect charges could not be deducted from the annual apportionment of funds to a State in any one fiscal year in excess of 3 percent. (See Section 6 of Title I of the bill [quoted above] for further explanation of these changes.) H.R. Rep. No. 91–1272, p. 14 (1970). See also S. Rep. No. 91–1284, pp. 7 and 9 (1970), and statement of Representative Dingell during debate on the 1970 amendments, 116 Cong. Rec. 24962–24963 (1970).

The Colorado Department of Natural Resources, to which the Deputy Solicitor refers, was created by the Colorado Administrative Organization Act of 1968, which established a number of divisions in DNR by transfers of the duties and functions of existing State agencies. Among the divisions was the—

Division of wildlife, the head of which shall be the director of the division of wildlife. The division of wildlife, the office of director thereof, and the wildlife commission, created by article 1 of title 33, C.R.S. 1973, and the powers, duties, and functions thereof concerning game and fish are transferred by a type 1 transfer to the department of natural resources as the division of wildlife. C.R.S. 1973, 24–1–124(3)(h).

A "type 1 transfer" is explained in C.R.S. 1973, 24–1–105(1):

Under this article, a type 1 transfer means the transferring intact of an existing department, institution, or other agency, or part thereof, to a principal department established by this article. When any department, institution, or other agency, or part thereof, is transferred to a principal department under a type 1 transfer, that department, institution, or other agency, or part thereof, shall be administered under the direction and supervision of that principal department, but it shall exercise its prescribed statutory powers, duties, and functions, including rule-making, regulation, licensing, and registration, the promulgation of rules, rates, regulations, and standards, and the rendering of findings, orders, and adjudications, independently of the head of the principal department. Under a type 1 transfer, any powers, duties, and functions not specifically vested by statute in the agency being transferred, including, but not limited to, all budgeting, purchasing, planning, and related management functions of any transferred department, institution, or other agency, or part thereof, shall be performed under the direction and supervision of the head of the principal department.

While a definitive determination of the relationship of one State body to the other should come from the Attorney General or other appropriate State authority, we offer the following observations. Based on our reading of the Colorado Statute, the program functions of the Division of Wildlife do not appear to be under the control of the head of the principal agency (DNR) (see *State Highway Commissioner of Colorado* v. *Haase*, 537 P. 2d 300 (Sup. Ct. Col. (1975)); only administrative support functions are apparently under the direction and supervision of the principal agency (DNR). Consequently, if this interpretation is correct, there is support for the contention that the Division of Wildlife, rather than DNR, is the "State agency having primary jurisdiction over the wildlife resources of the State" under the Pittman-Robertson Act, 16 U.S.C. § 669e(c).

Furthermore, both the Pittman-Robertson and Dingell-Johnson Acts define the term "State fish and game department" to mean:

> any department or *division of department of another name*, or commission, or official or officials, *of a State empowered under its laws to exercise the functions ordinarily exercised by a State fish and game department*. 16 U.S.C. §§ 669a and 777a(d) (1976). [Italic supplied.]

Thus, there is also support for the contention that "State fish and game department" as used in section 6(c) of the Dingell-Johnson Act, 16 U.S.C. § 777e(c), should be construed to mean the Division of Wildlife.

However, the 3 percent limitations refer to "administrative costs in the form of overhead or indirect costs for services provided by *State central service activities*." Unless the parent department performs nothing but Pittman-Robertson and Dingell-Johnson Act functions, there obviously will be administrative costs in the nature of indirect costs and overhead that will have to be allocated among the various programs within the department, no matter what its size or functions. It is inherent in the nature of a multi-purpose agency to provide its constituent elements some form of centralized administrative services. However, from the language of the statutory limitations and the legislative history of the two Acts, it was not these costs that the Congress sought to limit.

The kind of costs which are contemplated by the limitations are those incurred by an agency or department of the State—a "central service activity"—whose functions include regularly performing services not for its own constituent elements but for all agencies of the State. Otherwise, it would not be a *State* central service activity, but merely a Departmental central service activity. (One agency in Colorado which appears to fit the description of a central service activity is the Department of Administration. See C.R.S. 1973, 24–1–116.) Thus, if our interpretation of Colorado law is correct, even though the Division of Wildlife may exercise control over its programs, for administrative purposes it is a part of DNR, and any service provided by DNR to it is of an intra-departmental nature, not to be considered as being provided by a State central service activity. Only those costs provided by such central service activities are subject to the 3 percent limitation.

[B-193442]

Appropriations — Availability — Compensation — Transfer of Employee on Home Leave

Interior employee who satisfactorily completed an overseas tour of duty returned to the United States for home leave. He arranged transfer to AID while on home leave, effective on termination of leave. The salary charge to the Interior appropriation for the period of home leave was proper since the employee earned it as an Interior employee and it agreed to the effective date of the transfer.

In the matter of Donald E. Ryder — Transfer While on Home Leave, July 2, 1979:

By letter dated November 3, 1978, the Deputy Assistant Secretary, Policy, Budget and Administration, Department of the Interior, requested our decision as to which agency's appropriation is to be charged with the salary of an employee on home leave when the employee decides to transfer to another agency effective at the completion of his home leave. The Deputy Assistant Secretary reports the factual situation as follows:

Mr. Donald E. Ryder, a GS-13 supervisory auditor, was employed by the Office of the U.S. Government Comptroller for Guam/TTPI/NMI, Department of the Interior. Upon completion of his two year agreement for overseas duty at Guam on December 1, 1977, he became eligible for home leave. He departed Guam on June 30, 1978 and after leave-free travel time, began his home leave on July 3, 1978.

On or about July 17, 1978, the Agency for International Development (AID) contacted the Department of the Interior and requested that Mr. Ryder be dropped from Interior's rolls on August 13, 1978 so that AID could employ him effective August 14. Because the employee would not be returning to work for Interior, our office requested that the transfer date be set prior to August 14. However, the AID official indicated that it is not AID policy to effect such a transfer until home leave was completed. Interior did not wish to cause a break in the employee's service and compensation or jeopardize his employment opportunities with AID. Interior, therefore, reluctantly agreed to the August 14 transfer date which AID was requesting.

It is Interior's contention that once AID officially informed Interior of its plan to hire Mr. Ryder, Interior no longer had an obligation to carry him on home leave for the following reasons:

1. a condition for approving home leave is the employee's return to an overseas post, and
2. the purpose of home leave is to prepare an employee for further service abroad through re-acculturation to U.S. life and thought.

With respect to #1 above, on or about July 17, 1978 the condition for permitting home leave use could no longer be based on future service with Interior. In effect AID had then set the condition for use of home leave since upon assuming employment with AID, he was to be assigned to Pakistan. Therefore, we contend that Mr. Ryder's subsequent use of home leave and the attendant salary costs should have been AID's responsibility.

With respect to #2 above, AID rather than Interior is the agency that accrued the benefit from the employee's re-acculturation to the U.S. Reference is made to Comptroller General decision 44 CG 767 (B-144095), June 2, 1965. It appears to be the intent of that decision that the gaining agency bear the expenses from which it will benefit. * * *

In our decision 44 Comp. Gen. 767 (1965) we held as follows:

* * * Thus, if the employee has signed a renewal agreement for overseas duty with a different Government agency his old agency is not receiving any benefit from assuming his traveling expenses back to an overseas post. While the law is silent as to which agency must bear the expense of home leave travel and transportation under such circumstances, our view is that the law permits the expenses to be divided as suggested in the Under Secretary's letter, that is that the agency *from which* the employee transfers bear the expense of travel of the employee and transportation of his family to the actual place of residence in the United States, and that the agency *to which* the employee transfers after completion of a period of home leave pay such expenses from the actual place of residence in the United States to his new overseas duty station with that agency. * * *

We invited AID to comment upon the position of the Department of the Interior as set forth above. The Assistant General Counsel for Employee and Public Affairs, AID, replied by affirming AID's position that it was proper for the Department of the Interior to pay Mr. Ryder's salary during his home leave in the United States for the following reasons:

(1) A.I.D. has paid all of the personal travel and transportation of household effects for the employee from his place of residence to his new overseas assignment;
(2) The employee earned his home leave while serving with the Interior Department (to which he has re-employment rights) ; and
(3) A.I.D. should not pay the salary of the employee until his service with A.I.D. began on August 13, 1978.
We believe this interpretation is entirely consistent with the decision of Comptroller General in 44 Comp. Gen. 767. That opinion held that it was proper for the agency "to which the employee transfers *after completion of a home leave* pay such expenses [of travel and transportation]." [Italic supplied.]

Our decision in 44 Comp. Gen. 767 (1965), referred to by both agencies, did not specifically consider the question of which agency's appropriation would be chargeable with the salary of an employee while on home leave after having accepted a position with a different agency to which he will report immediately upon the completion of his home leave.

Under the provisions of 5 U.S.C. § 6305 (1976) a Federal employee generally is entitled to home leave after serving a tour of duty overseas for the required period. The specific requirements laid down for the granting of home leave are that the employee must have completed a basic service period of 24 continuous months abroad and that it is contemplated that he will serve another tour of duty abroad. 52 Comp. Gen. 860 (1973) ; 35 *id.* 655 (1956) ; B–147031, February 5, 1962. Also, see 5 C.F.R. § 630.601 *et seq.*

While the law and regulations are silent as to which agency must bear the expense of the employee's salary while on home leave, we concur generally with the views expressed by the AID Assistant General Counsel. Mr. Ryder completed an agreed period of service overseas of at least 24 months with the Department of the Interior and earned his home leave by virtue of such service. Since his home leave was calculated on the basis of the number of months of service provided to Interior, which received the benefit of that service, it was proper for that Department to pay the salary expense covering the period of home leave from its appropriations. However, while AID had no control over the granting of home leave in this case and it derived none of the benefit from the service rendered in earning the leave, we do not believe it would have been inappropriate to have charged its appropriations with the salary of Mr. Ryder while on home leave if an earlier transfer date had been set. This is so since home leave which is not used prior to transfer may be transferred to the acquiring agency and the effective date of a transfer is the date mutually agreed upon by the agencies involved. 5 C.F.R. § 630.607 and Federal Personnel Manual, ch. 315, § 5–4 (1969 ed. July 1969).

In the instant case Interior agreed to an effective date of transfer, although reluctantly, and the salary charge to its appropriation may not be changed.

[B-194342]

Leaves of Absence — Military Personnel — Payments for Unused Leave on Discharge, etc. — Additional Pay Not Included

An amendment to 37 U.S.C. 501(b) deleted inclusion of allowances in lump-sum leave payments to military members upon discharge; however, a saving provision retained entitlement to include the allowances for leave accrued prior to the amendment. Although the claimant contends that the services' regulation determining when a member will be charged with use of preamendment leave frustrates congressional intent of the saving provision, in view of the services' authority to prescribe regulations for accrual and use of leave, the language and legislative history of the amendment, the regulation is proper.

In the matter of Colonel William N. Jackomis, USAF, Retired, July 2, 1979:

A disbursing officer requests an advance decision as to whether basic allowance for subsistence (BAS) and basic allowance for quarters (BAQ) may be included in computing the lump-sum payment due Colonel William N. Jackomis, USAF, Retired, for 6 days' accrued leave. We conclude that BAS and BAQ may not be included in the computation.

The request for decision was presented by Major N. F. Heisey, USAF, Accounting and Finance Officer, Bolling Air Force Base, and has been assigned Submission No. DO–AF–1314 by the Department of Defense Military Pay and Allowance Committee.

Colonel Jackomis retired on January 31, 1979, at which time he received a payment for 60 days of accrued leave. The payment consisted of basic pay for all 60 days and BAS and BAQ for 54 of the days.

Colonel Jackomis argues that he was entitled to be paid BAS and BAQ for all 60 days. The basis of his claim is that the Department of Defense (DOD) regulation governing entitlement to payment for accrued leave upon release from active duty is inconsistent with the underlying statutory scheme enacted by the Congress. Specifically, the question is whether the current DOD system frustrates the congressional intent manifested in the 1976 amendments to 37 U.S.C. § 501 which repealed the provision authorizing the inclusion of BAS and BAQ in the computation of lump-sum leave payments. See Department of Defense Appropriation Authorization Act, 1977, Public Law 94–361, § 304(c), July 14, 1976, 90 Stat. 925.

In deleting the allowances from lump-sum leave payments, Congress saw fit to preserve inclusion of the allowances in payments for leave accrued before the effective date of the amendments to 37 U.S.C. § 501. This was done by including a saving provision in the amendments; that is, § 304(h), Public Law 94–361, 90 Stat. 926 which states:

> (h) Notwithstanding the provisions of section 501(b)(1) of title 37, United States Code, as amended by subsection (c), and subject to the limitations prescribed in section 501(b)(3) of such title, as amended by subsection (c), *any leave accrued* by any member of the Army, Navy, Air Force, Marine Corps, Coast Guard, or National Oceanic and Atmospheric Administration *prior to the first day of the second calendar month following the month in which this section is enacted* shall, at the option of such member, be paid for on the same basis such leave would have been paid for under the provisions of section 501(b) of title 37, United States Code, on the day prior to the first day of the second calendar month following the month in which this section is enacted. [Italic supplied.]

In explaining the elimination of BAS and BAQ from the leave computation, and the saving provision, the Senate Armed Services Committee, where those provisions originated, stated as follows:

> The committee amendment also deletes the authority for payment of the quarters and subsistence allowances as a part of terminal lump sum payment for unused leave for all military members. This is likewise not retroactive and only applies to leave accrued after the enactment of this provision. Thus, military members would continue to be paid the current authorized amounts for quarters and subsistence allowances in terminal lump sum payments for unused leave accrued prior to the date of enactment. Payment for all unused leave accrued after enactment would be limited to basic pay. S. Rep. No. 94–878, 94th Cong., 2d Sess. 135 (May 14, 1976).

Thus, for leave accrued prior to the amendment's effective date (September 1, 1976), a member is entitled to have included in the lump-sum payment basic pay, BAS and BAQ, whereas for leave accrued after the amendment's effective date, a member is entitled to have included only basic pay. Colonel Jackomis disagrees with the method devised by DOD to determine when leave should be charged to pre-amendment accruals. The specific DOD regulation is found in Department of Defense Military Pay and Allowances Entitlements Manual (DODPM), Part Four, Chapter 4, paragraph 40402 (change 49, September 2, 1977) which states:

Settlement for leave accrued as of 31 Aug. 1976 will include basic pay, BAQ, BAS, and PMA as appropriate. See Table 4-4-5. Settlement for leave accrued on and after 1 Sep 1976 will include basic pay only.

Example: On 31 Aug. 1976 a member has 65 days of accrued leave. The member takes leave from 5 through 24 Sep 1976 (20 days). As he accrued 2 days of leave 1-24 Sep 1976, he used 18 of his 65 days of saved leave reducing the saved balance to 47 days. Future leave accrued and used will be computed accordingly.

Colonel Jackomis carried over the allowable maximum of 60 days' accrued leave into the 1977 fiscal year (10 U.S.C. § 701(b) (1976)) which was all preamendment leave. Thus, he had a potential entitlement to receive a payment upon retirement which included 60 days' basic pay and 60 days' BAS and BAQ. However, at some point in a postamendment fiscal year prior to his retirement on January 29, 1979, he took 6 days more leave than he had accrued for that fiscal year. Accordingly, those 6 days were charged to his carried over amount which reduced it to 54 days. While Colonel Jackomis later increased his accrued leave balance to 60 days prior to his retirement, 6 of those days were postamendment accruals and, therefore, under paragraph 40402, DODPM, he was to be paid only basic pay for those 6 days upon his retirement.

The gist of Colonel Jackomis' argument is that it is inequitable that the loss of carried over leave with entitlement to inclusion of BAS and BAQ in his lump-sum payment may depend on when in the fiscal year a member takes leave. For example, the taking of extended leave in October 1976 (e.g. 15 days), the beginning of the fiscal year, would require the use of carried over leave, whereas taking 15 days' leave in September 1977, the end of the fiscal year, after having accrued additional leave, would not require the use of the carried over leave.

Colonel Jackomis takes issue with the regulation implementing the saving provision because of the potential for loss of entitlement to include BAS and BAQ solely due to when leave is taken. He questions whether the regulation frustrates the congressional intent behind the saving provision. He contends that only used leave which exceeds the amount which will be earned in a fiscal year should be charged to preamendment accruals. In effect, he is stating that advance leave should be given if the used leave is more than the member's current fiscal year accrual but less than the member's potential accrual for the fiscal year, thus preserving the leave previously accrued.

From the legislative history behind the amendments, it does not appear that Congress considered the precise question before us. However, both the saving provision and the legislative history base the determination as to whether allowance are to be included in the computation on when the leave is "accrued." The DOD regulations are consistent with the statute and legislative history in that regard. In addition, under 10 U.S.C. § 704 (1976) the Secretaries concerned have the authority to prescribe regulations providing for the computation of leave and the determination of the amount of leave to which members are entitled. See 33 Comp. Gen. 337 (1954).

As a general rule, in the absence of a clear indication of legislative intent, the administration construction by the agency responsible for implementing the statutory scheme is deemed to be consistent with the congressional intent unless it can be characterized as arbitrary or inconsistent with the statutory purpose. See *Forbes Federal Union v. National Credit Union Administration*, 477 F. 2d 777 (10th Cir. 1973) and citations therein; see also *Satty v. Nashville Gas Company*, 522 F. 2d 850 (6th Cir. 1975).

In our view the DOD regulation is in accord with the language of, and rationally effectuates the statutory purpose behind the amendment and the saving provision. Accordingly, we conclude that Colonel Jackomis is not entitled to BAS and BAQ for the 6 days' leave he claims.

[B-194170]

Compensation — Night Work — Summer Aids

Individuals who are hired as summer aids under 5 C.F.R. 213.3102(v), in the excepted service, with their pay set at the FLSA minimum wage, may be paid night differential under 5 U.S.C. 5545(a). Summer aids are not excluded from the definition of employees entitled to receive night differential, and, since there are no conflicting regulatory provisions, they should be paid night differential pay.

In the matter of Summer Aids — Night Differential, July 3, 1979:

We have been asked whether Summer Aids, who are in the excepted service, with their pay set at the equivalent of the highest minimum wage rate established by the Fair Labor Standards Act of 1938, as amended, 29 U.S.C. § 201 *et seq.* (1976), (FLSA), should be paid night differential pay under 5 U.S.C. § 5545(a) (1976). For the reasons set out below, we hold that payment of the night differential is proper.

The Administrator of the General Services Administration, by letter of February 8, 1979, requested our decision on whether Summer Aids hired under 5 C.F.R. § 213.3102(v) (1977), who were assigned to custodial labor positions on the night shift, should be paid night differential pay. Section 213.3102(v) provides that:

Temporary Summer Aid positions whose duties involve work of a routine nature not regularly covered under the General Schedule and requiring no specific knowledge or skills, when filled by youth appointed for summer employment under such economic or educational needs standards as the Commission may prescribe. A person may not be appointed unless he has reached his sixteenth but not his twenty-second birthday, or employed for more than 700 hours under this paragraph. This paragraph shall apply only to the positions whose pay is fixed at the equivalent of the highest minimum wage rate established by the Fair Labor Standards Act of 1938, as amended. However, during 1974 an agency shall not fix the pay at a rate less than that paid to Summer Aids by Federal agencies (other than the Postal Service) in the geographic area concerned in 1973.

We have been advised that there is no specific statutory authority for this program; it has been authorized yearly by Presidential order or memorandum. We have been unable to locate any specific guidance regarding payment of premium pay for individuals employed in this program.

Night differential pay for General Schedule employees is authorized by 5 U.S.C. § 5545(a) (1976). This section is part of Subchapter V of Ch. 55 of title 5, and provides that:

> Except as provided by subsection (b) of this section, nightwork is regularly scheduled work between the hours of 6:00 p.m. and 6:00 a.m., and includes—
> (1) periods of absence with pay during these hours due to holidays; and
> (2) periods of leave with pay during these hours if the periods of leave with pay during a pay period total less than 8 hours.
> Except as otherwise provided by subsection (c) of this section, an employee is entitled to pay for nightwork at his rate of basic pay plus premium pay amounting to 10 percent of that basic rate. This subsection and subsection (b) of this section do not modify section 180 of title 31, or other statute authorizing additional pay for nightwork.

For the purposes of Subchapter V, employee is defined in section 5541. The Summer Aids are included within the general definition of employee contained in that section, and they are not within any of the exclusions to the general definition.

In fact, it is easier to say what status these Summer Aids do not hold than it is to define what their actual status is. Their positions would seem to be within 5 U.S.C. § 5102(c)(19) (1976), as emergency or seasonal employees, thus excluding them from the General Schedule. However, since their pay is set at the FLSA minimum wage, instead of by a wage survey under 5 U.S.C. § 5343 (1976), and, under 5 U.S.C. § 5342(b)(1) (1976), which excludes most employees listed in section 5102(c) from the definition of prevailing rate employee, they are excluded from the coverage of the prevailing rate system. Therefore, even though their positions would generally be prevailing rate positions, they cannot be considered prevailing rate employees.

Since we can find nothing that specifically excludes these employees from the right to receive the night pay differential, we hold that they are entitled to that benefit. We are providing the Office of Personnel Management with a copy of this decision, and suggest that appropriate action be taken to more specifically delineate the status of individuals hired as Summer Aids under 5 C.F.R. § 213.3102(v) (1977).

[B-114874.115]

Postal Service, United States—Mails—Government—Registered Mail

Although as a matter of policy General Accounting Office (GAO) favors the exclusion of the cost of indemnity from the fee for registered mail as a cost savings to the Federal Government, GAO is not the appropriate forum to determine whether the U.S. Postal Service has authority to achieve this objective by establishing this special rate for Federal agencies only, to the exclusion of other users of registered mail, without violating the Postal Reorganizaiton Act.

General Accounting Office—Jurisdiction—Postal Matters

The authority of GAO to render binding decisions with respect to matters involving agency expenditures stems generally from its authority to adjust and settle agency accounts under section 305 of the Budget and Accounting Act of 1921, 81 U.S. Code 71. These settlements are final and conclusive upon the executive branch of the Government. 81 U.S.C. 44 and 74. Opinions of GAO are not binding on either the U.S. Postal Service (USPS) or the Postal Rate Commission (PRC), since 39 U.S.C. 410(a) and 3604(e) exempt the USPS and PRC from the provisions of the Budget and Accounting Act.

Postal Service, United States—Postal Rates and Classifications—Changes—Procedures

Where Postal Reorganization Act prescribes specific administrative procedures for consideration of proposed changes in mail classification and postal rates and fees and where question of whether a change will result in "undue or unreasonable discrimination among users of the mails" or "undue or unreasonable preferences to any such user" is such a pervasive and integral part of such decisions, GAO defers to agencies with primary jurisdiction on such matter, the USPS and the PRC, who can better resolve the issue after providing for opportunity for participation by the United States Government, as well as other users of registered mail, in a hearing on the record.

In the matter of Exclusion of cost of indemnity from registered mail rate payable by Federal agencies, July 6, 1979:

The Acting Administrator, General Services Administration (GSA), has requested a clarification of our decision B-114874, October 13, 1978, 58 Comp. Gen. 14. We held there that neither the Government Losses in Shipment Act, 40 U.S.C. § 726 (1976), nor the Government's general self-insurance policy prohibits Federal agencies from using registered mail where administratively determined necessary in order to obtain the "special" service of greater protection in the handling and delivery of mail, rather than to obtain the insurance coverage also offered by registered mail. However, Federal agencies are prohibited from using insured mail under both 40 U.S.C. § 726 (1976) and the Government's self-insurance policy, since insured mail provides no "special" or "additional" service aside from the indemnity offered.

The question now posed by GSA is whether the cost of indemnity should be excluded from the registered mail rate payable by Federal agencies, leaving the resulting Federal agency rate based on the cost of providing the "special" service of greater protection in the handling and delivery of mail.

GSA's stated view is that the U.S. Postal Service (USPS) should provide such a new Federal agency rate for registered mail and has the necessary authority to do so. On the other hand, in correspondence from the USPS to the Administrator of GSA, which has been forwarded to us, officials of the USPS stated:

> * * * we are evaluating the feasibility of selling indemnity as a separate feature of registered mail, rather than as a mandatory part of the fee structure. We have been advised on numerous occasions by our Law Department, however, that we can not establish separate fees for small groups (i.e., federal mailers) but must establish consistent fees that are applicable to everyone. Therefore, any new fee structure that is developed will be applicable to all registered mail users.

The apparent concern of the USPS is the policy of the Postal Reorganization Act, stated in 39 U.S.C. § 403(c) (1976), that:

> In providing services and in establishing classifications, rates, and fees under this title, the Postal Service shall not, except as specifically authorized in this title, make any undue or unreasonable discrimination among users of the mails, nor shall it grant any undue or unreasonable preferences to any such user.

We conclude that, although as a matter of policy GAO favors the exclusion of the cost of indemnity from the fee for registered mail as a cost savings to the Federal Government, GAO is not the appropriate forum to determine whether the USPS has authority to achieve this objective by establishing this special rate for Federal agencies only, to the exclusion of other users of registered mail, without violating the Postal Reorganization Act, 39 U.S.C. 101 note.

Initially, we note that a decision by GAO on the issue would not be legally binding on either the USPS or the Postal Rate Commission (PRC), the agencies having primary responsibility for mail classification and postal rates and fees. The authority of GAO to render binding decisions with respect to matters involving agency expenditures stems generally from its authority to adjust and settle agency accounts under section 305 of the Budget and Accounting Act of 1921, 31 U.S.C. § 71 (1976). These settlements are final and conclusive upon the executive branch of the Government. 31 U.S.C. §§ 44 and 74 (1976). We held in B–164786, October 8, 1970, that the Budget and Accounting Act of 1921, which includes these settlement provisions, was not applicable to the USPS as a consequence of the statutory exemptions set forth in 39 U.S.C. § 410(a) (1976). Accordingly, we have refrained from rendering certain opinions affecting the USPS. For example, we have not considered protests against the proposed award of contracts by the USPS. *E.g., Thomas S. Brown, Associates, Inc.*, B–188402, March 3, 1977, 77–1 CPD 161. Similarly, because of the provisions of 39 U.S.C. §§ 410(a) and 3604(e) (1976), GAO has determined that it has no jurisdiction to consider bid protests involving the Postal Rate

Commission, *E.g., Alderson Reporting Company, Inc.*, B–192653, October 10, 1978, 78–2 CPD 263; *Federal Data Retrieval Systems, Inc.*, B–187660, November 26, 1976, 76–2 CPD 448. Therefore, due to the inapplicability of our settlement authority, the opinion of GAO would not bind either the USPS or the PRC. See *Sierra Club* v. *U.S. Postal Service*, 386 F. Supp. 1102 (N.D. Cal. 1973), *affirmed* 549 F. 2d 1199 (9th Cir. 1976).

In addition, subchapter II of chapter 36 of the Postal Reorganization Act of 1970, as amended, 39 U.S.C. § 3621 *et seq.* (1976), establishes a specific, carefully delineated administrative procedure for developing a mail classification system and fixing postal rates and fees. Under this procedure the USPS requests the PRC to render a recommended decision on changes in rates of postage or fees for postal services. 39 U.S.C. § 3622(a) (1976). The PRC then renders a recommended decision to the Governors of the USPS in accordance with a particularized list of criteria and the general policies of the Postal Reorganization Act. 39 U.S.C. § 3622(b) (1976). A similar procedure is set forth with respect to changes in the mail classification schedule, except that the PRC also has authority to initiate changes in the mail classification schedule. 39 U.S.C. § 3623 (1976). In both instances, the PRC may not recommend a decision until the opportunity for a hearing on the record under the Administrative Procedure Act has been accorded to the USPS, users of the mails, and an officer of the PRC who is required to represent the interests of the general public. 39 U.S.C. § 3624 (1976). Once the Board of Governors of the USPS has received the PRC's recommendation, it may (1) approve the recommended decision and order it placed in effect; (2) allow a recommended decision of the PRC to take effect under protest, and seek judicial review; (3) reject a recommended decision and return it to the PRC for reconsideration; or (4) modify a second recommended decision stemming from a PRC reconsideration, but only unanimously and under very specific circumstances. 39 U.S.C. § 3625 (1976). If a judicial appeal is taken, the court may only affirm the decision or order that the entire matter be returned for further consideration. but the court may not modify the decision. 39 U.S.C. § 3628 (1976). Even within this narrow dispositional framework, a court has limited the scope of its review to determining whether there was a lack of substantial evidence, irrelevant considerations were taken into account, relevant considerations were omitted, a statutory command was flouted, a constitutional right was denied, or the agency acted ultra vires. *Association of American Publishers, Inc.* v. *Governors of U.S. Postal Service*, 485 F. 2d 768 (D.C. Cir. 1973). Thus a detailed administrative procedure has been prescribed for making changes in the mail classification schedule, postal rates or postal fees, and the roles and authorities of the participating entities have been carefully described and circumscribed.

It is our understanding that the establishment of a special rate for registered mail applicable only to Federal agencies, which would exclude the cost of indemnity, would involve both a change in the classification schedule and a change in the fees for postal services. Any change in the classification schedule must be recommended to the USPS by the PRC and would be invalid in the absence of such a recommendation. *National Retired Teachers Ass'n. v. U.S. Postal Service*, 430 F. Supp. 141 (D.C.D.C. 1977). In addition, changes in fees for the furnishing of, among other things, registry of mail and insurance of mail cannot be made without the scrutiny of a PRC proceeding. *Associated Third Class Mail Users* v. *U.S. Postal Service*, 405 F. Supp. 1109 (D.C.D.C. 1975), *affirmed sub nomine National Association of Greeting Card Publishers* v. *U.S. Postal Service*, 569 F. 2d 570 (D.C. Cir. 1976). Thus, regardless of whether GAO renders an opinion on the merits in this case, GSA's proposal could only be implemented after a proceeding before the PRC and a favorable conclusion of the administrative procedure described above.

With respect to the legal impact of these matters on other Federal agencies for which GAO does have settlement authority, in none of the three possible situations anticipated would a Federal agency's proper use of registered mail be precluded. If USPS and the PRC do not adopt any modification to the present fee structure for registered mail, our decision B–114874, October 13, 1978, 58 Comp. Gen. 14, permits Federal agencies to use registered mail where it is administratively determined to be necessary in order to obtain the "special" service of greater protection in the handling and delivery of mail, even though the cost of indemnity is included as part of the fee. If USPS and the PRC do establish a separate category and fee for registered mail which excludes the cost of indemnity, Federal agency use of this separate category of registered mail would likewise not be illegal under our past decisions, if otherwise proper, regardless whether the special rate were applicable to Federal agencies only or available to all mail users.

In these circumstances, where the statute prescribes specific administrative procedures for the consideration of proposed changes in mail classification and postal rates and fees and where the question of whether a change will result in "undue or unreasonable discrimination among users of the mails" or "undue or unreasonable preferences to any such user" is such a pervasive and integral part of such decisions, we defer to the agencies with primary jurisdiction on such matter. The USPS and the PRC can better resolve the issue after providing for an opportunity for participation by the United States

Government, as well as other users of registered mail, in a hearing on the record. In so concluding, we are not unaware that a court has stated that "Congress unmistakably delegated its ratemaking and classification prerogatives to the PRC." *National Retired Teachers Ass'n.* v. *U.S. Postal Service, supra*, at 146.

[B–193965]

Decedents' Estates — Compensation — Entitlement Determinations—Bankruptcy Order

At the time of his death a VA employee was subject to a Wage Earners' Plan under Chapter XIII of the Bankruptcy Act. The Bankruptcy Judge issued an order requiring unpaid compensation due the employee at the time of death to be paid to the Trustee of the Chapter XIII Plan. The VA had also received a claim from surviving children, under 5 U.S.C. 5582, seeking the same money. The order of the Bankruptcy Judge may not be followed since there is no waiver of sovereign immunity sufficient to permit enforcement of the order against United States in the face of the competing claim based upon a specific statutorily granted right.

In the matter of Harold S. Fenner — Bankruptcy Order, July 9, 1979:

This matter arises from a submission by the Veterans Administration (VA) Hospital in East Orange, New Jersey, in which they requested guidance regarding the disposition of unpaid compensation owed to a VA employee, Mr. Harold S. Fenner, Jr., at the time of his death on November 4, 1977.

The VA has received competing claims for the unpaid compensation from a Trustee in Bankruptcy and the deceased employee's children. We hold that the children are entitled to the compensation as provided in 5 U.S.C. § 5582 (1976).

On April 19, 1973, an order confirming a Wage Earners' Plan under Chapter XIII of the Bankruptcy Act, 11 U.S.C. §§ 1011 *et seq.*, submitted by Harold S. Fenner and Doris F. Fenner, his wife, was entered in the United States District Court for the District of New Jersey. However, prior to his death Mr. Fenner was divorced, and, thus, he left no surviving spouse. Under the terms of the order he was to make weekly payments of $32 to the Trustee appointed to administer his plan. We have ascertained that his salary checks were always sent to his home address and at no time did he execute an assignment authorizing the VA to send his salary directly to the Trustee.

As far as can be determined from the record before us, Mr. Fenner complied with the Wage Earners' Plan until the time of his death. By letter of May 30, 1978, Jerome J. La Penna, Esq., as counsel to Mr. Fenner in the bankruptcy proceeding, requested that the VA pay over to the Trustee the unpaid compensation owed to him at the time of his death, an amount described as "in excess of $800." The VA declined to voluntarily pay this amount to the Trustee because two of Mr. Fenner's surviving children, Deborah C. Lepore and Gregory S. Fenner, had filed a claim for the same fund. On or about July 26, 1978, Mr. Theodore S. Meth, the Trustee of Mr. Fenner's Wage Earners' Plan, applied to the Bankruptcy Judge for an order directing the VA to pay the unpaid salary to him as Trustee. An Order to that effect was entered on July 26, 1978, and forwarded to the VA by Mr. La Penna on August 1, 1978.

The disposition of money due at the time of death to an employee of the Government is controlled by the provisions of 5 U.S.C. § 5582 which provides in part:

> (b) In order to facilitate the settlement of the accounts of deceased employees, money due an employee at the time of his death shall be paid to the person or persons surviving at the date of death, in the following order of precedence, and the payment bars recovery by another person of amounts so paid:
>
> First, to the beneficiary or beneficiaries designated by the employee in a writing received in the employing agency before his death.
>
> Second, if there is no designated beneficiary, to the widow or widower of the employee.
>
> Third, if none of the above, to the child or children of the employee and descendants of deceased children by representation.
>
> Fourth, if none of the above, to the parents of the employee or the survivor of them.
>
> Fifth, if none of the above, to the duly appointed legal representative of the estate of the employee.
>
> Sixth, if none of the above, to the person or persons entitled under the laws of the domicile of the employee at the time of his death.

Mr. Fenner had not designated a beneficiary as permitted by that provision, nor, as we noted above, was he survived by a spouse. Therefore, his surviving children held the highest position in the order of precedence established by the statute. This statute has been considered in *Ashton* v. *Ashton*, 117 A. 2d 459 (D.C. Mun. Ct. App. 1955), which held that the disposition of the unpaid salary of a deceased Federal employee was governed by the quoted provision, not the local laws regarding decedents' estates. We have also reached that conclusion. See 51 Comp. Gen. 483 (1972).

The order entered by the Bankruptcy Judge is directly contradictory to the provisions of 5 U.S.C. § 5582, and it is, therefore, necessary to examine the force and effect of an order entered against the United States in a Bankruptcy proceeding. This issue was considered in *United States* v. *Krakover*, 377 F. 2d 104 (10 Cir. 1967), *cert. denied* 389 U.S. 845. In that case the Bankruptcy Referee ordered the United States, as the employer of the debtor, to pay over a certain sum from the debtor-employee's wages directly to the Trustee who was administering the Wage Earners' Plan. The Court of Appeals held that the Referee's order was not enforceable against the United States, since there was no waiver of sovereign immunity. The court went on to say that the same result could have been accomplished by ordering the employee to assign his salary checks to the Trustee. Such an order would then be enforceable against the employee.

In 47 Comp. Gen. 522 (1968), we were asked to rule on the propriety of an Air Force procedure of requiring finance officers to respond to court orders issued under Chapter XIII Wage Earners' Plan in light of *Krakover*. We held that the Air Force could continue to follow their policy since the orders would be enforceable against the employee, and, thus, the Government would get good acquittances against its employees. It must be remembered that there were no competing claims in that situation. The employee had voluntarily entered into the Wage Earners' Plan, and, if the Government did not respond to the order voluntarily, the same end could be achieved by entering an appropriate order against the employee himself, which could then be enforced by the court. In effect, the employee's filing of the Plan was treated as a voluntary assignment to the Trustee when the employee failed to comply with the Plan's provisions.

Here, on the other hand, there is a specific, competing claim, based upon a statute that has been uniformly held to be controlling as to the distribution of unpaid compensation due an employee at the time of his death. The informal policy endorsed in our decision cannot overcome the statutory mandate of 5 U.S.C. § 5582. Therefore, the compensation due Mr. Fenner at the time of his death should be paid not to the Trustee, but to the appropriate claimants under the statute who appear to be his surviving children.

Accordingly, the VA should dispose of the unpaid compensation due Mr. Fenner at the time of his death as is required by 5 U.S.C. § 5582, not as specified in the July 26, 1978 Order of the Bankruptcy Judge.

The children's claim form is, therefore, being returned to the VA. We are forwarding a copy of this decision to the Department of Justice should they deem it advisable to take appropriate action to dissolve the July 26, 1978 Order.

[B–193867]

Funds — Imprest — Availability — Partial and Emergency Salary Payments

General Accounting Office has no objection to Treasury Department proposal to authorize, in limited circumstances, use of imprest funds for partial salary payments to new employees and for certain emergency salary payments, as long as payments do not represent advance payments, proposal is coordinated with Office of Personnel Management and Office of Management and Budget to assure consistency of regulations, and time and attendance reporting requirements are satisfied.

In the matter of Use of imprest funds for partial and emergency salary payments, July 11, 1979:

This decision is in response to a request from the Commissioner, Fiscal Service, Department of the Treasury (Treasury), for our views on a proposal to permit the use of imprest funds (1) to make emergency salary payments without specific advance approval by Treasury, and (2) to make partial salary payments to new employees early in the week following the first week of employment.

Currently, Treasury permits agency use of imprest funds for emergency salary payments in the following situations:

1. Payments to employees who are not issued a check on the scheduled payday due to an administrative error or to a delay in processing necessary documents;

2. Payments to youths hired under special programs for the disadvantaged during the initial pay period when waiting for the normal payday would impose a serious financial hardship; and

3. Payments to employees who receive a salary check for less than 90 percent of the net amount due.

Under current procedures, each agency wishing to use imprest funds in this way must obtain Treasury's advance approval. Treasury further requires that such payments be entered on agency payroll records, that no payments be made prior to the time work has been performed and compensation earned, and that imprest funds be used only in locations not situated near a disbursing center. Treasury has informally advised us that approximately one-third of all Federal agencies have already requested, and been granted, approval to make emergency salary payments as outlined in this paragraph.

Treasury now states that many new Federal employees are faced with a hardship situation prior to receipt of their first salary check analogous to the situations of employees eligible for receipt of emergency salary payments. Although Treasury has not previously permitted partial salary payments to new employees, it notes that employees hired at the beginning of a pay period must generally wait a minimum of 3 weeks before receiving their first salary check. This lapse of time can impose financial hardship on an employee. The partial salary payments proposed by Treasury to be made in the second week of employment would be subject to the same guidelines presently imposed with respect to emergency salary payments.

We have reviewed titles 5 and 31 of the United States Code and know of no statutory impediment to Treasury's proposal. 5 U.S.C. § 5504 defines the basic pay period as "two administrative workweeks" but does not preclude the types of partial or emergency payments contemplated by the proposal. In addition, 31 U.S.C. § 529 generally prohibits advance payments. Thus, as Treasury recognizes, the partial or emergency salary payments may not represent advance payments (except as authorized by 5 U.S.C. § 5522).

As Treasury also recognizes, various regulations will have to be amended to implement the proposal. For example, the Treasury Fiscal Requirements Manual, title 4, section 3040.20, currently prohibits the use of imprest funds to make cash payments for personal services unless specifically authorized. Also, the proposal should be coordinated with the Office of Personnel Management (OPM), which is responsible for prescribing pay administration regulations under 5 U.S.C. § 5504 (c), and with the Office of Management and Budget (see, *e.g.*, OMB Circular No. A-36, October 25, 1948).

Section 112(a) of the Budget and Accounting Procedures Act of 1950 (31 U.S.C. § 66(a)) requires the Comptroller General to prescribe the principles, standards, and related requirements to be observed by Federal departments and agencies in the operation of their financial management systems. These principles, standards, and requirements are set forth in the General Accounting Office Policy and Procedures Manual for Guidance of Federal Agencies. The GAO Manual does not prohibit the use of imprest funds for the contemplated partial and emergency salary payments. In pertinent part, the Manual provides:

> An imprest fund should satisfy a definite and continuing need of an agency for making cash disbursements. Disbursements from imprest funds generally are made:
> 1. To vendors for goods and services.
> 2. To employees as advances for specifically authorized expenditures.
> 3. To employees as reimbursements for authorized expenditures. * * *
> * * * * *
> Agencies having imprest funds shall issue regulations and establish procedures for their use. Such regulations and procedures shall be consistent with regulations of the Treasury Department * * *. 7 GAO 27.3 and 27.8.

We would point out, however, that 6 GAO 16.2 requires time and attendance reports for each civilian employee, to "provide affirmative evidence that each employee is entitled to his normal pay or to a greater or lesser amount by a showing as to the number of hours of duty attendance and the nature and length of absences." Should the Treasury proposal be implemented, corresponding adjustments to the time and attendance procedures currently used by the various agencies would be necessary.

Subject to the qualifications mentioned above—prohibition on advance payments, appropriate coordination with OPM and OMB, and adherence to time and attendance reporting requirements—we have no objection to the Treasury Department's proposal.

[B-194057]

Travel Expenses—Air Travel—Foreign Air Carriers—Reimbursement Basis

Where U.S. air carriers were available from last point of official business, but where traveler combined personal business with his return travel and used a train and a foreign air carrier for segments of the journey, the traveler may not be reimbursed travel expenses representing revenues diverted from U.S. air carriers to foreign air carriers. Using the fare proration method set forth in 56 Comp. Gen. 209 (1977), the Fly America Act penalty is determined by subtracting the rail fare from the amount of revenues lost by U.S. air carriers determined under that formula.

In the matter of Kenneth M. Curtis—Indirect Travel by Foreign Air Carrier and Railroad, July 11, 1979:

This decision is in response to a request by the Chairman, United States Section, International Joint Commission (IJC), United States and Canada, to consider the disallowance of part of a travel voucher submitted by and paid to Governor Kenneth M. Curtis, one of the IJC's Commissioners. The disallowance was based on a determination by the Department of State that the Commissioner should be assessed a penalty for violating the statutory requirement to use U.S. air carrier service whenever available. That statute, commonly referred to as the Fly America Act, is Section 5 of the International Air Transportation Fair Competitive Practices Act of 1975, 49 U.S.C. § 1517 (1976).

The Commissioner was authorized to travel by air from Portland, Maine, to Penticton and Vancouver, British Columbia, and return to Portland. When the Commissioner completed his official duties in Vancouver, he traveled by rail at a cost of $46.84 to Calgary, Alberta, for personal business. He then returned to Portland by air, using a foreign air carrier between Calgary and Chicago, Illinois, because he believed that only foreign air carriers provided service from Calgary. The airfare from Calgary to Portland was $221.42. On his travel voucher, the Commissioner claimed the constructive airfare between Vancouver and Portland of $265.52, which was $2.34 less than the expense he incurred for his return travel by way of Calgary. The Department of State disallowed $106.01 of the amount claimed as a penalty for improper use of a foreign air carrier inasmuch as U.S. air carriers provided service between Vancouver and Portland. The Chairman of the IJC has asked that the penalty assessment be reconsidered in view of the fact that the Commissioner's decision to continue his travel from Calgary rather than to return to Vancouver was prudent, both in terms of time and cost.

The Fly America Act provides:

* * * The Comptroller General of the United States shall disallow any expenditure from appropriated funds for payment of such personnel or cargo transportation on an air carrier not holding a certification under Section 401 of this Act in the absence of satisfactory proof of the necessity therefor. * * *

Guidelines implementing the Act were issued by the Comptroller General. See B–138942, March 12, 1976. Among other things, they provide that a U.S. air carrier which can provide the service needed is considered available even though comparable or a different kind of service by a foreign air carrier costs less or is preferred by the traveler. Under the Guidelines, we have held that a traveler must take U.S. air carrier service available at point of origin to the furthest practicable interchange point. 55 Comp. Gen. 1230 (1976). Where the traveler does not properly route his travel, he is liable for any loss of revenues by U.S. air carriers which results from improper use of or indirect travel by noncertificated air carriers. 56 Comp. Gen. 209 (1977).

In B–188648, November 18, 1977, we held an employee liable under the Fly America Act for $16.02 where, incident to his official travel by way of London, he combined personal travel by trading in his ticket to obtain a substitute ticket permitting him a side trip between London and Edinburgh aboard a foreign flag carrier. In response to the traveler's arguments that there was no U.S. air carrier service between London and Edinburgh, that the travel was performed at no cost to himself or the Government, and that it was performed on his own time, we stated:

* * * where the employee takes a side trip or otherwise indirectly routes his travel, and where such indirect travel is wholly or in part subsidized by the fare payable by the Government in connection with the employee's official itinerary, the employee is responsible not only for any additional cost attributable to his personal travel but for any diversion of revenues from certificated U.S. air carriers. 56 Comp. Gen. 209 (1977). The opportunity that Government travel may afford an employee to augment his personal travel plans is purely fortuitous and is sanctioned only insofar as it does not result in additional cost to the Government or contravene otherwise applicable laws and regulations. To the extent that such personal travel results in a reduction in receipt of Government revenues by U.S. air carriers over revenues they would have earned had the employee performed only authorized travel, that personal travel does involve a violation of the requirement for use of certificated U.S. air carrier service imposed by 49 U.S.C. § 1517.

Under these authorities, the Commissioner is responsible for the portion of the airfare payable by the Government which his personal travel to Calgary diverted from U.S. to foreign air carriers. We note that his responsibility under the Fly America Act does not extend to amounts diverted to carriers providing other modes of transportation, such as railroads or vessels. B–190575, May 1, 1978. Contrary to the Commissioner's understanding, U.S. air carrier service to Portland, Maine, by way of Denver, Colorado, was available in Calgary on the morning he traveled. Had he taken that flight, he would not have been subject to a penalty since the only redistribution of revenues occasioned by his personal travel would have been from U.S. air carriers to the railroad which provided service between Vancouver and Calgary. However, the Commissioner traveled from Calgary to Chicago aboard a foreign air carrier. He is, therefore, responsible for the pro-rated portion of the $265.52 airfare from Vancouver that was transferred from U.S. air carriers to the foreign air carrier which provided service from Calgary to Chicago. The same penalty would pertain even if there had been no U.S. air carrier providing service from Calgary, since the Commissioner's travel to Calgary was personal rather than for official business.

Thus, we are in agreement with the Department of State's determination to assess the Commissioner a penalty for the use of a foreign air carrier occasioned by his personal travel to Calgary. Because the travel to Calgary was not for official business, the fact that it was less costly and more efficient in terms of the traveler's personal itinerary does not provide a basis to disregard the requirement to use otherwise available U.S. air carrier service. However, we are unable to verify the $106.01 penalty which appears to have been calculated by the Department of State on the basis of a proration of the fares involved. Using the fare proration method discussed in 56 Comp. Gen. 209 (1977) and subtracting the rail fare of $46.44 for travel from Vancouver to Calgary, the penalty for which the Commissioner is responsible is $90.51 and since the Commissioner already has been assessed a penalty of $106.01 by the Department of State, there is a refund of $15.50 due him.

Because a portion of the indirect travel involved was by rail, calculation of the penalty amount involves an additional step beyond application of the fare proration formula set forth in 56 Comp. Gen. 209 (1977). The dollar amount determined under that formula reflects revenues lost by U.S. air carriers as a result of improper or indirect travel. Because a portion of that amount represents Government revenues diverted to a rail carrier, for which there is no penalty, the rail fare of $46.44 is subtracted from the amount of revenues lost by U.S. air carriers to determine the amount of revenues lost as a result of the traveler's use of foreign air carriers. The following calculation is set forth as a matter of clarification:

Authorized route—Vancouver to Portland

	Date	City	Time	Flight No.	Fare
Lv	9/17/78	Vancouver	7:40a	UA404	
Ar	"	Chicago	1:30p		
Lv	"	Chicago	2:20p	UA216	
Ar	"	Boston	5:30p		
Lv	"	Boston	6:43p	DL518	
Ar	"	Portland	7:15p		

Fare payable by Government $265. 52

Actual route—Vancouver to Portland

	Date	City	Time	Flight No.	Fare
Lv	9/15/78	Vancouver	4:00p	CP Rail	
Ar	9/16/78	Calgary	1:15a		$46. 44
Lv	9/17/78	Calgary	11:15a	AC836	
Ar	"	Chicago	3:15p		93. 42
Lv	"	Chicago	4:45p	TW220	
Ar	"	Boston	7:54p		99. 00
Lv	"	Boston	8:50p	CL422	
Ar	"	Portland	9:22p		29. 00

Through fare paid $267. 86

Step 1. *Revenues Diverted from U.S. Air Carriers*

$$\frac{\text{Sum of certificated carrier segment fares authorized}}{\text{Sum of all segment fares authorized}} \times \frac{\text{Fare payable}}{\text{by Government}}$$

minus

$$\frac{\text{Sum of certificated carrier segment fares traveled}}{\text{Sum of all segment fares traveled (including rail)}} \times \frac{\text{Through fare paid}}{} =$$

$$\frac{\$265. 52}{\$265. 52} \times \$265. 52 - \frac{\$99+\$29}{\$267. 86} \times \$267. 86 =$$

$$1 \times \$265. 52 - . 48 \times \$267. 86 =$$

$$\$265. 52 - \$128. 57 \qquad = \$136. 95$$

Step 2. *Revenues Diverted to Foreign Air Carriers*

Revenues diverted from U.S. air carriers

minus

Revenues diverted to rail carrier =
$136. 95 − $46. 44 = $90. 51

[B–194509]

Officers and Employees — Transfers — Relocation Expenses — Temporary Quarters — Entitlement

Employee claims additional expenses for temporary quarters subsistence. Agency denied claim because employee had already been paid for a house-hunting trip. Agency exercised its discretion and followed policy outlined in Federal Travel Regulations to reduce period for occupying temporary quarters if house-hunting trip has been made. Even if method used resulted in reduced cost to Government, it does not furnish a basis for payment of temporary quarters subsistence. Claim is denied.

In the matter of John A. Orris—Relocation—Temporary Quarters Subsistence, July 11, 1979:

An advance decision has been requested by Claude F. Pickelsimer, Jr., an authorized certifying officer of the Public Health Service, Department of Health, Education, and Welfare (HEW), concerning the reclaim voucher of Mr. John A. Orris for additional temporary quarters subsistence expenses incident to a permanent change of station from Lansing, Michigan, to Atlanta, Georgia.

By travel order dated October 18, 1977, Mr. Orris was authorized one round trip to his new duty station to seek housing. Mr. Orris' travel order states in pertinent part as follows:

> * * * TRAVELER MUST TRAVEL IN ACCORDANCE WITH TRAVEL ORDERS. NO DEVIATIONS AUTHORIZED. Round trip via POA @ 10¢ per mile, 10/23–28/77, for employee and spouse from Lansing, MI to Atlanta, GA to seek housing authorized in accordance with F.T.R. (GSA Bulletin, FPMR, A–40) Part 4, subsistence—*temporary duty quarters at new duty station may be reduced by the amount of the round trip to seek housing or disallowed.* [Italic supplied.]

Mr. Orris' claim for reimbursement for a round trip to find housing was allowed. A portion of his claim, representing the 2-day period that he and his family awaited delivery of household goods, was allowed in the amount of $80.65. He is seeking an additional $339.37 for temporary quarters.

The certifying officer states that it is the policy of HEW's Center for Disease Control to authorize either a round trip to seek housing or temporary quarters, but not both. Mr. Orris, however, says that the total amount he claimed was less than what would have been claimed had the round trip not been utilized since charges for 2 months storage of household goods and 30 days temporary quarters would have been incurred. He requests reimbursement because he alleges that the method he used was more advantageous to the Government.

Under the provisions of section 5724a(a) of title 5, United States Code, an employee and his spouse traveling together may be authorized one round trip to seek permanent residence quarters at a new duty station, and the employee and his immediate family may be reimbursed for the expenses of occupying temporary quarters for a period of 30 days.

Paragraphs 2–4.1 and 2–5.1 of the Federal Travel Regulations (FPMR 101–7) (May 1973) establish the general policy for administering these provisions. They state that a round trip to seek residence quarters may be authorized when circumstances warrant it and that an appropriate official of the agency shall decide whether such a trip should be authorized. Thus, authorization for travel to seek residence quarters is discretionary with the agency. The agency, in the exercise of its discretion, issued travel orders and authorized Mr. Orris a round trip to seek housing with the stipulation, quoted above, that reimbursement for temporary quarters might be reduced or disallowed.

This stipulation by the agency is consistent with the policy contained in the Federal Travel Regulations, both as to travel to seek residence quarters and subsistence while occupying temporary quarters. Paragraph 2–4.1b states, as to travel to seek residence quarters, that this part shall be administered to minimize or avoid the expense involved whenever other satisfactory and more economical arrangements can be made. Paragraph 2–5.1 states that, as a general policy, the period for temporary quarters shall be reduced or avoided if a round trip to seek permanent residence quarters has been made. Assuming then that Mr. Orris is correct in his statement that the method he chose was less costly to the Government, this fact is apparently one of the reasons that such a policy has been implemented. Mr. Orris was apparently successful in his house-hunting trip and his travel orders put him on notice that subsistence expenses for temporary quarters might be reduced by the amount of the round trip to seek housing or disallowed.

Therefore, even if the method used resulted in reduced cost to the Government, it does not furnish a basis for payment of temporary quarters subsistence. *Matter of Patrick J. Twohig*, B–185511. March 3, 1976.

Accordingly, Mr. Orris may not be reimbursed the claimed expenses.

[B–195173]

Contracts — Cost-Plus — Cost-Plus-a-Percentage-of-Cost Prohibition—Payment Basis

Even though costs incurred under contracts awarded pursuant to grant projects were based on cost-plus-percentage-of-cost contracting, contractor can be paid on *quantum meruit/quantum valebat* basis as agency has determined costs to be reasonable and Government received benefit of services.

In the matter of Federal Aviation Administration—Request for Advance Decision, July 16, 1979:

The Rocky Mountain Region, Federal Aviation Administration (FAA), Department of Transportation (DOT), has requested our Office's opinion as to whether certain costs incurred under contracts awarded pursuant to two grant projects of the Airport Development Aid Program (ADAP) are payable.

The projects involved are ADAP Project No. 6–30–0046–04, Kalispell, Montana, and ADAP Project No. 6–30–0012–05, Butte, Montana.

Recent audits by the Office of the Inspector General, DOT, have disclosed that portions of the engineering contracts for the projects were based on a cost-plus–percentage-of-cost (CPPC) method of contracting.

Appendix "M" of the Federal Aviation Regulations, part 152, states that the CPPC method of contracting will not be used in connection with ADAP projects. FAA Order No. 2940.5, chapter 1, paragraph 9d, requires that the Comptroller General be consulted as to the propriety of payments under illegal contracts.

The FAA advises that at the time the contracts were approved, the contracts contained a "not to exceed" cost limitation and, therefore, it was concluded they were not CPPC type contracts. The FAA has also determined that the costs are reasonable in amount and that steps have been taken to prevent further occurrences of this nature.

The contracts in question provided that the firm's profits were to be based on 15 percent of actual direct labor and overhead costs.

The fourfold test utilized to determine if a certain contract is a CPPC type involves whether (1) payment is on a predetermined percentage rate; (2) the predetermined percentage rate is applied to actual performance costs; (3) contractor's entitlement is uncertain at the time of contracting; and (4) contractor's entitlement increases commensurately with increased performance costs. *Marketing Consultants International Limited*, 55 Comp. Gen. 554 (1975), 75–2 CPD 384. The instant contracts clearly meet these tests.

The presence of a cost limitation in the contract does not save the contract from violating the prohibition contained in the FAA regulations. 38 Comp. Gen. 38, 40 (1958).

However, our Office and the courts have recognized that where goods are furnished or services rendered but the contract under which the performance occurred is void, an obligation on the United States arises to pay the value of the goods or services actually furnished upon an implied contract for a *quantum meruit/quantum valebat*. 33 Comp. Gen. 533, 537 (1954) and *Pacific Maritime Association* v. *United States*, 123 Ct. Cls. 667, 675–677 (1952). We find this rule to have equal application here, where the question is the eligibility of costs under a grant–type arrangement, the purpose of which was fulfilled by the rendering of the services.

As the FAA has determined the costs in question to be fair and reasonable and the Government received the benefit of the service, the costs may be paid.

[B–193933]

Federal Procurement Regulations—Late Proposals—Consideration Propriety—Rule—"Only Proposal Received" Exception—Applicability

Manufacturers' late proposals, submitted after closing date for receipt of proposals and timely receipt of dealer's proposal for "identical" product, do not constitute "only proposal received" within meaning of Federal Procurement Regulation 1–3.802–1(c) which permits consideration of late proposals and may not be considered for award.

In the matter of Federal Sales Service, Inc., July 17, 1979:

Federal Sales Service, Inc. (Federal Sales) has protested against the solicitation and acceptance of proposals by the Federal Supply Service, General Services Administration (GSA), from K/Tronic, Inc. (K/Tronic) and Verbatim Corporation (Verbatim) after the closing date for receipt of proposals specified in request for proposals (RFP) No. FPHO–D–75051–N–3–9–78.

The RFP, issued on February 9, 1978, contemplates the award of indefinite quantity contracts for video and sound recording tapes, magnetic cards and digital cassettes for fiscal year 1979. GSA received 12 proposals by March 9, 1978, the closing date for receipt of proposals, and began negotiations with the offerors on April 12, 1978.

On June 22, 1978, GSA asked the protester to furnish a bona fide manufacturer's commercial price list for its cassettes. Federal Sales submitted a K/Tronic price list, stating that the cassettes are made by K/Tronic in accordance with an unwritten specification and sold under the protester's "Unicopy" label. On August 3, 1978, GSA requested a preaward survey of K/Tronic's facilities, pursuant to Federal Procurement Regulations (FPR) § 1–1.1205–4 (1964 ed. amend. 95) and GSA Procurement Regulations (GSPR) § 5A–1.1205–4 (1977 ed.), in order to verify the protester's statements. The Plant Facilities Report (PFR), dated August 25, 1978, stated that the K/Tronic and Unicopy cassettes are the same, except that the Unicopy cassette is of lower quality, and concluded that the protester is capable of performing under the RFP.

K/Tronic submitted a proposal on September 6, 1978. Although GSA had decided on the basis of the PFR to return the protester's proposal, after a September 14, 1978 conversation between Federal Sales and GSA personnel the firm's proposal was instead held in abeyance.

On November 8, 1978, Federal Sales added ¼-inch data cartridges manufactured by Verbatim to its original proposal. GSA contacted Verbatim on the same day. The firm expressed an interest in representing itself under the Federal Supply Schedule (FSS) and submitted a proposal for ¼-inch data cartridges on December 6, 1978.

GSA states that the protester, K/Tronic and Verbatim have offered identical products under GSA Special Item Number 165–25–Digital Cassettes/Cartridges. While five contracts for this item have been awarded to other offerors, no award has been made to any of the three firms involved. GSA has advised us that if Federal Sales' protest is denied, the protester, K/Tronic and Verbatim will be asked to submit their best and final offers and the offer which presents the most favorable discount advantage to Government and meets established benchmark criteria will be recommended for award.

Federal Sales essentially contends that the offers submitted by K/Tronic and Verbatim after the March 9 closing date should be rejected as late proposals and that award should be made to Federal Sales for both manufacturers' products.

GSA asserts that late proposals submitted in response to multiple-award FSS solicitations may be evaluated and considered for award in accordance with the agency's procedures. The RFP incorporates by reference GSA Form 1424, GSA Supplemental Provisions (June 1977 ed.); paragraph 62 sets forth the late proposal clause prescribed in FPR § 1–3.802–1(a) (1964 ed. amend. 194) which permits consideration of a late proposal received before award if "[i]t is the only proposal received." The term "only proposal received" is defined to include a proposal offering proprietary items where the RFP specifies that awards will be made on the basis of such items identified by the offeror by brand name, model, type or other identification. FPR § 1–3.802–1 (c)(3) (1964 ed. amend. 194). GSPR § 5A–3.802–1 (1978 ed.) implements that definition to include offers received in response to multiple-award FSS solicitations in accordance with FPR § 1–3.802–1(c)(3) in the term "only proposal received." GSA therefore concludes that the K/Tronic and Verbatim proposals, albeit late, fall within the "only proposal received" exception and were properly entitled to evaluation and consideration for award.

We cannot, however, agree with GSA's interpretation and proposed application of these regulations. GSA has stated that the products offered by the protester, K/Tronic and Verbatim, are identical and that in the event negotiations were reopened only one contract would be awarded. We therefore believe that the "only proposal exception" cannot be applied to the late proposal submitted by K/Tronic and Verbatim. GSA had already received a timely proposal, that of the protester, for the product by the March 9 closing date. Thus proposals for the "identical" product submitted after the closing date could hardly be considered the "only proposal received," nor does GSPR

§ 5A–3.802–1 expand that exception as it applies to FSS procurements because it pertains to proposals submitted *in accordance* with FPR § 1–3.802–1(c)(3). See *Office & Interior Furnishings*, B–191655, September 5, 1978, 78–2 CPD 168.

Because the proposals do not fall within any of the exceptions under which they may be considered, notwithstanding their lateness, they must be rejected as late. FPR § 1–3.802–1(b) (1964 ed. amend. 194). Although the Government may lose proposals which offer terms more advantageous than those timely received, the paramount consideration in applying the late proposal rules is the maintenance of confidence in the integrity of the Government procurement system rather than the possible advantage to be gained in a particular procurement. *Emergency Care Research Institute*, B–181204, August 23, 1974, 74–2 CPD 118.

K/Tronic and Verbatim, having failed to submit timely initial proposals, may not participate in further negotiations, and reopening negotiations without a valid reason tends to undermine the integrity of the competitor negotiation process. See *ILC Dover*, B–182104, November 29, 1974, 74–2 CPD 301; 50 Comp. Gen. 547, 552–53 (1971). We therefore recommend that GSA reject the late proposals of K/Tronic and Verbatim and make award to Federal Sales, if otherwise appropriate.

The protest is sustained.

[B–194318]

Contracts—Protests—Oral—To Procuring Agency

Oral protest to agency is permissible if intent to protest is clear. Intent to protest withdrawal of small business set-aside is not evident by protester's statement prior to bid opening merely expressing displeasure with withdrawal. Therefore, protest filed with General Accounting Office (GAO) after bid opening objecting to withdrawal of set-aside is untimely and not for consideration on the merits.

Contracts—Awards—Small Business Concerns—Set-Asides—Withdrawal—Procedural Compliance

Contracting officer's withdrawal of small business set-aside without notifying Small Business Administration (SBA) liaison representative, thereby denying SBA its right to appeal withdrawal to head of procuring agency, was contrary to regulation and to purpose and intent of Small Business Act. GAO recommends post-award referral of set-aside withdrawal to SBA with view toward possible termination of contract for convenience of the Government and resolicitation.

In the matter of Comprehensive Health Services, Inc., July 17, 1979:

Comprehensive Health Services, Inc. (Comprehensive), a small business, protests the withdrawal of a small business set-aside by the

Department of Commerce. Comprehensive alleges that the Department should not have removed the set-aside restriction and did not comply with the regulatory provisions and Departmental guidelines applicable to such withdrawals.

Although we find the first allegation to be untimely, we sustain the protest on the second ground.

The record shows that invitation for bids (IFB) BA–79–SA–C–00150 was originally issued as a total small business set-aside, but that an IFB amendment was issued to remove the restriction after the Department received a protest from another firm. Comprehensive alleges that it then filed an oral protest with the agency prior to bid opening and that its subsequent protest to this Office, filed after bid opening, is consequently timely.

However, an oral protest—permissible under Federal Procurement Regulations (FPR) 1–2.407–8(a) (1964 ed. amend. 139)—must be stated in such a fashion that the intent to lodge a protest is clear. *Joule Technical Corporation*, 58 Comp. Gen. 550 (1979), 79–1 CPD 364. Here, the contract specialist advises that after the amendment was issued Comprehensive's representative orally expressed his displeasure regarding the withdrawal of the small business set-aside. While the contract specialist acknowledges that the protester "complained" about the withdrawal, she did not conclude that Comprehensive was protesting this fact. According to the contract specialist, Comprehensive's representative ended this conversation by stating that the firm would submit a bid. The protester does not dispute this. In our opinion, an intent to protest is not evidenced by the mere expression of displeasure. For example, we have held that an offeror's mere assertion that a wage determination is incompatible with a solicitation does not reflect an intent to protest. *Joule Technical Corporation, supra.*

Under the circumstances, we believe Comprehensive's initial protest was that filed with GAO after bid opening. Since the removal of the set-aside by the IFB amendment relates to the solicitation itself, we view the protester's general objections to the removal as going to an alleged solicitation defect, which under our Bid Protest Procedures must be protested prior to bid opening. *See* 4 C.F.R. 20.2(b)(1) (1979). Since we cannot conclude that Comprehensive protested prior to bid opening, we find the protester's general objections to the set-aside withdrawal as untimely and therefore we will not consider them on the merits.

Comprehensive's second basis for protest, the Department's alleged failure to follow applicable regulations, is not related to a solicitation defect, however, and we view that portion of the protest as timely. We also find the record supports Comprehensive's allegations.

FPR 1–1.706–3(b) provides that a contracting officer shall initiate a withdrawal of a small business set-aside by giving notice to the Small Business Administration (SBA) representative. If that representative does not agree to the withdrawal, the matter ultimately may be appealed to the head of the agency. Such notice was not given to the SBA representative in this case.

The Small Business Act, 15 U.S.C. 631 *et seq.* (1976), reflects a national policy of furthering the interests of small business concerns and in awarding a fair proportion of procurement contracts to such concerns. The SBA, created by the Act, is charged with promoting policies and taking actions to assure that small businesses receive their fair share of Government procurement awards. To carry out this responsibility, SBA assigns representatives to procurement activities. These representatives are expected to screen agency decisions not to set aside procurements for small business and to process appeals to the agency head if SBA does not concur with negative decisions. *See* FPR 1–1.706–1, 1–1.706–2, and 1–1.706.3.

Those FPR sections, envisioning SBA participation in the set-aside decision process, implement the Small Business Act provision which authorizes the SBA to appeal to the procuring agency head a set-aside matter on which there is disagreement. *See* 15 U.S.C. § 644. Obviously, if the SBA representative is not properly notified of set-aside decisions, the SBA is denied the right to appeal in contravention of the statute. *See* 53 Comp. Gen. 58, 60 (1973). Here we think it is clear that the Department's failure to notify the SBA liaison representative of the set-aside withdrawal denied SBA that right and was inconsistent with the purpose and intent of the Act.

We are recommending that the contracting officer immediately refer the case to the SBA liaison representative so that he may pursue the matter as contemplated by the FPR. If a final determination is made that the set-aside should not have been withdrawn, the contract awarded to another firm (a large business) should be terminated for the convenience of the Government and the requirement resolicited as a set-aside.

This decision contains a recommendation for corrective action to be taken. Therefore, we are furnishing copies to the Senate Committees on Governmental Affairs and Appropriations and the House Committees on Government Operations and Appropriations in accordance with section 236 of the Legislative Reorganization Act of 1970, 31 U.S.C. § 1176 (1976), which requires the submission of written statements by the agency to the committees concerning the action taken with respect to our recommendation.

[B-193648]

Leaves of Absence—Without Pay—Substitution for Annual and Sick Leave

A Federal employee applied for disability retirement, waived military retired pay to increase his Civil Service annuity and spouse's survivor annuity to be effective when retirement is granted, but then went on extended sick leave and died in that status. While the agency has discretionary authority to place him in a leave-without-pay (LWOP) status because of retirement counseling errors or his misunderstanding, where there is nothing of record to show such counseling error or that he misunderstood that a sick leave status was not retirement, it would be improper to retroactively substitute LWOP for sick leave. B-190204, January 26, 1978, distinguished.

In the matter of Mr. Bartley T. Stokes, July 19, 1979:

The Navy has asked whether it may retroactively substitute leave without pay (LWOP) for sick leave for a period just prior to the death of an employee so that his military retired pay waiver may be given effect and his military service combined with civilian service to increase his spouse's survivor annuity.

Although the matter of substituting LWOP for sick leave charged (retroactively decreasing the deceased employee's pay entitlement) is within our jurisdiction, the Office of Personnel Management must determine how to compute the survivor annuity. 5 U.S.C. 8347. We have previously answered questions relating to leave charges and pay entitlement which have been asked primarily because of the effect on Civil Service Retirement benefits. Apparently the Civil Service Commission (now Office of Personnel Management) has paid benefits consistent with those decisions. While we cannot direct payment or withholding of payments from the Civil Service Retirement Fund, we have considered the leave substitution question and for the reasons given below have determined that substitution should not be allowed in this case.

Mr. Bartley Stokes was a civilian employee of the Federal Government from February 12, 1954, to March 25, 1977, the date of his death. Prior to that employment, he performed active duty in the United States Navy, for which he received retired pay.

On August 19, 1976, Mr. Stokes executed an application for disability retirement under the Civil Service retirement system and elected to provide his spouse with a survivor annuity. On September 7, 1976, he signed a letter to the Commanding Officer, Navy Finance Center, in which he stated that he wanted to waive his military retired pay "effective the day after my civilian disability retirement is approved by the Cvil Service Commission, to be combined with my Civil Service retirement." On September 10, 1976, his retirement application was forwarded by his agency to the Civil Service Commission and he went on extended sick leave. The record shows that he had in excess of 41 years of active Federal service and approximately 1 year of sick leave to his credit (to terminate on September 29, 1977) at that time.

By document dated October 1, 1976, the Civil Service Commission, in response to the employee's disability retirement application, advised the Accounting Support Center, Naval Air Station, that while the employee's disability retirement had been approved, his final SF 2806 "Individual Retirement Record" could not be forwarded for final action because he was still on the payroll of his agency in a sick leave status, confirming the September 29, 1977 termination date. Mr. Stokes died on March 25, 1977, while in that status.

Mr. Stokes had not elected coverage under the Survivor Benefit Plan, 10 U.S.C. 1447–1455, to provide an annuity for his wife based on his military retired pay. As a result, the only survivor annuity available to his spouse was that provided under the Civil Service system based on his civilian service. Since Mr. Stokes was not in a Civil Service retirement status at the time of his death but was on his agency's payroll, he was not able to combine his military service with his Civil Service time for the purpose of establishing an annuity at the higher rate. Thus, Civil Service survivor annuity for his spouse is not for computation on the basis of the higher rate.

Therefore, the agency asks whether it may retroactively substitute leave without pay for sick leave in Mr. Stokes' case and the employee's surviving spouse reimburse the agency for all sick leave payments made. The basis for that request is that while it appears that the employee completed all paperwork necessary for retirement and to combine both his military and civilian service for annuity purposes, it is claimed that there is an aura of uncertainty as to whether he fully understood that he was still on the Civil Service rolls as a full-time employee while in a sick leave status. In support of that request, the submission cites our decision B–190204, January 26, 1978.

In that decision, we considered the case of an employee on sick leave who, because of the critical nature of his illness, was unable to conduct his own affairs. He appointed his spouse to act on his behalf in the matter of his retirement. His spouse apparently received counseling and sought immediate disability retirement for her husband. Since the employee was receiving military retired pay, in order to maximize his retirement annuity and his spouse's survivor annuity he had to be on the Civil Service retirement rolls prior to his death. In order to accomplish this, his wife executed both his application for immediate disability retirement and a waiver of his military retired pay, delivering them to the agency. Apparently due to the anxieties of the moment, she failed to request a change in his status from sick leave to leave without pay and the failure to do so went unnoticed. The employee died shortly thereafter while in a sick leave status.

Based on the spouse's statement regarding her understanding of information given, the critical nature of her husband's illness, and the evidence of record corroborating the probable misunderstanding and error, we held that there was sufficient evidence to show that it was her intention to effect his immediate retirement, thereby maximizing his annuity and her survivor annuity. As a result, we concluded that it was appropriate for the agency to exercise their discretion and retroactively substitute leave without pay for sick leave in that case.

In general, the exercise of discretion in the granting of leave to an employee (annual, sick or leave without pay), within the limitation of applicable laws and regulations, is an administrative matter. When leave has been properly granted and compensation paid therefor by the agency, we are without jurisdiction to either review or direct any change in administrative records in the absence of any abuse of that authority. See 36 Comp. Gen. 183 (1956). Thus, where the administrative office changes the record to show an employee in a leave-without-pay status for all or any part of periods previously charged to annual or sick leave where the evidence of record shows that the original leave status to be in error, even after the employee's separation, by death or otherwise, we would not be required to object. See 24 Comp. Gen. 143 (1944). It is our view that the underlying basis for the exercise of sound administrative discretion in this area must be the existence of evidence of record which points up misunderstandings or mistakes, as was the case in B-190204, January 26, 1978.

The regulations governing Civil Service retirement are set forth in the Federal Personnel Manual (FPM) Supplement 831-1, Subchapter S10 of which applies to disability retirement. Paragraph S10-5 thereof, which discusses agency responsibility for counseling in disability retirement cases, provides in part:

a. *In general.* Generally, an employee who has a large accumulation of sick leave should defer filing an application for disability retirement until his or her leave reaches a balance of approximately 60 days. The agency should give every assistance to the employee in completing the application by helping him or her to select the type of annuity best suited to the circumstances * * *. If the employee is unable to work, the agency should carry him or her in a leave status (with or without pay) until notified by the Civil Service Commission of its action on the application.

In conjunction with the foregoing, paragraph S3-5 provides in part:

f. *Waiver of military retired pay.*

(1) An employee or employee-annuitant who is receiving military retired pay which bars credit for military service * * * may elect to waive the retired pay and have military service added to civilian service. * * *

     *   *   *   *   *   *   *

(4) In certain disability claims (where the nature of the disability appears to be very serious and the applicant is in receipt of military retired pay), the following procedure is suggested in order to ensure the maximum annuity benefits to the employee and spouse. Where unused sick leave is involved, and the applicant meets the age and service requirements for disability annuity, he or she may be placed on LWOP instead of sick-leave-with-pay status, and request a waiver of military retired pay. In the event of the applicant's death while the disability claim is pending, he or she can be considered to have completed a valid waiver of military retired pay after the commencing date of annuity because the annuity would commence the day following the last day in pay status.

In this way, credit for all honorable, active periods of military service will be included in computing both the annuity and the survivor benefits.

Paragraph S3–7g(3) of the same regulation provides in part:

a. *General rule.* The services of an employee who * * * dies leaving a widow or widower entitled to survivor annuity is increased by the days of unused sick leave to his or her credit under a formal leave system. * * *

g.(3) * * * In general, it is more advantageous to the employee to be separated as of the date sick leave expires than to be separated upon approval of the retirement application and receive retirement credit for his unused sick leave.

Under these regulations, while an agency is required to counsel an employee on retirement matters, including advising him as to the ramifications of taking certain courses of action, there is no requirement that the employee must follow the recommendations of the agency, since the choice is his to make. In other words, while the agency is to counsel the employee, it is the employee's responsibility to elect that course of action which he feels is in his best interest. The fact that subsequent events establish that the employee erred in his choice would not serve as a basis for an administrative change in his record.

In the present case, the employee acted for himself prior to actually going on sick leave on September 10, 1976. He executed his disability retirement application on August 19, 1976, as well as a waiver of his military retired pay on September 7, presumably based on retirement information administratively provided. When his disability retirement was approved he did not retire but continued on sick leave. Considering the fact that he had more than 41 years of creditable service and a year of sick leave to his credit, it may have appeared to him that receiving full pay in a sick leave status was more advantageous than receiving sick leave credit for retirement computation purposes. It is also noted that he had used more than 6 months of that leave before he died.

Unlike the situation in B–190204, January 26, 1978, no substantial evidence has been presented to show that the employee received incomplete or erroneous retirement counseling. Also, no evidence has been presented to show that during any of the period from August 1976 to his death in March 1977 Mr. Stokes intended to receive anything other than that which he was receiving or that he misunderstood that he was not retired while in a sick leave status. Therefore, based on the record before us, it is our view that it would be an abuse of discretion for the agency to retroactively substitute leave without pay for sick leave in this case.

[B–194053]

General Accounting Office—Jurisdiction—Contracts—Small Business Matters—Procurement Under 8(a) Program—Subcontractor Eligibility Determinations by SBA

Question of whether firm is eligible for assistance under section 8(a) of Small Business Act is basically matter for determination by Small Business Administration and is not subject to legal review by General Accounting Office.

Contracts — Awards — Small Business Concerns — Procurement Under 8(a) Program—Subcontractor Eligibility Standards—Statutory Changes

General Accounting Office review of Small Business Administration (SBA) action under 8(a) program is limited to determining whether SBA has followed its regulations. Where firm was determined eligible and accepted into 8(a) program based on social disadvantage alone and law and regulations were subsequently changed to require both social and economic disadvantage, recommendation is made to SBA to review firm's eligibility to determine if it should be allowed to continue to participate in 8(a) program or if participation should be terminated in accordance with present law and regulations.

In the matter of Orincon Corporation, July 19, 1979:

Orincon Corporation (Orincon) protests the award of a subcontract by the Small Business Administration (SBA) to Scientific Systems, Inc. (Scientific), under request for proposals F33615–79–R–3014 issued by Wright-Patterson Air Force Base, Ohio. The solicitation, which calls for a study to develop optimization techniques applicable to flight performance analysis methods, was set aside by the Air Force for minority business enterprises pursuant to section 8(a) of the Small Business Act, 15 U.S.C. § 637(a)(1) (1976).

Orincon contends that Scientific does not qualify as a section 8(a) minority business enterprise. In support of this contention, Orincon alleges that the principals of Scientific are not economically and socially deprived and that they are aliens, being citizens of India. In addition, Orincon claims that Scientific has become a self-sustaining, competitive entity and, therefore, does not need procurement assistance from the Government.

Scientific asserts that it is entitled to treatment as a disadvantaged small business. Scientific argues that it is in fact socially disadvantaged because its president is Asian in origin. Also, Scientific alleges that it is quite small, having net liquid assets of less than $60,000. Consequently, Scientific believes that its resources, capital, and credit opportunities are more limited than its competitors'. According to Scientific, the economic disadvantage of a small business should be evaluated on the basis of its position compared to its competitors and on the basis of its liquid net assets.

A sources-sought synopsis of the procurement was publicized in the July 12, 1978, issue of the Commerce Business Daily. All except one of the 24 firms that responded to the solicitation were considered qualified to perform the proposed contract. Scientific, one of the qualified firms, identified itself as a minority business enterprise. Therefore, the Air Force offered the contract to the SBA with Scientific listed as a technically qualified company indicating minority business status. The SBA agreed to accept the contract. The Air Force emphasizes, however, that it had no voice in determining whether Scientific was eligible to be a section 8(a) subcontractor.

The question of whether a firm is eligible for the 8(a) program is basically a matter for determination by the SBA and not this Office. *Steamatic by M & S Tolcser*, B–190799, December 22, 1977, 77–2 CPD 496. Furthermore, we have consistently stated that the question of how much aid a minority business needs to become self-sustaining is also a judgmental one for the SBA and not this Office. *Jets Services, Inc.*, B–186066, May 4, 1976, 76–1 CPD 300, and decisions cited therein.

Our review of the SBA action under the 8(a) program is limited to determining whether the SBA has followed its regulations. *Tidewater Protective Services, Inc.*, B–190957, January 13, 1978, 78–1 CPD 33. Because of the broad discretion afforded the SBA under the applicable statute, judgmental decisions under section 8(a), absent a showing of fraud or bad faith on the part of Government officials, will not be questioned. *Id.* Fraud or bad faith is not shown by the mere allegation of a violation of standard operating procedures since they may be waived or revoked. *Id.*

Orincon contends that the law presently requires that the principals of a concern be both economically and socially deprived in order for that concern to qualify as a minority small business under section 8(a). However, we note that Orincon also protested Scientific's section 8(a) status to the Air Force contracting officer. Because the SBA designates which eligible minority business is to perform its 8(a) contracts, the Air Force forwarded the protest to the SBA for resolution. By letter dated January 19, 1979, the SBA verified Scientific's eligibility and reaffirmed its intent to perform the contract entered into with the Air Force. In verifying Scientific's eligibility, the SBA specifically stated that the question of economic disadvantage was a "moot point" since the owner was found to be socially disadvantaged under the SBA's *then existing* eligibility criteria as set forth in the applicable standard operating procedure. The SBA verification letter further stated that persons were determined to be eligible who were either socially *or* economically disadvantaged.

The determination of whether Scientific's owner is socially disadvantaged is not reviewable by us. See *Wallace and Wallace Fuel Oil Company, Inc.*, B–182625, July 18, 1975, 75–2 CPD 48. As to Orincon's contention that both economic and social disadvantage is required for 8(a) eligibility, the SBA regulations at the time Scientific was determined eligible and accepted with the 8(a) program (March 6, 1978) provided instead that the concern must be owned and controlled by one or more persons who have been deprived of the opportunity to develop and maintain a competitive position in the economy because of social *or* economic disadvantage. See 13 C.F.R. § 124.8–1(c) (1978). Therefore, we find no indication that the SBA failed to follow its regulations in determining Scientific's eligibilty as an 8(a) concern.

We note that under P.L. 95–507, enacted October 24, 1978, 92 Stat. 1757, the standard for 8(a) eligibility was changed to require both economic and social disadvantage. See 15 U.S.C. 631(e)(2)(A). However, a firm previously granted 8(a) eligibility cannot be denied participation in the program for not meeting current eligibility requirements without first being afforded a hearing on the record in accordance with chapter 5 of title 5 of the United States Code. See sec. 202(a) of P.L. 95–507 (15 U.S.C. 637(a)) and implementing regulations, 44 Fed. Reg. 30672, May 29, 1979, sec. 124.1–1(e)(1)(i), (ii) and (2). In the absence of Scientific's eligibility being terminated by SBA in accordance with the law and implementing regulations, Scientific is eligible to participate in the 8(a) program. We understand that no contract has been entered into between the Air Force and the SBA. Therefore, by letter of today to the SBA, we are recommending that it review Scientific's eligibility based on social disadvantage alone to determine if it should be allowed to continue to participate in the 8(a) program in view of present law and regulations or if its participation should be terminated in accordance with the law and regulations.

Accordingly, the protest is denied in part and dismissed in part.

[B–194508]

Justice Department—Referrals—Compromises

Fine or penalty assessed administratively by State or local authority against Federal agency for violation of local air pollution law, atlhough it is claim against United States which local authority could sue to enforce, may not be referred to Attorney General for defense of imminent litigation if agency does not dispute basis for or amount of fine. Funds appropriated by 31 U.S.C. 724a for payment of compromise settlements, negotiated by Attorney General in connection with imminent litigation (28 U.S.C. 2414), are therefore not available to pay fine.

Appropriations — Availability — Expenses Incident to Specific Purposes—Necessary Expenses—Fines

Civil penalties imposed administratively on Federal facilities by State or local agencies for violations of local air pollution regulations must be paid from Federal agency's appropriation if incurred in the course of activities necessary and proper or incidental to fulfilling the purposes for which the appropriation was made. B–191747, June 6, 1978.

Courts — Judgments, Decrees, etc. — Payment — Indefinite Appropriation Availability—Judgments Against Government

Civil penalties imposed on Federal agencies by court after suit is brought against them for violation of local air pollution law, either in accordance with terms of consent decree or stipulated settlement, or as result of judgment on the merits, may be paid, upon proper certification by Attorney General (28 U.S.C. 2414), from permanent indefinite appropriation for judgments and compromise settlements established by 31 U.S.C. 724a.

In the matter of Civil Penalties Imposed on Federal Agencies for Violations of Local Air Quality Standards—Source of Funds for Payment, July 19, 1979:

The Assistant Attorney General, Land and Natural Resources Division, Department of Justice (Justice), requested our opinion on the available source of payment, in various circumstances, of civil penalties assessed against Federal facilities for violation of State or local air pollution regulations. (The United States was made subject to these penalties by section 118 of the Clean Air Act, as amended, 42 U.S.C. § 7418.)

The specific occurrences which precipitated Justice's request are the imposition of administrative penalties against the Department of the Navy (Navy) by two local air pollution control agencies, the Bay Area Air Pollution Control District in California and the Puget Sound Air Pollution Control Agency in Washington. The penalties were assessed for violations by several Navy vessels of the respective local air pollution regulations. Additionally, South Carolina has indicated that Navy's operation of steam-generating boilers in Charleston, South Carolina, has violated the State's air pollution regulations. South Carolina plans to file a civil action against Navy for such violations. In discussions of a negotiated settlement with Navy, the State apparently has said that it intends to require that Navy pay civil penalties as a condition of any settlement.

Navy has asked Justice to certify the penalties assessed in these three instances as compromise settlements to avoid imminent litigation, pursuant to 28 U.S.C. § 2414 (1976). Justice seeks our advice on whether administratively or judicially imposed penalties are payable under the procedures set forth in 28 U.S.C. § 2414.

Section 2414 of title 28 provides that compromise settlements by the Attorney General (or his designee) either of claims referred to him by Federal agencies for defense of imminent litigation, or of suits against the Government, shall be settled and paid in a manner similar to judgments, i.e., from the permanent indefinite appropriation made by 31 U.S.C. § 724a. Also, the Attorney General (or his designee) may certify that it is in the interest of the United States to pay "final judgments" by a State court or tribunal against the United States, upon which these also may be paid under the terms of 31 U.S.C. § 724a.

With a view to appropriate treatment of these and possible future situations, Justice has described four categories in which civil penalties for violation of State and local air pollution regulations may be assessed against Federal agencies and has asked which, if any, can be certified by the Attorney General under 28 U.S.C. § 2414. The first category consists of cases where the local administrative agency has the authority to impose a penalty by issuing a notice or an administrative order. Generally, payment is then due unless a request for a hearing is made. If the violator does not pay the penalty, the State usually has the right to go to court to collect the penalty. However, in the situation described by Justice, the Federal agency does not dispute its liability and agrees to pay the penalty. Thus, the question, as stated by Justice, is whether the payment of this kind of "purely administrative" fine can be accomplished as a compromise of imminent litigation within the meaning of 28 U.S.C. § 2414.

In the second category, the enforcement procedure is initiated by issuance of a notice of violation. Then a letter is sent to the violator notifying the violator that it is subject to a penalty under State law and that the State (or locality) may commence a civil action to assess penalties. The violator is advised that settlement may be made by payment of a penalty prior to filing of the civil suit. Again, the premise is that the Federal agency does not dispute its liability. Thus, the question is whether a fine assessed against a Federal agency (where the liability is undisputed) in order to avoid a threatened legal action to collect the fine is payable under 28 U.S.C. § 2414 as a compromise settlement.

The third category involves the payment of a fine in accordance with the terms of a consent decree or stipulated settlement filed in a State or Federal court. Justice has separated this category into three subcategories: (a) cases in which the civil suit seeks to collect an administratively assessed penalty which the violator has refused to pay; (b) cases in which there has been an attempt to settle on the part of the violator by payment of an agreed amount to the administrative agency prior to filing of the action; and (c) cases in which no attempt was made either to collect previously assessed fines or to settle the matter before the filing of an action seeking the imposition of a civil penalty for the violation. For each of these subcategories, the question is whether penalties paid in accordance with the terms of a consent decree or stipulated settlement are payable under 28 U.S.C. § 2414 as "final judgments" from the permanent indefinite "judgment fund" appropriation established by 31 U.S.C. § 724a.

Finally, the fourth category consists of cases in which a civil penalty is imposed against a Federal agency by a court after a trial or hearing on the merits of the case. This category is also subdivided into the three subcategories described above. As in category three, the question is whether penalties assessed against a Federal agency pursuant to a court order entered after a trial or hearing on the merits are "final judgments" within the meaning of 28 U.S.C. § 2414 and 31 U.S.C. § 724a.

Originally, judgments rendered against the United States were payable only upon enactment of specific appropriations for that purpose. Then, in 1956, section 1302 of the Supplemental Appropriation Act, 1957 (Pub. L. No. 84–814, 70 Stat. 694; 31 U.S.C. § 724a) was enacted, which established a permanent indefinite appropriation out of which judgments rendered against the United States not in excess of $100,000 were to be paid. In 1961, 31 U.S.C. § 724a and 28 U.S.C. § 2414 were amended to provide for the expeditious payment of compromise settlements made by the Attorney General or his designee in connection with imminent litigation in the same manner used to pay judgments. Pub. L. No. 87–187, August 30, 1961. (The $100,000 limit has since been removed.)

Justice asks whether what it describes as a "purely administrative" fine, in the first category, may be viewed as a compromise of imminent litigation within the meaning of 28 U.S.C. § 2414, and is therefore payable under the terms of that section. Section 2414 requires that there must be a compromise settlement of a claim, by the Attorney General (or his designee), by mutual concession. See generally *Newson* v. *Miller*, 42 Wash. 2d 727, 258 P.2d 812, 814 (1953). The compromise settlement must be made because resolution of the dispute otherwise seems possible only in court. That is, there must be a genuine disagreement or impasse. The claim must have been referred to the Attorney General "for defense of *imminent* litigation." *See* S. Rep. No. 733, 87th Cong., 1st Sess., *reprinted in* [1961] U.S. Code Cong. & Ad. News 2439, 2441. In the first category of cases described by Justice, there is no dispute as to liability, no reason to refuse to pay the fine, and therefore no reason for the agency to refer the matter to the Attorney General for defense of expected litigation. Agreement by the agency to pay the fine administratively assessed, therefore, is not a compromise settlement as contemplated by 28 U.S.C. § 2414, and funds from the permanent indefinite appropriation, 31 U.S.C. § 724a, are not available to pay it.

In the second category, Justice asks whether a State or locally assessed fine is payable under 28 U.S.C. § 2414 as a compromise settlement, where the State or locality serves notice on the Federal agency of the imposition of a penalty for a violation and of the State or locality's right to institute court proceedings to collect the penalty, assuming that the Federal agency does not dispute its liability. Only the Attorney General (or his designee) can enter into compromise settlements payable pursuant to 28 U.S.C. § 2414. In the circumstances which Justice describes as the second category, there are no issues to be resolved between the Federal and local agencies and therefore there is nothing to refer to the Attorney General. Hence the fine could not be paid pursuant to the procedure in 28 U.S.C. § 2414 in these circumstances.

In the first two categories, we find no significance, for present purposes, in the distinction between whether the fines are, as Justice characterizes the first category, "purely administrative," or whether, as in the second category, the State or locality assessing the fine advises that unless the penalty is paid, it may file suit. The important distinction, in terms of availability of funds under 31 U.S.C. § 724a, is not whether suit is expressly threatened as a collection procedure but whether the Federal agency contests its liability (or the amount of the assessment). If the agency concedes liability, then there is no controversy to be referred to the Attorney General for defense, as provided in 28 U.S.C. § 2414, and hence no basis for a compromise settlement by him.

In the first two categories, a penalty would be payable from the appropriate agency appropriation, assuming that the penalty was incurred in the course of activities necessary and proper or incidental to fulfilling the purposes for which the appropriation was made. *National Oceanic and Atmospheric Agency Payment of Civil Penalty for Violation of Local Air Quality Standards*, B–191747, June 6, 1978. If the agency requested an administrative hearing and after that hearing agreed to pay the penalty, that too would be payable from agency appropriations. However, if the agency disputed its liability for the levy, or if the agency and the State or local authority were unable to agree upon the amount to be paid, so that the matter was referred to the Attorney General for defense of an imminent law suit, and the Attorney General compromised the claim, the compromise settlement would be payable in accordance with 28 U.S.C. § 2414 and 31 U.S.C. § 724a. Payment of a compromise settlement under those circumstances, upon the Attorney General's submission to this Office, would be made from the permanent indefinite appropriation established by 31 U.S.C. § 724a.

Third, Justice asks whether a fine which is assessed against a Federal agency for air pollution violations in accordance with the terms of a consent decree or a stipulated settlement is payable under 28 U.S.C. § 2414 as a final judgment. As long as Justice (acting as the legal representative of the Federal agency in violation) and the State or local authority agree that the consent decree or stipulated settlement terminates the litigation, then payment of a consent decree or stipulated settlement may be made in the manner prescribed in 28 U.S.C. § 2414 from the appropriation established by 31 U.S.C. § 724a.

Justice asks if the answer to this question is changed by varying circumstances existing before suit is brought. These circumstances—whether the violator has either refused to pay or has unsuccessfully sought to settle, or whether there has been no previous attempt to collect or to settle (described above as subcategories (a), (b), and (c))—do not affect our answer.

Finally Justice asks whether civil penalties imposed against a Federal agency by a court after a trial or a hearing on the merits are payable as final judgments under 28 U.S.C. § 2414. The answer is yes, provided the Attorney General makes the required certification. As with the third question, this result is unaffected by circumstances existing before suit is brought. It is immaterial whether the court adopted the administratively determined fine in its disposition of the case or determined the amount of the fine *de novo*. A money judgment, when it is deemed final, is payable under 28 U.S.C. § 2414.

[B–195070]

Small Business Administration — Authority — Small Business Concerns—Allocation of 8(a) Subcontracts

Determination to set-aside procurement under section 8(a) of Small Business Act is matter for contracting agency and SBA, and will not be reviewed by General Accounting Office in absence of showing of fraud or bad faith on part of Government officials.

Contracts — Awards — Small Business Concerns — Procurement Under 8(a) Program—Civil Rights Act—Compliance

Although protester asserts that SBA 8(a) program violates Civil Rights Act of 1964 because of racial discrimination, courts have held that there is no merit to such assertion since eligibility standard of program is not defined racially but by social or economic disadvantage.

In the matter of American Laundry, July 23, 1979:

American Laundry, a nonminority firm, protests the setting aside for exclusive minority small business participation invitation for bids (IFB) No. DABT31–79–R–0101, issued by the Department of the Army (Army), Fort Leonard Wood, Missouri, for the operation of the base laundry/dry cleaning plant.

The protester asserts that the Army set-aside was improper because American Laundry allegedly received assurances from the Army in January 1977, after having furnished the Army a firm price quotation on the work, that it would be included in "any such potential contract." Further, American Laundry contends that the section 8(a) program illegally discriminates against nonminorities and violates the Civil Rights Act of 1964, 42 U.S. Code 2000a note.

Section 8(a) of the Small Business Act (15 U.S.C. § 637(a), as amended by Pub. L. 95–507, October 24, 1978, 92 Stat. 1757), authorizes the SBA to enter into contracts with any Government agency having procurement powers. The contracting officer of the procuring agency is authorized in his discretion to let the contract to SBA. In light of that discretionary authority, we do not review determinations to award contracts under section 8(a) unless there is a showing of fraud on the part of Government officials or such willful disregard of the facts as to necessarily imply bad faith. See *Chemical Technology, Inc.,* B–190165, January 18, 1978, 78–1 CPD 46; *Jets Services, Inc.,* B–186066, May 4, 1976, 76–1 CPD 300. No such showing has been made here.

The alleged promise made by the Army in January 1977 to include American Laundry in a potential contract and the instant action more than 2 years later, to set aside the procurement for small business participation, does not in our opinion constitute a *prima facie* case of bad faith or fraud.

With regard to American Laundry's allegation that the 8(a) program violates the Civil Rights Act of 1964, because it discriminates on the grounds of race, the court held in *Fortec Constructors v. Kleppe,* 350 F. Supp. 171 (1972), that the eligibility standard of the program is not defined racially but by social or economic disadvantage. The court further stated that there is no merit to an assertion that the program was designed for awarding contracts on the grounds of race, which would violate the Act.

We point out that the section 8(a) program is designed to encourage the fostering and promotion of minority business enterprises, and has been upheld by the courts. See *Ray Baillie Trash Hauling, Inc. v. Kleppe,* 477 F. 2d 696 (5th Cir. 1973). The fact that the program operates to the monetary detriment of a particular nonminority firm does not affect the validity of the program or of a specific set-aside.

See *Data Controls/North, Inc.*, B–192342, July 21, 1978, 78–2 CPD 62. The protest is dismissed.

[B–192975]

Military Personnel—Reservists—Retirement—Qualifying Service

Air Force Reserve major generals who have not been eliminated for years of service under 10 U.S.C. 8852 prior to reaching age 60 may receive retirement point credit for service performed after they have attained retirement eligibility under Chapter 67 of title 10, U.S. Code, only if their retention in active status thereafter is approved by the Secretary under 10 U.S.C. 676.

In the matter of Air Force Reserve Major Generals, July 25, 1979:

This action concerns the entitlement of Reserve major generals not on extended active duty to receive credit for service actually performed after they reach age 60 for the purpose of computing their Reserve retirement benefits under Chapter 67, title 10, United States Code.

The matter was presented in a letter dated September 20, 1978, from the Assistant Secretary of the Air Force (Manpower, Reserve Affairs and Installations), requesting an advance decision (DOD MPAC Control No. SS–AF–1307).

The following specific question is asked:

Is Secretary of the Air Force approval required (under 10 U.S.C. 676) for the award of creditable retirement points to Reserve major generals for service between ages 60 and 62?

Although most Air Force Reserve officers must retire at age 60, under the provisions of 10 U.S.C. 8844, commissioned officers of the Air Force in the Reserve grade of major general may remain in an active status under certain conditions until age 62. Age 60 is also the time when a Reserve otherwise eligible may qualify for retired pay under Chapter 67. However, it is suggested that sections 8844 and 8852 may permit credit for all service of Reserve major generals between ages 60 and 62 for Chapter 67 retirement computation purposes.

On the other hand it is pointed out that when those provisions are considered in connection with the provisions of 10 U.S.C. 676 and 1331, the same conclusion is not necessarily reached. Section 676 authorized the Secretary of the service concerned to retain on active duty any person who has qualified for retired pay under Chapter 67 and provides that "a member so retained shall be credited with that service for all purposes." Section 1331 of title 10—a part of Chapter 67—provides that the date of entitlement to such retired pay is the date upon which the individual has satisfied all of the conditions for such retired pay, among which is that the individual has attained age 60.

The Air Force has taken the position that Reserve major generals may not be authorized additional retirement credit for service beyond age 60 unless it is approved by the Secretary under 10 U.S.C. 676. The Air Force position is apparently based in part on certain language contained in several decisions of this Office, and reportedly is also supported by an opinion of the Office of the Army Judge Advocate General.

The crux of the matter is whether a Reserve major general, having qualified for retired pay, must be retained by the Secretary under 10 U.S.C. 676 after he reaches age 60 in order to qualify for further award of creditable service for retirement, or whether he has an independent right under 10 U.S.C. 8844 to credit for service until he reaches age 62.

The basic provisions regarding the retention of Air Force Reserve major generals are those in 10 U.S.C. 8844 and 8852. Those provisions were derived from sections 523(b) and 524(a) of the Reserve Officer Personnel Act of 1954, September 3, 1954, ch. 1257, 68 Stat. 1147, 1181–1182. Section 8844 provides for the elimination, by retirement if possible, of major generals at age 62; however, section 8852 requires the elimination (retirement) of major generals who have 35 years of service and 5 years in grade without regard to age. Exceptions to section 8852 have been authorized for State adjutant generals and assistant adjutant generals; also, 10 additional Reserve major generals may be retained by the Secretary of the Air Force, but not beyond the age of 62. Thus, a major general remains on active status until age 62 only if not sooner required to be removed under section 8852.

Regarding major generals who are not required to be removed prior to reaching age 62, the question is whether 10 U.S.C. 676 prevents crediting service after age 60 for retired pay computation under Chapter 67, in the absence of the Secretary's approval as required in that section.

Section 676, although not a part of Chapter 67 as codified, was enacted as section 302(e) of the Army and Air Force Vitalization and Retirement Equalization Act of 1948, approved June 29, 1948, ch. 708, 62 Stat. 1081, 1088. As such it was an integral part of the law which established Reserve retirement. We have consistently interpreted section 676 in that light and have held that credit for Reserve duty performed after qualification for Reserve retired pay at age 60 (assuming the individual is otherwise qualified) may not be given in the absence of approval by the Secretary concerned as provided for in that section. See 38 Comp. Gen. 647 (1959) ; 50 *id.* 428 (1970). Compare *Grahl* v. *United States*, 167 Ct. Cl. 80 (1964). Further, an individual is considered to have qualified for retired pay by meeting all requirements including attaining age 60 even though application for retired pay has not been made. 38 Comp. Gen. 159 (1958).

Therefore, major generals not retired prior to reaching age 60 and who are otherwise qualified for Chapter 67 retirement upon reaching age 60 are not entitled to credit for service performed after they reach that age for purposes of retirement pay computation unless they are retained in the service by the Secretary as provided in 10 U.S.C. 676. In that connection an individual specifically retained in service as one of the 10 major generals authorized to be retained until age 62, under 10 U.S.C. 8852(b), would also qualify as retained in service for purposes of 10 U.S.C. 676. See 38 Comp. Gen. 146, 152; 38 *id.* 647, 652.

The submission is answered accordingly.

[B-195163]

Appropriations—Fiscal Year—Availability Beyond—Federal Aid, Grants, etc.—Amendment

ACTION's proposed grant modification to expand the area from which enrollees in a demonstration youth employment project are drawn to include an additional county would not enlarge the grant's scope because the statutory authority for the grant (section 348(a) of the Comprehensive Employment and Training Act of 1973, as added by the Youth Employment and Demonstration Project Act of 1977, Pub. L. 95–93, 91 Stat. 645. 29 U.S.C.A. 849g) and the interagency agreement with the Department of Labor delegating this authority to ACTION support the conclusion that the proposed amendment is necessary to carry out the original purpose of the grant. Accordingly, such an amendment would not require the obligation of current fiscal year appropriated funds.

In the matter of ACTION—Availability of Appropriation—Grant Modification, July 25, 1979:

This decision to the Director of ACTION is in response to a request from the General Counsel of that agency for an opinion on whether a proposed modification would, in effect, constitute a new grant that requires the obligation of current fiscal year funds, or whether the prior year funds, originally obligated for the grant, may be used to fund the modification. Under the circumstances of this case and for the reasons given below, we do not believe a new grant will be created by the proposed modification; ACTION may therefore make the change without obligating current fiscal year funds.

In fiscal year 1978, the Youth Community Services Demonstration Project/Syracuse (YCS/S) received an ACTION grant to conduct a "community service volunteer program" that would provide 16 to 21 year old youths with an experience that would "aid their transition to regular employment." The grant is authorized under section 348(a) of the Comprehensive Employment and Training Act of 1973 (as added by section 201 of the Youth Employment and Demonstration Project

Act of 1977 (the Act), Pub. L. No. 95–93, 91 Stat. 645, August 5, 1977, 29 U.S.C.A. § 894g). Section 348(a) is a Department of Labor program, but ACTION made the grant, using funds appropriated to Labor, under an interagency agreement with Labor as expressly authorized by paragraph (3) of subsection 348(a). The funds in question are no longer available for obligation.

By the terms of the grant proposal, the grant program was to take place in the city of Syracuse and in Onondaga County, New York, but it was determined after the award that the grantee would be unable to recruit the specified number of volunteers without expansion of the geographical area. In order to allow the grantee to recruit the number of volunteers agreed to in the grant, ACTION, with the agreement of the Department of Labor and the grantee, proposes to expand the grant target area to include adjacent Oswego County.

The Director of Contracts and Grants Management for ACTION has questioned the grant amendment on the following basis:

> The purpose of the project was to establish a demonstration project to test the concept of a National Youth Service. To achieve this purpose the City of Syracuse and Onondaga County was chosen as the appropriate site. The Grant application submitted and funded includes the following excerpts:
>
> (a) "The purpose of the grant is to offer a vehicle to provide needed community services to youths of Syracuse and Onondaga County * * *"
>
> (b) "The target area encompassed by the proposed project is the area of Onondaga County in general and more specifically the City of Syracuse, hereinafter referred to as 'Greater Syracuse'."
>
> (c) "A YCS [Youth Community Service] Volunteer will be a 16 through 21 year old resident of the Greater Syracuse area * * *"
>
> (d) "Given both the needs and resources of Syracuse and Onondaga County the purpose of the YCS/S[yracuse] Demonstration Project is to offer a vehicle for youths to provide needed community services."
>
> (e) "Unemployed youth in Syracuse and Onondaga County will respond to the appeal of a full year of community service experience."
>
> The foregoing excerpts clearly illustrate that the funds obligated were intended for a demonstration project in Syracuse and Onondaga County. I can find no reference to indicate any intent to have the project encompass Oswego County. This would clearly indicate that the proposed expansion of the project to cover Oswego County constitutes the equiva'ent of "new procurement" and requires funds available for purposes of obligation when that obligation is effected.

A memorandum prepared by the ACTION General Counsel's staff, however, reaches a contrary conclusion.

> In summary, while the grant proposal unquestionably refers to the City of Syracuse and the surrounding Onondaga County as the target area, it appears that these geographic limitations were never perceived by any of the parties as essential elements of the purposes for which the grant was made. Selection of the target area referred to above appears to have been simply the best estimate of the project managers as to the population base which would produce the required number of volunteers. All grant documents are consistent in stating that the purposes of the grant were the placement of approximately 1650 young people in community service positions through a novel method of recruitment, and the testing of a model of youth community service which might later be used elsewhere in a projected national youth service program. The project documents are also clear in their recognition that changes might be required in non-essential elements of the project design to effect the desired result.

For the above reasons I conclude that the extension of the project into Oswego County is simply a modification of a non-essential element of the project model within the scope of the original grant of a kind which was authorized by the grant document, and does not amount to a change of scope which would require the obligation of additional funds.

The issue is whether the proposed modification of the geographical area from which project enrollees are recruited will change the scope of the grant.

We recently summarized the general rule in 57 Comp. Gen. 459, 460 (1978) as follows:

It is well established that agencies have no authority to amend grants so as to change their scope after the appropriations under which they have been made have ceased to be available for obligation. See, for example, 39 Comp. Gen. 296 (1959). The substitution of one grant for another extinguishes the old obligation and creates a new one. The new obligation is chargeable to the appropriation available at the time the new obligation is created. See 41 Comp. Gen. 134 (1961); 39 *id.* 296 (1959); 37 *id.* 861 (1958); and B–164031(5), June 25, 1976.

As we said in one of the cited cases (39 Comp. Gen. 296, 298 (1959)):

The execution of a grant based upon a proposal containing specific objectives, research methods to be followed, and estimates of project costs would ordinarily give rise to a definite and maximum obligation of the United States. To enlarge such a grant beyond the scope of the original is to create an additional obligation and must be considered as giving rise to a new grant.

A shift in the community served by a grant may also alter the scope of the grant. B–164031(5), June 25, 1976. We held in that case that where the originally intended recipient community was unable to use a grant, to make the grant to another community, for the same purpose, was not a "replacement" grant but a new and separate undertaking. This is not necessarily so in all cases, however. We have held that in the case of a joint application where the designated grantee was replaced by the other applicant that a new grant was not created because "the alternative proposal amounts to a replacement grant rather than a new and separate undertaking." 57 Comp. Gen. 205, 208–209 (1978).

In the instant case, there would be no change in the original grantee. Moreover, a total obligation has been recorded against funds which were available for the grant, in an amount sufficient to fund the participation of 1650 youths. Thus, the proposed modification of the grant would also not change the amount originally expected to be spent. Finally, the same geographical area originally named to receive services will continue to do so. The only question is whether that area may be expanded under the stated circumstances.

In order to determine the scope of this grant we look at the authorizing legislation, the interagency agreement as well as the actual grant documents.

Section 348(a) of the Act provides authority for the Government:

* * * to test new approaches for dealing with the unemployment problems of youth and to enable eligible participants to prepare for, enhance their prospects

for, or secure employment in occupations through which they may reasonably be expected to advance to productive working lives.

The interagency agreement between Labor and ACTION stated the purpose of the proposed project as follows:

> The purpose of the demonstration project covered by this Interagency Agreement is to explore the feasibility and the effectiveness of implementation of the "national youth service" concept by means of having an ACTION selected local non-profit organization arrange community service internships (a) for unemployed young persons residing in a selected area who are 16–21 years old, from all economic backgrounds, and wish to volunteer for such public service, and (b) designed to meet local community service needs, and at the same time, provide youth volunteers with an experience which will aid their transition to regular employment and advancement in the work world.

The ACTION General Counsel further summarizes the agreement in a staff memorandum as follows:

> The agreement then lists seven major objectives of the demonstration, and seven "major tasks of ACTION." None of these specific tasks or objectives involves geographic limitations. One of the tasks, however, is to arrange for "about 1650 community service volunteer internships for youth."

The grant proposal also emphasizes the demonstration aspects of the grant. The first sentence of the grantee's proposal says:

> The ACTION Agency proposes to test a national youth service concept by developing and implementing a Youth Community Services (YCS) Demonstration Project in an urban setting.

The introduction to the grantee's proposal also says that ACTION approached city and county officials to inform them that they were under consideration as a potential grant site for a demonstration project and that the grantee in preparing the proposal understands that—

> * * * because the YCS/S project is to be a demonstration of principles and procedures related to the development of a larger National Youth Service policy, changes in certain aspects of the proposal will be necessitated by the realities of experience as project implementation occurs.

Further, the project goals and objectives are generally described as follows:

> Given both the needs and resources of Syracuse and Onondaga County, the purpose of the YCS/S Demonstration Project is to offer a vehicle for youth to provide needed community services while enabling them to gain the necessary knowledge, skills and attitudes to assist in their subsequent transition into additional education/training or into the adult labor market while, at the same time, to test and demonstrate the concepts, policies, and procedures which would support the development of a nationwide youth service program.
>
> *The primary goal of the YCS/S Demonstration Project will be to enable up to 1650 youth, ages 16 through 21, to provide a year of quality service to their community.*
>
>   *   *   *   *   *   **
>
> The secondary goal of the YCS/S Demonstration Project will be to demonstrate that youth community service is an effective way of developing experiences which will aid the participants' transition to regular employment and advancement in the work world and, therefore, should be replicated on a national basis.
>
>   *   *   *   *   *   **
>
> A final goal of the YCS/S Demonstration Project is to develop in youth a feeling of self-esteem and self-worth, as well as to give them greater community awareness and responsibility. [Italic supplied.]

While it is not entirely clear how ACTION arrived at the figure of 1650 volunteers for the project, the figure seems to be related to the need for a large enough base of volunteers to provide meaningful demonstration test results. The ACTION proposal to Labor describes the demonstration objectives as follows:

1. To test the appeal of a full scale community service volunteer program among the unemployed youth of the respective community.
2. To determine the capability of a community to identify viable community service roles that volunteer youth could fill.
3. To identify successful components of the pilot program that could be replicated for a National Youth Service program.
4. To determine what effect the participation of youth in a volunteer community service program has on their post program employment.
5. To contrast the YCS pilot program with other traditional youth manpower programs.
6. To test the capacity of local agencies to cooperate in the implementation and management of the YCS project.
7. To assess the effect of in-service training and external education opportunities on the volunteer and on their performance in the community service environment.

At too low a level of volunteer presence, these goals, in ACTION's view, cannot be reached. As ACTION's proposal to Labor indicates, an earlier project of 372 young people in another city was too small for demonstration purposes. According to ACTION, YCS/S has only produced about 800 volunteers at the present time. ACTION has concluded, according to the General Counsel's staff memorandum, that the 800 existing volunteers do not reach "* * * the quantity or quality of participants needed to complete the demonstration." This 800 figure is less than half the consistently stated project goal, and we have no reason to question ACTION's judgment.

Further, the ACTION proposal to Labor and the YCS/S proposal to ACTION both discuss the placement of small groups of volunteers with 600 (ACTION) and 350 (YCS/S) local work stations that would provide enough placements for 1650 volunteers. The number of work sites, coupled with the project goal of providing "1650 volunteer work years to a medium size city" in order to "expand and provide needed community services" translate into a need for a sufficient number of volunteers to man the available work sites. Accordingly, efforts to expand the number of volunteers up to the project goal are consistent with the purposes of the grant.

Our earlier decisions concerning changes in grants after the period of availability of the grant funds for obligation has ended have identified three closely related areas of concern:

(1) whether a *bona fide* need for the grant project continues;
(2) whether the purpose of the grant will remain the same; and
(3) whether the revised grant will have the same scope as the original grant.

The scope of a grant grows out of the grant purposes. These purposes must be referred to in order to identify those aspects of a grant that make up the substantial and material features of a particular grant which in turn fix the scope of the Government's obligation. In this case, the *bona fide* need for the project continues. The Government's purpose in making the grant will not change if the amendment is accepted. The Government's purpose in making the grant is expressed most clearly in the interagency agreement. It is clear that the overriding purpose of this grant was to obtain test results for use by the Government from the demonstration. In defining this purpose, a specific number of volunteers—1650—was considered to be necessary. The geographic site specifications constitute an initial estimate of an area which was expected to produce the required number of volunteers, but which has not done so to date. Clearly, a larger recruitment area is necessary. According to the grant proposal, the Syracuse Standard Metropolitan Statistical Area covers Onondaga, Oswego and Madison Counties. Presumably the inclusion of one or all three of the counties in this metropolitan area would meet the requirements of the interagency agreement as explained in ACTION's proposal to the Department of Labor. Accordingly, if the scope of the grant is considered from the standpoint of the Government need and purpose in making it, the precise geographic boundaries would not appear to be a material aspect of the grant—one upon which approval or disapproval depended. Viewed as a whole, the proposed grant amendment if adopted will not create a new or separate undertaking, and will not enlarge the scope of the grant. Therefore, the proposed amendment will not require the obligation of current fiscal year funds.

[B–195443]

Bonds—Savings—Allotments—Conversion to Series EE Bonds

Incident to introduction of Series EE Savings Bonds to replace Series E Bonds being purchased by payroll allotment, Treasury proposes to substitute Series EE Bonds based on a "negative-response" method, whereby the Series EE Bonds will be substituted unless the employee terminates his allotment. Since the Series EE Bonds are a continuation without major substantive change of the Series E Bonds, the negative-response method of conversion is a proper means of continuing the employee's voluntary allotment under the Payroll Savings Plan. The proposal is approved.

In the matter of Department of the Treasury—Allotments for Series EE Savings Bonds, July 27, 1979:

On January 10, 1979, the Secretary of the Treasury announced the introduction of new Series EE and HH U.S. Savings Bonds to replace the current Series E and H Bonds. During the period from January

2 through June 30, 1980, payroll sales of Series E Bonds for Federal employees will be converted to the new Series EE Bonds. The Treasurer of the United States, by letter of July 16, 1979, has asked that this Office consider the legal sufficiency of the Department's proposal to use a "negative-response" method of automatic conversion whereby an employee who is currently being issued Series E Bonds under the Payroll Savings Plan will instead be issued Series EE Bonds unless the employee takes affirmative action to terminate the allotment. The Payroll Savings Plan is administered under Executive Order 9135, April 16, 1972.

To accomplish the conversion to Series EE Bonds, Treasury proposes to require that each individual employee be notified of the upcoming changes by means of a message to appear on or as an attachment to his Leave and Earnings Statement for at least four consecutive pay periods prior to the conversion date. During the same period a well-planned publicity campaign will be conducted to inform all Americans of the features of the new EE Bonds. We assume that Federal agencies will be advised that absent a Leave and Earnings Statement alternative methods should be used to inform employees of the change, and that supplemental notification procedures may be used to the extent deemed necessary. Any employee who is dissatisfied with the terms of the conversion may cancel his participation in the Payroll Savings Plan or may adjust his allotment. The Treasurer states that the Series EE Bonds are substantially similar to the Series E Bonds, with the interest rate and interest curve identical. She summarizes the main differences between the two series as follows:

Series EE Bonds will sell for 50 percent face value, compared to 75 percent for Series E Bonds.
The minimum denomination of Series EE Bonds will be $50. The current $25 E Bond will be eliminated.
Due to the increased discount purchase price the EE Bond will mature in 11 years, compared to five years for the current E Bond.
The retention period for Series EE Bonds will be increased to six months from the current two months for E Bonds.

Under the proposed conversion, Bond inscriptions on the Series EE Bonds would remain identical to those on the Series E Bonds the employee had been receiving, allotment amounts would remain the same or be decreased and, except in the case of employees now purchasing $25 Series E Bonds, employees would receive Series EE Bonds of the same purchase price or less. Also, the interest rate and interest curve will remain the same. With respect to those employees now purchasing $25 Series E Bonds, the Treasurer explains:

* * * A $25 Series E Bond is currently purchased for $18.75. However, the minimum denomination Series EE Bond will be $50, selling for $25. Although in this case the purchase price of a Bond would be increased by $6.25, the allotment amount per pay period will never be increased.

On June 28, 1979, the Department of the Treasury published in the Federal Register proposed regulations governing Savings Bonds, Series EE and HH. The Department intends the new Bonds to be a continuation of the old Bonds, without major substantive changes. As stated at 44 Fed. Reg. 37826 (1979):

> It is the intention and expectation of the Department of the Treasury that these new series of savings bonds will be treated similarly to the other series of savings bonds * * *. In other words, as mentioned, the new bonds are a continuation, without major substantive change, of the old bonds. The changes that are proposed to be made generally affect the ways in which owners may facilitate transactions involving bonds, rather than with the substantive property rights.

The Treasurer believes that the notice period of at least 2 months will give sufficient opportunity to any employee who is not satisfied with the terms of the conversion to cancel or adjust his allotment by submitting a new authorization for Standard Form 1192. The Treasurer requests our approval of the conversion plan on the basis of the foregoing information.

As precedent for the use of a negative-response system where an allotment is continued under different terms, the Treasurer refers to 5 C.F.R. § 890.301(k) which provides that when one option of a particular health benefits plan is discontinued, enrolled employees who do not change plans will be considered enrolled in the remaining option of the plan. While the Health Benefits Registration Form executed by an employee to enroll or change enrollment in a health benefit plan differs from the Standard Form 1192 executed by employees for purchase of U.S. Savings Bonds in that the latter is specific as to the dollar amount to be allotted each pay period and as to the Bond denomination and series, we believe that it is proper to treat substitution of Series EE Bonds for Series E Bonds in a similar manner.

By his execution of a Standard Form 1192 for the Series E Bond, the employee has expressed his desire to participate in the Payroll Savings Plan. Since the Series E Bonds will no longer be issued, the employee's participation will be terminated unless his allotment is converted to the Series EE Bond. Because the Series EE Bond is a continuation without major substantive change of the Series E Bonds, we believe that the negative-response method of conversion proposed by the Department of Treasury is proper insofar as proper steps are taken to notify the employees of the conversion plan. *Cf.* 42 Comp. Gen. 663 (1963).

There will undoubtedly be some cases in which employees do not receive notice in time to permit them to cancel their allotment because of dissatisfaction with the terms of the Series EE Bonds. Therefore, we believe that for a reasonable temporary period employees should be permitted to redeem Series EE Bonds at any time after the 2-month retention period required for Series E Bonds and prior to expiration of the 6-month redemption period for Series EE Bonds.

The proposal of the Department of Treasury for automatic conversion of payroll allotments from Series E Bonds to Series EE Bonds is approved in accordance with the foregoing.

[B-192494]

Leaves of Absence—Forfeiture—Administrative Error—Restored Leave

Approved leave was forfeited due to exigency of public business. Central Intelligence Agency employee's request for restoration was denied by CIA because exigency determination was not made by proper official in advance of cancellation of leave. Employee timely requested leave in writing and agency's failure to present case to proper official for exigency determination was administrative error which caused the loss of leave. Employee is entitled to restoration of forfeited leave. 5 U.S.C. 6304(d)(1)(A).

In the matter of Norbert A. Shepanek—Restoration of Forfeited Annual Leave, July 30, 1979:

This decision concerns the question of whether forfeited annual leave may be restored under provisions of 5 U.S.C. § 6304(d)(1).

Mr. Norbert A. Shepanek, an employee of the Central Intelligence Agency (CIA), claims restoration of previously scheduled annual leave that he forfeited due to exigencies of the public business. Mr. Shepanek's claim was forwarded for decision by our Claims Division. In connection with this claim, the CIA, through its Assistant General Counsel, John A. Rizzo, has requested our guidance concerning the standards the CIA should follow in formulating internal administrative policies governing the restoration of forfeited annual leave.

In January of 1975 Mr. Shepanek was assigned to the Coordination Staff of the Office of the Inspector General which was created to process CIA material for the Presidential Commission on Intelligence, otherwise known as the Rockefeller Commission. Although the Coordination Staff was abolished in August 1975, Mr. Shepanek continued to act as a liaison between the CIA and the Senate Select Committee on Intelligence, the House Select Committee on Intelligence, and the Department of Justice. On September 25, 1975, Mr. Shepanek submitted a Standard Form 71 requesting annual leave from October 20 to October 31, 1975. His supervisor approved this leave but later cancelled it due to the continuing House and Senate investigations. Subsequently, Mr. Shepanek submitted another Form 71 requesting annual leave from December 8, 1975, to January 2, 1976. His supervisor approved that request on November 6, 1975, but again found it necessary to cancel the leave. As a result Mr. Shepanek forfeited 104 hours of excess leave which could not be carried into the 1976 leave year.

On January 22, 1976, Mr. Shepanek made an application for restoration of his forfeited leave, supported by a statement from his supervisor that the leave had been cancelled due to a public exigency. On June 10, 1976, the Director of Finance approved the creation of a restored leave account. On January 7, 1977, however, the Director of Finance informed Mr. Shepanek that the June 1976 action was in error since the exigency determination had not been made in writing by the proper agency official in advance of the cancellation of leave.

For the reasons stated below, we hold that Mr. Shepanek is entitled to have the 104 hours of annual leave restored.

Forfeited annual leave can be restored under the limited circumstances set out in section 6304(d)(1) of title 5, United States Code (Supp. III, 1973), which provides:

> (d)(1) Annual leave which is lost by operation of this section because of—
> (A) administrative error when the error causes a loss of annual leave otherwise accruable after June 30, 1960;
> (B) exigencies of the public business when the annual leave was scheduled in advance; or,
> (O) sickness of the employee when the annual leave was scheduled in advance;
> shall be restored to the employee.

The Civil Service Commission (now Office of Personnel Management) regulations concerning restoration of leave are contained in Volume 5 of the Code of Federal Regulations. With regard to the officials authorized to make determinations of public exigency, section 630.305 provides that:

> Before annual leave may be restored under section 6304 of title 5, United States Code, the determination that an exigency is of major importance and that therefore annual leave may not be used by employees to avoid forfeiture must be made by the head of the agency or someone designated by him to act for him on this matter. The designated official may not be more than two organizational levels below the head of the agency at the central headquarters levels, or more than one organizational level below the head of a major field headquarters or major field installation. Except where made by the head of the agency, the determination may not be made by any official in the immediate organizational unit affected by the exigency or by any official whose leave would be affected by the decision.

Although the properly designated official ratified in writing the exigency determination made by Mr. Shepanek's supervisor, the CIA felt this did not qualify the leave for restoration in light of paragraph 5a(2)(c) of the attachment to FPM letter 630–22, January 11, 1974, which provides under the heading *"CSC Guidelines"* that:

> The determination that the exigency is of such importance that employees cannot be excused from duty for the duration is a separate decision. Normally this decision is to be made in advance of the cancellation of scheduled leave, or the assignment of employees who will be affected by the work requirement generated by the exigency. Only a bona fide emergency would preclude making the decision in advance.

In several recent cases we have allowed restoration of leave where an employee submitted a Form 71 requesting leave but the supervisor refused to schedule it due to a public exigency. We stated that the failure to schedule the leave constituted an administrative error and leave could therefore be restored under 5 U.S.C. § 6304(d)(1)(A). See *William D. Norsworthy*, 57 Comp. Gen. 325 (1978) and *John Connor*, B–189085, April 3, 1978. In an earlier case, *Michael Dana*, B–187104, April 1, 1977 (56 Comp. Gen. 470), we held that annual leave forfeited due to exigencies of the public business but not scheduled in advance by employees could not be restored under 5 U.S.C. § 6304(d)(1)(B) since the scheduling requirement was mandatory. We held that failure of the agency to inform the employees of the scheduling requirement did not constitute "administrative error" for purposes of 5 U.S.C. § 6304(d)(1)(A) stating that, "[e]ven if they have no actual knowledge, employees are charged with constructive knowledge of statutory requirements pertaining to them and of the implementing regulations authorized to be issued by statute."

The CIA feels that despite our holdings in *Norsworthy* and *Connor* the quoted guideline, requiring a determination of exigency prior to cancellation of leave, prevents restoration of Mr. Shepanek's leave. Furthermore, the CIA believes that in light of *Dana* Mr. Shepanek must be charged with constructive knowledge of the requirements of that regulation.

In our *Norsworthy* decision we affirmed the *Dana* decision, which held that, for restoration under subsection (B) or (C) of 5 U.S.C. § 6304(d)(1), the annual leave must have been scheduled in advance. However, we construed subsections (B) and (C) as creating a right to restoration of annual leave when it was lost because of a public exigency or sickness and was not lost due to the fault of the employee. Consequently, when an employee submits a "bona fide, formal and timely request for leave," there can be no discretion whether to schedule the leave or not. The agency must approve and schedule the leave either at the time requested by the employee or, if that is not possible because of the agency's workload, at some other time. In the case of an exigency of public business the matter must be submitted to the designated official for his determination. See Matter of *Joseph Hanyok*, B–187104, September 28, 1978. Since Mr. Shepanek submitted a formal and timely request for leave which was approved by his supervisor, the question of whether a public exigency existed should have been submitted to the proper official when his supervisor cancelled that leave. Therefore, because that question was not submitted, Mr. Shepanek is entitled to restoration of the forfeited leave under 5 U.S.C. § 6304(d)(1)(A). We do not feel that it is appropriate to charge an employee with constructive knowledge of a requirement which is the responsibility of an agency official to satisfy.

The CIA has also requested our guidance concerning the action it should take on a number of cases where it denied requests to restore leave from its employees on grounds substantially identical to the grounds upon which it denied Mr. Shepanek's request. The CIA is concerned about the proper disposition of these cases because the record in *Norsworthy* and *Connor* showed that the proper official would have determined an exigency existed had the matter been presented to him, while in the subject cases, the official who would have determined the existence of the exigency is in most instances no longer with the agency.

In *Hanyok* we held that if an agency is unable, due to a public exigency, to reschedule requested leave during the current leave year, the failure to submit the matter to the designated official for his determination of exigency constitutes an administrative error which would support a restoration of the requested leave pursuant to 5 U.S.C. § 6304(d)(1)(A). Therefore, it is not necessary for an employee, in order to have forfeited leave restored, to show that the proper official would have determined there was a public exigency. If there is no exigency, the agency has no discretion concerning whether or not to schedule the leave. Thus, even where there is no evidence in the record that the official would have made an exigency determination had the matter been presented to him, failure to submit the matter must be considered an administrative error.

If any of the employees concerned request that the CIA restore their leave, however, they must show that they submitted a formal and timely request for leave in order to satisfy the congressional intention that § 6304(d)(1) would authorize restoration of leave lost through no fault of the employee, but would not authorize restoration of leave lost because the employee of his own volition chose not to use it. See *Norsworthy* and *Hanyok*, *supra*.

[B-195418]

Federal Reserve—Board of Governors—Employees—Civil Service Reform Act of 1978—Applicability

Federal Reserve Act, as amended, expressly excepts the appointment and compensation of all employees of the Board of Governors, Federal Reserve System, from the provisions of the civil service laws and regulations. The Act must be given priority over a subsequently enacted statute applicable to Federal agencies generally, absent a clear indication that the Congress intended otherwise. Hence, the provisions of Civil Service Reform Act of 1978 establishing a Senior Executive Service do not apply to the employees of the Board.

In the matter of Federal Reserve Board—Applicability of Senior Executive Service, July 30, 1979:

By letter dated July 10, 1979, the General Counsel of the Office of Personnel Management (OPM) has requested our opinion whether the employees of the Board of Governors of the Federal Reserve System are subject to the provisions of Title IV of the Civil Service Reform Act of 1978, Public Law No. 95–454, October 13, 1978, 92 Stat. 1111, 5 U.S.C. § 3131 *et seq.*, establishing a Government-wide Senior Executive Service (SES), designed to insure the high quality of Government executives.

It is the position of OPM that the employees of the Board of Governors of the Federal Reserve System ("Federal Reserve Board") are subject to the provisions of Title IV of the Civil Service Reform Act governing the Senior Executive Service. OPM has found that the Board falls under the SES criteria contained in 5 U.S.C. § 3132(a), and thus is included under SES, unless excluded by the President pursuant to 5 U.S.C. § 3132(c). OPM points to Executive Order No. 9004, dated December 30, 1941, which placed all positions under the Board of Governors in Schedule A, Positions Excepted From Examination, which thereby excluded all Board employees from the competitive service. OPM argues that but for this Executive order, the Board's employees would have been swept into the competitive service by Executive Order No. 8743, dated April 23, 1941. Executive Order No. 8743 provided that all offices and positions in the executive civil service are covered into the classified civil service, unless excepted under Schedule A of the Civil Service Rules (and other exceptions not applicable).

OPM believes that the provisions in section 11(*l*) of the Federal Reserve Act of 1913, 12 U.S.C. 248(*l*), which states that "nothing herein shall prevent the President from placing said employees in the classified service," made the Board's independent status conditional and provided the statutory authority for a subsequent change in that status. As stated in a letter of June 15, 1979, to the Board, OPM's position is as follows:

> Under the condition, the Board positions could have been brought into the competitive service well before the reach of the Ramspeck Act [54 Stat. 1211, November 26, 1940] and Executive Order No. 8743, had the President elected to do so. The terms of the Executive Order No. 8743 superseding the Board's independent authority to place Board employees in the competitive service left the President no choice but the need to exercise his Presidential authority under the Federal Reserve Act's conditional provision if he wanted to avoid the competitive service reach of Executive Order No. 8743.

OPM concludes that the placement of the Board employees in Schedule A unequivocally placed them in the civil service, and "owing to the excepted service Schedule A status of the Board's employees, their posi tions would qualify as SES positions under the definition in 5 U.S.C. § 3132(a)."

The Board of Governors disagrees with the conclusions reached by OPM. In concluding that its employees are not subject to the Senior Executive Service, the Board relies on section 11(*l*) of the Federal Reserve Act of 1913, and section 6(b) of the Banking Act of 1933, 12 U.S.C. 244, both of which are set out below.

Section 11(*l*) of the Federal Reserve Act of 1913, 38 Stat. 251, 262, as enacted authorized the Board:

> (*l*) To employ such attorneys, experts, assistants, clerks, or other employees as may be deemed necessary to conduct the business of the board. All salaries and fees shall be fixed in advance by said board and shall be paid in the same manner as the salaries of the members of said board. All such attorneys, experts, assistants, clerks, and other employees shall be appointed without regard to the provisions of the Act of January sixteenth, eighteen hundred and eighty-three (volume twenty-two, United States Statutes at Large, page four hundred and three), and amendments thereto, or any rule or regulation made in pursuance thereof: *Provided, That nothing herein shall prevent the President from placing said employees in the classified service.* [Italic supplied.]

In 1933, Congress moved to strengthen the independence of the Federal Reserve Board. Section 6(b) of the Banking Act of 1933, 48 Stat. 162, 167, amended section 10 of the Federal Reserve Act, 12 U.S.C. § 244, to read in pertinent part as follows:

> * * * The Board shall determine and prescribe the manner in which its obligations shall be incurred and its disbursements and expenses allowed and paid, and may leave on deposit in the Federal Reserve banks the proceeds of assessments levied upon them to defray its estimated expenses and the salaries of its members and employees, whose employment, compensation, leave, and expenses shall be governed solely by the provisions of this Act, specific amendments thereof, and rules and regulations of the Board not inconsistent therewith; and funds derived from such assessments shall not be construed to be Government funds or appropriated moneys * * *.

The Board points out that these provisions expressly empowered the Board to appoint employees without regard to the provisions of the Civil Service Act of 1883 (5 U.S.C. 1101) "and amendments thereto or any rule or regulation made pursuant thereof." Further, section 6(b) states that the "employment, compensation, leave, and other expenses" of employees of the Board "shall be governed solely by the provisions" of the Federal Reserve Act, or "specific amendments thereof, and rules and regulations of the Board not inconsistent therewith." The Board's letter of March 12, 1979, to OPM states:

> The purpose of this amendment to the Act was to reinforce the importance of the Board's independence within the government and in particular to insure that the Board is able to exercise control over its own internal management policies. H. Rep. No. 150, 73d Cong., 1st Sess. [2] (1933) * * *. Furthermore, it is the Board's view that, under generally accepted rules of statutory construction, civil service legislation enacted after the Federal Reserve Act and applying to all federal employees in general does not repeal by implication the express language of that Act, which confers on the Board the sole authority to manage its own employees * * *. It should be noted that Congress has never acted to revoke those provisions of the Federal Reserve Act that established the Board's

independent status, nor has any such revocation been contained in any legislation dealing with the federal civil service in general.

We are of the opinion that the Board of Governors of the Federal Reserve System is not subject to Title IV, Senior Executive Service, of the Civil Service Reform Act for the following reasons.

The provisions of the Federal Reserve Act of 1913, 12 U.S.C. 226, as amended by the Banking Act of 1933, show a clear intent to give the Board independence in regard to its own personnel system. This intent is also reflected in the events that occurred in 1940 and 1941 following the passage of the Ramspeck Act of November 26, 1940, 5 U.S.C. 5102. The understandings between the President, the Federal Reserve Board, and the Civil Service Commission during the period in which the executive orders relied upon by OPM were issued do not support the interpretation that OPM has placed on the executive orders.

Specifically, our Office was furnished three documents which support a different interpretation of the President's actions. These documents consist of a draft letter prepared by the Board for signature by the President which was forwarded to the President on December 27, 1940, by the chairman of the Board.

The draft letter prepared for the President and addressed to the President of the Civil Service Commission reads as follows:

> The Chairman of the Board of Governors of the Federal Reserve System has conferred with me regarding the possibility of action under the Ramspeck Civil Service Act of November 26, 1940, to place the employees of his Board under the classified civil service and the Classification Act of 1923, as amended.
>
> I have advised him that it is not my intention to place the employees of the Board of Governors of the Federal Reserve System under the classified civil service or the Classification Act, as amended, in view of the desirability of avoiding a condition under which the employees of the Board of Governors would be placed in a different status in this regard from those of the Federal Reserve Banks and their branches, and in view also of the fact that the salaries of the Board's employees are paid from funds derived from assessments on the Federal Reserve Banks and not from appropriations by Congress.

According to a memorandum of December 30, 1940, in the Board's files the draft letter was retyped on White House stationery and signed by the President. The Commissioners replied to the President by letter dated January 3, 1941, which reads as follows:

> The Commission has received your letter of December 27, 1940, to the effect that it is not your intention to place the employees of the Board of Governors of the Federal Reserve System under the classified Civil Service Act or the Classification Act, as amended. The Commission, of course, will be guided accordingly.

Finally, a Board of Governors' memorandum, written for the files of the Board of Governors and dated March 10, 1941, summarized a conversation concluded that day between the Chairman of the Board of Governors, Mr. Eccles, and the Administrative Assistant to the President, Mr. McReynolds, with regard to the status of the Board under the Ramspeck Act and the proposed Executive Order [8743] of the

President. Chairman Eccles is reported to have related the substance of what Mr. McReynolds said in pertinent part as follows:

> He said that he was perfectly sure that we were not included. He said that there was nothing further for us to do, nothing whatever; just to forget it.

The memorandum concluded as follows:

> Chairman Eccles said that Mr. McReynolds said that he considered that we were not under the law because we are an independent agency reporting directly to Congress and that we do not get any appropriations from Congress. Mr. McReynolds went on to say that as far as he was concerned, it would be a big mistake to put us under because we have a special status in relation to Congress and that he thought that until the whole System is changed there would be no point in putting us under. He emphasized the fact that that was his view; that it was also the view of the Commission, and that the Attorney General's office agreed.

We find the exchange of letters between the President and the Civil Service Commission, along with the contemporaneous memorandum reporting the position of the White House, to be persuasive in showing a clear intent to keep the Board entirely independent of the civil service system. We believe that these documents contradict the interpretation placed by OPM on the intent of Executive Orders 8743 and 9004. Further, we find nothing inherent in either of these Executive orders which is inconsistent with the independence given the Board in hiring its employees and fixing their compensation under section 11(*l*) of the Federal Reserve Act of 1913 and by section 6(b) of the Banking Act of 1933. Further, in view of the history of these Executive orders we cannot envision the President intending that either of these Executive orders would provide the means by which future legislation, such as that creating the SES, would result in the Board losing its independence with respect to its employees.

There is nothing in the legislative history of the Civil Service Reform Act of 1978 indicating any intent to alter the Board's independent status in the Government or to eliminate the Board's autonomy in matters of personnel management. In enacting the Federal Reserve Act and in amending section 10 of the Act in 1933, Congress dealt specifically with the precise issue of the Board's relationship to the Federal civil service system. On the basis of an explicit finding that the Board's insulation from external influences was essential to the performance of its mandated functions, Congress provided that the Board's personnel policies and actions are to be governed solely by the provisions of the Federal Reserve Act. On the other hand, Title IV of the Civil Service Reform Act deals generally with senior management practices in the civil service at large and, consequently, Title IV cannot reasonably be viewed as repealing by implication the earlier congressional determination giving the Board exclusive authority over its own employees.

It is a basic principle of statutory construction that a statute dealing with a narrow, precise, and specific subject is not submerged by a later enacted statute covering a more generalized spectrum. "Where there is no clear intention otherwise, a specific statute will not be controlled or nullified by a general one, regardless of the priority of enactment." *Morton* v. *Mancari*, 417 U.S. 535, 550–551 (1974). The principle has also been stated as follows:

> The enactment of a general law broad enough in its scope and application to cover the field of operation of a special or local statute will generally not repeal a statute which limits its operation to a particular phase of the subject covered by the general law. * * * An implied repeal of prior statutes will be restricted to statutes of the same general nature, since the legislature is presumed to have known of the existence of prior special or particular legislation, and to have contemplated only a general enactment. Therefore, where the later general statute does not present an irreconcilable conflict the prior special statute will be construed as remaining in effect as a qualification of or exception to the general law. 1A J. Sutherland, Statutes and Statutory Construction § 23.15 (4th ed. C. Sands 1972). See *United States* v. *United Continental Tuna Corp.*, 425 U.S. 164, 168; *Pasadas* v. *National City Bank*, 296 U.S. 497, 503.

When Congress enacted the employee provisions of the Federal Reserve Act, it was focusing on the independence of the Board of Governors, specifically with regard to the hiring and compensating of its own employees. When Congress enacted the Civil Service Reform Act of 1978, its focus was on the objective of improving the quality of public service, and it enacted a general provision, creating the Senior Executive Service applicable to the broad universe of civil service employees not otherwise exempt. Thus, unless a "clear intention otherwise" can be discerned, the principle of statutory construction discussed above counsels that the specific provisions of the Federal Reserve Act are to be given effect.

We do not believe that the present situation falls into any of the categories of repeals by implication. The statutory provisions at issue here cannot be said to be in "irreconcilable conflict" in the sense that there is a positive repugnancy between them or that they cannot mutually coexist. "When two statutes are capable of co-existence, it is the duty of the courts * * * to regard each as effective." *Morton* v. *Mancuri*, *supra*, 417 U.S. at 551.

Here, the basic purposes of the Civil Service Reform Act can be fairly served by giving full effect to the provisions of the Federal Reserve Act. The primary purpose of the Civil Service Reform Act provisions establishing the SES "was to establish a Senior Executive Service to ensure that the executive management of the Government of the United States is responsive to the needs, policies, and goals of the Nation and otherwise of the highest quality." 5 U.S.C. § 3131. The purpose of the Banking Act of 1933 in amending the Federal Reserve Act was to leave "to the Board the determination of its own internal management policies." S. Rep. No. 77, 73d Cong., 1st Sess. 14 (1933).

By allowing the Board to continue to hire and compensate its employees outside of the civil service system, the purposes of the Federal Reserve Act will obviously be served. Yet continued application of 12 U.S.C. 244 and 248(*l*) will not unduly interfere with the operation of the Civil Service Reform Act and specifically the SES. Since it is possible for the statutes to coexist in this manner, they are not so repugnant to each other as to justify a finding of an implied repeal. Further, there is nothing in the legislative history of the Civil Service Reform Act to suggest that Congress gave any consideration to a repeal of these provisions of the Federal Reserve Act. We conclude, therefore, that the specific provisions of the Federal Reserve Act must prevail over the broader, more generally applicable SES provisions of the Civil Service Reform Act.

Accordingly, although we recognize that the scope of the Senior Executive Service was intended to be very broad, we believe, in the absence of contrary legislative history, that the statutory independence of the Federal Reserve System mandates the conclusion that the employees of the Board of Governors are not covered by the Senior Executive Service.

〔 B-192884 〕

Small Business Administration — Loans — Guaranteed Loan Programs — Refinancing of Defaulted Loan

Small Business Administration (SBA) has discretion in appropriate case, subject to applicable statutory or regulatory provisions, to approve refinancing of existing non-guaranteed loan by new SBA guaranteed loan. Therefore, Bank's failure to pay guarantee fee prior to default on initial loan, thereby extinguishing guarantee on that loan pursuant to our decision B-181432, March 13, 1975, may not necessarily defeat otherwise valid guarantee of subsequent refinancing loan. B-181432, July 7, 1978, modified (extended).

Small Business Administration — Loans — Guaranteed Loan Programs — Fiscal Agents — Errors

Where due to alleged clerical inadvertence date of note and date of disbursement of loan differ, it is not necessary to decide which date is controlling for purposes of determining whether guarantee fee was paid prior to default, because even assuming that default occurred prior to payment of guarantee fee, subsequent full payment by Borrower would have brought loan into fully paid, current status, thereby curing any existing default and enabling SBA to purchase guaranteed portion of loan.

In the matter of Chase Manhattan Bank—Small Business Administration Guaranteed Loan, July 31, 1979:

The Chase Manhattan Bank, N.A. (Chase) has requested the General Accounting Office (GAO) to authorize the Small Business Administration (SBA) to purchase the guaranteed portion of a $250,000 term loan made by Chase to the Digital Lighting Corporation (Digital). SBA previously declined to purchase the guaranteed portion of the loan because Chase had not paid the required guarantee fee prior to default by Digital.

A bank is not entitled, as a matter of law, to a formal decision from our Office. See 31 U.S.C. §§ 74, 82d (1976), and B–181432, November 12, 1975. However, since SBA's refusal to purchase the guaranteed portion of the loan was based on our decision B–181432, March 13, 1975, in which we held that SBA could not purchase the guaranteed portion of a loan if the guarantee fee had not been paid prior to the Borrower's default, we will consider the arguments presented by Chase. In accordance with our usual policy, we requested and have received the views of the Administrator of SBA on this matter. SBA now takes the position that the Government should honor its guarantee on the $250,000 term loan.

Based on the report submitted by SBA and the information provided by the Bank, the facts concerning the above-referenced loan appear to be as follows:

On April 5, 1976, Chase disbursed a $250,000, 90 percent SBA guaranteed loan (Loan 3) to Digital. This loan represented refinancing of two earlier loans made by Chase to the same Borrower. The first loan (Loan 1) was a $100,000, 90 percent SBA guaranteed term loan made in 1973. The second loan (Loan 2), a $150,000 line of credit loan with an 80 percent SBA guarantee, was disbursed in 1975.

Before addressing the question of whether the guaranteed portion of Loan 3 may be purchased by SBA, we must first consider the timeliness of the guarantee fees paid to SBA on the two initial loans which were subsequently refinanced by Loan 3. Based on the certified loan transcript provided by the Bank, Loan 1 was disbursed to Digital on April 18, 1973. The guarantee fee on Loan 1 was also paid to SBA on April 18, 1973, and was therefore timely and paid in accordance with paragraph 5 of the Blanket Guaranty Agreement which requires payment of the fee within 5 days of first disbursement of a term loan. However, we are unable to reach that same conclusion concerning the $150,000 line of credit loan.

Loan 2, which was approved by SBA in writing on January 22, 1975, was disbursed by Chase on February 27, 1975. However, Chase did not pay the required guarantee fee on that loan until June 18, 1975. The relevant terms of the Blanket Line of Credit Guaranty Agreement, governing line of credit loans, are similar to the provisions of the Blanket Guaranty Agreement upon which our March 13, 1975, decision was based. Paragraph 2 of the Line of Credit Agreement provides that "Any approved line of credit will not be covered by this agreement until Lender shall have paid the guaranty fee for said line of credit as provided for in paragraph 5 of this agreement." Paragraph 5 provides that "Within 5 days of written notice of SBA's approval of the guarantee of each line of credit, Lender shall pay SBA a guarantee fee amounting to ¼ of 1 percent of the total amount guaranteed by SBA."

Although it is clear that Chase did not pay the guarantee fee in accordance with paragraph 5 (which required payment by January 27, 1975), our decision of March 13, 1975, held that late payment of the guarantee fee did not necessarily preclude SBA from honoring the guarantee, provided the fee was paid prior to default by the Borrower. In the present case, the precise date on which Loan 2 first went into default is unclear. Digital apparently made interest payments on Loan 2 on March 1, and again on April 1, 1975. Following payment of the guarantee fee on June 18, only two additional payments are recorded for Loan 2—$2,000 on August 26, 1975 and $3,600 on January 2, 1976. Unfortunately, documents containing a record of the specific terms of the line of credit loan, including the schedule of interest and principal payments, are apparently missing from the SBA file. We do note that paragraph 3 of the Line of Credit Guaranty Agreement provides that:

The terms of the line of credit shall provide that non-payment of principal or interest on any note on any due date shall constitute a default. * * *

Based on this provision as well as the actual repayment record (and in the absence of any information to the contrary) it is reasonable to assume that interest payments on the loan were due at some regular interval beginning immediately after disbursal. Therefore, although the matter is not entirely free from doubt due to the incomplete record, it appears that Chase did not pay the guarantee fee on Loan 2 prior to Digital's default on that loan. Accordingly, it is our view that pursuant to the terms of the Blanket Line of Credit Guaranty Agreement between SBA and Chase, SBA's guarantee on Loan 2 was not in effect when that loan went into default.

The next question is whether a loan that "lost" its SBA guarantee because the guarantee fee was not paid prior to default can be refinanced by a new loan that is covered by SBA's guarantee. Hypothetically, the requirement that the guarantee fee be paid prior to default as a condition precedent to SBA's obligation to purchase the guaranteed portion of a loan (B-181432, October 20, 1978) would be meaningless if a Bank could simply refinance a defaulted loan in order

to obtain the SBA guarantee which it could not have secured on the
initial loan.

However, in a related case where the guarantee on the refinanced
loan was never secured, we considered the effect of a valid SBA
guarantee on the initial loan. That decision is relevant here. In
B–181432, July 7, 1978, the Lender contended that its rights under a
valid guarantee agreement applicable to an initial loan had vested and,
therefore, were not extinguished when the initial loan was repaid by
a refinancing loan. In that decision we responded to the Bank's argument as follows:

> From a legal perspective as well as a practical one it is clear that when funds
> from Loan II were used to repay Loan I, Loan I as well as SBA's concomitant
> responsibility to guarantee that loan had in fact terminated.

Extension of that rationale suggests the parallel conclusion that a
Bank's liability for failure to obtain a valid guarantee of the initial
loan would also terminate when that loan was repaid with funds from
the new loan. Accordingly, it could be argued that any effect of
Chase's failure to obtain a valid guarantee of Loan 2 should have
terminated when Loan 2 was repaid by Loan 3.

Furthermore, in the only case in which we addressed the specific
question of whether a loan with a lapsed guarantee could be refinanced
by a new guaranteed loan, we recognized that SBA does have a considerable degree of discretion in determining whether or not to permit
such a non-guaranteed loan to be refinanced and, in essence, reguaran-
teed. Thus, in B–181432, April 5, 1979, in which we first considered and
rejected the Lender's contention that a defaulted loan, for which the
guarantee fee had not been paid before default, had been cured by the
Borrower, thereby reviving the extinguished guarantee, we went on
to say the following:

> However, as to the possibility of a refinancing of this loan, should the Bank
> wish to make a new loan to the borrower to repay the existing one and request
> SBA to issue a new guarantee on the second loan, we express no opinion since
> we believe that this determination can best be made by SBA in accordance with
> whatever regulatory provisions or internal SBA guidelines might be applicable
> to a situation in which an existing non-guaranteed loan is to be refinanced by
> an SBA guaranteed loan. This of course assumes that the Bank's allegations as
> to the borrower's improved circumstances could be substantiated so that repay-
> ment of the loan was reasonably assured as required by 15 U.S.C. § 636(a)(7)
> (1976).

For these reasons, and because the record indicates that the refinancing of Digital's loans was primarily to assist the Borrower, we find
that Chase's failure to pay the guarantee fee prior to default on Loan
2 does not necessarily defeat a valid guarantee of Loan 3, either in its
entirety or for that portion of Loan 3 used to refinance Loan 2.

Turning now to the other major issue presented by this case, the relevant facts concerning the status of the guarantee on Loan 3 are as follows:

The note evidencing Loan 3 is dated March 24, 1976, the date originally scheduled for disbursement. However, because of delays by Digital in completing certain necessary forms, the loan was not disbursed by Chase until April 5, 1976. Chase alleges that due to a clerical error, the date which appears on the face of the note itself was never changed from March 24, 1976, to April 5, 1976. However, the loan was entered in the Bank's records as of April 5, 1976, and interest began to accrue from that date. (Although the funds representing Loan 3 were apparently not disbursed to Digital in the usual sense, we believe that the date on which Loans 1 and 2 were closed out and interest began to accrue on Loan 3 is equivalent to the date of disbursement.) Chase paid the guarantee fee for the $250,000 term loan on April 30, 1976.

The note representing Loan 3 stipulated that only monthly interest payments were due for the first year, and on May 17, 1976, Digital paid the interest due on that date in full. Assuming Digital's first monthly interest payment was to be computed from the date of the note itself, payment was due on April 24, 1976. In that event, Chase's payment of the guarantee fee on April 30, 1976, occurred after default by Digital. By letters of May 12, 1977, and June 10, 1977, SBA refused purchase of the guaranteed portion of the $250,000 term loan because, according to the SBA, Chase failed to pay the guarantee fee prior to default as required by the Comptroller General.

This conclusion rests on the premise that the loan was in default on April 30, 1976. However, Chase contends, and SBA now agrees, that the date of disbursement is controlling. If this is true, then Digital's first interest payment would not have been due until May 5, 1976, and Chase's guarantee fee payment on April 30, 1976, would have been made prior to default. -

We recognize that there may be some merit to this argument. The agreement covering Loan 3 is somewhat ambiguous in that it did not clearly indicate the day of the month on which each interest payment was due or whether the date of disbursement or the date of the note, assuming a difference between the two dates, was controlling. Also, it appears that except for the alleged clerical error by Chase, the date of disbursement and the date of the note would have been the same— April 5, 1976. This is somewhat analogous to the situation that was the subject of our decision B–191660, March 5, 1979, in which we held that a Bank's claim against the Government pursuant to Title I of the

National Housing Act, as amended (12 U.S.C. 1702), was not barred even though the term of the note exceeded the statutory maximum, because the record indicated that due to inadvertence, the note as written did not reflect the intention of the parties at the time the loan was made. However, in our view it is not necessary to determine which date is controlling or whether our decision in B–191660, March 5, 1979, is applicable to these facts, since the question of the validity of SBA's guarantee of Loan 3 can be resolved on an alternative basis.

Assuming the first payment was due on April 24, 1976, one month from the date of the note, the loan would have been in default prior to Chase's payment of the guarantee fee. However, in that case Digital's payment on May 17, 1976, would have brought the loan into a fully paid, current status, thereby curing the default that would have existed on April 30, 1976, the date the guarantee fee was paid. This issue was addressed at some length in B–181432, April 5, 1979, in which we said the following:

> * * * [It] is our view that the failure of a bank to pay the guaranty fee prior to a default by a borrower does not necessarily preclude SBA in all circumstances from reinstating its guaranty and even purchasing the loan if subsequently, the original default is completely cured by the borrower and the required guaranty fee is paid in full prior to the occurrence of another separate default. We believe in those circumstances that SBA would have authority to purchase the loan in accordance with paragraph 2 of the Guaranty Agreement, which provides that a loan is covered after the guaranty fee has been paid. We also believe that such a result is both fair and reasonable, especially upon consideration of the definition of default set forth at 13 C.F.R. § 122.10(b), * * * which provides that default "means non-payment of principal or interest on the due date." Otherwise, there would be a technical default under this definition whenever the borrower was late in making a payment. For example, the guaranty of a loan might be forever terminated if the borrower was one day late in making his first payment, or any subsequent payment, and the bank had not yet paid the fee. This result would obviously be inequitable as well as inconsistent with the basic purpose of the guaranteed loan program.

Therefore, pursuant to that decision, even if we had concluded that there was no valid guarantee of Loan 3 on April 30, 1976, because of a prior default by the Borrower, a valid guarantee would have come into existence on May 17, 1976, when that default was cured.

Accordingly, we do not believe that SBA is precluded by any of our decisions from purchasing the guaranteed portion of the $250,000 loan Chase made to Digital (Loan 3). We note that Chase has also requested payment of the accrued unpaid interest on the two prior loans as well. Although we would not object to SBA's payment of the accrued interest due on Loan 1, if otherwise correct, we do not believe that SBA would be authorized to pay any of the accrued interest on Loan 2, since, as explained herein, it appears that Chase had not paid the guarantee fee for that loan prior to default by the Borrower.

[B-185659]

Indian Affairs—Lumbee Indians—Federal Benefits

Final sentence of Pub. L. No. 84–570 states that nothing in Act will make Lumbee Indians eligible for Federal services performed for Indians and that none of Federal statutes affecting Indians because of their status as Indians shall be applicable to Lumbee Indians. Purpose of this provision is to assure that Act was not used in and of itself to acquire Federal benefits. However, provision does not deny to Lumbees benefits accorded Indians if they are otherwise entitled under the requirements of another Act.

Indian Affairs—Native American Programs Act—State Recognized Indian Tribes—Benefits Entitlement

Lumbee Indians are not entitled to or denied benefits of Native American Programs Act of 1974 (NAPA), 42 U.S.C. 2991 *et seq.*, by virtue of last sentence of sec. 1, Pub. L. No. 84–570. NAPA benefits can be extended to, among others, public and non-profit agencies including governing bodies of Indian tribes on State and Federal reservations, and to public and non-profit private agencies serving Indian organizations in urban or rural non-reservation areas. Dept. of Health, Education and Welfare (HEW) contends this indicates congressional intent to extend benefits to State recognized tribes as well as to other organizations serving Indians. Since neither statutory language nor its history gives clear indication of intended beneficiaries, views of agency charged with administering statute must be given great weight. Hence, we will not object to determination by HEW that NAPA programs are available to State recognized Indian tribes such as the Lumbees.

Indian Affairs—Native American Programs Act—State Recognized Indian Tribes—Benefits Entitlement

Department of the Interior states that unless otherwise provided, most statutes referring to "Indians" do so within a context which actually means "Indian tribes." HEW contends that statute authorizing benefits to, among others, governing bodies of Indian tribes on Federal and State reservations (including a reservation of a State recognized tribe) and to public and non-profit private agencies serving Indian organizations in urban or rural non-reservation areas confers benefits on Lumbee Indians, who are a State recognized, non-reservation tribe. In absence of clear indication in language or history of Native American Programs Act of 1974 of intended beneficiaries, General Accounting Office will not object to HEW's determination that the Lumbees are eligible to participate in the Act's programs.

In the matter of Lumbee Indians of North Carolina, August 1, 1979:

A bid protest was filed several years ago by United Southeastern Tribes, Inc. (USET) because its proposal to provide training and technical assistance to 40 grantees of the Office of Native American Programs (ONAP) was rejected by the Department of Health, Education and Welfare (HEW), Office of Human Development. HEW apparently rejected USET's proposal because of its refusal to furnish any assistance to one of the grantees, the Lumbee Regional Development Association, Inc. (LRDA), which serves the Lumbee Indians of North Carolina (Lumbees). By decision dated November 2, 1976, *United Southeastern Tribe, Inc.*, B–185659, this Office denied the protest on grounds of timeliness, but agreed to reserve the question of whether non-federally recognized or terminated Indian groups are eligible for programs funded under the Native American Programs Act of 1974 or other legislation aimed at benefitting Indians. This is the question we are now considering.

One of the grounds of USET's protest was the contention that "An Act Relating to the Lumbee Indians of North Carolina," Pub. L. No. 84–570, enacted June 7, 1956, 70 Stat. 254, renders the Lumbees ineligible for assistance under Title VIII (the Native American Programs Act of 1974, 42 U.S.C. § 2991 *et seq.* (1976) (hereafter referred to as title VIII)) of the Head Start, Economic Opportunity, and Community Partnership Act of 1974, as amended (Act), 42 U.S.C. § 270, as well as for assistance under any other legislation, the eligibility for which is dependent on the status of being an Indian.

After a number of "whereas" clauses and the enacting clauses, Pub. L. No. 84–570 provides in pertinent part as follows:

* * * That the Indians now residing in Robeson and adjoining counties of North Carolina, originally found by the first white settlers on the Lumbee River in Robeson County, and claiming joint descent from remnants of early American colonists and certain tribes of Indians originally inhabiting the coastal regions of North Carolina, shall, from and after the ratification of this Act, be known and designated as Lumbee Indians of North Carolina and shall continue to enjoy all rights, privileges, and immunities enjoyed by them as citizens of the State of North Carolina and of the United States as they enjoyed before the enactment of this Act, and shall continue to be subject to all the obligations and duties of such citizens under the laws of the State of North Carolina and the United States. *Nothing in this Act shall make such Indians eligible for any services performed by the United States for Indians because of their status as Indians, and none of the statutes of the United States which affect Indians because of their status as Indians shall be applicable to the Lumbee Indians.*

Sec. 2. All laws and parts of laws in conflict with this Act are hereby repealed. [Italic supplied.]

While we agreed that the immediate question was the eligibility of the Lumbees to receive Federal funds under title VIII, the language of Pub. L. No. 84–570 is similar to that contained in a number of termination statutes (see, e.g., Klamath Termination Act, 25 U.S.C. § 564q (1970)), and the rights of many other groups of Indians, both for title VIII benefits and other Federal assistance programs, would be affected by our determination of the Lumbee question. Accordingly, we solicited the views of other interested parties on the broader question of whether any legislation, which by its terms is applicable to "Indians" but which term is not otherwise defined, may be administratively determined to apply to the Lumbees or other non-federally recognized tribes.

Comments were received from a great many interested parties. A number of Indian organizations representing federally and non-federally recognized tribes, the North Carolina Commission of Indian Affairs, several individual tribes, HEW and the Department of the Interior, Bureau of Indian Affairs, have now responded with their views. The nature and number of the suggestions and comments have emphasized the myriad of considerations which are important in making determinations of eligibility for Federal services to Indians. All comments have received our careful consideration, but because of the number of responses received, we shall specifically address only those comments representative of the views submitted on the question of Lumbee eligibility for benefits under title VIII.

The initial question which we must discuss is whether the provisions of Pub. L. No. 84–570, which are quoted and italicized above, preclude the Lumbees from receiving benefits accorded by the United States to Indians. USET, among others, believes that the statute denies any and all benefits to the Lumbees which would be conferred because of their status as Indians.

We believe, however, that there is a different and better interpretation of this Act. This interpretation, set forth by the United States Court of Appeals for the District of Columbia Circuit in *Maynor* v. *Morton*, 510 F. 2d 1254 (1975), holds that "The whole purpose of this final clause of the one paragraph operative portion of the Lumbee Act was simply to leave the rights of the 'Lumbee Indians' unchanged." *Id.* at p. 1258.

The plaintiff in that case was certified by the Department of the Interior as an Indian within the meaning of the Indian Reorganization Act, even though he did not live on a reservation and was not a member of a recognized tribe. By virtue of the enactment of Public Law No. 84–570, the Department wished to refuse services under the Indian Reorganization Act (25 U.S.C. 461) to Mr. Maynor and 21 other persons previously identified by the Department as Indians. The court disagreed:

> True, the limited purposes of the legislation appears to be to designate this group of Indians as "Lumbee Indians" and recognize them as a specific group. Moreover, Congress was very careful not to confer *by this legislation* any special benefits on these people so designated as Lumbee Indians. But we do not see that Congress manifested any intention whatsoever to take away any rights conferred on any individuals by any *previous* legislation. *Id.* at 1257–1258. [Italic in original.]

In the words of the Court—

> The whole purpose of the clause, from whence arises the issue in this case, was simply to make sure that a simple statute granting the name "Lumbee Indian" to a group of Indians, which hitherto had not had such designation legally, was not used *in and of itself* to acquire benefits from the United States Government. *Id.* at 1259. [Italic supplied.]

Accordingly, it is our view that whether Federal benefits may be accorded to any or all of the Lumbees must be determined without regard to the provisions of Public Law No. 84–570. It constitutes neither congressional recognition of the Lumbees as Indians for the purpose of establishing eligibility for Federal benefits nor congressional direction that they be denied benefits if otherwise entitled. In other words, if entitlement to Federal benefits depends solely upon the status conferred by Public Law No. 84–570, the Lumbees cannot qualify. If they can base their entitlement on some other legislative authority, they can be included. It will thus be necessary to examine the authorizing legislation for each program in question on a case-by-case basis.

With regard to eligibility of the Lumbees for title VIII benefits by letter of August 5, 1977, HEW indicates that it relies on a legal memorandum dated April 3, 1975, in which the then Deputy Assistant Secretary of Human Development concluded that "(1) the Lumbees are eligible for funding under the Native American Programs Act of 1974 and (2) [the final clause of] Public Law No. 84–570 presents no legal bar to funding of the Lumbees by ONAP because financial assistance under that agency's program is predicated on economic and social conditions (being disadvantaged) rather than Indian status." As set forth in title 42, United States Code, the pertinent provisions of title VIII provide:

§ 2991a. Congressional statement of purpose.

The purpose of this subchapter is to promote the goal of economic and social self-sufficiency for American Indians, Hawaiian Natives and Alaskan Natives.

§ 2991b. Financial assistance for native American projects.

(a) The Secretary is authorized to provide financial assistance to public and nonprofit private agencies including but not limited to, governing bodies of Indian tribes on Federal and State reservations, Alaskan Native villages and regional corporations established by the Alaska Native Claims Settlement Act, and such public and nonprofit private agencies serving Hawaiian Natives, and Indian organizations in urban or rural nonreservation areas, for projects pertaining to the purposes of this subchapter. In determining the projects to be assisted under this subchapter, the Secretary shall consult with other Federal agencies for the purpose of eliminating duplication or conflict among similar activities or projects and for the purpose of determining whether the findings resulting from those projects may be incorporated into one or more programs for which those agencies are responsible.

§ 2992c. Definitions.

(2) "Indian reservation or Alaskan Native village" includes the reservation of any federally or State recognized Indian tribe, including any band, nation, pueblo, or rancheria, any former reservation in Oklahoma, and community under the jurisdiction of an Indian tribe, including a band, nation, pueblo, or rancheria, with allotted lands or lands subject to a restriction against alienation imposed by the United States or a State, and any lands of or under the jurisdiction of an Alaskan Native village or group, including any lands selected by Alaskan Natives or Alaskan Native organizations under the Alaska Native Claims Settlement Act;

HEW points out that section 2991b(a) provides the eligibility requirements to qualify as an "Indian" for the purposes of programs conducted pursuant to title VIII. It is stated that the Lumbees are not a federally recognized tribe and noted that they do not reside on a State reservation. However, the memorandum states:

* * * they have, however, been recognized by the State of North Carolina as Indians and would qualify for assistance under this provision as an Indian organization in a rural nonreservation area.

HEW also maintains that since ONAP provided services under the Economic Opportunity Act of 1964, as amended, 42 U.S.C. 2701 note, until its transfer to HEW by the Act, the Act operated only to transfer administrative responsibility for the original program and services. The memorandum cites H.R. Rep. No. 93–1043, 93d Cong., 2d Sess. (1974) in support of this proposition:

"The Act authorizes the Secretary of Health, Education, and Welfare to continue operation of the Native American Program in the same manner as that program is now being carried out under Title II of the Economic Opportunity Act under a delegation from the Director of Economic Opportunity * * *."

Senate Report No. 93–1292, 93d Cong., 2d Sess. (1974), also notes that:

"A major element for the variety of Native American projects is overcoming the problems of poverty * * *. The amount of the basic grants to reservations is based on the number of poor residents * * *. The Committee's bill continues the present focus of the Native American Program * * *."

The views of the National Tribal Chairman's Association (NTCA) on the subject of Lumbee eligibility for title VIII benefits were submitted June 30, 1976, as an interested party in the bid protest by the United Southeastern Tribes and are representative of the comments subsequently received from other interested parties who argue that the Lumbees are ineligible to receive title VIII services. NTCA is an organization of the elected or acknowledged leaders of tribal governments of 188 federally recognized Indian tribes. It disputes the HEW position that funding under title VIII may be predicated on the Lumbees' status as economically and socially disadvantaged in the absence of their being federally recognized Indians. While NTCA acknowledges that title VIII is a poverty program, it argues that it is designed to assist only those who are both economically disadvantaged *and* are American Indians, Hawaiian natives or Alaskan natives. Under this theory, the Lumbees either receive as (federally recognized) American Indians, or not at all. NTCA also takes issue with the HEW position that because the Lumbees are State recognized, they qualify for assistance as an Indian organization in a rural nonreservation area. Absent a specific congressional acceptance of State recognition as sufficient to establish eligibility, NTCA maintains that State recognition is irrelevant for purposes of determining eligibility for participation in Federal Indian programs.

The views of the Lumbees are contained in a position paper forwarded to this Office by letter of January 7, 1977, from the LRDA. The LRDA supports its contention that the Lumbees are eligible for assistance under title VIII as a federally recognized, nonreservation group of Indians by citing the decision in *Maynor* v. *Morton*, 510 F. 2d 1254 (1975), in which the court stated that Public Law No. 84–570 had the effect of "legislative recognition for the entire group." It also notes that the Lumbees are a State recognized nonreservation group of Indians.

The stated purpose of title VIII is to promote the economic and social self-sufficiency for, as pertinent here, American Indians. This class designation is a restriction on eligibility imposed in addition to those defined by the broader purposes of the Act. The various titles of the Act provide funds and services for specific groups for the broad purpose of aiding socially and economically disadvantaged persons. We are concerned here with a specific title carrying out the broad purposes of a comprehensive law. Benefits accorded by title VIII are available only to those otherwise eligible individuals who are Indians.

In presenting the views of the Department of the Interior, the Acting Commissioner of Indian Affairs stated that "in the absence of a preponderance of evidence to the contrary, most congressional statutes when referring to 'Indians' do so within a context which actually means 'Indian tribes.' " He notes that this flows from a special political relationship based upon the Constitution, treaties and/or congressional actions, which is established between the United States and the tribes. Generally, the special benefits and services to Indian tribes and their members have flowed from this special political relationship established by Federal recognition of a group of individuals as a tribe.

The practice of extending Federal recognition to Indian tribes arises from the unique legal status of those tribes under Federal law and from the plenary authority of Congress to legislate specifically for Indians. Federal legislation relating to Indians as such is not based upon racial classifications, but rather reflects the power of Congress "to regulate Commerce * * * with the Indian tribes." U.S. Const. Art. I. section 8, cl. 3. Federal legislation in behalf of Indians may also constitute an exercise of Congress' spending, war, property, or other constitutional powers. Federal recognition of a group of individuals as an Indian tribe can be accomplished either by legislation or by the Executive Branch. In this regard, the Secretary of the Interior is charged by 43 U.S.C. § 1457 (1976) with the supervision of public business relating to Indians. His responsibilities with respect to Indian affairs are defined by 25 U.S.C. § 2 (1976) :

The Commissioner of Indian Affairs shall, under the direction of the Secretary of the Interior, and agreeably to such regulations as the President may prescribe, have the management of all Indian Affairs and of all matters arising out of Indian relations.

The Secretary of the Interior, in discharge of his statutory responsibilities, has issued regulations to be followed for a group of Indians to receive Federal acknowledgement of existence as a tribe. 43 Fed. Reg. 39361 (1978) (to be codified in 25 C.F.R. § 54).

Of course, the Lumbees have not been federally recognized as an Indian tribe by the Secretary of the Interior, nor, for the reason discussed above, may the congressional recognition of the Lumbees as Indians in Public Law No. 84–570 be used as a basis for Lumbee entitlement to Indian benefits. However, as HEW points out, the Secretary of HEW is authorized by the Native American Programs Act of 1974 to provide financial assistance to public and non-profit agencies, including but not limited to, governing bodies of Indian tribes on Federal and State reservations. Section 803, 42 U.S.C. § 2991b(a). An Indian reservation is defined as a reservation of any federally or State recognized Indian tribe. Section 813, 42 U.S.C. § 2992c(2). The HEW Secretary is also authorized by section 803, *supra*, to provide assistance to public and non-profit private agencies serving Indian organizations in urban or rural nonreservation areas. (The Lumbees fall, if anywhere, in this latter category since they do not live on a reservation.)

HEW suggests that, at minimum, when sections 803 and 813 are read together, they indicate an intent on the part of Congress to extend benefits to State recognized tribes, as well as to other organizations serving Indians. These Indians might come from federally or State recognized tribes. The Lumbees are, of course, recognized as a tribe by the State of North Carolina.

The Department of the Interior declined to comment on the eligibility of the Lumbees for title VIII benefits. However, the Acting Commissioner of Indian Affairs noted that Congress has from time to time provided special benefits for groups with special social and/or economic needs. He stated that "[i]n some such instances, it seems likely that Congress intended that Indian people, as a racial entity, be among the special beneficiaries." The Acting Commissioner states that agencies charged with administering Indian legislation will have to determine for themselves "whether persons of Indian descent who do not enjoy a special political relationship with the United States are included among the beneficiaries."

As HEW points out, the entire Act is directed at improving the situations of socially and economically disadvantaged individuals, with title VIII directed at socially and economically disadvantaged Indians. Substantial arguments have been presented to us on both sides of the issue of whether the provisions of title VIII were specifically intended to provide benefits to persons of Indian heritage who are not members of federally recognized tribes but who are members of State recognized tribes. While the language of title VIII may be ambiguous, nevertheless there is a sufficient basis in the language used to support an interpretation that permits title VIII funds to be made available to State recognized tribes such as the Lumbees whether living on reservations or in urban or rural non-reservation areas. Further, where statutory language is ambiguous, great deference should be given to the views of the agency which is responsible for carrying out the Act's provisions.

In view of the broad ranging purposes of title VIII and the Act as a whole and since the language of the statute may readily be read to support HEW's position, we do not believe that that agency's position is unreasonable or unwarranted. Accordingly, we will not object to a determination by HEW that title VIII programs are available to State recognized Indians such as the Lumbees. In reaching this conclusion, however, we pass on the following caveat set forth by the Acting Commissioner of Indian Affairs:

> We do believe, however, that it is incumbent upon Agencies administering "Indian" programs to give close attention to this matter and not establish a relationship with such Indian groups which might unthinkingly lead to their developing a status not readily distinguished from those Indian tribes whose political relationship has been well defined. This could in the long run prove detrimental to those tribes to which the United States has special trust obligations.

[B-193740]

Subsistence—Per Diem—Rates—Lodging Costs—Distance From Temporary Duty Station

The fact that an employee on a temporary duty assignment stays in a motel which is 74 miles from the temporary duty station, and only 25 miles from his home, does not necessarily indicate imprudent conduct by the employee. Each case must be considered on its own facts. Here, since there is no showing of any increased cost to the Government and no indication that the distance impeded the employee in the performance of his assignment, the employee should be reimbursed for his lodging expenses.

In the matter of Robert C. Burden—Temporary Duty Travel—Lodging Expenses, August 6, 1979:

We have been asked to decide whether there is a maximum distance or range of distances from a temporary duty station within which an employee must obtain lodgings. In the case presented, we hold that the cost of the employee's lodging expenses may be allowed and we decline to prescribe any general rules regarding the distance between a temporary duty station and an employee's place of lodging as the Air Force requested.

By letter of November 8, 1978, the Chief, Accounting and Finance Branch, Headquarters Ogden Air Logistics Center, Hill Air Force Base, Utah, requested an advance decision on the reimbursement of lodging expenses of an employee on a temporary duty assignment. The matter was forwarded to us through the Per Diem, Travel and

Transportation Allowance Committee and was assigned PDTATAC Control Number 78-47.

By travel authorization dated June 21, 1978, Mr. Robert C. Burden and 21 other employees were authorized to perform repeated temporary duty travel from Hill Air Force Base to the Hill Air Force Base Test Range at Lakeside, Utah, to test fire weapons systems. For the period of time in question, Government quarters were not available at the temporary duty site. According to the submission, when on this temporary duty employees generally obtain lodging in Grantsville, Utah, which is 50 miles from the Lakeside test range. Mr. Burden, for three of the four nights involved, stayed in a motel in Salt Lake City, which was 74 miles from the Lakeside test range and 25 miles from his permanent duty station and home. The Air Force argues that Mr. Burden has not complied with the spirit of paragraph C4464 of Volume 2 of the Joint Travel Regulations (JTR) which requires an employee who is in a travel status to exercise prudence in incurring expenses.

There is nothing in the submission to indicate that Mr. Burden was in any way hindered in the performance of his duties because of the location of the lodgings he obtained during his temporary duty assignment. There is no indication that he was late for work, nor that any claim that he may have had for mileage reimbursement was increased by the location of his lodgings. Presumably, his action is questioned because, having traveled 74 miles from his temporary duty station, he did not continue another 24 miles so that he could have lodged at his home at no cost to the Government.

There is no restriction in the JTR or the Federal Travel Regulations, FPMR 101-7 (May 1973) (FTR), on where an employee should obtain lodging while in a temporary duty assignment. We have not previously considered this precise question but we have dealt with requests for reimbursement for local travel expenses when an employee lodges at a distance from his temporary duty station. See *Matter of Roland E. Groder*, B-192540, April 6, 1979, and B-178558, June 20, 1973. In both cases employees on temporary duty assignments in New York City stayed in lodgings outside the city at no cost (*Groder*) or lower cost. Each employee sought reimbursement of commuting expenses. In both cases the overall cost to the Government was less, so reimbursement was allowed.

In the instant case, there is nothing to indicate that Mr. Burden's choice of lodgings in any way increased the total cost to the Government of his travel expenses. In fact, we note that for the three nights questioned by the Air Force, Mr. Burden's cost of lodgings totalled $34 plus tax while the fourth night cost $24 plus tax. Absent some showing that the Government's costs were increased or Mr. Burden's performance of his temporary duty assignment was impaired by the location of his lodgings, we do not believe that it can be presumed that he acted in an imprudent manner simply because he did not travel the rest of the way to his home. Therefore, we see no basis for withholding reimbursement of Mr. Burden's lodging expenses from him.

The agency also asks us to respond to three specific questions concerning the distances between permanent duty stations, temporary duty stations, lodgings, and employees' homes. We do not believe that it is advisable or even possible to specify uniform rules in this area, and we decline to answer the specific questions posed. We believe that each case in this area must be considered on its own facts and the conduct of the employee must be individually evaluated, in light of the cost to the Government and the extent of the interference with the employee's assignment.

Accordingly, the voucher is returned and amounts claimed by Mr. Burden may be allowed, if otherwise correct.

[B–194542]

Leaves of Absence—Military Personnel—Advance Leave—Enlistment Extension Prior to Accrual

Marine Corps member, who takes 19 more days of leave than he would accrue prior to the expiration of his first extension of enlistment, had pay and allowances withheld from him upon return from leave for the 19 days pursuant to Department of Defense regulation. Although the member subsequently entered into a second reextension of enlistment which would enable him to earn more leave than the excess he used, there is no authority to repay him the withheld pay and allowances.

In the matter of Gunnery Sergeant Danny L. Radish, USMC, August 6, 1979:

The issue in this case is whether pay and allowances collected from a Marine Corps member for excess leave he used beyond what he would accrue in his extended enlistment may be refunded to him when he again extended his enlistment for a term sufficient to accrue enough leave to cover the excess.

The matter is presented by letter of February 22, 1979, from the Disbursing Officer, Marine Corps Air Station (Helicopter), New River, Jacksonville, North Carolina, requesting an advance decision as to whether the second extension of enlistment of Gunnery Sergeant Danny L. Radish, USMC, entitles him to reimbursement of pay and allowances previously withheld because of his taking excess leave. The request was assigned Control No. DO–MC–1317 and forwarded to us by the Department of Defense Military Pay and Allowance Committee.

On March 24, 1972, Sergeant Radish enlisted in the Marine Corps for 6 years. On March 16, 1977, he voluntarily extended his enlistment for 1 year until March 23, 1979. At this point, Sergeant Radish elected to receive payment for his unused accrued leave and his leave balance was reduced to zero. During the year's extension, Sergeant Radish requested and was granted leave which resulted in his using 19 days' leave in excess of the number of days he would earn until the expiration of his then current enlistment on March 23, 1979. In accordance with applicable regulation, pay and allowances for the excess leave were collected from him.

On February 16, 1979, Sergeant Radish entered into an agreement for a second extension of his enlistment for 2 years commencing March 24, 1979, and ending March 23, 1981. Because this second extension of enlistment (reextension) increases the leave Sergeant Radish will accrue prior to the normal expiration of his current enlistment to an amount greater than the total leave he previously used, the Disbursing Officer asks whether the pay and allowances previously withheld may be paid to Sergeant Radish.

The withholding of pay and allowances was done pursuant to the Department of Defense Military Pay and Allowances Entitlements Manual, Paragraph 10305a(6) which states in part:

10305.   Advance Leave Changed to Excess Leave

   a. *When Collection Required.* Collect pay and allowance from a member when advance leave becomes excess leave on date of:

       *   *   *   *   *   *   *

   (6) Return from a period of leave which was in excess of the number of days leave member will accrue prior to the normal expiration of his current enlistment or term of active service. * * *

This regulation implements the mandate of 37 U.S.C. § 502(b) (1976) which precludes payment for leave in excess of the amount (i.e., 2½ days' per month of active service) authorized in 10 U.S.C. § 701 (1976).

In line with the above statutes and similar regulation, we have held that a member who takes excess leave must have the pay and allowances for the excess leave collected from him and may not carry over excess leave into a first extension of an enlistment. 43 Comp. Gen. 539 (1964). The basis of this decision was that any leave taken by a member which exceeded the amount he normally would earn until the end of his obligated duty was properly regarded as excess leave and required collection of pay and allowances under the regulation. The nature of excess leave would not be changed by a subsequent act of extending (or reextending) an enlistment which would then increase the amount of leave normally earned until the end of the enlistment. See 43 Comp. Gen. 539, *supra*, at 542.

In Sergeant Radish's case the collection action was proper under the regulation promulgated under the authority contained in 10 U.S.C. § 704 (1976) which provides that the Secretaries concerned shall prescribe regulations for administering the military leave system. See 33 Comp. Gen. 337 (1954). There is no basis for retroactively changing the nature of his excess leave to advance leave due to his subsequent act of reextending his enlistment.

Accordingly, Sergeant Radish may not be repaid the previously withheld pay and allowances.

[B–194858]

Transportation—Travel Agencies—Restriction on Use

A member of the uniformed services, to take advantage of a low cost charter flight, purchased transportation for official travel with personal funds from a travel agency. Since traveler was not aware of the regulation which precludes use of travel agencies he may be reimbursed an amount not exceeding the cost of the transportation if it had been purchased directly from the carrier.

Insurance—Trip Cancellation Insurance—Travel Expense

A member of the uniformed services purchased trip cancellation insurance when he purchased charter flight accommodations. It is the policy of the Government to insure its own risks of loss. Trip cancellation insurance is not a reimbursable travel expense unless it can be shown that the insurance is an inseparable part of a travel package which provides special or reduced fares at a savings to the Government.

Subsistence — Per Diem — Delays — Awaiting Transportation — Excursion Rates

For purposes of qualifying for per diem a member of the uniformed services may be considered to be in a travel status for the extra time required to take advantage of a reduced air fare if it can be shown that the increased travel time will not interfere with the performance of official business, is not for personal convenience, and the cost of the extra per diem when added to the cost of the reduced fare does not exceed what the Government would have been required to pay had the reduced fare not been used.

In the matter of Dr. Kenneth J. Bart, USPHS, August 7, 1979:

Three issues are presented in this case. They are 1) whether a member of the uniformed services may be reimbursed travel expenses purchased through a travel agency in view of the prohibition contained in paragraph M2200–3 of Volume 1, Joint Travel Regulations (1 JTR); 2) whether a member of the uniformed services may be reimbursed for trip cancellation insurance purchased by him; and 3) whether a member of the uniformed services may be paid per diem for an additional day of travel required to take advantage of a reduced fare provided by a charter flight.

Questions one and three are answered in the affirmative. Question two is answered in the negative.

The issues arise from a request by the Director, Financial Management Office, Public Health Service, Center for Disease Control, Atlanta, Georgia, regarding reimbursement to Dr. Kenneth J. Bart for the payment of $365 to a travel agency for air fare, $15 paid for trip cancellation insurance and the claim of $45 for an extra day of per diem incident to a trip he took to Rome, Italy.

Dr. Bart, a commissioned officer of the United States Public Health Service (PHS), was authorized to travel on temporary duty from Atlanta, Georgia, to Rome, Italy, and return in August and September 1978. To take advantage of a charter flight by Capital Airways (United States registry) Dr. Bart, who was unaware of the Government's general prohibition against the use of travel agencies, paid to a travel agency from his personal funds the sum of $365 plus $15 for trip cancellation insurance. The charter flight was from New York, New York, to Rome, Italy, and return. It was therefore necessary for him to purchase a round-trip fare from Atlanta to New York which cost $116 (excursion fare). Upon the return from Rome, the charter flight arrived too late for Dr. Bart to take a flight to Atlanta the same day as his return. This delay necessitated his remaining in New York overnight and returning to Atlanta the next day. Had Dr. Bart taken a regular fare flight from Atlanta to Rome and return, the cost to the Government would have been $1,131. By use of an excursion fare (14–21 days) the cost could have been reduced to $850 for the round trip. Thus, by taking the charter flight Dr. Bart's air fare from New York to Rome was substantially less than it would have been otherwise.

As a commissioned officer of the PHS, Dr. Bart's travel allowances for temporary duty are governed by 37 U.S.C. 404 (1976) and by the implementing regulations of 1 JTR. Paragraph M2200–3 (change 276, February 1, 1976) provides that travel agencies may not be used to secure any passenger transportation service from the United States to foreign countries. However, in decision B–103315, August 1, 1978, we held that members of the uniformed services who inadvertently purchase official transportation with personal funds from a travel agency without prior approval by an administrative office may be reimbursed an amount not exceeding the cost of transportation if it had been purchased directly from the carrier. In that decision we also stated that to achieve more uniformity in regulations relating to travel, 1 JTR could be amended to permit procurement of passenger transportation by group or charter arrangements from travel agencies for travel by members of the uniformed services to the extent allowed civilian employees in the Federal Travel Regulations (FPMR 101–7) par. 1–3.4b(2).

The nonuse of travel agencies is premised on the determination that procurement directly from the carriers is more efficient and economical than purchases from the travel agencies. Flight reservations must generally be made and confirmed with the airlines and any cancellations or changes in flight plans can be effected more readily and with less likelihood of error by dealing directly with the carriers.

As Dr. Bart's use of the travel agency was inadvertent, his case falls within the exception noted in B–103315. Therefore, notwithstanding the fact that the JTRs had not been amended as approved in that decision at the time Dr. Bart traveled, he should be reimbursed an amount not exceeding cost of transportation if purchase was made directly from an airline carrier. See in this regard 1 JTR, paras. M4251, M4159–1 and 4, and M4150–4. Since the $365 air fare was lower than the Government would have otherwise paid, he may be reimbursed that amount.

It is the general rule that trip insurance is not a reimbursable item of travel expense. It is a longstanding policy of Government to self-insure its own risks of loss. See B–127343, December 15, 1976, and cases cited there. A limited exception to this rule has been applied when the insurance is an inseparable part of the contract. See 55 Comp. Gen. 1397 (1976) concerning insurance required in a rental car contract. However, in the present case it appears that the trip cancellation insurance was optional and, therefore, reimbursement for it may not be allowed.

An extra day's per diem is claimed due to scheduling requirements of the charter flight. To take advantage of the charter flight it was necessary for Dr. Bart to stop over in New York City upon his return from Rome since the charter flight arrived too late in the evening for him to make a connecting flight to Atlanta. Paragraph M3050, 1 JTR, provides that members shall be deemed to be in a travel status while performing travel away from their permanent duty station, upon public business, pursuant to competent travel orders, including necessary delays en route incident to mode of travel. Per diem is authorized for periods of temporary duty including periods of necessary delay awaiting further transportation. 1 JTR, para. M4200–1.

The travel time required to take advantage of special or reduced fares should also be viewed in light of the savings to the Government. If it can be shown that the increased travel time will not interfere with the performance of official business, is not solely for personal convenience, and the cost of the extra per diem when added to the cost of the special or reduced fares does not exceed what the Government would have been required to pay had the special or reduced fares not been used, the member should be considered to be in a travel status for the required extra time. In this case the extra travel time appears to satisfy those criteria. Therefore, payment of per diem for the extra day should be allowed.

Accordingly, the voucher submitted is being returned for payment, if otherwise correct, in accordance with this decision (excluding the trip insurance).

[B–194885]

Contracts — Protests — Timeliness — Solicitation Improprieties— Apparent Prior to Bid Opening

Protest, alleging procurement should not have been set aside for small business, which is filed after bid opening is untimely and not for consideration on the merits.

Contracts — Awards — Small Business Concerns — Self-Certification — Status Protests

Where bidder on procurement totally set aside for small business fails to check box on reverse side of Standard Form 33 to indicate whether or not it is certifying itself as small business concern, the procedures in 18 C.F.R. 181.3–5 and 121.3–8 do not apply; therefore, contracting officer acted reasonably and properly by telephoning bidder to give it an opportunity to cure deficiency which is considered a minor informality or irregularity in bid.

Contracts — Awards — Small Business Concerns — Set-Asides — Competition Sufficiency

Protest against solicitation restricting procurement as total small business set-aside is denied where record discloses that reasonable expectation of adequate competition existed and bid price was reasonable, notwithstanding that only one bid was received from small business concern.

Contracts — Awards — Small Business Concerns — Size — Status Determination — Small Business Administration

Protest concerning small business size status is not for consideration by General Accounting Office since by law it is matter for decision by the Small Business Administration.

Bidders — Qualifications — License Requirement — State, etc. Certifications

Whether contractor has obtained State and local permits is matter between contractor and State and local officials and has no bearing on bidder responsibility or award of contract.

Contracts—Protests—Allegations—Not Supported By Record— Award of Contract To Protester

Assertion that Government awarded valid contract to protester which subsequently was improperly canceled is not supported by record.

In the matter of Anderson-Cottonwood Disposal, August 8, 1979:

Anderson-Cottonwood Disposal (Anderson-Cottonwood) protests the award of a contract for garbage collection services to Red Bluff Disposal Co. (Red Bluff) under IFB R5–14–79–27 issued by the U.S. Forest Service.

Anderson-Cottonwood contends that the decision to totally set aside the procurement for small business concerns was arbitrary and capricious, that the contracting officer failed to follow proper procedures in determining it was not a small business, and that the firm awarded the contract may not be a small business. The protester also maintains that Red Bluff lacked the permits required to meet its obligations under the contract at the time award was made.

Finally, Anderson-Cottonwood maintains that the contracting officer awarded it a contract at the time of bid opening only to later award the contract to Red Bluff. Anderson-Cottonwood argues that under these facts the "Government was in breach even though no contract had been signed." As relief, Anderson-Cottonwood seeks money damages.

Bid opening occurred as scheduled on April 23, 1979, with two firms, Red Bluff and Anderson-Cottonwood, responding to the IFB. Anderson-Cottonwood bid $17,280 while Red Bluff bid $20,506. The IFB stated that the applicable size standard limited the size of firms eligible to bid on this procurement to those with average annual sales or receipts for the preceding 3 years not in excess of $3,500,000.

Red Bluff, upon learning that Anderson-Cottonwood was low bidder, telephoned the contracting officer on April 24, 1979, and protested Anderson-Cottonwood's size status. The contracting officer reviewed Anderson-Cottonwood's bid and found it had failed to indicate its size on the reverse side of Standard Form 33 but had indicated on the same form that Anderson-Cottonwood was either owned or controlled by Sunset Scavenger Company (Sunset Scavenger). The record indicates that the contracting officer then telephoned Anderson-Cottonwood's manager and asked him to verify his connection with Sunset Scavenger. The manager confirmed the relationship and informed the contracting officer that Sunset Scavenger's average annual sales exceeded the $3,500,000 size standard. The contracting officer then advised the manager that based on this information Anderson-Cottonwood was ineligible for award. The contracting officer also advised the manager that he had a right to appeal this size determination. When the manager did not appeal, the contracting officer awarded the contract to Red Bluff on April 26, 1979.

The first basis of protest, that the contracting officer's decision to set aside the procurement was improper, is untimely as the allegation relates to an impropriety in the solicitation which was apparent prior to bid opening. Section 20.2(b)(1) of our Bid Protest Procedures, 4 C.F.R. § 20.2(b)(1)(1979), provides that:

Protests based upon alleged improprieties in any type of solicitation which are apparent prior to bid opening * * * shall be filed prior to bid opening * * *.

Bid opening occurred on April 23, 1979, but the protester did not initially raise this issue until it filed its protest with our Office on May 17, 1979. Therefore, this basis of protest is untimely filed and will not be considered on the merits. *Triple "A" South*, B–193765, March 23, 1979, 79–1 CPD 300.

Anderson-Cottonwood's second basis of protest is that the contracting officer failed to follow appropriate procedures in determining that it was not a small business. Specifically, Anderson-Cottonwood complains that the contracting officer ignored 13 C.F.R. § 121.3–5 (1979) which sets forth "standards of procedural due process and orderly administration which were totally disregarded by the agency" and thereby effectively precluded the protester from presenting "critical information to a decision maker concerning its functional independence from Sunset Scavenger." Anderson–Cottonwood also contends that the contracting officer failed to follow the procedures set out in 13 C.F.R. § 121.3–8 in determining the protester's size status.

The procedures in 13 C.F.R. § 121.3–5 delineate the manner in which any bidder or other interested party may challenge the small business status of any bidder on a particular Government procurement. If a protest is timely filed within 5 days of bid opening, the contracting officer must promptly forward the protest to the appropriate Small Business Administration (SBA) district office. Further, the contracting officer may at any time after bid opening question the small business status of any bidder by filing a protest with the SBA.

The procedures in 13 C.F.R. § 121.3–8 provide that the contracting officer shall accept a small business self-certification at face value in the absence of a protest or other information which would cause him to question the veracity of the self certification. If the contracting officer has cause to question the veracity of a self-certification and elects to do so, he must refer the eligibility issue to the SBA by filing a formal protest pursuant to 13 C.F.R. § 121.3–5.

Both 13 C.F.R. §§ 121.3–5 and 121.3–8 contemplate a situation where a bidder has already certified itself as a small business and that self-certification is questioned. Neither regulation applies to the facts here where a bidder fails to check the box on the reverse side of Standard Form 33 to indicate whether or not it was certifying itself as small. Nevertheless, the contracting officer apparently believed he was required to contact the protester to verify whether or not it intended to designate itself as a small business concern for this procurement. In the circumstances, we believe the contracting officer acted reasonably and properly.

In the absence of the protester's self-certification, the contracting officer held a bid which was ineligible for award. Federal Procurement Regulations (FPR) § 1–1.703–1(b) (1964 ed.) provides that "no bidder * * * shall be eligible for award as a small business concern unless it has in good faith represented itself as a small business prior to the opening of bids * * *." However, the cited regulation refers to FPR § 1–2.405(b) (1964 ed.) which provides that the contracting officer shall give a bidder an opportunity to cure any deficiency resulting from a minor informality or irregularity in a bid such as a bidder's failure to furnish required information concerning the number of bidder's employees. By way of comparison, Defense Acquisition Regulation (DAR) 2–405 (1976 ed.) cites the same example but also lists failure to make a size status representation as an example of a minor informality which may be waived without prejudice to the bid. Moreover, the contracting officer had good reason to suspect that the protester had made an inadvertent mistake inasmuch as Anderson-Cottonwood was the incumbent contractor for this work which had been advertised the previous year in a solicitation totally set aside for small business. Consequently, we cannot object to the contracting officer's informally telephoning the protester in the fashion that he did since it appears he took this action to give the protester an opportunity to cure any oversight and not to circumvent the protested procedures discussed above.

Notwithstanding the contracting officer's determination that it was ineligible for award, the protester asserts that the contracting officer should have withdrawn the set-aside once it was apparent only one responsive bid, offering a price 15 percent higher than that offered by Anderson-Cottonwood, was received. We disagree. The contracting officer's decision to set aside a particular procurement exclusively for small business should be made on the basis of circumstances which exist at the time the decision is initially made. *U.S. Diver Company*, B–192867, February 26, 1979, 79–1 CPD 132; *DeWitt Transfer and Storage Company*, B–182635, March 26, 1975, 75–1 CPD 180. In making this decision, the contracting officer must determine that there is a reasonable expectation that bids will be obtained from a sufficient number of responsible small business concerns so that award will be made at a reasonable price. FPR § 1–1.706–5(a). This is basically a business judgment which requires the exercise of broad discretion by the contracting officer. *RCA Corporation, et al.*, 57 Comp. Gen. 809 (1978), 78–2 CPD 213. Thus, the reasonabless of the expectation will not be reevaluated in retrospect, and our Office will not substitute its judgment for that of the contracting officer in the absence of a clear showing of abuse of discretion. *U.S. Divers Company, supra.*

The record here reveals that there was a reasonable expectation of bids from a sufficient number of small business concerns at reasonable prices even though only one bid was received from a small business concern willing to certify itself as such. When the IFB was issued, it was sent to six firms, all of which the contracting officer believed to be small. The previous procurement for the same service resulted in the receipt of bids from both the protester and Red Bluff. The fact that only one acceptable bid was received does not affect the propriety of the determination to make the set-aside which was made prior to the issuance of the solicitation. *U.S. Divers Company, supra.*

With regard to the reasonableness of the award price, the previous contract was awarded for $13,244 and the Government estimate was $16,000. The protester bid $17,280 and the awardee bid $20,506, roughly 15 percent higher than the protester's bid. We have held that the Government may pay a premium price to small business firms on restricted procurements to implement the policy of Congress as expressed in the Small Business Act, 15 U.S.C. §§ 631 *et seq.* (1976). *Society Brand, Incorporated, et al.*, 55 Comp. Gen. 372 (1975), 75–2 CPD 225; *Tenco Construction Company*, B–187137, December 21, 1976, 76–2 CPD 512. In *Tenco Construction Company, supra*, a case where the awardee, the only small business to bid on the solicitation, bid $661,320 more than the protester, and $450,835 more than the Government estimate, we said:

> Simply because a bid exceeds other bids or the Government estimate does not necessarily mean that the bid is unreasonable. There can be a range over and above the low bid and the Government estimate which is a reasonable price range. The determination of price reasonableness requires a degree of discretion. Therefore, determinations dealing with price reasonableness will be sustained barring bad faith or fraud.

Consistent with this position, we have held that a contract price was not unreasonable even where it exceeded the "Government estimate by 22 percent and at an average 17 percent higher than other qualified firms, large and small business alike." *CDI Marine Company*, B–188905, November 15, 1977, 77–2 CPD 367.

The protester suggests that a contract price which is 15 percent higher than the bid price it offered is unreasonable. While we are not prepared to say that any contract price which falls within a predetermined percentage range of the next bid or the average of other bids must always be considered reasonable, a party attempting to demonstrate the unreasonableness of a contract price has the affirmative burden of proving its case. Here, Anderson-Cottonwood presents no facts or information beyond its bare allegation to support its position and so has not met its burden of demonstrating that the contract price was unreasonable. *Ads Audio Visual Productions, et al.*, B–193248, B–193248.2, April 18, 1979, 79–1 CPD 275.

There being no indication that the contracting officer was motivated by either bad faith or fraud when he awarded the contract to Red Bluff, we will not question the reasonableness of the contract price.

The protester's third basis of protest is that Red Bluff may not be a small business. Pursuant to 15 U.S.C. § 637(b)(6) (1976), the conclusive authority to determine small business size status of a business concern lies with the SBA and is not subject to review by this Office. *Cardan Company*, B–193839, January 31, 1979, 79–1 CPD 76. To protest a determination of small business status properly, a protester must file a protest within 5 days of "bid or proposal opening" to the contracting officer, who promptly forwards the protest to the appropriate SBA district office. 13 C.F.R. § 121.3–5.

The protester also argues that the firm awarded the contract lacked the permits required to meet the obligations of the contract. The Forest Service advises us that the solicitation contained the following provision:

It shall be the responsibility of the contractor to secure all licenses, permits, and to comply with all state and county health laws and regulations.

Compliance with such State regulatory and licensing requirements is a matter between the appropriate State officials and the contractor and will not be considered by our Office. Whether the awardee has met these requirements has no bearing on bidder responsibility or the award of the contract. *RCA Global Communications, Inc.*, B–191577, August 29, 1978, 78–2 CPD 150; *Burn Construction Company, Inc.*, B–192196, August 21, 1978, 78–2 CPD 139.

Finally, Anderson-Cottonwood protests the contracting officer's improper cancellation of the allegedly valid contract which it claims came into being once bids were opened and the contracting officer congratulated a representative of the protester in attendance that award would be made to his firm. The protester maintains that the contracting officer, under the holding in *Allen M. Campbell Company* v. *U.S.*, 467 F. 2d 931 (Ct. Cl. 1972), had no authority to cancel the contract allegedly awarded to it even though it was subsequently declared not to be a small business. As a remedy, Anderson-Cottonwood seeks money damages in the form of "lost profit unless a contractual provision sets out other relief."

We point out initially that, contrary to the protester's suggestion, the cited court case does not hold that the Government has no right to terminate a validly awarded contract; rather, the Court of Claims ruled that the Government should have terminated the contract under the Termination for Convenience clause. As relief, the Court denied recovery of anticipated profits and remanded the case for a determination of the amount of recovery in accordance with the Termination for Convenience clause.

Here we see no basis for the assertion that a contract with the protester came into being. The protester, insofar as the record indicates, did not act and does not claim to have acted as if it had believed it was the recipient of an award and indeed did not even make the assertion until well after the protest was filed. In any event, if the protester believes it is entitled to breach of contract damages, the matter should be pursued with the contracting officer pursuant to the Contracts Disputes Act of 1978, Public Law 95–563, approved November 1, 1978, 41 U.S.C. 601 note.

On the basis of the above, the protest is dismissed in part and denied in part.

[B–194891]

Details — Compensation — Higher Grade Duties Assignment — Classification Downgrade—Effect

A Federal employee appointed to a GS–13 position is detailed to perform duties of a GS–14 position and becomes entitled to a temporary promotion and backpay under 55 Comp. Gen. 539 (1975). Where the position is classified downward during the detail, and since an occupant of a position may only receive the salary authorized for that position, if the employee continues on the detail after it is reclassified downward to a GS–13 level, he may not continue to receive the pay at the higher level on and after the reclassification effective date.

In the matter of Mr. Jacob Klein, August 8, 1979:

This action is in response to a letter dated April 6, 1979, with enclosures, from Mr. Jacob Klein, appealing a settlement by our Claims Division, dated March 16, 1979, which disallowed his entitlement to backpay for the period March 4, 1974, through October 24, 1976, incident to a temporary promotion received effective May 2, 1973. We sustain the disallowance because after March 3, 1974, he was not serving in a position officially classified at the higher grade.

The file reflects that Mr. Klein, a grade GS–13 Chemical Engineer with the Department of the Army at Aberdeen Proving Ground, Maryland, was unofficially detailed to a grade GS–14 Supervisory Mechanical Engineer position (Chief) in the Flame Section on January 2, 1973, and officially detailed to the position on April 2, 1973. That position was officially classified at the GS–14 level until March 3, 1974, at which time it was reduced to a grade GS–13 level. The reason given for the classification reduction was that on administrative examination it was determined that the organizational structure of that section was such that it would not support a Chief of the section at the grade GS–14 level.

Based on our ruling in the *Turner-Caldwell* decisions, 55 Comp. Gen. 539 (1975) and 56 Comp. Gen. 427 (1977), our Claims Division authorized backpay for Mr. Klein based on a retroactive temporary promotion from May 2, 1973 (the 121st day of his detail) through March 3, 1974. The disallowance of his entitlement for the period subsequent to March 3, 1974, was due to the classification downgrading of the position at that time and that during the remainder of the period Mr. Klein did not occupy any position graded higher than grade GS–13.

Mr. Klein contends that the duties he performed before and after March 3, 1974, were the same; that there were no personnel realignments; and that the downgrading of the position was but a technicality. It seems to be his view that in order to be in consonance with the spirit of the *Turner-Caldwell* decisions, once an individual is detailed to a higher graded position and becomes entitled to the compensation of that position because of that detail, he is entitled to continue to receive the pay of the position until the duties and responsibilities of the position are altered or until he is removed, notwithstanding the fact that the position is classified downward.

We disagree. It was ruled in the *Turner-Caldwell* decisions that an employee detailed to a higher graded position for more than 120 days without Civil Service Commission approval (now Office of Personnel Management) is entitled to a temporary promotion with backpay for the period beginning with the 121st day of the detail until the detail in the higher grade is terminated. As it relates to the present case, the key element in those decisions was the existence of a position classified at a grade higher than the position to which the detailee was officially appointed. Pay entitlements arising from details to a position other than the position to which officially appointed, like the pay entitlements of the position to which the employee is officially appointed, are solely dependent on the actual classification of the position in question.

Chapter 51 of title 5, United States Code, provides a system whereby General Schedule positions in the Federal Government are grouped and identified by classes and grades based on their duties, responsibilities and qualification requirements. Individual agencies under the guidance of the Office of Personnel Management are authorized to place positions in appropriate classes and grades consistent with their needs and in conformance with standards published by the Commission. In this regard, CSC Bulletin No. 300–40, dated May 25, 1977, provided a reminder to all agencies in paragraph 4, citing to the United States Supreme Court decision in *United States* v. *Testan*, 424 U.S. 392

(1976). That paragraph indicated that in order for an employee to receive pay for the performance of particular duties that would qualify as a position, the position must be an established one, classified under an occupational standard to a particular grade or pay level.

It is fundamental that in order for an individual to be entitled to compensation for employment by the Federal Government in a particular position or grade level, the position or grade must be recognized and administratively established at the time the individual is performing the duties of that position or grade. This is true even where an individual is officially occupying a position at one grade level and is performing duties which would be performed by an employee classified at a higher grade.

In other words, a person serving on a detail to a position other than the one to which officially appointed, receives the salary of that position if the detail lasts more than 120 days. However, since it is within the authority of the agency to adjust the classification of any position regardless of the duties, the occupant of the position may only receive the salary authorized for the position at any one time.

Thus, it is our view that regardless of the length of detail beyond 120 days, if the position to which an employee is detailed is reclassified downward from a higher grade level to a grade level equal to the position that the detailee was officially appointed to, he is not entitled to the pay at the higher level on and after the effective date of that reclassification action.

Accordingly, the action taken by our Claims Division, disallowing that part of Mr. Klein's claim for the period following the position reclassification, is sustained.

Mr. Klein has also requested the opportunity to present oral testimony to us and to be assisted by counsel should it be of benefit to our reconsideration of his claim. While we are always willing to discuss matters with claimants, we do not hold formal hearings. Instead our decisions are based on the written record presented by the interested parties such as the agency and the claimant as in this case.

〔 B–194626 〕

Unions—Agreements—Legality

Federal Labor Relations Authority requests decision whether collective bargaining agreement provision conflicts with the Comptroller General's standards for waiver contained in 4 C.F.R. Part 91. Agreement requires agency to notify employee of error within 5 days of payment to employee or overpayment will be waived. Where agreement does not consider employee's obligation to inquire as to correctness of payment, it is inconsistent with standards for waiver and may not be implemented.

In the matter of National Treasury Employees Union and U.S. Customs Service, Region IX—Negotiated Agreement Concerning Waiver of Erroneous Payments, August 9, 1979:

This decision is in response to the request from the Federal Labor Relations Authority, FLRC No. 78A–29, concerning the legality of a provision in a locally negotiated collective bargaining agreement on waiver of erroneous payments of pay and allowances. The question presented for our decision is whether the provision in the negotiated agreement conflicts with the standards for waiver of claims issued by our Office and contained in 4 C.F.R. Part 91 *et seq*.

The Federal Labor Relations Authority is considering the negotiability of several provisions of a collective bargaining agreement entered into by the U.S. Customs Service, Region IX, and the National Treasury Employees Union. The provision of the agreement which is the subject of our decision provides, in Article 35, Section 3, as follows:

> The Employer agrees that where, through administrative error or oversight, an employee receives a monetary payment above that to which he or she would otherwise be entitled, said overpayment shall be waived upon a showing that:
> 1. The amount involved is not more than five hundred dollars ($500.00) or the equivalent;
> 2. The employee was not responsible for the error; and
> 3. Collection action under the claim would be against equity and good conscience and not in the best interests of the U.S. Government, that is, notice of the mistaken overpayment was not brought to the employee's attention by the Employer within five (5) calendar days of the payment.

The Customs Service argues that this provision is inconsistent with the standards for waiver issued by our Office, particularly 4 C.F.R. § 91.5(c), since the negotiated agreement would permit an employee who has not made reasonable inquiries as to the correctness of a payment to retain the overpayment. The union contends that the provision is consistent with the rules, regulations, and decisions of our Office with regard to the standards for waiver.

Under the authority of 5 U.S.C. § 5584 (1976) a claim of the United States arising out of an erroneous payment of pay or allowances may be waived if collection would be against equity and good conscience and not in the best interests of the United States. Such waiver may be made by the head of the agency when the claim is in an amount aggregating not more than $500 and by the Comptroller General for claims exceeding $500 provided "the waiver is made in accordance with standards which the Comptroller General shall prescribe." 5 U.S.C. § 5584(a). The law provides further that this authority for waiver may not be exercised if there exists, in connection with the claim, an indication of fraud, misrepresentation, fault, or lack of good faith on the part of the employee or any other person having an interest in obtaining a waiver of the claim. 5 U.S.C. § 5584(b).

The standards for waiver, promulgated by this Office under 5 U.S.C. § 5584, are contained in 4 C.F.R. Part 91 *et seq*. These regulations provide, in section 91.5(c), that a claim may be waived whenever:

(c) Collection action under the claim would be against equity and good conscience and not in the best interests of the United States. Generally these criteria will be met by a finding that the erroneous payment of pay or allowances occurred through administrative error and that there is no indication of fraud, misrepresentation, fault or lack of good faith on the part of the employee or member or any other person having an interest in obtaining a waiver of the claim. *Any significant unexplained increase in pay or allowances which would require a reasonable person to make inquiry concerning the correctness of his pay or allowances, ordinarily would preclude a waiver when the employee or member fails to bring the matter to the attention of appropriate officials.* Waiver of overpayments of pay and allowances under this standard necessarily must depend upon the facts existing in the particular case * * *. [Italic supplied.]

Our decisions have held that whether an employee who receives an erroneous payment is free from fault in the matter, can only be determined by a careful analysis of all pertinent facts, not only those giving rise to the overpayment but those indicating whether the employee reasonably could have been expected to have been aware that an error had been made. If under the circumstances involved a reasonable man would have made inquiry as to the correctness of the payment and the employee involved did not do so, then, in our opinion, the employee could not be said to be free from fault and the claim against him should not be waived. B–177629, February 22, 1973, and B–165663, June 11, 1969. See also *Gilbert G. Quintero*, B–183558, April 23, 1975.

In the present case, the collective bargaining agreement provision does not provide for an inquiry into the facts surrounding the overpayment. Instead, the agreement imposes a burden upon the agency to notify the employee within 5 days of the mistaken payment or lose its right to collect the overpayment. Furthermore, as the U.S. Customs Service has pointed out, the collective bargaining agreement does not take into consideration the obligation of the employee to make inquiries as to the correctness of a significant unexplained increase in pay or allowances. See 4 C.F.R. § 91.5(c).

As an example of the duty to make reasonable inquiries, we have held that where an employee has records which, if reviewed, would indicate an overpayment, and the employee fails to review such documents for accuracy or otherwise fails to take corrective action, he is not without fault and waiver will be denied. See *Roosevelt W. Royals*, B–188822, June 1, 1977, and decisions cited therein. An employee has the responsibility to verify the information provided on his payroll change slips or leave and earning statements, and where a reasonable man would have made inquiry but the employee did not, then he is not free from fault and the claim may not be waived. *John J. Doyle*, B–191295, July 7, 1978, and *Simon B. Guedea*, B–189385, August 10, 1977.

The provision of the collective bargaining agreement in question here makes no mention of the obligation of an employee to review records or documents in his possession for accuracy or to otherwise inquire as to the correctness of a significant unexplained increase in pay. The requirement that an overpayment be waived if the agency has not notified the employee of the error within 5 days does not take into consideration other facts which are relevant in determining if the employee is free from fault.

Accordingly, we conclude that the collective bargaining agreement provision is not consistent with the provisions of 5 U.S.C. § 5584 or the standards for waiver set forth in 4 C.F.R. Part 91, and such provision could not be legally implemented.

[B-194630]

Contracts—Specifications—Defective—Responsibility v. Responsiveness

Recommendation is made to cancel invitation for bids (IFB) and resolicit since record discloses that IFB was materially deficient and prevented fair and equal treatment of bidders by inclusion of "Reasonable Costs/Minimum Manning" clause which, by calling for bid rejection as unreasonably priced if below minimum manning cost, improperly converted matter of responsibility into responsiveness. Regulation cited as authority in clause (DAR 2–402.2(e) (1976 ed.)), which provides that bid may be rejected if unreasonable as to price, has been applied to permit rejection as nonresponsive of bid which is considered unreasonably high rather than low.

Contracts—Protests—Moot, Academic, etc. Questions—Solicitation to be Canceled

In view of recommendation that IFB be canceled, issues involving whether prebid conference should have been conducted to resolve questions with IFB or whether protest regarding alleged specific improprieties in IFB was timely will not be decided by General Accounting Office. Comment is offered that standard form of IFB provides mode to resolve such questions concerning IFB, and expectation that agency will take protester's specific complaints into account prior to resolicitation.

Contracts — Protests — Allegations — Burden of Proof — On Protester

Unsupported allegation of discrimination against minority contractors, which has been refuted by agency, does not meet protester's burden of affirmatively proving case.

In the matter of North American Laboratories of Ohio, Inc., August 9, 1979:

North American Laboratories of Ohio, Inc. (NAL), protests the proposed awards of contracts under invitation for bids (IFB) 33601–79–B0143, issued April 13, 1979, by the Base Contracting Branch, Wright-Patterson Air Force Base, Ohio. The IFB scheduled for opening on April 27, 1979, called for bids for custodial, janitorial and related services for various facilities at Wright-Patterson Air Force Base.

By letter dated April 10, 1979, NAL protested the procurement action to our Office. NAL sets forth four bases for protest. First, NAL contends that a prebid conference should have been held to permit bidders to ask questions regarding the IFB prior to bidding. Second, it is alleged that the IFB is constructed in such a poor and haphazard manner that it could force a contractor out of business or to commit fraud in attempting to comply with the requirements. NAL cites compliance with the minimum manning requirements as the problem, contending that in determining responsiveness to section D–3 of the IFB, the contracting activity is not assuring that sufficient cost has been included in the bid for taxes, insurance, supplies, equipment, vacation pay, G&A and profit. NAL next contends that the existing IFB provides the tools to contracting officers and inspectors to vary the quality of inspections so that some contractors would be allowed to provide less service than that required. NAL's final contention is that the history of contracting activities at Wright-Patterson Air Force Base shows a continuous pattern of discrimination against local black janitorial contractors.

Section D–3 of the IFB provides:

Reasonable Costs/Minimum Manning

In the evaluation of bids, the Government will compare the price bid for sub-items a. thru e. of each item to the total minimum cost established for each [of six] item[s]. The total minimum cost is established by multiplying the item minimum manning requirements (See Section F, paragraph 4–01) by the applicable minimum wage rates. Any bid which contains a price for sub-items a. thru e., which is less than the established item minimum costs, shall be determined to be unreasonable in accordance with DAR (ASPR) 2–404.2(e), and the bid for that item will be rejected as being non-responsive.

The Air Force states that this provision is used to ensure that the bidders have enough dollars in their bids to provide the required services and to preclude the contractor from offering a price that is so low that it will be forced out of business. Its experience has indicated that failure to include this provision results in awards of contracts to contractors who cannot satisfactorily accomplish its requirement, even though preaward surveys have been performed. Further, the agency argues that bidders are not precluded from including the costs cited by NAL. To the extent NAL is alleging "buying in" and "potential for selective enforcement," the Air Force views such statements as speculative and "GAO has repeatedly held that a below cost bid is not a legal basis for precluding or disturbing a contract award."

In our view, the subject IFB is materially deficient because section D–3 requires that noncompliance with this clause will result in a bid being rejected as nonresponsive. In our opinion, the Air Force has improperly converted a matter of responsibility into responsiveness. The Air Force's rationale for section D–3 relates to the ability and not the legal obligation of the bidder to perform the contract. We have stated that a matter of responsibility cannot be made into a question of responsiveness by the terms of the solicitation. *Reliable Building Maintenance Co.*, B–190167, February 17, 1978, 78–1 CPD 139; *Haughton Elevator Division, Reliance Electric Company*, 55 Comp. Gen. 1051 (1976), 76–1 CPD 294. We note here that the Air Force correctly states our position against rejecting below-cost or unprofitable bids other than in the context of responsibility. Yet, that is exactly the effect of the application of section D–3. Further, the section's specified authority to reject bids as nonresponsive is not authority to reject an unreasonably *low* bid. DAR § 2–404.2(e) (1976 ed.), which provides that a bid may be rejected if it is unreasonable as to price, applies only to reject for the benefit of the Government excessively *high* bids. Similarly, DAR § 2–404.1(b)(vi) permits cancellation of an invitation where otherwise acceptable bids are at unreasonable (i.e., high) prices. We find no support for a provision such as section D–3.

Moreover, the regulations provide measures to be taken if a bid is suspected of being too low. For example, the contracting officer should request verification as required by the mistake in bid procedures set forth in DAR § 2–406 (1976 ed.). Further, DAR § 1–311 (1976 ed.), dealing with the practice of "buying in," does not permit the contracting officer to reject as nonresponsive a bid suspected of being below cost. Rather, postaward and follow-on procurement safeguards are required to protect the Government.

We stated in *Edward B. Friel, Inc.*, 55 Comp. Gen. 231, 237 (1975), 75–2 CPD 164, that "The fact that the terms of an IFB are deficient in some way does not necessarily justify cancellation after bids have been opened and bidders' prices exposed." See *Joy Manufacturing Company*, 54 Comp. Gen. 237 (1974), 74–2 CPD 183. However, in determining if a cogent and compelling reason exists to justify cancellation, two factors must be examined: (1) whether the best interest of the Government would be served by making an award under the subject solicitation, and (2) whether bidders would be treated in an unfair and unequal manner if such an award were made. Here, we believe that the inclusion of the "Reasonable Costs/Minimum Manning" clause clearly prevented fair and equal treatment of bidders. See *Dyneteria, Inc. and La Tex Foods, Inc.*, B–190029, December 16, 1977, 77–2 CPD 475. Five of the 26 bids were determined to be nonresponsive as being below the minimum manning requirements to at least one of the six specified items, including the bids of two of the proposed awardees. In addition, the clause may very well have contributed to the "responsiveness" of the other 21 bids by forcing those bidders to exceed the minimum. Further, the inclusion of this clause may have discouraged other firms from submitting bids.

Accordingly, a cogent and compelling reason exists for the cancellation of the IFB and we recommend that the Air Force resolicit. Any new solicitation should eliminate the objections we noted in the "Reasonable Costs/Minimum Manning" clause.

NAL, prior to bid opening, contended generally that the contracting officer should have conducted a prebid conference to permit bidders to ask questions regarding the IFB. NAL, in a letter to our Office dated well after bid opening, refers to specific alleged improprieties in the IFB. Although it appears that the questions raised by counsel are untimely under our Bid Protest Procedures, 4 C.F.R. § 20.2(b) (1) (1979), since they were not raised prior to bid opening, we need not decide this issue or the necessity for a prebid conference in view of our recommendation that the subject IFB be canceled.

However, we offer the following comments. The requirement and scheduling of a prebid conference rests with the contracting officer. See DAR § 2-207 (1976 ed.). Further, the subject IFB, as will the resolicitation, in paragraph 3 of Standard Form 33A, Solicitation Instructions and Conditions, provides that "Any explanation desired by an offeror regarding the meaning or interpretation of the solicitation, drawings, specifications, etc., must be requested in writing and with sufficient time allowed for a reply to reach offerors before the submission of their offers." Bidders are required by this provision to specifically raise all questions they may have regarding the IFB prior to submitting a bid. In conclusion here, we trust the agency will take the protester's specific complaints into account prior to the resolicitation.

NAL makes an unsupported statement that section D-3 provides the tools to contracting officers and inspectors to vary the quality of inspection. In view of our conclusion that this section is objectionable, this matter is moot and will not be considered.

NAL further contends that the history of contracting activities at Wright-Patterson Air Force Base shows a continuous pattern of discrimination against local black janitorial contractors. No support for this statement appears in the record. Contrary to NAL's contention, the contracting officer states that over 56 percent of the previous year's custodial awards were made to minority contractors. Our Office does not conduct investigations for the purpose of verifying a protester's allegations and speculations. It is the responsibility of the protester to present probative evidence to affirmatively establish its position and

NAL has failed to do so in this case. See *Bowman Enterprises, Inc.*, B-194015, February 16. 1979, 79-1 CPD 121.

In view of our conclusion that the IFB is defective and thus no award should be made, by letter of today to the Secretary of the Air Force we are recommending resolicitation.

The protest is sustained.

[B-194388]

Bidders — Suspension — Validity — Procedural Requirements — Noncompliance

When agency decides to suspend contractor, it must independently follow applicable regulations since ongoing suspension by one agency does not suspend contractor at all other agencies, but only provides basis for other agencies to impose concurrent suspension.

In the matter of Opalack & Company, August 10, 1979:

Opalack & Company (Opalack) protests the award of a contract to Leonard G. Birnbaum and Company (Birnbaum) under request for proposals (RFP) No. ADA-0A-79-0001 issued by the National Institute of Mental Health, Department of Health, Education, and Welfare (HEW). Although its proposal was found to be within the competitive range, Opalack was eliminated from consideration when the contracting agency learned that the Department of Labor (DOL) had suspended Opalack from DOL contracting as a preliminary step in a debarment proceeding. Opalack argues, however, that if HEW also wants to disqualify Opalack from receiving any contracts it must in turn follow the proper procedures for the suspension of contractors and may not, as done here, summarily suspend Opalack based on the information received from DOL. For the reasons indicated below, we sustain Opalack's protest.

The RFP was issued on October 6, 1978, requesting proposals to provide financial advisory services for the Alcohol, Drug Abuse, and Mental Health Administration (ADAMHA). Specifically, these services are: (1) cost and price analyses of grant applications; (2) preaward and postaward surveys; (3) indirect cost verification; and (4) postaward reviews, reports and studies. Seven timely proposals were received and evaluated. As a result of this evaluation, the contracting officer established a competitive range consisting of four firms that included Opalack. However, prior to the opening of negotiations, the contracting officer learned that DOL had suspended Opalack as a preliminary step in a debarment proceeding. Acting upon the advice of his Office of General Counsel, the contracting officer decided that due to the DOL suspension he would not conduct negotiations with Opalack and would eliminate that firm from further consideration. Subsequently, negotiations were conducted with the three remaining offerors and on March 15, 1979, a contract was awarded to Birnbaum for the period of March 15 to September 30, 1979.

Upon learning of this award, Opalack filed a protest with our Office on March 16, 1979, arguing that once HEW decided to suspend Opalack the agency had to independently follow the procedures set forth in 41 C.F.R. Part 1-1.6 (1978) for the suspension of contractors and could not accept DOL's suspension of Opalack as also suspending Opalack from further contracts with HEW. In addition, Opalack maintains that this action violates the Small Business Act, as amended by Pub. L. No. 95–89, 15 U.S.C. 631 note, since as a small business Opalack was entitled to have this matter referred to the Small Business Administration (SBA) for a determination of responsibility.

HEW concedes that Opalack is qualified to perform the contract and that its proposal was lowest in estimated cost of those received. As to Opalack's contention that the contracting officer should have referred the matter to SBA for possible issuance of a certificate of competency (COC), HEW maintains that the validity of this argument is dependent on the merit of Opalack's allegation that it was improperly suspended. That is, if the suspension was proper then it is not a matter of responsibility and need not be referred to SBA for consideration under the COC program. In regard to the validity of the suspension, HEW agrees with Opalack that 41 C.F.R. §§ 1–1.605–1(b) and 1–1.605–3 indicate that the decision to suspend is an action which must be taken independently by individual agencies. However, HEW also maintains that a different conclusion may reasonably be reached by reading 41 CFR § 1–1.605–5(a) which states:

> Bids and proposals shall not be solicited from suspended contractors. If received, bids and proposals shall not be considered and awards for contracts shall not be made to suspended contractors unless it is determined by the agency to be in the best interest of the Government.

In HEW's opinion, since an agency imposing a suspension would have the authority to remove that suspension, the phrase "unless it is determined by the *agency* to be in the interest of the *Government*" can reasonably be construed as applying to agencies other than the one which suspended the contractor. [Italic supplied.] This means, according to HEW, that a suspension by one agency suspends the contractor from contracting with any Government agency. Therefore, in light of what it believes to be ambiguities in the regulations, HEW emphasizes that while the decision to eliminate Opalack from further consideration may have been erroneous, it was not arbitrary, capricious or in bad faith. Consequently, while conceding that Opalack's protest has merit, HEW believes that due to these alleged ambiguities in the regulations as well as the adverse impact of termination, the short duration of the current contract, and the fact that a new solicitation is currently in process for which Opalack is eligible for award, the Birnbaum contract should not be terminated for the convenience of the Government.

We must determine, therefore, what relief is appropriate under the circumstances.

The record indicates that upon being notified by DOL of its immediate suspension and proposed debarment, Opalack requested a hearing on the matter. This hearing was held before a DOL Administrative Law Judge who on March 16, 1979, issued an order which immediately terminated Opalack's suspension. The judge found that DOL had failed to comply with its own rules and regulations with respect to the suspension of contractors and that the evidence of Opalack's alleged misconduct was not of such a serious nature as to warrant suspension within the meaning of 41 C.F.R. § 1–1.605–1(a)(2). The debarment proceeding, however, was deferred until the judge could receive and consider both the hearing transcript and the briefs of counsel. We have been advised that this proceeding is still pending.

It is clear, therefore, that HEW's decision to eliminate Opalack from consideration for award of this contract was based upon an improper DOL suspension. While we do not question HEW's right to accept the validity of the DOL suspension when first notified of its existence, we also believe that the regulations for the suspension of contractors were established to help avoid problems such as the one that developed here.

A "suspension" is a disqualification from Government contracting for a temporary period because the contractor is suspected upon adequate evidence of engaging in criminal, fraudulent or seriously improper conduct. 41 C.F.R. § 1–1.601–1(b) (1978). The regulations recognize that suspension is a drastic action and, as such, should not be based upon an unsupported accusation. 41 C.F.R. § 1–1.605(b) (1978). However, a suspension invoked by one agency may be the basis for the imposition of a concurrent suspension by another. 41 C.F.R. § 1–1.605–1(b) (1978). But whatever the basis for the suspension, the Government is required to insure fundamental fairness to the firm or individual involved since the loss of Government business may cause a suspended contractor severe economic problems. *Horne Brothers, Inc. v. Laird*, 463 F. 2d 1268 (D.C. Cir. 1972). Such fairness requires that the contractor be given specific notice of at least some of the charges against it and be given, in the usual case, an opportunity to rebut those charges. *Horne Brothers, Inc. v. Laird, supra*, at 1271; see also 41 C.F.R. §§ 1–1.605–3 and 1–1.605–4 (1978). HEW's explanation for this failure is that it believes that 41 C.F.R. § 1–1.605–5(a) creates an ambiguity over whether the suspension of a contractor by one agency suspends that contractor at all other Government agencies.

We believe, however, the only reasonable interpretation of section 1–1.605–5(a) is that after an agency has followed the proper procedures for suspending a contractor, the agency shall not consider any bid or proposal submitted by that contractor or award it any contract unless the agency first determines that this action would be in the best interest of the Government. Nothing in this section relieves an agency of its duty to provide a suspended contractor with the procedural rights mentioned above. We believe, therefore, that read as a whole, the regulations pertaining to the suspension of contractors clearly indicate that each agency must determine on its own whether or not a particular contractor should be suspended. And although this determination may be based on a suspension imposed by another agency, each agency must follow the regulations in making that determination and in providing the contractor with the necessary procedural rights.

In Opalack's case, HEW had intended to suspend that firm at the time it decided to eliminate it from further consideration for award. Opalack was never notified of this action or given an opportunity to rebut the charges against it. As shown above, this was contrary to the regulations. Opalack now requests that the contract with Birnbaum be terminated for the convenience of the Government and the balance of that contract be awarded to it.

In our decision of *Opalack & Company*, B–193634, May 8, 1979, 79–1 CPD 319, we held that since DOL had found Opalack to be nonresponsible prior to any suspension or debarment, it was required under the Small Business Act (15 U.S.C. § 637(b)(7) (1976 & Supp. I 1977)) to refer the matter to SBA for consideration under the COC program because, under that act, the SBA is empowered to certify conclusively to Government procurement officials with respect to all elements of responsibility. Here, since the regulations were not followed, Opalack was never actually suspended, but was in effect found nonresponsible. HEW could not have rejected Opalack's proposal, if the best proposal after negotiations, without referring the matter to SBA for possible issuance of a COC. We note that the SBA recently issued Opalack a COC for the solicitation which was the subject of *Opalack & Company*, *supra*.

Since it would be necessary to reopen negotiations and subsequently reevaluate proposals before terminating the existing contract and since there is a brief time remaining before the completion of the contract on September 30, no recommendation is being made for corrective action at this time. However, by separate letter of today, we are advising the Secretary of HEW of the deficiency in the conduct of this procurement

and recommending that steps be taken to avoid any similar occurence
in the future.

Protest sustained.

[B-194897]

Liens—By Government—Release to Property Owner

Notwithstanding doubt that valid judgment lien exists, real property owner's
request for release of lien under 28 U.S.C. 2410(e) on basis that outstanding
judgment against former owner creates a cloud on title is denied, since applicant
holds title acquired in foreclosure sale and is not lien holder as required by
statute.

In the matter of Paul Waliga—Request for Release of Judgment Lien on Real Property, August 13, 1979:

Mr. Paul Waliga has requested a release of a lien on real property
owned by him and located in Leon County, Florida, arising from a
judgment entered in favor of the United States against Marvin V.
Scott, the former owner of the property. Mr. Waliga states that, in
the circumstances described below, the outstanding judgment against
Scott is a cloud on the property title. However, instead of filing suit
to quiet title, he asked the Department of Justice to issue a release of
the lien, and Justice has forwarded the request to us for consideration
under 28 U.S.C. § 2410(e) (1976). While it is doubtful that the United
States has a valid lien on Mr. Waliga's property, for the reasons that
follow, we are unable to honor Mr. Waliga's request.

The lien in question arose from a March 30, 1962, judgment in the
District Court for the Middle District of Alabama against Mr. Marvin
V. Scott in favor of the United States. Scott later moved to Florida,
and the Justice Department registered the Alabama judgment in
Florida on March 29, 1972. Under 28 U.S.C. §§ 1962 and 1963, a judgment obtained in the District Court of one State and registered in
another State creates a lien on property in the second State to the
same extent as a judgment in that State's own courts of general jurisdiction. Therefore, Florida law is controlling with respect to the
Government's lien interest, if any, in the property in question.

In January, 1972, Mr. Scott and his wife purchased the property
in question, taking title as tenants by the entirety. The Scotts subsequently defaulted on a second mortgage, and Mr. Waliga purchased
the property at a foreclosure sale in 1978. The judgment against
Marvin Scott remains outstanding.

Ordinarily, a judgment recorded in Florida creates a lien interest
in all the real property owned by the debtor. Fla. Stat. Ann. § 55.10
(West Supp. 1978). However, as noted, the property purchased by Mr.
Waliga at the foreclosure sale was previously owned by Marvin Scott

and his wife as tenants by the entirety. In Florida, property held by spouses under a tenancy by the entirety cannot be charged with the individual debts of either spouse, in the absence of fraud. E.g., *Ohio Butterine Co.* v. *Hargrave*, 79 Fla. 458, 84 So. 376 (1920). Therefore, a judgment lien cannot attach under Fla. Stat. § 55.10 to real property held by the entirety. *United States* v. *Gurley*, 415 F. 2d 144, 149 (5th Cir. 1969). Accordingly, we think it doubtful that in this case, a lien arising from the judgment against Marvin Scott ever attached to the property presently owned by Mr. Waliga.

Because Mr. Waliga nevertheless feels that the judgment casts a cloud on his title, he has requested the Government to release the property from the lien. We can honor such a request only in accordance with the provisions of 28 U.S.C. § 2410(e), which constitute the Comptroller General's sole authority to issue a certificate releasing liens of the United States. The requirements expressly stipulated by the statute which must be met before the Comptroller General can discharge a Government lien are (1) that a senior lien-holder apply for the release in writing to the officer responsible for the administration of the laws giving rise to the Government's lien, (2) that the applicant's lien be duly recorded, (3) that the Government's lien be junior and that it not be a tax lien, and (4) that the officer to whom the application is made, find and report that the proceeds from the property's sale would be insufficient to wholly or partly satisfy the lien, or that the Government's claim has been satisfied or that it is no longer enforceable because of lapse of time or for some other reason. Compliance with these conditions is a prerequisite to the exercise of our authority under the statute. See, *e.g.*, B–178601, June 4, 1973.

Since we have not received the responsible officer's (Secretary of the Army) report of findings, the procedural requirements of the statute have not been met in the present case. Moreover, even if the procedural requirements were met, we would be unable to issue a certificate of release since Mr. Waliga presently holds title to the property. As its owner, he does not qualify as one that "has a lien" on the property as required by the statute. B–194391, July 16, 1979. Accordingly, we do not have the authority to issue a certificate of release in this case, even if it is found that the United States does have a lien on this particular property.

In view of the doubts expressed above that the Government's lien attaches to property held by two persons as tenants by the entirety by reason of a debt owed to the Government by only one of the property owners, we suggest that Mr. Waliga seek legal advice as to the advantages of bringing an action to quiet title rather than continuing to seek a release of a lien on the property.

[B-191977]

Officers and Employees—*De Facto*—Compensation—Accrued

Claimant was hired from a certificate of eligibles and given a temporary appointment. Later, agency discovered he had been erroneously appointed due to a mistake of identity. He was removed and not paid his accrued pay or lump-sum annual leave. Since there was no absolute statutory bar to appointment and no fraud or misrepresentation by claimant, he is entitled to unpaid compensation and lump-sum leave payment. Prior inconsistent cases will no longer be followed.

In the matter of Victor M. Valdez, Jr., August 17, 1979:

Mr. Victor M. Valdez, Jr., has appealed our Claims Division's denial of his claim for payment of 1 week's salary and 57 hours of accrued annual leave. Mr. Valdez was removed from his temporary position as a Commissary Stock Handler, WG–4, at McClellan Air Force Base, California, on April 19, 1974, after his appointment was determined to be improper. As a result of that determination, his final salary payment was withheld and he was not paid for his unused annual leave.

The issue presented is whether an employee, whose appointment is found to have been improper, is entitled to receive unpaid compensation and payment for unused annual leave.

The hiring and removal of the claimant, Victor M. Valdez, Jr., involved a set of unusual circumstances. In April 1973, the area office of the U.S. Civil Service Commission sent a certificate of eligibles to the Headquarters, Sacramento Air Logistics Center, for use in considering candidates for Commissary Stock Handlers, WG–4, at McClellan Air Force Base. The certificate included a Victor M. Valdez of 4324 Cabrillo Way, Sacramento. The McClellan Employment Office sent a letter to Mr. Valdez at that address requesting an employment interview. On April 20, 1973, Victor M. Valdez, Jr., came in for the interview and was selected for the job. He was given a 1 year temporary appointment effective April 24, 1973.

Almost 1 year later, on April 17, 1974, the Civil Service Commission advised McClellan Air Force Base that the candidate it had certified was the claimant's father, Victor M. Valdez, Senior, based on his military service and associated veteran's preference rights. McClellan officials promptly notified Mr. Valdez, Jr., of the error and terminated his appointment effective April 19, 1974. Since the appointment had been improper, the base officials considered Mr. Valdez, Jr. to be in a "*de facto*" status and therefore entitled, under our decisions, to retain salary already received but not to be paid accrued pay or lump-sum leave.

We have extended our decisions to permit *de facto* employees serving in good faith with no fault on their part to be paid compensation equal to the reasonable value of their services during the *de facto* period. See 52 Comp. Gen. 700 (1973) and 55 *id.* 109 (1975). Our Claims Division denied Mr. Valdez's claim for unpaid compensation because it found that he was at least partially at fault in failing to question the propriety of his appointment since his father and he shared the same name and the letter requesting a preemployment interview did not specify whether it was intended for father or son. We shall discuss this point further below.

Although we have permitted *de facto* employees who serve in good faith to be paid unpaid compensation, we have, at the same time, adhered to the rule that there is no right to annual leave for *de facto* service. In *James C. Howard III*, 57 Comp. Gen. 406 (B–189741, April 4, 1978), we stated:

> We have recently extended the *de facto* rule to permit payment for the reasonable value of services rendered by persons who served in good faith. 52 Comp. Gen. 700 (1973) ; 55 *id.* 109 (1975) ; *Matter of William A. Keel, Jr.*, and *Richard Hernandez*, B–188424, March 22, 1977. However, because he is not an employee within the meaning of 5 U.S.C. § 2105, a *de facto* employee does not accrue any annual leave during the *de facto* period so as to be entitled to a lump-sum payment. See 31 Comp. Gen. 262 (1952).

See *James K. Saufley*, 57 Comp. Gen. 565 (B–189000, June 16, 1978).

In our cases, we have applied *de facto* status to an individual if there is no appointment or if an appointment is void. On the other hand, if there is an appointment and the period of service in question is determined to be "voidable" only and not "void *ab initio*," we have said that *de facto* status does not attach and the employee is entitled to all benefits of the position up to the date of separation, including lump-sum payment for annual leave. 37 Comp. Gen. 483 (1958); *Cherrold W. Seabrook*, 58 Comp. Gen. 197 (B–188693, January 5, 1979).

During the past year, we have reviewed our prior decisions in this area with a view toward adopting a rule that is easier to apply. There are several reasons for this review. The "void" versus "voidable" distinction, however clear in theory, has always been difficult to apply in practice and has led to confusion and uncertainty. Also, where a person has been appointed and has served in good faith for a period of time, it appears inconsistent to allow him to receive his unpaid compensation for the services, but not to receive lump-sum payment for unused annual leave.

Because of these considerations, we have decided to change our rule. Consequently, in those cases where a person has been appointed to a position by an agency and the appointment is subsequently found to have been improper or erroneous, the new rule is that the employee is entitled to receive unpaid compensation and to credit for good faith service for purposes of accrual of annual leave and to lump-sum payment for unused leave upon separation, unless—

(1) the appointment was made in violation of an absolute statutory prohibition, or

(2) the employee was guilty of fraud in regard to the appointment or deliberately misrepresented or falsified a material matter.

Our earlier decisions in conflict with this rule will no longer be followed. The new rule does not apply to persons who have never been appointed or who serve after their appointments have expired. Those persons do not satisfy the definition of "employee" in 5 U.S.C. § 2105 as "* * * an individual who is—appointed in the civil service by * * * [a designated official] * * *."

We must now apply this new rule to the claimant in the pending case. There was no statutory prohibition to his appointment and under the new rule we do not need to determine if his appointment was void or voidable. Hence, the remaining question is whether he engaged in fraud or misrepresentation of a material matter.

After the claimant's temporary appointment was terminated, the Air Force referred the matter to the Civil Service Commission to determine if any fraud had been involved. A Civil Service investigator contacted Mr. Valdez, Jr., and obtained an affidavit. Mr. Valdez, Jr., has furnished us with a copy of the affidavit he gave to the investigator.

In summary, the affidavit states the following. The claimant resided in April 1973 at his parent's home at 4324 Cabrillo Way. He had been out of work and had many applications on file, including one with the Civil Service Commission for a worker trainee position. When the letter arrived from McClellan Air Force Base addressed to Victor M. Valdez, he opened it because much of his mail was addressed that way. He assumed it was for him but he waited until his father returned from a trip and discussed it with his father. Mr. Valdez, Sr., said that the letter must be for the claimant because he, Mr. Valdez, Sr., had not indicated he was available for temporary work and also he was more interested in more technical assignments.

According to the affidavit, Mr. Valdez, Jr., thereupon filled out the application in his own name specifying "Jr.," and also indicated he was not a veteran, and included his draft board number. He went in for the interview, told the hiring clerk he was not a veteran, accepted the job offer, and went to work at the commissary as a stock handler. He had almost completed the one year temporary appointment when he first learned he had been improperly hired. He states that he had applied for the job honestly and was shocked to learn of the error.

The Air Force has not disputed Mr. Valdez, Jr.'s statements nor do we have any indication of fraud or misrepresentation on his part from the Civil Service Commission. In fact, the Air Force reports that following his termination on April 19, 1974, Mr. Valdez, Jr., was given another temporary appointment effective May 7, 1974, as an Aircraft Electrician Helper, WG–5. On the basis of all the facts presented, we believe that the claimant acted honestly and in good faith and was not responsible for the mistake regarding his identity. We find no fraud or misrepresentation on the part of Mr. Valdez, Jr.

Accordingly, since the erroneous appointment of Victor M. Valdez, Jr., did not involve any statutory prohibition or any fraud or misrepresentation on his part, he is entitled to receive his final week's unpaid compensation and a lump-sum payment for 57 hours of annual leave. Settlement will be made in due course.

[B–194643.2]

Foreign Aid Programs—Loan Programs—Procurements Using Borrowed Funds—Conducted By Foreign Government—Protest Status

Prior decision dismissing protest against procurement being conducted with Agency for International Development loan funds is affirmed as procurement is not by or for agency of Federal Government but being conducted by foreign government and is not governed by procurement regulations, thereby distinguishing instant situation from Foreign Military Sales procurements.

In the matter of Pettibone Corporation—Reconsideration, August 20, 1979:

Pettibone Corporation (Pettibone) has requested reconsideration of our decision in the matter of *Pettibone Corporation* (B–194643, May 2, 1979, 79–1 CPD 307) in which our Office declined to consider the merits of Pettibone's protest against invitation for bids No. 78/04 issued by the Alexandria Port Authority, Alexandria, Arab Republic of Egypt. The procurement is being conducted by the Government of Egypt using funds borrowed from and repayable with interest to the Agency for International Development (AID).

We dismissed the protest since the procurement involved neither a procurement by or for an agency of the Federal Government, nor a procurement by a Federal grantee. *Allis-Chalmers Corporation,* B–188514, April 5, 1977, 77–1 CPD 235, and *Bethlehem Steel Export Corporation,* B–189803, August 22, 1977, 77–2 CPD 139.

Pettibone's request for reconsideration is grounded on the contention that procurements under the AID loan program are no different than procurements conducted under the auspices of the Foreign Military Sales Program and, therefore, our Office should follow the same reasoning as that employed in our decision, *Procurements Involving Foreign Military Sales*, 58 Comp. Gen. 81 (1978), 78–2 CPD 349. In that decision we reconsidered our position relating to the review of procurements under Foreign Military Sales (FMS) and decided that we would entertain private party complaints in connection with the FMS procurements.

While both FMS procurements, especially section 23 transactions, and AID loan-funded procurements utilize appropriated funds, we believe there is a significant distinction which justified our not accepting jurisdiction over the latter category.

In FMS procurements, the Department of Defense conducts the procurements and, as noted in the 1978 FMS decision, the Defense Acquisition Regulation is applicable to the procurements. In the AID loan procurements, the foreign government which has secured the loan, repayable with interest, conducts the procurement. Therefore, the factual situation is more like that in *International Research Associates, Inc.*, B–192376, August 10, 1978, 78–2 CPD 113, wherein we declined jurisdiction of the protest of an award by the Federal Republic of Germany, financed with a loan of appropriated funds to NATO to be repaid by Germany, since it was not a procurement by or for an agency of the United States Government. See also *Central Construction, Inc.*, B–187699, February 23, 1977, 77–1 CPD 130.

Moreover, we acknowledge that 22 U.S.C. § 2393a (1976) provides that funds may not be expended after 35 days have elapsed following a request by our Office for any document, paper or other material in the custody of an agency carrying out a provision of the Foreign Assistance Act of 1961 (22 U.S.C. § 2251, *et seq.*) unless the document is furnished or the President certifies that he has forbidden the furnishing thereof and his reason for doing so. While that section would apply where a request for documents is made by our Office in an appropriate situation, we do not consider that section to require our Office to take jurisdiction of a complaint in circumstances as exist in this case. Further, we have not taken jurisdiction in the past in this kind of a case and we do not view the situation as requiring our involvement now.

Accordingly, we affirm our decision of May 2, 1979.

〔 B–170177 〕

Statutes of Limitation—Claims—Ten Year Period For Filing—Reduced to Six

Time limit for filing claims in General Accounting Office was changed from 10 to 6 years effective July 2, 1975, and claims received on that date which accrued prior to July 2, 1969, are barred.

Quarters Allowance—Civilian Overseas Employees—Entitlement—Administrative Discretion

General Accounting Office has no basis for overturning administrative determination, required by regulations, which fixed approved rent ceiling for employee's overseas private quarters at amount below rent he was actually paying and thereby disqualified employee for payment of living quarters allowance (LQA). Governing law and regulations give agencies considerable discretion concerning payment of LQA and there is no evidence of arbitrary and capricious exercise of discretion by agency.

In the matter of Wesley L. Goecker—Statute of Limitations—Living Quarters Allowance, August 23, 1979:

Mr. Wesley L. Goecker has requested review of the disallowance of his claim for a living quarters allowance (LQA) from February 25, 1966, to August 6, 1969. During this period he was a civilian employee of the U.S. Army Corps of Engineers stationed in Japan where he rented private quarters. The Army and the Air Force, which administered housing in the area, refused to grant him an LQA, initially on the ground that suitable Government quarters were available and later on the ground that the quarters he rented were not approved private housing as defined by governing regulations because the rent was in excess of the approved ceiling.

Mr. Goecker's claim was disallowed by the Claims Division of the General Accounting Office (GAO) because (1) it was received in GAO on July 2, 1975, the effective date of the change in the time limit for filing claims in GAO from 10 to 6 years and, therefore, that portion of the claim which accrued more than 6 years before receipt, i.e., prior to July 2, 1969, was barred, and (2) controlling regulations made the granting of an LQA discretionary with the employing agency and GAO had no authority to overrule the agency's determination regarding the claimant's entitlement in the absence of evidence that it was arbitrary or capricious.

Mr. Goecker contends that no part of his claim is barred because a letter dated March 14, 1975, from the Director, Transportation and Claims Division [United States General Accounting Office], indicates that claims received *on* or before July 2, 1975, will not be barred by the 6-year limitation. He further contends that regulations and implementing rental evaluation guides were defective, misinterpreted, and improperly applied to his situation, that some employees received an LQA even though their rent was known to be in excess of established ceilings, and that others obtained an LQA by understating the amount of their rent on their applications and paying the balance to their landlords "under the table" in violation of the regulations.

That portion of Mr. Goecker's claim which accrued prior to July 2, 1969, is in fact barred. The 10-year time limit for filing claims in GAO established by the Act of October 9, 1940, 54 Stat. 1061 (31 U.S.C. §§ 71a and 237) was changed to 6 years, effective July 2, 1975, by title VIII of Pub. L. No. 93–604, approved January 2, 1975, 88 Stat. 1965. B–185748, October 27, 1976. Since the claim was received in GAO on July 2, 1975, the effective date of this change, it is governed by the 6-year limitation. The letter of March 14, 1975, upon which Mr. Goecker relies is incorrect to the extent it indicates a different result.

Moreover, we can find no basis for allowing the remainder of Mr. Goecker's claim covering July 2 to August 6, 1969. Sections 5922(c) and 5923(2) of title 5, United States Code, provide that an LQA *may* be granted in accordance with regulations prescribed by the President. The President's authority was delegated to the Secretary of State by section 1(b) of Executive Order 10903, January 11, 1961, 26 F.R. 217. The Secretary's regulations, Standardized Regulations (Government Civilians, Foreign Areas) 1961, bestowed considerable discretion in the granting of an LQA upon heads of agencies and required them to withhold payment altogether when in their judgment circumstances warranted. Section 134.2 (TL:SR–144, 1–2–66). The Standardized Regulations also authorized heads of agencies to issue further implementing regulations. Section 013 (TL:SR–127, 1–6–63).

The implementing Air Force Regulations, 5 AFR 34–6, February 25, 1965, and its successor, 5 AFR 30–11, November 4, 1966, prohibited not only the payment of an LQA for, but also the occupancy of any other than "approved private housing." Approved private housing was defined as off-base private housing which met prescribed standards of construction, sanitation, and environment, and which rented for an amount not in excess of the ceiling approved for it under those regulations. Sections 2c, 8a, and 9.

The private housing occupied by Mr. Goecker was not approved and he was not granted an LQA because the rent he was paying—$100 per month plus utilities—exceeded the approved ceiling—initially $69.22 per month. As a result of his persistent complaints that his quarters had not been properly evaluated several additional evaluations were made and the ceiling was ultimately raised to $83.68 per month—still well below the amount he was paying.

We find nothing in the Air Force regulations inconsistent with the governing law or the Standardized Regulations. Neither do we find any substantial evidence that the Air Force abused its discretion and applied the regulations arbitrarily or capriciously to Mr. Goecker. On the contrary, it appears that considerable time and effort were devoted to determining the proper evaluation of his property—albeit not to his satisfaction. Accordingly, we have no basis for disturbing the determination that he was not entitled to an LQA. See B–161434, June 21, 1967, and February 20, 1970.

The file indicates that there may have been some misapplications and violations of the regulations as Mr. Goecker alleges. These of course should not have been permitted or condoned but they do not provide any basis for allowing his claim.

For the foregoing reasons the disallowance of Mr. Goecker's claim is sustained.

[B–195238]

Leaves of Absence—Sick—Recredit of Prior Leave—Evidence to Support Claim Missing

Employee may "buy back" sick leave taken in connection with a job-related illness in order to receive disability compensation under Federal Employees' Compensation Act, 5 U.S.C. 8101, *et seq.* Where there are no official records from which to determine amount of leave taken, leave may be credited and bought back on basis of secondary evidence determined to be acceptable by agency. Acceptable forms of secondary evidence include leave requests, Leave and Earnings Statements, Time and Attendance Reports, personal leave records, as well as certificates from supervisors and timekeepers.

In the matter of Oscar B. Bonner—"Buy back" of sick leave for leave without pay to accept compensation under the Federal Employees' Compensation Act, August 23, 1979:

Mr. Oscar B. Bonner has appealed the adjudication of our Claims Division in Settlement Certificate Z–2744941, dated March 16, 1979, denying his claim to "buy back" sick leave in order to accept compensation under the Federal Employees' Compensation Act for a work-related illness.

Fundamental to the adjudication by our Claims Division is the fact that the Federal Aviation Administration (FAA) stated that Mr. Bonner's official leave records for the period claimed have been destroyed. Thus, our Claims Division concluded that where the records necessary to either justify or refute a claim have been destroyed or become unavailable due to the lapse of time, the accounting officers of the Government, in the absence of clear and satisfactory evidence of validity, may not give the matter favorable consideration where the claimant has failed to act on his claim for a long period of years.

The claimaint has expressed dissatisfaction with this result, and in appealing the decision of our Claims Division Mr. Bonner contends that clear and satisfactory evidence of an amount of sick leave used in connection with his work-related illness is provided in the record in the form of correspondence drafted by the Personnel Management Specialist at the Miami Air Route Traffic Control Center (Miami ARTC Center) where Mr. Bonner was employed. We believe Mr. Bonner's contention is meritorious in the circumstances presented.

The record in support of Mr. Bonner's appeal presents the following chronology of events. In October 1967, Mr. Bonner received a flu shot given by the FAA. Subsequently, Mr. Bonner became ill and was hospitalized. However, it was not until Mr. Bonner visited the Mayo Clinic in August 1968 that his illness was correctly diagnosed. In October 1972, Mr. Bonner filed with the Office of Workers' Compensation Programs, claiming a job-connected illness. In July 1975, the Office of Workers' Compensation Programs informed both Mr. Bonner and the FAA that it had determined that Mr. Bonner's disability had been caused by the flu shot. Then, in August of 1976, the Office of Workers' Compensation Programs informed Mr. Bonner by letter that the injury entitled him to all compensation and medical benefits provided by the Federal Employees' Compensation Act for the inclusive periods from October 30, 1967, to February 1, 1968, and August 8 to August 23, 1968. This correspondence also advised Mr. Bonner in regard to the procedural requirements for effecting a "buy back" of the sick leave he had used during those periods.

In September of 1976, Mr. Bonner attempted to "buy back" the sick leave he had used by filing an "Application for Reinstatement of Leave" through the Office of Workers' Compensation Programs. In December of 1976, Mr. Bonner was notified that his employing agency was unable to provide the information necessary to permit restoration of sick leave because official records for the period in question had been destroyed. In January of 1977, the Personnel Management Specialist at the Miami Center—the facility at which Mr. Bonner was assigned— prepared a draft document based on facility records indicating that Mr. Bonner had used 530 hours of sick leave during the periods in question. However, following administrative review the agency determined that the application for restoration of leave could not be allowed on the basis of the information supplied and that no further action could be taken in the absence of Mr. Bonner's official sick leave records. Thereupon Mr. Bonner submitted his claim to our Claims Division for consideration.

An employee may not receive disability compensation under the Federal Employees' Compensation Act, 5 U.S.C. §§ 8101 *et seq.*, for a period that he is carried in a leave-with-pay status. Under 20 C.F.R. § 10.310, annual and/or sick leave taken in connection with a work-related illness or injury may be bought back and the employee may be placed in a leave-without-pay status so that he may receive disability compensation. See FPM chapter 630, S12–2(b)(4)(d) and FPM Supplement 990–2, Book 630, S12–2(b)(5)(e). While the FAA recognizes Mr. Bonner's right to buy back leave taken in connection with his work-related illness, it is of the opinion that it cannot properly determine the amount of leave taken in the absence of official records. Thus, the question presented for review in this appeal is the nature of evidentiary support required to substantiate a request for restoration of leave where official records are unobtainable.

Mr. Bonner's claim involves the certification of leave credits. In our decision in 32 Comp. Gen. 310 (1953) we held that the determination as to whether leave should be credited incident to transfer to an agency under a different leave system is the primary responsibility of the agency involved. We set forth the following rule for general application in instances where there are no official records from which to construct an employee's leave account:

* * * It is the view of this Office that the furnishing of *certifications* of leave credits based upon other than official records is not to be sanctioned. However, in lieu of a *certification*, where no official records are available, there should be furnished statements to requesting agencies of any other evidence which may be available in respect of employees' leave credits, including an estimate of his leave credit, if possible. Any such statements should clearly reflect the factors forming the basis of the estimate. The agency where the employee currently is employed may then determine whether upon the basis of such showing a credit of leave may be made.

More specifically, we have held that where an employee's leave records have been destroyed, an agency may accept as evidence of leave usage the officially approved leave requests. B–175742, June 20, 1972. In addition, we have held that acceptable secondary evidence which will serve as a basis for crediting leave includes Time and Attendance Reports, Leave and Earnings Statements, personal leave records, as well as certificates of former supervisors and timekeepers indicating leave earned and used. *Matter of Ruth L. Jones,* B–189288, November 23, 1977. See also B–171947, June 16, 1972, and B–164220, September 5, 1968.

The draft letter of the Personnel Management Specialist at the Miami ARTC Center presents the following partial reconstruction of Mr. Bonner's sick leave account in relation to the period of his illness:

In researching our facility records, we have positively established the use of five hundred thirty (530) hours. This determination was made as follows:

    (1) Standard Form 71 located in our employee's file establishes approval of three hundred ninety-four (394) hours of sick leave from October 30, 1967 through January 15, 1968 * * *;

    (2) We further establish ninety-six (96) hours from August 8, 1968 through August 23, 1968 while being diagnosed and treated at the Mayo Clinic located in Rochester, Minnesota. * * *;

    (3) In addition to above, supervisory personnel, Octavio Cowart, Assistant Chief, authorized sick leave for purposes of transportation to and from Mayo Clinic. These days were August 5, 6, 7, 26 and 27, 1968, for a total of forty (40) hours of sick leave.

We fully realize that Mr. Bonner used more sick leave in connection with this illness, but no records exist with which to substantiate leave in excess of five hundred thirty (530) hours.

The matter of establishing Mr. Bonner's leave usage does not directly involve a monetary claim payable by this Office. Thus, it is the employing agency rather than this Office that has responsibility for determining the acceptability of secondary evidence available from which to reconstruct an employee's leave account. We point out, however, that items 1 and 3 of the evidence referred to in the draft letter, quoted above, are in the nature of evidence which we have held to be acceptable in the absence of official records. Given the fact that Mr. Bonner was authorized sick leave for transportation to and from the Mayo Clinic in August 1968, it would be appropriate to rely on the bill from the Mayo Clinic referred to in item 2 as establishing his use of leave from August 8 to August 23, 1968.

Since the FAA's original conclusion that it is unable to provide information necessary to restore leave used by Mr. Bonner in connection with his job-related illness appears to have been based on the absence of official records, the employee's request for restoration of leave should be considered in light of the secondary evidence presented.

[B-194642]

Officers and Employees—Transfers—Relocation Expenses—New Appointees

New appointees cannot be reimbursed travel and relocation expenses from Washington, D.C., to next duty station. Record indicates that agency erroneously indicated Washington as permanent duty station instead of temporary duty station while appointees where trained for 4 months. New appointees must bear expense of reporting to first official duty station and such duty station must be where major part of employees' duties are performed and where they are expected to spend greater part of time. Government is not responsible for unauthorized acts of its agents. Erroneous payments must be collected.

Leaves of Absence — Annual — Charging — House Hunting Trip Upon Transfer

New appointees were erroneously authorized house-hunting trips from training site to first official station. Agency should charge employees annual leave for time spent on house-hunting trips. If leave charges result in negative leave balances, there are overpayments of pay which may be considered for waiver under 5 U.S.C. 5584. However, annual leave should not be charged for excess traveltime en route to appointees' first duty station required because of training.

Subsistence—Per Diem—Training Periods—Training Site Status

New hires and transferees may be authorized subsistence at Washington, D.C., since it is a training site and not a permanent duty station. Rate should be that authorized by Federal Travel Regulations. In this connection Washington has been designated as high-rate geographic area.

Travel Expenses—First Duty Station—Training Duty Prior To Reporting

New hires who traveled to training sites en route to first duty station may be authorized travel expenses in excess of what would have been incurred in traveling direct from employees' homes to their first duty station.

Officers and Employees — Transfers — Relocation Expenses — Temporary Quarters — Entitlement

Temporary quarters subsistence may not be paid incident to training. However, transferees would be entitled to that and other relocation allowances incident to permanent change of station.

In the matter of Cecil M. Halcomb, et al.—Reimbursement of New Appointees for Travel and Relocation Expenses, August 24, 1979:

This action is in response to a request from John E. O'Grady, an authorized certifying officer of the Fish and Wildlife Service (FWS), U.S. Department of the Interior, for an advance decision. The request involves reimbursement of travel and relocation expenses incurred by Cecil M. Halcomb, Michael A. Lucckino, David O. Cartwright, and James V. Klett, new appointees in a non-manpower-shortage category.

The four employees were assigned to the FWS Washington, D.C. office for a period of about 4 months. During that period they spent about 2 weeks in Washington. The remainder of the time was spent in training at Glynco, Georgia. The main issue is whether Washington was their duty station for the purpose of determining their entitlement to reimbursement of travel and relocation expenses. The agency has advised that it has paid similar claims and others are pending. Thus, our decision will be dispositive of similar past and present claims.

The record shows that the FWS Division of Law Enforcement uses Special Agents for the enforcement of Federal laws relating to wildlife. To meet the manpower requirements of law enforcement, FWS hires trainee Special Agents. In addition to the new hires, some of the trainees are transferred from within the agency or from other Government agencies. All of the trainees are considered by the Division of Law Enforcement to be Washington office employees and that office is designated as their official duty station. Travel orders are issued to this effect.

The trainees are normally directed to report to the Washington office for processing of employment papers and to take the Oath of Office prior to reporting to the Department of the Treasury Federal Law Enforcement Training Center (FLETC), Glynco, Georgia. Occasionally they may be directed to report directly to FLETC, in which case personnel from Washington go to Glynco to complete the paperwork and administer the Oath of Office. Prior to hiring, all candidates are told they will be sent to FLETC for a period of up to 4 months of training. A permanent duty location is to be determined prior to or upon completion of training.

Newly hired trainees are required to pay all of their expenses for travel to Washington. Trainees with prior continuous Government service are given orders transferring them to Washington at Government expense even though they have been informed that they will be assigned to a permanent duty station while at FLETC. In most cases such employees do not move their families until they are transferred again following training. All trainees, both new hires and transferees, pay their own subsistence expenses for the time spent in Washington, and receive a reduced per diem of $4 per day while at the FLETC.

The certifying officer questions the designation of Washington as the first official duty station because this results in the new employees being told that they will be entitled to moving and other travel expenses associated with a permanent change of station after they have completed training and have been assigned to another post of duty. He also believes that due to the nature of the assignment, and the short period of time involved, the Washington office should be designated only as an administrative headquarters for all trainees.

The certifying officer also states that prior claims of this nature have been authorized and paid. Also, without submitting any vouchers he has summarized the facts of four additional cases. Therefore, he raises the following specific questions:

1. If a determination is made that erroneous payments have been made will it be necessary to research prior payments and initiate collection action to recover amounts improperly paid, and charge annual leave accounts for the official duty time used for house-hunting trips and/or travel enroute to the official duty station?

2. If your answer to the first question is yes, may an allowance be made to new hires for subsistence expenses incurred for the time spent in Washington, D.C.? If so, at what daily rate?

3. If the answers to questions 1 and 2 are affirmative, are the transferees who were authorized PCS moves to Washington, D.C., entitled to subsistence? If not, are they entitled to temporary quarters under 5 USC 5724a(3) and FPMR 101-7.2-5.1?

QUESTION 1

The location of an employee's permanent duty station presents a question of fact and is not limited by the administrative designation. 57 Comp. Gen. 147 (1977). Such duty station must be where the major part of the employee's duties are performed and where he is expected to spend the greater part of his time. 32 Comp. Gen. 87 (1952); *Bertil Peterson*, B-191039, June 16, 1978. There must be some duties beyond taking the oath, physical examination, or job training. 22 Comp. Gen. 869 (1943). Also, see 41 Comp. Gen. 371 (1967). In the instant case the certifying officer says that at the mid-point in training at the FLETC, the trainees are brought to the Washington office for 1 week. That time, together with the time spent when the trainee first reports for swearing in, is normally the total time spent in the Washington office. Thus, the facts indicate that the agency designation of Washington as the first official duty station is erroneous.

The general rule is that an employee must bear the expenses of travel to his first permanent duty station in the absence of a statute to the contrary. 53 Comp. Gen. 313 (1973); 30 *id.* 373 (1951). Also, new appointees may not be authorized reimbursement of expenses which are authorized in the case of transfers, such as residence sale and purchase expenses, cost of househunting trip, etc. This is so even in cases where new appointees may be allowed travel and transportation expenses by statute. See Federal Travel Regulations (FPMR 101-7) paras. 2-1.5f(4) and 2-1.5g(2)(c) (May 1973). Moreover, an agency may not authorize expenses associated with a transfer of station based on the improper designation of a temporary duty station. B-166181, April 1, 1969.

It is unfortunate that the agency officials exceeded their authority by erroneously determining the employees' official duty station and authorizing travel and relocation expenses, but it is well established that the United States can be neither bound nor estopped by the unauthorized acts of its agents. 54 Comp. Gen. 747 (1975); *Kenneth P. Lindsley, Jr.*, B–194341, May 22, 1979; *Federal Crop Insurance Corporation* v. *Merrill*, 332 U.S. 380 (1947).

In view of the above the employees' claims for reimbursement for travel and relocation expenses based on Washington being their official station may not be paid, and the amount advanced to cover such expenses should be collected back in the usual manner. Also, since the payment of similar claims in the past would be erroneous under the well-established principles stated above, it will be necessary to research prior payments and initiate collection action when erroneous payments are identified. Such payments may not be waived since 5 U.S.C. § 5584 (1976) specifically states overpayments of transportation expenses and allowances may not be waived.

Under the principles stated above the authorization of house–hunting trips was not proper. Therefore, annual leave should be charged for the time spent by employees on improperly authorized house–hunting trips. In this connection we have held that waiver of a charge to annual leave under the provisions of 5 U.S.C. § 5584 is appropriate when, as a result of a later adjustment to an employee's leave account, it is shown that the employee has taken leave in excess of that to which he is entitled, thereby creating a negative balance in his annual leave account. Otherwise, there is no overpayment which may be considered for waiver under the waiver statute since the error is susceptible to correction through reduction of the employee's positive leave balance. 56 Comp. Gen. 824, 828 (1977); B–176020, August 2, 1972. Thus, it will be necessary to determine on a case-by-case basis if the employee has sufficient annual leave to his credit to cover the adjustment. If, after adjustment, it is shown that the employee took leave in excess of that to which he was entitled (resulting in a negative balance which cannot be brought forward to the following year's account), an overpayment is created for that year which may be considered for waiver. However, annual leave should not be charged for excess travel-time en route to the official duty station required because of the training.

Your first specific question is answered accordingly.

QUESTION 2

The new hires may be authorized subsistence at Washington since it is a training or temporary duty site, not a permanent duty station. 53 Comp. Gen. 313 (1973); 9 *id.* 359 (1930). The rate to be paid would be that authorized by the Federal Travel Regulations in effect at the time the employees performed such training. In this connection we point out that Washington has been listed as a designated high-rate geographic area since 1975. The new hires would also be authorized travel expenses in excess of what would have been incurred in going direct from the employee's home to his first duty station after completion of training. 22 Comp. Gen. 869 (1943) ; 10 *id*. 222 (1930).

Question number 2 is answered accordingly.

QUESTION 3

The transferees may be authorized subsistence to the same extent as the new hires as discussed in our reply to question number 2. Temporary quarters subsistence allowance may not be paid incident to training. However, as previously stated, the designation of Washington as a permanent duty station was in error. Thus, qualified transferees would be entitled to temporary quarters subsistence allowance incident to their permanent change of station. See *Robert V. Brown*, B–195281, May 24, 1976. Also, they may be authorized other relocation allowances incident to their transfer.

Question number 3 is answered accordingly.

GENERAL

The certifying officer questions the form of issuance of the travel orders. We would not object to any authorization which states the circumstances of travel as specifically as possible and the employees are not authorized reimbursement beyond the scope of the applicable statutes and regulations.

Accordingly, the agency should take such action as necessary consistent with the foregoing.

[B–194707]

Bids—Late—Nuclear Accident Effect

Where hand-carried bid was received one day after bid opening because common carrier closed its offices during emergency at nearby nuclear electric power generating plant, contracting officer properly rejected bid as late. Although facts of case are unique, they present no reason to depart from established rule, requiring rejection of late hand-carried bids, which has been applied where other extraordinary circumstances beyond bidder's control have disrupted delivery services.

In the matter of Unitron Engineering Co., Inc., August 27, 1979:

Unitron Engineering Co., Inc. (Unitron) protests the proposed award of a contract to Superior Steel Door & Trim Co., Inc., (Superior) under invitation for bids (IFB) No. N00104–79–B–0371, issued by the Navy Ships Parts Control Center (Navy), Mechanicsburg, Pa.

Bid opening was scheduled for 11:15 a.m., Monday, April 2, 1979, in Mechanicsburg. Unitron delivered its bid envelope to Airborne Freight's Chicago office on the afternoon of Thursday, March 29. The bid arrived at Harrisburg International Airport near the close of the working day on Friday, March 30. It was then transferred to the office of Central Penn Air Services, Inc. (Central Penn), at the airport terminal. From there it was to be delivered to the bid opening site the next work day.

Harrisburg International Airport is located in Middletown, Pa., approximately 20 miles from Mechanicsburg, but only about 2 miles from the Three Mile Island nuclear power generating facility. As a result of a nuclear emergency at Three Mile Island, Central Penn closed its office on the day of bid opening. However, the Ships Parts Control Center observed a normal work day and bids were opened as scheduled. Central Penn did not deliver Unitron's bid until April 3. The Navy later notified Unitron that its hand-carried bid was late and could not be considered under the terms of the late bid provision set forth in the IFB. Unitron contends that either its bid should be considered in spite of its lateness or the solicitation should be canceled and a new IFB issued. The Navy has withheld award of the contract pending our decision.

Unitron appears to concede that the late bid provision set forth in the solicitation precludes consideration of its hand-carried bid. Unitron contends, however, that the late bid provision is out-of-date and that the Government is responsible for not updating it to cover extraordinary circumstances such as nuclear accidents. In this regard, Unitron argues that an exception should be made to the late bid rules because the nuclear accident was "unique." Unitron also contends that the exception to the late bid rules relating to the use of certified or registered mail is unfair and prejudicial to the point of restricting transporting of bid documents to the U.S. Postal Service.

Our bid protest procedures require a protest based upon an alleged impropriety in an invitation for bids to be filed prior to bid opening. 4 C.F.R. § 20.2 (b)(1) (1979). To the extent that Unitron objects to the terms of the solicitation's late bid provision, its protest is untimely and will not be considered, since it was not filed prior to bid opening. However, we will consider the issue of the application of that provision to Unitron's bid.

We understand how in circumstances such as those present here, a bidder may consider as harsh the provision which prohibits consideration of late hand-carried bids. Nevertheless, we believe there is a strong policy reason which favors such a rule. Since bids are opened publicly, allowing consideration of a late bid, even one which is a few minutes late because of unusual circumstances over which the bidder had no control would lead to apprehension among timely bidders that the late bid was unfairly prepared after bid opening. The maintenance of the integrity and fairness of the procuring process is more important than the loss that a late bidder or the Government suffers from the rejection of a late, low bid. Therefore, we have held that all late bids must be rejected except for those permitted in the exact circumstances provided for in the invitation. *Southern Oregon Aggregate, Inc.*, B–190159, December 16, 1977, 77–2 CPD 477. We have applied this rule even when bids have arrived late under unusual circumstances over which the bidder had no control. For example, we have upheld an agency's refusal to consider a bid that was delivered late because of extreme weather conditions. *Hesse Machine & Mfg. Co., Inc.*, B–193984, February 23, 1979, 79–1 CPD 130. We have also upheld an agency's refusal to consider a bid that was delivered late when the bidder's representative was detained by the presence of a sniper in the area where bids were received. *Data Pathing Inc.*, B–188234, May 5, 1977, 77–1 CPD 311.

The specific circumstances of the present case appear to be unique in that Unitron's bid was delivered late because a common carrier closed its offices during an emergency at a nearby nuclear electric generating plant. Contracting officers do have authority to delay bid openings when unanticipated events indicate that bids "of an important segment of bidders have been delayed in the mails" or cause interruption of "normal governmental processes so that the conduct of bid openings as scheduled is impracticable." Defense Acquisition Regulation 2–402.3 (1976 ed.). The contracting officer reports, however, that mail deliveries were normal and, as stated above, the agency's normal workday was not affected. The contracting officer further advises that five bids were received and that it appears adequate competition was obtained. Under these circumstances, we do not believe that Unitron's bid should be treated any differently from a bid which is delivered late because of some other extraordinary and unforeseen circumstance such as a blizzard.

Since there is no legal requirement that Unitron's late bid be accepted or that the procurement be resolicited as Unitron has requested, the protest is denied.

[B–194322]

Contracts—Protests—Procedures—Bid Protest Procedures—Time For Filing—Initial Adverse Agency Action *v.* Solicitation Impropriety Provisions

Protest, initially filed with procuring agency, resulted in protester receiving notice of initial adverse agency action more than 10 working days before closing date for receipt of initial proposals—day that protest was filed with General Accounting Office (GAO). Section 20.2(a) of Bid Protest Procedures could reasonably be interpreted as permitting protest to be considered timely filed here so GAO will consider merits of protest. For future, to be considered timely, protest must be filed with GAO within 10 working days of initial adverse agency action even when initial closing date is more than 10 working days from such action.

Equipment — Automatic Data Processing Systems — Computer Service—Advertising v. Negotiation

GAO will not object to contracting officer's determination to negotiate on basis that it is impracticable to secure competition by advertising where, as here, reasonable basis exists. Here, procuring agency has shown that it must evaluate technical acceptability of proposals because, despite detailed request for proposals (RFP) specifications incorporating even more detailed references, all output situations have not, and cannot, be specified and offeror's technical flexibility to satisfy inevitable changes arising during contract must be ascertained.

Contracts—Negotiation—Evaluation Factors—Criteria—Adequacy

Protester contends that RFP's disclosed evaluation criteria failed to explain whether procurement was intended to achieve minimum standard at lowest price or whether price was secondary to quality. Contention is without merit where : (1) RFP states that award will be made to responsible offeror whose offer conforms to solicitation and is most advantageous to Government, price and other factors considered ; and (2) "price and other factors" is further defined as (a) extended unit prices, (b) prompt-payment discounts, and (c) net total annual price. RFP reasonably notified offerors that award would be made to responsible offeror who submitted low-priced, technically acceptable offer.

Contracts—Specifications—Restrictive—Minimum Needs Requirement—Start-Up Time

RFP requires that successful offeror be prepared for full production 90 days after award. Protester, who is unwilling to make preaward investment required for it to meet 90-day startup time, contends that requirement is unduly restrictive of competition. Agency believes that (1) time is reasonable for nonincumbent contractor and (2) Government will realize ultimate monetary savings by not extending time. Since GAO has recognized that agency can properly express its minimum needs in terms of reduced costs, and since there is nothing in record to show that agency's belief is incorrect, GAO has no basis to question startup time limit.

Contracts—Specifications—Restrictive—Minimum Needs Requirement—Administrative Determination—Reasonableness

Protester contends that RFP's suspense file requirement is in excess of agency's minimum needs, too costly and anticompetitive. Contention is without merit where (1) requirement does not prohibit protester from competing, (2) agency has shown that suspense file is frequently used, and (3) incumbent contractor has shown that file's effect on price is minimal.

In the matter of Informatics, Inc., August 28, 1979:

Table of Contents

Informatics, Inc., protests any award under request for proposals (RFP) No. PT–79–SA–C–00458 issued by the Department of Commerce for data processing services for the preparation of a full-text patent data base and related computer tapes. Basically, the data base constitutes a machine-format archive of patents issued during the contract term; the associated tapes are used to drive an automated typesetting machine, which produces camera-ready copy for published patents and the *Official Gazette*.

This contractual requirement has existed since 1970. Since that time, there has been only one contractor—the present incumbent. Informatics believes that because of the nature of the RFP, which is overly restrictive of competition, it is likely that the incumbent will retain this contract. Informatics notes that the predecessors of the RFP have been the subject of frequent—and usually successful—protests to our Office.

In essence, Informatics raises four bases of protest:

1. The solicitation was issued as a negotiated procurement; however, given the statutory preference accorded to advertised procurements, the solicitation should have been issued under the procedures for formal advertising.

2. In the alternative, if the issuance of a negotiated solicitation was proper here, it must then address the evaluation criteria provided in the RFP; those criteria are inordinately vague and fatally defective.

3. The RFP requires a startup period of 90 days; this is too short; the startup time should be at least 120 days.

4. The RFP contains a suspense file requirement, which is onerous, noncompetitive and confusing; it should be eliminated.

In response, Commerce explains its procurement choices and requests that our Office rule on the timeliness of the Informatics' protest.

A. TIMELINESS

Commerce reports that Informatics first complained to the contracting activity on January 25, 1979, requesting the relief outlined above. Commerce responded to the complaint on January 26, 1979, denying Informatics' request for relief.

Commerce cites § 20.2 of our Bid Protest Procedures, which provides that, if a protest has been filed initially with the contracting agency, any subsequent protest to the GAO shall be filed within ten (10) days of the informal notification or constructive knowledge of the initial adverse agency action.

Commerce concludes that since Informatics' protest to our Office was not filed until March 9, 1979, is based on the actual notice of adverse action provided on January 26, 1979, by the contracting agency, the protest is not timely.

In response, Informatics contends that Commerce's argument ignores clear and explicit portions of the Bid Protest Procedures such as:

§ 20.2 Time for filing.

(a) * * * If a protest has been filed initially with the contracting agency, any subsequent protest to the General Accounting Office filed within 10 days of formal notification of or actual or constructive knowledge of initial adverse agency action will be considered provided the initial protest to the agency was filed in accordance with the time limits prescribed in paragraph (b) of this section * * *. In any case, a protest will be considered if filed with the General Accounting Office within the time limits prescribed in paragraph (b).

(b)(1) Protests based upon alleged improprieties in any type of solicitation which are apparent prior to * * * the closing date for receipt of initial proposals shall be filed prior to * * * the closing date for receipt of initial proposals * * *.

Informatics states that this regulation prescribes rules which define a timely bid protest; untimely protests are determined solely by inference, i.e., as those protests which are not timely.

In the case of protests "filed initially with the contracting agency," Informatics argues that § 20.2(a) sets forth two independent methods of achieving timeliness: (1) the first method—protests filed within 10 days of notice of initial adverse agency action—is one route to timeliness; and (2) the final sentence of § 20.2(a) provides the second route— protests filed within the limits of paragraph (b), i.e., within the normal time limits for a protest filed directly with GAO. Informatics contends that the use of the words "[i]n any case" makes clear that this second route to timeliness is a freely available alternative.

Informatics notes that there is no dispute here that the protest was timely filed under the provisions of § 20.2(b). Informatics states that Commerce's argument is not persuasive because (1) it overlooks the location of the last sentence of paragraph (a); (2) it entirely ignores the beginning phrase "[i]n any case;" and (3) it converts the sentence into a mere surplusage, which adds nothing to the remaining text of paragraphs (a) or (b). Informatics contends that its protest is timely since Commerce's position violates the customary canons of legal construction and does violence to the words and phrasing of the procedures.

In reply, Commerce states that Informatics delayed a full month and waited until the closing date for the receipt of proposal to protest to GAO. Commerce argues that since a protest had been initially filed by Informatics before the contracting officer, the provisions of § 20.2 (a) govern; to hold that § 20.2(b) is applicable would place a premium on delay tactics frustrating essential Government objectives, especially in this procurement, where Commerce is carrying out constitutional requirements—"To promote the progress of science and useful arts, by securing for limited times to authors and inventors the exclusive right to their respective writings and discoveries." Commerce concludes that aside from the Bid Protest Procedures, common rules of fairness to all parties required a timely and expeditious filing of the Informatics protest with GAO.

GAO Analysis

We believe that reference to the predecessor to our Bid Protest Procedures, the "Interim Bid Protest Procedures and Standards," lends some insight to the matter. There, in § 20.2(a), it was stated:

Protestors are urged to seek resolution of their complaints initially with the contracting agency. * * * If a protest has been filed initially with the contracting agency, any subsequent protest to [GAO] filed within 5 days of notification of adverse agency action will be considered provided the initial protest to the agency was made timely. * * *

That language and our cases interpreting it (see, e.g., 52 Comp. Gen. 20 (1972)) clearly provided that a protester had 5 days after initial adverse agency action to protest here. Under the old rules, Informatics' protest would be clearly untimely.

When the "Bid Protect Procedures" were promulgated, however, we revised the language used in § 20.2(a), as quoted above. We can see that the addition of the last sentence of that section ("In any case * * *.") could reasonably lead to the belief that we intended to relax the timeliness requirement in the circumstances of this case. That was not our intention; our intention was expressly stated in the opening sentence of part 20—"the *expeditious* handling of bid protests is indispensable to the orderly process of Government procurement and to the protection of protesters and other parties." [Italic supplied.] Accordingly, for the future, Commerce's view—that complaints initially resolved adversely to the protestor must be filed here within 10 working days of actual or constructive knowledge of that action to be considered timely—will be the rule followed by our Office; however, fundamental fairness requires that we consider the merits of Informatics' protest under the circumstances.

B. USE OF NEGOTIATED PROCUREMENT

Informatics states that a substantially identical RFP was issued in 1977 by Commerce for the same basic patent data base preparation services. Informatics protested asserting as one ground that the RFP should properly have been issued as an IFB. Commerce believed that its action was justified under the exception for advertising described in 41 U.S.C. § 252(c)(10) (1976)—the procurement of property or services for which it is impracticable to obtain competition by formal advertising. Informatics also states, in our consideration of that protest (*Informatics, Inc.*, B-190203, March 20, 1978, 78-1 CPD 215, affirmed on reconsideration, 57 Comp. Gen. 615 (1978), 78-2 CPD 84), we examined each of the justifications offered by Commerce and rejected each. First, the decision held that:

* * * the record does not demonstrate the impossibility of drafting adequate specifications; in fact, the record shows that the "explicit and voluminous" specifications describe in detail what the agency wants and makes competition among bidders based on that specification feasible and practicable in an advertised procurement.

Next, regarding the issues of price comparability and compatibility with the existing data base, we found that the desired objective could be achieved under formal advertising and that the use of negotiation would "add nothing." Also, the opinion stated that the desire to conduct discussions in order to insure that offerors understand the specifications or to ascertain their responsibility "cannot, in our opinion, authorize a negotiated procurement."

Finally, miscellaneous points, such as the alleged absence of prejudice and the failure of past IFB's to result in a valid contract were dismissed. In conclusion, our Office held that "negotiation is improper and the RFP should be cancelled."

Informatics contends that nothing has happened since our decision to change this result; the instant RFP is identical to the old RFP and no circumstances, specifications or requirements have changed since that time in a way which would warrant a different conclusion. Competition under formal advertising is as practical under the subject RFP as it was under the former RFP. Therefore, Informatics concludes that our Office should again sustain the protest on this ground.

In response, Commerce reports that it is the contracting officer's determination that use of a negotiated procurement is proper in this instance because the Government is seeking proposals which will reveal the greatest value in terms of performance, timely delivery, desired product quality, utilization of the latest state-of-the-art technology and other factors advanced by offerors which could enhance performance and ultimately furnish superior products at no extra cost to the Government. Further, negotiation would permit the Government not only to point out areas of the technical proposal that fail to meet the minimum needs of the Government but also to point out areas which unnecessarily exceed such minimum requirements. Both conditions are most likely to occur when the specifications are not sufficiently precise for use in formal advertising. Award would not be made without regard to price merely because a prospective contractor proposes to furnish more desirable supplies or services provided a lower priced offer met the minimum needs of the Government.

Commerce also reports that the solicitation and technical references are only guides to what is required and are not specific instructions on how to do the work, since it is not possible to set out in detail, every specific process of production and precise quantities of codes. For example:

1. Quantities vary over the life of the contract and no firm estimate can be made. Offerors were required to study and analyze typical patent application files to determine the level of expertise required. Although the number of patent application files could remain constant from week to week, the level of complexities and number of codes can vary.

2. The solicitation requires submission of technical proposals "which shall describe in comprehensive detail the technical approach including intermediate processing steps which are intended to be used to furnish all of the production items required under the contract * * *." The Government required proposals on each offeror's plan to accomplish the work. Indeed, the solicitation states, "The magnetic tape format * * * must be designed by the Contractor, and approved by the COTR * * *." It has been the Government's desire to solicit the best method and alternatives for establishing and implementing this requirement.

3. Other factors which cannot be adequately defined because the methods used to accomplish these tasks will vary from offeror to offeror, and include, but are not limited to:

a. Establishing methods and control for implementing procedural changes, which history has shown, will be required for the life of the contract.

b. Full and detailed proposals for implementing "new data items," i.e., capture of new data necessitated by changing requirements of the U.S. Patent System.

c. Timely delivery of all deliverable products.

d. Provision for modification of the Weekly Issue size.

e. Processing of "excluded matter" for the Data Base File(s).

f. Specifics concerning offeror's proposed Inspection System for controlling production operations.

g. Incorporating corrections to deliverable items prior to delivery.

h. Security procedures for safeguarding patent application files and related computer operations.

i. Proposed plan for controlling overall production operations.

j. Processing of "Query" patent applications, i.e., patent applications returned to the Patent and Trademark Office for clarification of incomplete or ambiguous data.

k. Reworking of rejected issues (weekly work).

l. Complex Work Units (CWU's), counting of billable codes.

4. The solicitation requires submission of detailed plans for the methodology and approach which would be utilized by offerors; especially significant is the requirement that offerors show how they propose to incorporate changes in systems and procedures which are unique to each offeror.

International Computaprint Corporation (ICC), the incumbent, argues that the specifications are not complete and, moreover, never can be; no better proof exists for that than Informatics' failure, after three attempts, to meet the requirements of the Pilot Patent Production Demonstration (PPPD) in the 1975 procurement. ICC states that

Informatics made innumerable queries about processing situations which Informatics' system was unable to handle without additional guides and then the specifications were substantially similar to the instant ones. ICC cannot understand how these specifications (woefully inadequate—according to Informatics in 1974) became complete and accurate in 1978.

Further, ICC states that the specifications are subject to new conditions in the data and in Commerce's rules for the data so that it is impossible to draft adequate specifications anytime because of the thousands of possible conditions which exist in patents. ICC also states that the RFP contains 30 individual pricing items, each with its own peculiar format, but the only complete set of specifications would contain an annotated copy of most of the 600,000 patents produced since 1970, an insurmountable task requiring negotiation. ICC contends that Commerce must evaluate whether each offeror's system is flexible enough to meet the unforseen circumstances thus averting disruption of the Government's work flow.

ICC argues that Informatics' contention that the specifications are complete show its failure to grasp the complexity of the patent processing; that Commerce can only determine the offerors' knowledge, understanding and capability by a technical review and Commerce must negotiate with an offeror, in areas of concern, possible deficiency and alternate processing means capable of meeting new variations in patent data.

In conclusion, ICC points to the following statement in *International Computaprint Corporation*, 58 Comp. Gen. 395 (1979), 79–1 CPD 248:

Based on our analysis, it may well be that NASA and Commerce may have reached diametrically opposed technical judgments about the need for offerors to assist in the definition of reasonable needs for ADP support. Nevertheless, we will not substitute our opinion for that of a procuring agency in matters involving technical complexity and judgment even where other governmental units may advance differing technical judgments on similar matters so long as the particular agency judgment in question is reasonably founded. See *E. I. du Pont de Nemours & Company, et al.*, B–190611, September 22, 1978, 78–2 CPD 218.

ICC stresses that Commerce's highly complex and intricate requirements—more so than the NASA procurement—must be procured by negotiation and our Office should not substitute our opinion for Commerce's.

In rebuttal, Informatics argues that a dispassionate examination of the *International Computaprint* decision and of the NASA procurement it concerned demonstrates that it has no relevance to the instant RFP. The *International Computaprint* decision set forth four factors which were considered the crux of the decision in *Informatics, Inc.*, B–190203, *supra:*

1. The RFP set forth complete input and output specifications for the contract deliverables.

2. No technical evaluation factors were identified in the solicitation; the sole factor identified in the RFP was total evaluated price.

3. Prior solicitations for similar services had been formally advertised.

4. Commerce wanted to conduct a technical evaluation as part of a responsibility determination and not as part of a comparative evaluation of proposals.

Informatics contends that all four factors have equal viability in the context of this protest and the instant solicitation: (1) the input and output specifications, described as "complete," are largely the same; if anything, they are now even more complete; (2) in the subject RFP and the RFP protested in B–190203, the technical evaluation factors were excluded; (3) history has not changed—the record still shows that Commerce issued several formally advertised solicitations for this requirement; and (4) the technical evaluation still takes place solely in order to determine the offeror's responsibility.

Informatics also argues that a review of the NASA procurement shows that it is wholly distinguishable from the instant case. Informatics believes that the intent of the Commerce contract is to provide two types of deliverables: (1) computer tapes used to prepare camera-ready copy for the printing of published patents and the *Official Gazette*, and (2) computer tapes to be used as a machine-readable archive of published patents; the format of the finished tapes is controlled, in every respect, by explicit and detailed specifications.

In contrast, Informatics states that the NASA procurement involved contractor operation of a Government-owned facility, the Scientific and Technical Information Facility (STIF). This program is an integral part of an ongoing NASA effort to disseminate the results of its researches and experiments. In effect, the contractor staffs a facility which is a working part of the agency. The contractor-agency interface is extensive; about 32 NASA employees monitor performance on a day-to-day basis. On the other hand, Commerce has a single onsite inspector and an administrative assistant devoted to day-to-day contract administration.

Informatics also states that NASA needed to procure using negotiation rather than formal advertising because it was unable to define its ongoing and dynamic needs. The NASA contractor's tasks were:

1. Performing minor modifications, planning and estimating minor systems improvements, and implementing reliability enhancements.

2. Proposal of a plan for determining and analyzing the costs and benefits of NASA products and services.

3. Possible replacement of NASA's existing ADP software and hardware under an assumed increase in system users.

4. Proposal of a plan for more rapid document delivery, including the independent analysis of different online systems.

5. Presentation of a detailed approach of improved research system reliability.

Informatics further states that in addition to NASA's inability to define its needs, it obviously needed technical proposals to assess a prospective contractor's ability to undertake "level-of-effort" tasks of considerable sophistication, but of unspecified scope and extent; thus, the NASA RFP provided for a comparative evaluation of technical proposals based on detailed criteria, with numerical weights, to be used in point scoring.

Informatics concludes that the lessons of *International Computaprint* are not applicable here.

Reasonable Basis Test

All contracts for services are required by Federal procurement law to be made by formal advertising unless certain enumerated exceptions, permitting negotiation, are applicable; the tenth exception concerns services for which it is impracticable to secure competition. 41 U.S.C. § 252(c) (1976). Federal Procurement Regulations (FPR), implementing this provision, illustrate one circumstance in which it is impracticable to secure competition—when it is impossible to draft adequate specifications or any other adequately detailed description of the required services. FPR § 1–3.210(a) (13) (1964 ed. circ. 1). This is the primary basis for Commerce's determination to negotiate rather than using formal advertising. We will not object to a determination to negotiate on that basis where any reasonable ground for the determination exists. 41 Comp. Gen. 484, 492 (1962); *Informatics, Inc.*, B–190203, *supra.*

Specifically, Commerce contends that its detailed RFP incorporating even more detailed references does not, and cannot, cover all the output situations that will arise; it must review proposed technical approaches to determine whether an offeror is offering the flexibility to satisfy inevitable changes arising during the life of the contract. We note that Commerce's approach differs materially from that used last year (B–190203, *supra*)—there Commerce did not contend that it was necessary to evaluate an offeror's technical approach to ascertain the technical acceptability of its proposal and Commerce contemplated no discussions with offerors. All parties recognize the technical complexity involved and amount of discretion which must necessarily be exercised by procuring agencies in this type of procurement. Our office is reluctant to substitute our opinion for the procuring agency in these matters (*E.I. du Pont de Nemours & Company. et al., supra*)—even where procuring agencies may have opposing views on similar subject matter (see *International Computaprint Corp., supra*) or where, as here, the procuring agency switches from one approach to another from one procurement to the next.

Accordingly, we cannot conclude that the negotiation basis advanced by Commerce is unreasonable.

C. EVALUATION CRITERIA

Informatics states that our Office held in a landmark case:

[I]ntelligent competition requires, as a matter of sound procurement policy, that offerors be advised of the evaluation factors to be used and the relative importance of those factors. 49 Comp. Gen. 229 (1969). We believe that each offeror has a right to know whether the procurement is intended to achieve a minimum standard at the lowest cost or whether cost is secondary to quality. Competition is hardly served if offerors are not given any idea of the relative values of technical excellence and price. 52 Comp. Gen. 161, 164 (1972).

Judged by this standard, Informatics concludes that the solicitation is defective because: (1) it does not explain the relative importance of cost factors when compared with technical factors; and (2) it fails to set forth what technical factors will be evaluated and their relative weights.

Commerce contends that the "crucial interrelationship between price and technical factors" is more than adequately provided for in the solicitation, which states that "[t]he technical proposals shall be void of any price information to permit independent technical evaluation." Thus, Commerce intended to evaluate proposals in the competitive range with a view toward negotiating specific items not fully meeting the requirements of items proposed enhancing the value of the proposal. Additionally, Commerce notes that the FPR does not require specific numerical scores for evaluation criteria.

In essence, Commerce contemplated award to the low-priced, technically acceptable, responsible offeror and Informatics argues that it could not reach that conclusion from reading the language of the RFP, which provided:

C. *Contract Award*
    * * * [A] single award will be made on one offer only * * * to the offeror determined to be a responsible prospective contractor for the purposes of this procurement * * * whose offer, conforming to the Solicitation, will be most advantageous to the Government, price and other factors considered. Evaluation of price and other factors are included in "D" below.

D. *Selection of Offeror for Negotiation and Award*
    Proposals will be evaluated with a view to negotiation of a contract presenting the most favorable offer to the Government; therefore, proposals should be submitted initially on the most favorable terms, from a price and technical standpoint, which the offeror can submit to the Government.

●   ●   ●   ●   ●   ●   ●

Procedure for determining the most advantageous offer, price and other factors considered:
1. The unit prices offered * * * shall be used by the Government in making the calculation as indicated by the three price evaluation sheets * * *.
2. The most favorable discount offered, if any, for prompt payment shall be applied to each contract year price evaluation * * *.
3. * * * [T]he net total annual price for each 52-issue contract year is calculated as the "Price Evaluation Total" for each responsive offer.

We have held that the "other factors" portion of the "price and other factors" phrase, as used in the above context, relates to the technical acceptability. See *Wismer and Becker Contracting Engineers and Synthetic Fuel Corporation of America, A Joint Venture*, B–191756, March 6, 1979, 79–1 CPD 148; *TM Systems, Inc.*, 56 Comp. Gen. 300 (1977), 77–1 CPD 61. Moreover, Commerce expressly stated in the three subitems that they related to price only. Therefore, we must conclude that the RFP reasonably notified offerors that award would be made to the responsible offeror who submitted the low-priced, technically acceptable offer.

D. STARTUP TIME

This issue was also argued and adjudicated in B–190203, under the former RFP, where Commerce provided that a new contractor would have to gear up for full performance in a period of 60 days. Informatics persuasively showed that the startup period was unreasonably short and, therefore, unduly restrictive of competition.

In the instant procurement, Commerce established a 90-day startup time. Commerce believes that it is not unduly restrictive of competition and represents a reasonable period of time to formulate and implement work planning. Commerce reports that:

Becoming fully operational and ready to take over full responsibilities in 90 days would be less costly than needlessly stretching the process to 120 days. * * * We have concluded that the 90 day start-up is within the capability of competing firms and does not unduly restrict any serious offer.

In Commerce's view, 60 days would be adequate time to recruit and train necessary personnel and acquire required facilities and equipment. Commerce states that, if training starts too early, an idle and nonproductive staff is on hand whose cost can only add to the overall costs, since, obviously, the salaries and benefits of this workforce will be factored into the officer's price. Further, Commerce states that the crucial activities are completed prior to contract award; other activities can be post-contract award, but must be completed prior to start of performance.

Thus, after carefully and deliberately considering the primary activities which prospective offerors are likely to encounter, Commerce concludes that the startup period clearly permits orderly and timely acquisition of resources and that earlier than needed acquisition of these resources will only serve to add "front-end loading costs," since such resources are necessarily nonproductive because the nature of this work is highly specialized and not readily transferable to other income-producing work.

ICC notes that the determination of reasonable startup time cannot be left to the offerors or the Government may lose the ability to procure in a timely manner. ICC refers to the *International Computaprint* decision upholding the validity of a 60-day startup time:

> We will not question an agency's determination of what its actual minimum needs are unless there is a clear showing that the determination has no reasonable basis.

ICC states that Commerce's reasons for the 90-day startup time are sufficient, less costly and coinciding with the termination of the present contract.

Finally, ICC observes that, while the 1970 RFP required that the contractor begin with 100 patents a week and gradually build up to full volume, all the requirements, except full staffing, were achieved by ICC in 60 days despite the lack of any specifications. ICC reiterates that within 60 days in 1970 all facilities, all computers and auxilliary equipment, all software and peripheral procedures, all edit and quality assurance facilities had to be in place, whether the production load was 100 or 1200 for the first week. Thus, ICC disputes the conclusion in B-190203 that the original 1970 startup was not accomplished in 60 days.

In reply, Informatics first argues that the history of this procurement also shows that, when the difficult job of chemical formulas photocomposition was required, ICC, the incumbent contractor, could not add this task to its operation without significant disruption to contract performance, including: (1) rejection of 14 of the first 21 weekly patent issues; and (2) creation of a backlog of 2.200 unprocessed patents by May 1977. Informatics states that these problems took much longer than 90 days to resolve; indeed, they seem to have lasted for at least 5 months.

Secondly, Informatics argues that the *International Computaprint* decision involved a procurement that is not analogous. Informatics states that in the NASA contract the facility, computer, software and operations manual are all Government-furnished; experience has shown that 85 percent or more of the incumbent contractor's personnel will continue to work for a new contractor; and although a new contractor must furnish little more than a five or six person management team, it is still given 60 days to accomplish that task. In contrast, the Commerce contractor must furnish all facilities, computers, software and procedures, and must be able to hire and train its own staff.

Thirdly, Informatics states that the argument—made in the *International Computaprint* decision that a longer startup period would be more costly to the Government—was plausible in the context of a cost–reimbursable contract; it has no relevance in a fixed-price contract; hence, this contention carries no weight in the instant case.

Finally, Informatics notes that seven firms competed for the NASA contract, while only one—the incumbent—submitted a proposal for the Commerce contract; this underscores the anticompetitive impact of provisions like the 90-day startup time and distinguishes this matter from *International Computaprint*.

GAO Analysis

Since it is the procuring agency's primary responsibility to develop specifications which meet its reasonable minimum needs, we will not question such determination unless it is not reasonably based. *Informatics, Inc., supra.* Here the essence of Commerce's rationale for the 90 day startup is not only its belief that the time is reasonable for a nonincumbent offeror, but that the Government will realize ultimate monetary savings. There is nothing in the record to show that Commerce's position is erroneous and in the *International Computaprint* decision we recognized that an agency could express its minimum needs in terms of reduced costs. Accordingly, we have no basis to question Commerce's specification which is a good faith extension of the startup time by 30 days over the last RFP's time.

E. SUSPENSE FILE

Informatics states that the RFP, like the two preceding solicitations, requires that the contractor be prepared to establish and maintain a "suspense file" consisting of an automated system capable of storing up to an estimated 20,000 patent applications. The requirement that a contractor maintain such a file, without additional compensation, was protested by Informatics in B–190203. Our Office stated that Informatics had presented a "very convincing and uncontested case" that the suspense file was unnecessary and we suggested that Commerce "reconsider" the views of Informatics "before resoliciting for its future needs." Informatics contends that Commerce can easily meet its minimum needs without a suspense file.

The suspense file consists of nonfee-paid patents which are given to the contractor for preliminary processing in order to smooth out the workload since the rate of fee payment is random and unpredictable. In preparing issues for each week's publication, Commerce's policy is to keyboard fee-paid patents not previously processed and to withdraw patents from the suspense file as soon as their fee is paid. Thus, Informatics states that it would expect the number of patents withdrawn from the suspense file to be random; instead, the accounting of recent suspense file activity shows that, for 30 of the 69 weeks during which patents were taken off the suspense file, the number of patents removed were divisible by 10, which does not indicate random activity.

Moreover, Informatics notes that no patents were deleted from the suspense file during a 72-week period and the fact that none have been strongly supports the thesis that the suspense file is being used as an expensive and anticompetitive device to achieve a backlog of fee-paid patents.

In response Commerce states that the flexibility to stabilize the workload not only to the contractor performing the patent data base requirements, but also to the other publication subsystems, i.e, photocomposition and printing and distribution requirements, is necessary in order to minimize disruptions to these subsequent processes. Commerce reports that this requirement was more dramatically illustrated when recent budgetary limitations required the Government to drastically curtail its patent publishing program; the suspense file currently contains over 7,000 patent application files and is expected to contain 9,000 by the end of the current fiscal year. Thus, Commerce concludes that Informatics' allegation "that the Suspense File can no longer be justified as a legitimate need of the Department" is without merit.

ICC demonstrates that the suspense file is not costly because its update system which processes the weekly issue file was duplicated to process the suspense file, resulting in almost no development costs for the suspense file subsystem. ICC states that the RFP does, and always has, provided for suspense file processing in the item 5 unit prices; further, the suspense file will be given to the new contractor in Version II format, the same format specified for item 1 and item 5 under the RFP. The offerors at their own discretion may maintain the suspense file in the Version II format or can convert the Version II format to another format of their choosing.

ICC concludes that in revealing its proprietary design methods, it has proven that either Informatics has raised the suspense file issue as a smoke screen to torpedo the procurement process or it really does not fully comprehend the requirements of the suspense file.

GAO Analysis

As we noted in B–190203, the suspense file requirement does not keep Informatics from competing in this procurement. Moreover, this year ICC and Commerce have rebutted Informatics' contentions that the suspense file is unnecessary and too costly. After reviewing the current record, we cannot conclude that the suspense file requirement is unduly restrictive of competition.

F. CONCLUSION

Protest denied.

[B-194393]

Contracts — Specifications — Military — Approved Item Requirement — Removal From Listing—Notice Entitlement

No notice need be given manufacturer that product is removed from approved items list when defects are due to Government specification deficiencies and manufacturer's product conforms to those specifications.

Contracts — Specifications — Conformability of Equipment, etc. Offered — Defective Items Previously Furnished

Manufacturer does not submit technically acceptable proposal merely by offering to supply parts previously provided in prior solicitations. Parts must not only meet technical specifications but must also have performed in technically acceptable manner.

Contracts — Negotiation — Requests for Proposals — Solicitation of Approved Sources

It is not improper to remove manufacturer's part from approved items list and to procure item on source controlled basis where it is shown that adequate specification does not exist for competitive procurement purposes.

In the matter of Arista Devices Corp., September 5, 1979:

Arista Devices Corp. (Arista) protests the award of a contract to Control Products Division of the Amerace Corporation (Control) under request for proposals (RFP) DLA900–79–R–0925, issued by the Defense Logistics Agency (DLA). The procurement was for solenoid relays, NSN 5945–00–729–7813, to be manufactured in accordance with Control Products part number (P/N) SF–21WC3 for use in tank fire extinguishing systems. The procurement was limited to "approved item" sources whose product had current Government approval. Arista's P/N 7813 had previously been an "approved item." Arista bases its protest on the fact Arista P/N 7813 was removed from the approved items list because of deficiencies reported by the Army, without notice to Arista.

It is reported that the original relay manufacturer was Control's predecessor, Agistat Division of ESNA. Originally the part was a source controlled item because the technical data for this item was inadequate for competitive procurement. Although an attempt had been made to procure the item competitively in 1970, the contract which was awarded to a new supplier at that time was terminated prior to any deliveries because of specification deficiencies. Another data package was developed in 1974, and an invitation for bids was issued for the relay. Arista was awarded the contract. In early 1976, the Army received deficiency reports on the Arista part which showed that the cover to the relay became unsealed in certain situations. After evaluation of the deficiencies by the U.S. Army Tank Automotive Command, it was concluded that the technical data package was inadequate to assure that an item manufactured in accordance with the specification requirements would meet the Government's needs. As a result, Arista P/N 7813 was removed as an approved item, and the relay was redesignated a source controlled part.

Arista, while not conceding that it in fact was the supplier of the defective relays, suggests that the covers were not sealed properly at the supplier's factory. Arista admits that it encountered the same problem on the first run relays supplied under its earlier contracts but contends that the problem was rectified by soldering, even though the design specifications do not require the covers to be soldered to the units. Arista further asserts that it has supplied 765 units to the Government and has never received a notice of unsatisfactory material. Therefore, it claims that it should not have been removed from the approved items list. However, it is DLA's position that it does not know if Arista's changed manufacturing procedure will cure the problem because the agency lacks testing equipment and other data to make such a determination. Although the specification does not require a particular type of seal for the cover, the relays supplied by Control were apparently not subject to the problems encountered by the Arista unit. In any event Arista believes that it should have been given an opportunity to correct any defects in the products it previously supplied and that it was entitled to notice of those defects by Defense Acquisition Regulation (DAR) §§ 1–1110 and 14–406 (1976 ed.).

First, in view of Arista's admission that it supplied similarly defective items to DLA; the identification of Arista and its P/N on the Army's unsatisfactory material report; and the fact that the problem previously has not been encountered in relays supplied by Control (the only other approved source), we believe that it is clear that the defective relays were the protester's.

With respect to the notice issue, neither of the cited regulatory provisions provide support for Arista's position. DAR § 1–1110 deals with reporting unsatisfactory contract performance to "the activity that prepared the specification." DAR § 14–406 is concerned with supplies which do *not* conform to the Government's specifications; here Arista's parts do comply so that the defect is attributable to the specifications and not anything within Arista's control. We do not therefore believe that the agency was required by the regulations to notify Arista prior to dropping that firm's part from the approved items list.

It is our view that an offeror does not submit a technically acceptable offer under a solicitation merely by offering to provide parts previously supplied and accepted. Those parts must have not only met the specifications but must also perform in a technically acceptable manner. *See Joyce Teletronics Corporation*, B–190316, January 11, 1978, 78–1 CPD 24. Arista has not shown that its present sealing method will meet the Army's needs since there is no acceptable test to make that determination. Merely stating that no further complaints were received will not meet this burden.

In this vein, DAR § 1–313 provides that:

(a) Any part * * * for military equipment, * * * must be procured so as to assure the requisite safe, dependable, and effective operation of the equipment. * * * When it is feasible to do so without impairing this assurance, parts should be procured on a competitive basis * * *.

(b) * * *

(c) Parts * * * should be procured (either directly or indirectly) only from sources that have satisfactorily manufactured or furnished such parts in the past, unless fully adequate data * * * test results, and quality assurance procedures, are available * * * to assure the requisite reliability and interchangeability of the parts * * *. The exacting performance requirements of specially designed military equipment may demand that parts be closely controlled and have proven capabilities of precise integration with the system in which they operate, to a degree that precludes the use of even apparently identical parts from new sources, since the functioning of the whole may depend on latent characteristics of each part which are not definitely known.

Our Office has recognized that Government procurement officials, who are familiar with the conditions under which supplies, equipment, or services have been used in the past, and how they are to be used in the future, are generally in the best position to know the Government's actual needs. Consequently, we will not question an agency's determination of what its actual needs are or what products or equipment will satisfy those needs unless there is a clear showing that the determination has no reasonable basis. *Jarrel-Ash Division of the Fisher Scientific Company*, B–185582, January 12, 1977, 77–1 CPD 19; *Herley Industries, Inc.*, B–186947, September 30, 1977, 77–2 CPD 247. Thus, the fact that Arista disputes DLA's position on these matters does not invalidate it. *Julian A. McDermott Corporation*, B–191468, September 21, 1978, 78–2 CPD 214. In this connection, we point out that the protester, not the contracting agency, has the burden of affirmatively proving its case. *Reliable Maintenance Service, Inc.— request for reconsideration*, B–185103, May 24, 1976, 76–1 CPD 337.

Due to the limitations of the specifications available we cannot conclude that DLA acted improperly by removing the Arista item from the approved items list.

The protest is denied.

[B–192188]

Contracts—Awards—Propriety—Licensing-Type Requirements—General v. Specific Solicitation Requirement

Prior decision under same solicitation held that, since solicitation contained only general statements requiring contractor to obtain all necessary licenses and permits, failure of proposed awardee (protester in present decision) to obtain State license did not require contracting officer to find proposed awardee nonresponsible and would not affect validity of award if made. However, prior decision did not hold that State license statute and threatened enforcement thereof were irrelevant, nor that contracting officer was required to find proposed awardee responsible as protester alleges. Decision in *Inter-Con Security Systems, Inc.; Washington Patrol Service, Inc.*, B–192188, February 9, 1979, 79–1 CPD 86, clarified.

Contracting Officers—Determinations—Nonresponsibility—Small Business Concerns—Reasonableness of Determination

Contracting officer was notified after bid opening that State would try to enforce State license requirement on unlicensed bidder. Even though particular State license was not specifically incorporated into solicitation, contracting officer considered bidder's failure to obtain State license in 8 months since bid opening and likelihood that State would try to enforce licensing statute, and thereby interrupt or delay performance by unlicensed contractor, as factors affecting bidder's ability to perform. Determination that unlicensed bidder was nonresponsible in such circumstances was reasonable.

Bidders—Qualifications—Small Business Concerns—Nonreferral For Certification Justification—Military Procurement

Since Small Business Administration (SBA) has not issued regulations to resolve discrepancies between 1977 amendments to Small Business Act, which require referral to SBA before small business may be rejected as nonresponsible, and Defense Acquisition Regulation (DAR), General Accounting Office will not consider whether contracting officer properly relied on DAR exceptions to SBA referral procedure.

Contracts—Awards—Small Business Concerns—Certifications— Mandatory Referral to SBA—Exceptions Under DAR

Contracting officer did not refer nonresponsibility determination of small business to SBA as required under Small Business Act Amendments of 1977 because contracting officer interpreted DAR 1–903.1 (v) and DAR 1–705.4(c) (v) as creating exception to SBA referral procedure where small business concern was determined nonresponsible because it was not otherwise qualified and eligible under applicable State law. While we cannot find contracting officer's interpretation and failure to refer matter to SBA to be unreasonable in present case, it is our opinion that these DAR provisions create exception to SBA referral only where bidder is not otherwise qualified and eligible under Federal laws/regulations. Accordingly, in future decisions we will strictly limit use of DAR 1–903.1(v) to situations involving Federal laws/regulations in absence of clarifying regulations issued by SBA.

In the matter of What-Mac Contractors, Inc., September 6, 1979:

What-Mac Contractors, Inc. (What-Mac), protests award of a contract to Washington Patrol Service, Inc. (Washington), for the management and operation of base security services at the Los Angeles Air Force Station, Los Angeles, California. What-Mac contends that it was entitled to award of the contract as the lowest responsive, responsible bidder, and that the contracting officer improperly determined What-Mac to be nonresponsible in contravention of prior decisions of our Office including a decision under this same solicitation (*Inter-Con Security Systems Inc.; Washington Patrol Service, Inc.*, B–192188, February 9, 1979, 79–1 CPD 86). What-Mac further contends that, once the contracting officer determined What-Mac to be nonresponsible, the contracting officer was required to refer the matter of What-Mac's responsibility to the Small Business Administration (SBA) for a final determination as required under 15 U.S.C. § 637(b)(7)(A), (1976 & Supp. I, 1977).

BACKGROUND

Invitation for bids (IFB) No. F04693–78–B0002, a small business setaside, was issued by the Department of the Air Force on November 18, 1977. When bids were opened on June 12, 1978, it was determined that National Investigation Bureau, Inc. (National), was the low bidder. However, a preaward survey conducted by the Air Force on National resulted in a negative determination, and on September 8, 1978, SBA refused to issue a certificate of competency (COC) to National. Therefore, the contracting officer rejected National's bid after determining National to be nonresponsible.

The Air Force prepared to make award to What-Mac, the second low bidder, but the award was held in abeyance because several protests were filed with our Office contending, among other things, that What-Mac was not a responsible bidder since it did not possess a Private Patrol Operator license to perform security guard services in California as required in section 7520 of the California Business and Professions Code and by the IFB in paragraph 35, section "C," and paragraphs 15 and 21, section "J," entitled "Special Provisions."

Paragraph 35, section "C," stated:

Offerors without necessary operating authority may submit offers, but the offerors shall, without additional expense to the Government, be responsible for obtaining any necessary licenses and permits prior to award of a resultant contract and for complying with all laws, ordinances, statutes and regulations in connection with the furnishing of the services herein.

Paragraph 15 of the Special Provisions stated:

In performance of work hereunder, the Contractor shall procure and keep effective all necessary permits and licenses required by the Federal, State or local Government, or subdivision thereof, or of any other duly constituted public authority, and shall obey and abide by all applicable laws, regulations and ordinances.

Paragraph 21 of the Special Provisions provided in part that:

[T]he Contractor shall abide by and comply with all relevant statutes, ordinances, laws and regulations of the United States (including Executive Orders of the President) and any state * * *

In the earlier protests leading to our February 9, 1979, decision, the protesters contended that, since the contracting officer was familiar with California licensing requirements for security guard services and was aware that What-Mac did not have a mandatory Private Patrol Operator license, the contracting officer had no choice but to declare What-Mac to be nonresponsible in view of the above-quoted provisions of the IFB. Also protested was the fact that the contracting activity had extended the contract with the incumbent contractor several times pending resolution of the protests, thereby allowing What-Mac more time in which to obtain the California Private Patrol Operator license.

since What-Mac had applied for, but had not yet received, a license from the California Bureau of Collection and Investigative Services.

In our Februrary 9, 1979, decision, we held, among other things, that the contracting officer's actions in extending the contract with the incumbent were proper since the record showed that such extensions were related solely to delays involving resolution of the protests in our Office. Since the solicitation contained only general statements regarding compliance with State and local licensing requirements, we held also that the failure of What-Mac or any other bidder to meet State or local licensing requirements prior to award was a matter to be resolved between the contractor and State and local authorities. Accordingly, we held that the contracting officer was not required to reject What-Mac as nonresponsible and that the failure to meet State licensing requirements prior to award would not affect the validity of an award made to What-Mac.

Pending resolution of the prior protests, the contracting officer inquired of the California Bureau of Collection and Investigative Services (by telephone conversation of January 8, 1979, and by letter of January 9, 1979) whether the State licensing requirement would be enforced if award were made to What-Mac without a license. The Bureau of Collection and Investigative Services responded by letter of January 19, 1979, that What-Mac had applied for a Private Patrol Operator license but had not yet been issued one. The Bureau indicated that, if any firm attempted to operate in California without a license, it would initiate an investigation and recommend that appropriate action be taken by the local District Attorney. The Bureau also stated that unlicensed performance would be grounds for denying a license to a contractor. The contracting officer reports that a What-Mac representative informed him on February 14, 1979, that What-Mac's representative had failed the licensing examination taken on January 26, 1979, and that the next examination could not be rescheduled until March 30, 1979.

The contracting officer determined that award should be made by February 28, 1979, since the latest contract extension would expire at the end of March 1979, and the contract required a phase-in period of 1 month. Therefore, on February 15, 1979, just 6 days after our decision on the procurement was issued, the contracting officer determined What-Mac to be nonresponsible since What-Mac would not be able to obtain the Private Patrol Operator license before award. On February 21, 1979, the contract was awarded to Washington, the next low bidder. What-Mac was notified of the award to Washington on February 22, 1979, and filed a protest with our office on February 23, 1979. On May 15, 1979, the California Bureau of Collection and Investigative Services issued a Private Patrol Operator license to What-Mac.

LICENSING—GENERAL DISCUSSION

Our decisions on licensing requirements have taken different approaches depending on the license required in the performance of the Government contract.

We have drawn a distinction between Federal licenses or permits and State or local licenses or permits. It is well established by the decisions of this Office that failure to submit permits or licenses by the time of award or at the very latest by the time of contract performance, plus any leadtime which may be necessary in the particular case, shall affect the responsibility of a contractor in cases where the permit or license is a requirement of the Federal Government. See 34 Comp. Gen. 175 (1954), wherein a permit from the Interstate Commerce Commission was required; 39 *id.* 655 (1960), wherein operating authority from the Federal Aviation Administration was required; and 46 *id.* 326 (1966), wherein a license from the Atomic Energy Commission was required. See, generally, 51 Comp. Gen. 377 (1971). Since a contracting officer must make a determination that a bidder is responsible before he may make award to that bidder, we have held that a bidder may be held responsible if in the view of the contracting officer the bidder will be capable of performing and will have all necessary Federal authority and permits to perform at the time required for performance. 39 Comp. Gen. 655, *supra.* Award of the contract prior to the awardee obtaining the required Federal license is conditioned upon the awardee obtaining the Federal license prior to performance, and, if the condition is not met by the time of performance, the contract is void *ab initio.* 46 Comp. Gen. 326, *supra.*

We have treated State or local licensing requirements differently with respect to the effect they have on a bidder's responsibility. The crucial distinction in such cases has been whether the solicitation merely stated in general terms that the successful bidder must meet all requirements of Federal, State or city laws and regulations or whether the solicitation required that the successful bidder must have a particular State or local license. See *New Haven Ambulance Service, Inc.,* 57 Comp. Gen. 361 (1978), 78–1 CPD 225; 53 Comp. Gen. 51 (1973).

Where a solicitation contains only a general requirement that the contractor have all necessary licenses and permits to perform the contract but does not indicate a specific State or local license which is required, we have held that a contracting officer should not have to determine what the State or local requirements may be, and the responsibility for making such a determination is correctly placed with the prospective contractor. 53 Comp. Gen. 51, *supra.* We have held also that the failure of a low bidder to obtain a license required under State or local law was not a proper basis upon which to reject the low bidder where the solicitation merely stated in general terms that all State or local licenses must be obtained by the successful bidder, and that such a failure could not affect the eligibility of a bidder to be awarded a Government contract. See B–165274, May 8, 1969; B–125577, October 11, 1955. Further, we have recognized that, if a State determines that under its laws a Federal contractor must have a license or permit in order to be legally capable of performing the required services in that State, the State might be able to enforce its requirements against the contractor, provided the application of the State's laws does not interfere with the execution of Federal powers. See 51 Comp. Gen. 377, *supra*, and cases cited therein. In 51 Comp. Gen. 377, *supra*, we also held that, if as a result of State enforcement of the licensing requirement, the contractor chooses not to perform the contract or is prevented from doing so by an injunction won by the State, the contractor may be terminated for default by the contracting activity. We further held that the failure of a bidder to meet State or local licensing requirements prior to award, where the IFB contained only general statements regarding State or local licenses, was a matter between the State and local authorities and the awardee and would not affect the legality of the contract awarded.

In situations in which a contracting officer is aware of and familiar with local licensing requirements before issuance of the solicitation, we have held that he may incorporate those specific requirements into the solicitations, thereby making possession by the bidders of the particular licenses a prerequisite to affirmative determinations of responsibility. 53 Comp. Gen. 51, *supra*.

CONTRACTING OFFICER'S DETERMINATION OF WHAT-MAC'S NONRESPONSIBILITY

PROTESTER'S CONTENTIONS

What-Mac protests that the contracting officer's determination that What-Mac was nonresponsible was "arbitrary, capricious, recalcitrant" and was made in total disregard of our decision in *Inter-Con Security Systems, Inc.; Washington Patrol Service, Inc., supra*. What-Mac contends that our February 9, 1979, decision held that What-Mac was responsible under the protested IFB regardless of whether it was in possession of the California Private Patrol Operator license at the time of award. Referring to the February 9, 1979, decision, What-Mac states in pertinent part:

Without question, this decision held that What-Mac *could not be held nonresponsible due to a lack of the subject State license*. The protest alleged that the lack of the license made What-Mac nonresponsible. The protest was denied. Lack of a State license did not then, and does not now, make What-Mac nonresponsible.

The February 9, 1979, decision conclusively determined that possession of the subject license was not a matter of bidder responsibility under this IFB. * * * According to this decision, it is only in the former case [where the solicitation requires a specific State license] that possession of the license can be a responsibility factor. In the latter case, where the compliance statement is general, possession of a specific license is not a matter of bidder responsibility. [Italic supplied by protester.]

In support of its interpretation of our February 9, 1979, decision and of its position that possession of a State license is irrelevant to the issue of bidder responsibility where the solicitation contains only general statements that all licenses or permits are necessary, What-Mac cites a long line of our decisions, including: *New Haven Ambulance Service, Inc.*, 57 Comp. Gen. 361 (1978), 78-1 CPD 225; *McNamara-Lunz Warehouses, Inc.; Central Moving and Storage, Inc.*, B-188100, June 23, 1977, 77-1 CPD 448; *McNamara-Lunz Vans & Warehouses, Inc.*, B-185803, July 8, 1976, 76-2 CPD 20; *Mid South Fire Protection, Inc.*, B-180390, February 25, 1974, 74-1 CPD 102; *Paul's Line, Incorporated, et al.*, B-179605, February 7, 1974, 74-1 CPD 57; 53 Comp. Gen. 51, *supra;* 53 Comp. Gen. 36 (1973); 51 Comp. Gen. 377, *supra;* B-165274, *supra;* and B-125577, *supra.*

What-Mac also argues that the Air Force has acted improperly in determining What-Mac to be nonresponsible because the Air Force report on the earlier protests, dated November 27, 1978, indicated that the Air Force did not believe that What-Mac could be held to be nonresponsible because it did not have a California Private Patrol Operator license. Then, just 6 days after our decision was issued, the Air Force reversed its position, according to the protester, and held What-Mac to be nonresponsible.

What-Mac also contends that the Air Force acted improperly in rejecting What-Mac on February 15, 1979, for failure to possess a required State license because What-Mac was in the process of applying for a license and, therefore, should have been granted more time to obtain the Private Patrol Operator license. What-Mac contends that the Air Force did not need to award the contract by February 28, 1979, since the Air Force contract with the incumbent had already been extended for 8 months and the last contract extension was not due to expire until March 31, 1979.

What-Mac argues that the State of California could not successfully prohibit What-Mac or any other unlicensed firm from performing under a guard services contract within the confines of the Los Angeles Air Force Station. What-Mac points out that the California Bureau of Collection and Investigative Services merely stated in its letter of January 19, 1979, that it would investigate any unlicensed activity and would report such activity to the local District Attorney's office for appropriate action. The Bureau did not specifically state that any legal action would be taken to prevent unlicensed performance by

What-Mac if it attempted to perform guard services in California without the proper State license.

What-Mac also contends that the contracting officer's nonresponsibility determination was improper since it amounted to the addition of a definitive responsibility criterion by the contracting officer without expressly stating in the IFB that the State Private Patrol Operator license would be considered in determining a bidder's responsibility. What-Mac cites several decisions of this Office in support of the proposition that definitive responsibility criteria must be clearly stated in the solicitation.

AGENCY'S RESPONSE

The Air Force states that there was a significant change in circumstances between the issuance of its November 27, 1978, report on the previous protests and February 15, 1979 (the date on which the contracting officer held What-Mac to be nonresponsible. Essentially, the Air Force indicates that on November 27, 1978, What-Mac was in the process of applying for the California license and the contracting officer believed that What-Mac would be successful in obtaining the license prior to award of the contract. In such circumstances and in the face of our previously summarized licensing decisions, the Air Force did not believe that it could properly hold What-Mac to be nonresponsible. When our February 9, 1979, decision on this procurement was issued, the Air Force did not interpret that decision to hold that the California licensing statute was irrelevant to the issue of What-Mac's responsibility nor did the Air Force interpret that decision to mandate that What-Mac must be held responsible even without a State license. The Air Force states that, when the contracting officer learned that What-Mac had failed the licensing examination and would not be able to obtain the license by the time of award and that the State authorities were intent on enforcing the licensing statute if possible, the contracting officer was justified in finding What-Mac nonresponsible due to the changed circumstances.

Moreover, the Air Force points out that What-Mac was not issued the Private Patrol Operator license until May 15, 1979, well after the expiration of the contract extension on March 31, 1979. After our February 9, 1979, decision was issued, the Air Force did not feel that any further contract extensions could be justified. The Air Force also believed that the nature of the services being procured, security guards at an Air Force base, prevented the Air Force from making award to an unlicensed firm and then terminating the contract for default if the contractor could not secure the license and the State enforced its licensing laws. Lastly, the Air Force reports that the contracting officer consulted on many occasions with both the California Bureau of Collection and Investigative Services and with the Air Force Judge Advocate General's office in order to determine if the State would attempt to prevent performance of unlicensed security guard services and whether such enforcement could be imposed upon a Federal contractor. The contracting officer determined that enforcement attempts by the State were very likely and that there was a possibility that such enforcement attempts would either be successful or, at least, could interrupt and delay performance under the contract if awarded to an unlicensed contractor. Since the contract was for security services, the contracting officer did not feel that the Air Force could tolerate any interruptions in performance. Therefore, on February 15, 1979, the contracting officer held What-Mac to be nonresponsible and rejected its bid.

LEGAL DISCUSSION

Our cases hold, among other things, that the failure to hold a State/local license (in circumstances where the solicitation does not specify which State/local licenses are mandatory) is a matter to be settled between the contractor and the State or local authorities. Many of these cases also indicate that the proper procedure in such circumstances is for the contracting officer to make award to the unlicensed bidder and to terminate the contract for default if the contractor is unable to perform due to State interference. This rule developed in large part because State and municipal tax, permit, and license requirements vary almost infinitely in their details and legal effect. The validity of a particular State license as applied to the activities of a Federal contractor often cannot be determined except by the courts. 53 Comp. Gen. 51, *supra*. Where the contracting officer is aware of and familiar with local requirements prior to issuance of the solicitation, or bid opening at the latest, he should incorporate the local requirements into the solicitation if desired in order to make the holding of the particular licenses a prerequisite to an affirmative determination of responsibility. 53 Comp. Gen. 51, *supra*.

However, we believe that the circumstances in the present case are distinguishable from the circumstances of the above cases and that the actions of the contracting officer in determining What-Mac to be nonresponsible were, therefore, reasonable. There is no evidence in the record to show that the contracting officer was aware of or familiar with the California licensing statute at any time prior to bid opening.

Even though the Air Force argued in its November 27, 1978, report that it did not believe that it could find What-Mac to be nonresponsible at that time, the circumstances changed significantly by February 15,

1979, the date upon which What-Mac was actually determined to be nonresponsible. What-Mac had failed the examination and could not get a license before performance was to begin. The State indicated that it would enforce its licensing law on an unlicensed contractor, if necessary, and the Judge Advocate General's office indicated that there was a good possibility that the State of California could enforce its licensing statutes upon What-Mac. We are aware that in some instances State licensing requirements may not be enforceable against Federal Government contractors. *Leslie Miller, Inc.* v. *Arkansas*, 352 U.S. 187 (1956). However, we think it is reasonable for a contracting officer to be more concerned with whether the contract will be carried out properly and without interference than whether the contractor will ultimately prevail in litigation. 53 Comp. Gen. 51, *supra*. Therefore, we are not persuaded by the protester's argument that the State would ultimately fail in any attempt to enforce State licensing laws. The crucial question is whether contract performance may be prevented or delayed by State intervention. Moreover, since the contract was for security guard services at an Air Force base, the contracting officer's fear that State interference might interrupt or delay performance was reasonable.

We think that the failure of What-Mac to hold such license in these circumstances was relevant to What-Mac's ability to perform the contract in an efficient and uninterrupted fashion. Since the burden is on the prospective contractor to affirmatively demonstrate its ability to perform before being awarded a contract under section 1–902 of the Defense Acquisition Regulation (DAR) (1976 ed.), we believe that the possibility that the State authorities would attempt to prevent performance by What-Mac, or that What-Mac's performance might very well be delayed or interrupted by State attempts to prevent unlicensed activity, was clearly relevant to the issue of What-Mac's responsibility.

We also do not believe that What-Mac was entitled to have the incumbent's contract extended in order to allow What-Mac an opportunity to obtain the State license. The contract had been extended for 8 months pending resolution of several protests and What-Mac had not been able during this extended time to comply with the California license provision. There was no need for the contracting officer to extend the contract further. Under DAR section 1–902, the burden is on a prospective contractor to affirmatively demonstrate its "responsibility," i.e., the apparent ability to successfully meet the contract requirements, before being awarded the contract. In this case, What-Mac was unable to affirmatively demonstrate its ability to perform prior to award and was not, in fact, able to obtain the State license until several months after award, and 1½ months after performance was to begin. Accordingly, we find that the contracting officer properly exercised the administrative discretion entrusted to him in finding

What-Mac to be nonresponsible. See *Edw. Kocharian & Company, Inc.—request for modification*, 58 Comp. Gen. 516 (1979), 79-1 CPD 326.

REFERRAL TO SBA

Protester's contention and Agency response

What-Mac also protests that, since it is a small business concern, the contracting officer was required to refer the matter to the SBA for final disposition once What-Mac was found to be nonresponsible.

The Air Force responds that it was not necessary to refer the matter of What-Mac's responsibility to the SBA because the contracting officer's determination of nonresponsibility was made in accordance with DAR § 1–903.1 (1976 ed.) which states in pertinent part:

1–903.1 General Standards. Except as otherwise provided in this paragraph 1–903, a prospective contractor must:

*　　*　　*　　*　　*　　*　　*

(v) be otherwise qualified and eligible to receive an award under applicable laws and regulations, e.g., Section XII, Parts 6 and 8.

The applicable law under which What-Mac was not qualified was, according to the Air Force, section 7520 of the California Business and Professions Code—the State licensing statute. Under DAR § 1–705.4(c)(v) (DAC #76–15, June 1, 1978), a referral need not be made to the SBA if a contracting officer determines a small business concern nonresponsible pursuant to DAR § 1–903.1(v) and such determination is approved by the head of the procuring activity or his designee. The Air Force argues that since the determination was made and approved under these DAR sections, referral to the SBA for final disposition on responsibility was not appropriate.

LEGAL DISCUSSION

Section 501 of the Small Business Act Amendments of 1977, 15 U.S.C. § 637(b)(7) (1976 & Supp. I, 1977), provides that no small business concern may be precluded from award because of nonresponsibility without referral of the matter to the SBA for a final disposition under the COC procedures. No exceptions from this referral procedure are provided under the act. Thus, there is an apparent conflict between the terms of the Small Business Act which requires referral to the SBA with respect to "all elements of responsibility" with no exceptions and sections 1–705.4(c)(v) and 1–903.1 (v) which create an exception for nonresponsibility determinations where the bidder is not otherwise qualified and eligible for award under applicable laws and regulations. We have previously questioned similar conflicts between the Small Business Act, as amended by P.L.

95–89, and section 1–705.4 of DAR which creates exceptions to the mandatory referral to SBA on responsibility determinations. See *Applied Control Technology*, B–190719, September 1, 1978, 78–2 CPD 183; *X-Tyal International Corp.*, B–190101, March 30, 1978, 78–1 CPD 248. However, since the SBA has not yet issued appropriate implementing regulations to clarify these discrepancies, this Office will not consider whether the contracting officer properly relied on DAR § 1–705.4(c)(v) and DAR § 1–903.1(v) as an exception in the present case. *Applied Control Technology, supra.*

Nevertheless, in our opinion, DAR § 1–903.1(v) applies, if at all, only to Federal laws and regulations and not to State or local laws and regulations. In the absence of SBA regulations clarifying this matter, we will apply our view that DAR § 1–903.1(v) refers only to Federal statutes/regulations in any future protests arising under this DAR section. However, in the present case, we cannot find unreasonable the contracting officer's interpretation that DAR § 1–903.1(v) applies to State law and his failure to refer the matter to the SBA because of his interpretation, since it is not clear whether State law is included within the purview of the provision and because our Office had not provided any interpretation of the provision in any prior decision.

CONCLUSION

In view of the above discussion, the protest is denied.

[B–194383]

Debt Collections—Debtor Deceased—Liability of Distributee

Distributee of property from the estate of a deceased debtor of the United States is liable to repay debt resulting from overpayment of Supplemental Security Income Benefits to decedent debtor during her lifetime to the extent of assets received. Distributee is considered to constructively hold funds in trust for benefit of the United States. United States is not barred by Wisconsin nonclaim statute from satisfying its claim against decedent debtor through action against beneficiary, without participating in probate proceeding. Wisc. Stat. Ann. 859.01(3).

Debt Collections—More Than One Debtor—Joint and Several Liability

Among debtors jointly and severally liable to United States, Government is not required to collect proportionate share from each, but may collect in manner best calculated to liquidate indebtedness as quickly as possible even if this means collecting entire amount from one debtor. That debtor presumably can enforce legal right to contribution by fellow debtors.

In the matter of Jean Harris—Reconsideration of Collection Action, September 11, 1979:

This responds to a letter from Ms. Jean Harris, in effect asking for reconsideration of our Claims Division's determination that she is liable for the debt resulting from overpayments of Supplemental Security Income (SSI) Benefits made to her deceased mother.

Ms. Harris' mother, Mrs. Marion Doughty, received overpayments totaling $1,184.20 in SSI Benefits from April through November 1975. She never repaid the funds during her lifetime, so her estate became liable for the debt upon her death in September, 1976. Her estate consisted of about $1,000 in cash and a house worth approximately $20,000. Ms. Harris was one of three beneficiaries of the estate who were to divide the assets equally.

The Social Security Administration (SSA) notified the attorney for the estate of the Government's claim in a letter dated December 2, 1976. In the letter, SSA notified the attorney that the United States must be given priority over other creditors of the estate under the provisions of 31 U.S.C. § 191 (1976). It also pointed out that, under 31 U.S.C. § 192, a representative of an estate can become personally liable for a debt owed to the United States if he pays the general creditors of the estate without first satisfying the Government's claim. The letter concluded by requesting the attorney to furnish to SSA appropriate forms if it would be necessary to file a formal claim in order to collect the debt.

In place of the Government's filing a formal claim against Mrs. Doughty's estate, an agreement was made between representatives from the Department of Health, Education and Welfare (HEW), and the attorney for the estate, that Ms. Harris would pay the debt after the estate was closed, out of the proceeds from the sale of her mother's house. In a letter to HEW dated July 5, 1977, the attorney for the estate said:

Pursuant to our phone conversation, I hereby acknowledge, on behalf of my client, Jean Harris, who is one of the principal beneficiaries of the estate, the indebtedness of the estate to the United States Government in the amount of $1,184.20. Please be advised, however, that my client will not be able to pay this claim until after the estate has been closed. She fully intends to make payment at that time.

Then, in a letter dated February 3, 1978, to the SSA, the attorney stated:

The above estate has been closed. The arrangement which was made with representatives from HEW who I spoke to previously was that the daughter of the decedent would pay this claim after the estate was closed. This was agreed to by the daughter and by HEW. The daughter's name is Jean Harris, Route 7, Spooky Ridge Farm, Merrill, Wisconsin. The principal asset in the estate was a house which the beneficiaries of the estate intended to sell. I would suggest that you contact Ms. Harris directly about this.

The SSA attempted unsuccessfully to collect the debt from Ms. Harris after learning that the estate had been closed. It referred the case to the General Accounting Office's Claims Division for collection in July, 1978, which determined that Ms. Harris was liable for the debt and asked here to pay it. Our Claims Division explained this determination, and the rationale for it, in a January 2 letter to Senator Proxmire which was forwarded to Ms. Harris. She now asks for reconsideration of the decision that she must refund the overpayment.

Ms. Harris contends that it is unfair for the United States now to look to her alone to repay the entire debt, because HEW proceeded improperly following her mother's death. She argues that HEW should have filed a notice of the debt in the Probate Court having jurisdiction over her mother's estate, rather than informally making an arrangement with the attorney for the estate for satisfaction of the Government's claim. Ms. Harris points out that if HEW had submitted its claim to the Probate Court, then her mother's debt would have been satisfied from the estate and all three beneficiaries would in effect have shared the cost of repaying the Government. She says that she never authorized the attorney for the estate to agree that she would repay the entire debt, that in fact he did not represent her, that she did not know of the agreement until after her mother's estate was closed, and that she never would have agreed to the arrangement if HEW had proposed it to her. Ms. Harris contends, therefore, that it is inequitable to hold her solely responsible for the debt under the agreement.

We have no reason to change our determination that Ms. Harris is liable for her mother's debt notwithstanding the arguments she has presented. The rights of the United States are different from those of a private creditor seeking to collect a debt owed by a decedent. The Federal Government may look to Ms. Harris for satisfaction of its claim because she is a distributee of the estate, even though the Government did not participate in the Probate Proceedings. The United States can collect its debt from Ms. Harris even if HEW had not made the agreement with the attorney for the estate, because its rights stem from law and not the agreement.

Generally, a creditor must file a claim with the Probate Court within the time set by law in order to collect a debt owed by a deceased debtor whose estate is probated in Wisconsin (with exceptions not relevant here). Wis. Stat. Ann. § 859.01.(1). If the private creditor does not file his claim, he is forever barred from bringing it against the estate, the personal representatives and the heirs and beneficiaries of the decedent. *Id.*

However, the Wisconsin statute which bars a creditor's claim if it is not properly filed, does not apply to claims by the United States. *Id.* Subsection 859.01(3) of the Wisconsin Probate Code expressly provides that claims of the United States are not within the operation of subsection 859.01(1).

Wisconsin's law is thus in accord with the general principle that State "nonclaim" statutes (those statutes, usually found in the Probate Code, fixing the time within which claims against a decedent's estate must be filed or presented to the executor or administrator and which usually further provide that the claim will be barred unless presented within such time) do not apply to claims of the United States. *United States* v. *Deimer*, 140 F. Supp. 88 (D. Wyo. 1953) ; *Reconstruction Finance Corp.* v. *Faulkner*, 122 A. 2d 263 (1956). Individual states do not possess the power, under the Constitutional system, to invalidate a claim of the United States by statute or through State courts so that the claim cannot be enforced at all. *United States* v. *Summerlin*, 310 U.S. 414, 84 L. Ed. 1283, 60 S. Ct. 1019 (rev'g. 140 Fla. 475, 191 So. 842 (1940)). Accordingly, the SSA's failure to pursue its claim in the Probate Court does not terminate its right of action in this case, and the Government's claim remains valid and enforceable.

The Government may exercise its right of action against any or all persons who have inherited the debtor's property. *United States* v. *Anderson*, 66 F. Supp. 870 (1946) ; *United States* v. *Fisher et al.*, 57 F. Supp. 410 (1944) ; *United States* v. *Purdome*, 240 F. Supp. 221 (1963). They are considered, under the law, to receive and hold in trust funds belonging to the United States to the extent of assets received. Accordingly, Ms. Harris is liable for her mother's debt under the "trust fund" doctrine of the cited cases because she is a distributee of the estate.

As stated earlier, the Government could collect its debt from Ms. Harris even if HEW had not made the agreement with the attorney for the estate, since the basis of Ms. Harris' liability is a doctrine of law and not the agreement. Therefore, Ms. Harris' objections to the agreement are not material, even though, as may have been the case, the attorney for the estate was not authorized to make any agreement on behalf of Ms. Harris.

We see no impropriety in HEW's actions, following Ms. Harris' mother's death, in dealing informally with the attorney for the estate. HEW has a statutory duty to attempt collection of all claims of the United States arising out of HEW activities. 31 U.S.C. § 952 (1976). (Regulations require, to this end, "aggressive action, on a timely basis with effective followup." 4 C.F.R. § 102.1 (1978).) HEW's procedure is a legally recognized as well as administratively acceptable means for the Government to use to recover a debt owned by a deceased debtor.

Although the Government may, if it chooses, file and prosecute its claim in the same manner as any other creditor, as already discussed, the United States need not formally submit a claim in Probate Court in order to preserve its collection rights. However, if the Government does formally submit its claim in probate proceedings, it is bound by the determination made by the State Court. *United States* v. *Vibradamp Corp.*, 257 F. Supp. 931 (1966). On the other hand, if the United States chooses not to participate, then Federal law governs. If the Government notifies the representative of an estate that his decedent died owing a debt to the United States, the Government can look to the representative *personally* if he distributes the assets of the estate without paying the claim. 31 U.S.C. § 192 (1976).

Thus, the United States may file its claim in Probate Court, or notify the representative of the estate and then rely on him to preserve the priority accorded by sections 191 and 192 of title 31, United States Code. HEW apparently decided that it would be better in this case, as permitted by law, to deal with the estate directly and not to submit its claim to the risk and expense of litigation in Probate Court. Admittedly, if HEW had decided to file its claim in the Probate Court, the claim would presumably have been satisfied from the assets of the estate before distribution was made to the beneficiaries, but HEW's responsibility was to try to recover funds belonging to the United States through the most economical means legally available.

We do not agree that the Government's action has been inequitable. Ms. Harris does not now question that her mother owed $1,184.20 to the United States. Also, she would have a right to recover their proportionate shares of the debt by way of contribution from the other distributees of the estate. The fact that the other distributees are jointly liable, however, does not prevent the United States from looking to only one for full satisfaction of the debt and leaving it to that debtor to seek contribution from the others. In this regard, the Federal Claims Collection Standards require that—

When two or more debtors are jointly and severally liable collection action will not be withheld against one such debtor until the other or others pay their proportionate shares. The agency should not attempt to allocate the burden of paying such claims as between the debtors but should proceed to liquidate the indebtedness as quickly as possible. 4 C.F.R. § 103.6 (1978).

Moreover, in the Claims Division's January 2 letter to Senator Proxmire, it was agreed that we would initiate collection action against the other liable parties if Ms. Harris would advise us of their whereabouts, even though, as the above regulation indicates, there is no requirement that we do so. Ms. Harris did not provide the addresses, but we have now discovered a record of them and, as agreed, we will also try to collect the debt from the other two beneficiaries. One is Ms. Harris' brother and lives at the same address as she, and the other beneficiary, the executrix of her mother's estate lives in Milwaukee, according to the information we have. However, we reiterate that we will still hold Ms. Harris responsible for the entire debt as the law and regulations require us to do, should we be unable to locate or collect from the other two beneficiaries.

[B-195245]

Travel Expenses — Overseas Employees — Transfers — Agency Within U.S.

Air Force employee in Canal Zone, who was entitled to travel and transportation costs to home of record, transferred to Forest Service in Oregon. Air Force payments of travel and transportation expenses to new station before effective date of Forest Service appointment were proper to extent that they did not exceed constructive costs of travel and transportation to home of record. Principles of 46 Comp. Gen. 628 are not limited to transfers within the Department of Defense.

In the matter of Milton G. Parsons, September 12, 1979:

This action is in response to a request by the Secretary of Agriculture for an advance decision concerning the authority of the Department of the Air Force to pay the travel and transportation costs involved in the permanent change of station transfer of Mr. Milton G. Parsons.

While Mr. Parsons was employed at Howard Air Force Base, Canal Zone, he accepted an offer to transfer to the Siuslaw National Forest, U.S. Forest Service, Department of Agriculture, Corvallis, Oregon. Mr. Parsons served in the Canal Zone under an agreement providing for return transportation to his home of record in Bozeman, Montana, and he satisfactorily completed his tour of duty with the Air Force. The Air Force initially agreed to pay Mr. Parsons' travel costs and issued a travel authorization dated January 23, 1978. His travel was to begin on February 20 and the reporting date at his new station was indicated as February 26. The Forest Service issued a travel order authorizing allowable relocation expenses not covered by the Air Force order. That order also showed February 26, 1978, as the reporting date. Subsequently, after Mr. Parsons' family had moved pursuant to the order, the Air Force decided it was not authorized to pay the travel costs. While it paid the relocation expenses of Mr. Parsons and his dependents, it separated Mr. Parsons on February 20, 1978, and requested the Forest Service reimburse it for the expenses already paid.

Based on its interpretation of 5 U.S.C. § 5724(e) (1976) and paragraph C1052–2b(1)(a), volume 2 of the Joint Travel Regulations (JTR), the Air Force contends that Mr. Parsons' "selection for employment" by the Forest Service prior to his return requires the Forest Service (the acquiring agency) to pay his travel costs. The Air Force believes that the holding in 46 Comp. Gen. 628 (1967) is not applicable since that decision dealt with employee transfers between agencies within the Department of Defense (DOD). We hereby hold to the contrary that that decision is not limited to transfers within DOD exclusively, and its principles are applicable in the instant case.

In 46 Comp. Gen. 628 we considered three proposals forwarded by the Assistant Secretary of Defense relating to the overseas travel expenses of employees transferred from one agency to another under DOD. After quoting sections 5722(a)(1) and (2) and 5724(d) and (e) of title 5 of the United States Code, we held:

> There is no doubt that if the employee is *employed* by the new (acquiring) agency *prior to his return travel* to the United States the provisions of 5 U.S.C. 5724(e) would preclude the old (losing) agency from paying any part of such travel and transportation expenses. We understand that the first two proposals submitted by the Assistant Secretary relate to actual transfers effected prior to the return of the employee to the United States. If such be the case, we know of no legal basis upon which any part of the return travel expenses can be paid by the old (losing) agency.
>
> Concerning the third proposal, it is our understanding that the employee would be returned to the place of his actual residence or some other point in the United States for separation. *At the time of such return travel he would not have been employed by the new (acquiring) agency to which he later transfers.* See 44 Comp. Gen. 767. *In such a case it would be proper for the old (losing) agency to pay the expense incurred in traveling to the place of actual residence or some other selected point in the United States but not to exceed the constructive cost of travel to the place of actual residence.* [Italic supplied.]

We have followed the principles of 46 Comp. Gen. 628 with respect to transfers to agencies other than those within the Department of Defense. Our decision B–170639, July 29, 1971, dealt with the travel expenses of Mr. Isaac Rodrigues incident to his transfer from the Agency for International Development, Saigon, Vietnam, to the Department of Housing and Urban Development, Washington, D.C. A second case, B–163364, June 27, 1968, concerned the travel costs of Mr. William Cantelo, who was transferred from his position as an Entomology Advisor with the Agency for International Development in Bangkok, Thailand, to an appointment with the Agricultural Research Service, Department of Agriculture, St. Croix, Virgin Islands. In both cases, we cited 46 Comp. Gen. 628 to permit the losing agency to pay for the employees' travel not to exceed the cost of travel to their homes of record.

Also, there is nothing in the language of 46 Comp. Gen. 628 to indicate an intent to limit that case to DOD transfers exclusively. In this connection section 5721 of the subchapter on travel and transportation expenses in title 5, of the United States Code, on which 46 Comp. Gen. 628 is based, defines "agency" to include any executive agency.

The record in the instant case indicates that Mr. Parsons was not employed by the Forest Service prior to his travel and, therefore, section 5724(e) as interpreted in the above decisions does not preclude the Air Force from paying for his travel costs. Therefore, to the extent that Mr. Parsons' travel and transportation costs to his new station at the Siuslaw National Forest do not exceed the constructive cost of travel and transportation to his original residence at Bozeman, Montana, at the time of his initial assignment, the Air Force payments were proper.

In view of the above, the Air Force should change Mr. Parsons' separation date to February 26, 1978, the date shown on the original travel orders, and withdraw its request for reimbursement of the travel and transportation costs which do not exceed the costs of relocation to Mr. Parsons' home of record.

[B-194140]

Federal Grant and Cooperative Agreement Act of 1977 — Compliance — Grant, etc. Agreements v. Procurement Contract

Complaint that executive agency abandoned practice of awarding contracts under Federal procurement procedures in favor of grant awards in order to make sole-source award and avoid statutory requirements for competition is denied where record discloses agency awarded grant, rather than contract, for purpose of complying with requirements of Federal Grant and Cooperative Agreement Act of 1977.

In the matter of Burgos & Associates, Inc., September 13, 1979:

Burgos & Associates, Inc. (Burgos) protests the decision of the Department of Commerce's Office of Minority Business Enterprise (OMBE) to award a noncompetitive grant to the Greater Hartford Business Development Center, Inc. (GHBDC), to operate as a Business Development Organization (BDO) providing management and technical assistance to minority business firms in the Hartford, Connecticut area. Burgos contends that it should have been given an opportunity to compete for the award, particularly since it was OMBE's incumbent BDO contractor in the Hartford area for the previous year.

This Office generally does not consider complaints concerning the propriety of grant awards. *Washington State Department of Transportation*, B-193600, January 16, 1979, 79-1 CPD 25; 40 Fed. Reg. 42406 (1975). However, OMBE has previously conducted competitive procurements for BDO services, *see, e.g., National Puerto Rican Forum, Inc.*, B-189338, November 23, 1977, 77-2 CPD 400; *Decision Sciences Corporation*, B-183773, September 21, 1976, 76-2 CPD 260, and Burgos suggests that OMBE has abandoned that practice in favor of making grant awards to avoid the competitive requirements of Federal procurement and to deprive the protester of its right to compete.

OMBE explains that the shift to grant awards was prompted by the Federal Grant and Cooperative Agreement Act of 1977, Pub. L. No. 95-224, February 3, 1978, 92 Stat. 3, 41 U.S.C.A. §§ 501 *et seq.* (West Supp. 1978) (the Act). The Act defines and distinguishes among the terms "contract," "grant," and "cooperative agreement," and requires agencies to adhere to those distinctions when making awards. A procurement contract is to be used whenever the principal purpose of the relationship between the agency and its awardee is the acquisition by purchase, lease, or barter of property or services for the direct benefit or use of the Federal Government. On the other hand, when the relationship established is for the transfer of money, property, services, or anything of value to the recipient to accomplish a public purpose of support or stimulation, and the Federal role is passive or no substantial agency involvement is anticipated, the agency must use a grant agreement; if the Federal role is active or substantial agency involvement is anticipated the agency must enter into a cooperative agreement. Using these statutory standards, OMBE reports it determined that use of grant agreements is appropriate for BDO awards.

We find OMBE's position to be reasonable. Under the BDO program, OMBE funds public and private organizations which in turn render technical and management assistance to minority business enterprises. OMBE's determination that a grant instrument rather than a procurement is more appropriate to effect the program clearly is consistent with the Act.

The protest is denied.

We note that one of the purposes of the Act is to "encourage competition, where deemed appropriate, in the award of grants and cooperative agreeemnts * * *." 41 U.S.C.A. § 501(b)(3) (West Supp. 1978). Although a noncompetitive award was made in this case, we further note that OMBE in general intends to use a competitive approach and explains that it did not do so here because of its desire to coordinate this BDO program with other Department of Commerce funded programs in the Hartford area.

[B-193318]

Officers and Employees — Transfers — Relocation Expenses — Surveyor Fees, Reports, etc.—House Purchase and/or Sale

Employee may be reimbursed for $35 survey fee incident to financing purchase of a residence upon his relocation. Although assessed by the lending institution, the survey fee is expressly excluded from the definition of a finance charge by Regulation Z, 12 C.F.R. 226.4(e)(1), the fee is reasonable in amount, and all-inclusive fee, initially characterized as a "loan origination fee," is sufficiently itemized to show the portion allocable to the survey fee. See *Anthony J. Vrana*, B–189639, March 24, 1978.

Officers and Employees—Transfers—Relocation Expenses—House Purchase—Recording Fees

Although assessed by the lending institution as part of a charge initially characterized as a "loan origination fee," employee may be reimbursed for recording fees if they are customarily paid by purchaser in the area and do not exceed amounts customarily charged in the locality. Federal Travel Regulations 2–6.2c. While recording fees are not expressly excluded from the definition of a finance charge under 12 C.F.R. 226.4(e) they are not a condition for the extension of credit and, thus, are not part of the finance charge as defined by 12 C.F.R. 226.4(a).

Officers and Employees — Transfers — Relocation Expenses — Attorney Fees — Restrictions on Reimbursement

Employee may not be reimbursed for attorney fees assessed by lending institution and initially characterized as part of the "loan origination fee" unless certifying officer determines that such fees were incurred for the purposes specifically excluded from finance charges by Regulation Z, 12 C.F.R. 226.4(e), are reasonable in amount, and insofar as the attorneys fees are sufficiently itemized to show the portion of the origination fee allocable to each excluded item.

In the matter of Robert E. Whitney—Real Estate Expenses—Exclusions from Finance Charge, September 20, 1979:

This action is in response to a request dated October 20, 1978, from Elizabeth A. Allen, Chief, Accounting Section, of the Internal Revenue Service (IRS), regarding the propriety of certifying for payment a reclaim voucher in the amount of $460 in favor of Robert E. Whitney, representing real estate expense incurred in connection with the purchase of his residence in Schwartz, Louisiana. The purchase was pursuant to a permanent change of station from Baton Rouge, to Monroe, Louisiana, in March 1978.

Mr. Whitney's claim was denied by the IRS on the basis that the $460 amount was a loan origination fee, a cost incident to the extension of credit within the purview of Regulation Z, 12 C.F.R. § 226.4(a), which is not reimbursable under the Federal Travel Regulations (FTR) (FPMR 101–7) para. 2–6.2d (May 1973). The pertinent part of Regulation Z states:

§ 226.4 Determination of finance charge.

(a) *General Rule.* Except as otherwise provided in this section, the amount of the finance charge in connection with any transaction shall be determined as the sum of all charges, payable directly or indirectly by the customer, and imposed directly or indirectly by creditor as an incident to or as a condition of the extension of credit, whether paid or payable by the customer, the seller, or any other person on behalf of the customer to the creditor or to a third party, including any of the following types of charges :

*   *   *   *   *   *   *

(3) Loan fee, finder's fee, or similar charge.

*   *   *   *   *   *

(e) *Excludable charges, real property transactions.* The following charges in connection with any real property transaction, provided they are bona fide, reasonable in amount, and not for the purpose of circumvention or evasion of this part, shall not be included in the finance transaction :

(1) Fees or premiums for title examination, abstract of title, title insurance, or similar purposes and for required related property surveys.

(2) Fees for preparation of deeds, settlement statements, or other documents.

(3) Amounts required to be placed or paid into an escrow or trustee account for future payments of taxes, insurance, and water, sewer, and land rents.

(4) Fees for notarizing deeds and other documents.

(5) Appraisal fees.

(6) Credit reports.

Reimbursement of an amount that is a finance charge is precluded by the following provision of para. 2–6.2d of the FTR:

* * * no fee, cost, charge, or expense is reimbursable which is determined to be a part of the finance charge under the Truth in Lending Act, Title I, Public Law 90–321, and Regulation Z issued pursuant thereto by the Board of Governors of the Federal Reserve System. * * *

While the $460 amount is listed in the settlement documents as a "loan origination fee," Mr. Whitney has attached to his reclaim voucher a letter dated July 25, 1978, from the People's Homestead and Savings Association that states that the $460 loan origination fee included charges of $225 for attorneys fees, a survey fee of $35, and $16 for recording fees. Since the remaining $184 of the $460 amount is not characterized other than as a loan origination fee, that amount is for disallowance under FTR para. 2–6.2d, quoted above. The specifically identified charges, however, may be reimbursed if the charge is expressly excluded from the finance charge by Regulation Z, 12 C.F.R. § 226.4(e) and reasonable in amount, provided that the loan origination fee is itemized to show the portion of the fee allocable to each item. *Anthony J. Vrana*, B–189639, March 24, 1978.

An examination of Regulation Z, 12 C.F.R. § 226.4(e)(1) shows that fees for required property surveys are expressly excluded from the finance charge. The $35 survey fee is reasonable and is itemized sufficiently. Therefore, under the test established in *Anthony J. Vrana, supra*, the $35 survey fee may be certified for payment.

Although recovered as part of the fee charged by the lending institution and not expressly excluded from the finance charge under 12 C.F.R. § 226.4(e), recording fees are not part of a finance charge as defined by 12 C.F.R. § 226.4(a). They are assessed to meet the legal requirement for recording documentation essential to the transaction and not as a condition for extension of credit. They are not retained by the lender but are passed on to the local jurisdiction. Moreover, FTR para 2–6.2c (May 1973) specifically allows reimbursement for recording fees if they are customarily paid by the purchaser and if they do not exceed amounts customarily charged in the locality of the residence. Therefore, Mr. Whitney's claim for reimbursement of recording fees may be certified for payment if the requirements of FTR para. 2–6.2c are satisfied.

We have held that, under FTR para 2–6.2c, itemization is not generally required where legal fees are claimed. See *George W. Lay*, 56 Comp. Gen. 561 (1977). However, that decision is not applicable to this case because the reimbursement of the finance charge here is governed by FTR para. 2–6.2d and Regulation Z. Since these authorities prohibit reimbursement of finance charges, except for certain narrowly drawn specific services, we require an itemization of these fees in order to identify the services performed and whether they may be paid. *Charles W. Smith*, B–189381, December 15, 1977. Therefore, the requirements of *Anthony J. Vrana, supra*, must be satisfied before attorneys fees can be paid. Since the record does not indicate what service the attorneys fees covered, if it can be determined that the attorneys fees were for the purposes specifically excluded from the finance charge by Regulation Z, 12 C.F.R. § 226.4(e), reasonable in amount, and sufficiently itemized, then the attorneys fees can be certified for payment.

[B–194853]

Payments — Absence or Unenforceability of Contracts — Appropriation Availability — Fiscal Year Appropriations — Contract Ratification v. Performance Date

Payment may be made to a contractor for repair work to Government equipment even though formal contracting procedures were not followed because Government received the benefit and has specifically ratified the transaction. Appropriation available at time contractor was authorized to and actually performed the repair work should be charged, irrespective of fiscal year in which the transaction was ratified.

In the matter of Rust Tractor Company, September 21, 1979:

A certifying officer for the Bureau of Indian Affairs (BIA) in Albuquerque. New Mexico, has requested an advance decision from our Office as to whether he may certify a voucher in the amount of $22,875.36 to pay the Rust Tractor Company (Rust) for its services. He questions the propriety of making such a payment because formal procurement procedures were not followed and the transaction with Rust was not properly authorized.

Apparently, the instant situation arose as a result of a misunderstanding between personnel at the Ramah-Navajo Agency's Branch of Roads (Agency) and Rust. When repair work was needed for a Caterpillar Scraper, an estimate prepared by Rust was verbally quoted to the agency as $6,500. The Agency's branch chief authorized Rust to proceed with the repair work. Agency personnel did not realize until receiving Rust's invoices for the work that the quoted estimate was for labor only and did not cover parts. Rust was uncertain when it prepared the estimate what parts would actually be necessary.

The Agency had indicated that it would never have permitted Rust to proceed with the repair work if it had known that the total cost of the work was $22,875.36, since this amount exceeds its delegated procurement authority. However, the Agency has certified that the cost of repairing the equipment was valid and proper, that the repair work was necessary to place the equipment in operative condition and that the repair work has extended the useful life of the equipment for at least 5 additional years. The cost of replacing the equipment instead of repairing it would have been three times the total cost of the repair. The Agency also informs us that if proper procurement procedures had been followed, Rust would have received the authorized contract to do the repair work since it was the sole source for acquiring the necessary services. Based on these facts, a BIA contracting officer ratified in writing the unauthorized action as required by 41 CFR 1-1.405 and established a contract with Rust in the amount of $22,875.36 for services rendered. The certifying officer has withheld payment pending our decision as to whether the voucher may be certified.

The proper test to apply in a situation where there is no formal contract is whether the Government has received a benefit from the unauthorized procurement and whether this procurement has been either expressly or impliedly ratified by authorized contracting officials of the Government. *RCA Corporation*, B–183289, December 3, 1975, 75–2 CPD 369. If the outcome of this test is in the affirmative, then payment may be made for services rendered either under the unauthorized contract on a quantum meruit basis, which means that payment may be made for the reasonable value of work performed, 40 Comp. Gen. 447, 451 (1969), or under the later ratified contract for the contract price.

In the instant situation, the Government received the benefit of the work performed—the repaired equipment—and acknowledged this benefit. The contracting officer has specifically ratified the transaction. Therefore, payment may be made to Rust in the amount agreed to by the contracting officer who ratified the informal procurement. Under 31 U.S.C. §§ 628 and 701 the only proper appropriation to charge for the repair work would be the Fiscal Year 1978 appropriation because the need arose and the work was ordered and performed in that year.

[B–195757]

Bids—Responsiveness—Lot Bidding

Bidder which submits a low combination bid for drydock and topside overhaul work may not be rejected solely for failing to bid separately for both drydock and topside work. It is recommended that in future procurements agency revise provision in solicitation requiring bid rejection in such circumstances.

In the matter of Norfolk Shipbuilding & Drydock Corporation, September 21, 1979:

Norfolk Shipbuilding & Drydock Corporation (NORSHIPCO) protests any contract award to Sun Ship Building and Dry Dock Company (Sun Ship) under invitation for bids (IFB) N62678–79–

B–0067 issued by the Supervisor of Shipbuilding, Conversion and Repair, U.S. Navy, Portsmouth, Virginia (Navy) for the regular overhaul of the USS PORTLAND (LSD–37).

The protestor has filed suit in the United States District Court for the Eastern District of Virginia, Norfolk Division, Civil Action No. 79–743–N, requesting the court to enjoin the Navy from awarding a contract pending a decision by the Comptroller General on its protest. The court has enjoined the Navy from making an award, and we consider the court's action to be an expression of interest in obtaining our decision. 4 C.F.R. 20.10 (1979); *Dynalectron Corporation*, 54 Comp. Gen. 1009 (1975), 75–1 CPD 341.

In order to maximize competition the solicitation provided for three bidding lots, respectively, for drydock work, topside work and a combination of both. This division was intended to enable smaller ship repair facilities to compete for the topside overhaul work which does not require drydock facilities normally possessed only by the larger firms. Bids, however, were received only from larger firms with drydock facilities and the Navy proposes to accept Sun Ship's low bid for Lot III covering all work since no combination of Lot I and Lot II bids is lower priced.

NORSHIPCO argues that Sun Ship's bid must be rejected as non-responsive to the IFB because Sun Ship failed to bid on Lot II work, as required. For the reasons set forth herein, we deny the protest.

The solicitation provides, in part:

15. SPLIT BIDDING. The Government reserves the right to make award to any offeror on the basis of Lot I, Lot II, or Lot III as may be in the best interests of the Government, price and other factors considered. Offers submitted for Lot III (total job) will not be considered unless accompanied by offers for both Lot I (Drydock) and Lot II (Topside) * * *.

The bids received were as follows:

Bidder	Lot I	Lot II	Lot III
Sun Ship	$1,750,000	No bid	$9,760,000
NORSHIPCO	1,604,950	$11,197,000	11,505,950
Bethlehem Steel	2,394,029	11,137,373	12,572,004
Maryland Shipbuilding	2,490,000	No bid	No bid

The Navy argues that because NORSHIPCO and Sun Ship are in contention for award on the basis of their Lot III prices, the failure of Sun Ship to submit a bid on Lot II may be considered an immaterial deviation from the IFB's requirement and waived by the Navy under the provisions of Defense Acquition Regulation (DAR) 2–405 (1976 ed.).

In support of its contention, NORSHIPCO relies upon our decisions in a number of cases where we determined that a bidder which failed to include a price for every item as required by the IFB was nonresponsive and could not be considered for award. Two of the cited decisions are *Farrel Construction Company*, 57 Comp. Gen. 597 (1978), 78–2 CPD 45 and *Bayshore Systems Corporation*, 56 Comp. Gen. 83 (1976), 76–2 CPD 395. In both cases the protester failed to submit a price for an item which was to be added to other priced items in the IFB to determine the low bidder. We held the bids to be non-responsive because the bidders would not be contractually bound to perform the work required by the items for which bid prices had not been submitted. Therefore, the Government would not be receiving all of the work contemplated by the IFB.

However, in the case under consideration, the failure of Sun Ship to submit a bid for Lot II does not relieve Sun Ship from the obligation to perform topside work required by Lot II because its bid on Lot III covers all work required.

Generally, bids which do not conform to the requirements of a solicitation must be rejected as nonresponsive, unless the deviation is immaterial or is a matter of form rather than substance. Any deviation which affects price, quantity or quality is material and is cause for rejection. 30 Comp. Gen. 179 (1950). However, a requirement is not necessarily material simply because it is expressed in positive terms with a warning that failure to comply "may" or "will" result in rejection of the bid as nonresponsive. 39 Comp. Gen. 595 (1960).

In this connection we previously considered a similar IFB provision requiring the submission of separate bids on two portions of the work (Lot I and Lot II) if a combination bid (Lot III) was submitted and where only bidders who submitted combination bids were under consideration for award. We determined that a bidder for the combined work who failed to submit a bid for topside work only could be considered for award. B–173806, August 16, 1971. We stated that "since no small shipyard is in contention for award, the purpose sought to be achieved by lot bidding would not be violated," and "the failure * * * to bid on Lot 2 may be regarded as an immaterial deviation."

NORSHIPCO argues that our decision in B–173806, *supra*, has been impliedly overruled by our decision in *Coastal Drydock & Repair Corporation*, B–187048, September 28, 1976, 76–2 CPD 290 wherein we stated:

> We believe that when all of the IFB's "lot bidding" provisions quoted above are read together they require only that firms interested in bidding upon both dry dock and topside work must bid upon each type of work separately as well as a combined lot. * * *

The protester believes that we gave effect to the requirement that bidders for combined lots be required also to bid separately. However, it was not necessary to decide what effect we would have given that provision because the successful bidder bid only on drydock work and the quoted proscription applicable only to combined lot bidders did not apply in such circumstances.

We believe that the failure of Sun Ship to submit a bid for topside work had no effect on the price, quality, quantity or time of performance of any contract to be awarded for the combination of drydock and topside work covered in the firm's bid for Lot III. Moreover, it is clear that there is no valid purpose in the circumstances for rejecting a bid for combined drydock and topside work which was not accompanied by separate bids for both portions of the work because no smaller firm with only topside capabilities submitted a bid. *Cf.* B–168479, December 31, 1969. Furthermore, the protester is not prejudiced by the Government's nonenforcement of its "lot bidding" requirement because the protester was not low for either Lot III or for any combination with other bidders of its Lot I and Lot II bids.

Therefore, Sun Ship may be considered for award of Lot III if proper in other respects and the protest is denied.

However, we are concerned with the IFB provision that gave rise to the problem in this case. Although we have noted the concerns expressed by and on behalf of small businesses, that to ignore or eliminate a requirement to bid separately for drydock and topside work would make comparisons between large and small businesses impossible, we believe that in the absence of a determination to set aside the topside work for small business concerns, there is no authority to award a contract for all or part of the work other than on the basis of the lowest price bid in open competition.

We also question whether, as a practical matter, bidding restrictions effectively promote awards to smaller firms for topside work only. A bidder could submit an unreasonably inflated price for any lot of unwanted work. *See* B–168479, *supra*. Moreover, the requirement that combination bids be accompanied by separate bids for drydock as well as topside work could reduce competition among larger firms which have no interest in performing only the topside work but would be willing to perform drydock work with or without the topside work. Accordingly, we are recommending to the Secretary of the Navy that future solicitations be revised to eliminate the requirement for bidding separately for both drydock and topside overhaul work where a combination bid for all work is submitted.

[B–196007]

Bids—Mistakes—Verification—Refusal by Bidder to Verify

Bidder which refuses to verify bid price because it erroneously estimated costs to be substantially lower than price quotations subsequently received from suppliers may have bid withdrawn or rejected.

In the matter of Department of the Navy—Advance Decision, September 21, 1979:

The Department of the Navy, Naval Sea Systems Command (Navy) requests our advance decision as to whether Granite State Machine Co. (Granite) may be permitted to withdraw its bid or whether the contracting officer may reject the bid on invitation for bids (IFB) N0002479–B–4360 for anti-slack devices and related equipment. The basis for the request is that Granite has alleged a mistake in its bid price due to its incorrect estimates of certain items. We conclude that the bid may be withdrawn or rejected.

Bid opening revealed that Granite's bid of $576,600 was substantially lower than the three other bids received, which ranged from $950,374 to $1,237,900. In light of this sizeable price variance, the contracting officer requested Granite to verify its bid. Granite responded that is could not verify its bid. Granite states that it had been unable to obtain price quotations from the vendors of certain items prior to bid opening, and therefore had submitted a bid based on estimated costs. The quotations subsequently obtained after bid opening revealed that Granite had significantly underestimated the costs of these items. Granite states that its bid should have been $714,500. In support of its mistake, Granite submits a sworn statement detailing its efforts to obtain the correct prices prior to bid opening, its worksheets and quotations from the suppliers of the items mispriced, dated after bid opening.

The Navy believes that Granite's error was one of business judgment, as opposed to a mistake in the bid intended to be submitted, and it questions whether such an error justifies withdrawal or rejection of the bid.

The Navy is correct in that relief is not allowed for certain types of errors in judgment. These include such things as failing to foresee that an intended performance approach would not succeed, and incorrectly estimating the length of time it will take to complete performance. B–153279, October 21, 1964; 51 Comp. Gen. 18 (1971). The error involved here, however, is based on an erroneous assumption for which we have granted relief in cases where the bidder used an obsolete catalog or was ignorant of actual manufacturing costs. B–145192, March 16, 1961; B–162379, October 20, 1967. We allowed relief where, as here, the contracting officer was on notice of a possibility of mistake because the bid was significantly lower than the other bids received.

Where a bidder discovers that it made a mistake in its bid and furnishes evidence of such mistake to the contracting officer, after bid opening but before award, the bid may be withdrawn regardless of the bidder's negligence in making the mistake. The contracting officer would be overreaching to accept an unrealistic low bid with 'the knowledge that the bid was based on a mistake. *Ruggiero* v. *United States*, 190 Ct. Cl. 327, 420 F.2d 709 (1970).

There is no question that a mistake was made and the Government may not, in good faith, accept the bid as submitted which the bidder has refused to verify. The bid may be rejected or withdrawn from consideration for award. 41 Comp. Gen. 289 (1961).

[B-192117]

Pay—Retired—Survivor Benefit Plan—Spouse—Social Security Offset

The widow of a Survivor Benefit Plan (SBP) participator, who had some post-1956 Social Security covered military service, became entitled to Social Security payments based on the deceased member's total Social Security covered earnings, including the covered military service. For the purpose of the reduction in her SBP annuity required by 10 U.S.C. 1451(a) for Social Security payments attributable to military earnings, it is not necessary that the member acquire a fully insured status based solely on Social Security covered military earnings. Since generally Social Security payments received are enhanced by military covered quarters, the SBP annuity is to be reduced by the amount of the Social Security payment based on the member's military service.

In the matter of Mrs. Marjorie S. Nester, September 24, 1979:

The question to be decided here is whether the Social Security offset of a Survivor Benefit Plan (SBP) annuity is required by 10 U.S.C. 1451(a) based on the member's Social Security covered military earnings although the member did not acquire his Social Security insured status based on the military covered earnings alone. The answer is yes.

The member in the case before us, Lieutenant Colonel Norman W. Nester, USAR, was retired effective August 1, 1965, under the provisions of 10 U.S.C. 1331–1337, having elected survivor coverage for spouse only under the Retired Serviceman's Family Protection Plan (RSFPP). On December 1, 1972, Colonel Nester elected into the then newly enacted Survivor Benefit Plan, 10 U.S.C. 1447–1455, to provide maximum coverage for his spouse, and canceled his RSFPP coverage.

Colonel Nester died December 2, 1973, and an SBP annuity was established for his widow, Marjorie S. Nester, effective December 3, 1973. However, pursuant to 10 U.S.C. 1451(a), since Colonel Nester had Social Security covered earnings as a result of the performance of active military service after 1956, Mrs. Nester's SBP annuity was reduced.

Mrs. Nester expresses the view that her annuity should not be reduced. It is her contention that in order for her annuity to be reduced by Social Security benefits received, her deceased husband had to have acquired a fully insurable Social Security status based solely on his military service and that any coverage earned outside his military service is not to be taken into account in establishing that offset. According to Mrs. Nester, her husband would need 19 quarters of coverage to be eligible for Social Security coverage based solely on his military earnings. It is her position that since he had only four military covered quarters, there is no basis for reducing her SBP annuity.

The Army Finance Center, on the other hand, contends that 10 U.S.C. 1451(a), which requires offset, is to be applied whenever a widow is entitled to Social Security benefits. However, the computation for the offset is based only on the military earnings portion of the Social Security coverage.

We believe that the position taken by the Army Finance Center is the correct interpretation to be given the offset provision. Section 1451(a) provides for the reduction (offset) in the SBP annuity based on the Social Security benefit in part as follows:

> * * * the monthly annuity shall be reduced by an amount equal to the amount of the survivor benefit, if any, to which the widow * * * would be entitled * * * based solely upon [military] service by the person concerned * * *.

On page 30 of Senate Report 92–1089, 92d Cong., 2d Sess., the following statement is made regarding the Social Security offset:

> * * * when the widow reaches age 62. her [SBP] annuity based on her husband's military retired pay would be offset by the equivalent of the social security payment which is *attributable to her husband's military service*.

And on page 31, it is explained further that:

> There is no reduction because of the social security benefits that may have been earned as a result of the husband's employment in his post-retirement years * * *. It cannot be overemphasized that the only social security payments which are taken into account in this integration of benefits are the payments to the widow based on her husband's social security earned as a result of active duty in military service.

See also the similar statements in House Report No. 92–481, 92d Cong. 1st Sess., pages 14–15.

Enactment of the SBP did not modify Social Security entitlements. However, the SBP was intended to be integrated with Social Security and, therefore, it provides for reduction in SBP payments on account of the portion of Social Security payments predicated on the member's military service. It was also recognized that in many cases the member would have other Social Security covered earnings which are nonmilitary and which would not subject the SBP annuity to further reduction. See generally 57 Comp. Gen. 339 (1978).

When an individual, such as Mrs. Nester, becomes eligible for a widow's Social Security benefit, all quarters of her deceased husband's coverage, both military and nonmilitary, would be taken into account before the amount of the Social Security benefit to which she is entitled is established and paid. Generally, when military covered quarters are included, the Social Security benefit received is enhanced, whether or not the military covered earnings would be sufficient, alone, for the member to have achieved insured status. It is that enhancement to which the section 1451(a) required reduction is directed. See 53 Comp. Gen. 733 (1974) and 57 *id.* 339, 341–343, *supra.*

Thus, it is our view that the SBP annuity must be reduced by the amount of a widow's Social Security payment based on the deceased member's post-1956 military service.

Accordingly, deductions should continue to be made from Mrs. Nester's SBP annuity, if otherwise correct.

[B–193440]

Travel Expenses—Leaves of Absence—Temporary Duty—Notice of Duty Prior to Leave

Employee scheduled annual leave for vacation in Toronto, Canada, and made the necessary plans. Before departure from his permanent duty station (Boulder) he was directed to perform temporary duty in Norfolk before returning to his headquarters. Employee is entitled to be reimbursed the cost of his actual expenses not to exceed the cost of direct round-trip travel between headquarters and temporary duty point.

In the matter of Gregg Marshall, September 24, 1979:

The question presented is whether Mr. Gregg Marshall, an employee of the National Oceanic and Atmospheric Administration (NOAA), is entitled to be reimbursed the difference between the regular coach cost of air transportation expenses he incurred and the reduced air fare he would have incurred for his vacation had he not been required to perform temporary duty (TDY) prior to returning to his permanent duty station from his vacation point. He is entitled to receive the air transportation expenses he actually incurred not to exceed the cost of commercial air fare from his permanent duty station to his TDY site and return.

The question was presented by letter of October 12, 1978, from Mr. Ernest Martinez, Certifying Officer, NOAA, Boulder Field Finance Office.

Mr. Marshall, by Travel Order No. 20–8–RLO–99, dated July 27, 1978, was directed to travel from Boulder, Colorado, his permanent duty station, to Norfolk, Virginia, and return in order to perform temporary duty. At the time the travel order was prepared it was known that the claimant would be on annual leave status in Toronto, Canada. Prior to receiving his travel orders, Mr. Marshall, preparing to go on vacation made arrangements to fly from Denver to Toronto— travel from Boulder to Denver is not a part of the problem—and return using a super saver fare costing $156.60. As a result of his TDY assignment he was forced to cancel his reservations and obtain regular coach fare tickets from Denver to Toronto to Norfolk and return to Denver for $387.

Based upon our decision in 39 Comp. Gen. 611 (196``), NOAA reimbursed Mr. Marshall $119, which represents the difference between the coach fare from Toronto to Norfolk to Denver ($248) and the coach fare from Toronto to Denver ($129). The general rule stated in 39 Comp. Gen. 611, *supra*, is that when an employee proceeds to a point away from his official station on annual leave he assumes the obligation of returning at his own expense.

Mr. Marshall does not disagree with the above rule but contends that at a minimum he should be allowed the difference between his actual air transportation expenses of $387 and the $156.60, the cost of the super saver, since he would have been able to use the super saver but for the new orders requiring him to perform TDY prior to returning to Denver. We agree. Mr. Marshall, however, understates the extent of his entitlement.

Paragraph 1–2.5b of the Federal Travel Regulations (FTR) (FPMR 101–7) (1973) provides:

> When a person for his own convenience travels by an indirect route or interrupts travel by direct route, the extra expense shall be borne by him. Reimbursement for expenses shall be based only on such charges as would have been incurred by a usually traveled route. When transportation requests are used, they shall be issued only for that portion of the expense properly chargeable to the Government, and the employee shall pay the additional personal expense * * *.

Since Mr. Marshall was required to travel from Denver to Norfolk for the purpose of TDY and was notified of that requirement *before* his departure, his travel by way of Toronto is travel by indirect route within the meaning of FTR para. 1–2.5b, quoted above. Therefore, Mr. Marshall is entitled to reimbursement of his actual expenses not to exceed what he would have incurred had he traveled directly round trip between his permanent duty station and his TDY station. See *Richard B. Gentile*, B–188689, February 7, 1978; *Wallace W. Tanaka*, B–187926, June 8, 1977; and 24 Comp. Gen. 442 (1944). The cost of travel by usually traveled route from Denver to Norfolk and return would have been $312. Since his actual expenses of $387 exceeds that amount he is entitled to $312 less what he has already been reimbursed. Mr. Marshall's situation is distinguished from cases in which an employee, who is already away from his permanent duty station for a personal reason such as annual leave, is ordered to perform TDY there or at another location, interrupting, cancelling or following the taking of annual leave. See e.g., *Delbert C. Nahm*, B–191588, January 2, 1979, and *Paul B. Magallanes*, B–190646, January 25, 1978.

Furthermore, we recognize that there are times when an agency, for its own convenience, requests an employee, before he departs on annual leave, to perform TDY in conjunction with his vacation. In these instances, the agency request is based on the fact that the employee will be taking leave at or near the TDY site and but for this the request would not have been made. When this occurs the agency is not prohibited from reimbursing an employee only those costs attributable to performing TDY in excess of those the employee would have incurred for personal reasons. Mr. Marshall's travel does not fall into this category as his round-trip travel is specifically authorized in the travel order. The parenthetical notation that he would first go to Canada for leave is not viewed as diminishing his travel reimbursement.

Accordingly, Mr. Marshall is entitled to receive his actual air transportation expenses not to exceed the air transportation expenses he would have incurred had he traveled directly round trip between his permanent duty station and his TDY assignment. The voucher is returned for modification in accordance with our decision.

[B–192002]

Transportation — Freight — Charges — Delivery Requirement

Since there is no indication in legislative history that Congress in amending the Shipping Act, 1916, intended to repeal statutory and regulatory scheme which on shipments moving under Government bills of lading requires delivery to destination to earn freight charges, contrary provisions in carrier's LASH bill of lading are ineffective to support payment of additional freight charges.

In the matter of Delta Steamship Lines, Inc., September 26, 1979:

Delta Steamship Lines, Inc. (Delta), requests review by the Comptroller General of the General Services Administration's (GSA) settlement action which disallowed Delta's claim for additional freight. 4 C.F.R. 53.3 (1978). GSA's action was taken on eight shipments of Department of Defense cargo transported from New Orleans, Louisiana, to various points in South America under Government bills of lading (GBL).

While en route to Salvador, Brazil, the vessel performing the initial carriage, the SS *Delta Norte*, sustained machinery damage and had to be towed to Oranjestad, Aruba. Because parts necessary for repair would be unavailable for several months, the voyage was abandoned and the cargo was transshipped from Oranjestad, Aruba, to destination on the SS *Delta Brasil*. Delta claims that, pursuant to provisions 10 and 16 of its LASH bill of lading, transshipment of the cargo from Aruba to destination entitles it to receipt of a second freight. The shipper, Military Sealift Command Gulf Subarea, denied Delta's claim contending that under a Government bill of lading freight is at the risk of the vessel which means that cargo must be delivered to destination before freight is earned. It contends that

Delta must bear the cost of transshipment in order to earn the original freight. GSA concurs in the denial of Delta's claim for the cost of transshipment. Delta collected ocean freight charges of $4,242.98 under the original Government bills of lading and was denied additional ocean freight charges of $3,815.76 for the voyage from Aruba to destination.

The reverse of the covering GBL's Standard Form 1103, January 1974, provides that "[e]xcept as provided in 4 C.F.R. 52 or as otherwise stated hereon, this bill of lading is also subject to the same rules and conditions as govern commercial shipments made on the usual forms provided therefor by the carrier." Therefore the terms of the carrier's usual contract of carriage—here Delta's LASH bill of lading—are incorporated by reference and shipments of Government property are made subject to such terms except as provided by regulation or otherwise specifically provided on the GBL.

Conditions 10 and 16 of Delta's LASH bill of lading in effect provide that in any situation which threatens the ship or its cargo the goods may be unloaded at an alternate destination, which shall constitute full and satisfactory performance of the contract. Forwarding, or transshipment, of the goods to the designated destination is at the additional expense of the shipper and may be performed either by the shipper or by the carrier.

Delta contends that in 1961 Congress passed legislation converting tariffs and bills of lading of ocean carriers in foreign commerce into statutory tariffs binding on all parties thus making its LASH bill of lading contract paramount to the GBL contract.

Section 4 of Pub. L. 87-346, October 3, 1961, amended Section 18 of the Shipping Act, 1916, 46 U.S.C. 817, by adding a provision requiring carriers by sea in foreign commerce to file with the Federal Maritime Commission (FMC) and keep open to public inspection tariffs showing the rates, fares, charges, origins, and destinations, classifications, rules and regulations. The tariffs are required to include "specimens of any bill of lading contract of affreightment, or other document evidencing the transportation agreement." Subparagraph 3 prohibits any carrier from charging, demanding, collecting or receiving a greater or less or different compensation for transportation or any transportation service than is set forth in the published and filed tariff except as authorized by the FMC under specified circumstances. The rates, rules and other tariff provisions filed pursuant to this provision have the force and effect of law binding on both the carrier and the shipper. *Gilbert Imported Hardwoods, Inc. v. 245 Packages of Guatambu Squares, More or Less*, 508 F.2d 1116 (5th Cir. 1975); *Koninklijke Nedlloyd BV v. Uniroyal, Inc.*, 433 F. Supp. 121, 127 (S.D.N.Y. 1977).

However, Section 529 of Title 31 of the United States Code prohibits any advance of public money or any payment in excess of the value of the service rendered. This prohibition has been a part of statutory law since January 31, 1823. 3 Stat. 723. In recognition of the prohibition, Government regulations dealing with GBLs since 1907 have provided that in no case shall prepayment of charges be demanded by the carrier, and that the GBL properly certified or accomplished and attached to the voucher for transportation charges should be presented to the paying office. 14 Comp. Dec. 967 (1907). Until 1974 these provisions were set forth in full on the reverse of the GBL. 4 C.F.R. 8, 9 (1949) ; 4 C.F.R. 52 (1974). They now are published in 41 C.F.R. 101–41.302–3(a) (1978). They are statutory and, therefore, have the force and effect of law. *Farmer v. Philadelphia Electric Co.*, 329 F.2d 3 (3rd Cir. 1964).

The Attorney General has stated that the plain meaning of 31 U.S.C. § 529 is that, "no money shall be advanced to contractors; that is that no money shall be paid to them on account of their contracts before the actual performance of the service or the delivery of the articles stipulated for." 10 Ops. Atty. Gen. 288, 301 (1862). See also 32 Comp. Gen. 563 (1953) ; 43 *id.* 788 (1964), 50 *id.* 164 (1970).

Although the amendments to the Shipping Act give to a carrier's bill of lading the force and effect of law, there is no indication either in the amendments or in their legislative history that Congress intended to amend or repeal the statutory and regulatory scheme which on shipments moving under GBLs requires actual delivery to the specified destination on the GBL in order to earn freight charges. And to assume that the mere passage of a specific statute governing an area of conduct also regulated by a more general statute limits enforcement of the general statute by carving out an exception to it is, in effect, to accomplish by implication a partial repeal of the general statute, a type of repeal which is not favored. *United States v. Burnett*, 505 F.2d 815 (9th Cir. 1974) ; certiorari denied *Lyon v. United States*, 420 U.S. 966 (1975).

There is no indication in the legislative history that Congress intended to bar application of the general statute against advance payments when in 1961 it amended the Shipping Act, 1916, to require carriers to file tariffs containing "specimens of any bill of lading . . ." Therefore, the regulatory scheme to implement 31 U.S.C. § 529 which requires actual delivery to the destination specified on the GBL in order to earn freight charges makes the LASH bill of lading provisions 10 and 16 contrary to that statute and implementing regulations and ineffective to support payment of the additional freight charges. Cf. *Alcoa Steamship Co., Inc. v. United States*, 338 U.S. 421 (1949).

Since under the GBL freight is at the risk of the vessel there is no entitlement to a second freight or transshipment cost, which is dependent upon the freight having been earned at the alternate delivery. See Item 16 of the LASH bill of lading. In this connection in *Marine*

Insurance and General Average in the United States, Leslie J. Buglass, 1973, page 172 it is stated:

In such circumstances (justifiable abandonment of the voyage), the shipowner can either deliver the cargo at the port of refuge or (at cargo owners' request) arrange to forward it to destination at the expense of the cargo (assuming the original freight to have been guaranteed). Of course, if the freight was not guaranteed, the shipowner will no doubt pay the cost of forwarding to earn his original freight.

GSA's disallowance of the claim for additional freight charges is sustained.

[B–194201]

Officers and Employees—Contracting With Government—Public Policy Objectionability—Corporation—Substantial Ownership or Control Prohibition—Equitable Ownership Consideration

Federal Procurement Regulations (FPR) prohibit Government from contracting with corporations substantially owned or controlled by its employees. While Government employee shareholders of protester may have relinquished all corporate control by placing their stock in trust, Government employees have retained equitable ownership in protester so that procuring agency is justified in analyzing amount of their stockholdings to determine if they constitute substantial ownership for purposes of FPR.

Federal Procurement Regulations — Conflict of Interest Prohibitions — Contracting With Corporations, etc. Owned or Controlled by Government Employees, etc. — What Constitutes "Substantial Ownership"

Because issue of control is separate from issue of ownership for purpose of applying FPR, General Accounting Office (GAO) questions propriety of procuring agency's determination of substantial ownership by comparing percent of stock owned by Government employees with percent of stock owned by other individuals in protester. GAO believes that determination of substantial ownership for purposes of FPR should be made solely on basis of relationship of amount of Government employee stock to total amount of stock in protester. Nevertheless, if General Services Administration intends different meaning of substantial ownership, GAO suggests amending FPR to clarify any such meaning.

In the matter of Metro Electric, Inc., September 26, 1979:

Metro Electric, Inc. (Metro), protests the award of a contract to another bidder under solicitation No. ROC 88071 issued by the General Services Administration, Public Buildings Service (GSA). The solicitation was for the electrical renovation of steam tunnels in the Washington, D.C., steam distribution complex.

GSA determined that no contract could be awarded to Metro because of Federal Procurement Regulations (FPR) § 1–1.302–3 (1964 ed. amend. 95). This section of the FPR provides as follows:

Contracts between the Government and Government employees or business concerns substantially owned or controlled by Government employees.
(a) Contracts shall not knowingly be entered into between the Government and employees of the Government or business concerns or organizations which are substantially owned or controlled by Government employees, except for the most compelling reasons, such as cases where the needs of the Government cannot reasonably be otherwise supplied.

Metro has two Government employees, James L. Martin, Jr., and Leo Glascoe, who have 23½ percent of that company's stock between them. Both had placed their stock in trust prior to the issuance of the protested solicitation. Despite the trusts, however, GSA found that Metro was substantially owned by these two Government employees.

Metro states that it bid on the solicitation as the prime electrical contractor and was the lowest bidder. Metro also states that its problems with GSA on the matter of ownership began with a prior GSA solicitation for fire alarm systems. At the time of that solicitation, Metro had three directors and stockholders owning 38.99 percent of the company who were employed by the Government. According to Metro, after it had submitted a bid, GSA informed it that there was a possible conflict of interest. Consequently, Metro wrote a letter on May 4, 1978, to GSA concerning its stockholders. By letter dated May 26, 1978, GSA responded by stating that the point at which a company is not substantially owned by Government employees would be somewhat less than 25 percent.

Metro contends that two of the three Government employee stockholders subsequently divested themselves of ownership by placing their stock in trust. Under the trust of James L. Martin, Jr., the income from the trust is paid to his two children. The trustees are Mr. Martin's parents. The terms of the trust also provide that the trust will terminate in the event of the death of both children or 30 days after Mr. Martin ceases to work for the Government with the trust principal then being distributed to Mr. Martin. The terms of Leo Glascoe's trust are similar except that the income from the trust is to be paid to Mr. Glascoe's father-in-law and mother-in-law. Like Mr. Martin's trust, Mr. Glascoe's trust will terminate upon the death of both trust beneficiaries or 30 days after Mr. Glascoe ceases to work for the Government.

In addition, Metro states that prior to its bidding on the protested solicitation, it held a stockholders meeting where new officers were elected. Thus, Metro avers that two of the three Government employee stockholders now no longer hold office in the company. As to the third Government employee stockholder, Metro indicates that this individual has since retired from the Government.

With regard to whether Mr. Martin's and Mr. Glascoe's Government employment conflicts with their association with Metro, Metro has submitted with its protest two letters from their supervisors to the Small Business Administration. The first letter dated June 14, 1979, is from the Sergeant at Arms, United States House of Representatives, which declares that Leo Glascoe's interest in Metro would in no way present any conflict with his duties in the Office of the Sergeant at Arms. The second letter, undated, is apparently from Mr. James L. Martin's Supervisor at "DEA" stating that it is reasonable to assume that Mr. Martin's function with DEA would not allow him any advantages in assisting Metro in any possible means of obtaining that company's goals.

GSA takes the position that the purpose of FPR § 1–1.302–3 is to avoid any *appearance* of favoritism or preferential treatment by the Government toward its employees. See 41 Comp. Gen. 569 (1962). The only factors under this provision of the FPR are substantial ownership *or* control of a company by a Government employee. Consequently, GSA believes that the duties of the Government employee and the particular agency for which he works are not considerations.

GSA points out that FPR § 1–1.302–3 does not define substantial ownership or control. However, GSA refers to our decision in *Capital Aero, Inc.*, 55 Comp. Gen. 295 (1975), 75–2 CPD 201, in which we noted that the regulation does not speak of "majority" ownership, only "substantial" ownership. In that case we concluded that in light of the significant history which has discouraged contracting between the Government and its employees, a Government employee owning 39.95 percent of the stock in a corporation had substantial ownership in that corporation.

Nevertheless, GSA recognizes that we did not determine in *Capital Aero, supra,* whether the holding of a small amount of stock by Government employees is sufficient to bring the company within the general rule that it is undesirable for the Government to contract with its employees. Mr. Martin and Mr. Glascoe each own 11.76 percent of Metro's stock and thus cumulatively own 23.52 percent. GSA states that there are 16 stockholders in Metro, six of whom own 9 percent or more of the total stock. The largest single holding is 23.53 percent. Based on the relationship of the block of stock owned by these two Government employees to the percent of stock owned by the other Metro shareholders, GSA decided that 23.52 percent did constitute substantial ownership in the company. While GSA admits it had initially indicated to Metro that somewhat less than 25 percent would not be considered substantial ownership, it states that the final determintion that Metro was still substantially owned by Government employees was made because of the relationship of their 23.52 percent of stock ownership to the other stockholdings in the company.

GSA also contends that the trusts of Mr. Martin and Mr. Glascoe have to be analyzed from the point of view whether an appearance of impropriety still exists even though legal title to the stock no longer rests with these individuals. GSA asserts that Mr. Martin and Mr. Glascoe are, in effect, beneficiaries under their respective trusts and both have vested reverter interests in the trust corpus. While it is true that they will not receive any income from the stock during the period of their Government employment, GSA argues that they will enjoy the affected value of the stock later. Therefore, GSA believes even though Mr. Martin and Mr. Glascoe do not now have full legal title to the stock, the effect of their interest in the stock as far as the appearance of impropriety is concerned is the same as when their ownership of the stock was full.

With regard to whether Metro is controlled by Government employees, GSA contends that it is unnecessary to show control in addition to substantial ownership since the regulation is phrased in the alternative. In any event, by placing the authority to vote their stock in the trustees under the terms of their trusts, GSA believes Mr. Martin and Mr. Glascoe have divested themselves of any control over Metro during the period of their Government employment.

In rebuttal, Metro claims that GSA has interpreted FPR § 1–1.302–3 beyond the scope of any previous decision by this Office. Metro characterizes our decision in *Capital Aero, Inc., supra,* as involving a situation where *one* Government employee owned 39.95 percent of a company's stock. In Metro's opinion, GSA has interpreted the word "substantial" as being a far lower percent of ownership than 39.95 percent that we found in that decision. Further, Metro points out that GSA recognizes that Mr. Martin and Mr. Glascoe will not receive income on the stock placed in trust. According to Metro, the fact that these individuals will enjoy the affected value of the stock after their Government employment ceases is true for any Government employee who places his corporate stock in trust, including the President of the United States. Thus, Metro requests that the determinations made by GSA be rejected by us because they have no basis in law or fact.

Finally, Metro alleges that it has in the past entered into contracts with other governmental agencies. In support of this allegation, Metro has furnished us with copies of contracts entered into with the United States Soldiers' and Airmen's Home and Howard University. By entering into contracts with it, Metro believes that this implies that these agencies determined that there was no conflict of interest.

GAO ANALYSIS

We have stated that while contracts between the Government and its employees are not expressly prohibited by statute, they are undesirable and should be authorized only where the needs of the Government cannot be reasonably supplied otherwise. 55 Comp. Gen. 681 (1976), and the cases cited therein. Such contracts are open to criticism as to *alleged favoritism and possible fraud.* 41 Comp. Gen. 569 (1962). FPR § 1–1.302–3, then, is the regulatory implementation of well-established policy.

The prohibition against the Government entering into contracts with its employees is equally applicable to corporations owned by Government employees. *Capital Aero, Inc., supra.* Here, however, Metro takes the position that by placing their stock in trust, Metro's two Government employee shareholders have divested themselves of the ownership of such stock.

We believe that Metro has confused ownership of the stock with control over it. We agree with GSA that by placing the authority to vote their stock in the trustees, Mr. Martin and Mr. Glascoe have divested themselves of any control over the stock while they are employed by the Government. Also, as Metro points out, it is common practice for high-ranking Government officials to establish a temporary trust for their own benefit, usually lasting for the duration of their tenure in Federal office. S. Report No. 95–639, 85th Cong., 2nd Sess. (1978). These trusts, which are termed "blind trusts," serve important objectives. They relieve Government officials from day-to-day investment decisions on the trust assets, which decisions may conflict or interfere with Government duties. Further, they play an important role in reducing the appearance of a conflict of interest.

The placing of assets in a blind trust does not, however, mean that the Government employee trustor has divested himself of full ownership of the trust assets. Indeed, one of the primary reasons for the use of the blind trust is that actual divestiture of ownership of the Government employee's assets may result in burdensome tax consequences. S. Report No. 95–639, *supra.* Moreover, the fact that the trusts of Mr. Martin and Mr. Glascoe will terminate automatically 30 days after they cease to be employees of the Government, in our opinion, is in itself sufficient to show that there has not been a complete divestment of ownership of their trust assets (Metro's stock).

Moreover, we believe that the role of the Government employees in the management and control of the corporation is for purposes of the applicability of FPR § 1–1.302–3 a separate consideration from whether the Government employees substantially own that corporation. The rationale of the rule prohibiting the Government from contracting with its own employees is not merely to avoid any conflict of interest that might arise between the employees' interests and their Government duties. It is also to avoid possible criticism of favoritism or preferential treatment by the Government toward its employees. In this regard, if the Government employees have retained a substantial equitable ownership in the corporation, we think that this is enough in itself to invoke the above-described rule.

On the other hand, because the issue of control is separate from the issue of ownership for purposes of applying the regulation, we question the propriety of GSA's determination of substantial ownership by comparing the percent of stock owned by Mr. Glascoe and Mr. Martin to the percent of stock owned by each of the other stockholders. In *Capital Aero, Inc., supra,* we noted that the regulation does not speak of "majority" ownership, only "substantial" ownership. Nevertheless, we found in that case that the amount of stock owned by the Government employee was so significant in relation to the *total amount* of the corporation's stock as to constitute substantial ownership. While a comparison of the amount of stock owned by Government employees with the amount of the corporate stock owned by other individuals may be relevant to a determination of whether the Government employees have substantial control in the corporation, we do not believe such comparison is relevant to the determination of whether the corporation is substantially owned by the Government employees.

We believe that the determination of substantial ownership for purposes of FPR § 1–1.302–3 should be made solely on the basis of the relationship of the amount of Government employee stock to the total amount of the corporation's stock. Accordingly, Metro's protest is sustained. However, no purpose would be served by referring the matter back to GSA for a determination on this basis since the completion date for the contract repair work was August 28, 1979. If GSA intends a meaning of the term "substantial ownership" different from ours and if it anticipates that there will be a significant number of situations in the future involving the application of FPR § 1–1.302–3, we suggest amending the regulation to clarify any such meaning of this term.

[B–193893]

Travel Expenses — Transfers — Reimbursement — Foreign Air Carrier Use

Employee who transferred to Korea in May 1975, indirectly routed his travel by way of Paris, and used foreign airlines for all or a portion of his travel may be reimbursed for constructive air fare without penalty for travel by foreign air carrier. For the period following enactment of 49 U.S.C. 1517, but prior to the issuance of guidelines on June 17, 1975, we have not penalized employees for use of foreign air carriers unless an agency regulation specifically requires the assessment of a penalty.

Officers and Employees — Transfers — Relocation Expenses — Temporary Quarters — Time Limitation

Army employee who occupies temporary quarters for a 53-day period upon being transferred from Korea to Fort Sheridan, Illinois, claims reimbursement for the period beyond 30 days. Claim may not be allowed as 5 U.S.C. 5724a expressly limits reimbursement for temporary quarters to 30 days except where employee transfers to or from Alaska, Hawaii, the territories or possessions of the United States, Puerto Rico or the Canal Zone, for which an additional 30-day reimbursement may be allowed.

In the matter of Leslie H. Black — Fly America Act — penalty and temporary quarters subsistence expenses, September 27, 1979:

By letter dated November 21, 1978, Mr. Leslie H. Black, a civilian employee of the Department of the Army, has appealed our Claims Division's September 26, 1978 settlement which denied his claim for reimbursement of expenses incurred for travel by foreign air carrier incident to his transfer from Fort Sheridan, Illinois, to Waegwan, Korea. In addition, he appeals the denial of his claim for temporary quarters subsistence expenses in excess of 30 days incident to his subsequent transfer from Waegwan, Korea, to Fort Sheridan.

Upon review, we sustain our Claims Division's disallowance of Mr. Black's claim for additional reimbursement for temporary quarters subsistence expenses. However, we find that Mr. Black may be reimbursed for the constructive cost of his and his wife's travel to Korea without penalty for travel by foreign air carrier.

Claim for Travel Expenses

On March 25, 1975, Mr. Black was authorized travel and transportation expenses for himself and his wife incident to his transfer from Fort Sheridan, Illinois, to Waegwan, Korea, in May 1975. The usually traveled route from Fort Sheridan to Korea is by way of either Travis Air Force Base, California, or Seattle, Washington. Service by U.S. air carrier is available by either routing. Instead, Mr. Black and his wife flew from JFK International Airport in New York City to Paris, France, on May 1, 1975. He remained in Paris on leave until May 9, 1975, when he flew to Korea. While the record clearly indicates that Mr. Black and his wife used a foreign air carrier between Paris and Korea, there is some confusion as to whether they traveled by U.S. or foreign air carrier between New York and Paris. Mr. Black has stated that they traveled by U.S. air carrier for that portion of the journey. However, we have been advised by the Army Finance and Accounting Center that copies of airlines tickets that should resolve any doubt in the matter were not forwarded by the certifying officer as attachments to Mr. Black's travel voucher.

Mr. Black appears to have been assessed a penalty of approximately one-half the MAC fare for travel directly to Korea. On the basis of the record before us we are unable to verify the correctness of that penalty amount. Under the computational principles set forth at 56 Comp. Gen. 209 (1977), the penalty should equal the total MAC fare in the event foreign air carriers were used between New York and Paris as well as between Paris and Korea. If a foreign air carrier was used only between Paris and Korea, it does not appear that any penalty would be required. Under the formula, U.S. air carriers would be deemed to have received about 30 percent of the air fare of approximately $1,900 paid by Mr. Black, or $570. Since the record indicates that the MAC fare that was payable for their direct travel to Korea, and hence the revenues that should have been received by U.S. air carriers, did not exceed $570, there is no basis to assess a penalty for the employee's travel by foreign air carrier.

While we would ordinarily request further information from the Army to clarify the record, in this particular case the matter may be resolved in Mr. Black's favor on the basis of the record available. Section 5 of Public Law No. 93-623, 88 Stat. 2104, commonly referred to as the Fly America Act, was enacted on January 3, 1975. That section, now contained at 49 U.S.C. 1517, requires the Comptroller General to disallow expenditures from appropriated funds for travel by foreign air carriers in the absence of proof of the necessity therefor. Until the Comptroller General's guidelines for implementation of the Fly America Act, B–138942, were issued on June 17, 1975, there was no specific directive as to the circumstances under which U.S. air carrier service would be deemed available.

Mr. Black's travel occurred in May 1975, after the law was enacted but before guidelines had been issued. The language of the Act itself provides little assistance to agencies in determining when an employee should be penalized for travel by foreign air carrier. For this reason and because of documentation problems such as are involved in Mr. Black's case, employees need not be penalized for travel prior to June 17, 1975, in the absence of agency regulations specifically requiring the assessment of a penalty. In the case of the Department of Defense, Volume 2 of the Joint Travel Regulations (JTR) were not amended until July 1, 1975, to reflect enactment of the Fly America Act and paragraph C6204 as in effect prior to that date did not require assessment of a penalty or disallowance of air fare for unjustified travel by foreign air carriers. Accordingly, we hold that Mr. Black may be reimbursed for travel to Korea based on the constructive air fare without penalty for his use of a foreign air carrier for all or a portion of his travel by indirect route. That portion of the Claims Division settlement holding to the contrary is overruled.

Claim for Temporary Quarters

The record shows that Mr. Black was transferred from Waegwan, Korea, to Fort Sheridan, Illinois, in May 1977. He and his dependents occupied temporary quarters in the Fort Sheridan area from June 19, 1977, through August 10, 1977. He has been allowed temporary quarters subsistence expenses (TQSE) for the 30-day period through July 18, 1977. However, he has claimed TQSE for the additional 23-day period through August 10, 1977, based on the fact that he and his family were unable to occupy their residence until it was vacated by a tenant on September 30, 1977. Our Claims Division disallowed his claim on the basis that there is no authority to pay TQSE for a period in excess of 30 days.

The authority for entitlement to subsistence expenses while occupying temporary quarters is found at 5 U.S.C. 5724a(a)(3) which expressly provides that reimbursement for temporary quarters is limited to a period of 30 days except when the employee "moves to or from Hawaii, Alaska, the territories or possessions, the Commonwealth of Puerto Rico or the Canal Zone," an additional 30-day reimbursement may be allowed. Volume 2, JTR, para. C13001–2, in effect at the time of Mr. Black's transfer, contained the same authorization and limitations.

In view of the above limitation on the period of reimbursement for occupancy of temporary quarters and as Mr. Black transferred from a foreign post to a duty station in Illinois, there is no basis upon which to allow his claim for TQSE for an additional 23 days. 55 Comp. Gen. 1107 (1976). Accordingly, this portion of our Claims Division's disallowance is sustained.

[B-194197]

Subsistence — Per Diem — Actual Expenses — Fractional Days—Ten Hours or Less

Employee, whose duty station is in New York City, traveled to high-rate geographical area. Newark, New Jersey, from his home in Brooklyn, New York. Period of travel was less than 10 hours and he is not entitled to reimbursement of $2.75. cost of lunch incurred in Newark. Restriction in para. 1–7.6d(1), Federal Travel Regulations (FTR). that per diem is generally not allowable for periods of travel of 10 hours or less in a calendar day has application to employee being reimbursed actual subsistence expenses for travel to a high-rate geographical area. See FTR para. 1–8.1a. B–184489, April 16, 1976, distinguished.

In the matter of Nicholas M. Veneziano — Actual Subsistence Expense Status, September 27, 1979:

Mr. Nicholas M. Veneziano, an employee of the General Services Administration (GSA), has appealed our Claims Division's denial of his claim for actual subsistence expenses incurred incident to duty he performed in Newark, New Jersey, on July 20, 1977.

Mr. Veneziano, whose official duty station is New York, New York, and whose residence is in Brooklyn, New York, was ordered to perform official business in Newark, New Jersey, where he incurred the expense of $2.75 for lunch. Citing decision B–184489, April 16, 1976, and paragraph 1–8.6 of the Federal Travel Regulations (FTR) (FPMR Temporary Regulation A–11, Supp. 4, Attachment A) (1977), Mr. Veneziano claimed reimbursement for lunch. The GSA denied his claim. Our Claims Division also denied Mr. Veneziano's claim on the basis that GSA did not authorize or approve reimbursement on an actual-expense basis. Mr. Veneziano points out in his appeal, however, that a travel voucher which he submitted has been signed by the approving officer.

LAW AND REGULATIONS

Section 5702c of title 5, United States Code (1976), allows for the payment of actual expenses as follows:

Under regulations prescribed under section 5707 of this title, the Administrator of General Services, or his designee, may prescribe conditions under which an employee may be reimbursed for the actual and necessary expenses of official travel when the maximum per diem allowance would be less than these expenses, except that such reimbursement shall not exceed $50 for each day in a travel status within the continental United States when the per diem otherwise allowable is determined to be inadequate (A) due to the unusual circumstances of the travel assignment, or (B) for travel to high rate geographical areas designated as such in regulations prescribed under section 5707 of this title.

Paragraph 1–8.1 of the FTR, FPMR Temporary Regulation A–11, Supp. 4, Attachment A (April 29, 1977), is the basic regulatory authority providing for actual expenses and it states:

1–8.1 *Authorization or approval.*

  a. *General. Authority for reimbursement of actual and necessary subsistence expenses incurred during official travel is normally contingent upon the entitlement to per diem* (see 1–7) and the determination that the authorized maximum per diem allowance would be inadequate to cover the actual and necessary expenses of the traveler. A traveler may be reimbursed for the actual and necessary expenses of the official travel when the actual maximum per diem allowance otherwise allowable is determined to be inadequate due to the unusual circumstances of the travel assignment, or for travel to high rate geographical areas. Heads of those agencies defined in 5 U.S.C. 5701, or their designees (see 1–8.3), shall authorize or approve reimbursement for the actual and necessary subsistence expenses of a traveler incurred during official travel in accordance with the provisions of this part. [Italic of text supplied.]

  b. *Travel to high rate geographical areas.* Actual subsistence expense reimbursement shall normally be authorized or approved whenever temporary duty travel is performed to or in a location designated as a high rate geographical area (see 1–8.6), except when the high rate geographical area is only an enroute or intermediate stopover point at which no official duty is performed.* * *

Paragraph 1–8.6 of the FTR, FPMR Temporary Regulation A–11, Supp. 4, Attachment A (April 29, 1977), upon which Mr. Veneziano relies, provides:

1–8.6. *Designated high rate geographical areas.* Pursuant to the provisions of 1–8.1b and 1–8.2a(1), for temporary duty travel to or within the cities designated as high rate geographical areas below, a traveler automatically shall be placed in an actual subsistence expense status and shall be reimbursed for the actual and necessary subsistence expenses incurred not to exceed the maximum rate prescribed for the particular geographical area involved.

Designated High Rate Geographical Areas	Prescribed Maximum Daily Rates
* * * * * * *	
Newark, N.J. (all locations within the corporate limits thereof)_____	$42

There is also for consideration paragraph 1–7.6d(1) of the FTR which provides that "* * * per diem shall not be allowed when the travel period is 10 hours or less during the same calendar day, except when the travel period is 6 hours or more and begins before 6 a.m. or terminates after 8 p.m. * * *." There is no evidence that Mr. Veneziano's travel took place before 6 a.m. or terminated after 8 p.m.

ISSUE

The voucher submitted shows that Mr. Veneziano's luncheon expense has been approved by signature of the approving officer. The question, therefore, is whether the approving officer had the authority to approve the voucher under the above-cited law and regulations. If he did not have such authority the voucher may not be certified for payment.

Basically, Mr. Veneziano's argument is that since he traveled to a designated high-rate geographical area, Newark, he is automatically entitled to actual subsistence expenses he incurred in Newark. Further, even though his day's assignment and travel to Newark was completed within 10 hours, he cites B–184489, April 16, 1976, as support for the proposition that there is no bar to his receiving actual subsistence expenses under FTR para. 1–8–6.

OPINION

In decision B–184489, April 16, 1976, cited by Mr. Veneziano, we held that since the regulations pertaining to high-rate geographical areas did not contain special provisions for reimbursement of actual subsistence expenses for travel of 24 hours or less when no lodging is involved an agency could not set a per diem rate of $24 or less for such travel to a high-rate geographical area. The regulations have since been amended so that a per diem rate may be set in a high-rate geographical area when circumstances warrant it. See para. 1–8.1b(1) of the FTR. FPMR Temporary Regulation A–11, Supp. 4, Attachment A (April 29, 1977).

We do not think it follows, however, that the absolute prohibition against the payment of per diem for travel of 10 hours or less found in FTR para. 1–7.6d(1) has no application to employees' travel to high-rate geographical areas. The payment of actual expenses in high-rate geographical areas is normally contingent upon the entitlement to per diem. FTR para. 1–8.1a. Since per diem may not be allowed in cases of travel of 10 hours or less, actual expense reimbursement under Part 8 of the FTR is likewise limited. Decision B–184489, April 16, 1976, is distinguishable since in that case we held that the per diem method of reimbursing an employee had no application to an employee's reimbursement when his entitlement was under the distinct actual-expense mode. This was later corrected by an amendment to the regulations. In the case at hand, however, there is an absolute bar on the payment of per diem for travel of 10 hours or less and this bar is applicable to the payment of actual subsistence expenses in like situations.

Even though Mr. Veneziano's voucher was duly approved, the approving official acted beyond his authority because actual subsistence expenses may not be paid for travel of 10 hours or less. Accordingly, the disallowance of the claim by our Claims Division is sustained.

INDEX DIGEST

(OCTOBER 1, 1978–SEPTEMBER 30, 1979)

ADVERTISING—Continued

Advertising *v.* negotiation—Continued

Specifications availability

Page

GAO will not object to contracting officer's determination to negotiate on basis that it is impracticable to secure competition by advertising where, as here, reasonable basis exists. Here, procuring agency has shown that it must evaluate technical acceptability of proposals because, despite detailed request for proposals (RFP) specifications incorporating even more detailed references, all output situations have not, and cannot, be specified and offeror's technical flexibility to satisfy inevitable changes arising during contract must be ascertained_____ 750

Commerce Business Daily

Information

Constructive notice

Date determination

Publication *v.* mail receipt date

Where protester has actual notice of award of contract after timely receipt of Commerce Business Daily in ordinary course of business within a reasonable time after publication and mailing, timeliness of protest may be measured from date publication is received, allowing a few days for mailing and receipt of the CBD. Prior decisions are clarified to allow for reasonable time for protester to receive publication in ordinary course of business. B–182318, Jan. 27, 1975, and other cases following rule established therein, modified_____ 248

Publication requirement

Prior to ordering under basic ordering agreement

Spare parts procurement

Procuring activity is required, absent circumstances not applicable here, to publish spare parts procurement synopses in Commerce Business Daily (CBD) in timeframe prescribed by ASPR 1–1003.2 (1976 ed.); neither fact that items are deemed critical aircraft parts nor that agency now posts CBD synopses letters in bid room relieves agency of obligation to promptly synopsize proposed procurements_____ 149

AGENCY

Promotion procedures. (*See* **REGULATIONS, Promotion procedures**)

AGENCY FOR INTERNATIONAL DEVELOPMENT

Foreign aid programs. (*See* **FOREIGN AID PROGRAMS**)

AGENTS

Government

Authority

Contract matters

Since agency officials had no authority to contract for purchase of suggestion, doctrine of estoppel is not for application_____ 35

Government liability for acts beyond authority

Civilian personnel matters

New appointees cannot be reimbursed travel and relocation expenses from Washington, D.C., to next duty station. Record indicates that agency erroneously indicated Washington as permanent duty station instead of temporary duty station while appointees were trained for 4

AGENTS—Continued
  Government—Continued
    Government liability for acts beyond authority—Continued
      Civilian personnel matters—Continued   Page
months. New appointees must bear expense of reporting to first official
duty station and such duty station must be where major part of employees' duties are performed and where they are expected to spend
greater part of time. Government is not responsible for unauthorized acts
of its agents. Erroneous payments must be collected _____ 744

      Contract execution
Department of Interior questions the legality of appropriated fund
expenditure by Bureau of Mines, a subordinate agency, where EEO
officer, who lacked delegated procurement authority, procured services
of contractors and payment was eventually made for services rendered.
Agreements violated the prohibition against the provision of entertainment from appropriated funds and included payments for premiums
on insurance coverage of art objects exhibited incident to National
Hispanic Heritage Week, contrary to the longstanding policy of Government to assume its own risks of loss and not to purchase commercial insurance. The employee has been advised of the limits of his authority. In
view of the special facts and circumstances involved, we believe no useful purpose will be served by taking exceptions to these payments _____ 202

      Government liability for negligent or erroneous acts
Transferred employee reported to new duty station on May 4, 1976.
He purchased a residence there with settlement on May 5, 1978. He is
not entitled to reimbursement of real estate expenses since applicable
regulations limit maximum time for settlement to within 2 years. Error
of agency in extending initial year to May 5, 1978, provides no authority
to modify statutory regulations _____ 539

      Doctrine of estoppel
Government is not bound by its agents acting beyond their authority
and contrary to law, and the United States is not estopped to deny the
authority of its agents _____ 240

  Of private parties
    Authority
      Contracts
        Evidence to establish
          Administrative determination
Question of signer's authority is essentially factual determination to
be made upon consideration of all relevant evidence _____ 276

        Signatures
          Time for submitting evidence
Where authority of signer of bid is questioned by contracting agency,
burden rests on bidder to submit necessary documentation to demonstrate such authority. Preferably, such evidence would be included on
Standard Form 129 which would be on file prior to bid opening. However, furnishing evidence after bid opening is not legally prohibited. In
absence of timely submission of probative evidence, protester has failed
to satisfy its burden to substantiate authority of signer of bid _____ 276

AGRICULTURE DEPARTMENT
Farmers Home Administration
Energy Impacted Area Development
Assistance Program   Page

Under section 601(a) of the Powerplant and Industrial Fuel Use Act of 1978, a State Governor may designate an impacted area based on his finding that employment in coal or uranium production activities "increased for the most recent calendar year by 8 percent or more from the immediately preceding year." Both the plain meaning of the statute and its legislative history support the view that "the most recent calendar year" is determined with respect to the time of the Governor's finding, and not, with respect to any calendar year since 1975, of 8 percent increased employment. Final regulations of the Farmers Home Administration for the Energy Impacted Area Development Assistance Program should include an amended definition of "base year" consistent with this decision_____   541

ALLOTMENTS
Savings bonds
Conversion to Series EE Bonds

Incident to introduction of Series EE Savings Bonds to replace Series E Bonds being purchased by payroll allotment, Treasury proposes to substitute Series EE Bonds based on a "negative-response" method, whereby the Series EE Bonds will be substituted unless the employee terminates his allotment. Since the Series EE Bonds are a continuation without major substantive change of the Series E Bonds, the negative-response method of conversion is a proper means of continuing the employee's voluntary allotment under the Payroll Savings Plan. The proposal is approved_____   681

ALLOWANCES
Family. (*See* **FAMILY ALLOWANCES**)
Military personnel
Basic allowance for quarters (BAQ). (*See* **QUARTERS ALLOWANCE,**
Basic allowance for quarters (BAQ)))
Leaves of absence
Lump-sum payments

An amendment to 37 U.S.C. 501(b) deleted inclusion of allowances in lump-sum leave payments to military members upon discharge; however, a saving provision retained entitlement to include the allowances for leave accrued prior to the amendment. Although the claimant contends that the services' regulation determining when a member will be charged with use of preamendment leave frustrates congressional intent of the saving provision, in view of the services' authority to prescribe regulations for accrual and use of leave, the language and legislative history of the amendment, the regulation is proper_____   635

Quarters. (*See* **QUARTERS ALLOWANCE**)

ANNUAL LEAVE (*See* **LEAVES OF ABSENCE, Annual**)

APPOINTMENTS
Informal, irregular, etc.
Voidable v. void

Civil Service Commission (CSC) directed cancellation of employee's temporary appointment at GS–6 level because of violation of CSC requirements. Since employee had basic qualification for appointment and appointment was not contrary to law it was voidable only and corrective action as ordered by CSC is prospective only. Employee is entitled to all benefits of position to which appointed until separated or transferred. Modified in part by 58 Comp. Gen. 734_____

APPROPRIATIONS
Agriculture Department
Federal aid, grants, etc.
State matching contributions

Since 1967, Department of Agriculture has interpreted annual appropriation provision requiring "minimum matching by any State of at least 40 per centum" as allowing accumulation of all contributions by a State since 1963 to determine if matching requirement for brucellosis program has been met. For 1979, provision was changed to require matching "by the States" on a 60/40 basis. Agriculture believes this change authorizes aggregation of all State contributions since 1963 rather than on State-by-State basis. Provisions in annual appropriation acts, unless otherwise provided, apply only to that fiscal year and neither language nor legislative history of these provisions support Agriculture's interpretation. However, in view of longstanding practice we will not object to this practice for this year_____

Augmentation
Gifts, etc.

Some members of the United States Metric Board desire to waive their compensation while other members desire to accept it but return it as a gift to the Board. Here the statute authorizes payment of Board members at a rate not to exceed the daily rate currently being paid grade 18 of the General Schedule. Such pay is not considered salary fixed by or pursuant to statute which would preclude waiver. Also, since statute authorizes acceptance of gifts and donations, members may make gifts of their salary to the agency. However, the members would be liable for the income tax on such salary and would be entitled only to the limited deduction for charitable contributions prescribed by the Internal Revenue Service. 57 Comp. Gen. 423 and 54 id. 393, distinguished_____

Availability
Advance payments. (See PAYMENTS, Advance)
Attorney fees

Where an SEC investigation of charges of misconduct against three SEC employees was ultimately resolved in favor of the employees, the employees' legal fees may not be reimbursed. Attorney's fees may be awarded to the prevailing party only when there is express authority for the payment of such fees and there is no specific authority for award of attorney's fees in standards of conduct proceedings in the nature of those conducted by the SEC_____

APPROPRIATIONS—Continued
  Availability—Continued
    Compensation
      Transfer of employee on home leave   Page

Interior employee who satisfactorily completed an overseas tour of duty returned to the United States for home leave. He arranged transfer to AID while on home leave, effective on termination of leave. The salary charge to the Interior appropriation for the period of home leave was proper since the employee earned it as an Interior employee and it agreed to the effective date of the transfer_   633

  Entertainment. (*See* **ENTERTAINMENT**)
  Expenses incident to specific purposes
    Necessary expenses
      Fines

Civil penalties imposed administratively on Federal facilities by State or local agencies for violations of local air pollution regulations must be paid from Federal agency's appropriation if incurred in the course of activities necessary and proper or incidental to fulfilling the purposes for which the appropriation was made. B–191747, June 6, 1978_ _ _ _ _ _ _ _ _ _ _   667

  Insurance. (*See* **INSURANCE**)
  Judgments, decrees, etc. (*See* **COURTS, Judgments, decrees, etc., Payment**)
  Training
    Equal Employment Opportunity programs

In the absence of specific authority in statute or regulations, appropriated funds may not be expended to procure entertainment for Federal employees. Hence agencies without specific authority may not procure entertainment such as live ethnic music and artistic presentations, characterize it as training and present it in connection with EEO programs. We will not question past agency characterizations of EEO program entertainment as training; however, all future entertainment expenses whether or not in connection with EEO programs will not be allowed_   202

  Continuing resolutions
    Availability of funds

Term "current rate for operations" as used in Continuing Resolutions is equivalent to total funds which were available for obligation for program for previous fiscal year. Fiscal year 1979 Continuing Resolution appropriated amount of funds for CETA programs, which, when added to 1978 unobligated balances carried over, equals the total funds that were available for fiscal year 1978, including funds appropriated for fiscal year 1978 by Economic Stimulus Appropriations Act of 1977. B–194063, May 4, 1979, and B–194362, May 1, 1979, distinguished in part_ _ _ _ _ _ _ _ _   530

  Deficiencies
    Anti-Deficiency Act
      Expenditures beyond administrative control

Agency is prohibited by Anti-Deficiency Act from making payments in excess of funding limitations. Fact that limitations must be exceeded to make contract payments because of fluctuation in currency exchange rates, and not through fault of agency, does not justify exceptions to Act. In such situation, agency must ask Congress for deficiency appropriation_   46

APPROPRIATIONS—Continued

Federal aid, grants, etc., to States. (*See* **STATES**, Federal aid, grants, etc.)

Fiscal year
Availability beyond
Contracts
Two fiscal years

Norton Sound Health Corporation annually has entered into contracts with Indian Health Service (IHS), Health, Education and Welfare, to provide health care services during that fiscal year and desires to carry over into the succeeding fiscal year any unexpended funds to provide for medical services it will render in that year. Although provisions of 25 U.S.C. 13a (1976) make the funds available for 2 years, this authority has been overridden annually by provision in appropriation acts restricting use of funds to current fiscal year unless specifically provided for otherwise in the appropriation act involved. Appropriations made to IHS for fiscal year 1978 contain no such specific provision and funds lapse at end of that year. Appropriation act for fiscal year 1979 makes IHS funds appropriated therein available until the end of fiscal year 1980_ _ _ _ _ _ _ _ _ _

Federal aid, grants, etc.

Since 1967, Department of Agriculture has interpreted annual appropriation provision requiring "minimum matching by any State of at least 40 per centum" as allowing accumulation of all contributions by a State since 1963 to determine if matching requirement for brucellosis program has been met. For 1979, provision was changed to require matching "by the States" on a 60/40 basis. Agriculture believes this change authorizes aggregation of all State contributions since 1963 rather than on State-by-State basis. Provisions in annual appropriation acts, unless otherwise provided, apply only to that fiscal year and neither language nor legislative history of these provisions support Agriculture's interpretation. However, in view of longstanding practice we will not object to this practice for this year_ _

Amendment

ACTION's proposed grant modification to expand the area from which enrollees in a demonstration youth employment project are drawn to include an additional county would not enlarge the grant's scope because the statutory authority for the grant (section 348(a) of the Comprehensive Employment and Training Act of 1973, as added by the Youth Employment and Demonstration Project Act of 1977, Pub. L. 95–93, 91 Stat. 645, 29 U.S.C.A. 849g) and the interagency agreement with the Department of Labor delegating this authority to ACTION support the conclusion that the proposed amendment is necessary to carry out the original purpose of the grant. Accordingly, such an amendment would not require the obligation of current fiscal year appropriated funds_ _ _ _

Prior year performance of later ratified contract

Payment may be made to a contractor for repair work to Government equipment even though formal contracting procedures were not followed because Government received the benefit and has specifically ratified the transaction. Appropriation available at time contractor was authorized to and actually performed the repair work should be charged, irrespective of fiscal year in which the transaction was ratified_ _ _ _ _ _ _ _ _ _ _ _ _ _ _ _ _

APPROPRIATIONS—Continued
  Permanent indefinite—Continued
    Judgments—Continued
      Availability for retirement and insurance deductions   Pag

Employee recovered judgment in U.S. District Court providing for backpay and specifically calling for payment of Government's contribution to Civil Service Retirement Fund. Where judgment specifically provides for payment of Government's contribution to Civil Service Retirement Fund or similar funds, that contribution may be paid from Judgment Fund created by 31 U.S.C. 724a_____ 11£

  Typographical errors
    Enrolled act controlling

Public Law 95–480 appropriates $36,606,000 for the Office of Inspector General, Department of Health, Education, and Welfare, despite convincing evidence in legislative history showing that each House of Congress passed bill appropriating $1,000,000 less and that figure in enrolled bill was the result of typographical error. Enrolled act, signed by the Speaker of the House of Representatives and the President of the Senate, and approved by the President of the United States, is conclusive evidence of the contents of a law passed by Congress_____ 35£

ARBITRATION
  Award
    Retroactive promotion with backpay
      Entitlement

Promotion of employee in career-ladder position was delayed because the promotion request was clerically misplaced before it reached the authorized official. Arbitrator's finding of administrative mistake does not itself provide a basis for award of backpay to grievant. In the absence of a nondiscretionary requirement mandating promotion within a particular time frame or in accordance with specified criteria, loss of promotion request prior to approval by authorized official does not constitute such administrative error as will support award of retroactive promotion and backpay_____ 5£

ARMED SERVICES PROCUREMENT REGULATION
  Advertised procurements
    Small business set-asides
      Unreasonable prices
        Reduction by negotiation propriety

Negotiation with sole bidder for reasonable prices after small business restricted advertisement resulted in unreasonable bid is not authorized by law_____ 10£

  Basic ordering agreements
    Limitations on use

Procuring activity's use of basic ordering agreement (BOA) to exclude previously unapproved suppliers that may be capable of furnishing acceptable products and to effect sole-source procurements with BOA contractor contravenes ASPR 3–410.2(c)(1) (1976 ed.) prohibition against using BOA in any manner to restrict competition_____ 14£

BIDDERS—Continued

Qualifications—Continued

Small business concerns

Nonreferral for certification justification

Military procurement   Page

Since Small Business Administration (SBA) has not issued regulations
to resolve discrepancies between 1977 amendments to Small Business
Act, which require referral to SBA before small business may be rejected
as nonresponsible, and Defense Acquisition Regulation (DAR), General
Accounting Office will not consider whether contracting officer properly
relied on DAR exceptions to SBA referral procedure_____   767

Responsibility

Conclusive determination

Vested in SBA

Issuance of Certificate of Competency (COC) by Small Business Administration (SBA) will overcome special experience requirements (definitive responsibility criteria) specified in solicitation as COC is conclusive on contracting officers by law, and where record shows SBA fully
considered definitive responsibility criteria in determining to issue COC,
GAO would not recommend that SBA reconsider decision_____   509

Unsatisfactory on basis of preaward survey

Veterans Administration contracting officer's determination of nonresponsibility, based on preaward survey which concluded that small
business concern, otherwise in line for award, does not have capacity to
perform required work, must be referred to Small Business Administration for consideration under certificate of competency program since
applicable law and regulations no longer allow exception to this requirement based on urgency_____   316

Responsibility *v.* bid responsiveness

"Responsibility" is term of art employed in Federal procurement
and refers to proposed contractor's ability or "capacity" to perform
all contract requirements, while "responsiveness" of a bid concerns
whether bidder has unequivocally offered to provide requested items or
service in total conformance with terms of invitation for bid. Question
of application of regulation requiring bids to materially conform to specifications of invitation for bids is matter of responsiveness_____   509

Site visits

Where bid does not take exception to Government's requirements,
bidder's failure to make mandatory prebid site inspection does not
justify bid rejection as "nonresponsive," since acceptance of bid would
effectively bind bidder to perform at bid price in accordance with advertised terms and specifications. However, such failure may be considered by contracting officer in determining whether bidder is responsible, i.e., whether bidder is able to so perform. Reconsideration of decision
in 58 Comp. Gen. 214_____   516

BIDDERS—Continued
Suspension
Validity
Procedural requirements
Noncompliance   Page

When agency decides to suspend contractor, it must independently follow applicable regulations since ongoing suspension by one agency does not suspend contractor at all other agencies, but only provides basis for other agencies to impose concurrent suspension_____   728

BIDS
Acceptance time limitation
Omitted from invitation

Statement in solicitation that bids would be rejected if they allowed less than number of days specified in "Offer" portion of Standard Form 33 (SF 33) does not establish a minimum bid acceptance period where SF 33 is not altered to establish a minimum period which would eliminate the option provided bidders to offer less than a 60-day acceptance period.   409

Aggregate v. separable items, prices, etc.
Lot bidding v. total job

Bidder which submits a low combination bid for drydock and topside overhaul work may not be rejected solely for failing to bid separately for both drydock and topside work. It is recommended that in future procurements agency revise provision in solicitation requiring bid rejection in such circumstances_____   790

Alternative
Acceptability

Bid accompanied by letter which sets forth unqualified bid price and alternate approach bid price is responsive since Army's acceptance of bid as submitted would have effectively bound bidder to perform in accordance with terms and conditions of the invitation for bids. Alternate approach is merely an offer to be accepted or rejected by Army_____   276

Bidders, generally. (*See* **BIDDERS**)
Buy American Act
Buy American Certificate
Acceptance
Not reviewable by GAO
Exceptions

General Accounting Office (GAO) will review protest challenging successful bidder's intended compliance with representation in its Buy American Certificate that domestic end products will be supplied where basis of protest is that successful bidder's bid samples indicated that it is offering other than domestic end products_____   49

Construction contracts
Statement of foreign materials

General Accounting Office (GAO) decision in 51 Comp. Gen. 814 (1972) is distinguishable. Unlike bids of first and second low bidders, bid in that case did not include information pertaining to portion of nondomestic material to be used. Sufficient information as to nondomestic material offered was submitted here by low bidders_____   493

BIDS—Continued
  Evaluation—Continued
    Options
      Status   Page
      Termination of contract is not justified by improper evaluation of
options under invitation for bids in violation of Defense Acquisition
Regulation 1–1504(c)(ii) where there is no evidence that bidders submitted unbalanced bids or that bidders would have submitted lower
base bids had options not been evaluated, where no bidder was prejudiced
by evaluation, and where awarded contract would result in lowest cost
to Government. However, since it appears option provisions should not
have been included in solicitation, it is recommended that agency not
exercise options in reinstated contract_____ 225

    Testing costs
    Bidder's potential eligibility for waiver of first article testing does not
preclude addition of evaluation factor for such testing, absent determination that waiver will be granted_____ 340

  Invitation for bids
    Cancellation
      After bid opening
        Defective solicitation
        Recommendation is made to cancel invitation for bids (IFB) and
resolicit since record discloses that IFB was materially deficient and
prevented fair and equal treatment of bidders by inclusion of "Reasonable Costs/Minimum Manning" clause which, by calling for bid rejection as unreasonably priced if below minimum manning cost,
improperly converted matter of responsibility into responsiveness.
Regulation cited as authority in clause (DAR 2–402.2(e) (1976 ed.)),
which provides that bid may be rejected if unreasonable as to price,
has been applied to permit rejection as nonresponsive of bid which is
considered unreasonably high rather than low_____ 724

          Current affirmative action provisions omitted
          No award may properly be made under solicitation that does not
contain current affirmative action provisions required in federally
financed contracts or subcontracts since such omission is material, and
readvertisement is required_____ 160

      Not required
        Set-aside erroneous
          Withdrawal by amendment
          While bidders, actual or potential, may have been misled as to com-
petition contemplated by inadvertent set-aside provision in IFB, any
possible adverse impact on competition does not require corrective
action in view of exposure of prices and inadvertent nature of
deficiency_____ 307

  Labor stipulations. (See CONTRACTS, Labor stipulations)
  Late
    Nuclear accident effect
    Where hand-carried bid was received one day after bid opening be-
cause common carrier closed its offices during emergency at nearby
nuclear electric power generating plant, contracting officer properly
rejected bid as late. Although facts of case are unique, they present no
reason to depart from established rule, requiring rejection of late hand-
carried bids, which has been applied where other extraordinary circumstances beyond bidder's control have disrupted delivery services____ 748

BIDS—Continued
  Responsiveness—Continued
    Test to determine
      Unqualified offer to meet all solicitation terms   Page

Where bid does not take exception to Government's requirements, bidder's failure to make mandatory prebid site inspection does not justify bid rejection as "nonresponsive," since acceptance of bid would effectively bind bidder to perform at bid price in accordance with advertised terms and specifications. Purpose of site inspection provision must be viewed as warning bidders that site conditions could affect performance cost and bidders therefore assume risks of increased performance cost caused by observable site conditions, and to protect Government trom necessity of permitting bid withdrawal or claims after contract award__   214

Where bid does not take exception to Government's requirements, bidder's failure to make mandatory prebid site inspection does not justify bid rejection as "nonresponsive," since acceptance of bid would effectively bind bidder to perform at bid price in accordance with advertised terms and specifications. However, such failure may be considered by contracting officer in determining whether bidder is responsible, i.e., whether bidder is able to so perform. Reconsideration of decision in 58 Comp. Gen. 214_____   516

      Unqualified offer to meet all solicitation terms

Contention that low bid is nonresponsive since work called for by solicitation cannot be performed at level of effort reflected by bid price is meritless since test of whether bid is responsive is whether bid constitutes an offer to perform, without exception, the exact thing called for in solicitation and low bid does not take exception to solicitation___   405

  Signatures
    Agents
      Authority. (*See* **AGENTS, Of private parties, Authority, Contracts, Signatures**)

  Site surveys. (*See* **CONTRACTS, Specifications, Site visits**)

  Small business concerns
    Contract awards. (*See* **CONTRACTS, Awards, Small business concerns**)

  Sole-source procurement. (*See* **CONTRACTS, Negotiation**)

  Specifications. (*See* **CONTRACTS, Specifications**)

  Two-step procurement
    First step
      Protest timeliness

While protester might have known prior to opening of step-two bids that competitor's technical proposal was determined acceptable under step one of two-step procurement, protest alleging unacceptability of competitor's technical proposal filed after bid opening is timely since protester did not know specific grounds of protest until after bid opening. Protester is not required to file Freedom of Information Act request to discover grounds for protest before step-two bid opening_____   119

CIVIL RIGHTS ACT
  Application
    Contract awards
      Allocation of 8(a) subcontracts. (*See* **CONTRACTS**, **Awards**, **Small business concerns**, **Procurement under 8(a) program**)

CLAIMS
  Assignments
    Contracts
      Bar against assignment
      Waiver when in interest of Government

Although assignment of Government contract may violate Anti-Assignment Act, Government can recognize assignee as successor in interest if in best interests of United States_____

      Novation agreements

Contract "A" with Federal Aviation Administration (FAA) provided that it would run concurrently with contract "B" (also with FAA), and would expire upon expiration or termination of contract "B." Contract "B" was subsequently novated with FAA's approval. Since general legal effect of contract novation is extinguishment of contract and substitution of new one, resulting in discharge of transferor, FAA view that novation of contract "B" operated to cause expiration of contract "A" under cited provision was not improper_____

      Validity of assignment
        Assignee's right to payment

Government contractor's secured note, assigning accounts receivable to financial institution, which was executed during the period the instant Government contract was being performed, should be recognized under Assignment of Claims Act. Record includes contractor's schedule of accounts receivable which lists the instant contract account. B–120222, Oct. 27, 1955, modified_____

  By Government
    Collection (*See* **DEBT COLLECTIONS**)
    Compromises. (*See* **COMPROMISES**)

  Evidence to support
    Absence of record
      Allowance on basis of other information

Employee may "buy back" sick leave taken in connection with a job-related illness in order to receive disability compensation under Federal Employees' Compensation Act, 5 U.S.C. 8101, *et seq.* Where there are no official records from which to determine amount of leave taken, leave may be credited and bought back on basis of secondary evidence determined to be acceptable by agency. Acceptable forms of secondary evidence include leave requests, Leave and Earnings Statements, Time and Attendance Reports, personal leave records, as well as certificates from supervisors and timekeepers_____

  Judgments, decrees, etc. (*See* **COURTS**, **Judgments**, **decrees**, etc.)
  Set-off. (*See* **SET-OFF**)

CLASSIFICATION
Reclassification
Downgrade
Detailed employees   Page

A Federal employee appointed to a GS–13 position is detailed to perform duties of a GS–14 position and becomes entitled to a temporary promotion and backpay under 55 Comp. Gen. 539 (1975). Where the position is classified downward during the detail, and since an occupant of a position may only receive the salary authorized for that position, if the employee continues on the detail after it is reclassified downward to a GS–13 level, he may not continue to receive the pay at the higher level on and after the reclassification effective date_____   719

COLLECTIONS (*See* DEBT COLLECTIONS)

COMMERCE DEPARTMENT
National Bureau of Standards
Working Capital Fund
Impairment
Definition

National Bureau of Standards finances operations in part by charges to users of its services, paid into Working Capital Fund. Earned net income of the Fund must be paid into Treasury annually, except that it "may be applied first to restore any prior impairment" of the Fund. 15 U.S.C. 278b (1976). Impairments contemplated by this provision are operating losses. Bureau may not retain profits to offset increased costs—caused by inflation—of replacing equipment or facilities, nor can Bureau calculate depreciation of equipment and facilities based on replacement cost_____   9

COMMUNICATION FACILITIES
Lease *v.* purchase
Equipment

Solicitation which does not permit consideration of offers to lease to Government equipment needed for entirely new system is unduly restrictive where based solely on earlier analysis of comparative cost to upgrade existing system, because determination that alternative approach is not competitive as to price can only be made by competitive procurement_____   324

COMPENSATION
Additional
Environmental pay differential
Basis for payment

General Services Administration (GSA) questions legality of Federal Labor Relations Council decision requiring payment of environmental differential for "high work." GSA believes payment is unauthorized because of mistakes of fact concerning height of structure and existence of protective wall. Grievance agreement upheld by Council may be implemented since under Federal Personnel Manual the parties may determine entitlement through collective bargaining process. Furthermore, authorization of environmental differential in the present case does not appear to be contrary to law or regulation or to be arbitrary or capricious_____   331

COMPENSATION—Continued
Night work
Summer aids
Individuals who are hired as summer aids under 5 C.F.R. 213.3102(v), in the excepted service, with their pay set at the FLSA minimum wage, may be paid night differential under 5 U.S.C. 5545(a). Summer aids are not excluded from the definition of employees entitled to receive night differential, and, since there are no conflicting regulatory provisions, they should be paid night differential pay _____   638

Overpayments
Waiver. (*See* DEBT COLLECTIONS, Waiver)

Overtime
Compensatory time
Overtime v. compensatory time
National Security Agency solicited nonexempt employee under FLSA to volunteer to work overtime supervising cleaning crews in restricted area with understanding he would receive compensatory time off in lieu of overtime. No funds were available to pay overtime, and overtime would not have been performed without a volunteer willing to accept compensatory time off. There is no violation of the Fair Labor Standards Act, 29 U.S.C. 201 *et seq.* (Supp. IV, 1974), in giving compensatory time off under such circumstances_____   1

Experts and consultants. (*See* EXPERTS AND CONSULTANTS, Compensation, Overtime)
Fair Labor Standards Act
Compensatory time
Employee of the National Security Agency covered by Fair Labor Standards Act (FLSA) overtime pay requirements pursuant to solicitation by agency volunteered to work overtime. He knew that in lieu of overtime compensation he would receive compensatory time off under 5 U.S.C. 5543. He is not entitled to additional pay under FLSA, since he is also entitled to overtime pay under title 5, U.S. Code, equal to or greater than his FLSA entitlement. In such cases regulations provide that employee may voluntarily accept compensatory time as full remuneration for overtime performed_____   1

Training courses
Outside regular tour of duty
Prohibition
Exceptions
Customs Patrol Officers who attended special training course claim overtime pay under the Fair Labor Standards Act (FLSA) or overtime or night premium pay under title 5, United States Code, for regularly scheduled training sessions conducted after 6 p.m. Where training qualifies under exception to prohibition against payment of premium pay for training in 5 U.S.C. 4109(a), overtime under FLSA or overtime or night premium pay under title 5, United States Code, must be paid. Payment should be made to employees under title 5 or under FLSA, whichever law gives the greater benefit. 38 Comp. Gen. 363 (1958) clarified_____   547

COMPENSATION—Continued
  Overtime—Continued
    Work in excess of daily and/or weekly limitations

Army hospital has two work shifts: 0500–1330 and 1100–1930. Employees on 1100–1930 shift, who periodically work regular shift 1 day and 0500–1330 shift next day, claim overtime compensation for work in excess of 8 hours. Definition of "day" for purposes of overtime compensation is not limited to calendar day but may be any 24-hour period. See 42 Comp. Gen. 195 (1962). Thus, since Army agreed through negotiated agreement to treat workday as 24-hour period from start of shift, employees who work more than 8 hours during 24-hour period but not on same calendar day are entitled to overtime compensation_____

Payments
  Partial and emergency
    Imprest funds

General Accounting Office has no objection to Treasury Department proposal to authorize, in limited circumstances, use of imprest funds for partial salary payments to new employees and for certain emergency salary payments, as long as payments do not represent advance payments, proposal is coordinated with Office of Personnel Management and Office of Management and Budget to assure consistency of regulations, and time and attendance reporting requirements are satisfied_____

Periodic step-increases
  Eligibility

Pursuant to Public Law 94–484, health professionals are appointed in the National Health Service Corps for short-term employment in designated health manpower shortage areas. Such employees are given excepted appointments of not more than 4 years under civil service regulations. They are eligible for within-grade salary increases under 5 U.S.C. 5335 on same basis as term employees. See B–164031(4).50, October 26, 1972_____

Premium pay
  Entitlement determination

Individuals who are hired as summer aids under 5 C.F.R. 213.3102(v), in the excepted service, with their pay set at the FLSA minimum wage, may be paid night differential under 5 U.S.C. 5545(a). Summer aids are not excluded from the definition of employees entitled to receive night differential, and, since there are no conflicting regulatory provisions, they should be paid night differential pay_____

  Night work. (*See* **COMPENSATION, Night work**)
  Sunday work regularly scheduled

Employee's normal 40-hour basic workweek is Monday through Friday, midnight to 8 a.m., in an administrative workweek of Sunday through Saturday. His regularly scheduled administrative workweek includes daily overtime from 11 p.m. to midnight. Working this hour on Sundays does not entitle him to premium pay for the entire shift under 5 U.S.C. 5546(a), since that hour is considered overtime under 5 U.S.C. 5542(a) and 6101 and is thereby excluded. The fact that the employee is entitled to overtime for hours worked over 40 hours under the Fair Labor Standards Act does not operate to change the employee's normal basic workweek as established under 5 U.S.C. 6101 and implementing regulations_____

COMPENSATION—Continued

Prevailing rate employees. (*See* **COMPENSATION, Wage board employees, Prevailing rate employees**)

Promotions

Delayed

"Backpay" claim   Page

Promotion of employee in career-ladder position was delayed because the promotion request was clerically misplaced before it reached the authorized official. Arbitrator's finding of administrative mistake does not itself provide a basis for award of backpay to grievant. In the absence of a nondiscretionary requirement mandating promotion within a particular time frame or in accordance with specified criteria, loss of promotion request prior to approval by authorized official does not constitute such administrative error as will support award of retroactive promotion and backpay_____   59

Retroactive

Administrative error

Lacking

Employee grieved due to delay in processing promotion papers. Grievance Examiner found that although promotion papers reached personnel office and were acted upon by classification officers prior to beginning of new pay period, grievant's papers were not approved by Personnel Officer until after beginning of new pay period. Grievance Examiner concluded that classification officer acted for Personnel Officer and ordered retroactive promotion. Award may not be implemented since agency regulations delegate authority to approve promotions to Personnel Officer and he has not further delegated that authority in writing_____   51

Temporary

Detailed employees

Employee, who was temporarily promoted to higher grade position for 120 days, was returned to former grade but was then immediately detailed to same higher level position for additional 132 days. Under *Turner-Caldwell* decisions employee must be detailed to higher level position without compensation of higher level position for 120 days before entitlement to temporary promotion begins on 121st day. Therefore, the period the employee served on temporary promotion may not be included in computation of detail_____   401

A retired civilian employee of the Air Force claims retroactive temporary promotion and accompanying backpay under *Turner-Caldwell*, 56 Comp. Gen. 427 (1977), incident to details to higher grade military positions. There is no entitlement to backpay as the employee could not have been temporarily promoted into the military position. The *Turner-Caldwell* remedy is only available where the employee was able to satisfy requirements for a retroactive temporary promotion_____   438

Classification downgrade effect

A Federal employee appointed to a GS–13 position is detailed to perform duties of a GS–14 position and becomes entitled to a temporary promotion and backpay under 55 Comp. Gen. 539 (1975). Where the position is classified downward during the detail, and since an occupant of a position may only receive the salary authorized for that position, if the employee continues on the detail after it is reclassified downward to a GS–13 level, he may not continue to receive the pay at the higher level on and after the reclassification effective date_____   719

COMPENSATION—Continued
  Promotions—Continued
    Temporary—Continued
      Detailed employees—Continued
        Retroactive application   Page
        Employee of Federal Aviation Administration alleges he was detailed
to a higher grade position from July 1968 to July 1969. Employee's
claim is barred by the statute of limitation which precludes consideration
of a claim not received in our Office within 6 years after the date first
accrued. Claim accrues on the date services in question were performed,
not on the date that *Turner-Caldwell* was decided. 50 Comp. Gen. 607
and 34 Comp. Gen. 605, distinguished_____   3
  Quality increases. (*See* COMPENSATION, Increases, Quality increases)
  Rates
    Establishment
      Federal dependents' schools employees
      Section IV, Army Procurement Procedure, directed that a clause be
included in dependents' school personal service employment contracts
reserving to school officials the right to amend the rate of pay in conformity with the pay schedules of Department of the Army civilian
employees performing similar duties; hence, the Fort Rucker Elementary
School Board had the right to adopt a policy of having all clerical,
janitorial, and other non-teaching positions at the school classified and
equated to comparable civil service positions for pay purposes_____   430
    Limitations
      Imposed by statute
      Pay adjustment limitation of section 614(a) of Public Law 95-429
applies only to those employees whose pay is adjusted by one of methods
listed in that section. Since the pay of employees who negotiated their
wages under section 9(b) of Public Law 92-392 is not adjusted pursuant
to any of the methods listed, the section 614(a) limitation does not
apply to them_____   251
  Reassignments
    Two step-increases
      Entitlement
      Three employees were reassigned under competitive procedures to a
position at the same GS grade having greater promotion potential. Reassignment to a position at the same GS grade where a promotion is
only potential or expected some time after reassignment falls short of
an actual promotion or transfer to a "higher General Schedule position"
under 5 C.F.R. 531.204(a). Consequently, the reassignment did not entitle the three employees to a two-step increase under 5 U.S.C. 5334(b)__ 181
  Removals, suspensions, etc.
    Backpay
      Entitlement
        Unjustified or unwarranted personnel action
        The Fort Rucker Elementary School Board adopted a policy in 1969
of paying school support personnel on an equivalent basis with Federal
General Schedule (GS) and wage board (WG) employees, but support
personnel pay was "frozen" between April 1974 and March 1977 as the
result of an erroneous opinion by Army procurement officials that there
could be "no such thing as a GS/WG equated contract employee."
The support personnel therefore suffered an unjustified or unwarranted
personnel action within the terms of the Back Pay Act, 5 U.S.C. 5596,
and are entitled to backpay for cost-of-living and step increases withheld
from them_____   430

COMPENSATION—Continued
Step-increases. (*See* **COMPENSATION**, Periodic step-increases)
Training

Overtime compensation

Customs Patrol Officers who attended special training course claim overtime pay under the Fair Labor Standards Act (FLSA) or overtime or night premium pay under title 5, United States Code, for regularly scheduled training sessions conducted after 6 p.m. Where training qualifies under exception to prohibition against payment of premium pay for training in 5 U.S.C. 4109(a), overtime under FLSA or overtime or night premium pay under title 5, United States Code, must be paid. Payment should be made to employees under title 5 or under FLSA, whichever law gives the greater benefit. 38 Comp. Gen. 363 (1958) clarified_____ 547

Wage board employees
Prevailing rate employees
Entitlement to negotiate wages

Section 704(b)(B) of Pub. L. No. 95–454, Civil Service Reform Act of 1978, allows prevailing rate employees whose labor-management contract provisions are covered by section 9(b) of Pub. L. No. 92–392 to negotiate these contract provisions without regard to the restrictions in 5 U.S.C. 5544. Accordingly, decisions 57 Comp. Gen. 259 (1978) and 57 *id.* 575 are overruled insofar as they invalidated certain contract provisions concerning overtime for section 9(b) employees. Likewise, B–191520, June 6, 1978, and 56 Comp. Gen. 360 (1977) are overruled to the same extent_____ 198

Waivers
Prohibition

Some members of the United States Metric Board desire to waive their compensation while other members desire to accept it but return it as a gift to the Board. Here the statute authorizes payment of Board members at a rate not to exceed the daily rate currently being paid grade 18 of the General Schedule. Such pay is not considered salary fixed by or pursuant to statute which would preclude waiver. Also, since statute authorizes acceptance of gifts and donations, members may make gifts of their salary to the agency. However, the members would be liable for the income tax on such salary and would be entitled only to the limited deduction for charitable contributions prescribed by the Internal Revenue Service. 57 Comp. Gen. 423 and 54 *id.* 393, distinguished_____ 383

Withholding
Debt liquidation
Withholding prohibited

Government may not withhold current salary to satisfy general debts owed by employee and may not setoff against employee's retirement account until employee withdraws contribution or claims annuity. Government has right to setoff indebtedness administratively against annuity payments or refund of retirement contribution based upon common-law right long recognized by our Office and the Courts_____ 501

COMPENSATION—Continued
Withholding—Continued
Savings bonds
Conversion to Series EE Bonds

Incident to introduction of Series EE Savings Bonds to replace Series E Bonds being purchased by payroll allotment, Treasury proposes to substitute Series EE Bonds based on a "negative-response" method, whereby the Series EE Bonds will be substituted unless the employee terminates his allotment. Since the Series EE Bonds are a continuation without major substantive change of the Series E Bonds, the negative-response method of conversion is a proper means of continuing the employee's voluntary allotment under the Payroll Savings Plan. The proposal is approved_____ 681

Within-grade increases. (*See* COMPENSATION, Periodic step-increases)

COMPROMISES
Jurisdiction
Justice Department

Fine or penalty assessed administratively by State or local authority against Federal agency for violation of local air pollution law, although it is claim against United States which local authority could sue to enforce, may not be referred to Attorney General for defense of imminent litigation if agency does not dispute basis for or amount of fine. Funds appropriated by 31 U.S.C. 724a for payment of compromise settlements, negotiated by Attorney General in connection with imminent litigation (28 U.S.C. 2414), are therefore not available to pay fine_ 667

CONCESSIONS
Contracts
Modification
Consideration

Secretary of Interior has determined, and General Accounting Office (GAO) concurs, that provision in standard National Park Service concession contract requiring concessioner to furnish accommodations at reduced rates to Federal employees in parks on official business is not in best interest of Government, despite reduced cost, because of risk and appearance of improper conflict of interest. Although generally vested contract rights may not be waived without consideration, GAO will not object to elimination of clause in question where cost saving is determined to be outweighed by adverse effect on Government of clause. 40 Comp. Gen. 234, distinguished_____ 7

CONFLICT OF INTEREST STATUTES
Officers and employees. (*See* OFFICERS AND EMPLOYEES, Conflict of interest statutes)

CONGRESS
Resolutions
Continuing
Funding level

Term "current rate for operations" as used in Continuing Resolutions is equivalent to total funds which were available for obligation for program for previous fiscal year. Fiscal year 1979 Continuing Resolution appropriated amount of funds for CETA programs, which, when added to 1978 unobligated balances carried over, equals the total funds that were available for fiscal year 1978, including funds appropriated for fiscal year 1978 by Economic Stimulus Appropriations Act of 1977. B-194063, May 4, 1979, and B-194362, May 1, 1979, distinguished in part_____ 530

CONSTITUTIONALITY OF ACTS
Acceptance by GAO

CONTRACT DISPUTES OF 1978
Breach of contract
Damages, (*See* CONTRACTS, Damages, "Breach", Determination, Contract Disputes Act of 1978)

CONTRACTING OFFICERS
Determinations
Erroneous
Estoppel

Nonresponsibility
Small business concerns
Reasonableness of determination

CONTRACTORS
Conflicts of interest
Avoidance

Potential or theoretical

CONTRACTORS—Continued
Successors—Continued
Wages
Reduction
Job reclassification
Retained employees
Successful offeror is not guilty of "wage busting" (practice of lowering employee wages and fringe benefits by successor contractor to become low offeror when incumbent contractor's employees are retained to perform same jobs on successor contracts) if incumbent's retained employees are reclassified to lower paying jobs with different duties and responsibilities. However, where no statute, regulation or statement of policy in existence at time solicitation issued precludes "wage busting," no legal impediment exists to prevent lowering of wages for incumbent employees even if reduction can be categorized as "wage busting"_____

CONTRACTS
Advertising v. negotiation. (See ADVERTISING, Advertising v. negotiation)

Allegations
Burden of proof
On protester
Protester failed to meet its burden of proof on its allegations about its ability to supply urgently needed items in less time than offerors Army had solicited since only evidence on matter consisted of conflicting statements between Army and protester_____

Assignments. (See CLAIMS, Assignments, Contracts)

Automatic Data Processing Systems. (See EQUIPMENT, Automatic Data Processing Systems)

Awards
Advantage to Government
Requirement
Termination of contract is not justified by improper evaluation of options under invitation for bids in violation of Defense Acquisition Regulation 1-1504(c)(ii) where there is no evidence that bidders submitted unbalanced bids or that bidders would have submitted lower base bids had options not been evaluated, where no bidder was prejudiced by evaluation, and where awarded contract would result in lowest cost to Government. However, since it appears option provisions should not have been included in solicitation, it is recommended that agency not exercise options in reinstated contract_____

Equal or tie bids/offers
Evaluation
Additional criteria for consideration
Change of contractor impact
Source selection official's consideration of incumbency status of one offeror and of disruptive effect of changing contractors is reasonable under circumstances where proposals are viewed as "tied" and official seeks appropriate discriminators on which to base award selection_____

CONTRACTS—Continued
  Awards—Continued
    Equal or tie bids/offers—Continued
      Evaluation—Continued
        Additional criteria for consideration—Continued
          Labor surplus area concern status   Page

Solicitation provision permitting firm's status as labor surplus area concern to be considered in case of tie bids is intended for use primarily in formal advertising and in negotiated procurements where award is to be made on basis of price. Where, however, proposals are "tied" based on evaluation of both technical and price factors, consideration of labor surplus area concern status would not be improper and would not involve violation of Maybank Amendment_____ 263

      Erroneous
        Performance
          Payment basis

Even though costs incurred under contracts awarded pursuant to grant projects were based on cost-plus-percentage-of-cost contracting, contractor can be paid on *quantum meruit/quantum valebat* basis as agency has determined costs to be reasonable and Government received benefit of services_____ 654

          Termination of contract

Agency's failure to follow ASPR/DAR 1–502(b)(v) raises doubt as to whether Government is receiving items at lowest possible cost and whether integrity of competitive bidding system is being maintained. These considerations form basis for recommendation that contract be terminated for convenience of Government and requirement be resolicited_____ 586

    Labor surplus areas
      Performance
        Buy American Act application
          Federal Supply Schedule purchases

Federal Procurement Regulations provide that Buy American Act differential of 12 percent be applied to price of foreign-origin products where concern submitting low domestic bid or offer will substantially perform contract in labor surplus area. A 12-percent Buy American Act differential should not be applied where vendor under FSS contract produced equipment in labor surplus area facility but facility was closed before purchase order was issued for equipment because regulations contemplate contract performance in labor surplus area after issuance of purchase orders so as to help achieve regulatory objective of fostering employment in such area_____ 234

      Qualification of bidder/offeror
        Administrative determination
          Improper

Agency's reliance on offeror's claim to be labor surplus area concern by virtue of performing contract to be awarded in area of substantial unemployment was improper where Department of Labor (DOL) had removed designated area from list of such areas several months prior to evaluation and award and so informed Federal agencies. Fact that agencies were notified through monthly notices instead of revision to DOL's formal publication referenced by applicable agency regulation does not change fact that agency had duty to verify offeror's claim and in so doing to seek out latest available information. 45 Comp Gen. 471, distinguished_____ 263

CONTRACTS—Continued
  Awards—Continued
    Labor surplus areas—Continued
      Set-asides
        Withdrawal
          Protest timeliness

Procuring agency's consideration on the merits of protest not filed within the time limits established by General Accounting Office's (GAO) Bid Protest Procedures does not preclude GAO from dismissing protest when subsequently filed with it. Protest of cancellation of IFB initially filed with procuring agency more than 10 working days after protester knew the basis therefor, but filed with GAO 4 days after agency's denial of protest, is dismissed. _____

    Legality
      Award not plainly or palpably illegal
        Procurement *v.* sales contracts

Where Government administrative error in sale of surplus property results in notice of award to second highest bidder, award is unauthorized _____

    Negotiated contracts. (*See* CONTRACTS, Negotiation, Awards)
    Notice
      Advance of award

Where protester has actual notice of award of contract after timely receipt of Commerce Business Daily in ordinary course of business within a reasonable time after publication and mailing, timeliness of protest may be measured from date publication is received, allowing a few days for mailing and receipt of the CBD. Prior decisions are clarified to allow for reasonable time for protester to receive publication in ordinary course of business. B-182318, Jan. 27, 1975, and other cases following rule established therein, modified _____

      Form of notice
        Commerce Business Daily
          Sole-source procurements

Protest concerning sole source nature of a procurement filed more than 2 months after notice of intent to make contract award was published in the Commerce Business Daily is untimely under GAO Bid Protest Procedures, 4 C.F.R. 20.2(b)(2) (1978). Even if initial protest had been filed with procuring agency, protester delayed too long in pursuing matter with General Accounting Office—more than 2 months after publication _____

    Propriety
      Licensing-type requirements
        General *v.* specific solicitation requirement

Prior decision under same solicitation held that, since solicitation contained only general statements requiring contractor to obtain all necessary licenses and permits, failure of proposed awardee (protester in present decision) to obtain State license did not require contracting officer to find proposed awardee nonresponsible and would not affect validity of award if made. However, prior decision did not hold that State license statute and threatened enforcement thereof were irrelevant, nor that contracting officer was required to find proposed awardee responsible as protester alleges. Decision in *Inter-Con Security Systems, Inc.; Washington Patrol Service, Inc.*, B-192188, February 9, 1979, 79-1 CPD 86, clarified _____

CONTRACTS—Continued
  Awards—Continued
    Propriety—Continued
      Premature bid opening   Page

Termination of contract is not justified where purchasing agent prematurely opened all bids in private to ascertain if bids contained necessary papers, low bid was first received and opened, and all bids were kept in purchasing agent's exclusive possession until formal bid "opening," since evidence clearly indicates that no bidder was prejudiced by premature opening_____   225

    Small business concerns
      Acceptability of large business on basis of lower price
        Partial set-aside dissolved

Small business concern's unwillingness to accept set-aside quantity at substantially lower, allegedly below cost, bid of 'arge business upon which non-set-aside quantity was awarded properly resulted in dissolution of set-aside. Even if it were proven that large business bid below cost, that in itself would not bar award to that firm, and under partial set-aside procedure Government's obligation is simply to reserve a portion of its needs for award to small business firms at the same price obtained for the unrestricted portion_____   405

      Administrative determination
        Reasonable expectation of competition

Protest against solicitation restricting procurement as total small business set-aside is denied where record discloses that reasonable expectation of adequate competition existed and bid price was reasonable, notwithstanding that only one bid was received from small business concern_____   713

    Certifications
      Competency
        Urgency exception eliminated

Veterans Administration contracting officer's determination of non-responsibility, based on preaward survey which concluded that small business concern, otherwise in line for award, does not have capacity to perform required work, must be referred to Small Business Administration for consideration under certificate of competency program since applicable law and regulations no longer allow exception to this requirement based on urgency_____   316

      Failure to request

Since Small Business Administration (SBA) has not issued regulations to resolve discrepancies between 1977 amendments to Small Business Act, which require referral to SBA before small business may be rejected as nonresponsible, and Defense Acquisition Regulation (DAR), General Accounting Office will not consider whether contracting officer properly relied on DAR exceptions to SBA referral procedure_____   767

CONTRACTS—Continued
  Awards—Continued
    Small business concerns—Continued
      Certifications—Continued
        Mandatory referral to SBA
          Exceptions under DAR

Contracting officer did not refer nonresponsibility determination of small business to SBA as required under Small Business Act Amendments of 1977 because contracting officer interpreted DAR 1-903.1(v) and DAR 1-705.4(c)(v) as creating exception to SBA referral procedure where small business concern was determined nonresponsible because it was not otherwise qualified and eligible under applicable State law. While we cannot find contracting officer's interpretation and failure to refer matter to SBA to be unreasonable in present case, it is our opinion that these DAR provisions create exception to SBA referral only where bidder is not otherwise qualified and eligible under Federal laws/regulations. Accordingly, in future decisions we will strictly limit use of DAR 1-903.1(v) to situations involving Federal laws/regulations in absence of clarifying regulations issued by SBA_____ 767

        Referral necessity
          Responsibility-related criteria
Agencies are not prohibited from making relative assessments of responsibility-related factors in determining competitive range without regard to certificate of competency procedure. Rejection of protester's proposal from competitive range cannot be regarded as tantamount to nonresponsibility finding as found by GAO in 52 Comp. Gen. 47 (1972)_ 415

      Erroneous award
        Contractor suspension
          Validity
When agency decides to suspend contractor, it must independently follow applicable regulations since ongoing suspension by one agency does not suspend contractor at all other agencies, but only provides basis for other agencies to impose concurrent suspension_____ 728

        Price reasonableness
          Reduction of price propriety
Negotiation with sole bidder for reasonable prices after small business restricted advertisement resulted in unreasonable bid is not authorized by law_____ 103

        Procurement under 8(a) program
Determination to set aside procurement under section 8(a) of Small Business Act is matter for contracting agency and Small Business Administration, not GAO_____ 108

        Civil Rights Act
          Compliance
Although protester asserts that SBA 8(a) program violates Civil Rights Act of 1964 because of racial discrimination, courts have held that there is no merit to such assertion since eligibility standard of program is not defined racially but by social or economic disadvantage_____ 671

CONTRACTS—Continued
  Awards—Continued
    Small business concerns—Continued
      Procurement under 8(a) program—Continued
        Subcontractor eligibility standards
          Statutory changes   Page
General Accounting Office review of Small Business Administration
(SBA) action under 8(a) program is limited to determining whether
SBA has followed its regulations. Where firm was determined eligible
and accepted into 8(a) program based on social disadvantage alone and
law and regulations were subsequently changed to require both social
and economic disadvantage, recommendation is made to SBA to review
firm's eligibility to determine if it should be allowed to continue to
participate in 8(a) program or if participation should be terminated in
accordance with present law and regulations_____   665

        Qualifications. (See BIDDERS, Qualifications, Small business con-
          cerns)
        Responsibility to perform contract
          Conclusive determination vested in SBA
Issuance of Certificate of Competency (COC) by Small Business
Administration (SBA) will overcome special experience requirements
(definitive responsibility criteria) specified in solicitation as COC is
conclusive on contracting officers by law, and where record shows SBA
fully considered definitive responsibility criteria in determining to issue
COC, GAO would not recommend that SBA reconsider decision_____   509

        Self-certification
        Status protests
Where bidder on procurement totally set aside for small business fails
to check box on reverse side of Standard Form 33 to indicate whether
or not it is certifying itself as small business concern, the procedures
in 13 C.F.R. 131.3–5 and 121.3–8 do not apply; therefore, contracting
officer acted reasonably and properly by telephoning bidder to give it an
opportunity to cure deficiency which is considered a minor informality
or irregularity in bid_____   713

        Set-asides
        Administrative determination
Decision as to whether particular procurement should be set aside for
small business is within discretion of contracting agency_____   119

        Competition sufficiency
Protest against solicitation restricting procurement as total small business set-aside is denied where record discloses that reasonable expectation
of adequate competition existed and bid price was reasonable, notwithstanding that only one bid was received from small business concern____   713

        Eligibility
        Unacceptable
Bidder on total small business set-aside which certifies it is small and
that large business concern will manufacture, inspect, package, and ship
supplies indicates that it intends to furnish supplies manufactured or produced by large business without small business making significant contribution to manufacture or production of contract end item. Therefore,
bid would be nonresponsive under small business set-aside and bidder is
not prejudiced by withdrawal of set-aside by amendment allegedly issued
too close to time set for bid opening_____   307

CONTRACTS—Continued
  Awards—Continued
    Small business concerns—Continued
      Set-asides—Continued
        Withdrawal
          Erroneous set-aside   Page
          While bidders, actual or potential, may have been misled as to competi-
          tion contemplated by inadvertent set-aside provision in IFB, any possible
          adverse impact on competition does not require corrective action in view
          of exposure of prices and inadvertent nature of deficiency_____   307

          Partial set-asides
          Small business concern's unwillingness to accept set-aside quantity at
          substantially lower, allegedly below cost, bid of large business upon
          which non-set-aside quantity was awarded properly resulted in dissolu-
          tion of set-aside. Even if it were proven that large business bid below
          cost, that in itself would not bar award to that firm, and under partial set-
          aside procedure Government's obligation is simply to reserve a portion
          of its needs for award to small business firms at the same price obtained
          for the unrestricted portion_____   405

          Procedural compliance
          Where contracting officer erroneously and inadvertently fills out small
          business set-aside determination, small business set-aside withdrawal
          procedures are not for application. In any event, pre-bid-opening with-
          drawal of small business set-aside by contracting officer was subsequently
          approved by small business specialist_____   307
          Contracting officer's withdrawal of small business set-aside without
          notifying Small Business Administration (SBA) liaison representative,
          thereby denying SBA its right to appeal withdrawal to head of procuring
          agency, was contrary to regulation and to purpose and intent of Smal
          Business Act. GAO recommends post-award referral of set-aside with-
          drawal to SBA with view toward possible termination of contract for
          convenience of the Government and resolicitation_____   658
        Size
          Status determination
            Small Business Administration
            Protest concerning small business size status is not for consideration
            by General Accounting Office since by law it is matter for decision by
            the Small Business Administration_____   713
  Basic ordering agreements
    Military procurements. (See ARMED SERVICES PROCUREMENT REG-
      ULATION, Basic ordering agreements)
    Propriety. (See CONTRACTS, Specifications, Basic ordering agree-
      ments, Propriety)
  Bids, generally. (See BIDS)
  Breach of contract
    Damages. (See CONTRACTS, Damages)

CONTRACTS—Continued
Buy American Act
Foreign products
End product v. components

Competitive system
Price competitiveness
Determination basis

Lease v. purchase

Restrictions on competition
Automatic Data Processing, etc. acquisition
Demonstration tests

Prequalification of bidders
Relative v. adequate basis of qualification
####### Spare parts procurement

Spare parts military procurement

Concessions. (See CONCESSIONS)
Conflicts of interest prohibitions
Avoidance. (See CONTRACTORS, Conflicts of interest, Avoidance)
Negotiated contracts. (See CONTRACTS, Negotiation, Conflict of interest prohibitions)

CONTRACTS—Continued
  Default—Continued
    Reprocurement—Continued
      Government procurement statutes
        Applicability

Prior General Accounting Office (GAO) decision held that once contracting officer decides to conduct new competition for reprocurement he may not automatically exclude defaulted contractor from that competition. Prior GAO decision did not hold that defaulted contractor has automatic right to resolicitation. 56 Comp. Gen. 976 clarified_____

      Restrictive specifications
        Justification

Because of relatively short period of time in which reprocurement contract for critically needed item had to be consummated and because offerors solicited were familiar with contractual requirements, GAO finds no abuse of discretion by contracting officer in limiting reprocurement competition to prior producers_____

  Disputes
    Finality of administrative findings
      Review by the General Accounting Office

Protest against termination of contract is appropriate for review by General Accounting Office (GAO) where there are no material facts in dispute and only question concerning propriety of termination is one of law_____

  Federal-State contracts
    Commercial services
      Advance payments
        Prohibition
          Applicability

Payments to State under Federal contract for telephone services, executed by contracting officer of the United States and obligating annual appropriations of National Guard, are subject to statutory prohibition against advance payments contained in 31 U.S.C. 529_____

  Federal Supply Schedule
    Awards
      Propriety

Where vendor under Federal Supply Schedule (FSS) contract apprises procuring activity shortly before award that it offers "middle of the line" equipment and procuring activity only has specifications for vendor's "top of the line" equipment, procuring activity, in attempt to reduce procurement costs, should have attempted to obtain specifications from vendor or General Services Administration and determine if "middle of the line" equipment would satisfy Government's legitimate needs. However, since vendor should have advised agency of middle of line equipment earlier in procurement process and offered equipment met agency's minimum needs and has been delivered and installed, award will not be disturbed_____

CONTRACTS—Continued
  Legality
    Sales contracts. (See SALES, Legality)

  Minority subcontracting. (See CONTRACTS, Subcontracts, Minority sub-
    contracting)

  Mistakes
    Acceptance of contract under protest   Page
    Authority under Federal Procurement Regulations 1–2.406–3 in ex-
  ecutive agencies to determine whether a mistake in bid case is doubtful
  and therefore should be referred to General Accounting Office (GAO)
  does not foreclose GAO from reviewing that determination as well as
  agency determination regarding sufficiency of bidder's evidence_____   583

    Allegation before award. (See BIDS, Mistakes)
    Purchase orders
      Erroneous quotation
    Contracting officer's error detection and verification obligation with
  regard to mistake in quotation alleged after performance is measured by
  standards applicable to mistake in oral bid alleged after award. Advice by
  contracting officer that supplier's oral quotation appeared low in conjunction with request for verification was sufficient to communicate
  both existence and nature, to extent known, of suspected mistake. Post-
  verification performance in accordance with purchase order creates binding contract and no price adjustment may be authorized on basis of error.
  Price disparity of about 35 percent does not reflect unconscionable
  bargain_____   293

      Reservation of right for price, etc. revision
    Where bidder requests permission only to correct bid price, bidder may
  alternatively be allowed to withdraw its bid if evidence is clear and convincing only as to the mistake, but not as to the intended bid_____   583

  Modification
    Consideration
      Best interest of Government
    Secretary of Interior had determined, and General Accounting Office
  (GAO) concurs, that provision in standard National Park Service concession contract requiring concessioner to furnish accommodations at
  reduced rates to Federal employees in parks on official business is not in
  best interest of Government, despite reduced cost, because of risk and
  appearance of improper conflict of interest. Although generally vested
  contract rights may not be waived without consideration, GAO will not
  object to elimination of clause in question where cost saving is determined to be outweighed by adverse effect on Government of clause.
  40 Comp. Gen. 234, distinguished_____   7

  Negotiation
    Administrative determination
      Advertising v. negotiation
    GAO will not object to contracting officer's determination to negotiate
  on basis that it is impracticable to secure competition by advertising
  where, as here, reasonable basis exists. Here, procuring agency has shown
  that it must evaluate technical acceptability of proposals because, despite detailed request for proposals (RFP) specifications incorporating
  even more detailed references, all output situations have not, and cannot, be specified and offeror's technical flexibility to satisfy inevitable
  changes arising during contract must be ascertained_____   750

CONTRACTS—Continued
Negotiation—Continued
Changes, etc.
Cancellation and resolicitation not required

RFP for design and manufacture of electronic air navigation equipment comtemplated that offerors propose individual technical approaches to meeting agency's needs. After negotiations with sole offeror, RFP amendment made changes in equipment configuration, delivery schedule and various technical specifications. Agency position that changes in requirements are not so substantial as to warrant complete revision of RFP (i.e., cancellation and resolicitation) is not clearly shown to have no reasonable basis_ _

Reopening negotiations
Failure to reopen
Not materially prejudicial

Agency's actions allowing one offeror, during so-called "pre-award survey," to make its proposal more favorable by offering earlier starting date constituted discussions and should have resulted in new request for best and final offers from other offeror in competitive range. However, agency's actions, while procedurally deficient, appear not to have been materially prejudicial since record suggests that earlier starting date was not significant factor in selection decision_ _

Scope of permissible changes
Solicitation *v.* existing contract

Protester, seeking cancellation of RFP, relies on General Accounting Office decisions which found that modifications to contracts were so substantial that work covered by modifications should have been subject of new procurement. Argument is not persuasive, as scope of changes which may permissibly be made to RFP without requiring cancellation and initiation of new procurement is greater than scope of changes permitted to existing contract_ _

Specifications
Competition on changes
Test requirements

Assertion that protester was not prejudiced because it would have been unable to be price competitive had it known that procuring activity would relax requirements is rejected. Pricing may only be determined through competition_ _

Written amendment requirement
Noncompliance

Request for proposals (RFP) required Tempest certified equipment. After receipt of best and final offers, agency determined that no offeror proposed technically acceptable system that could meet Tempest certification requirement. Agency then deleted requirement but did not notify competitors and other qualified offerors. General Accounting Office (GAO) views relaxation of requirement as substantial change in agency's needs and agency's failure to amend RFP violated applicable procurement regulations and sound procurement policy_ _ _ _ _ _ _ _ _ _ _ _ _ _ _ _ _ _ _

CONTRACTS—Continued
  Negotiation—Continued
    Competition—Continued
      Equality of competition
        Incumbent contractor's advantage

Two-month phase-in period is appropriate limitation where it appears that phase-in period will cost less than longer phase-in and it is speculative that higher performance cost will necessarily follow 2-month phase-in when nothing in record of experience supports that view_____ 395

        Lacking

Where snowstorm closed agency on original closing date and agency extended closing date for only 24 hours, even though debilitating conditions continued beyond that time, agency should not reject proposal as late because there was no urgency to justify the informal rescheduling of the closing date and interested parties have not alleged or shown premature disclosure of other proposals. In the absence of any urgency, agency abused its discretion in extending closing date without informing prospective offerors of that fact_____ 573

        Maximum possible extent

Although Federal Judicial Center (FJC) is exempt from 41 U.S.C. 5 (1976) and civilian agency procurement statutues do not apply to FJC, examination of FJC's enabling legislation shows Congress' intent that FJC enter into contracts by "negotiation." Further, maximum practicable competition should be obtained as matter of sound Federal procurement whenever contracts utilizing appropriated funds are to be awarded. Therefore, FJC should award contracts by using competitive negotiation where practicable_____ 350

      Restrictions
        Lease alternative precluded

Solicitation which does not permit consideration of offers to lease to Government equipment needed for entirely new system is unduly restrictive where based solely on earlier analysis of comparative cost to upgrade existing system, because determination that alternative approach is not competitive as to price can only be made by competitive procurement_____ 324

      Prequalification of offerors
        Prior producer requirement

Because of relatively short period of time in which reprocurement contract for critically needed item had to be consummated and because offerors solicited were familiar with contractual requirements, GAO finds no abuse of discretion by contracting officer in limiting reprocurement competition to prior producers_____ 54

     Conflict of interest prohibitions
      Applicability
        Non-profit organizations

Where offeror has individual and corporate ties with gas and oil industry, agency rejection of proposal for services to assist agency review of gas curtailment because of organizational conflict of interest is sustained. Offeror's status as not-for-profit, tax-exempt organization does not preclude agency determination that conflict of interest does or might exist_____ 520

CONTRACTS—Continued
  Negotiation—Continued
    Evaluation factors—Continued
      Evaluators
        Improper influence, bias, etc.
          Not established

Suggestion that there may have been impropriety in evaluation of proposals because one member of evaluation team was hired by successful offeror shortly after contract award is not substantiated by record, which indicates only that awardee learned of member's retirement plans and made employment offer only after contract award_____ 550

      Technical competence
        Standard of GAO review

Protester, after reviewing qualifications of agency's sole technical evaluator, challenges his technical competency. Where protester essentially contends that an evaluator is appointed in bad faith, prior decisions indicated that GAO will make subjective judgment on evaluator's qualifications. Absent such allegation, GAO's standard of review is whether technical evaluation is rationally based. Here, after considering merits of protester's contentions, GAO has no basis to conclude that technical evaluation was not reasonably based_____ 440

      Factors other than price
        Experience

Based on review of record, GAO cannot take exception to Army's technical evaluation of protester's proposal—especially given complexity of procurement—or specific judgment that protester's proposal did not demonstrate understanding of requirements. Consequently, exclusion of protester's higher priced proposal (compared to initial and final prices proposed by awardee) from competitive range is not questioned. Furthermore, GAO finds that request for proposals did call for experience information found lacking in protester's proposal_____ 415

      Technical acceptability
        Performance requirements

Manufacturer does not submit technically acceptable proposal merely by offering to supply parts previously provided in prior solicitations. Parts must not only meet technical specifications but must also have performed in technically acceptable manner_____ 765

      Labor costs

While offeror is not legally obligated to pay wages paid by incumbent, where such offeror's proposal expressly states labor rates proposed are based on current wage rates for incumbent personnel, contracting officer should take such statement into account in consideration of proposed costs_____ 550

      Point rating
        Differences significance

Where solicitation does not require award to be made in accordance with results of numerical point scoring of proposals, agency is not required to award contract to offeror whose overall proposal is rated two points higher than competing proposal_____ 263

CONTRACTS—Continued
  Negotiation—Continued
    Requests for proposals—Continued
      Unsolicited proposals, etc.
        Propriety of consideration
          Assessment, etc. of procurement needs   Page
  Whether proposal based on licensing arrangement, submitted after
date for receipt of initial proposals under ongoing RFP, was solicited or
unsolicited is immaterial, because procurement activity is entitled to
receive information concerning procurement at any time and utilize
that information to assess or reassess its procurement needs_____   575

      Sole-source basis
      Justification
      Delay and technical risk factors
  While protester argues that it was not permitted to compete on equal
basis with sole-source awardee, there was no method whereby any firm
could compete because licensing arrangement offered by awardee has
been determined to be Government's need and it was only available to
awardee. Determination to award sole-source, in view of lower technical
risk and schedule requirements, was justified_____   575

      Protest timeliness
      Letter contract
  Where protester has actual notice of award of contract after timely
receipt of Commerce Business Daily in ordinary course of business within
a reasonable time after publication and mailing, timeliness of protest
may be measured from date publication is received, allowing a few days
for mailing and receipt of the CBD. Prior decisions are clarified to allow
for reasonable time for protester to receive publication in ordinary
course of business. B–182318, Jan. 27, 1975, and other cases following
rule established therein, modified_____:_____   248

      Source selection
      Preprocurement v. procurement actions
      Review by GAO
      Prime contractor procurement
  Argument that choice of licensing proposal as opposed to proposals
for development of second source was preprocurement action under
Maremont Corporation, 55 Comp. Gen. 1362, to preclude GAO review is
found to be without merit since Government and prime contractor were
not determining minimum needs so much as they were comparing alternative proposals for meeting those needs_____   218

    Specifications. (*See* CONTRACTS, Specifications)

    Specifications unavailable
      Basis for exception to formal advertising
      Offeror assistance in defining needs
  "Exception 10" negotiating authority for National Aeronautics and
Space Administration (NASA) computerized information processing
system has been justified because: (1) NASA needed offerors' approaches
to work requirements to evaluate proposed acceptability and to assist
in defining reasonable needs for service unlike negotiated procurement

CONTRACTS—Continued
 Negotiation—Continued
  Specifications unavailable—Continued
   Basis for exception to formal advertising—Continued
   Offeror assistance in defining needs—Continued   Page
in *Informatics, Inc.*, B–190203, March 20, 1978, 78–1 CPD 215, where
procuring agency intended to evaluate offerors' approaches only as part
of responsibility evaluation and not as part of proposal evaluation;
and (2) there is no indication NASA ever formally advertised prior
procurements for similar system unlike prior advertised procurement
history in *Informatics* decision. B–190203, March 20, 1978, modified in
part_____ 395

  Two-step procurement
   First step
    Purpose
Step one of two-step procurement is qualifying rather than competitive phase which contemplates qualification of as many sources as
possible_____ 119

   Technical proposal acceptability
    Acceptance propriety
     Protest timeliness
While protester might have known prior to opening of step-two bids
that competitor's technical proposal was determined acceptable under
step one of two-step procurement, protest alleging unacceptability of
competitor's technical proposal filed after bid opening is timely since
protester did not know specific grounds of protest until after bid opening.
Protester is not required to file Freedom of Information Act request to
discover grounds for protest before step-two bid opening_____ 119

     Administrative determination
      Reasonableness
Contracting officer's acceptance of technical proposal submitted under
first step of two-step procurement was proper exercise of discretion since
proposal was determined susceptible of being made acceptable and
there is no evidence that determination was unreasonable or made in bad
faith. In determining acceptability of proposal, contracting officer may
consider all circumstances, including magnitude of changes needed as
well as whether Government time and effort and accompanying technical
risk can be justified by resulting increase in price competition_____ 119

 Novation agreements
  Rule
Contract "A" with Federal Aviation Administration (FAA) provided
that it would run concurrently with contract "B" (also with FAA), and
would expire upon expiration or termination of contract "B." Contract
"B" was subsequently novated with FAA's approval. Since general legal
effect of contract novation is extinguishment of contract and substitution
of new one, resulting in discharge of transferor, FAA view that novation
of contract "B" operated to cause expiration of contract "A" under cited
provision was not improper_____ 108

CONTRACTS—Continued
  Options—Continued
    Not to be exercised—Continued
      Procedural deficiencies in procurement   Page
      Termination of contract is not justified by improper evaluation of
      options under invitation for bids in violation of Defense Acquisition
      Regulation 1–1504(c)(ii) where there is no evidence that bidders sub-
      mitted unbalanced bids or that bidders would have submitted lower base
      bids had options not been evaluated, where no bidder was prejudiced by
      evaluation, and where awarded contract would result in lowest cost to
      Government. However, since it appears option provisions should not
      have been included in solicitation, it is recommended that agency not
      exercise options in reinstated contract_____   225

      Requirements to be resolicited
      Where purchase option price was not evaluated in awarding initial
      contract but added by subsequent contract modification, procedures
      followed in exercising purchase option should comport as much as possible
      with competitive procurement norm. Interested suppliers should be
      afforded adequate notice and fair opportunity to have products and
      prices evaluated and normally this should be accomplished through
      competitive procurement_____   38

    Prices
      Added by contract modification
      Where purchase option price was not evaluated in awarding initial
      contract but added by subsequent contract modification, procedures
      followed in exercising purchase option should comport as much as possible
      with competitive procurement norm. Interested suppliers should be
      afforded adequate notice and fair opportunity to have products and
      prices evaluated and normally this should be accomplished through
      competitive procurement_____   38

  Payments
    Advance
      Lessor's capital cost at beginning of lease
      Advance payment of capital cost of telephone equipment under con-
      tract for telephone services with State would be in violation of 31 U.S.C.
      529, even though a State is the recipient, since services to be provided
      by State are commercial in nature_____   29

      Prohibition
        Applicability
      Payments to State under Federal contract for telephone services, ex-
      ecuted by contracting officer of the United States and obligating annual
      appropriations of National Guard, are subject to statutory prohibition
      against advance payments contained in 31 U.S.C. 529_____   29

    Contractor v. surety
      Payment to contractor
      Army, although a mere stakeholder, became liable to Miller Act surety
      where surety notified Army of unpaid claims against contractor and as-
      serted its prior rights to contract retainages, but where through clerical
      error, Army mailed final payments to contractor rather than to surety
      as agreed by all parties. Surety may be paid upon submission of evidence
      that all outstanding claims have been paid and surety assigns to Gov-
      ernment any right it may have to recoup erroneous payments made to
      contractor_____   64

CONTRACTS—Continued
  Protests—Continued
    Procedures—Continued
      Bid Protest Procedures—Continued
        Time for filing—Continued
          Contract award notice effect   Page

CONTRACTS—Continued
  Protests—Continued
    Subcontractor protests   Page
    Where prime contractor is conducting competitive procurement
designed to develop second source for subsystem and after proposals are
received Government encourages prime to consider alternate proposal
from licensee of subsystem contractor, participation by Government is
sufficient under *Optimum Systems* standard for General Accounting
Office (GAO) to hear protest by potential second source against cancellation of solicitation and proposed award of subcontract to licensee_____   218

      Interested party requirement
      General Accounting Office will consider protest by subcontractor that
requirement in prime contract solicitation directly affects subcontractor
and is unduly restrictive of competition_____   297

      Timeliness
      While protester knew alternative method was being considered at
least 2 months prior to final decision being made, protest is timely where
filed within 10 working days of final decision because to have protested
earlier would have been premature_____   218

      Prime contract specifications
        Allegedly restrictive
      Protest of Navy's allegedly restrictive approach to subcontracting is
timely where protester learned of approach after bid opening and filed
protest within 10 working days thereafter_____   297

    Timeliness
      Basis of protest
        Date made known to protester
          Doubtful
      Where record does not contain probative evidence concerning aware-
ness of protest basis, any doubt as to date on which knowledge was or
should have been obtained should be resolved in favor of protester. Therefore, matter of award is considered on merits_____   276

      Filing in other than General Accounting Office
        Agency consideration of untimely protest
          Dismissal by GAO
      Procuring agency's consideration on the merits of protest not filed
within the time limits established by General Accounting Office's (GAO)
Bid Protest Procedures does not preclude GAO from dismissing protest
when subsequently filed with it. Protest of cancellation of IFB initially
filed with procuring agency more than 10 working days after protester
knew the basis therefor, but filed with GAO 4 days after agency's denial
of protest, is dismissed_____   33

      Issues not related to protest basis
        First raised at conference on protest
      Protest allegation first raised at bid protest conference is untimely
since it was neither made within 10 working days after basis of protest
was known nor related to issues timely filed_____   119

CONTRACTS—Continued
  Specifications—Continued
    Failure to furnish something required—Continued
      Licensing-type requirement
Contracting officer was notified after bid opening that State would
try to enforce State license requirement on unlicensed bidder. Even
though particular State license was not specifically incorporated into
solicitation, contracting officer considered bidder's failure to obtain State
license in 8 months since bid opening and likelihood that State would
try to enforce licensing statute, and thereby interrupt or delay performance by unlicensed contractor, as factors affecting bidder's ability to
perform. Determination that unlicensed bidder was nonresponsible in
such circumstances was reasonable_____

      Military
        Approved item requirement
          Removal from listing
            Notice entitlement
No notice need be given manufacturer that product is removed from
approved items list when defects are due to Government specification
deficiencies and manufacturer's product conforms to those specifications_

      Restrictive
        Procurement method coding of spare parts
          Sole-source suppliers
Coding of spare parts to require sole-source procurement under "approved source" system within contemplation of Armed Services Procurement Regulation (ASPR) 1–313 (1976 ed.) cannot be used to preclude consideration of offers from previously unapproved sources which
could otherwise qualify_____

      Minimum needs requirement
        Administrative determination
Purchase of least costly dictating and transcribing systems which satisfied legitimate need of various field offices, as determined by agency, was
proper procurement practice_____

        Basis for determination
Where vendor under Federal Supply Schedule (FSS) contract apprises
procuring activity shortly before award that it offers "middle of the line"
equipment and procuring activity only has specifications for vendor's
"top of the line" equipment, procuring activity, in attempt to reduce
procurement costs, should have attempted to obtain specifications from
vendor or General Services Administration and determine if "middle
of the line" equipment would satisfy Government's legitimate needs.
However, since vendor should have advised agency of middle of line
equipment earlier in procurement process and offered equipment met
agency's minimum needs and has been delivered and installed, award
will not be disturbed_____

        Different approaches to achieve
Protest that certain provisions of Master Terms and Conditions
(MTC) program, for procuring brand name automated data processing
equipment (ADPE) from vendors in addition to the original equipment
manufacturers, are restrictive of competition is denied, since provisions
were determined to be minimum needs of Government and protester
has not shown that determination was unreasonable, or that provisions
unduly restrict competition_____

CONTRACTS—Continued
  Termination—Continued
    Convenience of Government—Continued
      Propriety of termination—Continued
        Reinstatement of contract recommended   Page
        Termination of contract is not justified by improper evaluation of
        options under invitation for bids in violation of Defense Acquisition
        Regulation 1–1504(c)(ii) where there is no evidence that bidders sub-
        mitted unbalanced bids or that bidders would have submitted lower base
        bids had options not been evaluated, where no bidder was prejudiced by
        evaluation, and where awarded contract would result in lowest cost to
        Government. However, since it appears option provisions should not
        have been included in solicitation, it is recommended that agency not
        exercise options in reinstated contract_____   225

        Recommendation
        Resolicitation
        Agency's failure to follow ASPR/DAR 1–502(b)(v) raises doubt as to
        whether Government is receiving items at lowest possible cost and
        whether integrity of competitive bidding system is being maintained.
        These considerations form basis for recommendation that contract be
        terminated for convenience of Government and requirement be
        resolicited_____   586

      Legal basis
      Novation
        Government approval
        Contract "A" with Federal Aviation Administration (FAA) provided
        that it would run concurrently with contract "B" (also with FAA), and
        would expire upon expiration or termination of contract "B." Contract
        "B" was subsequently novated with FAA's approval. Since general legal
        effect of contract novation is extinguishment of contract and substitution
        of new one, resulting in discharge of transferor, FAA view that novation
        of contract "B" operated to cause expiration of contract "A" under cited
        provision was not improper_____   108

  Tie bids/offers
    Evaluation. (See CONTRACTS, Awards, Equal or tie bids/offers,
      Evaluation)
  Timber sales. (See TIMBER SALES, Contracts)

COURTS
  Decisions
    Grismac Corp. v. U.S., 556 F.2d 494 (Ct. Cl. 1977). (See DEFENSE
      DEPARTMENT, Procurement, Authority, Copyrights, patents, de-
      signs, etc. acquisition)

  Judgments; decrees, etc.
    Appeals
      Dismissal
      Since a purpose of first proviso of 31 U.S.C. 724a was to provide
      compensation to a successful plaintiff whose judgment payment was
      delayed solely because the United States appealed and lost, interest may
      be allowed on a wrongful death judgment against the United States
      where the Government filed notice of appeal and appeal was subse-
      quently dismissed by stipulation of the parties because the Government
      did not pursue its appeal. B–145389, April 18, 1961, is overruled. This
      decision modified (extended) by 59 Comp. Gen. ——————— (B–193927,
      Feb. 13, 1980) _____   67

COURTS—Continued
Judgements, decrees, etc.—Continued
Interest
Authority Page

Wrongful death judgment against United States for $373,431, apportioned equally by court among four heirs, is subject to interest limitations in 31 U.S.C. 724a (applied as it existed at time of judgment, prior to 1977 amendment), since each judgment beneficiary received severable and distinct amount less than $100,000. This decision modified by 59 Comp. Gen.————(B-193927, Feb. 13, 1980) _ _ _ _ _ _ _ _ _ _ _ _ _ _ _ _ _ _ _   67

Payment
Agency appropriations
Retirement fund contributions

Where judgment entered in favor of employee calls for payment of back pay, but does not specifically mention or provide for payment of Government's contribution to Civil Service Retirement Fund, that contribution may be paid from agency appropriations. B-124720, May 15, 1961, overruled _   115

"Final judgment" requirement

Judgments against the United States awarding back pay under the Back Pay Act but not indicating the dollar amount to be paid are nevertheless money judgments against the United States and therefore payable from the permanent appropriation established by 31 U.S.C. 724a. However, since an agency's computation of back pay is subject to judicial review, a judgment without a dollar amount cannot be considered "final" for purposes of certification for payment until General Accounting Office has been furnished the agency's computation together with written indication, administrative or judicial, that the plaintiff will accept the amount in satisfaction of the judgment _   311

Indefinite appropriation availability
Judgments against Government

Even though the agency or unit head is the nominal defendant in an employment discrimination suit under Title VII of the Civil Rights Act of 1964, as amended, a suit under 42 U.S.C. 2000e-16 is nevertheless a suit against the United States. Judgments against the Federal Government in Title VII actions are therefore payable from the permanent appropriation established by 31 U.S.C. 724a _   311

Civil penalties imposed on Federal agencies by court after suit is brought against them for violation of local air pollution law, either in accordance with terms of consent decree or stipulated settlement, or as result of judgment on the merits, may be paid, upon proper certification by Attorney General (28 U.S.C. 2414), from permanent indefinite appropriation for judgments and compromise settlements established by 31 U.S.C. 724a _   667

Retirement fund contributions

Employee recovered judgment in U.S. District Court providing for backpay and specifically calling for payment of Government's contribution to Civil Service Retirement Fund. Where judgment specifically provides for payment of Government's contribution to Civil Service Retirement Fund or similar funds, that contribution may be paid from Judgment Fund created by 31 U.S.C. 724a _   115

CREDIT UNIONS
Federal. (*See* FEDERAL CREDIT UNIONS)

DEBT COLLECTIONS
Debtor deceased
Liability of distributee

Distributee of property from the estate of a deceased debtor of the United States is liable to repay debt resulting from overpayment of Supplemental Security Income Benefits to decendent debtor during her lifetime to the extent of assets received. Distributee is considered to constructively hold funds in trust for benefit of the United States. United States is not barred by Wisconsin nonclaim statute from satisfying its claim against decedent debtor through action against beneficiary, without participating in probate proceeding. Wisc. Stat. Ann. 859.01(3)_____ 778

Federal Claims Collection Act of 1966. (*See* FEDERAL CLAIMS COLLECTION ACT OF 1966)

More than one debtor
Joint and several liability

Among debtors jointly and severally liable to United States, Government is not required to collect proportionate share from each, but may collect in manner best calculated to liquidate indebtedness as quickly as possible even if this means collecting entire amount from one debtor. That debtor presumably can enforce legal right to contribution by fellow debtors_____ 778

Point of diminishing returns

Under Federal Claims Collection Act of 1966, 31 U.S.C. 951–953, Department of the Interior need not pursue collection action in cases of underpayments of $1 or less of reclamation fees paid by coal mine operators pursuant to Surface Mining Control and Reclamation Act of 1977. Further, it is General Accounting Office policy that refunds of overpayments of $1 or less should not be made unless specifically claimed_____ 372

Set-off. (*See* SET-OFF)

Waiver
Authority
Agency limitations

Federal Labor Relations Authority requests decision whether collective bargaining agreement provision conflicts with the Comptroller General's standards for waiver contained in 4 C.F.R. Part 91. Agreement requires agency to notify employee of error within 5 days of payment to employee or overpayment will be waived. Where agreement does not consider employee's obligation to inquire as to correctness of payment, it is inconsistent with standards for waiver and may not be implemented_____ 721

DEFENSE DEPARTMENT
Procurement
Authority
Copyrights, patents, designs, etc. acquisition
Unsolicited proposal status
Grismac-case holding
Claimant's unsolicited value engineering proposal recommending that Defense Logistics Agency require that faucets it procures be constructed of zinc-based material constitutes mere suggestion and is not within the exclusive list of intellectual property which can be purchased by Department of Defense under 10 U.S.C. 2386 (1976)

Goods and services from DOD nonappropriated fund instrumentalities
Since basic mission of Department of Defense (DOD) nonappropriated fund instrumentalities (NAFIs) is to promote morale and welfare of military personnel and dependents, as a general proposition sale by NAFIs to regular DOD operating activities would be regarded as outside scope of NAFIs' proper functions except where circumstances require that agency obtain goods or services from NAFI and such requirement is properly documented and justified as sole-source procurement

DEPARTMENTS AND ESTABLISHMENTS
Commercial activities
By contract
Guidelines (OMB Circular No. A-76)
GAO view is that OMB Circular A-76, March 3, 1966, as revised—statement of Executive branch policy which does not have force and effect of law—does not create right of action in disappointed bidder to sue in Federal Courts to enforce its provisions

Private *v.* Government procurement
Cost comparison
Section 601 of Economy Act does not require Commerce Department to perform comparative cost analysis of plaintiff's proposal versus cost of doing work via Commerce—U.S. Postal Service agreement, because Economy Act does not apply to agreement for furnishing property or services between Postal Service and executive agencies

Promotion procedures. (*See* REGULATIONS, Promotion procedures)
Services between
Appropriation obligation
Fiscal year 1978 funds obligated by Bureau of Alcohol, Tobacco and Firearms under Economy Act agreement with Air Force must be deobligated at the end of fiscal year 1978 to extent that Air Force has not incurred valid obligations under agreement during fiscal year. Air Force has validly obligated funds only to extent that performance by contractor satisfies *bona fide* need of fiscal year 1978

Intra- and inter-departmental
Section 601 of Economy Act does not appear to be applicable to Commerce Department's cancellation of RFP and determination to proceed with work in-house, as record does not indicate any inter- or intra-departmental orders for work and services involved

DEPARTMENTS AND ESTABLISHMENTS—Continued
  Services between—Continued
    Reimbursement
      Research and development costs

Under Economy Act agreement providing that contractor of Air Force is to provide research and development work and technical support to Bureau of Alcohol, Tobacco and Firearms, with Air Force paying for work and then being reimbursed by Bureau, only work actually performed by contractor during fiscal year 1978 satisfies *bona fide* need of that year. Work done by contractor during fiscal year 1979 may not be paid for from fiscal year 1978 funds_____

DETAILS
  Compensation
    Higher grade duties assignment
      Classification downgrade
        Effect

A Federal employee appointed to a GS–13 position is detailed to perform duties of a GS–14 position and becomes entitled to a temporary promotion and backpay under 55 Comp. Gen. 539 (1975). Where the position is classified downward during the detail, and since an occupant of a position may only receive the salary authorized for that position, if the employee continues on the detail after it is reclassified downward to a GS–13 level, he may not continue to receive the pay at the higher level on and after the reclassification effective date_____

        Excessive period

Employee, who was temporarily promoted to higher grade position for 120 days, was returned to former grade but was then immediately detailed to same higher level position for additional 132 days. Under *Turner-Caldwell* decisions employee must be detailed to higher level position without compensation of higher level position for 120 days before entitlement to temporary promotion begins on 121st day. Therefore, the period the employee served on temporary promotion may not be included in computation of detail_____

        Prior Civil Service Commission approval

Employee was detailed from her excepted service position to higher grade competitive service position for 2 years without prior approval from Civil Service Commission. Commission Rule VI requires that employee serving under excepted appointment shall be assigned to competitive service position only with prior approval of Commission. Therefore, although employee was improperly placed in overlong detail she may not receive retroactive temporary promotion. Our *Turner-Caldwell* and *Rankin* decisions make it clear that if certain regulatory requirements concerning an employee's entitlement to retroactive temporary promotion are not met there is no entitlement to retroactive temporary promotion_____

        Military position duties

A retired civilian employee of the Air Force claims retroactive temporary promotion and accompanying backpay under *Turner-Caldwell*, 56 Comp. Gen. 427 (1977), incident to details to higher grade military positions. There is no entitlement to backpay as the employee could not have been temporarily promoted into the military position. The *Turner-Caldwell* remedy is only available where the employee was able to satisfy requirements for a retroactive temporary promotion_____

DISASTER RELIEF
Loans. (*See* LOANS, Disaster)

DOCUMENTS
Incorporation by reference
Bid evaluation information. (*See* BIDS, Evaluation, Incorporation of terms by reference)

DONATIONS
Legality
Authority requirement   Page

Some members of the United States Metric Board desire to waive their compensation while other members desire to accept it but return it as a gift to the Board. Here the statute authorizes payment of Board members at a rate not to exceed the daily rate currently being paid grade 18 of the General Schedule. Such pay is not considered salary fixed by or pursuant to statute which would preclude waiver. Also, since statute authorizes acceptance of gifts and donations, members may make gifts of their salary to the agency. However, the members would be liable for the income tax on such salary and would be entitled only to the limited deduction for charitable contributions prescribed by the Internal Revenue Service. 57 Comp. Gen. 423 and 54 *id.* 393, distinguished_____   383

Officers and employees
Voluntary services. (*See* VOLUNTARY SERVICES, Officers and employees)

EASEMENTS, RIGHTS OF WAY, ETC.
Acquisition
Compensation

Nothing in the Uniform Relocation Assistance and Real Property Acquisition Policies Act of 1970, Pub. L. No. 91–646, 84 Stat. 1894, 42 U.S.C. 4601 *et seq.* (1976) affects long-standing definition of just compensation which requires landowner to be put in as good shape pecuniarily as he or she would have been if property had not been taken. Where taking of easements has, in fact, benefitted remainder of landowner's property which has not taken, accruing benefit is to be set off against value of property interest actually taken. When direct benefits to landowner exceed value of easement taken, no monetary compensation is required. In our view, the Environmental Protection Agency may use any widely accepted appraisal method which takes both direct benefits and damages into account_____   559

Method of acquisition

Title III of the Uniform Relocation Assistance and Real Property Acquisition Policies Act of 1970, Pub. L. No. 91–646, 84 Stat. 1894, 42 U.S.C. 4601 *et seq.* (1976), sets forth uniform and equitable procedures for the taking of real property by Federal Government or by State agencies receiving Federal financial assistance. Pursuant to section 305, provisions of Title III are mandatory, to the extent practicable, upon States as condition to their receipt of Federal financial assistance. Title III is applicable to acquisition of any interest in real property, including easements, even where acquisition is funded solely by local funds, if underlying program or project is Federally administered or assisted_____   559

ENERGY
  Department of Energy
    Contracts
    Conflict of interest prohibitions
  Where offeror has individual and corporate ties with gas and oil
industry, agency rejection of proposal for services to assist agency
review of gas curtailment because of organizational conflict of interest
is sustained. Offeror's status as not-for-profit, tax-exempt organization
does not preclude agency determination that conflict of interest does or
might exist _

ENLISTMENTS
  Bonus. (See GRATUITIES, Enlistment bonus)

ENTERTAINMENT
  Appropriation availability
    Equal Employment Opportunity programs
  In the absence of specific authority in statute or regulations, appropriated funds may not be expended to procure entertainment for Federal
employees. Hence agencies without specific authority may not procure
entertainment such as live ethnic music and artistic presentations, characterize it as training and present it in connection with EEO programs.
We will not question past agency characterizations of EEO program
entertainment as training; however, all future entertainment expenses
whether or not in connection with EEO programs will not be allowed _ _

  Department of Interior questions the legality of appropriated fund
expenditure by Bureau of Mines, a subordinate agency, where EEO
officer, who lacked delegated procurement authority, procured services
of contractors and payment was eventually made for services rendered.
Agreements violated the prohibition against the provision of entertainment from appropriated funds and included payments for premiums on
insurance coverage of art objects exhibited incident to National Hispanic
Heritage Week, contrary to the longstanding policy of Government to
assume its own risks of loss and not to purchase commercial insurance.
The employee has been advised of the limits of his authority. In view of
the special facts and circumstances involved, we believe no useful purpose will be served by taking exceptions to these payments _ _ _ _ _ _ _ _ _ _ _ _

ENVIRONMENTAL PROTECTION AND IMPROVEMENT
  Clean Air Act
    State and local air quality regulations
      Federal compliance
  In the absence of express Presidential exemption, the 1977 Amendment
to section 118 of the Clean Air Act requires Federal facilities to abide by
State and local laws regarding abatement and control of pollution, to
same extent as nongovernmental entity, including obtaining permits
and paying associated fees. Therefore, Air Force must pay permit fee
to municipal air pollution control authority for operation of equipment
which would be subject to municipality's air pollution control regulations
if operated by nongovernmental entity _

  Fine or penalty assessed administratively by State or local authority
against Federal agency for violation of local air pollution law, although
it is claim against United States which local authority could sue to

ENVIRONMENTAL PROTECTION AND IMPROVEMENT—Continued
  Clean Air Act—Continued
    State and local air quality regulations—Continued
      Federal compliance—Continued

  Water pollution. (*See* WATER, Pollution prevention)

EQUAL EMPLOYMENT OPPORTUNITY
  Contract provision. (*See* CONTRACTS, Labor stipulations, Nondiscrimination)

  Spanish-Speaking Program
    Establishment

EQUIPMENT
  Automatic Data Processing Systems
    Acquisition, etc.

    Brooks Act applicability
      Federal Judicial Center procurements

EQUIPMENT—Continued
  Automatic Data Processing Systems—Continued
    Tests
      Demonstration v. simulation
        Effect on competition

Procedures established for potential suppliers to demonstrate equipment were unduly restrictive because agency made no apparent effort either to examine whether acceptability of equipment could be established through simulation testing techniques as requested by protester or to attempt to provide access to Government equipment to facilitate testing. GAO recommends that protester be permitted to show acceptability of equipment, particularly in view of alleged successful performance of recent similar contract with other agency_____ 38

Requirement for operational prototype restricted offerors to propose existing equipment components capable of demonstrating essential solicitation requirements. Offeror's prior model did not meet requirement for operational prototype where solicitation expressly sought equipment capable of computational capabilities beyond prior model's capacity_____ 475

Lease v. purchase
  Propriety

Solicitation which does not permit consideration of offers to lease to Government equipment needed for entirely new system is unduly restrictive where based solely on earlier analysis of comparative cost to upgrade existing system, because determination that alternative approach is not competitive as to price can only be made by competitive procurement_____ 324

ESTOPPEL
  Against Government
    Not established

Since agency officals had no authority to contract for purchase of suggestion, doctrine of estoppel is not for application_____ 35

      Surplus sales
        Cancellation of erroneous award

Government is not bound by its agents acting beyond their authority and contrary to law, and the United States is not estopped to deny the authority of its agents_____ 240

Government liability for agents' acts. (*See* AGENTS, Government, Government liability for negligent or erroneous acts, Doctrine of estoppel)

  Prior actions
    Signature acceptance
      Contract matters

Where record does not contain probative evidence concerning awareness of protest basis, any doubt as to date on which knowledge was or should have been obtained should be resolved in favor of protester. Therefore, matter of award is considered on merits_____ 276

EVIDENCE
Presumptions
Death
A claim by a retired Navy member's wife for the member's retired pay accruing during the 7-year period from the date of his disappearance to the date he was declared dead by a State court may not be allowed since retired pay is payable only during the member's life and there is no showing whether he was alive after his disappearance or evidence of when he actually died, and the State court determination appears to be presumptive only and does not establish that the member lived for 7 years_____

Secondary in lieu of primary evidence
Employee may "buy back" sick leave taken in connection with a job-related illness in order to receive disability compensation under Federal Employees' Compensation Act, 5 U.S.C. 8101, *et seq.* Where there are no official records from which to determine amount of leave taken, leave may be credited and bought back on basis of secondary evidence determined to be acceptable by agency. Acceptable forms of secondary evidence include leave requests, Leave and Earnings Statements, Time and Attendance Reports, personal leave records, as well as certificates from supervisors and timekeepers_____

EXPERTS AND CONSULTANTS
Compensation
Overtime
Although an expert or consultant is not entitled to overtime compensation, if he is employed on a per diem basis he may be paid his rate of basic compensation for work on days outside his prescribed tour of duty, provided his compensation within any biweekly pay period does not exceed the rate of basic pay for level V of the Executive Schedule. Since the compensation of experts and consultants under 5 U.S.C. 3109 is set by administrative action under 5 U.S.C. 5307, it is subject to the limitation on compensation imposed by 5 U.S.C. 5308 which, by virtue of 5 U.S.C. 5504, is applicable on a pay-period basis_____

Leaves of absence
Accrual
Expert appointed on an intermittent basis is not entitled to leave even though he was compensated for 80 hours per day period for substantially the full term of his employment. His work was assigned on a project basis and the hours at which he worked were largely within his discretion. Since he was not required in advance to report at a definite and certain time within each workweek, he is not entitled to leave as a part-time employee with an established regular tour of duty. He is not entitled to leave as a de facto full-time employee since he was not required to work a standard workweek_____

FAIR LABOR STANDARDS ACT
Compensation
Overtime. (*See* COMPENSATION, Overtime, Fair Labor Standards Act)

FAMILY ALLOWANCES
Evacuation
Payment basis
Employees of Padre Island National Seashore and their families were ordered to leave the island and travel to a place of safety due to the threat of a hurricane. If the agency determines that an evacuation in fact occurred under its regulations, employees would be entitled to mileage for dependent transportation by private automobiles incident to the evacuation_____ 134

Separation
Eligibility basis
Base closure
"Enforced" separation
Where a base closure plan requires the transfer, using Government-furnished transportation, of dependents to the sponsor's next permanent duty station, while the sponsor remains behind to implement base closure, "enforced" separation exists within the contemplation of 37 U.S.C. 427(b)(1), and the granting of Family Separation Allowance, Type II, is authorized_____ 183

FARMERS HOME ADMINISTRATION (See AGRICULTURE DEPARTMENT, Farmers Home Administration)

FEDERAL AVIATION ADMINISTRATION
Airport development
Grant contracts
Even though costs incurred under contracts awarded pursuant to grant projects were based on cost-plus-percentage-of-cost contracting, contractor can be paid on *quantum meruit/quantum valebat* basis as agency has determined costs to be reasonable and Government received benefit of services_____ 654

FEDERAL CLAIMS COLLECTION ACT OF 1966
Compromise, waiver, etc. of claims
Collection expense excessive
Under Federal Claims Collection Act of 1966, 31 U.S.C. 951–953, Department of the Interior need not pursue collection action in cases of underpayments of $1 or less of reclamation fees paid by coal mine operators pursuant to Surface Mining Control and Reclamation Act of 1977. Further, it is General Accounting Office policy that refunds of overpayments of $1 or less should not be made unless specifically claimed_____ 372

FEDERAL CREDIT UNIONS
Services furnished by Government
Available space and services may be provided to Federal Credit Union Service Centers if approved by the appropriate officer or agency. 12 U.S.C. 1770 (1976). Also, General Accounting Office will not raise legal objection if credit union is allowed to use desks, chairs, and office machines without charge. However, agency funds are hereafter not available to furnish without charge telephone services for credit union_____ 610

FEDERAL GRANT AND COOPERATIVE AGREEMENT ACT OF 1977
Compliance
Grant, etc. agreements v. procurement contract

Complaint that executive agency abandoned practice of awarding contracts under Federal procurement procedures in favor of grant awards in order to make sole-source award and avoid statutory requirements for competition is denied where record discloses agency awarded grant, rather than contract, for purpose of complying with requirements of Federal Grant and Cooperative Agreement Act of 1977_____ 785

FEDERAL JUDICIAL CENTER
Contracts
Competitive negotiation where practicable requirement

Although Federal Judicial Center (FJC) is exempt from 41 U.S.C. 5 (1976) and civilian agency procurement statutes do not apply to FJC, examination of FJC's enabling legislation shows Congress' intent that FJC enter into contracts by "negotiation." Further, maximum practicable competition should be obtained as matter of sound Federal procurement whenever contracts utilizing appropriated funds are to be awarded. Therefore, FJC should award contracts by using competitive negotiation where practicable_____ 350

FEDERAL PROCUREMENT REGULATIONS
Applicability
Services "procured" from Postal Service

GAO does not agree with plaintiff's contentions in U.S. District Court litigation that Commerce Department, in canceling RFP, violated numerous provisions of Federal Procurement Regulations (41 C.F.R. 1-1.000 et seq. (1978)) including sections 1-1.009-1(e), 1-1.1001, 1-2. 404-1, 1-3.210, 1-3.302(c), 1-3.804, 1-3.805-1(b), and 1-3.802(c)(2)___ 451

Conflict of interest prohibitions
Contracting with corporations, etc. owned or controlled by Government employees, etc.
What constitutes "substantial ownership"

Because issue of control is separate from issue of ownership for purpose of applying FPR, General Accounting Office (GAO) questions propriety of procuring agency's determination of substantial ownership by comparing percent of stock owned by Government employees with percent of stock owned by other individuals in protester. GAO believes that determination of substantial ownership for purposes of FPR should be made solely on basis of relationship of amount of Government employee stock to total amount of stock in protester. Nevertheless, if General Services Administration intends different meaning of substantial ownership, GAO suggests amending FPR to clarify any such meaning___ 802

Late proposals
Consideration propriety
Rule
"Only proposal received" exception
Applicability

Even though costs incurred under contracts awarded pursuant to grant projects were based on cost-plus-percentage-of-cost contracting, contractor can be paid on *quantum meruit/quantum ralebat* basis as agency has determined costs to be reasonable and Government received benefit of services. _____ 656

FEDERAL PROCUREMENT REGULATIONS—Continued
Negotiated procurement
Cancellation
Guidelines
Availability

FEDERAL RESERVE
Board of Governors
Employees
Civil Service Reform Act of 1978
Applicability

Federal Reserve Act, as amended, expressly excepts the appointment and compensation of all employees of the Board of Governors, Federal Reserve System, from the provisions of the civil service laws and regulations. The Act must be given priority over a subsequently enacted statute applicable to Federal agencies generally, absent a clear indication

FEDERAL RESERVE—Continued
  Board of Governors—Continued
    Employees—Continued
      Civil Service Reform Act of 1978—Continued
        Applicability—Continued   **Page**

that the Congress intended otherwise. Hence, the provisions of Civil
Service Reform Act of 1978 establishing a Senior Executive Service do
not apply to the employees of the Board_____ 687

FEDERAL SUPPLY SCHEDULE CONTRACTS (*See* **CONTRACTS, Federal
Supply Schedule**)

FEES
  License, permit, etc. fees
    State
      Federal agency liability

Section 404(t), Federal Water Pollution Control Act, as amended,
requires Federal agencies to comply with State substantive or procedural requirements governing discharge in navigable waters of dredged
material to same extent as "any person." Section 67, Pub. L. No. 95–217.
Federal agencies must get permits if required by State for activity in
question, whether or not State has taken over from United States
administration of program for issuance of dredging permits. In present
case, however, Wisconsin permit requirement does not pertain to dredging activities. Therefore, section 404(t) does not apply and permit fee
may not be paid_____ 193

In the absence of express Presidential exemption, the 1977 Amendment to section 118 of the Clean Air Act requires Federal facilities to
abide by State and local laws regarding abatement and control of pollution, to same extent as nongovernmental entity, including obtaining
permits and paying associated fees. Therefore Air Force must pay
permit fee to municipal air pollution control authority for operation of
equipment which would be subject to municipality's air pollution control
regulations if operated by nongovernmental entity_____ 244

  User fees
    Retention
      Cost recovery

National Bureau of Standards finances operations in part by charges
to users of its services, paid into Working Capital Fund. Earned net
income of the Fund must be paid into Treasury annually, except that it
"may be applied first to restore any prior impairment" of the Fund. 15
U.S.C. 278b (1976). Impairments contemplated by this provision are
operating losses. Bureau may not retain profits to offset increased
costs—caused by inflation—of replacing equipment or facilities, nor
can Bureau calculate depreciation of equipment and facilities based on
replacement cost_____ 9

  Witnesses
    Payment
      Appropriation chargeable

Generally, fees and expenses of expert witnesses appointed by the
court in land condemnation proceedings, whether on motion of the court
or at request of a party, are considered to be expenses of litigation and

FUNDS—Continued
Nonappropriated
Contract awards
Protest status   Page

General Accounting Office (GAO), despite prior decisions holding otherwise, will undertake bid protest type reviews concerning propriety of contract awards under Department of Defense (DOD) foreign military sales (FMS) program. Change in position is based on recognition that appropriated funds are utilized in FMS procurements and that, in view of significant dollar amounts involved, area is appropriate for review. 55 Comp. Gen. 674 is modified. Other decisions, to the contrary, are overruled or modified, as appropriate_____ 81

GENERAL ACCOUNTING OFFICE
Contracts
Protests. (*See* CONTRACTS, Protests)

Decisions
Abeyance
Pending court, quasi-judicial, appellate board, etc. action
It is the policy of the General Accounting Office to decline ruling on matters in litigation. Hence, no action will be taken on questions of whether Variable Reenlistment Bonus payments may be made to members of the Armed Forces who (1) cancelled enlistment extension agreements on the basis of erroneous advice that they were not eligible for the previously authorized Variable Reenlistment Bonus, 37 U.S.C. 308 (1970), and (2) executed new enlistment extension agreements in order to become eligible for the new Selective Reenlistment Bonus, 37 U.S.C. 308 (1976), since those questions are the subject of pending litigation in the Federal courts_____ 282

Clarification
Prior decision under same solicitation held that, since solicitation contained only general statements requiring contractor to obtain all necessary licenses and permits, failure of proposed awardee (protester in present decision) to obtain State license did not require contracting officer to find proposed awardee nonresponsible and would not affect validity of award if made. However, prior decision did not hold that State license statute and threatened enforcement thereof were irrelevant, nor that contracting officer was required to find proposed awardee responsible as protestor alleges. Decision in *Inter-Con Security Systems, Inc.; Washington Patrol Service, Inc.*, B–192188, February 9, 1979, 79–1 CPD 86, clarified_____ 767

Overruled or modified
Prospective application
Department of the Navy asks if the intent of 56 Comp. Gen. 551 (1977) requires deduction of leave credited under 54 Comp. Gen. 662 (1975) but unused as of April 19, 1977, and whether related claims unresolved between the dates of the two decisions are valid. Such leave recredited prior to April 19, 1977, remains available for use. The determination in 56 Comp. Gen. 551 to forego collection action for lump-sum payments made for leave recredited, and not to require correction of leave records for recredited leave taken pursuant to 54 Comp. Gen. 662, did not validate all claims that arose or were presented for payment between the dates of the two decisions. Rather, it was to inform agencies that corrective action would not be required for actions allowing claims taken prior to April 19, 1977, pursuant to 54 Comp. Gen. 662_____ 345

GENERAL ACCOUNTING OFFICE—Continued
  Recommendations—Continued
    Reporting to Congress—Continued
      Contract matters—Continued
        Corrective action requested   Page

Since selection decision may have been influenced by erroneous view that awardee was labor surplus area concern, recommendation is made that source selection official reconsider his decision. If it is determined that award should have been made to protester, it is further recommended that contrast be terminated and award made to protester_   263

Contracting officer's withdrawal of small business set-aside without notifying Small Business Administration (SBA) liaison representative, thereby denying SBA its right to appeal withdrawal to head of procuring agency, was contrary to regulation and to purpose and intent of Small Business Act. GAO recommends post-award referral of set–aside withdrawal to SBA with view toward possible termination of contract for convenience of the Government and resolicitation_____   658

GENERAL SERVICES ADMINISTRATION
  Authority
    Procurement of goods and services
      Federal Supply Schedule
        Multiple award schedule contracts
          Single award for identical items

Manufacturers' late proposals, submitted after closing date for receipt of proposals and timely receipt of dealer's proposal for "identical" product, do not constitute "only proposal received" within meaning of Federal Procurement Regulation 1–3.802–1(c) which permits consideration of late proposals and may not be considered for award_____   656

  Services for other agencies, etc.
    Procurement
      Automatic Data Processing Systems

Protest that MTC violates Brooks Act mandate that Administrator of General Services Administration procure ADPE in economic and efficient manner is denied, since Administrator is given discretion to develop and implement ADPE procurement policies so long as policies are not contrary to law or otherwise detrimental to Government's interest, and protester has not shown either condition_____   73

      Brooks Act applicability
        Federal Judicial Center status

Federal Judicial Center (FJC), as establishment in judicial branch, is "Federal agency" as term is used in Brooks Act, 40 U.S.C. 759 (1976). Since no law expressly exempts FJC from Brooks Act, FJC must comply with Brooks Act and General Services Administration's implementing regulations in all automatic data processing equipment procurements___   350

GIFTS
  Donations. (*See* **DONATIONS**)

GOVERNMENT LOSSES IN SHIPMENT ACT
Insurance
Prohibition
Applicability

Neither the Government Losses in Shipment Act, 40 U.S.C. 726 (1970), nor the Government's general self-insurance policy prohibits Federal agencies from using registered mail where administratively determined necessary in order to obtain the "special" service of greater protection in the handling and delivery of mail rather than to obtain the insurance coverage also offered_____

GRANTS
Federal
Amendment
Appropriation availability

ACTION's proposed grant modification to expand the area from which enrollees in a demonstration youth employment project are drawn to include an additional county would not enlarge the grant's scope because the statutory authority for the grant (section 348(a) of the Comprehensive Employment and Training Act of 1973, as added by the Youth Employment and Demonstration Project Act of 1977, Pub. L. 95–93, 91 Stat. 645, 29 U.S.C.A. 849g) and the interagency agreement with the Department of Labor delegating this authority to ACTION support the conclusion that the proposed amendment is necessary to carry out the original purpose of the grant. Accordingly, such an amendment would not require the obligation of current fiscal year appropriated funds_____

To States. (*See* STATES, Federal aid, grants, etc.)

GRATUITIES
Enlistment bonus
Basis for payment

If an individual enlists in a Reserve component under the Delayed Entry Program with a concurrent commitment to serve in a Regular component for a period of at least 4 years in a skill designated as critical, the award level of the enlistment bonus authorized by 37 U.S.C. 308a (1976) must be fixed on the date of enlistment in the Delayed Entry Program, rather than on the date of entry on active duty. Payment of the bonus must, however, be contingent on the member's qualifying and serving in his designated military specialty. *United States* v. *Larionoff*, 431 U.S. 864 (1977); 52 Comp. Gen. 105 (1972)_____

Selective reenlistment bonus
Computation
Multiplier
Effective date

Selective Reenlistment Bonus payments for extensions of enlistments, authorized by 37 U.S.C. 308 (1976), must be based on the award level multiplier in effect on the date the extension agreement is executed rather than on the date the extension agreement becomes operative, in accordance with the Supreme Court's decision in *United States* v. *Larionoff*, 431 U.S. 864 (1977), concerning the similar Variable Reenlistment Bonus. 50 Comp. Gen. 515, B–175846, Oct. 4, 1972, and similar cases are overruled_____

HEALTH, EDUCATION AND WELFARE DEPARTMENT
Programs
Medicare, Medicaid, etc. (*See* SOCIAL SECURITY, Medicare, Medicaid, etc.)

HOLIDAYS
Annual leave charge. (*See* **LEAVES OF ABSENCE, Holidays**)

INDIAN AFFAIRS
Contracting with Government
Preference to Indian concerns   Page
   Indian Self-Determination and Education Assistance Act does not
require award to Indian-owned economic enterprises because statute and
regulations call for preference "to the greatest extent feasible," thus conferring broad, discretionary authority. Approval or disapproval by Department of Interior of proposed subcontract awards will not be disturbed
by General Accounting Office unless arbitrary, capricious, or in violation
of law or regulation_____   160

Lumbee Indians
Federal benefits
   Final sentence of Pub. L. No. 84-570 states that nothing in Act will
make Lumbee Indians eligible for Federal services performed for Indians
and that none of Federal statutes affecting Indians because of their
status as Indians shall be applicable to Lumbee Indians. Purpose of this
provision is to assure that Act was not used in and of itself to acquire
Federal benefits. However, provision does not deny to Lumbees benefits
accorded Indians if they are otherwise entitled under the requirements of
another Act_____   699

Native American Programs Act
State recognized Indian tribes
   Benefits entitlement
   Lumbee Indians are not entitled to or denied benefits of Native
American Programs Act of 1974 (NAPA), 42 U.S.C. 2991 *et seq.*, by
virtue of last sentence of sec. 1, Pub. L. No. 84-570. NAPA benefits can
be extended to, among others, public and non-profit agencies including
governing bodies of Indian tribes on State and Federal reservations,
and to public and non-profit private agencies serving Indian organizations
in urban or rural non-reservation areas. Dept. of Health, Education and
Welfare (HEW) contends this indicates congressional intent to extend
benefits to State recognized tribes as well as to other organizations serving Indians. Since neither statutory language nor its history gives clear
indication of intended beneficiaries, views of agency charged with administering statute must be given great weight. Hence, we will not object
to determination by HEW that NAPA programs are available to State
recognized Indian tribes such as the Lumbees_____   699

   Department of the Interior states that unless otherwise provided,
most statutes referring to "Indians" do so within a context which actually means "Indian tribes." HEW contends that statute authorizing
benefits to, among others, governing bodies of Indian tribes on Federal
and State reservations (including a reservation of a State recognized
tribe) and to public and non-profit private agencies serving Indian
organizations in urban or rural non-reservation areas confers benefits
on Lumbee Indians, who are a State recognized, non-reservation triber
In absence of clear indication in language or history of Native American
Programs Act of 1974 of intended beneficiaries, General Accounting
Office will not object to HEW's determination that the Lumbees are
eligible to participate in the Act's programs_____   699

INSURANCE
Government
Self-insurer

Federal agencies are prohibited from using insured mail under both 40 U.S.C. 726 and the Government's self-insurance policy since insured mail provides no "special" or "additional" service in addition to the indemnity offered. 3 Comp. Gen. 391 and 22 Comp. Gen. 832, modified__   14

Department of Interior questions the legality of appropriated fund expenditure by Bureau of Mines, a subordinate agency, where EEO officer, who lacked delegated procurement authority, procured services of contractors and payment was eventually made for services rendered. Agreements violated the prohibition against the provision of entertainment from appropriated funds and included payments for premiums on insurance coverage of art objects exhibited incident to National Hispanic Heritage Week, contrary to the longstanding policy of Government to assume its own risks of loss and not to purchase commercial insurance. The employee has been advised of the limits of his authority. In view of the special facts and circumstances involved, we believe no useful purpose will be served by taking exceptions to these payments_____   202

Trip cancellation insurance
Travel expense

A member of the uniformed services purchased trip cancellation insurance when he purchased charter flight accommodations. It is the policy of the Government to insure its own risks of loss. Trip cancellation insurance is not a reimbursable travel expense unless it can be shown that the insurance is an inseparable part of a travel package which provides special or reduced fares at a savings to the Government_____   710

INTEREST
Back pay
Statutory authority required

Pursuant to 5 C.F.R. 713.217, Securities and Exchange Commission (SEC) adjusted employee's complaint of discrimination by agreement to authorize retroactive promotion and accompanying backpay plus interest. The SEC has no authority to allow payment of interest. It is well-settled rule of law that interest may be assessed against Government only under an express statutory authority and neither Equal Employment Opportunity Act of 1972 nor the incorporated provisions of title VII provide express authorization of interest against Government____   5

Judgments. (*See* COURTS, Judgments, decrees, etc., Interest)

INTERIOR DEPARTMENT
National Park Service
Concessions
Discounts by concessioners

Secretary of Interior has determined, and General Accounting Office (GAO) concurs, that provision in standard National Park Service concession contract requiring concessioner to furnish accommodations at reduced rates to Federal employees in parks on official business is not in best interest of Government, despite reduced cost, because of risk and appearance of improper conflict of interest. Although generally vested contract rights may not be waived without consideration, GAO will not object to elimination of clause in question where cost saving is determined to be outweighed by adverse effect on Government of clause. 40 Comp. Gen. 234, distinguished_____   7

JOINT VENTURES
Status

Firms acting as joint venturers are answerable for acts done by their co-venturers, or other agents, and may be found nonresponsible because of deficient performance by joint venture in prior procurement_____ 303

JUDGMENTS, DECREES, ETC. (*See* **COURTS**, Judgments, decrees, etc.)

JUSTICE DEPARTMENT
Referrals
Compromises

Fine or penalty assessed administratively by State or local authority against Federal agency for violation of local air pollution law, although it is claim against United States which local authority could sue to enforce, may not be referred to Attorney General for defense of imminent litigation if agency does not dispute basis for or amount of fine. Funds appropriated by 31 U.S.C. 724a for payment of compromise settlements, negotiated by Attorney General in connection with imminent litigation (28 U.S.C. 2414), are therefore not available to pay fine_____ 667

LEAVES OF ABSENCE
Annual
Accrual
Irregular workweek employment

Expert appointed on an intermittent basis is not entitled to leave even though he was compensated for 80 hours per pay period for substantially the full term of his employment. His work was assigned on a project basis and the hours at which he worked were largely within his discretion. Since he was not required in advance to report at a definite and certain time within each workweek, he is not entitled to leave as a part-time employee with an established regular tour of duty. He is not entitled to leave as a de facto full-time employee since he was not required to work a standard workweek_____ 167

Charging
Excess compensatory time

Employee, who was erroneously granted compensatory time off in excess of the hours for which he could have received overtime pay under the aggregate salary limitation in 5 U.S.C. 5547, requests recredit of 47 hours of annual leave which agency charged to recover erroneous payments. Payments for the salary paid for excess compensatory time off must be recovered but are subject to waiver under 5 U.S.C. 5584 and 4 C.F.R. Part 91. Employee's annual leave balance may not be charged for compensatory time erroneously granted without employee's consent. Modified (amplified) by 59 Comp. Gen.————(B-196444, Feb. 8, 1980)_____ 571

House hunting trip upon transfer

New appointees were erroneously authorized house-hunting trips from training site to first official station. Agency should charge employees annual leave for time spent on house-hunting trips. If leave charges result in negative leave balances, there are overpayments of pay which may be considered for waiver under 5 U.S.C. 5584. However, annual leave should not be charged for excess travel time en route to appointees' first duty station required because of training_____ 744

LEAVES OF ABSENCE—Continued
Home leave travel of overseas employees
Transfers

Interior employee who satisfactorily completed an overseas tour of duty returned to the United States for home leave. He arranged transfer to AID while on home leave, effective on termination of leave. The salary charge to the Interior appropriation for the period of home leave was proper since the employee earned it as an Interior employee and it agreed to the effective date of the transfer_____ 633

Lump-sum payments
De facto employees

Claimant was hired from a certificate of eligibles and given a temporary appointment. Later, agency discovered he had been erroneously appointed due to a mistake of identity. He was removed and not paid his accrued pay or lump-sum annual leave. Since there was no absolute statutory bar to appointment and no fraud or misrepresentation by claimant, he is entitled to unpaid compensation and lump-sum leave payment. Prior inconsistent cases will no longer be followed_____ 734

Military personnel
Advance leave
Enlistment extension prior to accrual

Marine Corps member, who takes 19 more days of leave than he would accrue prior to the expiration of his first extension of enlistment, had pay and allowances withheld from him upon return from leave for the 19 days pursuant to Department of Defense regulation. Although the member subsequently entered into a second reextension of enlistment which would enable him to earn more leave than the excess he used, there is no authority to repay him the withheld pay and allowances_____ 708

Payments for unused leave on discharge, etc.
Additional pay not included

An amendment to 37 U.S.C. 501(b) deleted inclusion of allowances in lump-sum leave payments to military members upon discharge; however, a saving provision retained entitlement to include the allowances for leave accrued prior to the amendment. Although the claimant contends that the services' regulation determining when a member will be charged with use of preamendment leave frustrates congressional intent of the saving provision, in view of the services' authority to prescribe regulations for accrual and use of leave, the language and legislative history of the amendment, the regulation is proper_____ 635

Sick
Recredit of prior leave
Evidence to support claim missing

Employee may "buy back" sick leave taken in connection with a job-related illness in order to receive disability compensation under Federal Employees' Compensation Act, 5 U.S.C. 8101, *et seq.* Where there are no official records from which to determine amount of leave taken, leave may be credited and bought back on basis of secondary evidence determined to be acceptable by agency. Acceptable forms of secondary evidence include leave requests, Leave and Earnings Statements, Time and Attendance Reports, personal leave records, as well as certificates from supervisors and timekeepers_____ 741

LEAVES OF ABSENCE—Continued
Without pay
Substitution for annual and sick leave

A Federal employee applied for disability retirement, waived military retired pay to increase his Civil Service annuity and spouse's survivor annuity to be effective when retirement is granted, but then went on extended sick leave and died in that status. While the agency has discretionary authority to place him in a leave-without-pay (LWOP) status because of retirement counseling errors or his misunderstanding, where there is nothing of record to show such counseling error or that he misunderstood that a sick leave status was not retirement, it would be improper to retroactively substitute LWOP for sick leave. B–190204, January 26, 1978, distinguished_____

LEGISLATION
Statutory construction. (*See* STATUTORY CONSTRUCTION)

LICENSES
State and municipalities
Government contractors

Prior decision under same solicitation held that, since solicitation contained only general statements requiring contractor to obtain all necessary licenses and permits, failure of proposed awardee (protester in present decision) to obtain State license did not require contracting officer to find proposed awardee nonresponsible and would not affect validity of award if made. However, prior decision did not hold that State license statute and threatened enforcement thereof were irrelevant, nor that contracting officer was required to find proposed awardee responsible as protester alleges. Decision in *Inter-Con Security Systems, Inc.; Washington Patrol Service, Inc.*, B–192183, February 9, 1979, 79–1 CPD 86, clarified_____

LIENS
By Government
Release to property owner

Notwithstanding doubt that valid judgment lien exists, real property owner's request for release of lien under 28 U.S.C. 2410(e) on basis that outstanding judgment against former owner creates a cloud on title is denied, since applicant holds title acquired in foreclosure sale and is not lien holder as required by statute_____

LOANS
Disaster
Guaranteed
Direct sale

SBA is not authorized under existing legislation to sell direct disaster loans to Federal Financing Bank on guaranteed basis either individually or collectively. In absence of specific statutory authority or clear expression of congressional intent that SBA does have such authority to sell direct disaster loans in this manner, which, if allowed, could result in establishment of unlimited contingent liability against SBA without any congressional restraints, our Office cannot approve proposed procedure. Moreover, SBA's proposal to sell these loans with 100 percent guarantees is not consistent with its statutory authority to guarantee maximum of 90 percent of loans made in first instance by participating lending institutions_____

LOANS—Continued
  Sale
    Authority
      Small Business Administration (SBA) does have authority to issue certificates to Federal Financing Bank (FFB) evidencing ownership of group of SBA loans. Proposed financing arrangements, as well as SBA's current procedure of selling individual loans to FFB with recourse, is sufficiently similar from legal standpoint to financing arrangements our Office has approved in past. Also, SBA has some authority to sell loans to FFB with recourse as it has to sell to other purchasers_____ 138

    Small Business Administration. (*See* SMALL BUSINESS ADMINIS-TRATION, Loans)

MEDICARE AND MEDICAID (*See* SOCIAL SECURITY, Medicare, Medicaid, etc.)
MILEAGE Travel by privately owned automobile
  Dependents
    Evacuation
      Employees of Padre Island National Seashore and their families were ordered to leave the island and travel to a place of safety due to the threat of a hurricane. If the agency determines that an evacuation in fact occurred under its regulations, employees would be entitled to mileage for dependent transportation by private automobiles incident to the evacuation_____ 134

    More than one employee traveling
    Reimbursement basis
      Where an employee utilizes a privately owned vehicle as a matter of personal preference when such use is not determined to be advantageous to the Government, the employee's total reimbursement for the travel is limited to the total constructive cost of appropriate common carrier transportation. In the computation of the constructive costs, the employee is not entitled to include the cost by common carrier of transporting other Government employees who accompany the employee on the trip to determine maximum reimbursement when there is no order or administrative approval of additional payment_____ 305

MILITARY PERSONNEL
  Acceptance of foreign presents, emoluments, etc.
    Foreign government employment
      Prohibition
        The withholding of retired pay from a member of the uniformed services employed by a foreign government without the consent of Congress is based on the constitutional requirement for congressional consent to the receipt of emoluments from a foreign government, which requirement cannot be ignored. Substantial effect is given the constitutional mandate by withholding retired pay in an amount equal to the foreign emoluments received. The basis for the rule is that the emoluments are deemed accepted on behalf of the United States_____ 487

MILITARY PERSONNEL—Continued
National Guard. (*See* NATIONAL GUARD)

Pay
Retired. (*See* PAY, Retired)

Public Health Service. (*See* PUBLIC HEALTH SERVICE)

Quarters allowance. (*See* QUARTERS ALLOWANCE)

Record correction
Retirement status
Disability in lieu of years of service
Income tax refund
Where military records are corrected under 10 U.S.C. 1552 to show a portion of taxable retired pay as tax exempt disability retired pay, the claimant may be paid, under 10 U.S.C. 1552(c), the amounts of pay withheld for income taxes by the Air Force in years for which the Internal Revenue Service is barred from making tax refunds by the applicable statute of limitations. However, while 10 U.S.C. 1552(c) provides for certain types of payments pursuant to correction of military records, it does not authorize payment for tax refunds in derogation of the Internal Revenue Code statute of limitations beyond monies withheld for taxes by the military department concerned_____

Reservists
Retired pay. (*See* PAY, Retired pay, Reservists)
Retirement
Qualifying service
Air Force Reserve major generals who have not been eliminated for years of service under 10 U.S.C. 8852 prior to reaching age 60 may receive retirement point credit for service performed after they have attained retirement eligibility under Chapter 67 of title 10, U.S. Code, only if their retention in active status thereafter is approved by the Secretary under 10 U.S.C. 676_____

Selective reenlistment bonus. (*See* GRATUITIES, Selective reenlistment bonus)
Survivor Benefit Plan. (*See* PAY, Retired, Survivor Benefit Plan)

NATIONAL GUARD
Death or injury
While on training duty
Injury within scope of duties
A National Guard member is in a travel status for medical and disability entitlements for injury incurred while traveling to and from active training when he leaves his living quarters with the intention of going directly to the place where ordered to perform such duty and such travel status continues upon completion of his tour when he returns directly from his place of duty to his home until he has entered his living quarters_____

NONDISCRIMINATION
Discrimination alleged
Contract awards
Although protester asserts that SBA 8(a) program violates Civil Rights Act of 1964 because of racial discrimination, courts have held that there is no merit to such assertion since eligibility standard of program is not defined racially but by social or economic disadvantage_____

OFFICERS AND EMPLOYEES—Continued
De facto—Continued
Compensation
Accrued

Claimant was hired from a certificate of eligibles and given a temporary appointment. Later, agency discovered he had been erroneously appointed due to a mistake of identity. He was removed and not paid his accrued pay or lump-sum annual leave. Since there was no absolute statutory bar to appointment and no fraud or misrepresentation by claimant, he is entitled to unpaid compensation and lump-sum leave payment. Prior inconsistent cases will no longer be followed_____ 734

Death or injury
Compensation claims. (*See* DECEDENTS' ESTATES, Compensation)

Debt collections. (*See* DEBT COLLECTIONS)

Debts to U.S.
Satisfaction

Government may not withhold current salary to satisfy general debts owed by employee and may not setoff against employee's retirement account until employee withdraws contribution or claims annuity. Government has right to setoff indebtedness administratively against annuity payments or refund of retirement contribution based upon common-law right long recognized by our Office and the courts_____ 501

Deceased. (*See* DECEDENTS' ESTATES)

Details. (*See* DETAILS)

Equal employment opportunity
Spanish-Speaking Program

The Spanish-Speaking Program was established as a component of the Federal Equal Employment Opportunity Program by presidential proclamation on November 5, 1970. Under 42 U.S.C. 2000e–16(b), the Civil Service Commission promulgated Federal Personnel Manual letter 713–18, January 23, 1973, making the Spanish-Speaking Program a special emphasis area within the Federal EEO program. Accordingly, the Bureau of Mines, within the Department of Interior, is authorized to institute a Spanish-Speaking EEO program_____ 202

Federal dependents' schools employees
Civil service laws
Applicability

Under 20 U.S.C. 241(a), persons "may" be employed to work at Federal dependents' schools without regard to certain civil service laws, including those pertaining to the General Schedule pay rates, but the provisions of such laws may nevertheless be extended to school employees by operation of administrative directives and contract clauses_____ 430

Hours of work
Day defined
Twenty-four hour period

Army hospital has two work shifts: 0500–1330 and 1100–1930. Employees on 1100–1930 shift, who periodically work regular shift 1 day and 0500–1330 shift next day, claim overtime compensation for work in excess of 8 hours. Definition of "day" for purposes of overtime compensation is not limited to calendar day but may be any 24-hour period. See 42 Comp. Gen. 195 (1962). Thus, since Army agreed through negotiated agreement to treat workday as 24-hour period from start of shift, employees who work more than 8 hours during 24-hour period but not on same calendar day are entitled to overtime compensation_____ 347

OFFICERS AND EMPLOYEES—Continued
Intermittent. (*See* OFFICERS, AND EMPLOYEES, Status, Intermittent)

Leaves of absence. (*See* LEAVES OF ABSENCE)

Moving expenses. (*See* OFFICERS AND EMPLOYEES, Transfers, Relocation expenses)

Overseas
Home leave
Transfers   Page
Interior employee who satisfactorily completed an overseas tour of duty returned to the United States for home leave. He arranged transfer to AID while on home leave, effective on termination of leave. The salary charge to the Interior appropriation for the period of home leave was proper since the employee earned it as an Interior employee and it agreed to the effective date of the transfer_____ 633

Overtime. (*See* COMPENSATION, Overtime)

Per diem. (*See* SUBSISTENCE, Per diem)

Prevailing rate employees
Compensation. (*See* COMPENSATION, Wage board employees, Prevailing rate employees)

Promotions
Career-ladder
Promotions not mandatory
Provision of negotiated agreement calling for consistent and equitable application of merit promotion principles does not constitute a nondiscretionary agency policy requiring agency to make promotions at any specified time or under specified criteria. The inclusion of a provision in a negotiated agreement does not automatically make it nondiscretionary for purposes of the Back Pay Act. A nondiscretionary provision for such purposes is defined at 5 C.F.R. 550.802(d) to mean one requiring an agency to take prescribed action under stated conditions or criteria. 55 Comp. Gen. 42 is distinguished_____ 59

Retroactive promotions
Backpay
Promotion of employee in career-ladder position was delayed because the promotion request was clerically misplaced before it reached the authorized official. Arbitrator's finding of administrative mistake does not itself provide a basis for award of backpay to grievant. In the absence of a nondiscretionary requirement mandating promotion within a particular time frame or in accordance with specified criteria, loss of promotion request prior to approval by authorized official does not constitute such administrative error as will support award of retroactive promotion and backpay_____ 59

Compensation. (*See* COMPENSATION, Promotions)
Quality step increases
Action erroneously filed a supervisor's insufficiently documented recommendation of a Quality Step Increase (QSI) for an employee, thus causing a delay in the granting of the QSI. Retroactive granting of the QSI may not be made since Action had discretion to grant it and employee had no vested right to it at a particular time under statute or agency regulation_____ 290

OFFICERS AND EMPLOYEES—Continued

  Promotions—Continued

    Temporary—Continued

      Retroactive   **Page**

Employee was detailed from her excepted service position to higher grade competitive service position for 2 years without prior approval from Civil Service Commission. Commission Rule VI requires that employee serving under excepted appointment shall be assigned to competitive service position only with prior approval of Commission. Therefore, although employee was improperly placed in overlong detail she may not receive retroactive temporary promotion. Our *Turner-Caldwell* and *Rankin* decisions make it clear that if certain regulatory requirements concerning an employee's entitlement to retroactive temporary promotion are not met there is no entitlement to retroactive temporary promotion_ 88

Status

  Intermittent employees

Expert appointed on an intermittent basis is not entitled to leave even though he was compensated for 80 hours per pay period for substantially the full term of his employment. His work was assigned on a project basis and the hours at which he worked were largely within his discretion. Since he was not required in advance to report at a definite and certain time within each workweek, he is not entitled to leave as a part-time employee with an established regular tour of duty. He is not entitled to leave as a de facto full-time employee since he was not required to work a standard workweek_ 167

Temporary

  Cancellation of appointment

Civil Service Commission (CSC) directed cancellation of employee's temporary appointment at GS–6 level because of violation of CSC requirements. Since employee has basic qualification for appointment and appointment was not contrary to law it was voidable only and corrective action as ordered by CSC is prospective only. Employee is entitled to all benefits of position to which appointed until separated or transferred. Modified in part by 58 Comp. Gen. 734_ 197

Training

  Compensation payable

Customs Patrol Officers who attended special training course claim overtime pay under the Fair Labor Standards Act (FLSA) or overtime or night premium pay under title 5, United States Code, for regularly scheduled training sessions conducted after 6 p.m. Where training qualifies under exception to prohibition against payment of premium pay for training in 5 U.S.C. 4109(a), overtime under FLSA or overtime or night premium pay under title 5, United States Code, must be paid. Payment should be made to employees under title 5 or under FLSA, whichever law gives the greater benefit. 38 Comp. Gen. 363 (1958) clarified_ _ _ _ _ _ 547

OFFICERS AND EMPLOYEES—Continued
Training—Continued
Equal Employment Opportunity programs

In the absence of specific authority in statute or regulations, appropriated funds may not be expended to procure entertainment for Federal employees. Hence agencies without specific authority may not procure entertainment such as live ethnic music and artistic presentations, characterize it as training and present it in connection with EEO programs. We will not question past agency characterizations of EEO program entertainment as training; however, all future entertainment expenses whether or not in connection with EEO programs will not be allowed_____ 202

Expenses
Reimbursement
Where an employee is sent on a 2-year training assignment overseas under 5 U.S.C. 4109 and is authorized to have his immediate family accompany him, his entitlements to travel and transportation allowances at Government expense on their behalf are limited to those allowances specifically prescribed in that section not to exceed employee's estimated aggregate per diem payable, rather than those prescribed for permanent change-of-station assignments, since assignments for training purposes only are not permanent duty assignments. Since the terms "nontemporary storage of household goods" and "shipment of privately owned vehicles" are not allowances prescribed in that section, neither they, nor related costs, i.e., round-trip travel to pick up a shipped vehicle at port of debarkation, may be reimbursed under that section_____ 253

Transfers
Relocation expenses
Attorney fees
Restrictions on reimbursement
Employee may not be reimbursed for attorney fees assessed by lending institution and initially characterized as part of the "loan origination fee" unless certifying officer determines that such fees were incurred for the purposes specifically excluded from finance charges by Regulation Z, 12 C.F.R. 226.4(e), are reasonable in amount, and insofar as the attorneys fees are sufficiently itemized to show the portion of the origination fee allocable to each excluded item_____ 786

Eligibility
Employees of Postal Service contract compliance unit were transferred to General Services Administration (GSA) incident to a transfer of function. They are not eligible for relocation expenses under 5 U.S.C. 5724 and 5724a since those sections restrict reimbursement to employees of an agency. The term "agency," as defined in 5721(1) and 5 U.S.C. 105, excludes the United States Postal Service. Therefore, individuals who transfer to or from the Postal Service are not eligible for relocation expenses under 5 U.S.C. 5724 and 5724a_____ 13:

OFFICERS AND EMPLOYEES—Continued
  Transfers—Continued
    Relocation expenses—Continued
      House purchase
        Loan origination fee
          Itemization

Employee may be reimbursed for $35 survey fee incident to financing purchase of a residence upon his relocation. Although assessed by the lending institution, the survey fee is expressly excluded from the definition of a finance charge by Regulation Z, 12 C.F.R. 226.4(e)(1), the fee is reasonable in amount, and all-inclusive fee, initially characterized as a "loan origination fee," is sufficiently itemized to show the portion allocable to the survey fee. See *Anthony J. Vrana*, B–189639, March 24, 1978 _

        Recording fees

Although assessed by the lending institution as part of a charge initially characterized as a "loan origination fee," employee may be reimbursed for recording fees if they are customarily paid by purchaser in the area and do not exceed amounts customarily charged in the locality. Federal Travel Regulations 2–6.2c. While recording fees are not expressly excluded from the definition of a finance charge under 12 C.F.R. 226.4(e) they are not a condition for the extension of credit and, thus, are not part of the finance charge as defined by 12 C.F.R. 226.4(a) _ _

      House sale
        Actual residence at time of official transfer requirement

Entitlement to reimbursement for sale of residence incident to a transfer requires (under para. C14000.1–1 of 2 Joint Travel Regulations and para. 2–6.1 of Federal Travel Regulations) that it be the employee's actual residence when he is first definitely notified of the transfer. There was substantial compliance where illness of the employee's wife required living in an apartment pending notice of a transfer and where the employee had not entirely vacated the house before the transfer notice. Reimbursement for sales expense is allowable but subject to deduction of any previous reimbursement for lease termination expenses _ _ _ _ _ _ _ _ _

        Prior to official notice of transfer

Residence selling expenses in anticipation of transfer from Hawaii may be reimbursed where illness of employee's wife did not permit her to continue to live in Hawaii. There was a compelling reason for the transfer in the Government's interest at the time the expenses were incurred, and travel orders based on this compelling reason were subsequently issued authorizing expenses. Accordingly, there was substantial compliance with requirement that there be an administrative intention to transfer the employee when the real estate expenses are incurred. *James A. Colyer*, B–182840, February 18, 1975, modified _ _ _ _ _ _ _ _ _ _ _ _

        Incident to change of official duty station

The words "general local or metropolitan area" as used in paragraph 2–1.5b(1) of the Federal Travel Regulations (FTR) are descriptive rather than restrictive. These are general criteria rather than fixed rules to be narrowly applied in all cases involving transfer between official stations which are relatively close to each other. Therefore, it does not follow that for relocation to be incident to transfer of duty station it must invariably result in less commuting time and distance _ _ _ _ _ _ _ _ _ _ _

OFFICERS AND EMPLOYEES—Continued
Transfers—Continued
Relocation expenses—Continued
House sale—Continued
Mileage
Effect on relocation determination

Where the old duty station and the new duty station are located 77 miles apart and the employee's residence from which he commuted daily 43 miles to the old station is located midway between the two stations, fact that employee chose to relocate to the new station, rather than continue to commute 45 miles daily, does not preclude a determination that the relocation was incident to the transfer_____ 319

New appointees

New appointees cannot be reimbursed travel and relocation expenses from Washington, D.C., to next duty station. Record indicates that agency erroneously indicated Washington as permanent duty station instead of temporary duty station while appointees were trained for 4 months. New appointees must bear expense of reporting to first official duty station and such duty station must be where major part of employees' duties are performed and where they are expected to spend greater part of time. Government is not responsible for unauthorized acts of its agents. Erroneous payments must be collected_____ 744

Overseas employees
Temporary quarters

Army employee who occupies temporary quarters for a 53-day period upon being transferred from Korea to Fort Sheridan, Illinois, claims reimbursement for the period beyond 30 days. Claim may not be allowed as 5 U.S.C. 5724a expressly limits reimbursement for temporary quarters to 30 days except where employee transfers to or from Alaska, Hawaii, the territories or possessions of the United States, Puerto Rico or the Canal Zone, for which an additional 30-day reimbursement may be allowed_____ 807

Transferred to U.S.

Employee, who was transferred from Ankara, Turkey, to Detroit, Michigan, resigned in Washington, D.C. during a debriefing and did not report at Detroit, is not entitled to reimbursement of traveling expenses of himself and wife under relocation travel order since such obligation does not arise until the transfer is consummated by the employee's entrance on duty at his new official station. The employee's travel expenses to Washington do not have to be collected since his travel may be considered temporary duty travel incident to his debriefing_____ 385

Air Force employee in Canal Zone, who was entitled to travel and transportation costs to home of record, transferred to Forest Service in Oregon. Air Force payments of travel and transportation expenses to new station before effective date of Forest Service appointment were proper to extent that they did not exceed constructive costs of travel and transportation to home of record. Principles of 46 Comp. Gen. 628 are not limited to transfers within the Department of Defense_____ 799

OFFICERS AND EMPLOYEES—Continued
  Transfers—Continued
    Relocation expenses—Continued
      Surveyor fees, reports, etc.

OFFICERS AND EMPLOYEES—Continued
  Transfers—Continued
    Relocation expenses—Continued
      Training assignments—Continued
New appointees cannot be reimbursed travel and relocation expenses
from Washington, D.C., to next duty station. Record indicates that
agency erroneously indicated Washington as permanent duty station
instead of temporary duty station while appointees were trained for 4
months. New appointees must bear expense of reporting to first official
duty station and such duty station must be where major part of employees' duties are performed and where they are expected to spend
greater part of time. Government is not responsible for unauthorized
acts of its agents. Erroneous payments must be collected_____

      Transportation for house hunting
        Reimbursement basis
Employee claims additional expenses for temporary quarters subsistence. Agency denied claim because employee had already been paid
for a house-hunting trip. Agency exercised its discretion and followed
policy outlined in Federal Travel Regulations to reduce period for
occupying temporary quarters if house-hunting trip has been made.
Even if method used resulted in reduced cost to Government, it does not
furnish a basis for payment of temporary quarters subsistence. Claim is
denied_____

      Travel expenses. (See TRAVEL EXPENSES, Transfers)
      Travel expenses. (See TRAVEL EXPENSES)
OVERTIME
  Compensation. (See COMPENSATION, Overtime)
PAY
  Civilian employees. (See COMPENSATION)
  Gratuities. (See GRATUITIES)
  Medical and dental officers
    "Variable Incentive Pay"
      Agreement
        Renegotiation
An existing Variable Incentive Pay (VIP) agreement under 37 U.S.C.
313 may not be renegotiated to a lesser commitment by executing a
second VIP contract, even if it had been received by the proper officials.
Terms of the first VIP contract are binding on the parties and where
officer does not complete active service agreed to, he is subject to the
refund provisions of the contract, 37 U.S.C. 313, and the regulations
requiring repayment of amounts received for which service was not
performed_____

  Retired
    Death of member
      Court determination
A claim by a retired Navy member's wife for the member's retired pay
accruing during the 7-year period from the date of his disappearance to
the date he was declared dead by a State court may not be allowed since
retired pay is payable only during the member's life and there is no
showing whether he was alive after his disappearance or evidence of
when he actually died, and the State court determination appears to be
presumptive only and does not establish that the member lived for 7
years_____

PAY—Continued
 Retired—Continued
  Foreign citizenship effect Page

A retired Regular Army officer residing in Israel acquired Israeli citizenship by operation of Israeli law, but also remains a United States citizen. While the loss of United States citizenship is inconsistent with status as a retired Regular officer and thus results in loss of status as an officer and loss of entitlement to retired pay, dual Israeli/United States citizenship alone does not require loss of entitlement to retired pay_____ 566

  Foreign employment
   Congressional consent
    Pub. L. 95–105
     Prospective application

Section 509 of the Foreign Relations Authorization Act, Fiscal Year 1978, granting consent of Congress to the acceptance of foreign civil employment by certain officers of the United States, as required by Article I, section 9, clause 8 of the Constitution, cannot be retroactively applied to retirement pay withheld from an officer for a period he was employed by a foreign state without such consent which occurred prior to the effective date of section 509 _____ 487

The consent of Congress to the acceptance of foreign civil employment and compensation by certain retired members of the uniformed services, as required by Article I, section 9, clause 8 of the Constitution, is granted in section 509 of the Foreign Relations Authorization Act, Fiscal Year 1978, which consent is conditioned upon approval of the employment by the Secretary of State and the Secretary of the service concerned. Such approval is only effective prospectively from the date it is granted and may not be made retroactively to authorize foreign employment and compensation received before the approval is granted. However, once approval is granted withholding of retired pay may be terminated and the payment of retired pay resumed on the date of approval_____ 487

As with the constitutional provision prohibiting retired military officers from accepting emoluments from foreign governments without congressional consent, section 509 of the Foreign Relations Authorization Act, Fiscal Year 1978, which grants such consent, is silent as to any sanctions to be applied. Thus, the rule that retired pay is to be withheld in the amount of the foreign emoluments received is applicable to the law when approval is not granted. However, when approval is granted the legislative history is clear that Congress intended withholding of retired pay to terminate and payment of retired pay be resumed effective on the approval date_____ 487

  Foreign military service effect

A retired Regular Army officer residing in Israel who has dual Israeli/United States citizenship is subject to service in the Israel Defense Forces, the Israeli armed force. Such service in a foreign armed force by a retired Regular Officer appears inherently inconsistent with his position as a Regular Army officer, as well as being prohibited (without congressional consent) by Article I, section 9, clause 8 of the Constitution of the United States. Thus, service in the foreign armed force would make his status as a retired Army officer very doubtful. Retired pay may not be paid to him without authorizing legislation_____ 566

PAY—Continued
  Retired—Continued
    Reservists
      Eligibility   Page

The exceptions to the invocation of 10 U.S.C. 1406, preventing denial of retired pay entitlement due to erroneous written notice of entitlement, are limited to cases of direct fraud or misrepresentation on the part of the person to whom the notice is sent. Where the evidence fails to show that the member caused his service record to be altered or induced the erroneous notice to be sent, the statutory exceptions have not been met. A showing that the member possibly should have had reasonable doubt as to the propriety of the notice is insufficient to serve as a basis to deny entitlement to retired pay at age 60, if he is otherwise qualified.......... 390

      Erroneous notification of eligibility
        What constitutes

The written communication required by 10 U.S.C. 1331(d) as notice to a member of a Reserve component of an armed force advising that he has completed the years of service requirement for retired pay at age 60 need not be in any specific format. So long as the notice is from an authorized activity of his military service and uses appropriate words advising him that he has completed the service requirements for such retired pay at age 60, such notice satisfies the requirements of 10 U.S.C. 1331(d) so as to invoke 10 U.S.C. 1406, thereby preventing denial of retired pay due to administrative error_____ 390

    Survivor Benefit Plan
      Spouse
        Remarriage after age 60
          Loss of DIC eligibility

A deceased Navy officer's widow was receiving a reduced Survivor Benefit Plan (SBP) annuity because she was also entitled to Veterans Administration Dependency and Indemnity Compensation (DIC). She remarried in 1977 after reaching age 60 and thereby lost entitlement to DIC. Under the new provisions of 10 U.S.C. 1450(k), added by sec. 203 of Public Law 95–397, the full SPB annuity may be restored to her upon repayment of retired pay contributions she received when the SBP annuity was reduced. However, under sec. 210(a) of Public Law 95–397, the full annuity may not be paid for months prior to October 1, 1978__ 626

        Social Security offset

The widow of a Survivor Benefit Plan (SBP) participator, who had some post-1956 Social Security covered military service, became entitled to Social Security payments based on the deceased member's total Social Security covered earnings, including the covered military service. For the purpose of the reduction in her SBP annuity required by 10 U.S.C. 1451(a) for Social Security payments attributable to military earnings, it is not necessary that the member acquire a fully insured status based solely on Social Security covered military earnings. Since generally Social Security payments received are enhanced by military covered quarters, the SBP annuity is to be reduced by the amount of the Social Security payment based on the member's military service   795

PAY—Continued
  Retired—Continued
    Waiver for veterans benefits
      Effective date   Page

A retired Regular Air Force Officer employed in a Federal civilian position whose retired pay was subject to reduction under the Dual Compensation Act, 5 U.S.C. 5532, was advised by the Veterans Administration (VA) on February 23, 1978, that he was entitled to VA disability compensation retroactive to June 26, 1977. The officer filed a waiver of retired pay with the service department, pursuant to 38 U.S.C. 3105, on March 3, 1978. Waiver of retired pay upon notification of entitlement to VA compensation is effective from the earliest date of entitlement to VA compensation; but the additional amount due is payable as VA compensation, and not retired pay. *Matter of Lieutenant Colonel Oliver B. Larson*, 55 Comp. Gen. 1402 (1976), is modified_____ 622

    Withholding
      Foreign employment

Amounts of retired pay withheld from members of the uniformed services who accept foreign employment without congressional consent as required by the Constitution should be treated as though the members had no entitlement to them and should not be "held in trust" for them pending possible future congressional consent to their receipt_____ 487

  Selective reenlistment bonus. (*See* GRATUITIES, Selective reenlistment bonus)

  Service credits
    Retention after age and service qualification
      Reserves

Air Force Reserve major generals who have not been eliminated for years of service under 10 U.S.C. 8852 prior to reaching age 60 may receive retirement point credit for service performed after they have attained retirement eligibility under Chapter 67 of title 10, U.S. Code, only if their retention in active status thereafter is approved by the Secretary under 10 U.S.C. 676_____ 674

PAYMENTS
  Absence or unenforceability of contracts
    Acceptance of goods or services by Government
      Payment on *quantum meruit/quantum valebant* basis

Army's purchase of $40,000 worth of mattresses from Army and Air Force Exchange System, in lieu of following normal procurement procedures, is contrary to applicable law and regulations. Since record indicates Army has obtained and received benefit of mattresses, payment may be made on *quantum valebant* basis upon ratification of purchase by appropriate contracting official. Similarly, where record is not sufficient to indicate propriety of Army's obtaining services from NAFIs, payment for services may be made on *quantum meruit* basis pending resolution of the matter_____ 94

Even though costs incurred under contracts awarded pursuant to grant projects were based on cost-plus-percentage-of-cost contracting, contractor can be paid on *quantum meruit/quantum valebat* basis as agency has determined costs to be reasonable and Government received benefit of services_____ 654

PAYMENTS—Continued
  Absence or unenforceability of contracts—Continued
    Appropriation availability
      Fiscal year appropriations
        Contract ratification v. performance date   **Page**
        Payment may be made to a contractor for repair work to Government
equipment even though formal contracting procedures were not followed
because Government received the benefit and has specifically ratified the
transaction. Appropriation available at time contractor was authorized
to and actually performed the repair work should be charged, irrespective
of fiscal year in which the transaction was ratified_____   789

    Advance
      Contracts. (*See* CONTRACTS, Payments, Advance)
      Prohibition
        Payments to State under Federal contract for telephone services,
executed by contracting officer of the United States and obligating
annual appropriation of National Guard, are subject to statutory prohibition against advance payments contained in 31 U.S.C. 529_____   29

    Contracts. (*See* CONTRACTS, Payments)
    In lieu of taxes. (*See* TAXES, Federal payments in lieu of taxes)

PERSONAL SERVICES
  Contracts
    Federal dependents' schools employees
      Compensation
        Rate establishment
        Section IV, Army Procurement Procedure, directed that a clause be
included in dependents' school personal service employment contracts
reserving to school officials the right to amend the rate of pay in conformity with the pay schedules of Department of the Army civilian
employees performing similar duties; hence, the Fort Rucker Elementary
School Board has the right to adopt a policy of having all clerical, janitorial, and other non-teaching positions at the school classified and
equated to comparable civil service positions for pay purposes_____   430

POST EXCHANGES, SHIP STORES, ETC.
  Sales to Department of Defense
    Propriety
      Since basic mission of Department of Defense (DOD) nonappropriated
fund instrumentalities (NAFIs) is to promote morale and welfare of
military personnel and dependents, as a general proposition sale by
NAFIs to regular DOD operating activities would be regarded as outside scope of NAFIs' proper functions except where circumstances require
that agency obtain goods or services from NAFI and such requirement is
properly documented and justified as sole-source procurement_____   94

POSTAL SERVICE, UNITED STATES

Audit

The authority of GAO to render binding decisions with respect to matters involving agency expenditures stems generally from its authority to adjust and settle agency accounts under section 305 of the Budget and Accounting Act of 1921, 31 U.S. Code 71. These settlements are final and conclusive upon the executive branch of the Government. 31 U.S.C. 44 and 74. Opinions of GAO are not binding on either the U.S. Postal Service (USPS) or the Postal Rate Commission (PRC), since 39 U.S.C. 410(a) and 3604(e) exempt the USPS and PRC from the provisions of the Budget and Accounting Act_____ 640

Employees
Transfers
Relocation expenses
Eligibility

Employees of Postal Service contract compliance unit were transferred to General Services Administration (GSA) incident to a transfer of function. They are not eligible for relocation expenses under 5 U.S.C. 5724 and 5724a since those sections restrict reimbursement to employees of an agency. The term "agency," as defined in 5721(1) and 5 U.S.C. 105, excludes the United States Postal Service. Therefore, individuals who transfer to or from the Postal Service are not eligible for relocation expenses under 5 U.S.C. 5724 and 5724a_____ 132

Mails
Government
Insured mail

Federal agencies are prohibited from using insured mail under both 40 U.S.C. 726 and the Government's self-insurance policy since insured mail provides no "special" or "additional" service in addition to the indemnity offered. 3 Comp. Gen. 391 and 22 Comp. Gen. 832, modified__ 14

Registered mail

Neither the Government Losses in Shipment Act, 40 U.S.C. 726 (1970), nor the Government's general self-insurance policy prohibits Federal agencies from using registered mail where administratively determined necessary in order to obtain the "special" service of greater protection in the handling and delivery of mail rather than to obtain the insurance coverage also offered_____ 14

Although as a matter of policy General Accounting Office (GAO) favors the exclusion of the cost of indemnity from the fee for registered mail as a cost savings to the Federal Government, GAO is not the appropriate forum to determine whether the U.S. Postal Service has authority to achieve this objective by establishing this special rate for Federal agencies only, to the exclusion of other users of registered mail, without violating the Postal Reorganization Act_____ 640

Postal rates and classifications
Changes
Procedures

Where Postal Reorganization Act prescribes specific administrative procedures for consideration of proposed changes in mail classification and postal rates and fees and where question of whether a change will result in "undue or unreasonable discrimination among users of the

POSTAL SERVICE, UNITED STATES—Continued
  Postal rates and classifications—Continued
    Changes—Continued
      Procedures—Continued
  mails" or "undue or unreasonable preferences to any such user" is such
  a pervasive and integral part of such decisions, GAO defers to agencies
  with primary jurisdiction on such matter, the USPS and the PRC, who
  can better resolve the issue after providing for opportunity for participation by the United States Government, as well as other users of registered
  mail, in a hearing on the record _

  Services to executive agencies
    Sec. 601, Economy Act applicability
  Section 601 of Economy Act does not require Commerce Department
  to perform comparative cost analysis of plaintiff's proposal versus cost
  of doing work via Commerce—U.S. Postal Service agreement, because
  Economy Act does not apply to agreement for furnishing property or
  services between Postal Service and executive agencies _ _ _ _ _ _ _ _ _ _ _ _ _ _

PRESUMPTIONS (See EVIDENCE, Presumptions)

PROCUREMENT
  Authority
    Department of Defense. (See DEFENSE DEPARTMENT, Procurement,
      Authority)
  Regulations. (See REGULATIONS)
  Solicitation for informational purposes
    Demonstration tests
      Unduly restrictive of competition
        Computers, etc. acquisition
  Procedures established for potential suppliers to demonstrate equipment were unduly restrictive because agency made no apparent effort
  either to examine whether acceptability of equipment could be established through simulation testing techniques as requested by protester
  or to attempt to provide access to Government equipment to facilitate
  testing. GAO recommends that protester be permitted to show acceptability of equipment, particularly in view of alleged successful performance of recent similar contract with other agency _ _ _ _ _ _ _ _ _ _ _ _ _ _ _ _ _ _

PROPERTY
  Private
    Damage, loss, etc.
      Military Personnel and Civilian Employees' Claims Act of 1964
  Military Personnel and Civilian Employees' Claims Act of 1964 provides that claim may be allowed only if use of employee's property under
  the particular circumstances was reasonable, useful, or proper, and if
  damage to employee's property was not caused wholly or partly by
  employee's negligence. Settlement is final and conclusive if statutory
  conditions are met. Claim of National Labor Relations Board employee,
  for damage to motor vehicle resulting from accident where other participant in accident is compensated under Federal Tort Claims Act, is
  not cognizable under Military Personnel and Civilian Employees' Claims
  Act since settlement under Federal Tort Claims Act amounts to determination of employee's negligence _

  Real. (See REAL PROPERTY)

PROTESTS
Contracts. (*See* CONTRACTS, Protests)

PUBLIC HEALTH SERVICE
Commissioned personnel
Active service obligation
Failure to complete
Entitlements

A commissioned officer of the Public Health Service who does not complete a term of active service to which he agreed in writing may be divested of entitlement to lump-sum annual leave and travel and transportation entitlements in accordance with regulations promulgated by the Public Health Service under 37 U.S.C. 501(g) and paragraph M6457 of 1 Joint Travel Regulations, promulgated under 37 U.S.C. 404(b) and 406(c) _

Pay, etc.
Variable Incentive Pay

An existing Variable Incentive Pay (VIP) agreement under 37 U.S.C. 313 may not be renegotiated to a lesser commitment by executing a second VIP contract, even if it had been received by the proper officials. Terms of the first VIP contract are binding on the parties and where officer does not complete active service agreed to, he is subject to the refund provisions of the contract, 37 U.S.C. 313, and the regulations requiring repayment of amounts received for which service was not performed _

PURCHASES
Improper, etc.
Disregard of ASPR/DAR

Army's purchase of $40,000 worth of mattresses from Army and Air Force Exchange System, in lieu of following normal procurement procedures, is contrary to applicable law and regulations. Since record indicates Army has obtained and received benefit of mattresses, payment may be made on *quantum valebant* basis upon ratification of purchase by appropriate contracting official. Similarly, where record is not sufficient to indicate propriety of Army's obtaining services from NAFIs, payment for services may be made on *quantum meruit* basis pending resolution of the matter _

Purchase orders
Evaluation propriety

Where vendor under Federal Supply Schedule (FSS) contract apprises procuring activity shortly before award that it offers "middle of the line" equipment and procuring activity only has specifications for vendor's "top of the line" equipment, procuring activity, in attempt to reduce procurement costs, should have attempted to obtain specifications from vendor or General Services Administration and determine if "middle of the line" equipment would satisfy Government's legitimate needs. However, since vendor should have advised agency of middle of line equipment earlier in procurement process and offered equipment met agency's minimum needs and has been delivered and installed, award will not be disturbed _

QUARTERS ALLOWANCE
Basic allowance for quarters (BAQ)
Assigned to Government quarters
Partial allowance entitlement

A Navy member assigned Government single-type quarters (barracks), and who is ineligible for regular basic allowance for quarters (BAQ) under 37 U.S.C. 403(b), is entitled to "partial" BAQ under 37 U.S.C. 1009(d). Neither the member's temporary duty status, between permanent duty stations, nor his pay grade (E–4, less than 4 years' service, or below) precludes him from receiving partial BAQ_____ 136

Rate payable
Child support payments by separated or divorced member

A member paying child support to divorced or estranged spouse who is also a member of the uniformed services is not entitled to an increase in basic allowance for quarters based upon the child support if the former or estranged spouse and child are provided adequate family-type quarters by the Government. 45 Comp. Gen. 146, overruled in part_____ 100

Civilian overseas employees
Entitlement
Administrative discretion

General Accounting Office has no basis for overturning administrative determination, required by regulations, which fixed approved rent ceiling for employee's overseas private quarters at amount below rent he was actually paying and thereby disqualified employee for payment of living quarters allowance (LQA). Governing law and regulations give agencies considerable discretion concerning payment of LQA and there is no evidence of arbitrary and capricious exercise of discretion by agency_____ 738

Occupancy of quarters
Child support payments by separated or divorced member
Basic allowance for quarters

The basic allowance for quarters at the with dependent rate is not payable to a member living in adequate single-type Government quarters and paying child support to an estranged or divorced spouse when that spouse is also a service member and assigned to adequate family-type Government quarters. 45 Comp. Gen. 146, overruled in part_____ 100

REAL PROPERTY
Acquisition
Condemnation proceedings
Uniform Relocation Assistance and Real Property Acquisition Policies Act of 1970

Title III of the Uniform Relocation Assistance and Real Property Acquisition Policies Act of 1970, Pub. L. No. 91–646, 84 Stat. 1894, 42 U.S.C. 4601 *et seq.* (1976), sets forth uniform and equitable procedures for the taking of real property by Federal Government or by State agencies receiving Federal financial assistance. Pursuant to section 305, provisions of Title III are mandatory, to the extent practicable, upon States as condition to their receipt of Federal financial assistance. Title III is applicable to acquisition of any interest in real property, including easements, even where acquisition is funded solely by local funds, if underlying program or project is Federally administered or assisted_____ 559

REGULATIONS—Continued
Legality
Military personnel
Leaves of absence
Lump-sum payments

An amendment to 37 U.S.C. 501(b) deleted inclusion of allowances in lump-sum leave payments to military members upon discharge; however, a saving provision retained entitlement to include the allowances for leave accrued prior to the amendment. Although the claimant contends that the services' regulation determining when a member will be charged with use of preamendment leave frustrates congressional intent of the saving provision, in view of the services' authority to prescribe regulations for accrual and use of leave, the language and legislative history of the amendment, the regulation is proper_____ 635

Modification
Review by General Accounting Office

Under section 601(a) of the Powerplant and Industrial Fuel Use Act of 1978, a State Governor may designate an impacted area based on his finding that employment in coal or uranium production activities "increased for the most recent calendar year by 8 percent or more from the immediately preceding year." Both the plain meaning of the statute and its legislative history support the view that "the most recent calendar year" is determined with respect to the time of the Governor's finding, and not, with respect to any calendar year since 1975, of 8 percent increased employment. Final regulations of the Farmers Home Administration for the Energy Impacted Area Development Assistance Program should include an amended definition of "base year" consistent with this decision_____ 541

Procurement
General Services Administration
Legality
Multi-award FSS contracts
Late proposal consideration

Manufacturers' late proposals, submitted after closing date for receipt of proposals and timely receipt of dealer's proposal for "identical" product, do not constitute "only proposal received" within meaning of Federal Procurement Regulation 1–3.802–1(c) which permits consideration of late proposals and may not be considered for award_____ 656

Promotion procedures
Approval authority

Employee grieved due to delay in processing promotion papers. Grievance Examiner found that although promotion papers reached personnel office and were acted upon by classification officers prior to beginning of new pay period, grievant's papers were not approved by Personnel Officer until after beginning of new pay period. Grievance Examiner concluded that classification officer acted for Personnel Officer and ordered retroactive promotion. Award may not be implemented since agency regulations delegate authority to approve promotions to Personnel Officer and he has not further delegated that authority in writing_____ 51

SMALL BUSINESS ADMINISTRATION—Continued
  Loans—Continued
    Guaranteed loan programs
      Fiscal agents
        Errors
Where due to alleged clerical inadvertence date of note and date of disbursement of loan differ, it is not necessary to decide which date is controlling for purposes of determining whether guarantee fee was paid prior to default, because even assuming that default occurred prior to payment of guarantee fee, subsequent full payment by Borrower would have brought loan into fully paid, current status, thereby curing any existing default and enabling SBA to purchase guaranteed portion of loan_____

      Refinancing of defaulted loan
Small Business Administration (SBA) has discretion in appropriate case, subject to applicable statutory or regulatory provisions, to approve refinancing of existing non-guaranteed loan by new SBA guaranteed loan. Therefore, Bank's failure to pay guarantee fee prior to default on initial loan, thereby extinguishing guarantee on that loan pursuant to our decision B-181432, March 13, 1975, may not necessarily defeat otherwise valid guarantee of subsequent refinancing loan. B-181432, July 7, 1978, modified (extended)_____

    Sale
      Federal Financing Bank
Small Business Administration (SBA) does have authority to issue certificates to Federal Financing Bank (FFB) evidencing ownership of group of SBA loans. Proposed financing arrangements, as well as SBA's current procedure of selling individual loans to FFB with recourse, is sufficiently similar from legal standpoint to financing arrangements our Office has approved in past. Also, SBA has same authority to sell loans to FFB with recourse as it has to sell to other purchasers_____

SOCIAL SECURITY
  Medicare, Medicaid, etc.
    Reduction in Federal share
      Waiver
Under section 1903 (g) of the Social Security Act, 42 U.S.C. 1396b(g), as amended, the Secretary may waive otherwise required reductions in Medicaid payments to a State if he finds that the State's showing for the last quarter of calendar year 1977 was (1) on its face, satisfactorily in compliance with specified statutory requirements and (2) valid (i.e., actually in compliance with those requirements). In order to have a satisfactory showing, subsection 1903(g) (1) (D) requires an annual on-site evaluation by the State. Even though the State of Colorado may have complied with the other requirements, the Secretary has no authority to grant it a waiver of reductions since he has been unable to validate the State's compliance with that subsection_____

STATES

Contracts with Federal Government. (*See* CONTRACTS, Federal-State contracts)

Federal aid, grants, etc.
Administration
Cost limitations

The 3 percent administrative overhead and indirect cost limitations of the Pittman-Robertson and Dingell-Johnson Acts, 16 U.S.C. 669e(c) and 777e(c) respectively, apply to costs incurred by an agency or department—a central service activity—of the State whose functions include regularly performing services not for its own constitutent elements but all agencies of the State. Therefore, they do not apply to costs incurred by the Colorado Department of Natural Resources (DNR) in providing services to its Division of Wildlife even though the Division may exercise control over its programs, since for administrative purposes it is a part of DNR and any services provided by DNR to it are of an intra-departmental nature_____

Amendment, etc.
Appropriation availability

ACTION's proposed grant modification to expand the area from which enrollees in a demonstration youth employment project are drawn to include an additional county would not enlarge the grant's scope because the statutory authority for the grant (section 348(a) of the Comprehensive Employment and Training Act of 1973, as added by the Youth Employment and Demonstration Project Act of 1977, Pub. L. 95–93, 91 Stat. 645, 29 U.S.C.A. 849g) and the interagency agreement with the Department of Labor delegating this authority to ACTION support the conclusion that the proposed amendment is necessary to carry out the original purpose of the grant. Accordingly, such an amendment would not require the obligation of current fiscal year appropriated funds_____

Federal statutory restrictions

Under section 601(a) of the Powerplant and Industrial Fuel Use Act of 1978, a State Governor may designate an impacted area based on his finding that employment in coal or uranium production activities "increased for the most recent calendar year by 8 percent or more from the immediately preceding year." Both the plain meaning of the statute and its legislative history support the view that "the most recent calendar year" is determined with respect to the time of the Governor's finding, and not, with respect to any calendar year since 1975, of 8 percent increased employment. Final regulations of the Farmers Home Administration for the Energy Impacted Area Development Assistance Program should include an amended definition of "base year" consistent with this decision_____

STATES—Continued
    Federal aid, grants, etc.—Continued
        Matching fund activities
            Aggregation of state contributions   Page

Since 1967, Department of Agriculture has interpreted annual appropriation provision requiring "minimum matching by any State of at least 40 per centum" as allowing accumulation of all contributions by a State since 1963 to determine if matching requirement for brucellosis program has been met. For 1979, provision was changed to require matching "by the States" on a 60/40 basis. Agriculture believes this change authorizes aggregation of all State contributions since 1963 rather than on State-by-State basis. Provisions in annual appropriation acts, unless otherwise provided, apply only to that fiscal year and neither language nor legislative history of these provisions support Agriculture's interpretation. However, in view of longstanding practice we will not object to this practice for this year_____   524

        Relocation allowances and assistance
            Persons displaced by federally assisted programs
Title II of the Uniform Relocation Assistance and Real Property Acquisition Policies Act of 1970, Pub. L. 91–646, 84 Stat. 1894, 42 U.S.C. 4601 et seq. (1976), is inapplicable to Federal Government or State agency acquisition of property for a program or project undertaken by a Federal agency or with Federal financial assistance, where property owner is not displaced or relocated as a result of such acquisition _____   559

        Restrictions imposed by law
            Real property acquisition
Title III of the Uniform Relocation Assistance and Real Property Acquisition Policies Act of 1970, Pub. L. 91–646, 84 Stat. 1894, 42 U.S.C. 4601 et seq. (1976), sets forth uniform and equitable procedures for the taking of real property by Federal Government or by State agencies receiving Federal financial assistance. Pursuant to section 305, provisions of Title III are mandatory, to the extent practicable, upon States as condition to their receipt of Federal financial assistance. Title III is applicable to acquisition of any interest in real property, including easements, even where acquisition is funded solely by local funds, if underlying program or project is Federally administered or assisted_____   559

    Federal payments in lieu of taxes
        Distribution to single or special purpose districts
Payments to units of local government under section 2(a)(1) of the Payments in Lieu of Taxes Act of 1976, 31 U.S.C. 1601–1607, are to be reduced only by the amounts of payments actually received by the units of local government under the statutes specified in section 4 of the Act, 31 U.S.C. 1604. Thus, Federal revenues paid to a State under the statutes in section 4 and distributed by the State directly to a school district without being received or acted upon by a unit of local government should not be deducted from payments to that unit of local government under section 2(a)(1) of the Act, 31 U.S.C. 1602(a)(1). Payments to other single or special purpose districts should be treated in a similar manner_____   19

STATES—Continued
License, permit, etc. fees
Federal agency liability

Section 404(t), Federal Water Pollution Control Act, as amended, requires Federal agencies to comply with State substantive or procedural requirements governing discharge in navigable waters of dredged material to same extent as "any person." Section 67, Pub. L. No. 95–217. Federal agencies must get permits if required by State for activity in question, whether or not State has taken over from United States administration of program for issuance of dredging permits. In present case, however, Wisconsin permit requirement does not pertain to dredging activities. Therefore, section 404(t) does not apply and permit fee may not be paid _____ 193

In the absence of express Presidential exemption, the 1977 Amendment to section 118 of the Clean Air Act requires Federal facilities to abide by State and local laws regarding abatement and control of pollution, to same extent as nongovernmental entity, including obtaining permits and paying associated fees. Therefore Air Force must pay permit fee to municipal air pollution control authority for operation of equipment which would be subject to municipality's air pollution control regulations if operated by nongovernmental entity _____ 244

STATUTES OF LIMITATION
Claims
Date of accrual
Compensation payments
Back pay

Employee of Federal Aviation Administration alleges he was detailed to a higher grade position from July 1968 to July 1969. Employee's claim is barred by the statute of limitation which precludes consideration of a claim not received in our Office within 6 years after the date first accrued. Claim accrues on the date services in question were performed, not on the date that *Turner-Caldwell* was decided. 50 Comp. Gen. 607 and 34 Comp. Gen. 605, distinguished _____ 3

Ten year period for filing
Reduced to six

Time limit for filing claims in General Accounting Office was changed from 10 to 6 years effective July 2, 1975, and claims received on that date which accrued prior to July 2, 1969, are barred _____ 738

Set off right after action barred. (*See* SET-OFF, Statutes of limitation effect)

STATUTORY CONSTRUCTION
General and specific statutes
Precedence

Federal Reserve Act, as amended, expressly excepts the appointment and compensation of all employees of the Board of Governors, Federal Reserve System, from the provisions of the civil service laws and regulations. The Act must be given priority over a subsequently enacted statute applicable to Federal agencies generally, absent a clear indication that the Congress intended otherwise. Hence, the provisions of Civil Service Reform Act of 1978 establishing a Senior Executive Service do not apply to the employees of the Board _____ 687

STATUTORY CONSTRUCTION—Continued
Legislative intent
Typographical errors Page

Public Law 95-480 appropriates $36,606,000 for the Office of Inspector General, Department of Health, Education, and Welfare, despite convincing evidence in legislative history showing that each House of Congress passed bill appropriating $1,000,000 less and that figure in enrolled bill was the result of typographical error. Enrolled act, signed by the Speaker of the House of Representatives and the President of the Senate, and approved by the President of the United States, is conclusive evidence of the contents of a law passed by Congress_____ 358

STORAGE
Household effects
Overseas employees
Nontemporary

Where an employee is sent on a 2-year training assignment overseas under 5 U.S.C. 4109 and is authorized to have his immediate family accompany him, his entitlements to travel and transportation allowances at Government expense on their behalf are limited to those allowances specifically prescribed in that section not to exceed employee's estimated aggregate per diem payable, rather than those prescribed for permanent change-of-station assignments, since assignments for training purposes only are not permanent duty assignments. Since the terms "nontemporary storage of household goods" and "shipment of privately owned vehicles" are not allowances prescribed in that section, neither they, nor related costs, i.e., round-trip travel to pick up a shipped vehicle at port of debarkation, may be reimbursed under that section_____ 253

SUBCONTRACTS
Generally. (*See* **CONTRACTS, Subcontracts**)

SUBSISTENCE
Per diem
Actual expenses
Fractional days
Ten hours or less

Employee, whose duty station is in New York City, traveled to high-rate geographical area, Newark, New Jersey, from his home in Brooklyn, New York. Period of travel was less than 10 hours and he is not entitled to reimbursement of $2.75, cost of lunch incurred in Newark. Restriction in para. 1-7.6d(1), Federal Travel Regulations (FTR), that per diem is generally not allowable for periods of travel of 10 hours or less in a calendar day has application to employee being reimbursed actual subsistence expenses for travel to a high-rate geographical area. See FTR para. 1-8.1a. B-184489, April 16, 1976, distinguished_____ 810

Delays
Awaiting transportation
Excursion rates

For purposes of qualifying for per diem a member of the uniformed services may be considered to be in a travel status for the extra time required to take advantage of a reduced air fare if it can be shown that the increased travel time will not interfere with the performance of official business, is not for personal convenience, and the cost of the extra per diem when added to the cost of the reduced fare does not exceed what the Government would have been required to pay had the reduced fare not been used_____ 710

TAXES
Federal
Refunds
Military records correction
Disability in lieu of years of service

Where military records are corrected under 10 U.S.C. 1552 to show a portion of taxable retired pay as tax exempt disability retired pay, the claimant may be paid, under 10 U.S.C. 1552(c), the amounts of pay withheld for income taxes by the Air Force in years for which the Internal Revenue Service is barred from making tax refunds by the applicable statute of limitations. However, while 10 U.S.C. 1552(c) provides for certain types of payments pursuant to correction of military records, it does not authorize payment for tax refunds in derogation of the Internal Revenue Code statute of limitations beyond monies withheld for taxes by the military department concerned_____ 528

Federal payments in lieu of taxes
To units of local government
Deduction propriety

Payments to units of local government under section 2(a)(1) of the Payments in Lieu of Taxes Act of 1976, 31 U.S.C. 1601–1607, are to be reduced only by the amounts of payments actually received by the units of local government under the statutes specified in section 4 of the Act, 31 U.S.C. 1604. Thus, Federal revenues paid to a State under the statutes in section 4 and distributed by the State directly to a school district without being received or acted upon by a unit of local government should not be deducted from payments to that unit of local government under section 2(a)(1) of the Act, 31 U.S.C. 1602(a)(1). Payments to other single or special purpose districts should be treated in a similar manner_____ 19

Relocation expenses
Transfers
Officers and employees. (*See* OFFICERS AND EMPLOYEES, Transfers, Relocation expenses, Taxes)

TELEPHONES
Contract for services
Federal-State agreements
Advance payments
Legality

Advance payment of capital cost of telephone equipment under contract for telephone services with State would be in violation of 31 U.S.C. 529, even though a State is the recipient, since services to be provided by State are commercial in nature_____ 29

Furnished by Government
Without charge
Private organizations

Available space and services may be provided to Federal Credit Union Service Centers if approved by the appropriate officer or agency. 12 U.S.C. 1770 (1976). Also, General Accounting Office will not raise legal objection if credit union is allowed to use desks, chairs, and office machines without charge. However, agency funds are hereafter not available to furnish without charge telephone services for credit union_____ 610

TENNESSEE VALLEY AUTHORITY
Condemnation proceedings
Fees
Expert witnesses

Generally, fees and expenses of expert witnesses appointed by the court in land condemnation proceedings, whether on motion of the court or at request of a party, are considered to be expenses of litigation and are therefore pursuant to Rule 706, Federal Rules of Evidence, payable by the litigating agency. However, where Tennessee Valley Authority (TVA) is the litigating agency, courts have held that costs in condemnation case cannot be assessed against TVA. Courts have also held that costs may not be assessed against the condemnee. Since neither party may pay such costs, if court so orders, the Administrative Office of the United States Courts may pay litigation expenses from Judiciary appropriations. 52 Comp. Gen. 621 (1973) will no longer be followed......... 259

TIMBER SALES
Contracts
Modification
Mutual mistake
Reformation of contract

Bidder is justified in placing reasonable reliance on estimates stated in purchaser road credit portion of timber sale contract; if, as here, agency negligently states unreasonable estimate for road clearing, mutual mistake as to accuracy of estimate exists and reformation of contract to allow additional compensation for doing required clearing work is proper. Prior denial of claim is reversed; decision in B-193399, Dec. 5, 1978, overruled_____ 388

TORTS
Claims under Federal Tort Claims Act
Private property damage, etc.
Settlement
Effect

Military Personnel and Civilian Employees' Claims Act of 1964 provides that claim may be allowed only if use of employee's property under the particular circumstances was reasonable, useful, or proper, and if damage to employee's property was not caused wholly or partly by employee's negligence. Settlement is final and conclusive if statutory conditions are met. Claim of National Labor Relations Board employee, for damage to motor vehicle resulting from accident where other participant in accident is compensated under Federal Tort Claims Act, is not cognizable under Military Personnel and Civilian Employees' Claims Act since settlement under Federal Tort Claims Act amounts to determination of employee's negligence_____ 291

Wrongful death

Wrongful death judgment against United States for $373,431, apportioned equally by court among four heirs, is subject to interest limitations in 31 U.S.C. 724a (applied as it existed at time of judgment, prior to 1977 amendment), since each judgment beneficiary received severable and distinct amount less than $100,000. This decision modified (extended) by 59 Comp. Gen.————(B-193927, Feb. 13, 1980)_____ 67

TRANSPORTATION
Automobiles
Authority
Employee transferred in August 1977 from San Diego, California, to Denver, Colorado, drove to new station. Although authorized the use of a second automobile, his wife and children traveled by air and shipped the second car by commercial carrier. The transportation costs of the dependents and automobile plus per diem are less than the constructive entitlement of the dependents' travel by automobile. In the absence of specific statutory authorization required by 5 U.S.C. 5727(a), employee's claim for the cost of shipping his privately owned vehicle from San Diego to Denver may not be paid_____

Overseas employees
Reimbursement basis
Where an employee is sent on a 2-year training assignment overseas under 5 U.S.C. 4109 and is authorized to have his immediate family accompany him, his entitlements to travel and transportation allowances at Government expense on their behalf are limited to those allowances specifically prescribed in that section not to exceed employee's estimated aggregate per diem payable, rather than those prescribed for permanent change-of-station assignments, since assignments for training purposes only are not permanent duty assignments. Since the terms "nontemporary storage of household goods" and "shipment of privately owned vehicles" are not allowances prescribed in that section, neither they, nor related costs, i.e., round-trip travel to pick up a shipped vehicle at port of debarkation, may be reimbursed under that section_____

Freight
Charges
Delivery requirement
Since there is no indication in legislative history that Congress in amending the Shipping Act, 1916, intended to repeal statutory and regulatory scheme which on shipments moving under Government bills of lading requires delivery to destination to earn freight charges, contrary provisions in carrier's LASH bill of lading are ineffective to support payment of additional freight charges_____

More than one rate applicable
Where either of two rates may be applied the shipper is entitled to the rate which produces the lowest charges on the shipment_____

Mileage basis payment. (*See* MILEAGE)
Rates
Intrastate
Applicability
United States and carrier may contract independently of tariff filed with State regulatory commission although, in absence of contract, tariff applies. Government officers have no authority to contract for interstate or intrastate transportation at rates higher than those available to the general public for the same or similar services_____

TRANSPORTATION—Continued
  Rates—Continued
    Special agreements
      Special v. tariff rates   **Page**
      United States and carrier may contract independently of tariff filed
      with State regulatory commission although, in absence of contract, tariff
      applies. Government officers have no authority to contract for interstate
      or intrastate transportation at rates higher than those available to the
      general public for the same or similar services 375

  Travel agencies
    Restriction on use
      A member of the uniformed services, to take advantage of a low cost
      charter flight, purchased transportation for official travel with personal
      funds from a travel agency. Since traveler was not aware of the regula-
      tion which precludes use of travel agencies he may be reimbursed an
      amount not exceeding the cost of the transportation if it had been
      purchased directly from the carrier 710

TRAVEL EXPENSES
  Air travel
    Excursion rates
      Delay in travel to obtain
      For purposes of qualifying for per diem a member of the uniformed
      services may be considered to be in a travel status for the extra time
      required to take advantage of a reduced air fare if it can be shown that
      the increased travel time will not interfere with the performance of
      official business, is not for personal convenience, and the cost of the
      extra per diem when added to the cost of the reduced fare does not ex-
      ceed what the Government would have been required to pay had the
      reduced fare not been used 710

    Fly America Act
      Applicability
      Requirement to use U.S. Flag air carriers unless those carriers are
      "unavailable" applies to Government invitees even though traveler is
      unaware of statutory provisions and inviting agency fails to make
      proper travel arrangements. 49 U.S.C. 1517 612

      Foreign air carriers
        Reimbursement basis
        Where U.S. air carriers were available from last point of official
        business, but where traveler combined personal business with his return
        travel and used a train and a foreign air carrier for segments of the
        journey, the traveler may not be reimbursed travel expenses representing
        revenues diverted from U.S. air carriers to foreign air carriers. Using the
        fare proration method set forth in 56 Comp. Gen. 209 (1977), the Fly
        America Act penalty is determined by subtracting the rail fare from the
        amount of revenues lost by U.S. air carriers determined under that
        formula 649

      Employee who transferred to Korea in May 1975, indirectly routed
      his travel by way of Paris, and used foreign airlines for all or a portion
      of his travel may be reimbursed for constructive air fare without penalty
      for travel by foreign air carrier. For the period following enactment of

TREASURY DEPARTMENT
  Bureau of the Mint
    Contracts with foreign governments
      Coin manufacture   Page
      Buy American Act does not apply to Bureau of Mint purchases of
metal for use in manufacturing coins for foreign government because such
acquisitions are not for public use under terms of Buy American Act____   327

UNIONS
  Agreements
    Legality
      Federal Labor Relations Authority requests decision whether collec-
tive bargaining agreement provision conflicts with the Comptroller
General's standards for waiver contained in 4 C.F.R. Part 91. Agreement requires agency to notify employee of error within 5 days of payment to employee or overpayment will be waived. Where agreement
does not consider employee's obligation to inquire as to correctness of
payment, it is inconsistent with standards for waiver and may not be
implemented_____   721

VETERANS
  Compensation payments
    Retired pay
      Waiver
      A retired Regular Air Force Officer employed in a Federal civilian
position whose retired pay was subject to reduction under the Dual Compensation Act, 5 U.S.C. 5532, was advised by the Veterans Administration (VA) on February 23, 1978, that he was entitled to VA disability
compensation retroactive to June 26, 1977. The officer filed a waiver of
retired pay with the service department, pursuant to 38 U.S.C. 3105, on
March 3 1978. Waiver of retired pay upon notification of entitlement to
VA compensation is effective from the earliest date of entitlement to VA
compensation; but the additional amount due is payable as VA compensation, and not retired pay. *Matter of Lieutenant Colonel Oliver B.
Larson*, 55 Comp. Gen. 1402 (1976), is modified_____   622

VEHICLES
  Transportation. (*See* TRANSPORTATION, Automobiles)

VOLUNTARY SERVICES
  Officers and employees
    Waiver of portion or all of statutory salary
      Some members of the United States Metric Board desire to waive their
compensation while other members desire to accept it but return it as a
gift to the Board. Here the statute authorizes payment of Board members at a rate not to exceed the daily rate currently being paid grade 18 of
the General Schedule. Such pay is not considered salary fixed by or pursuant to statute which would preclude waiver. Also, since statute authorizes acceptance of gifts and donations, members may make gifts of
their salary to the agency. However, the members would be liable for
the income tax on such salary and would be entitled only to the limited
deduction for charitable contributions prescribed by the Internal
Revenue Service. 57 Comp. Gen. 423 and 54 *id.* 393, distinguished_____   383

WAIVERS
  Debt collection. (*See* DEBT COLLECTIONS, Waiver)

WATER

Pollution prevention
Water Pollution Control Act
State requirements

Section 404(t), Federal Water Pollution Control Act, as amended, requires Federal agencies to comply with State substantive or procedural requirements governing discharge in navigable waters of dredged material to same extent as "any person." Section 67, Pub. L. No. 95–217. Federal agencies must get permits if required by State for activity in question, whether or not State has taken over from United States administration of program for issuance of dredging permits. In present case, however, Wisconsin permit requirement does not pertain to dredging activities. Therefore, section 404(t) does not apply and permit fee may not be paid_____

WITNESSES

Fees. (See FEES, Witnesses)

WORDS AND PHRASES

"Adverse agency action"

Protest filed with General Accounting Office (GAO) more than 10 working days after receipt by protester of notice that another firm has been selected for award, despite pending protest filed with agency, is untimely since selection constituted adverse agency action as defined in GAO Bid Protest Procedures_____

"Agency"

Employees of Postal Service contract compliance unit were transferred to General Services Administration (GSA) incident to a transfer of function. They are not eligible for relocation expenses under 5 U.S.C. 5724 and 5724a since those sections restrict reimbursement to employees of an agency. The term "agency," as defined in 5721(1) and 5 U.S.C. 105, excludes the United States Postal Service. Therefore, individuals who transfer to or from the Postal Service are not eligible for relocation expenses under 5 U.S.C. 5724 and 5724a_____

"Base year"

Under section 601(a) of the Powerplant and Industrial Fuel Use Act of 1978, a State Governor may designate an impacted area based on his finding that employment in coal or uranium production activities "increased for the most recent calendar year by 8 percent or more from the immediately preceding year." Both the plain meaning of the statute and its legislative history support the view that "the most recent calendar year" is determined with respect to the time of the Governor's finding, and not, with respect to any calendar year since 1975, of 8 percent increased employment. Final regulations of the Farmers Home Administration for the Energy Impacted Area Development Assistance Program should include an amended definition of "base year" consistent with this decision_____

"Basic ordering agreement"

Procuring activity's use of basic ordering agreement (BOA) to exclude previously unapproved suppliers that may be capable of furnishing acceptable products and to effect sole-source procurements with BOA contractor contravenes ASPR 3–410.2(c)(1) (1976 ed.) prohibition against using BOA in any manner to restrict competition_____

WORDS AND PHRASES—Continued

"Government as stakeholder"

Army, although a mere stakeholder, became liab'e to Miller Act surety where surety notified Army of unpaid claims against contractor and asserted its prior rights to contract retainages, but where through clerical error, Army mailed final payments to contractor rather than to surety as agreed by all parties. Surety may be paid upon submission of evidence that all outstanding claims have been paid and surety assigns to Government any right it may have to recoup erroneous payments made to contractor_____ 64

"Grant agreement"

Complaint that executive agency abandoned practice of awarding contracts under Federal procurement procedures in favor of grant awards in order to make sole-source award and avoid statutory requirements for competition is denied where record discloses agency awarded grant, rather than contract, for purpose of complying with requirements of Federal Grant and Cooperative Agreement Act of 1977_____ 785

"High work"

General Services Administration (GSA) questions legality of Federal Labor Relations Council decision requiring payment of environmental differential for "high work." GSA believes payment is unauthorized because of mistakes of fact concerning height of structure and existence of protective wall. Grievance agreement upheld by Council may be implemented since under Federal Personnel Manual the parties may determine entitlement through collective bargaining process. Furthermore, authorization of environmental differential in the present case does not appear to be contrary to law or regulation or to be arbitrary or capricious_____ 331

"Impairment"

National Bureau of Standards finances operations in part by charges to users of its services, paid into Working Capital Fund. Earned net income of the Fund must be paid into Treasury annually, except that it "may be applied first to restore any prior impairment" of the Fund. 15 U.S.C. 278b (1976). Impairments contemplated by this provision are operating losses. Bureau may not retain profits to offset increased costs—caused by inflation—of replacing equipment or facilities, nor can Bureau calculate depreciation of equipment and facilities based on replacement cost_____ 9

"Indian tribes"

"Indians"

Department of the Interior states that unless otherwise provided, most statutes referring to "Indians" do so within a context which actully means "Indian tribes." HEW contends that statute authorizing benefits to, among others, governing bodies of Indian tribes on Federal and State reservations (including a reservation of a State recognized tribe) and to public and non-profit private agencies serving Indian organizations in urban or rural non-reservation areas confers benefits on Lumbee Indians, who are a State recognized, non-reservation tribe. In absence of clear indication in language or history of Native American Programs Act of 1974 of intended beneficiaries, General Accounting Office will not object to HEW's determination that the Lumbees are eligible to participate in the Act's programs_____ 699

WORDS AND PHRASES—Continued

"Leader Company Procurement"   Page

Where only one firm can supply system deemed necessary, there is no violation of "Leader Company Procurement" regulations (DAR 4–701)_   575

Lumbee Indians

Final sentence of Pub. L. No. 84–570 states that nothing in Act will make Lumbee Indians eligible for Federal services performed for Indians and that none of Federal statutes affecting Indians because of their status as Indians shall be applicable to Lumbee Indians. Purpose of this provision is to assure that Act was not used in and of itself to acquire Federal benefits. However, provision does not deny to Lumbees benefits accorded Indians if they are otherwise entitled under the requirements of another Act_____   699

"Maybank Amendment"

Solicitation provision permitting firm's status as labor surplus area concern to be considered in case of tie bids is intended for use primarily in formal advertising and in negotiated procurements where award is to be made on basis of price. Where, however, proposals are "tied" based on evaluation of both technical and price factors, consideration of labor surplus area concern status would not be improper and would not involve violation of Maybank Amendment_____   263

Most recent calendar year

Under section 601(a) of the Powerplant and Industrial Fuel Use Act of 1978, a State Governor may designate an impacted area based on his finding that employment in coal or uranium production activities "increased for the most recent calendar year by 8 percent or more from the immediately preceding year." Both the plain meaning of the statute and its legislative history support the view that "the most recent calendar year" is determined with respect to the time of the Governor's finding, and not, with respect to any calendar year since 1975, of 8 percent increased employment. Final regulations of the Farmers Home Administration for the Energy Impacted Area Development Assistance Program should include an amended definition of "base year" consistent with this decision_____   541

"Negative-response" method

Incident to introduction of Series EE Savings Bonds to replace Series E Bonds being purchased by payroll allotment, Treasury proposes to substitute Series EE Bonds based on a "negative-response" method, whereby the Series EE Bonds will be substituted unless the employee terminates his allotment. Since the Series EE Bonds are a continuation without major substantive change of the Series E Bonds, the negative-response method of conversion is a proper means of continuing the employee's voluntary allotment under the Payroll Savings Plan. The proposal is approved_____   681

"Only proposal received"

Manufacturers' late proposals, submitted after closing date for receipt of proposals and timely receipt of dealer's proposal for "identical" product, do not constitute "only proposal received" within meaning of Federal Procurement Regulation 1–3.802–1(c) which permits consideration of late proposals and may not be considered for award_____   656

WORDS AND PHRASES—Continued

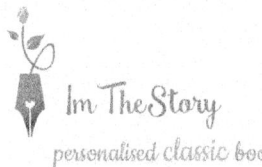

Im TheStory

personalised classic books

"Beautiful gift.. lovely finish.
My Niece loves it, so precious!"

Helen R Brumfieldon

⭐⭐⭐⭐⭐

UNIQUE GIFT

FOR KIDS, PARTNERS
AND FRIENDS

Timeless books such as:

Kids

Alice in Wonderland • The Jungle Book • The Wonderful Wizard of Oz
Peter and Wendy • **Robin Hood** • The Prince and The Pauper
The Railway Children • Treasure Island • A Christmas Carol

Adults

Romeo and Juliet • Dracula

Highly Customizable

Change Book's Title

Replace Characters names with your

Upload Photos and more under

Add Inscriptions

Visit
Im TheStory.com

and order yours today!

CPSIA information can be obtained
at www.ICGtesting.com
Printed in the USA
BVHW060222120819
555626BV00001B/34/P

9 780461 001785